Longman Annotated E

CW00794291

GENERAL EDITORS: JOHN BARNARI

FOUNDING EDITOR: F.

LONGMAN ANNOTATED ENGLISH POETS

General Editors: John Barnard and Paul Hammond
Founding Editor: F. W. Bateson

Titles available in paperback:

BLAKE: THE COMPLETE POEMS
(Third Edition)
Edited by W. H. Stevenson

DRYDEN: SELECTED POEMS
Edited by Paul Hammond and David Hopkins

THE POEMS OF ANDREW MARVELL
(Revised Edition)
Edited by Nigel Smith

MILTON: PARADISE LOST
(Second Edition)
Edited by Alastair Fowler

MILTON: COMPLETE SHORTER POEMS
(Second Edition)
Edited by John Carey

SPENSER: THE FAERIE QUEENE
(Revised Second Edition)
Edited by A. C. Hamilton

TENNYSON: A SELECTED EDITION
(Revised Edition)
Edited by Christopher Ricks

Frontispiece. John Dryden by Sir Godfrey Kneller (*c.* 1698).
Reproduced by permission of the Master and Fellows of
Trinity College, Cambridge.

DRYDEN

SELECTED POEMS

EDITED BY

PAUL HAMMOND

AND

DAVID HOPKINS

Harlow, England • London • New York • Boston • San Francisco • Toronto
Sydney • Tokyo • Singapore • Hong Kong • Seoul • Taipei • New Delhi
Cape Town • Madrid • Mexico City • Amsterdam • Munich • Paris • Milan

PEARSON EDUCATION LIMITED

Edinburgh Gate
Harlow CM20 2JE
United Kingdom
Tel: +44 (0)1279 623623
Fax: +44 (0)1279 431059
Website: www.pearsoned.co.uk

First edition published in Great Britain in 2007

© Pearson Education Limited 2007

The right of Paul Hammond and David Hopkins to be identified
as authors of this work has been asserted by them in accordance
with the Copyright, Designs and Patents Act 1988.

ISBN: 978-1-4058-3545-9 (paperback)

ISBN: 978-1-4058-3573-2 (cased)

British Library Cataloguing in Publication Data
A CIP catalogue record for this book can be obtained from the British Library

Library of Congress Cataloging in Publication Data
A CIP catalog record for this book can be obtained from the Library of Congress

10 9 8 7 6 5 4 3 2 1
11   10 09 08 07

Set by 35 in 10.5/11.5pt Bembo
Printed and bound in China
EPC/01

The Publishers' policy is to use paper manufactured from sustainable forests.

Contents

Note by the General Editors

Longman Annotated English Poets was launched in 1965 with the publication of Kenneth Allott's edition of *The Poems of Matthew Arnold*. F. W. Bateson wrote that the 'new series is the first designed to provide university students and teachers, and the general reader with complete and fully annotated editions of the major English poets'. That remains the aim of the series, and Bateson's original vision of its policy remains essentially the same. Its 'concern is primarily with the *meaning* of the extant texts in their various contexts'. The two other main principles of the series were that the text should be modernized and the poems printed 'as far as possible in the order in which they were composed'.

These broad principles still govern the series. Its primary purpose is to provide an annotated text giving the reader any necessary contextual information. However, flexibility in the detailed application has proved necessary in the light of experience and the needs of a particular case (and each poet is, by definition, a particular case).

First, proper glossing of a poet's vocabulary has proved essential and not something which can be taken for granted. Second, modernization has presented difficulties, which have been resolved pragmatically, trying to reach a balance between sensitivity to the text in question and attention to the needs of a modern reader. Thus, to modernize Browning's text has a double redundancy: Victorian conventions are very close to modern conventions, and Browning had firm ideas on punctuation. Equally, to impose modern pointing on the ambiguities of Marvell would create a misleading clarity. Third, in the very early days of the series Bateson hoped that editors would be able in many cases to annotate a *textus receptus*. That has not always been possible, and where no accepted text exists or where the text is controversial, editors have been obliged to go back to the originals and create their own text. The series has taken, and will continue to take, the opportunity not only of providing thorough annotations not available elsewhere, but also of making important scholarly textual contributions where necessary. A case in point is the edition of *The Poems of Tennyson* by Christopher Ricks, the Second Edition of which (1987) takes into account a full collation of the Trinity College Manuscripts, not previously available for an edition of this kind. Yet the series' primary purpose remains annotation.

The requirements of a particular author take precedence over principle. It would make little sense to print Herbert's *Temple* in the order of composition even if it could be established. Where Ricks rightly decided that Tennyson's reader needs to be given the circumstances of composition, the attitude to Tennyson and his circle, allusions, and important variants, a necessary consequence was the exclusion of twentieth-century critical responses. Milton, however, is a very different case. John

Carey and Alastair Fowler, looking to the needs of their readers, undertook synopses of the main lines of the critical debate over Milton's poetry. Finally, chronological ordering by date of composition will almost always have a greater or lesser degree of speculation or arbitrariness. The evidence is usually partial, and is confused further by the fact that poets do not always write one poem at a time and frequently revise at a later period than that of composition.

John Barnard
Paul Hammond

Preface

This volume presents a generous selection from the poetry of John Dryden drawn from our complete Longman Annotated English Poets edition of Dryden's non-dramatic poems (minus the translation of Virgil) together with their associated Prefaces and Dedications (5 vols, 1995–2005: henceforth cited as '*Poems*'). The selection contains Dryden's major historical, satirical, political, and religious poems of the 1660s, 1670s, and 1680s, together with some of the best verse translations and occasional poems from the 1680s and 1690s. It provides the serious student and general reader with the most comprehensive and fully annotated selection from Dryden's poetry to date.

The poems are printed in chronological order of publication – 'publication' being interpreted flexibly to include manuscript circulation and limited printing in broadsheet or pamphlet form. Texts are based on the early editions (usually the first) specified in the headnote to each poem. Verbal departures from the copy-text, and later substantive variants which might be the result of authorial revision, are recorded in the notes. Spelling is modernized (except in instances where it might seriously affect pronunciation or rhymes), with contractions or sounded final syllables being marked only in instances where a word is stressed differently from the modern norm or where the scansion of a line might be misread. Punctuation, too, is modernized, but in a way that seeks to avoid the over-rigorous imposition of modern grammatical structures on the more fluid contours of Drydenian syntax. Capitalization is preserved only for proper names and for nouns clearly intended as personifications. (For a fuller presentation and rationale of the edition's textual policy, see *Poems* i xii–xxi, and David Hopkins's essay in *John Dryden: Tercentenary Essays*, edited by Paul Hammond and David Hopkins (2000) 330–57). We have made a few minor adjustments to the capitalization and punctuation of the text for this selection.

A principal aim of the selection is to provide substantial, though concise, annotation designed to illuminate each poem's meaning, sources, and contexts (personal, historical, political, and literary). To this end, annotation from *Poems* is preserved in full, with extra material supplied where *Poems* makes cross-reference to texts and information not included in the selection. Though the notes have not been systematically revised for the selection, they have been occasionally expanded, to incorporate recent scholarship and provide additional glosses. Each poem is prefaced by a headnote, giving details of the poem's publication and the contexts within which it was originally composed, received, and interpreted. Under 'Sources' the headnote indicates the major sources for the poem, while 'Reception' records the most important responses of readers up to Dryden's death in 1700, and shortly beyond. Footnotes provide lexical glosses, illuminate echoes and allusions, and provide further information about the poem's sources and contexts, including cross-references to other related poems by Dryden. Quotations from works by Dryden included in *Poems* are taken from that edition. Cross-references to items in *Poems* which are not reprinted in this selection are given by short-title: these items can be easily identified and located by consulting the Index of Titles to the five-volume edition which is reprinted at the end of the present volume. Works by Dryden not included in *Poems* are quoted from the University of California Press edition of his *Works* (for details see the Bibliography). Notes on the historical, political, religious, and occasional poems chart the poems' relation to current pamphlet and controversial literature, and their dealings with eminent and lesser-known contemporaries. Annotation to the translations plots Dryden's response to his originals, indicating significant departures from and reshaping of his sources, and documenting – illustratively rather than exhaustively – his debts to scholarly editions and earlier translations. Dryden's practice as a translator is flexible and varied, and our shorthand note 'Dryden's addition' covers a range of effects from outright departures from the source-text (most notable in the translations from Chaucer and Boccaccio) to passages which, while having no direct equivalent in the original, develop meanings which might be thought latent or implicit in the earlier author.

Poems numbers 1–14, 16, 21, 23, and 27–8 were originally edited by Professor Hammond, and numbers 15, 17–20, 22, and 24–6 by Professor Hopkins, though we have checked each other's work and jointly prepared the present selected edition.

An edition of this kind is inevitably indebted to the work of numerous other scholars, past and present. Concise indications of our specific debts to existing scholarship are given in particular headnotes and footnotes. Our larger indebtedness to the many individuals and institutions that have assisted us in our work is fully registered in the Acknowledgements to *Poems* volume i and the Prefaces to volumes iii and v, but we should like to repeat here our special thanks to our partners, Nicholas and Sandra.

Paul Hammond and David Hopkins
May 2006

Chronological Table of Dryden's Life and Publications

For documentation and further details see Winn, Macdonald and *Letters*.

1631   (*9 August*) D. born at Aldwincle, Northamptonshire, the son of Erasmus Dryden and Mary Pickering; brought up in the nearby village of Titchmarsh; probably educated initially at the village school.

1644   Possible date of D.'s entry to Westminster School, London (scholars' conjectures range from 1642 to 1646).

1649   Publication of *Lachrymae Musarum*, a collection of elegies on the death of Lord Hastings, to which D. contributed.

1650   Admitted to Trinity College, Cambridge, as a Westminster scholar; his tutor was John Templer.
Contributes commendatory verses to John Hoddesdon's *Sion and Parnassus*.

1652   (*19 July*) D. punished by the Master and Seniors for his (unspecified) disobedience to the Vice-Master.
(*August*) D. writes 'Carmen Lapidarium' on the death of John Smith.

1654   (*February*) D. graduates BA and subsequently leaves Cambridge.
(*June*) Death of D.'s father, Erasmus (buried *14 June*). He leaves D. a farm, but insufficient income to make him financially independent.

1657   (*19 October*) D. signs a receipt for £50 from John Thurloe, Cromwell's Secretary of State; how long he had been employed by the government is not known, but he was probably introduced by his cousin Sir Gilbert Pickering, Cromwell's Lord Chamberlain.

1657–60   D. has some form of employment with the bookseller Henry Herringman during these years, and may have written occasional prefaces and advertisements for books published by him.

1658   (*3 September*) Death of Cromwell.
(*23 November*) D. walks in Cromwell's funeral procession along with Milton and Marvell as the Secretaries of the French and Latin Tongues.

1659   (*January*) 'Heroic Stanzas' printed in *Three Poems Upon the Death of his late Highness Oliver*.

1660   D. contributes a commendatory poem to Sir Robert Howard's *Poems*; he is lodging with Howard in London at around this time.
(*May*) Restoration of the monarchy and return of Charles Stuart as King Charles II.
(*June*) Publication of *Astraea Redux*.

1661	(*April*) Publication of *To His Sacred Majesty* on the coronation.
1662	(*January*) Publication of *To My Lord Chancellor*.

(*September*) Publication of commendatory verses in Walter Charleton's *Chorea Gigantum* (dated 1663).

(*19 November*) D. elected a Fellow of the Royal Society (proposed by Charleton).

1663 (*5 February*) First performance of D.'s first play, *The Wild Gallant*, at the Theatre Royal, Vere Street; subsequently performed at court 23 February, probably due to the influence of Lady Castlemaine; D.'s verses 'To the Lady Castlemaine' (circulated in MS) may date from this occasion, or from the play's printing in 1669.

(*1 December*) D. marries Elizabeth Howard, daughter of the Earl of Berkshire, and sister of Sir Robert Howard.

Late in 1663 or early in 1664 *The Rival Ladies* performed at the Theatre Royal, Bridges Street.

1664 (*January*) *The Indian Queen* performed at the Theatre Royal; first recorded performance on 25 January in the presence of the King.

(*c. November*) *The Rival Ladies* published.

1665 (*February/March*) *The Indian Emperor* performed at the Theatre Royal.

(*March*) *The Indian Queen* published in Sir Robert Howard's *Four New Plays*.

(*5 June*) London theatres close because of the plague. Around this time D. leaves with his wife for her father's country estate at Charlton, Wiltshire. During his year at Charlton D. works on *Secret Love, Of Dramatic Poesy* and *Annus Mirabilis*.

1666 (*27 August*) D.'s first son, Charles, born.

(*2–5 September*) Fire of London.

(*November*) London theatres reopen.

(*November/December*) Likely date for the performance of the revised version of *The Wild Gallant*, with a new Prologue and Epilogue.

1667 (*January*) *Annus Mirabilis* published.

(*March*) *Secret Love* performed at the Theatre Royal.

(*15 August*) *Sir Martin Mar-All* performed at Lincoln's Inn Fields.

(*Autumn*) *Of Dramatic Poesy* and *The Indian Emperor* published.

(*7 November*) *The Tempest* performed at Lincoln's Inn Fields.

1668 D.'s second son, John, born.

(*January*) *Secret Love* published.

(*February*) 'Prologue to *Albumazar*' spoken.

(*13 April*) D. appointed Poet Laureate.

(*Spring*) D. signs contract with the King's Company to write three plays a year in return for a share of the profits.

(*12 June*) *An Evening's Love* performed at the Theatre Royal.

(*Autumn*) *Sir Martin Mar-All* published. Shadwell's *The Sullen*

Lovers published with a preface attacking D.'s remarks on Jonson. Sir Robert Howard's *The Duke of Lerma* published with a preface attacking D.'s views on the use of rhyme in plays. D. replies in 'A Defence of *An Essay of Dramatic Poesy*' prefixed to the second edition of *The Indian Emperor* (*early September*).

1669   (*Spring*) *The Wild Gallant* published.
          (*2 May*) D.'s third son, Erasmus-Henry, born.
          (*June*) *Tyrannic Love* performed at the Theatre Royal.
1670   (*c. February*) *The Tempest* published.
          (*18 August*) D. appointed Historiographer Royal.
          (*Autumn*) *Tyrannic Love* published.
          (*December*) *The First Part of The Conquest of Granada* performed at the Theatre Royal.
1671   (*January*) *The Second Part of The Conquest of Granada* performed at the Theatre Royal.
          (*c. February*) *An Evening's Love* published.
          (*November*) *Marriage A-la-Mode* performed at the Theatre Royal.
          (*7 December*) First performance of Buckingham's *The Rehearsal*, in which D. is satirized as Mr Bayes.
1672   The song 'Farewell, fair Armida' appears in various printed miscellanies.
          (*25 January*) Theatre Royal destroyed by fire.
          (*February*) *The Conquest of Granada* published.
          (*26 February*) 'Prologue to *Wit without Money*' spoken.
          (*Summer: after 4 July*) 'Prologue and Epilogue to *Secret Love*, Spoken by the Women'.
          (*Summer or Autumn*) *The Assignation* performed at Lincoln's Inn Fields.
1673   (*Spring*) 'Prologue to *Arviragus* revived' spoken. Probable date of first performance of *Amboyna*. D.'s poems and plays extensively attacked in *The Censure of the Rota* and *The Friendly Vindication*; he is defended in *Mr Dreyden Vindicated* and *A Description of the Academy of the Athenian Virtuosi*.
          (*June*) *Marriage A-la-Mode* and *The Assignation* published.
          (*July*) 'Prologue and Epilogue at Oxford' spoken.
          (*Autumn*) *Amboyna* published.
1674   *Notes and Observations on the Empress of Morocco* published (written jointly by D., Crowne and Shadwell).
          (*26 March*) 'Prologue and Epilogue Spoken at the Opening of the New House'.
          (*Spring*) *The State of Innocence* written, but not staged, because of the expense.
          (*July*) 'Prologue and Epilogue at Oxford' spoken.
1675   (*February*) Epilogue written for a performance of *Calisto* at court.
          (*17 November*) *Aureng-Zebe* performed at Drury Lane.
          (*Winter*) Rochester's *An Allusion to Horace* (which includes an attack on D.) circulates in MS.

1676   (*February*) *Aureng-Zebe* published.
        (*11 March*) 'Epilogue to *The Man of Mode*' spoken.
        (*June*) Death of D.'s mother (buried *14 June*).
        (*July*) 'Prologue at Oxford' spoken. Publication of Shadwell's
        The Virtuoso; its Dedication has an implicit attack on D.
        (*July/August*) *Mac Flecknoe* composed, and put into circula-
        tion in MS.

1677   (*February*) *The State of Innocence* published.
        (*12 May*) 'Prologue to Circe' spoken.
        (*Autumn*) 'To Mr Lee, on his *Alexander*' published in Lee's
        The Rival Queens. D. writes 'Heads of an Answer to Rymer'
        on the endpapers of Thomas Rymer's *The Tragedies of the Last
        Age* (1677).
        (*December*) *All for Love* performed at the Theatre Royal.

1678   (*c. February*) 'Epilogue to *Mithridates*' spoken.
        (*11 March*) *The Kind Keeper* performed at Dorset Garden.
        (*March*) 'Prologue to *A True Widow*' spoken. *All for Love*
        published.
        (*Autumn*) *Oedipus* (by D. and Lee) performed at Dorset Garden.

1679   (*March*) *Oedipus* published.
        (*c. April*) *Troilus and Cressida* performed at Dorset Garden.
        (*July*) 'Prologue at Oxford' spoken.
        (*Summer*) 'Prologue to *Caesar Borgia*' spoken.
        (*Autumn*) *Troilus and Cressida* published by Tonson, marking the
        beginning of his association with D. *The Kind Keeper* published
        (dated 1680).
        (*c. December*) 'Prologue to *The Loyal General*' spoken.
        (*18 December*) D. attacked and badly injured in Rose Alley,
        probably because he was thought to have had a hand in
        Mulgrave's *An Essay upon Satire*.

1680   (*February*) *Ovid's Epistles* published, with Preface and three trans-
        lations by D.
        (*July*) 'Prologue at Oxford' spoken.
        (*November*) *The Spanish Friar* performed at Dorset Garden.

1681   (*c. February*) 'Epilogue to *Tamerlane the Great*' spoken.
        (*March*) *The Spanish Friar* published.
        (*19 March*) 'Epilogue Spoken to the King' at the Oxford
        Parliament.
        (*Spring*) 'Prologue and Epilogue to *The Unhappy Favourite*'
        spoken.
        (*June*) *His Majesties Declaration Defended* published.
        (*July*) 'Prologue at Oxford' spoken.
        (*October*) 'Prologue and Epilogue spoken at *Mithridates*'.
        (*November*) *Absalom and Achitophel* published, followed by many
        rejoinders.

1682   (*February*) 'Prologue and Epilogue to *The Loyal Brother*' spoken.
        (*15/16 March*) *The Medal* published, followed by rejoinders.
        (*21 April*) 'Prologue to His Royal Highness' spoken.

(*May*) Publication of *The Medal of John Bayes*, an outspoken attack on D., probably by Shadwell.

(*31 May*) 'Prologue to the Duchess' spoken.

(*July*) *The Duke of Guise* ready for performance, but banned by the Lord Chamberlain.

(*October*) *Mac Flecknoe* printed in a pirated edition.

(*November*) *The Second Part of Absalom and Achitophel* published. *Religio Laici* published. 'Prologue and Epilogue to the King and Queen' spoken.

(*28 November*) *The Duke of Guise* performed at the Theatre Royal.

(*c. December*) 'Prologue and Epilogue to *The Princess of Cleves*' spoken.

1683   Song 'High state and honours' printed in *Choice Ayres and Songs*.

(*February*) *The Duke of Guise* published, followed by pamphlets attacking it.

(*Spring*) *The Vindication of The Duke of Guise* published.

(*May*) Vol. I of *Plutarch's Lives* published, containing D.'s 'Life of Plutarch'.

(*Autumn*) Soame's *The Art of Poetry* published, with revisions by D.

(*November*) 'Epilogue to *Constantine the Great*' spoken.

1684   'To the Earl of Roscommon' published in Roscommon's *Essay on Translated Verse*. 'To Mr L. Maidwell' written and left in MS. First version of *King Arthur* composed.

(*February*) *Miscellany Poems* published, with contributions by D.

(*March*) Probable date of D.'s letter to Laurence Hyde, asking for help in securing payment of his salary.

(*April*) 'Prologue to *The Disappointment*' spoken.

(*July*) *The History of the League* published.

(*Autumn*) 'To the Memory of Mr Oldham' published in Oldham's *Remains*. *Albion and Albanius* staged before the King.

1685   (*January*) *Sylvae* published, with contributions by D.

(*6 February*) Death of Charles II; accession of James II.

(*March*) *Threnodia Augustalis* published.

(*3 June*) Revised version of *Albion and Albanius* performed at Dorset Garden.

(*11 June*) Duke of Monmouth lands at Lyme Regis; defeated at the Battle of Sedgemoor (*6 July*), and executed (*15 July*).

(*Summer*) Publication of commendatory verses in Northleigh's *The Triumph of our Monarchy*.

(*November*) Publication of 'To the Pious Memory of Mrs Anne Killigrew' in her *Poems* (dated 1686).

1686   D.'s conversion to the Church of Rome is not precisely datable, but probably occurred in 1685; on *19 January 1686* Evelyn recorded: '*Dryden* the famous play-poet & his two sonns, & Mrs. *Nelle* (Misse to the late . . .) were said to go to Masse; & such purchases were no greate losse to the Church.'

D. contributes to *A Defence of the Papers*, a work defending papers on Catholicism attributed to Charles II and Anne Hyde.

1687   (*May*) *The Hind and the Panther* published. D. says in the address 'To the Reader' that it had been written 'during the last Winter and the beginning of this Spring: though with long interruptions of ill health, and other hindrances'.

(*Summer*) Publication of commendatory verses in Higden's *A Modern Essay on the Tenth Satyr of Juvenal*.

(*July*) Publication of Montague and Prior's satirical *The Hind and the Panther Transvers'd*.

(*22 November*) St Cecilia's Day celebration, at which D.'s 'A Song for St Cecilia's Day' was performed; the printed text appeared around this time, and was probably distributed at the performance.

(*December*) Composition of 'On the Marriage of Anastasia Stafford'.

1688   Lines on Milton printed in Tonson's new edition of *Paradise Lost*. Publication of Tom Brown's attack on D., *The Reasons of Mr Bays Changing his Religion*.

(*June*) Publication of *Britannia Rediviva*, celebrating the birth of a son to James II and Queen Mary (on *10 June*).

(*July*) Publication of D.'s translation of Bouhours's *The Life of St Francis Xavier*.

(*5 November*) Prince William of Orange lands at Torbay.

(*11 December*) James II flees London, but is captured and returned; finally escapes to France.

1689   (*January*) Convention Parliament offers the crown to William and Mary. As a result of the Revolution, D. loses his offices as Poet Laureate and Historiographer Royal (replaced by Shadwell); he returns to the theatre to make a living.

(*November*) Contributes Prologue for performance of Behn's *The Widow Ranter*.

(*4 December*) *Don Sebastian* performed at the Theatre Royal.

1690   Tom Brown publishes another attack on D., *The Late Converts Expos'd*.

(*January*) *Don Sebastian* published.

(*May*) Politically controversial Prologue for Beaumont and Fletcher's *The Prophetess* spoken and immediately suppressed.

(*October*) *Amphitryon* performed at the Theatre Royal; printed at the end of the month.

(*December*) Prologue for Harris's *The Mistakes* spoken.

1691   D. contributes Preface to Walsh's *A Dialogue concerning Women*.

(*February/March*) Publication of Purcell's music for *The Prophetess*, with a dedication to the Duke of Somerset drafted for Purcell by D.

(*May/June*) *King Arthur* performed at Dorset Garden (originally written in 1684); published *early June*.

1692   (*c. February*) Publication of commendatory verses in Southerne's
        The Wives' Excuse.
        (*March*) Publication of *Eleonora*, mourning the Countess of
        Abingdon.
        (*April*) *Cleomenes* performed at the Theatre Royal: it is pub-
        lished in *May*. D. contributes a 'Character of Saint-Evremond'
        to a translation of his *Miscellaneous Essays*.
        (*September*) Contributes Prologue to the anonymous *Henry the
        Second*.
        (*October*) Publication of *The Satires of Juvenal and Persius*
        (dated 1693).

1693   D. contributes 'A Character of Polybius' to *The History of
        Polybius*.
        (*July*) Publication of *Examen Poeticum*, with contributions by D.
        (*December*) 'To My Dear Friend Mr Congreve' published in
        Congreve's *The Double Dealer* (dated 1694).

1694   (*January*) *Love Triumphant* performed at the Theatre Royal.
        (*March*) *Love Triumphant* published.
        (*15 June*) D. signs contract with Tonson for a complete trans-
        lation of Virgil, which occupies most of the next three years.
        (*July*) *Annual Miscellany for the Year 1694* published with con-
        tributions by D.

1695   (*June*) D.'s translation of Du Fresnoy's *De Arte Graphica*
        published.

1696   (*February*) Contributes Epilogue to *The Husband his own
        Cuckold* by his son John, and adds a Preface when it is
        printed in *July*.
        (*Spring: before June*) *An Ode on the Death of Mr Henry Purcell*
        published (Purcell died *21 November 1695*).

1697   (*July*) Publication of *The Works of Virgil*.
        (*22 November*) *Alexander's Feast* performed at the St Cecilia's
        Day celebration; the printed text appeared about this time,
        and was probably distributed at the performance.

1698   (*February*) Commendatory verses published in Granville's
        Heroick Love.
        (*March*) Publication of Jeremy Collier's *A Short View of the
        Immorality and Profaneness of the English Stage*, including criticism
        of D.'s plays.
        (*June*) Commendatory verses published in Motteux's *Beauty
        in Distress*. D.'s translation of *Annals* Book I published in *The
        Annals and History of Cornelius Tacitus*.

1699   (*20 March*) Contract for *Fables* drawn up with Tonson.
        (*October*) D. plans to translate Homer and seeks patronage for
        the project.

1700   (*March*) *Fables Ancient and Modern* published.
        (*April*) *The Pilgrim* performed (adapted from a play by Fletcher)
        with Prologue, Epilogue, Song, and Secular Masque by D.

(*1 May*) Death of D.; buried on *2 May* in St Anne's Church, Soho; reburied in Chaucer's grave in Westminster Abbey, *13 May*.

(*June*) *The Pilgrim* published.

Various poems published in memory of D., including *Luctus Britannici* (*June*) and *The Nine Muses*, by women admirers (*September*).

1704   *Poetical Miscellanies: The Fifth Part* includes material by D.

1709   *Ovid's Art of Love* includes Book I translated by D. (written in 1693).

1711   D.'s 'The Life of Lucian' (written *c.* 1696) published in *The Works of Lucian*.

1717   D.'s 'Aesacus transformed into a Cormorant' (written ?1699) published in *Ovid's Metamorphoses*.

Abbreviations

The Works of Dryden

AA	*Absalom and Achitophel*
2AA	*The Second Part of Absalom and Achitophel*
AM	*Annus Mirabilis*
EDP	*Of Dramatic Poesy, An Essay*
EP	*Examen Poeticum* (1693)
HP	*The Hind and the Panther*
MF	*Mac Flecknoe*
MP	*Miscellany Poems* (1684)
RL	*Religio Laici*

Journals

BJRL	*Bulletin of the John Rylands University Library of Manchester*
CQ	*Cambridge Quarterly*
DUJ	*Durham University Journal*
EA	*Études Anglaises*
ECS	*Eighteenth-Century Studies*
EIC	*Essays in Criticism*
ELH	*English Literary History* (now known as 'ELH')
ELN	*English Language Notes*
ES	*English Studies*
HJ	*Historical Journal*
HLQ	*Huntington Library Quarterly*
JEGP	*Journal of English and Germanic Philology*
JHI	*Journal of the History of Ideas*
JWCI	*Journal of the Warburg and Courtauld Institutes*
MLN	*Modern Language Notes*
MLQ	*Modern Language Quarterly*
MLR	*Modern Language Review*
MPh	*Modern Philology*
N & Q	*Notes and Queries*
PBSA	*Papers of the Bibliographical Society of America*
PLL	*Papers on Language and Literature*
PMLA	*Publications of the Modern Language Association of America* (now known as 'PMLA')
PQ	*Philological Quarterly*
PTRS	*Philosophical Transactions of the Royal Society*
RES	*Review of English Studies*
SB	*Studies in Bibliography*
SC	*Seventeenth Century*
SEL	*Studies in English Literature 1500–1900*
SP	*Studies in Philology*

Other abbreviations

Aen.	Virgil, *Aeneid*
BL	British Library, London
BodL	Bodleian Library, Oxford
Carm.	Horace, *Carmina* ('*Odes*')
CSPD	*Calendar of State Papers Domestic*
DNB	*Dictionary of National Biography*
Ecl.	Virgil, *Eclogues*
Ed.	The present editor
Eds	The general consensus among previous editors
Epist.	*Epistles*
FQ	Spenser, *The Faerie Queene*
Geo.	Virgil, *Georgics*
HMC	Historical Manuscripts Commission
Johnson	Johnson's *Dictionary*
LS	*The London Stage* (see Bibliography for details)
Met.	Ovid, *Metamorphoses*
NT	New Testament
ODNB	*Oxford Dictionary of National Biography*
OED	*Oxford English Dictionary* (The first edition was used for poems 1–14 and 16, the second edition (1989) for poems 15 and 17–28; there are occasional differences in the numbering of senses between the two editions.)
OLD	*Oxford Latin Dictionary*
OT	Old Testament
PL	Milton, *Paradise Lost*
POAS	*Poems on Affairs of State* (see Bibliography for details)
PR	Milton, *Paradise Regained*
Sat.	*Satires*
s.d.	stage direction
Serm.	Horace, *Sermones* ('*Satires*')
SR	*The Stationers' Register*
TC	*The Term Catalogues*
tr.	translated by
UL	University Library

Note on the use of abbreviated titles for Dryden's poems
Each poem has been given a standardized short title which is used throughout, except that the full original title is given at the beginning of each poem.

Bibliography

This bibliography lists only the editions used for principal references and quotations, and those works of scholarship and criticism which are cited by author or short title. In this bibliography the place of publication is London unless otherwise stated, but in the rest of this edition the place of publication is not given. Throughout the edition the date given for plays is the date of their appearance in print, unless first performance is specified.

The Works of Dryden

Christie	*The Poetical Works of John Dryden*, edited by W. D. Christie (1870)
Day	*The Songs of John Dryden*, edited by Cyrus Lawrence Day (New York, 1932)
Derrick	*The Miscellaneous Works of John Dryden*, edited by Samuel Derrick, 4 vols (1760)
Hales	*Alexander's Feast, Mac Flecknoe, and St Cecilia's Day*, edited by J. W. Hales (1883)
Ker	*Essays of John Dryden*, edited by W. P. Ker, 2 vols (Oxford, 1900)
Kinsley	*The Poems of John Dryden*, edited by James Kinsley, 4 vols (Oxford, 1958)
Letters	*The Letters of John Dryden*, edited by Charles E. Ward (Durham, NC, 1942)
Malone	*The Critical and Miscellaneous Prose Works of John Dryden*, edited by Edmond Malone, 3 vols (1800)
Noyes	*The Poetical Works of Dryden*, edited by George R. Noyes (Boston, Mass., 1909; 2nd edition 1950)
Poems	*The Poems of John Dryden*, edited by Paul Hammond and David Hopkins, 5 vols (1995–2005)
Scott	*The Works of John Dryden*, edited by Walter Scott, 18 vols (1808)
Walker	*The Oxford Authors: John Dryden*, edited by Keith Walker (Oxford, 1987)
Warton	*The Poetical Works of John Dryden*, with notes by Joseph Warton, John Warton and others, edited by H. J. Todd, 4 vols (1811)
Watson	John Dryden, *Of Dramatic Poesy and other critical essays*, edited by George Watson, 2 vols (1962)
Williams	*The Hind and the Panther*, edited by W. H. Williams (1900)
Works	*The Works of John Dryden*, edited by H. T. Swedenberg et al., 20 vols (Berkeley, Calif., 1956–2000)
Yonge	*Essays of John Dryden*, edited by C. D. Yonge (1892)

Dryden's writings, other than those appearing in *Poems*, are generally cited from *Works*. References to *Works* are given by line numbers for

the poetry (e.g. ll. 12–34), by act, scene, and line numbers for the plays
(e.g. I ii 34–56), and by volume and page number for the prose and for
the editorial commentary (e.g. i 2–3). When a note in the present
edition draws upon or discusses material in the equivalent note in *Works*,
this is signalled by a simple citation (*Works*) without further references.
The same applies to the citation of other editors.

Classical works
Classical writers are quoted from the Loeb Library, unless there is a
particular reason for citing the editions that Dryden is known to have
used (for these see Bottkol's article, and the headnotes to Dryden's translations). Translations are generally based on the Loeb versions, but are
adapted where necessary.

Seventeenth-century works

Boileau   *Oeuvres complètes de Boileau*, edited by Charles-H. Boudhors,
              7 vols (Paris, 1934–43)

Buckingham   George Villiers, Duke of Buckingham, *The Rehearsal*,
              edited by D. E. L. Crane (Durham, 1976)

Burnet   *Bishop Burnet's History of his Own Time*, 3rd edition, 4 vols
              (1766)

Burton   Robert Burton, *The Anatomy of Melancholy*, Everyman's
              Library (1932)

Bysshe   Edward Bysshe, *The British Parnassus*, 2 vols (1714)

Carew   *The Poems of Thomas Carew*, edited by Rhodes Dunlap
              (Oxford, 1949)

Cowley   Abraham Cowley, *Poems*, edited by A. R. Waller
              (Cambridge, 1905)
              Abraham Cowley, *Essays, Plays and Sundry Verses*, edited
              by A. R. Waller (Cambridge, 1906)

Danchin   *The Prologues and Epilogues of the Restoration 1660–1700*, edited
              by Pierre Danchin, 7 vols (Nancy, 1981–8)

Denham   *The Poetical Works of Sir John Denham*, edited by Theodore
              Howard Banks, 2nd edition (Hamden, Conn., 1969)

Dennis   John Dennis, *Critical Works*, edited by E. N. Hooker, 2 vols
              (Baltimore, Md, 1939–43)

Dorset   *The Poems of Charles Sackville, Sixth Earl of Dorset*, edited
              by Brice Harris (New York and London, 1979)

Downes   John Downes, *Roscius Anglicanus* [first published 1708],
              edited by Judith Milhous and Robert D. Hume
              (1987)

Etherege   *The Dramatic Works of Sir George Etherege*, edited by
              H. F. B. Brett-Smith, 2 vols (Oxford, 1927)

Evelyn   *The Diary of John Evelyn*, edited by E. S. de Beer, 6 vols
              (Oxford, 1955)

Fanshawe   *The Poems and Translations of Sir Richard Fanshawe*, edited
              by Peter Davidson, 2 vols (Oxford, 1997–9)

Godwyn   Thomas Godwyn, *Romanae Historiae Anthologia*, revised
               edition (Oxford, 1631)
Gondibert   Sir William Davenant, *Gondibert*, edited by David F. Gladish
               (Oxford, 1971)
Jonson   *Ben Jonson*, edited by C. H. Herford, Percy and Evelyn
               Simpson, 11 vols (Oxford, 1925–52)
Langbaine   Gerard Langbaine, *An Account of the English Dramatick Poets*
               (1691)
Lee   *The Works of Nathaniel Lee*, edited by Thomas B. Stroup
               and Arthur L. Cooke, 2 vols (New Brunswick, NJ,
               1954–5)
Luttrell   Narcissus Luttrell, *A Brief Historical Relation of State Affairs
               1678–1714*, 6 vols (1857)
Marvell   *The Poems of Andrew Marvell*, edited by Nigel Smith
               (2003)
Milton   *The Poems of John Milton*, edited by John Carey and
               Alastair Fowler (1968)
               The Complete Prose Works of John Milton, edited by Don
               M. Wolfe et al., 8 vols (New Haven, Conn., 1953–82)
Montaigne   Montaigne, *Œuvres complètes*, edited by Maurice Rat
               (Paris, 1962)
Oldham   *The Poems of John Oldham*, edited by Harold F. Brooks
               with Raman Selden (Oxford, 1987)
Otway   *The Works of Thomas Otway*, edited by J. C. Ghosh, 2 vols
               (Oxford, 1932)
Pepys   *The Diary of Samuel Pepys*, edited by Robert Latham and
               William Matthews, 11 vols (1970–83)
POAS   *Poems on Affairs of State*, edited by George deF. Lord et al.,
               7 vols (New Haven, Conn., 1963–75)
Rochester   *The Works of John Wilmot, Earl of Rochester*, edited by Harold
               Love (Oxford, 1999)
Ross   Alexander Ross, *Mystagogus Poeticus, or, The Muses Interpreter*
               (first published 1647; 5th edition 1672)
Rymer   *The Critical Works of Thomas Rymer*, edited by Curt A.
               Zimansky (New Haven, Conn., 1956)
Shadwell   *The Complete Works of Thomas Shadwell*, edited by Montague
               Summers, 5 vols (1927)
Shakespeare   *The Arden Edition of the Works of William Shakespeare*, in
               progress (1949–); third series cited where available
Southerne   *The Works of Thomas Southerne*, edited by Robert Jordan
               and Harold Love, 2 vols (Oxford, 1988)
Spence   Joseph Spence, *Observations, Anecdotes, and Characters of Books
               and Men*, edited by James M. Osborn, 2 vols (Oxford, 1966)
Spenser   *Spenser's Faerie Queene*, edited by J. C. Smith, 2 vols
               (Oxford, 1909)
               Spenser's Minor Poems, edited by Ernest de Selincourt
               (Oxford, 1910)

Spingarn	*Critical Essays of the Seventeenth Century*, edited by J. E. Spingarn, 3 vols (Oxford, 1908–9)
Sprat	Thomas Sprat, *The History of the Royal-Society of London* (1667)
Waller	*The Poems of Edmund Waller*, edited by G. Thorn Drury, 2 vols (1901)
Wycherley	*The Plays of William Wycherley*, edited by Arthur Friedman (Oxford, 1979)

Modern scholarship and criticism

This list provides the details of those works which it has been convenient to cite in this edition by author or short title. Readers wishing to find listings of Dryden scholarship and criticism might consult David J. Latt and Samuel Holt Monk, *John Dryden: A Survey and Bibliography of Critical Studies, 1895–1974* (Minneapolis, Minn., 1976); more recent work is listed in regular bibliographies in the periodicals *Restoration*, *The Scriblerian* and *The Year's Work in English Studies*, and in various electronic databases. Selective bibliographies are included in Paul Hammond, *John Dryden: A Literary Life* (Basingstoke, 1991), and David Hopkins, *John Dryden*, Writers and their Work (Tavistock, 2004).

Beal	Peter Beal, *Index of English Literary Manuscripts*, vol. 2, part 1 (1987)
Bottkol	J. McG. Bottkol, 'Dryden's Latin Scholarship', *MPh* xl (1943) 241–54
CH	*Dryden: The Critical Heritage*, edited by James and Helen Kinsley (1971)
Garrison	James D. Garrison, *Dryden and the Tradition of Panegyric* (Berkeley, Calif., 1975)
Haley	K. H. D. Haley, *The First Earl of Shaftesbury* (Oxford, 1968)
Hammond	Paul Hammond, *Dryden and the Traces of Classical Rome* (Oxford, 1999)
Hammond and Hopkins	*John Dryden: Tercentenary Essays*, edited by Paul Hammond and David Hopkins (Oxford, 2000)
Harth	Phillip Harth, *Contexts of Dryden's Thought* (Chicago, Ill., 1968)
	Phillip Harth, *Pen for a Party: Dryden's Tory Propaganda in its Contexts* (Princeton, NJ, 1993)
Hawkins	Edward Hawkins, *Medallic Illustrations of the History of Great Britain to the Death of George II*, 2 vols (1885)
Hoffman	Arthur W. Hoffman, *John Dryden's Imagery* (Gainesville, Fla., 1962)
Hutton	Ronald Hutton, *The Restoration: A Political and Religious History of England and Wales 1658–1667* (Oxford, 1985)
	Ronald Hutton, *Charles the Second: King of England, Scotland, and Ireland* (Oxford, 1989)

LS	*The London Stage 1660–1800, Part I: 1660–1700*, edited by William van Lennep (Carbondale, Ill., 1965)
Maccubbin and Hamilton-Phillips	*The Age of William III and Mary II: Power, Politics, and Patronage, 1688–1702*, edited by Robert P. Maccubbin and Martha Hamilton-Phillips (Williamsburg, Va, 1989)
Macdonald	Hugh Macdonald, *John Dryden: A Bibliography of Early Editions and of Drydeniana* (Oxford, 1939). (For corrections and additions to Macdonald's bibliography see James M. Osborn, *MPh* xxxix (1941) 69–98, 197–212)
Mason	J. R. Mason, 'To Milton through Dryden and Pope' (unpublished PhD thesis, Cambridge, 1987)
Miner	Earl Miner, *Dryden's Poetry* (Bloomington, Ind., 1967)
Ogg	David Ogg, *England in the Reign of Charles II*, 2nd edition (Oxford, 1956)
Osborn	James M. Osborn, *John Dryden: Some Biographical Facts and Problems*, revised edition (Gainesville, Fla., 1965)
Owen	Susan J. Owen, *Restoration Theatre and Crisis* (Oxford, 1996)
Reverand	Cedric D. Reverand II, *Dryden's Final Poetic Mode: 'The Fables'* (Philadelphia, Pa, 1988)
Spurr	John Spurr, *The Restoration Church of England, 1646–1681* (New Haven, Conn., 1991)
Tilley	M. P. Tilley, *A Dictionary of the Proverbs in England in the Sixteenth and Seventeenth Centuries* (Ann Arbor, Mich., 1950)
Verrall	A. W. Verrall, *Lectures on Dryden* (Cambridge, 1914)
Winn	James Anderson Winn, *John Dryden and his World* (New Haven, Conn., 1987) (cited as 'Winn') James Anderson Winn, *'When Beauty Fires the Blood': Love and the Arts in the Age of Dryden* (Ann Arbor, Mich., 1992) (cited with short title)

THE POEMS

1 Heroic Stanzas

Date and publication. Cromwell died on 3 September 1658. Because of ineffectual embalming, the body had to be buried privately at an unknown date before the state funeral on 23 November, at which an effigy was used. On 20 January 1659 Henry Herringman entered in *SR* 'a booke called *Three poems to the happy memory of the most renowned Oliver, late Lord Protector of this Commonwealth*, by Mr. Marvell, Mr. Driden, Mr. Sprat.' But Herringman did not proceed with publication, possibly because of changing political circumstances. It was William Wilson who at an unknown date in 1659 published *Three Poems Upon the Death of his late Highnesse Oliver Lord Protector of England, Scotland, and Ireland*, with Waller's 'Upon the Late Storm, and the Death of his Highness ensuing the same', already printed, replacing Marvell's poem. D.'s poem was reprinted in 1681 with the title *An Elegy on the Usurper O.C. by the Author of Absalom and Achitophel, published to shew the Loyalty and Integrity of the Poet*, which was evidently a Whig attempt to embarrass D.; there were two similar unauthorized reprints in 1682, and another in 1687, which described D. as 'the Author of *The H—d and the P—r*'. An authorized reprint was issued by Tonson in 1691 or 1692 as part of a uniform set of D.'s earlier poems.

An autograph MS of this poem survives in BL MS Lansdowne 1045 (hereafter '*MS*'), the only autograph MS of a poem by D. now known (apart from the verses in his letter to Honor Dryden). This was identified as being in D.'s hand by Anna Maria Crinò in *English Miscellany* xvii (1966) 311–20. Beal 403–4 lists fourteen other MSS of this poem, so it was evidently given some limited MS circulation through the Restoration period. A critical text based on *MS* was printed by Vinton A. Dearing et al. in *PBSA* lxix (1975) 502–26, and the texts of *MS*, *1659* and *1692* were compared (particularly in their use of accidentals) by Paul Hammond in *PBSA* lxxvi (1982) 457–70.

The relationship of *MS* to *1659* is not entirely clear: *MS* is probably a fair copy (perhaps intended for presentation) made before the poem was revised for its publication in *1659*. It is likely that the substantive variants in ll. 10, 67, 89, 90 and 145 are authorial revisions to the poem made for *1659*; it is possible that the same is true of the variants in ll. 57 and 138 (though Dearing regards them as errors made by *1659*). If the text in *MS* could be shown to have had any public circulation, the textual policy of this edition would point to the choice of *MS* as copytext; however, since the poem seems to have reached its first public in *1659*, the present edition follows *1659*, emending only at l. 63 (apart from the usual silent emendation of indubitable misprints). Substantive variants between *MS* and *1659* are recorded in the notes, and a reprint of *MS* is provided in *Poems* i, Appendix A.

Context. D. probably joined the service of the Protectoral government through his cousin Sir Gilbert Pickering, who was Cromwell's Lord Chamberlain. (Later, Shadwell wrote that D. had been 'Clerk to *Nolls* Lord Chamberlain': *The Medal of John Bayes* (1682) 8.) On 19 October 1657 D. received £50 from John Thurloe, Cromwell's Secretary of State, for unspecified services. In 1659 he was allocated 9s. for mourning and walked in Cromwell's funeral procession as one of the secretaries of Latin and French tongues, who also included Milton and Marvell (see Paul Hammond, *Transactions of the Cambridge Bibliographical Society* viii (1981) 130–6; Winn 557–8).

Sources. The stanza form had been used by Davenant in *Gondibert* (1651). Several similarities with Sprat's and Waller's poems on the death of Cromwell

suggest that D. saw them before writing his own. Garrison 149–55 describes
how the poem draws upon the arrangement of material favoured in classical
orations. For the classical elements see also Hammond 70–84.

Heroic Stanzas

Consecrated to the Glorious Memory
Of his most Serene and Renowned
Highness Oliver,
Late Lord Protector of this
Commonwealth, etc.
Written after the Celebration of his Funeral

I

And now 'tis time; for their officious haste
Who would before have borne him to the sky,
Like eager Romans, ere all rites were past
Did let too soon the sacred eagle fly.

2

5   Though our best notes are treason to his fame,
Joined with the loud applause of public voice,
Since heaven what praise we offer to his name
Hath rendered too authentic by its choice;

3

Though in his praise no arts can liberal be,
10 Since they whose Muses have the highest flown
Add not to his immortal memory,
But do an act of friendship to their own:

¶1. *Title. glorious*] glorious [& happy *deleted*] MS. *funeral*] Funeralls MS.
1–4. A reference to panegyrics written before the funeral. Waller wrote: 'So
Romulus was lost! / New Rome in such a tempest missed her king, / And from
obeying fell to worshipping' ('Upon the Late Storm, and of the Death of His
Highness Ensuing the Same' ll. 6–8).
3–4. At the deification of a Roman emperor an eagle was released from the top
of his funeral pile to carry his soul to heaven (Herodian IV ii).
8. authentic] duly authorized.
10–12. Cp. Sprat: 'thy mighty name / Wants not Addition of another's Beam; /
. . . The Muses are made great by Thee, not thou by Them' (*Three Poems* 13;
Works).
10. Since] And MS.

4

Yet 'tis our duty and our interest too,
Such monuments as we can build to raise,
15 Lest all the world prevent what we should do,
And claim a title in him by their praise.

5

How shall I then begin, or where conclude,
To draw a fame so truly circular?
For in a round what order can be shewed,
20 Where all the parts so equal perfect are?

6

His grandeur he derived from heaven alone,
For he was great ere Fortune made him so;
And wars, like mists that rise against the sun,
Made him but greater seem, not greater grow.

7

25 No borrowed bays his temples did adorn,
But to our crown he did fresh jewels bring;
Nor was his virtue poisoned soon as born
With the too early thoughts of being king.

8

Fortune (that easy mistress of the young,
30 But to her ancient servants coy and hard)

13. Cp. Sprat: 'but yet our Duty calls our Songs' (13; *Works*).
15. prevent] anticipate.
16. title] legal right.
17. Cp. Sprat: 'What shall I say, or where begin?' (14; *Works*).
18–20. The circle was a common seventeenth-century image of perfection: cp.
Jonson, *Epigrammes* xcviii 3 (drawing on Horace, *Serm.* II vii 86–8) and cxxviii
8; 'Upon the Death of the Lord Hastings' ll. 27–30, and *AA* ll. 838–9.
19. round] sphere (*OED* 1); circle (*OED* 6). *shewed*] The now obsolete form
of *showed*; a perfect rhyme with *conclude*.
22–4. Cp. Sprat: 'whilst yet / Thou only to thy self wert great; / . . . As bodyes,
in the Dark and Night, / Have the same Colours, the same Red and White, /
As in the open day and Light; / The Sun doth only show / That they are bright,
not make them so' (15–16; *Works*).
25. bays] laurels, forming the conqueror's crown.
25–8. Cromwell rejected the offer of the crown in 1657. Cp. Sprat: 'thou wast
not born unto a Crown, / Thy Scepter's not thy Fathers, but thy own' (16).
29–30. Echoes Machiavelli: 'Fortune is a mistresse; and it is necessary, to keep
her in obedience to ruffle and force her: and we see, that she suffers her self
rather to be mastered by those, than by others that proceed coldly. And

Him at that age her favourites ranked among
When she her best-loved Pompey did discard.

9

He private marked the faults of others' sway,
And set as sea-marks for himself to shun;
35   Not like rash monarchs who their youth betray
By acts their age too late would wish undone.

10

And yet dominion was not his design:
We owe that blessing not to him but heaven,
Which to fair acts unsought rewards did join,
40   Rewards that less to him than us were given.

11

Our former chiefs, like sticklers of the war,
First sought t' inflame the parties, then to poise;

---

therefore, as a mistresse, shee is a friend to young men, because they are lesse
respective, more rough, and command her with more boldnesse' (*The Prince*, tr.
Edward Dacres (1640), Tudor Translations xxxix (1905) 352). Some contemporaries accused Cromwell of Machiavellian deviousness: see *Oliver Cromwell and
the English Revolution*, edited by John Morrill (1990) 263–4. For links between
Marvell's 'An Horatian Ode' and Machiavelli see Blair Worden in *Politics of Discourse*,
edited by Kevin Sharpe and Steven N. Zwicker (1987) 162–8. For the importance of Fortune in D.'s thought see 'Horace: *Odes* III xxix' ll. 73–87*n*. Sprat
says of Cromwell that 'Fortune did hang on thy Sword' (23).
31–2. Cromwell was 45 when he won the Battle of Marston Moor in 1644, and
59 when he died. Pompey was 45 when he returned to Rome from the East at
the height of his fortunes, which declined until his death in 48 BC, in his fifty-
ninth year. Lucan says: *sed poenas longi Fortuna fauoris / exigit a misero* ('but Fortune
who had long favoured him [Pompey], now demands from her victim the penalty
of that favour': *Pharsalia* viii 21–2).
34. sea-marks] conspicuous objects distinguishable at sea, serving to guide or warn sailors.
38. Cromwell habitually ascribed his victories to divine providence (see Blair
Worden, *Past and Present* cix (1985) 55–99; essays by J. C. Davis and Anthony
Fletcher in *Oliver Cromwell*, edited by Morrill). Sprat says: 'when the Heavens
smil'd on thee in Fight, / When thy propitious God had lent / Successe and
Victory to thy Tent; / To Heaven again the Victory was sent' (23–4).
41–8. Some parliamentary leaders, such as the Earl of Manchester, were reluctant to press home the victory at Marston Moor and hoped to reach a settlement
with the King in favour of parliamentary rights and Presbyterian religion. On
25 November 1644 Cromwell accused Manchester of 'unwillingness . . . to have
this war prosecuted unto a full victory, and a design or desire to have it ended
by accommodation on some such terms to which it might be disadvantageous to
bring the King too low', and on 9 December he told the Commons: 'The important occasion now is no less than to save a Nation out of a bleeding, nay almost

The quarrel loved, but did the cause abhor,
And did not strike to hurt, but make a noise.

12
45   War, our consumption, was their gainful trade;
     We inward bled whilst they prolonged our pain:
     He fought to end our fighting, and essayed
     To stanch the blood by breathing of the vein.

13
     Swift and resistless through the land he passed,
50   Like that bold Greek who did the east subdue;
     And made to battles such heroic haste
     As if on wings of victory he flew.

14
     He fought secure of fortune as of fame,
     Till by new maps the island might be shown
55   Of conquests, which he strewed where'er he came,
     Thick as the galaxy with stars is sown.

dying, condition . . . casting off all lingering proceedings like soldiers of fortune beyond sea, to spin out a war' (*The Writings and Speeches of Oliver Cromwell*, edited by W. C. Abbott, 4 vols (1937–47) i 302, 314).
41. sticklers] umpires at tournaments, wrestling or fencing matches, who part the combatants when they have fought enough (*OED*).
48. The opening ('breathing' *OED* 8) of a vein in order to let blood was standard medical practice for many complaints. This line, which completes the image begun at l. 45, was later read by D.'s enemies as a reference to the execution of Charles I. *1681* prints the line in italics, and marks it with an initial dagger. Shadwell says D. 'prais'd his opening the Basilick Vein' (*The Medal of John Bayes* (1682) 8), and Robert Gould says that had Charles II been murdered, 'thou hadst prais'd the Fact; his Father Slain, / Thou call'dst but gently breathing of a Vein' (*The Laureat* [1687]). *Works* notes that Sprat has similar images to D.'s: 'Thy Country wounded 'twas, and sick before, / Thy Wars and Armes did her restore: / . . . like the Cure of Sympathy, / Thy strong and certain Remedy / Unto the Weapon didst apply' (18); and 'Thy hand . . . / Not only Lanc'd, but heal'd the Wound' (28).
50. that bold Greek] Alexander the Great.
52. The Greek goddess of victory, Nike, was represented as winged.
54–5. i.e. the island might be represented by new maps in which the sites of Cromwell's victories replace the features previously marked. A map in John Speed's *Theatre of the Empire of Great Britaine* (1631) marks 'The Invasions of England and Ireland With all their Civill Wars Since the Conquest', while Wenceslaus Hollar's *Comparison of the English and Bohemian Civil Wars* (print *c.* 1642) marks the battles of the Civil War on a map of England.
55–6. Cp. Sprat: 'Others' great Actions are / But thinly scatter'd here and there; / At best, all but one single Starr: / But thine the Milkie way' (14; *Works*).

15

His palms, though under weights they did not stand,
Still thrived; no winter could his laurels fade:
Heaven in his portrait showed a workman's hand,
60   And drew it perfect, yet without a shade.

16

Peace was the prize of all his toils and care
Which war had banished, and did now restore;
Bologna's walls thus mounted in the air
To seat themselves more surely than before.

17

65   Her safety rescued Ireland to him owes,
And treacherous Scotland, to no interest true,
Yet blessed that fate which did his arms dispose
Her land to civilize as to subdue.

57. *weights*] weight *MS*. It was commonly supposed that the palm tree thrives
when weighted down; hence it became an emblem of virtue, truth or constancy
overcoming hardships. The frontispiece to Ἐικὼν Βασιλική (1649) showed Charles
I at prayer, two palms (one heavily weighted) and the motto *Crescit sub Pondere
Virtus* ('Virtue rises under weight'). Another example, used to opposite political
effect, is in Matthew Mew's poem in *Musarum Oxoniensium Ἐλαιοφορία* (1654)
34: *Sed pressa, palmae par virenti, / Ponderibus melius resurgit* ('Weighed down like a
flourishing palm, [England] rises again better under weights').
59–60. This is the first of D.'s many references to painting, which he often saw
as a parallel art to poetry (e.g. in 'To Sir Godfrey Kneller', and 'A Parallel, of
Poetry and Painting' prefixed to his translation of Du Fresnoy's *De Arte Graphica*
(1695)). Cp. ll. 94–6; *Astraea Redux* ll. 125–8n; *Threnodia Augustalis* ll. 255–6. For
a discussion of D. and painting see Winn, *When Beauty, passim.*
61–4. Cp. Sprat: Cromwell made war 'That peace might land again upon the
shoare / Richer and better than before' (19; *Works*). The motto of the
Protectorate was *Pax Quaeritur Bello* ('Peace is sought through war').
63–4. Guicciardini recounts that during the siege of Bologna by the Spanish in
1512 a mine blew up part of the city wall on which was built a chapel dedicated
to the Virgin Mary. The chapel was lifted into the air by the explosion, but then
fell so exactly into its original place that the breach was completely filled (*The
Historie*, tr. Geffray Fenton (1579) 569).
63. *walls*] *MS*, 1692; wall 1659.
65–8. The native Irish had risen against the settlers in 1641; Cromwell said that
his Irish campaign of 1649–50 was undertaken by divine guidance in defence of
liberty and property (*Writings and Speeches* ii 36–9). Both sides in the English Civil
War would have regarded l. 66 as an apt summary of their experience with the
Scots, whose duplicity culminated in their sale of Charles I to Parliament in 1647.
Marvell in 'An Horatian Ode' had referred to the Pict's 'parti-coloured mind'

18

Nor was he like those stars which only shine
70 When to pale mariners they storms portend;
He had his calmer influence, and his mine
Did love and majesty together blend.

19

'Tis true, his count'nance did imprint an awe,
And naturally all souls to his did bow;
75 As wands of divination downward draw,
And point to beds where sovereign gold doth grow.

20

When past all offerings to Feretrian Jove
He Mars deposed, and arms to gowns made yield,
Successful counsels did him soon approve
80 As fit for close intrigues as open field.

(l. 106). Cromwell's conquest of Scotland was accomplished chiefly by the Battle of Dunbar on 3 September 1650. Cp. Waller: 'The Caledonians, armed with want and cold, / Have, by a fate indulgent to your fame, / Been from all ages kept for you to tame. / . . . So kind dictators made, when they came home, / Their vanquished foes free citizens of Rome. / Like favour find the Irish' ('A Panegyric to My Lord Protector' ll. 82–97; *Works*).
67. *Yet blessed*] May blesse MS.
68. The idea that Scotland needed to be civilized also appears in Waller's earlier poem 'To My Lord of Falkland': 'To civilize, and to instruct the north' (*Poems* i 75).
69–70. The rising and setting of Arcturus and the Hyades were associated with stormy weather (Horace, *Carm.* I iii 14; Virgil, *Aen.* iii 513–19).
71. *mine*] variant spelling of 'mien'.
75. 'A *Divining Wand* is a two-forked branch of an *Hazel-tree*, which is used for the finding out either of *Veins*, or hidden *Treasures* of *Gold* or *Silver*; and being carryed about, bends downwards (or rather is said to do so) when it comes to the place where they lye' (Cowley's note to his poem 'To Mr. Hobs': *Poems* 191; *Works*).
76. *grow*] See *AM* l. 553–6n.
77. *Feretrian Jove*] Romulus inaugurated the custom whereby arms taken personally by a Roman general from an enemy commander were offered to Jupiter Feretrius; his achievement was matched only twice (Livy I x; Propertius IV x).
78. Cicero applied the dictum *cedant arma togae* ('let arms yield to the toga') to his own consulship, in which sedition was defeated (*De Officiis* I xxii 77). *gowns*] togas, the dress of peace (*OED* 3). The antithesis is in Sprat: 'Or in thy Armes, or in thy Gown' (14).
79. *approve*] demonstrate (*OED* 1).

21

To suppliant Holland he vouchsafed a peace,
Our once bold rival in the British main,
Now tamely glad her unjust claim to cease,
And buy our friendship with her idol gain.

22

85   Fame of th' asserted sea through Europe blown
Made France and Spain ambitious of his love:
Each knew that side must conquer he would own,
And for him fiercely as for empire strove.

23

No sooner was the Frenchman's cause embraced
90   Than the light Monsieur the grave Don outweighed:
His fortune turned the scale where it was cast,
Though Indian mines were in the other laid.

81–4. The First Dutch War (1652–4) was provoked by commercial rivalry. The English Navigation Act (1651) prohibited imports which were not carried in ships belonging to England or to the exporting country, thus impeding Dutch trade. Dutch ships were also required to strike their flags and topsails to English ships in the Channel. The treaty of 1654 enforced these provisions, and exacted compensation from the Dutch for the massacre of English traders at Amboyna and damage to English merchantmen.

82. main] sea.

83–4. Cp. Waller: 'Holland, to gain your friendship, is content / To be our outguard on the continent' ('A Panegyric' ll. 101–2; *Works*).

85–8. 'His greatness at home was but a shadow of the glory he had abroad. It was hard to discover which feared him most, France, Spain, or the Low Countries, where his friendship was current at the value he put on it' (Clarendon, *The History of the Rebellion*, edited by W. D. Macray, 6 vols (1888) vi 94).

85. asserted sea] British claims to the sovereignty of the surrounding seas, including the whole of the Channel and North Sea, had been stated by John Selden in *Mare Clausum* (1635), a reply to *Mare Liberum* (1609) by the Dutchman Hugo Grotius. *assert*] lay claim to (*OED* 3, 4).

89–92. In 1656 England and France agreed to a joint campaign against Spain in Flanders, which led to the capture of Dunkirk in June 1658.

89. No] Nor MS.

90. the light] th' ayery MS.

91. European strategy was frequently viewed in terms of an imbalance of power brought about by shifting alliances between England, France and Spain, as in Waller's lines: 'Heaven . . . has placed this island to give law, / To balance Europe, and her states to awe' ('A Panegyric' ll. 21–2).

92. Spain's supplies of gold from the Americas had been disrupted by Admiral Blake's destruction of the plate fleet at Santa Cruz in 1657, which hampered her campaign in Flanders.

24

When absent, yet we conquered in his right,
For though some meaner artist's skill were shown
95   In mingling colours, or in placing light,
Yet still the fair designment was his own.

25

For from all tempers he could service draw;
The worth of each with its allay he knew,
And as the confidant of Nature saw
100 How she complexions did divide and brew.

26

Or he their single virtues did survey
By intuition in his own large breast,
Where all the rich ideas of them lay
That were the rule and measure to the rest.

27

105 When such heroic virtue heaven sets out,
The stars like commons sullenly obey;
Because it drains them when it comes about,
And therefore is a tax they seldom pay.

28

From this high spring our foreign conquests flow,
110 Which yet more glorious triumphs do portend,

96. designment] original design (OED 4).
97–100. For the alchemical implications of this imagery see Jack M. Armistead,
SEL xxvii (1987) 383.
98. allay] mixture of elements which detracts from the object's purity and value
(OED 4).
100. complexions] the four humours which determined the temperament of the
body (OED 1b).
101–4. Cp. Sprat on the young Cromwell: 'Then the same vertues did appear /
Though in a lesse, and more Contracted Sphear' (16). Cp. George Lawrence's
sermon on 13 October 1658: 'Those lines of Honour which by refractions ran
dispersedly in others, in him were knit up as their natural centre: and what made
others happy in division, was in him a Colledge of vertues solemnly met and
seated' (Peplum Olivarii (1658) 29). Lawrence cites Claudian: sparguntur in omnes,
/ in te mixta fluunt; et quae divisa beatos / efficiunt, collecta tenes ('To all other men
blessings come scattered, to you they flow commingled, and gifts that separately
make one happy are all together yours': De Consulatu Stilichonis i 33–5).
103. ideas] in the Platonic sense of eternal archetypes (OED 1); conception of
something in its highest perfection (OED 2). Cp. AM ll. 661–4.

Since their commencement to his arms they owe,
If springs as high as fountains may ascend.

29

He made us freemen of the continent,
Whom Nature did like captives treat before;
115 To nobler preys the English lion sent,
And taught him first in Belgian walks to roar.

30

That old, unquestioned pirate of the land,
Proud Rome, with dread the fate of Dunkirk heard,
And trembling wished behind more Alps to stand,
120 Although an Alexander were her guard.

31

By his command we boldly crossed the line,
And bravely fought where southern stars arise;
We traced the far-fetched gold unto the mine,
And that which bribed our fathers made our prize.

32

125 Such was our Prince; yet owned a soul above
The highest acts it could produce to show;

113–20. The capture of Dunkirk seemed to make Cromwell the arbiter of Europe: Thurloe said he 'carried the keys of the continent at his girdle, and was able to make invasions thereupon, and let in armies and forces upon it at his pleasure'. In particular, Cromwell renewed support for Protestants in Flanders, France and Piedmont, and pursued negotiations for a Protestant league against Catholic Austria (C. H. Firth, *Last Years of the Protectorate*, 2 vols (1909) ii 218–23). Cp. Marvell: 'Who once more joined us to the continent; / Who planted England on the Flandrick shoar' ('A Poem upon the Death of his Late Highness the Lord Protector' ll. 172–3).
115–16. Sprat says that after years when 'The Brittish Lyon hung his Main and droopt / . . . whose least voice before / . . . shook the World at every Roare /', Cromwell made him 'again afright the neighbouring Floods' (24–5).
118. heard] The spellings *h'ard* in MS and *har'd* in 1659 clearly indicate the required pronunciation.
120. Alexander] Alexander VII, Pope from 1655 to 1667; implicitly not as strong a defence as Alexander the Great.
121–3. An expedition commanded by Penn and Venables set out for the West Indies in 1654 to disrupt Spanish supplies of gold. Their attack on San Domingo in 1655 was an ignominious failure, but they did take Jamaica.
124. Spanish gold was thought to have corrupted the councillors of James I. In 1656 Captain Stayner captured part of the Spanish bullion fleet near Cadiz.

Thus poor mechanic arts in public move,
Whilst the deep secrets beyond practice go.

33
Nor died he when his ebbing fame went less,
130   But when fresh laurels courted him to live;
He seemed but to prevent some new success,
As if above what triumphs earth could give.

34
His latest victories still thickest came,
As near the centre motion does increase;
135   Till he pressed down by his own weighty name
Did like the vestal under spoils decease.

35
But first the ocean as a tribute sent
That giant prince of all her watery herd;
And th' isle, when her protecting genius went,
140   Upon his obsequies loud sighs conferred.

---

127. mechanic arts] practical applications of theory (*OED* mechanical 2b).
128. practice] calculation (*OED* 8).
129–31. Just before Cromwell's death a Spanish attempt to retake Jamaica failed; after it, the campaign in Flanders continued with the capture of Ypres on 27 September. Cp. Waller: 'Our dying hero from the continent / Ravished whole towns; and forts from Spaniards reft, / As his last legacy to Britain left' ('Upon the Late Storm' ll. 14–16).
131. prevent] anticipate.
134. 'Nature at the approaches of Death usually puts forth the utmost of her activity. A Stone in its descent increaseth in the celerity of its Motion, as it comes nearer the Center' (John Templer [D.'s tutor], *Reason of Episcopall Inspection* (1676) 26).
135. Cp. Spenser's image of Rome: 'With her own weight down pressed now she lies' ('The Ruines of Time' l. 76).
136. The vestal virgin Tarpeia betrayed Rome to the Sabines, and in recompense asked for what they had on their left arms, meaning their gold bracelets; instead they heaped their bucklers upon her and killed her (Livy I xi).
137–8. On 3 June 1658 a large whale appeared in the Thames; 'after a long Conflict it was killed with the harping yrons, & struck in the head . . . & after a horrid grone it ran quite on shore & died' (Evelyn, *Diary*). It was later interpreted as a portent: 'Flaming Comets *Divination* hold, / But *Whales*, extinct, *Divinity* unfold: / *Jonah's* Pulpit, (dead) turn'd Prophet, shew'd Thee / Thy Death, *swallow'd up into victorie*' (Samuel Slater, *A Rhetorical Rapture* (1658)).
138. her] the *MS*.
139–40. On 30 August, while Cromwell was on his deathbed, a great storm swept over England, which Waller made the theme of his memorial poem. James Heath later saw the whale and the storm as a 'prognostick that the great *Leviathan* of

36

No civil broils have since his death arose,
But faction now by habit does obey;
And wars have that respect for his repose
As winds for halcyons when they breed at sea.

37

145   His ashes in a peaceful urn shall rest,
His name a great example stands, to show
How strangely high endeavours may be blessed,
Where piety and valour jointly go.

men, that Tempest and overthrow of Government, was now going to his own place' (*Flagellum* (1663) 205; Firth).

139. genius] guardian spirit.

144. halcyons] Ovid records that for the seven days in winter when halcyons breed in a nest floating on the sea the winds are still (*Met.* xi 745–8, translated by D. in 'Ceyx and Alcyone' ll. 494–9). This image was frequently used in mid-seventeenth-century poetry for a period of peace against a background of war. It was chiefly applied to Stuart rule, but also to Cromwell's achievements by Marvell in 'The Character of Holland' ll. 127–30 and 'A Poem upon the Death of his Late Highness' ll. 79–82. See D. Palomo, *HLQ* xliv (1980–1) 205–21.

145. In peacefull Urne his sacred Ashes rest *MS*.

147. strangely] very greatly, to an exceptional degree (*OED* 4).

148. Cp. Waller: 'so much power, and piety, in one' ('A Panegyric' l. 124; quarto text).

2 Astraea Redux

Date and publication. Astraea Redux. A Poem On the Happy Restoration & Return Of His Sacred Majesty Charles the Second was published by Herringman in 1660 (advertised in *Mercurius Publicus* 21–8 June); George Thomason's copy in the BL is dated 19 June. There are two states of *1660*, the second incorporating press corrections, including one substantive change which is probably authorial (see l. 208*n*), and another which could have been made by the printing house (see l. 195*n*). The poem was reprinted in the 1688 edition of *AM*. The present edition follows *1660* with the two press corrections included.

Context. General George Monck (1608–70), commander of the army in Scotland, led his forces into England on 1 January 1660, and occupied London on 3 February. He recalled those members of the Long Parliament who had been excluded by Colonel Pride; an election was held, and on 25 April the new 'Convention Parliament' met. Charles Stuart's Declaration of Breda, which proposed the basis of a political settlement, was accepted, and he was proclaimed King on 8 May. On 25 May he landed at Dover, and entered London on the 29th, his thirtieth birthday. Monck was created Duke of Albemarle. For the political changes see Ogg 1–34; Hutton, *The Restoration* 3–123. For the rhetoric of sermons welcoming Charles see Caroline Edie, *BJRL* lxii (1979–80) 61–86.

Sources. Charles was greeted by scores of similar panegyrics; samples from these are quoted by H. T. Swedenberg in his account of the political context of D.'s poem (*SP* l (1953) 30–44), and by Nicholas Jose in *Ideas of the Restoration in English Literature, 1660–71* (1984) 1–66. D. definitely knew Martin Lluelyn, *To the King's most excellent Majesty* (Thomason's copy in the BL is dated 24 May); Thomas Higgons, *A Panegyrick to the King* (10 June); Cowley, *Ode upon the blessed Restoration and Returne* (31 May); and Waller, *To the King* (9 June). But many of D.'s images are the common stock of other panegyrics, notably in the two university collections, Oxford's *Britannia Rediviva* (7 July) and *Academiae Cantabrigiensis ΣΩΣΤΡΑ* (10 July). Winn 561 suggests some parallels with poems by Malherbe. For the poem's relation to the wider tradition of panegyric, see Garrison 155–64; and for its use of classical material see Howard Erskine-Hill, *The Augustan Idea in English Literature* (1983) 213–22, Hammond 84–92.

Astraea Redux

A Poem on the Happy Restoration and Return of His Sacred Majesty Charles the Second

Iam redit et virgo, redeunt Saturnia regna.

Virgil

Now with a general peace the world was blessed,
While ours, a world divided from the rest,
A dreadful quiet felt, and worser far
Than arms, a sullen interval of war:
5   Thus when black clouds draw down the labouring skies,
Ere yet abroad the wingèd thunder flies,

¶2. *Title. Astraea Redux* means 'Justice brought back'. Ovid in *Met.* i 89–150
(ll. 113–92 in D.'s translation, 'The First Book of Ovid's *Metamorphoses*' (1693))
recounts that the golden age of Saturn was succeeded by the increasingly degenerate ages of silver, brass and iron; in the latter Astraea (Justice) left the earth.
Virgil in *Ecl.* iv prophesies that the golden age is about to begin anew: *Iam redit
et virgo, redeunt Saturnia regna* (l. 6: 'now the virgin [Astraea] returns, the kingdom of Saturn returns'). This prophecy was associated with Augustus (cp. ll.
320–3*n* below), and was later read as a prophecy of the birth of Christ. In the
Renaissance, Astraea was associated with the monarch, particularly with
Elizabeth I (see Frances Yates, *Astraea* (1975)), though James I was also greeted
as Astraea in his coronation entry into London, when the motto from *Ecl.* iv
appeared on the Temple Bar arch. For the Augustan imagery see Swedenberg
and Erskine-Hill (cited in the headnote). D.'s handling (here and elsewhere) of
the myth of the Golden Age is discussed by Thomas H. Fujimura in *PLL* xi (1975)
149–67. The example of Astraea is also used by Samuel Willes, *To the King's
Most Sacred Majesty* (1660) 5, and in *Academiae Cantabrigiensis ΣΩΣΤΡΑ* sig. *3ᵛ.
1–2. D. echoes, and reverses, Sir Richard Fanshawe's 'An Ode Upon occasion
of His Majesties Proclamation in the yeare 1630', which opens: 'Now warre is
all the world about', and presents Britain as a haven of peace, 'A world without
the world' (Fanshawe i 55–6; Michael Cordner, *N & Q* ccxxix (1984) 341–2).
Cowley begins his poem by praising the stars which 'calm the stormy *World*, and
still the rage of *Warrs*' (*Poems* 420).
1. This hyperbole is understandable. The war between France and Spain had been
ended by the Treaty of the Pyrenees (7 November 1659) and this peace was sealed
by the spectacular wedding of Louis XIV and Maria Theresa in June 1660;
and the War of the North involving Sweden, Denmark and Brandenburg was
concluded by the Treaties of Oliva and Copenhagen (May and June 1660).
2. From Virgil, *Ecl.* i 66: *penitus toto divisos orbe Britannos* ('the Britons, completely
cut off from the whole world'). This motto was used on the Fenchurch arch in
James I's coronation entry, and in Jonson's *The Masque of Blacknesse* (1605) l. 248.
3. *dreadful quiet*] Echoes Tacitus: *ducemque terruit dira quies* ('a fearful quiet terrified
the general': *Annales* i 45; Christie). *worser*] a common seventeenth-century variant
of *worse*.
5. *labouring*] moving strenuously (*OED* labour 12); troubled (*OED* labour 15).

An horrid stillness first invades the ear,
And in that silence we the tempest fear.
Th' ambitious Swede like restless billows tossed,
10 On this hand gaining what on that he lost,
Though in his life he blood and ruin breathed,
To his now guideless kingdom peace bequeathed;
And heaven that seemed regardless of our fate,
For France and Spain did miracles create,
15 Such mortal quarrels to compose in peace
As nature bred and interest did increase.
We sighed to hear the fair Iberian bride
Must grow a lily to the lily's side,
While our cross stars denied us Charles his bed
20 Whom our first flames and virgin love did wed.
For his long absence church and state did groan,
Madness the pulpit, faction seized the throne;
Experienced age in deep despair was lost
To see the rebel thrive, the loyal crossed;
25 Youth that with joys had unacquainted been
Envied grey hairs that once good days had seen:
We thought our sires, not with their own content,
Had ere we came to age our portion spent.
Nor could our nobles hope their bold attempt

7. This line was ridiculed by several of D.'s critics: in *A Letter from a Gentleman to the Honourable Ed. Howard Esq* (1668) 6; in *The Censure of the Rota* (1673) 9; *The Friendly Vindication of Mr. Dryden* (1673) 16; and Martin Clifford, *Notes upon Mr. Dryden's Poems* (1687) 13. *Works* cites a comparable line from Cowley: 'A dreadful *Silence* fill'd the hollow place' (*Davideis* i; *Poems* 245).

9–12. Charles X of Sweden invaded Poland in 1655, but failed to secure it. In 1657–8 he twice invaded Denmark. He gained Scania, the island of Bornholm, and other territories which gave Sweden control of the Sound, but was forced to give up his claim to Prussia. At his death in February 1660 his son Charles XI was a minor, and his regents concluded peace in May–June 1660, returning Bornholm to Denmark. Contemporary English interest in his death is evidenced by *The Most Heavenly and Christian Speech of the Magnanimous and Victorious King of Sweden . . . on his Death-Bed* (1660) and the satirical *The Last Will and Testament of Carolus Gustavus* (1660).

9–10. Cp. Sir Robert Howard: 'So when the Trojan Prince was almost lost / In Storms, among ungentle billows tost' ('A Panegyrick to Generall Monck', *Poems* (1660) 283).

13–18. See l. 1n. The lily was the emblem of the French monarchy.

17. *Iberian bride*] Maria Theresa, daughter of Philip IV of Spain.

19. *cross*] adverse, unfavourable (*OED* 4). *Charles his*] i.e. Charles's.

27–8. D. applies the same image to pre-war dramatists in *EDP*: 'We acknowledge them our Fathers in wit, but they have ruin'd their Estates themselves before they came to their childrens hands' (*Works* xvii 73).

30   Who ruined crowns would coronets exempt:
      For when by their designing leaders taught
      To strike at power which for themselves they sought,
      The vulgar, gulled into rebellion, armed;
      Their blood to action by the prize was warmed.
35   The sacred purple then and scarlet gown
      Like sanguine dye to elephants was shown.
      Thus when the bold Typhoeus scaled the sky,
      And forced great Jove from his own heaven to fly,
      (What king, what crown from treason's reach is free,
40   If Jove and heaven can violated be?)
      The lesser gods that shared his prosperous state
      All suffered in the exiled Thunderer's fate.
      The rabble now such freedom did enjoy
      As winds at sea that use it to destroy:
45   Blind as the Cyclops, and as wild as he,
      They owned a lawless salvage liberty,

33. *The vulgar*] the common people.
35. The purple of bishops and scarlet of doctors, judges, and aldermen.
36. From Maccabees vi 34: 'And to the end they might provoke the elephants
to fight, they showed them the blood of grapes and mulberries' (Winn, privately).
37–44. Typhoeus or Typhon was the monstrous offspring of Earth and Hell, who
had a hundred heads which spoke with changeable voices. When he assaulted
Olympus the gods fled to Egypt; Zeus eventually buried him under Mount Etna,
where he generated winds which wreak havoc at sea (Hesiod, *Theogony* ll. 820–80;
Apollodorus I vi 3). The image is used similarly in *Academiae Cantabrigiensis ΣΩΣΤΡΑ*
sigs *4ʳ; B4ᵛ and D1ʳ. *Mercurius Publicus* (24–31 May) describing Charles's entry
into London recalled that '*Jupiter* himself was not quiet in Heaven till after a long
war with the Giants' (351). The myth of Typhon had been variously applied by
seventeenth-century writers. Francis Bacon interpreted it as an allegory of rebellion in his *De Sapientia Veterum* (1609) ch. 2.
45. *Cyclops*] Polyphemus, who was blinded by Odysseus (*Odyssey* ix 375–97). The
commonwealth without a king is compared to Polyphemus without an eye by
Ross 73; John Gauden, *Κακούργοι* (1660; sermon preached 28 February, printed
text dated 28 March by Thomason on his copy in BL) 63; and Waller, ll. 19–21.
D. uses the image again in *The Medal* ll. 226–7.
46–8. For this picture of man in the state of nature cp. Virgil's account of
society before the reign of Saturn: *Aen.* viii 314–18 (translated in D.'s 'The Eighth
Book of the *Aeneis*' ll. 417–24). In *AA* ll. 53–6 D. again associates the Commonwealth with the lawless state of nature. In *1 Conquest of Granada* D. has Almanzor
imagine the state of nature as a time of innocence, following Montaigne's essay
'Des Cannibales' and anticipating Rousseau by coining the phrase 'the noble
savage': 'I am as free as Nature first made man / 'Ere the base Laws of Servitude
began / When wild in woods the noble Savage ran.' (I i 207–9). See also 'To
Dr Charleton' l. 13.
46. *salvage*] variant form of *savage* (the spelling recalls the word's Latin origin from
silva, 'wood').

Like that our painted ancestors so prized
Ere empire's arts their breasts had civilized.
How great were then our Charles his woes, who thus
50 Was forced to suffer for himself and us!
He, tossed by Fate, and hurried up and down,
Heir to his father's sorrows with his crown,
Could taste no sweets of youth's desirèd age,
But found his life too true a pilgrimage.
55 Unconquered yet in that forlorn estate,
His manly courage overcame his fate.
His wounds he took like Romans on his breast,
Which by his virtue were with laurels dressed.
As souls reach heaven while yet in bodies pent,
60 So did he live above his banishment.
That sun which we beheld with cozened eyes
Within the water, moved along the skies.
How easy 'tis when Destiny proves kind
With full-spread sails to run before the wind;
65 But those that 'gainst stiff gales laveering go
Must be at once resolved and skilful too.
He would not like soft Otho hope prevent
But stayed and suffered Fortune to repent:
These virtues Galba in a stranger sought,

51. Cp. Higgons: 'Thus great Æneas when his Troy was lost, / And nought but ruine left of all that State, / Wander'd at Land, and on the Floods was tost, / And hurried up and down the World by Fate' (*A Panegyrick* 10). See also Cowley (st. xiii) and Robert Howard (*Poems* (1660) 283). *hurried*] driven rapidly (*OED* 1c); harassed (*OED* 3).
52. Apparently echoed by J. Ailmer in the anthology *Britannia Rediviva*: 'Heir to thy Fathers Sufferings, and his Crown' (sig. Bb3ʳ).
55. *estate*] condition.
57. Roman soldiers considered it a dishonour to receive wounds behind.
59. Referring either to the soul's capacity for mystical contact with God while still on earth, or to the bodily translation of some prophets to heaven (e.g. Enoch and Elijah).
61–2. i.e. we could see Charles's movements only indirectly, like people who see the sun's movements reflected in water.
61. *cozened*] deceived.
65. *laveering*] tacking.
67–70. Galba, Emperor of Rome AD 68–9, adopted Piso as his heir instead of the effeminate Otho. Otho revolted, had Galba and Piso murdered, and briefly gained power. But he was attacked by Vitellius, and after being defeated at Brixellum killed himself in despair (Suetonius).
67. *prevent*] cut off in advance (*OED* 6), frustrate, preclude, defeat (*OED* 10).
68. *suffered*] allowed.

70   And Piso to adopted empire brought.
       How shall I then my doubtful thoughts express
       That must his sufferings both regret and bless!
       For when his early valour heaven had crossed,
       And all at Worcester but the honour lost,
75   Forced into exile from his rightful throne
       He made all countries where he came his own;
       And viewing monarchs' secret arts of sway
       A royal factor for their kingdoms lay.
       Thus banished David spent abroad his time,
80   When to be God's anointed was his crime,
       And when restored made his proud neighbours rue
       Those choice remarks he from his travels drew.
       Nor is he only by afflictions shown
       To conquer others' realms, but rule his own:
85   Recov'ring hardly what he lost before,

74. Recalls the statement of François I of France to his mother after his defeat at Pavia (1525): 'all is lost except our honour'. Cp. Higgons: 'And won Renown, although you lost the field' (*A Panegyrick* 8). Charles was defeated by Cromwell at the Battle of Worcester in 1651 and subsequently escaped to France.

76–86. This passage resembles (and perhaps contributed to) T. Topping's verses in the anthology *Britannia Rediviva*: 'the Universe must be his School: / Thus Fate prov'd kind even against her will, / And whiles she did neglect him, taught him skill. / Thrice happy we! that our great Monarch thus / Must learn to Govern *Europe* first, then us. / While other Kings only their Crowns inherit, / The Crown is his by Birth-right and by Merit' (sig. Cc3ᵛ).

76–7. Cp. Waller: 'For, having viewed the persons and the things, / The councils, state, and strength of Europe's kings, / You know your work' (ll. 41–3); and cp. Jonson, 'To William Roe': 'th'art now, to goe / Countries, and climes, manners, and men to know, / T'extract, and choose the best of all these knowne, / And those to turne to bloud, and make thine owne' (ll. 1–4; *Epigrammes* cxxviii). D. commented again on the results of Charles's exile in his 'Defence of the Epilogue': 'His own misfortunes and the Nations, afforded him an opportunity, which is rarely allow'd to Sovereign Princes, I mean of travelling, and being conversant in the most polish'd Courts of *Europe*; and, thereby, of cultivating a Spirit, which was form'd by Nature, to receive the impression of a gallant and generous education. At his return, he found a Nation lost as much in Barbarism as in Rebellion: and as the excellency of his Nature forgave the one, so the excellency of his manners reform'd the other' (*Works* xi 216; Kinsley).

78. *factor*] deputy: i.e. by being a kind of understudy, Charles learned the art of government.

79. See 2 Samuel xv–xxi. For the comparison of David and Charles see the headnote to *AA*.

80. Cp. Lluelyn: 'But to be born our Prince, was all Thy Crimes' (*To the King's . . . Majesty* 3).

82. *remarks*] observations.

85. *hardly*] with difficulty (*OED* 6).

His right endears it much, his purchase more.
Inured to suffer ere he came to reign,
No rash procedure will his actions stain;
To business ripened by digestive thought,
90 His future rule is into method brought:
As they who first proportion understand
With easy practice reach a master's hand.
Well might the ancient poets then confer
On night the honoured name of counsellor,
95 Since struck with rays of prosperous fortune blind,
We light alone in dark afflictions find.
In such adversities to sceptres trained,
The name of Great his famous grandsire gained;
Who yet a king alone in name and right,
100 With hunger, cold and angry Jove did fight;
Shocked by a covenanting league's vast powers,
As holy and as catholic as ours,
Till Fortune's fruitless spite had made it known
Her blows not shook but riveted his throne.
105 Some lazy ages, lost in sleep and ease,
No action leave to busy chronicles;
Such whose supine felicity but makes
In story chasms, in epoches mistakes;

---

86. purchase] acquisition of property by one's own action, as distinct from inheritance (*OED* 5).

89. digestive] tending to methodize and reduce to order (*OED* 6; sole example).

91–2. An image from drawing.

93–4. Proverbial. In his comments on the adage *In nocte consilium* in his *Adagiorum Chiliades* Erasmus cites Sophocles, Plato and Plutarch. Cp. also Spenser, *FQ* 1 i 33.

98–104. Charles's maternal grandfather Henri IV of France (1553–1610) became nominal king in 1589. A Protestant, he was opposed by many of his subjects through the Catholic League, until he became a Catholic in 1593. Henri extended the powers of the crown and restored prosperity to the country. D.'s perception of a parallel with the English Solemn League and Covenant (1643) was anticipated by the royalist pamphlet *Mercurius Rusticus* (1646): 'the *holy League* in *France*, the *Prototype* of the present *Rebellion* in *England*' (sig. N1ʳ). D. said that he sketched a play about the Catholic League in 1660, which was completed in 1682 as *The Duke of Guise*. D. returns to the parallel in the Postscript to his translation of Maimbourg's *History of the League* (1684; *Works* xviii 393–415).

105–6. ease . . . chronicles] Christie notes that D. similarly rhymes *ease* and *articles* in 'To Sir George Etherege' ll. 36–7; for a comparable pronunciation of *miracles* see 'To the Memory of Anne Killigrew' l. 52.

107. supine] accented on the second syllable. D. frequently uses the word for the relaxed enjoyment of ease: cp. *MF* l. 28.

108. epoches] dates of historical events (*OED* 3); probably trisyllabic, as in the Greek ἐποχή.

O'er whom Time gently shakes his wings of down,
110 Till with his silent sickle they are mown:
Such is not Charles his too, too active age,
Which governed by the wild distempered rage
Of some black star infecting all the skies,
Made him at his own cost like Adam wise.
115 Tremble ye nations who, secure before,
Laughed at those arms that 'gainst ourselves we bore;
Roused by the lash of his own stubborn tail,
Our lion now will foreign foes assail.
With alga who the sacred altar strows?
120 To all the sea-gods Charles an offering owes:
A bull to thee, Portunus, shall be slain,
A lamb to you, the tempests of the main:
For those loud storms that did against him roar
Have cast his shipwracked vessel on the shore.
125 Yet as wise artists mix their colours so
That by degrees they from each other go,
Black steals unheeded from the neighbouring white
Without offending the well-cozened sight:
So on us stole our blessèd change, while we
130 Th' effect did feel, but scarce the manner see.
Frosts that constrain the ground, and birth deny
To flowers that in its womb expecting lie,

112. distempered] immoderate, intemperate (*OED* 5).
115–18. Cp. Waller, 'To My Lord of Falkland': 'our proud neighbours . . . ere long shall mourn / (Though now they joy in our expected harms) / . . . A lion so with self-provoking smart, / (His rebel tail scourging his noble part) / Calls up his courage; then begins to roar / And charge his foes, who thought him mad before' (ll. 34–40). With D.'s political viewpoint here contrast 'Heroic Stanzas' ll. 113–16.
119. alga] seaweed. *strows*] strews.
121. Portunus] the god of harbours (see *Aen.* v 241–3; Ovid, *Fasti* vi 545–8).
122. A lamb is sacrificed to the Tempests in *Aen.* v 772.
125–30. Sir Robert Howard also saw the Restoration as happening by degrees: 'Yet by degrees you mov'd, as after Night / The Sun begins to shew the World its light. / At whose approach, darknesse its place resignes, / And though it seems to move not, yet it shines. / So softly you began to spread your beams, / Through all our factions, dark in all extreams' ('A Panegyrick to Generall Monck', *Poems* (1660) 285).
125–8. This technique is advocated by William Sanderson: 'the sight must be sweetly deceived, by degrees, in breaking the Colours, by insensible passage, from higher Colours, to more dimme'; 'deceiving the Eye with a stealth of change' they 'lightly and smoothly coosin the Eye' (*Graphice* (1658) 23, 48).
130. Cp. Cowley: 'The manner *How* lies hid, th' *effect* we see' (*Davideis* ii; *Poems* 284).
131–6. Cp. *AM* ll. 1133–8.

Do seldom their usurping power withdraw,
But raging floods pursue their hasty thaw:
135   Our thaw was mild, the cold not chased away,
But lost in kindly heat of lengthened day.
Heaven would no bargain for its blessings drive,
But what we could not pay for, freely give.
The Prince of Peace would, like himself, confer
140   A gift unhoped without the price of war:
Yet as he knew his blessing's worth, took care
That we should know it by repeated prayer,
Which stormed the skies and ravished Charles from thence,
As heaven itself is took by violence.
145   Booth's forward valour only served to show
He durst that duty pay we all did owe:
Th' attempt was fair, but heaven's prefixèd hour
Not come; so like the watchful traveller
That by the moon's mistaken light did rise,
150   Lay down again, and closed his weary eyes.
'Twas Monck whom Providence designed to loose
Those real bonds false freedom did impose.
The blessèd saints that watched this turning scene
Did from their stars with joyful wonder lean
155   To see small clues draw vastest weights along,
Not in their bulk but in their order strong.
Thus pencils can by one slight touch restore

136. kindly] nurturing.
137–40. The idea of God's free gift comes from Romans v 15–18.
139. Prince of Peace] a title for the Messiah from Isaiah ix 6.
140. unhoped] not expected, not hoped for.
144. The phrasing is from Matthew xi 12 ('the kingdom of heaven suffereth violence'); the idea of prayer as importunate is from Luke xi 5–10.
145. Booth] In August 1659 Sir George Booth led a rising for Charles in Cheshire, but was defeated by the Republic's forces under John Lambert. *forward*] ready, prompt (*OED* 6).
147–8. hour / Not come] echoing John viii 20.
151. Monck] See headnote.
155. clues] threads. The image is of a pulley; D. could have found such machines described and illustrated in John Wilkins, *Mathematicall Magick* (1648) 86–102. This apparent paradox was the subject of University Act verses at Cambridge: see *Minima vis potest movere maximum pondus* [*c.* 1585–90], which has a large woodcut of cogwheels. Bacon said that historians must attend to the hidden causes of public events, for God 'doth hang the greatest weight upon the smallest wires' (*The Advancement of Learning* (1605) II ii 5). Cp. Cowley: 'Strange *Play* of *Fate!* when might'iest humane things / Hang on such small, *Imperceptible Strings!*' (*Davideis* iv; *Poems* 374).
156. order] arrangement.
157. pencils] paint brushes (*OED* 1).

Smiles to that changèd face that wept before.
With ease such fond chimeras we pursue
160   As fancy frames for fancy to subdue,
But when ourselves to action we betake
It shuns the mint like gold that chymists make.
How hard was then his task, at once to be
What in the body natural we see
165   Man's architect distinctly did ordain
The charge of muscles, nerves, and of the brain;
Through viewless conduits spirits to dispense,
The springs of motion from the seat of sense.
'Twas not the hasty product of a day,
170   But the well-ripened fruit of wise delay.
He like a patient angler, ere he strook
Would let them play a while upon the hook.
Our healthful food the stomach labours thus,
At first embracing what it straight doth crush.
175   Wise leeches will not vain receipts obtrude,
While growing pains pronounce the humours crude;
Deaf to complaints, they wait upon the ill
Till some safe crisis authorize their skill.
Nor could his acts too close a vizard wear
180   To scape their eyes whom guilt had taught to fear,
And guard with caution that polluted nest
Whence Legion twice before was dispossessed;

160. *fancy*] the imagination.
162. *It*] The antecedent is probably *fancy* (but possibly *chimera* or *action*).   *mint*]
place of assay; test.   *chymists*] alchemists.
163–8. i.e. 'How hard was it for Monck to perform [in the body politic] the
three functions which we see that God, in designing the natural body, has ordained
to be the separate responsibility of muscles, nerves, and brain: to send through
invisible channels of communication impulses from the brain which will stimulate action'. The image comes from contemporary physiology: 'The animal spirits
. . . resemble a very subtle wind, or rather a flame which is very pure and very
vivid, and which, continually rising up in great abundance from the heart to the
brain, thence proceeds through the nerves to the muscles, thereby giving the power
of motion to all the members' (Descartes, *Discours de la Méthode* (1637) V; *Philosophical
Works* tr. Elizabeth S. Haldane and G. R. T. Ross, 2 vols (1911) i 115).
167. *viewless*] invisible.
175–6. The medical metaphor is the theme of John Gauden's sermon Κακοῦργοι
(see l. 45*n*).   *leeches*] doctors.   *receipts*] recipes.   *humours*] bodily fluids which were
thought to determine health.   *crude*] undigested (*OED* 3).
179. *vizard*] mask.
181–2. Parliament was dissolved by Cromwell in 1653 and by Lambert in 1659.
Legion is the devil in Luke viii 26–36.

Once sacred house which when they entered in
They thought the place could sanctify a sin,
185   Like those that vainly hoped kind heaven would wink
While to excess on martyrs' tombs they drink:
And as devouter Turks first warn their souls
To part, before they taste forbidden bowls,
So these when their black crimes they went about
190   First timely charmed their useless conscience out.
Religion's name against itself was made;
The shadow served the substance to invade:
Like zealous missions they did care pretend
Of souls in show, but made the gold their end.
195   Th' incensèd powers beheld with scorn from high
An heaven so far distant from the sky,
Which durst with horses' hoofs that beat the ground
And martial brass belie the thunder's sound.
'Twas hence at length just Vengeance thought it fit
200   To speed their ruin by their impious wit.
Thus Sforza, cursed with a too fertile brain,

185. wink] close its eyes.
186. Probably a reference to the desecration of churches during the Civil War: soldiers quartered in Westminster Abbey 'set Formes about the Communion Table, there they eat, and there they drink Ale' (*Mercurius Rusticus* (1646) 216). Henry King's elegy for Charles I catalogues similar outrages (*Poems* (1664) 25–7). St Augustine knew of some early Christians who held sacrilegious banquets on tombs (*Patrologia Latina* xxxii 1342).
187–8. 'One [Turk] drinking wine . . . made great clamors; being asked the cause, he said he did it to warne his soule to flee into some corner of the bodie, or else be quite gone, lest it should be polluted with that sinne' (*Purchas his Pilgrimage* (1614) 294); cp. Burton, *Anatomy of Melancholy* 3. 4. 1. 3.
189–90. Commanders of the Parliamentary armies held prayer meetings before major actions.
190. timely] quickly (*OED* 1).
191. made] pressed into military service, enlisted (*OED* 15a).
195–8. Salmoneus tried to imitate the thunder and lightning of Jove by waving torches and driving his chariot over brass arches, in order to be worshipped as a god by his subjects. Jove struck him with a thunderbolt (Virgil, *Aen.* vi 585–94).
195. beheld] 1660 *second state*; behold 1660 *first state*.
200. wit] intelligence.
201–2. Lodovico Sforza, *il Moro* (1451–1508) poisoned his nephew Giovanni and succeeded him as Duke of Milan. He was betrayed by his own mercenaries to Louis XII of France in 1500, and died a prisoner. 'He carried a mind vaine, and full of thoughts busie and ambitious, and nourishing alwayes intentions dissembled, he kept no reckoning of his promises and faith. . . . This was a grosse error in his policie, to breed the storme, . . . fire suffered to runne, burnes without limite, even to the consuming of such as first kindled it' (Guicciardini, *Historie*, tr. G. Fenton, third edition (1618) 183, 30–1).

Lost by his wiles the power his wit did gain.
Henceforth their fogue must spend at lesser rate
Than in its flames to wrap a nation's fate.
205 Suffered to live, they are like helots set
A virtuous shame within us to beget:
For by example most we sinned before,
And glass-like, clearness mixed with frailty bore.
But since reformed by what we did amiss,
210 We by our sufferings learn to prize our bliss:
Like early lovers whose unpractised hearts
Were long the May-game of malicious arts,
When once they find their jealousies were vain,
With double heat renew their fires again.
215 'Twas this produced the joy that hurried o'er
Such swarms of English to the neighbouring shore,
To fetch that prize by which Batavia made
So rich amends for our impoverished trade.
O had you seen from Scheveline's barren shore
220 (Crowded with troops, and barren now no more)
Afflicted Holland to his farewell bring
True sorrow, Holland to regret a king;
While waiting him his royal fleet did ride,
And willing winds to their low'red sails denied,
225 The wavering streamers, flags and standard out,

---

203. fogue] fury, passion (*OED*'s first example); a borrowing from French.
205–6. The Spartans would sometimes make their slaves (helots) drunk and exhibit them to their young men to show them the evil of drunkenness (Plutarch, *Lycurgus* 28).
208. And glass-like] *1660 second state*; Like glass we *1660 first state*.
216. Clarendon recalled that 'Breda swarmed with English, a multitude repairing thither . . . with presents, and protestations how much they had longed and prayed for this blessed change, and magnifying their sufferings under the late tyrannical government, when many of them had been zealous ministers and promoters of it' (*History* xvi 234). One such was D.'s cousin John Pickering (Pepys, 16, 22 May 1660).
217. Batavia] Holland.
218. In 1660 English trade was depressed, partly because of competition from Holland for the conveyance of goods (Ogg 219–23).
219–20. Charles embarked from Sheveling (now Scheveningen) near The Hague on 23 May. Pepys noted on 22 May that 'the shore was so full of people . . . as that it was as black (which otherwise is white sand) as everyone would stand by another'.
222. The United Provinces of the Netherlands was a republic. (Holland was one of the chief constituent states, though its name was loosely applied in English to the whole federation.)

The merry seamen's rude but cheerful shout,
And last the cannons' voice that shook the skies, ⎫
And, as it fares in sudden ecstasies,   ⎬
At once bereft us both of ears and eyes.   ⎭
230   The *Naseby* now no longer England's shame,
But better to be lost in Charles his name
(Like some unequal bride in nobler sheets)
Receives her lord: the joyful *London* meets
The princely York, himself alone a freight;
235   The *Swiftsure* groans beneath great Gloucester's weight.
Secure as when the halcyon breeds, with these
He that was born to drown might cross the seas.
Heaven could not own a providence and take
The wealth three nations ventured at a stake.
240   The same indulgence Charles his voyage blessed
Which in his right had miracles confessed.
The winds that never moderation knew,
Afraid to blow too much, too faintly blew;
Or out of breath with joy could not enlarge
245   Their straitened lungs, or conscious of their charge.
The British Amphitrite smooth and clear
In richer azure never did appear;
Proud her returning Prince to entertain
With the submitted fasces of the main.

226. *rude*] rough.
227–9. 'My Lord fired all his guns round twice, and all the fleet after him; which in the end fell into disorder, which seemed very handsome. . . . Nothing in the world but going of guns almost all this day' (Pepys, 22 May).
228. *fares*] happens. *ecstasies*] trances.
230–1. 'After dinner, the King and Duke . . . altered the name of some of the Shipps, *viz*. the *Nazeby* into *Charles* . . .' (Pepys, 23 May).
232. *unequal*] of lower social status.
233–5. 'The Duke of Yorke went on board the *London*, and the Duke of Glocester the *Swiftsure*' (Pepys, 23 May).
235. From *Aen.* vi 412–13: *accipit alveo / ingentem Aenean. gemuit sub pondere cumba* ('[Charon] received great Aeneas in his boat. The boat groaned under the weight').
236. For halcyons see 'Heroic Stanzas' l. 144*n*.
238. *own a providence*] say that the world is governed by divine providence.
241. *confessed*] made known, revealed (*OED* 5).
243. Thomas Fuller writes that the wind 'fearing that his *Breath* might be too rough, / Prov'd *over-civil*, and was scarce enough' (*A Panegyrick to his Majesty* 8).
244–5. *Or . . . or*] Either . . . or.
246. *Amphitrite*] wife of Neptune and goddess of the sea.
249. *submitted fasces*] When the consul Publius Valerius appeared before the people to answer allegations of ambition, he ordered the lictors to walk with

250 And welcome now, great monarch, to your own;
Behold th' approaching cliffs of Albion;
It is no longer motion cheats your view:
As you meet it, the land approacheth you.
The land returns, and in the white it wears
255 The marks of penitence and sorrow bears.
But you, whose goodness your descent doth show,
Your heavenly parentage, and earthly too;
By that same mildness which your father's crown
Before did ravish, shall secure your own.
260 Not tied to rules of policy, you find
Revenge less sweet than a forgiving mind.
Thus when th' Almighty would to Moses give
A sight of all he could behold and live,
A voice before his entry did proclaim
265 Long-suffering, goodness, mercy in his name.
Your power to justice doth submit your cause,
Your goodness only is above the laws,
Whose rigid letter while pronounced by you
Is softer made. So winds that tempests brew
270 When through Arabian groves they take their flight,

---

lowered fasces (*submissis fascibus*) as a sign of the people's superior authority (Livy ii 7). Many panegyrists write of Neptune surrendering his trident (e.g. Robert Wild, *Iter Boreale* 19; *Britannia Rediviva* sigs B3ʳ, F4ʳ). For D.'s later uses of the image see 'Verses to her Highness the Duchess' (prefixed to *AM*) ll. 15–16; *AM* ll. 197–200; *Threnodia Augustalis* ll. 516–17; and his addition of the line 'And *Neptune* shall resign the Fasces of the Sea' to Virgil's praise of Augustus in 'The First Book of the *Georgics*' l. 42. *submitted*] lowered (*OED* 8). *fasces*] bundle of rods bound up with an axe in the middle, carried by Roman lictors in front of the chief magistrates as a symbol of their power.

250. A line space precedes this line in *1660*, marking a new section.

253. Hoffman 12 sees this as an accurate image for the Restoration, which was not a surrender, but a rapprochement on agreed terms.

254. *white*] The cliffs of Dover; to stand publicly in a white sheet was a form of penance for fornication or adultery.

258–65. For mercy as a characteristic of Charles II, cp. *AM* ll. 1053–6; *To My Lord Chancellor* ll. 55–60; *AA* ll. 146, 939; *Threnodia Augustalis* ll. 86–9.

260. *rules of policy*] As in Machiavelli, who wrote that an incoming ruler should decide what cruelty was necessary and inflict it immediately (*Prince* ch. 8). For Machiavelli, cp. 'Heroic Stanzas' ll. 29–30*n*.

261, 266–9. In the Declaration of Breda (14 April) Charles offered pardon to all except those whom Parliament decided to exclude; this was effected in the Act of Indemnity of 29 August.

262–5. See Exodus xxxiii 19 to xxxiv 10; and cp. *AA* ll. 1007–9*n*.

267. The idea may recall Cowley: 'To do much *Good* his *sole Prerogative*' (*Davideis* iv; *Poems* 377).

Made wanton with rich odours, lose their spite.
And as those lees that trouble it, refine
The agitated soul of generous wine,
So tears of joy for your returning spilt,
275 Work out and expiate our former guilt.
Methinks I see those crowds on Dover's strand,
Who in their haste to welcome you to land
Choked up the beach with their still growing store,
And made a wilder torrent on the shore;
280 While spurred with eager thoughts of past delight,
Those who had seen you court a second sight,
Preventing still your steps, and making haste
To meet you often wheresoe'er you passed.
How shall I speak of that triumphant day
285 When you renewed th' expiring pomp of May?
(A month that owns an interest in your name:
You and the flowers are its peculiar claim.)
That star that at your birth shone out so bright
It stained the duller sun's meridian light,
290 Did once again its potent fires renew,
Guiding our eyes to find and worship you.

272–3. *Trouble* and *agitate* are technical terms from fermentation (W. Hughes, *Compleat Vineyard* (1670) 53). *generous*] rich, strong; a common epithet for wine.
276–8. Pepys (25 May) noted: 'Infinite the Croud of people and the gallantry of the Horsmen, Citizens, and Noblemen of all sorts'. The scene is described by John Price in *A Letter written from Dover* (1660).
282. *Preventing*] going ahead of.
286–7. This idea is also used by Whichcote: *Mensis erat* Maius *quem Tu* nascendo *beasse / Diceris, & roseis condecorasse genis* ('It was the month of May which you are said to have blessed with your birth, and to have ornamented it with roses': *Academiae Cantabrigiensis ΣΩΣΤΡΑ* sig. A3ʳ).
287. *peculiar*] special.
288–9. On the day of Charles's birth in 1630 a bright star was seen in the midday sky. This is a commonplace of panegyrics on the Restoration, but D. particularly echoes Cowley: the star 'At *Charls* his *Birth*, did, in despight / Of the proud *Sun*'s Meridian Light, / His future *Glories*, and this *Year* foreshow / . . . Auspicious *Star* again arise' (*Poems* 421). Roettier's medal commemorating Charles's landing at Dover shows a star over the King's ship (Hawkins i 457–8).
289. *stained*] obscured the lustre of (*OED* 1b, c).
291. Evocations of the birth of Christ were likewise common; cp. 'I've seen *your Star*, and worship' (William Fairebrother, *An Essay of a Loyal Brest* (1660) 2; cp. *Britannia Rediviva* sigs a3ᵛ, Bb2ʳ). At his birth Herrick had written: 'At Noone of Day, was seene a silver Star, / Bright as the Wise-mens Torch, which guided them / To Gods sweet Babe, when borne at *Bethlehem*' ('A Pastorall upon the Birth of Prince *Charles*' ll. 20–2, in *Hesperides*; Kinsley). Cp. also the implications of D.'s epigraph (see note on title).

And now time's whiter series is begun,
Which in soft centuries shall smoothly run;
Those clouds that overcast your morn shall fly
295 Dispelled to farthest corners of the sky.
Our nation with united interest blessed,
Not now content to poise, shall sway the rest:
Abroad your empire shall no limits know,
But like the sea in boundless circles flow.
300 Your much-loved fleet shall with a wide command
Besiege the petty monarchs of the land:
And as old Time his offspring swallowed down,
Our ocean in its depths all seas shall drown.
Their wealthy trade from pirates' rapine free,
305 Our merchants shall no more adventurers be:
Nor in the farthest east those dangers fear
Which humble Holland must dissemble here.
Spain to your gift alone her Indies owes,
For what the powerful takes not, he bestows;
310 And France that did an exile's presence fear
May justly apprehend you still too near.

292–3. The renewal of time is a feature of the return of the golden age in Virgil's
Ecl. iv 4–7. Cp. Cowley: 'Such are the *years* (great *Charles*) which now we see
/ Begin their *glorious March* with Thee' (*Poems* 427); John Tatham, *London's Glory*
(1660) 1; and *AM* ll. 69–72; *AA* ll. 1028–9 (Kinsley).
292. whiter] more innocent (*OED* 7); more fortunate (*OED* 8); senses of the
Latin *alba.   series*] perhaps also a Latinism: cp. *innumerabilis annorum series et fuga
temporum* ('innumerable series of years and flight of time'; Horace, *Carm.* III xxx
5–6).
293. soft] The Latin *mollis* when applied to time can have the sense of 'propitious' (e.g. Virgil, *Aen.* iv 293).
297. See 'Heroic Stanzas' l. *91n.*
302. Chronos (Time) swallowed his children because it was prophesied that one
of his sons would dethrone him (Hesiod, *Theogony* ll. 453–67).
305. adventurers] Merchants will still be sharers in commercial enterprises (*OED*
adventurer 4), but they will no longer be waging war at their own risk (*OED* 3).
306–7. The Dutch had a virtual monopoly of the spice trade with the Far East;
now they will humbly have to pretend not to notice (*dissemble, OED* 3) the threats
to their economic survival posed by English naval dominance in the Channel.
308–9. Jamaica had been captured from Spain in 1655, and attempts were made
to colonize Guiana; but the only threat to the wealthy and extensive Spanish
possessions on the American mainland was to come from pirates.
310. Mazarin offered financial inducements to Charles to leave France for
Germany in 1654 as he was negotiating an alliance with Cromwell. Under this
treaty, signed on 24 October 1655, France excluded Charles, James and seventeen royalists from her territories.

At home the hateful names of parties cease
And factious souls are wearied into peace.
The discontented now are only they
315 Whose crimes before did your just cause betray:
Of those your edicts some reclaim from sins,
But most your life and blessed example wins.
O happy prince, whom heaven hath taught the way
By paying vows, to have more vows to pay!
320 O happy age! O times like those alone
By Fate reserved for great Augustus' throne!
When the joint growth of arms and arts foreshow
The world a monarch, and that monarch *you*.

312. The 1640s and 1650s had seen the proliferation of political and religious groups
with their own programmes for the country. Many had striking names, e.g. Levellers,
Diggers, Ranters, Quakers.
316. Sir Charles Firth saw that this refers to Charles's 'Proclamation against vicious,
debauched, and prophane persons' of 30 May 1660.
319. 'By keeping (*OED* pay 7a) your kingly vows of faithfulness to your people
and church you have attracted more vows of obedience from them, which you
must in turn honour' (and perhaps 'reward': *OED* pay 4).
320–3. In Virgil, *Aen.* vi 791–4 Anchises prophesies the return of the golden age
with Augustus: *hic vir, hic est, tibi quem promitti saepius audis, / Augustus Caesar,
divi genus, aurea condet / saecula qui rursus Latio regnata per arva / Saturno quondam*
('*Augustus*, promis'd oft, and long foretold, / Sent to the Realm that *Saturn* rul'd
of old; / Born to restore a better Age of Gold': tr. by D., ll. 1079–81). Higgons
also saw a parallel: 'When Rome was ruin'd with intestine hate, / Augustus took
the rudder of the State' (*A Panegyrick* 5).
322. *foreshow*] The spelling *foreshew* in 1660 provides a perfect rhyme with *you*.
323. Cp. Lluelyn: 'We still request a King, and that King, Thee' (*To the King's
. . . Majesty* 5; *Works*).

3 Annus Mirabilis

Date and publication. In 1665 D. left London to avoid the plague, perhaps soon
after the theatres closed on 5 June; the vivid description of the sounds of the
Battle of Lowestoft (3 June) at the opening of *EDP* suggests that he was still in
London then (see also the 'Verses to her Highness the Duchess' ll. 13–20, 30–2).
He retired to Charlton, Wiltshire, the seat of his father-in-law Thomas Howard,
Earl of Berkshire. He stayed there until the end of 1666, composing *Secret Love,
AM* and *EDP.* The poem depicts events from March 1665 to September 1666, and
was probably composed in the summer and autumn of 1666; the address to
Sir Robert Howard is dated 10 November 1666. On grounds of style and tone
Works (i 257) suggests that the verses on the fire were an afterthought, but this
is mere speculation. *Annus Mirabilis: The Year of Wonders, 1666* was licensed by
L'Estrange on 22 November 1666 and published by Herringman early in 1667
(*SR* 21 January). New light on the exact date and circumstances of the publication is shed by a letter from Sir Allen Brodrick to the Duke of Ormonde dated
29 December 1666: 'There is a Poem of the last Sumers Sea Fights by Mr Dreyden
in the Press, which I had hoped to inclose for your Graces divertisement, the
next shall certaynely bring it, for I suppose it deteyned only for the Ceremony
of a New Years guift to the Prince and Generall'. On 1 January 1667 he wrote
that 'I sent your Grace Mr Drydens by the last Post' (BodL MS Carte 35 ff. 191ʳ
and 232ʳ; information from Nicholas von Maltzahn, privately). Pepys bought a
copy on 2 February. Two alterations were made after the initial printing: in the
second issue C6 was cancelled and replaced with a leaf giving a revised version
of stanza 105; in the third issue C1 was also cancelled and a revised version of
l. 267 substituted (this C1 cancellans exists in two settings): for the variants see
the notes below. Since D. was in Wiltshire when *1667* was printed he asked
Sir Robert Howard to see it through the press. Howard failed to spot a number
of errors, and *1667* has a note 'To the Readers' (sig. a4ʳ) in which D. says:
'Notwithstanding the diligence which has been used in my absence, some faults
have escap'd the Press: and I have so many of my own to answer for, that I am
not willing to be charg'd with those of the Printer. I have onely noted the gross-
est of them, not such as by false stops have confounded the sense, but such as
by mistaken words have corrupted it'. An errata list follows. The present text is
from *1667*, third issue, with readings from the errata list silently incorporated. *AM*
was reprinted in 1668 (probably pirated) and 1688, but there is no evidence that
D. oversaw these editions. *1688* makes some necessary corrections (followed here)
but also adds many errors; some changes of wording could be attributable to D.
(see l. 649*n*), but they could easily have been made in the printing house.

Context. The euphoria of the Restoration soon gave way to dissension, and (in
1665–7) to a series of disasters (see Hutton, *The Restoration* 185–267). The year
1666 was widely expected to be a year of disaster, since 666 is the number of
the beast in Revelation xiii 18 (see D. Brady, *BJRL* lxi (1978–9) 314–36). As
Malone noted (ii 249) D.'s title echoes the titles of three pamphlets which reported
recent prodigies and held that these were divine judgements on England for the
ungodly behaviour of King and court: *Mirabilis Annus, the Year of Prodigies* (1661)
and *Mirabilis Annus Secundus; or, the Second Year of Prodigies,* in two parts (1662).
See also Gadbury, cited in l. 64*n*. E. N. Hooker (*HLQ* x (1946) 49–67) argued
that D. was responding to the apocalyptic prophecies of such opposition writers

by portraying the war and the fire not as judgements but as trials which a virtuous country and city should bear patiently, submissive to the King and providence. Nevertheless, apprehension about 1666 was not confined to dissidents: Sandwich told Pepys that he dreaded the issue of that year (25 February 1666), and Pepys himself bought a copy of Francis Potter's *An Interpretation of the Number 666* (1642), which, he said, 'whether it be right or wrong, is mighty ingenious' (18 February; 4, 10 November 1666). Moreover, D. was not reacting solely to dissident prophecy. Michael McKeon (in his *Politics and Poetry in Restoration England* (1975), a major study of *AM* and its context) points out that dissidents did not have a monopoly of prophecy, and some royalist writers expected good things from 1666. Almanacs anticipated a 'Year of Wonders', and the appendix to Vincent Wing's almanac has the running title 'Annus Mirabilis'. To McKeon's examples we may add that 'Anno Mirabili 1666' appears in the title of *A Short and Serious Narrative of Londons Fatal Fire* (1667; exact date of publication unknown). The two major events which made 1666 a year of wonders were the Dutch War and the Fire of London.

Dutch War. The Second Dutch War was provoked by commercial rivalry; Pepys reported Capt. Cocke as saying that 'the trade of the world is too little for us two, therefore one must down' (2 February 1664). The main engagements were the Battle of Lowestoft (3 June 1665), an English victory which was not followed through; the Four Days Battle (1–4 June 1666), a defeat, but inconclusive; and the St James's Day Fight (25 July 1666), a decisive English victory. D. describes these, together with the disastrous raid on Bergen and the successful raid on the Vly. (*AM* was published before the humiliating Dutch appearance in the Medway in 1667.) James Kinsley in *RES* vii (1956) 30–7 shows how D. presents the naval war in a favourable light, suppressing examples of cowardice and incompetence, and ignoring the criticisms of the conduct of the war which contemporaries such as Pepys heard and made (e.g. Pepys 10, 24 June 1666; 4 April 1667). Contemporary accounts are reprinted in *The Rupert and Monck Letter Book 1666*, edited by J. R. Powell and E. K. Timmings (1969), hereafter cited as *Letter Book*. See also Pepys, *passim*. For modern accounts see Hutton, *The Restoration* 214–25, 237–45, Richard Ollard in Pepys x 110–20, and W. L. Clowes, *The Royal Navy*, 7 vols (1897–1903) ii 252–85. The diplomatic context is explained by Keith Feiling, *British Foreign Policy 1660–1672* (1930). The Battle of Lowestoft and the Four Days Battle were drawn by Willem van de Velde (*Van De Velde Drawings*, edited by M. Robinson (1958) 352–3; 309); his drawing of the raid on the Vly, and Hollar's engraving of the St James's Day Fight are reproduced in Richard Ollard, *Man of War* (1969).

Fire of London. The best contemporary reports of the fire are by Pepys and Evelyn (2–7 September). For modern accounts see W. G. Bell, *The Great Fire of London in 1666* (1920; 1951) and Robert Latham in Pepys x 138–40. The extent of the disaster is shown in Hollar's engraving of London before and after the fire (reproduced in *Wenceslaus Hollar: Prints and Drawings*, edited by Antony Griffiths and Gabriela Kesnerová (1983) 70–1). The fire prompted many moral reflections: Samuel Rolle in *The Burning of London* (1667) and Thomas Vincent in *Gods Terrible Voice in the City* (1667) saw it as a punishment for the people's sins; the same view was taken in the official Anglican sermons on the Fast Day by Edward Stillingfleet (*A Sermon . . . Octob. 10* (1666)) and William Sancroft (*Lex Ignea* (1666)). For poems on the fire and rebuilding of London see *London in Flames, London in Glory*, edited by Robert Aubin (1943).

Royal Society. Although D.'s praise of the Royal Society is brief (ll. 656–64) and his own association with it inconsiderable (he was elected a member in 1662 but was inactive and expelled for non-payment of dues in 1666), *AM* does share the Society's interest in ores, tides, eclipses, longitude and shipping. It is also notable that Sprat in his *The History of the Royal-Society of London* (published 1667, though pages 1–319 were set up and printed in 1665, so possibly available to D.) claims that experimental philosophy will reduce men's dependence upon prophecy: he says that Englishmen are swayed too much by omens and prodigies, 'especially this last year, this gloomy, and ill-boding humor has prevail'd. So that it is now the fittest season for *Experiments* to arise, to teach us a Wisdome, which springs from the depths of *Knowledge*, to shake off the shadows, and to scatter the mists, which fill the minds of men with a vain consternation' (362). Sprat and D. also share a concern for language: D.'s interest in the terms proper to each art ('Account' ll. 88–109), though primarily related to literary discussions of decorum and poetic vocabulary, may also be compared with the Society's adoption of 'a close, naked, natural way of speaking; positive expressions; clear senses; a native easiness: bringing all things as near the Mathematical plainness, as they can: and preferring the language of Artizans, Countrymen, and Merchants, before that, of Wits, or Scholars' (113); and D.'s use of similes drawn from scientific discoveries is in line with Sprat's view that 'the *Works of Nature* . . . are one of the best and most fruitful Soils for the growth of *Wit*' (415). See also Helen M. Burke, *ELH* lvii (1990) 307–34 for a discussion of the ideology of science as represented in *AM*.

Sources. Since D. composed *AM* in Wiltshire, he would have relied upon documentary sources for his account of the war and the fire. The war was reported in the *London Gazette, Current Intelligence* and various pamphlets (see *Letter Book*). His account of the Four Days Battle is closest to that in the official pamphlet *A True Narrative of the Engagement between His Majesties Fleet, and that of Holland* (1666). The other engagements were described in *The Victory over the Fleet of the States General, obtained by His Majesties Navy Royal in the late Engagement, begun the 25 of July instant* (1666) and *A True and Perfect Narrative of the Great and Signal Success of a Part of His Majesties Fleet . . . Burning One hundred and Sixty Dutch Ships within the Ulie* (1666). For the fire he probably used the *London Gazette* lxxxv (3–10 September). The events of 1665–6 prompted a number of poems. Waller's *Instructions to a Painter* (1665) celebrated the Battle of Lowestoft, and drew a series of anonymous rejoinders: *Second Advice to a Painter* (Pepys saw a MS copy 14 December 1666; printed 1667); *Third Advice* (dated 1 October 1666; Pepys saw a MS copy 20 January 1667; printed 1667); *Fourth* and *Fifth Advice* and *Last Instructions* (the last by Marvell), these last three covering the period from September 1666 to late 1667. For all these see *POAS* i 20–156 and Marvell 321–6. There is evidence only for D.'s knowing Waller's poem (see l. 64*n*), but *AM* clearly responds defensively to the critical climate in which the others were written (even Pepys contemplated writing a satire on the Four Days Fight: see the entry for 15 July 1666). Waller's analogues from natural history (parodied in the *Second Advice*) may have suggested to D. his own use of georgic elements in *AM*. D. also used Waller's *Of a War with Spain* (1658). He also seems to have recalled William Smith's poems on the Battle of Lowestoft (see l. 228*n*) and the *Loyal London* (see ll. 17–20*n*). Simon Ford's thanksgiving sermon for Lowestoft, preached in Northampton, has some similarities with *AM*: it discusses the restriction of trade (9, 26; cp. *AM* ll. 5–6*n*), the ordering of tides (10), and the origins and development of shipping and navigation (14–15) (Θαυμάσια Κύριου ἐν Βυθῷ (1665)). D.'s stanza form, previously used in 'Heroic Stanzas', comes from Davenant's *Gondibert* (1651), as do some of the ideas in the 'Account'.

As the 'Account' shows, D. used several classical writers to help him define the appropriate mode for an historical poem. He tried to avoid the difficulties (exemplified for him in Lucan's *Pharsalia*) of taking too diverse a subject, and he used two Latin poets as his models. From Virgil's *Aeneid* he took a stress upon *pietas*, that submission to providence and dedication to one's country represented by Aeneas and by the protagonists of *AM* (see James D. Garrison, *Pietas from Vergil to Dryden* (1992) for this concept). D.'s poem thus suggests England's Augustan destiny, and sees the war with Holland in terms of Rome's struggle with Carthage. From the *Georgics* D. drew inspiration for his poem's delight in the ordinary, everyday world (both in nature, and in the details of human occupations), and its sense of the place of labour in a divinely ordered world. But while D. draws many images from Virgil, his wit is more akin to that of Ovid, whose ability to treat serious subjects wittily always influenced him. As his own notes show, D. draws upon other Latin authors for images or philosophical reflections. He also activates the Latinate roots of English, using many words of Latin origin in their primary meanings. See further, Hammond 92–105.

Reception. Pepys thought it 'a very good poem', but did not keep his copy (2 February 1667). Abraham Markland's 'Upon the Anniversary of His Majesties Birth and Restauration, May 29. (1667.)' uses the same stanza form as *AM*; other resemblances with *AM* include the King weeping at the fire, and the description of the wind which fanned the flames as 'a *Dutch* East-wind' (cp. *AM* l. 917) (*Poems on His Majestie's Birth and Restauration* (1667) 1–23). Many passages of *AM* were echoed in J[oseph] G[uillim]'s poem on the fire, Ἀκάματον Πῦρ (1667) (see Hammond and Hopkins 360–3), and there are echoes in [James Wright], *Ecclesia Restaurata* (1677), but other contemporaries were scathing about D.'s wit (see ll. 521–8*n*, 697*n*, 1121–4*n*).

Annus Mirabilis:
The Year of Wonders, 1666.
An Historical Poem:

Containing the progress and various successes of our naval war with Holland, under the conduct of His Highness Prince Rupert, and His Grace the Duke of Albemarle. And describing the Fire of London.

Multum interest res poscat, an homines latius imperare velint.
Trajan Imperator ad Plin.

Urbs antiqua ruit, multos dominata per annos.
Virg.

¶3. *Title.* See headnote, *Context.*
Epigraphs. Multum . . . velint.] '[The validity of a course of action] depends very much upon whether the occasion demands it, or men are [just] eager to extend their power more widely' (Pliny, *Epistulae* x 22).   Urbs . . . annos] 'The ancient city falls, having dominated for many years' (Virgil, *Aen.* ii 363).

To the Metropolis of Great Britain,
the most renowned and late flourishing
City of London,
in its representatives the Lord Mayor and
Court of Aldermen,
the Sheriffs and Common Council of it.

As perhaps I am the first who ever presented a work of
this nature to the metropolis of any nation, so is it likewise consonant to justice that he who was to give the
first example of such a dedication should begin it with
5   that city which has set a pattern to all others of true loyalty, invincible courage and unshaken constancy. Other
cities have been praised for the same virtues, but I am
much deceived if any have so dearly purchased their reputation; their fame has been won them by cheaper trials
10   than an expensive, though necesssary, war, a consuming
pestilence, and a more consuming fire. To submit yourselves with that humility to the judgements of heaven,
and at the same time to raise yourselves with that vigour
above all human enemies; to be combated at once from
15   above and from below, to be struck down and to triumph;
I know not whether such trials have been ever paralleled
in any nation: the resolution and successes of them never
can be. Never had prince or people more mutual reason
to love each other, if suffering for each other can endear
20   affection. You have come together a pair of matchless lovers,
through many difficulties; he, through a long exile, various traverses of Fortune, and the interposition of many

---

Dedication. Relations between the court and London had been difficult for many
years. During the Civil War London had provided a secure base of support for
Parliament, and after the Restoration it continued to nourish Protestant and, later,
Whiggish sentiments. During the plague many courtiers and clergy left London
for safer places, and pamphlets voiced the resentment of Londoners at their aban-
donment. Relations became particularly awkward for Charles II during the
Popish Plot (1678–9) and Exclusion Crisis (1680–1), and he moved Parliament
to Oxford to avoid Whig pressure from Londoners: this tension is registered by
D. in *AA*, and in *The Duke of Guise* (1683), which ridicules city sheriffs. Royal
control over the city was effected through a new charter in 1683, a victory which
D. celebrated in *Albion and Albanius* (1685).
22. *traverses*] obstructions, adversities (*OED* 7).

rivals, who violently ravished and withheld you from him; and certainly you have had your share in sufferings. But
25   Providence has cast upon you want of trade, that you might appear bountiful to your country's necessities; and the rest of your afflictions are not more the effects of God's displeasure (frequent examples of them having been in the reign of the most excellent princes) than occasions for
30   the manifesting of your Christian and civil virtues. To you therefore this *Year of Wonders* is justly dedicated, because you have made it so: you who are to stand a wonder to all years and ages, and who have built yourselves an immortal monument on your own ruins. You are now a phoenix
35   in her ashes, and, as far as humanity can approach, a great emblem of the suffering deity. But heaven never made so much piety and virtue to leave it miserable. I have heard indeed of some virtuous persons who have ended unfortunately, but never of any virtuous nation: Providence is
40   engaged too deeply, when the cause becomes so general. And I cannot imagine it has resolved the ruin of that people at home, which it has blessed abroad with such successes. I am therefore to conclude that your sufferings are at an end, and that one part of my poem has not
45   been more an history of your destruction than the other a prophecy of your restoration. The accomplishment of which happiness, as it is the wish of all true Englishmen, so is by none more passionately desired than by

The greatest of your admirers, and most humble of your
50   servants,

JOHN DRYDEN.

34–6. phoenix . . . suffering deity] The phoenix rising from the ashes of its parent was an obvious symbol for the city, and was included in the original design for the monument to the fire. It was also a traditional emblem of the passion and resurrection of Christ.

An Account of the Ensuing Poem,
in a letter to the Honourable Sir Robert
Howard

Sir,

I am so many ways obliged to you, and so little able to
return your favours, that, like those who owe too
much, I can only live by getting farther into your debt.
5   You have not only been careful of my fortune, which
was the effect of your nobleness, but you have been solicitous of my reputation, which is that of your kindness.
It is not long since I gave you the trouble of perusing a
play for me, and now, instead of an acknowledgement,
10   I have given you a greater, in the correction of a poem.
But since you are to bear this persecution, I will at least
give you the encouragement of a martyr: you could never
suffer in a nobler cause. For I have chosen the most heroic
subject which any poet could desire: I have taken upon
15   me to describe the motives, the beginning, progress and
successes of a most just and necessary war; in it, the care,
management and prudence of our King; the conduct and
valour of a royal admiral, and of two incomparable generals; the invincible courage of our captains and seamen;
20   and three glorious victories, the result of all. After this
I have, in the fire, the most deplorable, but withal the
greatest argument that can be imagined: the destruction being so swift, so sudden, so vast and miserable,

---

An Account of the Ensuing Poem. D.'s first critical essay was his Dedication to *The
Rival Ladies* (1664); the present essay is (with the closely preceding *EDP*) D.'s
first extended piece of literary criticism. He is concerned chiefly with decorum
– with the literary form which is appropriate for particular events, and with the
language which is appropriate to that form.

Howard] See headnote, *Date and publication*, and 'To Sir Robert Howard'.

5. careful of my fortune] Howard seems to have helped D. and his wife Elizabeth
in their negotiations with the Treasury to obtain the £3,000 dowry due to them
out of a grant from the King to the Earl of Berkshire (Winn 168–9).

8–9. a play] *Secret Love*, written during D.'s period at Charlton.

18. admiral] James, Duke of York.   *generals*] Prince Rupert and George Monck,
Duke of Albemarle.

21. deplorable] lamentable.

22. argument] topic.

as nothing can parallel in story. The former part of this
25   poem, relating to the war, is but a due expiation for my
not serving my King and country in it. All gentlemen
are almost obliged to it: and I know no reason we should
give that advantage to the commonalty of England to be
foremost in brave actions, which the noblesse of France
30   would never suffer in their peasants. I should not have
written this but to a person who has been ever forward
to appear in all employments whither his honour and generosity have called him. The latter part of my poem, which
describes the fire, I owe first to the piety and fatherly
35   affection of our monarch to his suffering subjects; and,
in the second place, to the courage, loyalty and magnanimity of the city: both which were so conspicuous that
I have wanted words to celebrate them as they deserve.
I have called my poem historical, not epic, though both
40   the actions and actors are as much heroic as any poem
can contain. But since the action is not properly one,
nor that accomplished in the last successes, I have judged
it too bold a title for a few stanzas which are little more
in number than a single *Iliad*, or the longest of the *Aeneids*.

26. *gentlemen*] Charles and James preferred gentlemen commanders to professional
seamen, but they were not always reliable under pressure (Ogg 273–4; Pepys
10 January 1666 and *n*).
28. *commonalty*] common people (*OED* 3).
29. *foremost*] formost *1688*; for most *1667*, *1668*.   *noblesse*] nobility (a long-standing English word).   *France*] The majority of the French nobility served in the
army, other pursuits being considered dishonourable.
32. *employments*] At the outbreak of the Civil War the young Howard joined
the royalist army, and in 1646 was knighted for his bravery. In October 1660
Howard was appointed a commissioner for investigating the dispersal of royal property during the Commonwealth; in November made colonel in the Hampshire
militia; in 1661 elected Member of Parliament for Stockbridge, Hampshire; in
1662 appointed a commissioner for reforming the streets and buildings of
London. He was also a partner in the building and ownership of the Theatre
Royal, Bridges Street, from 1661. Howard's prominence as a parliamentarian began
in 1666 with his opposition to court interests, though he soon changed sides
(H. J. Oliver, *Sir Robert Howard* (1963) 42–4, 131–2).   *generosity*] nobility (*OED* 1).
34. *piety*] partly in the Latin sense (from *pietas*) of 'dutiful care for one's country';
see headnote (*Sources*) and cp. *AM* l. 255*n*.
36–7. *magnanimity*] fortitude (*OED* 2).
41. *action is not properly one*] It is a basic classical principle that the subject of a poem
should have a unity (Aristotle, *Poetics* 1450b–51b; Horace, *Ars Poetica* ll. 1–23).
42. *last*] latest.
43–4. *little more in number*] *AM* has 1216 lines; Virgil, *Aen.* xii has 952; Homer,
Iliad v has 909.

45   For this reason (I mean not of length, but broken action,
      tied too severely to the laws of history) I am apt to agree
      with those who rank Lucan rather among historians
      in verse than epic poets: in whose room, if I am not
      deceived, Silius Italicus, though a worse writer, may
50   more justly be admitted. I have chosen to write my poem
      in quatrains, or stanzas of four in alternate rhyme,
      because I have ever judged them more noble, and of greater
      dignity, both for the sound and number, than any other
      verse in use amongst us; in which I am sure I have your
55   approbation. The learnèd languages have, certainly, a
      great advantage of us, in not being tied to the slavery of
      any rhyme, and were less constrained in the quantity
      of every syllable, which they might vary with spondees

47. Lucan] AD 39–65, author of *Bellum Civile* (or *Pharsalia*), a poem on the civil
war between Caesar and Pompey. D.'s critical estimate of him derives from
Quintilian, who thought him *magis oratoribus quam poetis imitandus* (X i 90; 'more
worthy of imitation by orators than poets'). Petronius concurred, saying that
historical events are better dealt with by historians than poets (*Satyricon* 118),
quoted by Fanshawe, translating Camões's *The Lusiad* (1655) (Fanshawe ii 8–9),
and by D. in *Of Heroique Playes* (1672; *Works* xi 11–12). J. C. Scaliger censured
Lucan for a lack of poetic unity caused by following too closely the events of
history, and contrasted him in this respect with Silius Italicus (*Poetices Libri Septem*
(1561) 325, 327). Davenant, in his Preface to *Gondibert* (1651) 4, wrote: 'Lucan,
who chose to write the greatest actions that ever were allowed to be true . . .
did not observe that such an enterprise rather beseem'd an Historian, then a Poet:
for wise Poets think it more worthy to seek out truth in the Passions, then
to record the truth of Actions'. In 1672 D. said that Lucan 'follow'd too much
the truth of history, crowded sentences [i.e. philosophical aphorisms] together,
was too full of points, and too often offer'd at somewhat which had more of
the sting of an Epigram, than of the dignity and state of an Heroick Poem'
(*Works* xi 11).
49. Silius Italicus] AD 26–101, writer of *Punica*, the longest Latin poem, 12,200
verses on the Second Punic War. A translation by Thomas Ross was published
in 1661; an epigram on the frontispiece portrait of Charles II says that the King
surpasses Scipio and Hannibal.
51. quatrains] the form of D.'s 'Heroic Stanzas', of Davenant's *Gondibert* and of
Sir John Davies's *Nosce Teipsum* (1599).
53. for] 1688; fro 1667; from 1668. *number*] metre or rhythm.
56–7. slavery of any rhyme] Milton's note on 'The Verse' added to the fourth issue
of *PL* (1668) also remarks on 'the troublesome and modern bondage of rhyming'.
D. had just defended the use of rhyme in drama in *EDP*. Latin hexameter
verse is scanned by quantity rather than stress, and permits spondees and dactyls.
The inflexions of Latin allow considerable liberty in word order.

or dactyls, besides so many other helps of grammatical
60   figures for the lengthening or abbreviation of them, than
the modern are in the close of that one syllable which
often confines and more often corrupts the sense of all
the rest. But in this necessity of our rhymes I have always
found the couplet verse most easy (though not so proper
65   for this occasion), for there the work is sooner at an end,
every two lines concluding the labour of the poet: but
in quatrains he is to carry it farther on, and not only so,
but to bear along in his head the troublesome sense of
four lines together. For those who write correctly in this
70   kind must needs acknowledge that the last line of the stanza
is to be considered in the composition of the first.
Neither can we give ourselves the liberty of making any
part of a verse for the sake of rhyme, or concluding with
a word which is not current English, or using the var-
75   iety of female rhymes, all which our fathers practised;
and for the female rhymes, they are still in use amongst
other nations: with the Italian in every line, with the
Spaniard promiscuously, with the French alternately,
as those who have read the *Alaric*, the *Pucelle*, or any of
80   their latter poems will agree with me. And besides this,
they write in alexandrines, or verses of six feet, such as
amongst us is the old translation of Homer by Chapman;
all which, by lengthening of their chain, makes the
sphere of their activity the larger. I have dwelt too long
85   upon the choice of my stanza, which you may remember is much better defended in the Preface to *Gondibert*,
and therefore I will hasten to acquaint you with my
endeavours in the writing. In general I will only say,

75. *female rhymes*] In the Preface to *Albion and Albanius* (1685) D. says: 'Female,
or double Rhyme . . . is not natural to our Tongue, because it consists too much
of Monosyllables, and those too, most commonly clogg'd with Consonants' (*Works*
xv 10).
79. Alaric] *Alaric, ou Rome vaincüe* (1654) by Georges de Scudéry. Pucelle] *La
Pucelle, ou la France délivrée* (1656) by Jean Chapelain.
82. *translation of Homer by Chapman*] His *Iliad* (1598–1611) is actually in lines of
seven feet, and his *Odyssey* (1614–15) in lines of five.
86. *better defended in the Preface to* Gondibert] 'I beleev'd it would be more pleasant to the Reader, in a Work of length, to give this respite or pause, between
every *Stanza* (having endeavour'd that each should contain a period) then to
run him out of breath with continu'd *Couplets*. Nor doth alternate Rime by any
lowliness of cadence make the sound less Heroick' (*Gondibert* (1651) 25).

I have never yet seen the description of any naval fight
90   in the proper terms which are used at sea; and if there
be any such in another language, as that of Lucan in the
third of his *Pharsalia*, yet I could not prevail myself of it
in the English, the terms of arts in every tongue bearing
more of the idiom of it than any other words. We hear,
95   indeed, among our poets of the thundering of guns, the
smoke, the disorder and the slaughter; but all these are
common notions. And certainly, as those who in a logical dispute keep in general terms would hide a fallacy,
so those who do it in any poetical description would veil
100   their ignorance.

> *descriptas servare vices operumque colores*
> *cur ego, si nequeo ignoroque, poeta salutor?*

For my own part, if I had little knowledge of the sea,
yet I have thought it no shame to learn; and if I have
105   made some few mistakes, 'tis only, as you can bear me
witness, because I have wanted opportunity to correct
them, the whole poem being first written and now sent
you from a place where I have not so much as the converse of any seaman. Yet, though the trouble I had in
110   writing it was great, it was more than recompensed by
the pleasure; I found myself so warm in celebrating the
praises of military men, two such especially as the Prince
and General, that it is no wonder if they inspired me
with thoughts above my ordinary level. And I am well
115   satisfied that as they are incomparably the best subject
I have ever had, excepting only the royal family, so also
that this I have written of them is much better than what

---

90. *proper terms*] As W. P. Ker noted, Ronsard advocated the use of 'les noms
propres des mestiers' in his *Abrégé de l'art poëtique françois* (1565). D.'s interest
here may be compared with the Royal Society's concern for style (see headnote,
Royal Society). D. returns to the subject of the poet being master of the appropriate languages in his note to 'The Second Book of the *Georgics*' (*Works* vi 814)
and his 'Dedication of the *Aeneis*' (*Works* v 337), where he now says that he has
followed Virgil in not using the proper terms of navigation and other professions.
91–2. *Lucan in the third of his* Pharsalia] *Pharsalia* iii 509–762.
92. *prevail*] avail (*OED* 4c); cp. *AA* l. 461.
98. Kinsley cites the tag *Fraus latet in generalibus*; cp. *HP* ii 79.
101–2. 'If I am ignorant of and fail to adhere to the established varieties and styles
of works, why should I be hailed as a poet?' (Horace, *Ars Poetica* ll. 86–7).
106. *wanted*] lacked.

I have performed on any other. I have been forced to
help out other arguments, but this has been bountiful
120 to me; they have been low and barren of praise, and
I have exalted them, and made them fruitful: but here
——*Omnia sponte sua reddit justissima tellus*. I have had a
large, a fair and a pleasant field, so fertile that without
my cultivating it has given me two harvests in a summer,
125 and in both oppressed the reaper. All other greatness in
subjects is only counterfeit, it will not endure the test
of danger; the greatness of arms is only real: other greatness burdens a nation with its weight, this supports it with
its strength. And as it is the happiness of the age, so is it
130 the peculiar goodness of the best of kings, that we may
praise his subjects without offending him: doubtless it
proceeds from a just confidence of his own virtue,
which the lustre of no other can be so great as to darken
in him, for the good or the valiant are never safely praised
135 under a bad or a degenerate prince. But to return from
this digression to a farther account of my poem, I must
crave leave to tell you, that as I have endeavoured to adorn
it with noble thoughts, so much more to express those
thoughts with elocution. The composition of all poems
140 is or ought to be of wit, and wit in the poet, or wit writing (if you will give me leave to use a school distinction)

122. Omnia . . . tellus] 'The most righteous earth returns everything of its own
free will': D.'s own hexameter, probably based on Virgil's *fundit humo facilem uictum
iustissima tellus* (*Geo.* ii 460), *omnis feret omnia tellus* (*Ecl.* iv 39), and Ovid's *tellus
animalia formis / sponte sua peperit* (*Met.* i 416–17; cp. *Fasti* iv 370).
124. two harvests in a summer] probably the praises of Prince Rupert and General
Monck.
139. elocution] See 'Account' l. 166.
139–49. Cp. Davenant: '*Wit* is the laborious, and the lucky resultances of
thought, having towards its excellence (as we say of the strokes of Painting) as
well a happiness, as care. . . . *Wit* is not only the luck and labour, but also the
dexterity of thought, rounding the world, like the Sun, with unimaginable motion;
and bringing swiftly home to the memory universall surveys' (Preface to
Gondibert (1651) 26–7; D. seems to have borrowed Davenant's terms 'laborious'
and 'lucky' to describe Shakespeare in *EDP* (*Works* xvii 55)). D. is developing
his earlier account of poetic creation: in the Dedication to *The Rival Ladies* (1664)
he said that the play was once 'a confus'd Mass of Thoughts, tumbling over one
another in the Dark: When the Fancy was yet in its first Work, moving the Sleeping
Images of things towards the Light, there to be Distinguish'd, and then either
chosen or rejected by the Judgment' (*Works* viii 95); cp. also 'To Sir Robert Howard'
ll. 1–34. The threefold analysis of the act of creation is derived from classical rhetoric
(see 'Account' ll. 162–6*nn*); D. has a similar division in his 'A Parallel of Poetry
and Painting' (*Works* xx 61–71).

is no other than the faculty of imagination in the writer,
which like a nimble spaniel beats over and ranges
through the field of memory, till it springs the quarry it
145   hunted after; or, without metaphor, which searches over
all the memory for the species or ideas of those things
which it designs to represent. Wit written is that which
is well defined, the happy result of thought or product
of that imagination. But to proceed from wit in the
150   general notion of it to the proper wit of an heroic or
historical poem, I judge it chiefly to consist in the
delightful imaging of persons, actions, passions or things.
'Tis not the jerk or sting of an epigram, nor the seeming contradiction of a poor antithesis (the delight of an
155   ill-judging audience in a play of rhyme), nor the jingle
of a more poor paronomasia: neither is it so much the
morality of a grave sentence, affected by Lucan, but
more sparingly used by Virgil; but it is some lively and
apt description, dressed in such colours of speech that
160   it sets before your eyes the absent object as perfectly
and more delightfully than nature. So then, the first
happiness of the poet's imagination is properly invention,
or finding of the thought; the second is fancy, or the

140–7. wit writing . . . Wit written] 'The school distinction which D. has in his
mind is that of *Natura naturans* and *Natura naturata*. So in the case of Wit he
distinguishes between Wit the faculty and Wit the product' (Ker).
141. school distinction] a distinction from scholastic philosophy.
143. spaniel] Cp. Hobbes: 'Sometimes a man knows a place determinate, within
the compasse whereof he is to seek; and then his thoughts run over all the parts
thereof, in the same manner . . . as a Spaniel ranges the field, till he find a
sent' (*Leviathan* (1651) 10). D. had used the image in the Dedication to *The Rival
Ladies*: 'Imagination in a Poet is a faculty so Wild and Lawless, that, like an
High-ranging Spaniel it must have Cloggs tied to it, least it out-run the
Judgment' (*Works* viii 101). For Shadwell's parody of this image in *The Humorists*
see Winn 223.
146. species] mental impressions; ideas (*OED* 5c). *ideas*] abstract or ideal forms
(ultimately from Plato).
148. happy] fortunate and skilful.
153. Cp. D.'s comment on Lucan, quoted in l. 47n.
156. paronomasia] play on words; pun.
157. grave sentence] Quintilian says that Lucan is *sententiis clarissimus* (X i 90; 'most
famous for his sentences' [i.e. moral aphorisms]).
162. invention] The finding out or selection of topics to be treated (*OED* 1d); a
standard rhetorical term, *inventio* in classical rhetoric. For this and the following
terms cp. the list of five elements of rhetoric (*inventio, dispositio, elocutio, memoria,
pronuntiatio*) in Cicero, *De Inventione* i 7 and *Ad Herennium* i 2.

variation, driving or moulding of that thought as the
165 judgement represents it proper to the subject; the third
is elocution, or the art of clothing and adorning
that thought so found and varied in apt, significant and
sounding words: the quickness of the imagination is seen
in the invention, the fertility in the fancy, and the accur-
170 acy in the expression. For the two first of these Ovid
is famous amongst the poets, for the latter Virgil. Ovid
images more often the movements and affections of the
mind, either combating between two contrary passions,
or extremely discomposed by one: his words therefore are
175 the least part of his care, for he pictures nature in disorder,
with which the study and choice of words is inconsistent. This is the proper wit of dialogue or discourse, and
consequently of the drama, where all that is said is to be
supposed the effect of sudden thought; which, though it
180 excludes not the quickness of wit in repartees, yet admits
not a too curious election of words, too frequent allusions
or use of tropes, or, in fine, anything that shows remote-
ness of thought, or labour in the writer. On the other side,
Virgil speaks not so often to us in the person of another,

164. variation] corresponds to *dispositio*. *driving*] *1667, 1668, Watson*; deriving *1688, Ker, Kinsley, Works*. 'Deriving' would be inappropriate, as it belongs to the first stage of composition; *driving* refers to the pursuit of the idea once found: it is either an elaboration of the hunting image from ll. 144–5 or an image from painting or metalwork (spreading a colour or beating a metal thinly (*OED* 12)). Cp. 'drive' in 'Preface to *Ovid's Epistles*' (*Poems* i 382).
166. elocution] oratorical or literary expression of thought (*OED* 1); from *elocutio*. *clothing*] That thoughts were 'clothed' in words was a contemporary commonplace (*OED* clothe 8b).
168. sounding] high-sounding, imposing (*OED* 2).
171–97. D.'s praise of Ovid's invention and fancy is probably derived from the classical critics' stress on his *ingenium* (Seneca, *Quaestiones Naturales* III xxvii 14; Quintilian X i 88, 98). D.'s l. 172 seems to echo Daniel Heinsius' remark on Ovid's *imitatio affectuum in quibus semper regnat* ('imitation of the affections, in which he always excels') in the Preface to his edition of 1629 (sig. ★4ᵛ). Heinsius also places Ovid second to Virgil (sig. ★3ʳ). Otherwise, D.'s comparison of Ovid and Virgil seems to be original. In *EDP* he again says that Ovid shows dramatic abil-ities in depicting 'the various movements of a Soul combating betwixt two dif-ferent Passions', and commends his stories of Myrrha and Byblis (*Works* xvii 30–1). For D.'s later comments on Ovid see the Prefaces to *Ovid's Epistles* (*Poems* i 376–91), *Sylvae* (*Poems* ii 241–2) and *Fables* (*Poems* v 60–7), and 'Dedication of the *Aeneis*' (*Works* v 322, 339).
181. curious] exact.
182. tropes] See l. 225.

185   like Ovid, but in his own; he relates almost all things as
       from himself, and thereby gains more liberty than the other
       to express his thoughts with all the graces of elocution,
       to write more figuratively, and to confess as well the labour
       as the force of his imagination. Though he describes his
190   Dido well and naturally in the violence of her passions,
       yet he must yield in that to the Myrrha, the Byblis, the
       Althaea of Ovid; for, as great an admirer of him as I am,
       I must acknowledge that if I see not more of their souls
       than I see of Dido's, at least I have a greater concern-
195   ment for them, and that convinces me that Ovid has
       touched those tender strokes more delicately than Virgil
       could. But when action or persons are to be described,
       when any such image is to be set before us, how bold,
       how masterly are the strokes of Virgil! We see the
200   objects he represents us with in their native figures, in
       their proper motions; but we so see them as our own
       eyes could never have beheld them so beautiful in them-
       selves. We see the soul of the poet, like that universal
       one of which he speaks, informing and moving through
205   all his pictures, *Totamque infusa per artus mens agitat molem,*
       et magno se corpore miscet; we behold him embellishing his
       images, as he makes Venus breathing beauty upon her son
       Aeneas:

            ——*lumenque juventae*
210   *purpureum, et laetos oculis afflarat honores:*
            quale manus addunt ebori decus, aut ubi flavo
            argentum, Pariusve lapis circundatur auro.

183–97. This comparative judgement was condemned as a 'soloecism of commendation' in *The Friendly Vindication of Mr. Dryden* (1673) 13–14.
188. confess] reveal.
191. Myrrha] She fell in love with her father: Ovid, *Met.* x 314–518, tr. D. as
'Cinyras and Myrrha' in *Fables* (below).   *Byblis*] She fell in love with her
brother: *Met.* ix 454–665, tr. John Oldham in his *Satyrs upon the Jesuits* (1681),
and again by John Dennis (1692) and Stephen Harvey (1694).
192. Althaea] She took vengeance on her son for killing her brothers: *Met.* viii
445–514, tr. D. as 'Meleager and Atalanta' in *Fables.*
198. be set] *1668, 1688;* beset *1667.*
205–6. Totamque . . . miscet] 'and mind, pervading the frame, moves the whole
mass, and mingles with the mighty body' (Virgil, *Aen.* vi 726–7).
206. molem] *1688;* motem *1667, 1668.*
209–12. lumenque . . . auro] '[Venus] had breathed on him the bright light of
youth and joyful glory on his eyes: such grace as hands give to ivory, or when
silver or Parian marble is encircled by yellow gold' (Virgil, *Aen.* i 590–3).

See his tempest, his funeral sports, his combat of Turnus
and Aeneas, and in his *Georgics*, which I esteem the divinest
215   part of all his writings, the plague, the country, the
battle of bulls, the labour of the bees, and those many other
excellent images of nature, most of which are neither great
in themselves, nor have any natural ornament to bear them
up; but the words wherewith he describes them are so
220   excellent that it might be well applied to him which was
said by Ovid, *materiam superabat opus*; the very sound of
his words has often somewhat that is connatural to the
subject, and while we read him we sit, as in a play, beholding the scenes of what he represents. To perform this he
225   made frequent use of tropes, which you know change
the nature of a known word by applying it to some other
signification, and this is it which Horace means in his
Epistle to the Pisos:

dixeris egregie notum si callida verbum
230   *reddiderit junctura novum*——

But I am sensible I have presumed too far, to entertain
you with a rude discourse of that art which you both
know so well, and put into practice with so much happiness. Yet before I leave Virgil, I must own the vanity
235   to tell you, and by you the world, that he has been my
master in this poem: I have followed him everywhere,
I know not with what success, but I am sure with diligence enough: my images are many of them copied from
him, and the rest are imitations of him. My expressions
240   also are as near as the idioms of the two languages would

213. tempest] *Aen.* i 84–156.   *funeral sports*] *Aen.* v 42–603.   *combat*] *Aen.* xi.
214. Georgics] For this opinion cp. 'Preface to *Sylvae*' ll. 272–4 (*Poems* ii 246)
and D.'s note to Virgil, *Geo.* i (*Works* vi 813–14).
215. plague] *Geo.* iii 478–566.   *country*] probably the praise of country life in *Geo.*
ii 458–542.
216. battle of bulls] *Geo.* iii 209–41.   *bees*] *Geo.* iv.
221. materiam superabat opus] 'The workmanship surpassed the material' (Ovid,
Met. ii 5).
229–30. dixeris . . . novum] 'You will have spoken well if a skilful method of
connecting makes a well-known word new' (Horace, *Ars Poetica* ll. 47–8).
231. sensible] aware.
232. rude] rough, unsophisticated.
234–6. Virgil . . . has been my master] See headnote (*Sources*).

admit of in translation. And this, sir, I have done with
that boldness for which I will stand accomptable to
any of our little critics, who perhaps are not better
acquainted with him than I am. Upon your first perusal
245 of this poem you have taken notice of some words
which I have innovated (if it be too bold for me to say
refined) upon his Latin; which, as I offer not to introduce into English prose, so I hope they are neither
improper nor altogether unelegant in verse; and in this
250 Horace will again defend me:

  et nova, fictaque nuper habebunt verba fidem, si
  Graeco fonte cadant, parce detorta——

The inference is exceeding plain: for if a Roman poet
might have liberty to coin a word, supposing only that
255 it was derived from the Greek, was put into a Latin ter-
mination, and that he used this liberty but seldom, and
with modesty; how much more justly may I challenge
that privilege to do it with the same prerequisites, from
the best and most judicious of Latin writers? In some places
260 where either the fancy or the words were his, or any
other's, I have noted it in the margin, that I might not
seem a plagiary; in others I have neglected it, to avoid
as well the tediousness as the affectation of doing it too
often. Such descriptions or images, well wrought, which
265 I promise not for mine, are, as I have said, the adequate
delight of heroic poesy, for they beget admiration,
which is its proper object; as the images of the burlesque,

242. *accomptable*] accountable.
246. *innovated*] D. makes Latinate innovations in both phrasing and vocabulary;
see ll. 251–2n, 1022n, 1028n, 1069n. Cp. 'Dedication of the *Aeneis*' (*Works* v 333–5),
and D.'s note to 'The Ninth Book of the *Aeneis*' l. 1095 (*Works* vi 828–9).
251–2. et . . . detorta] 'New words, and words recently made, will win acceptance if they spring from a Greek source, and are drawn sparingly' (*Ars Poetica*
ll. 52–3). cadant] Modern texts of Horace read *cadent*, but *cadant* is preferred by
some seventeenth-century editors, e.g. Lubinus, Bond, Marolles and Schrevelius.
265. *adequate*] appropriate, fitting (*OED* 2).
266. *admiration*] wonder, astonishment (*OED* 1).
267. *burlesque*] D.'s first use of the word, which seems to have established itself
slowly in England; it was used loosely at first, and then acquired a more
precise meaning. In Randle Cotgrave's *A Dictionarie of the French and English Tongues*
(1611) it is defined as 'jeasting . . . mocking, flouting', and in Thomas Blount's
Glossographia (1656) as 'drolish, merry, pleasant'. Burlesque poetry, which

which is contrary to this, by the same reason beget
laughter: for the one shows nature beautified, as in the
270   picture of a fair woman, which we all admire; the other
shows her deformed, as in that of a lazar, or of a fool
with distorted face and antic gestures, at which we cannot forbear to laugh because it is a deviation from
nature. But though the same images serve equally for the
275   epic poesy and for the historic and panegyric, which are
branches of it, yet a several sort of sculpture is to be used
in them: if some of them are to be like those of Juvenal,
stantes in curribus Aemiliani, heroes drawn in their triumphal
chariots, and in their full proportion, others are to be like
280   that of Virgil, *spirantia mollius aera*: there is somewhat more
of softness and tenderness to be shown in them. You
will soon find I write not this without concern. Some
who have seen a paper of verses which I wrote last year
to her Highness the Duchess, have accused them of that
285   only thing I could defend in them: they have said I did
humi serpere, that I wanted not only height of fancy, but
dignity of words to set it off; I might well answer with

mocked heroic poetry, was popular in Italy and France, a notable example being
Paul Scarron's *Le Virgile travesty en vers burlesques* (1648–53), imitated in English
by Charles Cotton as *Scarronides* (1664). The Prologue to *The Knight of the Burning
Pestle* explains the word carefully: 'our *Fletchers* wit, / Has here burlesqu'd all he
himself had writ. / Burlesqu'd, that is has turn'd to ridicule, / As one would say,
has wisely play'd the fool' (*Covent Garden Drolery* (1672) 78). Some succeeding
lines suggest that the word was also applied to personal abuse: 'Not only every
wit, Lampoons his brother, / But men are all burlosque [*sic*] to one another'. For
further definitions and discussions see *A Description of the Academy of the Athenian
Virtuosi* (1673) 34; Davenant's *The Play-house to be Lett* in *The Works of Sr William
D'avenant* (1673) 75–6; and Rymer 4, 89.
271. lazar] poor and diseased person, esp. leper. D. returns to the image in *Defence
of An Essay* (1668), discussing *Bartholomew Fair.* Jonson 'hath made an excellent
lazar of it; the copy is of price, though the original be vile' (*Works* ix 7). The
analogy of painting and poetry is a classical commonplace (e.g. Horace, *Ars Poetica*
l. 361) and recurs through D.'s criticism. Cp. 'Heroic Stanzas' ll. 59–60n.
272. antic] grotesque, ludicrous.
276. several] different.
278. stantes . . . Aemiliani] 'Aemiliani standing in their chariots' (*Satire* viii 3; actually 'Aemilianos': D. changes the case to suit his syntax).
280. spirantia mollius aera] '[Others will shape] more smoothly [statues of]
breathing bronze' (*Aen.* vi 847).
282. concern] self-interest.
286. humi serpere] 'creep on the earth' (*Ars Poetica* l. 28). *wanted*] lacked.

that of Horace, *nunc non erat hic locus*, I knew I addressed
them to a lady, and accordingly I affected the softness of
290   expression and the smoothness of measure, rather than
the height of thought; and in what I did endeavour, it
is no vanity to say I have succeeded. I detest arrogance,
but there is some difference betwixt that and a just
defence. But I will not farther bribe your candour or the
295   reader's. I leave them to speak for me, and, if they can,
to make out that character, not pretending to a greater,
which I have given them.

Verses to her Highness the Duchess, on the memorable victory gained by the Duke against the Hollanders, June the 3. 1665, and on her journey afterwards into the north

Madam,
When for our sakes your hero you resigned
To swelling seas, and every faithless wind;
When you released his courage, and set free
A valour fatal to the enemy,

288. nunc . . . locus] 'This was not now the place' (*Ars Poetica* l. 19; D. alters *his*
('for them') to *hic* ('this')).
289. affected] aimed at (*OED* 1).
294. candour] impartiality, justice (*OED* 3).
296. pretending to] claiming, aspiring to.

Verses. This poem was first printed as part of the prefatory material to *AM*; from
ll. 282–5 above, it appears that the verses circulated in MS, but no separate MS
copy is known. The Duchess of York (Anne Hyde: 1637–71) had visited the
fleet at Harwich in May 1665 (the *Second Advice* has a scathing account, ll. 55–74).
After James's narrow escape from death in the Battle of Lowestoft he was kept
on shore to avoid further risks to his life. On 5 August 1665 the Duke and Duchess
left plague-ridden London and made a triumphal progress to York, where rebel-
lions had been reported. Waller also has complimentary lines to the Duchess in
his *Instructions* ll. 81–90. D.'s lines are favourably alluded to in Christopher Wase's
Divination (1666; a rejoinder to the *Second Advice*); Wase rejects several possible
authors for the *Second Advice* including D.: 'Or else if love and honour crown
each page, / You well had read the champion of the stage: / Here the kind Duchess
is forbid to mourn / When her Lord parts, or joy at his return' (ll. 33–6; *POAS*
i 56). For D.'s defence of the Duchess's posthumously published religious papers
in 1686 see *Works* xvii 291–323.

5   You lodged your country's cares within your breast
    (The mansion where soft love should only rest);
    And ere our foes abroad were overcome,
    The noblest conquest you had gained at home.
    Ah, what concerns did both your souls divide!
10 Your honour gave us what your love denied;
    And 'twas for him much easier to subdue
    Those foes he fought with, than to part from you.
    That glorious day which two such navies saw
    As each unmatched might to the world give law,
15 Neptune, yet doubtful whom he should obey,
    Held to them both the trident of the sea:
    The winds were hushed, the waves in ranks were cast,
    As awfully as when God's people passed;
    Those yet uncertain on whose sails to blow,
20 These where the wealth of nations ought to flow.
    Then with the Duke your Highness ruled the day, ⎫
    While all the brave did his command obey,   ⎬
    The fair and pious under you did pray.   ⎭
    How powerful are chaste vows! The wind and tide
25 You bribed to combat on the English side.
    Thus to your much-loved lord you did convey
    An unknown succour, sent the nearest way.
    New vigour to his wearied arms you brought
    (So Moses was upheld while Israel fought).
30 While from afar we heard the cannon play
    Like distant thunder on a shiny day,
    For absent friends we were ashamed to fear
    When we considered what you ventured there.
    Ships, men and arms our country might restore,
35 But such a leader could supply no more.
    With generous thoughts of conquest he did burn,
    Yet fought not more to vanquish than return.

15–16. *obey* / . . . *sea*] Scott noted that *sea* is often pronounced in D. to rhyme
with *obey*, *way* etc. (cp. ll. 42–3). For the image cp. *Astraea Redux* l. 249*n*.
17. *cast*] thrown up, banked up (*OED* 30).
18. Exodus xiv 21–2.   *awfully*] inspiring awe.
29. When Joshua fought with Amalek, he was victorious so long as Moses
kept his arms raised; when Moses grew weary his arms were supported (Exodus
xvii 11–13).
30–1. Cp. the account of the naval battle at the opening of *EDP* (*Works*
xvii 8–9).
36. *generous*] noble.

Fortune and victory he did pursue
To bring them as his slaves to wait on you.
40   Thus beauty ravished the rewards of fame,
And the fair triumphed when the brave o'ercame.
Then, as you meant to spread another way
By land your conquests far as his by sea,
Leaving our southern clime you marched along
45   The stubborn north, ten thousand Cupids strong.
Like commons the nobility resort
In crowding heaps to fill your moving court;
To welcome your approach the vulgar run
Like some new envoy from the distant sun,
50   And country beauties by their lovers go,
Blessing themselves and wondering at the show.
So when the new-born phoenix first is seen,
Her feathered subjects all adore their queen,
And while she makes her progress through the east
55   From every grove her numerous train's increased;
Each poet of the air her glory sings,
And round him the pleased audience clap their wings.

And now, sir, 'tis time I should relieve you from the
tedious length of this account. You have better and more
300   profitable employment for your hours, and I wrong the
public to detain you longer. In conclusion, I must leave
my poem to you with all its faults, which I hope to find
fewer in the printing by your emendations. I know you
are not of the number of those of whom the younger

44. *along*] through (*OED* 1).
45. *stubborn north*] Opposition to Charles's rule was strong in the north of
England, as seen in the Yorkshire rebellion of 1663 (Hutton, *The Restoration* 204–9).
50. *go*] walk.
52–7. The progress of the new-born phoenix, attended by other birds, was first
recounted in the late Latin poem *Phoenix*, sometimes attributed to Lactantius
(ll. 151–8), and then in Claudian's *Phoenix* ll. 76–80. The former is closer to D.'s
passage. Claudian also makes a political application of the phoenix simile in *De
Consulatu Stilichonis* ii 414–20. The progress is described at length in Du Bartas
(tr. Sylvester, I v 645–712), which D. knew well as a boy. The phoenix is
normally masculine, but is feminine in 'Lactantius'; Sylvester changes the sex to
feminine in his translation of Du Bartas, probably as a compliment to Elizabeth
I (for the phoenix as an emblem of Elizabeth see Frances Yates, *Astraea* (1975)
58, 65–6). Cp. *Threnodia Augustalis* ll. 364–71, where Charles II is likened to the
phoenix; 'To the Memory of Anne Killigrew' l. 134; 'Of the Pythagorean
Philosophy' ll. 600–11.

305 Pliny speaks, *Nec sunt parum multi qui carpere amicos suos judicium vocant*; I am rather too secure of you on that side. Your candour in pardoning my errors may make you more remiss in correcting them, if you will not withal consider that they come into the world with your
310 approbation, and through your hands. I beg from you the greatest favour you can confer upon an absent person, since I repose upon your management what is dearest to me, my fame and reputation; and therefore I hope it will stir you up to make my poem fairer by many of your
315 blots: if not, you know the story of the gamester who married the rich man's daughter, and when her father denied the portion, christened all the children by his surname, that if, in conclusion, they must beg, they should do so by one name as well as by the other. But since the
320 reproach of my faults will light on you, 'tis but reason I should do you that justice to the readers, to let them know that if there be anything tolerable in this poem, they owe the argument to your choice, the writing to your encouragement, the correction to your judgement,
325 and the care of it to your friendship, to which he must ever acknowledge himself to owe all things, who is,

SIR,

From Charlton in The most obedient and most
Wiltshire, Novem. faithful of your servants,
10. 1666. JOHN DRYDEN.

305–6. Nec . . . vocant] 'There are not a few who call it discernment to disparage their friends' (*Epistulae* vii 28).

Annus Mirabilis:
The Year of Wonders,
MDCLXVI

I

In thriving arts long time had Holland grown,
Crouching at home, and cruel when abroad;
Scarce leaving us the means to claim our own;
Our King they courted, and our merchants awed.

2

5   Trade, which like blood should circularly flow,
Stopped in their channels, found its freedom lost;

1–24. Samuel Johnson noted that the opening of *AM* resembles the opening of
Waller's *Of a War with Spain, and Fight at Sea* (1658): 'Now, for some ages, had
the pride of Spain / Made the sun shine on half the world in vain; / While she
bid war to all that durst supply / The place of those her cruelty made die. / Of
nature's bounty men forbore to taste, / And the best portion of the earth lay
waste, / From the new world her silver and her gold / Came, like a tempest, to
confound the old; / . . . When Britain, looking with a just disdain / Upon this
gilded majesty of Spain, / And knowing well that empire must decline, / Whose
chief support and sinews are of coin, / Our nation's solid virtue did oppose /
To the rich troublers of the world's repose' (ll. 1–8, 13–18).
1. Holland] England was at war with the United Provinces of the Netherlands,
a republic made up of seven independent provinces; Holland was a powerful maritime province, and its name was often used loosely for the whole republic; 'Belgium'
was another loose seventeenth-century term for the same country (cp. l. 16 etc.).
2. Crouching] cringing, fawning (*OED* 2). *cruel*] The cruelty of the Dutch against
English traders had recently been recorded by Thomas Mun in *England's Treasure
by Forraign Trade* (1664) 206 and in *His Majesties Propriety, and Dominion on the
British Seas Asserted* (1665) (*Works*). The massacre of English sailors by the Dutch
at Amboyna in 1619 was still bitterly remembered, as in D.'s play *Amboyna* (1673).
4. After the Restoration Holland desired peace and a trade agreement with England;
inconclusive negotiations took place in 1660–2.
5–6. Simon Ford (Θαυμάσια Κύριου ἐν Βυθῷ (1665)) says that the Dutch
'think the *Trade* of the *whole World* ought to run in no other *channell* but that
which unloads it selfe into their *private purses*' (9), and compares restriction of
trade to illness in the body, where 'the *blood* and *spirits* being any way *infected* or
obstructed (though in *remoter* parts) quickly by *circulation* communicate their distempers to the *heart* it selfe' (26). The Speaker of the House of Commons said:
'we found our Body Politick entring into a Consumption, our Treasures, that
are the sinews of War, and the bond of Peace, are much exhausted; the great
aydes which are given to your Majesty for the maintenance of the War, are but
like the blood in its circulation, which will return again, and nourish all the parts'
(*The Speech of Sʳ. Edw. Turnor, Kᵗ . . . Delivered on Friday the Eighteenth day of
January 1666* [i.e. 1666/7] (1666) 2).
5. Perhaps echoed by Denham in 'Our knowledge, like our blood, must circu-
late' ('The Progress of Learning' l. 216, in his *Poems and Translations* (1668)).

Thither the wealth of all the world did go,
  And seemed but shipwrecked on so base a coast.

3
For them alone the heavens had kindly heat,
10 ᵃIn eastern quarries ripening precious dew;
For them the Idumaean balm did sweat,
  And in hot Ceylon spicy forests grew.

(a) In eastern quarries, etc: *Precious stones at first are dew, condensed and hardened by the warmth of the sun, or subterranean fires.*

4
The sun but seemed the labourer of their year;
  ᵇEach waxing moon supplied her watery store
15 To swell those tides which from the line did bear
  Their brim-full vessels to the Belgian shore.

(b) Each waxing, etc: *According to their opinion, who think that great heap of waters under the line is depressed into tides by the moon towards the poles.*

5
Thus mighty in her ships stood Carthage long,
  And swept the riches of the world from far;

8. shipwrecked] *1667*'s spelling *shipwracked* indicates seventeenth-century pronunciation. *base*] punning on the meaning 'low-lying' (*OED* 3); cp. the French name for the Netherlands, Les Pays-Bas.
9. kindly] favourable to growth (*OED* 5b).
10. The origin of metals and stones was a subject of contemporary debate. At a meeting of the Royal Society on 27 May 1663 some members argued 'that minerals were produced by certain subterraneous juices, which passing through the veins of the earth, and having mingled therewith, do afterwards precipitate and crystallize into stones, ores and metals of various kinds and figures, according to the various kinds of salts contained in the juices and the earth' (Thomas Birch, *History of the Royal Society*, 4 vols (1756–7) i 247) (*Works*).
11. From Virgil: *odorato . . . sudantia ligno / balsama* ('balsam sweating from the odorous wood'; *Geo.* ii 118–19). Idumaea was a region in southern Palestine occupied by the Edomites.
12. The Royal Society had enquired about the cinnamon trees in Ceylon (Sprat 169) (*Works*). *Ceylon*] stressed on the first syllable.
14–15. Descartes proposed in his *Principia* (1644) that tides result from lunar pressure, rather than lunar attraction; G. P. de Roberval further argued that the pressure of the moon being greatest at the equator, the waters are depressed there and pushed outwards towards the poles (reprinted by Marin Mersenne, *Novarum Observationum Physico-Mathematicarum tomus III* (1647) 31–2; C. W. Adams, *Isis* xliv (1953) 100–1).
15. line] equator.
17–20. The Second Punic War (218–201 BC) decisively established Rome as the dominant power in the Mediterranean; the Second Dutch War by no means

      Yet stooped to Rome, less wealthy but more strong:
20   And this may prove our second Punic War.

6

What peace can be where both to one pretend?
    (But they more diligent, and we more strong)
Or if a peace, it soon must have an end,
    For they would grow too powerful were it long.

7

25 Behold two nations then, engaged so far
      That each seven years the fit must shake each land;
    Where France will side to weaken us by war,
      Who only can his vast designs withstand.

8

    See how he feeds th' ʿIberian with delays,
30   To render us his timely friendship vain;
    And while his secret soul on Flanders preys,
      He rocks the cradle of the babe of Spain.

(c) Th' Iberian: *the Spaniard.*

9

    Such deep designs of empire does he lay
      O'er them whose cause he seems to take in hand;
35 And prudently would make them lords at sea
      To whom with ease he can give laws by land.

---

achieved a comparable result for England. The First Dutch War had been fought successfully under Cromwell in 1653–4. The same comparison is used by William Smith: 'With equall folly, and with equal fate / Mistaken *Carthage* urg'd the *Romane* State' (*A Poem on the famous ship called the Loyal London* (1666; licensed 15 June) 4). For further echoes of Smith's poem see ll. 601–16n, 1049–52n, 1205n. For comparisons of Holland and Carthage during the First Dutch War see Marvell, 'The Character of Holland' ll. 141–2, and L. S., *The Perfect Politician* (1660) 254–60 (a biography of Cromwell). For D.'s later use of the comparison see 'Epilogue to *Amboyna*' ll. 19–22.

21. pretend] claim.

27–36. Louis XIV was bound by the treaty of 1662 to aid the Dutch against aggression. His marriage with the Spanish princess Maria Theresa in 1660 seemed to promise peace and dynastic union between France and Spain. In June 1664 Clarendon sent Sir Richard Fanshawe as ambassador to Madrid in an effort to repair England's bad relations with Spain, but through Fanshawe's incompetence and Louis's influence this came to nothing. It was in Louis's interest for England and Holland to weaken each other, and Dutch domination of the sea in the event

10

This saw our King; and long within his breast
   His pensive counsels balanced to and fro;
He grieved the land he freed should be oppressed,
40   And he less for it than usurpers do.

11

His generous mind the fair ideas drew
   Of fame and honour which in dangers lay;
Where wealth, like fruit on precipices, grew,
   Not to be gathered but by birds of prey.

12

45   The loss and gain each fatally were great,
   And still his subjects called aloud for war;
But peaceful kings o'er martial people set
   Each other's poise and counterbalance are.

13

He first surveyed the charge with careful eyes,
50   Which none but mighty monarchs could maintain;
Yet judged, like vapours that from limbecks rise,
   It would in richer showers descend again.

---

of their victory would be counterbalanced by the proximity to Holland of Louis's
powerful army. When Philip IV of Spain died in September 1665, leaving the
throne to his infant son, Louis invaded the Spanish Netherlands (Flanders) and
claimed them for his wife.

38. Cp. the Latin idiom *consilia eventis ponderare* (Cicero, *Pro Rabirio Postumo* 1).

40. On the military achievements of Britain under Cromwell see 'Heroic
Stanzas' ll. 81, 96, 113–24.

41. *generous*] noble.

45–8. On 2 June 1664 Charles wrote to his sister Henriette-Anne: 'I never saw
so great an appetite to a war as is, in both this town and country, especially in
the Parliament men, who, I am confident, would pawn their estates to maintain
a war. But all this shall not govern me, for I will look merely [to] what is just
and best for the honour and good of England, and will be very steady in what
I resolve, and if I be forced to a war, I shall be ready with as good ships and
men as ever was seen, and leave the success to God' (*Letters of Charles II*, edited
by Arthur Bryant (1935) 159).

51. *limbecks*] alembics, apparatuses used in distilling; for the alchemical implications see l. 1169n.

52. Cp. Virgil: *tum pater omnipotens fecundis imbribus Aether / coniugis in gremium
laetae descendit* (*Geo.* ii 325–6: 'Then the almighty father, the Sky, descends in
fruitful showers upon the lap of his joyful consort'). Cp. 'The Sun exhales the
vapours from the earth, and then sends them down again in showres of plenty:

14

At length resolved t' assert the watery ball,
    He in himself did whole armadoes bring;
55 Him agèd seamen might their master call,
    And choose for general were he not their King.

15

It seems as every ship their sovereign knows,
    His awful summons they so soon obey;
So hear the scaly herd when ᵈProteus blows,
60 And so to pasture follow through the sea.

(d) When Proteus blows, *or* Caeruleus Proteus immania ponti armenta, et mag-
nas pascit sub gurgite phocas. *Virg.*

16

To see this fleet upon the ocean move,
    Angels drew wide the curtains of the skies;

So we to our great joy, do find that our obedience and affection to your Majesty
are returned upon our heads in plenty, peace and protection' (*The Several Speeches
of Sr. Edward Turner Kt.* (1661) 9). Cp. ll. 181–4.
53. assert] lay claim to (*OED* 3, 4); see 'Heroic Stanzas' l. 85*n*.
54–6. Charles took a keen interest in the navy: John Sheffield's *Character of Charles
II* says: 'The great and almost only pleasure of mind he appeared addicted to,
was shipping and sea-affairs; which seemed to be so much his talent both
for knowledge, as well as inclination, that a war of that kind was rather an
entertainment, than any disturbance to his thoughts' (*Works* (1723) ii 59–60). See
also 'To His Sacred Majesty' ll. 107–10; Robert Latham in Pepys, *Diary* x 56–8;
Hutton, *Charles the Second passim*. The anonymous *A Poem upon his Maiesties
Coronation* said: 'The Seamans Art, and his great end, Commerce / Through all
the corners of the Universe, / Are not alone the subject of Your care, / But
Your delight' (9).
54. Cp. Virgil: *magnum / agmen agens Clausus magnique ipse agminis instar* (*Aen.* vii
706–7: 'Clausus bringing a large army, and himself worth a large army').
58. awful] awe-inspiring.
59n. A version of *Geo.* iv 388, 394–5: *caeruleus Proteus . . . immania cuius / armenta
et turpis pascit sub gurgite phocas* ('sea-green Proteus drives his huge flock and ugly
seals to pasture under the sea'). The comparison of Charles with Proteus may
draw upon the use of Proteus as an emblem of the qualities of the wise ruler (see
Ross 371 and D.'s *Albion and Albanius* III i (*Works* xv 47–8)).
59. hear] Eds; here *1667, 1668, 1688*.
62–3. Cp. Du Bartas, tr. Sylvester: God 'Spred Heav'ns blew Curtains and those
Lamps . . . burnisht' (I i 463); and Sidney: '*Phoebus* drew wide the curtaines of
the skies' (*Astrophil and Stella* xiii 12).

And heaven, as if there wanted lights above,
For tapers made two glaring comets rise.

17

65 Whether they unctuous exhalations are,
Fired by the sun, or seeming so alone,
Or each some more remote and slippery star
Which loses footing when to mortals shown:

18

Or one that bright companion of the sun,
70   Whose glorious aspect sealed our new-born King;
And now a round of greater years begun,
New influence from his walks of light did bring.

63. there] *1668, 1688*; their *1667. wanted*] lacked.
64. The first comet was discovered in Spain in November 1664, and was last
seen in March 1665; the second was discovered at Aix in March 1665 and dis-
appeared in April (see Pepys 15, 17 December 1664, 1 March 1665). There had
been a comet in 1652 when the English defeated the Dutch at sea (John
Gadbury, *De Cometis* (1665) 43). Gadbury says: 'It is a thing so *rare* and *unusual,*
for to have *three Comets* in a *year*, nay, sometimes in an *Age*: that we may properly term *this*, wherein we live, not only, ANNUS (*sed* AETAS) MIRABILIS!
not only, a WONDERFUL YEAR, but AGE' (62); but he also thought that
the first comet portended 'shipwracks and sea-fights; Wars . . . destruction of
Governments, Laws, Customs and Constitutions'; and the second 'Famine, the
Plague, Exile', and he carefully leaves in Latin the implication that the King may
die (45–8). D. omits these dire implications, as did Waller: 'Make Heaven concerned, and an unusual star / Declare the importance of the approaching war'
(*Instructions* ll. 7–8).
65–72. D. offers four explanations for comets: (i) they are produced by vapours
drawn up by the sun: this is the traditional theory, originating with Aristotle, and
held by Gadbury ('not so much *enflamed*, as *illustrated* of the Sun' (6)); (ii) they
are illusions, as suggested by Galileo in 1623, and recorded by Gadbury (5);
(iii) they are falling stars: cp. Song I in *Tyrannic Love* ll. 12–13; Shakespeare, *The
Rape of Lucrece* l. 1525 and *A Midsummer Night's Dream* II i 153; (iv) one of
the comets is that which greeted the birth of Charles II and has now returned
(cp. *Astraea Redux* ll. 288–9n).
67. slippery] Probably from Latin usage; *labor* ('slide') is often used of stars (e.g.
Geo. i 366).
71. Cp. *Astraea Redux* ll. 292–3n.
72. influence] In astrology an emanation from a heavenly body which acts upon
human life (*OED* 2). *walks*] region where something moves (*OED* 8b); probably rendering *solisque vias* ('walks of the sun') in *Aen.* vi 796.

19

Victorious York did first, with famed success,
　　To his known valour make the Dutch give place:
75　Thus heaven our monarch's fortune did confess,
　　Beginning conquest from his royal race.

20

But since it was decreed, auspicious King,
　　In Britain's right that thou shouldst wed the main,
Heaven as a gage would cast some precious thing,
80　And therefore doomed that Lawson should be slain.

21

Lawson amongst the foremost met his fate,
　　Whom sea-green Sirens from the rocks lament;
Thus as an offering for the Grecian state
He first was killed who first to battle went.

22

85　*Their chief blown up, in air not waves expired,
　　To which his pride presumed to give the law;

73–4. The Duke of York took command of the fleet on 25 March 1665, and put to sea in May with ninety-eight warships. The Dutch fleet was engaged off Lowestoft on 2–3 June, and although both sides incurred heavy losses, the Dutch suffered worst and withdrew. The news was received with delight in London: see Pepys 8 June, and the opening of *EDP*.

75. *confess*] reveal by circumstances (*OED* 5).

77. *auspicious*] favoured by heaven (*OED* 3); cp. *AA* l. 230, *Threnodia Augustalis* l. 373.

78. *wed the main*] As in the annual ceremony on Ascension Day when the Doge of Venice married the sea and cast a ring into it. The *Second Advice* sarcastically says that this ceremony was eclipsed by the splendour of the Duchess of York's visit to the fleet at Harwich (ll. 73–4; *POAS* i 40).

79. *gage*] pledge.

80–1. *Lawson*] Vice-Admiral Sir John Lawson commanded ships in the service of Parliament from 1642 to 1656, and in 1659–60 was Vice-Admiral of the fleet which brought Charles from Holland. He served against the corsairs in the Mediterranean 1661–4. At Lowestoft he was wounded in the knee; gangrene set in and he died on 29 June.

80. Cp. 'They therefore doom that *Dargonet* must fall' (Davenant, *Gondibert* I iv 18).

83–4. Protesilaus was the first Greek to land at Troy, and the first to be killed (*Iliad* ii 695–702). Lawson's ship was in the van of the fleet.

85. The Dutch commander Opdam's flagship, *De Eendracht*, blew up during an engagement with the Duke of York's ship *Royal Charles*. This was the

The Dutch confessed heaven present, and retired,
      And all was Britain the wide ocean saw.
*The Admiral of Holland.

                              23
      To nearest ports their shattered ships repair,
90   Where by our dreadful cannon they lay awed:
      So reverently men quit the open air
            When thunder speaks the angry gods abroad.

                              24
                                        The attempt at Bergen.
      And now approached their fleet from India, fraught
            With all the riches of the rising sun;
95   And precious sand from ᶜsouthern climates brought
            (The fatal regions where the war begun).

(e) Southern climates: *Guinea.*

                              25
      Like hunted castors, conscious of their store,
            Their waylayed wealth to Norway's coasts they bring;

---

turning-point in the battle. D. omits to mention that the Dutch were allowed
to retire unharried into the Texel because James's secretary Henry Brounker, weary
of the pursuit, fabricated an order from James to slacken sail while the Duke was
asleep.
91–2. Cp. D.'s contemporaneous *Secret Love*: 'as, when it thunders / Men reverently quit the open Air / Because the angry Gods are then abroad' (III i 13–15)
(*Works*).
93–124. In July 1665 the English fleet, commanded by the Earl of Sandwich,
was cruising about the Dogger Bank waiting to intercept the rich fleet
from the Indies under the Dutch admiral De Ruyter. An arrangement was negotiated with the King of Denmark to allow the English to attack the fleet in the
neutral port of Bergen, in return for half the spoils. Sandwich dispatched
Teddiman with fifteen ships, but the governor of Bergen urged delay pend-
ing firm orders from his king. Impatient, Teddiman entered the harbour on
2 August, was bombarded by the shore forts, and withdrew with the loss of
118 men.
95–6. *southern climates*] The valuable gold-bearing reefs on the coast of West Africa
had been fought over by Dutch and English factors for fifty years. The immediate
trigger of the Second Dutch War was the dispatch in August 1664 of a Dutch
fleet under De Ruyter to retake the Gold Coast which had been captured
earlier that year by Sir Robert Holmes.
97. *castors*] beavers, who were hunted for the substance in their sacs which was
used in making perfumes and medicines.

There first the north's cold bosom spices bore,
100   And winter brooded on the eastern spring.

26

By the rich scent we found our perfumed prey,
    Which flanked with rocks did close in covert lie;
And round about their murdering cannon lay,
    At once to threaten and invite the eye.

27

105 Fiercer than cannon, and than rocks more hard,
    The English undertake th' unequal war:
Seven ships alone, by which the port is barred,
    Besiege the Indies and all Denmark dare.

28

These fight like husbands, but like lovers those:
110   These fain would keep, and those more fain enjoy;
And to such height their frantic passion grows
    That what both love, both hazard to destroy.

29

Amidst whole heaps of spices lights a ball,
    And now their odours armed against them fly:
115 Some preciously by shattered porcelain fall,
    And some by aromatic splinters die.

30

And though by tempests of the prize bereft,
    In heaven's inclemency some ease we find:
Our foes we vanquished by our valour left,
120   And only yielded to the seas and wind.

---

107. Seven ships] 'I got 8 sail in a line, and brought our broadsides on the ships in the harbour, which spread from one side to the other, the other 7 I placed against the Castle' (Teddiman's report to Sandwich, in *Journal of Edward Montagu* (1929) 262).

109. lovers] Cp. Waller: 'These dying lovers' (*Of a War with Spain* l. 89).

110–12. enjoy . . . destroy] Cp. Waller: 'glad to see the fire destroy / Wealth that prevailing foes were to enjoy' (ll. 77–8).

113–16. Cp. Waller: 'Spices and gums about them melting fry, / And, phoenix-like, in that rich nest they die' (ll. 83–4).

120. The wind was blowing from the south, out of the port, so Teddiman could not send in his fireships (*Journal* 262).

31
Nor wholly lost we so deserved a prey,
  For storms, repenting, part of it restored,
Which, as a tribute from the Baltic Sea,
  The British Ocean sent her mighty lord.

32
125 Go, mortals, now, and vex yourselves in vain
  For wealth which so uncertainly must come,
When what was brought so far, and with such pain,
  Was only kept to lose it nearer home.

33
The son who, twice three months on th' ocean tossed,
130   Prepared to tell what he had passed before,
Now sees in English ships the Holland coast,
  And parents' arms in vain stretched from the shore.

34
This careful husband had been long away,
  Whom his chaste wife and little children mourn,

121–4. The Dutch ships were scattered by a storm on their way home from Bergen, and Sandwich captured seven warships, two East Indiamen and other merchantmen (*Journal* 277–81).

125–40. D.'s note to l. 137 cites Petronius, *Satyricon* 115 ('If you consider it rightly, shipwreck is everywhere'). In this note *1667* reads *naufragiunt est* in the text, which is corrected to *fit naufragium* in the errata; it is a peculiar correction, since the proper reading in Petronius is *naufragium est*, and the correction of *nt* to *m* is all that was needed. Christie noted that D.'s ll. 125–36 also draw upon the same passage: *Hunc, forsitan, proclamo, in aliqua parte terrarum secura expectat uxor, forsitan ignarus tempestatis filius, aut patrem utique reliquit aliquem, cui proficiscens osculum dedit. Haec sunt consilia mortalium, haec vota magnarum cogitationum. . . . Ite nunc, mortales, et magnis cogitationibus pectora implete. Ite cauti, et opes fraudibus captas per mille annos disponite. Nempe hic proxima luce patrimonii sui rationes inspexit, nempe diem etiam, quo venturus esset in patriam, animo suo fixit. Dii deaeque, quam longe a destinatione sua iacet.* ('Perhaps somewhere, I say, a carefree wife waits for him; perhaps a son, not knowing about the storm; or he left a father, or someone whom he kissed as he set out. Such are the plans of mortals, such are our great designs. . . . Go now, mortals, and fill your hearts with great schemes. Go and carefully invest your ill-gotten gains for a thousand years. Yesterday he must have looked at the accounts of his investments, he must have imagined the day he would reach his home town. O heavens, how far away he lies from his destination!'). Thomas Flatman paraphrases the same passage in his *Poems and Songs* (1674) 36–7. Cp. Waller, *Of a War with Spain* ll. 51–60.

134. Cp. also Lucretius iii 894–6 (tr. D. in 'Lucretius: Against the Fear of Death' ll. 76–80) and *Geo.* ii 523–4, esp. Virgil's *casta* ('chaste').

135   Who on their fingers learned to tell the day
          On which their father promised to return.

                              35
          ᶠSuch are the proud designs of human kind,
             And so we suffer shipwreck everywhere!
          Alas, what port can such a pilot find,
140   Who in the night of fate must blindly steer!

(f) Such are etc: *From Petronius*: Si bene calculum ponas ubique fit naufragium.

                              36
          The undistinguished seeds of good and ill
             Heaven in his bosom from our knowledge hides,
          And draws them in contempt of human skill,
             Which oft for friends mistaken foes provides.

                              37
145   Let Münster's prelate ever be accursed,
          In whom we seek the ᵍGerman faith in vain:
          Alas, that he should teach the English first
             That fraud and avarice in the church could reign!

(g) The German faith: *Tacitus saith of them*, Nullos mortalium fide aut armis ante
Germanos esse.

                              38
          Happy who never trust a stranger's will,
150   Whose friendship's in his interest understood,
          Since money giv'n but tempts him to be ill
             When power is too remote to make him good.

141. 'Good and evill we know in the field of this World grow up together almost
inseparably; . . . those confused seeds which were impos'd on *Psyche* as an incessant labour to cull out, and sort asunder, were not more intermixt' (Milton,
Areopagitica (1644); *Complete Prose Works* ii 514).   *undistinguished*] not separated
or kept distinct (*OED* 1).
145. In June 1665 a treaty was made with Bernhard von Galen, Bishop of Münster,
whereby he would invade Holland in return for subsidies from England. No peace
was to be made without agreement. He did invade, but was soon under pressure from French armies and from his German enemies. English subsidies dried
up, and he was forced to make peace unilaterally in April 1666.
146n. 'No men exceed the Germans in loyalty or arms', *Annales* xiii 54. (The
usual text is *armis aut fide*.)

39

War declared by France.

Till now, alone the mighty nations strove:
The rest at gaze without the lists did stand;
155   And threatening France, placed like a painted Jove,
Kept idle thunder in his lifted hand:

40

That eunuch guardian of rich Holland's trade,
Who envies us what he wants power t' enjoy;
Whose noiseful valour does no foe invade,
160   And weak assistance will his friends destroy.

41

Offended that we fought without his leave,
He takes this time his secret hate to show;
Which Charles does with a mind so calm receive
As one that neither seeks nor shuns his foe.

42

165   With France to aid the Dutch the Danes unite,
France as their tyrant, Denmark as their slave;
But when with one three nations join to fight,
They silently confess that one more brave.

43

Louis had chased the English from his shore,
170   But Charles the French as subjects does invite.

---

154. at gaze] gazing in wonder or fascination (*OED* 3b).
155–62. For the early part of 1665 Louis's attitude was uncertain. He sent an embassy to try to reconcile England and Holland, but as the year wore on it became apparent that Louis would honour his treaty obligations to Holland, and he declared war on 6 January 1666. Louis was beginning to assert his claim to the Spanish Netherlands, and at this point wanted the friendship of the Dutch; neither did he want to see England strengthened.
165–6. After the fiasco at Bergen, England tried to cement an alliance with Denmark by threats and promises; but in February 1666 Denmark joined the other side, the decision being eased by a French subsidy.
169–76. Louis had given English residents in France three months to leave; Charles promised protection to any French or Dutch nationals who wished to leave their countries, particularly oppressed Protestants, in *His Majesties Declaration against the French* (9 February 1666); cp. Pepys 11 February.

Would heaven for each some Solomon restore,
   Who by their mercy may decide their right.

44

   Were subjects so but only by their choice,
     And not from birth did forced dominion take,
175 Our Prince alone would have the public voice,
     And all his neighbours' realms would deserts make.

45

   He without fear a dangerous war pursues,
     Which without rashness he began before:
   As honour made him first the danger choose,
180   So still he makes it good on virtue's score.

46

   The doubled charge his subjects' love supplies,
     Who in that bounty to themselves are kind:
   So glad Egyptians see their Nilus rise,
     And in his plenty their abundance find.

47
Prince Rupert and Duke Albemarle sent to sea.

185 With equal power he does two chiefs create,
     Two such, as each seemed worthiest when alone;
   Each able to sustain a nation's fate,
     Since both had found a greater in their own.

48

   Both great in courage, conduct, and in fame,
190   Yet neither envious of the other's praise;

171–2. See 1 Kings iii 16–28 for the judgement of Solomon.
176. deserts] 1667's spelling *desarts* indicates seventeenth-century pronunciation.
181–4. Cp. l. 52n.
181. doubled charge] On 9 February 1665 the House of Commons, in bellicose mood, voted £2,500,000 for the war, which was to be raised by a three-year assessment. In October 1665 the House voted a further £1,250,000.
185–6. Rupert and Albemarle were placed in joint command of a fleet of eighty ships (Pepys 23 April 1666).
188. i.e. their own lives had already demonstrated their capacity to triumph over adversity (see ll. 193–4n, 197–8n).
190. But see the quotation in ll. 197–8n below.

Their duty, faith, and interest too the same,
    Like mighty partners equally they raise.

49

The Prince long time had courted Fortune's love,
    But once possessed did absolutely reign;
195 Thus with their Amazons the heroes strove,
    And conquered first those beauties they would gain.

50

The Duke beheld, like Scipio, with disdain
    That Carthage which he ruined rise once more;
And shook aloft the fasces of the main
200   To fright those slaves with what they felt before.

51

Together to the watery camp they haste,
    Whom matrons passing to their children show:

192. *raise*] rise (*OED* 35).
193–4. Prince Rupert (1619–82) was the son of the Queen of Bohemia and the
Elector Palatine, and shared their exile in Holland and England during 1620–37.
After he and his father lost the Battle of Vlotho (1638) he was imprisoned until
1641. During the Civil War he served his uncle Charles I as a successful but rash
and brutal general, though he lost the Battle of Marston Moor. From 1649 to
1653 he harassed the Commonwealth's fleet.
193. For the image cp. 'Heroic Stanzas' ll. 29–30n.
194. i.e. dominated Fortune like an autocratic (*absolute*) ruler.
195–6. For Theseus' campaign against the Amazons and his marriage to their Queen
Antiope, see Plutarch, *Theseus* 26–7.
196–7. D. also links stanzas by repeating a rhyme at ll. 296–7, 524–5, 576–7,
1024–5, 1116–17.
197–8. Monck (for whom see *Astraea Redux*, headnote) had been a successful
commander of the fleet in the First Dutch War. Scipio Africanus defeated the
Carthaginians in Spain, and ended the Second Punic War by defeating Hannibal
at Zama (202 BC). One contemporary viewed Monck's fortune more critically:
'It was reported, before the General went from Whitehall, that he had said he
would undertake with forty sail of ships, to beat the Dutch out of the sea. Fortune
had so long attended him at sea and land, that perhaps he took her for his slave,
and she would now let him know to his cost, she was his commandress . . . it is
not unlikely, that he was greedy to engross all the glory of besting the Dutch to
himself' (MS account in *Letter Book* 212).
199. *fasces of the main*] Cp. *Astraea Redux* l. 249n.
200. The Scythians suppressed a slave rising by brandishing horse-whips instead
of spears; the slaves were awed, and fled (Herodotus iv 3–4).
201. *watery camp*] The Latin *campus* means 'plain'; cp. Virgil's *campos liquentis*
('liquid plains'; *Aen.* vi 724).

Infants' first vows for them to heaven are cast,
And ʰfuture people bless them as they go.

(h) Future people: Examina infantium futurusque populus. *Plin. Jun. in pan. ad Traj.*

52

205   With them no riotous pomp nor Asian train
          T' infect a navy with their gaudy fears,
      To make slow fights, and victories but vain—
          But war, severely, like itself appears.

53

      Diffusive of themselves where'er they pass,
210   They make that warmth in others they expect:
      Their valour works like bodies on a glass,
          And does its image on their men project.

54

                              Duke of Albemarle's battle, first day.
      Our fleet divides, and straight the Dutch appear,
          In number and a famed commander bold;
215   The narrow seas can scarce their navy bear,
          Or crowded vessels can their soldiers hold.

55

      The Duke, less numerous, but in courage more,
          On wings of all the winds to combat flies;
      His murdering guns a loud defiance roar,
220   And bloody crosses on his flagstaffs rise.

204n. From Pliny, *Panegyricus* 26: 'swarms of children, the future populace'.
205. Asian] proverbially luxurious.
211–12. For the image of the optic glass cp. 'Epilogue Spoken to the King' ll. 1–4.
213–16. On 29 May Rupert, with twenty ships, sailed to intercept the French
fleet which was wrongly reported to be entering the Channel. Albemarle was left
in the Downs with about sixty ships, and this division of the fleet was much criticized after the event. At the same time, the Dutch fleet of eighty-four warships
under De Ruyter was leaving harbour. Orders for the recall of Rupert were delayed,
but Albemarle moved to a new anchorage off the North Foreland. On 1 June
Albemarle decided (against the advice of some of his officers) to engage the Dutch,
who were sighted at anchor off Ostend. Thus began the Four Days Battle.
220. Each ship flew the Union Jack at the jack staff; an ensign of the squadronal
colour (red, white or blue) with the red St George's cross in the canton at the
ensign staff; and all except the admiral's ships flew long pennants with the St
George's cross in the hoist at the main mast (Timothy Wilson, *Flags at Sea* (1986)
21–2).

56

Both furl their sails, and strip them for the fight,
    Their folded sheets dismiss the useless air:
ᶦTh' Elean plains could boast no nobler sight,
    When struggling champions did their bodies bare.

(i) Th' Elean etc: *Where the Olympic games were celebrated.*

57

225 Borne each by other in a distant line
        The sea-built forts in dreadful order move;
    So vast the noise, as if not fleets did join
        ᵏBut lands unfixed and floating nations strove.

(k) Lands unfixed: *From Virgil:* Credas innare revulsas Cyclades.

58

    Now passed, on either side they nimbly tack,
230   Both strive to intercept and guide the wind,
    And in its eye more closely they come back
        To finish all the deaths they left behind.

59

    On high-raised decks the haughty Belgians ride,
        Beneath whose shade our humble frigates go:

221–2. In preparation for action 'they use to strip themselves into their short sailes, or fighting sailes, which is onely the fore sail, the maine and fore top sailes, because the rest should not be fired nor spoiled' (John Smith, *The Sea-Mans Grammar* (1653) 60) (*Works*).
225–44. Ogg 267 explains that the usual practice was 'for each fleet to file past the other, firing into the enemy hulls and rigging; the ships in the van, having fired their volleys, then bore round to take up position behind the rearmost ships so as to repeat the attack. This was continued until the order of battle was broken, when there was likely to be a general mêlée in which the disabled ships might be boarded or burnt by fire-ships'. On this occasion, the English ships passed twice through the Dutch fleet, 'the *Dutch* being on the Leewards, their Guns mounted so high, that they onely shot our Rigging, but did little execution on the Men or Hulls . . . they had much holed and torn the Admirals Rigging' (*London Gazette* lviii).
228n. Virgil, *Aen.* viii 691–3: 'you would think that the Cyclades, torn from their roots, were floating on the sea, or that high mountains were clashing with mountains, so huge are the towered ships on which the heroes stand'. revulsas] *1688;* revultas *1667, 1668.* The comparison with the Cyclades is used in William Smith's poem on the Battle of Lowestoft, *Ingratitude Reveng'd* (1665), which includes the line 'Or two unfixed *Towns,* or floating *Woods*' (3); the poem ends with an address to the City of London.
230. guide] manage (*OED* 4b).

235   Such port the elephant bears, and so defied
          By the rhinoceros her unequal foe.

60

          And as the built, so different is the fight:
             Their mounting shot is on our sails designed;
          Deep in their hulls our deadly bullets light,
240   And through the yielding planks a passage find.

61

          Our dreaded admiral from far they threat,
             Whose battered rigging their whole war receives:
          All bare, like some old oak which tempests beat,
             He stands, and sees below his scattered leaves.

62

245   Heroes of old, when wounded, shelter sought,
             But he, who meets all danger with disdain,
          Ev'n in their face his ship to anchor brought,
             And steeple-high stood propped upon the main.

63

          At this excess of courage, all amazed
250   The foremost of his foes a while withdraw:

235–6. A traditional idea: see Pliny, *Naturalis Historia* viii 29; Du Bartas tr. Sylvester
I vi 41–50.
235. port] bearing, demeanour.
237. built] style of construction, esp. of a ship (*OED*).
239–40. Cp. Waller: 'Through yielding planks the angry bullets fly' (*Of a War
with Spain* l. 47).
241–8. 'Several other of our ships, had their Rigging and Sails very much shattered, and especially the Admiral (his Courage carrying him foremost to all Dangers)
to such a degree, as she was forced in the sight of the Enemy to chop to an
Anchor, till she had brought new Sayls to the Yards, the old being rendred
useless' (*True Narrative* 4).
243–4. Delicately recalling that 'The Duke had all his Tackle taken off by
Chain-shot, and his Breeches to his Skin were shot off' (*London Gazette* lix). The
incident is less sympathetically recorded in *Third Advice* ll. 123–30 (*POAS* i 73).
D. is also adapting Virgil: *ac velut annoso validam cum robore quercum / Alpini Boreae
nunc hinc nunc flatibus illinc / eruere inter se certant; it stridor, et altae / consternunt
terram concusso stipite frondes* ('And as when Alpine North winds strive with each
other to uproot a mighty oak of aged strength, with blasts now on this side, now
on that, a creaking ensues, and the lofty leaves strew the ground, as the trunk is
shaken'; *Aen.* iv 441–4). John Ogilby's translation here includes the words
'Tempests . . . some old Oake . . . scatter'd Leavs' (1654) 278; differently worded
in his 1649 and 1665 texts.

With such respect in entered Rome they gazed,
Who on high chairs the godlike fathers saw.

64

And now, as where Patroclus' body lay,
Here Trojan chiefs advanced, and there the Greek:
255 Ours o'er the Duke their pious wings display,
And theirs the noblest spoils of Britain seek.

65

Meantime his busy mariners he hastes,
His shattered sails with rigging to restore;
And willing pines ascend his broken masts,
260 Whose lofty heads rise higher than before.

66

Straight to the Dutch he turns his dreadful prow,
More fierce th' important quarrel to decide:
Like swans in long array his vessels show,
Whose crests advancing do the waves divide.

67

265 They charge, re-charge, and all along the sea
They drive and squander the huge Belgian fleet;
Berkeley alone who nearest danger lay
Did a like fate with lost Creüsa meet.

251–2. When the Gauls sacked Rome in 387 BC they were awed by the sight of the elders sitting in their chairs of state 'like gods' (*simillimos diis*; Livy v 41). *entered Rome*] a Latinate participial construction. *fathers*] rendering *patres*, the Roman honorific for senators.

253–4. The battle over the body of Patroclus is related in *Iliad* xvii.

255. *pious*] faithful in the duties owed to a friend or superior (*OED* 2); cp. Latin *pius*, frequently applied by Virgil to Aeneas. *display*] spread out (*OED* 1).

259. *willing*] perhaps a Latinate usage: cp. *volentia rura* ('willing Ground' in D.'s translation) in *Geo*. ii 500.

265. 'We tackt and stood through the Body of their Fleet, . . . then tackt to the Westward again' (*True Narrative* 4). *all along*] throughout (*OED* 1).

266. *squander*] scatter (*OED* 2).

267–8. *who nearest danger lay*] 1667 third issue; *not making equal way* 1667 first and second issues. The alteration was probably made to avoid any imputation of cowardice, of which Sir William Berkeley (1639–66) had been accused in the Battle of Lowestoft: cp. *Second Advice*, 'But judg'd it safe and decent (cost what cost) / To lose the day, since his dear brother's lost. / With his whole squadron straight away he bore, / And like good boy, promis'd to fight no more' (ll. 193–6; *POAS*

68

The night comes on, we eager to pursue
270   The combat still, and they ashamed to leave:
Till the last streaks of dying day withdrew,
    And doubtful moonlight did our rage deceive.

69

In th' English fleet each ship resounds with joy,
    And loud applause of their great leader's fame;
275 In fiery dreams the Dutch they still destroy,
    And slumbering smile at the imagined flame.

70

Not so the Holland fleet, who tired and done
    Stretched on their decks like weary oxen lie:
Faint sweats all down their mighty members run,
280   (Vast bulks which little souls but ill supply).

71

In dreams they fearful precipices tread,
    Or shipwrecked labour to some distant shore;
Or in dark churches walk among the dead:
    They wake with horror, and dare sleep no more.

---

i 45; cp. i 72). Berkeley now led the van in the *Swiftsure*, which was cut off and surrounded. He fought heroically, and died from a wound in the throat. One account says: 'Sir William Berkley had from the June fight the year before, undergone the aspersion of a Coward . . . [which] lay like a load upon his mind, and his valour, or his rage, engaged him so far among the enemies, that neither his discretion nor his friends knew how to bring him off' (*Notes upon the June Fight* in *Letter Book* 213). But *A True Narrative* 4 confirms (and was probably the source for) D.'s original phrasing: 'the *Swiftsure* [and others] . . . staying a little behind, were cut from our Fleet'. The revision makes l. 268 less apt: Creüsa became separated from her husband Aeneas in their escape from Troy, and was killed (*Aen.* ii 735–95).

269–72. 'continuing so long as there was light enough to distinguish friends from enemies' (*An Account of the Battle* in *Letter Book* 238).

272. Cp. *per incertam lunam sub luce maligna* ('by the doubtful and malignant light of the moon'; *Aen.* vi 270). *deceive*] frustrate (*OED* 3b).

278. Homer compares the death-throes of a warrior with those of an ox (*Iliad* xiii 571).

280. Perhaps reversing Virgil's description of the warrior bees: *ingentis animos angusto in pectore* ('great souls in narrow breasts'; *Geo.* iv 83). *supply*] furnish with an occupant (*OED* 7b).

281–4. Perhaps suggested by Lucan's account of soldiers' dreams in an interval in the Battle of Pharsalus (vii 764–76).

72

285 The morn they look on with unwilling eyes,
       Till from their maintop joyful news they hear
     Of ships, which by their mould bring new supplies,
       And in their colours Belgian lions bear.

73

     Our watchful General had discerned from far
290   This mighty succour which made glad the foe;
     He sighed, but like a father of the war
       ¹His face spake hope, while deep his sorrows flow.

(l) His face etc: Spem vultu simulat premit alto corde dolorem. *Virg.*

74

     His wounded men he first sends off to shore,
       Never till now unwilling to obey;
295 They not their wounds but want of strength deplore,
       And think them happy who with him can stay.

75

     Then to the rest, 'Rejoice', said he, 'today
       In you the fortune of Great Britain lies:
     Among so brave a people you are they
300   Whom heaven has chose to fight for such a prize.

76

     If number English courages could quell
       We should at first have shunned, not met our foes,

286–8. There is no evidence that the Dutch were reinforced on the morning
of the second day, though they did receive sixteen extra ships that evening
(*London Gazette* lix). However, *A True Narrative* 4 says that early on the second
morning 'we . . . discovered . . . 12. sayl on our Weather-bow, which we supposed a supply'.
287. mould] structural type (*OED* 11).
288. The flag of the States General of the United Provinces of the Netherlands
showed a lion holding a sword and a bunch of seven arrows, one for each province
(*Flags at Sea* 58–9).
291. father of the war] Davenant has the phrase 'The Father of those fights we
Lombards fought' (*Gondibert* I v 4), but D. seems only to wish to stress
Albemarle's paternal care (*Works*).
292n. Aeneas 'feigns hope in his face, and presses his grief deep down in his heart';
Aen. i 209.

Whose numerous sails the fearful only tell:
   Courage from hearts, and not from numbers grows.'

77

305 He said; nor needed more to say: with haste
   To their known stations cheerfully they go;
And all at once, disdaining to be last,
   Solicit every gale to meet the foe.

78

Nor did th' encouraged Belgians long delay,
310   But bold in others, not themselves, they stood:
So thick our navy scarce could shear their way,
   But seemed to wander in a moving wood.

79

Our little fleet was now engaged so far
   That like the swordfish in the whale they fought:
315 The combat only seemed a civil war,
   Till through their bowels we our passage wrought.

80

Never had valour, no not ours before,
   Done aught like this upon the land or main,
Where not to be o'ercome was to do more
320   Than all the conquests former kings did gain.

81

The mighty ghosts of our great Harries rose,
   And armèd Edwards looked with anxious eyes
To see this fleet among unequal foes,
   By which Fate promised them their Charles should rise.

---

303. tell] count.
314. The story of the swordfish attacking the whale is traditional (see Donne, 'The Progresse of the Soule' ll. 351–60; Spenser, 'Visions of the Worlds Vanitie' ll. 62–8). No story has been found of the swordfish inside the whale, though Donne writes of fish swimming inside the whale (ll. 316–27). One report to the Royal Society spoke of 'a certain horny Fish . . . who runs its horn into the Whal's belly, . . . [and] is known, sometimes to run its horn into Ships (perhaps taking them for Whales)' (*PTRS* i (1665–6) 133) (*Works*).
321–2. Kings such as Henry V, Henry VIII, Edward I and Edward III, and Edward the Black Prince: warriors and nationalistic rulers.

82

325 Meantime the Belgians tack upon our rear,
　　And raking chase-guns through our sterns they send;
　　Close by their fireships like jackals appear,
　　　Who on their lions for the prey attend.

83

　　Silent in smoke of cannons they come on
330　(Such vapours once did fiery Cacus hide);
　　In these the height of pleased revenge is shown,
　　　Who burn contented by another's side.

84

　　Sometimes from fighting squadrons of each fleet
　　(Deceived themselves, or to preserve some friend)
335　Two grappling Etnas on the ocean meet,
　　　And English fires with Belgian flames contend.

85

　　Now at each tack our little fleet grows less,
　　And like maimed fowl swim lagging on the main;
　　Their greater loss their numbers scarce confess,
340　While they lose cheaper than the English gain.

86

　　Have you not seen when, whistled from the fist,
　　Some falcon stoops at what her eye designed,
　　And with her eagerness, the quarry missed,
　　　Straight flies at check, and clips it down the wind:

325–40. 'The manner of fighting at that time was, that each fleet lay in a line, and when the ships of one fleet lay with their heads to the northward, the heads of the other lay to the southward, the headmost ships of our fleet engaging first the headmost of theirs: so passing on by their fleet in a line, firing all the way, and as soon as the rear of one fleet was clear from the rear of the other, then each fleet tacked in the van, standing almost stem for stem with one another to engage again' (*An Account* in *Letter Book* 239).
326. chase-guns] guns mounted in the bows of a ship, used when pursuing an enemy.
327. jackals] They were supposed to go ahead of lions to hunt up their prey for them. The word was stressed on the second syllable (*OED*).
330. fiery Cacus] Cacus, the son of Vulcan, stole cattle from Hercules, and when pursued vomited smoke to conceal himself (*Aen.* viii 251–5).
341–4. A hawk is released from the hand by whistling, cast off against the wind in pursuit of prey, or downwind when turned loose. *stoops*] descends swiftly on

87

345   The dastard crow, that to the wood made wing,
           And sees the groves no shelter can afford,
       With her loud caws her craven kind does bring,
           Who safe in numbers cuff the noble bird.

88

       Among the Dutch thus Albemarle did fare:
350   He could not conquer, and disdained to fly;
       Past hope of safety, 'twas his latest care
           Like falling Caesar decently to die.

89

       Yet pity did his manly spirit move
           To see those perish who so well had fought;
355   And generously with his despair he strove,
           Resolved to live till he their safety wrought.

90

       Let other Muses write his prosperous fate,
           Of conquered nations tell, and kings restored;
       But mine shall sing of his eclipsed estate,
360   Which like the sun's more wonders does afford.

---

its prey (*OED* 6).   *flies at check*] forsakes the proper prey and pursues baser game
which crosses her flight (*OED* 6).   *clips it*] flies rapidly (*OED* 6). For D.'s precise ornithological vocabulary cp. 'Virgil's Ninth Eclogue' ll. 16–17.
345. Cp. 'the crow / Makes wing to th' rooky wood' (*Macbeth* III ii 50–1) (*Works*).
dastard] coward.
348. cuff] buffet with their wings (*OED* 2).
352. decently] fittingly.
353–80. 'At a Council of Flagg-Officers, his Grace the Lord Generall resolved
to draw our Fleet into a Reer-line of Battel, and make a fair Retreat of it. Here
his Grace's accustomed and excellent Conduct, as well as his invincible Courage,
was eminently seen; for, by placing his weak and disabled Ships before in a Line,
and 16. of his greatest and best in a Rank in the Reer, as a Bulwark for
them, keeping his own Ship nearest the Enemy, such of the *Dutch* Fleet that
were the best saylers of them, came first in parties upon him, and finding it too
hot service to attaque him, staid for the rest of their Fleet' (*A True Narrative* 5).
355. generously] nobly.
357–8. Referring to the panegyrics on Monck at the Restoration (e.g. by Sir Robert
Howard and Robert Wild).
360. There was an eclipse of the sun on 22 June 1666; observations of it were
printed in *PTRS* i (1665–6) 295–7 (9 September 1666) and 369–72 (21 January
1667).

91

He drew his mighty frigates all before,
  On which the foe his fruitless force employs;
His weak ones deep into his rear he bore,
  Remote from guns as sick men are from noise.

92

365 His fiery cannon did their passage guide,
  And following smoke obscured them from the foe:
Thus Israel safe from the Egyptian's pride
  By flaming pillars and by clouds did go.

93

Elsewhere the Belgian force we did defeat,
370   But here our courages did theirs subdue:
So Xenophon once led that famed retreat
  Which first the Asian empire overthrew.

94

The foe approached: and one for his bold sin
  Was sunk, as he that touched the ark was slain;
375 The wild waves mastered him, and sucked him in,
  And smiling eddies dimpled on the main.

95

This seen, the rest at awful distance stood,
  As if they had been there as servants set,
To stay or to go on as he thought good,
380   And not pursue, but wait on his retreat.

96

So Libyan huntsmen on some sandy plain,
  From shady coverts roused, the lion chase;

367–8. Exodus xiii 21: when escaping from the Egyptian pharaoh the Israelites
were led through the wilderness by pillars of cloud by day and fire by night.
371–2. After the defeat of Cyrus's attempt to seize the throne of Persia, his troops
were extricated by Xenophon, who led them on the long retreat described in
his *Anabasis*.
374. 1 Chronicles xiii 9–10; see *AA* l. 804n.
377. *awful*] respectful, awe-struck.
381–4. The simile is used by Virgil of Turnus who 'retraces his unhurried steps'
in *Aen.* ix 791–8; it is also Homeric (*Iliad* xi 548–55; xvii 657–64).
381. *Libyan*] may recall the hunt in *Aen.* iv 151–9.

The kingly beast roars out with loud disdain,
    ᵐAnd slowly moves, unknowing to give place.

(m) *The simile is Virgil's*: Vestigia retro improperata refert, etc.

97

385 But if some one approach to dare his force,
         He swings his tail, and swiftly turns him round;
     With one paw seizes on his trembling horse,
         And with the other tears him to the ground.

98

     Amidst these toils succeeds the balmy night;
390   Now hissing waters the quenched guns restore,
     ⁿAnd weary waves, withdrawing from the fight,
         Lie lulled and panting on the silent shore.

(n) Weary waves: *From Statius*, Sylv.: Nec trucibus fluviis idem sonus: occidit
horror aequoris, ac terris maria acclinata quiescunt.

99

     The moon shone clear on the becalmèd flood,
         Where, while her beams like glittering silver play,
395 Upon the deck our careful General stood,
         And deeply mused on the ᵒsucceeding day.

(o) *The third of June, famous for two former victories.*

100

     'That happy sun', said he, 'will rise again,
         Who twice victorious did our navy see;
     And I alone must view him rise in vain,
400   Without one ray of all his star for me.

384. unknowing to give place] Cp. *cedere nescii* (Achilles 'not knowing how to yield';
Horace, *Carm.* I vi 6; George Loane, *N & Q* clxxxv (1943) 273).
389–93. 'At Night it proved calm' (*A True Narrative* 5).
391n. 'The boisterous waves roar no longer; the raging sea is stilled; the sea is
pillowed on the shore in slumber' (Statius, *Sylvae* V iv 5–6).
395. careful] full of cares.
396n. The two former victories were those over the Dutch in 1653 and 1665.
397. happy] propitious.

101

Yet like an English general will I die,
 And all the ocean make my spacious grave;
Women and cowards on the land may lie,
 The sea's a tomb that's proper for the brave.'

102

405 Restless he passed the remnants of the night,
 Till the fresh air proclaimed the morning nigh,
And burning ships, the martyrs of the fight,
 With paler fires beheld the eastern sky.

103

Third day.

But now, his stores of ammunition spent,
410　His naked valour is his only guard:
Rare thunders are from his dumb cannon sent,
 And solitary guns are scarcely heard.

104

Thus far had Fortune power; here forced to stay,
 Nor longer durst with virtue be at strife:
415 This as a ransom Albemarle did pay
 For all the glories of so great a life.

105

For now brave Rupert from afar appears,
 Whose waving streamers the glad General knows;
With full spread sails his eager navy steers,
420　And every ship in swift proportion grows.

402. Cp. *nunc tibi pro tumulo Carpathium omne mare est* ('now the whole Carpathian sea is your tomb', Propertius III vii 12; Loane 272–81).
415. ransom] fine (*OED* 3).
417–20. 1667 second issue; For now brave *Rupert's* Navy did appear, / Whose waving streamers from afar he knows: / As in his fate something divine there were, / Who dead and buried the third day arose. *1667 first issue.* D. probably made the change to remove the blasphemous comparison; but cp. ll. 453–4 and 560.
417. In the afternoon of 3 June, the third day of the battle, Prince Rupert's squadron was sighted.

106

The anxious Prince had heard the cannon long,
    And from that length of time dire omens drew
Of English overmatched and Dutch too strong,
    Who never fought three days but to pursue.

107

425 Then, as an eagle (who with pious care
    Was beating widely on the wing for prey)
To her now silent eyry does repair,
    And finds her callow infants forced away;

108

Stung with her love she stoops upon the plain,
430   The broken air loud whistling as she flies;
She stops, and listens, and shoots forth again,
    And guides her pinions by her young ones' cries:

109

With such kind passion hastes the Prince to fight,
    And spreads his flying canvas to the sound;
435 Him whom no danger, were he there, could fright,
    Now absent every little noise can wound.

110

As in a drought the thirsty creatures cry,
    And gape upon the gathered clouds for rain,

423. overmatched] defeated by superior strength.
425–32. Cp. *The Indian Emperor* (performed 1665): 'As Callow Birds— /Whose Mother's kill'd in seeking of the prey, / Cry in their Nest, and think her long away; / And at each leaf that stirs, each blast of wind, / Gape for the Food which they must never find: / So cry the people in their misery' (IV ii 39–44).
425. pious] Cp. l. 255*n*.
428. callow] unfledged.
429. stoops] See ll. 341–4*n*.
432. pinions] wings.
433. kind] responding to the bonds of kinship.
435–6. From Virgil: *et me, quem dudum non ulla iniecta mouebant / tela neque aduerso glomerati examine Grai, / nunc omnes terrent aurae, sonus excitat omnis / suspensum* ('And I [Aeneas], whom previously no hurled weapons could move, nor hostile ranks of Greeks, am now terrified by all noises, every sound holds me in suspense, and I fear equally for my companion [Ascanius] and my burden [Anchises]'; *Aen.* ii 726–9; Loane (see l. 402*n*)).
437–40. Cp. Virgil: *bucula caelum / suspiciens patulis captauit naribus auras, / aut arguta lacus circumuolitauit hirundo* ('the cow looking up into the sky caught the breeze in extended nostrils, or the graceful swallow swooped round the lake'; *Geo.* i 375–7).

And first the martlet meets it in the sky,
440   And with wet wings joys all the feathered train:

111

With such glad hearts did our despairing men
    Salute the appearance of the Prince's fleet;
And each ambitiously would claim the ken
    That with first eyes did distant safety meet.

112

445 The Dutch, who came like greedy hinds before
    To reap the harvest their ripe ears did yield,
Now look like those when rolling thunders roar
    And sheets of lightning blast the standing field.

113

Full in the Prince's passage hills of sand
450   And dangerous flats in secret ambush lay,
Where the false tides skim o'er the covered land,
    And seamen with dissembled depths betray.

114

The wily Dutch, who like fall'n angels feared
    This new Messiah's coming, there did wait,
455 And round the verge their braving vessels steered
    To tempt his courage with so fair a bait.

115

But he unmoved contemns their idle threat,
    Secure of fame whene'er he please to fight;

---

439. martlet] swift.
443. ken] look, gaze (*OED*).
445. hinds] farm workers.
449–56. Albemarle's fleet fell 'unluckily upon a tail of the Galloper sand; where most of the great ships struck, and the *Royal Prince* stuck fast, and could not be got off. . . . So the General made sail to join with the Prince, sending him timely notice of the dangerous sand, for his Highness had a mind to attack the enemy then; and they had drawn out a squadron of ships, making as if they had an intention to fight the Prince, purposely to decoy him upon the said sand' (*An Account* in *Letter Book* 239–40).
455. braving] challenging, defiant (*OED* 1); vaunting (*OED* 7).
457. contemns] despises.

His cold experience tempers all his heat,
460   And inbred worth does boasting valour slight.

116

Heroic virtue did his actions guide,
     And he the substance not th' appearance chose:
To rescue one such friend he took more pride
     Than to destroy whole thousands of such foes.

117

465 But when approached, in strict embraces bound
     Rupert and Albemarle together grow:
He joys to have his friend in safety found,
     Which he to none but to that friend would owe.

118

The cheerful soldiers, with new stores supplied,
470   Now long to execute their spleenful will;
And in revenge for those three days they tried
     Wish one like Joshua's when the sun stood still.

119

Fourth day's battle.

Thus reinforced, against the adverse fleet
     Still doubling ours, brave Rupert leads the way;
475 With the first blushes of the morn they meet,
     And bring night back upon the new-born day.

120

His presence soon blows up the kindling fight,
     And his loud guns speak thick like angry men;

460. *slight*] disdain, disregard.
465. As D. implies, Albemarle and Rupert met on the evening of the third day (*pace Works* i 294); *meet* in l. 475 refers to the encounter with the Dutch.
470. *spleenful*] courageous (*OED* spleen 5).
471. *tried*] underwent (*OED* 14).
472. In Joshua x 12–14 the sun stands still while Joshua and the Israelites kill their enemies.
474. *doubling ours*] The odds were about 80:50.
476. Cp. 'And with their smoky cannons banish day' (Waller, *Of a War with Spain* l. 44).
478. *thick*] rapidly; confusedly (*OED* 3, 4).

It seemed as slaughter had been breathed all night,
480   And death new pointed his dull dart again.

121

The Dutch too well his mighty conduct knew,
    And matchless courage since the former fight;
Whose navy like a stiff-stretched cord did show
    Till he bore in and bent them into flight.

122

485 The wind he shares while half their fleet offends
        His open side, and high above him shows;
    Upon the rest at pleasure he descends
        And, doubly harmed, he double harms bestows.

123

    Behind, the General mends his weary pace,
490   And sullenly to his revenge he sails:
    ᵖSo glides some trodden serpent on the grass,
        And long behind his wounded volume trails.

(p) So glides etc. *From Virgil*: Cum medii nexus, extremaeque agmina caudae
solvuntur; tardosque trahit sinus ultimus orbes, etc.

124

    Th' increasing sound is borne to either shore,
        And for their stakes the throwing nations fear:
495 Their passion double with the cannons' roar,
        And with warm wishes each man combats there.

479. breathed] refreshed by being given a breathing space (*OED* 13).
481–90. 'The Prince thought fit to keep the Wind, and so led the whole Line
through the middle of the Enemy, the General with the rest of the Fleet following in good order . . . the Prince . . . in this Pass was environ'd with as many
dangers as the Enemy could apply unto him, they raked him Fore and Aft, plyed
him on both sides' (*True Narrative* 6–7).
485. offends] attacks (*OED* 5).
490. sullenly] slowly.
491n. 'While the central coils and the moving tip of his tail untwine, and his last
fold drags its slow coils' (Virgil, *Geo.* iii 423–4). Cp. *Aen.* v 273–9, where the
damaged ship *Centaur* is compared to an injured snake.
492. volume] coil; from Latin *volumen* (coil), as in *Aen.* ii 208; it later becomes a
piece of poetic diction (see *OED* 11).
495. passion double] *Christie, Noyes*; passion, double *1667, 1668, 1688*; passions
double *Scott, Kinsley, Works*. The sense seems to be 'their passion [is *or* becomes]
double'.

125

Plied thick and close as when the fight begun,
    Their huge unwieldy navy wastes away:
So sicken waning moons too near the sun,
500   And blunt their crescents on the edge of day.

126

And now reduced on equal terms to fight,
    Their ships like wasted patrimonies show,
Where the thin scattering trees admit the light,
    And shun each other's shadows as they grow.

127

505 The warlike Prince had severed from the rest
    Two giant ships, the pride of all the main,
Which with his one so vigorously he pressed
    And flew so home they could not rise again.

128

Already battered, by his lee they lay,
510   In vain upon the passing winds they call:
The passing winds through their torn canvas play,
    And flagging sails on heartless sailors fall.

129

Their opened sides receive a gloomy light,
    Dreadful as day let in to shades below;
515 Without, grim death rides bare-faced in their sight,
    And urges entering billows as they flow.

---

500. crescents] also a common battle-formation for ships. The line was ridiculed in *The Censure of the Rota* (1673) 8–9.
501. on equal terms] The Dutch were 'reduced from Eighty four, to under the number of Forty sayl' (*True Narrative* 8).
502. patrimonies] inherited estates. The image is of ancestral woods partly felled to provide ready money.
505–12. No source for this episode has been traced, unless D. is thinking of Rupert's encounter with two fireships (*True Narrative* 7).
508. so home] so precisely to his target.
512. heartless] dispirited.
513–14. Perhaps recalling *Aen.* viii 241–6, where light is let into the cave of Cacus.
516. urges] drives onward (*OED* 6).

130

When one dire shot, the last they could supply,
   Close by the board the Prince's mainmast bore,
All three now helpless by each other lie,
520   And this offends not, and those fear no more.

131

So have I seen some fearful hare maintain
   A course, till tired before the dog she lay,
Who, stretched behind her, pants upon the plain,
   Past power to kill as she to get away:

132

525   With his lolled tongue he faintly licks his prey,
   His warm breath blows her flix up as she lies;
She, trembling, creeps upon the ground away,
   And looks back to him with beseeching eyes.

133

The Prince unjustly does his stars accuse,
530   Which hindered him to push his fortune on:
For what they to his courage did refuse,
   By mortal valour never must be done.

518–19. 'His Main-stay, and Main-top-mast, being terribly shaken, came all by the Board' (*True Narrative* 7). *Close*] completely (*OED adv.* 5). *by the board*] overboard.

520. offends] See l. 485n.

521–8. From Ovid, *Met.* i 533–42 (the pursuit of Daphne by Apollo): *ut canis in vacuo leporem cum Gallicus arvo / vidit, et hic praedam pedibus petit, ille salutem; / alter inhaesuro similis iam iamque tenere / sperat et extento stringit vestigia rostro, / alter in ambiguo est, an sit conprensus, et ipsis / morsibus eripitur tangentiaque ora relinquit: / sic deus et virgo est hic spe celer, illa timore, / qui tamen insequitur pennis adiutus Amoris, / ocior est requiemque negat tergoque fugacis / imminet et crinem sparsum cervicibus adflat.* ('Just as when a Gallic hound has seen a hare in an open plain, and seeks his prey on flying feet, but the hare, safety; he, just about to fasten on her, now, even now thinks he has her, and grazes her very heels with his outstretched muzzle; but she knows not whether she be not already caught, and barely escapes from those sharp fangs and leaves behind the jaws just closing on her: so ran the god and maid, he sped by hope and she by fear. But he ran the more swiftly, borne on the wings of love, gave her no time to rest, hung over her fleeing shoulders and breathed on the hair that streamed over her neck.') For D.'s translation of these lines in *EP* (1693) see 'The First Book of Ovid's *Metamorphoses*' ll. 719–33. The simile was misquoted and ridiculed in *The Friendly Vindication of Mr. Dryden* (1673) 2–3, and defended in *Mr. Dreyden Vindicated* (1673) 3.

526. flix] dialect word for fur of hare, rabbit or cat (first example in *OED* and *English Dialect Dictionary*).

134
This lucky hour the wise Batavian takes,
    And warns his tattered fleet to follow home;
535 Proud to have so got off with equal stakes,
    ^qWhere 'twas a triumph not to be o'ercome.

(q) *From Horace*: Quos opimus fallere et effugere est triumphus.

135
The General's force, as kept alive by fight,
    Now, not opposed, no longer can pursue;
Lasting till heaven had done his courage right,
540   When he had conquered he his weakness knew.

136
He casts a frown on the departing foe,
    And sighs to see him quit the watery field;
His stern, fixed eyes no satisfaction show
    For all the glories which the fight did yield.

137
545 Though, as when fiends did miracles avow,
    He stands confessed ev'n by the boastful Dutch,
He only does his conquest disavow,
    And thinks too little what they found too much.

138
Returned, he with the fleet resolved to stay,
550   No tender thoughts of home his heart divide:

533. De Ruyter withdrew his fleet to the Dutch coast in the evening of 4 June.

535. equal stakes] The Four Days Battle cost England fourteen ships, 5,000 killed and wounded, and 3,000 prisoners. The cost to Holland was four ships and 2,000 casualties. After initial reports of an English victory, Pepys noted that 'all give over the thoughts of it as a victory, and do reckon it a great overthrow' (9 June).

536n. [The wolves] 'which it is the richest triumph for us to deceive and escape', *Carm.* IV iv 51–2. Spoken by Hannibal, it refers to the indestructible Romans who gain strength from every trial (see Horace's ll. 45–76). *opimus*] Eds; opinius *1667, 1668, 1688*.

545. Mark iii 11, where unclean spirits call Jesus 'Son of God'.

547. He only] Only he.

Domestic joys and cares he puts away,
For realms are households which the great must guide.

139
As those who unripe veins in mines explore,
On the rich bed again the warm turf lay,
555 Till time digests the yet imperfect ore,
And know it will be gold another day:

140
So looks our monarch on this early fight,
Th' essay and rudiments of great success,
Which all-maturing time must bring to light,
560   While he, like heaven, does each day's labour bless.

141
Heaven ended not the first or second day,
Yet each was perfect to the work designed:
God and kings work when they their work survey
And passive aptness in all subjects find.

142
His Majesty repairs the fleet.
565 In burdened vessels, first, with speedy care
His plenteous stores do seasoned timber send;

552. Another example of D. stressing the paternal concept of rule, which was a commonplace long before Filmer's *Patriarcha* (1680): see (e.g.) Hooker, *Of the Lawes of Ecclesiasticall Politie* (1593) I x 4, citing Aristotle, *Politics* i 2; James I, *Basilicon Doron* (1599), edited by James Craigie, 2 vols (1944–50) i 54; and cp. l. 291; 'Account' l. 34; *To His Sacred Majesty* ll. 93–4n.
553–6. The idea that metals grew underground, gradually evolving into gold, was a contemporary commonplace.
558. *essay*] rehearsal (*OED* 2); first effort or draft (*OED* 7); accented on the second syllable.
560–2. See Genesis i.
565–72. The Royal Society had 'employ'd much time in examining *the Fabrick of Ships*, the forms of their *Sails*, the shapes of their *Keels*, the sorts of Timber, the planting of Firr, the bettering of Pitch, and Tarr, and Tackling. And in all *Maritime* affairs of this Nature, his *Majesty* is acknowledg'd to be the best *Judge* amongst Seamen, and Shipwrights, as well as the most powerful amongst *Princes*' (Sprat 150) (*Works*).
565. On 9 June Pepys noted 'the haste requisite to be made in getting the fleet out again', and on 13 July the fleet was 'now in all points ready to sail'.

Thither the brawny carpenters repair,
And as the surgeons of maimed ships attend.

143

With cord and canvas from rich Hamburg sent
570   His navy's moulted wings he imps once more;
Tall Norway fir their masts in battle spent
And English oak sprung leaks and planks restore.

144

All hands employed, 'the royal work grows warm:
Like labouring bees on a long summer's day,
575   Some sound the trumpet for the rest to swarm,
And some on bells of tasted lilies play;

(r) Fervet opus: *the same similitude in Virgil.*

145

With gluey wax some new foundation lay
Of virgin combs which from the roof are hung;
Some armed within doors upon duty stay,
580   Or tend the sick, or educate the young.

146

So here, some pick out bullets from the sides,
Some drive old oakum through each seam and rift;
Their left hand does the caulking-iron guide,
The rattling mallet with the right they lift.

569. Various naval supplies were imported from Hamburg (Pepys, e.g. 30 May 1665n, 18 March 1666n, 3 May 1669).
570. imps] Another image from falconry: to *imp* is to engraft new feathers on to the wing of a bird to improve its flight.
571. For the use of Norwegian fir see Pepys 23 June 1662 and *n.*
573n. Fervet opus] 'The work glows'; from *Aen.* i 430–6, where Virgil compares the Carthaginians building the walls of their city to bees.
574–6. Cp. *Aen.* vi 707–9: *ubi apes aestate serena / floribus insidunt variis, et candida circum / lilia funduntur* ('Where bees in serene summer creep into various flowers, and pour round white lilies') (*Works*).
577–80. Cp. *Geo.* iv 160–3: *lentum de cortice gluten / prima fauis ponunt fundamenta, deinde tenacis / suspendunt ceras; aliae spem gentis adultos / educunt fetus* ('lay down gluey gum from tree-bark as the first foundation of the comb, then hang aloft clinging wax; others lead out the full-grown young, the nation's hope').
578. virgin] See 'Horace: *Epode* II' l. 27n.
582–7. 'Calking is beating Okum into every seame or betwixt Planke and Planke and Okum is old Ropes torn in pieces like a Towze Match, or Hurds of Flax,

147

585 With boiling pitch another near at hand
    (From friendly Sweden brought) the seams instops,
Which well paid o'er the salt-sea waves withstand,
    And shakes them from the rising beak in drops.

148

Some the galled ropes with dauby marling bind,
590   Or cerecloth masts with strong tarpaulin coats;
To try new shrouds one mounts into the wind,
    And one below their ease or stiffness notes.

149

Our careful monarch stands in person by,
    His new-cast cannons' firmness to explore:
595 The strength of big-corned powder loves to try,
    And ball and cartridge sorts for every bore.

150

Each day brings fresh supplies of arms and men,
    And ships which all last winter were abroad;
And such as fitted since the fight had been,
600   Or new from stocks were fall'n into the road.

---

which being close beat into every seame with a calking Iron and a Mallet, which
is a hammer of wood and an Iron chissell, being well payed over with hot pitch'
(John Smith, *The Sea-Mans Grammar* (1653) 13) (*Works*).
586. Tar was imported for the navy from Stockholm (Pepys 21 July 1662*n*). *instops*]
the only example recorded in *OED*.
587. paid] *pay* (*OED v.*²) is a nautical term: to cover with pitch as a protection
against water.
588. beak] prow.
589. galled] frayed. *dauby*] like daub; sticky: apparently D.'s coinage. *marling*]
marline, a tarred line wound round ropes to prevent fraying.
590. cerecloth] (verb) wrap in waterproof material.
595. big-corned] large-grained; this powder was used for cannons, finer powder
for small arms. The manufacture of gunpowder is described in Sprat 282–3.
600. The English fleet now had twenty-three new ships. *fall'n into*] took
their place in (*OED* 62c); cp. 'Ships from *Chatham, Harwich, &c.* come daily
to encrease our strength, and some few in the River, though not yet com-
pleatly fitted, yet are falling down, for fear they should have no share of the
honour of the next Engagement' (*Current Intelligence* viii, 25–8 June 1666).
road] anchorage.

151

Loyal London described.

The goodly *London* in her gallant trim
   (The phoenix daughter of the vanished old)
Like a rich bride does to the ocean swim,
   And on her shadow rides in floating gold.

152

605 Her flag aloft spread ruffling to the wind,
   And sanguine streamers seem the flood to fire;
The weaver charmed with what his loom designed
   Goes on to sea, and knows not to retire.

153

With roomy decks, her guns of mighty strength
610   (Whose low-laid mouths each mounting billow laves),
Deep in her draught, and warlike in her length,
   She seems a sea-wasp flying on the waves.

154

This martial present, piously designed,
   The loyal city gave their best-loved King;
615 And with a bounty ample as the wind
   Built, fitted and maintained to aid him bring.

155

Digression concerning shipping and navigation.

By viewing Nature, Nature's hand-maid Art
   Makes mighty things from small beginnings grow:
Thus fishes first to shipping did impart
620   Their tail the rudder, and their head the prow.

601–16. The *London* had blown up on 7 March 1665; in her place the City built
the *Loyal London*, which was to be burnt by the Dutch in the Medway in June
1667. D. may have taken some hints from William Smith, *A Poem on the famous
ship called the Loyal London* (1666): cp. his 'This mightier *Phoenix*' (1) and 'laves
. . . waves' rhyme (5).
609. The guns in fact exploded when tested, and the ship joined the fleet without
them (Pepys 26 June 1666).
610. laves] washes against (*OED* 2).

156

Some log, perhaps, upon the waters swam
    An useless drift, which rudely cut within
And hollowed, first a floating trough became,
    And cross some riv'let passage did begin.

157

625 In shipping such as this the Irish kern
        And untaught Indian on the stream did glide,
    Ere sharp-keeled boats to stem the flood did learn,
        Or fin-like oars did spread from either side.

158

Add but a sail, and Saturn so appeared
630   When from lost empire he to exile went,
    And with the golden age to Tiber steered,
        Where coin and first commerce he did invent.

159

Rude as their ships was navigation then,
    No useful compass or meridian known;
635 Coasting they kept the land within their ken,
        And knew no north but when the pole-star shone.

160

Of all who since have used the open sea,
    Than the bold English none more fame have won:
ᶳBeyond the year and out of heaven's highway
640   They make discoveries where they see no sun.

(s) Extra anni solisque vias. *Virg.*

621–4. Cp. *Geo.* i 136: *tunc alnos primum fluvii sensere cavatas* ('then rivers first felt the hollowed alders') (*Works*).
622. drift] floating mass (*OED* 9).
624. riv'let] This is the spelling in *1667*; other seventeenth-century spellings (*rivlet, rivelet*: see *OED*) show that the word was often pronounced as disyllabic.
625. kern] rustic, peasant (*OED* 2).
626. untaught Indian] Cp. *Astraea Redux* ll. 46–8n. D. repeats the adjective *untaught* from *The Indian Emperor* I i 9–10: 'No useful Arts have yet found footing here; / But all untaught and salvage does appear.'
629–32. Saturn, dethroned by his son Jove, fled to Italy, where he established the golden age of peace and justice (*Aen.* viii 319–25).
632. commerce] Seventeenth-century pronunciation stressed the second syllable.
639n. Aen. vi 796: 'beyond the paths of the year and the sun'; cp. *Threnodia Augustalis* l. 353.
639. highway] Stressed on the second syllable.

161

But what so long in vain, and yet unknown,
    By poor mankind's benighted wit is sought,
Shall in this age to Britain first be shown,
    And hence be to admiring nations taught.

162

645   The ebbs of tides, and their mysterious flow,
    We as art's elements shall understand;
And as by line upon the ocean go,
    Whose paths shall be familiar as the land.

163

'Instructed ships shall sail to quick commerce,
650   By which remotest regions are allied,
Which makes one city of the universe,
    Where some may gain, and all may be supplied.

(t) *By a more exact knowledge of longitudes.*

164

Then we upon our globe's last verge shall go,
    And view the ocean leaning on the sky;
655   From thence our rolling neighbours we shall know,
    And on the lunar world securely pry.

641–4. Cp. Sprat: 'And it is a good sign, that Nature will reveal more of its secrets to the English, than to others; because it has already furnish'd them with a Genius so well proportion'd, for the receiving, and retaining its mysteries' (114–15) (*Works*).
644. admiring] marvelling.
645. Sir Robert Moray's account of tides in the Western Isles appeared in *PTRS* i (1665–6) 53–5 (5 June 1665). John Wallis's paper presenting a universal theory of tides was read to the Royal Society on 16 May 1666 and printed in *PTRS* i (1665–6) 263–89 (6 August), occasioning great interest.
646. elements] elementary knowledge; basic principles.
647. by line] with great accuracy (*OED* 4b).
649n. knowledge of longitudes] *1667, 1668*; measure of Longitude *1688* (a possible revision). Despite various attempts, there was as yet no sound way of measuring longitude at sea. Major Holmes reported a successful experiment using pendulum watches to determine longitude (*PTRS* i (1665–6) 13–15 (6 March 1665)). The King was 'most ready to reward those, that shall discover the *Meridian*' (Sprat 150).
653. last verge] utmost limit.
655. rolling neighbours] planets.
656. M. Auzout's proposals for a closer study of the moon appeared in *PTRS* i (1665–6) 120–3 (4 December 1665).   *pry*] investigate closely (*OED* 2b); not pejorative.

165

Apostrophe to the Royal Society.

This I foretell from your auspicious care,
　　Who great in search of God and nature grow;
　　Who best your wise Creator's praise declare,
660　Since best to praise his works is best to know.

166

O truly royal! who behold the law
　　And rule of beings in your Maker's mind,
And thence, like limbecks, rich ideas draw
　　To fit the levelled use of human kind.

167

665　But first the toils of war we must endure,
　　And from th' injurious Dutch redeem the seas:
War makes the valiant of his right secure,
　　And gives up fraud to be chastised with ease.

168

Already were the Belgians on our coast,
670　Whose fleet more mighty every day became
By late success which they did falsely boast,
　　And now by first appearing seemed to claim.

169

Designing, subtle, diligent and close,
　　They knew to manage war with wise delay;
675　Yet all those arts their vanity did cross,
　　And by their pride their prudence did betray.

657–64. For D.'s association with the Royal Society see headnote. Sprat noted
that the Society 'principally consulted the advancement of *Navigation*' (150). Like
Sprat (345–62) D. refutes allegations of atheism and impracticality which had been
made against the Society.
657n. *Apostrophe*] address.
663. *limbecks*] See l. 51n.
664. *levelled*] aimed, directed (*OED* 6b).
669–72. De Ruyter put to sea again on 25 June, and on 1 July anchored off the
King's Channel. On 22 July the English fleet assembled at the Gunfleet.

170

Nor stayed the English long; but well supplied
    Appear as numerous as th' insulting foe:
The combat now by courage must be tried,
680   And the success the braver nation show.

171

There was the Plymouth squadron new come in,
    Which in the Straits last winter was abroad;
Which twice on Biscay's working bay had been,
    And on the midland sea the French had awed.

172

685 Old expert Allin, loyal all along,
    Famed for his action on the Smyrna fleet,
And Holmes, whose name shall live in epic song,
    While music numbers, or while verse has feet:

173

Holmes, the Achates of the generals' fight,
690 Who first bewitched our eyes with Guinea gold;
    As once old Cato in the Romans' sight
    The tempting fruits of Afric did unfold.

678. 'On the 25th. the fight began with equal numbers, 90 Men of War, and 17 Fireships on each side' (*The Victory over the Fleet of the States General* (1666) 7). *insulting*] vaunting, triumphing insolently (*OED* 1); attacking (*OED* 3).
680. success] result (*OED* 1).
681–4. The Plymouth squadron under the command of Sir Jeremy Smith sailed in December 1665 for Tangier and the Straits of Gibraltar. It prevented the French Atlantic and Mediterranean (*midland*) fleets from joining.
683. working] agitated, tossing (*OED* 4).
685–6. Sir Thomas Allin (1612–85) now led the van as Admiral of the White. In December 1664 he had attacked the Dutch merchant fleet returning from Smyrna.
687–92. Sir Robert Holmes (1622–92), Rear Admiral of the Red, led a small expedition to the Gold Coast in 1661, and a larger one in 1664 which captured Dutch settlements and returned with great wealth (Pepys 10 December 1664).
689. Achates] The faithful companion of Aeneas. Holmes accompanied the generals, who led the Red squadron. *generals'*] Ed.; Gen'rals *1667*, which could be singular or plural. *Works* prefers the singular, referring to Rupert, on the grounds that Holmes was not on good terms with Albemarle. But D. gives no hint of this, and in *AM* 'General' in the singular always refers to Albemarle, while Rupert is always 'the Prince'.
691–2. When the Roman senators admired the figs which Cato the Censor dropped in the Senate, he told them that 'the country where that fine fruit grew was but three days sail from Rome' (Plutarch, *Marcus Cato* 27). He was urging Rome into the Third Punic War.

174
With him went Spragge, as bountiful as brave,
   Whom his high courage to command had brought;
695 Harman, who did the twice-fired *Harry* save,
   And in his burning ship undaunted fought.

175
Young Holles, on a Muse by Mars begot,
   Born, Caesar-like, to write and act great deeds;
Impatient to revenge his fatal shot,
700   His right hand doubly to his left succeeds.

176
Thousands were there in darker fame that dwell,
   Whose deeds some nobler poem shall adorn;
And, though to me unknown, they, sure, fought well
   Whom Rupert led, and who were British born.

177
705 Of every size an hundred fighting sail,
   So vast the navy now at anchor rides,
That underneath it the pressed waters fail,
   And with its weight it shoulders off the tides.

178
Now anchors weighed, the seamen shout so shrill
710   That heaven and earth and the wide ocean rings;
A breeze from westward waits their sails to fill,
   And rests in those high beds his downy wings.

693–4. Sir Edward Spragge (d. 1673), Vice-Admiral of the Blue, had been
knighted for gallantry in the Battle of Lowestoft.
695–6. In the Four Days Battle, the *Henry*, commanded by Sir John Harman
(d. 1673) was twice set on fire by fireships; he continued to fight, killed the
Dutch admiral with a broadside, and brought his ship into Harwich.
697–700. Sir Frescheville Holles (1642–72), son of the royalist officer and
antiquary Gervase Holles, lost his left arm in the Four Days Battle. His literary
talents are unrecorded, though he is said to have recited poetry during a storm
at sea (*ODNB*). Unflattering opinions of him are noted by Pepys (14, 17, 25
June 1667, etc.).
697. Ridiculed in *The Friendly Vindication of Mr. Dryden* (1673) 9, and by
Buckingham in *Poetical Reflections on . . . Absalom and Achitophel* (1681) 1.
699. fatal] destructive (*OED* 6).
701. Cp. *Aen.* v 302: *multi praeterea, quos fama obscura recondit* ('many besides, whom
dark report hides').

179

<blockquote>

The wary Dutch this gathering storm foresaw,
  And durst not bide it on the English coast:
715 Behind their treacherous shallows they withdraw,
  And there lay snares to catch the British host.

</blockquote>

180

<blockquote>

So the false spider, when her nets are spread,
  Deep ambushed in her silent den does lie;
And feels far off the trembling of her thread,
720 Whose filmy cord should bind the struggling fly:

</blockquote>

181

<blockquote>

Then, if at last she find him fast beset,
  She issues forth and runs along her loom;
She joys to touch the captive in her net,
  And drags the little wretch in triumph home.

</blockquote>

182

<blockquote>

725 The Belgians hoped that with disordered haste
  Our deep-cut keels upon the sands might run;
Or if with caution leisurely were past
  Their numerous gross might charge us one by one.

</blockquote>

183

<blockquote>

But with a fore-wind pushing them above,
730 And swelling tide that heaved them from below,
O'er the blind flats our warlike squadrons move,
  And with spread sails to welcome battle go.

</blockquote>

184

<blockquote>

It seemed as there the British Neptune stood,
  With all his host of waters at command,

</blockquote>

715. After the St James's Day Fight (25 July) the Dutch retreated to their coast, taking advantage of the sandbanks that deterred the English ships, which had a deeper draught. As Kinsley notes, D. places this retreat before the beginning of the action, so as to emphasize Dutch cowardice and cunning.
718. *ambushed*] lying in wait, lurking (*OED* 2).
728. *gross*] main body (a military term).
729. *fore-wind*] wind which blows a ship forwards (*OED*).
731. *blind flats*] translating *vada caeca* (*Aen.* i 536; Kinsley).   *blind*] covered, concealed from sight (*OED* 9).   *flats*] level ground covered by shallow water (*OED* 6).

735 Beneath them to submit the officious flood,
       ᵘAnd with his trident shoved them off the sand.

(u) Levat ipse tridenti, et vastas aperit syrtes, etc. *Virg.*

                        185
     To the pale foes they suddenly draw near,
       And summon them to unexpected fight:
     They start like murderers when ghosts appear,
740   And draw their curtains in the dead of night.

                        186
                                              Second battle.
     Now van to van the foremost squadrons meet,
       The midmost battles hasting up behind,
     Who view far off the storm of falling sleet,
       And hear their thunder rattling in the wind.

                        187
745 At length the adverse admirals appear
       (The two bold champions of each country's right);
     Their eyes describe the lists as they come near,
       And draw the lines of death before they fight.

                        188
     The distance judged for shot of every size,
750   The linstocks touch, the ponderous ball expires;

735. submit] bring under control (*OED* 4).   *officious*] helpful, dutiful.
736n. Aen. i 145–6: 'With his trident [Neptune] himself lifts [the Trojan ships
off the rocks] and opens the huge quicksands'.
740. Cp. Shakespeare: 'Even such a man, so faint, so spiritless, / So dull, so dead
in look, so woe begone, / Drew Priam's curtain in the dead of night, / And
would have told him, half his Troy was burned' (*2 Henry IV* I i 70–3; Loane
(see l. 402*n*)).
741. The English fleet intended to 'engage them Van to Van'; 'half an hour after
nine, the Vans on each side came near' (*London Gazette* lxxv).   *van*] the detachment of ships at the front of the fleet.
742. battles] A *battle* is the main body of a naval force, as distinct from the van
or rear (*OED* 9).
743. sleet] i.e. shot from the guns falling like sleet.
747. describe] i.e. descry (*OED* 7), perceive.
748. Hollar's engraving shows each fleet drawn up in a line (reproduced in Ollard,
Man of War).
750. linstocks] staves for holding lighted matches.   *expires*] rushes forth (*OED* 3).

The vigorous seaman every porthole plies,
    And adds his heart to every gun he fires.

189

Fierce was the fight on the proud Belgians' side,
    For honour, which they seldom sought before;
755 But now they by their own vain boasts were tied,
    And forced, at least in show, to prize it more.

190

But sharp remembrance on the English part,
    And shame of being matched by such a foe,
Rouse conscious virtue up in every heart,
760   ᵂAnd seeming to be stronger makes them so.

(w) Possunt quia posse videntur. *Virg.*

191

Nor long the Belgians could that fleet sustain
    Which did two generals' fates and Caesar's bear:
Each several ship a victory did gain,
    As Rupert or as Albemarle were there.

192

765 Their battered admiral too soon withdrew,
    Unthanked by ours for his unfinished fight;
But he the minds of his Dutch masters knew,
    Who called that providence which we called flight.

752. Cp. *dant animos plagae* (*Aen.* vii 383: 'give their souls to the blow').
759. *conscious virtue*] Cp. Virgil: *pudor incendit viris et conscia virtus* (*Aen.* v 455: 'shame and awareness of his manhood fire his strength'); and cp. *Aen.* xii 666–8. *conscious*] present to one's consciousness, felt (*OED* 10; first example from *PL* (1667)). *virtue*] manliness, courage (*OED* 7).
760n. *Aen.* v 231: 'they are able because they seem to be able'. D. echoes this line again in *2 Conquest of Granada* II iii 106.
762. When Caesar was in a ship on the rough river Aoüs the pilot was about to turn back when Caesar revealed his identity and said, 'Go boldly on, and fear nothing; you carry Caesar and his fortune in your boat' (Plutarch, *Caesar* 38; cp. Lucan, *Pharsalia* v 568–93).
763. *several*] individual.
765. De Ruyter's ship was closely engaged for several hours, and lost her topmast. 'About four *De Ruyter* made all the sail he could, and ran for it, but made frequent Tacks to fetch off his maymed ships'; his ship was 'much battered' in the retreat (*London Gazette* lxxv). This was in fact an hour after his van had turned and fled.

193

Never did men more joyfully obey,
770   Or sooner understood the sign to fly:
With such alacrity they bore away
   As if to praise them all the States stood by.

194

O famous leader of the Belgian fleet,
   Thy monument inscribed such praise shall wear
775 As Varro, timely flying, once did meet,
   Because he did not of his Rome despair.

195

Behold that navy which a while before
   Provoked the tardy English to the fight,
Now draw their beaten vessels close to shore,
780   As larks lie dared to shun the hobby's flight.

196

Whoe'er would English monuments survey
   In other records may our courage know;
But let them hide the story of this day,
   Whose fame was blemished by too base a foe:

197

785 Or if too busily they will enquire
   Into a victory which we disdain,
Then let them know the Belgians did retire
   ˣBefore the patron saint of injured Spain.

(x) Patron saint: *St James, on whose day this victory was gained.*

198

Repenting England this revengeful day
790   ʸTo Philip's *manes* did an offering bring:
England, which first by leading them astray
   Hatched up rebellion to destroy her King.

(y) Philip's *manes: Philip the Second of Spain, against whom the Hollanders rebelling were aided by Queen Elizabeth.*

772. States] The States General was the parliament of the United Provinces.
775–6. When Varro returned to Rome after his defeat by Hannibal at the Battle of Cannae, he was thanked by the Senate for not despairing of the state (Livy xxii 41).
780. dared] terrified, fascinated with fear.   *hobby*] a small falcon, used to fly above larks and scare them into nets.
790. manes] shade, ghost (Latin); disyllabic.

199

Our fathers bent their baneful industry
　　To check a monarchy that slowly grew;
795　But did not France or Holland's fate foresee,
　　Whose rising power to swift dominion flew.

200

In Fortune's empire blindly thus we go,
　　And wander after pathless destiny,
Whose dark resorts since prudence cannot know
800　In vain it would provide for what shall be.

201

But whate'er English to the blessed shall go,
　　And the fourth Harry or first Orange meet,
Find him disowning of a Bourbon foe,
　　And him detesting a Batavian fleet.

202

805　Now on their coasts our conquering navy rides,
　　Waylays their merchants, and their land besets:
Each day new wealth without their care provides,
　　They lie asleep with prizes in their nets.

203

So close behind some promontory lie
810　The huge leviathans to attend their prey,
And give no chase, but swallow in the fry
　　Which through their gaping jaws mistake the way.

793–6. i.e. late Tudor and early Stuart foreign policy had aimed at containing
the power of Spain, but had not foreseen the commercial rise of the Dutch Republic,
or the military strength of France under Louis XIV.
801–4. The *Bourbon foe* is Louis XIV, disowned by Henri IV his grandfather as a
foe to the English. William the Silent, the *first Orange*, detests the fleet of Holland
as employed against his benefactors (Verrall).
804. *Batavian*] Dutch.
805–8. After 25 July the English fleet cruised off the Dutch coast capturing
shipping.
809–12. Cp. Du Bartas tr. Sylvester: 'One (like a Pirate) onely lives of prizes /
That in the Deepe he desperately surprises; / Another haunts the shoare, to feed
on foame' (I v 149–51).

204

Burning of the fleet in the Vly by Sir Robert Holmes.

Nor was this all: in ports and roads remote
Destructive fires among whole fleets we send;
815 Triumphant flames upon the water float,
And out-bound ships at home their voyage end.

205

Those various squadrons, variously designed,
Each vessel freighted with a several load;
Each squadron waiting for a several wind,
820 All find but one, to burn them in the road.

206

Some bound for Guinea, golden sand to find,
Bore all the gauds the simple natives wear;
Some for the pride of Turkish courts designed
For folded turbans finest Holland bear.

207

825 Some English wool, vexed in a Belgian loom
And into cloth of spungy softness made,
Did into France or colder Denmark doom
To ruin with worse ware our staple trade.

208

Our greedy seamen rummage every hold,
830 Smile on the booty of each wealthier chest,

813–16. On 8 August Holmes attacked 170 merchantmen off Vly island; he burnt
150 and sacked the town of Terschelling.
813. roads] sheltered waters where ships may anchor in safety.
819. several] separate, different.
822. gauds] ornaments.
824. Holland] i.e. Holland linen.
825–8. Kinsley notes that English wool, being finer than that of the continent,
was greatly in demand, and smuggled abroad in defiance of a prohibition on its
export; the French re-exported goods made from this wool to England, thus spoiling the market for home-manufactured goods. See Ogg 71–2.
825. vexed] worked (*OED* 6).
827. doom] i.e. some ships condemned English wool to be carried into France or
Denmark.
829. rummage] a nautical term: to scrutinize and sort the contents of a ship's hold.
829–32. Holmes's own account says that 'the common Seamen and Soldiers

And, as the priests who with their gods make bold,
   Take what they like, and sacrifice the rest.

209

Transitum to the Fire of London.

But ah! how unsincere are all our joys!
   Which sent from heaven, like lightning make no stay:
835 Their palling taste the journey's length destroys,
   Or grief sent post o'ertakes them on the way.

210

Swelled with our late successes on the foe,
   Which France and Holland wanted power to cross,
We urge an unseen Fate to lay us low,
840 And feed their envious eyes with English loss.

211

Each element his dread command obeys,
   Who makes or ruins with a smile or frown;
Who as by one he did our nation raise,
   So now he with another pulls us down.

212

845 Yet, London, Empress of the northern clime,
   By an high fate thou greatly didst expire:

[returned with] their pockets well lined with Duckets and other rich spoil, which was found in great plenty, as well on board the Merchants ships, as in the Town they burnt, and was freely abandoned to them' (*London Gazette* lxxix).

833. unsincere] impure, not unmixed. For the idea that human happiness is not unmixed, see also *AA* l. 43n; 'Lucretius: The Beginning of the Second Book' l. 22; 'Lucretius: Concerning the Nature of Love' l. 42; 'The Second Book of Virgil's *Georgics*' l. 584; and 'Cinyras and Myrrha' l. 259. By contrast, the medal commemorating the plague and the Fire of London bore the inscription *Mera Bonitas* ('pure goodness'), referring to God's providence (Hawkins i 525). Transitum] Not recorded in *OED*, either separately or as a seventeenth-century spelling of *transition*. It appears to be unnaturalized Latin, but the Latin noun is *transitus*; it is not clear why D. uses the accusative, unless he mistakenly thinks it to be the nominative of a neuter noun. *1688* has *Transit*.

834. lightning] Cp. ll. 849–60n for a possible echo of Marvell here.

836. post] post-haste.

841. his] The gender which D. gives to Fate is peculiar: in Latin it is neuter (*fatum*), in Greek feminine (μοῖρα). He may intend a partial assimilation to Christian Providence or God.

843–4. i.e. England, made mighty on the water, is laid low by fire.

846. fate] here means 'end', 'death'.

> [z]Great as the world's, which at the death of time
>   Must fall, and rise a nobler frame by fire.

(z) Cum mare cum tellus correptaque regia coeli ardeat, etc. *Ovid.*

213

> As when some dire usurper heaven provides
850   To scourge his country with a lawless sway;
>   His birth perhaps some petty village hides,
>   And sets his cradle out of Fortune's way:

214

> Till fully ripe his swelling fate breaks out,
>   And hurries him to mighty mischiefs on;
855 His prince surprised at first no ill could doubt,
>   And wants the power to meet it when 'tis known.

215

> Such was the rise of this prodigious fire,
>   Which in mean buildings first obscurely bred,

847n. In Ovid's *Met.* i 257 – 8, Jove, about to hurl his thunderbolts at the world, remembers that it is in the fates that a time will come 'when sea and land, the royal palace of heaven will catch fire and burn'.

849–60. This passage echoes Marvell's lines on the rise of Cromwell in 'An Horatian Ode': 'like the three-forked lightning, first / Breaking the clouds where it was nursed, / Did thorough his own side / His fiery way divide. / . . . Then burning through the air he went, / And palaces and temples rent; / And Caesar's head at last / Did through his laurels blast. / 'Tis madness to resist or blame / The force of angry heaven's flame: / . . . Who, from his private gardens, where / He lived reservèd and austere, / . . . Could by industrious valour climb / To ruin the great work of time' (ll. 13–34) (G. deF. Lord in *John Dryden*, edited by Earl Miner (1972) 172–3). Since D. worked with Marvell in the same office in Cromwell's government he could easily have seen a MS of the poem, which was written in 1650 but first printed in Marvell's *Miscellaneous Poems* (1681), and even then excised from most copies. For D.'s other echoes of this poem see *To My Lord Chancellor* ll. 39–42 (cp. Marvell ll. 19–20, 41–2) and 105–6 (cp. Marvell ll. 9–10); *AA* ll. 295n, 353–4n, 387–8n, 805–8n, 887n; *The Medal* l. 316n; *Threnodia Augustalis* ll. 230–5 (cp. Marvell ll. 119–20, 79–84); *HP* i 454–5n; 'Of the Pythagorean Philosophy' ll. 264–5 (cp. Marvell ll. 34–6); and see Hammond 74–84.

853. Cp. 'Some unborn sorrow ripe in Fortune's womb' (Shakespeare, *Richard II* II ii 10).

855. doubt] suspect (*OED* 6b).

857–60. The Great Fire of London broke out early in the morning of 2 September 1666 in the King's baker's shop in Pudding Lane. It burnt for four days, covered 436 acres, destroyed 89 churches and about 13,200 houses and gutted St Paul's, the Guildhall and the Royal Exchange.

857. prodigious] ominous, portentous (*OED* 1).

From thence did soon to open streets aspire,
860   And straight to palaces and temples spread.

216

The diligence of trades, and noiseful gain,
    And luxury, more late, asleep were laid:
All was the night's, and in her silent reign
    No sound the rest of nature did invade.

217

865 In this deep quiet, from what source unknown,
    Those seeds of fire their fatal birth disclose;
And first, few scattering sparks about were blown,
    Big with the flames that to our ruin rose.

218

Then in some close-pent room it crept along,
870   And smouldering as it went, in silence fed;
Till th' infant monster, with devouring strong,
    Walked boldly upright with exalted head.

219

Now like some rich or mighty murderer
    Too great for prison, which he breaks with gold,
875 Who fresher for new mischiefs does appear,
    And dares the world to tax him with the old:

220

So scapes th' insulting fire his narrow jail,
    And makes small outlets into open air;
There the fierce winds his tender force assail,
880   And beat him downward to his first repair.

---

862. luxury] lasciviousness, lust, sensual indulgence (*OED* 1, 3).
863. All was the night's] From *omnia noctis erant, placida composta quiete* ('all was the night's, lulled to quiet rest', Varro cited in Seneca, *Controversiae* VII i 27).
866. seeds of fire] Cp. *semina flammae* (Ovid, *Met.* xv 347), and 'Horace: *Odes* I iii' l. 39. *fatal*] bringing death (cp. l. 846).
868. Big] pregnant.
869–72. Cp. Ovid, *Met.* xv 218–24; tr. D. in 'Of the Pythagorean Philosophy' ll. 330–3.
874. Too] *1668, 1688*; To *1667*.
877. insulting] See l. 678*n*; also 'leaping' (*OED* 5; rare, from Latin *insultare*).
880. repair] dwelling place.

221

^aThe winds like crafty courtesans withheld
His flames from burning but to blow them more,
And every fresh attempt he is repelled,
With faint denials, weaker than before.

(a) Like crafty etc.: Haec arte tractabat cupidum virum, ut illius animum inopia
accenderet.

222

885 And now no longer letted of his prey
He leaps up at it with enraged desire,
O'erlooks the neighbours with a wide survey
And nods at every house his threatening fire.

223

The ghosts of traitors from the bridge descend
890 With bold fanatic spectres to rejoice;
About the fire into a dance they bend,
And sing their sabbath notes with feeble voice.

224

Our guardian angel saw them where he sate
Above the palace of our slumbering King;

881n. Terence, *Heautontimorumenos* ll. 366–7 ('She handled the longing man
with skill, so as to fire his heart by his failure'). Although seventeenth-century
editions of Terence vary here, D. does seem to misquote: those closest to D.'s
text have *virum, / Cupidum . . . incenderet.*
882. but] only.
885. letted of] hindered from attaining.
887. survey] Stressed on the second syllable.
889–90. The heads of traitors were impaled on the Southwark gate tower of London
Bridge; the fire reached the bridge on the first night, but did not spread to the
south bank. *fanatic spectres*] fifth-monarchy men and other radical insurgents
executed in 1661–2.
890–2. Winn 177 suggests an echo of Psalm c in the version by Sternhold and
Hopkins: 'Sing to the Lord with cheerful voice, / . . . Come ye before him and
rejoice'. The description of the *fanatic spectres* thus ironically evokes one of the
puritans' favourite psalms.
891. bend] direct themselves, turn, proceed (*OED* 20).
892. sabbath] Perhaps associating the witches' sabbath with the puritans, who strictly
observed the sabbath.
893. guardian angel] D. discusses the difficulty which Christian poets have in deploy-
ing supernatural figures in epic poetry in his 'Discourse Concerning Satire' (*Poems*
iii 340–8). *sate*] sat (common seventeenth-century form).

895   He sighed, abandoning his charge to Fate,
         And drooping, oft looked back upon the wing.

                              225
         At length the crackling noise and dreadful blaze
            Called up some waking lover to the sight,
         And long it was ere he the rest could raise,
900   Whose heavy eyelids yet were full of night.

                              226
         The next to danger, hot pursued by Fate,
            Half-clothed, half-naked, hastily retire,
         And frighted mothers strike their breasts too late
            For helpless infants left amidst the fire.

                              227
905   Their cries soon waken all the dwellers near:
            Now murmuring noises rise in every street;
         The more remote run stumbling with their fear,
            And in the dark men jostle as they meet.

                              228
         So weary bees in little cells repose,
910   But if night-robbers lift the well-stored hive
         An humming through their waxen city grows,
            And out upon each other's wings they drive.

                              229
         Now streets grow thronged and busy as by day:
            Some run for buckets to the hallowed choir,
915   Some cut the pipes, and some the engines play,
            And some more bold mount ladders to the fire.

896. *looked*] *1688*; look *1667, 1668.*
903. *mothers*] *1688*; Mother *1667, 1668.*
909–12. The simile is appropriate because those collecting honey use smoke to
drive out the bees: *Geo.* iv 230.
914–15. Fire buckets were kept in churches. It was usually necessary to cut
the wooden water-pipes to obtain water for fire-fighting. *engines*] brass hand-
squirts with a capacity of about a gallon (Bell 34–6). But 'this lamentable Fire in
a short time became too big to be mastered by any Engines' (*London Gazette*).

230

In vain: for from the east a Belgian wind
  His hostile breath through the dry rafters sent;
The flames impelled soon left their foes behind
920   And forward with a wanton fury went.

231

A quay of fire ran all along the shore
  ᵇAnd lightened all the river with the blaze;
The wakened tides began again to roar,
  And wondering fish in shining waters gaze.

(b) Sigaea igni freta lata relucent. *Virg.*

232

925 Old father Thames raised up his reverend head,
  But feared the fate of Simois would return;
Deep in his ooze he sought his sedgy bed,
  And shrunk his waters back into his urn.

233

The fire, meantime, walks in a broader gross,
930   To either hand his wings he opens wide:
He wades the streets, and straight he reaches 'cross
  And plays his longing flames on th' other side.

234

At first they warm, then scorch, and then they take;
  Now with long necks from side to side they feed:
935 At length grown strong their mother fire forsake,
  And a new colony of flames succeed.

---

917. 'A violent Easterly wind fomented it' (*London Gazette*); it was actually north-east (Bell 34).
922n. Aen. ii 312: 'the straits of Sigaeum light up far and wide from the fire'.
925–8. Cp. Virgil: *amnis / rauca sonans, revocatque pedem Tyberinus ab alto* (*Aen.* ix 124–5: 'Old Tyber roar'd; and raising up his Head, / Call'd back his Waters to their Oozy Bed'; tr. D. ll. 151–2).
926. The river Xanthus (near Troy) called on its tributary Simois for help and tried to drown Achilles; it was attacked by Hephaestus with fire, tormenting the fish (cp. D.'s l. 924) (*Iliad* xxi 305–82).
929. gross] body, mass.

235

To every nobler portion of the town
  The curling billows roll their restless tide;
In parties now they straggle up and down
940   As armies unopposed for prey divide.

236

One mighty squadron, with a side wind sped,
  Through narrow lanes his cumbered fire does haste,
By powerful charms of gold and silver led
  The Lombard bankers and the Change to waste.

237

945 Another backward to the Tower would go,
  And slowly eats his way against the wind;
But the main body of the marching foe
  Against th' imperial palace is designed.

238

Now day appears, and with the day the King,
950   Whose early care had robbed him of his rest;
Far off the cracks of falling houses ring,
  And shrieks of subjects pierce his tender breast.

239

Near as he draws, thick harbingers of smoke
  With gloomy pillars cover all the place;
955 Whose little intervals of night are broke
  By sparks that drive against his sacred face.

938. Cp. *propiusque aestus incendia volvunt* (*Aen.* ii 706: 'and waves roll the fires nearer').

941–8. On 3 September the fire spread north (burning the Royal Exchange and the houses of bankers around Lombard Street) and west (towards Whitehall). It also made some progress eastwards, against the prevailing wind, and drew close to the Tower on 4 September.

949–72. The King spent the whole of 4 September in the city directing the fire-fighting (Bell 113–15). 'It is not indeede imaginable how extraordinary the vigilance & activity of the King & Duke was, even labouring in person, & being present, to command, order, reward, and encourage Workemen; by which he shewed his affection to his people, & gained theirs' (Evelyn, 6 September).

949. Perhaps recalling Cowley: 'up rose the *Sun* and *Saul*' (*Davideis* ii; *Poems* 284); and cp. 'Palamon and Arcite' iii 190.

953–4. Observers were awed by the thick pall of smoke which hung over the city; Evelyn (3 September) thought it extended for fifty miles (Bell 67).

240

More than his guards his sorrows made him known,
    And pious tears which down his cheeks did shower;
The wretched in his grief forgot their own,
960   So much the pity of a king has power.

241

He wept the flames of what he loved so well,
    And what so well had merited his love:
For never prince in grace did more excel,
    Or royal city more in duty strove.

242

965 Nor with an idle care did he behold:
    Subjects may grieve, but monarchs must redress.
He cheers the fearful and commends the bold,
    And makes despairers hope for good success.

243

Himself directs what first is to be done,
970   And orders all the succours which they bring:
The helpful and the good about him run
    And form an army worthy such a King.

244

He sees the dire contagion spread so fast
    That where it seizes all relief is vain;
975 And therefore must unwillingly lay waste
    That country which would else the foe maintain.

245

The powder blows up all before the fire:
    Th' amazèd flames stand gathered on a heap,
And from the precipice's brink retire,
980   Afraid to venture on so large a leap.

246

Thus fighting fires awhile themselves consume,
    But straight, like Turks, forced on to win or die,

965. *idle*] ineffectual.
977–88. The desperate measure of blowing up houses to clear a way before the flames was eventually used on 4 September.

They first lay tender bridges of their fume
And o'er the breach in unctuous vapours fly.

247

985   Part stays for passage till a gust of wind
        Ships o'er their forces in a shining sheet;
      Part creeping under ground their journey blind,
        And climbing from below their fellows meet.

248

      Thus to some desert plain or old wood side
990   Dire night-hags come from far to dance their round,
      And o'er broad rivers on their fiends they ride,
        Or sweep in clouds above the blasted ground.

249

      No help avails: for hydra-like the fire
        Lifts up his hundred heads to aim his way;
995   And scarce the wealthy can one half retire
        Before he rushes in to share the prey.

250

      The rich grow suppliant, and the poor grow proud;
        Those offer mighty gain, and these ask more:
      So void of pity is th' ignoble crowd
1000   When others' ruin may increase their store.

982. Turkish foot-soldiers in battle were half-enclosed by their cavalry, who had
orders to kill any trying to retreat (Henry Blount, *A Voyage into the Levant*, third
edition (1638) 71) (*Works*).
983. *fume*] smoke.
987. *blind*] conceal, make difficult to trace (*OED* 3); a verb here.
989. *desert*] 1667's spelling *desart* indicates seventeenth-century pronunciation.
993–4. *hydra*] The monster with many heads (100 according to Diodorus Siculus
IV xi 5), which was killed by Hercules. It is used as an image for rebellion on
Rubens's ceiling in the Banqueting House, Whitehall, and in *Coriolanus* III i 93,
and so continues the image of the fire as a rebel. Cp. *AA* l. 541.
995. *retire*] remove (*OED* 8); a transitive verb here.
997–1000. 'Any money is given for help, 5l. 10l. 20l. 30l. for a cart, to bear
forth into the Fields some choice things, which were ready to be consumed;
and some of the countries [i.e. countrymen] had the Conscience to accept of the
highest price, which the Citizens did then offer in their extremity' (Thomas Vincent,
God's Terrible Voice in the City (1667) 53). It was a common complaint: cp. Samuel
Rolle, *The Burning of London* (1667) iii 28–33.
999. *ignoble crowd*] Cp. Virgil's *ignobile vulgus* (*Aen.* i 149).

251

As those who live by shores with joy behold
  Some wealthy vessel split or stranded nigh,
And from the rocks leap down for shipwrecked gold,
  And seek the tempest which the others fly:

252

1005 So these but wait the owners' last despair,
  And what's permitted to the flames invade;
Ev'n from their jaws they hungry morsels tear,
  And on their backs the spoils of Vulcan lade.

253

The days were all in this lost labour spent,
1010   And when the weary King gave place to night
His beams he to his royal brother lent,
  And so shone still in his reflective light.

254

Night came, but without darkness or repose,
  A dismal picture of the general doom,
1015 Where souls distracted when the trumpet blows
  And half unready with their bodies come.

255

Those who have homes, when home they do repair,
  To a last lodging call their wandering friends;
Their short, uneasy sleeps are broke with care,
1020   To look how near their own destruction tends.

1001–8. Rolle also condemns 'those that stole what they could in the time of
the Fire' and says: 'Some living upon the Sea-coast, may, perchance, gain now
and then by racks, bringing rich goods to their hands; but then, it is presumed,
the owners are cast away, or cannot be known' (iii 33–5).
1006. invade] seize, usurp (*OED* 4b).
1008. Vulcan] Roman god of fire.   *lade*] load.
1011–12. Cp. *To My Lord Chancellor* ll. 45–8.
1011. The Duke of York spent 4 September directing firefighting late into the
night (Bell 115).
1014–16. It was believed that at the Last Judgement (*general doom*) souls and
bodies would be reunited (cp. Cowley, 'The Resurrection'; *Poems* 183).
1014. dismal] Perhaps used with overtones of its Latin origin in *dies mali* (unlucky,
evil days); there were twenty-four unlucky days in the medieval calendar, including 3 September (see *OED*).
1020. tends] approaches (*OED* 1).

256

Those who have none sit round where once it was,
　　And with full eyes each wonted room require,
Haunting the yet warm ashes of the place,
　　As murdered men walk where they did expire.

257

1025　Some stir up coals and watch the Vestal fire,
　　Others in vain from sight of ruin run,
And while through burning labyrinths they retire
　　With loathing eyes repeat what they would shun.

258

The most in fields like herded beasts lie down,
1030　　To dews obnoxious on the grassy floor;
And while their babes in sleep their sorrows drown,
　　Sad parents watch the remnants of their store.

259

While by the motion of the flames they guess
　　What streets are burning now, and what are near;
1035　An infant, waking, to the paps would press,
　　And meets, instead of milk, a falling tear.

260

No thought can ease them but their sovereign's care,
　　Whose praise th' afflicted as their comfort sing:
Even those whom want might drive to just despair
1040　　Think life a blessing under such a King.

1022. require] seek for (*OED* 9); perhaps also 'look in vain for, miss', one of the
senses of the Latin *requiro*. Like *repeat* in l. 1028, this is a somewhat unusual usage in
English, and shows D.'s consciousness of Latin roots; cp. 'Account' ll. 245–9 above.
1025. Vestal fire] Vesta was the Roman goddess of the household and hearth; her
cult was centred on a fire which never went out.
1028. repeat] encounter again (*OED* 4), recalling *urbem repeto* ('I seek the city again';
Aen. ii 749). Cp. Waller: 'the pious Trojan . . . / Repeats the danger of the burning town' ('Battle of the Summer Islands' ll. 62–4); and D.'s 'Dedication of
the *Aeneis*': '*Æneas . . .* repeated all his former Dangers to have found his Wife'
(*Works* v 291).
1029–32. The refugees assembled at Moorfields (Bell 89–90).
1030. obnoxious] exposed to (*OED* 1).

261

Meantime he sadly suffers in their grief,
    Out-weeps an hermit, and out-prays a saint:
All the long night he studies their relief,
    How they may be supplied, and he may want.

262

King's Prayer.

1045 'O God', said he, 'thou patron of my days,
    Guide of my youth in exile and distress!
Who me unfriended brought'st by wondrous ways
    The kingdom of my fathers to possess;

263

Be thou my judge, with what unwearied care
1050   I since have laboured for my people's good,
To bind the bruises of a civil war,
    And stop the issues of their wasting blood.

264

Thou who hast taught me to forgive the ill,
    And recompense as friends the good misled,
1055 If mercy be a precept of thy will,
    Return that mercy on thy servant's head.

265

Or if my heedless youth has stepped astray,
    Too soon forgetful of thy gracious hand;
On me alone thy just displeasure lay,
1060   But take thy judgements from this mourning land.

266

We all have sinned, and thou hast laid us low
    As humble earth from whence at first we came;

1045–60. Cp. David's prayer in the pestilence, 1 Chronicles xxi 17.
1049–52. Cp. Smith (see ll. 601–16n): 'Your watchful thoughts, and your unwearied care, / Succeeding ages will with joy declare; / Tell, how without th' expence of their own bloud, / Or sweat, You wisely have contriv'd their good' (*A Poem on . . . The Loyal London* 9).
1053–6. For mercy as a characteristic of Charles cp. *Astraea Redux* ll. 258–65n.
1061. We all have sinned] See headnote, *Fire.*

Like flying shades before the clouds we show,
And shrink like parchment in consuming flame.

267
1065 O let it be enough what thou hast done,
When spotted deaths ran armed through every street
With poisoned darts which not the good could shun,
The speedy could out-fly, or valiant meet.

268
The living few, and frequent funerals then,
1070 Proclaimed thy wrath on this forsaken place;
And now those few who are returned again
Thy searching judgements to their dwellings trace.

269
O pass not, Lord, an absolute decree,
Or bind thy sentence unconditional;
1075 But in thy sentence our remorse foresee,
And in that foresight this thy doom recall.

270
Thy threatenings, Lord, as thine, thou may'st revoke;
But if immutable and fixed they stand,
Continue still thyself to give the stroke,
1080 And let not foreign foes oppress thy land.'

1063. 'Man . . . fleeth also as a shadow' (Job xiv 1–2).
1064. From Cowley: 'The wide-stretcht *Scrowl* of *Heaven* . . . / Shall crackle, and the parts together shrink / Like *Parchment* in a fire' ('The 34. Chapter of the Prophet *Isaiah*'; *Poems* 212) (Loane (see l. 402*n*)).
1066. D. diplomatically avoids other references to the plague of 1665, when the King, courtiers and clergy left Londoners largely to the care of dissenting ministers.
1069. *frequent funerals*] i.e. numerous corpses (*funeral* is not recorded in this sense in *OED*); D. repeats the phrase when translating *plurima corpora* (*Aen.* ii 364–5). For the Latin poetic use of *funera* (funerals) to mean 'corpses' cp. Horace, *Carm.* I xxviii 19.
1073–6. The vocabulary is from theological discussions of predestination; cp. 'The Cock and the Fox' ll. 507–52.
1076–82. Cp. 1 Chronicles xxi 13–16 (David's prayer).
1080. See quotation in l. 1084*n*.

271

Th' Eternal heard, and from the heavenly choir
   Chose out the cherub with the flaming sword;
And bad him swiftly drive th' approaching fire
   From where our naval magazines were stored.

272

1085 The blessèd minister his wings displayed,
     And like a shooting star he cleft the night;
  He charged the flames, and those that disobeyed
     He lashed to duty with his sword of light.

273

The fugitive flames, chastised, went forth to prey
1090   On pious structures by our fathers reared,
By which to heaven they did affect the way
    Ere faith in churchmen without works was heard.

274

The wanting orphans saw with watery eyes
    Their founder's charity in dust laid low,
1095 And sent to God their ever-answered cries,
    For he protects the poor who made them so.

1081. The *London Gazette* also speaks of divine intervention: 'his miraculous and never enough to be acknowledged Mercy in putting a stop to it when we were in the last despair, and that all attempts for the quenching it, however industriously pursued, seemed insufficient'.

1082. From Genesis iii 24, where Eden is guarded by cherubim and a flaming sword.

1084. The navy's gunpowder, which had been stored in the Tower of London, was moved to safety by Sir John Robinson, Lieutenant of the Tower. The Tower was saved by blowing up adjoining houses (Bell 160). The *London Gazette* said: 'And we have further this infinite cause particularly to give God thanks that the fire did not happen in any of those places where his Majesties Naval stores are kept, so as tho it hath pleased God to visit with his own hand, he hath not, by disfurnishing us with the means of carrying on the War, subjected us to our enemies'.

1090–2. Churches and almshouses built before the Reformation, when the doctrine of justification by faith alone, without the need for good works, was promoted by Protestant theologians. The Restoration Church of England was moving away from this position (see Spurr 305, 321).

1091. Cp. *Geo.* iv 562: *viamque adfectat Olympo* ('he seeks the way to Olympus'). *affect*] seek, aim at (*OED* 1); cp. *AA* l. 178.

1093–6. Parts of Christ's Hospital were burnt on 4 September; the Governors had taken the precaution of moving the children to safety (Bell 141–2).

275

Nor could thy fabric, Paul's, defend thee long,
    Though thou wert sacred to thy maker's praise;
Though made immortal by a poet's song,
1100   And poets' songs the Theban walls could raise.

276

The daring flames peeped in, and saw from far
    The awful beauties of the sacred choir;
But since it was profaned by civil war
    Heaven thought it fit to have it purged by fire.

277

1105 Now down the narrow streets it swiftly came,
    And widely opening did on both sides prey:
This benefit we sadly owe the flame,
    If only ruin must enlarge our way.

278

And now four days the sun had seen our woes,
1110   Four nights the moon beheld th' incessant fire;
It seemed as if the stars more sickly rose,
    And farther from the feverish north retire.

279

In th' empyrean heaven (the blessed abode)
    The thrones and the dominions prostrate lie,
1115 Not daring to behold their angry God,
    And an hushed silence damps the tuneful sky.

1097–104. St Paul's Cathedral caught fire on 4 September. The fabric was in poor
condition, and Wren had already made plans for its repair. He then designed the
new cathedral, which was built from 1675 to 1710.
1099. poet's song] Waller's 'Upon His Majesty's Repairing of Paul's'.
1100. Amphion built the walls of Thebes by drawing stones after him by the
magical music of his lyre. Cp. Waller (ibid, ll. 11–12): the King 'like Amphion,
makes those quarries leap / Into fair figures from a confused heap'.
1102. awful] awesome.
1103. Horses were stabled in the cathedral during the Civil War.
1108. The various plans for the rebuilding of London envisaged wide, straight
streets to replace the narrow winding streets of the old city.
1114. thrones . . . dominions] orders of angels (Colossians i 16).

280

At length th' Almighty cast a pitying eye,
 And mercy softly touched his melting breast;
He saw the town's one half in rubbish lie,
1120 And eager flames give on to storm the rest.

281

An hollow crystal pyramid he takes,
 In firmamental waters dipped above;
Of it a broad extinguisher he makes,
 And hoods the flames that to their quarry strove.

282

1125 The vanquished fires withdraw from every place,
 Or full with feeding sink into a sleep;
Each household genius shows again his face,
 And from the hearths the little Lares creep.

283

Our King this more-than-natural change beholds;
1130 With sober joy his heart and eyes abound:
To the All-good his lifted hands he folds,
 And thanks him low on his redeemèd ground.

284

As when sharp frosts had long constrained the earth
 A kindly thaw unlocks it with mild rain;

1120. give on] assault.
1121–4. The owner of the copy of *1667* now in the library of Trinity College, Cambridge, wrote two parodies of this stanza on the endpaper; one reads: 'An Hollow far-fetcht Metaphor he takes / In non-sense dipt of his fantastick braine / Of which a broad extinguisher he makes / Which hoods his witt & stifles all his flame'. The volume was presented to Thomas Smith by Richard Duke in 1684, so the parody may be by Duke or Smith. The stanza is also criticized in *A Letter from a Gentleman to the Honourable Ed. Howard* (1668) 8–9.
1122. firmamental] of the heavens.
1127. genius] in classical religion a tutelary god or attendant spirit allotted to a person or place.
1128. Lares] Roman gods of the home and hearth (disyllabic).
1133. constrained] constricted, contracted (*OED* 9); cp. 'When Winter Frosts constrain the Field with Cold' ('The Second Book of the *Georgics*' l. 430).
1134. kindly] nurturing, fruitful (as well as 'benign').   *unlocks*] Cp. 'Lucretius: The Beginning of the First Book' l. 15, where *unlocks* is D.'s adaptation of Lucretius' *reserata aura* ('loosened [or unlocked] wind').

1135 And first the tender blade peeps up to birth,
      And straight the green fields laugh with promised grain:

285
      By such degrees the spreading gladness grew
      In every heart which fear had froze before;
      The standing streets with so much joy they view
1140   That with less grief the perished they deplore.

286
      The father of the people opened wide
      His stores, and all the poor with plenty fed:
      Thus God's Anointed God's own place supplied,
      And filled the empty with his daily bread.

287
1145 This royal bounty brought its own reward,
      And in their minds so deep did print the sense,
      That if their ruins sadly they regard,
      'Tis but with fear the sight might drive him thence.

288
                        City's request to the King not to leave them.
      But so may he live long that town to sway
1150   Which by his auspice they will nobler make,

1136. laugh] The Latin *laetus* ('joyful') was used of crops and fields, meaning 'abundant' or 'fertile'.
1140. deplore] lament.
1141–8. On 5 and 6 September the King issued proclamations for the supply and distribution of bread, and 'commanded the Victualler of his Navy to send bread into *Moore-fields* for the relief of the poor' (*London Gazette*). On 6 September he rode out to Moorfields to address the homeless.
1141. father of the people] The title *pater patriae* ('father of the country') was conferred on Augustus in 2 BC (Suetonius, *Divus Augustus* 58).
1145–56. The *London Gazette* told enemies abroad that 'a greater instance of the affections of this City could never be given then hath been now given in this sad and deplorable Accident, when if at any time disorder might have been expected from the losses . . . yet nevertheless there hath not been observed so much as a murmuring word to fall from any, but on the contrary, even those persons whose losses rendered their conditions most desperate, and to be fit objects of others prayers, beholding those frequent instances of his Majesties care of his people, forgot their own misery, and filled the streets with their prayers for his Majesty, whose trouble they seemed to compassionate before their own'.
1150. auspice] prosperous lead; propitious influence (*OED* 3).

As he will hatch their ashes by his stay,
And not their humble ruins now forsake.

289
They have not lost their loyalty by fire,
Nor is their courage or their wealth so low
1155 That from his wars they poorly would retire,
Or beg the pity of a vanquished foe.

290
Not with more constancy the Jews of old
By Cyrus from rewarded exile sent,
Their royal city did in dust behold
1160   Or with more vigour to rebuild it went.

291
The utmost malice of their stars is past,
And two dire comets which have scourged the town
In their own plague and fire have breathed their last,
Or dimly in their sinking sockets frown.

292
1165 Now frequent trines the happier lights among,
And high-raised Jove from his dark prison freed
(Those weights took off that on his planet hung)
Will gloriously the new-laid work succeed.

1151. hatch] bring to full development (*OED* 6).
1157–60. Ezra i–iii.
1162. dire] boding ill.
1164. socket] part of a candlestick into which the candle is placed (*OED* 3).
1165–8. A *trine* is the relative position of two planets which are 120° (one-third of the zodiac) apart; this 'aspect' is benign. Jupiter is a propitious planet. In 1666 Jupiter had been in Pisces, its negative sign (each planet rules two signs, manifesting well in one and badly in the other). Pisces is also a sign linked with places of confinement (Simon Bentley, privately). In 1667, however, Jupiter was in Aries, where it is strongly placed, and Aries rules England. William Lilly wrote: 'The positure of *Jupiter* in *Aries*, seems to give some probability of Peace . . . it is the most promising position of Heaven for his Majesties successes against all Enemies whatsoever . . . *Mars* is . . . in a partile Trine Aspect unto the place of the last Conjunction of *Saturn* and *Jupiter*, and the benevolent *Jupiter* in Trine to the place of *Venus* in that Conjunction' (*Merlini Anglici Ephemeris* (1667) sigs B1^r, B5^r).
1168. succeed] give success to (*OED* 14).

293

Methinks already from this chymic flame

1170   I see a city of more precious mould:

Rich as the town which gives the ʿIndies name,

With silver paved, and all divine with gold.

(c) *Mexico.*

294

Already, labouring with a mighty fate,

She shakes the rubbish from her mounting brow,

1175   And seems to have renewed her charter's date

Which heaven will to the death of time allow.

295

More great than human, now, and more ᵈAugust,

New deified she from her fires does rise:

Her widening streets on new foundations trust,

1180   And opening, into larger parts she flies.

(d) *Augusta, the old name of London.*

296

Before, she like some shepherdess did show

Who sate to bathe her by a river's side;

Not answering to her fame, but rude and low,

Nor taught the beauteous arts of modern pride.

1169–80. After the fire, Wren, Evelyn, and Hooke all produced plans for a model
city, but in the event rebuilding proceeded piecemeal.

1169–72, 1179. Cp. the description of the New Jerusalem in Revelation xxi 18–19:
'the city was pure gold . . . And the foundations of the wall of the city were gar-
nished with all manner of precious stones'.

1169. chymic] alchemic, transmuting. The author of *London Undone* (1666) said of
London that 'She was not so much *ruin'd*, as *refin'd*'. The alchemical images
in *AM* are discussed by B. A. Rosenberg in *PMLA* lxxix (1964) 254–8,
J. M. Armistead, *SEL* xxvii (1987) 384–5, and Lyndy Abraham, *Marvell and
Alchemy* (1990) 46, 115, 147, 301, 315.

1170. mould] earth (for its alchemical implications see Abraham 46).

1175. date] duration, limit (*OED* 5).

1177. The name Augusta was recorded by Camden (*Britain* (1610) 80) and
revived by Edmund Bolton in *London, King Charles, his Augusta* (1648).

1183. answering] corresponding.   *rude*] unsophisticated.

297

1185 Now like a maiden queen she will behold
  From her high turrets hourly suitors come:
 The east with incense and the west with gold
  Will stand like suppliants to receive her doom.

298

 The silver Thames, her own domestic flood,
1190 Shall bear her vessels like a sweeping train,
 And often wind (as of his mistress proud)
  With longing eyes to meet her face again.

299

 The wealthy Tagus and the wealthier Rhine
  The glory of their towns no more shall boast;
1195 And Seine, that would with Belgian rivers join,
  Shall find her lustre stained and traffic lost.

300

 The venturous merchant who designed more far,
  And touches on our hospitable shore,
 Charmed with the splendour of this northern star
1200 Shall here unlade him and depart no more.

301

 Our powerful navy shall no longer meet
  The wealth of France or Holland to invade:
 The beauty of this town, without a fleet,
  From all the world shall vindicate her trade.

1185. maiden queen] The phrase here suggests the return of the golden age of Queen
Elizabeth, the Virgin Queen.
1188. doom] verdict, decision.
1193. Tagus] 'a famous river in Spain, which discharges itself into the ocean near
Lisbon in Portugal. It was held of old to be full of golden sands' (D.'s note to
'The Third Satire of Juvenal' l. 97).
1195. A reference to Louis XIV's expansionist designs on the Netherlands.
1200. unlade] unload.
1204. vindicate] defend against encroachment (*OED* 4).

302

1205   And while this famed emporium we prepare,
           The British ocean shall such triumphs boast
        That those who now disdain our trade to share
           Shall rob like pirates on our wealthy coast.

303

        Already we have conquered half the war,
1210   And the less dangerous part is left behind:
        Our trouble now is but to make them dare,
           And not so great to vanquish as to find.

304

        Thus to the eastern wealth through storms we go,
           But now, the Cape once doubled, fear no more:
1215   A constant trade-wind will securely blow,
           And gently lay us on the spicy shore.

1205. emporium] Cp. Smith (see ll. 601–16*n*): 'Thou always wert the great / *Emporeum* of our Kings, and royal Seat' (*A Poem on . . . the Loyal London* 10). The word appears to have first been applied to London by Bede (*Historia Ecclesiastica* ii 3); it is repeated by Camden (*Britannia* (1607) 304; not in the translation). Edward Waterhouse lamented 'the spoil and loss of that once famous place, which *Tacitus* so long ago terms, *Nobilissimum emporium & commeatu negotiatorum maxime celebre*' (*A Short Narrative of the late Dreadful Fire in London* (1667) 3). Waterhouse adds *emporium* to Tacitus' text in *Annales* xiv 33.
1209. Cp. Virgil, *Ecl.* ix 59: *hinc adeo media est nobis via* ('here we have half our way').

4 Mac Flecknoe

Date and publication. Written July–August 1676. The date of *MF* has been much debated, but was definitively established by David M. Vieth in *Evidence in Literary Scholarship*, edited by René Wellek and Alvaro Ribiero (1979) 63–87. Vieth shows that *MF* alludes to a number of Shadwell's works up to and including the printed text of *The Virtuoso* (advertised in the *London Gazette* 3–6 July 1676), but none thereafter; the reference to Ogilby (l. 174), who died on 4 September 1676, implies that he is still alive; and there are probable borrowings from *MF* by Settle in the Preface to *Ibrahim* (licensed 4 May 1676; *SR* 7 July; *TC* November). George McFadden (*PQ* xliii (1964) 55–72) suggested that D. borrowed from Settle's Preface, and that *MF* was conceived over a period of several years, after the controversy over Settle's *Empress of Morocco* (1673); this is unlikely, for *MF* is richly specific to Shadwell and to 1676, as Vieth shows.

Soon after its composition *MF* was given a restricted form of publication by being circulated in MS copies. Seventeen MSS are known to survive: Beal 407–8 lists fifteen, to which should be added National Library of Ireland MS 2093, and Badminton MS FmE 3/12 (described by Michael Brennan and Paul Hammond in *English Manuscript Studies* v (1993) 171–207). Of particular interest is BodL MS Rawl. Poet 123, transcribed in 1678 by John Oldham. Two have been published in facsimile: Leeds UL Brotherton Collection MS Lt 54, reproduced by Paul Hammond in *Proceedings of the Leeds Philosophical and Literary Society: Literary and Historical Section* xviii (1982) 287–96, and Royal Library Stockholm MS Vu. 69 reproduced as *The Gyldenstolpe Manuscript Miscellany of Poems by John Wilmot, Earl of Rochester, and other Restoration Authors*, edited by Bror Danielsson and David M. Vieth, *Stockholm Studies in English* 17 (1967). The poem reached print in a pirated text of no authority in 1682 entitled *Mac Flecknoe, or a Satyr upon the True-Blew-Protestant Poet, T.S.*; the subtitle is the bookseller's attempt to make the poem politically topical in the light of the controversy between D. and Shadwell in 1682 over *The Medal*, and is not attributable to D. himself. *MF* was printed in an authorized text in *MP* 1684 (reprinted 1692), and reprinted in 1692 as part of Tonson's uniform series of D.'s major poems. The relationship between the MSS and printed texts is established by David M. Vieth in *Harvard Library Bulletin* xxiv (1976) 204–45, supplemented by the discussions by Paul Hammond and Michael Brennan. Vieth's discussion corrects and supersedes the provisional piece by G. B. Evans in *Harvard Library Bulletin* vii (1953) 32–54 and the mistaken argument for extensive authorial revision propounded by Vinton A. Dearing in *SB* vii (1955) 85–102 and again in *Works* ii 428–30. The collation and stemma given in *Works* ii 430–9 are also superseded by those of Vieth and Hammond. Comparison of *1684* with the MSS and *1682* shows that the only indisputable revision which D. made for *1684* was to change *rustic* to *Norwich* in l. 33. It is possible that the original 1676 text may also have read *poppy* (l. 126), *heaven* (l. 139) and *after ages* (l. 159). Otherwise D. did not revise *MF* between 1676 and 1684. In the 1676 text all the proper names were spelt out in full, whereas *1684* prints many simply as initials and dashes. In order to present *MF* as it was first read in 1676, the present text is based on *1684* but restores *rustic* and spells out the names.

Context. Thomas Shadwell (1642–92), a leading dramatist with the Duke's Company, was the author of *The Sullen Lovers* (1668), *The Royal Shepherdess* (1669), *The Hypocrite* (produced 1670? not printed), *The Humorists* (1671), *The Miser* (1672), perhaps the operatic adaptation of *The Tempest* (1674), the opera *Psyche* (1675), *The Libertine* (1676) and *The Virtuoso* (1676). He continued to write plays after the appearance of *MF*, but had none produced from the union of the Duke's and the King's Companies in 1682 until 1688. We know of no personal animosity between D. and Shadwell before 1676, nor is there yet any political difference: that does not become apparent until 1682, with Shadwell's *The Medal of John .Bayes* and D.'s lines on Shadwell in *2AA* ll. 457–509. The dispute is a literary one, and *MF* is the culmination of a critical debate between D. and Shadwell which had begun in 1668. The debate is well summarized by R. Jack Smith in *RES* xx (1944) 29–44, and the relevant documents are reproduced with an introduction by Richard L. Oden in *Dryden and Shadwell* (1977). As Smith says, the matters at issue were: (i) the relative merits of the comedy of repartee, practised by D., and the comedy of humours, advocated by Shadwell; (ii) the right of an author to borrow from ancient and modern writers; (iii) the proper estimate of Ben Jonson; (iv) the rationale of heroic tragedy; (v) the relative importance of pleasing the public and instructing it. The debate begins with the Preface to *The Sullen Lovers*. Here Shadwell derides heroic tragedy, where 'they strein Love and Honour to that Ridiculous height, that it becomes Burlesque', and the comedy of wit, where 'the two chief persons are most commonly a Swearing, Drinking, Whoring, Ruffian for a Lover, and an impudent ill-bred *tomrig* for a Mistress'; by contrast, the Jonsonian comedy of humours offers 'perfect Representations of Humane Life' (Shadwell, *Works* i 11). He attacks those who had been 'so Insolent to say, that *Ben Johnson* wrote his best *Playes* without Wit', replying to D.'s *EDP*, published earlier that year, where D. said of Jonson that 'one cannot say he wanted wit, but rather that he was frugal of it' (*Works* xvii 57; and cp. 'Prologue to *The Tempest*'). To Shadwell, however, Jonson 'is the man, of all the World, *I* most passionately admire for his Excellency in Drammatick-*Poetry*' (i 11). In his Preface to *The Royal Shepherdess* Shadwell returned to his attack on the comedy of repartee, which encourages vice 'by bringing the Characters of debauch'd People upon the Stage, and making them pass for fine Gentlemen, who openly profess Swearing, Drinking, Whoring, breaking Windows, beating Constables, &c.' (i 100); the creators of such characters plead that they are pleasing the people, but 'he that debases himself to think of nothing but pleasing the Rabble, loses the dignity of a Poet, and becomes as little as a Jugler, or a Rope-Dancer' (i 100). D. replied in the Preface to *An Evening's Love* (1671), saying that in comedy 'the faults and vices are but the sallies of youth, and the frailties of humane nature, and not premeditated crimes'; consequently such characters need not be punished. As for pleasing the people, 'the first end of Comedie is delight, and instruction only the second'. D. says that he is not an enemy of Jonson, but 'I do not admire him blindly, and without looking into his imperfections: . . . I admire and applaud him where I ought: those who do more do but value themselves in their admiration of him: and, by telling you they extoll *Ben Johnson*'s way, would insinuate to you that they can practice it' (*Works* x 209, 205). Nor is D. a plagiarist: he may take the outline of his story from romance, novel or play, but he transforms it, as others, including Shakespeare and Jonson, have done. The exchange continued along these lines in Shadwell's Preface to *The Humorists* (1671), D.'s 'Epilogue to *2 Conquest of Granada*' and its 'Defence' (1672), Shadwell's Epilogue to *The Miser* (1672), D.'s 'Prologue at Oxford, 1673', Shadwell's Prologue to *Psyche* (1675) and Prologue and Epilogue to *The Virtuoso* (1676). All of these critical issues are taken up in *MF*: (i) wit, repartee and humours: ll. 12, 21, 89, 150, 161, 181–2, 188–90, 196; (ii) plagiarism: ll. 157–64, 183–6; (iii) Jonson: ll. 80, 172–96, and several verbal echoes; (iv) heroic tragedy: ll. 75–8 and the imagery of kingship made burlesque throughout; (v) comedy pleasing or instructing: ll. 150–6, 182, and the imagery of dullness throughout. Shadwell had claimed to be the heir of Ben Jonson, and through his frequent quotations from Horace had appropriated the classical heritage; D. in MF derides that claim by casting him as the true heir not of Jonson but of Flecknoe.

As Vieth saw, the immediate occasion of MF was the publication of The Virtuoso. Its Dedication (dated 26 June 1676) attacks comedies which rely upon 'downright silly folly' or 'the affectation of some French words', and defends his work against 'some Women, and some Men of Feminine understandings, who like slight Plays onely, that represent a little tattle sort of Conversation, like their own; but true Humour is not liked or understood by them, and therefore even my attempt towards it is condemned by them. But the same people, to my great comfort, damn all Mr. Johnson's Plays, who was incomparably the best Drammatick Poet that ever was, or, I believe, ever will be; and I had rather be Authour of one Scene in his best Comedies, than of any Play this Age has produced' (iii 101–2). Vieth (1979) 85–6 notes that MF is not only a review of Shadwell's career, but also a selective review of the theatrical season of 1675–6, in which the most successful plays were Etherege's The Man of Mode (performed in March with an Epilogue by D.) and The Virtuoso; there had also been three performances of Psyche, and a revival of D.'s Tyrannic Love (cp. l. 78). Shadwell may have irritated D. in other ways. Aline M. Taylor suggests that Shadwell's possible role in the lucrative adaptation of the D.–Davenant Tempest into an opera in 1674 may have rankled (SP extra series iv (1967) 39–53). Michael W. Alssid argues that the character Drybob in The Humorists was a humours portrayal of D. which prompted D. to turn Shadwell into a humour (of dullness) in MF (SEL vii (1967) 387–402). Richard Perkin (unpublished PhD thesis, Leeds 1980) notes that the MS of The Humorists included the part of Button, Drybob's mistress, which is missing from the printed text. If performed, it would clearly have irritated D., whether or not he was already involved with Anne Reeves. Perkin also suggests that the poet Crambo in Newcastle's The Triumphant Widow (partly written by Shadwell: performed 1674; printed 1677) may be a caricature of D. Crambo constantly laments how dull he is; when he falls sick, Codshead jokes that he is 'big with Muse, and cannot be delivered' (55: cp. MF ll. 41, 148), and the doctor, having suggested applying various poets as remedies, finally suggests applying Jonson's works 'to the head'. Crambo recoils: 'Oh, I hate Johnson, oh oh, dull dull, oh oh no Wit'. The doctor says that Jonson will purify his language. Characters also accuse Crambo of plagiarism (60–1).

Richard Flecknoe (c. 1605–c. 77) is the other chief figure in MF. Though Pope (Dunciad ii 2n) says he was Irish, he was probably born in Northamptonshire (ODNB); he is often said to have died in 1678, but this claim is based on two errors, (i) that MF was written in 1678, (ii) that MF is concerned with his death. He was a Roman Catholic priest, traveller and writer. His epigrams and prose characters appeared in many editions from 1653 to 1677; he wrote the plays Love's Dominion (1654; cp. ll. 122–5n) and Erminia (1661), satirical attacks upon Thomas Killigrew (The Life of Tomaso the Wanderer (1667)) and Sir William Davenant (S' William D'avenant's Voyage to the Other World (1668)), and A True and Faithful Account of . . . Ten Years Travels (1665). He has sometimes been credited with the attack on D. by one 'R. F.', A Letter from a Gentleman to the Honourable Ed. Howard Esq. (1668); the attribution may be wrong, but we do not know D.'s view. Flecknoe included laudatory verses on D. in his Epigrams of all Sorts (1670) 70: 'DReyden the Muses darling and delight, / Than whom none ever flew so high a flight. / Some have their vains so drosie, as from earth, / Their Muses onely seem to have

MAC FLECKNOE

126

tane their birth. / Others but *Water-Poets* are, have gon / No farther than to th' *Fount of Helicon*: / And they're but *aiery ones*, whose *Muse* soars up / No higher than to mount *Pernassus* top; / Whilst thou, with thine, dost seem to have mounted higher, / Then he who fetcht from *Heaven* Celestial fire: / And dost as far surpass all others, as / *Fire* does all other Elements surpass'. But there were several reasons why D. might have regarded Flecknoe as an archetypally bad writer: (i) his prolific output included the recycling of old material and the reissuing of sheets of unsold books under new titles; (ii) he had attacked D.'s colleagues Killigrew and Davenant, and suggested that Shakespeare would have resented the alteration of his plays by Davenant (and, implicitly, by D., his collaborator on *The Tempest*); (iii) he contributed to the debate between D. and Shadwell by attacking Jonson's critics and defending him against modern 'wit' (*Epigrams. Of All Sorts* (1671) 51–2); (iv) his output of epigrams and criticism lays claim to the classical heritage in the Jonsonian mould. It was Flecknoe's claim to be an heir of Jonson which allowed D. to cast Shadwell in the role of son of Flecknoe instead of son of Jonson. Flecknoe provided an apt image for the writer about to retire, since he had announced his retirement in 'L'Envoy' (*Epigrams Made at Several Times* (1673) 98; Novak (see below)) and three times subsequently. Flecknoe was already a byword for a bad writer. Marvell had written of him in 'Flecknoe, an English Priest at Rome'; this encounter would have been *c.* 1646, but the date of the poem's composition is unknown, and it was first printed in Marvell's *Miscellaneous Poems* (1681); however, D. could have seen a copy in MS (as he did with Marvell's 'An Horatian Ode'). Flecknoe was 'very well jeer'd' in *The Session of the Poets* (in MS, 1668; *POAS* i 329), and a poem on Edward Howard begins: 'Thou damn'd antipodes to common sense! / Thou foil to Flecknoe! Prithee tell from whence / Does all this mighty stock of dullness spring' (in MS, 1671; *POAS* i 340). Shadwell in his verse letter to Wycherley in 1671 derides Flecknoe (v 228). Shadwell owned a copy of Flecknoe's *Enigmaticall Characters* (1658), now in Cambridge UL (E. E. Duncan-Jones, privately). For the links between D., Shadwell and Flecknoe see further Maximillian E. Novak, *Bulletin of the New York Public Library* lxxii (1968) 499–506; Paul Hammond, *EIC* xxxv (1985) 315–29; Ian Donaldson, *Southern Review* xviii (1985) 314–27; for Flecknoe's life, see his *Prose Characters*, edited by Fred Mayer (1987) ix–cxix, and *ODNB*.

Authorship. Only two MSS (Illinois MS and Yale MS Osborn b. 105) attribute *MF* to D., so the poem probably circulated anonymously at first. *1682* describes it as being 'By the Author of *Absalom & Achitophel*'. Mulgrave attributes *MF* to 'The Laureat' in *An Essay upon Poetry* (1682) 10. It was printed anonymously in *1684*, but following on from *AA* and *The Medal*, forming a clearly defined group; in the 1692 reprint of *MP* the three satires were attributed to D. on the contents page but not in the text, and in the following year (after Shadwell's death) D. acknowledged his authorship of *MF* in the 'Discourse Concerning Satire' (*Poems* iii 389), For the significance of the anonymous publication see Paul Hammond, *The Making of Restoration Poetry* (2006) 50–2.

Sources. The chief sources for *MF* are the works of Shadwell and Flecknoe themselves, as the notes show. Shadwell's claim to be heir to the classical heritage in general, and to Jonson's achievement in particular, gave D. the reason for using the classical references and the image of succession. Jonson himself had called his followers 'sons'. Flecknoe had announced his retirement more than once (ll. 7–10n), and had also provided an image of himself as king at a Twelfth Night feast in a letter to Mademoiselle de Beauvais: 'Think me not now one of those who change their natural Condition, with the condition of Fortune, and wax proud with their honours. . . . I promise you on my *Royal* word, my Subjects here shall have cause to rejoice whilst I reign over them, my raign shall be nothing but one continued Feast, which they shall celebrate with joyful acclamation, nothing shall be consum'd but in the Kitchen; and nothing be exhausted but the Cellar'; the lady replied with an address 'To his Flecknotique Majesty' (*A Relation Of ten Years Travells* [1656] 137–9).

The idea of a poet being crowned goes back to the coronation of Petrarch as laureate in 1341, but D. may have known about two burlesque poetic coronations which took place later under the aegis of Pope Leo X (1475–1521). Camillo Querno came from Apulia to Rome to make his fortune, and was invited to a symposium at which he was made to drink and sing alternately. He was then crowned with a wreath of vine leaves, cabbage and laurel, and given the title of arch-poet. Baraballo of Gaeta considered himself a second Petrarch, and rode through the streets of Rome mounted on an elephant; after reciting his verses to the Pope he was led away to the sound of drums and trumpets, but on the return journey the elephant shied on the bridge of St Angelo and deposited the poet on the pavement. The stories are told by Paulo Giovio in *Elogia Doctorum Virorum* (1557).

The question of MF's genre and antecedents is complex. D. himself included *MF* in a discussion of Varronian satire in his 'Discourse Concerning Satire' in 1692 (*Poems* iii 389); other examples which he mentions include Petronius' *Satyricon*, some of Lucian's dialogues, Apuleius' *Golden Ass*, Seneca's *Apocolocyntosis* (the mock deification of the Emperor Claudius), Barclay's *Euphormio*, Erasmus' *Moriae Encomium* and Spenser's *Mother Hubbard's Tale*. Michael West (*SEL* xiii (1973) 437–49) points to the continental background to *MF*. The poem has affinities with the paradoxical encomium (on which see Henry Knight Miller, *MPh* liii (1956) 145–78), exemplified not only by Erasmus' *Moriae Encomium* but by other humanists' panegyrics to the louse, ant, ass, elephant, egg, shade, and gout. In his 'Discourse' (*Poems* iii 439–41) D. praises *Le Lutrin* (1674) by Nicolas Boileau-Despréaux, a satire on a battle for precedence in a chapel, and the *Secchia Rapita* (1622) by Alessandro Tassoni; according to an anecdote by Lockier D. once said that he valued *MF* 'because 'tis the first piece of ridicule written in heroics' and was then forced by Lockier to admit the precedence of Tassoni and Boileau (Spence i 274–5).

There had already been several verse satires on Restoration writers before *MF*, including the *Sessions of the Poets* (in MS, 1668; *POAS* i 327–37), some satires on Edward Howard (*POAS* i 338–41), ?Etherege's *Ephelia to Bajazet* and Rochester's reply *A Very Heroical Epistle in Answer to Ephelia* (in MS, 1675; *POAS* i 342–7), Rochester's *An Allusion to Horace* (in MS, 1675–6) and his *An Epistolary Essay from M.G. to O.B.* (in MS, 1676). McFadden has shown that *MF* has some ideas in common with D.'s contributions to *Notes and Observations on the Empress of Morocco* (1674). Michael West (*SEL* xviii (1978) 457–64) suggests that D. may have been influenced by the example of Thomas Duffett's burlesque dramas; the operatic *Tempest* was travestied in Duffett's *The Mock Tempest* (performed 1674), and Shadwell's opera *Psyche* was burlesqued by Duffett in *Psyche Debauch'd* (performed 1675). Both burlesques are set amid London low-life.

As these examples indicate, *MF* can be thought of as combining a number of modes or genres: the paradoxical encomium, the personal lampoon and the satirical discussion of literary values and writers. Ian Jack in *Augustan Satire* (1952) 43–52 defines *MF* as 'mock heroic'; in this mode heroic language and incident are applied to an unworthy subject. This is distinct from burlesque, exemplified by Butler's *Hudibras* (1663–78), which employs a low style. *MF* may be the

first poem in English to attempt quite this manner, though Boileau's *Le Lutrin*
showed what might be done, and its first appearance in his *Oeuvres diverses* (1674)
just two years before D. wrote *MF* may have been an important stimulus to D.'s
imagination. In his 'Discourse Concerning Satire' D. commented that the double rhyme used in *Hudibras* 'is not so proper for manly satire, for it turns earnest
too much to jest, and gives us a boyish kind of pleasure . . . when we know he
could have given us a better and more solid'. He compares this form of satire
with that of Boileau, who 'had read the burlesque poetry of Scarron with some
kind of indignation, as witty as it was . . . he writes it in the French heroic verse,
and calls it an heroic poem; his subject is trivial, but his verse is noble. I doubt
not but he had Virgil in his eye, for we find many admirable imitations of him,
and some parodies. . . . This I think . . . to be the most beautiful and most noble
kind of satire. Here is the majesty of the heroic finely mixed with the venom of
the other, and raising the delight which otherwise would be flat and vulgar by
the sublimity of the expression' (*Poems* iii 439–41). This seems to describe the
effect which D. aimed at in both *MF* and *AA*.

The heroic manner of *MF* is indebted to Virgil (see R. A. Brower, *PQ*
xviii (1939) 211–17, *PMLA* lv (1940) 119–38, *ELH* xix (1952) 38–48); to
Milton (see Michael Wilding, *EIC* xix (1969) 355–70; and J. R. Mason); and to
Cowley (see A. L. Korn, *HLQ* xiv (1950–1) 99–127), whose *Davideis*, along with
the Bible, provides the images of Flecknoe and Shadwell as prophets, priests,
and kings.

Reception. There are probable borrowings from *MF* in the Preface to Settle's *Ibrahim*
(1676): see above. If 'A Session of the Poets' is correctly dated to November or
December 1676, then the description of Shadwell in ll. 26–36 may owe something to *MF* (*POAS* i 353). The date on Oldham's transcript, 1678, is probably
the year in which he copied the poem; there are echoes of *MF* in his *Satyrs upon
the Jesuits* iii 657–63, 665 (written summer 1679), and 'A Satyr, in Imitation of
the Third of Juvenal' ll. 176–7 (written 1682), while 'A Satyr' ["Spenser's Ghost"]
(written 1682–3) has some comparable material. Vieth (1979) 67–9 collects
echoes of *MF* in D'Urfey's *Sir Barnaby Whigg* (performed 1681?), *The Tory-Poets*
(1682) and *Rochester's Farewell* (in MS, written 1680), and an apparent allusion in
Advice to Apollo (written 1677; *POAS* i 392–4). *The Loyal Protestant*, 9 February
1682, remarks: 'he would send him [Shadwell] his Recantation next morning,
with a *Mac-Flecknoe*, and a brace of Lobsters for his Breakfast; All which he
knew he had a singular aversion for'. See also Hammond and Hopkins 383. This
relatively meagre evidence, and the comparatively small number of extant MSS
(few of which can be dated with certainty to before 1682), suggests that the
circulation of *MF* before 1682 was confined to London literary circles, and
perhaps Oxford and Cambridge. It seems not to have made a great impact in
these early years. Mulgrave in *An Essay upon Poetry* (1682) 10 commends *MF* as
an example of how to write sharp satire in an elegant way. *MF* l. 178 is echoed
by Tonson in his poem on Oldham in *Sylvae* (1685) 473.

Mac Flecknoe

All human things are subject to decay,
And, when Fate summons, monarchs must obey:
This Flecknoe found, who like Augustus young
Was called to empire, and had governed long;
5   In prose and verse was owned without dispute
Through all the realms of nonsense absolute.

4. *Title. Mac*] Son [of] (Gaelic). Shadwell protested at D. 'giving me the *Irish*
name of *Mack*, when he knows I never saw *Ireland* till I was three and twenty
years old, and was there but four Months' (Dedication of *The Tenth Satyr of Juvenal*
(1687); v 292). The Irish have been proverbially represented by the English as
comic failures lacking intelligence and culture; Rochester included 'Hibernian learning' in his poem 'Upon Nothing' l. 47. See also l. 213n below.

1. Cp. Waller: 'Well sung the Roman bard, "All human things / Of dearest value
hang on slender strings"' ('Of the danger His Majesty . . . escaped' ll. 163–4;
the reference is to Ovid, *omnia sunt hominum tenui pendentia filo* (*Ex Ponto* IV
iii 35).

3. This Flecknoe found] Echoes 'This Caesar found' (Waller, 'A Panegyric to my
Lord Protector' l. 149).   *Augustus*] Gaius Octavius (63 BC to AD 14), first of the
Roman emperors, whose leading role in Rome began with his appointment as
consul in 43 BC.

3–4. young / Was called to empire] Flecknoe's first book was his poem *Hiero-
thalamium. Or, the heavenly nuptialls of our Saviour* (1626), published when he was
about 21.

4, 6. empire . . . realms] For the image cp. Shadwell's Preface to *Psyche* where he
says that some writers 'are very much offended with me, for leaving my own
Province of *Comedy*, to invade their Dominion of *Rhime*' (ii 279; Alssid). D. plays
later with the titles of Flecknoe's plays *Love's Dominion* and *Love's Kingdom* (ll. 122,
141, 143). See also headnote, *Sources*, for a tradition of poetic coronations.
Thomas Carew had said that Donne ruled 'The universall Monarchy of wit' (*Poems*
74). Cowley also uses the image of the poet's empire in 'To Sir *William Davenant*'
and 'On *Orinda's* Poems' (*Poems* 42–3, 406).

6. nonsense] This word is first used by Jonson: in *Bartholomew Fair* the game of
vapours 'is *non sense*. Euery man to oppose the last man that spoke: whether it
concern'd him, or no' (IV iv 27n), and in *Discoveries* he says: 'Many Writers
perplexe their Readers, and Hearers with meere *Non-sense*. Their writings need
sunshine' (ll. 1868–70). Shadwell in his Preface to *The Humorists* laments the fact
that the rabble are 'more pleased with the extravagant and unnatural actions
the trifles, and fripperies of a Play, or the trappings and ornaments of Nonsense,
than with all the wit in the world' (i 185), and in the Epilogue he says: 'Yet if
you hiss, he knows not where the harm is, / He'll not defend his Nonsence *Vi
& Armis*' (ll. 40–1). For Jonson the spectacles produced by Inigo Jones were instances
of nonsense because they lacked the profound art of the poet: 'O Showes! Showes!
Mighty Showes! / The Eloquence of Masques! What need of prose / Or Verse,
or Sense t' express Immortall you?' ('An Expostulation with Inigo Jones' ll. 39–41);
whereas 'In all speech, words and sense, are as the body, and the soule.

This agèd prince, now flourishing in peace,
And blessed with issue of a large increase,
Worn out with business, did at length debate
10   To settle the succession of the state;
And pondering which of all his sons was fit
To reign, and wage immortal war with wit,
Cried, ' 'Tis resolved; for Nature pleads that he
Should only rule who most resembles me:
15   Shadwell alone my perfect image bears,

The sense is as the life and soule of Language, without which all words are dead.
Sense is wrought out of experience, the knowledge of humane life, and actions,
or of the liberall Arts' (*Discoveries* ll. 1884–9). Shadwell is an enemy of sense
(ll. 20, 89, 117, 156, 194) and, like Inigo Jones, has devoted his energies to spectacle in his opera *Psyche* (Donaldson). The contrasting idea of *sense* is complex.
In part it has echoes of the French principle of *le bon sens* (see Boileau, *L' Art
poétique* (1674) i 28). As J. R. Crider notes (*Brno Studies in English* ix (1970) 11–16),
in neo-classical criticism wit (or imagination) and sense (or judgement) were the
two elements in the creative process. Shadwell does not possess the steady, restrain-
ing quality of sense or judgement. But neither does he possess *wit* (ll. 12, 89),
which denotes both 'imagination' (*OED* 7), 'verbal brilliance' (*OED* 8) and,
more generally, 'intelligence' (*OED* 5). So Shadwell is presented as an enemy
not only of the comedy of wit (see headnote) but also of poetic inventiveness
and intelligence. For D.'s deployment of these terms in his criticism see John M.
Aden, *PMLA* lxxiv (1959) 28–40 and Robert D. Hume, *RES* xxi (1970)
295–314.   *absolute*] (i) perfect, free from deficiency (*OED* 4); (ii) having absolute power (*OED* 8).
7–10. Flecknoe announced his own retirement in 'The *Remembrance*': 'Now aged
grown, does in some *hermitage*, / Desire to end the *remnant* of his age' (*A Treatise
of the Sports of Wit* (1675) 15 bis; cp. 'The Adue', ibid. 7).
8. Flecknoe published over thirty books. The phrasing may come from
Deuteronomy xvi 15: 'the Lord thy God shall bless thee in all thine increase'
(Korn).   *increase*] The noun was stressed on the second syllable.
9. *business*] with a play on the meaning 'sexual intercourse' (*OED* 19b); perhaps
also recalling Charles II's tireless devotion to such 'business'.   *debate*] deliberate, consider with himself (*OED* 5b).
10. In 1676 the question of the succession to Charles II was not yet as contentious
as it was to be from 1679, though anxiety about the religion of James and his
children was voiced in Parliament in 1674 (Haley 358–60).
12. Satan in *PL* resolves 'to wage by force or guile eternal war' against God
(i 121; *Works*) and vows 'immortal hate' (i 107; Wilding). *wit*] See l. 6n.
15–17. Korn (185–6) notes that these lines echo Cowley's repetition of the name
Abdon in *Davideis* iv: '*Abdon* alone his gen'erous purpose knew; / . . . *Abdon* alone
did on him now attend' (*Poems* 385).
15. *Shadwell*] all MSS independent of 1684; Shad— 1682; Sh— 1684. Although the
form 'Sh—' is particularly effective here (and at ll. 47–8, 103) in associating Shadwell
with shit (as Wilding observes), the MS evidence shows that D. originally spelt

Mature in <u>dullness</u> from his tender years;   *Shadwell is sublimely awful?*
Shadwell alone, of all my sons, is he
Who stands <u>confirmed</u> in full stupidity.
The rest to some faint meaning make pretence,   *to be praised for consistency at least?*
20 But Shadwell never deviates into sense.
Some beams of wit on other souls may fall,
Strike through and make a lucid interval,
But Shadwell's <u>genuine</u> night admits no ray,   *he can do nothing but write such rubbish?*
His rising fogs prevail upon the day.
25 Besides, his goodly fabric fills the eye,   *oversight?*
And seems designed for <u>thoughtless</u> majesty: *Even 'mindless' the while'?*

---

out the name in full (Vieth (1976) 227). *perfect image*] Sin is the 'perfect image'
of Satan (*PL* ii 764), and Christ is the 'image' of God the Father (*PL* iii 63;
PR iv 596).
16. *dullness*] Rochester had described D.'s poetry as dull in *An Allusion to Horace*
(in MS, 1675–6) l. 2, and said that D. called Jonson dull (l. 81). Crambo laments
his own dullness, and calls Jonson dull (*The Triumphant Widow* 22, 37, 46, 61;
see headnote). D. repeats the charge of Shadwell's dullness in *2AA* l. 477.
20. *sense*] See l. 6n.
21–4. Echoes the description of hell in Cowley's *Davideis*: 'There is a place deep,
wondrous deep below, / Which genuine *Night* and *Horrour* does o'reflow; / . . .
Here no dear glimpse of the *Suns* lovely face, / Strikes through the *Solid* darkness of the place; / No dawning *Morn* does her kind reds display; / One slight
weak beam would here be thought the *Day*' (*Poems* 244; Mark Van Doren,
John Dryden (rev. ed. 1946) 20–1). Cp. also Boileau: 'Il est certains Esprits, dont
les sombres pensées / Sont d'un nuage épais toûjours embarrassées. / Le jour de
la raison ne le sçauroit percer' (*L' Art poétique* (1674) i 147–9). Ken Robinson
and Clare Wenley cite Burton's account of windy, hypochondriacal melancholy:
'from these crudities, windy vapours ascend up to the brain, which trouble the
imagination, and cause fear, sorrow, dullness, heaviness, many terrible conceits
and chimeras, as Lemnius well observes, *lib.* 1, *cap.* 16: "As a black and thick
cloud covers the sun, and intercepts his beams and light, so doth this melancholy
vapour obnubilate the mind, enforce it to many absurd thoughts and imagina-
tions"' (*Anatomy of Melancholy* 1.3.2.2; *DUJ* lxxv (1983) 25–30).
22. *lucid interval*] period of temporary sanity between attacks of lunacy (*OED* lucid
3). The idea that the urge to write is a form of madness may be traced back to
Horace (*Epist.* II i 117–18; Gillian Manning, *N & Q* ccxxxv (1990) 295–6).
23. *genuine*] natural, not acquired (*OED* 1); cp. D. and Lee's *Oedipus* (1679):
'a sudden darkness covers all, / True genuine Night' (III i 293–4).
24–5. Pandaemonium, 'a fabric huge / Rose like an exhalation' (*PL* i 710–11).
25. *goodly*] of good appearance (*OED* 1); of considerable size (*OED* 2). It was
often applied to 'fabric' or 'frame' in admiration of the earth and heavens (*OED*
fabric 3a; *PL* vii 15; *Hamlet* II ii 298). *fabric*] frame (*OED* 3b; the first example
of 'fabric' used for the body is from 1695). D. ridicules Shadwell's size again in
2AA ll. 456–65.
26. *thoughtless*] unmindful, careless (*OED* 1); devoid of ideas (*OED* 2, first example).

unsentical ?

Thoughtless as monarch oaks that shade the plain,
And, spread in solemn state, supinely reign.
Heywood and Shirley were but types of thee,
prophet ; giving him Abbol being   30   Thou last great prophet of tautology:
Ev'n I, a dunce of more renown than they,
as John the Baptist   Was sent before but to prepare thy way,
And coarsely clad in rustic drugget came
To teach the nations in thy greater name.

27. For the oak see *Geo.* ii 290–7, translated in 'The Second Book of the *Georgics*'
ll. 397–409. Adding to Virgil, D. says that '*Joves* own Tree . . . holds the Woods
in awful Sov'raignty' and 'His Shade protects the Plains'. Flecknoe had compared
his patron to 'some goodly Oak . . . / Long time the pride and glory of the Wood'
('The Portrait of William Marquis of Newcastle', *Heroick Portraits* (1660) sig. E6ʳ).
There is probably also a reference to the Royal Oak in which Charles hid during
his escape from the Battle of Worcester; it was featured in one of the arches
in his coronation entry: see John Ogilby, *The Entertainment of his Most Excellent
Majestie Charles II* (1662) 37.
28. supinely] indolently (*OED* 2).
29. Heywood] Thomas Heywood (*c.* 1574–1641), prolific writer of plays and of
pageants for the Lord Mayor's Show.   *Shirley*] James Shirley (1596–1666), also
a prolific dramatist, particularly noted for comedy. Tom H. Towers argues that
D.'s references to Heywood, Shirley and Dekker (l. 87) link Shadwell to the
theatrical tradition exemplified by Christopher Beeston's company at the Red Bull,
which specialized in spectacular and vulgar productions; in the Restoration the
Duke's Company (for which Shadwell wrote) used more spectacle than the less
well-equipped King's Company for which D. wrote (*SEL* iii (1963) 323–34).
types] A 'type' is a person, object or event in the OT which is taken to prefigure
some person or thing fully revealed in the NT.
30. tautology] D. implies that the repetition of the same idea is a characteristic of
Shadwell's plays and prefaces. Shadwell admitted that 'Another Objection, that
has been made by some, is, that there is the same thing over and over' (*The
Sullen Lovers*; i 10). Repetition is certainly a characteristic of Flecknoe. Settle was
also accused of tautology in *Notes and Observations* (*Works* xvii 90, 92).
32. So John the Baptist preceded Christ as 'the voice of one crying in the wilderness, Prepare ye the way of the Lord' (Matthew iii 3).
33. coarsely clad] 'And the same John had his raiment of camel's hair, and a
leathern girdle about his loins' (Matthew iii 4). The homely dress is appropriate
for Flecknoe, who had commented on the simple dress worn by the King
of Portugal: 'the *King* is an honest plain man . . . faring as homely as any *Farmer*,
and going as meanly clad as any *Citizen*, neither did he ever make use of any of
the Crown Wardrope, since he came unto the Crown' (*A Relation of Ten Years
Travells* [1656] 56; Hammond in *EIC* (1985)). Flecknoe assigned different clothing
to different styles of satire: 'I would cloath *Satyr* in hair-cloath, *jeering* in homespun-
stuff, *jesting* in motley, and *Raillerie* in silk' ('Of Railerie', *Prose Characters* 102).
rustic] all MSS independent of *1684* (with some corruptions), *1682*; Norwich *1684*. This
change from *rustic* in the original text to *Norwich* in *1684* is D.'s only undoubted
revision in *MF*. Shadwell was a Norfolk man (though Flecknoe, who is wearing
the drugget, was from Northamptonshire).   *drugget*] Cloth of wool, wool and silk,

35   My warbling lute, the lute I whilom strung
      When to King John of Portugal I sung,
      Was but the prelude to that glorious day
      When thou on silver Thames didst cut thy way
      With well-timed oars before the royal barge,
40   Swelled with the pride of thy celestial charge,
      And big with hymn, commander of an host,
      The like was ne'er in Epsom blankets tossed.

---

or wool and linen; not necessarily coarse at this date (see *OED*). There seems to
be no evidence for the statement (Scott, Kinsley, *Works*) that 'Norwich drugget'
was a coarse cloth. A writer in *The Gentleman's Magazine* xv (1745) 99 drew on
this line when recalling that D. in his early years in London wore 'one uniform
clothing of *Norwich* drugget' (Scott).

35–6. In *A Relation* Flecknoe recalls how in Portugal the Secretary of State noticed
his lute and informed the king: 'he sent for me to Court . . . where after some
two or three hours tryal of my skill, (especially in the composative part of Musick,
in which his Majesty chiefly exceeded) I past *Court* Doctor' (50–1); and in 'The
Remembrance' he says: '*His Majesty* never danc'd, nor *Dutchess* sung; / But he with's
Lute or *Viol* still was one' (*A Treatise of the Sports of Wit* (1675) 15 *bis*). Marvell
described Flecknoe playing his lute in 'Flecknoe, an English Priest at Rome' (printed
1681) ll. 36–44. Wilding observes that the lute of Flecknoe and Shadwell is a
parody of the biblical King David's lyre.

37–42. The episode referred to here is unknown, but Mrs E. E. Duncan-Jones
points out (privately) that the royal barge which Shadwell was accompanying might
well have carried Queen Catharine, who was Portuguese, thus providing a pointed
comparison with Flecknoe's serenading of the King of Portugal. The passage also
alludes to Aeneas' voyage up the Tiber (Virgil, *Aen.* viii 86–101). Shadwell refers
to his own musical ability in the Preface to *Psyche*: 'In all the words which are
sung, I did not so much take care of the Wit or Fancy of 'em, as the making
of 'em proper for Musick; in which I cannot but have some little knowledge,
having been bred, for many years of my Youth, to some performance in it'
(ii 280). See also the Prefaces to *The Sullen Lovers* and *The Humorists*.

38. Cp. Waller: 'On the smooth back of silver Thames to ride' ('Of the danger'
l. 62; Noyes, citing N. H. Oswald; also for the following references to Waller).

39–40. Cp. Waller: 'These mighty Peers plac'd in the guilded Barge, / Proud
with the burden of so brave a charge; / With painted oars . . .' ('Of the danger'
ll. 39–41).

40. celestial charge] If the speculation in ll. 37–42n is correct, this would refer
to the Queen (who would be degraded by being named in a satire). *charge*]
responsibility (*OED* 12); person for whom one has responsibility (*OED* 14).

41. big with hymn] Echoing the description of the poet Crambo as 'big with Muse'
(see headnote). *hymn*] Primarily Shadwell's song of praise to the personage in
the royal barge; possibly also associating him with the inspiration (suspect in D.'s
opinion) claimed by Protestant zealots, since hymn singing was associated with
radical nonconformist sects (see Christopher Hill, *A Turbulent, Seditious, and Factious
People* (1988) 261–3).

42. On 17 June 1676 in Epsom a group of rakes including Rochester, Etherege
and Capt. Downs tossed in a blanket some fiddlers who refused to play for them;

[handwritten marginal note: ḱ will be thrown overboard?]
[handwritten marginal note: who & why chosen in this scene?]

Methinks I see the new Arion sail,
The lute still trembling underneath thy nail:
45   At thy well-sharpened thumb from shore to shore

[handwritten marginal note: no decorum, no skill?]
[handwritten marginal note: all England?]

The treble squeaks for fear, the basses roar;
Echoes from Pissing Alley "Shadwell" call,
And "Shadwell" they resound from Aston Hall.

[handwritten marginal note: listening? or dead?]

About thy boat the little fishes throng,
50   As at the morning toast that floats along.
Sometimes as prince of thy harmonious band

[handwritten marginal note: inhibiting his performance? or generally flailing?]

Thou wield'st thy papers in thy threshing hand:

---

the subsequent skirmish with the watch led to Downs's death (David M. Vieth, *Attribution in Restoration Poetry* (1963) 143). There is a subsidiary reference to Act II of Shadwell's *The Virtuoso*, where Sir Samuel Hearty, who 'by the help of humourous, nonsensical By-Words, takes himself to be a Wit', is tossed in a blanket. Editors have seen a further reference to Shadwell's *Epsom-Wells*, but this seems to lack any point.

43. Cp. Waller: 'While to his harp divine, *Arion* sings' ('Of the danger' l. 11). *Arion*] In Greek legend a musician, expert on the lyre; when he returned by ship from a music festival his prizes excited the greed of the sailors, who decided to force him overboard. Arion mounted on the prow of the ship, and sang a song which attracted a school of dolphins, one of which carried him safely ashore. Arion appears in the preface to Flecknoe's *Ariadne Deserted by Theseus* (1654; Towers).

45–6. Cp. Waller: 'Healths to both Kings attended with the rore / Of Cannons eccho'd from th' affrightèd shore' ('Of the danger' ll. 7–8).

47–8. Echoes Virgil, *Geo.* iv 526–7: *a miseram Eurydicen! anima fugiente uocabat: / Eurydicen toto referebant flumine ripae* (' "ah wretched Eurydice" [Orpheus] cried with his last voice; "Eurydice" the banks replied along the whole river') (Legouis).

47. Pissing Alley] John Ogilby and William Morgan list three Pissing Alleys in *London Survey'd* (1677) 22, 34, 35; the nearest one ran between the Strand and the Thames.

48. Aston Hall] most MSS, 1682; Ashton Hall *some MSS*; A— Hall *1684*. It is clear that D. wrote *Aston* or *Ashton*, so no emendation is required (*pace* Pat Rogers, who suggests 'Arm'rers Hall' (*Scriblerian* xvi (1984) 184–5)). No such place has been found in London. The reference is probably to Col. Edmund Ashton, the minor satirist and rake, who in May 1671 entertained Shadwell at his home in Lancashire; from this '*Hall* yclepped *Chaderlon*' Shadwell sent Wycherley a verse letter (G. deF. Lord in *POAS* i 388; David M. Vieth, *Attribution* 257, 264; q.v. 249–70 for a life of Ashton).

49. Cp. Waller: 'With the sweet sound of this harmonious lay / About the keele delighted Dolphins play:' ('Of the danger' ll. 33–4). Flecknoe says that on his voyage from Lisbon to Brazil 'our ship being all incompast with *Dorado's* or shining Fishes (somewhat like *Dolphins*) hunting the Flying Fishes, which you might see on Top of the water, fluttering to escape . . . nor wanted we Musick to our Feast . . . the Mariners having some *Fiddles* amongst them' (*A Relation* 61–3; Hammond in *EIC* (1985)).

52. threshing] beating violently as with a flail (simply a variant spelling of 'thrashing' which some MSS have).

St André's feet ne'er kept <u>more equal time</u>,
Not ev'n the feet of thy own *Psyche*'s rhyme,
55 Though they in number <u>as</u> in sense excel:
So just, so like tautology they fell,
That pale with envy Singleton forswore ⎫
The lute and sword which he in triumph bore, ⎬
And vowed he ne'er would act Villerius more.' ⎭
60 Here stopped the good old sire, and wept for joy
In <u>silent raptures</u> of the hopeful boy.
All arguments, but most his plays, persuade
That for anointed dullness he was made.
     Close to the walls which fair Augusta bind
65 (The fair Augusta, much to <u>fears</u> inclined),
An ancient fabric raised t' inform the sight
There stood of yore, and Barbican it hight:
A watchtower once, but now, <u>so Fate ordains</u>,

53–4. Shadwell's opera *Psyche* was staged by the Duke's Company at Dorset Garden
in February 1675, with music by Draghi, elaborate scenery, machines, and dances
arranged by the French dancing master St André. In the Preface, Shadwell
apologized for his venture into rhyme, and said that 'the great Design was to
entertain the Town with variety of Musick, curious Dancing, splendid Scenes
and Machines: And that I do not, nor ever did, intend to value my self upon
the writing of this Play' (ii 279). As Donaldson notes, Jonson would have heartily
despised this production (cp. l. 6*n*).
55. they] the feet.   *number*] rhythm.
56. they] the papers.
57–9. John Singleton (d. 1686) was one of the King's musicians, who were often
employed in the theatre (see Pepys 20 November 1660). Villerius is a character
in Davenant's *The Siege of Rhodes* (1656; restaged at Whitehall some time before
1673). The combination of lute and sword had been ridiculed in *The Rehearsal*
(1672), where Bayes makes two soldiers 'come out in Armor *Cap-a-pea*, with their
Swords drawn' but with each holding a lute, to 'play the battel in *Recitativo*'
(V 186–98).
61. hopeful] promising (*OED* 2).   *boy*] Shadwell was 34 (b. 1642). He is described
as 'so bonny a lad' in *A Session of the Poets* l. 30 (in MS, *c.* November 1676;
POAS i 353).
64–73. West 442–3 suggests that this setting is reminiscent of hell in Quevedo's
The Visions.
64–5. Cp. Crowne: '*Augusta* is inclin'd to fears' ('Prologue to *Calisto*' (1675)
l. 45).   *Augusta*] the ancient name for London: see *AM* l. 1177*n*.   *fears*] of plots
by Catholics or radical Protestants, as well as foreign invasion.
66–9. The Barbican was in the parish of St Giles, Cripplegate, which also included
Grub Street; the area was associated with nonconformity, plague, licentiousness
and madness: see Pat Rogers, *Grub Street* (1972) 18–37.
66. inform] inspire, impress (*OED* 3).
67. hight] was called.

Of all the pile an empty name remains.
From its old ruins brothel-houses rise,
Scenes of lewd loves, and of polluted joys;
Where their vast courts the mother-strumpets keep,
And undisturbed by watch, in silence sleep.
Near these a nursery erects its head,
75 Where queens are formed, and future heroes bred;
Where unfledged actors learn to laugh and cry,
Where infant punks their tender voices try,
And little Maximins the gods defy.
Great Fletcher never treads in buskins here,
80 Nor greater Jonson dares in socks appear;
But gentle Simkin just reception finds

72–3. Echoes Cowley's description of hell in the *Davideis*: 'Where their vast *Court*
the *Mother-waters* keep, / And undisturb'd by *Moons* in silence sleep' (*Poems* 244;
Christie). That the reference was familiar is shown by the reversion to the reading 'mother waters' in MS Harvard fMS Eng 636. D. had previously echoed these
lines in *To His Sacred Majesty* ll. 113–14. In 'The Authors Apology for Heroique
Poetry, and Poetique Licence' prefixed to *The State of Innocence* (1677), D. quotes
these lines by Cowley and says: 'How easie 'tis to turn into ridicule, the best
descriptions, when once a man is in the humour of laughing, till he wheezes at
his own dull jest! but an Image which is strongly and beautifully set before the
eyes of the Reader, will still be Poetry, when the merry fit is over: and last when
the other is forgotten' (*Works* xii 96).
74. *nursery*] A theatre for the training of young actors was built in the Barbican
by Lady Davenant in 1671, despite opposition from the residents (Leslie Hotson,
The Commonwealth and Restoration Stage (1928) 176–94). On 23 November 1671
Joseph Williamson noted that the two nurseries in Barbican and Bunhill were a
source of opposition to the government (*CSPD* 1671 581; W. J. Cameron).
75. *queens*] punning on 'quean' (also spelt 'queen'), prostitute.
76–7. Echoes Cowley: 'Beneath the dens where *unfletcht Tempests* lye, / And infant
Winds their tender *Voyces* try' (*Poems* 244). For a subsequent echo see 'The Tenth
Book of the *Aeneis*' ll. 149–50.
77. *punks*] prostitutes.
78. Maximin is the ranting, atheist emperor in D.'s *Tyrannic Love* (1670). In his
dedication to *The Spanish Friar* (1681) D. expresses regret for Maximin's ex-
travagances (*Works* xiv 100; Kinsley).
79–80. John Fletcher (1579–1625) and Ben Jonson (?1572–1637), the major Jacobean
dramatists to whom Restoration criticism looks back (e.g. in D.'s *EDP* (1668)).
buskins] boots supposedly worn by actors in Greek tragedy. *socks*] low shoes
supposedly worn by actors in Greek comedy. Buskins and socks stand for tragedy
and comedy in Jonson's 'To the memory of my beloved, The Author Mr. William
Shakespeare' ll. 36–7; and cp. Milton, 'L' Allegro' l. 132.
81. *gentle*] well-born (ironic here). *Simkin*] the clown in *The Humours of Simpkin*
(printed in Francis Kirkman's *The Wits, or Sport upon Sport* (1672)); generally, a
simpleton (*OED*). In Shadwell's *The Miser* Timothy enjoys '*Simkin* in the Chest'
and other 'Pretty harmless Drolls' (ii 53; Kinsley).

Amidst this <u>monument of vanished minds</u>.
Pure clinches the suburbian Muse affords,
And Panton waging harmless war with words.
85   Here Flecknoe, as a place to <u>Fame</u> well known,
Ambitiously designed his Shadwell's throne;
For ancient Dekker <u>prophesied</u> long since
That in this pile should reign a mighty prince,
Born for a <u>scourge of wit</u>, and <u>flail of sense</u>,

82. In Davenant's *Gondibert* (1651) there is a repository of books, 'a structure . . . long knowne to Fame, / And cald, *The Monument of vanish'd Mindes*' (II v 36; Noyes, citing J. C. Collins).

83. clinches] puns, word-play (*OED*).   *suburbian*] At this period the suburbs were often associated with squalor and licentiousness; cp. Flecknoe: 'He is so far from a courtly Wit, as his breeding seems only to have been i'th' Suburbs; or at best, he seems onely graduated good companion in a Tavern' (*Prose Characters* 42); see also examples in *OED*, and Pat Rogers, *Grub Street passim*.

84. Panton] Probably Capt. Edward Panton (suggested by E. E. Duncan-Jones, privately). He wrote *Speculum Juventutis* (1671), a treatise on the education of the nobility which stresses the need for the rulers of empires not to be ignorant, and says that their natural abilities should be improved by art. However, he also argues for the precedence of arms over arts, and devotes much attention to the proper conduct of duels. In 1676 (the year of *MF*) he published *A Publick and Pious Design for the Preserving the Generous Youth, and Consequently the Nation from Ruine*, in which he sets out plans to found a 'Royal Academy' at Chelsea or another place near London to educate the sons of the nobility; his scheme includes a promise to teach them 'to Speak & Write Proper and Short, Without Tautology or Repetition' (3; cp. *MF* ll. 30, 56).

85. a place to Fame well known] Cp. l. 82*n*.

86. Ambitiously] Ambition is a characteristic of Satan (*PL* i 262 etc.).   *designed*] *design* also has Satanic connotations (*PL* i 646 etc.).

87. Dekker] Thomas Dekker (*c.* 1572–1632), dramatist and City poet (cp. l. 29*n*). Dekker, once a rival and antagonist of Jonson, is seen as a forerunner and prophet of Shadwell. In Dekker's *Satiromastix* (1602), an attack on Jonson, Horace (who represents Jonson) prophesies 'That we to learned eares should sweetly sing, / But to the vulger and adulterate braine, / Should loath to prostitute our Virgin straine' (II ii 57–9). G. B. Evans notes that *Satiromastix* (which means 'a whipping of the satire', cp. *flail* in l. 89) was performed by the Children of Paul's, and may therefore have been associated by D. with an earlier kind of nursery (*MLN* lxxvi (1961) 598–600). When attacking Settle in *Notes and Observations on the Empress of Morocco* (1673; *Works* xvii 84) D. had said: 'I knew indeed that to Write against him, was to do him too great an Honour: But I consider'd *Ben. Johnson* had done it before to *Decker*, our Authors Predecessor, whom he chastis'd in his *Poetaster* . . . and brought him in Vomiting up his Fustian and Non-sense' (Donaldson).

89. flail] Pace S. H. Monk (*N & Q* ccv (1960) 67–8) *MF* is too early for this to allude to the 'Protestant flail' which was used during the Popish Plot (1678–9). *sense*] See l. 6*n*.

~theatre

90　To whom <u>true dullness</u> should some *Psyches* owe,
　　But worlds of *Misers* from his pen should flow;
　　Humourists and *Hypocrites* it should produce,
　　Whole Raymond families, and tribes of Bruce.

does anything yet published in London?

95　Now Empress Fame had <u>published</u> the renown
　　Of <u>Shadwell's coronation</u> through the town.

grandiloquent, he again wholly inappropriate?

　　Roused by report of Fame, the <u>nations</u> meet
　　From near Bunhill and distant Watling Street.
　　No Persian carpets spread th' <u>imperial</u> way,

using all puns of other poets? plagiarism?

100　But scattered limbs of mangled poets lay:
　　From dusty shops neglected authors come,

their prizes?
already used or today purses?

　　Martyrs of pies, and relics of the bum. *what either --*
　　Much Heywood, Shirley, Ogilby there lay,
　　But loads of Shadwell almost choked the way.
　　Bilked stationers for yeomen stood prepared,
105　And Herringman was captain of the guard.

could he rusty corrupt
metaphoric? becomes literal rather disorderly...

　　The <u>hoary prince</u> in majesty appeared,
　　High on a throne o<u>f his</u> own labours <u>reared</u>.

this surely echoes the 'bung; making his own labours his shit?

90–3. Alludes to Shadwell's plays *Psyche* (see ll. 53–4n), *The Miser*, based on Molière's *L'Avare*, *The Hypocrite* (never printed), presumably based on Molière's *Tartuffe*, and *The Humorists*. Raymond and Bruce are gentlemen of wit in *The Humorists* and *The Virtuoso* respectively.

94. *Fame*] Rumour, as in Virgil, *Aen.* iv 173–7.

97. *Bunhill*] Bunhill Fields, on the edge of Cripplegate, a burial ground for nonconformists (not, *pace Works*, for plague victims: see Rogers, *Grub Street* 29). It was already associated with bad poetry by Dekker in his preface to *Satir-omastix*, where he writes of the world of poetry from 'all mount *Helicon* to *Bun-hill*' (Evans). *Watling Street*] in the heart of the City.

101. *Martyrs of pies*] In *EDP* (1668) D. said of Robert Wild: 'they have bought more Editions of his Works then would serve to lay under all their Pies at the Lord Mayor's *Christmass*' (*Works* xvii 12; Kinsley). *relics of the bum*] In his Advertisement to *Poems, and Translations* (1683) Oldham says: 'If it be their Fate to perish, and go the way of all mortal Rhimes, 'tis no great matter . . . whether *Ode, Elegy*, or *Satyr* have the honor of Wiping first' (*Poems* 161).

102. *Ogilby*] John Ogilby (1600–76), friend of Shirley, dancing master, Master of the Revels in Ireland, founder of the theatre in Dublin; translator of Virgil (1649), Aesop (1651), the *Iliad* (1660) and *Odyssey* (1665); publisher of atlases (1670–5; cp. l. 47n); author of 'the poetical part' of *The Entertainment of . . . Charles II* (1662) describing the King's coronation entry and ceremony.

104. *Bilked*] cheated, unpaid. *stationers*] publishers.

105. *Herringman*] Henry Herringman was the publisher of D.'s works to 1678, of Shadwell's plays from *Epsom-Wells* (1673) to *Timon of Athens* (1678), and of Flecknoe's *The Diarium* (1656).

107. Echoes *PL* ii 1, where Satan sits 'High on a throne of royal state'.

At his right hand our young Ascanius sate,
Rome's other hope, and pillar of the state:
110 His brows thick fogs, instead of glories, grace,
And lambent dullness played around his face.
As Hannibal did to the altars come,
Sworn by his sire a mortal foe to Rome,
So Shadwell swore, nor should his vow be vain,
115 That he till death true dullness would maintain,
And in his father's right, and realm's defence,
Ne'er to have peace with wit, nor truce with sense.
The king himself the sacred unction made,
As king by office, and as priest by trade:
120 In his sinister hand, instead of ball
He placed a mighty mug of potent ale;

108–9. Echoes Virgil, Aen. xii 168: *iuxta Ascanius, magnae spes altera Romae* ('And by his [Aeneas'] side *Ascanius* took his place, / The second Hope of *Rome*'s Immortal Race': 'The Twelfth Book of the *Aeneis*' ll. 253–4). The phrase *Magnae Spes Altera Romae* is said to have been used of Virgil by Cicero (see Knightly Chetwood's 'Preface to the Pastorals' in *Works* v 41), and is inscribed on a medal of Virgil reproduced in D.'s copy of *P. Virgilii Maronis Opera* (1636) acquired in 1685 (now in Cambridge UL). 'Spes Altera' was the motto assigned to the Duke of York in the coronation entry (Ogilby, *The Entertainment* 93).
108. *Ascanius*] the son of Aeneas. *sate*] common seventeenth-century spelling of 'sat'.
109. *pillar of the state*] Beelzebub is called 'a pillar of state' (*PL* ii 302; Wilding).
110–11. Echoes Virgil, Aen. ii 682–4: *ecce leui summo de uertice uisus Iuli / fundere lumen apex, tactuque innoxia mollis / lambere flamma comas et circum tempora pasci* ('from young *Iulus* [i.e. Ascanius'] Head / A lambent Flame arose, which gently spread / Around his Brows, and on his Temples fed.': 'The Second Book of the *Aeneis*' ll. 930–2). The flame around the head of Ascanius is a sign of divine approval and protection. For the phrasing of l. 111 cp. Cowley: 'Like harmless *Lambent Fires* about my Temples play' (The Extasie', *Poems* 204).
110. *glories*] circles of light, haloes (*OED*).
111. *lambent*] playing lightly over the surface (*OED*; first example is from Cowley, 1647).
112–13. When Hannibal was about nine years old, his father Hamilcar took him to the altar and made him swear that he would become an enemy to Rome (Livy xxi 1).
118. *unction*] the oil used to anoint the king as part of the coronation ceremony.
119. Kings were traditionally held to have priestly attributes (see E. H. Kantorowicz, *The King's Two Bodies* (1957)). Flecknoe was himself a Roman Catholic priest, here seen as merely a 'trade'; cp. the pejorative 'priestcraft' in *AA* l. 1.
120–3. In the coronation ceremony the orb ('ball') is placed in the monarch's left hand, and the sceptre in the right.
120. *sinister*] left; accented on the second syllable in the seventeenth century.
121. *potent ale*] Flecknoe's reign as king at Twelfth Night was characterized by abundant drink (see headnote), and he wrote an epigram 'In Execration of small [i.e. weak] Beer' (*Epigrams of All Sorts* (1669) 13–14). Shadwell's verse letter to

Love's Kingdom to his right he did convey,
At once his sceptre and his rule of sway,
Whose righteous lore the prince had practised young,
125 And from whose loins recorded *Psyche* sprung.
His temples last with poppies were o'erspread,
That nodding seemed to consecrate his head.
Just at that point of time, if Fame not lie,
On his left hand twelve reverend owls did fly:
130 So Romulus, 'tis sung, by Tiber's brook
Presage of sway from twice six vultures took.
Th' admiring throng loud acclamations make,
And omens of his future empire take.

Wycherley begins with an invocation of ale: 'Inspir'd with high and mighty Ale, / That does with stubborn Muse prevail: / Ale, that makes Tinker mighty Witty, / And makes him Droll out merry Ditty' (v 227; Wilding). Shadwell and Flecknoe are Jonson's heirs in their drinking, if not in their wit (Hammond in *EIC* (1985)). D. has a portrait of Shadwell drunk in *2AA* ll. 457–66.

122–5. Love's Kingdom] Flecknoe's 'Pastoral Trage-Comedy', originally published as *Love's Dominion* (1654), was revised, retitled and printed in 1664; reissued 1674. When staged by the Duke's Company in 1664 'it had the misfortune to be damn'd by the Audience' (Langbaine). *Psyche*, as a pastoral opera, is its offspring.

123. Cp. Cowley: 'At once his *Murder* and his *Monument*' (*Davideis* i; *Poems* 247).

124. *righteous lore*] The title page of *Love's Dominion* claims: 'Full of Excellent Moralitie; Written as a Pattern for the Reformed Stage'. In his Preface Flecknoe says: 'I have endeavoured here the clearing of it [the stage], and restoring it to its former splendor, and first institution; (of teaching *Virtue*, reproving *Vice*, and amendment of *Manners*,)' (sig. A4ᵛ). *Love's Kingdom* is prefaced by 'A Short Discourse of the English Stage'. Flecknoe's emphasis on the moral responsibility of the drama is consistent with the line taken by Shadwell in his debate with D.

125. *recorded*] rendered in song, warbled (*OED* 2); probably facetious, since the word was applied mainly to birds, and was becoming obsolete. James Winn (privately) notes that Matthew Locke's music for *Psyche* has prominent parts for recorders. In his Preface to *Psyche*, Shadwell says that 'in all the words which are sung, I did not so much take care of the Wit or Fancy of 'em, as the making of 'em proper for Musick' (ii 280).

126. *poppies*] The poppy is (i) soporific (e.g. *Aen.* iv 486, and the cave of sleep in *Met.* xi 605); (ii) parching and sterilizing (e.g. *Geo.* i 78); (iii) aphrodisiac but not fertilizing (e.g. Thomas Browne, *Pseudodoxia Epidemica* (1646) vii 7; Kinsley). Shadwell was addicted to opium (*2AA* l. 482; Scott).

129. *owls*] signifying apparent wisdom but actual stupidity (*OED* 2).

130. Romulus and Remus agreed to settle a dispute about the site of Rome by observing the flight of birds of omen. Remus saw six vultures and Romulus twelve (Plutarch, *Romulus* ix 4–5).

132. *admiring throng*] Wilding notes echoes of the devils entering Pandaemonium in *PL*: 'the hasty multitude / Admiring entered', and 'all access was thronged' (i 730–1, 761). *admiring*] wondering, marvelling.

The sire then shook the honours of his head,
135 And from his brows damps of oblivion shed
Full on the filial dullness; long he stood.
Repelling from his breast the raging god;
At length burst out in this prophetic mood:
    'Heavens bless my son: from Ireland let him reign
140 To far Barbados on the western main;
Of his dominion may no end be known,
And greater than his father's be his throne.
Beyond *Love's Kingdom* let him stretch his pen;'
He paused, and all the people cried, 'Amen'.

134–6. Echoes Cowley's *Davideis*: 'He saw the reverend *Prophet* boldly shed /
The *Royal Drops* round his *Enlarged Head*', and 'He tells the mighty *Fate* to him
assign'd, / And with great rules fills his *capacious mind*. / Then takes the sacred
Viol, and does shed / A *Crown* of mystique drops around his head' (*Poems* 245,
375, describing the anointing of David by Samuel; Korn). Wilding observes that
'the "damps" and "dullness" have extinguished and darkened the dignity of the
light and enlightenment of *Paradise Lost*, where the Father "on his Son with Rays
direct / Shon full" prior to Christ's enthronement' (*PL* vi 719–20).
134. shook the honours] '*Honours*, that is, *Beauties*, which make things *Honoured*'
(Cowley, *Davideis* ii *n*. 1; *Poems* 306). The usage is Virgilian, as in *laetos oculis
adflarat honores* (*Aen.* i 591; 'she had breathed beauty into his eyes'). In 'The Tenth
Book of the *Aeneis*' l. 172 D. says that Jupiter 'shook the sacred Honours of his
Head' (translating *adnuit*, 'he nodded': *Aen.* x 115).
135. damps] fogs (*OED* 2).
136. the filial dullness] For the Miltonic echoes cp. 'the filial Godhead' (*PL* vi 722,
vii 175) and 'the filial power arrived, and sate him down' (*PL* vii 587).
137–8. Echoes Virgil, *Aen.* vi 77–82, on the Sibyl, the frenzied prophetess: *at Phoebi
nondum patiens immanis in antro / bacchatur uates, magnum si pectore possit / excussisse
deum; tanto magis ille fatigat / os rabidum, fera corda domans, fingitque premendo.* ('Strugling
in vain, impatient of her Load, / And lab'ring underneath the pond'rous God, /
The more she strove to shake him from her Breast, / With more, and far superior Force he press'd: / Commands his Entrance, and without Controul, / Usurps
her Organs, and inspires her Soul.': 'The Sixth Book of the *Aeneis*' ll. 120–5;
Brower).
139. Ireland] See Title, *n*.
140. Echoes Cowley, *Davideis*: 'From sacred *Jordan* to the *Western main*' (*Poems*
366; Korn).   *Barbados*] probably thought of as the setting for the D.–Davenant
version of *The Tempest* (1674) which Shadwell had turned into an opera (Taylor);
also proverbially remote and uncivilized (cp. Wycherley, *The Gentleman Dancing-
Master* (1672) II i 460–6; Alan Roper in *Works*). Flecknoe's journeys took him
to Brazil, but not to Barbados.
141. Echoes Isaiah ix 7: 'Of the increase of his government and peace there shall
be no end' (interpreted as a prophecy of the Messiah).   *dominion*] See l. 6*n*.
143. pen] For the pun on 'penis' cp. 'I'll mar the young clerk's pen' (*The Merchant
of Venice* V i 237).
144. Cp. Nehemiah viii 6: 'And all the people answered, Amen' (Korn).

145   Then thus continued he, 'My son, advance
        Still in new impudence, new ignorance.
        Success let others teach; learn thou from me
        Pangs without birth, and fruitless industry.
        Let *Virtuosos* in five years be writ,
150   Yet not one thought accuse thy toil of wit.
        Let gentle George in triumph tread the stage,
        Make Dorimant betray, and Loveit rage;
        Let Cully, Cockwood, Fopling charm the pit,
        And in their folly show the writer's wit;
155   Yet still thy fools shall stand in thy defence,
        And justify their author's want of sense.
        Let 'em be all by thy own model made
        Of dullness, and desire no foreign aid,

145. *Ed.*; Then thus, continued he, my Son advance *1684*. The commas in *1684* (which does not use inverted commas to mark speech) imply that *Then thus* are the opening words of Flecknoe's speech, but *1682* and all the MSS have no comma after *thus*, which is therefore probably a compositorial error. *advance*] Cp. Shadwell's 'Prologue to the King and Queen' from *Epsom-Wells*: 'Poets and Souldiers used to various chance, / Cannot expect they should each day advance' (ll. 1–2; ii 105).

147–8. Echoes Aeneas' advice to Ascanius in *Aen.* xii 435–6: *disce, puer, uirtutem ex me uerumque laborem, / fortunam ex aliis* ('boy, learn virtue and true labour from me, good fortune from others'; G. C. Loane, *N & Q* clxxxv (1943) 275).

148. Echoes Shadwell's Epilogue to *The Virtuoso*: 'You know the pangs and many labouring throws, / By which your Brains their perfect births disclose' (ll. 36–7; iii 182; Noyes, citing Oswald). Cp. Crambo's supposed pregnancy in *The Triumphant Widow* (see headnote).

149. In his Prologue to *The Virtuoso*, Shadwell says that wit 'requires expence of time and pains, / Too great, alas, for Poets slender gains. / For Wit, like *China*, should long buri'd lie, / Before it ripens to good Comedy: / . . . Now Drudges of the Stage must oft appear, / They must be bound to scribble twice a year' (ll. 7–14; iii 103). Rochester in *An Allusion to Horace* (in MS, winter 1675–6; l. 46) calls Shadwell 'hasty'. Shadwell claimed that *The Libertine* took him three weeks (iii 21). The suggestion that *The Virtuoso* took five years may be a deliberate misreading of Shadwell's reference in his Dedication to 'the *Humorists*, written five Years since' (iii 102) (Kinsley).

151–4. These lines refer to Sir George Etherege (?1636–?92) and several characters from his plays: Dorimant, Mrs Loveit and Sir Fopling Flutter from *The Man of Mode* (staged 11 March 1676), Sir Nicholas Cully from *The Comical Revenge, or, Love in a Tub* (1664), and Sir Oliver Cockwood from *She wou'd if She cou'd* (1668).

151. *gentle*] This epithet is again applied to Etherege in *A Session of the Poets* l. 16 (in MS *c*. November 1676; *POAS* i 353).

155–6. This is a retort to Shadwell's comment on himself in the Prologue to *The Virtuoso*: 'He's sure in Wit he cann't excel the rest, / He'd but be thought to write a Fool the best' (ll. 23–4; iii 103; *Works*).

That they to future ages may be known
160 Not copies drawn, but issue of thy own.]→
Nay, let thy men of wit too be the same,
All full of thee, and differing but in name.
But let no alien Sedley interpose
To lard with wit thy hungry Epsom prose,
165 And when false flowers of rhetoric thou wouldst cull,
Trust nature, do not labour to be dull;
But write thy best, and top, and in each line
Sir Formal's oratory will be thine:

160. Vieth compares the Epilogue to *The Humorists*: 'All that have since [Jonson] been writ, if they be scan'd, / Are but faint Copies from that Master's Hand' (ll. 24–5; i 254). Donaldson observes that Jonson had said of Shakespeare: 'Looke how the fathers face / Liues in his issue' ('To the memory of . . . Mr. William Shakespeare' ll. 65–6).

163–4. Rumour had it that *Epsom-Wells* was not Shadwell's unaided work, and in his 'Prologue to the King and Queen' he said: 'If this for him had been by others done, / After this honour sure they'd claim their own' (ll. 16–17), and printed it with this note: 'These two Lines were writ in answer to the calumny of some impotent and envious Scriblers, and some industrious Enemies of mine, who would have made the Town and Court believe, though I am sure they themselves did not, that I did not write the Play; but at last it was found to be so frivolous a piece of malice, it left an impression upon few or none' (ii 105). Sir Charles Sedley wrote a Prologue for *Epsom-Wells*; later he corrected Shadwell's *A True Widow* (1679) for him (Noyes; Kinsley). Vieth notes that Rochester's *Timon* (in MS, 1674) refers to 'Shadwells, unassisted former Scenes' (l. 16).

164. Burton says of writers who pilfer from others: 'They lard their lean books with the fat of others' works' ('Democritus to the Reader', *The Anatomy of Melancholy* i 23).   *hungry*] not satisfying one's hunger (*OED* 3a); not rich or fertile (*OED* 6).

165. flowers of rhetoric] See l. 168n.

166. Shadwell in the Preface to *The Virtuoso* writes of 'those, who are not Coxcombs by Nature, but with great Art and Industry make themselves so' (iii 102). Cp. Rochester: 'Shadwells unfinisht works doe yet impart / Great proofs of force of Nature, none of Art' (*An Allusion to Horace* ll. 44–5). Flecknoe in 'Of a Dull-fellow' says: 'if he say any thing like a *pump*, he labours for it', and in 'Of Wit': 'it is . . . not acquired by *Art* and *Study*, but *Nature* and *Conversation*' (*Prose Characters* 269, 521). Flecknoe admitted that writing epigrams and characters suited him because they are 'a short and easy kind of writing; and therefore most fit for me, who Love not long discourses, and cannot take pains in anything' (*Epigrams of All Sorts* (1669) sig. A3^{r-v}). See also ll. 175–6n and Shadwell's Preface to *Timon of Athens*. The basic antithesis between art and nature in poetic creativity goes back to Horace, *Ars Poetica* ll. 408–18; for its use in the critique of Shakespeare by D. and others see Paul Hammond in *John Dryden (1631–1700): His Politics, His Plays, and His Poets*, edited by Claude Rawson and Aaron Santesso (2004) 158–79. See also ll. 175–6n. Tonson echoed D.'s line in 'On the Death of Mr. Oldham': 'sweated not to be correctly dull' (*Sylvae* (1685) 472); cp. l. 178n.

168. Sir Formal Trifle in *The Virtuoso* is 'the greatest Master of Tropes and Figures: The most *Ciceronian* Coxcomb: the noblest Orator breathing; he never speaks

Sir Formal, though unsought, attends thy quill,
170 And does thy northern dedications <u>fill</u>.
Nor let <u>false friends</u> seduce thy mind to fame
By arrogating Jonson's <u>hostile</u> name:
Let father Flecknoe fire thy mind with praise,
And uncle Ogilby thy envy raise.
175 <u>Thou art my blood, where Jonson has no part</u>;
What share have we in nature or in art?
Where did his <u>wit on learning</u> fix a brand,

---

without Flowers of Rhetorick: In short, he is very much abounding in words, and very much defective in sense' (iii 107).

170. northern dedications] Shadwell dedicated *The Sullen Lovers, Epsom-Wells, The Virtuoso* and *The Libertine* to the Duke of Newcastle. Flecknoe had dedicated *Love's Kingdom* to the Duke, *A Farrago of Several Pieces* (1666) to the Duchess, and *The Damoiselles A La Mode* (1667) to both Duke and Duchess; he also addressed several poems to them. The Duke returned the compliment with commendatory poems for *Rich. Flecknoe's Ænigmaticall Characters* (1665). Newcastle had been patron of Jonson and Shirley; he had collaborated with D. on *Sir Martin Mar-all* (1668), and D. dedicated *An Evening's Love* (1671) to him. See further Harold Love, *PLL* xxi (1985) 19–27, though Love's suggestion that *MF* was originally a satire on Newcastle is implausible.

173–4. Echoes *Aen.* iii 342–3: *ecquid in antiquam uirtutem animosque uirilis / et pater Aeneas et auunculus excitat Hector?* ('do his father Aeneas and his uncle Hector rouse him [Ascanius] to ancient virtue and manly spirit?'; Kinsley).

174. envy] desire to equal another in achievement (without malevolent feelings) (*OED* 4).

175–6. Echoes Jonson on Shakespeare: 'Yet must I not giue Nature all: Thy Art, / My gentle *Shakespeare*, must enioy a part' ('To the memory of . . . Mr. William Shakespeare' ll. 55–6; Donaldson). The antithesis between nature and art had informed the debate over the relative merits of Shakespeare and Jonson; Flecknoe wrote: '*Shakespear* excelled in a natural Vein, . . . *Johnson* in Gravity and ponderousness of Style; whose onely fault was, he was too elaborate; and had he mixt less erudition with his Playes, they had been more pleasant and delightful then they are. Comparing him with *Shakespear*, you shall see the difference betwixt Nature and Art' (*Love's Kingdom* sig. G5ʳ). Cp. also D.'s 'Prologue to *The Tempest*' ll. 5–8, and l. 166n.

177–8. (i) As in Flecknoe's criticism of Jonson's learning (see ll. 175–6n); (ii) as in *The Virtuoso*, in so far as it might be construed as caricaturing the new science (for an argument that the play does not attack true virtuosi see Joseph M. Gilde, *SEL* x (1970) 469–90); (iii) as in Shadwell's disparagement of the art of heroic drama, e.g. in the Epilogue to *The Virtuoso*: 'sniveling Heroes sigh, and pine, and cry. / Though singly they beat Armies, and huff Kings, / Rant at the Gods, and do impossible things' (ll. 14–16; iii 181; Vieth); (iv) as in Shadwell's criticism of the comedy of wit in his debate with D. (see headnote).

177. brand] Jonson had written of Inigo Jones: 'Thy Forehead is too narrow for my Brand' ('To a ffriend an Epigram Of Him' l. 14), and cp. Martial XII lxi i 11 (Donaldson).

178. understand] Jonson frequently stressed the need for readers to understand his work, e.g. 'Pray thee, take care, that tak'st my booke in hand, / To read it well:

And rail at <u>arts</u> he <u>did not understand?</u>
Where made he love in Prince Nicander's vein,
180   Or swept the dust in *Psyche's* humble strain?
Where sold he bargains, "whip-stitch, kiss my arse",
Promised a <u>play</u> and dwindled to a <u>farce?</u>

that is, to vnderstand' (*Epigrammes* i), and the preface to *The Alchemist*: 'To the Reader. If thou beest more, thou art an Vnderstander, and then I trust thee.' (v 291). Donaldson notes that in the Dedication to *The Assignation* (1673) D. said: 'I know I honour *Ben Johnson* more than my little Critiques, because without vanity I may own, I understand him better' (*Works* xi 322). Snarl in *The Virtuoso* says of young men that 'they are all forward and positive in things they understand not; they laugh at any Gentleman that has Art or Science' (iii 131). D.'s line was echoed by Tonson on Oldham: 'And censur'd what they did not understand' (*Sylvae* 473).
179. Nicander pursues Psyche with 'Industrious Love' and high rhetoric (Kinsley). D.'s phrase echoes Falstaff, who promises to play Henry IV 'in King Cambyses' vein' (*1 Henry IV* II iv 383); and cp. Buckingham's Prologue to *The Rehearsal* (1672): 'There strutting Heroes, with a grim fac'd train, / Shall brave the Gods, in King *Cambyses* vein' (ll. 9–10).
180. humble] Shadwell says in the Prologue to *Psyche*: 'You must not here expect exalted Thought, / Nor lofty Verse, nor Scenes with labor wrought: / His Subject's humble, and his Verse is so' (ll. 12–14; ii 281; Noyes, citing Oswald).
181. i.e. 'Where did Jonson use coarse repartee such as "whip-stitch, kiss my arse"?' D. is continuing the debate with Shadwell over wit and humours (see headnote). D. had used repartee in his comedies, and defended it; here he convicts the would-be Jonsonian Shadwell of using repartee coarser than D.'s, and without precedent in Jonson.   *sold . . . bargains*] To sell someone bargains was to make a fool of them (*OED* 7), specifically to give a coarse reply to a question: in the Prologue to *The Debauchee* (1677), boorish men are told: 'to be brisk, and free, / You sell 'em Bargains for a Repartee' (ll. 42–3; Danchin no. 229), and Sir Carr Scrope's Prologue to Lee's *The Rival Queens* (1677) says that the sparks in the theatre 'with loud Non-sense drown the Stages Wit: / . . . And witty Bargains to each other sell' (ll. 24–6; Danchin no. 231.   *"whip-stitch, kiss my arse"*] Quoting Sir Samuel Hearty in *The Virtuoso*: 'Prethee, *Longvil*, hold thy peace, with a whip-stitch, your nose in my breech' (iii 119). From being a stitch in needlework, *whip-stitch* came to mean 'suddenly' (*OED*). Kinsley notes that Settle says that 'Whip stitch, your Nose in my Breech' are 'Link-boy phrases' (Preface to *Ibrahim* (1677) sig. a3ʳ).
182. In the Dedication to *The Virtuoso* Shadwell says: 'I have endeavoured, in this Play, at Humour, Wit, and Satyr, which are . . . the life of a Comedy. . . . Nor do I count those Humours which . . . consist in using one or two By words . . . I say nothing of impossible, unnatural Farce Fools, which some intend for Comical, who think it the easiest thing in the World to write a Comedy' (iii 101; Noyes). D. had expressed his contempt for the contemporary fashion for farce in the Preface to *An Evening's Love* (1671; *Works* x 202–4) and 'Prologue to *1 Conquest of Granada*' ll. 35–9, and his *Marriage A-la-Mode* (1673) is an attempt to elevate the tone of comedy (see R. D. Hume, *The Development of English Drama in the Late Seventeenth Century* (1976) 277). For verbal parallels to l. 182 cp. 'this Huff, like all those in his Play, dwindles, when examin'd, into non-sense or nothing' and 'has debased Tragedy into farce' (*Notes and Observations*; *Works* xvii 88, 90).

When did his Muse from Fletcher scenes purloin,
As thou whole Eth'rege dost transfuse to thine?
185 But so transfused as oil on water's flow,

184. Noyes shows that there are similarities between some characters and plot-
devices in Etherege's *She wou'd if She cou'd* (1668) and *Epsom-Wells* (1673); Vieth
(1979) 75 shows that similar roles and incidents are used again in *The Virtuoso*
(1676), and points out that *She wou'd* was revived *c.* February 1676 and would
therefore have been fresh in the minds of the audience of *The Virtuoso*. Ironically,
Flecknoe had attacked Etherege's play as offering 'sparks of wit, as much as you'd
desire, / But sparks alone, as far from solid fire' ('On the Play, of she wou'd, if
she cou'd', *Epigrams of All Sorts* (1669) 10–11). *transfuse*] Vieth (1979) 75 suggests that D. alludes to Sir Nicholas Gimcrack's transfusions of blood between a
mangy spaniel and a sound bulldog in *The Virtuoso* (iii 128).
185–6. Perhaps recalling Cowley: 'That *Oyl* mixt with any other liquor, still gets
uppermost, is perhaps one of the chiefest *Significancies* in the *Ceremony of
Anointing Kings* and *Priests*' (*Davideis* iv *n.* 28; *Poems* 399; Korn).
185. oil on water's flow] Noyes; Oyl on Waters flow *1684*. The line has always
been problematic, as Vieth's collation of the MSS shows. *1684* is either (i) textually correct and grammatically correct; or (ii) textually correct but grammatically incorrect; or (iii) textually corrupt and grammatically incorrect. If (i), then
Noyes's proposal that *flow* is a noun is the only possible interpretation of the line.
In this case *1684* requires no emendation but only modernization (*Waters* could
be modernized to either *water's* or *waters*'). Elsewhere D. does use *flow* as a noun,
meaning the opposite of ebb (e.g. *AM* l. 645), but he more frequently uses it as
a verb (e.g. 'Prologue to *All for Love*' ll. 25–6, q.v. for a parallel), while in *RL*
l. 341 it could be taken either way. If (ii), then D. wrote *Oyl . . . flow*, wrongly
allowing the verb *flow* to take a plural form under the influence of *Waters* and
of the rhyme. In seventeenth-century English, plural subjects often take singular
verbs, but the reverse is very rare (Manfred Görlach, *Introduction to Early Modern
English* (1991) 88 has only one example, from 1591; information from Jonathan
Hope); though unlikely, this interpretation is possible. Both (i) and (ii) assume
that *Oyl* is the textually correct reading. In favour of this is the fact that *Oyl* is
supported by three MSS independent of *1684*, and (as Vieth (1976) 228 argues)
the agreement of *1684* with one or more independent MSS is good testimony
that their reading was present in the original 1676 text. If (iii), then *flow* is a verb,
and *Oyl* is a textual corruption of *Oyls*, as Evans argues. In favour of this is that
1682 and nine MSS read *Oyls*. But in textual criticism the number of witnesses
to a reading is no indication of its authority, and *Oyls* is a suspiciously easy
resolution of the crux (which other MSS attempt to solve by emending *on* to
and, *of* or *in*). If the original reading was indeed *Oyls* it is difficult to explain
how *1684* and three MSS arrived at the harder reading *Oyl*. The textual evidence
therefore points to D. having written *Oyl* in 1676; this produced a difficult
line which most MSS tried to regularize in various ways; and the line stood unrevised in *1684*. On textual grounds, then, (iii) seems the least likely explanation.
The grounds for deciding between (i) and (ii) can only be one's assumptions about
D.'s grammar. In favour of (i) is that a grammatical error is unlikely to have eluded
D. both in 1676 and when rereading *MF* for *1684*; in favour of (ii) is that the
syntax leads one to expect a verb, and D. was not infallible. The argument is
inconclusive, and Noyes's solution is adopted here since it produces a grammatical line without altering *1684*. Kinsley and *Works* are silent on this crux.

His always floats above, thine sinks below.
This is thy province, this thy wondrous way,
New humours to invent for each new play.
This is that boasted bias of thy mind,
190   By which one way, to dullness, 'tis inclined,
Which makes thy writings lean on one side still,
And in all changes that way bends thy will.
Nor let thy mountain belly make pretence
Of likeness; thine's a tympany of sense:
195   A tun of man in thy large bulk is writ,
But sure thou'rt but a kilderkin of wit.
Like mine thy gentle numbers feebly creep,

---

186. sinks below] When Sir Formal disappears down the trap in Act III of *The Virtuoso* the stage direction reads 'He sinks below' (iii 145).

187. province] See ll. 4, 6n.

188. Cp. the Preface to *The Virtuoso*: 'Four of the Humors are entirely new; and (without vanity) I may say, I ne'er produc'd a Comedy that had not some natural Humour in it not represented before, nor I hope I ever shall' (iii 101; Noyes).

189–92. Parodies Shadwell's Epilogue to *The Humorists*: 'A Humor is the Byas of the Mind, / By which with violence 'tis one way inclin'd: / It makes our Actions lean on one side still, / And in all Changes that way bends the Will' (ll. 15–18; i 254; Noyes).

193. mountain belly] Jonson refers to his 'mountaine belly' in 'My Picture left in Scotland' l. 17 (*The Vnder-wood* ix). For Shadwell's bulk see l. 25n. Flecknoe describes a man with a mountain belly in *The Diarium* (1656) 44–6.

194. likeness] i.e. to Jonson.   *tympany*] swelling, tumour (OED 1); figuratively something big or pretentious but empty or vain; often used of style (OED 2).

195. A tun of man] Echoes the description of Falstaff: 'a tun of man is thy companion' (*1 Henry IV* II iv 442).   *tun*) a large cask for wine, ale or beer, usually holding 210 gallons (OED).

196. kilderkin] cask holding 16 or 18 gallons (OED).

197–208. This passage seems to represent Shadwell as a fusion of the two bad poets (generally thought to be Robert Wild and Flecknoe) discussed in *EDP*: 'I ask you if one of them does not perpetually pay us with clenches upon words and a certain clownish kind of raillery . . . wresting and torturing a word into another meaning . . . one who is so much a well-willer to the Satire, that he intends, at least, to spare no man . . . though he cannot strike a blow to hurt any . . . my other extremity of Poetry . . . is one of those who having had some advantage of education and converse, knows better then the other what a Poet should be, but puts it into practice more unluckily then any man; his stile and matter are every where alike; he is the most calm, peaceable Writer you ever read: he never disquiets your passions with the least concernment, but still leaves you in as even a temper as he found you; he is a very Leveller in Poetry, he creeps along with ten little words in every line . . . when he writes the serious way, the highest flight of his fancy is some miserable *Antithesis*, or seeming contradiction; and in the Comick he is still reaching at some thin conceit, the ghost of a Jest, and that too flies before him, never to be caught' (*Works* xvii 10–11).

wrong effect both times?

P. unhurt..?

Thy tragic Muse gives smiles, thy comic sleep.
With whate'er gall thou sett'st thyself to write,
200   Thy <u>inoffensive satires never bite</u>:
In thy felonious heart though venom lies,
It does but touch thy Irish pen, and dies.
Thy genius calls thee not to purchase fame

P. has the higher art form?

In <u>keen</u> iambics, but mild anagram.

F. actually did so good volume? 205   Leave writing plays, and choose for thy command
Some peaceful province in acrostic land:

197. Cp. Shadwell's Prologue to *Psyche*: 'He would not soar too high, nor creep too low' (l. 31; ii 281; Noyes, citing Oswald). In commendatory verses prefixed to *A Relation Of ten Years Travells* the Marquis of Newcastle had commended the lofty flight of Flecknoe's Muse: '*Flecknoe* thy verses are too high for me, / Though they but justly fit thy Muse and thee, / . . . Though *Homers* blush, and *Virgils* lofty stile: / For thy Poetique Flame is so much higher, / Where it should warm, 't consumes us with thy fire. / Thy vaster fancy does imbrace all things' (sig. A4ʳ). Flecknoe's epigram on D. commends his high-flying Muse (see headnote), and the 1675 revision of it adds these lines: 'Nor ever any's *Muse* so high did soar / Above the Poets *Empyreum* before. / Some are so *low* and *creeping*, they appear / But as the *reptils* of Parnassus were;' (*Euterpe Revived* (1675) 77).

198. Cp. Buckingham's Prologue to *The Rehearsal* (1672): 'Our Poets make us laugh at Tragoedy, / And with their Comedies they make us cry' (ll. 13–14; Michael Wilding in *John Dryden*, edited by Earl Miner (1972) 194–5).

200, 204. bite . . . keen iambics] Cp. Cleveland: 'Come keen *Iambicks*, with your Badgers feet, / And Badger-like, bite till your teeth do meet' ('The Rebell *Scot*' ll. 27–8; W. J. Cameron, *N & Q* cciii (1957) 39); *keen iambics* may be a translation of *celeres iambos* (Horace, *Carm.* I xvi 24; R. Martin, *N & Q* ccii (1956) 505).

201. venom] 'Iambus' was falsely derived from the Greek 'ἰός 'poison' (R. C. Elliott, *The Power of Satire* (1960) 23).

202. Irish] Probably because St Patrick was said to have banished snakes from Ireland, so there was no venom there; cp. Cleveland: 'No more let *Ireland* brag, her harmless Nation / Fosters no Venome' ('The Rebell *Scot*' ll. 37–8). See also Title *n* for alleged Irish characteristics.

204–8. One of Robert Burton's remedies for melancholy was: 'he may apply his mind, I say, to heraldry, antiquity, invent impresses, emblems; make epithalamiums, elegies, epitaphs, epigrams, *palindroma epigrammata*, anagrams, chronograms, acrostics upon his friends' names . . . and rather than do nothing, vary a verse a thousand ways with Putean, so torturing his wits' (*The Anatomy of Melancholy* 2. 2. 4; *Works*). Figure poems originated in Greek poetry, and were given currency in the Renaissance in the *Planudean Anthology* (1494). Poems in the shape of wings and altars abound in English Renaissance Latin poetry; in English the best-known examples are George Herbert's poems 'Easter-wings' and 'The Altar' in *The Temple* (1633). Flecknoe in *A Treatise of the Sports of Wit* (1675) describes the word-games which he devised for the amusement of his royal patrons: 'The next Nights sport . . . was the Acting of Proverbs . . . some which cause laughter without any *Wit*, others more studious then delightful as *Ridles, Rebus's*, and *Anagrams*' (25; Hammond in *EIC* (1985)).

206. province] See ll. 4, 6n.

There thou mayest wings display and altars raise,
And torture one poor word ten thousand ways.
Or if thou wouldst thy different talents suit,
210 Set thy own songs, and sing them to thy lute.'
He said; but his last words were scarcely heard,
For Bruce and Longvil had a trap prepared,
And down they sent the yet declaiming bard,
Sinking he left his drugget robe behind,
215 Born upwards by a subterranean wind.
The mantle fell to the young prophet's part
With double portion of his father's art.

211–13. In *The Virtuoso* Act III Clarinda and Miranda dispose of Sir Formal through a trapdoor while he is in the middle of a flight of oratory; E. E. Duncan-Jones points out (privately) that Bruce and Longvil are merely spectators, not authors, of the trick.
213. bard] Michael Wilding (*John Dryden*, edited by Earl Miner (1972) 193–4) notes that *bard* at this date specifically applied to Irish poets (*OED* 1), who according to Spenser praised licentious and lawless men: 'Theare is amongst the Irishe a certen kinde of people Called Bardes which are to them in steade of Poets whose profession is to sett fourthe the praises and dispraises of menne in their Poems or Rymes. . . . But these Irishe Bardes are for the moste parte . . . so farre from instructinge yonge men in morrall discipline that they themselues doe more deserue to be sharpelye discipled for . . . whom soeuer they finde to be moste . . . daungerous and desperate in all partes of disobedience and rebellious disposicion him they set vp and glorifye in their Rymes' (*A View of the Present State of Ireland* (1633) in *Spenser's Prose Works*, edited by Rudolf Gottfried (1949) 124–5).
214–17. Echoes the disappearance of Elijah: 'Elijah said unto Elisha, Ask what I shall do for thee, before I be taken away from thee. And Elisha said, I pray thee, let a double portion of thy spirit be upon me . . . and Elijah went up by a whirlwind into heaven. . . . And Elisha saw it, and he cried, My father, my father. . . . He took up also the mantle of Elijah that fell from him' (2 Kings ii 9–13). Unlike Elijah, Flecknoe disappears downwards. The rapid disappearance of a butt of satire is also a feature of Seneca's *Apocolocyntosis*, Erasmus' *Julius Exclusus* and Marvell's 'Tom May's Death'.
214. See l. *186n.*
215. subterranean wind] A. S. Borgman (*Thomas Shadwell* (1928) 51) notes an echo of a song sung by a devil in Shadwell's operatic *Tempest*: 'Arise, arise! ye subterranean winds, / More to disturb their guilty minds. / And all ye filthy damps and vapours rise, / Which use t' infect the Earth, and trouble all the Skies; / Rise you, from whom devouring plagues have birth: / You that i' th' vast and hollow womb of Earth, / Engender Earthquakes, make whole Countreys shake, / And stately Cities into Desarts turn; / . . . Cause Fogs and Storms' (ii 224). Wilding observes an echo of *PL*, where Satan lands on ground which appears as if wrecked by 'the force / Of subterranean wind' (i 231).

5 Absalom and Achitophel

Date and publication. The statement in *The Second Part of Miscellany Poems* (1716) that *AA* was begun 'in the year 1680' has been accepted by some scholars (e.g. Howard H. Schless, *POAS* iii 278–9), but is unlikely. Malone took it to mean before 25 March 1681 (i.e. 1680 in the old calendar), which would be before the dissolution of the Oxford Parliament. It is more probable that the dissolution prompted D. to begin the poem, and that he worked at it over the summer of 1681. *Absalom and Achitophel. A Poem* was published by Tonson in 1681 (advertised in *The Loyal Protestant* 19 November; Luttrell's copy (in the Huntington) is dated 17 November, and was given him by Tonson). This first edition, in folio (siglum: *F*) had one misprint on p. 5 and four (plus an incorrect catchword) on p. 6. The errors on p. 6 were corrected as the book was going through the press, resulting in four different issues (Macdonald nos. 12a (i)–(iv)). The folio edition was reprinted (partly reset) in 1681 (*F2*), and some copies of this printing have an extra leaf with commendatory verses by Nathaniel Lee and Richard Duke (Macdonald 12d). 'The Second Edition; Augmented and Revised', in quarto (*Q*), was published in 1681, adding twelve lines on Shaftesbury (ll. 180–91) and four on Monmouth (ll. 957–60), and making several verbal alterations which appear to be D.'s revisions (Macdonald 12e (i)–(ii)). Noyes 959 conjectured that ll. 180–91 might have been in D.'s original MS but omitted in order to sharpen the satire on Shaftesbury; Vinton A. Dearing (*Works* ii 411–12) developed this into an elaborate hypothesis about royal censorship and last-minute revision; a rival hypothesis about revision was proposed by E. L. Saslow (*SB* xxviii (1975) 276–83). Another hypothesis is that ll. 180–91 and 957–60 were added when D. saw that it was both safe and advantageous for the King's supporters to appear reasonable and magnanimous. The present editors think that Noyes was right in supposing that ll. 180–91 were in the original MS, but suggest that they may have been omitted accidentally: ll. 180–91 do not form a coherent unit, since ll. 180–5 are a strongly worded development of the point in l. 179 about private ambition masquerading as public service, while ll. 186–91 make a generous concession about Shaftesbury's probity as a judge, and lead smoothly into ll. 192–3. It is therefore unlikely that this passage would have been seen as a unit and omitted in *F* to sharpen the satire, or composed as a block to be added in *Q* to show magnanimity. It is more likely that ll. 180–91 were in D.'s original MS but accidentally omitted in *F* (they would have come between the foot of p. 6 and the top of p. 7, and other errors and signs of haste affected p. 6); they would then have been restored when the poem was reset in a new format for *Q*. Lines 957–60 need not have had the same textual history as ll. 180–91: they could well have been added in *Q* to soften the presentation of Monmouth. *Q* was reprinted in 1682 with the addition of verses by Nahum Tate (Macdonald 12f), and twice again in the same year (Macdonald 12g and h). *AA* was then reprinted in *MP* (1684; reprinted 1692) and again in 1692 along with *The Medal* and *MF* as part of Tonson's series of D.'s poems in a uniform format. Two undated editions appeared, probably in Dublin (Macdonald 12b and c), and there is a pirated edition called *Absalom and Achitpohel* [sic] (1681). The poem was also reprinted (n.p., n.d.) with a key (Macdonald 12l). The present text is based on *F*, incorporating the press corrections, but emended from *Q* to include the additional lines and revisions within square brackets. There is no evidence that D. revised the poem after *Q*.

Paragraphing has been added at ll. 150, 543 and 630. For the commendatory poems
see *Poems* i 540–3.

Context. In the late 1670s there was growing anxiety about the succession to
Charles II, who had no legitimate children. His heir, his brother James, Duke
of York, was a Roman Catholic, and the prospect of a Catholic king made many
Englishmen fear for their political and religious liberties. Fears were accentuated
by the allegations made by Titus Oates in October 1678 that there was a Popish
Plot to assassinate Charles and establish Catholicism. Proposals were discussed for
excluding James from the succession: either by enabling Charles to divorce Catherine
of Braganza and remarry; or by making Charles's son James, Duke of Monmouth,
legitimate; or by establishing a regency over James, Duke of York; or by
having the crown pass to either James's daughter Mary or her husband William
of Orange. Exclusion Bills were debated by Parliament in April–May 1679 and
November 1680; in March 1681 the King summoned Parliament to meet at Oxford,
but dissolved it before another Exclusion Bill could be passed. Opposition to the
court had begun to take the form of a loose party which became known as
the Whigs. One of the chief Whigs, though not a formal leader, was the Earl
of Shaftesbury, and after the political tide turned in favour of Charles in the
summer of 1681 Shaftesbury was arrested on 2 July and imprisoned in the Tower
of London on a charge of treason. A preliminary hearing of his case began on
24 November, and a jury picked by Whig sheriffs returned a verdict of *ignoramus*
('we do not know'), by which the crown's evidence was rejected as insufficient
for the case to proceed to a full trial by the House of Lords, which would almost
certainly have convicted him. The publication of *AA* on 17 November seems
timed to influence public opinion at a critical moment (the first edition shows
signs of hasty production), but Phillip Harth (*Studies in Eighteenth-Century Culture*
iv (1975) 13–29) refutes the common notion that *AA* was written or published
to affect the outcome of Shaftesbury's trial: a verdict favourable to Shaftesbury
was regarded as inevitable a few weeks before *AA* was published, so the poem
was designed to influence public opinion generally. A detailed account of the
relation of *AA* to the contemporary political crisis is provided by Harth, *Pen for
a Party* (1993). For studies of the political machinations of this period see Ogg
559–631; J. R. Jones, *The First Whigs* (1970); Haley; Tim Harris, *London Crowds
in the Reign of Charles II* (1987); and Hutton, *Charles the Second*. For the debate
over political theory see Richard Ashcraft, *Revolutionary Politics and Locke's 'Two
Treatises of Government'* (1986); and Jonathan Scott, *Algernon Sidney and the
Restoration Crisis, 1677–1683* (1991). Some contemporary political materials are
reprinted in *Contexts 3: Absalom and Achitophel*, edited by Robert W. McHenry
Jr (1986). Tonson in *The Second Part of Miscellany Poems* (1716) reported that *AA*
was written 'upon the Desire of King *Charles* the Second'; a letter from Richard
Mulys in November 1681 claims that Edward Seymour commissioned it (*HMC
Ormonde* vi 233; Wallace Maurer, *PQ* xl (1961) 130–8); another report says that
D. was paid £100 for it (*HMC* X iv 175; Winn).

Authorship. *AA* was published anonymously, and never appeared over D.'s name
in his lifetime (it was attributed to him on the contents page of *MP* (1692) but
not in the text); for the significance of this see Paul Hammond, *SC* viii (1993)
138–9. D.'s authorship was quickly guessed (by Mulys, cited above; and in
Correspondence of the Family of Hatton (1878) ii 10, dated 22 November 1681), but
D. acknowledged it (with *MF*) only in 'A Discourse Concerning Satire' (1693).

Sources. The story of Absalom's rebellion against King David comes from 2 Samuel xiii–xviii, though D. adds some names from other parts of the OT and there are many allusions to both OT and NT (see Barbara K. Lewalski, *ELN* iii (1965) 29–35). The names which D. adopts vary in the precision with which they suit the contemporary characters, and some of the allusions are not clearly determinable. Robert Aylett's poem *David's Troubles Remembred* (1638) is a possible source for *AA* (see Barbara K. Lewalski, *N & Q* ccix (1964) 340–3), as is Cowley's *Davideis* (1656). The application of the story to English politics is not new, as R. F. Jones showed (*MLN* xlvi (1931) 211–18). Nathaniel Carpenter in *Achitophel, or the Picture of a Wicked Politician* (1627) wrote of '*David* an anointed King: *Absolon* an ambitious prince: *Achitophel* a wicked politician, and *Hushai* a loyal subject'. During the parliamentary debates on the eve of the Civil War 'Achitophel' was applied to some of Charles I's ministers; and Henry King's 'An Elegy upon the most Incomparable King *Charls* the First' employs many OT parallels, including Absalom, David and Zimri (*Poems, Elegies, Paradoxes, and Sonnets* (1664) 18–38). At the Restoration the parallel between Charles II and David was used widely in sermons and poems (see *Astraea Redux* l. 79; Carolyn A. Edie, *BJRL* lxii (1979–80) 81). Simon Ford remarked: 'It is a matter of greatest wonder to me to observe how exactly the *two Histories* run *parallel*. Insomuch that it were no hard matter for an *ingenious phancy*, by altering the Names of *David, Absalom, Joab, Abishai, Zadock, Abiathar, Ziba, Mephibosheth, Jordan,* &c. into others proper to our late affairs, to insert *verbatim* the *greatest part of the Chapter* into a *Chronicle of these Times*' (Παράλληλα; . . . *A Sermon Preached at All-Saints Church in Northampton, Jun. 28. 1660* (1660) 1–2). The form of service for 29 May (Charles's birthday and return) in the *Book of Common Prayer* (1662) includes verses from the Psalms which give thanks for David's preservation, and the first lesson is from 2 Samuel xix. In 1667 Robert Creighton, who had been at Westminster and Trinity with D., preached a sermon before the King 'against the sins of the Court, and particularly against adultery, over and over instancing how for that single sin in David, the whole nation was undone' (Winn 185). In 1677 Nathaniel Lee, in a poem prefixed to D.'s *The State of Innocence*, had suggested that D. should 'The troubles of majestic Charles sat [i.e. set] down: / Not David vanquish'd more to reach a crown. / Praise him as Cowley did that Hebrew King; / Thy theme's as great, do thou as greatly sing.' (E. S. de Beer, *RES* xvii (1941) 300). In his 5 November commemorative sermon in 1678 Aaron Baker implied a connection between Absalom and Monmouth, without naming the Duke (*Achitophel befool'd* (1678) 3–4) and said that Achitophel was 'of *David*'s Privy-Councill, a great Statesman, and a cunning Politician, and therefore a very dangerous and remarkable Conspirator' (11); see also l. 163*n*. In Thomas Jordan's 1678 Lord Mayor's Show, *London in Luster*, the story of David and Bathsheba is linked with that of Cain and Abel as a topical comment on Exclusion (Owen 284–5).

During the Exclusion Crisis the story was used several times in pamphlets. *A Letter to His Grace the D. of Monmouth, this 15th. of July, 1680* warns Monmouth against advisers who would have him seek the crown, comparing them with the advisers of Absalom: 'these Principled Men were they that set on *Absalom* to steal away the Hearts of the People from the King; . . . And These were the Men that led him into Actual Rebellion against his Father, and to be destroy'd by some of the very Hands that had assisted him in those pernicious Councels' (3). The writer of *Absalom's Conspiracy; or, The Tragedy of Treason* (1680; dated June in Cambridge UL copy) cites the story as 'a particular Caveat to all young men, to beware of such Counsellors, as the old *Achitophel*, lest while they are tempted

with the hopes of a Crown, they hasten on their own Destiny, and come to an
untimely End' (1). Shaftesbury is linked with Achitophel in *An Answer to a Paper*
(1681; probably July) and in the Whig pamphlet *Some Memoirs* (1681; October
or November, according to Wood's MS note in BodL copy): 'What was said of
Achitophel (that bad man, yet of a deep reach) may better be said of this better
Gentleman (*That his Counsel was as if a Man had enquired at the Oracle of God*)'
(4). This pamphlet also has an extensive comparison of Shaftesbury with Job, and
remarks: 'This *Comparison* must not therefore be accounted ridiculous, because it
cannot *in omnibus quadrare* [be an exact parallel at all points], or have a happy Hit
in ev'ry punctilio. . . . There is never a *congruity*, either in Civil or sacred History,
which will not well enough admit of some unlikeness thereunto in some circum-
stantial Adjuncts' (7). See also the citations from *A Seasonable Invitation* in ll. 229*n*
and 267–9*n* below. Several poems used these references. Thomas D'Urfey's
The Progress of Honesty (1680; Luttrell's copy dated 11 October) calls Shaftesbury
Achitophel and gives OT names to some of his followers. *Satyr Unmuzzled*
(in MS, 1680; *POAS* ii 209–16) characterizes Monmouth and Shaftesbury as
Absalom and Achitophel in ll. 86–101; so too does *The Waking Vision* (1681; probably April–June; *POAS* ii 419–24) in ll. 7–19. In *A Vision in the Tower* (1681;
dated 22 July on Luttrell's copy; *POAS* ii 435–9), l. 8 refers to Shaftesbury as
Achitophel. [John Dean's] *The Badger in the Fox-Trap* (?July 1681; see R. H. Levy,
ELN (1964) 253–6) reports that some call Shaftesbury Achitophel. *A Dialogue
between Nathan and Absolome* (in MS, 1680; *POAS* ii 269–72; see Howard H.
Schless, *PQ* xl (1961) 139–43) casts Monmouth as Absalom. These and other
contemporary poems supplied D. with hints, particularly for the characters of the
opposition leaders, as the notes below indicate. The idea of a series of character
sketches may go back to the *Advice to a Painter* genre, while previous political
allegories using OT stories were John Caryll's *Naboth's Vinyard* (1679), 'E. P.
Philopatris', *News from Hell* (1680), and Anon, *A Poem on the History of Queen
Hesther* [1680]. For discussions of D.'s use of biblical imagery see Hoffman
72–91; Miner 106–43; Steven N. Zwicker, *Dryden's Political Poetry* (1972)
83–101; G. R. Levine, *ECS* i (1968) 291–312; L. M. Guilhamet, *SEL* ix (1969)
395–413; Dustin Griffin, *PQ* lvii (1978) 359–82. For the relation of *AA* to contemporary political pamphlets see W. K. Thomas, *The Crafting of 'Absalom and
Achitophel'* (1978) and Phillip Harth, *Pen for a Party* (1993). Altogether the ideas,
images and rhetoric of *AA* are much more indebted to contemporary polemics
than has previously been realized, and the notes below illustrate this. However,
it is not always possible, particularly with the many works dated 1681, to know
whether a particular parallel constitutes a source for *AA*, an analogue to it, or a
borrowing from it.

   AA also draws upon classical poetry and history: the use of classical allusion is
discussed by Reuben A. Brower in *ELH* xix (1952) 38–48; of Virgil by Brower,
PMLA lv (1940) 132–3; of Virgil and Sallust by R. G. Peterson, *PMLA* lxxxii
(1967) 236–44; and of Ovid by A. Poyet, *N & Q* ccxxvi (1981) 52–3. The roll
call of champions on each side is a classical device, e.g. in *Aen.* vii. D.'s use of
Milton, esp. *PL*, was pointed out by A. W. Verrall; Morris Freedman sketched
the relationship between *AA* and Milton's epics in *JEGP* lvii (1958) 211–19;
A. B. Chambers briefly noted the associations of Achitophel with the Miltonic
Satan in *MLN* lxxiv (1959) 592–6. L. L. Brodwin (*JEGP* lxviii (1969) 24–44) discusses in detail the extensive parallels with *PL*, *PR* and *Samson Agonistes*, suggesting
that the first part of *AA* (ll. 1–753) is structured on *PL* i, and that D.'s allusions
ironically enlist Milton in the campaign against his own political heirs. A. D. Ferry

in *Milton and the Miltonic Dryden* (1968) discusses the different kinds of Miltonic allusion and imitation which D. uses in *AA*, and suggests that the seductive rhetoric of Achitophel has a Satanic precedent. For a wider discussion of D.'s use of Milton see J. R. Mason.

The form and genre of *AA* have been much debated; affinities have been noted with epic, classical oration, and painting: for a survey and bibliography see A. E. Wallace Maurer, *PLL* xxvii (1991) 320–37.

Reception. Many readers annotated their copies with identifications of the characters and brief comments; these are discussed by Alan Roper, *HLQ* lxiii (2001) 98–138. Particularly interesting marginalia from a Whig reader are on Folger Shakespeare Library, Washington, copy D2212, printed in Hammond and Hopkins 368. On 3 December 1681 the Duke of Beaufort wrote to his wife: 'I most humbly thanke you for the bookes I like Mr Dreyden very well, I hope hee will goe on wth it, tis somewhat obrupt as it is an I am sure hee hath left out some of the Kings best friends; I wish his patron may make out the carac- ter hee gives of him' (Badminton Muniments Room MS FmE 4/1/14; refer- ence supplied by Michael Brennan). *AA* attracted a number of rejoinders: [Henry Care ?], *Towser The Second A Bull-Dog* (1681; Luttrell's copy dated 10 December); *Poetical Reflections on a Late Poem Entituled Absalom and Achitophel* (1681; Luttrell's copy dated 14 December); *A Panegyrick On the Author of Absolom and Achitophel, occasioned by his former writing of an Elegy in praise of Oliver Cromwell, lately reprinted* (1681; Luttrell's copies dated 19 and 20 December; reprinted 1682); Christopher Nesse, *A Whip for the Fools Back* (1681; Luttrell's copy dated 24 December), and *A Key (With the Whip) To open the Mystery & Iniquity of the Poem called, Absalom & Achitophel* (1682; Luttrell's copy dated 13 January); [Samuel Pordage], *Azaria and Hushai* (1682; Luttrell's copy dated 17 January; reprinted 1682); *Absolon's IX Worthies* ([1682]; Luttrell's copy dated 10 March); [Elkanah Settle], *Absalom Senior: or, Achitophel Transpros'd* (1682; Luttrell's copy dated 6 April; reprinted 1682). In *A Loyal Congratulation to the Right Honourable Anthony, Earl of Shaftsbury* (1681), published soon after the *ignoramus* verdict, the writer says: 'Let them with their Poetick Malice swell, / Falsly apply the Story, known so well, / Of *Absalom*, and of *Achitophel*'. There are also adverse comments on D. and *AA* in *Directions to Fame, about an Elegy On the Late Deceased Thomas Thynn, Esq.* (1682). 'A short Reply to *Absalon* and *Achitophel*' appeared in *Rome Rhym'd to Death* (1683). As *A Panegyrick* states, D.'s enemies attempted to embarrass him by reprinting his 'Heroic Stanzas' as *An Elegy on the Usurper O. C. By the Author of Absalom and Achitophel, published to shew the Loyalty and Integrity of the Poet* (1681; two other reprints in 1682), with a self-incriminating postscript attributed to D. Two Latin translations of *AA* were published in 1682, one by William Coward, the other by Francis Atterbury and Francis Hickman. A few examples must suffice to illus- trate the wide influence of the rhetoric of *AA*. The name 'Achitophel' is used in many pamphlets and poems. *A Congratulatory Poem Upon the Happy Arrival of . . . James Duke of York* (1682) 2 echoes *AA* ll. 82–4 and uses the names Absalom and Corah. The sermon *Ahitophel's Policy Defeated* (1683) applies the biblical story to the Rye House Plot. The prose attack on Shaftesbury in the form of a novel, *The Fugitive Statesman* (1683), makes substantial use of *AA* (see Paul Salzman, *Restoration* iv (1980) 11–13). The verse satire *Massinello* (1683) echoes *AA* verbally and structurally. Thomas D'Urfey's *The Malecontent* (1684) 22 echoes *AA* l. 547, and its roll call of heroes and villains also recalls *AA*, while other echoes of *AA* may be found in *The Polititian's Downfall; or Potapski's Arrival at the Netherlands* (1684). See further Hammond and Hopkins 368–98.

Absalom and Achitophel
A Poem

—Si propius stes
Te capiet magis—

To the Reader

'Tis not my intention to make an apology for my poem:
some will think it needs no excuse, and others will receive
none. The design, I am sure, is honest, but he who draws
his pen for one party must expect to make enemies of the
5 other: for wit and fool are consequents of Whig and Tory,
and every man is a knave or an ass to the contrary side.
There's a treasury of merits in the fanatic church as well
as in the papist; and a pennyworth to be had of saintship,
honesty and poetry for the lewd, the factious and the
10 blockheads: but the longest chapter in Deuteronomy has
not curses enough for an Anti-Bromingham. My comfort
is, their manifest prejudice to my cause will render their
judgement of less authority against me. Yet if a poem have

¶5. *Epigraph*. Si . . . magis] 'If you stand nearer, it will please you more' (Horace, *Ars Poetica* ll. 361–2).
5. *consequents*] consequences. *Whig and Tory*] This is D.'s first use of these words. Both terms seem to have been applied to the emerging parties in the first months of 1681, and popularized by L'Estrange in *The Observator* from 2 July 1681 onwards (R. Willman, *HJ* xvii (1974) 247–64, correcting *OED*). *Whig* was originally applied to the Scottish rebels of 1648; *Tory* originally applied to the dispossessed Irish who became outlaws, thence to any Irish Catholic or Royalist in arms. Luttrell wrote in September 1681: 'Ever since the dissolution of the last parliament, the presse has abounded with pamphlets of all sorts, so that there has been a violent paper scuffle; some, on the one side, branding the two late parliaments, and standing very highly for the church; the other side defending the parliament, and cryeing up (as they call it) the true protestant religion, and opposing a popish successor: whence the latter party have been called by the former, whigs, fanaticks, covenanters, bromigham protestants, &c.; and the former are called by the latter, tories, tantivies, Yorkists, high flown church men, &c.' (i 124).
7. *treasury of merits*] The Roman Catholic doctrine that the merits of Christ and the saints are laid up as a treasury which can be drawn upon in aid of ordinary sinners. *fanatic*] extreme Protestant; dissenting.
10. *the longest chapter in Deuteronomy*] ch. xxviii, containing curses for disobedience to the law.
11. *enough*] Q; enow F. *Anti-Bromingham*] Tory; cp. 'Prologue to *The Spanish Friar*' l. 11. Tories 'styled the adversary *Birmingham* Protestants, alluding to false Groats counterfeited at that Place' (Roger North, *Examen* (1740) 321; Kinsley).

a genius it will force its own reception in the world: for
15 there's a sweetness in good verse which tickles even while
it hurts; and no man can be heartily angry with him who
pleases him against his will. The commendation of adversaries is the greatest triumph of a writer, because it never
comes unless extorted. But I can be satisfied on more
20 easy terms: if I happen to please the more moderate sort
I shall be sure of an honest party, and, in all probability,
of the best judges, for the least concerned are commonly
the least corrupt; and, I confess, I have laid in for those by
rebating the satire (where justice would allow it) from car-
25 rying too sharp an edge. They who can criticize so weakly
as to imagine I have done my worst may be convinced, at
their own cost, that I can write severely with more ease
than I can gently. I have but laughed at some men's follies
when I could have declaimed against their vices; and
30 other men's virtues I have commended as freely as I have
taxed their crimes. And now, if you are a malicious
reader, I expect you should return upon me that I affect
to be thought more impartial than I am. But if men are
not to be judged by their professions, God forgive you
35 Commonwealthsmen for professing so plausibly for the
government. You cannot be so unconscionable as to
charge me for not subscribing of my name, for that would
reflect too grossly upon your own party, who never dare,
though they have the advantage of a jury to secure them.
40 If you like not my poem, the fault may, possibly, be in
my writing (though 'tis hard for an author to judge against
himself): but, more probably, 'tis in your morals, which
cannot bear the truth of it. The violent on both sides will
condemn the character of Absalom, as either too favour-

---

14. genius] power appropriate for its task (*OED* 4).
15. sweetness] pleasing artistic effect (*OED* 5).
23. laid in] provided.
24. rebating] blunting (*OED* 4b).
34. professions] professed aims and beliefs.
35. Commonwealthsmen] Cp. l. 82*n*.
38–9. There had been several recent convictions of Whig writers and publishers,
notably of the booksellers Francis Smith and Benjamin Harris; in January 1681
'an indictment was brought against Francis Smith the elder, for publishing a seditious paper entituled A Speech of a noble Peer, (pretended to be a speech of the
earl of Shaftesburies in the lords house;) but the jury brought in an ignoramus
thereon' (Luttrell i 64). London juries were selected by the Whig sheriffs.

45 ably or too hardly drawn. But they are not the violent
whom I desire to please. The fault, on the right hand, is to
extenuate, palliate and indulge; and, to confess freely, I have
endeavoured to commit it. Besides the respect which I owe
his birth, I have a greater for his heroic virtues, and David
50 himself could not be more tender of the young man's life
than I would be of his reputation. But since the most excellent natures are always the most easy, and, as being such,
are the soonest perverted by ill counsels, especially when
baited with fame and glory, 'tis no more a wonder that he
55 withstood not the temptations of Achitophel than it was
for Adam not to have resisted the two devils, the serpent
and the woman. The conclusion of the story I purposely
forbore to prosecute, because I could not obtain from myself
to show Absalom unfortunate. The frame of it was cut out
60 but for a picture to the waist, and if the draft be so far
true, 'tis as much as I designed.

Were I the inventor, who am only the historian, I should
certainly conclude the piece with the reconcilement of
Absalom to David. And who knows but this may come to
65 pass? Things were not brought to an extremity where I left
the story. There seems yet to be room left for a composure;
hereafter there may only be for pity. I have not so much
as an uncharitable wish against Achitophel, but am content to be accused of a good natured error, and to hope
70 with Origen that the devil himself may, at last, be saved.
For which reason, in this poem he is neither brought to
set his house in order, nor to dispose of his person afterwards,
as he in wisdom shall think fit. God is infinitely merciful,
and his vicegerent is only not so because he is not infinite.
75 The true end of satire is the amendment of vices by correction. And he who writes honestly is no more an enemy

52. *easy*] easily persuaded, compliant (*OED* 12).
57. *conclusion*] In 2 Samuel xviii Absalom, riding on a mule, is caught in the branches
of an oak tree, and killed by Joab.
66. *composure*] agreement, settlement (*OED* 4).
70. *Origen*] The Alexandrian theologian and biblical critic (*c.* 185–*c.* 254); he believed
that the devil was a fallen angel, and that the evil powers had retained freedom
and reason; no being is totally depraved, and even Satan can repent at the end.
Cp. *RL* Preface ll. 48–50*n*.
72. In 2 Samuel xvii 23 'when Ahitophel saw that his counsel was not followed,
he . . . put his household in order, and hanged himself'.
74. *his vicegerent*] the King. *vicegerent*] deputy.

to the offender than the physician to the patient when he
prescribes harsh remedies to an inveterate disease: for those
are only in order to prevent the chirurgeon's work of an
80 *ense rescindendum*, which I wish not to my very enemies.
To conclude all, if the body politic have any analogy to
the natural, in my weak judgement an Act of Oblivion were
as necessary in a hot, distempered state as an opiate would
be in a raging fever.

Absalom and Achitophel
A Poem

In pious times, ere priestcraft did begin,
Before polygamy was made a sin,
When man on many multiplied his kind,

---

79. *chirurgeon*] surgeon.
80. ense rescindendum] *cuncta prius temptanda, sed inmedicabile curae / ense rescindendum, ne pars sincera trahatur* ('all means should first be tried, but what does not
respond to treatment must be cut away with the knife, lest the untainted part
also draw infection': Ovid, *Met.* i 190–1; the context is Jove's speech after the
rebellion of the giants and the rejection of piety and justice by men). The usual
reading of seventeenth-century and modern editions of Ovid is *recidendum*: evidently D. was quoting from memory. The two verbs *recido* and *rescindo* are approximately synonymous.
82. *Act of Oblivion*] In 1660 the Act of Indemnity and Oblivion pardoned offences
committed during the Civil War and Commonwealth (see ll. 323–4n).

1–10. G. B. Evans suggests a parallel with Plutarch's life of Antony, translated
by North: 'Nobility was multiplyed [cp. l. 3] amongst men by the Posterity of
Kings, when they left of their seed in divers places: and that by this means his
first Ancestor was begotten of *Hercules*, who had not left the hope and continuance of his Line and Posterity in the womb of one onely woman, fearing *Solons*
Laws, or regarding the Ordinances of men touching the procreation of children:
but that he gave it unto nature, and established the foundation of many noble
Races and Families in divers places' (*Lives of the Noble Grecians and Romans* (1676)
767; *N & Q* ccxxxii (1987) 331).
1–6. Kinsley compares Donne: 'How happy were our Syres in ancient time, /
Who held plurality of loves no crime! / With them it was accounted charity /
To stirre up race of all indifferently;' ('Variety' ll. 37–40). Cp. also Don John
in Otway's *Don Carlos* (1676): 'How vainly would dull Moralists Impose / Limits
on Love, whose Nature brooks no Laws: / Love is a God, and like a God
should be / Inconstant: with unbounded liberty / Rove as he list.- . . . How
wretched then's the man who . . . Confin'd to one, / Is but at best a pris'ner on
a Throne.' (III i 1–5, 18–20); for another parallel see ll. 19–20n.

Ere one to one was cursedly confined;
5   When nature prompted, and no law denied
Promiscuous use of concubine and bride;
Then Israel's monarch, after heaven's own heart,
His vigorous warmth did variously impart
To wives and slaves: and wide as his command
10   Scattered his maker's image through the land.
Michal, of royal blood, the crown did wear,
A soil ungrateful to the tiller's care:
Not so the rest, for several mothers bore
To godlike David several sons before;

1. This is an example of D.'s ambiguous chronology and selective use of biblical material, since the priestly caste originated with Aaron, long before David
(Lewalski in *ELN* 30).   *priestcraft*] (i) the profession of priesthood; (ii) the deceitful cunning of priests. This is the *OED*'s first example, but Mark Goldie cites an
instance in James Harrington's *Pian Piano* (1657), and argues that it is part of the
vocabulary of Whig anticlericalism; he suggests that in *AA* D. uses it to allude
to 'the scoffing Whig's habit of treating the laws of marriage as amongst priestly
inventions' (*Political Discourse in Early Modern Britain*, edited by Nicholas
Phillipson and Quentin Skinner (1993) 216–18). It may therefore be an instance
not of D.'s anticlericalism, but of his habit of turning his opponents' vocabulary
against them.
2. Polygamy was practised in early Judaism, but monogamy had become the
norm by the time of Christ. Milton and others had advocated polygamy during
the Commonwealth (Christopher Hill, *Milton and the English Revolution* (1977)
136–9, 287–8). D. often discussed the relation between nature and law in
the field of sexual behaviour, e.g. in *Aureng-Zebe* IV i 71–167; *Oedipus, passim*;
'The Cock and the Fox' ll. 56–64 (q.v. for its political allusions); and 'Cinyras
and Myrrha' (on which see David Hopkins, *MLR* lxxx (1985) 786–801).
4. Cp. 'Since Liberty, Nature for all has design'd, / A pox on the Fool who to
one is confin'd' (Shadwell, *The Libertine* (1676); iii 43). Winn (*When Beauty* 17)
notes that D.'s line is echoed by Creech in his translation of Lucretius (1682)
171: 'When One to One confin'd in chast embrace'; cp. ll. 53–6*n.*
6. Promiscuous] without distinction (*OED* 2); English law, however, distinguished
between the children of a wife and those of a mistress.
7. Israel's monarch] Here Charles II. King David had several wives, including
Bathsheba, whose previous husband Uriah had been killed at David's instigation
(2 Samuel xi). Samuel told Saul that 'the Lord hath sought him a man after his
own heart' (1 Samuel xiii 14).
11. Michal] Catherine of Braganza (1638–1705), the Portuguese princess who
married Charles in 1662. She had no children. The biblical Michal was Saul's
daughter, and 'had no child unto the day of her death' (2 Samuel vi 23).
12. The image was a commonplace: cp. Shakespeare, *Sonnets* iii 5–6.   *ungrateful*] not responding to cultivation (*OED* 1c, first example; a sense of the Latin
ingratus). Cp. ground 'ungrateful to the Plough' ('The Second Book of the *Georgics*'
l. 262).
13–14. Charles had fourteen acknowledged illegitimate children (GEC, *Complete
Peerage*, 13 vols (1910–40) vi 706–8). His affection for them was well known.

15   But since like slaves his bed they did ascend,
      No true succession could their seed attend.
      Of all this numerous progeny was none
      So beautiful, so brave as Absolon:
      Whether, inspired by some diviner lust,
20   His father got him with a greater gust,
      Or that his conscious destiny made way
      By manly beauty to imperial sway.
      Early in foreign fields he won renown,
      With kings and states allied to Israel's crown:
25   In peace the thoughts of war he could remove,
      And seemed as he were only born for love.
      Whate'er he did was done with so much ease,
      In him alone 'twas natural to please:
      His motions all accompanied with grace,
30   And paradise was opened in his face.

17–18. Cp. 'In all the kingdoms of the east not one / Was found, for beauty, like to Absalon' (Aylett 2; Schilling).
18–30. Absolon] A variant seventeenth-century spelling which D. uses for the rhyme; it is kept here in the form given in F. James Scott (1649–85), son of Charles II and Lucy Walter; created Duke of Monmouth in 1663. 2 Samuel iv 25 says that 'in all Israel there was none to be so much praised as Absalom for his beauty: from the sole of his feet even to the crown of his head there was no blemish in him'. Evelyn wrote of Monmouth that he was 'the darling of his Father, and the Ladys, being extraordinarily handsome, and adroit: an excellent souldier, & dauncer, a favorite of the people, of an Easy nature, debauched by lust, seduc'd by crafty knaves' (*Diary* 15 July 1685). Monmouth served at sea in 1664–6; he commanded the English troops fighting with the French against the Dutch in 1672–3, and those fighting with the Dutch against the French in 1678. In 1679 he defeated the Scottish rebels at the battle of Bothwell Bridge. His military career was characterized by his personal bravery. In 1678–9 Monmouth became a focus for opposition to the court, and was sent to Holland by Charles in September 1679, but returned in November, probably at the instance of Shaftesbury. He received an enthusiastic welcome from the people of London, but incurred the wrath of the King, who stripped him of all his posts and pensions. After rumours that the King had been married to Lucy Walter, and that Monmouth was therefore legitimate, Charles issued a declaration on 2 June 1680 that he had never been married to anyone but the Queen. In July 1680 Monmouth embarked on a popular tour of the West Country (see ll. 729–44*nn*); in November he voted for the Exclusion Bill, making a speech about the dangers to Charles's life, which caused the King to remark, 'The kiss of Judas!' (Haley 602). See further Elizabeth D'Oyley, *James Duke of Monmouth* (1938). D. had dedicated *The Indian Emperor* (1667) to the Duchess of Monmouth, who acted with the Duke in a performance of the play at court in 1668 (Winn 188); D. dedicated *Tyrannic Love* (1670) to the Duke, saying: 'Heaven has already taken care to form you for an Heroe. You have all the advantages of Mind and Body, and an Illustrious Birth, conspiring

With secret joy indulgent David viewed
His youthful image in his son renewed;
To all his wishes nothing he denied,
And made the charming Annabel his bride.
35 What faults he had (for who from faults is free?)
His father could not, or he would not see.
Some warm excesses which the law forbore
Were construed youth that purged by boiling o'er;
And Amnon's murther by a specious name
40 Was called a just revenge for injured fame.

---

to render you an extraordinary Person . . . Youth, Beauty, and Courage (all which
you possess in the height of their perfection) are the most desirable gifts of Heaven:
and Heaven is never prodigal of such Treasures, but to some uncommon purpose.
So goodly a Fabrick was never framed by an Almighty Architect for a vulgar
Guest. He shewed the value which he set upon your Mind, when he took care
to have it so nobly and so beautifully lodg'd. To a graceful fashion and deportment
of Body, you have joyned a winning Conversation, and an easie Greatness,
derived to you from the best, and best-belov'd of Princes' (*Works* x 107−8). In
The Vindication . . . of . . . The Duke of Guise (1683) D. acknowledges his obligations to Monmouth for 'his Countenance, his Favour, his good Word, and his
Esteem; all which I have likewise had in a greater measure from his excellent
Dutchess, the Patroness of my poor unworthy Poetry' (*Works* xiv 325).
19−20. Cp. the King's illegitimate son Don John in Otway's *Don Carlos*: 'My
Glorious Father got me in his heat, / When all he did was eminently great'
(II i 10−11); Cp. ll. 1−6*n*.
19. by] Q; with F.
20. gust] keen relish (*OED* 4).
21. conscious] aware of itself (*OED* 10).
30. Cp. 'Paradis stood formed in hire yën' (Chaucer, *Troilus and Criseyde* v 817);
Dante, *Paradiso* xviii 21; Samuel Pordage, *Mundorum Explicatio* (1661) 77: 'Paradise
doth open in the heart'. D.'s line was parodied as 'For Baud is always open'd in
thy Face' in 'M^{rs}. Nelly's Complaint, 1682' (BodL MS Firth c 15 p. 131).
34. Annabel] Anne, Countess of Buccleuch (1651−1732), who married Monmouth
in 1663. Shadwell in *The Medal of John Bayes* (1682) 9−10 says that the Duchess's
patronage brought D. the favour of the court, and that his only gratitude to her
was to traduce her husband. See further Winn (*When Beauty* 408−11).
38. construed] accented on the first syllable until the nineteenth century (*OED*).
purged] purified itself (*OED* 7, first example).
39−40. Amnon's murther . . . injured fame] Amnon's murder was arranged by
Absalom to avenge the rape of his sister Tamar by Amnon (2 Samuel xiii). There
are two possible contemporary applications: (i) In the early hours of 26 February
1671 a beadle named Peter Vernell was murdered in a brothel in Whetstones
Park by the Dukes of Monmouth, Albemarle and Somerset, and Viscount
Dunbar; they received pardons, but the affair became a scandal: see 'On the Three
Dukes Killing the Beadle' and 'Upon the Beadle' in *POAS* i 172−6. 'Upon the
Beadle' ll. 43−54 presents Monmouth as being enraged by the beadle's effrontery
in opposing him. (ii) A savage, but not fatal, attack on Sir John Coventry

Thus praised and loved the noble youth remained,
While David undisturbed in Sion reigned.
But life can never be sincerely blessed:
Heaven punishes the bad, and proves the best.
45   The Jews, a headstrong, moody, murmuring race
As ever tried th' extent and stretch of grace,
God's pampered people, whom, debauched with ease,
No king could govern, nor no god could please
(Gods they had tried of every shape and size
50   That god-smiths could produce, or priests devise);

was carried out on 21 December 1670 by the King's Horseguards, of which
Monmouth was captain; he is blamed for the assault in 'A Song' in BodL MS
Don.b.8 pp. 210–11. In this case the 'injured fame' would be that of Charles II:
when a proposal in the Commons for a tax on the playhouses was objected to
because 'the Players were the King's servants, and a part of his pleasure',
Coventry asked 'If the King's pleasure lay among the men or women Players?'
(*Debates of the House of Commons, From the Year 1667 to the Year 1694*, edited by
Anchitell Grey, 10 vols (1763) i 332). Kinsley (*RES* vi (1955) 292) notes that
Coventry was attacked on his way home from a tavern, while Amnon was murdered when he was 'merry with wine'; neither Absalom nor Monmouth actually took part in the assault, but exhorted their followers to action; and both David
and Charles condemned the offence. It seems impossible to choose between these
two explanations, both of which would have occurred to contemporaries (see
Roper 127–9).
42. Sion] a biblical name for Jerusalem; here applied to London.
43. sincerely] completely, purely (*OED* 4b).
44. proves] tests.
45. The Jews] The English. Supporters of the Commonwealth had often represented England as an elect nation, a second Israel (Zwicker 84; and Zwicker in
Millenarianism and Messianism . . . 1650–1800, edited by Richard H. Popkin (1988)
42–7). Sir Edward Turner had used this parallel to describe the ingratitude of the
English people: 'The *Children of Israel*, when they were in the Wilderness, though
they were fed with Gods own hand . . . yet they surfeited, and murmured, and
rebelled against *Moses*. The same unthankfull spirit dwelt in this Nation for divers
years last past; the men of that Age were weary of the Government' (*The Several
Speeches of Sr. Edward Turner Kt. Speaker of the honourable House of Commons* (1661)
7). Some writers at the Restoration had compared those who were responsible
for Charles I's execution with the Jews who called for Jesus' crucifixion (see
Jonathan Sawday, *SC* vii (1992) 192–3).
47. Cp. 'no Disease / Is like a Surfeit of Luxurious Ease' (*A Dialogue Between the
Ghosts of the Two last Parliaments* (1681)). *pampered*] Cp. the quotation from *The
Character of a Leading Petitioner* (1681) in ll. 51–6n. *debauched*] (i) corrupted morally
(*OED* 2); (ii) seduced from proper allegiance (*OED* 1), as in 'the People are
debauched with false Representations, and Rebellious Principles' (*The Character
of a Rebellion* (1681) 4).
50. god-smiths] apparently D.'s coinage.

These Adam-wits, too fortunately free
Began to dream they wanted liberty,
And when no rule, no precedent was found
Of men, by laws less circumscribed and bound
55   They led their wild desires to woods and caves,

51–6. In the Epistle Dedicatory to *All for Love* (1678) D. expresses 'a loathing to that specious Name of a *Republick*: that mock-appearance of a Liberty, where all who have not part in the Government, are Slaves: and Slaves they are of a viler note than such as are Subjects to an absolute Dominion. For no Christian Monarchy is so absolute, but 'tis circumscrib'd with Laws. . . . And yet there are not wanting Malecontents amongst us, who surfeiting themselves on too much happiness, wou'd perswade the People that they might be happier by a change. 'Twas indeed the policy of their old Forefather, when himself was fallen from the station of Glory, to seduce Mankind into the same Rebellion with him, by telling him he might yet be freer than he was: that is, more free than his Nature wou'd allow, or (if I may so say) than God cou'd make him. We have already all the Liberty which Free-born Subjects can enjoy; and all beyond it is but License' (*Works* xiii 6–7); cp. *Astraea Redux* ll. 43–8 (Kinsley). Sir Edward Turner said of the English under the Commonwealth: 'Liberty they called it, but it was *Libertas quidlibet audendi* [a liberty of daring to do what they liked] (*Several Speeches* 8). Sir Robert Filmer objected to those 'who magnify liberty as if the height of human felicity were only to be found in it, never remembering that the desire of liberty was the cause of the fall of Adam' (*Patriarcha* (1680), edited by Peter Laslett (1949) 53). The charge that the Whigs are pursuing a specious liberty is common in contemporary Tory pamphlets, e.g.: 'I chang'd True Freedom for the Name of Free, / And grew Seditious for Variety' (*A Dialogue Between the Ghosts of the Two last Parliaments* (1681)); 'How greadily this Petitional *Animal* catcheth at the seeming gilded bait of that imaginary *Liberty* that betrays him; He repines when he's hungry, and murmurs when he's full, no sooner has a *Moses* redeliver'd him from slavery, and pamper'd him with the *Manna* of peace and plenty, but the Highfled Blockhead grows senseless of his happiness, and industriously contrives for misery and want' (*The Character of a Leading Petitioner* (1681) 1–2); 'where he can find no real Faults, he Feigns imaginary ones . . . He Amuses the freest Nation in the *Universe*, with wild Rumours and extravagant Apprehensions of *Slavery*' (*The Character of a Disbanded Courtier* (1681) 1). For discussions of the Whig rhetoric of 'liberty' see Ashcraft, *passim*, but esp. 208–14, and Tim Harris in *The Politics of Religion in Restoration England*, edited by Tim Harris, Paul Seaward and Mark Goldie (1990) 217–41.

51. Adam-wits] Those who, like Adam, were not satisfied with their God-given freedom, and rebelled against their imagined constraint. For the image of the Fall cp. ll. 202–3*n*.   *too fortunately free*] Echoes Virgil: *O fortunatos nimium, sua si bona norint* ('O how exceptionally [or 'too'] fortunate, if only they had known their good fortune!': *Geo.* ii 458, referring to the happy life of farmers). Cp. *The Medal* l. 123.

52. wanted] lacked.

53–6. Echoes Lucretius' account of primitive man: *nemora atque cavos montis silvasque colebant . . . nec commune bonum poterant spectare, neque ullis / moribus inter se scibant nec legibus uti* (*De Rerum Natura* v 955, 958–9: 'they dwelt in the woods and forests and mountain caves, . . . they could not look to the common good,

And thought that all but savages were slaves.
They who when Saul was dead, without a blow,
Made foolish Ishbosheth the crown forgo,
Who banished David did from Hebron bring
60   And with a general shout proclaimed him King:
Those very Jews, who, at their very best
Their humour more than loyalty expressed,
Now wondered why so long they had obeyed
An idol monarch which their hands had made;
65   Thought they might ruin him they could create,
Or melt him to that golden calf, a state.
But these were random bolts: no formed design
Nor interest made the factious crowd to join;

they did not know how to govern their intercourse by custom and law'). Cp.
also *Aen.* v 667–8, describing the flight of the women who had madly burnt
Aeneas' ships: *silvasque et sicubi concava furtim / saxa petunt* ('Dispers'd, to Woods
and Caverns take their flight': 'The Fifth Book of the *Aeneis*' l. 885).

56. See *Astraea Redux* ll. 46–8n. D. can also imagine savages as innocent and noble
(perhaps following Montaigne in *Des Cannibales*), as in *1 Conquest of Granada* I
i 203–9, which is probably the first occurrence in English of the phrase 'the noble
savage', anticipating Rousseau.

57–60. After his death, Saul was succeeded as King of Israel by his son
Ishbosheth, who ruled for two years, while David became King of Judah and
ruled in Hebron for seven and a half years; after the murder of Ishbosheth the
tribes of Israel came to David in Hebron and anointed him King of Israel (2 Samuel
ii–v). Oliver Cromwell was succeeded as Lord Protector in September 1658 by
his son Richard, who ruled for eight months; Charles II was recalled from exile
in Holland in May 1660.

58. Ishbosheth] Q; Isbosheth *F.*

59. Hebron] Either Scotland (as in *2AA* l. 320), since Charles was crowned King
of Scots on 1 January 1651, nine and a half years before his recall to England; or
(stressing '*from* Hebron') Brussels, whence Charles was summoned in 1660,
though his place of exile is called 'Gath' at l. 264.

62. humour] temporary mood (*OED* 5); whim, caprice (*OED* 6).

64. idol] The Jews were forbidden to worship idols (Exodus xx 4). *which their
hands had made*] Whereas early Stuart political theory had insisted that kings were
appointed by God and were not accountable to the people (see James I, *The Trew
Law of Free Monarchies* (1598)), the theories which were prevalent during the
Commonwealth tended to argue that rulers were created by the people, who
transferred their rights to them (thus Hobbes, *Leviathan* (1651)) or entrusted them
with authority which could be taken back by the people if the rulers abused their
trust (thus Milton, *The Tenure of Kings and Magistrates* (1649)); cp. ll. 409–12.

66. golden calf] While Moses was receiving instructions from God on Mt Sinai,
the Israelites built a golden calf, which they worshipped (Exodus xxxii). *state*]
republic (*OED* 28b).

67. bolts] shots; ventures (*OED* 1b).

68. crowd] For the importance of the London crowd in contemporary politics,
see Harris, *London Crowds.*

The sober part of Israel, free from stain,
70 Well knew the value of a peaceful reign,
And looking backward with a wise affright
Saw seams of wounds dishonest to the sight;
In contemplation of whose ugly scars
They cursed the memory of civil wars.
75 The moderate sort of men, thus qualified,
Inclined the balance to the better side,
And David's mildness managed it so well
The bad found no occasion to rebel.
But when to sin our biased nature leans,
80 The careful devil is still at hand with means,
And providently pimps for ill desires:
The Good Old Cause revived a plot requires;
Plots, true or false, are necessary things
To raise up commonwealths and ruin kings.

71–4. The parallel between 1641 and 1681 was frequently made on all sides. *The Weekly Discovery of the Mystery of Iniquity* recounted events in England in 1641 in thirty issues from February to August 1681, while 'Theophilus Rationalis' compared the 1640s' and 1680s' parliaments in *Multum in Parvo* (1681).
71. *affright*] fear, terror (*OED* 2).
72. *seams*] the joining of the edges of a wound by sewing (*OED* 1b). *dishonest*] hideous (*OED* 3); from *inhonesto vulnere* (*Aen.* vi 497; cp. 'The Sixth Book of the *Aeneis*' l. 668; Kinsley).
75. *qualified*] moderated (*OED* 8); calmed (*OED* 9); brought into a proper condition (*OED* 10).
79. *biased*] the image is from the bias in a bowl which makes it run in a curve away from the straight path; cp. *MF* l. 189.
82. *The Good Old Cause*] The Commonwealth. The Whigs were often accused of working for the restoration of a republic. Shaftesbury himself wanted a monarchy rather than a republic, but said in the Privy Council on 7 June 1679 that 'if the King so governed as that his estate might with safety be transmitted to his son, as it was by his father to him, and he might enjoy the known rights and liberties of the subjects, he would rather be under kingly government, but if he could not be satisfied of that he declared he was for a Commonwealth' (Haley 536; cp. 312, 517). In *The Waking Vision* (1681) Shaftesbury (as 'Achitophel') boasts that he 'fought and prosper'd in the Good Old Cause', and says that to stir up fears of Popery 'of a Bad Old Cause a Good one makes' (ll. 24, 63; *POAS* ii 420–1). Cp. the title of *The Good Old Cause Revived* (MS date 2 February 1680 on BL copy).
83. *Plots*] (i) The Popish Plot of 1678–9 (see l. 108n); (ii) the alleged Popish Plot of 1640, in which the Jesuits were supposedly plotting to kill Charles I and bring England under the Church of Rome; this allegation strengthened suspicion of Charles I in the Commons (see *A True Narrative of the Popish-Plot against King Charles I. and the Protestant Religion* (1680); Caroline Hibbard, *Charles I and the Popish Plot* (1983)).

85   Th' inhabitants of old Jerusalem
        Were Jebusites, the town so called from them,
        And theirs the native right——
        But when the chosen people grew more strong,
        The rightful cause at length became the wrong,
90   And every loss the men of Jebus bore
        They still were thought God's enemies the more.
        Thus worn and weakened, well or ill content,
        Submit they must to David's government:
        Impoverished, and deprived of all command,
95   Their taxes doubled as they lost their land,
        And, what was harder yet to flesh and blood,
        Their gods disgraced, and burned like common wood.
        This set the heathen priesthood in a flame,
        For priests of all religions are the same:
100   Of whatsoe'er descent their godhead be,
        Stock, stone, or other homely pedigree,
        In his defence his servants are as bold
        As if he had been born of beaten gold.
        The Jewish rabbins, though their enemies,
105   In this conclude them honest men and wise;
        For 'twas their duty, all the learnèd think,
        T' espouse his cause by whom they eat and drink.

86. Jebusites] Roman Catholics (perhaps with a pun on 'Jesuits'). 'As for the Jebusites the inhabitants of Jerusalem, the children of Judah could not drive them out: but the Jebusites dwell with the children of Judah at Jerusalem unto this day' (Joshua xv 63). Jerusalem is called Jebus in Judges xix 10–11 and 1 Chronicles xi 4. D. also recalls England's Catholic past in *His Majesties Declaration Defended* (1681; *Works* xvii 210).
87. An imitation of the Virgilian hemistich (Brower); but in his 'Dedication of the *Aeneis*' (1697) D. argues that Virgil's half-lines were simply unfinished, not deliberate effects (*Works* v 332). In his own copy of Virgil D. added a phrase to complete the half-line at *Aen.* iii 340 (Paul Hammond, *N & Q* ccxxix (1984) 345).
88. the chosen people] Protestants, recalling Calvin's doctrine of election.
94–5. Under an Act of James I the crown had power to seize two-thirds of recusants' estates; the Test Act of 1673 barred all who were not Anglican communicants from holding office under the crown; and Catholics paid double taxes.
97. There was widespread destruction of religious images, particularly wooden statues, at the Reformation.
101. Stock] block of wood (*OED* 1b).
104. Jewish rabbins] Anglican theologians.

From hence began that plot, the nation's curse,
Bad in itself, but represented worse;
110   Raised in extremes, and in extremes decried,
With oaths affirmed, with dying vows denied;
Not weighed or winnowed by the multitude,
But swallowed in the mass, unchewed and crude.
Some truth there was, but dashed and brewed with lies,
115   To please the fools and puzzle all the wise.
Succeeding times did equal folly call
Believing nothing, or believing all.
Th' Egyptian rites the Jebusites embraced,
Where gods were recommended by their taste:
120   Such savoury deities must needs be good
As served at once for worship and for food.
By force they could not introduce these gods,

108. plot] The Popish Plot. On 13 August 1678 Charles was informed by Israel
Tonge of a plot to assassinate him; Tonge was working in an uneasy alliance with
Titus Oates (see ll. 632–81nn). The allegations widened to implicate many
Catholics in a conspiracy against the King and the Protestant religion, master-
minded by the Jesuits. Most of the allegations were lies, but there were enough
correct details and lucky guesses for the whole story to alarm a nation always
susceptible to rumour and afraid of a Catholic coup. Oates was examined by
the Privy Council on 28–9 September, and when Parliament assembled on
21 October it established committees to investigate. The papers of Edward
Coleman, secretary to the Duchess of York (and previously to the Duke) were
seized and proved highly suspicious: he was tried for treason and executed on
3 December 1678. Altogether some 35 people had been executed by July 1681.
Charles told Burnet in December 1678 that 'the greatest part of the evidence was
a contrivance. But he suspected, some had set on Oates, and instructed him: And
he named the Earl of Shaftesbury' (ii 54). Shaftesbury is unlikely to have mani-
pulated Oates directly, but the affair suited his political purposes. See further
J. P. Kenyon, *The Popish Plot* (1972).
111. Oates gave his evidence on oath to the Privy Council, to Sir Edmund Berry
Godfrey, and at the trials; many of those convicted protested their innocence at
their execution.
113. crude] raw, uncooked (*OED* 2).
114. dashed] mingled (*OED* 5).   *brewed*] diluted (*OED* 2).
118–21. Egyptian] Catholic French. D. also alludes to the Egyptians' animal gods
derided by Juvenal (*Satire* xv 1–13). The Catholic doctrine of transubstantiation
was often mocked during the Popish Plot trials, e.g. by Chief Justice Scroggs:
'They eat their God, they kill their King, and saint the murderer!' (Kenyon
146); cp. John Oldham, *Satyrs upon the Jesuits* (1681) iv 259–72; Oldham,
Poems 52.
120–1. Such . . . As] i.e. deities of such a kind which.
121. As] Q; And *F*.

For ten to one in former days was odds,
So fraud was used (the sacrificer's trade):
125 Fools are more hard to conquer than persuade.
Their busy teachers mingled with the Jews,
And raked for converts ev'n the court and stews;
Which Hebrew priests the more unkindly took
Because the fleece accompanies the flock.
130 Some thought they God's anointed meant to slay
By guns, invented since full many a day:
Our author swears it not, but who can know
How far the devil and Jebusites may go?
This plot, which failed for want of common sense,
135 Had yet a deep and dangerous consequence:
For, as when raging fevers boil the blood
The standing lake soon floats into a flood,
And every hostile humour which before
Slept quiet in its channels, bubbles o'er;
140 So several factions from this first ferment
Work up to foam, and threat the government.

---

123. *ten to one*] In the mid-seventeenth century there were roughly 60,000
Catholics in England and Wales out of a population of about 5 million, i.e. 1 per
cent; only in Lancashire and Monmouth did the proportion approach 10 per cent
(John Bossy, *The English Catholic Community 1570–1850* (1975) 188–9, 404–5). *odds*]
balance of advantage, superior position (*OED* 4).
127. *stews*] brothels.
130–1. According to Oates's and Tonge's first allegations, the Benedictine Thomas
Pickering and a Jesuit lay brother, John Grove, had vowed to shoot Charles.
136–9. For the disease imagery cp. 'I can by no ways approve of those of our
Physitians who use such violent means to wake us out of our Security, as if there
were no Cure for a Lethargy but casting us into a Raving Frenzy. And indeed
such has been the Physick of our State Mountebanks . . . since they have possest
the people with so desperate a madness' (*An Answer to a late Pamphlet; Entituled,
A Character of a Popish Successor* (1681) 2); and in *The Badger in the Fox-Trap* [July
1681], Shaftesbury is made to say that some call him 'the Scab, from whence
the Infection Breeds' (1). Cp. 'Theophilus Rationalis', *Multum in Parvo* (1681):
'To see how boldly you infect the blood / Of Prince and People, which much
like a floud / Of lofty Billows, purposely to drown / Our Ship, our Pilate, and
our Captains Crown'. For the political connotations of the image of a river
overflowing its banks cp. Denham, *Cooper's Hill* ll. 173–6.
137. *lake*] channel of water (*OED sb.*³). *floats*] undulates.
138. *humour*] one of the fluids in the human body thought to determine physical
and mental qualities.
140. *several factions*] See ll. 491–4n. *ferment*] The noun was accented on the second
syllable (cp. Jonson, *The Alchemist* II ii 3).
141. *Work up to*] are agitated into (*OED* 39l, first example, but cp. *OED* 32, 'ferment', used of liquor; and *OED* 34 where a stormy sea 'works').

Some by their friends, more by themselves thought wise,
Opposed the power to which they could not rise.
Some had in courts been great, and thrown from thence
145 Like fiends, were hardened in impenitence.
Some by their monarch's fatal mercy grown
From pardoned rebels, kinsmen to the throne,
Were raised in power and public office high—
Strong bands, if bands ungrateful men could tie.
150   Of these the false Achitophel was first:

144–5. Homer's story of how Hephaistos was thrown from heaven by Zeus (*Iliad* i 591–5) is echoed in Milton's account of the fallen angels throwing themselves over the walls of heaven (*PL* vi 864–6; cp. i 740–2).

146. fatal mercy] For Charles II's possibly unwise tendency to show mercy to his opponents cp. Thomas Otway: 'Mercy shou'd pardon, but the sword compell. / Compassion's else a Kingdom's greatest harm, / Its Warmth engenders Rebels till they swarm' (*Windsor Castle* (1685) 3).

150–99. Achitophel] Anthony Ashley Cooper (1621–83) fought initially on the royalist side in the Civil War, but went over to Parliament in 1644, and held various military and civil posts in Dorset. In January 1652 he was appointed to Parliament's commission on legal reform, and in July 1653 was elected to the Council of State, which he left in January 1655. He rejected overtures from Charles II, then in exile. The recalled Rump Parliament elected him to the new Council of State in May 1659, and he was instrumental in persuading Monck to force it to readmit the secluded members. Early in 1660 he began to incline towards the restoration of the monarchy, and responded positively to an emissary from Charles in April. He sat in the Convention Parliament as Member of Parliament for Wiltshire, and was one of twelve commissioners sent to The Hague to invite Charles to return. He was appointed a Privy Councillor, and in April 1661 created Lord Ashley and appointed Chancellor of the Exchequer; in May 1667 he became one of the commissioners of the Treasury. He was created Earl of Shaftesbury in March 1672, and in September made President of the new Council of Trade and Plantations, an area in which he already had private interests as one of the proprietors of Carolina (cp. 'Prologue to the King and Queen' ll. 2–5); in November he became Lord Chancellor, but was dismissed on 9 November 1673. Thereafter he was a member of the opposition, or 'country party'. In February 1677 Shaftesbury was one of four lords (including Buckingham) who argued that Parliament stood dissolved, as it had been prorogued for more than twelve months, but the House of Lords disagreed and committed all four to the Tower; Shaftesbury was not released until February 1678. He was one of the organizers of the Exclusion Bills, and was not converted when the King attempted to defuse the opposition by bringing Shaftesbury and some others back into the Privy Council. The parliamentary attempts to exclude James from the succession were accompanied by vigorous propaganda which Shaftesbury encouraged, assisted by John Locke. After the sudden dissolution of the Oxford Parliament in March 1681 the Whigs' position weakened, and Shaftesbury was arrested on a charge of high treason on 2 July. The jury at the preliminary hearing on 24 November refused to find a true bill, and he was released on bail (Monmouth offering surety, which was refused). The year 1682 saw the struggle for control of the City of London

A name to all succeeding ages cursed.
For close designs and crooked counsels fit,
Sagacious, bold, and turbulent of wit;
Restless, unfixed in principles and place,
155   In power unpleased, impatient of disgrace.
A fiery soul, which working out its way   ⎤
Fretted the pigmy body to decay,   ⎬
And o'erinformed the tenement of clay.   ⎦

(cp. 'Prologue and Epilogues to *The Duke of Guise*'), and the Rye House Plot
to assassinate Charles laid by Shaftesbury's associates. In danger of arrest, he went
into hiding and left secretly for Holland in late November 1682. He died in
Amsterdam on 21 January 1683. See Haley *passim*.

152–5. This is a partisan view, shared by the author of *The Character of a Disbanded Courtier* (1681; second edition 1682): He 'thought all the Favors, and Honours,
he enjoy'd, were less then the reward of his Merit; that Thought puff'd him up
with Pride, such a sort of Pride, as is usually attended with an irrecoverable fall
. . . like that of *Lucifer*, his Predecessor. . . . He would fain be reputed as constant
as the *Sun*; and yet this Age has produced nothing beneath the *Moon*, more fickle
and variable, for he never was, and 'tis like never will be true to anything; save
onely the Eternal Resolution of doing Mischeif' (1–3; *Works*). L'Estrange agreed:
'his very *Inclination* prompted him to *Mischief*, Even for *Mischiefs* sake. It was his
Way, and his *Humour*, to *Tear All to pieces*, where he could not be the *First Man
in Bus'ness Himself*. And yet All this while, his *Faculty*, was rather a *Quirking* way
of *Wit*, then a *Solidity of Judgment*; and he was *much Happier* at *Pulling-down*, then
at *Building-up*. In One Word; He was a man of *Subtlety*, not of *Depth*; and his
Talent was *Fancy*, rather than *Wisdom*' (*A Brief History of the Times* (1687) i 131–2).
But Shaftesbury's own view of himself was of 'one that, in all these variety of
changes of this last Age, was never known to be either bought or frighted out
of his publick Principles' (*A Letter from a Person of Quality, to his Friend in the
Country* (1675) 9; probably written by Locke at Shaftesbury's direction). A supporter concurred: his 'Policy was always founded upon the solid Basis of
Piety and Judgment; upon which firm Foundation he endeavour'd to raise the
admirable superstructure of Royal Government in the Prince, free from all manner of arbitrary severity, and a willing subjection in the People, without any kind
of force or compunction; so uniting the Interest of the Governour with that
of the governed' (*Rawleigh Redivivus* (1683) 4; *Works*). The latter view is probably
closer to the truth.

152–3. Echoes John Caryll, *Naboth's Vinyard* (1679): 'nature furnish'd him
with parts and wit, / For bold attempts and deep intriguing fit' (ll. 145–6, on
Scroggs; *POAS* ii 88).

152. counsels] Q; Counsell F.

153. Peterson suggests an echo of Sallust's character of Catiline: *animus audax,
subdolus, varius, cuius rei lubet simulator ac dissimulator* ('a bold spirit, crafty, changeable,
able to simulate and dissimulate'; *Bellum Catilinae* 5); cp. l. 545*n*.

154. principles] Q; Principle F.

156–8. Cp. Carew: 'The purest Soule that e're was sent / Into a clayie tenement /
Inform'd this dust, but the weake mold / Could the great guest no longer hold'
(Second 'Epitaph on the Lady Mary Villiers' ll. 1–4). J. D. Jump also cites uses

A daring pilot in extremity:
160 Pleased with the danger, when the waves went high
He sought the storms; but for a calm unfit
Would steer too nigh the sands to boast his wit.

---

of 'tenement of clay' in Thomas Philipott, *Poems* (1646) 6, 11 (*N & Q* cxcvi
(1951) 535–6). Winn (311–12) suggests that D. had previously caricatured
Shaftesbury in the character of Creon in *Oedipus* (1679): 'Creon. Am I to blame
if Nature threw my body / In so perverse a mould? . . . to revenge / Her
bungled work she stampt my mind more fair: / And as from Chaos, huddled and
deform'd, / The God strook fire, and lighted up the Lamps / That beautify the
sky, so he inform'd / This ill-shap'd body with a daring soul: / . . . *Euryd*. No;
thou art all one errour; soul and body; / . . . Thy crooked mind within hunch'd
out thy back' (I i 145–59). Mulgrave in *An Essay upon Satire* (circulating in MS,
1679) writes of Shaftesbury: 'His limbs are crippl'd and his body shakes, / Yet
his hard mind, which all this bustle makes, / No pity of his poor companion
takes. / What gravity can hold from laughing out / To see that drag his feeble
legs about / . . . Yet this false comfort never gives him o'er, / That whilst he
creeps his vig'rous thoughts can soar' (ll. 104–14; *POAS* i 406–7). Cp. also *The
Cabal* (in MS, 1680): 'Double with head to tail he crawls apart, / His body's th'
emblem of his double heart' (ll. 87–8; *POAS* ii 331); *The Badger in the Fox-Trap*:
'A perfect Monster both in Soul and Body' (1); and D'Urfey, *The Progress of Honesty*
16–17. Shaftesbury was short in stature, and suffered from poor health throughout his life; in June 1668 he was operated on at the direction of his friend John
Locke for a hydatid cyst of the liver. D. drew attention to Shaftesbury's body
again in *Albion and Albanius* (1685) III ii *s.d.* (*Works* xv 53). The emphasis on
Shaftesbury's deformity (and that of Oates in ll. 646–9) suggests that these opposition leaders will deform the body politic and rival the sacred body of the King
(see Paul Hammond, *The Making of Restoration Poetry* (2006) 132–3).
157. Fretted] devoured, consumed (*OED* 3b). *pigmy*] He is called a 'Pigmy Lord'
in *Sejanus: or the Popular Favourite* [summer 1681] 3.
158. o'erinformed] over-animated (*OED*'s first example; from 'inform' 3c, 'to
impart life or spirit to'). *tenement*] often applied to the body as the dwelling place
of the soul (*OED* 3b).
159. daring] Shaftesbury had applied this epithet to himself: 'the E. of *Schaftsbury*,
a man as daring but more able' (*A Letter from a Person of Quality* 3). Cp. also the
quotation from *Oedipus* in ll. 156–8n.
159–62. The image of the ship of state which needs to be carefully steered recurs
in the pamphlet literature; several writers picture Shaftesbury as an unreliable pilot:
'Like a vile sculler he abjures the realm, / And sinks the bark 'cause he's not
chief at helm; / . . . if he got through / Secure himself, he drowns the ship and
crew. / If to the ocean back again he's bent, / The rabble, he's in his own element' (*The Cabal* ll. 65–74; *POAS* ii 331–2); 'being injoyn'd by duty, and qualyfi'd
by education, to shew himself an industrious *Terpawlin* [i.e. common sailor], when
the billows of the troubl'd State furiously heave, yet He'l saucily presume to give
directions to his *Pilate*, and regardless of his own respective Office, will boldly
aym at the management of the Helm' (*The Character of a Leading Petitioner* 1);
'Whilst on the Purpl'd Ocean thou didst ride, / And Tack about still with the
Wind and Tide: / This floating Bark, he now again would Steer, / Ah! treacher-

Great wits are sure to madness near allied,
And thin partitions do their bounds divide:
165   Else why should he, with wealth and honour blessed,
Refuse his age the needful hours of rest?
Punish a body which he could not please,
Bankrupt of life, yet prodigal of ease?
And all to leave what with his toil he won
170   To that unfeathered, two-legged thing, a son:
Got while his soul did huddled notions try,

ous Pilot, and false Mariner; / The Kingdom's yet scarce mended Hulk to save, / Would launch again into the Purple wave:' (*Sejanus* 2). For other applications of the image cp. *A Dialogue Between the Ghosts of the Two last Parliaments*; *A Congratulatory Poem on the meeting together of the Parliament* (1680); *The Good Old Cause Revived*. The image also belongs in a moralist tradition: Joseph Hall's presumptuous man 'hois[t]eth saile in a tempest, & sayth never any of his Ancestors were drowned' (*Characters of Vertues and Vices* (1608) 141). See also *The Medal* ll. 79–80*n*.
161. He sought the storms] Cp. Virgil: *in patriam, loca feta furentibus Austris, / Aeoliam uenit* (*Aen.* i 51–2: 'Thus rag'd the Goddess, and with Fury fraught, / The restless Regions of the Storms she sought'; 'The First Book of the *Aeneis*' ll. 76–7).
163. Echoes Seneca: *nullum magnum ingenium sine mixtura dementiae fuit* ('there was no great wit without an element of madness'; *De Tranquillitate Animi* xvii 10, following Aristotle, *Problemata* xxx 1). In *Sir Martin Mar-all* (1668) Rose says: 'your greatest wits have ever a touch of madness and extravagance in them' (V i 61–2). Joseph Hall had commented on the 'mixture . . . of wisdom and madness' in the biblical Achitophel (*Contemplations upon . . . the Old Testament* in his *Works* (1837) i 437–8; Chambers 593). Aaron Baker said of Achitophel: 'The greatest Wits prove most Pernicious, when they are misimploy'd' (*Achitophel befool'd* (1678) 11). Ruth Wallerstein relates D.'s character of Shaftesbury to Renaissance attitudes towards melancholy and the imagination (*HLQ* vi (1942–3) 445–71).
165–6. In 1676 Charles had told Shaftesbury to cease his involvement in public affairs and retire to his home in the country; Shaftesbury declined (Haley 404).
168. ease] Often used by D. with positive connotations of rest and refreshment (cp. 'Horace: *Epode* II' l. 54), unlike the 'ignoble ease' advocated by Belial in *PL* ii 227. Classical and Renaissance writers were divided as to whether *ease* (*otium* in Latin; the opposite of *negotium*, 'business') was to be approved or censured: see Brian Vickers, *Renaissance Studies* iv (1990) 1–37, 107–54.
170. Applying the definition of man as 'a two-legged unfeathered animal', which is attributed to Plato by Diogenes Laertius (vi 40). Cp. 'The Cock and the Fox' ll. 459–62. Shaftesbury's son Anthony (1652–99) had poor health and was politically insignificant (Haley 221–2).
171–2. For a comparable jibe cp. *The Character of a Modern Whig* (1681): 'his Father begetting him in the hot Zeal of this Persuasion, and his Dam all that while fixing her teeming Fancy with Adulterous lust on their able Holderforth, he was moulded a strong *Presbyterian* in the very Womb' (1). In Crowne's *The Ambitious Statesman* (1679) 52 the villainous Constable envisages producing chaotic children:

And born a shapeless lump, like anarchy.
In friendship false, implacable in hate,
Resolved to ruin or to rule the state;
175 To compass this the triple bond he broke, ⎫
The pillars of the public safety shook, ⎬
And fitted Israel for a foreign yoke. ⎭
Then, seized with fear, yet still affecting fame,
Usurped a patriot's all-atoning name.

'I ought not to get Children of a Woman, / I ought to mix with nothing but a
Chaos, / And get Confusion to the Universe, / And then the Children wou'd
be like the Father'.
171. huddled] concealed (*OED v.* 1); heaped in confusion (*OED v.* 2).
172. lump] Used of the unformed mass of the body without shape or soul:
cp. Cowley: '*Nature* herself, whilst in the *womb* he was, / Sow'd *Strength* and
Beauty through the *forming Mass*, / They mov'ed the *vital Lump* in every part'
('Nemeæan Ode', *Poems* 172). Cp. D.'s 'Lucretius: Against the Fear of Death'
l. 10 and 'The First Book of Ovid's *Metamorphoses*' ll. 10–11.
174. Cp. the quotations from L'Estrange in ll. 152–5*n*, and *The Cabal* in ll. 159–62*n*.
175. The Triple Alliance between England, Holland and Sweden had been
formed in 1668, but in May 1670 Charles (with the knowledge of Arlington and
Clifford) signed the secret Treaty of Dover with Louis XIV, under which
Charles was to receive 1 million livres (£150,000) from Louis, to declare himself a Catholic when circumstances permitted (receiving 6,000 French troops to
suppress any revolt), and to join the French in a war against the Dutch. In December
a treaty with France was signed by Shaftesbury along with Clifford, Arlington,
Buckingham and Lauderdale; this *traité simulé* committed England to an alliance
with France without revealing the secret clauses in the earlier treaty. Shaftesbury
seems to have been the last of Charles's ministers to accept this switch of
alliances, though he became particularly associated with it in the popular mind,
largely through his vehement speech against the Dutch on 5 February 1673 (cp.
'Epilogue to *Amboyna*' ll. 19–22); the responsibility for initiating the change was,
however, the King's, and the secret treaty tied him to France in ways that Shaftesbury
could not suspect and would have repudiated (Haley 282–3). For the charge that
Shaftesbury and his colleagues 'gave rise to the present greatness of the *French*'
see D.'s *His Majesties Declaration Defended* (1681; *Works* xvii 202). *compass this*]
bring this about.
176. For the image cp. *The Character of a Disbanded Courtier*: Shaftesbury knew
'that the *Mighty Fabrick* can never be shaken, till its Main Pillars and Supporters
be by Cunning and Sly Stratagem, either destroy'd or undermined' (2).
178. affecting] aiming at (*OED* 1).
179. Cp. 'Having lost his Honour with his Prince, and Reputation with the best
of Men, he Cringes, and Creeps, and Sneaks, to the lowest and Basest of the
People; to procure himself among them an empty, vainglorious, and undeserved
name, the *Patriot* of his Country' (*The Character of a Disbanded Courtier* 2; Kinsley).
The rhetoric of patriotism was part of the Whig claim to be defending the country against subversion. D. had already attacked this rhetoric in *Troilus and Cressida*
(1679): 'While secret envy, and while open pride, / Among thy factious Nobles
discord threw; / While publique good was urg'd for private ends, / And those

180   [So easy still it proves in factious times
       With public zeal to cancel private crimes:
       How safe is treason, and how sacred ill,
       Where none can sin against the people's will;
       Where crowds can wink, and no offence be known,
185   Since in another's guilt they find their own.
       Yet fame deserved no enemy can grudge:
       The statesman we abhor, but praise the judge.
       In Israel's courts ne'er sat an Abbethdin
       With more discerning eyes, or hands more clean:
190   Unbribed, unsought, the wretched to redress,
       Swift of despatch, and easy of access.]
       O, had he been content to serve the crown
       With virtues only proper to the gown,
       Or had the rankness of the soil been freed
195   From cockle that oppressed the noble seed,

---

thought Patriots, who disturb'd it most;' (V ii 317–20). For another echo of this
speech see ll. 1028–31n. D.'s suspicion of politicians' claims to patriotic motives
continued: cp. 'such only merit to be call'd Patriots, under whom we see their
Country Flourish' ('Dedication of the *Georgics*'; *Works* v 141) and 'Some Patriot
Fools to pop'lar Praise aspire, / By Publick Speeches, which worse Fools admire'
('The Second Book of the *Georgics*' ll. 730–1). Cp. ll. 497, 965–8. *Usurped*] Q;
Assumed F. H. Buchan notes that both words occur in Adam's denunciation of
the tyrant Nimrod: 'to himself assuming / Authority usurped, from God not given'
(*PL* xii 65–6; *Yearbook of English Studies* vii (1977) 87). *patriot's*] Q, F *corrected
state*; Patron's F *uncorrected state*. Buchan argues that 'patron' in the sense of protector or advocate is likely to have been D.'s first idea, but it seems more likely
to have been a compositorial error, as D. uses *patriot* again in l. 965.
180–91. Added in Q; not in F. See headnote, *Date and publication*.
181. *zeal*] a quality associated with extreme Protestants.
184. *wink*] close one's eyes (*OED* 1), e.g. to something improper.
187–91. Shaftesbury's record as Lord Chancellor does seem to have been credit-
able (Haley 309–10); his integrity as a judge is emphasized in the Whig broadside
The Character of a Loyal Statesman (1680).
188. *Abbethdin*] 'father of the court of justice', one of two presiding judges of the
Jewish civil court. D. could have found the term in Thomas Godwin, *Moses and
Aaron* (1625) (de Beer 303).
190. *unsought*] To *seek* (*OED* 5) is to approach someone for help; i.e. he did not
need to be bribed or begged before helping someone.
191. *access*] accented on the second syllable in the seventeenth century.
194. *rankness*] fertility (*OED* rank 11).
195. *cockle*] A weed which grows in cornfields (see *OED*). D. echoes the parable
of the wheat and the tares, where 'the good seed are the children of the kingdom; but the tares are the children of the wicked one' (Matthew xiii 24–30, 38–40).
Kinsley notes a reference to 'the cockle of rebellion, insolence, sedition' in *Coriolanus*
III i 69.

David for him his tuneful harp had strung,
And heaven had wanted one immortal song.
But wild ambition loves to slide, not stand,
And fortune's ice prefers to virtue's land.
200 Achitophel, grown weary to possess
A lawful fame and lazy happiness,
Disdained the golden fruit to gather free,
And lent the crowd his arm to shake the tree.
Now, manifest of crimes contrived long since,
205 He stood at bold defiance with his prince;
Held up the buckler of the people's cause
Against the crown, and skulked behind the laws.
The wished occasion of the plot he takes,
Some circumstances finds, but more he makes.

196–7. i.e. 'David would have sung his praises instead of writing a psalm, and so Heaven would have had one immortal song the less' (Nichol Smith). The song may be either Psalm cix, which some seventeenth-century commentators saw as a prediction of God's judgements on Absalom and Achitophel (H. Hammond, *RES* v (1954) 60–2), or 2 Samuel xxii, David's song of thanksgiving towards the end of his reign (W. Maurer, *N & Q* cciii (1958) 341–3). *wanted*] lacked.

198–9. Cp. 'Greatnesse, on Goodnesse loues to slide, not stand, / And leaues for Fortunes ice, Vertues firm land' (Richard Knolles, *The Generall Historie of the Turkes* (1621) 1370, lines under a portrait of Mustapha I; Macaulay, 'Sir William Temple' in *Lord Macaulay's Essays* (1899) 454). Hall's presumptuous man 'walks on weake ice, and never thinks, what if I fall? but, What if I runne over, and fall not?' (*Characters* 141).

198. wild ambition] D. had used this phrase in Ulysses' speech on 'the observance due to rule' in *Troilus and Cressida* I i 45. Ambition is also the force which drives Creon in D. and Lee's *Oedipus* (1679): see V i 393, and cp. ll. 156–8*n* above. Ambition is frequently denounced in Tory writing, e.g. Otway, *The History and Fall of Caius Marius* (1680) 9, 66. D. returns to the topic in *The Medal* and in 'Horace: *Odes* I iii'.

199. fortune] See ll. 252–61*n*.

202–3. Cp. 'In his whole Paradice one only Tree / He had excepted by a strict Decree; / A *Sacred Tree* which *Royal Fruit* did bear, / Yet It in pieces I Conspir'd to tear;' (*A Dialogue between the Ghosts of the Two last Parliaments*). Like Milton (*PL* iv 250) D. associates the fruit of the forbidden tree in Eden with the golden apples of the Hesperides gathered by Heracles.

204. manifest of] evidently guilty of (*OED* 2, first example; a Latinate construction).

207. skulked behind the laws] The Whigs used carefully picked juries to frustrate Charles's attempts to use the courts against the opposition (see ll. 584–629*n*, 606–9*n*).

208–9. Shaftesbury did not instigate Oates's revelations, but took full advantage of them, particularly to discredit James; he was active in the House of Lords committees which investigated the Plot, and may have encouraged Oates behind the scenes, though some of Oates's testimony was tangential or unhelpful to

210   By buzzing emissaries fills the ears
       Of listening crowds with jealousies and fears
       Of arbitrary counsels brought to light,
       And proves the King himself a Jebusite.
       Weak arguments! which yet he knew full well
215   Were strong with people easy to rebel:
       For, governed by the moon, the giddy Jews
       Tread the same track when she the prime renews;
       And once in twenty years, their scribes record,
       By natural instinct they change their lord.
220   Achitophel still wants a chief, and none
       Was found so fit as warlike Absolon:
       Not that he wished his greatness to create
       (For politicians neither love nor hate),

Shaftesbury's interests. Oates's *The Popes Ware-house, or the Merchandise of the Whore of Rome* (1679) was dedicated to Shaftesbury as his 'affectionate good Friend, and singular good Lord' (sig. A^r) as were his *An Exact Discovery of the Mystery of Iniquity* (1679) and *The Witch of Endor* (1679). The Tory pamphlet *A Brief Account of the Commitment of the Earl of Sh.* (1681) comments: 'But now People begin to find out the Mystery, and are pretty well satisfyed, that his Lordship did not promote the Discovery of the *Popish* Plot out of any extraordinary Zeal he had for the good either of the King or Kingdom, but was resolv'd to make a good hand of this Hellish Conspiracy, to advance another of his own' (1).
210. *buzzing*] To *buzz* is to move about busily (*OED* 2); murmur busily (*OED* 3); spread a rumour (*OED* 5); incite by suggestions (*OED* 7). Cp. *Titus Andronicus*: 'these disturbers of our peace / Buzz in the people's ears' (IV iv 6–7).
211. *jealousies*] indignation (*OED* 1); suspicions, apprehensions of evil, mistrust (*OED* 5).
212–13. One of the charges against Shaftesbury when he was arrested was that 'he used great endeavours to possess the People that His Majesty is a *Papist*, and designs to introduce *Popery* and *Arbitrary Power*' (*A Brief Account* 1).   *arbitrary*] absolutist.
215. *easy*] not unwilling, ready (*OED* 12b).
217. *prime*] the lunar cycle of nineteen years (*OED* 4b).
218. *once in twenty years*] i.e. at the outbreak of the Civil War in 1641–2, at the restoration of the monarchy in 1660, and now in 1680–1.
219. *instinct*] stressed on the second syllable in the seventeenth century.
220–1. Monmouth was not a consistent supporter of exclusion, nor did Shaftesbury ever commit himself to Monmouth's succession, though he did propose it privately to the King during the Oxford Parliament. But the two men were close politically and met frequently (Haley 633–4; Ashcraft 177).
220. *wants*] lacks.
222, 224. *he*] Shaftesbury.   *his*] Monmouth's.
223. *politicians*] predominantly a pejorative word in the seventeenth century: 'schemers, plotters' (*OED* 1).

But for he knew his title not allowed
225 Would keep him still depending on the crowd,
That kingly power, thus ebbing out, might be
Drawn to the dregs of a democracy.
Him he attempts with studied arts to please,
And sheds his venom in such words as these:
230 'Auspicious Prince! at whose nativity
Some royal planet ruled the southern sky;
Thy longing country's darling and desire,

224–5. An Appeal from the Country to the City (1679) advocated the claims of Monmouth, since 'his Life and Fortune depends upon the same bottom with yours: he will stand by you, therefore ought you to stand by him. And remember, the old Rule is, *He who hath the worst Title, ever makes the best King*; as being constrain'd by a gracious Government, to supply what he wants in Title; that instead of *God and my Right*, his Motto may be, *God and my People*' (25; Kinsley).
224. allowed] acknowledged to be valid (*OED* 4).
227. Echoes Marchamont Needham: 'It is decreed, we must be drain'd (I see) / Down to the dregs of a *Democracie*' (*Lachrymae Musarum* (1649) 81), in which D.'s 'Upon the Death of the Lord Hastings' also appeared; and cp. *HP* i 211.   *Drawn*] contracted, shrunk (*OED* 6); made to flow (like beer from a cask) (*OED* 40). *democracy*] often pejorative in the seventeenth century, implying mob rule, as when Shaftesbury said that without the secure privileges of the House of Lords 'the *Monarchy* cannot long support, or keep it self from tumbling into a *Democratical Republique*' (*Two Speeches. I. The Earl of Shaftesbury's Speech in the House of Lords the 20th of October, 1675* . . . (1675) 7).
229. venom] Cp. '*Caballing Devils*; who, like cursed *Achitophel*, are ever pouring Poison in the Ears of Young *Absolom*' (*A Seasonable Invitation for Monmouth to Return to Court* (1681) 1). Satan sheds his 'venom' into the ear of Eve in *PL* iv 804.
230–61. Bruce King (*EA* xvi (1963) 251–4) suggests that this speech echoes *The Prince*, chs xxv–xxvi, in which Machiavelli writes of Fortune, and urges Cesare Borgia to liberate Italy. Garrison relates it to the tradition of panegyric (228–36).
230–1. The royal planet would be the sun, moon or Jupiter; the southern sky is the zenith or midheaven of the horoscope. Monmouth, born on 9 April 1649, had the sun in Aries, its exaltation sign. William Lilly writes: '[The Sun] and [the Moon] in the very degree of their Exaltation . . . are arguments unto the Native of obtaining a Kingdom, if he be capable thereof' and they portend 'Kingly Preferment, if the Native be of Kingly Progeny' (*Christian Astrology* (1659) 617; *Works*; Simon Bentley, privately).
230. Auspicious] well-omened. Garrison 230 identifies the term as a common feature of panegyric, e.g.: *Auspiciis iterum sese regalibus annus / induit et nota fruitur iactantior aula* ('Once more the year opens under royal auspices and enjoys in fuller pride its famous prince'; Claudian, *Panegyricus De Quarto Consulatu Honorii Augusti* ll. 1–2); 'Auspicious *Star* again arise', Cowley, *Ode Upon His Majesties Restoration and Return* l. 23. For D.'s usage of the word see Paul Hammond, *MLR* lxxx (1985) 772–3.

Their cloudy pillar and their guardian fire;
Their second Moses, whose extended wand
235   Divides the seas, and shows the promised land;
Whose dawning day in every distant age
Has exercised the sacred prophets' rage;
The people's prayer, the glad diviner's theme,
The young men's vision, and the old men's dream!
240   Thee, saviour, thee, the nation's vows confess,
And never satisfied with seeing, bless.
Swift, unbespoken pomps thy steps proclaim,
And stammering babes are taught to lisp thy name.
How long wilt thou the general joy detain,
245   Starve and defraud the people of thy reign;
Content ingloriously to pass thy days
Like one of virtue's fools that feeds on praise,
Till thy fresh glories which now shine so bright
Grow stale and tarnish with our daily sight?
250   Believe me, royal youth, thy fruit must be
Or gathered ripe, or rot upon the tree.
Heaven has to all allotted, soon or late,

233–5. The Israelites were led through the wilderness by a pillar of cloud by day and fire by night; when they came to the Red Sea, God told Moses: 'lift thou up thy rod, and stretch out thine hand over the sea, and divide it' (Exodus xiii 21, xiv 16).

235. Divides] Q; Shuts up *F* (echoing Job xxxviii 8).

237. rage] prophetic enthusiasm or inspiration (*OED* 8).

239. From Joel ii 28: 'your old men shall dream dreams, your young men shall see visions'.

240. Thee, saviour, thee] Cp. 'Thee, goddess, thee the clouds and tempests fear' ('Lucretius: The Beginning of the First Book' l. 7), echoing Spenser, *FQ* IV x 44 (*Works*) and *The State of Innocence* II iii 30; cp. also 'Palamon and Arcite' iii 135. *confess*] acknowledge.

242. unbespoken] not arranged, spontaneous (*OED*'s first example).   *pomps*] triumphal processions; splendid displays along a route (*OED* 2).

244. detain] hinder, delay (*OED* 5).

251. Or . . . or] Either . . . or.

252–63. Achitophel's stress on Fortune (or 'Occasion'), rather than divine Providence, associates him with Machiavelli's advice to the Prince to seize his opportunities (see *The Prince* ch. xxv, and 'Heroic Stanzas' ll. 29–30n). His assumption in l. 263 that Charles II was given his crown by Fortune is a denial of the hand of God in his restoration. This passage uses details from the emblem-book tradition. G. E. Wilson cites the emblem 'Of Occasion' in Geoffrey Whitney's *A Choice of Emblemes* (1586) 181: 'What creature thou? *Occasion I doe showe.* / On whirling wheel declare why doste thou stande? / *Bicause, I still am tossed too, and froe.* / . . . What meanes long lockes before? *that suche as meete, / Maye houlde at firste, when they occasion finde.* / Thy head behinde all balde, what telles it more? /

Some lucky revolution of their fate;
Whose motions, if we watch and guide with skill
255 (For human good depends on human will),
Our Fortune rolls, as from a smooth descent,
And from the first impression takes the bent:
But if unseized, she glides away like wind,
And leaves repenting folly far behind.
260 Now, now she meets you with a glorious prize,
And spreads her locks before her as she flies.
Had thus old David, from whose loins you spring,
Not dared, when Fortune called him, to be King,
At Gath an exile he might still remain,
265 And heaven's anointing oil had been in vain.
Let his successful youth your hopes engage,
But shun th' example of declining age:
Behold him setting in his western skies,
The shadows lengthening as the vapours rise.

That none shoulde houlde, that let me slippe before'; cp. *1 Conquest of Granada* III
i 265–7 (*PLL* xi (1975) 199–203). For this and other examples of D.'s thinking
about Fortune see Hammond in *MLR* 769–85. The motif of Fortune's dealings
with Monmouth is used in 'On the Election of yᵉ Duke of Monmouth to be
Chancellor of yᵉ University of Cambridge' (1674; BodL MS Don.b.8 pp. 506–7).
Milton's Satan, tempting Christ 'to sit upon thy father David's throne', says: 'zeal
and duty are not slow; / But on occasion's forelock watchful wait' (*PR* iii 153,
172–3).
253. revolution] alteration (*OED* 6).
257. bent] direction of motion (*OED* 6d).
262–5. To escape Saul, David went into exile in Gath (1 Samuel xxvii 1–7). Charles
II's exile was spent chiefly in Germany and the Netherlands, particularly Brussels.
265. heaven's anointing oil] After God rejected Saul, Samuel anointed the boy David
(1 Samuel xvi 13).
266. engage] invite (*OED* 8).
267–9. Cp. *A Seasonable Invitation*: Achitophel tells Absalom: 'The *King* (his Father)
grows Old and Weak, and that He is easily subdued; that the *Mobile* grow weary
of His Government, and fall off from Him; that he himself hath so much the
Hearts of the People, as that he can immediately Raise *Twelve* Thousand Men
and that the *King* being left Desolate, he will strike Him: And all this, that *Absolom*
may be King, and the People may live in Peace' (1).
267. declining age] Charles (b. 29 May 1630) was 51, old in seventeenth-century terms.
268–9. Kinsley compares *Aureng-Zebe* (1676) I i 74–81: '*Solyman.* [He] Wishes,
each Minute, he could unbeget / Those Rebel-Sons, who dare t' usurp his
Seat: / To sway his Empire with unequal Skill, / And mount a Throne, which
none but he can fill. / *Arimant.* Oh! had he still that Character maintain'd, / Of
Valour, which in blooming Youth he gain'd! / He promis'd in his East a Glorious
Race; / Now, sunk from his Meridian, sets apace'.
269. vapours] mists (*OED* 2b).

270 He is not now, as when on Jordan's sand ⎫
The joyful people thronged to see him land, ⎬
Cov'ring the beach, and black'ning all the strand: ⎭
But like the Prince of Angels from his height
Comes tumbling downward with diminished light;
275 Betrayed by one poor plot to public scorn
(Our only blessing since his cursed return):
Those heaps of people which one sheaf did bind
Blown off and scattered by a puff of wind.
What strength can he to your designs oppose,
280 Naked of friends, and round beset with foes?
If Pharaoh's doubtful succour he should use,
A foreign aid would more incense the Jews:
Proud Egypt would dissembled friendship bring,
Foment the war, but not support the King;
285 Nor would the royal party e'er unite
With Pharaoh's arms t' assist the Jebusite;
Or if they should, their interest soon would break,
And with such odious aid make David weak.
All sorts of men by my successful arts
290 Abhorring kings, estrange their altered hearts
From David's rule; and 'tis the general cry
"Religion, Commonwealth and Liberty".
If you as champion of the public good
Add to their arms a chief of royal blood,
295 What may not Israel hope, and what applause
Might such a general gain by such a cause?

270–2. Cp. Virgil: *migrantis cernas totaque ex urbe ruentis: / ac velut ingentem form- icae farris acervum / cum populant hiemis memores tectoque reponunt, / it nigrum campis agmen* (*Aen.* iv 401–4; 'The Beach is cover'd o're / With *Trojan* Bands that blacken all the Shore: / On ev'ry side are seen, descending down, / Thick swarms of Souldiers loaden from the Town. / Thus, in Battalia, march embody'd Ants, / Fearful of Winter, and of future Wants', 'The Fourth Book of the *Aeneis*' ll. 578–83; R. M. Ogilvie, *N & Q* ccxv (1970) 415–16); cp. *Astraea Redux* ll. 276–9.
270. *Jordan's sand*] Dover beach; see 2 Samuel xix 15.
273–4. 'How art thou fallen from heaven, O Lucifer, son of the morning! how art thou cut down to the ground, which didst weaken the nations! For thou hast said in thine heart, I will ascend into heaven, I will exalt my throne above the stars of God' (Isaiah xiv 12–13; cp. Luke x 18).
281. *Pharaoh*] Louis XIV.
287. *interest*] participation (*OED* 1d). *break*] dissolve (*OED* 8b, quoting this line).
295. *What may not Israel hope*] Cp. Marvell: 'What may not then our isle presume' ('An Horatian Ode' l. 97); and the rhyme *break/weak* in ll. 287–8 also occurs in Marvell ll. 39–40. See also ll. 353–4n. *applause*] Distrusted by D.; cp. 'Lucretius: Against the Fear of Death' l. 203.

Not barren praise alone, that gaudy flower
Fair only to the sight, but solid power:
And nobler is a limited command
300 Given by the love of all your native land,
Than a successive title, long and dark,
Drawn from the mouldy rolls of Noah's ark.'
    What cannot praise effect in mighty minds,
When flattery soothes, and when ambition blinds!
305 Desire of power, on earth a vicious weed,
Yet, sprung from high, is of celestial seed:
In God 'tis glory; and when men aspire
'Tis but a spark too much of heavenly fire.
Th' ambitious youth, too covetous of fame,
310 Too full of angel's metal in his frame,
Unwarily was led from virtue's ways,
Made drunk with honour, and debauched with praise.
Half loath, and half consenting to the ill
(For loyal blood within him struggled still),
315 He thus replied: 'And what pretence have I
To take up arms for public liberty?
My father governs with unquestioned right,
The faith's defender, and mankind's delight:
Good, gracious, just, observant of the laws,
320 And heaven by wonders has espoused his cause.
Whom has he wronged in all his peaceful reign?
Who sues for justice to his throne in vain?

302. rolls] The descent of English kings was shown in genealogical parchment rolls
(e.g. BodL MS Rolls 3).
310. angel] (i) ominously, in view of the Luciferian precedent; (ii) with a pun
on the gold coin, last minted by Charles I, which was presented to patients touched
by the monarch for the King's Evil (*OED*; W. K. Thomas, *The Crafting of 'Absalom
and Achitophel'*). *metal*] 'metal' and 'mettle' are originally the same word, and
both could be spelt 'metal' in the seventeenth century, as here.
312. debauched] See l. 47*n*.
318. The faith's defender] echoing the King's title *Fidei Defensor*, originally granted
to Henry VIII by Pope Leo X for his treatise against Luther. *mankind's delight*]
Suetonius calls Titus *amor ac deliciae generis humani* ('the love and delight of mankind',
viii 1; Christie). Thomas D'Urfey has the same comparison: '*Titus* the Second
reigns, he whose celestial mind / Stiles him the joy of human kind' (*The Progress
of Honesty* (1681) 7). Cp. also George Berkeley, *Historical Applications*, third edition (1680) 90–1. For the phrasing cp. 'Lucretius: The Beginning of the First
Book' l. 1 (used of Venus).
320. For a supporter of Charles, such *wonders* would have included his escape
after the Battle of Worcester in 1651, his restoration in 1660 (see *Astraea
Redux* l. 241), and the course taken by the Fire of London (see *AM* l. 1081*n*).

What millions has he pardoned of his foes,
Whom just revenge did to his wrath expose?
325   Mild, easy, humble, studious of our good,
Inclined to mercy, and averse from blood.
If mildness ill with stubborn Israel suit,
His crime is God's belovèd attribute.
What could he gain, his people to betray,
330   Or change his right for arbitrary sway?
Let haughty Pharaoh curse with such a reign
His fruitful Nile, and yoke a servile train.
If David's rule Jerusalem displease,
The dog-star heats their brains to this disease.
335   Why then should I, encouraging the bad,
Turn rebel, and run popularly mad?
Were he a tyrant who by lawless might
Oppressed the Jews and raised the Jebusite,
Well might I mourn; but nature's holy bands
340   Would curb my spirits and restrain my hands:
The people might assert their liberty,
But what was right in them were crime in me.

Cp. *Threnodia Augustalis* ll. 90–1. The anonymous *A True Relation of the Late Kings Death* (1685) would represent Charles himself exclaiming '*Almighty God, what good Planet governs me, that all my Life is Wonders and Miracles?*'

323–4. The general pardon offered by Charles in the Declaration of Breda (4 April 1660) was implemented in the Act of Indemnity and Oblivion (29 August 1660) which offered a general pardon for all treasons, felonies and numerous other offences committed since 1 January 1637; 51 individuals, chiefly regicides, were excepted from the pardon (Ogg 154–5).

326. Although Charles allowed the law to take its usual course during the Popish Plot, he regretted some of the executions, and occasionally remitted the more savage punishments for treason. 'The King like a Just and Excellent Prince, who like Heavens Monarch delights in Mercy, suspends the Rigors and Severities of the Penal Laws against them; this they construe to be Fear and not Favour' (*The Character of a Rebellion* (1681) 2).

329–30. In his speech to the Oxford Parliament on 20 March 1681 Charles said: 'I, who will never use arbitrary government myself, am resolved not to suffer it in others . . . It is much my interest, and it shall be as much my care as yours, to preserve the liberty of the subject; because the Crown can never be safe when that is in danger. And I would have you likewise be convinced, that neither your liberties nor properties can subsist long, when the just rights and prerogatives of the Crown are invaded, or the honour of the government brought low and into disreputation' (*Letters, Speeches and Declarations of King Charles II*, edited by Arthur Bryant (1935) 317–18; Kinsley).

334. Sirius, the Dog Star, rises around 11 August, and the previous forty days (dog days) were said to bring unpleasantly hot weather and malignant influences.

336. run popularly mad] run mad and pander to the people.

His favour leaves me nothing to require,
Prevents my wishes, and outruns desire.
345 What more can I expect while David lives?
All but his kingly diadem he gives,
And that—' But there he paused, then sighing said,
'Is justly destined for a worthier head.
For when my father from his toils shall rest,
350 And late augment the number of the blessed,
His lawful issue shall the throne ascend,
Or the collateral line where that shall end.
His brother, though oppressed with vulgar spite,
Yet dauntless and secure of native right,
355 Of every royal virtue stands possessed,
Still dear to all the bravest, and the best.
His courage foes, his friends his truth proclaim,

344. *Prevents*] anticipates.
349. *toils*] Charles II notoriously preferred pleasure to business. For the sexual connotations of *toil* cp. Lady Fidget in Wycherley's *The Country-Wife*: 'I have been toyling and moyling, for the pretti'st piece of China' (IV iii 177–8).
353–60. James, Duke of York, 'cunningly unnamed' by D. (Winn 357). Suspicion of him intensified during the Popish Plot; though he was not alleged to be implicated personally, the discovery of Coleman's correspondence was embarrassing, and it was fortunate that no one discovered that there had in fact been a meeting of the Jesuits in James's own apartments. On 3 November 1678 it was decided that James should cease to attend the Privy Council and its committees, and on 27 April 1679 the House of Commons resolved 'That the Duke of *Yorke's* being a Papist, and the Hopes of his coming such to the Crown, has given the greatest Countenance and Encouragement to the present Conspiracies and Designs of the Papists against the King, and the Protestant Religion' (*Commons' Journals* ix 605). James spent some time away from London: March to September 1679 in Brussels, and November 1679 to February 1680 and October 1680 to March 1681 in Scotland. D. had praised James in the Dedication of *The State of Innocence* (1677) to the Duchess of York, as a prince 'whose Conduct, Courage, and Success in War, whose Fidelity to His Royal Brother, whose Love for His Countrey, whose Constancy to His Friends, whose Bounty to His Servants, whose Justice to Merit, whose Inviolable Truth, and whose Magnanimity in all His Actions, seem to have been rewarded by Heaven by the gift of You' (*Works* xii 82). Lines in *The Duke of Guise* (1683) also reflect on James: '*King*. I know my Brother's nature, 'tis sincere, / Above deceit, no crookedness of thought, / Says, what he means, and what he says performs: / Brave, but not rash; successful, but not proud; / So much acknowledging that he's uneasie / Till every petty service be o're paid. / *Archb*. Some say revengeful. / *King*. Some then libel him: / But that's what both of us have learn't to bear. / He can forgive, but you disdain Forgiveness' (V i 220–8). Cp. also 'Epilogue to *Albion and Albanius*' (Kinsley).
353–4. Echoing Marvell: 'Nor called the Gods with vulgar spite / To vindicate his helpless right' ('An Horatian Ode' ll. 61–2, of Charles I). This is one of a cluster of echoes of the Ode in *AA*; see also ll. 295n, 387–8n, 805–8n, 887n; and *AM* ll. 849–60n.

His loyalty the King, the world his fame.
His mercy ev'n th' offending crowd will find,
360   For sure he comes of a forgiving kind.
Why should I then repine at heaven's decree,
Which gives me no pretence to royalty?
Yet O that Fate, propitiously inclined,
Had raised my birth, or had debased my mind;
365   To my large soul not all her treasure lent,
And then betrayed it to a mean descent.
I find, I find my mounting spirits bold,
And David's part disdains my mother's mould.
Why am I scanted by a niggard birth?
370   My soul disclaims the kindred of her earth,
And made for empire whispers me within,
"Desire of greatness is a godlike sin." '
        Him staggering so when hell's dire agent found,
While fainting virtue scarce maintained her ground,
375   He pours fresh forces in, and thus replies:
'Th' eternal God, supremely good and wise,
Imparts not these prodigious gifts in vain;
What wonders are reserved to bless your reign!
Against your will your arguments have shown
380   Such virtue's only given to guide a throne.

360. kind] race (*OED* 10).
362. pretence] claim (*OED* 1).
363–72. Cp. Torrismond in *The Spanish Friar* (1681) II ii 103–8: 'Good Heav'ns,
why gave you me a Monarch's Soul, / And crusted it with base Plebeian Clay?
/ Why gave you me Desires of such extent, / And such a Span to grasp 'em?
Sure my lot / By some o'er-hasty Angel was misplac'd / In Fate's Eternal Volume!'
(Kinsley).
363–4. Cp. 'Ah mighty prince! By too great Birth betray'd, / Borne to those
Fortunes, which you might have made; / Had Fate been kind, she would have
plac'd you lowe, / That to your selfe you might your Greatnesse owe' ('On the
Election of yᵉ Duke of Monmouth . . .', BodL MS Don.b.8. p. 506).
366. mean] lowly.
368. mould] (i) earth, regarded as the material of the body (*OED sb.*¹ 4; cp. *earth*
in l. 370); (ii) the body as a matrix for creating a child (*OED sb.*² 4).
369. scanted] inadequately supplied (*OED* 3); confined, restricted (*OED* 6).
373. A quasi-Miltonic line. *staggering*] beginning to doubt or waver (*OED* 2).
hell's dire agent] D. associates Shaftesbury with the Satan of *PL*, for which cp. the
Epistle Dedicatory to *All for Love*, quoted in ll. *51–6n*; but he had already been
presented as a devil in the pamphlet literature, most viciously in *A Seasonable Invitation*
2. Cp. 'Some call me Devil, some his Foster-Brother' (*The Badger in the Fox-Trap* 1).
Monmouth is seduced by 'Hells curst Agents' in *The Progress of Honesty* 11.
376–80. Cp. D.'s Dedication to *Tyrannic Love*, quoted in ll. *18–30n* (Bruce
King, *ES* xlvi (1965) 332–3).

Not that your father's mildness I condemn,
But manly force becomes the diadem.
'Tis true, he grants the people all they crave,
And more perhaps than subjects ought to have:
385 For lavish grants suppose a monarch tame,
And more his goodness than his wit proclaim.
But when should people strive their bonds to break,
If not when kings are negligent or weak?
Let him give on till he can give no more,
390 The thrifty Sanhedrin shall keep him poor:
And every shekel which he can receive
Shall cost a limb of his prerogative.
To ply him with new plots shall be my care,
Or plunge him deep in some expensive war;
395 Which when his treasure can no more supply
He must with the remains of kingship buy.
His faithful friends our jealousies and fears
Call Jebusites, and Pharaoh's pensioners;
Whom when our fury from his aid has torn
400 He shall be naked left to public scorn.
The next successor, whom I fear and hate,
My arts have made obnoxious to the state,
Turned all his virtues to his overthrow,
And gained our elders to pronounce a foe.
405 His right for sums of necessary gold
Shall first be pawned, and afterwards be sold;

385. suppose] imply, presuppose (*OED* 10).
386. wit] intelligence.
387–8. Echoing Marvell: 'But those [ancient rights] do hold or break, / As men are strong or weak' ('An Horatian Ode' ll. 39–40).
390. Sanhedrin] The highest court of justice in Jerusalem; applied here to Parliament. None of the last three parliaments (March–May 1679; October 1680 to January 1681; March 1681) had voted money for the King's use; see 'Epilogue to *The Unhappy Favourite*' l. 8.
392. prerogative] power which the monarch can exercise without the consent of Parliament.
394–6. Recalling the Third Anglo-Dutch War (1672–4) which Shaftesbury had helped to promote. The Commons voted money for it, but at the same time challenged the King's prerogative right to suspend penal laws against dissenters; Charles cancelled his Declaration of Indulgence, and the Money Bill was passed. Another outcome of this session was the Test Act, which disqualified from public office anyone refusing to take the oath of allegiance and supremacy and the Anglican sacrament (Ogg 365–8).
398. Pharaoh's pensioners] Louis XIV's ambassadors in London spent considerable sums of money to influence both court and Parliament.

Till time shall ever-wanting David draw
To pass your doubtful title into law:
If not, the people have a right supreme
410   To make their kings, for kings are made for them.
All empire is no more than power in trust,
Which when resumed can be no longer just.
Succession, for the general good designed,
In its own wrong a nation cannot bind:
415   If alt'ring that the people can relieve,
Better one suffer than a nation grieve.
The Jews well know their power: ere Saul they chose
God was their King, and God they durst depose.
Urge now your piety, your filial name,
420   A father's right, and fear of future fame;
The public good, that universal call
To which ev'n heaven submitted, answers all.
Nor let his love enchant your generous mind:
'Tis nature's trick to propagate her kind.
425   Our fond begetters, who would never die,
Love but themselves in their posterity.
Or let his kindness by th' effects be tried,
Or let him lay his vain pretence aside.
God said he loved your father: could he bring
430   A better proof than to anoint him King?

409–12. See ll. *759–810nn.*

412. i.e. when the people take back the power which they had entrusted to a ruler, he no longer has any just claim to it.

414. i.e. a nation cannot be bound by arrangements for the succession which will cause it harm.

416. Echoes John xviii 14: 'it was expedient that one man [i.e. Christ] should die for the people'. Sir Thomas Player, a Whig, used a similar argument in the Commons on 4 January 1681: 'I have read *That one man died for the People,* but never that three Kingdoms must die for one man' (Grey viii 236). *nation*] Q; Million F.

417–18. Saul was the first king of Israel, and the people's demand for a king was seen as a rejection of the rule of God (1 Samuel viii 4–8, 18–19). D. refers to the replacement of the Commonwealth by the quasi-monarchical Protectorate under Cromwell ('Saul') on 16 December 1653. Vavasor Powell denounced the change, saying: 'Lord wilt Thou have Oliver Cromwell or Jesus Christ to reign over us?' (*CSPD 1653–4* 306).

419. piety] reverence and obedience to God (*OED* 2) and parents (*OED* 3); cp. *AM* l. 255n.

421–2. Applying the dictum *salus populi suprema lex* ('the safety of the people is the supreme law').

423. generous] noble.

427–8. Or . . . Or] Either . . . Or.

It surely showed he loved the shepherd well
Who gave so fair a flock as Israel.
Would David have you thought his darling son?
What means he then to alienate the crown?
435 The name of godly he may blush to bear:
'Tis after God's own heart to cheat his heir.
He to his brother gives supreme command:
To you, a legacy of barren land;
Perhaps th' old harp on which he thrums his lays,
440 Or some dull Hebrew ballad in your praise.
Then the next heir, a prince severe and wise,
Already looks on you with jealous eyes;
Sees through the thin disguises of your arts,
And marks your progress in the people's hearts.
445 Though now his mighty soul its grief contains,
He meditates revenge who least complains;
And like a lion slumbering in the way,

431. shepherd] David had been a shepherd boy (1 Samuel xvi 11); the reference also carries connotations of Christ as the good shepherd (John x 11–15).
434. alienate] transfer to the ownership of another (*OED* 2).
435–6. i.e. 'Charles may blush to call himself "godly" when he declines to cheat the Duke of York of his succession, to do which would be "after God's own heart"' (Christie). The 'cheat' would be acceptable to God because it would preserve Protestantism. D. may be recalling that David had his son Solomon anointed king to thwart his elder son Adonijah, who had begun to behave as king (1 Kings i).
438. Probably a reference to the Border estates of Monmouth's wife (Kinsley).
439. Charles was a lover of music, particularly of the guitar: see Richard Luckett, 'Music' in Pepys, *Diary* x 264–7, 274.
441. severe] not inclined to indulgence: often seen as a proper attribute of princes: cp. 'He who the sword of heaven will bear / Should be as holy as severe' (*Measure for Measure* III ii 254–5).
442. jealous] See l. 211*n.*
445. grief] feeling of having been wronged; displeasure; anger (*OED* 4).
447–54. Cp. Lucan: *sicut squalentibus arvis / Aestiferae Libyes viso leo comminus hoste / Subsedit dubius, totam dum colligit iram; / Mox, ubi se saevae stimulavit verbere caudae / Erexitque iubam et vasto grave murmur hiatu / Infremuit* ('So on the untilled fields of sultry Libya, when the lion sees his foe at hand, he crouches down at first uncertain till he gathers all his rage; but soon, when he has maddened himself with the cruel lash of his tail, and made his mane stand up, and sent forth a roar from his cavernous jaws . . .'; *Pharsalia* i 205–10; Ogilvie). D.'s rhymes also point to a recollection of Cowley's *Davideis*: 'A *Lyon* prickt with rage and want of food, / Espies out from afar some well-fed beast, / And brustles up preparing for his feast; / If that by swiftness scape his gaping jaws; / His bloody eyes he hurls round, his sharp paws / Tear up the ground; then runs he wild about, / Lashing his angry tail, and roaring out. / . . . *Silence* and *horror* fill the place around. / *Eccho* it self dares scarce repeat the sound' (Cowley, *Poems* 258). For the comparison of James with a lion cp. Col. Titus's speech in the Commons, 7 January

Or sleep dissembling while he waits his prey,
His fearless foes within his distance draws,
450 Constrains his roaring and contracts his paws;
Till at the last, his time for fury found,
He shoots with sudden vengeance from the ground,
The prostrate vulgar passes o'er and spares,
But with a lordly rage his hunters tears.
455 Your case no tame expedients will afford:
Resolve on death, or conquest by the sword,
Which for no less a stake than life you draw;
And self-defence is nature's eldest law.
Leave the warm people no considering time,
460 For then rebellion may be thought a crime:
Prevail yourself of what occasion gives,
But try your title while your father lives;
And that your arms may have a fair pretence,
Proclaim you take them in the King's defence,
465 Whose sacred life each minute would expose
To plots from seeming friends and secret foes.
And who can sound the depth of David's soul?
Perhaps his fear his kindness may control.
He fears his brother though he loves his son

1681: 'If a Lion was in the Lobby, and we were to consider which way to secure
ourselves from him, and conclude it is best to shut the Door, and keep him out,
"No," says another, "let us chain him, and let him come in;" but I should be
loth to put the chain on' (Grey viii 279). James is referred to as 'the Popish Lyon'
in the Tory beast-fable *Grimalkin, or, the Rebel-Cat* (1681); and *The White Rose:
or A Word for the House of York* (1680) remarks: 'From the secret instincts of *Nature*,
Birds and Beasts are taught to obey the *Eagle* and the *Lyon*' (2). For examples of
political beast-fables at this period see Paul Hammond, *N & Q* ccxxvii (1982) 55–7;
Ashcraft 401; and ll. 527–8n.
448. sleep dissembling] F2; Sleep-dissembling F, Q.
453. From Pliny: *Leoni tantum ex feris clementia in supplices; prostratis parcit* ('The
lion alone of wild animals shows mercy to suppliants; it spares persons prostrated
in front of it'; *Naturalis Historia* viii 19 (Kinsley)); so too Edward Topsell, *The
History of Four-footed Beasts* (1658) 365.
458. So Hobbes: 'The Right of Nature . . . is the Liberty each man hath, to use
his own power, as he will himselfe, for the preservation of his own Nature; that
is to say, of his own Life' (*Leviathan* (1651) 64; Kinsley). See 'Palamon and Arcite'
ii 337n.
461. Prevail] avail (*OED* 4c). *occasion*] See ll. 252–61n.
464. This claim had been made by Parliament in the early stages of the Civil
War.
468. i.e. Perhaps his fear of James may restrain the natural affection arising from
his kinship to you.

470   For plighted vows too late to be undone.
      If so, by force he wishes to be gained,
      Like women's lechery, to seem constrained.
      Doubt not, but when he most affects the frown
      Commit a pleasing rape upon the crown;
475   Secure his person to secure your cause:
      They who possess the prince possess the laws.'
          He said; and this advice above the rest
      With Absalom's mild nature suited best:
      Unblamed of life (ambition set aside),
480   Not stained with cruelty, nor puffed with pride;
      How happy had he been if destiny
      Had higher placed his birth, or not so high!
      His kingly virtues might have claimed a throne,
      And blessed all other countries but his own;
485   But charming greatness since so few refuse
      'Tis juster to lament him than accuse.
      Strong were his hopes a rival to remove,
      With blandishments to gain the public love;
      To head the faction while their zeal was hot,
490   And popularly prosecute the plot.
      To farther this, Achitophel unites

470. plighted vows] See ll. 18–30*n*.
472. Proverbial: Tilley W 660; Ovid, *Ars Amatoria* i 664, 672, 698 (Poyet).
473. Doubt] hesitate, scruple, delay (*OED* 3).
474. rape] (i) violent theft (*OED* 1); (ii) sexual violation (*OED* 3c). The latter
sense was commonly used politically, e.g. in *King John*: 'Thou hast under-wrought
[i.e. undermined] his lawful king, / Cut off the sequence of posterity, / . . . and
done a rape / Upon the maiden virtue of the crown' (II i 95–8). Rape was used
as a political trope in the Exclusion Crisis by several dramatists, as Susan Owen
shows: to the Whigs it could figure tyranny, to the Tories, rebellion. Examples
are Creon in *Oedipus*, a rebel leader who contemplates rape in a temple; the tyrant
Tarquin who rapes Lucrece in Lee's *Lucius Junius Brutus*; and the attempted rape
of Belvidera by Renault in Otway's *Venice Preserv'd* (Owen 175–6, 231–2 and
SEL xxxi (1991) 474–6).
479. Unblamed of life] a Latin construction, translating *integer vitae* (Horace, *Carm.*
I xxii 1).
481–2. Cp. ll. 363–4*n*.
491–4. The Whigs were a coalition of different interests. J. R. Jones (10–16)
divides them into five groups: (i) 'The old Presbyterians', distinguished by zeal
for religious reform and Protestant unity, sympathetic to dissenters, and advocates
of toleration; (ii) 'The country opposition', who valued the law, honest government, consultation with parliament, financial retrenchment and the defence of
Protestantism: cp. D.'s ll. 495–500; (iii) 'The adventurers', who criticized ministers in the hope of supplanting them: cp. D.'s ll. 501–4; (iv) 'Monmouth and his
circle', bound together by personal interests; (v) 'The radicals', the survivors and

The malcontents of all the Israelites,
Whose differing parties he could wisely join
For several ends, to serve the same design.
495 The best, and of the princes some were such,
Who thought the power of monarchy too much,
Mistaken men, and patriots in their hearts,
Not wicked, but seduced by impious arts:
By these the springs of property were bent,
500 And wound so high they cracked the government.
The next for interest sought t' embroil the state,
To sell their duty at a dearer rate;
And make their Jewish markets of the throne,
Pretending public good, to serve their own.
505 Others thought kings an useless, heavy load,
Who cost too much, and did too little good:
These were for laying honest David by
On principles of pure good husbandry.
With them joined all th' haranguers of the throng
510 That thought to get preferment by the tongue.
Who follow next a double danger bring,
Not only hating David, but the King—
The Solymæan rout, well versed of old
In godly faction, and in treason bold;
515 Cowering and quaking at a conqueror's sword,
But lofty to a lawful prince restored,

successors of the republicans of the 1650s: cp. D.'s ll. 511–14. Ashcraft says of
L'Estrange's propaganda that 'like Dryden, L'Estrange perceived the "contradictory" interests united in the Whig political movement, and he hoped to break
apart the unity of the movement by showing that some classes (tradesmen and
merchants) would benefit greatly at the expense of others (nobility and gentry)
if the Whigs achieved their political objectives' (242). See also Gary S. De Krey
in Harris, Seaward and Goldie (cited in ll. 51–6n) 133–62, for the London Whigs.
497. *patriots*] a designation claimed by the Whigs: cp. l. 179n, ll. 965–8.
499. *property*] See l. 536n.
501–4. The Whigs drew strong support from merchants and traders, and much
Whig propaganda was aimed at their interests (Ashcraft 230–3).
501. *interest*] advantage, profit (OED 2b); faction, political party (OED 4); selfish
pursuit of one's own welfare (OED 5). *embroil the state*] Echoes [Roger
L'Estrange]: 'Nor is't at all th' *Intent* of *Their Debate* / To fix Religion, but t'
embroyl the *State*' (*The Committee; or Popery in Masquerade* (1680)). *embroil*] throw
into uproar or tumult (OED 2).
513. *Solymæan rout*] London rabble. Tory pamphleteers often accused the Whigs
of appealing to the rabble (Ashcraft 301–3). See Harris, *London Crowds, passim.*
Solymæan] of Jerusalem (from the Latin *Solyma* for *Hierosolyma*, Jerusalem),
OED's only example.

Saw with disdain an ethnic plot begun,
And scorned by Jebusites to be outdone.
Hot Levites headed these, who pulled before
520 From th' ark, which in the Judges' days they bore,
Resumed their cant, and with a zealous cry
Pursued their old beloved theocracy,
Where Sanhedrin and priest enslaved the nation,
And justified their spoils by inspiration;
525 For who so fit for reign as Aaron's race
If once dominion they could found in grace?
These led the pack, though not of surest scent
Yet deepest-mouthed against the government.
A numerous host of dreaming saints succeed,
530 Of the true old enthusiastic breed;
'Gainst form and order they their power employ,
Nothing to build, and all things to destroy.
But far more numerous was the herd of such
Who think too little, and who talk too much.
535 These, out of mere instinct, they knew not why,
Adored their fathers' god, and property;

517. ethnic] Gentile (*OED* 1); here, Roman Catholic.
519. Levites] Jewish priests; here, the dissenting clergy who were deprived of their benefices by the Act of Uniformity (1662).
520. Judges] the leaders of Israel between the death of Joshua and the election of Saul as king.
521. cant] peculiar phraseology of a religious sect (*OED* 4c; first example).
522. theocracy] form of government in which God is recognized as king, and the country is administered by a priestly order; applied particularly to Israel from the Exodus to the election of Saul (*OED*); here, the Commonwealth of England.
525. Aaron's race] The clergy; the Jewish priesthood was hereditary in the line of Aaron.
526. Cp. *The Character of a Fanatick* (1675): 'he makes his Doctrine suitable to his Text, and owns above-board, that Dominion is founded in Grace, not Nature: That the Goods of this World are properly the Elects' (Kinsley).
527–8. Cp. *The Progress of Honesty*: 'Their deep mouth'd Oaths to th' lofty Skies were sent / That there would be a Change in Government' (12); the image is also applied to the Tories in *The Character of a Tory* (1681) 2: 'Whilst we were Hunting down their *Plot* with a full Cry, they slipt in their *Deep-mouth'd* Hound, who spending on a *false Scent* diverted the Chase, and so the *Popish Puss squats safe in her Form*'. *deepest-mouthed*] with the deepest or most sonorous voices (of dogs).
530. enthusiastic] 'Enthusiasm' first meant possession by a god, supernatural inspiration (*OED* 1); thence fancied inspiration, extravagant religious fervour (*OED* 2, from 1660). See Susie I. Tucker, *Enthusiasm: A Study in Semantic Change* (1972).
535. instinct] accented on the second syllable.
536. The Whigs 'included a considerable proportion of both the landed nobility and the landed gentry, as well as many city merchants and rich Dissenters. From

And by the same blind benefit of fate
The devil and the Jebusite did hate:
Born to be saved, ev'n in their own despite,
540 Because they could not help believing right.
Such were the tools, but a whole hydra more
Remains, of sprouting heads too long to score.
Some of their chiefs were princes of the land:
In the first rank of these did Zimri stand;

these constituent elements can be deduced two of their fundamental principles –
sanctity of private property and religious toleration' (Ogg 611; Kinsley). The Whigs
feared that James as king would appropriate the former church lands which had
been in private ownership since the Reformation, and generally would not respect
property rights (Ashcraft 202–3). Buckingham voiced this fear in the Lords in
1675: 'There is a thing called *Property*, (whatever some men may think) *that* the
People of *England* are fondest *of*. It is *that* they will never part with, and it is *that*
His *Majesty* in his *Speech* has promised to take particular care of. *This*, my Lords,
in my opinion, can never be done, without an *Indulgence to all Protestant dissenters'*
(*Two Speeches* . . . 13); cp. 'Think how your Magistrates are murder'd before your
eyes, for supporting that Liberty and Property whereby alone you subsist! That
Property which entitles you to something you may call your own, which having
enjoy'd your self, you may bequeath to your Posterity after you: That Property
which satisfies your hunger and thirst with wholesom and substantial food, as
good Beef, Mutton, &c. meats unknown to any in an absolute Monarchy, under
the degree of the Nobility' (*A Character of Popery and Arbitrary Government* [early
1681] 2); cp. also *The Case of Protestants in England under a Popish Prince* (1681)
10; Henry Neville, *Plato Redivivus* (1681) 134, 141. See further Harris, cited in
ll. 51–6*n*; Ashcraft 255–7; and Judith Richards et al., *JHI* xlii (1981) 29–51.
539–40. The Calvinist doctrine that the righteous are justified by faith, not works,
and are elected for salvation from before their birth.
541. hydra] The mythical many-headed snake whose heads grew as fast as they
were cut off; it was eventually killed by Heracles. In *The Badger in the Fox-Trap*
Shaftesbury says: 'Some call me *Hydra* with a hundred Heads' (1). Cp. *Threnodia
Augustalis* l. 464. It was traditionally an image of the unruly mob, e.g. in
Coriolanus III i 92; see further C. A. Patrides, *Shakespeare Quarterly* xvi (1965) 241–6.
542. score] count.
544–68. Zimri] George Villiers (1628–87), second Duke of Buckingham. There
are two biblical Zimris: (i) In Numbers xxv 6–15 Zimri is 'a prince of a chief
house among the Simeonites' who openly takes a Midianite mistress, Cozbi; they
are both killed by the outraged priest Phinehas. This parallel suggests a reference
to Buckingham's notoriously open affair with the Countess of Shrewsbury,
which led to her husband's death after a duel with Buckingham in 1668. Kinsley
notes that this reference is developed in *Absolon's IX Worthies* (1682): 'T' enjoy
his *Cosbi*, He her Husband kill'd; / The rest 'oth story waits to be fulfill'd'. (ii)
In 1 Kings xvi 8–20 Zimri is the servant of Elah, king of Israel, and captain of
half his chariots; he conspired against Elah, killed him, and reigned as king for
seven days; when the people rose up against him, Zimri 'went into the palace
of the king's house, and burnt the king's house over him with fire, and died'.
In 2 Kings ix 31 Jezebel asks, 'Had Zimri peace, who slew his master?'

Buckingham had been a close friend of Charles II in boyhood and exile, and became his chief minister after the fall of Clarendon in 1667 (see Pepys 27 November), though as a member of the 'Cabal' ministry he was less important than he imagined. In January 1674 the Commons voted to ask the King to remove Buckingham 'from all his employments that are held during his Majesty's pleasure, and from his Presence and Councils for ever'; the main charges were that he had broken the Triple Alliance (see l. 175*n*), arranged the alliance with France, and endeavoured 'to take away the affections of the King's good subjects, by saying, "that the King was an arrant knave, and unfit to govern"'; he was also accused of attempting 'a horrid sin not to be named; not to be named at *Rome*, where their other practices are horrid' (Grey ii 270, 245–6); the 'horrid sin' was sodomy: see *POAS* i 187. Buckingham aligned himself with the opposition, cultivated radical associates (Harris (cited in ll. 51–6*n*) 11), and was one of the lords committed to the Tower in 1677 (see ll. 150–99*n*). He was prominent in the investigations into the Popish Plot, but his political power waned; he was not among the opposition leaders brought into the Privy Council in 1679, and did not attend the Oxford Parliament of 1681. His character was described thus by Burnet: 'He had a great liveliness of wit, and a peculiar faculty of turning all things into ridicule with bold figures and natural descriptions. He had no sort of literature: Only he was drawn into chymistry: And for some years he thought he was very near the finding the philosopher's stone . . . He had no principles of religion, virtue, or friendship. Pleasure, frolick, or extravagant diversion was all that he laid to heart. He was true to nothing, for he was not true to himself. He had no steadiness nor conduct . . . He could never fix his thoughts, nor govern his estate, tho' then the greatest in England . . . And he at length ruined both body and mind, fortune and reputation equally . . . since at last he became contemptible and poor, sickly, and sunk in his parts, as well as in all other respects, so that his conversation was as much avoided as ever it had been courted' (i 137–8). Samuel Butler wrote: 'Continual Wine, Women, and Music put false Values upon Things, which by Custom become habitual, and debauch his Understanding so, that he retains no right Notion nor Sense of Things . . . He is as inconstant as the Moon, which he lives under . . . His Mind entertains all Things very freely, that come and go; but like Guests and Strangers they are not welcome, if they stay long— This lays him open to all Cheats, Quacks, and Imposters, who apply to every particular Humour while it lasts, and afterwards vanish . . . His Ears are perpetually drilled with a Fiddlestick. He endures Pleasures with less Patience, than other Men do their Pains' ('A Duke of Bucks' in *Genuine Remains* (1759) ii 73–5). Members of Parliament commented in the Commons in January 1673 on the beliefs and wit of Buckingham and his associates: Mr Russel feared 'the danger the King and the nation are in, from a knot of persons that meet at the Duke's, who have neither Morality nor Christianity, who turn our Saviour and Parliaments into ridicule'; while Mr Sawyer said: 'This new light, a thing called wit, is little less than fanaticism, one degree below madness— Of *Democritus*'s family, he laughs always at all Religion and true Wisdom— We come here to take away examples of such things; such as this Duke, as great as any. This kind of Wit's best ornament is most horrid blasphemy, oaths, and imprecations' (Grey ii 256–7). Buckingham satirized D. in *The Rehearsal* (performed 1671). In 1673 D. wrote to Rochester about Buckingham: 'I hope your Lordship will not omitt the occasion of laughing at the Great Duke of B— who is so oneasy to [him]self by pursueing the honour of Lieutenant Generall which flyes him, that he can enjoy nothing he possesses. Though at the same time, he is so unfit to command an Army, that he is the onely Man in the three Nations who does not know it. Yet he still

545   A man so various that he seemed to be
       Not one, but all mankind's epitome.
       Stiff in opinions, always in the wrong,
       Was everything by starts, and nothing long;
       But in the course of one revolving moon
550   Was chemist, fiddler, statesman, and buffoon:

---

picques him self, like his father, to find another Isle of Rhe in Zealand: thinkes
this dissappointment an injury to him which is indeed a favour, and will not be
satisfyed but with his own ruine and with ours. Tis a strange quality in a man
to love idlenesse so well as to destroy his Estate by it; and yet at the same time
to pursue so violently the most toilesome, and most unpleasant part of
businesse. These observations would easily run into lampoon, if I had not forsworn that dangerous part of wit' (*Letters* 9–10). In 1692 D. commented: 'The
character of "Zimri" in my *Absalom* is, in my opinion, worth the whole poem:
'tis not bloody, but 'tis ridiculous enough; and he for whom it was intended
was too witty to resent it as an injury. If I had railed, I might have suffered for
it justly; but I managed my own work more happily, perhaps more dextrously.
I avoided the mention of great crimes, and applied myself to the representing of
blind sides and little extravagancies; to which, the wittier a man is, he is generally the more obnoxious [i.e. liable]. It succeeded as I wished: the jest went round,
and he was laughed at in his turn who began the frolic' ('Discourse Concerning
Satire', *Poems* iii 424). But Buckingham himself wrote lines 'To Dryden' in his
commonplace book: 'As witches images of wax invent / To torture those theyr
bid to Represent. / And as the true live substance do's decay / Whilst that slight
Idoll melts in flames away / Such, & no lesser witchcraft wounds my name / So
thy ill made Resemblance wasts my fame. / So as the charmed brand consumd
ith' fire / So did Meleagers vitall heat expire. / Poor name! wᵗ medicine for
thee can I finde / But thus with stronger charms, thy charme t' unbinde?'
(*Buckingham: Public and Private Man*, edited by Christine Phipps (1985) 168). See
further J. H. Wilson, *A Rake and His Times* (1954); Winn esp. 178–89.
545–52. This passage is modelled on Juvenal's character of the timeserving Greek
in Rome: *quemuis hominem secum attulit ad nos: / grammaticus, rhetor, geometres, pic-
tor, aliptes, / augur, schoenobates, medicus, magus, omnia nouit / Graeculus esuriens* (*Satire*
iii 75–8: 'Who bears a nation in a single man? / A cook, a conjurer, a rhetori-
cian, / A painter, pedant, a geometrician, / A dancer on the ropes, and a physician.
/ All things the hungry Greek exactly knows', 'The Third Satire of Juvenal'
ll. 136–40). Buckingham's volatility is similarly described in several earlier satires:
'At variance with himself, whose youth and age / Confronted in a mortal feud
engage, / A court-spy and an evil counsellor, / A soph-divine, a mock-philosopher,
/ Many in one, one from himself another, / Two States, two Churches in
the same false brother' (Christopher Wase, *Divination* (in MS, 1666) ll. 105–10;
POAS i 59–60); 'Would fain be something if he knew but what? / A commonwealth's man he owns himself to be, / And, by and by, for absolute monarchy, / Then neither likes, but, some new knicknacks found, / Nor fish nor flesh,
nor square is nor yet round. / Venetian model pleaseth him at night; /
Tomorrow, France is only in the right. / Thus, like light butterflies, much flutter
makes, / Sleeps of one judgment, and of another wakes. / Zealous in morn, he
doth a bishop make, / Yet before night all bishops down he'd take. / He all
things is, but unto nothing true, / All old things hates, but can abide no new'

(*On the Prorogation* (in MS, 1671) ll. 77–89; *POAS* i 182–3); 'First, let's behold
the merriest man alive / Against his careless genius vainly strive; / Quit his dear
ease some deep design to lay / 'Gainst a set time, and then forget the day. / Yet
he will laugh at his best friends and be / Just as good company as Nokes or Lee.
/ But when he aims at reason or at rule / He turns himself the best in ridicule;
/ Let him at business ne'er so earnest sit, / Show him but mirth, and bait that
mirth with wit, / That shadow of a jest shall be enjoyed / Though he left all
mankind to be destroy'd:' (Mulgrave, *An Essay upon Satire* (in MS, 1679) ll. 84–95;
POAS i 405–6); 'Like the late Duke who from a glorious bully / Retir'd from
Court to be the City's cully; / The City's minion, now their scorn and sport, /
There more despis'd than once ador'd at Court; / Who did his fall so wittily
contrive, / In quaint disguise to riot, rant, and swive; / And when he's lost himself in infamy, / Revile the state and rail at monarchy; / The only means true
glory to pursue, / And must be the best way, because 'tis new' (*The Cabal* (in
MS, November 1679, printed February 1680) ll. 78–87; *POAS* ii 332). There
may also be an echo of Sir Positive At-all (a caricature of Sir Robert Howard)
in Shadwell's *The Sullen Lovers* (1668), who says: 'I have considered all mankind . . . and I find you may be a Poet, a Musitian, a Painter, a Divine, a
Mathematician, a States-man'; later he forces a clerk to admit that he is 'a Poet,
Mathematician, Divine, Statesman, Lawyer, Phisitian, Geographer, Musician, and
indeed a *Unus in Omnibus* through all the Arts and Sciences' (i 27, 53).

545. various] versatile in knowledge (*OED* 3a); changeable in character, vacillating
in opinions (*OED* 2a, b). Cp. *varius* in Sallust's character of Catiline (see l. 153*n*).
546. Adapted from the gloss to *Satire* iii 75 in the edition of Juvenal by Lubinus
(1603): *Non vnus homo est, sed ad omnia promtus est & paratus* ('he is not one man,
but is ready and eager for all things': Paul Hammond, *N & Q* ccxxiii (1978) 26).
epitome] not necessarily complimentary: cp. 'He is the *Epitome* of all sorts of
villanies' (*The Character of a Leading Petitioner* 2).
548. Like Hall's 'The Unconstant', who 'is in possibilitie any thing, or everie thing;
nothing in present substance' (*Characters* 110–11).
550. Adapted from Richard Flecknoe's gibe that Killigrew was 'one born to
discredit all the Professions he was of; the *Traveller, Courtier, Soldier, Writer*, and
the *Buffoon*' (*The Life of Tomaso the Wanderer* (1667) 6; Paul Hammond, *EIC* xxxv
(1985) 326–7). *chemist*] Buckingham established a laboratory at Fairfax House in
York, and a factory for making crystal glass at Lambeth; the chemist who devised
the formula for crystal, M. Le Cann, is said to have led him to spend £20,000
(J. H. Wilson (1954) 17). *fiddler*] Buckingham was an accomplished violinist
(Wilson 20); but the word has other connotations: a trifler (*OED* 2), a frivolous
person (*OED* fiddle *v.* 3a), one who fritters away resources (*OED* *v.* 3c), a swindler
(*OED* *v.* 4a). The musical sense had already been applied figuratively to politics
in an attack on L'Estrange: 'He is also a noted Fidler, for he is always playing on
the Strings of the State, which he screws up to a great height, and would stretch
beyond the *Gamut*' (*An Hue and Cry after R.Ls.* [n.d., early 1680s] 3). *statesman,
and buffoon*] This combination is exemplified by the incident during the debate
in the Lords on the Test Act, when Buckingham 'coming last out of the Field,
made a Speech late at night of Eloquent, and well placed Non-sense, showing
how excellently well he could do both ways, and hoping that might do, when
Sense (which he often before used with the highest advantage of Wit, and Reason)
would not' (*A Letter from a Person of Quality* 31). Clarendon noted that in Parliament
Buckingham 'assumed a liberty of speaking when and what he would in a dialect
unusual and ungrave, his similes and other expressions giving occasion of much
mirth and laughter' (*Life* (1827) iii 147).

Then all for women, painting, rhyming, drinking,
Besides ten thousand freaks that died in thinking.
Blessed madman, who could every hour employ
With something new to wish, or to enjoy!
555 Railing and praising were his usual themes,
And both, to show his judgement, in extremes:
So over-violent, or over-civil,
That every man with him was god or devil.
In squandering wealth was his peculiar art:
560 Nothing went unrewarded but desert.
Beggared by fools, whom still he found too late,
He had his jest, and they had his estate.
He laughed himself from court, then sought relief
By forming parties, but could ne'er be chief;
565 For, spite of him, the weight of business fell
On Absalom and wise Achitophel.
Thus wicked but in will, of means bereft,
He left not faction, but of that was left.
    Titles and names 'twere tedious to rehearse
570 Of lords below the dignity of verse.
Wits, warriors, Commonwealthsmen were the best,
Kind husbands and mere nobles all the rest.
And therefore in the name of dullness be
The well-hung Balaam and cold Caleb free;

551. rhyming] Buckingham's mediocre verse is printed in Phipps.
552. freaks] whims (*OED* 1).
559. Reputedly the wealthiest man in England at the Restoration, he spent lavishly (e.g. £30,000 on a suit for Charles's coronation); in August 1671 he owed £123,140 plus £9,097 interest, and a group of friends, including Shaftesbury, were appointed trustees to pay him an annual allowance and settle his debts (J. H. Wilson (1954) 188–9). *peculiar*] particular, special.
560. desert] pronounced 'desart', giving a perfect rhyme.
561–2. Cp. 'From being still cheated by th' same undertakers, / By Levellers, bawds, saints, chemists, and Quakers, / Who make us gold-finders and themselves gold-makers, / *Libera nos*' (*The Litany: of the D. of B.* [1679–80] ll. 28–30; *POAS* ii 195).
562. Cp. 'Wittie to wrong himselfe, a guest in his own house' (Hall, *Characters* 111).
564. In 1668 Pepys heard a rumour that Buckingham 'hath a mind . . . to overthow all the Kingdom and bring in a Commonwealth, wherein he may think to be General of their Army, or to make himself King' (23 November); in 1674 he tried to assemble a following from Presbyterians and old Commonwealthsmen, but with little success (Ogg 526).
572. kind] complacent, tacitly conniving in their wives' adulterous affairs (sense not recorded in *OED*); cp. 'Prologue Spoken at *Mithridates*' l. 13.
574. Balaam] The prophet who followed a path contrary to God's will, but repented (Numbers xxii–xxiv; seen in the NT as an example of sexual errancy: Jude 8–11,

575 And canting Nadab let oblivion damn,
Who made new porridge for the paschal lamb.
Let friendship's holy band some names assure;

Revelation ii 14); here probably Theophilus Hastings, seventh Earl of Huntingdon (1650–1701), whose elder brother D. had commemorated in 'Upon the Death of the Lord Hastings'. One of the peers in Shaftesbury's faction, he proposed a health to Monmouth at a dinner with the Lord Mayor on 1 December 1679, and was instrumental in organizing the petitions which in December 1679 and January 1680 urged the King to meet Parliament. In October 1681 he was received back into Charles's favour. (W. Maurer's identification of Balaam with Sir Francis Winnington is unconvincing (*RES* x (1959) 398–401).) *well-hung*] with large genitals (the meaning 'fluent of tongue', preferred by some editors, is irrelevant here). Huntingdon was credited with this endowment by several contemporaries: in *A Modest Vindication of the Earl of S—y* (1681) 3 he is nicknamed 'Tarsallan'; in *The Quarrel between Frank and Nan* (in MS, 1681) he appears thus: 'Huntingdon with his long tool, / Not as his mark of man but fool, / Whose tail and follies make his life / Only useful to his wife' (ll. 61–4; *POAS* ii 238); cp. also 'The Vindication. 1686' (BodL MS Firth c 15 p. 200); *The Lovers' Session* (in MS, 1687), ll. 175–8 (*Court Satires of the Restoration*, edited by J. H. Wilson (1976) 184); and Roper 115–16. *Caleb*] In Numbers xiii–xiv Caleb holds to his faith in God's providence, and is rewarded by the promise that only he and Joshua shall enter the Promised Land. Two applications have been proposed: (i) Arthur Capel, Earl of Essex (1631–83); he was considered a model Lord Lieutenant of Ireland (1672–7) and on his return allied himself with Shaftesbury. Arrested after the Rye House Plot, he committed suicide in the Tower in July 1683. Evelyn wrote: 'he is a sober, wise, judicious & pondering person, not illiterate beyond the rate of most noble-men in this age, very well Versed in our English Histories & Affaires, Industrious, frugal, Methodical, & every way accomplished' (18 April 1680). Christopher Nesse could not understand the name Caleb for Essex: ''Tis (Hebrew) Hearty, and doth well denote / This *Hearty* lover of his Liege, and Land, / What e're black-mouths to th' contrary him brand: / Yet *Cordial Caleb* is reproach'd as *cold*, / Is it, because for Children he's too old?' (*A Key* 30). See also A. M. Baumgartner, *RES* xiii (1962) 394–7. (ii) Ford, Lord Grey of Warke (1655–1701), identified as Caleb by the Key of 1716; an associate of Monmouth, his wife was rumoured to be Monmouth's mistress (see *A True Relation of a Strange Apparition which appear'd to the Lady Gray* (1681), which is partly an attack on the Whigs, and *Sophronia. Verses Written occasionally by Reading a Late Scandalous Libel Designed, an Aspersion upon the Lady G.* (MS date 19 October 1681 on BL copy)). A later scandal was fictionalized by Aphra Behn in *Love-Letters between a Nobleman and his Sister* (1684–7). Grey was responsible for the House of Lords passing the Habeas Corpus Act when as a teller he jestingly counted a fat lord as ten. See further Cecil Price, *Cold Caleb* (1956). Price infers that Grey was 'cold' because of his manner (71), but it is better to read it as an antithesis to 'well-hung', and thus a reference to Grey's apparent acquiescence in his wife's adultery. It seems impossible to adjudicate between the claims of Essex and Grey for this reference. For other conjectures by contemporary readers see Roper 116–17. *free*] i.e. from the satirist's attention.
575–6. *Nadab*] Nadab and Abihu, the sons of Aaron, 'offered strange fire before the Lord, which he commanded them not. And there went out fire from the Lord, and devoured them, and they died before the Lord' (Leviticus x 1–2). Here,

Some their own worth, and some let scorn secure.
Nor shall the rascal rabble here have place,
580   Whom kings no titles gave, and God no grace:
Not bull-faced Jonas, who could statutes draw
To mean rebellion, and make treason law.
But he, though bad, is followed by a worse,
The wretch who heaven's anointed dared to curse:

William Howard, third baron Howard of Escrick (1626–94), a former Anabaptist
preacher, 'a man of wit and learning, bold and poor, who had run thro' many
parties in religion; . . . He was a man of a pleasant conversation: But he railed so
indecently both at the King and the Clergy, that I was very uneasy in his company' (Burnet i 525, ii 147). In June 1681 Howard was committed to the Tower
on the charge that he was the author of a seditious draft pamphlet found in the
possession of Edward Fitzharris, who was executed for treason. In the Tower
Howard is said to have taken the sacrament in lamb's wool (hot ale mixed with
the pulp of roasted apples) instead of wine: cp. *Absolon's IX Worthies* (1682): 'Then
Prophane *Nadab*, that hates all Sacred things / And on that score abominateth
Kings / With *Mahomet* Wine he damneth; with intent / T' erect his *Paschal-
Lambs-Wool-Sacrament*'. See also Roper 115.
575. *canting*] using religious language affectedly, esp. of Puritans (*OED* 4).
576. *porridge*] soup made from stewed vegetables or meat (*OED* 1); hotchpotch,
unsubstantial stuff, contemptuously applied to the Prayer Book since 1642 (*OED*
3a); in 1662 Pepys heard that 'there hath been a disturbance in a church in Friday-
street; a great many young [people] knotting together and crying out "porridge"
often and seditiously in the church; and took the Common Prayer-Book, they
say, away; and some say did tear it' (24 August).
579. *rascal*] belonging to the rabble (*OED* B1).
581. *Jonas*] Jonah, who was angry when God spared Ninevah after he had prophesied its destruction. Here, Sir William Jones (1631–82); as Attorney-General 1675–9
he directed the Plot prosecutions, and as Member of Parliament 1680–1 promoted, and perhaps drafted, the Exclusion Bills. He was reputedly the author
of *A Just and Modest Vindication of the Proceedings of the Two Last Parliaments* (1682)
which answered *His Majesties Declaration* defending the dissolution of the Oxford
Parliament. Burnet wrote: 'He was raised to that high post merely by merit, and
by his being thought the greatest man of the law: For, as he was no flatterer, but
a man of a morose temper, so he was against all the measures that they took at
Court' (i 558). Referring to Jones's promotion of the Exclusion Bill, a Tory pamphleteer wrote: 'Since *He* the *Jonas* is that rais'd the *Storm*, / Fling Him o'er-
Board' (*A Vote for Moderate Counsels* (1681; Luttrell's copy dated 11 May) 12; W. K.
Thomas 121–2). See also 'On the Bishops throwing out the Bill of Exclusion'
(1679) in BodL MS Firth c 15 p. 45. The Jonah/Jones parallel hardly extends
beyond the verbal echo, but a possible link is their ingratitude: 'Ungrateful *Jonas*
next to *Nineveh* / Pleads Treason *gratis*, that's without his Fee; / Which he n'eer
did before for King or Clown; / That got most by't, yet most disgrac'd the Crown'
(*Absolon's IX Worthies*).
584–629. *Shimei*] When David was fleeing after Absalom's rebellion, he was cursed
by Shimei, one of the house of Saul, who said, 'come out, thou bloody man,
and thou man of Belial . . . the Lord hath delivered the kingdom into the hand
of Absalom thy son'. David prevented one of his followers from killing him,

585 Shimei, whose youth did early promise bring
     Of zeal to God, and hatred to his King,
     Did wisely from expensive sins refrain,
     And never broke the sabbath but for gain:
     Nor ever was he known an oath to vent,

saying, 'It may be . . . that the Lord will requite me good for his cursing this day'
(2 Samuel xvi 5–13). In *The True Presbyterian Without Disguise* (1680) the Presbyterian is described thus: '*Shimei* like, to all the Men he meets, / He spews his
Frantick Venom in the streets: / And tho' he sayes the spirit moves him to it, /
The Devil is that spirit made him do it'. D.'s Shimei is Slingsby Bethel
(1617–97), a successful merchant who lived in Hamburg from 1637 to December
1649; elected Member of Parliament for Knaresborough in 1659 he opposed the
Protectorate of Richard Cromwell on republican grounds. A member of the Council
of State in January 1660, he lived a retired life after the Restoration; on 24 June
1680 he and Henry Cornish were elected sheriffs for London and Middlesex, but
they were unable to serve because they had not sworn the oaths of allegiance
required by the Corporation Act. A second election took place on 14 July, by
which time they had qualified, and both were elected again. The sheriffs were
responsible for the selection of juries, and notoriously Whig juries returned *ignoramus* verdicts, refusing to indict Stephen College in July 1681 and Shaftesbury
in November (cp. 'Prologue to *The Duke of Guise*' ll. 42–3). In February 1681,
with Buckingham's support, Bethel stood for election to Parliament for
Southwark, but came bottom of the poll. The polling was rowdy, as one Tory
pamphlet relates: 'He must thank himself, if by threatening to pull the King's
Watermans Coat over his Ears, he provok'd him to reply, *Ay, Sir, so perhaps you
would my Masters too, if it were in your Power*' (*How and Rich* (1681) 2). Tried in
October for his assault on the waterman, Bethel was convicted, but fined only
five marks by the jury. Burnet wrote: 'Bethel was a man of knowledge, and had
writ a very judicious book of the interests of Princes: But as he was a known
republican in principle, so he was a sullen and wilful man; and turned from the
ordinary way of a Sheriff's living into the extream of sordidness, which was very
unacceptable to the body of the citizens, and proved a great prejudice to the
party . . . The Court was very jealous of this, and understood it to be done on
design to pack juries: So that the party should be always safe, whatever they might
engage in. It was said that the King would not have common justice done him
hereafter against any of them, how guilty soever. The setting up Bethel gave a
great colour to this jealousy; for it was said, he had expressed his approving
the late King's death in very indecent terms. These two persons had never
before received the Sacrament in the Church, being Independents: But they did
it now to qualify themselves for this office, which gave great advantages against
the whole party: It was said, that the serving an end was a good resolver of all
cases of conscience, and purged all scruples' (ii 115–16). On D.'s presentation of
Bethel, see Robert McHenry, *HLQ* xlvii (1984) 253–72.
585. youth did early] Q; early Youth did F.
586. hatred to his King] In *The Vindication of Slingsby Bethel Esq.* (1681) Bethel denied
the allegation that 'being at *Hambrough* at such time as the late Kings Death was
resolved of in *England*, I did there say, That rather than he should want an
Executioner, I would come thence to perform the Office' (3).
589. oath] playing on Bethel's not having taken the oath of allegiance.

590   Or curse, unless against the government.
        Thus heaping wealth by the most ready way
        Among the Jews, which was to cheat and pray;
        The city to reward his pious hate
        Against his master, chose him magistrate:
595   His hand a vare of justice did uphold,
        His neck was loaded with a chain of gold.
        During his office treason was no crime,
        The sons of Belial had a glorious time:
        For Shimei, though not prodigal of pelf,
600   Yet loved his wicked neighbour as himself.
        When two or three were gathered to declaim ⎫
        Against the monarch of Jerusalem,   ⎬
        Shimei was always in the midst of them;   ⎭
        And if they cursed the King when he was by,
605   Would rather curse than break good company.

595. vare] staff carried as a symbol of office.
598. sons of Belial] (i) rebels (e.g. in Deuteronomy xiii 13; 1 Samuel x 27; 2 Samuel
xx 1; 2 Chronicles xiii 7); (ii) false witnesses (1 Kings xxi 10: the story of Naboth's
vineyard, which John Caryll used in his poem about the perjured witnesses to
the Plot; Robert McHenry, *ELN* xxii.2 (1984) 27–30); (iii) the other connota-
tion, of debauchery, seems irrelevant (Judges xix 22; Milton, *PL* i 500–5). Cp.
the collect at Evening Prayer on 30 January, the commemoration of King
Charles the Martyr: 'We thy sinful people fall down before thee, confessing that
thy judgments were right in permitting cruel men, sons of Belial, this day to imbrue
their hands in the bloud of thine Anointed; we having drawn down the same
upon our selves, by the great and long provocations of our sins against thee' (*Book
of Common Prayer* (1662); *Works*). Several Tory pamphlets use the phrase: *A Letter
to the Earl of Shaftesbury . . . From Tom Tell-Troth* (1680) attributes the execution
of Charles I and the Civil War to 'such pernicious Counsels and Designs, as are
now hatching by these Sons of *Belial*, to the present disturbance, if not ruine of
our flourishing Church and Kingdoms' (1); Oates is called 'the *First Son* of *Belial*'
(*The Character of an Ignoramus Doctor* (1681) 1); the Parliamentarian armies are referred
to as 'those Sons of *Belial* [who] fought / Against their King' (*The Glory of the
English Nation* (1681); MS date 30 May 1681 on BL copy); and in *The Progress of
Honesty* 'Two wretched Sons of *Belial* rose / Unhappy *Resolution* to oppose' (12).
But the Whigs also used the phrase, as in *The Freeholders Choice* [1681]: ''Tis these
Sons of *Belial* who in all ages have endeavoured to corrupt and stain the generous minds of Princes with Arbitrary and unmanly Maxims of Government and
State, and have framed for them the weak Policies of Cruelty, Craft, Treachery,
and formal Devotion, instead of Protection, Wisdom, Justice, and Righteousness,
which alone can establish a Nation' (3).
599. pelf] riches.
600. Playing on Matthew xix 19.
601–3. Playing on Christ's promise, 'For where two or three are gathered
together in my name, there am I in the midst of them' (Matthew xviii 20).

If any durst his factious friends accuse,
He packed a jury of dissenting Jews,
Whose fellow-feeling in the godly cause
Would free the suffering saint from human laws;
610   For laws are only made to punish those
Who serve the King, and to protect his foes.
If any leisure time he had from power
(Because 'tis sin to misemploy an hour)
His business was, by writing, to persuade
615   That kings were useless, and a clog to trade:
And that his noble style he might refine,
No Rechabite more shunned the fumes of wine.
Chaste were his cellars, and his shrieval board
The grossness of a city feast abhorred:
620   His cooks with long disuse their trade forgot;
Cool was his kitchen, though his brains were hot.

606–9. When the jury returned a verdict of *ignoramus* in the case of Stephen College,
tried in London in July 1681 for seditious words and actions, 'The Lord Chief
Justice asked the foreman if he did not believe the evidence. He answered he
was not bound to give any reasons. The foreman was one John Wilmer, a professed fanatic, and hackney-bail for all almost that of late have been committed
for treason and have had bail . . . The Lord Chief Justice told the Sheriffs that it
was not fit that such a person should be a juryman. Bethel answered he was a
stranger in the City, and therefore must take others advice' (*HMC Ormonde*,
n.s. vi 96; McHenry, *HLQ* 260).

614–15. Bethel wrote a series of tracts exploring the political and social conditions which advance trade. He does not make the argument attributed to him
here, though he does say that the Netherlands flourished more as a federation of
autonomous provinces than when they were under the rule of a standing General
or Governor (*The Interest of Princes and States* (1680) 110–11; *Works*). An approx-
imation to D.'s charge may be found in *The Present Interest of England Stated* (1671),
where Bethel says that 'the Domestick Interest of *England* . . . lyeth in the
advancement of Trade, by removing all obstructions both in City and Country
. . . especially in giving Liberty of Conscience to all Protestant Non-conformists,
and denying it to Papists' (34).

617. The Rechabites, following the command of their ancestor, drank no wine
(Jeremiah xxxv).

617–21. Bethel had attacked the custom of public feasting long before becoming
sheriff: 'I am not of their opinion, who think popular feastings and good fellowship, called Hospitality, to be the Interest of the Nation . . . For, besides the
provoking of the Judgments of God by such inordinate living, Excess weakens
mens bodies, spends vainly their time, dulls their wits, and makes them unfit for
action and business' (*The Present Interest* 12). Answering the charge that '*I live in
a Garret, and keep no House*', Bethel said: 'The Truth is, being a single Person (as
I have been for many years) and having neither the Concerns of a Family nor
of Trade lying upon me, that I might have a settled and known Being for
such time of the Year as I commonly spend in Town, without the trouble and

Such frugal virtue malice may accuse,
But sure 'twas necessary to the Jews,
For towns once burnt such magistrates require
625   As dare not tempt God's providence by fire.
With spiritual food he fed his servants well,
But free from flesh that made the Jews rebel;
And Moses' laws he held in more account
For forty days of fasting in the mount.
630   To speak the rest, who better are forgot,
Would tire a well-breathed witness of the plot.
Yet Corah, thou shalt from oblivion pass:

---

inconveniency which commonly attends the shifting of Lodgings: I took the House
I now live in, (not the Garrets but) all save the Garrets, Cellars, and one small
Room upon the first Floor, with accommodations suffiecient for a Gentleman
of better Quality than my self' (*The Vindication* 4–5). At the Southwark election
'some Waggs, by the Emblematical Black-Pudding and the famish'd Mouse, intended
an abusive Representation of the Gentleman-Strangers Nine-penny Ordinary abroad,
and his empty Cupboard at home' (*How and Rich* 2).
618. shrieval] of the sheriff.
629. See Exodus xxxiv 28.
630–2. Echoes *Dr. Otes his Vindication* (1680): 'Let not the name of *Otes* live, let
it dye, / And in the Grave of dark Oblivion lye: / Let *Bedloe*, *Otes* and *Dugdale*
be forgot, / For they were not discoverers of this Plot'.
631. well-breathed] well exercised; in training.
632–77. Corah] Korah, Dathan and Abiram rebelled against the priestly authority
of Moses and Aaron, and were punished: 'the earth opened her mouth, and swallowed them up, and their houses, and all the men that appertained unto Korah,
and all their goods' (Numbers xvi). Moses prayed God not to destroy the people
who had followed Korah, and urged them to stand apart. Abraham Wright
commented thus on the passage: 'The same Tongue that prayed against the
Conspirators prayes for the people: as lewd men think to carry it with number;
Corah had so far prevail'd, that he had drawn the multitude to his side. God the
avenger of Treasons would have consumed them at once; *Moses* and *Aaron* pray
for the Rebels; although they were worthy of Death, and nothing but Death
could stop their mouths, yet their merciful Leaders will not buy their own peace
with the loss of such Enemies. O rare and inimitable mercy! the people rise up
against their Governors, their Governors fall *on their faces to God for the people*' (*A
Practical Commentary or Exposition upon the Pentateuch* (1662) 158; *Works*). D.'s Corah
is Titus Oates (1649–1705), the chief witness in the Popish Plot. His father, Samuel,
was a weaver, a chaplain in the New Model Army, and an Anabaptist, who in
1660 was presented to the living of All Saints, Hastings. Titus attended
Westminster School and Merchant Taylors' School, from which he was expelled;
then Gonville and Caius College, Cambridge, from which he was expelled after
two terms, and St John's College, which he left without a degree in 1669 after
a dispute with his tutor over a tailor's bill. He then took orders, and after a curacy
at Sandhurst, Surrey, was presented to the living of Bobbing, Kent, in March
1673. His parishioners complained of his drunkenness and his 'very indecent expressions concerning the mysteries of the Christian religion', and before the end of

Erect thyself, thou monumental brass,
High as the serpent of thy metal made,
635   While nations stand secure beneath thy shade.

the year he was ejected. Joining his father in Hastings, he took up Samuel's quarrel with the local Parker family, accusing the elder Parker of treasonable words,
and his son of sodomy. The former charge was dismissed by the Privy Council,
and the latter by local magistrates; Oates then faced an action for £1,000 damages from the son, and a charge of perjury. He promptly signed up as chaplain
on a frigate bound for Tangier, but on its return was dismissed for sodomy. Early
in 1677 he was appointed chaplain to the Catholic Earl of Norwich's household
in London, was dismissed, and on 3 March 1677 was received into the Roman
Catholic Church. He was sent to Valladolid to study, but was soon sent back to
England when his ignorance of Latin was discovered; after a month in London
he entered the college at St Omer in northern France in December, but was
expelled in June 1678. Returning to London, he took up with his old acquaintance Israel Tonge, and the two concocted the allegations of a Popish Plot which
were put before the King in August 1678 (see l. 108n). Though Oates received
a pension and lodgings in Whitehall during the height of the panic, his standing
declined in the summer of 1681; his evidence for the defence at College's trial
in August was sarcastically handled by Judge Jeffreys; he was moved out of his
lodgings in Whitehall, and was said to have taken lodgings with a Quaker in
Lombard Street; in September his allowance from the King was stopped (cp.
'Prologue Spoken at *Mithridates*' ll. 26–30). In May 1684 Oates was convicted of
scandalum magnatum for calling James a traitor, and fined £100,000, and in May
1685 he was convicted of perjury, fined, whipped, pilloried and imprisoned
for life. Released in December 1688 he was granted a pension by William III.
See Kenyon, *The Popish Plot*, *passim*, and Jane Lane, *Titus Oates* (1949).
633–5. When the people of Israel complained against God and Moses for bringing them out of Egypt into the wilderness, God punished them by sending fiery
serpents; the people repented, and Moses 'made a serpent of brass, and put it
upon a pole, and it came to pass, that if a serpent had bitten any man, when he
beheld the serpent of brass, he lived' (Numbers xxi 5–9). Robert Rowles notes
(privately) that the example of the brazen serpent was used in the *Homily against
Idolatry* (in *Certain Sermons or Homilies* (1676) 139) in an official Anglican argument against Catholic claims for miracles wrought by relics and images; its use
here may therefore imply that Oates has become an idol, about whose salvific
powers specious claims are being made.
633. Erect thyself] This *double entendre* is the closest D. comes to joining in the
vilification of Oates's homosexuality which was frequent in Tory pamphlets,
particularly after the tide had turned against him, e.g. *A Hue and Cry after Dr.
T.O.* (1681): 'He seldom frequents the Company of Women, but keeps private
Communication with four *Bums*, to make good the old Proverb, *Lying together
makes Swine to love . . . with a Masculine Chamber-maid, which he keeps to scour his*
Yard'. See further Paul Hammond, *Figuring Sex between Men from Shakespeare to
Rochester* (2002) 155–71. George McFadden, *Dryden the Public Writer 1660–1685*
(1978) 261–2 notes that Corah is associated with the men of Sodom in the Epistle
of Jude (4–11), where they are denounced as 'ungodly men, turning the grace
of our God into lasciviousness'.   *brass*] This has several connotations: (i) effrontery, impudence (*OED* 4); cp. 'In his *Brazen Forehead* is writ *ABOMINATION*'

What though his birth were base, yet comets rise
From earthy vapours ere they shine in skies:
Prodigious actions may as well be done
By weaver's issue as by prince's son.
640   This arch-attestor for the public good
By that one deed ennobles all his blood.
Who ever asked the witnesses' high race
Whose oath with martyrdom did Stephen grace?
Ours was a Levite, and as times went then
645   His tribe were God Almighty's gentlemen.
Sunk were his eyes, his voice was harsh and loud,

(*The Character of an Ignoramus Doctor* (1681) 1); (ii) in the OT it denotes people
impudent in sin, e.g. in Jeremiah vi 28: 'They are all grievous revolters, walking
with slanders: they are brass and iron; they are all corrupters' (Kinsley); (iii) in
the Civil War, royalist propaganda called a parliamentary spokesman a 'brazen
Head as often as they bid Him speak in defamation of the Kings side' and 'the
states trumpet; for then he does not preach, but is blown; proclaims news, very
loud, the trumpet and his forehead being both of one metal' (P. W. Thomas, *Sir
John Berkenhead* (1969) 119); (iv) echoes Horace, *Carm.* III xxx 1: *exegi monu-
mentum aere perennius* ('I have completed a monument more durable than brass';
Reuben A. Brower, *ELH* xix (1952) 42).

636–7. Comets were thought ominous, often portending national disaster; the
one which appeared in December 1680 was interpreted thus by one Whig writer:
'This present Comet (it's true) is of a menacing Aspect, but if the *New Parliament*
(for whose Convention so many good men pray) continue long to sit, I fear not
but the *Star* will lose its virulence and malignancy' (*The Petitioning-Comet* (1681)
sig. Aʳ). For contemporary views of the origins of comets see *The Wonderful Blazing
Star* (1681) and *AM* ll. 65–72n.

639. *weaver's issue*] 'He is one that preached B—y before the Weavers, in respect
to his Father being one of the same Trade and Tribe' (A *Hue and Cry*); 'The
Monster was begot (as some will have it) by the Gyant *Typhon*, in the shape of a
Broken Tub-preaching Weaver' (*The Character of an Ignoramus Doctor* 1).

641. Embarrassed by his origins, Oates 'would needs be descended from some
Ancient and worshipful stock . . . Heralds were sent for, to make out his
Pedigree, and give him a Blazon . . . And it was engraved on his Table and other
Plate' (Roger North, *Examen* (1740) 223 (Kinsley); cp. Lane, *Titus Oates* 167–8;
William Smith, *Intrigues of the Popish Plot Laid Open* (1685) 15 *bis*).

642–3. Acts vi 9–15.

644–5. Korah was a Levite, one of the tribe which provided the priests.

646–9. The Jesuit John Warner recalled: 'Oates had an extremely stupid mind,
a babbling tongue, the speech of the gutter, and a strident and singsong voice,
so that he seemed to wail rather than to speak. His memory was bad, never repeating accurately what had been said; his brow was low, his eyes small and sunk
deep in his head; his face was flat, compressed in the middle so as to look like
a dish or a discus; on each side were prominent ruddy cheeks; his nose was snub,
his mouth in the very centre of his face, for his chin was almost equal in size to
the rest of his face. His head scarcely protruded from his body and was bowed
towards his chest. The rest of his figure was equally grotesque; more like a beast's
than human, it filled people with contempt' (*The History of English Persecution of*

Sure signs he neither choleric was, nor proud:
His long chin proved his wit, his saintlike grace
A church vermilion and a Moses face.
650   His memory, miraculously great,
Could plots exceeding man's belief repeat;
Which therefore cannot be accounted lies,
For human wit could never such devise.
Some future truths are mingled in his book,
655   But where the witness failed, the prophet spoke.
Some things like visionary flights appear:
The Spirit caught him up, the Lord knows where,
And gave him his rabbinical degree
Unknown to foreign university.

Catholics and the Presbyterian Plot, edited by T. A. Birrell, tr. J. Bligh, Catholic
Record Society xlvii–xlviii (1953–5) ii 415–16; Kinsley). Caricature seems super-
fluous, but cp. *Hue and Cry*: 'His marks are as followeth; The off Leg behind
something shorter than the other, and cloven Foot on the nether side; His Face
Rain-bow-colour, and the rest of his Body black: Two slouching Ears, ready to
be cropp'd the next Spring, if they do not drop off before; His Mouth is in the
middle of his Face, exactly between the upper part of his Forehead and the lower
part of his Chin; He hath a short Neck, which makes him defie the Pillory; A
thin Chin, and somewhat sharp, bending up almost to his Nose; He hath few or no
Teeth on the upper Jaw, but bites with his *Tongue*; His voice something resembles
that of the *Guinney-Pigs*. . . . His eyes are very small, and sunk, and is suppos'd to
be either thick-ey'd, or Moon-blind'; and *The Character of an Ignoramus Doctor*:
'His Eyes are *Murdering* as the *Basilisk*'s; tho' *Blindish* too as the *Batt*'s. With his
Screech-Owl's Voice, he bodes Death and Destruction' (1). But these portraits also
correspond to a literary type, e.g. *The Phanatick Anatomized* (1672): 'His forehead
high, and hard beyond all Story: / His Chin is an extended Promontory. /
His Eyes are small, yet one bigger then t' other, / . . . His Nose is sharp, and
very quick of scent, / . . . His Ears are long, one always hanging down'.
647. choleric] Choler was one of the four humours, causing irascibility. Burton
characterized choleric men as 'bold and impudent, and of a more hairebraine disposition . . . furious, impatient in discourse, stiffe, irrefragable and prodigious in
their tenents, and if they be moved, most violent, outrageous, and ready to disgrace,
provoke any, to kill themselves and others, Arnoldus [adds,] starke mad by fits'
(*The Anatomy of Melancholy* (1621) I. 3. 1. 3; Kinsley).
649. church vermilion] Clerical countenances have traditionally been depicted as rosy.
Moses face] When Moses came down from Mount Sinai 'the skin of his face shone'
(Exodus xxxiv 29).
654. his book] *A True Narrative of the Horrid Plot* (1679).
655. L'Estrange commented: 'He has certainly a strange *Fore-sight*' (*The Observator*
xxxv (20 July 1681)).
656–9. Cp. 'he should (like Dr. *Faustus*) fly over the World, *Unseen*; and converse *Invisibly* with *Grandees* at *Rome, Paris, Madrid, Salamanca*' (*The Character of
an Ignoramus Doctor* 2). Oates claimed to hold the degree of Doctor of Divinity
from Salamanca, but the university denied it. L'Estrange printed the university's
denial (dated 30 April 1682) in *The Observator* ccxxv (17 October 1682).

660   His judgement yet his memory did excel,
       Which pieced his wondrous evidence so well,
       And suited to the temper of the times
       Then groaning under Jebusitic crimes.
       Let Israel's foes suspect his heavenly call,
665   And rashly judge his writ apocryphal;
       Our laws for such affronts have forfeits made:
       He takes his life who takes away his trade.
       Were I myself in witness Corah's place,
       The wretch who did me such a dire disgrace
670   Should whet my memory, though once forgot,
       To make him an appendix of my plot.
       His zeal to heaven made him his prince despise,
       And load his person with indignities:
       But zeal peculiar privilege affords,
675   Indulging latitude to deeds and words;
       And Corah might for Agag's murther call

661. *pieced*] put together from pieces (*OED* 2).

665. *writ*] Q; wit F.

666–71. It was dangerous to cross Oates. In 1679 his former servant John Lane charged him with sodomy; when the jury returned a verdict of *ignoramus*, Oates had Lane indicted and convicted on a charge of trying to stifle the discovery of the Plot, and sued him for heavy damages. See *The Reputation of Dr. Oates . . . Clear'd* (1679) and *An Exact and Faithful Narrative of the Horrid Conspiracy of Thomas Knox, William Osborne, and John Lane, to Invalidate the Testimonies of Dr. Titus Oates, and Mr. William Bedloe* (1680). Adam Elliot also became embroiled with Oates: see his *A Modest Vindication of Titus Oates the Salamanca-Doctor from Perjury: or an Essay to Demonstrate him only forsworn in several Instances* (1682).

667. Cp. 'you take my life / When you do take the means whereby I live' (*The Merchant of Venice* IV i 372–3), and Ecclesiasticus xxxiv 22. Kenyon reckons that Oates gained comparatively little financial reward from the Plot: the lodgings and a maintenance allowance, £116 17s in expenses, royal bounty of £297 10s, and some money from his publications; but none of this lasted (277–8).

671. *appendix*] Oates appended a list of the alleged conspirators to his *A True Narrative of the Horrid Plot* (1679).

672–3. Oates made no direct charges against the King, but he did accuse the Queen of high treason, and her physician Sir George Wakeman with complicity in a plot to poison Charles with her approval (Kinsley).

676–7. *Agag's murther*] Samuel told Saul that God commanded him to destroy Israel's enemies, the Amalekites; Saul did so, but spared their king, Agag. Samuel then rejected Saul for disobeying God, and Samuel himself 'hewed Agag in pieces before the Lord in Gilgal' (1 Samuel xv). D.'s application of this story has been much disputed. There are several general problems: (i) how close a parallel with the OT story should we expect? (ii) how much emphasis is to be put on 'might' (but did not?), 'call' for (but not achieve?), 'coarse' (do we have to find examples of coarse words from Oates? indeed, were Samuel's words coarse?), and 'murther' (literally, or metaphorically?)? (iii) is 'Agag' Oates's opprobrious term, which we

In terms as coarse as Samuel used to Saul.
What others in his evidence did join
(The best that could be had for love or coin)
680 In Corah's own predicament will fall,
For witness is a common name to all.
    Surrounded thus with friends of every sort,
Deluded Absalom forsakes the court;
Impatient of high hopes, urged with renown,
685 And fired with near possession of a crown;

see to be inappropriate, or is it D.'s identification, like the other names? (iv) does
the poem's mode demand a single clear reference, or does it admit of general-
ities, or mischievously contrived ambiguities? Four candidates for 'Agag' have been
proposed: (i) Sir Edmund Berry Godfrey, suggested in contemporary MS annotations and in the 1716 Key. But Godfrey was not the leader of an enemy people
or group, and Oates did not call for his murder – rather, he called for it to be
avenged. Nevertheless, many seventeenth-century readers evidently thought that
D. was implying that Oates arranged Godfrey's murder in order to blame it on
the Catholics. (ii) Lord Chief Justice Scroggs, proposed by E. S. de Beer (*RES*
xvii (1941) 298–309). After Scroggs had cast doubts on Oates's evidence at
Wakeman's trial, Oates brought a charge of misdemeanour before the Privy Council,
which was rejected. Yet this scarcely amounts to a call for his murder, nor is
there any apparent parallel between Scroggs and Agag. (iii) Lord Stafford, proposed by Kinsley (*RES* vi (1955) 295–6, and debate in vii (1956) 411–15); see
also Roper 105. Oates gave the testimony to the Commons on which Stafford
was arrested, and was a witness at his trial; he was therefore instrumental in Stafford's
death. As a Catholic Stafford would be seen by Oates as one of a hostile faction,
though he was by no means their leader. It is not clear that D. would have regarded
Stafford's death as murder. (iv) James, Duke of York, identified as Agag by
Christopher Nesse: 'Where did he [Oates] with affronts the *King* Annoy, / Or
threaten him *his Brother* to Destroy? / As *Samuel* did *Saul* for *Agags* Death' (*A
Key* 34). W. K. Thomas (135–6) supports this identification by saying that 'Oates
repeatedly called for his murder or execution for treason'. Thomas cites no evidence, but Roger L'Estrange quotes Oates as having called James a traitor and
said 'He shall be hang'd' (*A Brief History of the Times* (1687) i 151–2), and *The
Account of the Manner of Executing a Writ of Inquiry* (1684) 12–13, which reports
Oates's trial for *scandalum magnatum*, cites evidence that Oates had called for James
to be hanged. Thomas suggests that by making Oates refer to James as Agag, D.
exposes Oates's exaggerated view of Roman Catholics as enemies. J. R. Crider
notes that Charles I had been called 'Agag' by his opponents, so that Oates's attack
on James is associated with the execution, or murder, of Charles I (*ELN* xxi (1983)
34–42). It is impossible now to be certain about this reference, but James seems
the best suggestion, particularly since the immediately preceding lines refer to Oates's
offensive handling of the King and Queen: this charge is the culmination of the
passage on Oates, and an allusion to anyone but James would be anticlimactic.
679. *coin*] See l. 922n.
681. Echoes '*Homo*, is a commune name to all men', William Lily and John Colet,
A Shorte Introduction of Grammar (1549) 7; a familiar seventeenth-century tag, as
in *1 Henry IV* II i 94.

Th' admiring crowd are dazzled with surprise,
And on his goodly person feed their eyes.
His joy concealed, he sets himself to show,
On each side bowing popularly low;
690   His looks, his gestures and his words he frames,
And with familiar ease repeats their names.
Thus, formed by nature, furnished out with arts,
He glides unfelt into their secret hearts;
Then with a kind compassionating look,
695   And sighs bespeaking pity ere he spoke,
Few words he said, but easy those and fit,
More slow than Hybla drops, and far more sweet:
            'I mourn, my countrymen, your lost estate,
Though far unable to prevent your fate;
700   Behold a banished man, for your dear cause
Exposed a prey to arbitrary laws!
Yet O that I alone could be undone,
Cut off from empire, and no more a son!
Now all your liberties a spoil are made,   ⎫
705   Egypt and Tyrus intercept your trade,   ⎬
And Jebusites your sacred rites invade.   ⎭
My father, whom with reverence yet I name,
Charmed into ease, is careless of his fame;

---

686. *admiring*] wondering.

688. *His joy concealed*] Q; Dissembling Joy F.

690. *frames*] adapts to the occasion.

693–7. Cp. Spenser: Despair's 'subtill tongue, like dropping honny, mealt'th / Into the hart, and searcheth euery vaine' (*FQ* I ix 31 ll. 5–6).

697. *Hybla*] a town in Sicily celebrated for its honey (cp. Virgil, *Ecl.* vii 37).

698. *estate*] legal right to property (*OED* 11); political constitution (*OED* 8).

699. *far unable*] far from able (*OED* far 4b, a seventeenth-century idiom).

700. *a banished man*] Monmouth had been banished from England by Charles in 1679, but his absence from London in 1680 was part of his campaign to attract popular support (see ll. 18–30n, 729–38n).

701. *arbitrary laws*] The Whigs alleged that Charles was intent upon arbitrary government, i.e. rule without consultation with Parliament, and using the royal prerogative to suspend laws.

705. *Egypt and Tyrus*] France and Holland. Dutch merchant ships had established a strong position in transporting the products of other countries; this commercial rivalry led to three Dutch wars (see *AM* ll. 1–6 and headnote; Ogg 221–2). From France many luxury goods were imported into England, resulting in an annual trade deficit of about £1 million (Ogg 221). Ezekiel xxvii describes the glories of Tyre as a trading city, and its destruction.

And bribed with petty sums of foreign gold
710   Is grown in Bathsheba's embraces old;
Exalts his enemies, his friends destroys,
And all his power against himself employs.
He gives, and let him give my right away,
But why should he his own, and yours, betray?
715   He only, he can make the nation bleed,
And he alone from my revenge is freed.

709. Charles received extensive subsidies from Louis XIV, and although these were secret, the fact that he had asked for them was revealed in the House of Commons on 19 December 1678, when Ralph Montagu, formerly ambassador in Paris, produced letters which he had received earlier that year from the Earl of Danby, saying that the King expected to have 6 million livres (£300,000) annually for three years on making peace with France (Grey vi 348).

710. Bathsheba] The biblical Bathsheba was one of David's wives; the parallel does not extend to the way David acquired her, which was by arranging the death of her husband Uriah (2 Samuel xi). Here, Louise de Kéroualle (1649–1734). A Breton, she was maid of honour to Charles's sister Henrietta (1668–70) and then to Queen Catherine. She became Charles's mistress in October 1671. In 1673 she was created Duchess of Portsmouth, with apartments in Whitehall and an income of some £10,000 a year. She was suspected of influencing Charles in the French interest. During the Popish Plot she was subjected to much abuse: some Members of Parliament drafted articles of impeachment against her, and there was an attempt to prosecute her as a common prostitute. She contemplated leaving for France, but stayed and weathered the storm. Although she had advised Charles to exile Monmouth in 1679, she effected a rapprochement with Monmouth and Shaftesbury in 1680, and favoured Exclusion (Haley 502–3, 588, 599). She was the subject of many satires directed particularly against her influence over the King. *Britannia and Raleigh* (in MS, 1674–5), perhaps by John Ayloffe, says that Charles's 'fair soul, transform'd by that French dame, / Had lost all sense of honor, justice, fame. / Like a tame spinster in's seragl' he sits, / Besieg'd by whores, buffoons, and bastard chits; / Lull'd in security, rolling in lust, / Resigns his crown to angel Carwell's trust' (ll. 117–22; *POAS* i 233). *Colin*, by the Earl of Dorset (in MS, 1679; *POAS* ii 167–75), depicts her selling her place as royal mistress. The *Satire on Old Rowley* (in MS, 1680) refers to 'slimy Portsmouth's creatures / . . . Who would reform this brutal nation, / And bring French slavery in fashion' (ll. 20–4), and the same poem presents Charles in terms which state more viciously Absalom's charge in *AA* ll. 708–10: 'Silly and sauntering he goes / From French whore to Italian; / Unlucky in what'er he does, / An old ill-favor'd stallion. / Fain the good man would live at ease, / And ev'ry punk and party please' (ll. 7–12; *POAS* ii 184–5). *Rochester's Farewell* (in MS, 1680) comments on her political moves: 'O Portsmouth, foolish Portsmouth! not to take / The offer the great faction once did make, / When cringing at thy feet e'en Monmouth bow'd, / The golden calf that's worship'd by the crowd: / But then for York (who now despises thee) / To leave both him and pow'rful Shaftesbury!' (ll. 206–11; *POAS* ii 227). See also *The King's Answer* and *A Satire* (*POAS* ii 255, 291). Some early readers thought that the reference was to Charles's previous mistress, the Duchess of Cleveland (Roper 109).

Take then my tears' (with that he wiped his eyes),
"'Tis all the aid my present power supplies.
No court informer can these arms accuse,
720   These arms may sons against their fathers use;
And 'tis my wish the next successor's reign
May make no other Israelite complain.'
      Youth, beauty, graceful action seldom fail,
But common interest always will prevail:
725   And pity never ceases to be shown
To him who makes the people's wrongs his own.
The crowd (that still believe their kings oppress)
With lifted hands their young Messiah bless,
Who now begins his progress to ordain
730   With chariots, horsemen and a numerous train.
From east to west his glories he displays,
And like the sun the promised land surveys.
Fame runs before him as the morning star,
And shouts of joy salute him from afar;
735   Each house receives him as a guardian god,
And consecrates the place of his abode:
But hospitable treats did most commend
Wise Issachar, his wealthy western friend.

717. Cp. the gesture of the duplicitous Ulysses in Ovid, *Met.* xiii 132–3 (David
Hopkins, *N & Q* ccxxiv (1979) 523).
723. *action*] gesture, oratorical management of the body and features (*OED* 6a);
histrionic personation (*OED* 12).
727. *believe*] Q; believes F.
728. *With lifted hands*] the OT posture for blessing (e.g. in Leviticus ix 22).
729–38. In July and August 1680 Monmouth made a triumphal progress from
London through the West Country, defying Charles's prohibition (D'Oyley 168–74;
Ogg 645; *A True Narrative of the Duke of Monmouth's Late Journey into the West*
(1680)). Cp. 2 Samuel xv 1–6: 'Absalom prepared him chariots and horses, and fifty
men to run before him . . . Absalom said moreover, Oh that I were made judge
in the land, that every man which hath any suit for cause might come unto me,
and I would do him justice! . . . so Absalom stole the hearts of the men of Israel'.
733. *morning star*] The planet Venus, which precedes the rising of the sun; Christ
is described as the morning star in Revelation xxii 16, and Satan is a misleading
morning star in *PL* v 708–10.
738. *Issachar*] Early readers proposed various identifications (see Roper 107–8), but
the reference is probably to Thomas Thynne (1648–82), of Longleat, Wiltshire,
a wealthy supporter of Monmouth who entertained him on his western progress.
In Genesis xlix 14–15 Jacob describes his son Issachar as 'a strong ass couching
down between two burdens: And he saw that rest was good, and the land that
it was pleasant; and bowed his shoulder to bear, and became a servant unto
tribute'. Kinsley suggests that Thynne's 'two burdens' were his financial support
of Monmouth and his unhappy marriage to Lady Ogle (*RES* vi (1955) 296–7).

This moving court that caught the people's eyes,
740   And seemed but pomp, did other ends disguise:
Achitophel had formed it with intent
To sound the depths, and fathom, where it went,
The people's hearts, distinguish friends from foes,
And try their strength before they came to blows.
745   Yet all was coloured with a smooth pretence
Of specious love, and duty to their prince;
Religion, and redress of grievances,
Two names that always cheat and always please,
Are often urged; and good King David's life
750   Endangered by a brother and a wife.
Thus in a pageant show a plot is made,
And peace itself is war in masquerade.
O foolish Israel! never warned by ill,
Still the same bait, and circumvented still!
755   Did ever men forsake their present ease,
In midst of health imagine a disease,
Take pains contingent mischiefs to foresee,
Make heirs for monarchs, and for God decree?
What shall we think? Can people give away,
760   Both for themselves and sons, their native sway?
Then they are left defenceless to the sword

741–4. It seems likely that Shaftesbury planned Monmouth's expedition in order
to demonstrate his popular support (Haley 586–7).
742. depths] Q; depth F.
747. These had been Parliament's concerns before the outbreak of the Civil War.
749–50. Oates did not include James among the Popish Plot conspirators, but
Stephen Dugdale did implicate him in March 1679, and the resulting alarm led
to the Commons' resolution of 27 April (see ll. 353–60*n*; Kenyon, *The Popish
Plot* 176–7). The Queen was implicated by Oates in Sir George Wakeman's alleged
plot to poison the King (Kenyon 125–31).
752. masquerade] Whigs accused Tories of being 'masqueraders' in concealing their
political and religious aims: see D'Urfey's Prologue to *Sir Barnaby Whigg* (staged
autumn 1681) l. 23 (Danchin no. 308).
754. circumvented] outwitted (*OED* 3).
759–810. In this passage D. examines the political theories underlying the
Exclusion Crisis. The discussion falls into four parts: see ll. 759–64*n*; ll. 765–76*n*;
ll. 777–94*n*; ll. 795–810*n*. The passage is well analysed by M. J. Conlon, *JEGP*
lxxviii (1979) 17–32.
759–64. D. begins with one of the main Whig arguments, that the fundamental
rights of the people need to be safeguarded against the threat of arbitrary power
represented by James. One Whig wrote: 'Our Ancestors might refrain and limit
us in the usage of those things which we derive from them; yet they could not
refrain and limit us in those things which we have a right unto by the Law of

Nature' (*A Letter from a Gentleman in the City* (1680) 14; Conlon 21). D. concedes that there is a danger in the absolutist monarchical theory as expounded by Hobbes in *Leviathan* (1651), who had argued that the people emerge from a state of nature (in which every man had a right to everything) by transferring their natural rights to a single sovereign; this theory makes the people completely vulnerable to their sovereign, since his power is unbounded and he is accountable only to God. Such a view was still held by some Tories: 'After the People have conveyed their Power unto a person to be King; there remains no superintendent power in them over him; for they have divested themselves of all power by the conveyance; if it were conveyed with conditions, then under those conditions it may be held against them; if absolutely, then it may be held absolutely over them' (*Antidotum Britannicum* (1681) 19). D. dissociates himself from such extreme positions, and 'by affirming the native rights and privileges of English subjects, Dryden gains a moral frame of reference for his subsequent argument against Exclusion. Rights and privileges conferred by the law of nature cannot be limited or resumed arbitrarily from one generation to the next. This much the reader must grant, and Dryden can now apply this shared assumption to the subject of Exclusion, an act that implied the power of subjects to revoke or resume the king's title from one generation to the next' (Conlon 21).

759–60. D. returns to this point in 'The Tenth Satire of Juvenal' ll. 128–9.

765–76. D. now considers the Whig argument that kings are only entrusted with power by the people, who may resume it at will (cp. ll. 409–12); this argument assumes that the people had included terms allowing for their resumption of power in the original contract by which kingship was set up (which D. implies is unlikely). Rather, D.'s view is that all succeeding generations are bound by the original establishment of government as firmly as they are implicated in the original sin of Adam (and many seventeenth-century writers thought that it was the Fall which rendered government necessary in the first place: Conlon 23–5). The idea that kings are only entrusted with power had a republican ancestry. Conlon notes that John Bradshaw told Charles I at his trial that the King was 'but an officer in trust and he ought to discharge that trust for the people, and if he do not they are to take order for the . . . punishment of such an offending governor' (22–3). Milton, in *The Tenure of Kings and Magistrates* (1649), insisted that 'the power of Kings and Magistrates is nothing else, but what is only derivative, transferr'd and committed to them in trust from the People, to the Common good of them all, in whom the power yet remaines fundamentally, and cannot be tak'n from them, without a violation of thir natural birthright' (*Complete Prose Works* iii 202). For the influence of Milton on Whig thought see George F. Sensabaugh, *That Grand Whig Milton* (1952). Henry Neville in *Plato Redivivus* (1681) says: 'our Prince has no Authority of his own, but what was first intrusted in him by the Government, of which he is Head' (119; and cp. the reply to Neville, *Antidotum Britannicum* 14). The idea was also advanced by Locke in his *Two Treatises of Government* (composed 1679–80; published 1689; edited by Peter Laslett (1970) 444–5; for Locke on 'trust' see 112–14). Whig thinkers argued that because the King had abrogated the people's right to redress of grievances through Parliament, he had forfeited his trust and could therefore be resisted as a private individual who had no authority (Ashcraft 322; 336; 403–4). This argument is countered by W. P., who says that 'The King hath His Title to the Crown, and to His Kingly Office and Power, not by way of Trust from the People, but by inherent Birthright, immediately from God, Nature, and the Law' (*The Divine Right of Kings Asserted* [*c.* 1680] 2). Conlon notes that D. uses the conventional explanation for the origins of government in Adam's fall to undermine the idea of an original contract or

Of each unbounded arbitrary lord:
And laws are vain by which we right enjoy,
If kings unquestioned can those laws destroy.
765 Yet if the crowd be judge of fit and just,
And kings are only officers in trust,
Then this resuming cov'nant was declared
When kings were made, or is for ever barred:
If those who gave the sceptre could not tie
770 By their own deed their own posterity,
How then could Adam bind his future race?
How could his forfeit on mankind take place?
Or how could heavenly justice damn us all,
Who ne'er consented to our father's fall?
775 Then kings are slaves to those whom they command,
And tenants to their people's pleasure stand.
Add that the power for property allowed
Is mischievously seated in the crowd:
For who can be secure of private right
780 If sovereign sway may be dissolved by might?
Nor is the people's judgement always true:

covenant, invoking a providential view of history which is at odds with the voluntarist principles of trust, covenant and consent (24–5).

765, 778. *crowd*] a sly shift from 'people'.

772. *take place*] take effect (*OED* 27a).

777–94. Milton in *The Tenure* had argued that 'to say, as is usual, the King hath as good right to his Crown and dignitie, as any man to his inheritance, is to make the Subject no better than the Kings slave, his chattel, or his possession that may be bought and sould' (iii 203). According to the Whig view, no man can be secure and free in a system where sovereign power is the birthright of one man. But D. now turns this question on its head, suggesting that 'if the king can be deprived of his right by a *de facto* power, then no man's right is secure. This was another royalist tactic, designed to show that the king's prerogatives were the best guarantee of the subject's privileges . . . These lines effect a deliberate inversion of the commonwealth argument, suggesting that the threat of arbitrary rule comes from Whig attempts to transform the king's office into a fiduciary power, not from the Stuart succession' (Conlon 25–6). D. also counters the Whig stress on 'property' (see l. 536n). One Tory writer had represented a Whig as arguing: 'the natural part of the Government of *England*, which is Power, is by means of Property in the hands of the People; and they having the greatest interest in the Property, they will and must have it in the Empire' (*Antidotum Britannicum* 30). D.'s argument shows that Whig theory would actually lead to the destruction of 'property' – in the sense both of 'material possessions' and 'political rights' – by mob rule.

777. *Add that the power*] Q; That Pow'r, which is *F*.

> The most may err as grossly as the few,
> And faultless kings run down by common cry
> For vice, oppression and for tyranny.
> 785 What standard is there in a fickle rout,
> Which flowing to the mark runs faster out?
> Nor only crowds, but Sanhedrins may be
> Infected with this public lunacy,
> And share the madness of rebellious times
> 790 To murther monarchs for imagined crimes.
> If they may give and take whene'er they please,
> Not kings alone (the Godhead's images)
> But government itself at length must fall
> To nature's state, where all have right to all.
> 795 Yet grant our lords the people kings can make,

784. These charges had been levelled at Charles in many poems from the late 1660s onward; see *POAS* i and ii *passim*, and Hammond, *Making of Restoration Poetry* 107–36.

785. standard] principle, means of judgement (*OED* 10b).

786. i.e. which fluctuates like the tides: 'the higher the tide and consequently the greater the distance between high and low water-mark (the interval of time between tides remaining the same), the more rapid is the fall of the water at the ebb' (Verrall 87). *mark*] boundary, limit (*OED* 1).

788. lunacy] The moon was thought to produce madness as well as influencing the tides (Verrall).

794. Cp. Hobbes's description of the state of nature: 'during the time men live without a common Power to keep them all in awe, they are in that condition which is called Warre; and such a warre, as is of every man, against every man. . . . It is consequent also to the same condition, that there be no Propriety [i.e. property], no Dominion, no *Mine* and *Thine* distinct; but onely that to be every mans that he can get; and for as long, as he can keep it' (*Leviathan* (1651) 62–3). Whig thinkers made the concept of the state of nature an important part of their political philosophy, since it implied a contractual theory of government (e.g. Henry Neville, *Plato Redivivus* 29). Locke considered that England in 1681 had been reduced to a state of nature, since the King was governing by force without Parliament; similarly one of the arguments for Exclusion was that a Catholic king would be at war with his people, returning the country to a state of nature (Ashcraft 330–1, 190–6 and *passim*). The Whigs saw absolutism returning England to a state of nature: D. typically reverses his opponents' point, seeing the state of nature resulting from their policies.

795–810. Finally D. appeals for peace and quiet (cp. *RL* ll. 446–50); minor reforms may be permissible, but to change a settled government runs the risk of destroying it completely. D. 'proceeds to locate monarchy within the tradition of England's ancient constitution in a manner that mutes the absolutist implications of divine right but retains the divine source of the king's authority . . . The idea of an ancient constitution had evolved out of the history of English common law. Both the king and parliament were thought to be subject to the fundamental or common laws of the realm, which, in turn, formed and informed its constitution. Throughout the seventeenth century, moderate royalists accepted the idea of the

What prudent men a settled throne would shake?
For whatsoe'er their sufferings were before,
That change they covet makes them suffer more.
All other errors but disturb a state,
800   But innovation is the blow of Fate.
If ancient fabrics nod, and threat to fall,
To patch the flaws and buttress up the wall
Thus far 'tis duty; but here fix the mark,
For all beyond it is to touch our ark.
805   To change foundations, cast the frame anew,
Is work for rebels who base ends pursue,
At once divine and human laws control,
And mend the parts by ruin of the whole.
The tampering world is subject to this curse,
810   To physic their disease into a worse.
        Now what relief can righteous David bring?
How fatal 'tis to be too good a king!
Friends he has few, so high the madness grows;
Who dare be such must be the people's foes.

---

ancient constitution, but insisted that the king's prerogatives were as essential to
the constitution as were the powers of parliament' (Conlon 28; see also J. G. A.
Pocock, *The Ancient Constitution and the Feudal Law* (1957, 1987)). Kinsley cites
the Epistle Dedicatory to *All for Love* (1678) where D. says: 'Neither is it enough
for them to answer that they only intend a Reformation of the Government, but
not the Subversion of it: On such pretences all Insurrections have been founded:
'Tis striking at the Root of Power, which is Obedience. Every Remonstrance
of private Men, has the seed of Treason in it' (*Works* xiii 7).
799. but] only.
800. innovation] (i) the alteration of what is established (*OED* 1 and 2; all its
sixteenth- and seventeenth-century examples are pejorative); (ii) revolution,
insurrection (*OED* 1b and 2b).
801. nod] sway away from the perpendicular (*OED* 3).
803. mark] boundary, limit (*OED* 1).
804. touch our ark] The Ark of the Covenant was a wooden coffer containing the
stone tablets of the law which Moses had brought down from Mount Horeb.
When it was being moved by David to Jerusalem, Uzzah put out his hand to
steady it, as the oxen were making it tilt, and was struck dead by God for presuming to touch it (1 Chronicles xiii 9–10); cp. Preface to *RL* l. 14. In this case
the *ark* stands for the ancient constitution.
805–8. Echoing Marvell: 'To ruin the great work of time, / And cast the kingdoms old / Into another mould' ('An Horatian Ode' ll. 34–6); D. echoes Marvell's
lines again in 'Of the Pythagorean Philosophy' ll. 264–5.
807. control] challenge, find fault with (*OED* 3b).
809. tampering] scheming, plotting (*OED* 2); meddling (esp. medically, *OED* 4b;
cp. l. 810).
810. physic] medicate.

815   Yet some there were, ev'n in the worst of days,
      Some let me name, and naming is to praise.
        In this short file Barzillai first appears:
      Barzillai crowned with honour and with years.
      Long since the rising rebels he withstood
820   In regions waste beyond the Jordan's flood,
      Unfortunately brave to buoy the state,
      But sinking underneath his master's fate.
      In exile with his godlike prince he mourned,
      For him he suffered, and with him returned.
825   The court he practised, not the courtier's art;
      Large was his wealth, but larger was his heart,
      Which well the noblest objects knew to choose,
      The fighting warrior and recording Muse.
      His bed could once a fruitful issue boast,
830   Now more than half a father's name is lost.
      His eldest hope, with every grace adorned,

817–59. Barzillai] In the OT an old man of Gilead loyal to David during Absalom's rebellion (2 Samuel xvii 27–9; xix 31–9). Here, James Butler, Duke of Ormonde (1610–88). He commanded Charles I's army against the Irish rebels in 1641, and was Lord Lieutenant of Ireland from 1644 until he was forced into exile in 1650. During the Commonwealth he was a close adviser to Prince Charles, and suffered severe financial hardship; in 1660 he was rewarded with a dukedom and recouped some of his losses. He served again as Lord Lieutenant 1661–9 (removed at Buckingham's instigation) and 1677–85, surviving strong Whig criticism. Thomas Carte recorded that 'Once in a quarter of a year, he used to have the Marquis of *Hallifax*, the Earls of *Mulgrave*, *Dorset* and *Danby*, Mr. *Dryden*, and others of that set of men at supper, and then they were merry and drank hard' (*An History of the Life of James, Duke of Ormonde*, 3 vols (1735–6) ii 554). In 1683 D. dedicated to Ormonde the collaborative translation of Plutarch which he had supervised.

825. practised] performed the duties of (*OED* 2; cp. 'to practise religion'), rather than 'frequent, haunt' (*OED* 7b, citing this line; Kinsley). Ormonde was punctilious in maintaining the dress and hospitality appropriate to his position. Burnet commented: 'A man every way fitted for a Court: Of a graceful appearance, a lively wit, and a cheerful temper: A man of great expense, decent even in his vices, for he always kept up the form of religion' (i 130; Kinsley).

829–30. Seven of Ormonde's eight sons had now died; his two daughters survived him (Carte, *An History* ii 551).

831–53. Thomas, Earl of Ossory (1634–80), Ormonde's eldest son. He distinguished himself in the Second and Third Dutch Wars, and fighting for the Dutch against France in 1677–8. Ossory defended his father vigorously against attacks by Shaftesbury in the Lords. On his death Evelyn wrote: 'Surely his Majestie never lost a worthier Subject; nor Father, a better, & more dutifull sonn, a loving, good-natured, generous and perfectly obliging friend, & one who had don innumerable kindnesses to severall persons, before they so much as knew it; nor advanc'd he any but such as were worthy; None more brave, more modest, none more humble, sober, & every way virtuous: O unhapy *England*! in this illustrious

By me (so heaven will have it) always mourned,
And always honoured, snatched in manhood's prime
By' unequal Fates, and providence's crime.
835 Yet not before the goal of honour won,
All parts fulfilled of subject and of son;
Swift was the race, but short the time to run.
O narrow circle, but of power divine,
Scanted in space, but perfect in thy line!
840 By sea, by land, thy matchless worth was known,
Arms thy delight, and war was all thy own:
Thy force infused the fainting Tyrians propped,
And haughty Pharaoh found his fortune stopped.
O ancient honour, O unconquered hand,
845 Whom foes unpunished never could withstand!

---

persons losse' (*Diary*, 26 July 1680). In 1683 D. wrote to Ormonde: 'Never was one Soul more fully infus'd into anothers breast: Never was so strong an impression made of vertue, as that of your Graces into him: But though the stamp was deep, the subject which receiv'd it was of too fine a composition to be durable. Were not priority of time and nature in the case, it might have been doubted which of you had been most excellent: But Heaven snatch'd away the Copy to make the Original more precious. I dare trust my self no farther on this subject, for after years of mourning, my sorrow is yet so green upon me, that I am ready to tax Providence for the loss of that Heroick Son: Three Nations had a general concernment in his Death, but I had one so very particular, that all my hopes are almost dead with him; and I have lost so much that I am past the danger of a second Shipwreck. But he sleeps with an unenvy'd commendation: And has left your Grace the sad Legacy of all those Glories which he deriv'd from you' (*Works* xvii 229–30). D. dedicated the *Fables* (1700) to Ossory's son, the second Duke of Ormonde.

832–4. From Virgil: *iamque dies, nisi fallor, adest, quem semper acerbum, / semper honoratum (sic di voluistis) habebo* (*Aen.* v 49–50; 'already, if I am not mistaken, the day is at hand which I shall keep always as a day of grief, always as one of honour (such, O gods, was your will)'; Christie).

834. unequal Fates] From Virgil's *fatis iniquis* (*Aen.* ii 257, x 380). *unequal*] unjust, unfair (*OED* 4).

835–7. Cp. 'To the Memory of Mr Oldham' ll. 7–10n.

836. Cp. 'Hee entered well, by vertuous parts, / . . . A perfect Patriot, and a noble friend, / But most, a vertuous Sonne' (Ben Jonson, 'To the immortall memorie, and friendship of that noble paire, Sir Lucius Cary, and Sir H. Morrison' ll. 33, 46–7).

838–9. The circle was an image of perfection; cp. Jonson, *Epigrammes* xcviii 3 (drawing on Horace, *Serm.* II vii 86–8) and cxxviii 8; and D.'s 'Upon the Death of the Lord Hastings' l. 27; 'Heroic Stanzas' ll. 18–20; *Eleonora* ll. 272–3.

839. Scanted in space] Cp. 'For, what is life, if measur'd by the space, / Not by the act?' (Jonson, 'To the immortall memorie' ll. 21–2). *Scanted*] limited (*OED* 3c).

844–5. Cp. Virgil's tribute to Marcellus: *heu pietas, heu prisca fides invictaque bello / dextera! non illi se quisquam impune tulisset / obvius armato* (*Aen.* vi 878–80; 'alas for piety, alas for ancient honour and the right hand invincible in war! no one

But Israel was unworthy of thy name:
Short is the date of all immoderate fame.
It looks as heaven our ruin had designed,
And durst not trust thy fortune and thy mind.

850 Now free from earth, thy disencumbered soul
Mounts up and leaves behind the clouds and starry pole.
From thence thy kindred legions may'st thou bring
To aid the guardian angel of thy King.
Here stop my Muse, here cease thy painful flight;

855 No pinions can pursue immortal height:
Tell good Barzillai thou canst sing no more,
And tell thy soul she should have fled before:
Or fled she with his life, and left this verse
To hang on her departed patron's hearse?

860 Now take thy steepy flight from heaven, and see
If thou canst find on earth another he;
Another he would be too hard to find,
See then whom thou canst see not far behind.
Zadok the priest, whom, shunning power and place,

865 His lowly mind advanced to David's grace;

would have advanced unscathed against him in arms'; Reuben A. Brower,
PMLA lv (1940) 133).

846–7. name . . . fame] Q; Birth . . . Worth F.

847. Translates Martial VI xxix 7: *immodicis brevis est aetas, et rara senectus* ('short
is the life of those who are uncommonly endowed, and they rarely reach old
age'); cp. 'To the Memory of Anne Killigrew' l. 147.

850–1. Echoes Virgil: *Candidus insuetum miratur limen Olympi / sub pedibusque videt
nubes et sidera Daphnis* (*Ecl.* v 56–7: 'Daphnis in radiant beauty marvels at heaven's
unfamiliar threshold, and beneath his feet beholds the clouds and the stars'; Brower
133).

855. pinions] wings.

858–9. Friends often attached epitaphs to a hearse, the structure which was erected
over a bier to carry arms and devices (Kinsley).

860. steepy] precipitous (*OED*'s first example of the word applied to movement
rather than place).

864–5. Zadok] When David fled during Absalom's rebellion, Zadok the priest
and the Levites took the ark and followed him, but David sent them back to
Jerusalem (2 Samuel xv 24–9). D.'s Zadok is William Sancroft (1617–93),
appointed Dean of St Paul's in 1664, where he was energetic in promoting the
rebuilding of the cathedral after the Great Fire, and Archbishop of Canterbury
in 1678. Burnet wrote sourly of him: 'He was a man of solemn deportment, had
a sullen gravity in his looks, and was considerably learned. He had put on a mona-
stick strictness, and lived abstracted from company. These things, together with
his living unmarried, and his being fixed in the old maxims of high loyalty, and
a superstitious valuing of little things, made the Court conclude, that he was a
man, who might be entirely gained to serve all their ends; or, at least, that he

With him the Sagan of Jerusalem,
Of hospitable soul and noble stem;
Him of the western dome, whose weighty sense
Flows in fit words and heavenly eloquence:
870   The prophets' sons by such example led,
To learning and to loyalty were bred,
For colleges on bounteous kings depend,
And never rebel was to arts a friend.
To these succeed the pillars of the laws,
875   Who best could plead, and best can judge a cause.
Next them a train of loyal peers ascend:
Sharp-judging Adriel the Muses' friend,

---

would be an unactive speculative man, and give them little opposition in any
thing that they might attempt . . . He was a dry, cold man, reserved, and peevish;
so that none loved him, and few esteemed him: Yet the high church party were
well pleased with his promotion' (i 553–4). But D. is correct in saying that Sancroft
lacked personal ambition; he was a devoted guardian of the Church of England
who attempted to convert James from Catholicism, and, after 1688, was a courageous non-juror.

866–7. the Sagan of Jerusalem] Henry Compton (1632–1713), son of the Earl of
Northampton; Bishop of London since 1675. Burnet commented: 'He was an
humble and modest man. He applied himself more to his function, than Bishops
had commonly done . . . He was a great patron of the Converts from Popery . . .
He was a property to Lord Danby, and was turned by him as he pleased. The
Duke [of York] hated him. But Lord Danby persuaded both the King and him,
that, as his heat did no great hurt to any person, so the giving way to it helped
to lay the jealousies of the Church party' (i 553). He supervised the Protestant
education of James's children, but was an opponent of Exclusion. Compton was
well known for his hospitality and charity (*DNB*).   *Sagan*] the Jewish high priest's
deputy.

868–9. Him of the western dome] John Dolben (1625–86), Dean of Westminster
since 1662 (later Archbishop of York 1683–6); though some early readers made
other identifications: see Roper 110. He fought for the King in the Civil War,
and was wounded at Marston Moor and at the siege of York. Burnet, who bore
him a grudge, said that he was 'a man of more spirit than discretion, and an excellent preacher, but of a free conversation, which laid him open to much censure
in a vitious Court' (ii 260). His preaching was much admired; Evelyn called it
'most passionat & pathetic' (*Diary*, 28 March 1673).   *dome*] church (from Latin
domus dei, 'house of God'; *pace OED* 2, not specifically a cathedral: Thomas Otway
calls St George's Chapel, Windsor, a 'dome' in *Windsor Castle* (1685) 11; and cp.
D.'s *To His Sacred Majesty* l. 61; 'Dido to Aeneas' l. 109.

870. The prophets' sons] the boys at Westminster School.

872–3. P. W. Thomas notes that this link between culture and political allegiance
has its roots in Civil War propaganda (*Sir John Berkenhead* (1969) 102–3). Cp. *To
My Lord Chancellor* ll. 17–18.

877. Adriel] Saul's son-in-law (1 Samuel xviii 19). There is no apparent point
in D.'s choice of this name for John Sheffield, Earl of Mulgrave (1648–1721).

Himself a Muse; in Sanhedrin's debate
True to his prince, but not a slave of state;
880   Whom David's love with honours did adorn
That from his disobedient son were torn.
Jotham, of piercing wit and pregnant thought,

D. had dedicated *Aureng-Zebe* (1676) to him, thanking him for 'the care you have taken of my Fortune; which you have rescu'd, not onely from the power of others, but from my worst of Enemies, my own modesty and Laziness' (*Works* xii 151). Mulgrave showed the draft of *Aureng-Zebe* to the King, and also gave D. an opportunity of discussing his plans for an epic poem on English history with the King and the Duke of York (*Works* xii 154–5). Mulgrave was the author of *An Essay upon Satire* (in MS, 1679) and *An Essay upon Poetry* (1682); D. was suspected of having a hand in the former, and this was the probable cause of the attack on him in Rose Alley on 18 December 1679 (see *POAS* i 396–401). The two men collaborated on 'Helen to Paris' in *Ovid's Epistles* (1680) and D. dedicated his *Aeneis* to Mulgrave in 1697. In 1701 John Dennis praised Mulgrave for his patronage of D.: 'you generously began to espouse him, when he was more than half oppress'd, by a very formidable Party in the Court of King *Charles* II. a Faction that wanted neither Power nor Authority to crush him [e.g. Buckingham and Rochester] . . . Your Lordship, in Consideration of that rising Merit, cherish'd his Person, notwithstanding his pretended Frailties; and while others, to express their Malice to the Man, would have hindred the Advancement, even of that Art, which they pretended to esteem so much; your Lordship . . . cherish'd the Man on purpose, to make him instrumental in advancing the Art' (Dennis i 198).

879. not a slave of state] D. told Mulgrave: 'Your mind has always been above the wretched affectation of Popularity. A popular man is, in truth, no better than a Prostitute to common Fame, and to the People' (Dedication to *Aureng-Zebe*; *Works* xii 151).

880–1. When Charles deprived Monmouth of his offices in 1679, Mulgrave was made Lord Lieutenant of the East Riding, and Governor of Hull.

882–7. Jotham] In Judges ix Jotham protests against the attempt by the men of Shechem to make the usurper Abimelech king. Here, George Savile (1633–95), created Viscount (1668) and Marquis of Halifax (1682). 'He was a man of a great and ready wit; full of life, and very pleasant; much turned to satyr . . . A severe jest was preferred by him to all arguments whatsoever. And he was endless in consultations: For when after much discourse a point was settled, if he could find a new jest, to make even that which was suggested by himself seem ridiculous, he could not hold, but would study to raise the credit of his wit, tho' it made others call his judgment in question' (Burnet i 375–6). Halifax had been associated with Shaftesbury, his uncle by marriage, and supported the impeachment of Danby, but they parted company in 1679 (Haley 530–1). Although he had remarked that no man would use the hereditary principle to select his coachman, Halifax opposed the Exclusion Bill, and spoke energetically against it in the Lords in November 1680, when 'He gained great honour in the debate; and had a visible superiority to Lord Shaftesbury in the opinion of the whole House' (Burnet ii 118). D. dedicated *King Arthur* (1691) to Halifax, remarking that Halifax had been a trusted friend of Charles II in the King's last years, and recalling that 'formerly I have shadow'd some part of your Virtues under another Name; but

Endued by nature, and by learning taught
To move assemblies, who but only tried
885   The worse awhile, then chose the better side;
Nor chose alone, but turned the balance too—
So much the weight of one brave man can do.
Hushai, the friend of David in distress,
In public storms of manly steadfastness;
890   By foreign treaties he informed his youth,
And joined experience to his native truth.
His frugal care supplied the wanting throne,
Frugal for that, but bounteous of his own;
'Tis easy conduct when exchequers flow,
895   But hard the task to manage well the low,
For sovereign power is too depressed or high
When kings are forced to sell, or crowds to buy.
Indulge one labour more, my weary Muse,

<hr />

the Character, though short and imperfect, was so true, that it broke through the Fable, and was discover'd by its Native Light' (*Works* xvi 7).

882. piercing] Q; ready F.

887. Echoing Marvell: 'So much one man can do, / That does both act and know' ('An Horatian Ode' ll. 75–6).

888–97. The OT Hushai offered to join David in exile during Absalom's rebellion, but David persuaded him to stay in Jerusalem and provide intelligence of Absalom's plans; he did so, and also gave Absalom misleading advice to destroy him (2 Samuel xv 32–7, xvi 16–19, xvii 5–16). Here, Laurence Hyde (1642–1711), Clarendon's son, first Earl of Rochester of the second creation (1682). In 1676 he was sent as ambassador to the King of Poland and assisted in negotiating a settlement with the Turks; in 1677 he was one of the ambassadors at the negotiations at the Congress of Nijmegen. Hyde was First Lord of the Treasury 1679–84, and opposed Exclusion at the cost of being accused of popery by the Commons. Burnet wrote: 'He was thought the smoothest man in the Court: And during all the dispute concerning his father, he made his Court so dextrously, that no resentments ever appeared on that head. When he came into business, and rose to high posts, he grew violent: But was thought an incorrupt man. He has high notions of Government, and thinks it must be maintained with great severity' (i 362). D. wrote to him *c.* 1683 in an attempt to have part of his salary paid (*Letters* 20–2); in 1685 he referred to his 'particular obligations' to Hyde ('Preface to *Sylvae*'; *Poems* ii 255) and dedicated 'Horace: *Odes* III xxix' to him. D. also dedicated *The Duke of Guise* (1683) and *Cleomenes* (1692) to Hyde; in the latter D. wrote: 'I shall be proud to hold my Dependance on you in Chief, as I do part of my small Fortune in *Wiltshire*. Your Goodness had not been wanting to me, during the Reign of my two Masters. And even from a bare Treasury, my Success has been contrary to that of Mr. *Cowley*; and *Gideon*'s Fleece has then been moisten'd, when all the Ground has been dry about it' (*Works* xvi 75).

898. Cp. Virgil: *extremum hunc, Arethusa, mihi concede laborem* (*Ecl.* x 1; 'concede to me this final labour, Arethusa'; Brower, *PMLA* lv (1940) 132).

For Amiel, who can Amiel's praise refuse?
900   Of ancient race by birth, but nobler yet
        In his own worth, and without title great:
        The Sanhedrin long time as chief he ruled,
        Their reason guided and their passion cooled;
        So dexterous was he in the crown's defence,
905   So formed to speak a loyal nation's sense,
        That as their band was Israel's tribes in small,
        So fit was he to represent them all.
        Now rasher charioteers the seat ascend,
        Whose loose careers his steady skill commend:
910   They like th' unequal ruler of the day

899–913. *Amiel*] The father of Machir, who with Barzillai brought David supplies
(2 Samuel xvii 27–9; alternatively, the gatekeeper mentioned in 1 Chronicles xxvi 5).
Here, Edward Seymour (1633–1708), a descendant of the first Duke of Somerset,
Protector to Edward VI. He was Navy Treasurer 1673–81. As Speaker of the
House of Commons 1673–8 he was adept at managing business to the advantage
of the court: 'He knew the House and every man in it so well, that by looking
about he could tell the fate of any question. So, if any thing was put, when the
Court party was not well gathered together, he would have held the House from
doing any thing, by a wilful mistaking or mistating the question. By that he
gave time to those, who were appointed for that mercenary work, to go about
and gather in all their party. And he would discern when they had got the majority. And then he would very fairly state the question, when he saw he was sure
to carry it' (Burnet ii 538). When Parliament met in March 1679 Seymour was
again elected Speaker, but Danby, with whom Seymour had quarrelled, persuaded
Charles to veto the nomination, provoking a furious reaction from the MPs.
Seymour was active in opposing Exclusion, and in the course of 1681 attempted
unsuccessfully to make himself Charles's chief minister (Haley 504; J. R. Jones,
Charles II: Royal Politician (1987) 141, 174–5).
908–11. Seymour was succeeded as Speaker by William Gregory in March 1679;
that Parliament was prorogued in May and dissolved in July. When the new
Parliament that was elected in October 1679 eventually met in October 1680,
William Williams was elected Speaker, and was re-elected for the Oxford
Parliament of March 1681. He was no friend of the court, and attracted particular notice for the blunt terms in which he expelled Sir Robert Peyton from the
House after his alleged complicity in the Meal Tub Plot (Grey viii 148–9; *POAS*
ii 305–8).
910–11. Phaëton, son of Apollo, persuaded his father to allow him to drive the
chariot of the sun across the sky for one day; he was unable to control it, and
was on the verge of destroying the earth when Jupiter killed him with a thunderbolt (Ovid, *Met.* ii 1–328). The story had been given a political application
by Henry King in 'An Elegy upon the most Incomparable King *Charls* the First':
'Whilst blind Ambition by successes fed / Hath You beyond the bound of Subjects
led, /... Needs must you with unskilfull *Phaeton* / Aspire to guid the Chariot
of the Sun, / Though your ill-govern'd height with lightning be / Thrown headlong from his burning Axle-tree' (ll. 309–10, 16–18; Kinsley).
910. *unequal*] inadequate for the task (*OED* 2).

Misguide the seasons and mistake the way,
While he withdrawn at their mad labour smiles,
And safe enjoys the sabbath of his toils.
        These were the chief, a small but faithful band ⎫
915   Of worthies, in the breach who dared to stand, ⎬
And tempt th' united fury of the land. ⎭
With grief they viewed such powerful engines bent
To batter down the lawful government,
A numerous faction with pretended frights
920   In Sanhedrins to plume the regal rights,
The true successor from the court removed,
The plot by hireling witnesses improved.
These ills they saw, and as their duty bound
They showed the King the danger of the wound:
925   That no concessions from the throne would please,
But lenitives fomented the disease;
That Absalom, ambitious of the crown,
Was made the lure to draw the people down;
That false Achitophel's pernicious hate
930   Had turned the plot to ruin church and state;
The council violent, the rabble worse,
That Shimei taught Jerusalem to curse.
        With all these loads of injuries oppressed,
And long revolving in his careful breast
935   Th' event of things, at last his patience tired,
Thus from his royal throne by heaven inspired
The godlike David spoke: with awful fear
His train their maker in their master hear:

---

915. worthies] men of courage and noble character (*OED* 1).
916. tempt] confront, risk the dangers of (*OED* 2c; first example from *PL* ii 404).
920. plume] pluck the feathers from (*OED* 2).
922. hireling witnesses] Hired witnesses figured prominently in the Popish Plot trials. Luttrell reports that the Catholic David Fitzgerald 'has been often heard to say that he could have as many witnesses as he pleased from Ireland to forswear themselves for 2s. 6d. each' (i 89–90). For Shaftesbury's use of hired witnesses see l. 679, and for the use of them on the King's side see l. 1012 and *n*. See also 'Epistle to the Whigs' l. 186*n*, prefixed to *The Medal*.
926. lenitives] soothing medicines.
928. An image from hawking: the lure is an artificial bird from which the hawk is fed, used to draw down the hawk.
931. The Privy Council, which had been enlarged in 1679 to include opposition leaders, was often the forum for heated discussions (Haley 536–7).
935. event] outcome.

'Thus long have I, by native mercy swayed,
940   My wrongs dissembled, my revenge delayed;
So willing to forgive th' offending age,
So much the father did the King assuage.
But now so far my clemency they slight,
Th' offenders question my forgiving right.
945   That one was made for many they contend,
But 'tis to rule, for that's a monarch's end.
They call my tenderness of blood my fear,
Though manly tempers can the longest bear.
Yet since they will divert my native course,
950   'Tis time to show I am not good by force.
Those heaped affronts that haughty subjects bring
Are burthens for a camel, not a King:
Kings are the public pillars of the state,
Born to sustain and prop the nation's weight;
955   If my young Samson will pretend a call
To shake the column, let him share the fall.
[But O that yet he would repent and live,

939–1025. David's speech has resemblances to *His Majesties Declaration to all His Loving Subjects* (8 April 1681; reprinted in *Works* xvii 513–16), rather than to the King's speech opening the Oxford Parliament, as Spence reported (Spence 28–9, 614; see G. Davies, *HLQ* x (1946) 69–82). D. was probably responsible for the anonymous tract *His Majesties Declaration Defended* (June 1681; *Works* xvii 195–225).

942. Cp. Ovid: *in rege tamen pater est* ('however the father is in the king'; *Met.* xiii 187; Poyet).

944. In an attempt to prevent the trial of the Earl of Danby, Charles gave him a pardon on 1 March 1679. When the King informed the Commons of this on 22 March he told them: 'I never denied it to any of my servants or Ministers, when they quitted their places, as Lord *Shaftsbury* and the Duke of *Buckingham* well know'. But the Commons attacked the pardon, and disputed the King's right to grant it (Grey vii 19–30). When Viscount Stafford was condemned in December 1680 the King commuted the penalty of hanging, drawing and quartering to one of beheading; the sheriffs Cornish and Bethel disputed the validity of the King's action and sought the advice of the Commons, which directed them to follow the King's writ (Grey viii 204–5, 209–10).

945. Cp. 'all his actings without himself are only as a King, and in his Politick capacity he ought not to Marry, Love, Hate, make War Friendship or Peace, but as a King and agreeable to the People, and their Interest he governs' (*A Letter from a Person of Quality to his Friend concerning His Majesties late Declaration* [1681] 6; *Works*).

955–6. Samson destroyed both himself and the Philistines by pulling down the two pillars which supported their house (Judges xvi 21–31).

957–60. Q; *not in* F. Cp. 'Prologue to His Royal Highness' ll. 27–9.

How easy 'tis for parents to forgive!
With how few tears a pardon might be won
960 From nature, pleading for a darling son!]
Poor pitied youth, by my paternal care
Raised up to all the height his frame could bear:
Had God ordained his fate for empire born,
He would have given his soul another turn;
965 Gulled with a patriot's name, whose modern sense
Is one that would by law supplant his prince;
The people's brave, the politician's tool,
Never was patriot yet, but was a fool.
Whence comes it that religion and the laws
970 Should more be Absalom's than David's cause?
His old instructor, ere he lost his place,
Was never thought endued with so much grace.
Good heavens, how faction can a patriot paint!
My rebel ever proves my people's saint.
975 Would they impose an heir upon the throne?
Let Sanhedrins be taught to give their own.
A king's at least a part of government,
And mine as requisite as their consent;
Without my leave a future king to choose
980 Infers a right the present to depose:
True, they petition me t' approve their choice,
But Esau's hands suit ill with Jacob's voice.

965–6. See l. 179n.
966. supplant] Q; destroy F.
967. brave] warrior (*OED* 1); bravo, bully, hired assassin (*OED* 1b).
976. their own] what is theirs to give (Kinsley).
979–80. Cp. 'We have reason to believe, by what pass'd in the last Parliament at *Westminster*, that if We could have been brought to give Our consent to a Bill of Exclusion, the Intent was not to rest there, but to pass further, and to attempt some other Great and Important Changes even in Present' (*His Majesties Declaration*; Kinsley). L'Estrange made the same point: 'His Majesty will not agree to the Disinheriting his Brother, contrary to Honour, Justice and Conscience; nor to the Erecting of such a Doctrine or Precedent, in the Excluding of his Royall Highness, as may be apply'd, in Consequence, to the Deposing of Himself' (*Observator* xxvi (22 June 1681); *Works*).
982. Jacob tricked his blind father Isaac into giving him the blessing which was due to his elder brother Esau, by covering his hands and neck with goatskin to make them feel like Esau's; Isaac 'felt him, and said, The voice is Jacob's voice, but the hands are the hands of Esau' (Genesis xxvii). The image had been used in the Whig poem *The Protestants Congratulation to the City for their Excellent Choice of Members to Serve in Parliament* (1679): 'But Thanks, brave *City*, which well Understands, / To Judge 'twixt *Jacob's* Voice and *Esau's* Hands'.

My pious subjects for my safety pray,
Which to secure they take my power away.
985   From plots and treasons heaven preserve my years,
But save me most from my petitioners.
Unsatiate as the barren womb or grave;
God cannot grant so much as they can crave.
What then is left, but with a jealous eye
990   To guard the small remains of royalty?
The law shall still direct my peaceful sway,
And the same law teach rebels to obey.
Votes shall no more established power control,
Such votes as make a part exceed the whole:
995   No groundless clamours shall my friends remove,
Nor crowds have power to punish ere they prove.

983–4. Cp. 'while they pretended a care of his Person on the one hand, were
plucking at his Scepter with the other' (*His Majesties Declaration Defended*; *Works*
xvii 209).
986. petitioners] Affirmations of support for the Whig cause were called 'petitions'.
A royal proclamation of 12 December 1679 forbade petitions against the prorogation or dissolution of Parliament, but on 27 October 1680 the Commons resolved
that petitioning was the inalienable right of the subject (Ogg 602). Shaftesbury
orchestrated a Whig campaign of petitioning for Parliament to be allowed to meet
in January 1680; a petition 300 feet long with some 50,000 names from Westminster and Southwark was presented to the King on 13 January, and another
with 30,000 names from Wiltshire was presented by Thomas Thynne nine days
later. Others followed (Haley 559–64). In July 1681 Luttrell commented on the
different reception which the King gave to 'addressers [Tories who offered declarations of support for the King's actions] and petitioners: those meet with a kind
reception at any time, these are alwaies distasteful; these petition him in these
times of danger to call the representative body of the nation, and those give him
thanks for dissolving them' (Luttrell i 108). Cp. D'Urfey's Prologue to *The Royalist*
(1682): the Tory '*Addresses* loves, to all Mankind is civil; / But hates *Petitions* as
he hates the Devil' (ll. 28–9; Danchin no. 315).
987. From Proverbs xxx 15–16: 'four things say not, It is enough: The grave;
and the barren womb; the earth that is not filled with water; and the fire that
saith not, It is enough' (Christie).
993–4. Cp. 'By which Vote, without any regard to the Laws establish'd, they
[the Commons] assumed to themselves a Power of Suspending Acts of Parliament' (*His Majesties Declaration*).
995–6. His Majesties Declaration refers to 'Strange illegal Votes, declaring divers
eminent Persons to be enemies to the King and Kingdom, without any Order
or Process of Law, any hearing of their Defence, or any Proof so much as offer'd
against them'. Whig objections to this passage were countered by D. in *His Majesties
Declaration Defended*: 'They who will have a thing done, and give no reason for
it, assume to themselves a manifest Arbitrary Power. Now this Power cannot be
in the Representatives, if it be not in the People: or if it be in them, the People
is absolute' (*Works* xvii 215).

     For gods and godlike kings their care express,
     Still to defend their servants in distress.
     O that my power to saving were confined;   ⎫
1000 Why am I forced like heaven, against my mind ⎬
     To make examples of another kind?   ⎭
     Must I at length the sword of justice draw?
     O cursed effects of necessary law!
     How ill my fear they by my mercy scan;
1005 Beware the fury of a patient man.
     Law they require; let law then show her face:
     They could not be content to look on grace
     Her hinder parts, but with a daring eye
     To tempt the terror of her front, and die.
1010 By their own arts 'tis righteously decreed
     Those dire artificers of death shall bleed.
     Against themselves their witnesses will swear,
     Till viper-like their mother plot they tear,

1004. scan] form an opinion of.
1006. require] demand.
1007–9. i.e. 'They could not be content with experiencing just grace and mercy, which are the hind parts of the law, but insisted on challenging the law face to face'. The image is based on Exodus xxxiii 20–3, where God says to Moses: 'Thou canst not see my face: for there shall no man see me, and live. And the Lord said, Behold, there is a place by me, and thou shalt stand upon a rock: And it shall come to pass, while my glory passeth by, that I will put thee in a clift of the rock, and will cover thee with my hand while I pass by: And I will take away mine hand, and thou shalt see my back parts: but my face shall not be seen'. Cp. *Astraea Redux* ll. 262–5. *tempt*] See l. 916*n*.
1010–11. From Ovid: *neque enim lex aequior ulla, / quam necis artifices arte perire sua* (*Ars Amatoria* i 655–6: 'for there is no juster law than that contrivers of death should perish by their own contrivances'; translated by D. as: 'A rightful doom, the laws of nature cry, / 'Tis, the artificers of death should die' ('Ovid's *Art of Love*, Book I' ll. 739–40)).
1012. Several of those who had been used by the Whigs as witnesses against Catholics in earlier trials (including Dugdale and Turberville who had sworn against Stafford) found it expedient and profitable to testify in the King's interest at the trial of Stephen College in August 1681, and were now being prepared to testify at Shaftesbury's trial (Haley 652–4). Cp. *The Medal*, 'Epistle' l. 186.
1013–15. Cp. 'Oh! of *themselves*, they're e'en a *Vip'rous Brood*; / *Begot* in *Discord*, and *brought up* with *Blood*. / . . . *the Ungrateful Brats* devour'd their *Dam*.' ([Sir Roger L'Estrange], *The Committee; or Popery in Masquerade* (1680)). The idea that the viper's young are born by eating their way out of their mother's belly is traditional (see Edward Topsell, *The History of Four-footed Beasts and Serpents* (1658) 802). James I cites the viper as an image of rebellion in *The Trew Law of Free Monarchies* (1598) (*The Political Works of James I*, edited by C. H. McIlwain (1918) 65). Du Bartas cites the viper as an example of God's providence in setting man's

And suck for nutriment that bloody gore
1015   Which was their principle of life before.
Their Belial with their Belzebub will fight,
Thus on my foes my foes shall do me right.
Nor doubt th' event, for factious crowds engage
In their first onset all their brutal rage;
1020   Then let 'em take an unresisted course,
Retire and traverse, and delude their force:
But when they stand all breathless, urge the fight,
And rise upon 'em with redoubled might;
For lawful power is still superior found,
1025   When long driv'n back, at length it stands the ground.'
        He said. Th' Almighty, nodding, gave consent,
And peals of thunder shook the firmament.
Henceforth a series of new time began,
The mighty years in long procession ran;
1030   Once more the godlike David was restored,
And willing nations knew their lawful lord.

---

enemies mutually at strife (*Divine Weeks and Works*, tr. Sylvester (1605) I vi 233–40).
For other allegorical applications see Spenser, *FQ* I i 25–6 (Error) and Milton,
PL ii 653–9 (Sin).
1018. event] outcome.
1021. retire] i.e. let us retire.   *traverse*] tack (*OED* 14); move from side to side,
dodge (*OED* 15).   *delude*] elude, evade, frustrate the purposes of (*OED* 4).
1026. nodding] as in Homer, Virgil (*Aen.* ix 106) and Ovid (*Met.* i 179–80; Poyet).
1028–31. Cp. the end of D.'s *Troilus and Cressida* (1679): 'Now peacefull order
has resum'd the reynes, / Old time looks young, and Nature seems renew'd: /
Then, since from homebred factions ruine springs, / Let Subjects learn obedience to their kings' (V ii 323–6).
1028–9. Cp. Virgil: *magnus ab integro saeclorum nascitur ordo* ('the great order of
the centuries starts again from the beginning': *Ecl.* iv 5; Brower, *PMLA* lv (1940)
132); and cp. *Astraea Redux* ll. 292–3n.

6 The Medal

Date and publication. When Shaftesbury was indicted on a charge of high treason at the Old Bailey on 24 November 1681 the jury returned the bill marked *ignoramus* ('we do not know'). To celebrate, a medal was struck by George Bower, embosser in ordinary to the Mint since 1664, who had previously produced medals for Charles II's restoration, his marriage, and the Popish Plot. The date of issue of the medal is uncertain, but it seems to be alluded to in Christopher Nesse's *A Key* (Luttrell's copy is dated 13 January 1682; Macdonald 225) and so probably appeared in mid-December 1681. Edmund Hickeringill (*The Mushroom* (March 1682) 16) says that D.'s poem is of 'three months birth' (Winn 601). The medal carried a bust of Shaftesbury on the obverse, with the inscription 'Antonio Comiti de Shaftesbury', and on the reverse a view of London Bridge and the Tower, with the rising sun breaking through a cloud, and the inscriptions 'Laetamur' ('we rejoice') and '24 Nov 1681'. Spence reported (from a priest whom he met at Pope's house) that the idea for the poem was suggested to D. by Charles: 'One day as the King was walking in the Mall and talking with Dryden, he said: "If I were a poet (and I think I'm poor enough to be one) I would write a poem on such a subject in the following manner—"; and then gave him the plan for it. Dryden took the hint, carried the poem as soon as it was written to the King, and had a present of a hundred broadpieces [pound coins] for it' (Spence 28). Politically, by early 1682 the tide was turning against the Whigs: 'A month before the verdict, the court had succeeded in promoting the election of a moderate Tory, Sir John Moore, as Lord Mayor; ten members of Shaftesbury's jury were defeated in the December elections for the Common Council of London; and the King now felt strong enough to begin an action of *quo warranto* that would allow him to alter the City's charter . . . the Duke of York was recalled from Scotland; he arrived at Yarmouth a week before the publication of *The Medall*' (Winn 365). *The Medall. A Satyre Against Sedition. By the Author of Absalom and Achitophel* was published by Jacob Tonson in 1682 (16 March according to Malone (I i 163) citing Luttrell; a letter from Lenthall Warcupp to his father dated 15 March says 'wee expect the Poem vpon my Lord S. Meddall to come out this morning' (G. Thorn-Drury, *RES* i (1925) 324)). Some press corrections were made; the present text is taken from a corrected copy of *1682*. The poem was reprinted in Edinburgh, 1682; Dublin, 1682; in *MP* 1684 and 1692; and in 1692. The first edition carried anonymous commendatory verses by Nahum Tate and T. Adams: see *Poems* ii Appendix B.

Authorship. The poem appeared anonymously, but by now D.'s authorship of *AA* was no secret; see *AA*, headnote (*Authorship*). *The Medal* was attributed to D. on the contents page of *MP* (1692), but not in the text.

Sources. W. O. S. Sutherland showed that many images in the poem are paralleled in contemporary pamphlets and newspapers (*University of Texas Studies in English* xxxv (1956) 123–34). A. E. Wallace Maurer pointed out that the design of the poem echoes the design of the medal, so that D. is coining his own medal. After an introduction (ll. 1–21), on the obverse D.'s portrait of Shaftesbury (ll. 22–144); then on the reverse, not one but five emblematic scenes: Shaftesbury's followers in confusion (ll. 145–66), London in a precarious condition (ll. 167–204), the Association (ll. 205–55), Shaftesbury corrupting the nation (ll. 256–86), and the future should the Whigs succeed (ll. 287–322). The poem concludes with a Latin motto, a rejoinder to *Laetamur* on the medal. Maurer notes that D. draws on the 'Advice to a Painter' convention of satire, and also on the emblem tradition for many of his images, e.g. ll. 27, 31, 35, 79–80, 119–22 (Maurer, *PLL* ii (1966) 293–304). M. A. Doody suggests that D. may have recalled the Interregnum ballad 'The States New Coyne', printed in *Rump* (1662) i 289–90 (*The Daring Muse* (1985) 40).

Reception. There were several swift replies: *The Mushroom* [by Edmund Hickeringill] (Luttrell's copy dated 23 March according to Malone); *The Medal Revers'd* [by Samuel Pordage] (Luttrell's copy (Dyce Collection) dated 31 March); *The Loyal Medal Vindicated* (Luttrell's copy (Huntington) dated 6 April); and *The Medal of John Bayes*, almost certainly by Shadwell (Luttrell's copy (Dyce Collection) dated 15 May). Pordage doubted whether the author of *AA* also wrote *The Medal*, 'since the stile and painting is far different, and their *Satyrs*, are of a different hew, the one being a much slovenlier Beast than the other' (2–3). Shadwell said that D. had mistaken the difference between satire and libel: 'For Libel and true *Satyr* / different be; / This must have *Truth*, and *Salt*, with *Modesty*. / Sparing the Persons, this does tax the Crimes, / Gall's not great Men, but Vices of the Times / With Witty and Sharp, not blunt and bitter rimes. / Methinks the Ghost of *Horace* there I see, / Lashing this *Cherry-cheek'd Dunce* of Fifty three; / Who, at that age, so boldly durst profane, / With base hir'd Libel, the free *Satyr*'s Vein. / Thou stil'st it Satyr, to call Names, Rogue, Whore, / Traytor, and Rebel, and a thousand more' (2). BodL MS Firth c 16 has an anonymous poem 'Uppon the Author of the Poem yᵉ Medall' (pp. 50–1), printed in Hammond and Hopkins 376–7.

The Medal

A Satire against Sedition

Per Graiûm populos, mediaeque per Elidis urbem
Ibat ovans; divumque sibi poscebat honores.

Epistle to the Whigs

For to whom can I dedicate this poem with so much justice as to you? 'Tis the representation of your own hero: 'tis the picture drawn at length which you admire and prize so much in little. None of your ornaments are
5   wanting, neither the landscape of the Tower, nor the rising sun, nor the *anno domini* of your new sovereign's

¶6. *Epigraph.* 'Through the Greek people, and through the city in the heart of Elis, he went triumphant, claiming for himself the honours due to the gods' (*Aen.* vi 588–9, of Salmoneus who sought to emulate Jove).

coronation. This must needs be a grateful undertaking
to your whole party, especially to those who have
not been so happy as to purchase the original. I
10   hear the graver has made a good market of it: all his
kings are bought up already, or the value of the remainder
so enhanced that many a poor Polander who would
be glad to worship the image is not able to go to the cost
of him, but must be content to see him here. I must
15   confess I am no great artist, but signpost painting will
꙳ serve the turn to remember a friend by, especially when
better is not to be had. Yet for your comfort the linea-
ments are true, and though he sate not five times to me,
as he did to B., yet I have consulted history, as the
20   Italian painters do when they would draw a Nero or a
Caligula: though they have not seen the man, they can
help their imagination by a statue of him, and find out
the colouring from Suetonius and Tacitus. Truth is,

---

12. Polander] The sixteenth- and seventeenth-century debate over the advantages
of elective and hereditary monarchies cited the ancient custom among the
Germanic tribes of electing their rulers; Denmark, Sweden and Poland were current examples of this practice. But by 1660 Denmark and Sweden had become
hereditary monarchies, leaving Poland as the only example of an elective monarchy (E. R. Wasserman, *MLN* lxxiii (1958) 165–7). Tory propaganda alleged that
Shaftesbury had sought election to the throne of Poland in 1674 when Jan Sobieski
was chosen, thus implying that he favoured an elective monarchy for England.
There seems to be no historical basis for this report, and he would have been
ineligible anyway, since the Poles chose only from reigning European houses.
The story is carried in *A Modest Vindication of the Earl of S—y* (1681), where his
poet laureate is to be 'John Drydenurtzitz . . . for writing Panegyricks upon
Oliver Cromwel, and Libels against his present Master King *Charles* II' (4). In Aphra
Behn's *The City Heiress* (*c.* April 1682) Sir Timothy Treat-all has his head meas-
ured for the crown of Poland; cp. also Otway's Prologue to *Venice Preserv'd*
(February 1682) ll. 36–9; *Scandalum Magnatum: or, Potapski's Case. A Satyr against
Polish Oppression* (which has echoes of *AA*, and an attack on Shadwell); and 'The
Last Will and Testament of Anthony King of Poland' (BL MS Burney 390).
15. signpost painting] Maurer 298 suggests an echo of Marvell's *Last Instructions to a
Painter* (in MS, 1667): 'canst thou daub a signpost, and that ill? / 'Twill suit our
great debauch and little skill' (ll. 7–8). Cp. 'The Tenth Satire of Juvenal' l. 254.
18. he sate not five times] Cp. *Last Instructions*: 'After two sittings, now our Lady
State, / To end her picture, does the third time wait' (ll. 1–2; Maurer).
19. B.] George Bower (see headnote).
20–1. Nero . . . Caligula] Nero Claudius Caesar, Emperor AD 54–68, and Gaius
Julius Caesar Germanicus ('Caligula'), Emperor AD 37–41, were two of the most
cruel and tyrannical of Roman emperors.
23. Suetonius and Tacitus] Suetonius (b. *c.* AD 69) was the author of *De Vita Caesarum*,
which included lives of Nero and Caligula. Tacitus (b. *c.* AD 56) included accounts
of Caligula and Nero in his *Annales*, though the former is lost.

you might have spared one side of your medal: the head
25 would be seen to more advantage if it were placed on a
spike of the Tower, a little nearer to the sun, which
would then break out to better purpose. You tell us in
your preface to the *No Protestant Plot* that you shall be
forced hereafter to leave off your modesty: I suppose
30 you mean that little which is left you, for it was worn to
rags when you put out this medal. Never was there
practised such a piece of notorious impudence in the
face of an established government. I believe when he is
dead you will wear him in thumb-rings as the Turks did
35 Scanderbeg, as if there were virtue in his bones to preserve you against monarchy. Yet all this while you pretend not only zeal for the public good, but a due
veneration for the person of the King. But all men who
can see an inch before them may easily detect those
40 gross fallacies. That it is necessary for men in your circumstances to pretend both is granted you, for without them there could be no ground to raise a faction.
But I would ask you one civil question: what right has
any man among you, or any Association of men (to
45 come nearer to you), who out of Parliament cannot be
considered in a public capacity, to meet, as you daily
do, in factious clubs, to vilify the government in your

28. No Protestant Plot] The Whig tract *No Protestant Plot* (three parts, 1681–2)
by Robert Ferguson; the address to the reader in part three (published February
1682 (Haley 691)) says: 'if our Enemies persevere in their ways of impudence,
we hope all mankind will acquit us, if from henceforth we lay aside bashfulness
and modesty' (sig. A4ᵛ).
35. *Scanderbeg*] George Castriota *alias* Iskander Beg (c. 1404–67), an Albanian who
deserted the Turkish service and fought for his country's independence. 'The Turkes
hauing gotten the towne of *Lissa*, did with a vehement and earnest desire search
out the bodie of *Scanderbeg*: . . . ioyfull was he that could get or cary away any
peece of his bodie were it neuer so litle: and those that had any part thereof,
caused the same most religiously to be set and curiously enchased, some in siluer,
some in golde, bearing it about them vpon some part of their bodies as a thing
most holy, diuine, and fatall' (*The Historie of George Castriot* (1596) 496; Kinsley).
44. *Association*] In 1680 the Whigs in Parliament proposed a Protestant Association
against popery and the succession of the Duke of York; a paper outlining such an
association was discovered in Shaftesbury's rooms and used at his trial (cp. 'Prologue
to *The Duke of Guise*' l. 14).
47. *factious clubs*] There were many Whig clubs in London, most importantly
the Green Ribbon Club, through which Whig activities were co-ordinated (see
J. R. Jones, *DUJ* xlix (1956) 17–20; D. Allen, *HJ* xix (1976) 561–80; Ashcraft
143–5; 2*AA* ll. 524–33).

discourses and to libel it in all your writings? Who made
you judges in Israel? Or how is it consistent with your
50   zeal of the public welfare to promote sedition? Does
your definition of loyal, which is to serve the King
according to the laws, allow you the licence of tradu-
cing the executive power with which you own he is
invested? You complain that His Majesty has lost the
55   love and confidence of his people, and by your very
urging it you endeavour what in you lies to make him
lose them. All good subjects abhor the thought of arbitrary power, whether it be in one or many: if you were
the patriots you would seem, you would not at this rate
60   incense the multitude to assume it; for no sober man can
fear it, either from the King's disposition or his practice,
or even, where you would odiously lay it, from his
ministers. Give us leave to enjoy the government and the
benefit of laws under which we were born, and which
65   we desire to transmit to our posterity. You are not the
trustees of the public liberty, and if you have not right
to petition in a crowd, much less have you to intermeddle
in the management of affairs, or to arraign what you
do not like—which in effect is everything that is done
70   by the King and Council. Can you imagine that any
reasonable man will believe you respect the person of
His Majesty, when 'tis apparent that your seditious
pamphlets are stuffed with particular reflections on
him? If you have the confidence to deny this, 'tis easy to
75   be evinced from a thousand passages, which I only forbear to quote because I desire they should die and be
forgotten. I have perused many of your papers, and to
show you that I have, the third part of your *No Protestant Plot* is much of it stolen from your dead author's
80   pamphlet called *The Growth of Popery*, as manifestly as

49. *judges in Israel*] The judges were the rulers of Israel in the period between
Joshua and the kings; this reference echoes the application of OT history to contemporary politics in *AA* (cp. ll. 119, 177–8 below).
59. *patriots*] See *AA* l. 179n.
66–7. *you have not right to petition in a crowd*] In 1661 Parliament passed an Act
against tumultuous petitioning, making it illegal to obtain more than twenty
signatures, or for more than ten persons to present a petition to Parliament
(Kinsley). Cp. *AA* l. 986n.
79–80. *your dead author's pamphlet*] *An Account of the Growth of Popery and Arbitrary
Government in England* (1677) by Andrew Marvell (1621–78). Ferguson's pamphlet

Milton's *Defence of the English People* is from Buchanan
De Jure Regni apud Scotos, or your first Covenant and
new Association from the Holy League of the French
Guisards. Anyone who reads Davila may trace your
85 practices all along. There were the same pretences for
reformation and loyalty, the same aspersions of the
King, and the same grounds of a rebellion. I know not
whether you will take the historian's word, who says it
was reported that Poltrot, a Huguenot, murthered
90 Francis Duke of Guise by the instigations of Theodore
Beza; or that it was a Huguenot minister, otherwise
called a Presbyterian (for our church abhors so devilish

does not seem particularly indebted to Marvell's, though they share basic
assumptions about a papist threat to English liberties. Allegations of plagiarism
were standard polemical devices: Marvell was accused of lifting *The Rehearsal
Transpros'd* from Milton's pamphlets (George F. Sensabaugh, *That Grand Whig
Milton* (1952) 37; cp. 77–88).

81. Milton . . . Buchanan] Milton's *Defensio pro populo Anglicano* (1651) and *Defensio
Secunda* (1654) are defences of the new English republic against the attack
mounted by Salmasius. It is particularly in *The Tenure of Kings and Magistrates* (1649)
that Milton follows George Buchanan (1506–82) who in his *De Jure Regni apud
Scotos* (1579) argued that the people only entrust power to their ruler, and may
remove or kill a tyrant if that trust is abused. Buchanan's work appeared in an
English translation in 1680, and is discussed in Sir William Dugdale's *A Short View
of the Late Troubles in England* (1681), on which D. may have been drawing
(J. H. Smith, *HLQ* xx (1957) 233–43). Milton's work had a significant influence
upon Whig political thought: see Sensabaugh. Milton, Buchanan and Suarez (see
l. 201*n* below) are cited together as advocates of the killing of tyrants in George
Hickes, *A Sermon preached before the Lord Mayor . . . 30th of January, 1681/2* (1682)
17–19.

82–3. Covenant . . . Holy League] Dugdale 600–50 compared the Holy League of
the sixteenth-century Guisards with the opposition to Charles I, which produced
the Solemn League and Covenant. D. exploited the parallel further in *The Duke
of Guise.* In 'The Vindication of *The Duke of Guise*' (1683) D. says that the play
is 'a Parallel, betwixt the *Holy League* plotted by the House of *Guise* and its *Adhærants,*
with the *Covenant* plotted by the *Rebels* in the time of King *Charles* the *First,* and
those of the *new Association,* which was the Spawn of the *old Covenant*' (*Works*
xiv 314). Cp. also 'Prologue to *The Duke of Guise*' ll. 1–2.

84. Davila] Historian of the French civil wars; D. used the translation of his work,
The Historie of the Civill Warres of France (1647–8) for *The Duke of Guise.*

90–1. Theodore Beza] Beza (1519–1605) was Calvin's associate and successor as
leader of the Genevan Protestants. The allegation that he persuaded Poltrot to
kill the Duke of Guise is reported by Davila (*Historie* i 176; *Works*).

91. a Huguenot minister] Davila reports that a Huguenot minister 'printed a book
in which he maintained, That the people of France were no longer obliged to
be obedient to the King, because he was turned Idolator; and for this reason affirmed,
that it was lawful to kill him' (*Historie* i 216–17; *Works*).

a tenent) who first writ a treatise of the lawfulness of
deposing and murthering kings of a different persuasion
95 in religion. But I am able to prove from the doctrine of
Calvin and principles of Buchanan that they set the
people above the magistrate, which if I mistake not is
your own fundamental, and which carries your loyalty
no farther than your liking. When a vote of the House
100 of Commons goes on your side, you are as ready to
observe it as if it were passed into a law; but when you
are pinched with any former and yet unrepealed Act of
Parliament, you declare that in some cases you will not
be obliged by it. The passage is in the same third part of
105 the *No Protestant Plot*, and is too plain to be denied. The
late copy of your intended Association you neither
wholly justify nor condemn, but, as the papists when
they are unopposed fly out into all the pageantries of
worship, but in times of war, when they are hard
110 pressed by arguments, lie close entrenched behind the
Council of Trent, so now, when your affairs are in a
low condition, you dare not pretend that to be a legal
combination, but whensoever you are afloat I doubt not
but it will be maintained and justified to purpose. For
115 indeed there is nothing to defend it but the sword: 'tis
the proper time to say anything when men have all things
in their power.

93. tenent] tenet.
96. Calvin . . . Buchanan] Calvinist political theory, exemplified by Calvin himself, Beza and Buchanan, developed the argument that it was lawful to resist and
kill a tyrant, particularly one who persecuted the godly (see Quentin Skinner,
The Foundations of Modern Political Thought, 2 vols (1978) ii 302–48).
99–102. vote . . . unrepealed Act] The Bill to exclude James from the succession,
and the Bill to exempt Protestant dissenters from the Elizabethan and Jacobean
statutes still in force against dissenters, which passed the Commons but did not
become law, were reprinted as part of Whig propaganda in *A Collection of the
Substance of several Speeches and Debates* (1681).
104. The passage] Ferguson argues that dissenters are not bound by the Acts which
'*prevent and suppress Seditious Conventicles*' since their meetings are not seditious;
and also that if the Parliament which met on 8 May 1673 were found to have
assembled after the statutory interval between sessions, then 'the Laws by which
the Phanaticks are Disturbed, Fined and Imprisoned, will not be found to have
the Legality, Force and Power that some men do imagine' (*The Third Part of No
Protestant Plot* (1682) 34–5).
111. Council of Trent] The Council (1545–63) which renewed Roman Catholic
doctrine and discipline in response to the attacks made on the church by
Protestantism.

In the meantime you would fain be nibbling at a
parallel betwixt this Association and that in the time
120   of Queen Elizabeth. But there is this small difference
betwixt them, that the ends of the one are directly opposite to the other: one with the Queen's approbation and
conjunction, as head of it; the other without either the
consent or knowledge of the King, against whose
125   authority it is manifestly designed. Therefore you do
well to have recourse to your last evasion, that it was
contrived by your enemies, and shuffled into the papers
that were seized: which yet you see the nation is not so
easy to believe as your own jury; but the matter is not
130   difficult, to find twelve men in Newgate who would
acquit a malefactor.

I have one only favour to desire of you at parting,
that when you think of answering this poem, you
would employ the same pens against it who have com-
135   bated with so much success against *Absalom and Achitophel*: for then you may assure yourselves of a clear
victory, without the least reply. Rail at me abundantly,
and, not to break a custom, do it without wit. By
this method you will gain a considerable point, which is
140   wholly to waive the answer of my arguments. Never
own the bottom of your principles, for fear they should
be treason. Fall severely on the miscarriages of government, for if scandal be not allowed, you are no freeborn
subjects. If God has not blessed you with the talent of
145   rhyming, make use of my poor stock and welcome: let
your verses run upon my feet, and for the utmost refuge
of notorious blockheads, reduced to the last extremity
of sense, turn my own lines upon me, and in utter
despair of your own satire, make me satirize myself.
150   Some of you have been driven to this bay already; but
above all the rest commend me to the nonconformist
parson who writ the *Whip* and *Key*. I am afraid it is not

---

120. *Queen Elizabeth*] The Whigs' proposed Association echoed that of 1585, which
was designed to protect Elizabeth against assassination by promising to avenge
her death on the Catholics.
130. *Newgate*] a prison in London.
134. *the same pens*] For the replies to *AA* see the headnote to that poem.
148. *turn my own lines upon me*] as in Pordage's *Azaria and Hushai*.
151–2. *the nonconformist parson*] Christopher Nesse, author of *A Whip* and *A Key*.

read so much as the piece deserves, because the bookseller is every week crying help at the end of his gazette
155 to get it off. You see I am charitable enough to do him
a kindness, that it may be published as well as printed,
and that so much skill in Hebrew derivations may not
lie for waste paper in the shop. Yet I half suspect he
went no farther for his learning than the index of
160 Hebrew names and etymologies which is printed at the
end of some English bibles. If Achitophel signify the
brother of a fool, the author of that poem will pass with
his readers for the next of kin. And perhaps 'tis the
relation that makes the kindness. Whatever the verses
165 are, buy 'em up, I beseech you, out of pity; for I hear
the conventicle is shut up, and the brother of Achitophel
out of service.

Now footmen, you know, have the generosity to
make a purse for a member of their society who has had
170 his livery pulled over his ears, and even protestant socks
are bought up among you out of veneration to the
name. A dissenter in poetry from sense and English will
make as good a protestant rhymer as a dissenter from
the Church of England a protestant parson. Besides, if
175 you encourage a young beginner, who knows but he
may elevate his style a little above the vulgar epithets of
'profane', and 'saucy Jack' and 'atheistic scribbler' with
which he treats me when the fit of enthusiasm is strong
upon him: by which well-mannered and charitable
180 expressions I was certain of his sect before I knew his
name. What would you have more of a man? He has
damned me in your cause from Genesis to the
Revelations, and has half the texts of both the testaments
against me, if you will be so civil to yourselves as to
185 take him for your interpreter, and not to take them for
Irish witnesses. After all, perhaps you will tell me that

161–2. the brother of a fool] Nesse says that 'Achitophel' in Hebrew means 'A Foole
my Brother' (A Key 24).
176. vulgar epithets] A Key calls AA 'that Prophane, and Blasphemous Poem' ('To
the King') and 'Sawcy Satyr Verse' (25).
178. enthusiasm] See AA l. 530n.
186. Irish witnesses] See AA l. 922n. After Shaftesbury's trial the witnesses left in
guarded coaches, 'and it was but necessary, for a rabble of above six hundred
men followed them very tumultuously, and with very ill language' (HMC
Ormonde n.s. vi 237). The Whigs attempted to discredit these turncoat informers:

you retained him only for the opening of your cause,
and that your main lawyer is yet behind. Now if it so
happen he meet with no more reply than his pre-
190 decessors, you may either conclude that I trust to the
goodness of my cause, or fear my adversary, or disdain
him, or what you please; for the short on't is, 'tis indifferent to your humble servant whatever your party says
or thinks of him.

The Medal

A Satire against Sedition

Of all our antic sights and pageantry
Which English idiots run in crowds to see,
The Polish medal bears the prize alone:
A monster, more the favourite of the town
5   Than either fairs or theatres have shown.
Never did art so well with nature strive,
Nor ever idol seemed so much alive;
So like the man: so golden to the sight,
So base within, so counterfeit and light.
10 One side is filled with title and with face,
And, lest the king should want a regal place,
On the reverse a tower the town surveys,
O'er which our mounting sun his beams displays.

'their *Notorious Adventures*, their *Swearing, Counter-swearing, Quarrels* amongst
themselves, *Suborning*, and being *Suborn'd*, Endeavours to *drop* the Popish Plot,
and *Sham* another upon Protestants, &c. are become the Common themes of
every Table-talk, and the Subject matter of *Play-House Drolls*' ([William
Hetherington], *The Irish-Evidence Convicted by their Own Oaths* (1682) 3; Kinsley).
The Third Part of No Protestant Plot attacks the credibility of these witnesses in
great detail.

1. antic] grotesque, bizarre (*OED* 2).
3–16. For a description of the medal see headnote, and also S. A. Golden, *N &
Q* ccvii (1962) 383–4.
3. Polish] See 'Epistle' l. 12*n*.
8. golden] Surviving examples of the medal are in silver, but some must have been
silver gilt: Richard Duke writing to Otway calls it 'a fine gilt Thing' (Macdonald
26).
10. face] also meaning 'impudence, effrontery' (*OED* 7).
11. the king] i.e. Shaftesbury. *want*] lack. *place*] residence (*OED* 5b).
13. mounting sun] The sun is in the east, therefore rising (S. A. Golden).

The word, pronounced aloud by shrieval voice,
15 *Laetamur*, which in Polish is 'rejoice'.
The day, month, year to the great act are joined,
And a new canting holiday designed.
Five days he sate for every cast and look,
Four more than God to finish Adam took.
20 But who can tell what essence angels are,
Or how long heaven was making Lucifer?
O could the style that copied every grace
And ploughed such furrows for an eunuch face,
Could it have formed his ever-changing will,
25 The various piece had tired the graver's skill!
A martial hero first, with early care
Blown like a pigmy by the winds to war:
A beardless chief, a rebel ere a man
(So young his hatred to his prince began).
30 Next this (how wildly will ambition steer!)
A vermin wriggling in th' usurper's ear:
Bart'ring his venal wit for sums of gold,

14. *shrieval*] The Whig sheriffs were responsible for the selection of the jury which returned the *ignoramus* verdict on Shaftesbury (cp. *AA* ll. 584–629*n*).
15. The Latin *laetamur* means 'we rejoice'.
17. Days of fasting and prayer were proclaimed by Parliament in the 1640s in thanksgiving for victories over the King (Schless, *POAS* iii 47). *canting*] using religious language affectedly, esp. of puritans.
19. God created Adam on the sixth day (Genesis i 27).
21. *Lucifer*] For the application of satanic imagery to Shaftesbury see *AA* l. 373*n*.
22. *style*] engraving tool (*OED* 2).
23. *furrows*] Bower's portrait shows deep lines from the side of the nose down to the chin (Schless). *eunuch*] reworking the idea of Shaftesbury's unproductive sexuality from *AA* ll. 170–2.
24. *ever-changing will*] Cp. *AA* ll. 152–5*n*. For a summary of Shaftesbury's career, which is discussed in the following lines, see *AA* ll. 150–99*n*.
25. *various*] changeable in character and opinions (*OED* 2a, b); cp. *AA* l. 545*n*.
27. *pigmy*] Cp. *AA* l. 157*n*.
28–9. Shaftesbury fought for Parliament in the Civil War, holding various military and civil posts in Dorset while in his twenties.
30–1. From 1653 to 1655 Shaftesbury served on Cromwell's Council of State.
30. For the image cp. *AA* l. 162.
31. 'Earwig' was a common metaphor for a parasite or whisperer (*OED* 2; Kinsley).
32–3. 'It is quite unnecessary to suppose that Ashley Cooper had to put on any hypocritical act in order to impress Cromwell, and there is no evidence to suggest that he did in fact pretend to be one of the "Saints". Dryden's lines refer to nothing more than the common Tory view that the Barebones Parliament was composed entirely of extreme religious enthusiasts, and that any member of it must have been either a religious maniac or a hypocrite' (Haley 67).

He cast himself into the saint-like mould:
Groaned, sighed and prayed, while godliness was gain,
35   The loudest bagpipe of the squeaking train.
But as 'tis hard to cheat a juggler's eyes,
His open lewdness he could ne'er disguise.
There split the saint: for hypocritic zeal
Allows no sins but those it can conceal.
40   Whoring to scandal gives too large a scope:
Saints must not trade, but they may interlope.
Th' ungodly principle was all the same,
But a gross cheat betrays his partner's game.
Besides, their pace was formal, grave and slack:
45   His nimble wit outran the heavy pack.
Yet still he found his fortune at a stay,
Whole droves of blockheads choking up his way.
They took, but not rewarded, his advice:
Villain and wit exact a double price.
50   Power was his aim, but thrown from that pretence ⎫
The wretch turned loyal in his own defence,   ⎬
And malice reconciled him to his prince.   ⎭
Him in the anguish of his soul he served,
Rewarded faster still than he deserved.
55   Behold him now exalted into trust,
His counsel's oft convenient, seldom just:
Ev'n in the most sincere advice he gave
He had a grudging still to be a knave;

---

35. bagpipe] Alluding to puritan claims to speak by inspiration of the Holy Spirit.
Cp. L'Estrange: [Whig] 'Common Pamphleteers . . . [are] no more then the Caballs
Bag-Pipe to the Faction' (*Observator* lxxxii (21 December 1681); W. O. S.
Sutherland). Maurer 299 notes that in *The Ship of Fools* the bagpipe is chosen
over the lute and the harp by the impatient fool who will not abide correction
(*Stultifera Nauis . . . The Ship of Fooles*, tr. Alexander Barclay (1570) 100).
36. juggler] L'Estrange called the Whigs spiritual jugglers (*Observator* lxvii (2 November 1681), lxxii (19 November 1681); W. O. S. Sutherland).
37. lewdness] Enemies frequently accused Shaftesbury of lewdness, especially after
the tide had turned against the Whigs in 1682, but Haley 211–15 finds no actual
evidence to support these allegations.
38. split] foundered, was wrecked.
41. interlope] trade without a licence (*OED* 1).
44. slack] slow (*OED* 4).
46. at a stay] at a standstill.
51–2. At the Restoration, Shaftesbury was appointed a Privy Councillor and served
Charles as Chancellor of the Exchequer, Commissioner of the Treasury, and Lord
Chancellor, until his dismissal in November 1673.
58. grudging] secret inclination (*OED* 4).

The frauds he learned in his fanatic years
60   Made him uneasy in his lawful gears;
     At best as little honest as he could,
     And like white witches mischievously good;
     To his first bias longingly he leans,
     And rather would be great by wicked means.
65   Thus framed for ill, he loosed our triple hold
     (Advice unsafe, precipitous and bold).
     From hence those tears! that Ilium of our woe!
     Who helps a powerful friend forearms a foe.
     What wonder if the waves prevail so far
70   When he cut down the banks that made the bar?
     Seas follow but their nature to invade,
     But he by art our native strength betrayed.
     So Samson to his foe his force confessed,
     And to be shorn lay slumbering on her breast.
75   But when this fatal counsel, found too late,
     Exposed its author to the public hate,
     When his just sovereign by no impious way
     Could be seduced to arbitrary sway,
     Forsaken of that hope he shifts the sail,   ⎫
80   Drives down the current with a pop'lar gale,   ⎬
     And shows the fiend confessed without a veil.   ⎭

---

60. gears] harness (*OED* 3b).
62. white witches] ones who use witchcraft benevolently.
63. bias] Cp. *AA* l. 79.
65. loosed our triple hold] broke the Triple Alliance; see *AA* l. 175*n*.
67. Ilium] Troy, which was betrayed by the duplicity of Sinon.
68. The breaking of the Triple Alliance helped France (always thought of as England's principal potential enemy) in its war against Holland.
73–4. Samson told Delilah that his strength depended on his never having cut his hair; then as he slept on her knees Delilah had his hair cut off (Judges xvi 17–19).
77–80. On 15 March 1672 Charles issued the Declaration of Indulgence suspending the execution of all penal laws against nonconformists and recusants; when the Commons objected to the King's suspending power Shaftesbury defended it, but Charles decided to cancel the Declaration in March 1673. Shaftesbury's strong support later that month for the Test Act (which excluded all but Anglicans from public office) established his reputation as 'a Protestant hero' (Haley 323).
79–80. Cp. *AA* ll. 159–62*n*. Maurer 299 notes that in *The Ship of Fools* 224 a fool guilty of 'the despising of misfortune' tugs frantically at the sail of a boat which is cracking in the middle.
80. Drives] drifts (*OED* 26).
81. confessed] revealed.

He preaches to the crowd that power is lent,
But not conveyed, to kingly government;
That claims successive bear no binding force;
85   That coronation oaths are things of course;
Maintains the multitude can never err,
And sets the people in the papal chair.
The reason's obvious: interest never lies;
The most have still their interest in their eyes;
90   The power is always theirs, and power is ever wise.
Almighty crowd, thou shorten'st all dispute,
Power is thy essence, wit thy attribute!
Nor faith nor reason make thee at a stay,
Thou leap'st o'er all eternal truths in thy Pindaric way!
95   Athens, no doubt, did righteously decide
When Phocion and when Socrates were tried;
As righteously they did those dooms repent:
Still they were wise, whatever way they went.
Crowds err not, though to both extremes they run,
100   To kill the father, and recall the son.
Some think the fools were most, as times went then,

82–7. See *AA* ll. 759–810*nn.*

85. things of course] matters of mere custom.

87. i.e. makes the people infallible.

88. interest never lies] The Tory paper *Heraclitus Ridens* used this phrase as the motto for the issue reporting the *ignoramus* verdict (no. xliv, 29 November 1681; W. O. S. Sutherland). Cp. *AA* l. 501*n*, and *His Majesties Declaration Defended* (1681; *Works* xvii 205).

92. wit] cleverness, ingenuity (*OED* 5); here a suspect attribute, as in *AA* ll. 153, 162–3.

94. A fourteener. Tom Brown has D. say: 'I measur'd it not by my Fingers, but a pair of Compasses; and I dare safely say 'tis the longest line except one in Christendom' (*The Reasons of Mr. Bays Changing his Religion* (1688) 17; *Works*). *Pindaric*] The poems of Pindar (Greek, 518–438 BC), with their apparently inexplicable versification and lack of connections, were thought of as quintessential examples of poetic inspiration untrammelled by reason; the link between irrational 'enthusiasm' in poetry and in religion had been made by Thomas Rymer in *The Tragedies of the Last Age Consider'd* (1678) 8: 'Those who object against reason are the Fanaticks in Poetry, and are never to be sav'd by their good works' (see also Oldham, *Poems* 414, 456).

95–7. The Athenians executed the philosopher Socrates for impiety (399 BC) and the general Phocion for treason (317 BC); on each occasion they repented and punished the accusers of the condemned men. Plutarch noted that 'Phocion's fate reminded the Greeks anew of that of Socrates; they felt that the sin and misfortune of Athens were alike in both cases' (*Phocion* 38),

100. The execution of Charles I in 1649, and the recall of his son in 1660.

But now the world's o'erstocked with prudent men.
The common cry is ev'n religion's test:
The Turk's is, at Constantinople, best,
105   Idols in India, Popery at Rome,
And our own worship only true at home:
And true but for the time: 'tis hard to know
How long we please it shall continue so;
This side today, and that tomorrow burns,
110   So all are God-a'mighties in their turns.
A tempting doctrine, plausible and new:
What fools our fathers were, if this be true!
Who to destroy the seeds of civil war
Inherent right in monarchs did declare,
115   And that a lawful power might never cease
Secured succession to secure our peace.
Thus property and sovereign sway at last
In equal balances were justly cast:
But this new Jehu spurs the hot-mouthed horse,

103–6. Martin Clifford (an associate of the Duke of Buckingham) wrote in his
A Treatise of Humane Reason (1674) that every man should be allowed quietly to
follow his own religion, and that each religion is mistaken in thinking its own
sacred texts to be an infallible guide to the truth: 'The Jew says, I cannot err, for
I follow the Old Testament, which is infallible, and only that. The Christian assures
himself of the Truth as long as he is guided by the Evangelists and Apostles, whose
Writings are the infallible dictates of the Holy Ghost. The Turk assumes the same
from the Alcoran; and the Heathen from Oracles, Sybill's Books, and the like.
What shall I do? None of all these Books can be believed by their own Light,
for there are things equally strange in them all' (79, 87–8). The nonconformist
and future Whig pamphleteer Robert Ferguson replied: 'I know not an Opinion
more pernicious in its Consequences, than that Men may be as safe in the Event
by embracing Turcism as Christianity. . . . Should Persons conspire to overthrow
all Revelation, they could not fall upon a Method more likely to effect it, than by
endeavouring to persuade the World that there are things equally as strange in the
Bible as in the Alcoran' (*The Interest of Reason in Religion* (1675) sig. a4ᵛ) (*Works*).
103. i.e. popular opinion is the arbiter even of the truth of religion.
117–18. The Whigs, however, argued that the actions of the King were encroaching upon the property and freedom of the people: see *AA* ll. 536n, 777–94n.
119. *Jehu*] leader of a revolt against King Joram; 'and the driving is like the driving of Jehu the son of Nimshi; for he driveth furiously' (2 Kings ix 20). Cp.
Settle: 'besides the specious flattery, *That Kings can do no ill*, and *That all Crimes
are cancelled in a Crown*, he has Religion to drive the Royal Jehu on' (*The Character
of a Popish Successour* (1681) 11; W. O. S. Sutherland). The story of Jehu had
generally been used in the seventeenth century to show that revolt against a
ruler could be justified on religious grounds; D. reinterprets Jehu as an anarchic
revolutionary (see Laura B. Kennelly, *Restoration* xiv (1990) 91–6). D.'s lines also

120 Instructs the beast to know his native force,
     To take the bit between his teeth and fly
     To the next headlong steep of anarchy.
     Too happy England, if our good we knew,
     Would we possess the freedom we pursue!
125 The lavish government can give no more,
     Yet we repine, and plenty makes us poor.
     God tried us once: our rebel fathers fought;
     He glutted 'em with all the power they sought,
     Till mastered by their own usurping brave
130 The free-born subject sunk into a slave.
     We loathe our manna, and we long for quails;
     Ah, what is man, when his own wish prevails!
     How rash, how swift to plunge himself in ill,
     Proud of his power, and boundless in his will!
135 That kings can do no wrong we must believe:
     None can they do, and must they all receive?
     Help heaven! or sadly we shall see an hour
     When neither wrong nor right are in their power!
     Already they have lost their best defence,
140 The benefit of laws which they dispense;
     No justice to their righteous cause allowed,
     But baffled by an arbitrary crowd;
     And medals graved their conquest to record,
     The stamp and coin of their adopted lord.

---

draw upon the traditional image of the ruler controlling the people like a rider
controlling a horse, as in Renaissance equestrian statues and paintings; the image
of horse and rider also serves traditionally for the control of the passions by
reason. Maurer 299 notes that one of Alciati's emblems shows a driver of a
wagon who has lost control of the reins and bits of two furious horses who are
dragging him over a cliff (*Emblematum Flumen* (1551) no. 63).
122. steep] precipice (*OED* B 1).
123. Echoes Virgil: *O fortunatos nimium, sua si bona norint, / agricolas!* ('O too happy
farmers, if they knew their good!'; *Geo.* ii 458–9). Cp. *AA* l. 51*n*.
129. usurping brave] Oliver Cromwell. *brave*] bravo, bully, assassin (*OED* 1b).
131. During their journey through the wilderness the Israelites were given manna
from heaven to eat; when they complained at the lack of meat, God provided
quails, but punished the people with a plague (Numbers xi).
142. The Whigs charged that Charles's government had become arbitrary (as
in Marvell's *An Account of the Growth of Popery and Arbitrary Government* (1677);
cp. *AA* ll. 212, 330, 701, 762). D. replies here that power granted to the crowd
will produce arbitrary government (cp. *AA* ll. 777–94*n*). *baffled*] treated with
scorn (*OED* 2); brought to nothing, thwarted (*OED* 7).
144. stamp] medal (*OED* 15). *coin*] device, impress (*OED* 4).

145   The man who laughed but once, to see an ass
        Mumbling to make the cross-grained thistles pass,
        Might laugh again to see a jury chaw
        The prickles of unpalatable law.
        The witnesses that, leech-like, lived on blood,
150   Sucking for them were med'cinally good;
        But when they fastened on *their* festered sore, ⎫
        Then justice and religion they forswore, ⎬
        Their maiden oaths debauched into a whore. ⎭
        Thus men are raised by factions, and decried,
155   And rogue and saint distinguished by their side.
        They rack ev'n scripture to confess their cause,
        And plead a call to preach in spite of laws.
        But that's no news to the poor injured page:
        It has been used as ill in every age,
160   And is constrained, with patience, all to take,
        For what defence can Greek and Hebrew make?
        Happy who can this talking trumpet seize,
        They make it speak whatever sense they please!
        'Twas framed at first our oracle t' enquire, ⎫
165   But since our sects in prophecy grow higher ⎬
        The text inspires not them, but they the text inspire. ⎭

145–6. The story is told of Crassus by Lucillius (see Thomas Browne, *Pseudodoxia Epidemica* VII xvi 2; Saintsbury).

146. Mumbling] chewing softly (*OED* 3).

147–8. As Charles gained mastery of the political situation in 1681–2 he used the law increasingly to the discomfort of the Whigs, e.g. in the trial of Stephen College (executed August 1681) and the legal attack on the charters by which London and other cities were governed. *chaw*] chew, esp. roughly (*OED*).

149–53. See 'Epistle to the Whigs' l. 186*n.*

151. festered sore] With an allusion to the open wound in Shaftesbury's side, left after an operation in 1668 to remove a hydatid cyst of the liver, which was drained through a pipe. Tory propagandists called him 'Tapski', and the final scene in D.'s *Albion and Albanius* (1685) shows a man '*incompast by several Phanatical Rebellious Heads, who suck poyson from him, which runs out of a Tap in his Side*' (III ii *s.d.*).

154–5. Cp. *AA* 'To the Reader' ll. 5–6.

156–7. Nonconformist preachers claimed the authority of divine inspiration, against Anglican insistence that only ministers ordained in the legally established Church of England had authority to preach.

158–9. Cp. *RL* ll. 400–8.

162. talking trumpet] megaphone.

164. enquire] seek information from (*OED* 3a; citing this as its last example).

London, thou great emporium of our isle,
O thou too bounteous, thou too fruitful Nile,
How shall I praise or curse to thy desert,
170   Or separate thy sound from thy corrupted part!
I called thee Nile; the parallel will stand:
Thy tides of wealth o'erflow the fattened land,
Yet monsters from thy large increase we find
Engendered on the slime thou leav'st behind.
175   Sedition has not wholly seized on thee,
Thy nobler parts are from infection free:
Of Israel's tribes thou hast a numerous band,
But still the Canaanite is in the land;
Thy military chiefs are brave and true,
180   Nor are thy disenchanted burghers few;
The head is loyal which thy heart commands,
But what's a head with two such gouty hands?
The wise and wealthy love the surest way,
And are content to thrive and to obey,
185   But wisdom is to sloth too great a slave;

167. London] London was the seat of Whig opposition to the court, and the theatre in which much of the drama of the Popish Plot and Exclusion Crisis took place. Charles Blount's Whig pamphlet *An Appeal from the Country to the City* (1679) opens with an encomium of London as 'the great Metropolis and Soul of our once flourishing and glorious Kingdom' and continues with a lurid vision of the destruction of the city by papists (1–3). *emporium*] principal centre of commerce; cp. *AM* l. 1205*n*.
168. Cp. *AM* ll. 183–4.
169–70. desert . . . part] a perfect rhyme in seventeenth-century pronunciation.
173–4. Ovid recounts that monstrous half-live forms were discovered in the slime left by the receding Nile (*Met.* i 422–9). D. reverses Settle's application of the image: 'the very Name of a Popish Monarch has the Influence of the Sun in *Egypt*, and daily warms our Mud into Monsters, till they are become our most threatening and most formidable *Enemies*' (*The Character of a Popish Successour* (1681) 3; W. O. S. Sutherland). *increase*] The noun was stressed on the second syllable.
174. Engendered on] *1682 corrected state*; Enlivened by *1682 uncorrected state*.
178. Canaanite] zealot, fanatic (*OED* 2, citing Matthew x 4).
179–82. Control of the City of London was being wrested from the Whigs during 1681–2 (see 'Prologue to *The Duke of Guise*' l. 3*n*). Some of London's *burghers* had become *disenchanted* (freed from magical enchantment or illusion (*OED*'s first example apart from Cotgrave's French dictionary)) with the Whig cause; its *head* was the Tory Lord Mayor Sir John Moore (elected September 1681), but its two *gouty hands* were the Whig sheriffs Thomas Pilkington and Benjamin Shute (elected June 1681). In *1682 uncorrected state* the present ll. 179–80 follow ll. 181–2.
182. a] *1682 corrected state*; the *1682 uncorrected state*.

None are so busy as the fool and knave.
Those let me curse; what vengeance will they urge
Whose ordures neither plague nor fire can purge,
Nor sharp experience can to duty bring,
190   Nor angry heaven, nor a forgiving King!
In gospel phrase their chapmen they betray,
Their shops are dens, the buyer is their prey.
The knack of trades is living on the spoil;
They boast ev'n when each other they beguile.
195   Customs to steal is such a trivial thing,
That 'tis their charter to defraud their King.
All hands unite of every jarring sect,
They cheat the country first, and then infect.
They for God's cause their monarchs dare dethrone,
200   And they'll be sure to make his cause their own.
Whether the plotting Jesuit laid the plan
Of murthering kings, or the French Puritan,
Our sacrilegious sects their guides outgo,
And kings and kingly power would murther too.
205   What means their trait'rous combination less,
Too plain t' evade, too shameful to confess.
But treason is not owned when 'tis descried:
Successful crimes alone are justified.

187. urge] provoke (*OED* 7a).
188. The plague of 1665 and the fire of 1666.
191. i.e. they cheat their customers ('chapmen': *OED* 4) while using phrases from the gospels.
195. Customs duties were often evaded, and in 1680 the soldiers assisting customs officers in seizing contraband were themselves imprisoned by the Lord Mayor of London (Ogg 422).
201. Jesuit] The Spanish Jesuit Juan Mariana (1536–1623) justified tyrannicide in his *De Rege et Regis Institutione* (1559), and another Spanish Jesuit Francisco Suarez (1548–1617) in his treatise *Defensio Catholicae Fidei contra Anglicanae Sectae Errores* (1613) argued that a heretical king, once deposed by decree from the Pope, could be killed by a private individual; the murder of kings was popularly regarded as a Jesuit speciality, e.g. in John Oldham's *Satyrs upon the Jesuits* (1681). The similar regicidal tenets of Jesuits and Protestant fanatics were often noted, e.g. in the sermons on the anniversary of Charles I's execution, 30 January 1682, by Henry Maurice (*A Sermon Preached* . . . (1682) 32) and Edward Pelling (*A Sermon Preached* . . . (1682) 13–14).
202. French Puritan] See 'Epistle to the Whigs' ll. 90–1*n*.
205. combination] The Association (see 'Epistle to the Whigs' l. 44*n*). *less*] less than tyrannicide.
207. i.e. traitors do not admit their plans to be treason when they are discovered.

The men who no conspiracy would find,
210   Who doubts, but had it taken, they had joined:
Joined in a mutual cov'nant of defence,
At first without, at last against their prince.
If sovereign right by sovereign power they scan,
The same bold maxim holds in God and man:
215   God were not safe, his thunder could they shun
He should be forced to crown another son.
Thus when the heir was from the vineyard thrown,
The rich possession was the murtherers' own.
In vain to sophistry they have recourse:
220   By proving theirs no plot, they prove 'tis worse —
Unmasked rebellion, and audacious force;
Which though not actual, yet all eyes may see
'Tis working in th' immediate power to be:
For from pretended grievances they rise,
225   First to dislike, and after to despise;
Then Cyclop-like in human flesh to deal,
Chop up a minister at every meal;
Perhaps not wholly to melt down the King,
But clip his regal rights within the ring;
230   From thence t' assume the power of peace and war,
And ease him by degrees of public care.
Yet to consult his dignity and fame
He should have leave to exercise the name,
And hold the cards while Commons played the game.

209. *The men*] the jury who rejected the charge of treason against Shaftesbury.
213. i.e. if they define sovereignty by its power rather than its legitimacy.
217–18. In the parable of the wicked husbandmen the owner of a vineyard sent his son to receive the fruits of it, but the husbandmen said, 'This is the heir; come, let us kill him, and let us seize on his inheritance. And they caught him, and cast him out of the vineyard, and slew him' (Matthew xxi 33–41).
220. As in *No Protestant Plot* (see 'Epistle to the Whigs' l. 28*n*).
223. *working*] plotting (*OED* 22); striving (*OED* 25); perhaps also 'fermenting' (*OED* 32), for which cp. *AA* l. 141*n*.
226–7. The Cyclopes were giants who had no assemblies or laws; one of them cut up and ate two of Odysseus' companions at each meal (*Odyssey* ix 113, 289–344; cp. *Astraea Redux* l. 45*n*). D. refers here to the Commons' attacks on Charles's ministers, e.g. the moves to impeach Clarendon in 1667 and Danby in 1679, recalling also the Act of Attainder against Charles I's minister Strafford, who was executed in 1641.
229. Coins which were clipped within the ring or circle surrounding the King's head were not legal tender.
230. Only the King could declare war and make peace treaties.
232. *consult*] have respect for (*OED* 5).

235 For what can power give more than food and drink,
     To live at ease, and not be bound to think?
     These are the cooler methods of their crime,
     But their hot zealots think 'tis loss of time:
     On utmost bounds of loyalty they stand,   ⎫
240 And grin and whet like a Croatian band   ⎬
     That waits impatient for the last command. ⎭
     Thus outlaws open villainy maintain:
     They steal not, but in squadrons scour the plain,
     And if their power the passengers subdue,
245 The most have right, the wrong is in the few.
     Such impious axioms foolishly they show,
     For in some soils republics will not grow:
     Our temperate isle will no extremes sustain
     Of pop'lar sway or arbitrary reign,
250 But slides between them both into the best,
     Secure in freedom, in a monarch blessed:
     And though the climate, vexed with various winds,
     Works through our yielding bodies on our minds,
     The wholesome tempest purges what it breeds
255 To recommend the calmness that succeeds.
         But thou, the pander of the people's hearts
     (O crookèd soul, and serpentine in arts),
     Whose blandishments a loyal land have whored,
     And broke the bonds she plighted to her lord,
260 What curses on thy blasted name will fall,   ⎫
     Which age to age their legacy shall call;   ⎬
     For all must curse the woes that must descend on all. ⎭

243. *scour*] move across, looking for enemies.
244. *passengers*] travellers, passers-by.
252–5. Cp. Halifax: 'Our Government is like our climate. There are winds which are sometimes loud and unquiet, and yet with all the trouble they give us, we owe great part of our health unto them; they clear the air, which else would be like a standing pool, and instead of refreshment would be a disease unto us. There may be fresh gales of asserting liberty, without turning into such storms or hurricanes, as that the state should run any hazard of being cast away by them. These strugglings, which are natural to all mixed governments, while they are kept from growing into convulsions do by a mutual agitation from the several parts rather support and strengthen than weaken or maim the constitution; and the whole frame, instead of being torn or disjointed, cometh to be the better and closer knit by being thus exercised.' ('The Character of a Trimmer' (in MS, 1684–5) in *Complete Works*, edited by J. P. Kenyon (1969) 63; cp. Burton, *Anatomy of Melancholy* 1.2.2.5; 2.2.3; Kinsley).
252. *vexed*] agitated, tossed about (*OED* 6).

Religion thou hast none: thy mercury
Has passed through every sect, or theirs through thee;
265   But what thou giv'st, that venom still remains,
And the poxed nation feels thee in their brains.
What else inspires the tongues and swells the breasts
Of all thy bellowing renegado priests,
That preach up thee for God, dispense thy laws,
270   And with thy stum ferment their fainting cause,
Fresh fumes of madness raise, and toil and sweat
To make the formidable cripple great?
Yet should thy crimes succeed, should lawless power
Compass those ends thy greedy hopes devour,
275   Thy canting friends thy mortal foes would be:
Thy God and theirs will never long agree.
For thine (if thou hast any) must be one
That lets the world and humankind alone;
A jolly God that passes hours too well
280   To promise heaven, or threaten us with hell,
That unconcerned can at rebellion sit,
And wink at crimes he did himself commit.

---

263. This was a common charge against Shaftesbury: cp. 'There is no body swears
against my L. *Shaftesbury* . . . for being a Protestant, or being publickly engaged
against *Popery*; I never heard that he was accused for being of any Religion' (*Heraclitus
Ridens* xxxvii (11 October 1681); Kinsley); and 'Being a Gentleman of no Religion
himself, he seems for all that, to Espouse every Devision, and Sub-division of it;
every Faction, and Person, who are bold enough, to stand stiff in opposition to the
Ancient and *Well Setled Government*' (*The Character of a Disbanded Courtier* (1682) 3;
Works). In his later years, Shaftesbury inclined to Deism (Haley 67, 732).   *mercury*]
This is the *OED*'s first example of the metal being used figuratively for liveliness, volatility and inconstancy (*OED* 9). Mercury was used in the treatment of
syphilis (cp. l. 266). W. O. S. Sutherland 128 notes a pun on mercury meaning
newspaper (as in the Whig papers *The True Protestant Mercury* and *The Impartial
Protestant Mercury*), citing the pun in *Heraclitus Ridens* (no. iii; 15 February 1681):
'whether taking so much *Mercury* so ill prepared by the Quacks of *Goatham*-Colledg,
is not the reason why so many People are troubled with Ulcers in their Mouths,
and a continual Salivation of Sedition'.
268. renegado priests] Nonconformist ministers, formerly Anglican clergy, who
could not accept the Act of Uniformity (1662) or the Test Act (1673) (Schless).
renegado] renegade: apostate, turncoat.
270. stum] must used for renewing vapid wine (*OED* 1b).
271–2. Cp. 'Lucretius: Against the Fear of Death' ll. 204–5.
272. cripple] For other denigrations of Shaftesbury's physical form see *AA* ll. 156–8n.
274. Compass] bring about.
278–82. A caricature of the Epicurean notion of the gods as explained by
Lucretius: *omnis enim per se divom natura necessest / immortali aevo summa cum pace
fruatur / semota ab nostris rebus seiunctaque longe; / nam privata dolore omni, privata*

A tyrant theirs; the heaven their priesthood paints
A convent'cle of gloomy sullen saints,
285 A heaven, like Bedlam, slovenly and sad,
Foredoomed for souls with false religion mad.
    Without a vision poets can foreshow
What all but fools by common sense may know:
If true succession from our isle should fail,
290 And crowds profane with impious arms prevail,
Not thou, nor those thy factious arts engage ⎤
Shall reap that harvest of rebellious rage   ⎬
With which thou flatt'rest thy decrepit age. ⎦
The swelling poison of the several sects
295 Which, wanting vent, the nation's health infects,
Shall burst its bag, and fighting out their way
The various venoms on each other prey.
The presbyter, puffed up with spiritual pride,
Shall on the necks of the lewd nobles ride,
300 His brethren damn, the civil power defy,
And parcel out republic prelacy.
But short shall be his reign: his rigid yoke
And tyrant power will puny sects provoke,

---

periclis, / ipsa suis pollens opibus, nil indiga nostri, / nec bene promeritis capitur neque tangitur ira. (*De Rerum Natura* i 44–9: 'For whatsoere's *Divine* must live in Peace, / In undisturb'd and everlasting ease: / Not care for us, from fears and dangers free, / Sufficient to its own felicity: / Nought here below, Nought in our power it needs; / Nere smiles at good, nere frowns at wicked deeds', tr. Creech (1682)).

282. Zeus rebelled against and deposed his father Chronos (Pierre Legouis, *TLS* (15 July 1965) 602).

284. convent'cle] clandestine meeting of Nonconformist Protestants. *OED* only records a pronunciation stressing the second syllable, but D. also stresses the word on the first syllable in 'Prologue to *The Disappointment*' l. 64, where it again has a hypermetrical extra syllable: 'They make it bawdier than a conventicle'.

286. Foredoomed] according to the Calvinist doctrine that the godly elect are pre-destined to eternal salvation.

293. decrepit age] Shaftesbury was sixty and in poor health.

297. Cp. *AA* ll. 1012–15.

298. presbyter] Puritan ministers preferred this Greek NT term (meaning 'elder') to 'priest'.

299. lewd nobles] e.g. the Duke of Buckingham (*AA* ll. 544–68n), the Earl of Huntingdon (*AA* l. 574n), Lord Howard of Escrick (*AA* ll. 575–6n).

301. republic prelacy] quasi-republican government of the church by presbyters instead of hierarchical government by bishops.

303. puny] later, i.e. newly emerging (*OED* 2); small, feeble (*OED* 4).

And frogs and toads and all the tadpole train
305 Will croak to heaven for help from this devouring crane.
The cut-throat sword and clamorous gown shall jar
In sharing their ill-gotten spoils of war:
Chiefs shall be grudged the part which they pretend, ⎫
Lords envy lords, and friends with every friend   ⎬
310 About their impious merit shall contend.   ⎭
The surly Commons shall respect deny,
And jostle peerage out with property.
Their general either shall his trust betray
And force the crowd to arbitrary sway,
315 Or they suspecting his ambitious aim   ⎫
In hate of kings shall cast anew the frame,   ⎬
And thrust out Collatine that bore their name. ⎭
    Thus inborn broils the factions would engage,   ⎫
Or wars of exiled heirs, or foreign rage,   ⎬
320 Till halting vengeance overtook our age,   ⎭
And our wild labours, wearied into rest,
Reclined us on a rightful monarch's breast.
                    —*Pudet haec opprobria, vobis*
    Et dici potuisse, et non potuisse refelli.

304–5. In Aesop's fable the frogs ask Jove for a king, and he gives them a log; dissatisfied, they ask for an active leader, and he sends a stork, which devours them. They ask Jove to remove 'This cruel Prince that made his Will a Law', but Jove refuses. The moral is that 'No Government can th' unsetled Vulgar please, / Whom Change delights, think Quiet a disease. / Now Anarchy and Armies they maintain, / And wearied, are for King and Lords again' (*The Fables of Æsop*, tr. John Ogilby, second edition (1668) 32). Settle also uses this story (*The Character of a Popish Successour* (1681) 16; W. O. S. Sutherland), as do other writers against royal power (see *POAS* i 189, 251, 281, ii 343).
306. *jar*] fight.
308. *pretend*] claim (*OED* 4b).
311. *surly*] haughty, arrogant (*OED* 2).
316. Cp. 'And cast the kingdoms old / Into another mould' (Marvell, 'An Horatian Ode' ll. 35–6; see *AM* ll. 849–60).
317. Lucius Tarquinius Collatinus took part in the expulsion from Rome of the King Tarquinius Superbus, and was elected consul. Later when a law was passed banishing the entire Tarquin family, he too went into exile (Livy i 50, ii 2). D. suggests that a similar fate awaits the Duke of Monmouth should he become king. Kinsley notes that D. makes the same point in *His Majesties Declaration Defended* (1681; *Works* xvii 212).
320. *halting*] limping.
323–4. Added in *1682 corrected state*. From Ovid, *Met.* i 758–9: 'It is shameful that this opprobrium could be said of you, and that it could not be answered' (D. changes *nobis* ('us') to *vobis* ('you')).

7 Religio Laici

Date and publication. Religio Laici or A Laymans Faith. A Poem was published
by Tonson in late November 1682: Luttrell's copy is dated 28 November
(Macdonald 33), and the poem was advertised in *The Observator* on 30 November. There were three issues of the first edition (siglum: '*1682a*'), and
reprints in 1682 ('*1682b*') and 1683. The present text is from *1682a*, second issue,
which includes revisions in the Preface and l. 456. The first edition includes two
commendatory poems, one anonymous (apparently by John Vaughan: see
Richard H. Perkinson, *PQ* xxviii (1949) 517–18), and one by Thomas Creech;
1683 adds one by Roscommon (see *Poems* ii Appendix B). Although D. considered including *RL* in *Sylvae* (see *Letters* 23), it was not reprinted in D.'s lifetime.

Context. The immediate occasion of *RL* was the publication of *A Critical
History of the Old Testament*, a translation by Henry Dickinson of the *Histoire
Critique du Vieux Testament* (1678) by the French Catholic priest Richard
Simon (1638–1712). This pioneering work of biblical criticism studied the
textual problems of the OT, discussing the corruptions which had crept into
the text in the process of its transmission, and evaluating modern translations.
Simon thought that this demonstration of the unreliability of the text of scripture had grave consequences for the Protestant reliance on scripture as the sole
authoritative source of Christian teaching (see ll. 276–81*n*). But Simon had criticized Catholic as well as Protestant authorities, and copies of the first edition of
the book were seized and burnt in Paris before it was officially published. It was
reprinted in 1680 in Amsterdam (three impressions). Rejoinders soon appeared:
Charles Marie Du Veil (1678) pointed out the dangerous implications of Simon's
work for Protestant reliance on the Bible, and Friedrich Spanheim (1679) argued
that Simon's work was dangerous to Christianity generally. For Simon see
further Jean Steinmann, *Richard Simon et les origines de l'exégèse biblique* (1960) and
Paul Auvray, *Richard Simon* (1974). For the relationship of *RL* to Simon's work
see Phillip Harth, *Contexts of Dryden's Thought* (1968), which provides a detailed
and authoritative discussion of the poem's contexts and arguments, and Gerard
Reedy, *The Bible and Reason* (1985) 90–118.

Around May 1681 Tonson began negotiations with Dickinson for a translation
of Simon's work, but after the translation was complete he withdrew from what
he now considered to be a dangerous project; the English version was published
with the imprint of Walter Davis late in 1681 (dated 1682). After poor sales, Tonson
took the book over and reissued it with his own name on the title page, adding
Dickinson's translation of Simon's reply to Spanheim, and including commendatory poems from Richard Duke, Nathaniel Lee and Nahum Tate; another
appeared in *Sylvae* (1685). Harth 194 suggests that *RL* may have originated as
D.'s commendatory poem for this volume (perhaps the extant ll. 228–51). D.
might have been motivated not only by his intellectual interest in the work, and
loyalty to Tonson, but also by the Cambridge connection with Dickinson, who
was a graduate of D.'s college, Trinity (matric. 1673, LLB 1678). For the publishing history of the translation see Charles E. Ward, *MLN* lxi (1946) 407–12.
Dickinson saw the translation as a means of combating deism, by 'giving in English
a Piece of so much Learning, and from whence we may draw convincing Arguments
for the confuting of all the atheistical Opinions of our Age. There are a sort of
half-learned men . . . searching out of the Bible those things onely which at

the first sight seem to destroy the authority of it. . . . We have a fresh example of what I have been saying in the person of him, who, not many years ago, occasion'd the publishing of that excellent Piece, intituled, *A Letter to A Deist*' (sig. A2^{r-v}). Reaction to the translation included a letter from John Evelyn to John Fell, Bishop of Oxford, on 19 March 1682, expressing concern that Simon's book would be seen as undermining the Protestant claim to rest faith on scripture alone (*Diary and Correspondence of John Evelyn*, edited by William Bray, 4 vols (1854) iii 264–7; Harth 185–6). Dissenters were also worried, and William Lorimer's *An Examination of a Considerable Part of Pere Simon's Critical History of the Old Testament* appeared in 1682 with a preface by Richard Baxter.

The wider context for *RL* is that of religious controversy in the Restoration period. The principal guide to this is Harth's book, though Sanford Budick's *Dryden and the Abyss of Light* (1970) and Victor M. Hamm's article on D. and Catholic apologists, *PMLA* lxxx (1965) 190–8, are also useful. (Louis I. Bredvold's *The Intellectual Milieu of John Dryden* (1934) includes interesting material, but his argument that *RL* is almost Catholic in spirit is misguided, and has been refuted by Thomas H. Fujimura, *PMLA* lxxvi (1961) 205–17.) Four questions of particular concern to *RL* may be distinguished. (i) The poem places great emphasis upon the right use of reason in religious matters. Anglican theology had come to stress the importance of rational enquiry as an aid to religious understanding: in different ways this was a concern of the Tew Circle in the 1630s (whose members included Viscount Falkland and William Chillingworth), the Cambridge Platonists in the 1650s (including Benjamin Whichcote, Ralph Cudworth, Henry More and John Smith), and the group which was now being called Latitudinarian (including Edward Stillingfleet and John Tillotson: for their beliefs see Simon Patrick, *A Brief Account of the New Sect of Latitude-Men* (1662)). For discussions of the importance of reason in Restoration religion see R. W. McHenry, *Mosaic* vii (1974) 69–86; Spurr 249–69 (a useful brief context for the debates in *RL*) and in *JHI* xlix (1988) 563–85; Lotte Mulligan in *Occult and Scientific Mentalities in the Renaissance*, edited by Brian Vickers (1984) 375–401; Gillian Manning, *SC* viii (1993) 99–121; and *Philosophy, Science and Religion in England 1640–1700*, edited by Richard Kroll et al. (1992). D. argues that reason has an important place in the understanding of religious matters, but it cannot produce all the answers, and has to give way to faith at the appropriate point. (ii) The poem combats the deist position, according to which human reason is sufficient to discover that there is a God, and that man is to serve him through worship. Deism in England is generally traced back to Lord Herbert of Cherbury and his treatises *De Veritate* (1624) and *De Religione Laici* (1645; edited by and tr. Harold R. Hutcheson (1944)). In Restoration England deist ideas had some currency, but not in printed form until *The Oracles of Reason* (1693), a collection of tracts edited by Charles Blount, though Harth notes that two of the pieces in this collection are found in MS (bound with printed tracts in BL 873.b.3) and might therefore have been available to D. in MS form when writing *RL*. For a discussion of seventeenth-century deism see Hutcheson 55–81 and Harth 56–94, and for contemporary views of deism see Edward Stillingfleet's *A Letter to a Deist* (1677), and William Stephens's *An Account of the Growth of Deism in England* (1696). D. argues against the deist that human intuition is insufficient, and only supernatural revelation can inform us truly and fully of God and his will; in any case, human reasoning is itself only the afterglow of revelation. (iii) The poem combats the Roman Catholic position that church tradition, specifically that embodied in the papacy, provides the only authoritative guide that God has given mankind. Against this claim D. argues that scripture is the only authoritative word

of God, and that this, carefully interpreted, gives man all he needs to know.
This is the common tenor of Protestant apologetics throughout the seventeenth
century. (iv) The poem also combats the nonconformists, who rely upon the
inspiration of the spirit to guide them in interpreting scripture, and who will admit
no human authority external to themselves. Although the dissenting sects
had been marginalized and contained by the Restoration settlement, they still
flourished, and the upheaval of the Exclusion Crisis in 1680–2 had been fuelled
partly by adherents to 'the Good Old Cause', who combined republicanism in
politics with Nonconformity in religion. All in all, RL argues for a non-Calvinist,
Anglican position, which insists that the use of reason in matters of religion is
necessary but insufficient; man's natural reason and intuition need to be corrected
and completed by revelation; God's revelation is found definitively in the Bible;
the Bible may be troubled by textual errors but is clear from doubt at all *but more how?*
important points; interpretation should take tradition into account, but cannot
rely upon it; and private reason or inspiration must be checked by tradition and
consensus.

Structure. These topics are organized into a carefully designed argument, the first
part of which Harth (96) outlines thus:

    I.   *Necessity of Revelation* (ll. 1–125).
        (a) Inadequacy of natural religion (ll. 1–92).
        (b) Our dependence on revelation for the means of atonement (ll. 93–125).
    II. *Proofs that this Revelation is Contained in the Bible* (ll. 126–67).
        (a) Superiority of its teachings to those of other religions in answering the ends of human life (ll. 126–33).
        (b) Antiquity of its laws (ll. 134–7).
        (c) Character and circumstances of its authors (ll. 138–45).
        (d) Confirmation of its doctrines by miracles (ll. 146–51).
        (e) Its remarkable reception, in spite of so many hindrances, internal and external (ll. 152–67).
    III. *Answer to the Objection of the Deist* (ll. 168–223).

At this point D. turns to Simon's book, and we may summarize the argument
of the rest of the poem thus:

    ll. 224–51: Commendation of Simon's book and Dickinson's translation.
    ll. 252–75: If the text of the Bible (upon which Protestants rely) has suffered through the process of transmission over the centuries, all the more so has oral tradition (upon which Catholics rely).
    ll. 276–81: Interjection of the Catholic argument that only church tradition can provide a reliable guide when the text of the Bible is uncertain.
    ll. 282–369: The Anglican rejoinder that the text of the Bible is sufficiently clear at all essential points, and if it needs to be interpreted by reference to tradition, the most reliable tradition is the most ancient one, i.e. the interpretations of scripture provided by the early church fathers, not by the modern papacy.
    ll. 370–97: During the Middle Ages the Catholic Church kept the Bible in the hands of the priests; at the Reformation the people discovered what it was of which they had been deprived.

ll. 398–426: The widespread availability of the Bible had the unfortunate effect of permitting individual interpretations of scripture, and encouraging the proliferation of sects.

ll. 427–50: The safest way to proceed is to rely upon the clear passages of scripture, and to seek guidance from authoritative tradition, setting aside idiosyncratic personal opinions in the interests of public harmony.

Sources. Many of the arguments in *RL* are commonplaces of seventeenth-century religious debate, but Harth established that D. made extensive use of Sir Charles Wolseley's *The Reasonablenes of Scripture-Belief* (1672), which he followed closely in the arguments against deism in the first half of *RL*. D. may also have used Wolseley's *The Unreasonablenesse of Atheism Made Manifest* (1669). Other likely sources were Richard Burthogge's *Causa Dei* (1675) (see Budick (1970) 85–92) and Hamon L'Estrange's *Considerations, upon Dr Bayly's Parenthetical Interlocution* (1651) (Sanford Budick, *N & Q* ccxiv (1969) 375–9). D.'s knowledge of deism might have derived from reading Lord Herbert of Cherbury, but Harth showed that D.'s formulation of the seven catholic articles is closest to that found in the tract 'Of Natural Religion', first printed in 1693 but possibly available to D. in MS (see above and ll. 42–61n). Since Stephens in *An Account of the Growth of Deism in England* says that he has gained his knowledge of deist principles from enquiry and conversation among acquaintances in London, rather than from reading, D. may likewise have been able to draw upon personal contacts. For the second part of *RL*, which discusses the issues raised by Simon's book, D. evidently read at least some parts of the *Critical History* attentively. D.'s passages defending the Protestant reliance on the authority of scripture against the Catholic adherence to church tradition draw upon a debate in which many writers had been embroiled for decades (see Harth 199–200); since most of their arguments had become commonplaces, it is impossible to establish D.'s sources here with any confidence, though he evidently knew Hooker (see Preface l. 324). The records of D.'s purchases at book auctions on 19 April 1680 and 15 May 1682 show that he was reading extensively in Protestant and Catholic theology: for details see T. A. Birrell, *ES* xlii (1961) 193–217. K. W. Gransden (*SEL* xvii (1977) 397–406) argues for the general influence of Latin satire on *RL*.

Reception. Contemporary reception seems to have been muted. Luttrell wrote 'Atheisticall' on his copy (Macdonald 33). For Henry Care's response see Preface l. 300n. Charles Blount's *Religio Laici* (1683) is addressed to D. and commends *RL*, but is largely derived from Herbert of Cherbury (see Harth 92–4). Two poems in *MP* (1684) commend *RL*, one by Roscommon and the other anonymous. Robert Gould in *The Laureat* [1687] derides D.'s discussion of Athanasius, and J. R.'s *Religio Laici* (1688) borrows D.'s title for an attack on his change of religion. William Lowth's *A Vindication of the Divine Authority and Inspiration of the Writings of the Old and New Testaments* (1692) refers to D.'s treatment of Simon in *RL* (sigs. b^r-b2^r); reprinted in Hammond and Hopkins 392–3; see also 371, 379, 388–9.

Religio Laici
or
A Layman's Faith
A Poem

Ornari res ipsa negat; contenta doceri.
didactic; not striving to be b

The Preface

A poem with so bold a title, and a name prefixed from
which the handling of so serious a subject would not be
expected, may reasonably oblige the author to say
somewhat in defence both of himself and of his under-
5   taking. In the first place, if it be objected to me that
being a layman I ought not to have concerned myself
with speculations which belong to the profession of
divinity, I could answer that perhaps laymen, with
equal advantages of parts and knowledge, are not the
10   most incompetent judges of sacred things; but in the
due sense of my own weakness and want of learning,
I plead not this: I pretend not to make myself a judge of
faith in others, but only to make a confession of my
own; I lay no unhallowed hand upon the ark, but wait
15   on it, with the reverence that becomes me, at a distance.
In the next place, I will ingenuously confess that the
helps I have used in this small treatise were many of
them taken from the works of our own reverend
divines of the Church of England, so that the weapons
20   with which I combat irreligion are already consecrated;
though I suppose they may be taken down as lawfully

¶**7**. *Title. Religio Laici*] 'The religion of a layman'. The title has precedents in
Lord Herbert of Cherbury's *De Religione Laici* (1645; its running title is *Religio
Laici* (Harth 62)), Sir Thomas Browne's *Religio Medici* (1642) and Sir George
Mackenzie's *Religio Stoici* (1665).
Epigraph. 'The subject itself refuses to be ornamented; it is content to be
explained' (Manilius, *Astronomica* iii 39). In the 'Dedication of the *Aeneis*' (1697)
(*Works* v 318) D. quotes this line again, and applies it to Horace's satires and
epistles.
9. parts] abilities, talents.
14. lay no unhallowed hand upon the ark] Uzzah was struck dead by God for touching the ark in order to stop it toppling (1 Chronicles xiii 9–10; cp. *AA* l. 804*n*).

as the sword of Goliah was by David, when they are to
be employed for the common cause against the enemies
of piety. I intend not by this to entitle them to any of
25   my errors, which yet I hope are only those of charity to
mankind; and such as my own charity has caused me to
commit, that of others may more easily excuse. Being
naturally inclined to scepticism in philosophy, I have no
reason to impose my opinions in a subject which is
30   above it; but whatever they are I submit them with all
reverence to my mother church, accounting them no
further mine than as they are authorized, or at least
uncondemned, by her. And indeed, to secure myself
on this side, I have used the necessary precaution of
35   showing this paper before it was published to a judicious
and learned friend, a man indefatigably zealous in the

22. *sword of Goliah*] David, fleeing from Saul, took the sword of Goliath whom
he had killed (1 Samuel xxi 8–9; cp. *HP* ii 599–600).
24. *entitle them to*] impute to them (*OED* 5c).
28. *scepticism*] Harth 1–31 argues convincingly that this refers to modesty and
diffidence in enquiry, as advocated by the Royal Society and by others in the
Restoration, rather than to the sceptical approach to epistemology which derives
from Greek philosophy and is exemplified in Montaigne. The opposite to *scepticism* in this Restoration sense would be dogmatism. 'He is drawing our attention to his way of reasoning, not to his theory of knowledge' (Harth 7). Cp. D.'s
Defence of EDP (1667): 'my whole Discourse was Sceptical, according to that way
of reasoning which was used by *Socrates, Plato*, and all the Academiques of old,
which *Tully* and the best of the Ancients followed, and which is imitated by the
modest Inquisitions of the Royal Society . . . it is a Dialogue sustain'd by persons
of several opinions, all of them left doubtful, to be determined by the Readers'
(*Works* ix 15). In the 'Life of Plutarch' prefixed to *Plutarchs Lives* (1683), D. writes
approvingly of Plutarch's rejection of both the dogmatism of the Epicureans and
Stoics, and the excessive scepticism of the Pyrrhonists: he 'was content . . . only
to propound and weigh opinions, leaving the Judgment of his Readers free without presuming to decide Dogmatically. Yet it is to be confess'd, that in the midst
of this moderation, he oppos'd the two extreams of the *Epicurean* and *Stoick* Sects:
Both which he has judiciously combatted in several of his treatises, and both upon
the same account, because they pretend too much to certainty, in their Dogma's;
and to impose them with too great arrogance; which he, who (following the
Academists,) doubted more and pretended less, was no way able to support. The
Pyrrhonians, or grosser sort of *Scepticks*, who bring all certainty in question, and
startle even at the notions of Common sense, appear'd as absurd to him on the
other side; for there is a kind of positiveness in granting nothing to be more
likely on the one part than on another, which his Academy avoided by inclin-
ing the ballance to that hand, where the most weighty reasons, and probability
of truth were visible' (*Works* xvii 249).
29–30. *a subject which is above it*] i.e. theology.
35–6. *a judicious and learned friend*] Identified as John Tillotson (1630–94) by David
Nichol Smith (*John Dryden* (1950) 88–9); see further David D. Brown, *MLR* lvi

service of the church and state, and whose writings have
highly deserved of both. He was pleased to approve the
body of the discourse, and I hope he is more my friend
40 than to do it out of complaisance. 'Tis true he had too
good a taste to like it all, and amongst some other faults
recommended to my second view what I have written,
perhaps too boldly, on St Athanasius, which he advised
me wholly to omit. I am sensible enough that I had
45 done more prudently to have followed his opinion, but
then I could not have satisfied myself that I had done
honestly not to have written what was my own. It has
always been my thought that heathens who never did,
nor without miracle could hear of the name of Christ,
50 were yet in a possibility of salvation. Neither will it
enter easily into my belief, that before the coming of
our Saviour, the whole world, excepting only the Jewish
nation, should lie under the inevitable necessity of everlasting punishment, for want of that revelation which
55 was confined to so small a spot of ground as that of
Palestine. Among the sons of Noah we read of one only

(1961) 66–9. Tillotson was a notable preacher, Dean of Canterbury 1672–89,
Dean of St Paul's 1689–91, and Archbishop of Canterbury 1691–4. (Kinsley and
Works follow Smith in giving wrong dates here.) His treatise *The Rule of Faith*
(1666) was a work of Protestant apologetics which stressed the role of reason in
matters of religion, and his many published sermons traversed similar ground. He
was not comfortable with the Athanasian Creed, and in a letter to Gilbert Burnet
in 1694 said 'I wish we were well rid of it' (BodL MS Add D. 23 f. 62; Kinsley).
40. complaisance] mere desire to please.
43. Athanasius] See Preface ll. 130–75.
44. sensible] conscious, aware.
48–50. heathens . . . were yet in a possibility of salvation] Christian theologians
had long been divided on the question of whether virtuous heathens who had
had no opportunity to learn of Christ could be saved. The view taken by D. had
some support from contemporaries, e.g. Martin Clifford: 'Certainly in the two
contrary excesses of belief in this matter, that on the side of Mercy hath the appearance of greater safety; and I had rather think with *Origen, That the Devils themselves, by the excessive kindness of their Judge, shall at last be exempted from damnation*,
than that he himself shall be damn'd for that Opinion'; furthermore, 'so small a
part of Mankind hath submitted to the Obedience of the Christian Faith: Now
to condemn all those Millions of persons . . . is so wild an uncharitableness, that
few have been so barbarously severe, as to be guilty of it' (*A Treatise of Humane
Reason* (1675) 30–2); cp. also Tillotson, Wilkins and Burthogge, quoted in Harth
163–4, and Harth's discussion generally, 156–73.
56. sons of Noah] After the flood God blessed the sons of Noah, though Ham
was subsequently cursed because he saw his father's nakedness (Genesis ix 1, 22–5).
Noah's son Japheth was said to be the ancestor of the Gentiles, and their

who was accursed, and if a blessing in the ripeness of
time was reserved for Japhet (of whose progeny we are),
it seems unaccountable to me why so many genera-
60   tions of the same offspring as preceded our Saviour in
the flesh should be all involved in one common condemnation, and yet that their posterity should be entitled to the hopes of salvation: as if a Bill of Exclusion
had passed only on the fathers, which debarred not the
65   sons from their succession. Or that so many ages had
been delivered over to hell, and so many reserved for
heaven, and that the devil had the first choice and God
the next. Truly I am apt to think that the revealed
religion which was taught by Noah to all his sons might
70   continue for some ages in the whole posterity: that
afterwards it was included wholly in the family of Sem
is manifest, but when the progenies of Cham and Japhet
swarmed into colonies, and those colonies were sub-
divided into many others, in process of time their des-
75   cendants lost by little and little the primitive and purer
rites of divine worship, retaining only the notion of
one deity, to which succeeding generations added others
(for men took their degrees in those ages from conquerors to gods). Revelation being thus eclipsed to almost
80   all mankind, the light of nature as the next in dignity
was substituted, and that is it which St Paul concludes to
be the rule of the heathens, and by which they are
hereafter to be judged. If my supposition be true, then
the consequence which I have assumed in my poem
85   may be also true, namely, that deism, or the principles
of natural worship, are only the faint remnants or dying
flames of revealed religion in the posterity of Noah, and

---

knowledge to be the dimly remembered instructions of Noah to his sons (see
Don Cameron Allen, *The Legend of Noah* (1949) 116 and Harth 121).
63. *Bill of Exclusion*] Alluding to the Whig attempts in 1680–1 to pass a bill excluding James, Duke of York, from the succession to the throne.
78. *took their degrees*] graduated (i.e. successful conquerers were deified).
81. *St Paul*] In Romans ii 14–15: 'For when the Gentiles, which have not the
law, do by nature the things contained in the law, these, having not the law, are
a law unto themselves: Which shew the work of the law written in their hearts,
their conscience also bearing witness'.
85. *deism*] Belief in the existence of a God, based upon the testimony of reason,
but rejecting revelation (*OED*'s first example). See headnote, *Context*.

that our modern philosophers, nay, and some of our
philosophizing divines, have too much exalted the
90 faculties of our souls, when they have maintained that
by their force mankind has been able to find out that
there is one supreme agent or intellectual being which
we call God, that praise and prayer are his due worship,
and the rest of those deducements, which I am confid-
95 ent are the remote effects of revelation, and unattain-
able by our discourse—I mean as simply considered,
and without the benefit of divine illumination. So that
we have not lifted up ourselves to God by the weak
pinions of our reason, but he has been pleased to
100 descend to us; and what Socrates said of him, what Plato
writ, and the rest of the heathen philosophers of several
nations, is all no more than the twilight of revelation,
after the sun of it was set in the race of Noah. That there

88–9. our modern philosophers . . . philosophizing divines] Those thinkers who
emphasized the capacity of unaided human reason to form some conception of
God. Among such philosophers would be the deist Lord Herbert of Cherbury
(see headnote); René Descartes, whose *Meditationes de Prima Philosophia* (1641)
argued that the concept of a supremely perfect being proved the existence of that
being; and Walter Charleton, D.'s friend, and a follower of Gassendi (the
addressee of 'To Dr Charleton'). The philosophizing divines would primarily be
the Cambridge Platonists, such as Ralph Cudworth, who thought that religious
truths, once they were revealed by God, were amenable to rational inquiry. D.
is arguing that reason, while having its proper place in religious discourse, is
ultimately incapable of understanding religious truths fully. See further Harth 129–34.
90. faculties of our souls] Renaissance philosophers, developing Aristotle's *De
Anima*, divided the soul into the vegetative, the sensitive and the intellective, each
with its appropriate faculties; the intellective soul had the faculties of intellect,
will and memory (see *The Cambridge History of Renaissance Philosophy*, edited by
Charles B. Schmitt (1988) 455–534, esp. 466–7).
92. intellectual being] a being who can be apprehended only by the intellect, not
by the senses (*OED* 2).
93. praise and prayer are his due worship] For these, and the other inferences of
natural religion, see headnote, *Context*, and ll. 42–61*n*.
94. deducements] deductions.
95–7. Cp. Wolseley: 'So *Plato* and others having spoken somewhat of *One God*
(Though it ought to be noted that the Being of *One God* was never generally
and distinctly acknowledged in any *Heathen Country*, nor was there ever a *Law*
made in any *Heathen State* to establish the Being and Worship of *one God*. Nay,
some have supposed that no particular *Person* did ever purely by *Natural Light*,
determine that there was *but one God*: But that such who have spoken of it had
it from a *Tradition* originated in *Revelation*)' (*Reasonablenes* 109–10; Harth 124–5).
96. discourse] reasoning (*OED* 2); the word is used frequently by Wolseley
(e.g. 83).
99. pinions] wings.

is something above us, some principle of motion, our
105   reason can apprehend, though it cannot discover what it
is by its own virtue. And indeed 'tis very improbable
that we, who by the strength of our faculties cannot
enter into the knowledge of any being, not so much as
of our own, should be able to find out by them that
110   supreme nature which we cannot otherwise define than
by saying it is infinite, as if infinite were definable, or
infinity a subject for our narrow understanding. They
who would prove religion by reason do but weaken the
cause which they endeavour to support: 'tis to take
115   away the pillars from our faith, and to prop it only with
a twig; 'tis to design a tower like that of Babel, which
if it were possible (as it is not) to reach heaven, would
come to nothing by the confusion of the workmen.
For every man is building a several way, impotently
120   conceited of his own model and his own materials:
reason is always striving, and always at a loss, and of
necessity it must so come to pass, while 'tis exercised
about that which is not its proper object. Let us be
content at last to know God by his own methods, at
125   least so much of him as he is pleased to reveal to us in
the sacred scriptures; to apprehend them to be the word
of God is all our reason has to do, for all beyond it is
the work of faith, which is the seal of heaven impressed
upon our human understanding.

---

104. *principle of motion*] Aristotle introduced the idea of a first mover, the origin
of all motion in the universe, which is itself unmoved. This became the first of
Aquinas' five ways of deducing the existence of God from general facts about
the universe. The point applies not to a creator who initiates the universe and
then leaves it (e.g. to run like a clock), but to one who continues as a sustain-
ing cause of the universe, for according to Aristotelian physics (in contrast to
Newton's physics, to be described in his *Principia* (1687)), the continuation of
motion requires explanation, just as much as its initiation does.   *principle*] fundamental source, cause (*OED* 3).
106. *virtue*] strength.
116. *Babel*] The builders of the tower of Babel intended it to reach to heaven;
God decided to 'confound their language, that they may not understand one
another's speech' (Genesis xi 1–9).
119. *several*] different.
120. *conceited of*] possessed with a good opinion of (*OED* 2b).
128. *seal*] D. adapts and reapplies the image of sealing, which was common in
Calvinist writing to indicate those whom God had predestined for eternal salvation (based on Ephesians iv 30 and Revelation vii 4).

0   And now for what concerns the holy bishop Athanasius,
        the preface of whose creed seems inconsistent with
        my opinion, which is that heathens may possibly be
        saved. In the first place, I desire it may be considered
        that it is the preface only, not the creed itself, which (till
135   I am better informed) is of too hard a digestion for my
        charity. 'Tis not that I am ignorant how many several
        texts of scripture seemingly support that cause, but
        neither am I ignorant how all those texts may receive a
        kinder and more mollified interpretation. Every man
140   who is read in church history knows that belief was
        drawn up after a long contestation with Arius concern-
        ing the divinity of our blessed Saviour, and his being
        one substance with the Father; and that thus compiled
        it was sent abroad among the Christian churches as a
145   kind of test, which whosoever took was looked on as an
        orthodox believer. 'Tis manifest from hence that the
        heathen part of the empire was not concerned in it, for
        its business was not to distinguish betwixt pagans and
        Christians, but betwixt heretics and true believers. This
150   well considered takes off the heavy weight of censure
        which I would willingly avoid from so venerable a
        man, for if this proportion, 'whosoever will be saved',
        be restrained only to those to whom it was intended,

0–75. *Athanasius*] St Athanasius (*c.* 296–373) was Bishop of Alexandria, and the
leading opponent of Arianism (which denied the divinity of Christ, and taught
that the Son of God was not eternal, but created by the Father). The Athanasian
Creed (no longer attributed to the saint following the researches of Gerard Voss
(1642)), is prefaced by the assertion: 'Whosoever will be saved: before all things
it is necessary that he hold the Catholick Faith. Which Faith except every one
do keep whole and undefiled: without doubt he shall perish everlastingly'.
Various seventeenth-century divines were troubled by the damnatory clauses in
this creed. Harth 172–3 notes that D.'s arguments here are paralleled by (and
may derive from) those of the distinguished Anglican divine Henry Hammond,
quoted by Gabriel Towerson in his *A Briefe Account of Some Expressions in Saint
Athanasius His Creed* (1663) 8–9: 'I suppose they must be interpreted by their
opposition to those *Heresies* that had invaded the *Church* . . . against the *Apostolick
Doctrine* . . . and were therefore to be *anathematiz'd* after this manner and with
detestation branded and banished out of the *Church*; Not that it was hereby defin'd
to be a *damnable sin*, to faile in the *understanding*, or *believing* the full matter of
any of those *explications* before they were *propounded*'.
141. contestation] disputation, controversy.
151. avoid] remove (*OED* 4).
152. proportion] part of the whole.
153. restrained] restricted.

and for whom it was composed (I mean the Christians),
155   then the anathema reaches not the heathens, who had
never heard of Christ, and were nothing interessed in
that dispute. After all, I am far from blaming even that
prefatory addition to the creed, and as far from cavilling
at the continuation of it in the liturgy of the church,
160   where on the days appointed 'tis publicly read: for I suppose there is the same reason for it now, in opposition to the Socinians, as there was then against the
Arians, the one being a heresy which seems to have
been refined out of the other, and with how much more
165   plausibility of reason it combats our religion, with so
much more caution to be avoided, and therefore the
prudence of our church is to be commended which has
interposed her authority for the recommendation of
this creed. Yet to such as are grounded in the true
170   belief, those explanatory creeds, the Nicene and this of
Athanasius, might perhaps be spared; for what is supernatural will always be a mystery in spite of exposition,
and for my own part the plain Apostles' Creed is most
suitable to my weak understanding, as the simplest diet
175   is the most easy of digestion.

    I have dwelt longer on this subject than I intended,
and longer than perhaps I ought; for having laid down,
as my foundation, that the scripture is a rule, that in all
things needful to salvation it is clear, sufficient and
180   ordained by God Almighty for that purpose, I have left
myself no right to interpret obscure places such as concern the possibility of eternal happiness to heathens,

156. *interessed*] implicated, involved (*OED* 2).

160. *on the days appointed*] The *Book of Common Prayer* (1662) prescribes the use
of the Athanasian Creed in place of the Apostles' Creed at Morning Prayer on
thirteen holy days.

162. *Socinians*] Unitarian belief, which dates from the Reformation, rejects the
doctrines of the Trinity and the divinity of Christ; it became particularly associated with the names of Lelio and Fausto Socini (uncle and nephew, 1525–62 and
1539–1604). See H. J. McLachlan, *Socinianism in Seventeenth-Century England* (1951).
D. bought Johan Crell's Socinian treatise *Ethica Aristotelia. Ethica Christiana* (1681)
in 1682 (Birrell 209).

170. *Nicene*] The Nicene Creed was drawn up at the Council of Nicaea (325) to
defend the orthodox faith against the Arians; a longer version of this creed is
commonly used in the eucharist. Its statements on the person of Christ and the
work of the Holy Spirit are more explanatory than those of the terser Apostles'
Creed.

because whatsoever is obscure is concluded not necessary to be known.

185   But, by asserting the scripture to be the canon of our
faith, I have unavoidably created to myself two sorts of
enemies: the papists, indeed, more directly, because
they have kept the scripture from us, what they could,
and have reserved to themselves a right of interpreting
190   what they have delivered under the pretence of infallibility; and the fanatics more collaterally, because they
have assumed what amounts to an infallibility in the
private spirit, and have detorted those texts of scripture
which are not necessary to salvation to the damnable
195   uses of sedition, disturbance and destruction of the civil
government. To begin with the papists, and to speak
freely, I think them the less dangerous (at least, in
appearance) to our present state, for not only the penal
laws are in force against them, and their number is
200   contemptible, but also their peerage and commons are
excluded from parliaments, and consequently those
laws in no probability of being repealed. A general and
uninterrupted plot of their clergy ever since the Reformation, I suppose all Protestants believe; for 'tis not
205   reasonable to think but that so many of their orders as
were outed from their fat possessions would endeavour

185. canon] standard of judgement or authority (*OED* 2c).
188. kept the scripture from us] Translation of the Bible into English was forbidden
at the Council of Oxford (1407); Tyndale's translation of the NT was printed
abroad in 1525–6, as was his Pentateuch in 1529–30. As the Reformation took
hold in England several translations were made; the first one authorized by Henry
VIII appeared in 1537. *what they could*] as far as they could.
191–3. fanatics . . . private spirit] Members of extreme Protestant sects claimed to
be directly and individually inspired by the Holy Spirit.
191. collaterally] secondarily, indirectly.
193. detorted] twisted.
198–9. penal laws] See *AA* ll. 94–5n.
199. number] See *AA* l. 123n.
201. excluded from parliaments] The Test Act of 1673 excluded all but adherents
to the Church of England from public office, and that of 1678 imposed an affirmation of Anglican belief on Members of both Houses of Parliament.
203. plot] Many seventeenth-century Protestants supposed that Roman Catholic
clergy (esp. the Jesuits) were plotting to overthrow Protestantism in England; episodes
such as the Gunpowder Plot (1605) and the Popish Plot (1678–9) fuelled such fears.
206. outed] ousted. *fat possessions*] After the dissolution of the monasteries,
abbey lands were sold or given to laymen. The supposed desire of the Roman
Catholic religious orders to recover them was a standard topic in seventeenth-
century Protestant polemic.

a re-entrance against those whom they account heretics.
As for the late design, Mr Coleman's letters, for aught
I know, are the best evidence, and what they discover,
210   without wire-drawing their sense, or malicious glosses,
all men of reason conclude credible. If there be anything
more than this required of me, I must believe it as well
as I am able, in spite of the witnesses, and out of a
decent conformity to the votes of Parliament. For I sup-
215   pose the fanatics will not allow the private spirit in this
case: here the infallibility is at least in one part of the
government, and our understandings as well as our wills
are represented. But to return to the Roman Catholics,
how can we be secure from the practice of Jesuited
220   papists in that religion? For not two or three of that
order, as some of them would impose upon us, but
almost the whole body of them, are of opinion that
their infallible master has a right over kings, not only in
spirituals but temporals. Not to name Mariana, Bellar-
225   mine, Emmanuel Sa, Molina, Santarel, Simancha, and

208. *the late design*] The Popish Plot to kill Charles II and impose Catholicism by
force; it was uncovered (but largely invented) by Titus Oates in the autumn of
1678.   *Mr Coleman's letters*] Edward Coleman, secretary to the Duchess of York
and previously to the Duke, corresponded with Louis XIV's Jesuit confessor François
La Chaise and others on the ways of promoting 'the conversion of three kingdoms, and by that perhaps the subduing of a pestilent heresy which has domi-
neered over a greater part of this northern world a long time' (J. P. Kenyon,
The Popish Plot (1972) 101). The letters were discovered during the Popish Plot
crisis; Coleman was found guilty of treason, and executed on 3 December 1678.
210. *wire-drawing*] straining, forcing by subtle argument (*OED* 3c).
213. *witnesses*] The witnesses at the Popish Plot and Exclusion Crisis trials were
frequently suborned: see *AA* l. 922n.
219–20. *Jesuited papists*] The Jesuits were regarded as the leading proponents of
the idea that rulers could be resisted, deposed or even killed in the interests of
the Roman Catholic Church. They were suspected of masterminding the assassination of Henri IV of France, the Gunpowder Plot, and the Popish Plot. For
a contemporary Protestant view of them see John Oldham, *Satyrs upon the Jesuits*
(1681). D. bought John Barnes's anti-Jesuit book *Dissertatio contra Aequivocationes*
(1625) in 1680 (Birrell 199).
224. *Mariana*] Juan Mariana (1536–1623), Spanish Jesuit, whose book *De Rege et
Regis Institutione* (1559) justified tyrannicide.   *Bellarmine*] Roberto Bellarmino
(1542–1621), Italian Jesuit, who was one of the most prominent Roman
Catholic controversialists. Although he defended the temporal authority of the
Pope, he held that the Pope had only an indirect power in temporal matters. D.
bought his *Dottrina Christiana* (1603) in Italian in 1680 (Birrell 208).
225. *Emmanuel Sa*] Manoel Sa (*c.* 1530–96), Portuguese Jesuit, whose works included
a manual of casuistry.   *Molina*] Luis de Molina (1535–1600), Spanish Jesuit, whose

at the least twenty others of foreign countries, we can produce of our own nation Campion, and Doleman or Parsons, besides many are named whom I have not read, who all of them attest this doctrine, that the Pope
230   can depose and give away the right of any sovereign prince, *si vel paulum deflexerit*, if he shall never so little warp; but if he once comes to be excommunicated, then the bond of obedience is taken off from subjects, and they may and ought to drive him like another
235   Nebuchadnezzar, *ex hominum Christianorum dominatu*, from exercising dominion over Christians: and to this they are bound by virtue of divine precept, and by all the ties of conscience under no less penalty than damnation. If they answer me (as a learned priest has lately written)
240   that this doctrine of the Jesuits is not *de fide*, and that consequently they are not obliged by it, they must pardon me if I think they have said nothing to the purpose, for 'tis a maxim in their church, where points of faith are not decided, and that doctors are of contrary
245   opinions, they may follow which part they please, but more safely the most received and most authorized. And their champion Bellarmine has told the world in his *Apology* that the King of England is a vassal to the

---

De Justitia et Jure (1592) argued that rulers' actions are limited by natural law. *Santarel*] Anton Santarelli (1569–1649), Italian Jesuit, whose *Tractatus de haeresi* (1625) created a storm at the University of Paris because of his remarks on the power of popes over kings.   *Simancha*] Jacobus Simancas, late sixteenth-century Spanish theologian and jurist.

227. Campion] Edmund Campion (1540–81), who was part of the first Jesuit mission to England in 1580; he was arrested and executed in 1581 for conspiracy against the crown.   *Doleman or Parsons*] Robert Parsons (1546–1610), who led the mission of 1580 with Campion; he escaped to the continent in 1581. His book *A Conference about the Next Succession to the Crowne of Ingland* (1594), published under the name of R. Doleman, argued that bad kings may lawfully be deposed by their people, and that the church has power over rulers; it was reprinted in 1681.

235. Nebuchadnezzar] The King of Babylon, who was driven out from human society and made to eat grass, because he would not acknowledge that God 'ruleth in the kingdom of men, and giveth it to whomsoever he will' (Daniel iv 31–7).

239. a learned priest] Probably Peter Walsh, an Irish Franciscan, who wrote that the Jesuits' 'deposing Doctrine is not a point of Faith' (*An Answer to Three Treatises Publisht under the Title of The Jesuites Loyalty* (1678) 83; see Perkinson).

240. de fide] a matter of faith.

248. Apology] Bellarmine's *Apologia . . . pro responsione sua ad librum Jacobi Magnae Britanniae Regis* (1610), a reply to James I's defence of the oath of allegiance of

Pope, *ratione directi dominii*, and that he holds in villein-
250   age of his Roman landlord: which is no new claim put
in for England. Our chronicles are his authentic witnesses that King John was deposed by the same plea,
and Philip Augustus admitted tenant. And, which
makes the more for Bellarmine, the French King was
255   again ejected when our King submitted to the church,
and the crown received under the sordid condition of a
vassalage.

'Tis not sufficient for the more moderate and well-
meaning papists (of which I doubt not there are many)
260   to produce the evidences of their loyalty to the late
King, and to declare their innocency in this plot: I will
grant their behaviour in the first to have been as loyal
and as brave as they desire, and will be willing to hold
them excused as to the second (I mean, when it comes
265   to my turn, and after my betters, for 'tis a madness to be
sober alone, while the nation continues drunk), but that
saying of their Father Cress. is still running in my head,
that they may be dispensed with in their obedience to

---

subjects to their sovereign in *Triplici Nodo, Triplex Cuneus* (1607). Bellarmine argues,
from a series of medieval examples, that English kings acknowledged that they
were subject to the Pope (*Opera Omnia*, 12 vols (1870–4) xii 126–8).

249. ratione directi dominii] 'by reason of the right of seignory': i.e. the King
holds his kingdom from the Pope just as a vassal holds his lands *in villeinage* from
his feudal lord.

252. King John] In 1208 Pope Innocent III placed England under an interdict (which
excluded the people from the benefits of the church's offices), because King John
refused to recognize his appointment of Stephen Langton to the see of
Canterbury. In 1212 the Pope issued a bull excommunicating John and deposing him from the throne, and entrusted its execution to Philip of France. The
following year John submitted to the Pope and placed the kingdom under his
suzerainty.

260–1. loyalty to the late King] In *An Apology for the Catholics* (1666; revised 1674)
Roger Palmer, Earl of Castlemaine, listed the Catholic gentry and lords who were
killed fighting for Charles I.

267. Father Cress.] Hugh Paulinus Cressy (1605–74), Benedictine monk and
servant to Queen Catherine; his *Exomologesis* (1647) gave an account of his
conversion to Rome. He wrote various historical and controversial works, and
the *Reflexions upon the Oathes of Supremacy and Allegiance* (1661) was attributed to
him. In this book (60–78) he denies that the Pope's power to depose princes is
held as an article of faith (*de fide*), and observes that books by Suarez, Mariana,
Bellarmine and Santarelli 'which maintained the *Popes temporal Jurisdiction* and *power
to deprive Princes*, and *to absolve Subjects from their Obedience*' have been condemned
in Catholic countries (65). He says that while some Catholics are prepared to
renounce this view, they cannot swear that this position is actually heretical.

an heretic prince while the necessity of the times shall
270   oblige them to it: for that (as another of them tells us)
is only the effect of Christian prudence, but when once
they shall get power to shake him off, an heretic is no
lawful king, and consequently to rise against him is no
rebellion. I should be glad therefore that they would
275   follow the advice which was charitably given them by a
reverend prelate of our church, namely that they would
join in a public act of disowning and detesting those
Jesuitic principles, and subscribe to all doctrines which
deny the Pope's authority of deposing kings and releas-
280   ing subjects from their oath of allegiance: to which
I should think they might easily be induced, if it be true
that this present Pope has condemned the doctrine of
king-killing (a thesis of the Jesuits) amongst others *ex
cathedra* (as they call it) or in open consistory.

285   Leaving them, therefore, in so fair a way (if they
please themselves) of satisfying all reasonable men of
their sincerity and good meaning to the government,
I shall make bold to consider that other extreme of our
religion, I mean the fanatics or schismatics of the Eng-
290   lish church. Since the Bible has been translated into our
tongue, they have used it so as if their business was not
to be saved but to be damned by its contents. If we
consider only them, better had it been for the English
nation that it had still remained in the original Greek
295   and Hebrew, or at least in the honest Latin of St Jerome,

---

270. another] unidentified.
276. prelate of our church] *Works* plausibly suggests Edward Stillingfleet (1635–99),
Dean of St Paul's since 1678, although as a dean he was not a *prelate*. In the
Preface to *The Jesuits Loyalty* (1677), a collection of Catholic tracts, Stillingfleet
challenges Catholics to renounce the Pope's power of deposing princes, and to
take the oath of allegiance, but he also argues that the Catholic tracts which he
reprints are a sufficiently clear indication of Catholics' real beliefs, and that the
country cannot afford to relax its legal tests against them.
282. this present Pope] Innocent XI (1611–89) condemned sixty-five propositions
from casuist moral theology in his bull *Sanctissimus Dominus* (1679), including some
which allowed equivocation under questioning about crimes, and mental reservations when taking an oath of allegiance (*A Decree made at Rome* (1679) 11–13).
283–4. ex cathedra] 'from the throne': used of pronouncements made by the Pope
with the full weight of his office.
284. consistory] the assembly of cardinals convoked by the Pope.
295. Latin of St Jerome] St Jerome (*c.* 342–420) produced a Latin text of the Bible,
partly by revising the Old Latin text, and partly by translating afresh from the

than that several texts in it should have been prevaricated to the destruction of that government which put
it into so ungrateful hands.

300   How many heresies the first translation of Tyndale
produced in few years, let my Lord Herbert's *History of
Henry the Eighth* inform you, insomuch that for the
gross errors in it, and the great mischiefs it occasioned,
a sentence passed on the first edition of the Bible too
shameful almost to be repeated. After the short reign
305   of Edward the Sixth (who had continued to carry on
the Reformation on other principles than it was begun)

Hebrew and Greek. This formed the basis of the Vulgate, the standard Latin text
used by the Roman Catholic Church.
296–7. prevaricated] twisted from their true meaning (*OED* 6).
299. Tyndale] William Tyndale (*c.* 1494–1536) published translations of the NT
(1525), the Pentateuch (1530) and Jonah (1531). His translations were banned
in 1543.
300. Herbert] In his *The Life and Raigne of King Henry the Eighth* (1649; reprinted
1682) Lord Herbert of Cherbury reports Henry VIII's speech of 1545: 'And be
not Judges of your selves, of your phantastical opinions and vain Expositions. In
such high Causes you may lightly erre; and although you be permitted to read
holy Scriptures, and to have the Word of God in your Mother-Tongue, you
must understand, that it is licensed you so to do, onely to inform your own consciences, and to instruct your children and Family; and not to dispute, and make
Scripture a railing or taunting stock against Priests and Preachers, as many light
persons do. I am very sorry to know and hear, how unreverently that most
precious Jewel, the Word of God, is disputed, rimed, sung, and jangled in every
Ale-house and Tavern' (1649 edn. 536; *Works*). The Whig propagandist Henry
Care objected that any Protestant should 'dare brand this good and holy mans
endeavours with causless *Aspersions*, as Mr. *Dryden* (the *Play-maker*) has lately done
in a *Preface* to a Pamphlet which he calls *Religio Laici*, wherein he suggests many
Haeresies produced in few years by *Tyndals* Translation, and that for the *gross Errours
and the great mischiefs it occasion'd, a sentence pass'd on the first Edition of the Bible,
too shameful* (he says) *almost to be repeated*. – Too *shameful*! I pray, Sir! to whom?
If to those that gave it, why then have you no more Manners to Authority, no
more Respect to Truth, than to revive the memory of a thing so *shameful* and
better buried in Oblivion? If to *Tindal*, or his Work, why is not *one* Haeresie
named that it produced, or one of those *shameful* passages Instanc'd in? The World
is not unacquainted with a certain mercenary *Versificator*, whose *Obscure* and *Atheistical*
Sheets (and yet half *Stoln* too, as this very *Preface* is from a little Pamphlet of
George Cranmers, publisht about 41.) has done abundantly more *shameful mischief*
than ever *Tyndals* Translation of the *Holy Bible*. . . . 'Tis perhaps *necessary* that *Cromwels
Panegyrist* and so passionate an Admirer of *Pere Simon*, should cast a *Squint Eye*
not only on Poor *Tyndal*, but all English *Bibles*, and in a word the whole *Reformation*'
(*The Weekly Pacquet of Advice from Rome* v 21 (12 January 1682/3) 165–6; *Works*).
306. on other principles] During the reign of Edward VI (1547–53) the
Reformation was promoted vigorously in a Calvinist direction; the subsequent

everyone knows that not only the chief promoters of
that work but many others whose consciences would
not dispense with popery, were forced for fear of
310   persecution to change climates; from whence returning
at the beginning of Queen Elizabeth's reign, many of
them who had been in France and at Geneva, brought
back the rigid opinions and imperious discipline of
Calvin to graff upon our Reformation: which, though
315   they cunningly concealed at first (as well knowing how
nauseously that drug would go down in a lawful monarchy which was prescribed for a rebellious commonwealth)
yet they always kept it in reserve, and were never wanting to themselves either in court or Parliament, when
320   either they had any prospect of a numerous party of
fanatic members in the one, or the encouragement of
any favourite in the other, whose covetousness was
gaping at the patrimony of the church. They who will
consult the works of our venerable Hooker, or the
325   account of his life, or more particularly the letter
written to him on this subject by George Cranmer, may
see by what gradations they proceeded: from the dislike
of cap and surplice, the very next step was admonitions
to the Parliament against the whole government ecclesi-
330   astical; then came out volumes in English and Latin in
defence of their tenets; and immediately practices were

reign of the Catholic Queen Mary (1553–8) saw the persecution and martyrdom
of many Protestants, including Archbishop Cranmer and Bishops Latimer and Ridley.
312. Geneva] The city of John Calvin (1509–64), whose theology included
the doctrine of predestination. Opposition from some citizens to his exercise of
dictatorial power over Geneva was met with torture and executions.
314. graff] graft.
324. Hooker] Richard Hooker (*c.* 1554–1600) was the principal apologist for the
Elizabethan Church of England. *The Works of Mr. Richard Hooker* (1666) included
his *Laws of Ecclesiastical Polity*, Walton's *Life* and Cranmer's *Letter* of 1598.
Cranmer wrote: 'the first degree was only some small difference about Cap and
Surplice. . . . This was peaceable; the next degree more stirring. *Admonitions* were
directed to the Parliament in peremptory sort against our whole Form of
Regiment; in defence of them, Volumes were published in English, and in Latin;
yet this was no more than writing, Devices were set on foot to erect the Practice
of the Discipline without Authority: yet herein some regard of Modesty, some
moderation was used; Behold, at length it brake forth into open outrage, first in
writing by *Martin* . . . it was imagined that by open rayling (which to the vulgar
is commonly most plausible) the State Ecclesiastical might have been drawn in
to such contempt and hatred, as the overthrow thereof should have been most
grateful to all Men' (32; *Works*).

set on foot to erect their discipline without authority.
Those not succeeding, satire and railing was the next,
and Martin Mar-Prelate (the Marvell of those times)
335   was the first Presbyterian scribbler who sanctified libels
and scurrility to the use of the Good Old Cause, which
was done (says my author) upon this account, that,
their serious treatises having been fully answered and
refuted, they might compass by railing what they had
340   lost by reasoning; and when their cause was sunk in
court and Parliament, they might at least hedge in a
stake amongst the rabble: for to their ignorance all
things are wit which are abusive; but if church and state
were made the theme, then the doctoral degree of wit
345   was to be taken at Billingsgate: even the most saintlike
of the party, though they durst not excuse this contempt and villifying of the government, yet were
pleased, and grinned at it with a pious smile, and called
it a judgement of God against the hierarchy. Thus sec-
350   taries, we may see, were born with teeth, foul-mouthed
and scurrilous from their infancy, and if spiritual pride,
venom, violence, contempt of superiors and slander had
been the marks of orthodox belief, the presbytery and
the rest of our schismatics, which are their spawn, were
355   always the most visible church in the Christian world.
    'Tis true, the government was too strong at that time
for a rebellion, but to show what proficiency they had
made in Calvin's school, even then their mouths
watered at it: for two of their gifted brotherhood
360   (Hacket and Coppinger) as the story tells us, got up into

334. Martin Mar-Prelate] The pen-name of the author of scurrilous puritan tracts
against episcopacy published in 1588–9.   *Marvell*] Andrew Marvell (1621–78) wrote
for the Whig cause, especially in his *An Account of the Growth of Popery and Arbitrary
Government in England* (1677); cp. *The Medal*, 'Epistle to the Whigs' ll. 79–80*n*.
336. Good Old Cause] Presbyterianism, and, more generally, puritan republicanism.
341–2. hedge in a stake] secure oneself against loss in one speculation by betting
on the other side (*OED* 8).
345. Billingsgate] the London fishmarket; a by-word for foul language.
360. Hacket and Coppinger] In 1591 Edmund Coppinger and Henry Arthington
proclaimed that William Hacket had come as Christ's representative to establish
the gospel and rule over Europe. Hacket was executed. Cranmer writes: 'Certain
Prophets did arise, who deeming it not possible that God should suffer that to
be undone, which they did so fiercely desire to have done, Namely, that his
holy Saints, the favourers and Fathers of the Discipline, should be enlarged, and
delivered from persecution; and seeing no means of deliverance Ordinary, were
fain to perswade themselves that God must needs raise some extraordinary means;

a pease-cart and harangued the people to dispose them
to an insurrection, and to establish their discipline by
force; so that however it comes about that now they
celebrate Queen Elizabeth's birthnight as that of their
365 saint and patroness, yet then they were for doing the
work of the Lord by arms against her, and in all probability they wanted but a fanatic Lord Mayor and two
sheriffs of their party to have compassed it.

Our venerable Hooker, after many admonitions
370 which he had given them, toward the end of his preface
breaks out into this prophetic speech: 'There is in every
one of these considerations most just cause to fear, lest
our hastiness to embrace a thing of so perilous consequence' (meaning the Presbyterian discipline) 'should
375 cause posterity to feel those evils which as yet are more
easy for us to prevent than they would be for them to
remedy'.

How fatally this Cassandra has foretold we know too
well by sad experience: the seeds were sown in the time
380 of Queen Elizabeth, the bloody harvest ripened in the
reign of King Charles the Martyr, and because all the
sheaves could not be carried off without shedding some
of the loose grains, another crop is too like to follow;
nay, I fear 'tis unavoidable if the conventiclers be per-
385 mitted still to scatter.

A man may be suffered to quote an adversary to our
religion when he speaks truth; and 'tis the observation
of Maimbourg in his *History of Calvinism*, that wherever

---

and being perswaded of none so well as of themselves, they forthwith must needs
be the instruments of this great work. Hereupon they framed unto themselves
an assured hope that upon their Preaching out of a Pease Cart, all the multitude
would have presently joyned unto them' (*Works of Hooker* 32; *Works*).
361. pease] pea.
364. Queen Elizabeth's birthnight] Elizabeth I's accession day, 17 November,
was celebrated with processions by the more Whiggish Protestants: see Sheila
Williams, *JWCI* xxi (1958) 104–18.
367–8. Lord Mayor and two sheriffs] The Lord Mayor of London and the two
sheriffs, whose duties included the nomination of grand juries, played important
parts in the Exclusion Crisis: cp. *AA* ll. 584–629n, *The Medal* l. 14n.
371–7. 'There is . . . remedy'] *Works of Hooker* sig. D4^r.
384. conventiclers] The Nonconformist Protestants who gathered for worship in
separate congregations or conventicles.
388. Maimbourg] Louis Maimbourg, in his *Histoire du Calvinisme* (1682). D.'s translation of another work by Maimbourg, *The History of the League*, was published

that discipline was planted and embraced, rebellion,
390   civil war and misery attended it. And how indeed
should it happen otherwise? Reformation of church and
state has always been the ground of our divisions in
England. While we were papists, our holy father rid us,
by pretending authority out of the scriptures to depose
395   princes; when we shook off his authority, the sectaries
furnished themselves with the same weapons, and out
of the same magazine, the Bible. So that the scriptures,
which are in themselves the greatest security of
governors, as commanding express obedience to them,
400   are now turned to their destruction, and never since the
Reformation has there wanted a text of their interpreting to authorize a rebel. And 'tis to be noted by the
way, that the doctrines of king-killing and deposing,
which have been taken up only by the worst party of
405   the papists, the most frontless flatterers of the Pope's
authority, have been espoused, defended and are still
maintained by the whole body of nonconformists and
republicans. 'Tis but dubbing themselves the people of
God, which 'tis the interest of their preachers to tell
410   them they are, and their own interest to believe; and
after that they cannot dip into the Bible but one text or
another will turn up for their purpose. If they are under
persecution (as they call it) then that is a mark of their
election; if they flourish, then God works miracles for
415   their deliverance, and the saints are to possess the earth.

in 1684; in his Postscript D. says that the political tenets of Jesuits and of Protestant
sectaries are similar (*Works* xviii 399).
393. our holy father] the Pope.   *rid*] rode.
394. pretending] claiming.
395. princes] *1682a* (*second and third issues*); Princes, (a Doctrine which, though some
Papists may reject, no Pope has hitherto deny'd, nor ever will,) *1682a* (*first issue*).
The reason for this change is unclear.
399. commanding express obedience] e.g. 'Let every soul be subject unto the higher
powers. For there is no power but of God: the powers that be are ordained of
God. Whosoever therefore resisteth the power, resisteth the ordinance of God'
(Romans xiii 1–2).
401. wanted] been lacking.
402. to authorize a rebel] Calvinist political thought authorized subjects to resist
an ungodly ruler: see Quentin Skinner, *The Foundations of Modern Political
Thought*, 2 vols (1978) ii 189–348; and cp. *AA* ll. 765–76n.
405. frontless] brazen, shameless.
414. election] as those predestined by God ('elected') to eternal salvation, according to Calvinist teaching.

They may think themselves to be too roughly
handled in this paper, but I who know best how far
I could have gone on this subject, must be bold to
tell them they are spared; though at the same time I am
420 not ignorant that they interpret the mildness of a writer
to them as they do the mercy of the government: in
the one they think it fear, and conclude it weakness in
the other. The best way for them to confute me is, as
I before advised the papists, to disclaim their principles
425 and renounce their practices. We shall all be glad to think
them true Englishmen when they obey the King, and
true Protestants when they conform to the church
discipline.
      It remains that I acquaint the reader that the verses
430 were written for an ingenious young gentleman my
friend, upon his translation of *The Critical History of the
Old Testament*, composed by the learned Father Simon:
the verses therefore are addressed to the translator of
that work, and the style of them is, what it ought to be,
435 epistolary.
      If anyone be so lamentable a critic as to require the
smoothness, the numbers and the turn of heroic poetry
in this poem, I must tell him that if he has not read
Horace, I have studied him, and hope the style of his
440 *Epistles* is not ill imitated here. The expressions of a
poem designed purely for instruction ought to be plain
and natural, and yet majestic, for here the poet is presumed to be a kind of law-giver, and those three qualities which I have named are proper to the legislative
445 style. The florid, elevated and figurative way is for the
passions, for love and hatred, fear and anger are begotten in the soul by showing their objects out of their true
proportion, either greater than the life, or less; but
instruction is to be given by showing them what they

---

427. *true Protestants*] 'True Protestant' was a title assumed by the Whigs.
430–2. young gentleman . . . Father Simon] See headnote, *Context*.
432. composed] *1682a* (*second and third issues*); written *1682a* (*first issue*).
437. numbers] harmonious rhythms.   *turn*] particular style (*OED* 31, 32).
439. Horace] Cp. Epigraph *n* and *RL* ll. 453–4*n*. However, K. W. Gransden argues
that the manner of *RL* is more akin to that of Juvenal or Lucretius, who argue
a particular case, and offer a *consolatio*, a way of understanding life philosophically
(*SEL* xvii (1977) 397–406).

450   naturally are. A man is to be cheated into passion, but
             to be reasoned into truth.

450–1. Echoes Wolseley, who says that belief in Christianity 'is not to be
imposed upon any man, but all men reasoned and discoursed into an assent to
it' (*Reasonablenes of Scripture-Belief* 78).

1–11. The use of the imagery of light in spiritual writing is very ancient; John
i 1–14 is the starting-point for the image of Christ as the light of the world, and
behind this stands a tradition of Jewish and Hellenistic mysticism (see C. H. Dodd,
The Interpretation of the Fourth Gospel (1953)). Light is widely used as an image
for spiritual understanding in man: the Cambridge Platonists frequently quoted
Proverbs xx 27: 'The spirit of man is the candle of the Lord' (see *The Cambridge
Platonists*, edited by C. A. Patrides (1969) 11–13). The image of reason as a light
is a commonplace of the seventeenth century, and those who would dissuade
from too great a reliance upon reason sometimes liken reason to an *ignis fatuus*,
the phosphorescent light which hovers over marshy ground and leads travellers
astray (e.g. Rochester, *Satire Against Reason and Mankind* (in MS, *c.* 1674) ll. 12–15
(noted by P. J. C. Field, *N & Q* ccxv (1970) 259–60); and Martin Clifford, *A
Treatise of Humane Reason* (1675) 3–4, 63). The comparison which D. makes here
between the light of nature within human beings and that of the moon, and of
revealed Christian religion to that of the sun, is also found in Donne: 'That Light
which issues from the Moone doth best represent and expresse that which in our
selves we call the Light of Nature; For as that in the Moone is permanent and
ever there, and yet it is unequall, various, pale, and languishing, So is our Light
of Nature changeable. . . . And then those artificiall Lightes, which our selves make
for our use and service here, as Fires, Tapers, and such, resemble the light of
Reason. . . . But because of these two kindes of light, the first is too weake, and
the other false . . . we have therefore the Sunne; which is the fountayne and
treasure of all created Light, for an Embleme of that third best light of our understanding, which is the Word of God' (*Biathanatos* [1647], edited by Ernest W.
Sullivan (1984) 109; Kinsley). Harth 117 also compares Richard Burthogge: 'All
the *Light* before Christ, whether that among the Jews, or that among the
Gentiles, was but *Moon*, or *Star-light*, designed only for the *night* preceding; but
it is the *Sun* must Rule by *Day*, and *Christ* the Sun that makes it; by whose
Alone Light we must walk. For as in Nature, the *Light* afforded by the Moon
and Stars, which is of great Advantage, and very much administers to our
Direction, and Comfort in a Journey by night, yet in the day is *none*; The Moon
and Stars that shine by night, and then make other things Visible, they are Invisible
themselves, and Dark by day; So in the *Moral* world, not only the *Law* of *Moses*
to the Jews, but that *Philosophy* and Wisdom among the Gentiles, that before the
coming of the Lord Christ, while it was yet extream Dark, was of extraordinary
Use and Benefit, *It* is no longer *now* of any to them, nor to be insisted on, since
He is come. For now 'tis *broad Day*. One would be glad of Moon-light, or Star-
light, that is to travel by night; but he delires, and is out of his Wits, that would
preferr it before the Sun by Day' (*Causa Dei* (1675) 195–6). Budick (1969) cites
a comparable passage in Henry More's *Conjectura Cabbalistica* (1662) 31. Wolseley
says that no man who 'searches by the Candle-light of *Nature*' will find answers
to spiritual questions (*Reasonablenes* 153). Jeanne H. Welcher, *SEL* viii (1968) 391–6,
suggests that these lines also echo Virgil, *Aen.* vi 268–72, where Aeneas and the
Sibyl begin their descent to the underworld: *ibant obscuri, solo sub nocte per umbram /
perque domos Ditis vacuas et inania regna: / quale per incertam lunam sub luce maligna /*

Religio Laici

Dim as the borrowed beams of moon and stars
To lonely, weary, wandering travellers
Is reason to the soul; and as on high
Those rolling fires discover but the sky
5 Not light us here, so reason's glimmering ray ⎫
Was lent, not to assure our doubtful way,   ⎬
But guide us upward to a better day: ⎭
And as those nightly tapers disappear
When day's bright lord ascends our hemisphere,
10 So pale grows reason at religion's sight,
So dies, and so dissolves in supernatural light.

---

est iter in silvis, ubi caelum condidit umbra / *Iuppiter, et rebus nox abstulit atra colorem*
('Obscure they went thro dreery Shades, that led / Along the waste Dominions
of the dead: / Thus wander Travellers in Woods by Night, / By the Moon's
doubtful, and malignant Light: / When *Jove* in dusky Clouds involves the Skies;
/ And the faint Crescent shoots by fits before their Eyes': 'The Sixth Book of
the *Aeneis*' ll. 378–83).

1–3. D. is not dismissing reason, but assigning it to a secondary role in matters
of religion, where divine revelation must be the primary guide to our understanding. For the imagery cp. the Catholic apologist John Serjeant's description
of reason as 'like a dimsighted man who us'd his Reason to find a trusty Friend
to lead him in the twi-light, and then reli'd on his guidance rationally without
using his own Reason at all about the Way it self' (*Sure-Footing in Christianity*
(1665) 183; quoted by Tillotson in *The Rule of Faith* 153).

2. Perhaps an echo of Spenser's Mutability Cantos, where the moon and the evening
star light the way 'to weary wandring travailers' (*FQ* VII vi 9.9; Budick (1970)).
travellers] Herbert of Cherbury describes his enquiring layman as a *viator* ('traveller') (*De Religione Laici* 86 etc.).

4. rolling] performing a periodic revolution (*OED* 15).   *fires*] stars (*OED* 10b).
discover but the sky] afford a view only of the sky.

5–7. This argument is denied by A. W. in the deist tract 'Of Natural Religion':
'The next Objection against the Sufficiency of Natural Religion to Happiness
eternal, is only a bare Affirmation of our Adversaries, That Natural Religion is
but an imperfect Light, which God gives us so far, as that by improving it, we
may arrive at a Supernatural Knowledge. . . . But I wholly deny any Natural Light
can lead one to a Supernatural; there is no proportion betwixt those two
extreams: There is a Gulph betwixt, a μέγα χάσμα' (*The Oracles of Reason* (1693)
201–2).

5. reason's glimmering ray] Cp. 'Our glim'ring knowledge, like the wandring Light
/ In *Fenns*, doth to incertainties direct' (Davenant, 'The Philosophers
Disquisition' ll. 261–2, in his *Works* (1673)).

8–11. In *The Indian Emperor* (1667), Montezuma argues that Christian teaching
is like a taper, an unnecessary addition to the sunlight, while the Christian priest
sees it as a heavenly beam: the priest says, 'That which we worship, and which
you believe, / From Natures common hand we both receive: / All under

Some few, whose lamp shone brighter, have been led
From cause to cause, to nature's secret head,
And found that one first principle must be;
15   But what, or who that universal he—
Whether some soul encompassing this ball,
Unmade, unmoved, yet making, moving all,
Or various atoms' interfering dance
Leaped into form, the noble work of chance,

---

various names, Adore and Love / One power Immense, which ever rules above.
/ . . . But here our Worship takes another way. / *Mont.* Where both agree 'tis
there most safe to stay: / For what's more vain then Publick Light to shun, / And
set up Tapers while we see the Sun? / *Chr. Pr.* Though Nature teaches whom
we should Adore, / By Heavenly Beams we still discover more' (V ii 61–72).
12–22. This passage refers to the attempts of classical philosophers to understand
the origins of the universe.
12–14. Cp. Wolseley: 'The single exercise of natural reason, in such an inquiry,
will safely conduct a man to the conclusion of some *first cause*, and some one
Supreme Being the cause of all Beings, which we call God. . . . If we can happily
bring mankind to God by this high-way of their reason, and light a man to his
Creator by this *Lamp* that continually burns in his own soul, we shall then prove
Atheism a very lye' (*Unreasonablenesse* 45).
13. D.'s interest in how man may understand the secret origins of life, and the
often inscrutable causes of events, is evident in many poems, e.g. in the account
of the naval war and the causes of the Fire of London in *AM* ll. 137–44, 661–4,
797–800, 849–68; in the injunction to leave alone those things which God has
hidden ('Horace: *Odes* III xxix' ll. 40–9); in the encomium of the knowledge-
able farmer in 'The Second Book of the *Georgics*': 'Happy the Man, who, studying Nature's Laws, / Thro' known Effects can trace the secret Cause' (ll. 698–9);
throughout 'Of the Pythagorean Philosophy', which celebrates Pythagoras who
'discoursed of heaven's mysterious laws, / The world's original, and nature's cause'
(ll. 89–90); and in Theseus' philosophical summation of life in 'Palamon and Arcite'
iii 1024–83.   *head*] source (*OED* 16).
14. one first principle] The prime mover, which creates the world and sets it in
motion; cp. Preface l. 104*n*. The idea derives from Aristotle (*Metaphysics* XII
1071b–1073a), who argued that the prime mover is eternal, and cannot itself change
or move (cp. l. 17).
15. Cp. Wolseley: 'That God is, and that he is to be *Served*, my *Reason* will tell
me; But *What* he is! and after what *Manner* he *Exists* . . . I must be taught from
above' (*Reasonablenes* 128–9; Harth 126).
16. soul] Plato thought of the soul as the primary source of all things: 'Of all the
planets, of the moon, of years and months and all seasons, what other story shall
we have to tell than just this same, that since soul, or souls, and those souls good
with perfect goodness, have proved to be the causes of all, these souls we hold
to be gods, whether they direct the universe by inhabiting bodies, like animated
beings, or whatever the manner of their action?' (*Laws* 899b; tr. A. E. Taylor).
18–19. Epicurus taught that the world was brought about by the chance collocation of atoms; see headnote to 'Lucretius: Against the Fear of Death'.
He is cited repeatedly by Christian apologists in the Restoration, who use him

20   Or this great all was from eternity—   ⎫
      Not ev'n the Stagirite himself could see; ⎬
      And Epicurus guessed as well as he.   ⎭
      As blindly groped they for a future state,
      As rashly judged of Providence and Fate.

as the chief atheistic adversary who must be refuted: e.g. Edward Stillingfleet, *Origines Sacrae* (1662) *passim*, John Tillotson, *The Wisdom of Being Religious* (1664) 18–20, and Wolseley in *Reasonablenes*, who has an extensive refutation of Epicureanism.

18. interfering] colliding (*OED* 2).   *dance*] Wolseley uses this image when writing scathingly of Epicurus' theory: 'If the *dancing motion* of these *Atoms*, in this fancied space, did by chance first dance the World into this *Form*, and *caper'd* the Sun, and the Moon, and the Starres into their stations above us, and placed every thing in the posture it is in About us, and Below us; what is the reason these *Atoms* never danced themselves into any thing since?' (*Unreasonablenesse* 91).

19. Leaped] Lucretius says that the atoms 'leap' (*dissiliant: De Rerum Natura* ii 87); cp. 'Lucretius: Against the Fear of Death' l. 20; 'A Song for St Cecilia's Day' l. 9.

20. Aristotle (in *De Caelo*) argued that the world is eternal, and cannot be said ever to have been generated. His view was much contested by Restoration writers, e.g. Stillingfleet in *Origines Sacrae* 423–40, Tillotson in *The Wisdom of Being Religious* 17–18 and Wolseley, who devotes much of *The Unreasonablenesse of Atheism* to contesting the argument that the world is eternal, seeing it as supporting atheism: 'The Atheist usually objects, in this matter, and pleads for the worlds eternity, by urging that *maxim* of *Aristotle*, so much renowned by him, that he saies, all *Philosophers* did agree to it; which is, that *ex nihilo nihil fit*, out of *nothing, nothing can be produced*. And therefore they infer from thence, either an eternity in the world, or in some pre-existing matter' (63). Wolseley regards this as one of the dangerous elements in pagan philosophy which are leading astray contemporary youth: 'Whatever can be fetched from *Aristotle* and others to make good the worlds eternity, is greedily embraced: and all the notions of *Epicurus*, to make good the *Hypothesis of Atoms*, are not only revived and justified, but improved, to the total denial of a God, in the height of all Atheistical principles . . . that he is thought a freshman in the highest sort of learning, that has not imbibed some of this kind of Philosophy' (37–8).

21. Stagirite] Aristotle, who was born at Stagira in Macedonia.

23. future state] Plato's ideas concerning the future state are set out in the *Phaedo*, in which Socrates argues that the soul is immortal because it can perceive and share in truth, goodness and beauty, which are eternal; moreover, only in another life can God's justice be shown. Aristotle, however, argued in *De Anima* that the soul is simply the form of organization of a living body, and therefore it is nonsensical to suggest that this might survive the dissolution of the body. Epicurus thought that after death the body dissolved into its constituent atoms (see 'Lucretius: Against the Fear of Death'). Charles Blount surveys classical opinion on this issue in *Anima Mundi: or, an Historical Narration of the Opinions of the Ancients Concerning Mans Soul after this Life: According to unenlightened Nature* [1679].

24. Providence and Fate] Although Plato sometimes uses the idea of God as providence (e.g. *Letters* VIII 353b), and Aristotle argues that the good is present in the universe both as the order of the parts and as their ruler (*Metaphysics* XIII

25   But least of all could their endeavours find   *Opinions of*
      What most concerned the good of human kind: *the several*
      For happiness was never to be found,   *sects of*
      But vanished from 'em like enchanted ground.   *philosophers*
      One thought content the good to be enjoyed: *concerning*
30   This every little accident destroyed.   *the*
      The wiser madmen did for virtue toil,   summum
      A thorny, or at best a barren soil.   bonum.
      In pleasure some their glutton souls would steep, ⎫
      But found their line too short, the well too deep, ⎬
35   And leaky vessels which no bliss could keep.   ⎭

1074b–1076a), these ideas are far removed from the Christian understanding of the operation of God in the world. Epicurus taught that the universe was a collection of atoms in random motion, without any guiding principle.

25–35. This passage considers the attempts of classical philosophers to establish the highest good. Although Stoics, Aristotelians and Epicureans seem to be aimed at, the representation of their positions is somewhat imprecise.

25. *marginal note*] Begins by l. 24 in *1682*; positioned here by this edition.   *summum bonum*] highest good.

29. *content*] Not 'satisfaction, pleasure' (*OED* 1) but 'acceptance of conditions or circumstances' (*OED* 2). This is probably an allusion to the Stoic philosophy (propounded originally by Zeno *c.* 300 BC), which taught that the supreme good was to live in consistency with Nature; in its Roman form (e.g. with Epictetus) it taught detachment from everything which is not in our power, and this became an influential philosophy in the Renaissance (e.g. with Lipsius): peace of mind can only be achieved through control of one's emotions. But *pace* D. in l. 30, the true Stoic would not have his peace of mind destroyed by every little accident (quite the opposite), and would have regarded his aim as being virtue rather than content in any solipsistic or hedonistic sense. A sympathy for true Stoic values is seen in D.'s praise of Persius' Stoicism in his 'Discourse Concerning Satire' (1692; *Poems* iii 400–2), though he criticizes Stoicism in the Dedication to *Don Sebastian* (1690; *Works* xv 62).

30. *accident*] unexpected occurrence.

31. *virtue*] Probably a reference to Aristotelianism: Aristotle in his *Nicomachean Ethics* argues that man should pursue the golden mean that is the virtue which lies between two opposite vices.

32. The imagery comes from the parable of the sower: some seeds 'fell upon stony places, where they had not much earth: and forthwith they sprung up, because they had no deepness of earth: And when the sun was up, they were scorched; and because they had no root they withered away. And some fell among thorns; and the thorns sprung up, and choked them' (Matthew xiii 5–7).

33. *pleasure*] Clearly a reference to Epicureanism, though a tendentious and pejorative interpretation of the Epicurean notion of pleasure, which was properly a state of bodily and mental tranquillity (see headnote to 'Lucretius: Against the Fear of Death', and Paul Hammond, *MLR* lxxviii (1983) 5–6).

35. *leaky vessels*] See 'Lucretius: Against the Fear of Death' l. 220*n.*

Thus anxious thoughts in endless circles roll,
Without a centre where to fix the soul:
In this wild maze their vain endeavours end.
How can the less the greater comprehend,
40   Or finite reason reach infinity?
For what could fathom God were more than he.
    The deist thinks he stands on firmer ground,   *System of*
Cries, 'εὕρηκα, the mighty secret's found: *deism.*

36. anxious thoughts] The anxiety of the unsatisfied search for knowledge is a theme
of *Sylvae*: see 'Horace: *Odes* III xxix' l. 44; 'Horace: *Epode* II' l. 55.
38. Wolseley says that 'the more Refined part lost themselves in a Wilderness of
Abstracted Speculations about what they could never distinctly comprehend'
(*Reasonablenes* 113). *wild*] desolate (*OED* 4); wayward, unruly (*OED* 7); going
beyond reasonable limits (*OED* 13). *maze*] The rebel angels, debating philosophical problems in hell, end 'in wandering mazes lost' (*PL* ii 561).
39–40. Cp. Tiresias in *Oedipus* (1679): 'But how can Finite measure Infinite? /
Reason! alas, it does not know it self! / Yet Man, vain Man, wou'd with this
short-lin'd Plummet, / Fathom the vast Abysse of Heav'nly justice' (III i 240–3);
and cp. *HP* i 104–5. Wolseley says: 'This is to measure out *Infiniteness* (which
can have no measure) by *Finiteness*. 'Tis in short, to measure out God to our
selves by our *own Line*' (*Reasonablenes* 52).
42–61. For the history of deism, see headnote, *Context*. D.'s account of the principles of deism follows the catholic articles originally propounded by Lord
Herbert of Cherbury in *De Veritate* (1624) and *De Religione Laici* (1645), but (as
Harth points out, 84–94) the order and wording of D.'s passage are closest to the
version of the articles set out in the essay by 'A. W.' called 'Of Natural Religion,
as opposed to Divine Revelation', which was first printed in *The Oracles of Reason*
(1693) 195–209. Since this tract also survives in MS (BL 873.b.3), it is possible that D. had access to it, or to a similar MS account, when composing *RL*.
The articles in this version are: 'Natural Religion is the Belief we have of an
eternal intellectual Being, and of the Duty which we owe him, manifested to us
by our Reason, without Revelation or positive Law: The chief Heads whereof
seem contain'd in these few Particulars. *1. That there is one infinite eternal God,
Creator of all Things. 2. That he governs the World by Providence. 3. That 'tis our Duty
to worship and obey him as our Creator and Governor. 4. That our Worship consists in
Prayer to him, and Praise of him. 5. That our Obedience consists in the Rules of Right
Reason, the Practice whereof is Moral Virtue. 6. That we are to expect Rewards and
Punishments hereafter, according to our Actions in this Life; which includes the Soul's
Immortality, and is proved by our admitting Providence.* Seventhly, *That when we err
from the Rules of our Duty, we ought to Repent, and trust in God's mercy for Pardon.*'
(*The Oracles of Reason* 195–6).
43. εὕρηκα] Eds; ἕυρεκα 1682. 'I have found it' (the cry attributed to Archimedes);
pronounced 'héureká' here (three syllables). The correct spelling is εὕρηκα, with
an eta rather than an epsilon before the kappa. As Kinsley notes, the spelling in
1682 and the metre of the line show that D.'s pronunciation of Greek was based
on accent rather than quantity; this was common in the seventeenth century (see
Ben Jonson ix 486). Herbert said that in formulating the articles of deism he thought
himself happier than Archimedes (*De Religione Gentilium* (1663) 218; Hutcheson 57).

God is that spring of good, supreme and best,
45   We made to serve, and in that service blessed;
If so, some rules of worship must be given,
Distributed alike to all by heaven,
Else God were partial, and to some denied
The means his justice should for all provide.
50   This general worship is to praise and pray,
One part to borrow blessings, one to pay;
And when frail nature slides into offence,
The sacrifice for crimes is penitence.
Yet since th' effects of providence we find
55   Are variously dispensed to human kind,
That vice triumphs, and virtue suffers here
(A brand that sovereign justice cannot bear)
Our reason prompts us to a future state,
The last appeal from Fortune, and from fate,
60   Where God's all-righteous ways will be declared,
The bad meet punishment, the good reward.'
      Thus man by his own strength to heaven would
         soar,   *Of revealed*
And would not be obliged to God for more.   *religion.*
Vain, wretched creature, how art thou misled
65   To think thy wit these godlike notions bred!
These truths are not the product of thy mind,
But dropped from heaven, and of a nobler kind.
Revealed religion first informed thy sight,
And reason saw not till faith sprung the light.
70   Hence all thy natural worship takes the source:

51. borrow] obtain by request (*OED* 2).   *pay*] render something which is due (*OED*
7a).
52. slides] lapses morally (*OED* 9).
56. triumphs] The verb was often accented on the second syllable in the seventeenth century (cp. *PL* ix 948, x 572, and many of *OED*'s quotations).
57. brand] mark of disgrace (*OED* 4b).
59. Fortune] Fortune is a capricious power which awards and withdraws gifts arbitrarily, with no concern for justice: for D.'s interest in fortune see 'Horace: *Odes*
III xxix' ll. 73–87*n*.   *fate*] Here probably 'death' (*OED* 4b) rather than 'destiny'.
62–3. i.e., the deist relies upon his own reason, and rejects revelation.
66–71. For the argument that the principles of natural religion are not discovered
by the unaided reason, but instead are the traces of revelation, see Preface ll. 95–7*n*.
69. sprung] caused to appear (*OED* 17).
70–1. Cp. Wolseley: 'some have supposed that no particular *Person* did ever purely
by *Natural Light*, determine that there was *but one God*: But that such who have
spoken of it had it from a *Tradition* originated in *Revelation*' (*Reasonablenes* 110).

'Tis revelation what thou think'st discourse.
Else how com'st thou to see these truths so clear
Which so obscure to heathens did appear?
Not Plato these, nor Aristotle found,
75   Nor he whose wisdom oracles renowned.   *Socrates.*
Hast thou a wit so deep, or so sublime,
Or canst thou lower dive, or higher climb?
Canst thou by reason more of godhead know
Than Plutarch, Seneca or Cicero?
80   Those giant wits, in happier ages born,
When arms and arts did Greece and Rome adorn,
Knew no such system, no such piles could raise
Of natural worship, built on prayer and praise,
To one sole God.
85   Nor did remorse to expiate sin prescribe,
But slew their fellow creatures for a bribe:
The guiltless victim groaned for their offence,
And cruelty and blood was penitence.
If sheep and oxen could atone for men,
90   Ah, at how cheap a rate the rich might sin!
And great oppressors might heaven's wrath beguile
By offering his own creatures for a spoil!

71. *discourse*] reasoning (*OED* 2); stressed on the second syllable.
75. Socrates' follower Chaerephon asked the Delphic oracle whether anyone was wiser than Socrates, and was told that no one was (Plato, *Apology* 21a).
76. *wit*] intellect.
79. *Plutarch*] Greek philosopher (*c.* AD 50–*c.* 120), whose works include moral treatises and dialogues of religious speculation.   *Seneca*] The Roman Stoic philosopher (*c.* AD 1–65), author of moral essays.   *Cicero*] The Roman philosopher (106–43 BC), author of moral and theological treatises, including *De Natura Deorum* ('On the nature of the gods').
80. From Virgil: *magnanimi heroes nati melioribus annis* ('high-minded heroes, born in better years'; *Aen.* vi 649; Kinsley).   *wits*] men of intellect.
82. *piles*] heaps of wood on which sacrifices are burnt (*OED* 3e); large buildings, e.g. temples (*OED* 4).
86–8. Greeks and Romans tended to regard sacrifice as a gift to the gods (thus Plato, *Euthyphro* 14c), and although some sacrifices were propitiatory or purificatory, they were not normally conducted out of remorse for sin in the way D. implies: that was a Jewish understanding of sacrifice, according to which the animal sacrificed took upon itself the sins of the penitent who offered it.
86. *bribe*] i.e. to the gods.
89–90. D. adapts Wolseley: 'What a *trifle* is the *Blood* of a *Sheep* or an *Oxe* to satisfie for an Offence against an Infinite Justice! At how *easie* and *cheap* a rate might men *Sin*, and God be *satisfied*! And what a publick *tolleration* of evil were it, if the Blood of Bulls and Goats might take away sin, and the lives of *unreasonable* Creatures *Commute* for the sins of *Men*!' (*Reasonablenes* 162; Harth).

> Dar'st thou, poor worm, offend infinity,
> And must the terms of peace be given by thee?
95 Then thou art justice in the last appeal:
> Thy easy God instructs thee to rebel,
> And like a king remote and weak must take
> What satisfaction thou art pleased to make.
> But if there be a power too just and strong
100 To wink at crimes, and bear unpunished wrong,
> Look humbly upward, see his will disclose
> The forfeit first, and then the fine impose:
> A mulct thy poverty could never pay
> Had not eternal wisdom found the way,
105 And with celestial wealth supplied thy store:
> His justice makes the fine, his mercy quits the score.
> See God descending in thy human frame,
> Th' offended suffering in th' offender's name;
> All thy misdeeds to him imputed see,
110 And all his righteousness devolved on thee.
> For granting we have sinned, and that th' offence

93–110. Cp. Wolseley: 'the terms of our pardon must come from God. 'Tis not in man to find out how God shall forgive him, or to Chalk out the Tracks of Divine Justice and Mercy toward himself; nor will his guilt be removed, nor his thoughts be at rest, till he know Gods mind about it. Nothing can assure us of reconciliation with God, but what is from Heaven appointed as the means of it. No natural knowledg can give us any certain direction about it' (*Reasonablenes* 160).
93. *worm*] a biblical expression of the humility of man: cp. Psalm xxii 6: 'But I am a worm, and no man'.
95. *justice*] judge.
98. *satisfaction*] performance by a penitent of the acts prescribed as payment of the temporal punishment for sin.
100. *wink at*] close their eyes to.
102. *forfeit*] transgression (*OED* 1).
103. *mulct*] fine.
105–10. This passage refers to the Christian doctrine of the atonement, that mankind is redeemed through the incarnation and death of Christ, who took man's sins upon him, and whose death provided the only possible satisfaction to God the Father for man's sinfulness.
107. i.e. God becomes incarnate as a man in Christ.
109–10. The vocabulary here invokes the Lutheran version of the doctrine of atonement, according to which man is justified by the imputation of the righteousness of Christ, without becoming possessed of any personal righteousness of his own.
111–14. The development of the doctrine of atonement made by Anselm in *Cur Deus Homo* (1098), and followed by the scholastic theologians, stressed that since sin is an infinite offence against God, it requires an infinite satisfaction; since no finite being, man or angel, could offer such satisfaction, it was necessary for an

Of man is made against omnipotence,
Some price that bears proportion must be paid,
And infinite with infinite be weighed.
115 See then the deist lost, remorse for vice
Not paid, or, paid, inadequate in price.
What farther means can reason now direct,
Or what relief from human wit expect?
That shows us sick, and sadly are we sure
120 Still to be sick, till heaven reveal the cure.
If then heaven's will must needs be understood
(Which must, if we want cure, and heaven be good),
Let all records of will revealed be shown,   ⎫
With scripture all in equal balance thrown, ⎬
125 And our one sacred book will be that one.   ⎭
     Proof needs not here, for whether we compare
That impious, idle, superstitious ware
Of rites, lustrations, offerings (which before
In various ages, various countries bore)
130 With Christian faith and virtues, we shall find

---

infinite being, God himself, to take the place of man, and through his death to
make complete satisfaction to divine justice. Wolseley says: 'nothing of less Dignity
then the *Offender* can compensate for the *Offence*, if any thing but the *Offender*
himself' (*Reasonablenes* 159).
119. That] i.e. human intellect.
123–5. Cp. Wolseley: 'If it be acknowledged there is any where extant a
Revelation from *God* to the *World*, let it be produced. Let the best *rival* to the
Bible upon that account, or all its *Competitors* together be brought forth . . . and
the *Bible* must needs be *Predominant*, and prevail against all *Competition*'
(*Reasonablenes* 178; Harth).
123. records] accented on the second syllable in the seventeenth century.
126–67. D. now turns to arguments for the reliability of the Bible. Harth 141–5
argues that D. is drawing on Wolseley's *The Reasonablenes of Scripture-Belief* for
this material; the arguments are also paralleled in other contemporary writers
(see Harth's footnotes). Sanford Budick (1969) argues that D.'s awareness that the
status of scripture cannot be proved may be indebted to Hamon L'Estrange's
Considerations, upon Dr Bayly's Parenthetical Interlocution (1651), which D. bought
at auction in May 1682 (Birrell 215). L'Estrange says: 'I do not exclude reason,
as a guide. . . . Arguments she hath many, and ponderous to perswade that the
Scriptures are of Divine inspiration; that they are not so, to diswade she hath and
can frame none. But yet those Arguments are but soluble, no Demonstrations;
for in Demonstrations the understanding is so clearly convinced by reason, that
it can possibly incline no other way then one . . . so that impossible it is for us
to *know* that the Scriptures are the word of God' (85–6; Budick (1969)).
127. idle] worthless (*OED* 2). *ware*] trash (*OED* 4).
128. lustrations] expiatory sacrifices, purificatory rites.

None answ'ring the great ends of human kind
But this one rule of life: that shows us best
How God may be appeased, and mortals blessed.
Whether from length of time its worth we draw
135   (The world is scarce more ancient than the law;
Heaven's early care prescribed for every age,
First in the soul, and after in the page),
Or whether more abstractedly we look
Or on the writers, or the written book,
140   Whence but from heaven could men unskilled in arts,
In several ages born, in several parts,
Weave such agreeing truths? Or how, or why
Should all conspire to cheat us with a lie?
Unasked their pains, ungrateful their advice,
145   Starving their gain, and martyrdom their price.
     If on the book itself we cast our view,
     Concurrent heathens prove the story true;

131. Wolseley argues that the Bible best answers 'all the great *Ends of Mankind* relating to *this life* and a *future*' (*Reasonablenes* 181).
135. Wolseley points to 'the *Antiquity* of those things it relates to us, and informs us of: And Secondly, the *Antiquity* of this *Book it self*. . . . If we consider the Revelation Historically contained in this Book, 'tis what was from the *beginning*, and of the same *Date* with the *World* it self' (*Reasonablenes* 200). Budick (1969) 378 cites a similar argument from L'Estrange 90–1.
136. Wolseley supposes that 'Gods Revelations were as early as mans *necessities*, That there was no time wherein man stood in need of Supernatural Instruction and help, but that God affords it to him' (*Reasonablenes* 223).
137. Many seventeenth-century theologians thought that certain innate ideas were inscribed by God on man's heart or soul: see Budick (1970) 46–72.
139. *Or . . . or*] Either . . . or.
140. Cp. Wolseley: 'Many of the *Prophets*, and most of the *Apostles* were men Illiterate, and of Parts and Education so *mean*, that they seem no way *capable* to write so profoundly, to lay so *deep* a Contrivement of mischief, or by the single strength of their own abilities to bid so fair to delude the World' (*Reasonablenes* 229).
141–3. Cp. Wolseley: 'The world affords not an instance, that ever so many *Men* that lived in so many several and *distinct Ages*, so exactly agreed about *any one thing*, much less to *cheat* and *abuse* the *World*' (*Reasonablenes* 233).
141. *several*] separate.
144–5. Cp. Wolseley: 'The most of those that God imploied in that work actually exposed themselves by the doing of it to all the *Persecutions, Hazards*, and *Contempts* imaginable; And some of them . . . with the *loss* of their own *Lives* published their Doctrine' (*Reasonablenes* 230–1).
144. *ungrateful*] disagreeable (*OED* 2).
145. *price*] reward.
147. Wolseley 325–47 adduces the testimony of pagan writers to corroborate the historical material in the Bible.

The doctrine, miracles, which must convince,
For heaven in them appeals to human sense;
150 And though they prove not, they confirm the cause
When what is taught agrees with nature's laws.
        Then for the style: majestic and divine,
It speaks no less than God in every line,
Commanding words, whose force is still the same
155 As the first fiat that produced our frame.
All faiths beside or did by arms ascend,
Or sense indulged has made mankind their friend:
This only doctrine does our lusts oppose,
Unfed by nature's soil in which it grows,
160 Cross to our int'rests, curbing sense and sin,
Oppressed without, and undermined within;
It thrives through pain, its own tormentors tires,
And with a stubborn patience still aspires.
To what can reason such effects assign

148–51. Wolseley discusses the question 'whether *Miracles* simply in themselves are always an unquestionable proof of that Doctrine they are brought in to Confirme', and concludes that if the doctrine is not 'opposite to that Natural Duty we owe [God], They *are*. But if otherwise, if they come in direct Competition with the Law of Nature, They are *not*' (*Reasonablenes* 243).

148. i.e. miracles prove the doctrine to be true.

152–5. Wolseley says: 'no Book nor Writing has so much as attempted to *Command* the world in so *Majestick* a way, nor indeed in any way becoming the *Greatness* and *Sovereignty* of God. . . . Not one of them having been clothed with such a *Divine & Majestick Authority*' (*Reasonablenes* 180; and cp. 179, 291).

155. first fiat] 'Fiat lux' is the Latin form of God's command 'Let there be light' (Genesis i 3). Longinus cites this phrase as an example of the sublime (*On the Sublime* ch. 9; widely read in the translations by Boileau (1674) and John Pulteney (1680)).   *frame*] the universe, regarded as a structure (*OED* 8).

156–63. Cp. Wolseley: 'Never was there at first any Force used to compel men, nor any Arts practised to deceive men about this matter. No man can prove out of any story that ever the Apostles or the Primitive Professors of this Religion raised Arms to introduce or promote it'. Internally it was 'a Religion directly opposite to the whole corrupt interest of humane Nature, and calling men to the highest Mortification and Self-denial, upon the account of an Invisible World to come'; externally 'all the force of the *Roman Empire* was every where violently at work for its total Suppression and Extirpation'; never 'was any Religion so begun and propagated by such indefatigable sufferings' (*Reasonablenes* 289–91).

156–7. or . . . Or] either . . . Or.

157. sense] sensuality.

158. This only doctrine] this doctrine alone.

160. Cross to] counter to.

164–5. Cp. Wolseley: 'To no other Cause, but its own Innate worth, and the Divine evidence from Heaven attending it, can it with any tolerable colour of reason be ascribed' (*Reasonablenes* 290).

165 Transcending nature, but to laws divine?
   Which in that sacred volume are contained,
   Sufficient, clear, and for that use ordained.
      But stay: the deist here will urge anew   *Objection*
   No supernatural worship can be true,   *of the deis*
170 Because a general law is that alone
   Which must to all and everywhere be known;
   A style so large as not this book can claim,
   Nor aught that bears revealed religion's name.
   'Tis said the sound of a messiah's birth
175 Is gone through all the habitable earth,
   But still that text must be confined alone
   To what was then inhabited and known;
   And what provision could from thence accrue
   To Indian souls, and worlds discovered new?
180 In other parts it helps that ages past
   The scriptures there were known, and were embraced,
   Till sin spread once again the shades of night;
   What's that to these who never saw the light?
      Of all objections this indeed is chief   *The*
185 To startle reason, stagger frail belief.   *objection*
   We grant, 'tis true, that heaven from human sense   *answered.*
   Has hid the secret paths of providence,
   But boundless wisdom, boundless mercy may

168–83. The deist objects that Christianity cannot be definitive because not all times and places have had access to the Bible, and so many generations and races are excluded from the salvation which it promises. Harth 87 points out that the arguments are similar to those in the essay 'Of Natural Religion' (see ll. 42–61*n*): 'That Rule which is necessary to our future Happiness, ought to be generally made known to all men. But no Rule of Revealed Religion was, or ever could be made known to all men. Therefore no Revealed Religion is necessary to future Happiness . . . the Minor of the . . . Syllogism is matter of Fact, and uncontrovertible, that no Religion supernatural has been conveyed to all the World; witness the large Continent of *America*, not discover'd till within this two Hundred Years; where if there were any Reveal'd Religion, at least it was not the *Christian*' (*The Oracles of Reason* 196). The problem of the salvation of those who had had no opportunity to learn of Christ is discussed in the Preface: see ll. 48–50*n*. *172. style*] title, designation (*OED* 18).

179. D. explored the religion of the American Indians, and their clash with European Christianity, in *The Indian Queen* (1665) and *The Indian Emperor* (1667).

182. shades of night] From *PL* iv 1015, where they are associated with Satan.

185. startle . . . stagger] Both mean 'cause to waver, unsettle' (*OED* startle 7d; stagger 6).

186–7. Cp. 'Horace: *Odes* III xxix' ll. 45–7*n*.

Find ev'n for those bewildered souls a way:
190   If from his nature foes may pity claim,
        Much more may strangers who ne'er heard his name;
        And though no name be for salvation known
        But that of his eternal Son's alone,
        Who knows how far transcending goodness can
195   Extend the merits of that Son to man?
        Who knows what reasons may his mercy lead,
        Or ignorance invincible may plead?
        Not only charity bids hope the best,
        But more the great apostle has expressed:
200   That if the gentiles (whom no law inspired)
        By nature did what was by law required,
        They who the written rule had never known
        Were to themselves both rule and law alone;
        To nature's plain indictment they shall plead,
205   And by their conscience be condemned or freed.
        Most righteous doom! because a rule revealed
        Is none to those from whom it was concealed.
        Then those who followed reason's dictates right,
        Lived up, and lifted high their natural light,

189. bewildered] lost in pathless places; *OED*'s first example is from 'Lucretius: The Beginning of the Second Book' l. 11.

192–3. 'Neither is there salvation in any other: for there is none other name under heaven given among men, whereby we must be saved' (Acts iv 12).

193. Son's] Noyes; *Sons 1682, 1683.* This is a pleonastic genitive, not a plural.

194–5. Cp. Martin Clifford: 'I may very well believe withal, that there are secret and wonderful waies, by which God may be pleased to apply his [i.e. Christ's] Merits to mankind, besides those direct, open, and ordinary ones of *Baptism* and *Confession*' (*A Treatise of Humane Reason* (1675) 34).

195. merits] The work of man's salvation performed by Christ through the cross (cp. ll. 105–10n).

199–205. For the apostle (St Paul) see Preface l. 81n. The law in l. 200 is the law given to Moses by God, which prescribed the terms on which the behaviour of the Jewish people would be acceptable to God. According to Christian teaching, the demands of the Mosaic law are replaced through the atonement, which establishes a different way in which man's sins may be forgiven. D. suggests that the gentiles who are not subject to the Jewish law, and do not partake in the salvation wrought through the atonement, may be judged in terms of whether they have acted in accordance with that law which was available to them (i.e. the law of nature), and may be saved if they have honestly followed it. Lines 200–5 are italicized in *1682*, indicating that they are a paraphrase of St Paul.

206. doom] decree (*OED* 1).

209. Lived up] lived on a high level, took a high moral position (*OED* 4f (first example)).

210 With Socrates may see their Maker's face,
     While thousand rubric-martyrs want a place.
        Nor does it balk my charity to find
     Th' Egyptian bishop of another mind;
     For though his creed eternal truth contains,
215 'Tis hard for man to doom to endless pains
     All who believed not all his zeal required,
     Unless he first could prove he was inspired.
     Then let us either think he meant to say
     This faith, where published, was the only way,
220 Or else conclude that, Arius to confute,
     The good old man, too eager in dispute,
     Flew high, and as his Christian fury rose,
     Damned all for heretics who durst oppose.
        Thus far my charity this path has tried   *Digres*
225 (A much unskilful, but well-meaning guide),   *to the*
     Yet what they are, ev'n these crude thoughts were   *transla*
        bred   *Father*
     By reading that which better thou hast read—   *Simon*
     Thy matchless author's work; which thou, my friend, Critic
     By well translating better dost commend.   Histor
230 Those youthful hours which, of thy equals most   the O
     In toys have squandered, or in vice have lost,   Testan
     Those hours hast thou to nobler use employed,
     And the severe delights of truth enjoyed.
        Witness this weighty book, in which appears
235 The crabbèd toil of many thoughtful years

---

211. rubric-martyrs] Those who have become martyrs for some fine point of ecclesiastical procedure. The rubrics are the passages in prayer books and missals, properly printed in red, which give directions governing the performance of the liturgy.
want] lack.
212. balk] place an obstacle in the way of.
213. th' Egyptian bishop] Athanasius: see Preface ll. 130–75n.
220. Arius] Christian theologian, c. 250–c. 336. For Arianism see Preface ll. 130–75n.
224. charity] Christian love of one's fellow men (*OED* 1c).
228. author . . . friend] For Richard Simon and his translator Henry Dickinson see
headnote.
230. equals] contemporaries (*OED* B 1c).
231. toys] things of no value, trifles (*OED* 5).
233. severe] serious (*OED* 5, a Latin sense). Cp. *Musas colimus severiores* ('we cul-
tivate more serious Muses': Martial IX xi 17).
235. crabbèd] difficult, intricate (*OED* 7).

Spent by thy author in the sifting care
Of rabbins' old sophisticated ware
From gold divine, which he who well can sort
May afterwards make algebra a sport;
240   A treasure which if country curates buy,
They Junius and Tremellius may defy,
Save pains in various readings and translations,
And without Hebrew make most learn'd quotations;
A work so full with various learning fraught,
245   So nicely pondered, yet so strongly wrought,
As nature's height and art's last hand required,
As much as man could compass uninspired;
Where we may see what errors have been made
Both in the copier's and translator's trade,
250   How Jewish, Popish interests have prevailed,
And where infallibility has failed.
    For some who have his secret meaning guessed
Have found our author not too much a priest:
For fashion sake he seems to have recourse

236. *sifting care*] careful sifting.
237. *rabbins*] rabbis, chief Jewish authorities on law and doctrine.   *sophisticated*]
mixed (*OED* 1), falsified (*OED* 3).
241. *Junius and Tremellius*] Franciscus Junius (1545–1602) and John Immanuel
Tremellius (1510–80) were Protestant scholars who translated the Bible into Latin
(NT 1569, OT 1575–9). Simon criticizes the translation in his *Critical History* 155.
D. repeats his joke in the 'Dedication of the *Aeneis*': 'If I desired to appear more
Learned than I am, it had been as easie for me to have taken their Objections and
Solutions [from Macrobius and Pontanus], as it is for a Country Parson to take
the Expositions of the Fathers out of *Junius* and *Tremellius*' (*Works* v 309; Harth).
244–5. Echoes Richard Duke's commendatory poem: 'With various learning,
knowledge, strength of thought. / Order and art, and solid judgment fraught;'
(*Critical History*, unsigned preliminary pages).
244. *fraught*] loaded.
245. *nicely*] carefully, exactly.
246. *last hand*] final touch, finishing stroke (*OED* 6b).
247. *uninspired*] without divine inspiration.
250. Simon discusses the ways in which various Jewish and Christian scholars have
made the text and interpretation of the Bible serve sectional interests.
251. *infallibility*] The claim (made particularly by Roman Catholics) that the church
is incapable of error when teaching revealed doctrine. See ll. 276–94.
253. Simon was attacked for undermining the Christian faith both by the
Catholic Bossuet and the Calvinist Spanheim (Harth 180–2). In England, Evelyn
was worried about the implications of the book (see letter cited in headnote, above).
Dickinson in his Preface says: 'I could wish this Criticism had been made by
some of our own Communion, who might have alter'd nothing of the substance
of it, but have left out onely some small reflexions upon the Protestants; Father
Simon however is less inveterate and makes fewer of his reflexions than could be

255   To Pope and councils, and tradition's force,
      But he that old traditions could subdue
      Could not but find the weakness of the new:
      If scripture, though derived from heavenly birth,
      Has been but carelessly preserved on earth,
260   If God's own people (who of God before
      Knew what we know, and had been promised more,
      In fuller terms, of heaven's assisting care,
      And who did neither time nor study spare
      To keep this book untainted, unperplexed)
265   Let in gross errors to corrupt the text,
      Omitted paragraphs, embroiled the sense,
      With vain traditions stopped the gaping fence,
      Which every common hand pulled up with ease,
      What safety from such brushwood helps as these?
270   If written words from time are not secured,
      How can we think have oral sounds endured?
      Which thus transmitted, if one mouth has failed,
      Immortal lies on ages are entailed;
      And that some such have been is proved too plain,
275   If we consider interest, church and gain.
        'O but', says one, 'tradition set aside,   *Of the*
      Where can we hope for an unerring guide?   *infallibility*
      For since th' orig'nal scripture has been lost,   *of tradition*
      All copies disagreeing, maimed the most,   *in general.*

expected from a Roman Catholick Doctour; which thing is yet more pardonable
in him in that he spares not even them of his own Church' (*Critical History* sig.
A2ᵛ; Harth).
260. *God's own people*] the Jews.
264. *unperplexed*] without doubts or difficulties.
266. *embroiled*] confused, made unintelligible (*OED* 1).
271. *oral sounds*] Simon points out that 'the Gospel was established in many Churches
before any thing of it was writ', and notes that the Council of Trent 'made the
not written Traditions to be of equal authority with the word of God contain'd
in the Holy Scriptures, because it suppos'd that those Traditions which were not
writ proceeded from our Saviour who communicated them to his Apostles, and
from thence they at last came down to us' (*Critical History* sigs. (*b*)ʳ, *b*ᵛ). The
Council of Trent (1545–63) declared that unwritten (*non scripta*) tradition shared
equal authority with scripture, but this tradition was understood to be 'unwritten'
in the special sense that its doctrines were not originally written down by their
authors. D. follows many English theologians (both Catholic and Protestant) in
assuming that this unwritten tradition is an oral tradition (Harth 202–4; Tillotson,
The Rule of Faith 7–10).
276–81. This speaker urges a Catholic position, that church tradition provides a
reliable guide when scripture fails because of its textual corruption. Cp. Simon:

280   Or Christian faith can have no certain ground,
       Or truth in church tradition must be found.'
           Such an omniscient church we wish indeed,
       'Twere worth both testaments, and cast in the creed:
       But if this mother be a guide so sure
285   As can all doubts resolve, all truth secure,
       Then her infallibility as well
       Where copies are corrupt or lame can tell,
       Restore lost canon with as little pains
       As truly explicate what still remains;
290   Which yet no council dare pretend to do,   ⎤
       Unless like Esdras they could write it new. ⎬
       Strange confidence, still to interpret true, ⎦
       Yet not be sure that all they have explained
       Is in the blessed original contained.
295   More safe, and much more modest 'tis, to say
       God would not leave mankind without a way,

'The great alterations which have happened, as we have shewn in the first Book
of this Work, to the Copies of the Bible since the first Originals have been lost,
utterly destroy the Protestants and Socinians Principle, who consult onely these
same Copies of the Bible as we at present have them. If the truth of Religion
remain'd not in the Church, it would be unsafe to search for it at present in
Books which have been subject to so many alterations, and have in many things
depended upon the pleasure of Transcribers' (*Critical History* sig. (a)4ᵛ).
280–1. Or . . . / Or] Either . . . Or.
282–9. Line 282 does not suggest that D. is already longing for the infallible guide
which he was later to find in Rome. Rather, as Harth argues, D. is contesting
the Catholic Church's claim to *infallibility* (i.e. to be an unerring guide in
matters of faith) by equating it with *omniscience* (i.e. the ability to know and
pronounce truly upon every matter) (Harth 208–9). John Serjeant had claimed
that tradition provided the Roman Church with an infallible guide by which to
interpret scripture: 'Tradition establisht, the Church is provided of a certain and
Infallible Rule to preserve a Copy of the Scripture's Letter truly significative of
Christs sence' (*Sure-Footing in Christianity* 116–17; a similar passage is quoted by
Tillotson in *The Rule of Faith* 13).
283. cast in] throw in, add (*OED* 78b).
291. Esdras] Simon notes that the extensive editorial work performed by Esdras
on the text of the OT after the books had been corrupted during the Babylonian
captivity went beyond the usual degree of collation and correction: 'For *Esdras*
could not re-establish those Books, which . . . had been corrupted in time of
Captivity, but in quality of Prophet or publick Writer' (*Critical History* 23, and
cp. 32–3).
295–304. Against the Catholic adherence to church tradition, D. now proposes
the standard Protestant reliance upon scripture and private judgement (but cp.
ll. 447–50n).
296. Harth 210 notes that the argument that Providence would have preserved
the essential parts of scripture from corruption was familiar in Anglican apologetics.

> And that the scriptures, though not everywhere
> Free from corruption, or entire, or clear,
> Are uncorrupt, sufficient, clear, entire
> 300   In all things which our needful faith require.
> If others in the same glass better see,
> 'Tis for themselves they look, but not for me:
> For my salvation must its doom receive
> Not from what others, but what I believe.
> 305   Must all tradition then be set aside?   *Objection*
> This to affirm were ignorance or pride.   *in behalf of*
> Are there not many points, some needful sure   *tradition,*
> To saving faith, that scripture leaves obscure?   *urged by*
> Which every sect will wrest a several way   *Father*
> 310   (For what one sect interprets, all sects may).   *Simon.*

William Chillingworth wrote that 'the watchfull eye of divine providence . . . will never suffer, that the Scripture should be depraved and corrupted, but that in them should alwaies be extant a conspicuous and plain way to eternall happinesse' (*The Religion of Protestants a Safe Way to Salvation* (1638) 61; cp. Tillotson, *The Rule of Faith* 25).

299–300. This is a standard Protestant position; cp. Tillotson: 'the Books of Scripture are sufficiently plain, as to all things necessary to be believed, and practised' (*The Rule of Faith* 20). Simon disagreed: 'Those Protestants without doubt are either ignorant or prejudic'd who affirm that the Scripture is plain of it self. As they have laid aside the Tradition of the Church, and will acknowledge no other principle of Religion but the Scripture it self, they were obliged to suppose it plain and sufficient for the establishing the truth of Faith without any Tradition. But if we but consider the conclusions which the Protestants and Socinians draw from the same principle, we shall be convinc'd that their principle is not so plain as they imagin, since these conclusions are so different and the one absolutely denies what the other affirms' (*Critical History* sig. (b)ʳ).

300. i.e. in all things which we are required to believe, as necessary to salvation.
303. doom] judgement.

305–15. D. adopts, but to a different purpose, an argument from Simon: 'There is no Religion which is not at least in appearance, grounded upon the pure Word of God. Upon this Foundation all the new Heresies are grounded, and it is strange that all the Patriarchs of these new Sects agree in their Principle, and yet draw such different Conclusions from the same Principle. The *Socinians* agree with the Protestants, whether *Lutherans, Zuinglians,* or *Calvinists,* that the Holy Scripture is the only true Principle of Religion, and that we ought to search for it only in the Old and New Testament, and that there is no need of having recourse either to Tradition or the Fathers. But when any Fundamental Point in Religion comes to be decided by this Principle, the latter are as much wide from the former, as Heaven from Earth. Which is a certain sign that the Principle they make use of, is not sufficient for the deciding of the differences which daily arise about Matters of Religion, and therefore that we ought with the Catholicks to have recourse to something else' (*Critical History* 114).

309. several] separate.

We hold, and say we prove from scripture plain, ⎫
That Christ is God; the bold Socinian   ⎬
From the same scripture urges he's but man. ⎭
Now what appeal can end th' important suit?
315 Both parts talk loudly, but the rule is mute.
          Shall I speak plain, and in a nation free
     Assume an honest layman's liberty?
     I think (according to my little skill,
     To my own mother church submitting still)
320 That many have been saved, and many may,
     Who never heard this question brought in play.
     Th' unlettered Christian, who believes in gross,
     Plods on to heaven, and ne'er is at a loss:
     For the strait gate would be made straiter yet
325 Were none admitted there but men of wit.
     The few, by nature formed, with learning fraught,
     Born to instruct, as others to be taught,
     Must study well the sacred page, and see
     Which doctrine, this or that, does best agree
330 With the whole tenor of the work divine,
     And plainliest points to heaven's revealed design;
     Which exposition flows from genuine sense,
     And which is forced by wit and eloquence.

312. Socinian] See Preface l. 162n.

315. rule] the biblical text, considered to be the rule of life.

318. skill] knowledge, understanding (*OED* 7).

322. in gross] in a general way, without going into details (*OED* B 2).

324. strait gate] From Matthew vii 14: 'strait is the gate, and narrow is the way, which leadeth unto life, and few there be that find it'. *strait*] narrow.

325. wit] intellect.

334–41. D. adopts the usual Anglican view that ancient church traditions are a useful guide to faith and to the interpretation of scripture. Kinsley cites Hooker to exemplify this position: 'Lest therefore the name of Tradition should be offensive to any, considering how far by some it hath been, and is abused, we mean by Traditions, Ordinances made in the prime of Christian Religion, established with that Authority which Christ hath left to his Church for matters indifferent; and in that consideration requisite to be observed, till like authority see just and reasonable cause to alter them' (*Of the Lawes of Ecclesiasticall Politie* v 65; Hooker, *Works* (1666) 245). Similarly the Restoration Latitudinarians based their teaching upon scripture interpreted through the early church Fathers: 'they derive it . . . from the Sacred writings of the Apostles and Evangelists, in interpreting whereof, they carefully attend to the sense of the ancient Church, by which they conceive the modern ought to be guided: and therefore they are very conversant in all the genuine Monuments of the ancient Fathers, those especially of the first and purest ages' (Simon Patrick, *A Brief Account of the New Sect of Latitude-Men* (1662) 9).

Not that tradition's parts are useless here,
335   When general, old, disinteressed and clear:
That ancient fathers thus expound the page
Gives truth the reverend majesty of age,
Confirms its force by biding every test,
For best authorities next rules are best,
340   And still the nearer to the spring we go
More limpid, more unsoiled the waters flow.
Thus first traditions were a proof alone,
Could we be certain such they were, so known;
But since some flaws in long descent may be,
345   They make not truth, but probability.
Ev'n Arius and Pelagius durst provoke
To what the centuries preceding spoke.
Such difference is there in an oft-told tale,
But truth by its own sinews will prevail.
350   Tradition written therefore more commends
Authority than what from voice descends;
And this, as perfect as its kind can be,
Rolls down to us the sacred history,
Which, from the universal church received,
355   Is tried, and after for itself believed.
          The partial papists would infer from hence   *The second*
Their church in last resort should judge the sense;   *objection.*

334. parts] roles (*OED* 9b); capacities (*OED* 12).
335. disinteressed] disinterested.
339. Ed.; For best *Authority's* next *Rules* are *best 1682*. The reading *Authority's* could
be understood either as *authorities* or *authorities'* or *authority's*. The first is probably preferable, so that the line means 'next to the rules, the best guides are the
best authorities' (thus *Works*), rather than 'the rules of the best authority, nearest ('next') in time to the original text, are best' (thus Noyes; Kinsley).
346. Arius] See l. 220*n*.   *Pelagius*] British theologian active in the late fourth and
early fifth centuries AD, who taught that man can take the initial steps towards
salvation by his own efforts, independently of divine grace. Opposed by St Augustine,
his views were condemned as heretical.   *provoke*] appeal (*OED* 2, citing this
example); not 'challenge' as *Works* says.
349. From *magna est veritas et praevalet* ('Great is truth and it prevails': 3 Esdras iv
41 (Vulgate)). For the idea that truth is strong in itself, cp. Cicero: *O magna vis
veritatis, quae . . . facile se per se ipsa defendat!* ('O great is the power of truth, which
may easily defend itself on its own': *Pro Caelio* xxvi 63).
350. commends] invites acceptance [of its] (approximately *OED* 2).
353. Rolls down] causes to flow onwards (*OED* 3).
355. tried] tested.
356. partial] favouring their own party, biased.

But first they would assume, with wondrous art,   *Answer*
Themselves to be the whole, who are but part   *to the*
360 Of that vast frame, the church. Yet grant they were   *objection.*
The handers down, can they from thence infer
A right t' interpret? Or would they alone
Who brought the present claim it for their own?
The book's a common largess to mankind,
365 Not more for them than every man designed;
The welcome news is in the letter found,
The carrier's not commissioned to expound;
It speaks itself, and what it does contain
In all things needful to be known is plain.
370   In times o'ergrown with rust and ignorance,
A gainful trade their clergy did advance,
When want of learning kept the laymen low,
And none but priests were authorized to know,
When what small knowledge was, in them did dwell,
375 And he a god who could but read or spell;
Then mother church did mightily prevail,
She parcelled out the Bible by retail,
But still expounded what she sold or gave,
To keep it in her power to damn and save.
380 Scripture was scarce, and as the market went
Poor laymen took salvation on content,
As needy men take money, good or bad:
God's word they had not, but the priest's they had.
Yet whate'er false conveyances they made,
385 The lawyer still was certain to be paid.
In those dark times they learned their knack so well
That by long use they grew infallible.
At last a knowing age began t' enquire

370. *rust*] moral corruption (*OED* 2); deteriorating influence of inactivity upon character and abilities (*OED* 5).
377. *by retail*] in small quantities (*OED* 4b).
381. *on content*] without question or examination (*OED* 2).
382. Much of the coinage circulating in the Restoration was clipped or adulterated; D. himself had difficulty with the bad coinage in which Tonson paid him (*Letters* 75, 77, 80–2).
384. *whate'er*] accented on the first syllable.   *conveyances*] legal documents by which property is transferred. Harth 219 notes that William Laud's *Relation of a Conference betweene William Lawd and Mr. Fisher the Jesuite* (1639) 194 cites the use of this legal metaphor by several early church fathers, who (unlike the Roman clergy) 'appeale to the *Written* Will, and make that the *Judge* without any Exception, when a matter of Faith comes in Question'.

If they the book, or that did them inspire;
390   And making narrower search they found, though late,
      That what they thought the priest's, was their estate;
      Taught by the will produced (the written word)
      How long they had been cheated on record.
      Then every man who saw the title fair
395   Claimed a child's part, and put in for a share,
      Consulted soberly his private good,
      And saved himself as cheap as e'er he could.
         'Tis true, my friend (and far be flattery hence),
      This good had full as bad a consequence;
400   The book thus put in every vulgar hand
      Which each presumed he best could understand,
      The common rule was made the common prey,
      And at the mercy of the rabble lay.
      The tender page with horny fists was galled,
405   And he was gifted most that loudest bawled.
      The spirit gave the doctoral degree,   ⎫
      And every member of a company   ⎬
      Was of his trade, and of the Bible free.   ⎭
      Plain truths enough for needful use they found,
410   But men would still be itching to expound;
      Each was ambitious of th' obscurest place,
      No measure ta'en from knowledge, all from grace.
      Study and pains were now no more their care,

---

389. Cp. *The Medal* l. 166.

391. estate] Cp. *HP* ii 384.

393. record] written evidence of legal proceedings (*OED* 1). The word was accented on the second syllable in the seventeenth century.

394. fair] clear (*OED* 17).

398. my friend] Dickinson.

400–22. This passage is directed at the nonconformist Protestant sects.

400. vulgar] of the common people (*OED* 8); coarse, uncultured (*OED* 13b; first example 1678).

406. Cp. *AA* ll. 657–9.

407. company] the trade and craft guilds.

408. i.e. as free to interpret the Bible as to practise his trade.

411. ambitious of] eager for the credit [to be gained by interpreting].

412. Kinsley cites Hooker to exemplify the Anglican position: 'An opinion hath spred it self very far in the World; as if the way to be ripe in Faith, were to be raw in Wit and Judgment; as if Reason were an enemy unto Religion, childish simplicity the Mother of Ghostly and Divine Wisdom. . . . The Apostle teacheth . . . that Nature hath need of Grace, whereunto I hope we are not opposit, by holding, that Grace hath use of Nature' (*Of the Lawes of Ecclesiasticall Politie* iii 8; Hooker, *Works* (1666) 73–4).

Texts were explained by fasting and by prayer.
415 This was the fruit the private spirit brought,
Occasioned by great zeal, and little thought.
While crowds unlearn'd, with rude devotion warm,
About the sacred viands buzz and swarm,
The fly-blown text creates a crawling brood,
420 And turns to maggots what was meant for food.
A thousand daily sects rise up, and die,
A thousand more the perished race supply.
So all we make of heaven's discovered will
Is not to have it, or to use it ill.
425 The danger's much the same, on several shelves
If others wreck us, or we wreck ourselves.
    What then remains, but waiving each extreme,
The tides of ignorance and pride to stem?
Neither so rich a treasure to forgo,
430 Nor proudly seek beyond our power to know.
Faith is not built on disquisitions vain:
The things we must believe are few, and plain;

417–20. Cp. Samuel Butler, *Hudibras* (1678): 'The Learned Write, *An Insect Breeze,* / Is but a Mungrel Prince of *Bees,* / That Falls, before a Storm, on Cows, / And stings the Founders of his House; / From whose Corrupted Flesh, that Breed / Of Vermine, did at first proceed: / So ere the Storm of war broke out / Religion spawn'd a various Rout, / Of Petulant Capricious Sects, / The Maggots of Corrupted Texts, / That first Run all Religion down, / And after every swarm its own' (III ii 1–12). For the association of 'Sects, and Insects' cp. Denham, 'The Progress of Learning' l. 161. Budick (1970) 153 notes that Francisco Redi's recent experiments with blowflies had destroyed the hypothesis of spontaneous generation (reported in *PTRS* v (1670) 1175–6).
418. viands] The image of the Bible as meat which nourishes believers was much used by nonconformists; it derives from Hebrews v 12–14.
420. maggots] with a play on the meaning of *maggot* as 'whimsical fancy' (*OED* 2).
425–6. For the image cp. 'Horace: *Epode* II' l. 101n.
427. What then remains] See 'The First Book of Homer's *Ilias*' ll. 85–6n.
428. stem] make headway against (*OED* v.³ 1b).
430. Cp. 'Horace: *Odes* III xxix' ll. 44–7nn.
431–2. Cp. St Catharine in *Tyrannic Love* (1670): 'Faith's necessary Rules are plain and Few; / We, many, and those needless Rules pursue: / Faith from our hearts into our heads we drive; / And make Religion all Contemplative. / You, on Heav'ns will may witty glosses feign; / But that which I must practise here, is plain:' (IV i 548–53). Harth 222–3 notes that the Latitudinarians considered that there were few things which had to be believed: 'They made this one of their main Doctrines; That *The principles which are necessary to Salvation are very few, and very plain, and generally acknowledg'd among Christians.* . . . They saw . . . That *Papism* . . . would drop to the ground, if it were believed, That the *necessary principles of Religion were few,* and *plain,* and those *agreed* on: For then there would be no need of an *Infallible Interpreter,* and *Judge*' (Joseph Glanvill, *Essays on Several Important Subjects* (1676) 25–6).

But since men will believe more than they need,
And every man will make himself a creed,
435 In doubtful questions 'tis the safest way
To learn what unsuspected ancients say;
For 'tis not likely we should higher soar
In search of heaven than all the church before;
Nor can we be deceived, unless we see
440 The scripture and the fathers disagree.
If after all they stand suspected still
(For no man's faith depends upon his will)
'Tis some relief that points not clearly known
Without much hazard may be let alone;
445 And after hearing what our church can say,
If still our reason runs another way,
That private reason 'tis more just to curb,
Than by disputes the public peace disturb.
For points obscure are of small use to learn,
450 But common quiet is mankind's concern.
        Thus have I made my own opinions clear,
Yet neither praise expect, nor censure fear;
And this unpolished, rugged verse I chose,
As fittest for discourse, and nearest prose.
455 For while from sacred truth I do not swerve,
Tom Sternhold's or Tom Sha—ll's rhymes will serve.

436. unsuspected] not regarded with suspicion.

447–50. Harth 224 observes that even after the Act of Uniformity (1662) expelled dissenters from the Church of England, Anglican clerics continued to stress the need for private judgement to be restrained, as their predecessors had done: 'Wee teach all Inferiors . . . when they finde cause of doubt or question . . . to instruct their owne reason, and rather rely upon the publick Judgement then their owne in every doubtfull case. . . . If they cannot finde satisfaction so, as inwardly to acquiesce, yet to yeild externall obedience, and peaceable subjection' (Henry Ferne, *Of the Division between the English and Romish Church* (1652) 49–50).

450. Herbert ends *De Religione Laici* by hoping that his work will help *Pacem Communem stabiliendam* ('to establish the common peace': edited by Hutcheson 132). Cp. *AA* ll. 795–810.

453–4. Cp. Wolseley: 'Thus, *my Lord*, I have led you through . . . a discourse unpolished' (*Unreasonablenesse* 189). Horace says that he writes lines which are more fitted for prose (*sermoni propriora: Serm.* I iv 42). Cp. Preface ll. 433–51. *discourse*] rational argument; stressed on the second syllable.

456. Sternhold] Thomas Sternhold (d. 1549), author with John Hopkins of a metrical translation of the Psalms (cp. *2AA* l. 403). Settle had called Shadwell 'our *Hopkin Rhimer*' (Preface to *Ibrahim* (1677) sig. a3ᵛ). *Sha—ll*] *1682a* (*second and third issues*), *1682b*, *1683*; *Shadwell 1682a* (*first issue*). For Shadwell see headnote to *MF*. His attack on D., *The Medal of John Bayes*, had appeared in May 1682. *rhymes*] verses (*OED* 1).

8 To the Earl of Roscommon

Date and publication. This is the first of the commendatory poems in *An Essay on Translated Verse. By the Earl of Roscommon*, published by Jacob Tonson in 1684; second edition 1685.

Context. Wentworth Dillon, fourth Earl of Roscommon (1637–85), was born in Ireland and educated at the Protestant academy in Caen during the Commonwealth, returning to a place of favour at court after the Restoration. Around 1680 he formed an academy which was particularly concerned with translation and the refinement of the English language; members included the Marquis of Halifax (who began to translate Tacitus), Lord Maitland (who began to translate Virgil), the Earl of Dorset, and D. himself (see Carl Niemeyer, *MLN* xlix (1934) 432–7; Greg Clingham, *Restoration* xxvi (2002) 15–26; Andrew Barclay, *Restoration* xxvi (2002) 119–26). Knightly Chetwood wrote that 'they aim'd at refining our Language, without abating the force of it, & therefore insted of making a laborius Dictionary, they proposed severally to peruse our best writers, & mark such words, as they thought vulgar, base, improper, or obsolete'; he also recorded that Roscommon thought D. 'a naturall rather than a correct Poet' ('A Short Account of Some Passages of the Life & Death of Wentworth late Earl of Roscommon', edited by Greg Clingham, *Restoration* xxv (2001) 117–38, at 130). Roscommon himself published a translation of Horace's *Ars Poetica* in 1680 (reprinted 1684), a commendatory poem for the 1683 issue of D.'s *RL*, translations of Virgil's *Ecl.* vi and Horace's *Carm.* I xxii and III vi in *MP*, and other poems (for the canon see Carl Niemeyer, *SP* xxxvi (1939) 622–36). The other commendatory poems printed with the *Essay* were by D.'s son Charles (in Latin), Knightly Chetwood and J. Amherst. D. praised Roscommon in the 'Preface to Ovid's Epistles' (*Poems* i 385), the 'Preface to *Sylvae*' (*Poems* ii 237, 244, 250) and the 'Dedication of the *Aeneis*' (*Works* v 325), and dedicated 'Horace: *Odes* I iii' to him. D. wrote to Tonson *c.* August 1684: 'For my Lord Roscommons Essay, I am of your opinion, that you shou'd reprint it, & that you may safely venture on a thousand more' (*Letters* 22–3). Roscommon's interest in translation in the early 1680s coincides with that shown by D. and Tonson in *Ovid's Epistles* (1680), *MP* (1684) and *Sylvae* (1685), and Roscommon specifically praises recent translations of Ovid, Theocritus and Horace (*Essay* 2, 4; see H. A. Mason, *N & Q* ccxxxv (1990) 296).

To the Earl of Roscommon on his
Excellent *Essay on Translated Verse*

Whether the fruitful Nile, or Tyrian shore,
The seeds of arts and infant science bore,
'Tis sure the noble plant, translated first,
Advanced its head in Grecian gardens nursed.
5   The Grecians added verse, their tuneful tongue
Made nature first, and nature's God their song.
Nor stopped translation here: for conquering Rome
With Grecian spoils brought Grecian numbers home,
Enriched by those Athenian Muses more
10 Than all the vanquished world could yield before;
Till barb'rous nations, and more barb'rous times,
Debased the majesty of verse to rhymes:

¶8. *1–10.* D. probably had in mind Denham's 'The Progress of Learning' (1668):
'From thence [Chaldaea] did Learning into Ægypt pass; / . . . From Ægypt Arts
their Progress made to *Greece*, / . . . Flying from thence, to *Italy* it came, / . . .
Till both their Nation and their Arts did come / A welcom Trophy to
Triumphant *Rome*; / Then wheresoe're her Conquering Eagles fled, / Arts, Learning,
and Civility were spread' (ll. 16, 21, 47, 49–52; *Poetical Works* 115–16).
2. science] learning.
3–4. The image is used by Roscommon: 'The noblest Fruits Transplanted,
in our Isle / With early Hope, and fragrant Blossoms smile' (2); cp. Amherst's
commendatory poem: 'a generous understanding Muse / Does richer fruits
from happier Soils Translate' (sig. a2ʳ). The image goes back to Denham:
'Transplanted wit, / All the defects of air and soil doth share' ('To Sir Richard
Fanshaw upon his translation of *Pastor Fido*' (1648) ll. 10–11).
4. Grecian gardens] The Greeks often taught and debated outdoors.
6. nature] It was a contemporary commonplace that the Greek poets, particularly
Homer, had a specially close contact with, and insight into, 'nature', in its wide
sense of 'the fundamental principles of life': see Kirsti Simonsuuri, *Homer's Original
Genius* (1979), and Pope: '*Nature* and *Homer* were, he found, the *same*' (*An Essay
on Criticism* l. 135). D. uses the same idea in complimenting Shakespeare: 'All the
Images of Nature were still present to him . . . he needed not the spectacles of
Books to read Nature; he look'd inwards, and found her there' (*EDP* in *Works*
xvii 55). See *MF* l. 166n, and cp. 'Prologue to *The Tempest*' ll. 7–8.
7–8. Rome gained control of parts of Greece in 229 BC and completed her
domination in 146 BC. Greek poets and philosophers had an important influence
on their Roman successors. See also ll. 41–8n. Chetwood writes in his commendatory poem that Englishmen 'Search'd all the *Treasuries* of *Greece*, and *Rome*,
/ And brought the *precious spoils* in Triumph *home*' (sig. A3ᵛ).
11–12. Rhyme was not used in classical poetry, and was introduced into Latin
verse in the early Middle Ages. Milton, in his prefatory note in the fourth issue
of the first edition of *PL* (1668), calls rhyme 'the invention of a barbarous age,
to set off wretched matter and lame metre'. In the *Essay* Roscommon says: 'Of
many faults, *Rhyme* is (perhaps) the *Cause*, / Too *strict* to *Rhyme* We slight more
useful Laws. / For *That*, in *Greece* or *Rome*, was never *known*, / 'Till By *Barbarian*

Those rude at first, a kind of hobbling prose
That limped along, and tinkled in the close;
15   But Italy, reviving from the trance
Of Vandal, Goth, and monkish ignorance,
With pauses, cadence, and well-vowelled words,
And all the graces a good ear affords,
Made rhyme an art; and Dante's polished page
20   Restored a silver, not a golden age.
Then Petrarch followed, and in him we see   ⎫
What rhyme improved in all its height can be: ⎬
At best a pleasing sound, and fair barbarity.   ⎭
The French pursued their steps, and Britain last
25   In manly sweetness all the rest surpassed.
The wit of Greece, the gravity of Rome,
Appear exalted in the British loom;
The Muses' empire is restored again
In Charles his reign, and by Roscommon's pen.
30   Yet modestly he does his work survey,
And calls a finished poem an 'essay':
For all the needful rules are scattered here,   ⎫
Truth smoothly told, and pleasantly severe   ⎬
(So well is art disguised, for nature to appear). ⎭
35   Nor need those rules to give translation light:
His own example is a flame so bright
That he who but arrives to copy well
Unguided will advance, unknowing will excel.

Deluges oreflown' (23). In the second edition he adds a passage in blank verse
in imitation of *PL* (24–5). D. had given up using rhyme in his plays with *All For
Love* (1678).

15–23. D.'s admiration for the Italian language is expressed in the Preface to *Albion
and Albanius* (1685) (*Works* xv 6–7) (Kinsley).

17. pauses] breaks in the line of verse, caesuras.   *cadence*] rhythm and metre.   *well-
vowelled*] well supplied with vowels; OED quotes Playford (1662): 'The Italian
language is more smooth and better vowelled than the English'.

19–21. Dante Alighieri (1265–1321) and Francesco Petrarch (1304–74) were instrumental in pioneering vernacular Italian poetry.

31. essay] accented on the second syllable; a tentative treatment, a rough draft
(OED 7, 8).

32. needful rules] Rules were a feature of neo-classical literary criticism, which tended
to develop and codify the principles offered less systematically by Aristotle and
Horace. Contemporary interest in this approach is evident in the translations of
Horace's *Ars Poetica* by Roscommon (1680), Oldham (1681) and Creech (1684),
the translation of Boileau's *Art poétique* by Soame and D. (1683), and Mulgrave's
An Essay upon Poetry (1682).

36. His own example] See headnote.

37. arrives to] reaches his object (OED).

Scarce his own Horace could such rules ordain,
40   Or his own Virgil sing a nobler strain.
How much in him may rising Ireland boast,
How much in gaining him has Britain lost!
Their island in revenge has ours reclaimed,
The more instructed we, the more we still are shamed.
45   'Tis well for us his generous blood did flow
Derived from British channels long ago,
That here his conquering ancestors were nursed,
And Ireland but translated England first:
By this reprisal we regain our right,
50   Else must the two contending nations fight
A nobler quarrel for his native earth
Than what divided Greece for Homer's birth.
To what perfection will our tongue arrive,
How will invention and translation thrive,
55   When authors nobly born will bear their part,
And not disdain th' inglorious praise of art!
Great generals thus descending from command
With their own toil provoke the soldiers' hand.
How will sweet Ovid's ghost be pleased to hear
60   His fame augmented by an English peer;   *The Earl of*
How he embellishes his Helen's loves,   *Mulgrave.*

39. Roscommon had translated Horace (see headnote), and says in the *Essay* that
he has 'serv'd him more than twenty years' (4).
40. Roscommon had translated Virgil (see headnote), and his reverence for Virgil
is evident in the *Essay* (11–12).
41–8. Works notes that this passage is based on Horace's epistle to Augustus: *Graecia
capta ferum victorem cepit et artes / intulit agresti Latio* ('Greece, the captive, made her
savage victor captive, and brought the arts into rustic Latium': *Epist.* II i 156–7).
41. Roscommon had estates in Ireland, but after spending a period there after
the Restoration, he returned to England.
45–7. Roscommon's mother came from Yorkshire, and was the sister of the Earl
of Strafford; his father's family had lived in Ireland for at least five generations,
but had presumably come over as part of the Tudor settlement of Ireland.
45. generous] noble.
47. were] *1685*; was *1684*. Writing to Tonson D. said: 'pray let the printer mend
his errour, & let the line stand thus, That heer his Conque'ring Ancestors were
nursd' (*Letters* 23).
49. reprisal] regaining, recovery (*OED* 3c).
52. Greek cities had contended for the honour of having been Homer's birthplace; Chios and Smyrna were the chief candidates.
53. The perfecting of the English language was one of the aims of Roscommon's
academy (see headnote). For D.'s anxieties about the inexactitude and instability
of English see his Dedication to *Troilus and Cressida* (1679) (*Works* xiii 222–4).
56. i.e. artistic achievement brings the artist no glory.
58. provoke] call forth, from the Latin *provocare* (*Works*).

Outdoes his softness, and his sense improves!
When these translate, and teach translators too,
Nor firstling kid, nor any vulgar vow
65   Should at Apollo's grateful altar stand:
Roscommon writes; to that auspicious hand,
Muse, feed the bull that spurns the yellow sand.
Roscommon, whom both court and camps commend,
True to his prince, and faithful to his friend;
70   Roscommon, first in fields of honour known,
First in the peaceful triumphs of the gown,
He both Minervas justly makes his own.
Now let the few beloved by Jove, and they
Whom infused Titan formed of better clay,
75   On equal terms with ancient wit engage,
Nor mighty Homer fear, nor sacred Virgil's page:
Our English palace opens wide in state,
And without stooping they may pass the gate.

60. John Sheffield, Earl of Mulgrave (1648–1721) was D.'s patron. They had collaborated on 'Helen to Paris' in *Ovid's Epistles.* Roscommon's *Essay* begins with a compliment to Mulgrave, whose *Essay upon Poetry* 'Repairs so well our Old *Horatian* way' (1). *English*] *1685*; Brittish *1684.*
64. vow] votive offering (*OED* 6).
65. grateful] pleasing (*OED* 1).
67. Works notes an echo of Virgil's *Ecl.* iii 86–7, where sacrifice is offered to the Roman general, critic and poet Pollio: *pascite taurum / iam cornu petat et pedibus qui spargat harenam* ('feed a bull, able even now to butt with the horn and to churn up the sand with his hoofs').
68. Cp. Amherst: 'A Muse inur'd to Camps, in Courts refin'd' (sig. a2ᵛ).
70–1. Roscommon had held several military positions, and was now a captain in Arran's Regiment of Horse, and Master of the Horse to the Duchess of York. He had received honorary doctorates from both Cambridge and Oxford.
72. both Minervas] Minerva was goddess of wisdom and of war.
73–4. Cp. Roscommon: 'But, few, oh, few, Souls, praeordain'd by *Fate,* / The Race of *Gods,* have reach'd that *envy'd* Height. / No *Rebel-Titan's sacrilegious Crime,* / By heaping Hills on Hills can *thither climb*' (10–11).
74. D. echoes Juvenal, *Satire* xiv 34–5: *Forsitan haec spernant iuvenes, quibus arte benigna / et meliore luto finxit praecordia Titan* ('Perhaps *one* youth, or *two,* untainted live, / . . . whose hearts *Tytan* may / Have fram'd with more art, and of better clay': Stapylton's translation (1647) 255) (Kinsley). *infused*] divinely inspired; accented on the first syllable. *Titan*] Prometheus, who according to Greek myth created mankind, and taught them arts and crafts.
75–8. D.'s lines are in tune with the ending of the *Essay:* Britain will be 'what *Rome* or *Athens* were *Before.* / O may I Live to see that glorious Day, / And sing loud *Paeans* through the Crowded way / When in Triumphant state the *British Muse* / True to her *self* shall *Barb'rous* aid *refuse.* / And in that *Roman Majesty* appear, / Which none knows better and none *Comes* so *near*' (24).
78. Perhaps recalling Aeneas' entrance into the palace of Evander: 'stooping, through the Narrow Gate they press'd' ('The Eighth Book of the *Aeneis*' l. 475; Donald C. Mell, *PLL* xvii (1981) 153).

9 To the Memory of Mr Oldham

Date and publication. Printed in 1684 as the first of the memorial poems prefixed to *Remains of Mr. John Oldham in Verse and Prose,* published by Joseph Hindmarsh in 1684 (*TC* November; Wood's memorial poem is dated 26 May 1684); second edition 1687.

Context. John Oldham (1653–83) was born in Shipton Moyne, Gloucestershire, and educated at St Edmund Hall, Oxford. In 1676 he became an usher at Whitgift School, Croydon, where he is said to have 'received a Visit from the Earl of *Rochester,* the Earl of *Dorset,* Sir *Charles Sedley,* and other Persons of Distinction, merely upon the Reputation of some of his Verses, which they had seen in Manuscript' (anonymous life in Oldham's *Works* (1722) v). From 1679 to 1681 he was a tutor in the household of Sir Edward Thurland, and later tutor to the son of Sir William Hickes. At some stage, perhaps in 1682, he set up independently in London, and if he knew D. personally it would have been at this time. Oldham found a new patron in the Earl of Kingston, and died at his house at Holme Pierrepont, Nottinghamshire, being buried on 7 December 1683. Oldham's poetry includes pindaric verses in the manner of Cowley, erotic poems influenced by Rochester and his circle, the *Satyrs upon the Jesuits* inspired by the Popish Plot, poems which lament the poor status of the poet in Restoration England, and translations from Greek, Latin and French poetry. Some poems show the influence of D.'s poetry and heroic plays, and his transcript of *MF* (dated 1678) is preserved in BodL MS Rawl. Poet. 123. It is often assumed (e.g. in *Works* iii 385) that the race which D. says Oldham won (ll. 7–10) was for the publication of heroic satire on national themes, since his *Satyrs upon the Jesuits* (1681; *TC* November 1680) appeared a year before *AA.* But it is also possible (given D.'s special interest in translation in the early 1680s, and the markedly classical temper of this poem) that D. had in mind Oldham's translations. His versions of Horace's *Ars Poetica, Serm.* I ix, and *Carm.* I xxxi and II xiv appeared in *Some New Pieces* (1681), while his *Poems, and Translations* (1683) included versions of Juvenal's *Satires* III and XIII, and Boileau's *Satires* V and VIII; all these renderings transpose the setting to contemporary England. It may be no coincidence that it was in 1684 which D. began his serious work as a translator. There are several thematic and verbal parallels between this poem and D.'s other poems of 1684–5, notably those which discuss the writer's vocation ('Virgil's Ninth Eclogue', 'To the Earl of Roscommon' and 'To Mr L. Maidwell') and those which contemplate death ('Nisus and Euryalus', 'Lucretius: Against the Fear of Death'): for a discussion of the significance of this poem to D.'s understanding of himself as a writer see Dustin H. Griffin, *MLQ* xxxvii (1976) 133–50. For Oldham's work generally see his *Poems,* and Paul Hammond, *John Oldham and the Renewal of Classical Culture* (1983). The other contributors of memorial verses to *Remains* were Thomas Flatman, Nahum Tate, Thomas D'Urfey, Thomas Andrews, and Anon; and in the second edition Jacob Tonson (anonymously, first printed in *Sylvae*) and Robert Gould.

Sources. The poem is full of echoes (including echoes of D.'s own work), but no single source dominates. D. draws on two pieces in Oldham's *Poems, and Translations*: one celebrated a male friendship, 'David's Lamentation for the Death of Saul and Jonathan' and the other an English classical poet, 'Upon the Works of Ben. Johnson'. (Both poems are singled out for praise by other elegists in the

Remains.) D. also draws on Milton's *Lycidas* (see Bruce King, *EA* xix (1966) 60–3) and on Cowley's *Davideis* and 'On the Death of Mr. *William Hervey*'. There are several echoes of Roman poetry too – appropriately, given Oldham's classical interests: see Hoffman 92–8 and R. G. Petersen, *MPh* lxvi (1969) 232–6. Two passages in Virgil came to D.'s mind: the story of Nisus and Euryalus from *Aen.* v and ix (see ll. 9–10, and ll. 3–4*n*, 7*n*); and the vision of Marcellus in *Aen.* vi (see l. 23*n*). These allusions counteract the note of Augustan promise which D. sounds in 'Virgil's Fourth Eclogue', but are in keeping with the almost despairing tone of 'Virgil's Ninth Eclogue'. Virgil's passage on Marcellus is an acknowledged masterpiece of the Latin literature of grief, and had probably inspired D.'s eulogy for the young Ossory in *AA* ll. 831–53. There may be another Latin source in the *Noctes Atticae* of Aulus Gellius: Leonard Moskovit (*N & Q* ccxvii (1972) 26–7) cites XIII ii 3–6 where Accius says, 'it is with the mind as it is with fruits; those which are at first harsh and bitter, later become mild and sweet; but those which at once grow mellow and soft, and are juicy in the beginning, presently become, not ripe, but decayed. Accordingly it has seemed to me that something should be left in the products of the intellect for time and age to mellow'. There are also several classical turns of phrase in the poem (see notes).

Reception. Apart from those cited in ll. 15–16*n*, there are no contemporary comments on this poem, but it was echoed by the anonymous author of 'The Vision' (BL MS Add 28276 f. 86ᵛ), and imitated by H. Hall in his memorial poem for Purcell (*Orpheus Britannicus* (1696) vi).

To the Memory of Mr Oldham

Farewell, too little and too lately known,
Whom I began to think and call my own;
For sure our souls were near allied, and thine

¶9. *1.* Echoes 'Too early seen unknown, and known too late' (*Romeo and Juliet* I v 141); cp. also Andrews: 'Fled e'er his Worth or Merit was half known;/ No sooner seen, but in a Moment gone' (*Remains* sig. A4ʳ); and cp. Cowley, quoted in l. 11*n*. There is no evidence as to whether D. knew Oldham personally. The fact that all Oldham's work was published anonymously would have impeded recognition.
3–4. Echoes Oldham: 'Oh, dearer than my Soul! if I can call it mine,/ For sure we had the same, 'twas very thine' ('David's Lamentation' ll. 204–5). There are verbal parallels between ll. 3–5 here and 'Nisus and Euryalus' ll. 249–54. D. also echoes his own earlier line: 'For Noble Souls in Nature are alli'd' (*Aureng-Zebe* (1676) IV i 73). *souls*] Perhaps from *animae duae, animus unus* ('two souls, one soul'), the gloss on *Aen.* ix 182 (describing Nisus' love for Euryalus) in Emmenessius' edition (1680); D. echoes the present lines when translating Ascanius' address to Euryalus in 'Nisus and Euryalus' ll. 249–54. *near allied*] Anna Battigelli points out that since Oldham and D. shared the same birthday of 9 August they would have shared the same astrological sign (*N & Q* ccxxxiii (1988) 174–5); however, we do not know that D. knew this. *allied*] Echoes Oldham's 'Both excellent they were, both equally alli'd' ('David's Lamentation' l. 119).

Cast in the same poetic mould with mine.
5   One common note on either lyre did strike,
     And knaves and fools we both abhorred alike:
     To the same goal did both our studies drive,
     The last set out the soonest did arrive.
     Thus Nisus fell upon the slippery place,
10   While his young friend performed and won the race.
     O early ripe! to thy abundant store

5–6. Echoes Cowley: 'Thus when two *Brethren strings* are set alike, / To *move* them *both*, but *one* of them we *strike*, / Thus *Davids Lyre* did *Sauls* wild rage controul. / And tun'd the harsh disorders of his *Soul*' (*Davideis*; *Poems* 254).

7–10. D. echoes his earlier lines: 'It seems my soul then mov'd the quicker pace, / Yours first set out, mine reach'd her in the race' (*The Indian Emperor* (1667) I ii 147–8), and he echoes these lines again in Evander's lament for his son Pallas, 'The Eleventh Book of the *Aeneis*' ll. 244–5. D. had used the image of the writer's life as a race in 'Prologue to *Tyrannic Love*' ll. 19–23 and 'To Mr Lee, on his *Alexander*' ll. 43–4, and writes of praise as a race in 'To Mr L. Maidwell' ll. 39–40. For the image of life as a race see Hebrews xii 1 and *OED* race 1c.

7. studies] Cp. *eorum studio flagrabant* ('they were inflamed with study'): Servius' gloss on *Aen.* ix 182, quoted in Emmenessius.

9–10. In *Aen.* v the young Euryalus wins a race as a result of his friend Nisus falling and impeding a rival; the allusion also implicitly evokes the death of the pair in *Aen.* ix. D. translated both passages in 1684 for *Sylvae*; for verbal parallels with that translation see ll. 3–4*n*, 11*n*. The story had also been used as an example of friendship by Otway in a poem to Richard Duke in *MP* (1684). Nisus here represents D., but, as Griffin notes, many readers momentarily assume that Nisus, being the fallen runner, stands for Oldham, which strengthens the suggestion that the two poets share a similar fate. Exactly why D. thought of himself as having fallen is unclear.

9. slippery] In Virgil the ground is wet with sacrificial blood, but D. probably retains the word here because it had become the standard epithet for the position of the courtier, deriving from Seneca's *Thyestes* ll. 391–2: *stet quicunque volet potens / aulae culmine lubrico* ('Upon the slippery tops of humane State / . . . Let others proudly stand': tr. Cowley, *Essays* 399–400). D. uses its connotations again in 'The slipp'ry state of human-kind, / And fickle fortune' ('The Tenth Book of the *Aeneis*' ll. 225–6; cp. *Threnodia Augustalis* l. 400). The phrasing of the line thus associates D. with the slippery life of the courtier; for his growing distrust of such a role see 'Horace: *Epode* II' l. 15*n*.

11–14. Tonson speculated that Oldham would have equalled D. himself: 'Had Fate allow'd his Life a longer thread, / Adding experience to that wondrous fraught / Of Youthful vigour, how wou'd he have wrote! / Equal to mighty *Pan*'s Immortal Verse, [marginal note: '*Mr. Dryden.*'] / He that now rules with undisputed sway' (*Sylvae* 472–3).

11. Echoes Cowley's 'On the Death of Mr. *William Hervey*': 'Wondrous young Man, why wert thou made so good, / To be snatcht hence ere better *understood*? / Snatcht before half of thee enough was seen! / *Thou Ripe*, and yet thy *Life* but *Green*!' (*Poems* 36). D. uses Cowley's poem again in 'Nisus and Euryalus' ll. 251, 253. D. also adapts Oldham: 'Rich in thy self, to whose unbounded

What could advancing age have added more?
It might (what Nature never gives the young)
Have taught the numbers of thy native tongue;
15   But satire needs not those, and wit will shine
Through the harsh cadence of a rugged line:
A noble error, and but seldom made,
When poets are by too much force betrayed.

---

store / Exhausted Nature could vouchsafe no more' ('Upon the Works of *Ben.
Johnson*' ll. 171–2). For the sentiment and rhymes see D.'s addition to Virgil in
'Mezentius and Lausus' ll. 101–2. Cp. also *2AA* ll. 949–50; 'Lucretius: Against
the Fear of Death' ll. 138–9; 'To My Dear Friend Mr Congreve' ll. 61–3 and *n*.
early ripe] Thomas Sprat had described the young Cowley's talents as 'early-ripe'
(*Works of Mr Abraham Cowley* (1668) sig. A2ʳ).

14. numbers] rhythm and metre. For discussions of D.'s understanding of prosody
see R. D. Jameson, *MPh* xx (1923) 241–53 and George McFadden, *Duquesne
Studies, Philological Series* v (1964) 87–109.

15–16. D. adapts Roscommon's *Essay on Translated Verse* (1684) 15: 'Be not too
fond of a Sonorous Line; / *Good Sence* will through a *plain expression* shine.' Raman
Selden (*MLR* lxvi (1971) 264–72) suggests an echo of Horace's verdict on Lucilius:
facetus, / emunctae naris, durus componere versus (*Serm.* I iv 7–8: 'Witty he was, and
of keen-scented nostrils, but harsh in framing his verse'). Selden also observes
that in associating satirical and metrical asperity Oldham and D. were closer
to the views of J. C. Scaliger and Joseph Hall than to those of their Restoration colleagues. (For D.'s later rejection of the association of satire with metrical
harshness – which depended on a false etymological connection of 'satire' with
'satyr' – see the 'Discourse Concerning Satire', *Poems* iii 357–9.) Oldham defended
himself against the charge of excessive harshness in the Advertisement to *Some
New Pieces*, saying that his work showed that he was capable of melodious verse
when it was appropriate, but that in satire 'I did not so much mind the Cadence,
as the Sense and expressiveness of my words' (ll. 82–3). In their contributions
to *Remains* D'Urfey and Andrews stress Oldham's ability at both rough and 'easie
Numbers', and Gould (perhaps replying to D.) objects to such criticism: 'How
wide shoot they, that strive to blast thy Fame, / By saying, that thy Verse was
rough and lame?' (*Remains* (1687) sig. B5ᵛ). Tom Brown said that D. here kicked
over the milk he had given: 'you tell the World that he was a very fine ingenious Gentleman, but still did not understand the cadence of the *English* Tongue'
(*The Late Converts Exposed* (1690) 33). Tonson found Oldham's roughness to be
artistically appropriate: 'Sometimes becoming negligence adorn'd / His Verse, and
nature shew'd they were her own, / Yet Art he us'd, where Art cou'd useful
be, / But sweated not to be correctly dull' (*Sylvae* 472).

17–18. D. had praised Lee's vigour, defending him against criticisms that he was
too fiery, in 'To Mr Lee, on his *Alexander*' ll. 37–48; cp. also 'Prologue to *Tyrannic
Love*' l. 21. In the 'Dedication of the Georgics' (1697) D. says of Virgil's description of a colt: 'His beginnings must be in rashness; a Noble Fault: But Time and
Experience will correct that Errour, and tame it into a deliberate and well-weigh'd
Courage; which knows both to be cautious and to dare, as occasion offers' (*Works*
v 140).

18. Echoes Roscommon: 'With how much ease is a *young Muse Betrayed*' (*Essay* 7).

> Thy generous fruits, though gathered ere their prime ⎫
> 20　Still showed a quickness; and maturing time ⎬
> But mellows what we write to the dull sweets of rhyme. ⎭
> Once more, hail and farewell; farewell thou young,
> But ah too short, Marcellus of our tongue;
> Thy brows with ivy, and with laurels bound;
> 25　But fate and gloomy night encompass thee around.

19–21. Echoes *Lycidas* ll. 3–8: 'I come to pluck your berries harsh and crude, / And with forced fingers rude, / Shatter your leaves before the mellowing year / . . . For Lycidas is dead, dead ere his prime'. D'Urfey has a similar image: 'That *Oldham* honour'd for his early Worth, / Was cropt, like a sweet Blossom from the earth' (*Remains* sig. A3ʳ). Cp. also *2AA* ll. 963–4.

19. generous] abundant (*OED* 4); strong, rich (a metaphor from wine; *OED* 5).

20. quickness] liveliness; sharpness of taste (*OED* 5).

21. sweets] pleasures (*OED* 3). Cp. 'Preface to *Sylvae*' (*Poems* ii 241).

22. Cp. Catullus ci 10: *in perpetuum, frater, ave atque vale* ('for ever, my brother, hail and farewell'). R. G. Petersen notes the Roman custom of bidding a triple farewell to a corpse.

23. Marcellus] The nephew and adopted son of Augustus, who died in 23 BC, his twentieth year, of great and unfulfilled promise. In *Aen.* vi 860–86 Aeneas sees the shade of Marcellus in the underworld. Anchises describes him as 'Admir'd when living, and Ador'd when lost! / Mirror of ancient Faith in early Youth! / Undaunted Worth, Inviolable Truth!' ('The Sixth Book of the *Aeneis*' ll. 1213–15). D. implies that Oldham was the lost heir to the classical tradition of English poetry, as Marcellus was the lost heir to Augustus. The same comparison is used by the anonymous contributor to *Remains* (sig. A5ᵛ).

24. ivy . . . laurels] In antiquity laurel denoted conquest, ivy immortality. Virgil awards Pollio this mixed crown in *Ecl.* viii 11–13; Petersen notes that in *Ecl.* vii 25 Virgil assigns ivy to a *crescentem poetam* ('rising poet'). Horace (*Carm.* I i 29) was responsible for the further association of ivy with learning; see also Ovid's elegy for Tibullus (*Amores* III xxix 61–2). For classical garlands see further J. B. Trapp, *JWCI* xxi (1958) 227–55.

25. Echoes Virgil's description of Marcellus: *sed nox atra caput tristi circumuolat umbra* (*Aen.* vi 866: 'But hov'ring Mists around his Brows are spread, / And Night, with sable Shades, involves his Head': 'The Sixth Book of the *Aeneis*' ll. 1198–9). At *Aen.* vi 869 Fate allows Aeneas only a brief glimpse of Marcellus. D. uses 'compass him around' again in l. 1196; the phrasing is biblical: cp. 'The sorrows of hell compassed me about' (Psalm xviii 5). The ending not only offers no hope of Christian immortality, it also omits the injunction to fortitude common in classical elegies (e.g. Horace, *Carm.* I xxix). *fate*] destiny (*OED* 1); death (*OED* 4b).

10 Lucretius: Against the Fear of Death (from Book III)

Date and publication. Printed in 1685 in *Sylvae: Or, The Second Part of Poetical Miscellanies* (*SR* 10 January; advertised in *The Observator* 1 January); reprinted 1692; reprinted, along with the part of the Preface to *Sylvae* discussing Lucretius, as an appendix to Creech's *Lucretius . . . and Manilius . . . Translated* (1700). D.'s five translations from Lucretius were probably composed in the summer and autumn of 1684 (see *Letters* 23, *Poems* ii 234).

Context. Sylvae is a volume of major importance in D.'s career (for its contents see *Poems* ii Appendix A). It is the second of the miscellanies published by Tonson with some editorial supervision by D., the first being *MP* in 1684. (For a bibliographical analysis of the way in which the two collections were assembled see Paul Hammond, *PBSA* lxxxiv (1990) 402–12.) Whereas *MP* collected many items which had previously been published separately, *Sylvae* includes only new pieces. D. wrote to Tonson: 'Your opinion of the Miscellanyes is likewise mine: I will for once lay by the Religio Laici, till another time. But I must also add, that since we are to have nothing but new, I am resolvd we will have nothing but good, whomever we disoblige' (*Letters* 23). *Sylvae* begins with a substantial group of translations by D.: three translations from the *Aeneid* (the story of Nisus and Euryalus from Books V and IX; the story of Mezentius and Lausus from Book X; and the speech of Venus to Vulcan from Book VIII); five translations from Lucretius ('The Beginning of the First Book'; 'The Beginning of the Second Book'; 'Against the Fear of Death' from Book III; 'Concerning the Nature of Love' from Book IV; and a short extract from Book V); translations of Theocritus' *Idylls* XVIII and XXIII; and four versions of Horace: *Odes* I iii, I ix, III xxix, and *Epode* II. These verse translations are preceded by a critical Preface in which D. defines the distinctive characteristics of the four poets. The remaining pieces by other hands (including D.'s son Charles and his brother-in-law Sir Robert Howard) are mainly classical translations, though the volume also includes a poem on the translation of Fr Simon's *Critical History* (see headnote to *RL*), and Tonson's poem on the/death of Oldham. *Sylvae* marks an important stage in the development of D.'s work as a translator, demonstrating a serious commitment which goes beyond that of *Ovid's Epistles* (see Hammond 150–79). It is partly a response to the interest that several gifted contemporaries had shown in poetic translation in the 1680s. Thomas Creech published his complete translation of Lucretius in 1682 to considerable acclaim, and followed it with a Horace and Theocritus, both in 1684. John Oldham had printed some fine translations of Horace in *Some New Pieces* (1681) and of Juvenal in *Poems, and Translations* (1683) (see Paul Hammond, *John Oldham and the Renewal of Classical Culture* (1983), and D.'s 'To the Memory of Mr Oldham'). The Earl of Roscommon and his circle were interested in translation, and the Earl published an *Essay on Translated Verse* in 1684 (see 'To the Earl of Roscommon'). D.'s translations in *Sylvae* share concerns and common influences. Recurring topics are the confrontation of death (with links to D.'s contemporary poem 'To the Memory of Mr Oldham'), the power of sexual desire, the corrupting influence on the soul of involvement in court and commerce, the attractions of the retired country life, and the need to make use of the present. There are many echoes between the poems, and when translating one piece D. frequently recalled other comparable passages in classical and Renaissance poetry,

as H. A. Mason has shown (see headnotes to the Horatian translations). Besides
the examples of Creech, Oldham and Roscommon, noted above, Cowley's *Essays*
helped to shape D.'s thinking about freedom and retirement, and Milton is an
influential presence (see J. R. Mason).

De Rerum Natura ('On the Nature of Things'), the only work of Titus
Lucretius Carus (94–55 BC), is a poem on the phenomena of the physical world,
following the philosophy of Epicurus. This philosophy attracted renewed interest in England in the mid-seventeenth century (see Howard Jones, *The Epicurean
Tradition* (1989); T. H. Mayo, *Epicurus in England 1650–1725* (1934); C. T. Harrison,
Harvard Studies in Classical Philology xlv (1934) 1–79). This revival was particularly aided by the work of Pierre Gassendi, e.g. his *De Vita et Moribus Epicuri*
(1647). The materialism of Epicurus, and his teaching that pleasure is the highest good, shocked Christian moralists (see *RL* ll. 18–19*n*) and encouraged the
vulgar idea that he advocated mere libertinism; but, as Gassendi showed,
Epicurus thought of pleasure as a state of tranquillity in which the mind was untroubled by passions and desires. This view of Epicureanism was promoted by
Walter Charleton in *Epicurus' Morals* (1656). An example of Epicurus' philosophy
is provided in his epistle to Menoeceus, translated by Charleton: 'when we say;
that Pleasure in the Generall is the end of a happy life, or the Chiefest Good;
we are very far from understanding those Pleasures, which are so much admired,
courted and pursued by men wallowing in Luxury, or any other pleasures that
are placed in the meer motion or action of Fruition [i.e. sex], wereby, the sense
is pleasantly tickled . . . but onely this . . . Not to be pained in body, nor per-
turbed in Mind. For, it is not perpetuall Feastings and Drinkings; it is not the
love of, and Familiarity with beautifull boyes and women; it is not the Delicacies
of rare Fishes, sweet meats, rich Wines, nor any other Dainties of the Table, that
can make a Happy life: But, it is Reason, with Sobriety, and consequently a serene
Mind; investigating the Causes, why this Object is to be Elected, and that to be
Rejected; and chasing away those vain, superstitious and deluding opinions, which
would occasion very great disquiet in the mind' (23). This philosophy is apparent in the passages which D. has selected from Lucretius, which particularly stress
two of the chief disturbances to the tranquillity of the mind: the fear of death,
and sexual desire. D.'s selection is consistent with his other classical translations
in *Sylvae*, which also urge moderate, contented enjoyment of nature's gifts, and
the need for freedom from anxiety and care. In the Preface to *Sylvae* (*Poems* ii
245–52) D. comments on his selection from Lucretius, noting that he has laid
by his 'natural diffidence and scepticism for a while' to adopt the 'dogmatical'
tone, the 'noble pride, and positive assertion of his opinions' and the 'magisterial
authority' which he found characteristic of the Roman poet.

Lucretius had never been one of the most popular classical poets in England,
but his reputation grew during the seventeenth century. He was translated by
Lucy Hutchinson (MS in BL; modern edition by Hugh de Quehn (1996)) and
John Evelyn (MS of Books i and iii–vi in BL; Book i printed 1656; modern edition by Michael M. Repetzki (2000)). Creech's complete translation was published in 1682 and reprinted three times in 1683. Rochester translated two fragments
from Book i, and D. refers to Rochester's interest in Lucretius when writing to
him in 1673 (*Letters* 9). Sir Robert Howard published a translation from part of
Book v in *Sylvae*. Although D. had been interested in the Epicurean atomic theory as early as 1660 (see 'To Sir Robert Howard' ll. 29–34), and may have planned
a translation of Lucretius then (see 'Preface to *Sylvae*'; *Poems* ii 251), his reading
of Lucretius first becomes evident in *Tyrannic Love* (1669), where arguments drawn
from Lucretius are debated between St Catharine and the Romans (see III i 40–73;
IV i 380–406). In *Aureng-Zebe* (1676) the Emperor voices a debased version of

Epicureanism (Act III), while lines from Nature's speech in Book iii are adapted in Act IV (see 'Lucretius: Against the Fear of Death' ll. 126–34n). In the Dedication of *Aureng-Zebe* to the Earl of Mulgrave (*Works* xii 153–4) D. quotes *De Rerum Natura* ii 1–4 (see 'Lucretius: The Beginning of the Second Book' ll. 1–4) and says: 'I am sure his Master *Epicurus*, and my better Master *Cowley*, prefer'd the solitude of a Garden, and the conversation of a friend to any consideration, so much as a regard, of those unhappy People, whom in our own wrong, we call the great. True greatness, if it be any where on Earth, is in a private Virtue; remov'd from the notion of Pomp and Vanity, confin'd to a contemplation of it self, and centring on it self: *Omnis enim per se Divum natura, necesse est/ Immortali aevo summa cum pace fruatur;/ . . . Cura semota, metuque/ Ipsa suis pollens opibus*' (from ii 646–50: 'For the very nature of divinity must necessarily enjoy immortal life in the deepest peace . . . remote from care and fear, mighty through its own resources'; 'remote from care and fear' is D.'s alteration of the Latin, taken from ii 19 and consonant with the recurring stress on this point throughout *Sylvae*). He continues: 'If this be not the life of a Deity, because it cannot consist with Providence; 'tis at least a godlike life: I can be contented . . . with an humbler station in the Temple of Virtue, than to be set on the Pinacle of it', and quotes ii 9–10 (see ll. 10–11 in D.'s version). There are several echoes of Lucretius in *The State of Innocence* (1677) (see Paul Hammond, *SC* xvi (2001) 158–76). RL takes issue with Epicureanism (see ll. 18–33nn). D. alludes to Lucretius' theory of creation in the Dedication to *Plutarchs Lives* (1683) (*Works* xvii 227). There is also an undated letter in which D. adjudicates in a dispute about the sense of some lines in Creech's translation (*Letters* 14–16). For D.'s aims and methods in his translations from Lucretius see Paul Hammond, *MLR* lxxviii (1983) 1–23, and for their association with the seventeenth-century tradition of poems on the theme of the 'Happy Man' see Maren-Sofie Røstvig, *The Happy Man* (1962) 229–310.

   D. had previously taken some material from this present portion of Lucretius for speeches in *Oedipus* (1679) III i 41–65. Montaigne had used the passage extensively in his essay 'Que Philosopher, c'est apprendre à mourir'. George Sandys had translated ll. 972–1010 in the commentary to his *Ovid's Metamorphosis Englished* (1632) 163–4. Lines 843–52 were quoted by Charles Blount in his *Anima Mundi* [1679] 11–12. Lines 894–6 were translated by Thomas Flatman in his *Poems and Songs* (1682) 140. Lucretius' denial of the immortality of the soul made this a controversial passage, particularly since churchmen were currently campaigning against atheism (for contexts see Michael Hunter, *Transactions of the Royal Historical Society* xxxv (1985) 135–57, chiefly on the early seventeenth century, and Gillian Manning, *SC* viii (1993) 99–121 on Rochester and the current religious debate). In the 'Preface to *Sylvae*' (*Poems* ii 247–8) D. rejects Lucretius' dismissal of the immortality of the soul, and in this he is following Renaissance commentators otherwise sympathetic to Epicureanism, such as Lucretius' editor Lambinus. Mortalism was not unknown in England: it was espoused by Milton and other radicals (see Christopher Hill, *Milton and the English Revolution* (1977) 317–23), by Hobbes, and by Rochester in his translation from Seneca's *Troades* (*c.*1674). But, as D. says in the 'Preface to *Sylvae*', it was possible to believe in the immortality of the soul and still find the passage valuable as a *consolatio*, a dissuasion from the fear of death and an encouragement to the proper use of the gifts of nature. For such reasons the passage figured prominently in Walter Charleton's *Epicurus' Morals* (1656) even though Charleton was simultaneously staging a debate with Lucretius in *The Immortality of the Human Soul Demonstrated* (1656), which used arguments from natural philosophy of the kind to which D. refers in the 'Preface to *Sylvae*' (*Poems* ii 247).

Sources. D. translates *De Rerum Natura* iii 830–1094. For his translations from Lucretius D. relied chiefly upon the edition by Lambinus (1570) and the translation by Creech (1682). He often drew upon the Latin glosses in Lambinus, and took words, phrases, and rhymes from Creech. Other minor parallels suggest that he may also have consulted the French translation by Marolles (1650). For the extract from Book III he also evidently had access to John Evelyn's translation, which was still in MS.

Translation of the Latter Part of the Third Book of Lucretius: Against the Fear of Death

What has this bugbear death to frighten man,
If souls can die, as well as bodies can?
For, as before our birth we felt no pain
When Punic arms infested land and main,
5   When heaven and earth were in confusion hurled
For the debated empire of the world,
Which awed with dreadful expectation lay,
Sure to be slaves, uncertain who should sway:
So, when our mortal frame shall be disjoined,
10   The lifeless lump uncoupled from the mind,
From sense of grief and pain we shall be free;
We shall not feel, because we shall not be.
Though earth in seas, and seas in heaven were lost,
We should not move, we only should be tossed.

¶**10.** *Title. Against the Fear of Death*] thus Creech (margin).
1. bugbear] Object of needless (especially superstitious) terror; Eurydice calls death a bugbear in *Oedipus* (1679) III i 75.
2. The distinction between soul and body is added by D.; Lucretius has: *quandoquidem natura animi mortalis habetur* ('since the nature of the mind [or 'soul'] is understood to be mortal'). *souls can die*] thus Creech.
4–8. The three Punic Wars in which Rome and Carthage contended for supremacy in the western Mediterranean (264–241, 218–201 and 149–146 BC).
4. infested] attacked, harassed (*OED* 1).
6–8. Translating *in dubioque fuere utrorum ad regna cadendum / omnibus humanis esset* ('and was in doubt under which domination all men were destined to fall'). For D.'s stress on fear and slavery in the poems in *Sylvae* cp. 'Horace: *Epode* II' ll. 16–17n.
6. debated] contested, fought for (*OED* 2).
9. Cp. 'Let the frame of things disjoint' (*Macbeth* III ii 16).
10. lifeless lump] for *corporis* ('body'). *lump*] See *AA* l. 172n.
11, 14. D.'s additions.

15   Nay, ev'n suppose when we have suffered fate,
     The soul could feel in her divided state,
     What's that to us? for we are only we
     While souls and bodies in one frame agree.
     Nay, though our atoms should revolve by chance,
20   And matter leap into the former dance;
     Though time our life and motion could restore,
     And make our bodies what they were before,
     What gain to us would all this bustle bring?
     The new-made man would be another thing;
25   When once an interrupting pause is made,
     That individual being is decayed.
     We, who are dead and gone, shall bear no part
     In all the pleasures, nor shall feel the smart,
     Which to that other mortal shall accrue,
30   Whom of our matter time shall mould anew.
     For backward if you look on that long space
     Of ages past, and view the changing face
     Of matter, tossed and variously combined
     In sundry shapes, 'tis easy for the mind
35   From thence t' infer, that seeds of things have been
     In the same order as they now are seen:
     Which yet our dark remembrance cannot trace,
     Because a pause of life, a gaping space
     Has come betwixt, where memory lies dead,
40   And all the wandering motions from the sense are fled.
     For whosoe'er shall in misfortunes live

15–17. Cp. Creech: 'But now suppose the *Soul*, when separate, / Could live, and think, in a *divided state*: / Yet what is that to *us*'.

15. *fate*] death, destruction (*OED* 4b,c).

19. *revolve*] turn back again. *OED* quotes Sir Thomas Herbert (1665): 'And the four Elements . . . shall maintain a dreadful fight, so long and so fiercely . . . that at last all will be revolved into a dark confusion'.

20. *leap . . . dance*] D.'s images; cp. *RL* ll. 18–19, and 'Song for St Cecilia's Day' ll. 3–9.

24, 26. D.'s additions.

28. From Lambinus' gloss: *aut me ulla voluptate, vel molestia afficit* ('affects me with either any pleasure or hurt').

30. D. translates *Quos de materia nostra proferet aetas*, which modern editors omit.

32. *face*] With biblical overtones: 'And the earth was without form, and void; and darkness was upon the face of the deep' (Genesis i 2); cp. Milton, *PL* vii 278, 316, 636.

35. *seeds*] literal translation of *semina*, Lucretius' word for atoms.

39. *where memory lies dead*] D.'s addition.

40. *sense*] consciousness (*OED* 6b); also at ll. 55, 113–14, and cp. *senseless* (l. 67).

Must *be* when those misfortunes shall arrive;
And since the man who *is* not, feels not woe
(For death exempts him, and wards off the blow,
45 Which we the living only feel and bear),
What is there left for us in death to fear?
When once that pause of life has come between,
'Tis just the same as we had never been.
And therefore if a man bemoan his lot,
50 That after death his mouldering limbs shall rot,
Or flames, or jaws of beasts devour his mass,
Know he's an unsincere, unthinking ass.
A secret sting remains within his mind,
The fool is to his own cast offals kind;
55 He boasts no sense can after death remain, ⎱
Yet makes himself a part of life again: ⎰
As if some other he could feel the pain. ⎰
If while he live this thought molest his head,
'What wolf or vulture shall devour me dead?',
60 He wastes his days in idle grief, nor can
Distinguish 'twixt the body and the man;
But thinks himself can still himself survive,
And what when dead he feels not, feels alive.
Then he repines that he was born to die,
65 Nor knows in death there is no other he;
No living he remains his grief to vent,
And o'er his senseless carcass to lament.

48. Cp. 'Who are perished as though they had never been' (Ecclesiasticus xliv 9).

52. *unsincere*] unsound (*OED* 2). *unthinking ass*] D.'s addition. Cp. 'our sphere of Action is Lifes happiness / And he who thinks beyond, thinks like an Asse' (Rochester, *Satire against Reason and Mankind* (in MS *c*.1674; printed 1679) ll. 96–7).

54. D.'s addition. *offals*] carrion; also (opprobriously) the bodies of the slain (*OED* 2b).

57. D.'s addition.

58. *this thought molest his head*] J. R. Mason compares Milton: 'nor with perplexing thoughts / To interrupt the sweet of life, from which / God hath bid dwell far off all anxious cares, / And not molest us, unless we our selves / Seek them with wandering thoughts, and notions vain' (*PL* viii 183–7). Cp. 'Horace: *Odes* III xxix' ll. 45, 49*n*; 'Horace: *Epode* II' l. 55*n*; 'Lucretius: Concerning the Nature of Love' l. 19. *molest*] Cp. also l. 28*n*.

60. *idle*] futile.

64. Cp. Creech: 'And hence he grieves, that he was born to dye'. *repines*] complains.

If after death 'tis painful to be torn
By birds and beasts, then why not so to burn,
70   Or drenched in floods of honey to be soaked,
Embalmed to be at once preserved and choked;
Or on an airy mountain's top to lie
Exposed to cold and heaven's inclemency,
Or crowded in a tomb to be oppressed
75   With monumental marble on thy breast?
But to be snatched from all thy household joys,
From thy chaste wife, and thy dear prattling boys,
Whose little arms about thy legs are cast,
And climbing for a kiss prevent their mother's haste,
80   Inspiring secret pleasure through thy breast;
All these shall be no more: thy friends oppressed
Thy care and courage now no more shall free: →
'Ah wretch', thou criest, 'ah! miserable me,
One woeful day sweeps children, friends, and wife,
85   And all the brittle blessings of my life!'
Add one thing more, and all thou say'st is true:
Thy want and wish of them is vanished too,
Which well considered were a quick relief
To all thy vain imaginary grief.
90   For thou shalt sleep and never wake again,
And quitting life, shall quit thy living pain.
But we thy friends shall all those sorrows find
Which in forgetful death thou leav'st behind;
No time shall dry our tears, nor drive thee from our
        mind.
95   The worst that can befall thee, measured right,
Is a sound slumber, and a long good night.

68–9. Cp. Creech: 'But if 'tis miserable to be torn / By Beasts when dead, why
is't not so to burn?'.
72. D.'s addition.
73–4. Creech has: 'expos'd to cold' and 'To be opprest'.
76–9. Cp. Creech: 'Ay, but he now is snatch'd from all his joys: / No more
shall his chast wife, and pratling boyes / Run to their Dad with eager hast, and
strive / Which shall have the first kiss, as when alive'.
78. D.'s addition.
79. prevent] anticipate.
84–5. children . . . life] for Lucretius' tot praemia vitae ('so many prizes of life').
91. quitting] giving up, letting go of (OED 5).
92. Future tense because Lambinus prints deflebimus ('we shall lament') where modern editors have deflevimus ('we have lamented').

attacking the pushing of a fashionable sect?

      Yet thus the fools, that would be thought the wits,
      Disturb their mirth with melancholy fits,
      When healths go round, and kindly brimmers flow,
100 Till the fresh garlands on their foreheads glow,

carpe diem?

      They whine, and cry, 'Let us make haste to live,

a never-ending?
though their indecisions toast?

      Short are the joys that human life can give'.
      Eternal preachers, that corrupt the draught,
      And pall the god that never thinks with thought;
105 Idiots with all that thought, to whom the worst

devils, epicures?

      Of death is want of drink, and endless thirst,
      Or any fond desire as vain as these.
      For ev'n in sleep, the body wrapped in ease
      Supinely lies, as in the peaceful grave,
110 And wanting nothing, nothing can it crave.
      Were that sound sleep eternal, it were death;

Lucretius science?

      Yet the first atoms then, the seeds of breath

97–8. D.'s addition. Lucretius is attacking mere hedonism, false 'epicureanism'. D.'s *wits* suggests a reference to Restoration rakes, who combined sensual indulgence with versifying and moralising (cp. ll. 103–5n), though the word can also mean 'men of intelligence', as in Tillotson's attack on Epicureans who 'assume to themselves to be the *Men of Reason*, the *great Wits* of the World, the onely *cautious* and wary persons, that hate to be imposed upon, that must have convincing evidence for every thing, and can assent to nothing without a clear Demonstration for it' (*The Wisdom of Being Religious* (1664) 16). See further Manning 105–6.

99. Cp. 'whilst frequent Healths go round' (Creech).   *brimmers*] brimming cups (perhaps a vogue word, since *OED*'s first example is from 1663).

101 whine] D. makes Lucretius' sarcasm explicit.   *make haste to live*] from Cowley: 'None ever yet, made Haste enough to Live' ('Mart. Lib. 2. Ep. 90', *Essays* 455).

103–5. Eternal . . . thought] D.'s addition. D. may be alluding to works such as Rochester's *Satire against Reason and Mankind*, which attempts to correct the relationship between reason and appetite: 'His Wisedome did his Happiness destroy, / Ayming to know that World he should enjoy; / . . . The Pleasure past, a threatning doubt remains, / That frights th' enjoyer with succeeding pains: / . . . But Thoughts are given for Actions government, / Where Action ceases, Thought's impertinent' (ll. 33–4, 39–40, 94–5).

104. pall] particularly, to make wine flat or stale (*OED* 8).   *god*] Bacchus, god of wine.

107. fond] foolish.

108. wrapped in ease] Cp. Cowley: 'wrapt in th' Arms of Quiet' ('Seneca, ex Thyeste, Act. 2. Chor.', *Essays* 400).   *ease*] See *AA* l. 168n.

110. wanting] lacking.

112. Translating *primordia* ('first beginnings'). Cp. Lambinus' note: *corpora prima, ex quibus animus noster constat* ('the first beginnings, from which our soul [or 'breath'] is made up').

Are moving near to sense, we do but shake
And rouse that sense, and straight we are awake.
115 Then death to us, and death's anxiety
Is less than nothing, if a less could be.
For then our atoms, which in order lay,
Are scattered from their heap, and puffed away,
And never can return into their place,
120 When once the pause of life has left an empty space.
And last, suppose great Nature's voice should call
To thee, or me, or any of us all,
'What dost thou mean, ungrateful wretch, thou vain,
Thou mortal thing, thus idly to complain,
125 And sigh and sob, that thou shalt be no more?
For if thy life were pleasant heretofore,
If all the bounteous blessings I could give
Thou hast enjoyed, if thou hast known to live,
And pleasure not leaked through thee like a sieve,
130 Why dost thou not give thanks as at a plenteous feast,
Crammed to the throat with life, and rise and take thy
rest?
But if my blessings thou hast thrown away,
If indigested joys passed through and would not stay,
Why dost thou wish for more to squander still?
135 If life be grown a load, a real ill,
And I would all thy cares and labours end,
Lay down thy burden, fool, and know thy friend.

123. *ungrateful wretch . . . vain*] D.'s addition.
126–34. D. had already adapted this passage in *Aureng-Zebe* (1676) IV i 344–8: 'If you have liv'd, take thankfully the past: / Make, as you can, the sweet remembrance last. / If you have not enjoy'd what Youth could give, / But life sunk through you like a leaky Sieve, / Accuse yourself you liv'd not while you might'.
126. *pleasant*] pleasing (*OED* 1, stronger than in modern usage); merry (*OED* 2).
128. *known to live*] D.'s addition. Lambinus' note on l. 961 cites the parallel passage in Horace, *Epistulae* II ii 213–16, including *vivere si recte nescis, decede peritis* ('if you do not know how to live, make way for those who do'). *live*] The emphatic positioning of this word stresses its importance for D.; for other strong uses of *live* see 'Horace: *Odes* III xxix' l. 68 and 'Palamon and Arcite' iii 1114.
130–1. Cp. Creech: 'Why dost thou not then like a *thankful* Guest / Rise chearfully from *Life's abundant* Feast, / And with a *quiet* mind go take thy *rest*?'.
133. D.'s addition, adapting Lambinus' gloss: *sin ea omnia . . . tibi e memoria effluxerunt, vel te non expleuerunt* ('if all things . . . passed out of your memory, or did not fill you').
136–7. D. expands Lucretius' *non potius vitae finem facis atque laboris?* ('why not rather make an end of life and trouble?'). *burden*] from Creech.

Nature finite

will life is limited so as to avoid repetition?

         To please thee I have emptied all my store,
         I can invent, and can supply no more,
140   But run the round again, the round I ran before.
         Suppose thou art not broken yet with years,
         Yet still the self-same scene of things appears,
         And would be ever, could'st thou ever live;

rather ironical, I fear: is D's addition

         For life is still but life, there's nothing new to give.'
145   What can we plead against so just a bill?
         We stand convicted, and our cause goes ill.
         But if a wretch, a man oppressed by fate,
         Should beg of Nature to prolong his date,

personification of Nature again in course we further?

         She speaks aloud to him with more disdain,
150   'Be still thou martyr fool, thou covetous of pain.'
         But if an old decrepit sot lament,

troubling with these types

         'What thou', she cries, 'who hast outlived content!
         Dost thou complain, who hast enjoyed my store?
         But this is still th' effect of wishing more!

on discontent thought life

155   Unsatisfied with all that Nature brings,
         Loathing the present, liking absent things;

we ourselves self-deceived?

         From hence it comes thy vain desires at strife
         Within themselves, have tantalized thy life,
         And ghastly death appeared before thy sight
160   Ere thou had'st gorged thy soul and senses with delight.

diff. ages deserve diff. things?

         Now leave those joys unsuiting to thy age

138–40. Translating *nam tibi praeterea quod machiner inveniamque, / quod placeat, nil est: eadem sunt omnia semper* ('for there is nothing else I can devise and invent to please you: everything is always the same'). Cp. *To His Sacred Majesty* ll. 21–2; 'To the Memory of Mr Oldham' ll. 11–12.

140. Cp. Creech: 'My *Pleasures* always in a *Circle* run'.

141–2. Cp. Evelyn (in MS): 'Suppose thy body be not dry'd with yeares / Nor thy parts languid, yet each thing appears / The same'.

144. D.'s addition.

145. bill] charge, indictment.

147. Cp. Creech: 'But if a *Wretch*, if one *opprest* by fate'.

148. date] allotted span of life (*OED* 4).

150–2. D. follows the order of lines in Lambinus (*aufer . . . / grandior . . . / omnia . . .*), which differs in modern editions.

150. martyr . . . covetous of pain] D.'s additions, adapting Lambinus' gloss *avidissime* ('very covetous').

157–8. Translating *imperfecta tibi elapsast ingrataque vita* ('life has slipped by for you incomplete and ungratifying'). *at strife / Within themselves*] For D.'s stress on the mind divided against itself cp. l. 269, and 'Lucretius: Concerning the Nature of Love' l. 114. *tantalized*] D.'s only use of this word; see ll. 185–8.

161–2. Cp. Creech: 'Yet leave these toyes, that not befit thine age, / *New* Actors now come on; *resign* the Stage'. D. applies this advice to himself in 'To Mr Granville' (1698) ll. 1–10.

To a fresh comer, and resign the stage.'
Is Nature to be blamed if thus she chide?
No, sure; for 'tis her business to provide,
165   Against this ever-changing frame's decay,
New things to come, and old to pass away.
One being worn, another being makes,
Changed but not lost; for Nature gives and takes:]
New matter must be found for things to come,
170   And these must waste like those, and follow Nature's
doom.
All things, like thee, have time to rise and rot,
And from each other's ruin are begot;
For life is not confined to him or thee—
'Tis giv'n to all for use, to none for property.]
175   Consider former ages past and gone,
Whose circles ended long ere thine begun,
Then tell me fool, what part in them thou hast?
Thus may'st thou judge the future by the past.
What horror seest thou in that quiet state,
180   What bugbear dreams to fright thee after fate?
No ghost, no goblins that still passage keep,
But all is there serene in that eternal sleep.
For all the dismal tales that poets tell
Are verified on earth, and not in hell.

163. *if thus she chide*] from Creech.
164–74. D. returns to the universal processes of change in 'Of the Pythagorean Philosophy', esp. ll. 374–97.
166, 168. Cp. 'The Lord geueth, and the Lord taketh awaie . . . so cummeth thynges to passe' (Job i 21; text from the burial service in the pre-1662 Book of Common Prayer).
170. *doom*] judgement, decision.
171. *rise and rot*] Cp. 'we ripe and ripe, / And then from hour to hour we rot and rot' (*As You Like It* II v 26–7).
173–4. Cp. Evelyn (in MS): 'And life to none is given save to be / Made use of; but is no mans propertie'.
173. D.'s addition.
174. *property*] *proprietas* is Lambinus' gloss for Lucretius' *mancipium* ('right of ownership').
176. *circles*] D.'s addition; cp. 'Virgil's Fourth Eclogue' l. 8.
180–1. D.'s addition.
180. *fate*] death.
181. *goblins*] demons. *passage*] [transition to] death (*OED* 2). *keep*] guard.
184. *verified*] made true.

185 No Tantalus looks up with fearful eye,
Or dreads th' impending rock to crush him from on high:
But fear of chance on earth disturbs our easy hours,
Or vain imagined wrath, of vain imagined powers.
No Tityus torn by vultures lies in hell,
190 Nor could the lobes of his rank liver swell
To that prodigious mass for their eternal meal;
Not though his monstrous bulk had covered o'er
Nine spreading acres, or nine thousand more;
Not though the globe of earth had been the giant's
    floor;
195 Nor in eternal torments could he lie,
Nor could his corpse sufficient food supply.
But he's the Tityus, who by love oppressed,
Or tyrant passion preying on his breast,
And ever-anxious thoughts is robbed of rest.
200 The Sisyphus is he, whom noise and strife
Seduce from all the soft retreats of life,
To vex the government, disturb the laws,
Drunk with the fumes of popular applause;
He courts the giddy crowd to make him great,

185–6. Lucretius follows the version of the legend in which Tantalus is punished for stealing the gods' nectar and ambrosia by having a large stone suspended over him, for fear of which he dares not drink.
186. impending] hanging threateningly (OED 2).
188. Lucretius has: divom metus urget inanis mortalis ('the fear of gods oppresses mortals without cause').
189. Two vultures fed eternally on the liver of Tityos, who had tried to rape Leto (Odyssey xi 576–81).
190. lobes] the technical term for the divisions of the liver (OED 1a).
198. tyrant] D.'s addition. Cowley frequently calls a passion a tyrant (e.g. Essays 388, 390, 442).
199. ever-anxious thoughts] A close translation, but also a recurring topic in Sylvae: see 'Lucretius: Concerning the Nature of Love' l. 114 and 'Horace: Odes III xxix' l. 10n.
200–5. D. expands from qui petere a populo fasces saevasque secures / imbibit et semper victus tristisque recedit ('athirst to solicit from the people the lictor's rods and cruel axes, and always retiring defeated and full of gloom').
200. Sisyphus] D. described himself as 'the Sisyphus of the Stage' in the Dedication to Aureng-Zebe (1676) (Works xii 154). He returns to the character of the ambitious man in the Dedication to Don Sebastian (1690) (Works xv 60).
202. vex] trouble, harass (OED 1); stronger in seventeenth-century usage than now.
203. D. repeats this line in HP iii 1092.
204–5. Cp. The Medal ll. 271–2.
204. giddy] D.'s epithet for the Jews in AA l. 216.

205 And sweats and toils in vain to mount the sovereign seat.
For still to aim at power, and <u>still to fail,</u>
Ever to strive and never to prevail,
What is it, but in <u>reason's</u> true account
To heave the stone against the rising mount;
210 Which urged, and laboured, and forced up with pain,
Recoils and rolls impetuous down, and smokes along the <u>plain?</u>
Then still to treat thy <u>ever</u>-craving mind
With <u>every</u> blessing, and of <u>every</u> kind,
Yet never fill thy ravening appetite,
215 Though years and seasons vary thy delight,
Yet nothing to be seen of all the store,
But still <u>the wolf within thee</u> barks for more:
This is the <u>fable's moral</u> which they tell
Of fifty foolish virgins damned in hell
220 To leaky vessels, which the liquor spill—
To vessels of their sex, which none could ever fill.
As for the dog, the Furies, and their snakes,

206–11. Cp. Creech: 'For still to seek, and still in Hopes devour, / But never to enjoy desired Power, / What is it, but to roll a *mighty* stone / Against the *hill*, which streight will tumble down? / Almost at *top*, it must *return* again, / And with *swift* force roll thro the *humble* Plain'.
210–11. Lucretius (ll. 1000–2, following *Odyssey* xi 598) also makes his rhythm appropriate to the ascent and descent of the stone.
211. impetuous] with violent motion (*OED* 1). *smokes*] moves rapidly (*OED* 2c, where the first example is from 'The Seventh Book of the *Aeneis*' l. 909); sends up dust (*OED* 2). Homer says that dust rose up from the head of Sisyphus (*Odyssey* xi 600).
214. Cp. Creech: 'And never fills the *greedy* Appetite'.
217. D.'s image.
219–21. Cp. Evelyn (in MS): 'This I think is by those young Virgins meant / Who in a Vessel pierc't powre liquor still / Which yet with all their paines they cannot fill'.
219. The Danaids were condemned to carry water in perforated vessels as a punishment for murdering their husbands on their wedding night. *foolish virgins*] The phrasing recalls the parable in Matthew xxv 1–13 of the girls who made improvident use of the oil in their lamps.
220. leaky vessels] The image had been applied to insatiable desire by Plato: 'that part of the soul in foolish people where the desires reside . . . he likened to a leaky jar, because it can never be filled' (*Gorgias* 493). Cp. 'Lucretius: Concerning the Nature of Love' l. 20; *RL* l. 35.
221. D.'s addition.
222. dog] Cerberus, who guarded the entrance to the underworld. *snakes*] Not in Lucretius, but the Furies were regularly depicted as or with snakes, e.g. in Aeschylus, *Choephoroi* l. 1049.

The gloomy caverns, and the burning lakes,
And all the vain infernal trumpery,
225 They neither are, nor were, nor e'er can be.
But here on earth the guilty have in view
The mighty pains to mighty mischiefs due:
Racks, prisons, poisons, the Tarpeian rock,
Stripes, hangmen, pitch, and suffocating smoke,
230 And last, and most, if these were cast behind,
Th' avenging horror of a conscious mind,
Whose deadly fear anticipates the blow,
And sees no end of punishment and woe,
But looks for more, at the last gasp of breath:
235 [This makes an hell on earth, and life a death.
Meantime, when thoughts of death disturb thy head,
Consider, Ancus great and good is dead;
Ancus, thy better far, was born to die,
And thou, dost thou bewail mortality?
240 So many monarchs with their mighty state,
Who ruled the world, were overruled by fate.
That haughty king, who lorded o'er the main,
And whose stupendous bridge did the wild waves restrain
(In vain they foamed, in vain they threatened wreck,
245 While his proud legions marched upon their back),
Him death, a greater monarch, overcame,
Nor spared his guards the more, for their immortal name.

223. *burning lakes*] Not in Lucretius; see Revelation xix 20 and *PL* i 210.
224. D.'s addition.
225. This line is reused in 'The Cock and the Fox' l. 332.
228. *Racks*] *numella* (l. 1015, an alternative reading to *luella* ('punishment')) is glossed by Lambinus as a wooden machine for torturing criminals. *Tarpeian rock*] a cliff in Rome from which murderers and traitors were thrown to their deaths.
229. *Stripes*] lashes from a whip.
231. *conscious*] guilty (*OED* 4b).
237. *Ancus*] according to tradition, the fourth king of Rome.
239. D.'s addition.
241. *overruled by fate*] D.'s addition. *fate*] Probably 'death' rather than 'destiny'.
242. Xerxes, King of Persia, who in 480 BC built a wooden bridge across the Hellespont to attack Greece.
243. *stupendous bridge*] from *PL* x 351 (J. R. Mason).
244–5. *wreck / . . . back /*] a perfect rhyme in seventeenth-century pronunciation.
244. *they²*] 1700; *thy* 1685, 1692.
245. *upon their back*] D.'s addition, prompted by *dorso* in Lambinus' quotation here from *Geo.* iii 116.
247. D.'s addition. The 10,000 men of the royal Persian bodyguard were known as the Immortals because their number was kept constantly replenished.

The Roman chief, the Carthaginian dread,
Scipio, the thunderbolt of war is dead,
250 And like a common slave by Fate in triumph led.
The founders of invented arts are lost,
And wits who made eternity their boast;
Where now is Homer who possessed the throne?
Th' immortal work remains, the mortal author's gone.
255 Democritus perceiving age invade,
His body weakened, and his mind decayed,
Obeyed the summons with a cheerful face,
Made haste to welcome death, and met him half the race.
That stroke ev'n Epicurus could not bar,
260 Though he in wit surpassed mankind as far
As does the midday sun the midnight star.
And thou, dost thou disdain to yield thy breath,
Whose very life is little more than death?
More than one half by lazy sleep possessed,
265 And when awake, thy soul but nods at best,
Day-dreams and sickly thoughts revolving in thy breast.
Eternal troubles haunt thy anxious mind,
Whose cause and cure thou never hop'st to find;
But still uncertain, with thyself at strife,
270 Thou wander'st in the labyrinth of life.
O, if the foolish race of man, who find
A weight of cares still pressing on their mind,
Could find as well the cause of this unrest,
And all this burden lodged within the breast,

249. *Scipio*] Roman general (236–184/3 BC) who defeated the Carthaginian armies in Spain and North Africa.
250. Cp. Creech: 'like the meanest *common* Slave'. *by Fate in triumph led*] D.'s addition. *Fate*] Probably 'death' personified, rather than 'destiny'.
251. *invented arts*] From Virgil, *Aen.* vi 663: *inuentas aut qui uitam excoluere per artis* ('or those who refined life through the arts they invented').
252. Cp. Creech: '*Wits*, and *Poets* too, that give, / *Eternity* to others'. See ll. 97–8n.
254. D.'s addition.
255. *Democritus*] Philosopher of the fifth century BC who was an early proponent of the atomic theory of the universe. He advised living cheerfully within bounds, and counselled against the fear of death.
257–8. Translating *sponte sua leto caput obvius obtulit ipse* ('of his own free will himself offered his head to death'). For the image of the race as 'the course of life' (*OED* 1c) cp. 'To the Memory of Mr Oldham' ll. 7–10n.
257. Cp. Creech: 'obey thy *summons*'.
260. *wit*] intelligence.
269. *with thyself at strife*] D.'s addition; cp. ll. 157–8n.
270. *labyrinth*] D.'s image.

275 Sure they would change their course, nor live as now,
Uncertain what to wish or what to vow.
Uneasy both in country and in town,
They search a place to lay their burden down.
One restless in his palace walks abroad,
280 And vainly thinks to leave behind the load;
But straight returns, for he's as restless there,
And finds there's no relief in open air.
Another to his villa would retire,
And spurs as hard as if it were on fire;
285 No sooner entered at his country door,
But he begins to stretch, and yawn, and snore,
Or seeks the city which he left before.
Thus every man o'erworks his weary will
To shun himself, and to shake off his ill;
290 The shaking fit returns and hangs upon him still.
No prospect of repose, nor hope of ease,
The wretch is ignorant of his disease,
Which known would all his fruitless trouble spare,
For he would know the world not worth his care:
295 Then would he search more deeply for the cause,
And study nature well, and nature's laws:
For in this moment lies not the debate,
But on our future, fixed, eternal state,
That never-changing state which all must keep
300 Whom Death has doomed to everlasting sleep.
Why are we then so fond of mortal life,
Beset with dangers and maintained with strife?
A life which all our care can never save;
One fate attends us, and one common grave.

277. D.'s addition.

290. D.'s addition.

294. Translating *rebus relictis* ('having abandoned his business'). Cp. 'Believe me, Son, and needless trouble spare; / 'Tis a base World, and is not worth our care' (*Aureng-Zebe* (1676) III i 180–1); and 'The World's not worth my care' (*All for Love* (1678) I i 123).

295–6. Translating *naturam primum studeat cognoscere rerum* ('first study to learn the nature of things'). The stress on the *laws* of nature is D.'s own; cp. 'Happy the Man, who, studying Nature's Laws, / Thro' known Effects can trace the secret Cause' ('The Second Book of the *Georgics*' ll. 698–9, translating *felix qui potuit rerum cognoscere causas* ('happy he who can understand the causes of things': *Geo.* ii 490)); and 'To learn the laws / Of nature, and explore their hidden cause' ('Of the Pythagorean Philosophy' ll. 8–9). See 'Palamon and Arcite' ii 337*n.*

303. D.'s addition; cp. 'whosoever will save his life shall lose it', Mark viii 35.

305 Besides we tread but a perpetual round,
     We ne'er strike out, but beat the former ground,
     And the same mawkish joys in the same track are
        found.
     For still we think an absent blessing best,
     Which cloys, and is no blessing when possessed;
310 A new arising wish expels it from the breast.
     The feverish thirst of life increases still,
     We call for more and more, and never have our fill;
     Yet know not what tomorrow we shall try,
     What dregs of life in the last draught may lie.
315 Nor, by the longest life we can attain,
     One moment from the length of death we gain;
     For all behind belongs to his eternal reign.
     When once the Fates have cut the mortal thread,
     The man as much to all intents is dead
320 Who dies today, and will as long be so,
     As he who died a thousand years ago.

307. *mawkish*] nauseating (*OED* 2; first example 1697). The *OED*'s first examples for the adjective, in the sense 'inclined to sickness' or 'without appetite' (*OED* 1a, b) are both from D. The word comes from *mawk*, a maggot.
308–12. D. had adapted these lines from Lucretius in *Tyrannic Love* (1670): 'You roam about, and never are at rest, / By new desires, that is, new torments, still possest; / Qualmish and loathing all you had before, / Yet with a sickly appetite to more. / As in a fev'rish dream you still drink on; / And wonder why your thirst is never gone' (IV i 384–9).
308. Lambinus, annotating l. 1082, quotes Horace, *Carm.* III xxix 41–4 (see 'Horace: Odes III xxix' ll. 65–9).
314. D.'s addition, adapting Rochester's description of love: 'That Cordiall dropp Heav'n in our Cup has throwne, / To make the nauseous draught of Life goe downe' (*Artemiza to Chloe* (in MS 1674; printed 1679) ll. 44–5).
317. *behind*] still to come, in the future (*OED* 4).
318. D.'s addition.

11 Lucretius: Concerning the Nature of Love (from Book IV)

Date and publication. Printed in 1685 in *Sylvae* (*SR* 10 January; advertised in *The Observator* 1 January); reprinted 1692; reprinted as an appendix to Creech's *Lucretius . . . and Manilius . . . Translated* (1700). The translation was probably made in autumn 1684 (*Poems* ii 234).

Context. For D.'s Lucretian translations generally, see headnote to 'Lucretius: Against the Fear of Death'. See also D.'s discussion of this passage in 'Preface to *Sylvae*' (*Poems* ii 248–50). As he says there, one of the attractions of this part of the poem was its argument against being enslaved to sexual desire, and many of D.'s additions and emphases underline the powerful force of love and the mental agitation which it provokes. George Sandys had translated ll. 1074–113 in the commentary to his *Ovid's Metamorphosis Englished* (1632) 160.

Sources. D. translates *De Rerum Natura* iv 1052–287. For the editions and translations used by D. see headnote to 'Lucretius: Against the Fear of Death'.

Lucretius: The Fourth Book
Concerning the Nature of Love

Beginning at this line,
Sic igitur, Veneris qui telis accipit ictum, etc.

Thus therefore, he who feels the fiery dart
Of strong desire transfix his amorous heart,
Whether some beauteous boy's alluring face,
Or lovelier maid with unresisted grace
5 From her each part the wingèd arrow sends,
From whence he first was struck he thither tends;
Restless he roams, impatient to be freed,
And eager to inject the sprightly seed.
For fierce desire does all his mind employ,

¶**11.** *1–2.* For *sic igitur Veneris qui telis accipit ictus* ('so, therefore, he who receives a blow from the weapons of Venus').
3. Cp. Creech: '*beauteous* face'.   *alluring face*] rendering *membris mulieribus* ('girlish limbs').
4. unresisted] irresistible; D.'s addition.
7. D.'s addition.
8. sprightly] lively; cp. l. 29*n*.
9. D.'s addition.

10   And ardent love assures approaching joy.
      Such is the nature of that <u>pleasing smart</u>
      Whose <u>burning drops</u> distil upon the heart,
      The fever of the soul shot from the fair,
      And the cold ague of succeeding care.
15   If absent, <u>her idea still appears</u>,
      And her sweet name is chiming in your ears;
      But strive those pleasing phantoms to remove,
      And <u>shun th' aerial images of love</u>
      That feed the flame: when one molests thy mind
20   Discharge thy loins on all the leaky kind;
      For that's a wiser way than to restrain
      Within thy <u>swelling</u> nerves that hoard of pain.
      For every hour some deadlier symptom shows,
      And by delay the gathering venom grows
25   When kindly applications are not used;
      The scorpion, love, must on the wound be bruised:
      On that one object 'tis not safe to stay,
      But force the tide of thought some other way:
      The squandered spirits prodigally throw,

12. distil] trickle down (*OED* 1).

13. D.'s addition.

15. idea] mental image (*OED* 8a).

18. aerial] imaginary; trisyllabic, and always stressed on the second syllable in D.'s poetry, as in l. 62.

19. molests] From Lambinus' *amoris molestias* ('vexations of love'); cp. also 'Lucretius: Against the Fear of Death' l. 58*n*.

20. Discharge thy loins] From Marolles' *se decharger*, translating *iactere umorem conlectum* ('cast the collected liquid').   *all the leaky kind*] i.e. women, but Lucretius has *corpora quaeque* ('any body').   *leaky*] (i) talkative (*OED* 1c); the Wife of Bath says: 'Like leaky sieves no secrets we can hold' ('The Wife of Bath her Tale' l. 155); (ii) menstruating (cp. 'as leaky as an unstanched wench', Shakespeare, *The Tempest* I i 47–8, kept in the version by D. and Davenant); (iii) sexually insatiable (cp. 'Lucretius: Against the Fear of Death' ll. 219–21).

22. swelling nerves] D.'s addition. Here and at l. 84 D. may be using *nerve* in the modern physiological sense, or to mean 'sinew' (*OED* 1a), but he elsewhere uses *nerve* for 'penis', which is one sense of the Latin *nervus* (see *OED* 1b; 'The Sixth Satire of Juvenal' l. 285; 'The Tenth Satire of Juvenal' l. 328; 'The Fourth Satire of Persius' l. 108, and D.'s note). For the plural cp. Lucretius l. 1043: *in loca conveniens nervorum certa* ('gathering in fixed parts in the loins').

26. scorpion] D.'s image. *1685* reads *Viper*, but D. corrects this in the Preface (*Poems* ii 250). *Works* cites the cure for scorpion stings in Thomas Muffet's *The Theatre of Insects*: 'Lay on a Scorpion bruised, to recall / The venome' (in Edward Topsell, *The History of Four-footed Beasts and Serpents* (1658) 1057).

29–30. For *volgivagaque vagus Venere* ('wandering with roving love').

29, 86, 123. spirits] fluids supposed to permeate the blood and organs of the body

30 And in the common glebe of nature sow.
Nor wants he all the bliss that lovers feign,
Who takes the pleasure and avoids the pain;
For purer joys in purer health abound,
And less affect the sickly than the sound.
35 When love its utmost vigour does employ,
Ev'n then, 'tis but a restless wandering joy:
Nor knows the lover in that wild excess,
With hands or eyes what first he would possess;
But strains at all, and fastening where he strains,
40 Too closely presses with his frantic pains;
With biting kisses hurts the twining fair,
Which shows his joys imperfect, unsincere:
For stung with inward rage he flings around,
And strives t' avenge the smart on that which gave the
wound.
45 But love those eager bitings does restrain,
And mingling pleasure mollifies the pain.
For ardent hope still flatters anxious grief,
And sends him to his foe to seek relief:
Which yet the nature of the thing denies,
50 For love, and love alone of all our joys,
By full possession does but fan the fire;
The more we still enjoy, the more we still desire.
Nature for meat and drink provides a space,
And when received they fill their certain place;
55 Hence thirst and hunger may be satisfied,
But this repletion is to love denied:

(OED 16); cp. 'The Second Book of the *Georgics*' ll. 155–8: 'For when his Blood no Youthful Spirits move, / He languishes and labours in his Love. / And when the sprightly Seed should swiftly come, / Dribling he drudges, and defrauds the Womb'. For the specifically sexual senses see Hugh Ormsby-Lennon, *Swift Studies* iii (1988) 97–8, and cp. 'Epilogue to *The Loyal Brother*' l. 12, and Shakespeare, *Sonnet* cxxix l. 1; *Romeo and Juliet* II i 24.
30. *common glebe*] lands held in common; here meaning prostitutes.
31. *wants*] lacks.
34. *sickly*] i.e. the lovesick.
42. *unsincere*] not unmixed, not pure (OED 2), translating *non pura*; cp. *AM* l. 833.
47. For *namque in eo spes est* ('here lies the hope'). *anxious*] See l. 114n. *grief*] pain, suffering (OED 1).
56–62. D.'s expansion of *ex hominis vero facie pulchroque colore / nil datur in corpus praeter simulacra fruendum / tenuia; quae vento spes raptast saepe misella* ('But from

Form, feature, colour, whatsoe'er delight
Provokes the lover's endless appetite,
These fill no space, nor can we thence remove
60 With lips, or hands, or all our instruments of love:
In our <u>deluded</u> grasp we nothing find
But <u>thin aerial shapes</u> that fleet before the mind.
As he who in a dream with drought is cursed,
And finds no real drink to quench his thirst,
65 Runs to imagined lakes his heat to steep,
And vainly swills and labours in his sleep;
So love <u>with phantoms</u> cheats our longing eyes,
Which hourly seeing never satisfies;
Our hands pull nothing from the parts they strain,
70 But wander o'er the lovely limbs in vain:
Nor when the youthful pair more closely join,
When hands in hands they lock, and thighs in thighs
      they twine,
Just in the raging foam of full desire,
When both press on, both murmur, <u>both expire</u>,
75 They gripe, they squeeze, their humid tongues they dart,
As each would force their way to t' other's heart—
In vain; they only cruise about the coast,
For bodies cannot pierce, nor be in bodies lost:
As sure they strive to be, when both engage
80 In that tumultuous <u>momentany</u> rage;

---

man's aspect and beautiful bloom nothing comes into the body to be enjoyed
but thin images; and this poor hope is often snatched away by the wind').
62. *fleet*] float, drift (*OED* 3), dissolve, vanish (*OED* 9). *mind*] Possibly a
misprint for *wind*, since its equivalent in Lucretius is *vento*, but D. could have
settled on *mind* after beginning with the literal translation.
68. *hourly*] D.'s addition.
69. *strain*] clasp tightly (*OED* 2).
72. Lucretius has *membris conlatis* ('with limbs joined').
73. Replaces ll. 1106–7 ('when the body foretastes its joy, and Venus is on the
point of sowing the woman's field'). *foam*] a traditional metaphor, from its being
a sign of fury or madness. *OED* (1b) cites Bonner (1555): 'the fome or rage of
concupiscence'.
75. *gripe*] clutch (*OED* 3a); enclose in a tight embrace (*OED* 3c).
76. D.'s addition.
77. *cruise about the coast*] D.'s addition. *cruise*] often used of men-of-war on the
lookout for prizes (*OED* 1a, citing Etherege's *She Wou'd if She Cou'd* (1668) II
i 73–4).
80. D.'s addition. *momentany*] momentary; a common seventeenth-century word,
not a misprint.

So tangled in the nets of love they lie,
Till man dissolves in that excess of joy.
Then, when the gathered bag has burst its way,
And ebbing tides the slackened nerves betray,
85 A pause ensues; and nature nods a while,
Till with recruited rage new spirits boil;
And then the same vain violence returns,
With flames renewed th' erected furnace burns.
Again they in each other would be lost,
90 But still by adamantine bars are crossed;
All ways they try, successless all they prove,
To cure the secret sore of lingering love.
Besides———
They waste their strength in the venereal strife,
95 And to a woman's will enslave their life;

81. *tangled in the nets*] D.'s image, adapting Lambinus' gloss *vinculis* ('chains'), and perhaps recalling the net in which Vulcan caught his wife Venus making love to Mars. See also l. 133.

82–8. D. makes this passage refer specifically to the man (whereas Lucretius writes of the couple), and increases the physiological precision.

82. *dissolves*] A common Restoration word for achieving orgasm: cp. 'In liquid raptures I dissolve all o're' (Rochester, 'The Imperfect Enjoyment' l. 15, a male speaker; also in l. 10); Oldham, 'The Passion of Byblis' l. 69, where the woman says: 'I all dissolv'd in reeking pleasures lay!'; and cp. D.'s 'The Speech of Venus to Vulcan' l. 38.

83. *gathered bag*] For *conlecta cupido* ('gathered desire'); cp. Rochester: 'Nor doe you thinke it worth your care / How empty and how dull / The heads of your Admirers are, / Soe that their bags be full' ('To a Lady in a Letter' ll. 21–4; Love's text, but substituting the reading of *A New Collection of the Choicest Songs* (1676) which prints 'bags' where other texts have 'Codds' or 'Veins').

84–6. D.'s addition, apart from *A pause ensues*.

84. *nerves*] See l. 22n.

86. *recruited*] For the specifically sexual usage cp. P.M., *The Cimmerian Matron* (1668): 'with a thousand parting kisses [she] dismiss'd him to recruit his spirits lost in the conflict' (*Restoration Prose Fiction*, edited by C. C. Mish (1970) 155). *spirits*] See l. 29n.

88. D.'s addition.

89–90. For *cum sibi quod cupiunt ipsi contingere quaerunt, / nec reperire malum id possunt quae machina vincat: / usque adeo incerti tabescunt volnere caeco* ('when they seek to attain what they desire, and can find no device to master the trouble: in such uncertainty do they pine with their secret wound').

90. *adamantine*] impenetrable (from 'adamant', a very hard rock).

93–4. Cp. Creech: 'Besides, they wast their *strength*'. Creech has several lines consisting solely of 'Besides' in Books iv and v.

95. For *alterius sub nutu degitur aetas* ('one lives at the nod of another'): D.'s stress continues to be on the man's experience. *enslave*] For D.'s concern with freedom and enslavement in *Sylvae* see 'Horace: *Epode* II' ll. 16–17n, and 'Lucretius: Against the Fear of Death' ll. 6–8n.

Th' estate runs out, and mortgages are made,
All offices of friendship are decayed,
Their fortune ruined, and their fame betrayed.
Assyrian ointment from their temples flows,
100　And diamond buckles sparkle at their shoes;
The cheerful emerald twinkles on their hands,
With all the luxury of foreign lands,
And the blue coat that with embroidery shines
Is drunk with sweat of their o'er-laboured loins.
105　Their frugal fathers' gains they misemploy,
And turn to point, and pearl, and every female toy.
French fashions, costly treats are their delight;
The Park by day, and plays and balls by night.
In vain———
110　For in the fountain where their sweets are sought,
Some bitter bubbles up, and poisons all the draught.
First guilty conscience does the mirror bring,
Then sharp remorse shoots out her angry sting,
And anxious thoughts within themselves at strife
115　Upbraid the long misspent, luxurious life.
Perhaps the fickle fair one proves unkind,
Or drops a doubtful word that pains his mind,
And leaves a rankling jealousy behind.
Perhaps he watches close her amorous eyes,

96. *mortgages*] closely translates *vadimonia* in Lambinus' text; modern editors print *Babylonica*.
97. *offices*] kindnesses, attentions (*OED* 1); duties (*OED* 2); translating *officia*.　*of friendship*] D.'s addition.
99–100. For *unguenta et pulchra in pedibus Sicyonia rident* ('Fine Siconian slippers laugh on his mistress' perfumed feet').
102. D.'s addition.
103. *that with embroidery shines*] D.'s addition.
106–8. D. finds approximate modern equivalents. *point*] lace. *toy*] trifle. *Park*] i.e. St James's Park, London, a place of fashionable resort.
110. *sweets*] pleasures.
111. *bitter*] bitterness (*OED* B1). *draught*] For the image of a drink (D.'s addition) cp. 'Lucretius: Against the Fear of Death' l. 314n.
112–15. For *cum conscius ipse animus se forte remordet / desidiose agere aetatem lustrisque perire* ('when his conscious mind chances to sting him with the thought that he is passing his life in sloth and perishing in debauches').
114. For D.'s stress on anxiety see 'Horace: *Odes* III xxix' l. 10n, and for the mind at strife within itself see 'Lucretius: Against the Fear of Death' ll. 157–8n, 199.
116, 119. D.'s additions.

120   And in the act of ogling does surprise,
      And thinks he sees upon her cheeks the while
      The dimpled tracks of some foregoing smile;
      His raging pulse beats thick, and his pent spirits boil.
      This is the product ev'n of prosperous love,
125   Think then what pangs disastrous passions prove!
      Innumerable ills: disdain, despair,
      With all the meagre family of care.
      Thus, as I said, 'tis better to prevent
      Than flatter the disease, and late repent;
130   Because to shun th' allurement is not hard
      To minds resolved, forewarned, and well prepared:
      But wondrous difficult, when once beset,
      To struggle through the straits, and break th'
          involving net.
      Yet thus ensnared, thy freedom thou may'st gain,
135   If, like a fool, thou dost not hug thy chain;
      If not to ruin obstinately blind,
      And wilfully endeav'ring not to find
      Her plain defects of body and of mind.
      For thus the bedlam train of lovers use
140   T' enhance the value, and the faults excuse.
      And therefore 'tis no wonder if we see
      They dote on dowdies and deformity;
      Ev'n what they cannot praise, they will not blame,
      But veil with some extenuating name:
145   The sallow skin is for the swarthy put,

120. *ogling*] *OED*'s first example is from Shadwell (1682), who glosses it as 'a fool-ish Word among the Canters for glancing'.
123. D.'s addition.
124–5. Cp. Creech: 'Such mischeifs happen e'en in *prosperous* Love, / But those that *cross*, and *adverse* passion prove'.
125. *disastrous*] unlucky, ill-fated (*OED* 1). *prove*] experience, suffer (*OED* 3).
127. D.'s addition. *meagre*] emaciated (*OED* 1b); cp. 'Horace: *Odes* I iii' l. 42.
129. D.'s addition. *flatter*] soothe, gloss over (*OED* 6).
131. D.'s addition.
133. *straits*] Lucretius' *rete* ('net') may have recalled *fretum* ('strait'). *involving*] wrapping round, entangling; D.'s addition.
135. *hug thy chain*] D.'s image.
136. D.'s addition.
139. *bedlam*] mad. *use*] are accustomed.
142. *dowdies*] implies both plain features and shabby dress.
143–4. Replaces ll. 1157–9, which Lambinus marks for possible omission.
145. Here Lucretius begins a list of pet names borrowed from Greek.

And love can make a slattern of a slut;
If cat-eyed, then a Pallas is their love,
If freckled she's a particoloured dove.
If little, then she's life and soul all o'er;
150 An Amazon, the large two-handed whore.
She stammers, O what grace in lisping lies!
If she says nothing, to be sure she's wise.
If shrill, and with a voice to drown a choir,
Sharp-witted she must be, and full of fire.
155 The lean, consumptive wench with coughs decayed,
Is called a pretty, tight, and slender maid.
Th' o'er-grown, a goodly Ceres is expressed,
A bed-fellow for Bacchus at the least.
Flat-nose the name of satyr never misses,
160 And hanging blubber lips but pout for kisses.
The task were endless all the rest to trace:
Yet grant she were a Venus for her face
And shape, yet others equal beauty share,
And time was you could live without the fair:
165 She does no more, in that for which you woo,
Than homelier women full as well can do.
Besides she daubs, and stinks so much of paint,
Her own attendants cannot bear the scent,
But laugh behind, and bite their lips to hold,
170 Meantime excluded, and exposed to cold,
The whining lover stands before the gates,
And there with humble adoration waits,

146. slattern] untidy, slovenly woman.   *slut*] like *slattern*, but with the additional implication 'prostitute' (*OED*). The two words were virtually interchangeable in Restoration usage.
147. Homer's epithet for Pallas Athene is γλαυκῶπις ('grey-blue eyed, bright-eyed').
148. Lucretius has *nervosa et lignea dorcas* ('the sinewy and wooden a "gazelle"'). D. adopts the variant *naevosa* ('freckled'), noted but rejected by Lambinus.
149. life and soul] D.'s addition, recalling the phrase ζωή καί ψυχή; cp. 'The Sixth Satire of Juvenal' l. 278.
150. two-handed] bulky, strapping (*OED* 3).
156. tight] lively (*OED* 3); smart, shapely (*OED* 4).
157. o'er-grown] For *tumida et mammosa* ('swollen, with large breasts').   *Ceres*] goddess of the crops.
158. Bacchus] god of wine.
159. Because satyrs were depicted with flat noses (Lambinus).
163. Cp. Creech: 'yet others *equal* beauties'.
165–6. D.'s innuendo; Lucretius has 'she does all the same things as the ugly woman does' (i.e. painting and perfuming).
172. D.'s addition.

Crowning with flowers the threshold and the floor,
And printing kisses on th' obdurate door;
175 Who if admitted in that nick of time,
If some unsavoury whiff betray the crime,
Invents a quarrel straight, if there be none,
Or makes some faint excuses to be gone;
And calls himself a doting fool to serve,
180 Ascribing more than woman can deserve:
Which well they understand like cunning queans,
And hide their nastiness behind the scenes
From him they have allured and would retain;
But to a piercing eye 'tis all in vain,
185 For common sense brings all their cheats to view,
And the false light discovers by the true:
Which a wise harlot owns, and hopes to find
A pardon for defects that run through all the kind.
Nor always do they feign the sweets of love,
190 When round the panting youth their pliant limbs they
        move,
And cling, and heave, and moisten every kiss;
They often share, and more than share the bliss:
From every part, ev'n to their inmost soul,
They feel the trickling joys, and run with vigour to the
        goal.
195 Stirred with the same impetuous desire,
Birds, beasts, and herds, and mares their males require:
Because the throbbing nature in their veins
Provokes them to assuage their kindly pains:
The lusty leap th' expecting female stands,
200 By mutual heat compelled to mutual bands.
Thus dogs with lolling tongues by love are tied,
Nor shouting boys, nor blows their union can divide;
At either end they strive the link to loose—
In vain, for stronger Venus holds the noose:

177–8. Cp. Creech: 'none, / But seeks some *fit excuses* to be gone'.
177. D.'s addition, adapting *querela* ('complaint') in l. 1182.
181. *like cunning queans*] D.'s addition.   *queans*] prostitutes.
187. D.'s addition.
188. *the kind*] the female sex.
196. *require*] invite (OED 3e); seek for (OED 9).
198. D.'s addition.   *kindly*] natural.
201. *with lolling tongues*] D.'s addition.
202. D.'s addition.

205 Which never would those wretched lovers do,
     But that the common heats of love they know;
     The pleasure therefore must be <u>shared in common too.</u>
     And when the woman's more prevailing juice
     Sucks in the man's, the mixture will produce
210 The mother's likeness; when the man prevails,
     His own resemblance in the seed he seals.
     But when we see the new-begotten race
     Reflect the features of each parent's face,
     Then of the father's and the mother's blood
215 The <u>justly tempered seed</u> is understood:
     When both conspire, with equal ardour bent,
     From every limb <u>the due proportion</u> sent,
     When neither party foils, when neither foiled,
     This gives the blended features of the child.
220 Sometimes the boy the grandsire's image bears,
     Sometimes the more remote progenitor he shares,
     Because the genial atoms of the seed
     Lie long concealed ere they exert the breed,
     And after sundry ages past produce
225 The tardy likeness of the latent juice.
     Hence families such different figures take,
     And represent their ancestors in face, and hair and make:
     Because of the same seed the voice, and hair,
     And shape, and face, and other members are,
230 And the same antique mould the likeness does prepare.
     Thus oft the father's likeness does prevail
     In females, and the mother's in the male.
     For since the seed is of a double kind,
     From that where we the most resemblance find
235 We may conclude the strongest <u>tincture</u> sent,
     And that was in conception prevalent.
     Nor can the vain decrees of powers above
     Deny <u>production</u> to the act of love,
     Or hinder fathers of that happy name,
240 Or with a barren womb the matron shame;

216. *conspire*] combine to effect something (*OED* 3); also, evoking its Latin root,
'breathe together' (*OED* 6).
222. *genial*] generative.
223. *exert*] exhibit, reveal (*OED* 1b).
224–5. D.'s addition.
227. *make*] build (*OED* 2b).
230. D.'s addition.

As many think, who stain with victims' blood
The mournful altars, and with incense load,
To bless the showery seed with future life,
And to impregnate the well-laboured wife.
245 In vain they weary heaven with prayer, or fly
To oracles, or magic numbers try:
For barrenness of sexes will proceed
Either from too condensed or watery seed;
The watery juice too soon dissolves away,
250 And in the parts projected will not stay;
The too condensed, <u>unsouled</u>, unwieldly mass
Drops short, nor carries to the destined place:
Nor pierces to the parts, nor, though injected home,
Will mingle with the kindly moisture of the womb.
255 For nuptials are unlike in their success:
Some men with fruitful seed some women bless,
And from some men some women fruitful are,
Just as their constitutions join or jar;
And many seeming barren wives have been,
260 Who after matched with more prolific men
Have filled a family with prattling boys;
And many not supplied at home with joys
Have found a friend abroad to ease their smart,
And to perform the <u>sapless</u> husband's part.
265 So much it does import, that seed with seed
Should of the kindly mixture make the breed;
And thick with thin, and thin with thick should join,
So to produce and propagate the line.
Of such concernment too is drink and food,
270 T' incrassate or attenuate the blood.
Of like importance is the <u>posture</u> too,
In which the genial feat of love we do:
For as the females of the four-foot kind
Receive the leapings of their males behind,

244. well-laboured] thoroughly tilled; for the metaphor cp. l. 283.
250. the parts projected] the parts into which it has been thrown forward.
251. unsouled] unanimated; lacking life. *unwieldly*] variant form of 'unwieldy'.
254, 266. kindly] favourable to growth (*OED* 5b).
258. D.'s addition.
262–4. D.'s addition, replacing ll. 1254–6 on husbands who eventually find a fruitful mate.
270. incrassate] thicken; Lucretius has the adjective *crassus* here.
274. D.'s addition.

275 So the good wives, with loins uplifted high,
     And leaning on their hands the fruitful stroke may try:
     For in that posture will they best conceive,
     Not when supinely laid they frisk and heave;
     For active motions only break the blow,
280 And more of strumpets than of wives they show,
     When answering stroke with stroke, the mingled
          liquors flow.
     Endearments eager, and too brisk a bound,
     Throws off the ploughshare from the furrowed
          ground;
     But common harlots in conjunction heave,
285 Because 'tis less their business to conceive
     Than to delight, and to provoke the deed—
     A trick which honest wives but little need.
     Nor is it from the gods, or Cupid's dart,
     That many a homely woman takes the heart;
290 But wives well-humoured, dutiful, and chaste,
     And clean, will hold their wandering husbands fast;
     Such are the links of love, and such a love will last.
     For what remains, long habitude and use
     Will kindness in domestic bands produce,
295 For custom will a strong impression leave;
     Hard bodies which the lightest stroke receive,
     In length of time will moulder and decay,
     And stones with drops of rain are washed away.

276, 278, 280. D.'s additions.
291. *hold their wandering husbands fast*] For *facile insuescat te secum degere vitam* ('easily accustoms you to live with her').
292 D.'s addition.
293–4. For *quod superest, consuetudo concinnat amorem* ('moreover, it is habit that breeds love').
295. D.'s addition.

12 Horace: *Odes* I ix

Date and publication. Printed in 1685 in *Sylvae* (*SR* 10 January; advertised in *The Observator* 1 January); reprinted 1692. The poem had been written by August 1684 (*Letters* 23).

Context. Horace had been popular with translators throughout the seventeenth century; in the Restoration the composite translation of *The Poems of Horace* edited by Alexander Brome appeared in 1666 (revised 1671, 1680), and Thomas Creech's complete translation was published in 1684. Restoration writers who translated some of Horace's *Carmina* (Odes) included Cowley, Oldham, and Roscommon. In his comments on Horace in the 'Preface to *Sylvae*' (*Poems* ii 253–6) D. notes the 'noble and bold purity' of Horace's style, and the 'secret happiness' (Petronius' *curiosa felicitas*) that characterizes Horace's choice of words. 'But the most distinguishing part of all [Horace's] character', says D., 'seems to me to be his briskness, his jollity, and his good humour, and those I have chiefly endeavoured to copy'.

Sources. It is not easy to establish which editions of Horace D. used, since the textual variants are minimal, and editors take their notes from one another. Bottkol came to no conclusion; *Works* speculated (without evidence) that D. used Heinsius' 1629 edition. The notes in the present edition show that D. used the Latin prose interpretation and glosses in the editions by Lubinus (1612) and Schrevelius (1653), and the French edition and translation by Dacier (1681–9); other minor evidence suggests that he may also have consulted Cruquius (1578). For further evidence of D.'s use of particular editions of Horace see Paul Hammond in *Horace Made New*, edited by Charles Martindale and David Hopkins (1993) 127–47, 294–7, esp. 294. D. evidently used as many previous translations as he could find, and the following seem to have supplied him with occasional words (including rhymes): John Ashmore, *Certain Selected Odes of Horace Englished* (1621); Alexander Brome (ed.), *The Poems of Horace* (1666, revised 1671 and 1680); Richard Fanshawe, *Selected Parts of Horace, Prince of Lyricks* (1652); J. H[arrington], *The Odes and Epodes of Horace* (1684); Thomas Hawkins, *Odes of Horace, the Best of Lyrick Poets* (1635); Barten Holyday, *Horace, the Best of Lyrick Poets* (1652); Henry Rider, *All the Odes and Epodes of Horace* (1638). There are also parallels between D.'s versions and those of Creech, *The Odes, Satyrs, and Epistles of Horace* (1684), which have previously (and probably rightly) been taken to be D.'s borrowings, but the relative dates of the two translations are uncertain. For an account of D.'s methods and aims in this translation see H. A. Mason, *CQ* xiv (1985) 205–39.

Horace Lib. 1. Ode 9

I

Behold yon mountain's hoary height
    Made higher with new mounts of snow;
Again behold the winter's weight
    Oppress the labouring woods below;
5 And streams with icy fetters bound,
    Benumbed and cramped to solid ground.

II

With well-heaped logs dissolve the cold,
    And feed the genial hearth with fires;
Produce the wine that makes us bold,
10   And sprightly wit and love inspires:
For what hereafter shall betide,
    God, if 'tis worth his care, provide.

III

Let him alone with what he made,
    To toss and turn the world below;
15 At his command the storms invade,
    The winds by his commission blow;
Till with a nod he bids 'em cease,
    And then the calm returns, and all is peace.

¶**12.** *1. mountain*] Horace specifically writes of Soracte. *hoary*] greyish white (*OED* 2); venerable (*OED* 1c).
4. labouring] burdened (*OED* 15), i.e. with snow; from Horace's *laborantes*.
5–6. fetters . . . ground] D.'s expansion of *constiterint* ('stand'). *bound*] thus Creech.
7. dissolve] translating *dissolve*.
8. genial] festive (*OED* 2). On the significance of *genial* (which combines religious and joyful feelings about the hearth as the focus of the good life) see H. A. Mason 213–22. For a parallel with this passage see 'The Fifth Satire of Persius' ll. 220–3.
9–10. that . . . inspires] D.'s addition. D. gives no equivalent for Horace's address to Thaliarchus.
11–12. Translating *permitte divis cetera* ('entrust the rest to the gods').
13. D.'s addition.
14. Biblical: Isaiah xxii 18 says that God 'will surely violently turn and toss thee' (H. A. Mason).

IV

Tomorrow and her works defy,
20   Lay hold upon the present hour,
And snatch the pleasures passing by,
        To put them out of Fortune's power;
Nor love, nor love's delights disdain:
Whate'er thou get'st today is gain.

V

25   Secure those golden early joys
        That youth unsoured with sorrow bears,
Ere withering time the taste destroys
        With sickness and unwieldy years!
For active sports, for pleasing rest,
30   This is the time to be possessed;
The best is but in season best.

VI

The pointed hour of promised bliss,
        The pleasing whisper in the dark,
The half-unwilling, willing kiss,
35   The laugh that guides thee to the mark,
When the kind nymph would coyness feign,
And hides but to be found again:
These, these are joys the gods for youth ordain.

19. Translating *quid sit futurum cras fuge quaerere* ('forbear to ask what tomorrow will be').
20–3. Translating *quem Fors dierum cumque dabit lucro / appone* ('credit to your account whatever days Fortune gives you'). Cp. 'Horace: *Odes* III xxix' ll. 50–1, and l. 73*n*. H. A. Mason 222 suggests an influence from Horace's *Carm*. III viii: *dona praesentis rape laetus horae ac / linque severa* ('snatch joyfully what the present hour gives, and leave gloomier matters to the future'), and compares 'The Seventh Book of the *Aeneis*' ll. 179–82.
24. Cp. Dacier: 'comme si vous aviez dû mourir aujourd'huy, comtez que vous gagnez' (Stuart Gillespie, privately).
28. *unwieldy*] feeble, infirm (*OED* 1).
30–1. D.'s elaboration of *nunc . . . nunc* ('now . . . now').
30. Probably not 'now is the time to possess such blessings' (*Works*) but 'this is the time which must be possessed' (cp. the tag *carpe diem* ('seize the day') and l. 20).
32. *pointed*] appointed (*OED*).
34. *half-unwilling, willing*] For *male pertinaci* ('hardly resisting'). *willing*] in Creech.
35. *that . . . mark*] D.'s addition. Cp. Denham: 'Not a Spark / Left to light me to the mark' ('Martial. Epigram' ll. 14–15, *Poems and Translations* (1668)).
36–8. D.'s addition.

13 Horace: *Odes* III xxix

Date and publication. Printed in 1685 in *Sylvae* (*SR* 10 January; advertised in *The Observator* 1 January); reprinted 1692. The poem had been written by August 1684 (Letters 23). In the present text the indentation has been regularized to reflect the number of syllables in each line.

Context. For Restoration translations of Horace generally see headnote to 'Horace: *Odes* I ix'. Buckingham translated ll. 46–64 of *Carm.* III xxix in 1680 (BL MS Add 34362).

Sources. For the editions and translations used by D. see headnote to 'Horace: *Odes* I ix'. In addition, Cowley's *Essays*, with their stress on liberty and retirement, are an important influence on this poem. For an account of the aims and methods of D.'s translation see H. A. Mason, *CQ* x (1981) 91–129.

Horat. Ode 29. Book 3.
Paraphrased in Pindaric Verse
and
Inscribed to the Right Honourable
Laurence, Earl of Rochester

I
Descended of an ancient line
That long the Tuscan sceptre swayed,
Make haste to meet the generous wine

¶13. *Title. Paraphrased*] This indicates that D. is not attempting a close translation; he actually blends Roman and contemporary references. See further 'Preface to *Ovid's Epistles*' (*Poems* i 384–5). *Pindaric Verse*] See 'Preface to *Sylvae*' (*Poems* ii 255–7). *Laurence, Earl of Rochester*] Laurence Hyde (1641–1711), second son of Edward Hyde, Earl of Clarendon (see *To My Lord Chancellor*); previously celebrated in *AA* (see ll. 888–97n); see 'Preface to *Sylvae*' (*Poems* ii 255). *1–2. Works* comments that these lines apply awkwardly to Rochester's family, since his father had been ennobled only in 1660. But D. does not refer specifically to membership of the peerage, and Clarendon had served Charles I (if not actually swayed his sceptre) since before the Civil War, and served his son since 1645, first as his guardian and subsequently as Lord Chancellor. The original is addressed to Horace's patron Maecenas, a member of the ancient Etruscan (hence *Tuscan*) aristocracy; he was a friend and confidant of Augustus. *1.* From Dacier's 'qui descendez d'une des plus anciennes Familles' (H. A. Mason). *3. generous*] rich and strong (*OED* 5); the English application of the word to wine comes from Horace's use of *generosus* in *Epist.* I xv 18.

Whose piercing is for thee delayed:
5   The rosy wreath is ready made,
And artful hands prepare
The fragrant Syrian oil that shall perfume thy hair.

II

When the wine sparkles from afar,
And the well-natured friend cries, 'Come away',
10   Make haste, and leave thy business and thy care;
No mortal interest can be worth thy stay.

III

Leave for a while thy costly country seat,
And, to be great indeed, forget
The nauseous pleasures of the great:
15   Make haste and come;
Come and forsake thy cloying store,
Thy turret that surveys from high
The smoke, and wealth and noise of Rome,

4. piercing] To *pierce* (*OED* 2) was to broach a cask. Creech has 'pierc'd' and Dacier 'percé'.
7. Syrian] Not named by Horace, but suggested by Schrevelius.
8–11. D.'s addition.
10. thy business and thy care] This translates Lubinus' gloss *curis ac negotijs*. These are key words for D. in *Sylvae*. He frequently mentions the burdens of business (often aware of the element 'busy'): cp. ll. 19, 52; 'Horace: *Epode* II' ll. 4, 59; 'Lucretius: The Beginning of the First Book' l. 45. Business is seen as a curse in Cowley's *Essays* (e.g. 387–8, 390). Stuart Gillespie (in *Horace Made New*, edited by Charles Martindale and David Hopkins (1993) 298) notes that *business* means both 'professional duties' (*OED* 12) and 'anxiety, care' (*OED* 5). For its opposite, *ease*, see *AA* l. 168*n*. D. returns to the need for release from anxious care in 'Horace: *Epode* II' ll. 12, 55, 60; 'Lucretius: The Beginning of the Second Book' ll. 22, 35, 51; 'Lucretius: Against the Fear of Death' ll. 82, 136, 199, 272, 294, 303; 'Lucretius: Concerning the Nature of Love' l. 127.
11. interest] This word had been used frequently by D. for the narrow self-interest pursued by the Whigs at the expense of public peace (e.g. in *AA* ll. 501, 724; *The Medal* ll. 88–9). *worth thy stay*] Another leading idea in *Sylvae* is the question of what is worth man's attention: cp. 'Lucretius: Against the Fear of Death' l. 294; 'Horace: *Odes* I ix' l. 12.
13. D.'s addition.
16. cloying store] From Harrington.
17. turret] From *turrim* ('tower') in Lubinus and Schrevelius; in Horace this is Maecenas' town house.
18. Cp. 'The Wealth, the noise, and smoak of *Rome*' (Creech). Contemporaries were concerned at the atmospheric pollution in London; Evelyn proposed remedies in *Fumifugium: or The Inconvenience of the Aer and Smoak of London Dissipated* (1661).

And all the busy pageantry
20   That wise men scorn, and fools adore:
Come, give thy soul a loose, and taste the pleasures of the
poor.

                              IV
      Sometimes 'tis grateful to the rich to try
A short vicissitude, and fit of poverty;
      A savoury dish, a homely treat,
25   Where all is plain, where all is neat,
      Without the stately spacious room,
      The Persian carpet, or the Tyrian loom,
Clear up the cloudy foreheads of the great.

                              V
      The sun is in the lion mounted high;
30   The Sirian star
                Barks from afar,
      And with his sultry breath infects the sky;
The ground below is parched, the heavens above us fry.
      The shepherd drives his fainting flock
35   Beneath the covert of a rock;
      And seeks refreshing rivulets nigh:
      The Sylvans to their shades retire,

19–21. D.'s addition.
21. give . . . a loose] give freedom, allow free rein (*OED* 3b, first example);
perhaps translating *solveret animum* from Horace's *Serm.* II vi 83 (David Hopkins
in *Horace Made New* 118).
22. grateful] pleasing, welcome (*OED* 1).
23. vicissitude] change (*OED* 3); from *vices* in Horace and *vicissitudines* in Lubinus
and Cruquius. *fit*] short period (*OED* 4d).
24. savoury] appetising (*OED* 1). *a homely treat*] thus Creech.
26–7. Cp. Cowley: 'Behind a hanging in a spacious room, / (The richest work
of *Mortclakes* noble Loom)' ('The Country Mouse'; *Essays* 415; Stuart Gillespie,
privately).
27. Cp. Creech: 'Purple wrought in *Tyrian* Looms'.
28. cloudy foreheads] cp. 'clouded forhead' (Rider). *cloudy*] darkened by trouble,
frowning (*OED* 6).
29. lion] the sign of Leo.
30–1. Sirius, the Dog Star, associated with hot, sultry summer weather.
33–4. parched . . . fainting] Many translators have these words.
33. fry] suffer intense heat, burn (*OED* 4).
36. rivulets] Probably pronounced 'riv'lets'; cp. *AM* l. 624*n*.
37. Sylvans] wood spirits.

Those very shades and streams, new shades and streams
   require,
And want a cooling breeze of wind to fan the raging fire.

VI

40   Thou, what befits the new Lord Mayor,
         And what the city faction dare,
         And what the Gallic arms will do,
         And what the quiver-bearing foe,
         Art anxiously inquisitive to know;
45   But God has wisely hid from human sight
         The dark decrees of future fate,
         And sown their seeds in depth of night;
         He laughs at all the giddy turns of state,
         When mortals search too soon, and fear too late.

VII

50   Enjoy the present smiling hour,
         And put it out of Fortune's power.

---

38. require] seek (*OED* 9).

39. want] lack (translating *caret*).

40–3. D. finds modern equivalents for Horace's topical allusions. For this practice see 'Preface to *Sylvae*' (*Poems* ii 238).

40–1. Lord Mayor . . . city faction] London politics, dominated by the Whigs, had an important effect on national affairs: see *AA* ll. 513*n*, 584–629*n*.

42. Gallic arms] Louis XIV was conducting a vigorous military campaign against Spain and the Holy Roman Empire, and achieved a dominating position in Europe by the Truce of Ratisbon (August 1684).

43. quiver-bearing foe] Possibly the Turks, whose invasion of Europe had been halted at the gates of Vienna in 1683. Creech has 'quiver'd *Persian*'.

44. anxiously] From Lubinus' *anxius*; cp. 'Horace: *Epode* II' l. 55*n*; *RL* l. 35.

45, 49. wisely hid from human . . . search . . . fear] D. takes several words from Raphael's speeches to Adam in *PL* viii (which themselves draw on this ode in Horace): cp. 'To ask or search I blame thee not' (66); 'the rest / From man or angel the great architect / Did wisely to conceal' (71–3); 'Solicit not thy thoughts with matters hid, / Leave them to God above, him serve and fear' (167–8); 'God to remove his ways from human sense' (119); and cp. vii 118–25 (J. R. Mason).

47. sown their seeds] D.'s addition. For his interest in the unknowable origins of events cp. *AM* ll. 865–6.

48. at all the giddy turns of state] D.'s addition.

49. Translating *si mortalis ultra fas trepidat* ('if a mortal is alarmed beyond what is lawful').

50–1. Translating *quod adest memento componere aequus* ('be sure to deal calmly with what is at hand'); cp. 'Horace: *Odes* I ix' ll. 20–2. D. may have been prompted by Schrevelius' glosses: *futura in nostra non sunt potestate* ('future things are not in our power'), *quod praesens est* ('what is present'), and *nihil fortunae tribuere*

The tide of business, like the running stream,
  Is sometimes high, and sometimes low,
  A quiet ebb, or a tempestuous flow,
55   And always in extreme:
  Now with a noiseless, gentle course
  It keeps within the middle bed;
  Anon it lifts aloft the head,
And bears down all before it with impetuous force,
60   And trunks of trees come rolling down,
  Sheep and their folds together drown;
  Both house and homestead into seas are borne,
  And rocks are from their old foundations torn,
And woods made thin with winds their scattered
    honours mourn.

VIII

65 Happy the man, and happy he alone,
  He who can call today his own:
  He who secure within can say,
'Tomorrow do thy worst, for I have lived today.
  Be fair, or foul, or rain, or shine,

('give nothing to Fortune': gloss on l. 42). D. returns to this topic in the Dedication to *Don Sebastian* (*Works* xv 60) and 'Palamon and Arcite' iii 1096.
present . . . hour] Creech has 'present Hours'. *Fortune*] D.'s addition; see ll. 73–87*n*.
52. Cp. Cowley: 'The stream of Business does begin, / And a Spring-Tide of Clients is come in' ('Ode. Upon Liberty', *Essays* 389; Stuart Gillespie). *business*] translating *cetera* ('other things'); cp. l. 10*n*.
53–5, 58–9. D.'s additions.
59. *impetuous*] violent (*OED* 1).
63. *from their old foundations torn*] D.'s addition. Cp. 'The First Book of the *Georgics*' l. 455: 'The Rocks are from their old Foundations rent'.
64. Translating *clamore vicinaeque silvae* ('the roar of the neighbouring wood'). *honours*] ornaments (*OED* 6b).
65–7. Translating *ille potens sui / laetus deget, cui licet in diem / dixisse* ('he lives happy and master of himself, who can say each day'). For the phrasing cp. Cowley: 'He's no small Prince who every day / Thus to himself can say' ('Ode. Upon Liberty', *Essays* 390).
65. *he alone*] D.'s addition; Creech has 'alone'.
66. The phrasing recalls Cowley: 'The ground he holds, if he his own, can call' ('Martial. Lib. 2.', *Essays* 386); cp. 'Horace: *Epode* II' l. 9*n*.
68. Translating *vixi* ('I have lived'); cp. Creech: 'for I have liv'd to day', and Cowley: 'To morrow let my Sun his beams display, / Or in clouds hide them; I have liv'd to Day' ('Of My self', *Essays* 457; H. A. Mason). For the strong force of *lived* see 'Lucretius: Against the Fear of Death' l. 128*n*.

70   The joys I have possessed, in spite of Fate, are mine:
      Not heaven itself upon the past has power,
      But what has been has been, and I have had my hour.'

IX

      Fortune, that with malicious joy
        Does man her slave oppress,
75   Proud of her office to destroy
        Is seldom pleased to bless;
      Still various and unconstant still,
    But with an inclination to be ill,
      Promotes, degrades, delights in strife,
80   And makes a lottery of life.
      I can enjoy her while she's kind,
      But when she dances in the wind
      And shakes her wings, and will not stay,
      I puff the prostitute away:
85 The little or the much she gave is quietly resigned;
      Content with poverty, my soul I arm,
      And virtue, though in rags, will keep me warm.

70. *in spite of Fate*] D.'s addition, perhaps from Schrevelius' *non pendet ex fortunae inconstantia* ('it does not depend upon the inconstancy of Fortune').
71. Cp. Dacier: 'la Fortune n'a aucun pouvoir sur le passé' (H. A. Mason).
73–87. *Fortune*] Fortune is a significant figure in D.'s translations from Horace (cp. ll. 50–1; 'Horace: *Odes* I ix' l. 23), and in his poetry generally (e.g. 'Heroic Stanzas' ll. 29–32; *AM* ll. 797–800; *AA* ll. 252–61). She stands for the capricious power of chance, but also for the world of transitory and beguiling material rewards. See Paul Hammond, *MLR* lxxx (1985) 769–85.
73–80. Translates *Fortuna saevo laeta negotio et / ludum insolentem ludere pertinax / transmutat incertos honores, / nunc mihi, nunc alii benigna* ('Fortune is pleased with her savage work, and persists in playing her insolent game, changes her untrustworthy honours, kind now to me, now to another').
73–5. Cp. 'Sigismonda and Guiscardo' ll. 187–8 (Stuart Gillespie).
73. *malicious*] Creech has 'maliciously'.
74. For D.'s stress on man's servility cp. 'Horace: *Epode* II' l. 17.
75. *office*] duty, function.
77. Adapted from Virgil's *varium et mutabile semper femina* ('woman is a fickle and changeable thing': *Aen.* iv 569).
81–2. *kind / . . . wind /*] a perfect rhyme in seventeenth-century pronunciation.
82, 84. D.'s additions. For the idea of Fortune as a prostitute cp. Machiavelli, who describes her as a mistress (see 'Heroic Stanzas' ll. 29–30*n*).
86. *I arm*] D.'s addition, from Schrevelius' *munio*.

X

What is't to me,
Who never sail in her unfaithful sea,
90   If storms arise, and clouds grow black;
If the mast split and threaten wrack,
Then let the greedy merchant fear
For his ill-gotten gain,
And pray to gods that will not hear,
95   While the debating winds and billows bear
His wealth into the main.
For me, secure from Fortune's blows
(Secure of what I cannot lose),
In my small pinnace I can sail,
100   Contemning all the blustering roar,
And running with a merry gale,
With friendly stars my safety seek
Within some little winding creek,
And see the storm ashore.

89. D.'s addition.   *unfaithful*] A common classical epithet for the sea (e.g. *freta perfida*: Seneca, *Medea* l. 302). Cowley has 'faithless main' in his translation from Virgil's *Geo.* ii (*Essays* 410).
91. wrack] Ed.; wreck *1685*. The two words were close in pronunciation and meaning.
93. ill-gotten] D.'s addition.
95. debating] fighting, quarrelling (*OED* 1).
97–8. D.'s addition.
100. Contemning] despising, scorning.
101. merry] pleasant, favourable (*OED* 1d).
103–4. D.'s addition. For the idea of watching a storm from shore cp. 'Lucretius: The Beginning of the Second Book' ll. 1–4. D. returns to the image in the 'Dedication of the *Georgics*' (1697) (*Works* v 143).
104. ashore] Ed.; a shore *1685*.

14 Horace: *Epode* II

Date and publication. Printed in 1685 in *Sylvae* (*SR* 10 January; advertised in *The Observator* 1 January); reprinted 1692. The poem had been written by August 1684 (*Letters* 23). The indentation used here follows that in *Sylvae* (with some adjustments), which marks out the rhyme scheme.

Context. For Restoration interest in Horace see headnote to 'Horace: *Odes* I ix'. Horace's poem was a major source for the seventeenth-century tradition of celebrating rural retirement as an alternative to the corruptions of life in the city or at court; see Maren-Sofie Røstvig, *The Happy Man* (1954; second edition 1962). As Cowley's *Essays* and Marvell's 'The Garden' illustrate, the subject continued to fascinate Restoration writers. Recent instances which D. would have known include Oldham's translation of Horace's *Carm.* I xxxi and his 'A Letter from the Country to a Friend in Town' (in *Some New Pieces* (1681)), Creech's Dedication to his Theocritus (1684), and several poems in *MP*: Roscommon's translation of Horace's *Carm.* I xxii and III vi; Otway's 'Epistle To *R.D.* from *T.O.*'; Chetwood's translation of *Carm.* II xv; Otway's translation of *Carm.* II xvi; and an anonymous version of *Epode* I. D.'s own 'Horace: *Odes* III xxix' explores similar themes of seeking integrity through retirement.

Sources. For the editions and translations used by D. see headnote to 'Horace: *Odes* I ix'. In addition, for *Epode* II D. consulted O. van Veen's *Q. Horatii Flacci Emblemata* (1612), Jonson's translation in his *Under-wood* (1640), and Cowley's in his *Essays* (published in the 1668 *Works*). He also turned to various writers on the pleasures of country life, and to Milton's account of the garden of Eden, to guide him in his careful choice of vocabulary. The aims and methods of D.'s translation are discussed by H. A. Mason, *CQ* viii (1978) 11–55 and ix (1980) 218–71.

From Horace,
Epod. 2d

> How happy in his low degree,
> How rich in humble poverty is he
> Who leads a quiet country life!

¶**14.** *1–4.* Cp. 'To John Driden of Chesterton' ll. 1–2.
1. How happy] Translating *Beatus* ('blessed'). Most English translators have 'happy', which is a recurring epithet in the poems explored by Røstvig, e.g. Sir Henry Wotton's 'How *happy* is he born and taught, / That serveth not an others *will*?' ('The Character of a Happy Life' in *Reliquiae Wottonianae* (1651) 522), and Cowley's 'Happy the Man, who his whole time doth bound / Within th'enclosure of his little ground' ('Claudian's Old Man of Verona', *Essays* 447). *in his low degree*] D.'s addition. *degree*] social status.
2–3. D.'s addition. He also explores the idea of living content with little in 'Lucretius: The Beginning of the Second Book'; 'Horace: *Odes* III xxix'; *HP* ii 675–9; 'The Wife of Bath her Tale' ll. 464–84; and 'Baucis and Philemon'.

    Discharged of business, void of strife,
 5   And from the griping scrivener free.
     (Thus ere the seeds of vice were sown,
        Lived men in better ages born,
     Who ploughed with oxen of their own
        Their small paternal field of corn.)
 10 Nor trumpets summon him to war,
        Nor drums disturb his morning sleep,
     Nor knows he merchants' gainful care,
        Nor fears the dangers of the deep.
     The clamours of contentious law,

H. A. Mason notes that an illustration of Baucis and Philemon is provided in van
Veen, opposite quotations from *Epode* ii.
2. poverty] not destitution, but the state of having just the necessities of life (like
the Latin *paupertas*).
3. quiet] This word is common in the seventeenth-century tradition of 'Happy
Man' poems, and associates the aural peace of the countryside with man's
mental, spiritual and emotional peace. Cp. Cowley: 'Here wrapt in th'Arms of
Quiet let me ly' ('Seneca, ex Thyeste, Act. 2. Chor.', *Essays* 400; translating
dulcis quies in Seneca); and D.'s 'easie Quiet, a secure Retreat' in 'The Second
Book of the *Georgics*' l. 655 (translating *secura quies* in *Geo.* ii 467).
4. discharged] unburdened; for *procul* ('far from'), probably from 'déchargé
d'affaires' in van Veen (H. A. Mason). *business*] thus Jonson, Cowley and Creech;
see 'Horace: *Odes* III xxix' l. 10*n*. *void of strife*] D.'s addition; used again in 'The
Second Book of the *Georgics*' l. 688. *void of*] free from (*OED* 11b); thus Brome.
5. Cp. 'Free from the griping Scriveners bands' (Sir Richard Fanshawe, 'An Ode
Vpon occasion of His Majesties Proclamation in the yeare 1630' in *Il Pastor Fido*
(1648) 228). *griping*] clutching, grasping; many translators have this. 'Gripe' is
the name of the scrivener in James Howard's *The English Mounsieur* (1674). *scrivener*]
money-lender (*OED* 3); cp. 'Prologue to *Amboyna*' ll. 1–2.
6–7. For *ut prisca gens mortalium* ('like the first race of mortals').
6. seeds] Cp. 'Horace: *Odes* III xxix' l. 47*n*. D. echoes Spenser: 'the wicked seede
of vice / Began to spring which shortly grew full great' (*FQ* V i 1), and *semina
nequitiae* in Ovid (*Amores* III iv 9; *Tristia* ii 279) (H. A. Mason).
7. Added from *magnanimi heroes nati melioribus annis* ('great heroes born in better
times'; Virgil, *Aen.* vi 649); and cp. *RL* l. 80; (H. A. Mason).
9. small] D.'s addition, perhaps from Cowley: 'The ground he holds, if he his
own can call, / He quarrels not with Heaven because 'tis small' ('Martial. Lib. 2.',
Essays 386); cp. 'Horace: *Odes* III xxix' l. 66*n*. *field of corn*] For *rura* ('country');
cp. Cowley: 'A Field of Corn, a Fountain and a Wood, / Is all the Wealth by
Nature understood' ('A Paraphrase on an ode in Horace', *Essays* 442).
11. D.'s addition.
12. D.'s addition, possibly from Lubinus' *lucri spe* ('hope of gain'); cp. 'Horace:
Odes III xxix' ll. 10*n*, 92–3; 'Virgil's Fourth Eclogue' l. 38.
14–15. For *forumque vitat* ('he avoids the forum'). The forum was a market place,
as well as a place for public assemblies and law courts.
14. Cp. Shadwell, *The Libertine* (1676) where the shepherds dismiss 'the clamorous Courts of tedious Law' (Act IV; Shadwell, *Works* iii 75).

15   And court and state he wisely shuns,
        Nor bribed with hopes nor dared with awe
        To servile salutations runs:
        But either to the clasping vine
        Does the supporting poplar wed,
20   Or with his pruning hook disjoin
        Unbearing branches from their head,
        And grafts more happy in their stead;
        Or climbing to a hilly steep
        He views his herds in vales afar,
25   Or sheers his overburdened sheep;
        Or mead for cooling drink prepares
        Of virgin honey in the jars.

15. court] Though Horace seems to be thinking of law courts, D.'s singular *court* refers rather to the King's entourage. Although D. praised Charles II and many courtiers, there is a notable element in his work which rejects the corruption and strife associated with court politics: see Dedication to *Marriage A-la-Mode* (1672; *Works* xi 221–3); 'Epilogue at Oxford, 1674' ll. 1–6; Dedication to *Aureng-Zebe* (1676; *Works* xii 149–55); Dedication to *All for Love* (1678; *Works* xiii 8–9); Dedication to *Don Sebastian* (1690; *Works* xv 60); Dedication of the *Georgics* (*Works* v 141–4).
16–17. For *superba civium / potentiorum limina* ('the proud thresholds of powerful citizens'), with hints from Lubinus' *tanquam cliens & adulator* ('like a client and flatterer'). For other cases where D. stresses the servility of those who pay court to great men see *All for Love* III i 141–2; and 'The Tenth Satire of Juvenal' ll. 144–7.
16. dared] dazed, paralysed (*OED* 5); larks are 'dared' with mirrors in order to catch them (see ll. 51–2, and cp. *AM* l. 780).
17. salutations] H. A. Mason notes that D. has recalled the parallel passage in Virgil's *Geo.* ii 462: *mane salutantum totis uomit aedibus undam* ('a tide of clients spews in to greet him in the morning').
18. clasping] Cp. the 'clasping ivy' in Milton's paradise (*PL* ix 217; J. R. Mason).
21. Unbearing] unfruitful (*OED* has no example between 1200 and this one).
23. D.'s addition, from Lubinus' *ex editiore loco* ('from a loftier place'). *steep*] slope of a hill, cliff.
24. Pace *Works*, not an addition.
25. overburdened sheep] Thus Holyday and Hawkins.
26. D.'s addition. Mead was declining in importance in late seventeenth-century London, with tea, coffee, chocolate, wine and spirits becoming more fashionable, but it remained popular in the countryside, and enjoyed a revival among the gentry after the Restoration. Sir Kenelm Digby collected fifty-six recipes for mead (Jennifer Stead, privately; C. Anne Wilson, *Food and Drink in Britain* (1973) 403). *cooling*] Sir Kenelm Digby called it 'a most pleasant, quick, cooling, smoothing drink' (*The Closet of the Eminently Learned Sir Kenelme Digby Kt Opened* (1671) 93; H. A. Mason).
27. virgin honey] 'Virgin-honey . . . is the best . . . [it comes] of Bees that swarmed the Spring before, and are taken up in Autumn; and it is made best by chusing the whitest Combs of the Hive, and then letting the Honey run out of

Or in the now declining year,
  When bounteous Autumn rears his head,
30 He joys to pull the ripened pear,
  And clustering grapes with purple spread.
The fairest of his fruit he serves,
  Priapus, thy rewards;
Sylvanus too his part deserves,
35   Whose care the fences guards.
Sometimes beneath an ancient oak,
  Or on the matted grass he lies;
No god of sleep he need invoke,
  The stream that o'er the pebbles flies
40 With gentle slumber crowns his eyes.
The wind that whistles through the sprays
  Maintains the consort of the song,
And hidden birds with native lays
  The golden sleep prolong.
45 But when the blast of winter blows,

---

them lying on a Seive, without pressing it, or breaking of the Combs' (Digby 4;
H. A. Mason 47–8); cp. *AM* l. 578.
28. D.'s addition.
29. his] Autumnus is masculine in Latin.
31. clustering grapes] Cp. 'clustering vine' in *PL* vii 320 (J. R. Mason).
32. D.'s addition. *fairest . . . fruit*] Cp. 'goodliest trees loaden with fairest fruit'
(*PL* iv 147, and cp. ix 851; J. R. Mason).
33. Priapus] the god of procreation; also of gardens and vineyards, where his statue
was placed.
34. Sylvanus] the god of the woods.
38. D.'s addition. The god of sleep, Morpheus, comes from Ovid's *Met.* xi.
39. o'er the pebbles] D.'s addition, perhaps from Virgil, *Ecl.* v 84, where the rivers
flow through stony valleys (*saxosas uallis*: 'the scarce cover'd Pebbles'; 'Virgil's
Fifth Pastoral' l. 132).
40. D.'s addition. *crowns*] blesses (*OED* 11). H. A. Mason notes an echo
of Shakespeare: 'on your eyelids crown the god of sleep' (*I Henry IV* IV i
210).
41–2. D.'s addition. H. A. Mason notes an echo of 'How, with their drowsie
tone, the whistling Air / (Your sleep to tempt) a Consort does prepare!' (Virgil
Ecl. i, tr. John Caryll in *MP* (1684) 6). Mason also observes that the sound of
the wind contributes to the music of several paradisal scenes in Tasso, and in
Spenser's Bower of Bliss (*FQ* II xii 70–1). Cp. also Cowley: 'The whistling Winds
add their less artful strains' (Verses in 'The Garden', *Essays* 424).
42. Maintains] supports (*OED* 11, 12). *consort*] harmony (*OED* 3), perhaps from
concert in Dacier.
44. prolong] D.'s addition. He also adds the idea that a voice prolongs sleep in
'Virgil's First Pastoral' l. 76.

And hoary frost inverts the year,
Into the naked woods he goes,
        And seeks the tusky boar to rear
        With well-mouthed hounds and pointed spear;
50   Or spreads his subtle nets from sight,
        With twinkling glasses to betray
The larks that in the meshes light,
        Or makes the fearful hare his prey.
Amidst his harmless easy joys
55   No anxious care invades his health,
Nor love his peace of mind destroys,
        Nor wicked avarice of wealth.
But if a chaste and pleasing wife,
To ease the business of his life,
60   Divides with him his household care,
        Such as the Sabine matrons were,
Such as the swift Apulian's bride,
        Sunburnt and swarthy though she be,
Will fire for winter nights provide,
65   And without noise will oversee
        His children and his family,
And order all things till he come

46. *inverts the year*] D. adapts *inversum annum* ('the inverted [i.e. completed] year')
from Horace's *Serm.* I i 36 (H. A. Mason).
47. D.'s addition.
48. *rear*] rouse from covert (*OED* 4b): the technical term for dislodging a boar
(Nicholas Cox, *The Gentleman's Recreation* (1677) 10).
49. *well-mouthed*] capable of baying loudly; thus Cowley.   *and pointed spear*] D.'s
addition.
50. *subtle*] of fine texture (*OED* 2); thus Jonson.
51–2. D.'s addition, replacing Horace's thrushes with larks; cp. l. 16*n*.
51. *glasses*] mirrors.
54–6. For *quis non malarum, quas amor curas habet, / haec inter obliviscitur?* ('who,
amongst such things, would not forget the ills and cares which love brings?').
54. *harmless*] D.'s addition, stressing the innocence of the pastoral life. He adds the
same word in 'The Second Book of the *Georgics*' l. 656.   *easy*] See *AA* l. 168*n*.
55. *anxious care*] Cp. 'God hath bid dwell far off all anxious cares' (*PL* viii 185;
J. R. Mason); and cp. 'Horace: *Odes* III xxix' ll. 10*n*, 44; 'To John Driden of
Chesterton' l. 2.
57, 59. D.'s additions.
59. *business*] See 'Horace: *Odes* III xxix' l. 10*n*.
61. Cp. Creech: 'Such as the ancient *Sabines* were'. The Sabines lived north-east
of Rome, where Horace had his farm.
62. The Apulians lived in south-east Italy.

Sweaty and overlaboured home;
    If she in pens his flocks will fold,
70   And then produce her dairy store,
    With wine to drive away the cold,
        And unbought dainties of the poor;
    Not oysters of the Lucrine lake
        My sober appetite would wish,
75   Nor turbot, or the foreign fish
    That rolling tempests overtake,
        And hither waft the costly dish;
    Not heathpout, or the rarer bird
        Which Phasis or Ionia yields,
80 More pleasing morsels would afford
        Than the fat olives of my fields,
    Than shards or mallows for the pot,
        That keep the loosened body sound;
    Or than the lamb that falls by lot
85   To the just guardian of my ground.
    Amidst these feasts of happy swains,
        The jolly shepherd smiles to see
    His flock returning from the plains;
        The farmer is as pleased as he
90 To view his oxen, sweating smoke,
    Bear on their necks the loosened yoke;

68. *sweaty and overlaboured*] For *lassi* ('tired').
69. Cp. Milton: 'The folded flocks penned in their wattled cotes' (*A Masque* l. 343; and cp. *PL* iv 185–7; J. R. Mason).
73. *Lucrine lake*] a shallow lagoon off the Bay of Naples, famous for its oysters.
75. *turbot*] Exactly translating *rhombus*. Turbot caught near Tynemouth were conveyed in tanks on board ship to the London market, so it was an expensive fish (Wilson, *Food and Drink in Britain* 47; Jennifer Stead, privately).   *the foreign fish*] For Horace's *scar*, a fish much prized by the Romans.
78. *heathpout*] grouse.   *rarer bird*] In Horace, the heathcock. After the passing of the 1671 Act restricting the killing of game, these would have been rarities in London (Wilson 108; Stead).
79. *Phasis*] Not in Horace; an area in Colchis (east of the Black Sea) noted for pheasants.   *Ionia*] part of Asia Minor on the Aegean Sea.
82. *shards*] chard beet: ''Tis of quality Cold and Moist, and naturally somewhat Laxative' (John Evelyn, *Acetaria: A Discourse of Sallets* (1699) 11; Stead).   *mallows*] the marsh mallow: held by Pythagoras to reduce the passions and cleanse both stomach and mind; also a laxative (Evelyn 35–6; Stead).
85. *guardian*] Terminus, the god of boundaries. D. omits Horace's kid snatched from the wolf.
90. *sweating smoke*] D.'s addition.   *smoke*] steam (*OED* 3).

To look upon his menial crew
   That sit around his cheerful hearth,
. And bodies spent in toil renew
95   With wholesome food and country mirth.
This Morecraft said within himself,
   Resolved to leave the wicked town
   And live retired upon his own;
     He called his money in:
100 But the prevailing love of pelf
   Soon split him on the former shelf,
     And put it out again.

92. menial] household, domestic (*OED* 1; not derogatory).   *crew*] company (*OED* 3).

94–5. D.'s addition.

96–102. Some translators (e.g. Cowley) omit the ironic ending to Horace's poem, where it is revealed that this eloquent praise of the country life is spoken by a moneylender. In order to preserve the element of surprise which both Horace and D. have, the inverted commas which should mark out ll. 1–95 as Morecraft's speech are not added in this edition.

96–7. Echoes Oldham's 'A Satyr in Imitation of the Third of Juvenal' ll. 35–6, where the character who is about to move from the town to the country says: ''Tis my Resolve to quit the nauseous Town / Let thriving *Morecraft* chuse his dwelling there' (published in *Poems, and Translations* (1683)).

96. Morecraft] the usurer in Beaumont and Fletcher's *The Scornful Lady* (1616, frequently revived in the Restoration); also referred to in 'Prologue to *Marriage A-la-Mode*' l. 29.

97–8. For *iam iam futurus rusticus* ('already a future countryman').

98. his own] his own resources, own estate.

99. Thus Creech.

100–1. D.'s addition. Cp. '*This love of Pelf, / Makes this vile Slave an enemy to himself*' (Horace, *Serm.* I ii, tr. Brome (1666) 192).

100. pelf] money (*OED* 3; generally derogatory).

101. For the religious connotations of the image cp. Jonson: 'God wisheth, none should wracke on a strange shelf' ('To Sir Robert Wroth' l. 95), and *RL* ll. 425–6. *split*] wrecked (*OED* 1).   *shelf*] sandbank; submerged ledge of rock (*OED* 1).

15 To the Memory of Anne Killigrew

Date and publication. Probably written October 1685 (Winn 611). First printed as
a prefatory poem to *Poems by Mrs Anne Killigrew*, published by Samuel Lowndes
and dated 1686 (licensed 30 September 1685; advertised in *The Observator* 2
November 1685; *SR* 2 October; *TC* November). Reprinted with revisions in *EP*
(1693). The present text is based on *1686*, with the *EP* revisions (at ll. 12, 124,
128, 139–40, 141, 148) given in the notes (siglum: *1693*). Indentation has been
rationalized to correspond with the length of the lines, and additional triplet braces
supplied at ll. 68–70, 77–9, 146–8, 165–7, and 193–5. *Pace Works*, there is no
evidence for believing that the italicization in either *1686* or *1693* is authorial.

Context. Anne Killigrew (1660–1685), described by Anthony à Wood as 'a Grace
for beauty, and a Muse for Wit' (*Athenae Oxonienses*, edited by P. Bliss, 5 vols
(1813–20) iv 623), was a maid of honour to Maria Beatrice of Modena, Duchess
of York (subsequently Queen to James II), and an amateur painter and poet. She
died aged 25 in 1685, a victim of the particularly virulent smallpox epidemics of
that year (for which see Evelyn iv 463), 'to the unspeakable reluctancy of her
relations' (Wood 623). Her father's epitaph (printed in her *Poems*) gives the date
of her death as 16 June, but according to the register of the chapel of St John
the Baptist at the Savoy Hospital her burial there occurred on 15 June. Her father,
Dr Henry Killigrew (1613–1700), a former chaplain to Charles I's army, was the
author of a tragedy, *The Conspiracy* (1638; revised as *Palantus and Eudora* (1653))
which was said to have been praised by Ben Jonson (Wood 622). After the
Restoration, he was appointed almoner to the Duke of York and superintendent of the affairs of his chapel, as well as being reinstated as a prebendary of
Westminster and appointed master of the Savoy Hospital. Anne's uncle, Thomas
Killigrew (1612–1683), Groom of the Bedchamber and Master of the Revels to
Charles II, had been D.'s associate in the King's Company during the 1660s and
early 1670s. Winn 417 suggests that it was D.'s personal association with the Killigrew
family (and his probable acquaintance with Anne herself) that led to his involvement with the collection of poems designed as her memorial, in the prefatory
material to which, according to Wood, 'is nothing spoken of her, which (allowing only for the poetical dress) she was not equal to, if not superior' (623).

    Poems by Mrs Anne Killigrew consists of two prefatory poems (by 'The Pub-
lisher' and Dr Killigrew) in addition to D.'s, plus 29 poems by Anne Killigrew
herself in a variety of genres and metres: pastorals, occasional poems (several in
praise of virtuous ladies), epigrams, a fragment from an unfinished juvenile epic
on Alexander the Great, and poems of general (and often firmly moral) reflection on love, wealth, and worldly joys and pains. An appendix contains three
further poems '*found among* Mrs Killigrews *Papers . . . though none of hers*' (*Poems*
84). Three of Anne Killigrew's poems refer to her own paintings: of St John the
Baptist in the wilderness, of Salome presenting Herodias with the head of John
the Baptist, and of two nymphs of Diana, '*one in a posture to Hunt, the other Batheing*'
(*Poems* 28). George Vertue (BL MS Add. 23070, fol. 52^v, reprinted in *The Walpole
Society* xx (1931–2) 58) records that six more of her paintings were included in
a sale of her brother Admiral Henry Killigrew's collection in 1727: a 'Venus and
Adonis', a 'Satyr Playing the Pipe', a 'Judith and Holofernes', 'A Woman's Head',
'Venus attired by the Graces', and a self-portrait. She clearly also painted landscapes
(see below, ll. 108–26 and *nn*), but neither these, nor the biblical paintings, nor
the painting of Diana's nymphs seem to have survived. Her portrait of James II,

however (formerly attributed to Lely; see below, ll. 127–33), exists in the Royal Collection at Windsor and is reproduced as Plate 1 in *Poems* iii and in the *Burlington Magazine* xxviii (1915–16) 113, which also includes (116) a photograph of the 'Venus attired by the Graces' from a private collection. A full-length self-portrait in an allegorical setting is housed at Berkeley Castle, Gloucestershire. A mezzotint after a smaller self-portrait (now lost) forms the frontispiece to the 1686 *Poems* (see *Poems* iii, Plate 2). Both amply confirm D.'s tribute to Anne Killigrew's 'beauteous frame'. A photograph of a portrait in a private collection, said to be of the Duchess of York (see below, ll. 134–41), and said to be signed by Anne Killigrew, exists in the files of the National Portrait Gallery (Reyahn King, privately).

D.'s poem has no specific source, but draws on traditions and treats topics which are to be found both in the work of previous poets and in his own earlier poems and prefaces. A number of its procedures and concerns are indebted, in a general way, to Donne's two poems on the death of Elizabeth Drury (see Barbara Kiefer Lewalski, *Donne's 'Anniversaries' and the Poetry of Praise* (1973) 345–8) and to Ben Jonson's panegyrics (see Richard Luckett, *Proceedings of the British Academy* lxvii (1981) 294). A more specific and immediate precedent is provided by Abraham Cowley's pindaric eulogies, particularly his two poems on the poet Katherine Philips ('the matchless Orinda') (1631–64), to whom D. was distantly related, and with whom he had been acquainted (see *Letters* 125, 186). D. seems also to have remembered other commemorations of Katherine Philips's work, notably the poem 'To the Memory of the Excellent Orinda' by James Tyrell, prefixed to her *Poems* (1667) (see Luckett 295, and below, ll. 1–22, 33, 160–4*nn*). Like Anne Killigrew, Katherine Philips was renowned for her virtuous life, and had died prematurely from smallpox. The Preface and several of the commendatory verses to Philips's *Poems* had compared her with the Greek female poet Sappho (see below, l. 33*n*). Anne Killigrew had herself praised Katherine Philips (*Poems* 46).

At several points D. reveals his first-hand acquaintance with Anne Killigrew's own work (see ll. 70, 83, 116–18, 147–8, 162 and *nn* below). He also addresses topics – the connection of religion with poetry, the poet's role as moral reformer, the relation of poetic to saintly immortality, the continuity of the poetic community down the ages, the relation of poetic rules to nature – which he had previously dealt with in both prose and verse, notably in the Preface to *Tyrannic Love* and in 'Upon the Death of the Lord Hastings', 'To John Hoddesdon', 'To Sir Robert Howard', 'To Mr Lee, on his *Alexander*', 'To the Earl of Roscommon' and 'To the Memory of Mr Oldham' (on D.'s use of the elegiac tradition, see Ruth Wallerstein, *SP* xliv (1947) 519–28; on D. and the community of poets, the links between poetry and religion, and the connections with the poems on Hoddesdon, Howard, Lee and Oldham, see Robert Daly, *Texas Studies in Language and Literature* xviii (1976) 184–97; also Winn 419). The treatment of the relationship between poetry and painting in stanzas 7 and 8 anticipates that in 'To Sir Godfrey Kneller' and in the 'Parallel betwixt Painting and Poetry' prefixed to the translation of Charles Du Fresnoy's *De Arte Graphica* (1695). Many of the virtues for which Anne Killigrew is praised can be seen as opposites of the vices for which Shadwell is castigated in *MF* (see Mother Mary Eleanor, *PQ* xliii (1964) 47–54). In stanza 4, D. voices regrets about the prostitution of his own and his contemporaries' talents in writing for the Restoration stage; these have some precedent in his earlier expressions of misgiving at having pandered to the low tastes of his audiences: see, for example, 'Prologue to *The Rival Ladies*' ll. 21–2; Preface to *An Evening's Love* (*Works* x 202–3); Dedication to *Aureng-Zebe* (*Works* xii 154); 'Prologue to *Caesar Borgia*' ll. 1–6; Dedication to *The Spanish Friar* (*Works* xiv 100–1). D. was to voice misgivings about his former stage 'obscenities' and 'wantonnesses' in several later works (see 'To Peter Motteux'; 'Preface to *Fables*' (*Poems* v 88); 'Cymon and Iphigenia' ll. 1–41; 'Epilogue to *The Pilgrim*'). D.'s cynical humouring of his audiences' taste was noted by several contemporaries (see, for example, Rochester, *An Allusion to Horace* ll. 1–15, 71–6; Aphra Behn, 'Prologue to *Sir Patient Fancy*' ll. 20–8 (*The Works of Aphra Behn*, edited by Janet Todd, 7 vols (1992–6) vi 7); George Granville, Lord Lansdowne, 'An Essay upon Unnatural Flights in Poetry' (*Poems upon Several Occasions* (1712) 172–8); Charles Gildon, *The Laws of Poetry* (1721) 213, 350; John Oldmixon, *The Arts of Logick and Rhetorick* (1728) 238–40).

Reception. The pindaric form and subject matter of 'To the Memory of Anne Killigrew' are recalled in an elegy on Anne Killigrew by John Chatwin (or Chattins), preserved in BodL MS Rawl. Poet. 94 fols. 149–52 (printed and discussed by Stuart Gillespie in *Restoration* xx (1996) 31–5). D.'s emphasis on the challenge presented to the immorality of the age by Anne Killigrew's piety perhaps inspired another contemporary MS elegy, written *c.* 1689 by Edmund Wodehouse and entitled 'Anagram on Mistress Ann Killigrew who wrote one or more divine Poeme. My rare wit killing sin': 'Rare wit, more rarely us'd, her noble ayme / Was to reforme the Age; from sin reclame; / She slighted those low ends, her own high praise; / Shouts of applause, or wreaths of verdant bays. / She virtue's cause espous'd; bold vice defy'd, / Her life & deathlesse (*or* living) works its pow'r destroy'd' (Leeds UL, Brotherton Collection MS Lt 40, fol. 124ᵛ).

To the Pious Memory of the Accomplished Young Lady Mrs Anne Killigrew, Excellent in the Two Sister-Arts of Poesy and Painting.

An Ode

I

Thou youngest virgin-daughter of the skies,
Made in the last promotion of the blessed;

¶**15.** *Title. Mrs*] A standard seventeenth-century equivalent for the modern 'Miss' (*OED* 2b). *Sister-Arts*] Cp. D.'s Preface to his translation of Du Fresnoy's *De Arte Graphica* (1695): 'a Treatise twice as large as this of Painting cou'd not contain all that might be said on the Parallel of these two Sister Arts'. The translation itself begins: 'Painting and Poesy are two Sisters, which are so like in all things, that they mutually lend to each other both their Name and Office' (*Works* xx 47, 84).
1–22. Tyrell (see headnote) (ll. 1–25) depicts Philips as a saint and himself as a mortal votary offering Pindaric tribute to her 'Virtue' and 'Wit' (Luckett 295).
2. *promotion of the blessed*] exaltation to sainthood. In the Roman Catholic Church, the 'Promotor Fidei' is the member of the Congregation of the Causes

> Whose palms, new plucked from paradise,
> In spreading branches more sublimely rise,
> Rich with immortal green above the rest:
> Whether, adopted to some neighbouring star,
> Thou roll'st above us in thy wandering race,
> Or in procession fixed and regular,
>   Moved with the heavens' majestic pace;

5

---

of Saints appointed to examine the credentials of candidates for beatification or canonization. A beatified person is allowed public veneration after his or her death in a particular church, diocese, country or religious order, and receives the title 'blessed'. A previously beatified person may then be canonized (declared by the Pope to have entered eternal glory and thus to merit the status of 'saint' throughout the church). From the earliest Christian times, sainthood was particularly associated with virginity.

3. palms] In antiquity the palm was a sign of victory or triumph, and hence in the Christian era became associated with sainthood and martyrdom (see Revelation vii 9). The palm was commonly employed in emblem books to signify virtue and the triumph of righteousness and unwavering devotion over hardships. It featured in the frontispiece to Ἐικών Βασιλική (1649), the volume purporting to record the last meditations of Charles I ('King Charles the Martyr'). Cp. 'Heroic Stanzas' l. 57. *paradise*] the heaven of the blessed (as in 2 Corinthians xii 4 and Revelation ii 7), but also associated in the Christian tradition with the 'garden' of Genesis ii and iii. The palm is particularly associated with Eden by Milton in *PL* iv 139, ix 435.

4. sublimely] loftily.

6–13. E. M. W. Tillyard (*Five Poems, 1470–1870* (1948) 60) compares Virgil's speculation about the future habitation of the deified Augustus (*Geo.* i 24–42). *Works* compares Musaeus' description of the ever-changing habitation of the 'happy souls' (*Aen.* vi 669–75). D. was perhaps remembering the general rhetorical shape of ll. 1–22 of William Cartwright's 'To the Memory of a Shipwreckt Virgin', which has repeated speculations on the present whereabouts of the addressee, followed by an offer of tribute (*The Plays and Poems of William Cartwright*, edited by G. Blakemore Evans (1951) 705).

6–9. Ptolemaic astronomy depicted a geocentric universe in which the earth was at rest, and the 'fixed' stars moved round it together as a sphere; this offered a geocentric explanation of the movements of the apparently 'erratic' (wandering or uncertain) stars (the planets) within the larger sphere of 'fixed' stars.

6. adopted] taken up, assumed (*OED* 2). *neighbouring star*] one of the planets, relatively close to earth. The allusion is to the Neoplatonic belief that angels controlled each planetary sphere of the Ptolemaic heavens. Angels and saints were regularly confused or identified one with the other from early Christian times onwards.

7. roll'st] revolve (*OED* 15). *wandering*] with separate, individual motion (*OED* 1d). *race*] movement, orbit (*OED* 5).

9. i.e. carried along with the regular movement of the 'fixed' stars.

10   Or called to more superior bliss,
        Thou tread'st with seraphims the vast abyss.
        Whatever happy region be thy place,
        Cease thy celestial song a little space
        (Thou wilt have time enough for hymns divine,
15   Since heaven's eternal year is thine).
        Hear then a mortal Muse thy praise rehearse,
            In no ignoble verse;
        But such as thy own voice did practise here,
        When thy first fruits of poesy were given
20   To make thyself a welcome inmate there,
            While yet a young probationer,
            And candidate of heaven.

                        II

        If by traduction came thy mind,
        Our wonder is the less to find
25   A soul so charming from a stock so good;
        Thy father was transfused into thy blood:

---

10. more superior] (i) more heavenly, more celestial, closer to God (*OED* superior 1); (ii) outside the sphere of the 'fixed' stars in Ptolemaic astronomy (*OED* superior 9).
11. tread'st] walk in, go about in (*OED* 1), perhaps with the suggestion of stately movement (Johnson 3).   *seraphims*] the highest class of angels, distinguished by the fervour of their love (*OED* 2). Dr Henry Killigrew's epitaph on his daughter (see her *Poems* sig. C1ᵛ) describes her death as a 'blessed and Seraphique End' which 'Angels in Triumph did attend'.   *the vast abyss*] the unfathomable void (*OED* 2) of the heavenly regions. The phrase is used by Milton (*PL* i 21) of the massive gulf which is impregnated by the Holy Spirit at creation, and (vii 211) of the wild region calmed by the Son before his circumscription of the universe (J. R. Mason). In *HP* i 66 D. describes God's throne as 'darkness in th' abyss of light' (*Works*).
12. be] is 1693.
13. space] length of time (*OED* 1).
16. a mortal Muse] i.e. a living poet.   *rehearse*] relate, declare (*OED* 2).
19. first fruits] lit. offering of earliest crops to God (*OED* 1). Killigrew's poems are seen as a sacred tribute. D. refers to Oldham's poems as 'generous fruits' which were 'gathered ere their prime' ('To the Memory of Mr Oldham' ll. 19–21).
21. probationer] candidate, novice.
22. candidate] catechumen (someone preparing for Christian confirmation) (*OED* 2, citing this example). The word derives from the Latin *candidus* ('white', 'pure') and is thus appropriate to Anne Killigrew's virgin state.
23. traduction] transmission or propagation from parent to child (*OED* 3).   *mind*] spiritual part, soul (*OED* 17).
25. charming] (i) pleasing, delightful (*OED* 2); (ii) musical, melodious (*OED* 3).
26. Thy father] Dr Henry Killigrew, himself a poet (see headnote), as well as a staunch royalist.   *transfused*] (i) poured (*OED* 1); (ii) transferred, injected (the modern medical usage (*OED* 3; first example given 1666)).

> So wert thou born into the tuneful strain
> (An early, rich, and inexhausted vein).
>   But if thy pre-existing soul
> 30   Was formed, at first, with myriads more,
>   It did through all the mighty poets roll
>   Who Greek or Latin laurels wore,
>   And was that Sappho last, which once it was before.
>   If so, then cease thy flight, O heaven-born mind!
> 35   Thou hast no dross to purge from thy rich ore,
>   Nor can thy soul a fairer mansion find
>   Than was the beauteous frame she left behind:
> Return, to fill or mend the choir of thy celestial kind.

III

> May we presume to say that at thy birth
> 40   New joy was sprung in heaven, as well as here on earth?

27. *strain*] (i) race, stock (*OED* 6); (ii) melody (*OED* 12).

29. *pre-existing*] An allusion to the Pythagorean doctrine of metempsychosis, or transmigration of souls. In Plato's version of this doctine (*Timaeus* 41e), the number of souls was fixed at creation; birth, therefore, is never the creation of a soul, but the transmigration of an already-existing soul from one body to another. D. was to translate Ovid's account of Pythagoras' teaching in 'Of the Pythagorean Philosophy' in *Fables* (1700). Cp. also 'The Sixth Satire of Persius', D.'s note on ll. 21–6.

33. *Sappho*] The most famous female poet of antiquity (b. *c.* 612 BC). Only two of her complete poems, plus a number of fragments, were known before the nineteenth century. Katherine Philips (see headnote) had been compared to Sappho in the Preface to her *Poems* (1667) and in the two prefatory poems to that edition by Cowley (Cowley, *Poems* 405, 442). Winn (*When Beauty* 93–4) notes that D. is here placing Anne Killigrew in a lineal succession of female poets analogous to the poetical family tree in which he locates himself in the 'Preface to *Fables*' (*Poems* v 49–50). *last*] i.e. in the poems of Anne Killigrew.

35. An allusion to the Platonic doctine (see *Phaedo* 81b–84b) that the immortal soul is contaminated and adulterated by its residence in a mortal body. For Plato, only the philosopher who has striven to free his soul from corporeal taint can hope to dwell permanently in the realm of truth and spirit. The idea was drawn upon by Virgil in *Aen.* vi 724–51 (translated by D. in 'The Sixth Book of the *Aeneis*' ll. 980–1020). D. depicts Anne Killigrew as having attained a similar purity. *dross*] scum or impurities thrown off from metals when melting.

37. *frame*] bodily form (*OED* 9).

38. *mend*] improve (i.e. make even more harmonious) (*OED* 7).   *kind*] kindred (*OED* 12), alluding to the belief that in heaven the saints and angels praise God in perpetual song (cp. Milton, 'At a Solemn Music' ll. 6–16).

For sure the milder planets did combine ⎫
On thy auspicious horoscope to shine, ⎬
And ev'n the most malicious were in trine. ⎭
  Thy brother-angels at thy birth
45   Strung each his lyre, and tuned it high,
   That all the people of the sky
  Might know a poetess was born on earth.
   And then if ever, mortal ears
   Had heard the music of the spheres!
50   And if no clustering swarm of bees
  On thy sweet mouth distilled their golden dew,
   'Twas that such vulgar miracles
   Heaven had not leisure to renew:
  For all the blessed fraternity of love
55 Solemnized there thy birth, and kept thy holiday above.

IV

O gracious God, how far have we
Profaned thy heavenly gift of poesy!

41–3. For D.'s interest in astrology, see W. B. Gardner, *SP* xlvii (1950) 506–21; Simon Bentley and Paul Hammond, *Restoration* ix (1985) 57–60.

42. auspicious] bearing good omen (*OED* 1). *horoscope*] the configuration of the planets (and thus the disposition of the heavens) at one's birth.

43. in trine] at an angle of 120° from one another, and thus, astrologically, in their most benign 'aspect' (or relative position), 'because the rays of the two planets fall obliquely and yield to one another' (Kinsley). Cp. *AM* l. 1165; 'Palamon and Arcite' iii 389 (Noyes); *Britannia Rediviva* l. 327 (Kinsley).

44. brother-angels] Cp. l. 6*n*.

45. tuned it high] played loudly and vigorously (*OED* tune 4; high 10, 13).

48–9. Alluding to the belief that the music produced by the heavenly 'spheres' could not be heard by mortals after the Fall (see Milton, *Prolusion* ii). Some believed, however, that it had been heard again at the birth of Christ (see Milton, 'On the Morning of Christ's Nativity' ll. 125–40) (*Works*).

50–1. In antiquity, tales of infants miraculously fed by bees (a portent of their future eloquence) were told not only of Plato but of various mythological characters, and of the poets Homer, Hesiod, Pindar, Sophocles, Menander, Virgil and Lucan (see Cicero, *De Divinatione*, edited by A. S. Pease (1920) 229). The image had been applied by Sir John Beaumont to James I (Wallerstein 527).

52. vulgar] ordinary, commonplace (*OED* 10). *miracles*] Probably pronounced 'miraclees', to rhyme with 'bees' (cp. *Threnodia Augustalis* ll. 410, 414) (Christie).

55. Solemnized] celebrated, commemorated (*OED* 1; here stressed on the second syllable). *holiday*] consecrated day, festival (*OED* 1; spelt 'Holyday' in both *1686* and *1693*).

56–66. See headnote, and cp. *HP* iii 281–90. Winn 417–19 suggests that D.'s reflections may have been partly prompted by Anne Killigrew's denunciation of 'the Laurel'd Fool . . . that doats on Fame' in 'The Discontent' (*Poems* 54). Thomas Flatman

Made prostitute and profligate the Muse,
Debased to each obscene and impious use,
60   Whose harmony was first ordained above
For tongues of angels, and for hymns of love!
O wretched we, why were we hurried down
      This lubric and adulterate age
(Nay added fat pollutions of our own)
65   T' increase the steaming ordures of the stage?
What can we say t' excuse our second Fall?
Let this thy vestal, heaven, atone for all;
Her Arethusian stream remains unsoiled,
Unmixed with foreign filth, and undefiled;
70   Her wit was more than man, her innocence a child!

---

had contrasted Katherine Philips's pure and virtuous talents with the 'Short-liv'd
Nothings of the Stage' of 'this dull Age' (*The Collected Works of Katherine Philips*,
edited by Patrick Thomas, G. Greer and R. Little, 3 vols (1990–3) iii 213).
58. prostitute and profligate] Winn (*When Beauty* 107, drawing on A. K.
Ramanujan) points out that D.'s vocabulary here suggests a combination of both
male and female sexual excess.
60–1. Cp. 'To Peter Motteux' ll. 3–4. Anne Killigrew (*Poems* 22–3) had described
a fictional poet, Alexis, progressing from pastoral to amatory and then to religious poetry, thus proving 'Love to be, / As the Worlds Soul, the Soul of Poetry'.
Elsewhere she had offered her own passionate vows to the 'Sacred *Muse*' (44).
61. tongues of angels] Perhaps echoing 1 Corinthians xiii 1 (*Works*).
62. hurried down] driven by impetuous passions (*OED* 1b).
63. lubric] lascivious, wanton (*OED* 3). *adulterate*] counterfeit, base, corrupted
(*OED* 2).
64. fat] coarse, gross (Johnson 2, citing this example).
66. second Fall] Cp. ll. 48–9n.
67. vestal] The vestal virgins were the priestesses who tended the sacred fire in
the Roman temple of Vesta, goddess of the hearth, and thus of the ties of family and citizenship. *atone*] As Christ was believed to have atoned for man's sin
from the first Fall.
68. Arethusian] The nymph Arethusa had been transformed by Diana, goddess of
chastity, into a fountain, to rescue her from the amorous advances of the river-
god Alpheus (Ovid, *Met.* v 572–641). The fountain of Arethusa was on the island
of Ortygia, near Syracuse in Sicily; Virgil (*Ecl.* x 1) and Milton (*Arcades* ll. 30–1;
Lycidas l. 85) refer to Arethusa as one of the Sicilian Muses, the inspiring deities
of pastoral poetry (*Works*). Several of Anne Killigrew's poems were in the pastoral genre (see headnote).
69. foreign] alien (i.e. to its own purity) (*OED* 5).
70. Cp. Anne Killigrew, 'To My Lady Berkeley', praising Lady Berkeley's son:
'He then did Things, were Worthy to be writ! / Stayd not for Time, his Courage
that out-ran / In Actions, far before in Years, a Man. / Two *French* Campagnes
he boldly courted Fame, / While his Face more the Maid, than Youth became. /
Adde then to these a Soul so truly Mild, / Though more than Man, Obedient

V

Art she had none, yet wanted none;
For nature did that want supply;
So rich in treasures of her own,
She might our boasted stores defy:
75   Such noble vigour did her verse adorn,
That it seemed borrowed, where 'twas only born.
Her morals too were in her bosom bred, ⎫
    By great examples daily fed, ⎬
What in the best of books, her father's life, she read. ⎭
80   And to be read herself she need not fear;
Each test, and every light, her Muse will bear,
Though Epictetus with his lamp were there.

---

as a Child' (*Poems* 26); and cp. D., 'On the Death of Amyntas' l. 36: 'And more than man was given us in a child' (*Works*). Winn (*When Beauty* 104–6) notes D.'s use of the phrase 'more than man' in *1 The Conquest of Granada* I i 48, III i 268 and *Troilus and Cressida* III ii 421 to express his 'habitual equation between martial prowess and erotic grandeur'. D. used the phrase in *Threnodia Augustalis* l. 449 when comparing James to Hercules.   *wit*] intelligence, perspicacity.

71–6. Cp. D.'s praise of his addressee's 'natural' art in 'Upon the Death of the Lord Hastings' ll. 25–6; 'To Sir Robert Howard' ll. 1–8; and see *MF* l. 166n. Winn (*When Beauty* 89) also compares the lines with D.'s praise of Charles II's magical acquisition of knowledge without study in *Threnodia Augustalis* ll. 337–45. In his biography (419) Winn suggests that Anne Killigrew's disavowal of 'Art' and 'Labour', and her mention of the 'rude', 'unpolisht' and 'rugged' 'Measures' of her verse in 'The Discontent' (*Poems* 51) would have reminded D. of his own praise of Oldham's 'harsh' and 'rugged' qualities in 'To the Memory of Mr Oldham' ll. 15–16. Winn also proposes (*When Beauty* 90) that D.'s somewhat disingenuous disavowal of Anne Killigrew's learning may be designed in part to protect her against the misogynistic tradition of satire on learned women.

71. wanted] lacked.

74. our boasted stores] the resources of art on which poets like D. so pride themselves.

76. borrowed] In 'Upon the saying that my VERSES were made by another' (*Poems* 44–7) Anne Killigrew had responded to the charge that she had not written the poems attributed to her.

80. to be read herself] (i) to have the morality of her own life inspected; (ii) to have her work read (her poems have a consistently high ethical and religious tone).

81. test] The Test Act of 1673 had required potential civil and military officeholders to affirm their membership of the Church of England (*OED* 3). Anne Killigrew's credentials were impeccable, by virtue both of her strictly observed Anglicanism and of her wider moral purity.

82. Epictetus with his lamp] The Stoic philosopher Epictetus (*c.* AD 55–135) was much admired in the Christian era, and his writings were sometimes used as a guide for monastic ascetics. He 'had an iron lamp which was stolen, and thereafter he contented himself with an earthenware lamp. When he died, the lamp

Ev'n love (for love sometimes her Muse expressed)
Was but a lambent flame which played about her breast,
85   Light as the vapours of a morning dream:
So cold herself, whilst she such warmth expressed,
'Twas Cupid bathing in Diana's stream.

VI

Born to the spacious empire of the Nine,
One would have thought she should have been content
90   To manage well that mighty government;
But what can young ambitious souls confine?
  To the next realm she stretched her sway, ⎫
  For painture near-adjoining lay, ⎬
A plenteous province, and alluring prey. ⎭

---

was bought by an antiquarian for three thousand drachmas. [It] . . . had become
a symbol of the wisdom, simplicity of life, and moral integrity of Epictetus' (Hoffman
108). The ultimate source of the story seems to be Lucian's *The Ignorant Book-
Collector* xiii (Derrick).

83. Anne Killigrew had written about love on several occasions (see her *Poems*
11–13, 19–23, 57–75). Her 'Love the Soul of Poetry' depicts the poet Alexis,
moved to 'Enlarg[e] his Fancy, and set free his Muse' by the 'new Flame' of love,
which then leads him on to celebrate 'Acts Divine' (*Poems* 22–3).

84. lambent flame] a flame which plays lightly and brilliantly, without burning (*OED*
1); a positive application of an image used mockingly of Shadwell in *MF* l. 111.
The image had been used by Cowley in 'Destinie' (*Poems* 193) and 'The Exstasie'
(*Poems* 204).

87. Alluding to Anne Killigrew's poem 'On a Picture Painted by her self, representing two Nimphs of *DIANA'S*, one in a posture to Hunt, the other Batheing'
(*Poems* 28–9): 'We Bathe in Springs, to cleanse the Soil, / Contracted by our
eager Toil; / In which we shine like glittering Beams, / Or Christal in the Christal
Streams; / Though *Venus* we transcend in Form, / No wanton Flames our Bosomes
warm!' (*Works*). Luckett 294 also notes that in Nathaniel Lee's *Theodosius* (1680)
the hero reports seeing the maiden Athenais bathing with 'naked glory' like Venus,
but in a manner of which Diana would have approved (I i 168–200). Winn (*When
Beauty* 100) suggests that D. and Anne Killigrew both probably remembered the
performance in 1675 by an all-female cast of John Crowne's *Calisto*, which contains
an account of the purity of Calisto, who 'flies the very Shadow of a Man' (I i).

88–105. D. develops a running analogy between Anne Killigrew's conquest of
the arts of painting and the expanding imperialist ambitions of monarchs, particularly those of Louis XIV. Oldham had drawn analogies between poetic and
imperial conquest in his poems on Homer and Jonson (Oldham 123–4, 194–5).
Anne Killigrew's *Poems* begins with her fragmentary epic on the world conqueror
Alexander the Great (1–5).

88. the Nine] the Muses, patron deities of literature, music, dance, philosophy and
astronomy, but not of painting.

92. next realm] Alluding to Louis XIV's territorial ambitions against surrounding
countries.

93. painture] the art of painting (*OED* 1; a gallicism).

95   A chamber of dependences was framed
                (As conquerors will never want pretence,
                    When armed, to justify th' offence),
            And the whole fief in right of poetry she claimed.
                The country open lay without defence,
100   For poets frequent inroads there had made,
                    And perfectly could represent
                The shape, the face, with every lineament;
            And all the large domains which the dumb sister swayed,
                    All bowed beneath her government,
105   Received in triumph wheresoe'er she went.
                Her pencil drew whate'er her soul designed,
            And oft the happy draught surpassed the image in her mind.
                The sylvan scenes of herds and flocks,
                And fruitful plains and barren rocks;
110   Of shallow brooks that flowed so clear
                The bottom did the top appear;
                Of deeper too, and ampler floods,
                Which as in mirrors showed the woods;
                Of lofty trees with sacred shades,

95. chamber of dependences] An allusion to the *Chambres de Réunion* established by Louis XIV after the Treaty of Nijmegen (1678) to extend French authority over areas of disputed and uncertain territory by legal means.

96. want] lack.   *pretence*] the assertion of a right, claim, or title (*OED* 1).

97. offence] attack, assault (*OED* 3).

98. fief] a feudal estate, held (normally by males only) on condition of service to a superior lord, by whom it is granted, and in whom the ownership remains (*OED* 1, citing this example).   *in right of poetry*] on the grounds that poetry had a legally justified claim upon it (*OED* right 7b).

102. lineament] facial feature (*OED* 3).

103. the dumb sister] Cp. Epistle Dedicatory to *The Vocal and Instrumental Musick of the Prophetess* (*Works* xvii 324): 'Painting is, indeed, another Sister, being like them, an Imitation of Nature: but I may venture to say she is a dumb Lady, whose charmes are onely to the eye: a Mute actour upon the Stage, who can neither be heard there nor read afterwards' (Kinsley).

106. pencil] paintbrush (*OED* 1) (as in 'To Sir Godfrey Kneller' l. 176).   *designed*] conceived in her mind (*OED* 1).

108–18. A description of the characteristic forms, constituent elements and tranquil atmospheric effects of the idealized classical pastoral landscape perfected in the seventeenth century by the French painter Claude Gellée (known in England as Claude Lorrain) (1600–1682). Three of Claude's paintings were in the collection of Sir Peter Lely and would almost certainly have been known to both Anne Killigrew and D. (Michael Liversidge, privately). Winn (*When Beauty* 99–100, drawing on David Vieth, *SP* lxiii (1965) 91–100) notes a specific allusion to Anne Killigrew's poem on two nymphs of Diana (see l. 87*n*).

108. sylvan scenes] Echoing *PL* iv 140 (*Works*).   *sylvan*] wooded.

112. floods] rivers, streams (*OED* 2).

114. sacred shades] Echoing *PL* vii 331 (J. R. Mason).

115   And perspectives of pleasant glades,
             Where nymphs of brightest form appear, ⎫
             And shaggy satyrs standing near,   ⎬
             Which them at once admire and fear. ⎭
             The ruins too of some majestic piece,
120   Boasting the power of ancient Rome or Greece,
             Whose statues, friezes, columns broken lie,
             And though defaced, the wonder of the eye;
             What nature, art, bold fiction e'er durst frame,
             Her forming hand gave shape unto the name:
125   So strange a concourse ne'er was seen before,
             But when the peopled ark the whole creation bore.

                                    VII

             The scene then changed, with bold erected look
             Our martial King the eye with reverence strook:
             For not content t' express his outward part,

115. *perspectives*] views, pictures giving the effect of distance (*OED* 4; the word
is here stressed on the first syllable).
116–18. C. Anderson Silber (*Studies in Eighteenth-Century Culture* xiv (1985) 194)
compares the claim of Diana's nymphs in Anne Killigrew's poem 'On a Picture
Painted by her self' (*Poems* 28–9; cp. l. 87*n* above): 'We *Fawns* and Shaggy *Satyrs*
awe'. Later in the same poem, the nymphs claim to 'shine like glittering Beams,
/ Or Christal in the Christal Streams'. Nymphs and satyrs also feature prominently
in the work of the Dutch Italianate landscape painter Cornelis van Poelenburg
(*c.* 1595–1667). Poelenburg's paintings were popular with English collectors in the
1630s (Michael Liversidge, privately).   *admire*] wonder at, marvel at (*OED* 2).
119–24. An allusion to a particular kind of imaginary composition of picturesque
ruins in an overgrown landscape which became a popular form of 'furniture'
or decorative painting, much employed from the Restoration to the end of the
seventeenth century in the embellishment of panelled interiors, for overmantels,
overdoors and chimney pieces. Among the artists producing such pictures in
England the best known were Adriaen van Diest (1655–1704), Hendrick
Danckerts (*c.* 1625–*c.* 1680) and Jan Griffier senior (*c.* 1645/?1652–1718) (Michael
Liversidge, privately).
119. piece] fortress (*OED* 10b).
123. fiction] feigning, inventing imaginary objects, incidents, etc. (*OED* 3).
124. forming hand] Used of God in *PL* viii 470 (J. R. Mason).   *shape unto*] feature to *1693*.
125–6. Cp. Cowley, 'Ode. Of Wit' (*Poems* 18): 'In a true piece of *Wit* all things
must be, / Yet all things there *agree*. / As in the Ark, joyn'd without force or
strife, / All *Creatures* dwelt; all *Creatures* that had *Life*' (*Works*).   *concourse*] assem-
blage, gathering together (*OED* 4).
127. changed] i.e. from landscape- to portrait-painting.
128. For Anne Killigrew's portrait of James II, see headnote.   *Our martial King*]
D. noted James's soldierly qualities in the Dedication to *The State of Innocence*
(*Works* xii 82) (Kinsley); *Threnodia Augustalis* ll. 429–30, 465–90; *Britannia
Rediviva* l. 333 (*Works*). James had fought with distinction in French and Spanish

130   Her hand called out the image of his heart:
      His warlike mind, his soul devoid of fear,
      His high-designing thoughts, were figured there, ⎫
      As when by magic ghosts are made appear.   ⎬
      Our phoenix Queen was portrayed too so bright,⎭
135   Beauty alone could beauty take so right:
          Her dress, her shape, her matchless grace,
      Were all observed, as well as heavenly face.
      With such a peerless majesty she stands,
      As in that day she took from sacred hands
140   The crown; 'mongst numerous heroines was seen,
      More yet in beauty than in rank the Queen!
      Thus nothing to her genius was denied,
      But like a ball of fire the further thrown,
          Still with a greater blaze she shone,
145   And her bright soul broke out on every side.
      What next she had designed, heaven only knows; ⎫
      To such immoderate growth her conquest rose   ⎬
      That fate alone their progress could oppose. ⎭

---

campaigns of the 1650s, and had shown great ability as a naval commander against
the Dutch in 1665.   *eye*] sight *1693*.
132. figured] (i) brought into determinate shape (*OED* 1); (ii) represented in
pictorial form (*OED* 2).
134. phoenix] of unique excellence and beauty (*OED* 2). The phoenix was a unique
mythical bird with gorgeous plumage. On the origin of the phoenix legend and
the bird's gender, see 'Verses' in Preface to *AM* ll. 52–7*n*. Queen Mary, like Anne
Killigrew, was noted for her beauty as well as her virtue (see Dedication to *The
State of Innocence* (*Works* xii 81); 'Prologue to the Duchess'; *Britannia Rediviva* ll. 304–
15 (Kinsley)). For Anne Killigrew's portrait of Mary, see headnote. Her poem on
Mary is included in *Poems* 6–10.   *portrayed*] Here stressed on the first syllable.
139–40.] As in that Day she took the Crown from Sacred hands: / Before a Train
of Heroins was seen, *1693*. D.'s revisions seem designed to remove the awkward
elisions of the original l. 140.
139. The coronation of James and Mary (by the Archbishop of Canterbury, William
Sancroft) took place on 23 April 1685.
140. numerous heroines] the peeresses, whose gracefulness in procession with the Queen
at the coronation was even noted by the hostile Gilbert Burnet (*History* ii 308).
141. More yet in beauty than] In *Beauty* foremost, as *1693*.
143. a ball of fire] a ball filled with explosives and used as a projectile (*OED* fire-
ball 2).
147. Kinsley and *Works* compare the epigraph from Martial (VI xxix 7) on
the title page of Anne Killigrew's *Poems*: *immodicis brevis est aetas, et rara senectus*
('Short is the life of those who are uncommonly endowed, and they rarely reach
old age'). *Works* notes that the line had also formed the epigraph to Cowley's
'On the Death of Mr. *William Hervey*' (*Poems* 32) and had been translated by D.
in *AA* l. 847.
148. their] its *1693*.

VIII

Now all those charms, that blooming grace,
150   The well-proportioned shape, and beauteous face,
Shall never more be seen by mortal eyes;
In earth the much-lamented virgin lies!
Not wit, nor piety could fate prevent;
Nor was the cruel Destiny content
155   To finish all the murder at a blow,
To sweep at once her life and beauty too;
But like a hardened felon took a pride
   To work more mischievously slow,
   And plundered first, and then destroyed.
160   O double sacrilege on things divine,
To rob the relic, and deface the shrine!
   But thus Orinda died:
Heaven by the same disease did both translate;
As equal were their souls, so equal was their fate.

IX

165   Meantime her warlike brother on the seas ⎫
His waving streamers to the winds displays, ⎬
And vows for his return with vain devotion pays. ⎭
   Ah, generous youth, that wish forbear;

149–50. *Works* notes that in Anne Killigrew's *Poems*, D.'s poem follows soon after the engraving of Anne Killigrew's self-portrait.
149. *blooming*] in the prime of youth, flourishing (*OED* 2).
153. *fate*] death.
154. *the cruel Destiny*] one of the Fates (see l. 181*n*), using smallpox (see head-note) as her instrument.
160–4. For the comparison between Anne Killigrew and Katherine Philips ('the matchless Orinda'), see headnote and ll. 1–22, 33*nn*. Cp. also Cowley, 'On the Death of Mrs Katherine Philips': 'thou, profane Disease, / Didst on this Glorious Temple seize . . . / Wast not enough thus rudely to defile / But thou must quite destroy the goodly Pile? / And thy unbounded Sacriledge commit / On th' inward Holiest Holy of her Wit?' (*Poems* 441) (Kinsley, *Works*).
163. *translate*] transport to heaven (*OED* 1b; used of the souls of the righteous).
164. Perhaps echoing 'To the Memory of Mr Oldham' l. 3 and 'Nisus and Euryalus' ll. 252–4.
165. *her warlike brother*] Anne Killigrew's brother Henry (*d*. 1712), a naval officer (later to become an admiral), was at this time serving in the Mediterranean as commodore of a small squadron which had been sent to suppress piracy.
166. *streamers*] flags, pennons (on the ship's masts).
168. *generous*] gallant, courageous, noble (*OED* 2b). *forbear*] withhold, refrain from uttering or exercising (*OED* 7). The word was sometimes used as a nautical command (*OED* 6b).

The winds too soon will waft thee here!
170   Slack all thy sails, and fear to come;
Alas, thou know'st not thou art wrecked at home!
No more shalt thou behold thy sister's face;
Thou hast already had her last embrace.
But look aloft, and if thou ken'st from far
175   Among the Pleiads a new-kindled star;
If any sparkles than the rest more bright,
'Tis she that shines in that propitious light.

                              X

When in mid air the golden trump shall sound
          To raise the nations under ground;
180   When in the valley of Jehosaphat
The judging God shall close the book of fate,

170–1. D. inverts Anne Killigrew's sentiment in 'On a young Lady Whose *LORD* was Travelling' (*Poems* 78): 'Return young Lord, while thou abroad dost rome / The World to see, thou loosest Heaven at Home' (Winn, *When Beauty* 105).
174. ken'st] see, catch sight of (*OED* ken 6).
175. Pleiads] A group of stars into which the seven daughters of Atlas were said to have been transformed. They rose at the beginning of May, and some accounts derive their name from the Greek πλεῖν ('to sail'), because navigation began at the time of their rising. They also had poetic associations. The seven tragic poets who flourished in the reign of Ptolemy Philadelphus (288–247 BC) were known as the Pleiad, as were three groups of French poets: the Pleiad of Charlemagne, the circle centred on Pierre de Ronsard in the reign of Henri III (1574–89), and a group of neo-Latin poets in the reign of Louis XIII (1610–43).
177. propitious] favourably inclined (*sc.* to mankind) (*OED* 1; used by astrologers of the planets).
178–95. Contemporary readers would have remembered the treatment of the Last Judgment in 1 Corinthians xv 52 (*Works*); cp. *A Song for St Cecilia's Day* ll. 59–63.
178–9. Echoing Wentworth Dillon, Earl of Roscommon, 'On the *Day* of *Judgment*': 'The Last loud Trumpet's wondrous Sound / Shall through the cleaving Graves rebound, / And Wake the Nations under Ground' (first published in *Miscellanea Sacra: or, Poems on Divine and Moral subjects, Vol. 1, Collected by N. Tate* (1696) 138, but presumably shown to D. in MS; Roscommon died in 1685) (Samuel Johnson, *Lives of the Poets*, edited by G. Birkbeck Hill, 3 vols (1905) i 238).
180. Jehosaphat] The valley of Jehosaphat (or Jehoshaphat, meaning 'Jehovah has judged') was the traditional scene of the Last Judgement (see Joel iii 2, 12).
181. the book of fate] D. blends biblical allusions to the Last Trumpet and Last Judgement with a classical image. In Greek mythology, the Moirae (Latin: *Parcae*; English: Fates or Destinies) were the three goddesses who assigned to human beings their fate or lot. Clotho, one of the Fates, was frequently represented in art with

And there the last assizes keep
For those who wake and those who sleep;
When rattling bones together fly
185   From the four corners of the sky;
When sinews o'er the skeletons are spread,
Those clothed with flesh, and life inspires the dead;
The sacred poets first shall hear the sound,
    And foremost from the tomb shall bound
190   (For they are covered with the lightest ground);
And straight, with inborn vigour, on the wing
Like mounting larks to the new morning sing.
There thou, sweet saint, before the choir shalt go
As harbinger of heaven, the way to show;
195   The way which thou so well hast learned below.

a spindle or a roll (the book of fate) on which the goddesses' decrees were inscribed. For English allusions to the book of fate, see *2 Henry IV* III i 45; Beaumont and Fletcher, *A King and No King* V iv 53–8. D. had previously mentioned the book of fate in 'Song I' from *The Indian Emperor* ll. 1–2. In Renaissance mythography the decrees of the Fates were sometimes assimilated to those of the Christian God, e.g. in Alexander Ross, *Mystagogus Poeticus* 355–6.

184–7. Hoffman 127–8 notes the echoes of Ezekiel's prophecy of the resurrection of the Jewish people in the Valley of Dry Bones (Ezekiel xxxvii 7–9): 'As I prophesied, there was a noise, and behold a shaking, and the bones came together, bone to his bone. And when I beheld, lo, the sinews and the flesh came up upon them, and the skin covered them above: but there was no breath in them. Then said he unto me, Prophesy unto the wind, prophesy, son of man, and say to the wind, Thus saith the Lord GOD; Come from the four winds, O breath, and breathe upon these slain, that they may live'.

185. Hoffman 129 suggests an echo of John Donne, *Holy Sonnets* iv ll. 1–2: 'At the round earths imagin'd corners, blow / Your trumpets, Angells'.

187. inspires] breathes life into (*OED* 2b).

190. '*Sit tibi terra levis* ['May the earth lie light upon you'], the familiar classical epitaph [from Martial, *Epigrams* IX xxix], was often cut on English tombstones of the period' (Hoffman 117).

194. harbinger] someone who goes ahead to prepare lodgings for those who follow (*OED* 2).

16 The Hind and the Panther

Date and publication. D. says in the prefatory epistle 'To the Reader' (ll. 74–5) that *HP* 'was written during the last winter and the beginning of this spring', i.e. the winter and spring of 1686–7, and was finished about a fortnight after the publication of James II's *Declaration* on 4 April (for this see below under *Context*). Tonson's staying entry in *SR* on 12 January 1687 ('that noe person enter the poem called the Hinde and ye Panther') suggests that the poem was well advanced by then; it was licensed on 11 April. D.'s epistle 'To the Reader' cites an address published on 2 May (see ll. 43–4*n*), so the epistle must have been written after that date. Scott thought that because the portrait of the Pigeons (the Anglican clergy; iii 946–90) is sharper than that of the Panther (the Church of England in general) it may have been added after the Declaration, once James had abandoned hopes of conciliating the Anglican hierarchy; but Kinsley rightly comments that D. was never greatly impressed by clergy of any persuasion.[1] Noyes thought that the references to the penal laws (ii 268; iii 380–1, 633–4) were unrevised elements predating the Declaration, which suspended those laws; but Kinsley again points out that the moderate Catholic party to which D. belonged regarded the suspension as only a temporary respite from the threat of persecution. Kinsley himself plausibly suggests that iii 811–12, 892–7 and 1233–55 are likely to have been added after the Declaration. Miner in *Works* proposes that the passage on the Buzzard (iii 1120–94) may have been added or modified at a very late stage. Two country houses have traditionally claimed to be the place where D. composed the poem: (i) Ugbrooke, Devon, home of Lord Treasurer Clifford, which had a private chapel where Catholic services were permitted; (ii) Rushton Hall, Northamptonshire, owned by Viscount Cullen; for these see Osborn 219–20. Winn 612 suggests that D. sought the country air for his health (see 'To the Reader' l. 76*n*) in the autumn of 1686.

The Hind and the Panther. A Poem, In Three Parts was published by Jacob Tonson in 1687, probably on 27 May (entered in *SR* on 27 May; Part I was sent on the same day to Etherege (Macdonald p. 46)); siglum: *1687a*; reprinted twice in 1687 in London (*1687b*, *1687c*); also reprinted in Edinburgh 1687, and Dublin 1687. The errata to *1687a* make some obvious corrections, and may also include a revision by D. (see iii 188*n*). Press corrections were made to *1687a* on p. 137, part of the portrait of the Buzzard, probably as a result of late revisions by D. (recorded in the notes to iii 1147–54). The present text follows *1687a*, incorporating corrections from the errata and the press corrections. Some variants introduced in *1687b* may be D.'s further revisions or corrections (see ii 630*n*, iii 482*n*, iii 1045*n*). A MS of *HP* at Traquair House (hereafter 'MS') was transcribed in 1689 from a printed text, though omitting the prefatory epistle, and has many marginal notes which provide evidence as to how the poem was understood by a contemporary reader with Catholic and Jacobite loyalties. It was described and collated by Richard Eversole in *PBSA* lxxv (1981) 179–91. Selections from these annotations are included in the notes below.

Authorship. The poem was published anonymously (cp. 'To the Reader' l. 9), but more as a rhetorical strategy than as a practical attempt at concealment: its authorship seems to have been no secret.

Context. D.'s earlier religious apologia, *RL* (1682), had been a defence of the Church of England against Catholic, Nonconformist, and deist positions. At some point between *RL* and *HP* he had been received into the Church of Rome by the Benedictine monk James Maurus Corker (see T. A. Birrell, *ES* liv (1973) 461–8). The date of D.'s conversion to Catholicism is unknown: Tom Brown assigned it to 1685 (*The Reasons of Mr. Bays Changing his Religion* (1688) 21), while Evelyn recorded in his *Diary* for 19 January 1686 that 'Dryden the famous play-poet & his two sonns, & Mrs. *Nelle* [Gwyn] (Misse to the late . . . [i.e. Charles II]) were said to go to Masse; & such purchases were no great losse to the Church'. Though neither is an unbiased witness, the date of 1685 for the conversion is entirely plausible (see further Edward L. Saslow, *SEL* xx (1980) 373–84). While D.'s enemies characterized his conversion as opportunist, as it appeared to follow the accession of the Catholic King James II in February 1685, there is no reason to accept this slur, and there are good reasons to reject it. In 1680 and 1682 D. had bought at auction a number of books of Catholic theology, liturgy and church history: see T. A. Birrell, *ES* xlii (1961) 193–217. His poems and plays had shown D. to be a thoughtful student of theology and philosophy, at once principled and open-minded. As Winn comments: 'His circle of acquaintances since the Restoration had included prominent Catholics, and works of Catholic controversy had frequently been on his desk during the last several years. The accession of James probably increased his direct contact with apologists for Rome'. Moreover, D.'s wife may have been a Catholic (Winn 414–15). In 1686 D.'s *Defence of the Papers* replied to an attack by Edward Stillingfleet on papers by, or attributed to, Charles II and Anne Hyde, late Duchess of York, defending their conversions to Rome.

HP reflects the changing fortunes of the English Catholics in the first two years of James's reign. As Kinsley notes, they initially hoped for a reconciliation between the Anglican and Roman Churches (see *HP* i 327–30; iii 607–9), and so sought common cause against the Nonconformists, who are satirized sharply in the first part of *HP*. But by the beginning of 1687 James had alienated many Anglicans, particularly by using the royal prerogative to appoint Catholics in the army and universities, and on 4 April 1687 he issued *His Majesty's Gracious Declaration to all his Loving Subjects for Liberty of Conscience*, which applied equally to Catholics and to Protestant dissenters (see 'To the Reader' l. 4*n*). This suspended the penal laws which excluded all but Anglicans from public office and punished non-attendance at Anglican service, and instead permitted freedom of religious assembly. For a summary, see *HP* iii 1228–55*n*, and for the text, *English Historical Documents 1660–1714*, edited by Andrew Browning (1953) 395–7. For some of the poems prompted by the *Declaration* see *POAS* iv 100–8.

The history of the English Catholic community which D. joined at his conversion is described in John Bossy, *The English Catholic Community 1570–1850* (1975). D.'s new spiritual regimen would have been based upon regular attendance at mass, and would have made him familiar with the Roman missal, with its liturgical prayers and readings for the principal days of the Church's year, particularly the feasts of the saints. Both the liturgical year and the cult of the saints feature in *Britannia Rediviva*, while his translation of Bouhours's *Life of St Francis Xavier* was published in 1688. He would have known other devotional material in Latin, including the hymn 'Veni Creator Spiritus', translated in *EP* (1693). The Catholic emphasis on the importance of works of charity is reflected in *Eleonora*. An ignorant caricature of Catholicism haunted English politics throughout the seventeenth century: it was often represented (with some, but far from sufficient, justification) as a threat to the security of the state and the Protestant religion, as evidenced in the Gunpowder Plot of 1605, and the Popish Plot of 1678–9 (for the role of Catholicism in Restoration politics see John Miller, *Popery and Politics in England 1660–1688* (1973), and *AA*, esp. ll. 86, 108, 632–77*nn*). Contemporary Catholic theology is studied in George H. Tavard, *The Seventeenth-Century Tradition: A Study in Recusant Thought* (1978). The theological controversy which raged between Anglican and Catholic writers in the later seventeenth century was fierce and extensive: it was catalogued at the time by William Clagett in *The Present State of the Controversie between the Church of England and the Church of Rome* (1687) and more extensively by William Wake in *A Continuation of the Present State of the Controversy* (1688). Wake arranges the pamphlets thematically, identifying the principal topics of controversy as the Eucharist (especially the real presence and transubstantiation), the marks of the true church (drawing on Bellarmine's *De Notis Ecclesiae*), the authority of the church (especially the authority of the Pope), and the rule of faith (the claims of scripture and tradition to provide a secure guide in matters of faith). All of these topics feature prominently in *HP*. For a more extensive list of the controversial literature see Thomas Jones, *A Catalogue of the Collection of Tracts for and against Popery Published in or about the Reign of James II*, 2 vols, Chetham Society 48 and 64 (1859–65).

Sources. This controversial literature was so extensive that it is rarely possible to identify with certainty those works which D. used: many of the arguments and illustrations became commonplaces; the opposition's arguments were often quoted extensively in the course of attempts to rebut them; and D. would have held theological discussions with other Catholics, and probably had access to works in MS. The quotations from contemporary controversial literature in the following annotations may be sources for D.'s ideas or phrasing, or may simply be analogues; but they do at least illustrate the issues and language which were the common currency of contemporary debate, and show that D. was well versed in the arguments. Scott's edition has substantial extracts from contemporary materials, and shows a deep (if not unbiased) understanding of D.'s religious and political milieu. The most valuable modern attempt to identify D.'s sources is Victor M. Hamm in *PMLA* lxxxiii (1968) 400–15. Phillip Harth's *Contexts of Dryden's Thought* (1968) is also useful, as is Louis I. Bredvold's *The Intellectual Milieu of John Dryden* (1934), though some of his conclusions have been disputed. See also Raymond D. Tumbleson, *JHI* lvii (1996) 131–56. Anne Barbeau Gardiner charts the poem's engagement with both the traditional thinking and the contemporary concerns of the Catholic community in *Ancient Faith and Modern Freedom in John Dryden's 'The Hind and the Panther'* (1998), and suggests that the biblical Song of Solomon (and its traditional allegorical interpretation) was an important source for details of the fable.

For the sources of D.'s allegorical use of beast fable, the principal account is provided by James Kinsley, *RES* iv (1953) 331–6, supplemented by further research by Earl Miner presented in his *Dryden's Poetry* (1967) and in his commentary in *Works*. D. probably found material for his accounts of the characteristics and behaviour of the animals in Edward Topsel's *The History of Four-footed Beasts and Serpents* (1658), John Swan's *Speculum Mundi* (1635), and Wolfgang Franzius' *Historia Animalium* (1612; 1687), the first part of which, dealing with mammals, was translated as *The History of Brutes* (1670); Part II, dealing with birds, was available only in Latin (subsequent references to Franzius are to the English translation unless stated otherwise). Much of this beast lore would also have been proverbial, and whether or not D. knew Sir Thomas Browne's *Pseudodoxia Epidemica* (1646) he would have been familiar with the popular traditions which Browne discusses. William Oldys recorded that D. 'had collected many volumes of old ballads and penny story books' (D. F. McKenzie, privately), and Malone noted that D. read with pleasure 'the History of Reynard the Fox, and the numerous collection of old English ballads possessed by his patron, the Earl of Dorset', an interest for which he was ridiculed by Montague and Prior (Malone I i 512–13). *HP* has its roots partly in this popular material. Aesop's *Fables* contributed some hints for *HP*: these were an elementary school text in English, Latin or Greek, and D. may also have consulted John Ogilby's adaptation *The Fables of Aesop Paraphras'd in Verse* (second edition 1668). Beast fable was a flourishing literary genre in the period, and had become a favoured form for political commentary (see Annabel Patterson, *Fables of Power* (1991), Jayne Elizabeth Lewis, *The English Fable* (1996), and Mark Loveridge, *A History of Augustan Fable* (1998)). Among precedents for *HP* which D. might have known are John Hepwith's *The Calidonian Forrest* (1641), an allegory of the reigns of James I and Charles I in which the lion represents the kings and the hart the Duke of Buckingham; and W. B.'s *Experiences & Tears* (1652), a beast fable on the Civil War in which the lion represents Charles I and the bear Parliament (the bear is a complimentary portrait). In the Restoration the tradition of allegorical beast fable includes James Howell's social satire Θηρολογία: *The Parly of Beasts* (1660); John Cotgrave's beast fable of the Civil War, 'The Lyons Tale', in his *The Muses Mistresse* (1660); Sir Robert Howard's *The Duell of the Stags* (1668), also an allegory of the Civil War; *The Irish Hieroglyphick, or, A Dialogue between a Reverend Rattle-Snake, and a Dublin Swan* (n.d.), in which the snake represents the Church of Rome; and *The Swearers* (1681), which presents Aesop's fable of the dog and the sheep as a comment on Titus Oates and the perjured witnesses of the Popish Plot. One probable source for *HP* is the broadside from the Exclusion Crisis called *The Fanaticks Dream* [1680], in which the sheep (members of the Church of England) are protected by a hart (Charles II) from the attacks of a panther (the Pope). D. seems to have adopted the outlines of this allegory but changed its application (for this and other politicized beast fables see Paul Hammond, *N & Q* ccvii (1982) 55–7). Animals had also been drawn into the controversial literature in other ways: Toussaint Bridoul's *The School of the Eucharist* collected stories of animals venerating the sacrament (including a hind); this was translated into English in 1687 by a Protestant in order to discredit Catholic claims for the miraculous nature of the eucharist, and was the subject of much ridicule from Protestant writers. Margaret Duggan also suggests that various stories in Ovid's *Met.* influenced the presentation of the two principal animals (*Comparative Literature* xxvi (1974) 110–23).

Structure. The structure of *HP* may be summarized thus:

The First Part
This part concentrates upon the characteristics of the various animals in the fable; the need for an infallible guide in matters of faith; and the nature of Protestantism, seen as at best confused, at worst predatory and anarchic.

1–61   The characters of the animals:
      1–34   Hind (Church of Rome)
      35–6   Bear (Independents)
      37–8   Hare (Quakers)
      39–42 Ape (Atheists)
      43–52 Boar (Baptists)
      52–61 Fox (Socinians).

62–149   Excursus prompted by Socinian reliance upon reason: why the Christian should take the Church of Rome as his guide in matters of faith, rather than *[margin annotation]* trust to his own senses and reason:

    62–72   The Church of Rome as unerring guide
    73–8   The Poet's spiritual autobiography
    79–105 Catholic doctrine of the Eucharist
    106–49 Need for man to rely on faith rather than his senses and reason.

150–510   The characters of the animals (resumed):

    150–52   Fox (Socinians) concluded
    153–96   Wolf (Presbyterians); then the wolfish nature of Protestant sects
    197–283 Protestant sects are destroyers of church and state
    284–326 Catholic rulers, by contrast, protect their subjects, and in England the Catholic Church is preserved from her enemies by James II
    327–510 Panther (Church of England); the principal elements in this description are:

        327–46   her mixed nature
        347–91   her origin and history, and the nature of the Reformation
        392–409 her claims to be both reformed and apostolic
        410–29   her muddled Eucharistic doctrine
        430–52   her instability
        453–510 her lack of authority.

510–72   The Hind and the Panther seen among the other animals; their conversation begins.

The Second Part
This part concentrates upon the question of where one finds a reliable guide in matters of faith: Protestants rely upon scripture, Catholics upon tradition as embodied in the church; the Church of England reverences both scripture and tradition, but that position is exposed as untenable. The argument in Part II is dominated by the Hind, with the Panther given relatively brief questions or rejoinders, sometimes almost like those in a catechism which are designed to elicit a pre-arranged exposition (e.g. ll. 213–15). The following summary omits some brief interjections.

1–59   The Hind and the Panther review their experience of the recent past, including the Civil War and Popish Plot.

60–69   The Panther opens the theological debate by asking where infallibility is located.

70–104   Hind: Infallibility is located in pope and councils, and in church tradition.

105–36   Hind: Protestant reliance on scripture interpreted by individuals is precarious, and opens the way to disputes.

137–44   Panther: Scripture alone provides all that is necessary to salvation.

145–67   Hind: This reliance upon scripture permits heresy and promotes disputes; tradition is a safer guide.

168–80   Panther: The Church of England acknowledges the apostolic tradition, but tests tradition by reference to scripture.

a conservative religion

181–212   Hind: It is better to interpret scripture by reference to tradition, because otherwise there is no authority which can settle disputes.

213–15   Panther: How can true and false tradition be distinguished?

216–96   Hind: Only by relying on the church. The Anglican attempt to rely on both scripture and tradition is fatally muddled.

305–88   Hind: The nature of <u>oral tradition,</u> and its capacity to decide on obscurities in scripture.

is the C of E sacred a crime of the Creed who? resisted to be a means of confirming order?

395–473   Hind: The Church of Rome is the guide promised by Christ. No Protestant sect could be worthy of that role. Protestantism is <u>divided</u> in doctrine and organization.

474–525   Hind: The only unerring guide is the Church of Rome.

526–86   Hind: The marks (or 'notes') of the true church (unity, sanctity, catholicity and apostolicity), which the Church of England cannot claim.

587–638   Hind: The Church of Rome rests upon secure foundations, and preserves the pure faith through its unbroken link to the source.

639–48   The Hind offers to accept the return of a penitent Church of England.

654–62   The Hind's words are confirmed by a heavenly light, like that which the poet saw at the time of James II's victory over Monmouth at Sedgemoor.

663–722   The Hind invites the Panther to her cell; celebration of the Hind's <u>poverty</u>.

in England? but in Italy?

The Third Part
This part deals with the conditions which now prevail under James II, as the two protagonists debate their relative political power and material security. The Panther's <u>fable</u> of the Swallows warns Catholics that by taking too triumphalist an attitude, and exploiting their current opportunities too rashly, they may come to grief; the Hind replies with her <u>fable</u> of the Pigeons, warning the Church of England not to be disloyal to James by seeking a champion such as William of Orange.

1–15   The Poet defends his fable.

16–54   The Hind entertains the Panther; they review their common history and the dangers which they have shared.

55–134   The Panther is said to envy the Hind's newly found good fortune under James; the Hind points out that the Church of England still occupies its property, and that her own position is comparatively precarious.

135–250   The Panther maintains her principle of passive obedience to the reigning monarch; but the Hind says that the Panther has many rebellious sons (including Latitudinarians and Presbyterians) and many who seek worldly advancement regardless of principle. By contrast, the Hind's sons gain little material advantage from James.

251–357   Hind: The satirical controversy between champions of the two churches has gone too far; she disciplines her son (implicitly, D. himself) and the Church of England should do likewise.

358–419   The Hind and the Panther debate which of the two is the more dis-
advantaged under James.

419–638   The Panther's fable of the Swallows (for a summary see iii 419–
638*n*).

638–899   The Hind's reaction to the fable; the Church of England should
stop persecuting Catholics, because they pose no danger to the state; the Panther
says that she wishes to maintain the penal laws against Catholics because her conscience requires it. The Panther's equivocal position vis-à-vis James is revealed.

899–1288   The Hind's fable of the Pigeons and the Buzzard, expounding the
dangers of the Church of England opposing the authority of James.

1289–98   Conclusion.

Reception. *HP* soon drew a number of hostile responses, some of which are printed
in *POAS* iv 116–50. By the middle of July 1687 Charles Montague and Matthew
Prior had published *The Hind and the Panther Transvers'd*, with Montagu com-
posing a second attack which remained in MS (printed by Helene Maxwell Hooker,
ELH viii (1941) 51–73). There then followed *The Revolter*, and various pamphlets
which included comments on *HP*: Thomas Heyrick's *The New Atlantis*, Martin
Clifford's *Notes upon Mr. Dryden's Poems*, and Robert Gould's *The Laureat* (all
1687). Also in 1687 the anonymous *The Lay-Mans Answer to the Lay-Mans
Opinion* replied with a different fable about a revengeful Panther (see A. D. Burnett,
N & Q ccxiii (1968) 378–80; Gardiner 178). In 1688 Tom Brown brought out
The Reasons of Mr. Bays Changing his Religion, while anonymous writers produced
A Poem, in Defence of the Church of England (mischievously attributed to D.),
The Hind in the Toil, and J. R.'s *Religio Laici*. There is a single sheet of verses
on *HP* in Nottingham UL, MS PwV 1212, printed in Hammond and Hopkins
380–1; that volume also includes some briefer allusions to *HP*. Thereafter the
Revolution seems to have changed the agenda, though *HP* is mentioned in pass-
ing in many of the subsequent attacks on D. Tom Brown's *The Late Converts
Exposed* (1690) uses a beast fable to attack D. The poem left some traces on
contemporary theological controversy, e.g. in Robert Jenkin's *An Historical
Examination of the Authority of General Councils* (1688) (see John T. Shawcross,
ELN xi (1973–4) 110–12). Wake comments that *HP* shows D.'s equal lack of
talent for argument in verse as in prose (*A Continuation of the Present State of the
Controversy* 28).

The Hind and the Panther
A Poem

In Three Parts

A cross is heading to Rome too

—*Antiquam exquirite matrem.* ⎫
Et vera, incessu, patuit dea.— ⎭ Virg.

To the Reader

preparing for a post 1688 world?

The nation is in too high a ferment for me to expect either
fair war, or even so much as fair quarter, from a reader of
the opposite party. All men are engaged either on this side
or that, and though conscience is the common word which
5 is given by both, yet if a writer fall among enemies, and
cannot give the marks of *their* conscience, he is knocked down
before the reasons of his own are heard. A preface, therefore, which is but a bespeaking of favour, is altogether use-

is it autobiographical to some extent?

less. What I desire the reader should know concerning me,
10 he will find in the body of the poem, if he have but the

¶16. *Title. Hind*] The Church of Rome.   *Panther*] The Church of England. See
further i 1n and i 327n. For the quasi-proverbial linking of the two animals cp.
Titus Andronicus I i 493 ('To hunt the panther and the hart') and Sir Philip Sidney,
The Old Arcadia, ed. Jean Robertson (1973) 256: 'The fearful hind the leopard
did kiss'.
Epigraphs. Antiquam exquirite matrem] 'seek your ancient mother' (Virgil, *Aen.*
iii 96). These words are addressed by the oracle of Apollo to Aeneas, who is
searching for his destined homeland.   *Et vera, incessu, patuit dea*] 'and the true
goddess is revealed by her gait' (Virgil, *Aen.* i 405); this refers to Venus, mother
of Aeneas, who has been talking to her son unrecognized by him; he perceives
her true identity as she turns to leave. For the practice of referring to the Catholic

and associates x protects the believer

Church as 'mother' see *OED* church 8 and mother 2c.
To the Reader.
1. *ferment*] For the contemporary religious and political controversies, see headnote, *Context*.
2. *quarter*] conduct, treatment (*OED* 17).
4. *conscience*] James's *Declaration for Liberty of Conscience* (see headnote, *Context*) had
asserted his belief that 'conscience ought not to be constrained, nor people forced
in matters of mere religion' (*English Historical Documents 1660–1714*, ed. Andrew
Browning (1953) 395–6).   *word*] password.
6. *marks*] distinguishing features.
8. *bespeaking*] requesting.
9. *What I desire the reader should know concerning me*] *HP* was published anonymously, and is generally less of a personal apologia than *RL* had been.

patience to peruse it. Only this advertisement let him take
beforehand, which relates to the merits of the cause. No general characters of parties (call 'em either sects or churches)
can be so fully and exactly drawn as to comprehend all the
15   several members of 'em; at least all such as are received under
that denomination. For example, there are some of the church
by law established who envy not liberty of conscience to
dissenters, as being well satisfied that according to their own
principles they ought not to persecute them. Yet these, by
20   reason of their fewness, I could not distinguish from the
numbers of the rest with whom they are <u>embodied</u> in one
common name. On the other side there are many of our
sects, and more indeed than I could reasonably have hoped,
who have withdrawn themselves from the communion of
25   the Panther, and embraced this gracious indulgence of His
Majesty in point of toleration. But neither to the one nor
the other of these is <u>this satire</u> any way intended; 'tis aimed
only at the refractory and disobedient on either side: for those
who are come over to the royal party are consequently sup-
30   posed to be out of gunshot. Our physicians have observed
that in process of time some diseases have abated of their
virulence, and have in a manner worn out their malignity,
so as to be no longer mortal: and why may not I suppose
the same concerning some of those who have formerly been
35   enemies to kingly government, as well as Catholic religion?
I hope they have now another notion of both, as having
found by comfortable experience, that the doctrine of persecution is far from being an article of our faith.
      'Tis not for any private man to censure the proceedings
40   of a foreign prince, but without suspicion of flattery I may
praise our own, who has taken contrary measures, and those

11. *advertisement*] notification (*OED* 4).
14. *comprehend*] include.
16–17. *the church by law established*] the Church of England.
17. *envy*] begrudge, refuse to give (*OED* 3).
23. *sects*] Many Protestant Nonconformist groups welcomed James's *Declaration* and submitted addresses thanking him; but others, particularly the more moderate groups, were cool, and wary of the King's motives (John Miller, *James II* (1978) 171–2).
37. *comfortable*] encouraging, reassuring (*OED* 1).
39–40. *the proceedings of a foreign prince*] The persecution of the French Protestants (Huguenots) by Louis XIV culminated in October 1685 in the revocation of the Edict of Nantes, which had given them toleration. Many were forcibly converted prior to the revocation (cp. l. 50 below).

more suitable to the spirit of Christianity. Some of the dissenters in their addresses to His Majesty have said that 'he
has restored God to his empire over conscience': I confess

45 I dare not stretch the figure to so great a boldness, but I may
safely say, that conscience is the royalty and prerogative of
every private man. He is absolute in his own breast, and
accountable to no earthly power, for that which passes only
betwixt God and him. Those who are driven into the fold

50 are, generally speaking, rather made hypocrites than converts.
     This indulgence being granted to all the sects, it ought
in reason to be expected that they should both receive it
and receive it thankfully. For at this time of day to refuse
the benefit, and adhere to those whom they have esteemed

55 their persecutors, what is it else, but publicly to own that
they suffered not before for conscience sake, but only out
of pride and obstinacy to separate from a church for those
impositions which they now judge may be lawfully obeyed?
After they have so long contended for their classical ordina-

60 tion (not to speak of rites and ceremonies) will they at
length submit to an episcopal? If they can go so far out of
complaisance to their old enemies, methinks a little reason
should persuade 'em to take another step, and see whither
that would lead 'em.

65   Of the receiving this toleration thankfully, I shall say no
more than that they ought, and I doubt not they will consider from what hands they received it. 'Tis not from a Cyrus,
a heathen prince and a foreigner, but from a Christian king,
their native sovereign; who expects a return *in specie* from

43–4. *'he has restored God to his empire over conscience'*] Quoted from the address
presented by the Presbyterians of London, published in *The London Gazette* 28
April–2 May 1687 (*English Historical Documents* 398).

46. *royalty*] prerogative, right or privilege pertaining to the sovereign (*OED* 5).
prerogative] It was the royal prerogative power to suspend laws that James II used
in issuing his *Declaration of Indulgence*.

55. *their persecutors*] Anglican clergy.

59–60. *classical ordination*] ordination by a meeting ('classis') of Presbyterian elders,
rather than by a bishop, as in the Church of England.

62. *complaisance*] desire to please.

63. *take another step*] i.e. if Nonconformists were to accept Anglican episcopal jurisdiction, it would be a short step from there to accepting Roman Catholicism.

67. *Cyrus*] Cyrus, King of Persia, issued a proclamation encouraging the Israelites
to return to Jerusalem from their captivity in Babylon and rebuild the Temple
(Ezra i 1–4).

69. *in specie*] in a similar fashion (*OED* 4b); i.e. as Christians and Englishmen.

70   them, that the kindness which he has graciously shown them
      may be retaliated on those of his own persuasion.
         As for the poem in general, I will only thus far satisfy the
      reader: that it was neither imposed on me, nor so much as
      the subject given me by any man. It was written during the
75   last winter and the beginning of this spring, though with long
      interruptions of ill health, and other hindrances. About a
      fortnight before I had finished it, *His Majesty's Declaration*
      for Liberty of Conscience came abroad: which, if I had so soon
      expected, I might have spared myself the labour of writ-
80   ing many things which are contained in the third part of it.
      But I was always in some hope that the Church of England
      might have been persuaded to have taken off the penal laws
      and the Test, which was one design of the poem when I
      proposed to myself the writing of it.
85   'Tis evident that some part of it was only occasional, and
      not first intended; I mean that defence of myself to which

71. retaliated] repaid in kind (*OED* 1).

76. ill health] No more is known of D.'s health at this date, but it may have caused
him to leave London for his friends' country estates (see headnote, *Date and*
publication).   *other hindrances*] Various distractions might have hindered progress
on *HP*. In addition to the continuing controversy over *A Defence of the Papers*
(see l. 85*n* below), D. seems to have spent part of 1686 fruitlessly translating the
Histoire des révolutions arrivées dans l' Europe en matière de religion (1686–9) by Antoine
Varillas: a translation by D. was entered in *SR* by Tonson on 29 April 1686, but
publication was abandoned, probably due to Gilbert Burnet's *Reflections on*
Mr Varillas's History, published late in 1686. (For Burnet's possible contribution to
the character of the Buzzard see *HP* iii 1121*n*.) In his subsequent *A Defence of the*
Reflections (August/September 1687) 138, Burnet said that after three months' work
D. had given up the translation because of his criticism of Varillas's credibility.
D.'s translation is now lost. In the early months of 1687 rumours circulated that
D. would be appointed Warden of All Souls College, Oxford, or President of
Magdalen College, Oxford (see Roswell G. Ham, *MLN* xlix (1934) 324–32). As
Winn notes (613), two MS satires on his conversion were also circulating in the
period just before the publication of *HP*: 'To Mr Bays' and 'Heroic Scene' (printed
in *POAS* iv 79–90).

82–3. penal laws and the Test] For laws affecting Roman Catholics see i 5–8*n*,
ii 230*n*, iii 381–2*n*.

85. some part of it was only occasional] In 1686 James II ordered the publication of
Copies of Two Papers Written by the Late King Charles II. Together with a Copy of a
Paper written by the late Duchess of York. The first two papers, certified by James
to be printed from originals in the hand of Charles II, set out arguments against
the Church of England. James had shown these to Pepys, and told him that his
brother had lived and died a Catholic (Evelyn, *Diary*, 2 October 1685). The third
paper, attributed to James's first Duchess, Anne Hyde, and dated 20 August 1670,
sets out the reasons for her conversion to Rome. Edward Stillingfleet, Dean
of St Paul's, wrote *An Answer* to these papers (1686), which drew a rejoinder

every honest man is bound, when he is injuriously attacked
in print: and I refer myself to the judgement of those who
have read the *Answer to the Defence of the Late King's Papers*,

90   and that of the Duchess (in which last I was concerned) how
charitably I have been represented there. I am now informed
both of the author and supervisors of his pamphlet, and will
reply when I think he can affront me: for I am of Socrates'
opinion that all creatures cannot. In the meantime let him

95   consider whether he deserved not a more severe reprehen-
sion than I gave him formerly for using so little respect to
the memory of those whom he pretended to answer: and,
at his leisure look out for some original treatise of humility written by any Protestant in English (I believe I may say

100   in any other tongue); for the magnified piece of Duncomb
on that subject, which either he must mean or none, and
with which another of his fellows has upbraided me, was
translated from the Spanish of Rodriguez, though with the

---

entitled *A Defence of the Papers . . . Against the Answer made to Them*, of which the
third part, concerning the Duchess's apologia, was by D. (For the debate as to
whether D. also wrote, or contributed to, the first two parts, see Winn 612.)
Stillingfleet replied in *A Vindication of the Answer* (imprimatur 10 January 1687),
making the attack on D. to which he refers here. D. returns to this controversy
in the poem itself: see iii 197–217*nn*. For Stillingfleet as a controversialist see Tavard
209–18.

85–6. occasional . . . intended] Cp. ii 339*n*.   *occasional*] arising out of a particular
occasion.

92. supervisors] those who revise and correct a work (*OED* 3, citing this example).

93. affront] insult (*OED* 1); offend one's self-respect (*OED* 2).

93–4. Socrates' opinion] In Plato's *Apology* (30d) Socrates says that the law of God
does not permit a better man to be harmed by a worse.

98–9. treatise of humility] In his *Defence* D. had commented that 'the Spirit
of Meekness and Humble Charity would become our Author [i.e. Stillingfleet]
better than his boasts for this imaginary Victory, or his Reflections upon Gods
Anointed; but it is the less to be admir'd that he is such a Stranger to that Spirit,
because, among all the Volumes of Divinity written by the Protestants, there
is not one Original Treatise, at least, that I have seen, or heard of, which has
handled distinctly and by it self, that Christian Vertue of Humility' (*Works* xvii
323). Stillingfleet replied that this was false, for 'within a few years (besides what
hath been printed formerly) such a Book hath been published in London' (118).
As Earl Miner suggested (*HLQ* xxviii (1964–5) 93–8), Stillingfleet was probably
referring to W[illiam] A[llen]'s *A Practical Discourse of Humility* (1681), whereas D.
in this present passage is thinking of *A Treatise of Humilitie* (1654; reprinted 1673)
'Published by E. D., Parson (sequestered)', which was a translation from *Exercicio
de Perfecion y Virtudes Cristianas* (1609) by the Spanish Jesuit Alphonsus Rodriguez
(1526–1616), omitting the chapters which D. mentions (which were explicitly
Catholic). Miner proposes that 'E.D.' may have been the Laudian clergyman Eleazor
Duncon. D. returns to the subject in the poem itself: see iii 212–17, 328–40.

100. magnified] praised, glorified.

omission of the 17th, the 24th, the 25th, and the last chap-
105 ter, which will be found in comparing of the books.

He would have insinuated to the world that her late
Highness died not a Roman Catholic: he declares himself
to be now satisfied to the contrary; in which he has given
up the cause, for matter of fact was the principal debate
110 betwixt us. In the meantime he would dispute the motives
of her change: how preposterously let all men judge, when
he seemed to deny the subject of the controversy, the
change itself. And because I would not take up this ridiculous challenge, he tells the world I cannot argue: but he
115 may as well infer that a Catholic cannot fast because he will
not take up the cudgels against Mrs James, to confute the
Protestant religion.

I have but one word more to say concerning the poem
as such, and abstracting from the matters either religious
120 or civil which are handled in it. The first part, consisting
most in general characters and narration, I have endeavoured
to raise, and give it the majestic turn of heroic poesy. The
second, being matter of dispute, and chiefly concerning church
authority, I was obliged to make as plain and perspicuous
125 as possibly I could: yet not wholly neglecting the numbers,
though I had not frequent occasions for the magnificence of
verse. The third, which has more of the nature of domestic
conversation, is, or ought to be, more free and familiar than
the two former.

---

109. matter of fact] D. implies that Stillingfleet was primarily disputing the fact of
the Duchess's conversion (about which, as *Works* notes, there had been a controversy in 1669–70).

116. Mrs James] Elinor James, widow of a London printer, and a theological controversialist. In *May it please Your Most Sacred Majesty* [1685] she had asked James
II to oversee a fasting competition between herself and a Roman Catholic representative in order to test the Catholic Church's claim to be the one true church
(facsimile edition in *The Early Modern Englishwoman: series II volume 11: Elinor James*,
edited by Paula McDowell (2005) 23). She said of D.'s reference to her that 'though
some blame him for using my Name, I do not; because he hath used it civilly.
Indeed, I do not know him, nor never read his Book, but I am told that he doth
Abuse the *CHURCH* of *ENGLAND*, for which I blame him: For I count it not
Wisdom for a Wit, to Reflect on that he so lately own'd' (*Mrs James's Vindication
of the Church of England* (1687) sig. A1ᵛ).

119. abstracting from] leaving out of consideration, apart from (*OED* 3b).

124. perspicuous] clear, lucid.

125. Cp. D.'s description of the appropriate style for *RL*, 'Preface' ll. 436–51.
numbers] rhythm and verse-music.

126. magnificence] grand or beautiful appearance (*OED* 5b, citing only D. for the
application of this to language: 'The Third Book of the *Georgics*' ll. 456–7).

130   There are in it two episodes or fables which are inter-
        woven with the main design, so that they are properly parts
        of it, though they are also distinct stories of themselves. In
        both of these I have made use of the commonplaces of satire,
        whether true or false, which are urged by the members of
135   the one church against the other: at which I hope no reader
        of either party will be scandalized, because they are not of
        my invention, but as old, to my knowledge, as the times of
        Boccace and Chaucer on the one side, and as those of the
        Reformation on the other.

[marginal note: Judging too much ironic]

The Hind and the Panther

The First Part

A milk-white Hind, immortal and unchanged,

130. two episodes or fables] The Panther's fable of the Swallows (iii 427–638) and
the Hind's fable of the Pigeons (iii 906–1288).
138. i.e. the anti-clerical, anti-papal commonplaces date back to the days of Giovanni
Boccaccio (1313–75) and Geoffrey Chaucer (c. 1343–1400), while the anti-
Protestant ones are as old as the Reformation (early sixteenth century).

The First Part
i *Title.* The First Part *Ed.; not in 1687.*
i 1. *milk-white Hind*] A hind is a female deer, and here represents the Church of
Rome. The commentaries on the animal in classical and seventeenth-century
beast lore suggest several respects in which the hind is an appropriate figure for
the Catholic Church. The hart (male deer) or roe of the Song of Solomon ii 9
was interpreted as an allegory of the church, though D.'s gendering of the hind
as female allows her more easily to be seen as the bride of Christ, as in the
allegorical interpretations of the Song of Solomon iv (Gardiner 36). The hart is
compared with the soul thirsty for God in Psalm xlii 1. Wolfgang Franzius says
that the hatred of harts for serpents symbolizes the destruction of the devil by
Christ, and develops other emblematic meanings: '1. The *Hart* is meek, and a very
sociable Creature, loving the company of his fellows; thus the Church hath received
from *Christ* the spirit of meekness. 2. As the *Hart*, when surrounded and beset
with the *Hounds*, seeing no way to escape them, he will run to the Huntsman,
rather then be made a prey to the *Hounds*; thus the Church in her greatest
danger runneth for help to God . . . As there is a natural *Antipathy* and enmity
between the *Hart* and the *Serpent*; thus the Church in all Ages hath always had
implacable Enemies, Tyrants, Hereticks, &c.' (*The History of Brutes* (1670) 124–5).
Franzius also adds that the deer is prudent, safe from danger, without gall, and
liable to assault (116–26). Paulus Aringhus discusses the significance of the hart
in early Christian art, noting that it was frequently represented in the catacombs,
especially on lamps, representing Christ, or mutual aid and charity, or the apostles
and fathers of the church because they drink at the fountains (cp. *HP* ii 277n)

Fed on the lawns, and in the forest ranged;
Without unspotted, innocent within,

(Paulus Aringhus, *Roma Subterranea Novissima*, 2 vols (1659) ii 321–4; for the importance of this book see *HP* ii 67*n*). Indeed, the Christian interpretation of the hart
may be traced back to the allegorical bestiary of Physiologus (*c.* 2nd–4th cent.
AD): see the edition of the Latin text by Francis J. Carmody in *University of California
Publications in Classical Philology* xii (1933–44) 95–134. Sanford Budick notes that
a deer features in the legend of St Chad (*Dryden and the Abyss of Light* (1970)).
It was also seen more generally as having spiritual or mystical qualities. In classical mythology it was the emblem or companion of Artemis/Diana, goddess of
chastity. Plutarch records that Quintus Sertorius had a white hind which he said
had supernatural power to reveal the future (Plutarch, *Sertorius* 11; Kinsley). In
the alchemical tradition (and thence in emblem books) the deer was a symbol of
the soul, intermediate between earth and heaven, and it was said that the deer
and the unicorn inhabited the wood as the soul and spirit inhabit in the body
(Gareth Roberts, *The Mirror of Alchemy* (1994) 52–3; Lyndy Abraham, *Marvell and
Alchemy* (1990) 248–50). Petrarch used the white hind as an image of his beloved
(*Rime Sparse* 190). Sir John Denham's *Cooper's Hill* (1642) had developed a parallel between a hunted stag and a fallen statesman chased out of the land where
he used to rule, and hunted down by his opponents. Edward Topsel provided
another political dimension to the significance of the hind when he reported that
there are fewer deer in Switzerland than there used to be, 'because *Democraties*
do not nourish game and pleasures like unto Monarchies, and therefore they are
daily killed by the vulgar sort, there being no law against it' (*The History of Four-
footed Beasts and Serpents* (1658) 97). Topsel also notes that 'it is the property of
all Harts to love their native soils above all other places' (97). Milton described
the hind as 'Goodliest of all the forest' (*PL* xi 189). *milk-white*] pure white. Topsel
says that deer are mostly sand-coloured, but sometimes 'intermingled with some
white spots, especially the Hindes and their Calves, and sometimes milk-white'
(97). *milk*] appropriate for the church as mother; also contrasting with the Protestant
emphasis on 'the milk of the word', i.e. scripture (1 Peter ii 2). *white*] morally
and spiritually pure and innocent (*OED* 7); free from evil intentions, harmless
(*OED* 7a); happy, fortunate, well-omened (*OED* 8; cp. *Astraea Redux* l. 292);
dear, precious (*OED* 9). *immortal*] The deer was thought to be extremely long-
lived: Pliny said that deer have a long life, recording that some had been caught
100 years later wearing the gold collars which Alexander the Great had put round
their necks (*Naturalis Historia* viii 50; Topsel 102 reports other stories of longevity
taking the lifespan over 2000 years; see also Sir Thomas Browne, *Pseudodoxia
Epidemica*, edited by Robin Robbins, 2 vols (1985) i 189–95). *immortal and
unchanged*] The Church of Rome, which D. would have seen as the immortal
church established by Christ and essentially unchanging in its teachings, is implicitly contrasted with the Church of England, a mortal creation dating from
the sixteenth century, and an institution which had changed its doctrines and
practices: cp. iii 150–1.
i 2. lawns] glades, open spaces between woods (*OED* 1).
i 3. Without] on the outside.   *unspotted*] By contrast with the Panther (cp. i 328).
The church is described as 'not having spot' [i.e. spot of sin] in Ephesians v 27.
innocent] sinless, holy (*OED* 1); guileless, devoid of cunning (*OED* 3); doing no
harm (*OED* 5). Various popes took the name 'Innocent', including the current
pope, Innocent XI, for whom see i 288*n*.

> She feared no danger, for she knew no sin.
> 5   Yet had she oft been chased with horns and hounds,
>   And Scythian shafts, and many wingèd wounds
>   Aimed at her heart; was often forced to fly,
>   And doomed to death, though fated not to die.
>   Not so her young, for their unequal line

i 4–8. The hind was said to be able to cure injuries which it sustained: 'These creatures are said to be their own Physicians, and (as it were) not needing the help of man, can cure themselves through a secret instinct of nature, and the providence of God their maker: for by feeding on that precious herb *Dictamnum*, or *Dittanie . . .* they cure themselves of their cruell wounds, and so become whole again' (John Swan, *Speculum Mundi* (1635) 479).

i 4. Cp. 'To the Reader' ll. 93–4*n*. *Works* compares *Aureng-Zebe* (1676): 'With all th' assurance Innocence can bring, / Fearless without, because secure within' (III i 202–3). *she knew no sin*] she was without sin (*OED* know 5c). 'She taught no error in faith or Morality' *MS*.

i 5–8. The church had been persecuted in the early Roman Empire, and Catholics suffered discrimination and harassment in seventeenth-century England, where priests had been outlawed and sometimes executed, and the laity had been subjected to double taxation and exclusion from public office: see further iii 381–2*n*.

i 6. Scythian shafts] The Scythians were nomadic tribes of north Europe and Asia beyond the Black Sea, with a cruel and barbarous reputation (see *King Lear* I i 115). Their arrows were proverbially swift (Ovid, *Met.* x 588) and dipped in poison to make their wounds fatal (Pliny, *Naturalis Historia* xi 115). *wounds*] By metonymy for 'arrows' or 'spears'; Virgil similarly employs *vulnere* ('wound') for 'weapon' in *Aen.* ii 529 (Williams).

i 8. This line was ridiculed by Montague and Prior in *The Hind and the Panther Transvers'd* (Matthew Prior, *Works*, edited by H. Bunker Wright and Monroe K. Spears, 2 vols (1971) i 40): 'are not *doom* and *fate*, much the same thing?' But as Scott noted, *doomed* means 'sentenced' (*OED* 1), while *fated* means 'predestined': D. is contrasting human pronouncements against the church with the decrees of divine providence which protect her. Similarly *MS* glosses *doomed to death* 'by Infidels' and *fated not to die* 'never to fail'. Topsel said: 'The whole nature and disposition of every part of this beast is against poison and venemous things' (103).

i 9–16. 'I easily perceive, You, and the greatest part of Honest *Thinking Protestants* . . . begin . . . to suspect, That *Catholicks* have *Wrongfully Suffered* the loss of their *Fame*, their *Goods*, their *Fortunes*, and many their *Lives*. Nor do I wonder to see you touch'd with some Concern at our *Miseries*; For besides the sad Spectacles of *Bloodshed* . . . the *Prisons* have been filled with Us, whole *Families* Ruined and Exiled; poor *Widows* and Innocent *Orphans* have *Perished* through *Distress*, the very *Woods* and *Desarts* have not wanted *Men* Dying with *Cold* and *Hunger*' (James Maurus Corker, *Roman-Catholick Principles* (1680) 1).

i 9. her young] Individual Catholics, as distinct from the church herself. Franzius says that the hind 'hath a very tender care of her young ones, teaching them to avoyd the snares of the Huntsman, & inureth them to running while young' (117), and Swan regards deer as 'a fit embleme of carefull parents, who teach their children whilest their yeares be green, the right way wherein they ought to walk' (480). *unequal line*] mixed genealogical descent.

10   Was hero's make, half human, half divine.
      Their earthly mould obnoxious was to fate,
      Th' immortal part assumed immortal state.
      Of these a slaughtered army lay in blood
      Extended o'er the Caledonian wood,
15   Their native walk; whose vocal blood arose
      And cried for pardon on their perjured foes.
      Their fate was fruitful, and the sanguine seed
      Endued with souls increased the sacred breed.
      So captive Israel multiplied in chains,
20   A numerous exile, and enjoyed her pains.

i 10. hero] In classical mythology, one regarded as intermediate between the gods and
humans, or the offspring of a god and a mortal.   make] constitution (OED 2b).
i 11. earthly mould] earth regarded as the material of the human body (OED mould¹
4); body, bodily form (OED mould³ 10).   obnoxious] liable, vulnerable (OED 1).
fate] death.
i 12. assumed] took on (OED 4; cp. Milton, PL iii 318–19).
i 13. slaughtered army] The Catholic priests and laity executed for their faith (or for
alleged treason), esp. at the Reformation, after the Gunpowder Plot, and during
the Popish Plot (see i 563n).
i 14. Caledonian] Normally means 'Scottish', but D. is using it more generally to
mean 'ancient British', and creating a symbolic geography and history. He is aided
in this by echoes of 'Calydonian', referring to Calydon in ancient Greece, which
was ravaged by a monstrous boar (Ovid, Met. viii 270–424). See also Topsel quoted
in i 35n and i 43n below. D. may have been influenced here by John Hepwith's
The Calidonian Forrest (see headnote, Sources). For an application of the image to
recent political history cp. Carew Reynell: 'How tranquill are we grown, who
heretofore / Were haras'd by the ⁽ᵃ⁾ Caledonian Boar! [marginal note: ⁽ᵃ⁾ The Covenant,
which was the cause of our distempers, had its Origine from Scotland]' (The Fortunate Change: Being a Panegyrick to his Sacred Majesty . . . on his Coronation (1661)
1).   wood] Pliny refers to the Caledonian wood (silvae Caledoniae (Naturalis
Historia iv 16)), as does Lucius Florus, for whom it is proverbially pathless (i 12).
i 15. Their native walk] D. is claiming that the Catholics have a native right to
Britain (as in AA l. 87) as the original inhabitants (cp. l. 26).   walk] usual haunt
(OED 8).   vocal blood] Cp. God's words to Cain after he had murdered Abel: 'the
voice of thy brother's blood crieth unto me from the ground' (Genesis iv 10).
i 16. pardon] Rather than vengeance, so demonstrating forgiveness.   their perjured
foes] 'Oats, Bedlow &c' MS. Titus Oates and William Bedloe were instigators of
the Popish Plot in 1678–9, and their lies led to the deaths of many Catholic priests
and laymen (see i 563n). D. probably intends a wider reference to persecution,
including the Elizabethan period.
i 17–20. Referring to the exile of the Israelites in Egypt: 'And the children
of Israel were fruitful, and increased abundantly' (Exodus i 7).   fate] death.
sanguine seed] Echoing the proverbial idea that the blood of the martyrs is the
seed of the church (Tilley B 457): cp. Britannia Rediviva ll. 159–62.   exile] Since
Israel is a collective noun for the Israelites, exile here probably means 'exiled
person or group' rather than 'condition of exile'.

With grief and gladness mixed, their mother viewed
Her martyred offspring, and their race renewed;
Their corpse to perish, but their kind to last,
So much the deathless plant the dying fruit surpassed.
25   Panting and pensive now she ranged alone,
And wandered in the kingdoms once her own.
The common hunt, though from their rage restrained
By sovereign power, her company disdained,
Grinned as they passed, and with a glaring eye
30   Gave gloomy signs of secret enmity.
'Tis true, she bounded by, and tripped so light
They had not time to take a steady sight:
For truth has such a face and such a mien
As to be loved needs only to be seen.
35   The bloody Bear, an Independent beast,

---

i 23. corpse] bodies (probably 'living bodies' (*OED* 1) rather than 'dead bodies'
(*OED* 2). *1687* has *Corps*, which could be singular but is probably plural here (see
OED 2c). *kind*] race (*OED* 10).
i 24. deathless plant] 'Catho: Religion' MS. *the dying fruit*] 'professors of it' MS.
i 25. pensive] anxious, apprehensive (*OED* 2).
i 27. common hunt] 'all yᵉ Sects' MS. *common*] Perhaps by contrast with the deer,
a royal beast (*Works*). *hunt*] body of people, horses and dogs engaged in hunting
(*OED* 2, citing this example).
i 29. Grinned] bared their teeth. *glaring*] staring fiercely or wildly (*OED* 1).
i 33–4. Contrast iii 1040–1. *mien*] appearance.
i 35. Bear] The Independents, who had emerged during the 1640s, and had been
influential in Parliament and the army, worshipped in individual congregations
without a set form of service or a national organization (hence *Unlicked to form*).
Their most famous preacher was Bunyan. According to Pliny the bear's breath
is pestilent, and no creature can survive contact with it (*Naturalis Historia* xi 115;
Kinsley). In the Bible the Antichrist in Revelation xiii has bear's feet, and a bear
is one of the devouring beasts seen in a vision in Daniel vii 5. As Kinsley notes,
Butler had this vision in mind when calling Puritan synods 'mystical *Bear-gardens*
/ . . . This to the *Prophet* did appear, / Who in a Vision saw a *Bear*, / Prefigur-
ing the beastly rage / Of *Church-rule* in this later Age: / . . . *Bears* naturally are
beasts of Prey, / That live by rapine, so do they' (*Hudibras* I iii 1095, 1117–24).
Topsel's epithets for the bear include '*Calydonian* . . . bloudy' (28), and he
observes that 'they are very hardly tamed, and not to be trusted though they
seem never so tame' (32). Franzius says that bears 'love to be in Caves and secret
places' (56; *Works*), so this is an apt emblem of the Independents who met
in semi-secret conventicles. For W. B.'s use of the Bear as an image for Parliament see headnote, *Sources*. *bloody*] The Independents had been active
in the Parliamentarian army, and some Independent ministers had supported
the execution of Charles I. Butler wrote that the Independents were 'Free of
ev'ry Spiritual Order, / To *Preach*, and *Fight*, and *Pray*, and *Murther*' (*Hudibras* III
ii 117–18).

Unlicked to form, in groans her hate expressed.
Among the timorous kind the Quaking Hare
Professed neutrality, but would not swear.
Next her the buffoon Ape, as atheists use,
40   Mimicked all sects, and had his own to choose:

i 36. Unlicked to form] Pliny reported that bear cubs were born shapeless, and were licked into form by their parents (*Naturalis Historia* viii 54). Though known in the seventeenth century to be false (it is recorded but contradicted by Topsel, by Franzius 55, and by Browne i 178–80), the idea retained a proverbial force. *groans*] Parodying the groans in which extreme Protestants expressed their sense of their sinfulness.

i 37. Quaking Hare] The hare was proverbially timorous, and so provides a suitable symbol for the Quakers, or Society of Friends, which developed as a movement in the early 1650s. Their nickname alludes to their supposed habit of trembling when inspired by the Holy Spirit. Topsel says that there can be no peace between the hare and her enemies, 'but she rather trusteth the scratching brambles, the solitary woods, the ditches and corners of rocks or hedges, the bodies of hollow trees, and such like places, then a dissembling peace with her adversaries' (210): this provides an apt description of the Quakers' refusal to dissemble or compromise, and their practice of meeting for worship in secret or remote places. Kinsley notes that the hare was reputed to be melancholy (Tilley H 151), and to dislike music and merriment. George Fox, the leader of the Quakers, recorded that he 'was moved . . . to cry against all sorts of music' (*Journal*, edited by John L. Nickalls (1952) 38).

i 38. would not swear] The Friends refused to swear oaths, following Matthew v 34–7.

i 39. Ape] The cunning time-server who mimics religious devotion from motives of political expediency. Topsel says that the ape is 'a subtill, ironicall, ridiculous and unprofitable Beast . . . made for laughter' and given to 'wicked wasts, deceits, impostures and flatteries' (2). Franzius says that the ape may stand for 'all Flatterers and Dissemblers, and even the Devil himself, who may not unfitly be called God's *Ape* . . . most of them are to be found in great mens houses, and Princes Courts . . . *Apes* are so impudent, that they will not fear to disturb a *Lion*' (209–10). *Works* suggests that D. may have been influenced here by Spenser's story of the Ape at the court of the Lion in *Mother Hubberds Tale*. Scott saw a possible allusion to the Earl of Sunderland, of whose conversion to Catholicism Burnet wrote: 'the change he made looked too like a man who, having no religion, took up one, rather to serve a turn, than that he was truly changed' (Burnet ii 483). But if any one courtier was in D.'s mind here, it was more probably John Wilmot, Earl of Rochester, who was pictured in a portrait by Huysmans in the company of a monkey, over whose head he is holding a laurel wreath, a satirical allusion to D. as Poet Laureate. Rochester was noted for his mimicry, his professions of atheism, and his deathbed conversion in 1680. Even so, the reference is primarily to a type rather than an individual. *MS* has 'Latitudinarians' (for these see *HP* iii 160*n*). *buffoon*] comic actor, clown, mimic (*OED* 2); accented on the first syllable in the seventeenth century. *use*] are accustomed to do.

i 40. to choose] by preference (*OED* 12).

Still when the Lion looked, his knees he bent,
And paid at church a courtier's compliment.
  The bristled Baptist Boar, impure as he
  (But whitened with the foam of sanctity)
45 With fat pollutions filled the sacred place, ⎫
  And mountains levelled in his furious race: ⎬
  So first rebellion founded was in grace. ⎭

i 41. Still] always, constantly.   *Lion*] The king of beasts, so here James II. For earlier, hostile, representations of James as a lion which threatened English liberties, see *AA* l. 447*n*.

i 43. Baptist Boar] The Baptist movement within English Protestantism is generally traced back to John Smyth, who when exiled in Amsterdam in 1609 instituted the custom of baptizing conscious believers (rather than infants) as the basis of a gathered church. When the Baptists became prominent in England in the 1640s, their opponents associated them (as D. does here) with the German Anabaptists (see *Radical Religion in the English Revolution*, edited by J. F. McGregor and B. Reay (1984) 25–6). The most famous Anabaptist group was the one which attempted to establish a Kingdom of the Saints in Münster in 1533–5 led by Jan Matthys and Jan Bockelson, whose reign of terror became notorious. D. had already given his view of the German Anabaptists in the Postscript to his translation of *The History of the League* (1684) (*Works* xviii 396–9). The violence and indiscipline of the Anabaptists, though not the lives of English Baptists, are appropriately figured by the boar, which Topsel says is 'not capable of any discipline or instruction' (540). Topsel's epithets for it include 'woodwanderer . . . bristle-bearer, foaming . . . mountain-liver . . . *Calydonian*' (538). Franzius compares the enemies of the church to wild boars destroying the vineyard (135; alluding to Psalm lxxx 8–13; *Works*). See also Reynell, quoted in i 14*n*.   *impure*] Rejecting the claim of the Baptists (and other sectaries) to possess a special spiritual purity as a result of their divine election and their separation from established churches. Topsel calls the boar 'filthy' (538).

i 44. foam] Suggesting that the Baptists rage with madness rather than with divine inspiration. Topsel says that when the boar rages 'at his foaming white mouth, he desireth nothing but copulation' (540; *Works*); this suggests a parallel with the notorious sexual licence of the Anabaptists in Münster.   *sanctity*] Because the Anabaptists held that every true believer attains perfect freedom from sin while still on earth (Williams).

i 45. The Anabaptists soiled their supposedly pure and sacred city of Münster with murder and sexual licence; obscene parodies of the mass were staged in the cathedral. *fat pollutions*] The phrase is used by D. to refer to Restoration plays (including his own) in 'To the Memory of Anne Killigrew' l. 64.   *fat*] gross (a sense not given by the *OED*, but cp. *OED* 4c 'indecent', 7c 'dense').

i 46. mountains levelled] This ironically echoes John the Baptist's prophecy that 'every mountain and hill shall be brought low' (Luke iii 5; Gardiner).   *levelled*] The private ownership of money was abolished in Münster, and steps were taken towards common ownership of commodities and the abolition of private property. The word also recalls the English Levellers of the 1650s.   *race*] onset, charge (*OED* 2).

i 47. grace] In Christian teaching, the supernatural assistance of God bestowed on man not because of his desert but because of his need. Augustine (AD 354–430)

But since the mighty ravage which he made
In German forests had his guilt betrayed,
50   With broken tusks, and with a borrowed name,
He shunned the vengeance, and concealed the shame;
So lurked in sects unseen. With greater guile
False Reynard fed on consecrated spoil:

---

taught that since man is utterly corrupt he can produce nothing but sinful acts,
so grace is essential for the performance of good works; however, the British
theologian Pelagius (late 4th–early 5th cent. AD) argued that man could take
steps towards salvation by his own efforts, and that grace was not essential for the
performance of good works; rather, grace made the commands of God easier to
fulfil. Subsequent church teaching steered between these positions, but Reformation leaders such as Luther and Calvin emphasized the Augustinian view, and
Protestant belief, particularly among the more extreme sects, stressed the importance of grace, which they often imagined to favour them particularly.

i 50. broken tusks] The siege of Münster ended with the massacre of almost all
the Anabaptists. Bockelson was led by his captors on a chain, like a performing
bear, and after his execution his body was exhibited in a cage.   *borrowed name*]
Radical sects often varied their nomenclature: the Diggers were also called
'True Levellers', while 'Quakers' and 'Ranters' were pejorative terms used by
their opponents: they called themselves 'Friends' and 'My one flesh' respectively.
Individuals often moved from one sect to another, sometimes changing their
own names: the Ranter Abiezer Coppe became Higham (= 'I am').

i 52. Anabaptist ideas, especially the principle of adult baptism, passed into various English sects. The doctrine of the inner light, developed by the Anabaptist
Thomas Münzer, reappeared in Quaker thought.

i 53. Reynard] The Socinians. Unitarian (or Socinian) belief, which dates from
the Reformation, rejects the doctrines of the Trinity and the divinity of Christ;
it became particularly associated with the names of Lelio Sozini (1525–1562) and
his nephew Fausto Sozzini (1539–1604). See H. J. McLachlan, *Socinianism in
Seventeenth-Century England* (1951). D. says in *RL*, Preface ll. 160–4, that Socinianism is a development of Arianism. This school of thought (deriving from
Arius (*c.* AD 250–*c.* 336)) denied the divinity of Christ, and taught that the Son
of God was not eternal but created by the Father. Its leading opponent was St
Athanasius (*c.* AD 296–373), Bishop of Alexandria. In AD 325 at the Council of
Nicaea (Anglicized as *Nice* in l. 55) the Nicene Creed was adopted, which defended
the orthodox faith against Arianism. For D.'s earlier discussion of these issues
see *RL*, Preface ll. 130–75 and poem ll. 312–13; the subject is resumed in *HP*
ii 150–67. In *The Protestants Plea for a Socinian* (1686) the Catholic writer Abraham
Woodhead argued that the Socinians based their beliefs on the same attitudes
to scripture and church authority as the Protestants (cp. *HP* ii 150–5, 280*n*). Similarly
Hugh Serenus Cressy argued that 'upon Protestants groundes it is impossible
they should rationally call *any doctrine Haeresy*, or *any separation Schisme*, without
condemning themselves' (*Exomologesis* (1647) 481; Hamm). Kinsley observes that
the fox's cunning is a commonplace, and so he aptly typifies a heresy which had
its roots in an ancient intellectual controversy and influenced some distinguished
Restoration intellectuals, including Locke and Newton. According to Franzius, the
fox typifies craft, subtlety, hypocrisy and heresy, and Arius is for him an eminent

The graceless beast by Athanasius first
55   Was chased from Nice; then by Socinus nursed
His impious race their blasphemy renewed,
And nature's King through nature's optics viewed.
Reversed they viewed him lessened to their eye,
Nor in an infant could a God descry:
60   New swarming sects to this obliquely tend,
Hence they began, and here they all will end.
      What weight of ancient witness can prevail
If private reason hold the public scale?
But, gracious God, how well dost thou provide
65   For erring judgements an unerring guide!

---

example of the truth that 'as those little *Foxes* which lye hid under ground do most mischief to the Vines, thus the greatest Enemies of the Church lye in her very bosome' (137–40, 147; *Works*).   *False Reynard*] Spenser uses this phrase in *Mother Hubberds Tale* l. 883 (Williams).

i 57–8. D. says that the Socinians use man's natural faculties (i.e. reason) to attempt to comprehend God, who is the creator of nature; implicitly, reason should instead give way to divine revelation and grace (cp. *graceless*, l. 54). Like looking through the wrong end of a telescope, this reliance upon reason reduces God by confining him within the narrow limits of human understanding. The ultimate result of this is 'natural religion', which rejects any supernatural revelation, and relies entirely upon innate human reason to discover the principles of religious duty and observance: cp. D.'s account of deism in *RL* ll. 42–61. *MS* comments: 'God made man with natural reason, but not Sufficient without faith'.   *optics*] telescope (*OED* 2).

i 59. an infant] the infant Christ, regarded as God incarnate in orthodox Christianity.   *descry*] discern.

i 60. swarming] Cp. *RL* l. 419, where sectarian interpreters of scripture 'About the sacred viands buzz and swarm'.   *obliquely*] indirectly, by implication; not straightforwardly, dishonestly (*OED* 2).

i 61. i.e. new heresy and schism begin by denying the incarnation, and end by being merely forms of natural religion.

i 62–5. D. returns here to issues discussed from a different standpoint in *RL*: the danger of relying upon private reason to determine matters of faith, and the need for an unerring guide to decide such matters. Contrast *RL* ll. 276–89.   *ancient witness*] Roman Catholic doctrine held that matters of belief should be determined by reference to church tradition going back to the early Christian fathers; cp. *RL* ll. 282–9n.

i 64–5. MS comments: 'Christ and the H: Ghost, the Spirit of truth is alwise with The Cath: Church' and cites Matthew xxviii [20] and John xiv [13–21, 26].   *guide*] As Hamm notes (410), this is an important word in *HP* (cp. i 88, 365; ii 347 etc.), and the question of whether there was an infallible guide in matters of faith featured prominently in contemporary controversy, especially in the books by Abraham Woodhead, including *The Guide in Controversies* (1667), *A Rational Account of the Doctrine of Roman-Catholicks concerning the Ecclesiastical Guide in Controversies of Religion* (1673) and *A Discourse of the Necessity of Church-Guides* (1675).

Thy throne is darkness in th' abyss of light,
A blaze of glory that forbids the sight;
O teach me to believe thee thus concealed,
And search no farther than thyself revealed;
70 But her alone for my director take
Whom thou hast promised never to forsake!
My thoughtless youth was winged with vain desires,

i 66. This line boldly fuses several traditional ideas into a startling paradox. The idea that God is surrounded by darkness is biblical, e.g. in Psalm xviii 11–12: 'He made darkness his secret place; his pavilion round about him were dark waters and thick clouds of the skies. At the brightness that was before him his thick clouds passed, hail stones and coals of fire'. See also Exodus xx 21, where 'Moses drew near unto the thick darkness where God was'. God is also said to dwell 'in the light which no man can approach unto' (1 Timothy vi 16). Light and dark are combined in Exodus xxiv 16–17, where God 'called unto Moses out of the midst of the cloud. And the sight of the glory of the Lord was like devouring fire'. Pseudo-Dionysius (*c.* AD 500) writes that 'The divine darkness is unapproachable light, in which God is said to dwell' (*Patrologia Graeca* iii 1073–4). Milton writes (in a passage which may have supplied some of D.'s vocabulary): 'Fountain of light, thy self invisible / Amidst the glorious brightness where thou sit'st / Throned inaccessible, but when thou shadest / The full blaze of thy beams . . . / Dark with excessive bright thy skirts appear' (*PL* iii 375–80; cp. *PL* ii 264–7).   *abyss of light*] A possible precedent is 'abyss of brightness' in John Collop's 'On servile Will' (*Poems*, edited by Conrad Hilberry (1962) 52). D. had already used the phrase in 'Thou tread'st th' Abyss of light!' (*Tyrannic Love* (1670) IV i 175), which was ridiculed in *The Censure of the Rota* (1673) 15.
i 67. In Exodus xxxiii 20 God says to Moses: 'Thou canst not see my face: for there shall no man see me, and live'.   *forbids*] prohibits (*OED* 1); renders impossible (*OED* 2a).   *the sight*] MS interprets this specifically as 'Natural Reason'.
i 70. her alone] the Roman Catholic Church.
i 71. In Matthew xxviii 20 Christ promises the apostles: 'I am with you alway, even unto the end of the world'.
i 72. winged with] i.e. driven swiftly by (*OED* 4).
i 72–8. While this striking passage is autobiographical in its idiom, it is also an important part of the poem's rhetorical strategy, diminishing the merely human authority of the narrative voice, and pointing beyond personal experience and understanding to the authority of divine revelation and Catholic tradition. In some respects it is a corrective counterpart to Puritan conversion narratives and auto-biographical testimonies to the work of the Holy Spirit in the individual believer. However, in so far as the passage is D.'s personal confession, it is an account both of a specifically theological and philosophical journey (through childhood Puritanism, the Anglicanism of *RL*, explorations of Hobbism in the plays and of Epicureanism in the Lucretian translations), and of a period of reflection in the mid-1680s, during which D. seems to have thought deeply about his mortality (in 'To the Memory of Mr Oldham' and the poems in *Sylvae*) and the use or misuse of his talents to serve the questionable tastes of the court and theatrical audiences: cp. *HP* iii 281–97*n* and 'To the Memory of Anne Killigrew' ll. 56–66. H. A. Mason points out (in unpublished notes) that there is a literary model for

My manhood, long misled by wandering fires,
Followed false lights; and when their glimpse was gone,
75 My pride struck out new sparkles of her own.
Such was I, such by nature still I am,
Be thine the glory, and be mine the shame.
Good life be now my task: my doubts are done
(What more could fright my faith than Three in One?).
80 Can I believe eternal God could lie ⎫
Disguised in mortal mould and infancy?   ⎬
That the great maker of the world could die? ⎭

---

this passage in the shepherd's speech in *FQ* VI ix 24–5 (itself modelled on Tasso's *Gerusalemme Liberata* vii 8–13), stanzas which offer both a general parallel to D.'s life and specific verbal sources: 'The time was once, in my first prime of yeares, / When pride of youth forth pricked my desire, / That I disdain'd amongst mine equall peares / To follow sheepe, and shepheards base attire: / For further fortune then I would inquire. / And leaving home, to roiall court I sought; / Where I did sell my selfe for yearely hire, / And in the Princes gardin daily wrought: / There I beheld such vainenesse, as I neuer thought. // With sight whereof soone cloyd, and long deluded / With idle hopes, which them doe entertaine, / After I had ten yeares my selfe excluded / From natiue home, and spent my youth in vaine, / I gan my follies to my selfe to plaine, / And this sweet peace, whose lacke did then appeare. / Tho backe returning to my sheepe againe, / I from thenceforth haue learn'd to loue more deare / This lowly quiet life, which I inherite here'.
i 73–5, 89–90. The imagery here recalls that in *RL* ll. 1–11, where D. describes the unreliable light which reason brings to matters of religious belief.
i 73. wandering fires] Milton calls the *ignis fatuus* a 'wandering fire' in *PL* ix 633, when Eve is being misled by Satan (J. R. Mason).
i 74. glimpse] momentary shining, flash (*OED* 1).
i 76. by nature] (i) by personal character; (ii) by human nature. Implicitly, therefore, human reason and natural religion can accomplish little: only divine grace and Catholic tradition can change him.
i 78–86. D. argues that the believer whose reason can be subordinated to his faith so as to accept the fundamental tenets of Christianity which are common to both Protestant and Catholic, such as the doctrines of the Trinity (l. 79), the incarnation (ll. 80–81), and the crucifixion (l. 82), should not recoil when faced with the Roman Catholic Church's requirement that he also believe other doctrines which are difficult for human reason to accept, such as transubstantiation (l. 86), which Protestants reject. Various pamphlets were published in 1686–7 debating the Roman Catholic claim that the doctrine of transubstantiation was as evident and reasonable as that of the Trinity, e.g. *A Dialogue Between a New Catholic Convert and a Protestant, Shewing the Doctrin of Transubstantiation to be as Reasonable to be Believ'd as the Great Mystery of the Trinity by all good Catholicks* (1686); for others see Jones, *Catalogue* 374–9.
i 78. Good life] Roman Catholic teaching stressed the importance of good works (which D. emphasizes in *Eleonora*), whereas in Protestant (especially Calvinist) teaching works were without merit, since salvation came by faith alone.
i 81. mould] See i 11*n*.

And after that, trust my imperfect sense
Which calls in question his omnipotence?
85   Can I my reason to my faith compel,
And shall my sight, and touch, and taste rebel?
Superior faculties are set aside:
Shall their subservient organs be my guide?
Then let the moon usurp the rule of day,
90   And winking tapers show the sun his way;
For what my senses can themselves perceive
I need no revelation to believe.

i 83–6. D. argues that since the believer subordinates his reason to his faith in important matters of doctrine, the even more imperfect human senses of sight, touch and taste should not be allowed to override faith and judge what God is capable of doing in respect of transubstantiation. This was the Catholic doctrine that the bread and wine in the mass are turned into the body and blood of Christ; Protestants held that they were instead symbols of Christ's body and blood. Abraham Woodhead, from a Catholic standpoint, summarizes the four principal current views as to the real presence of Christ's body and blood in the Eucharist: (i) 'That it is *Present* to the Worthy or Faithful Receiver, in all the *Efficacy* and *Benefits* thereof . . . by a communication to us of Christ's *Spirit*'; (ii) 'a *real Presence* of Christs Body, not only in its *vertue*, but in its very *substance*; but in this, not after a *natural* or *carnal*, but *spiritual*, manner'; (iii) real presence by consubstantiation: 'a *real presence* of Christ's *body with* or *under* the *signs*; meaning by them, the *substances* of the bread and wine still remaining after consecration'; (iv) real presence by transubstantiation: 'the *real presence* of Christ's body *with*, or *under* the signs, meaning by them only the *accidents*, or *properties*, or all that is any way to be perceived by *sight* or any other *sense*, *of the bread and the wine*': this latter is the Roman Catholic doctrine (*A Compendious Discourse on the Eucharist* (1688) 1). There was an extensive debate on transubstantiation in this period, as this was probably the principal doctrinal issue which was contested between Protestants and Catholics (and was the shibboleth used by the Test Acts to identify Catholics: see ii 30*n*); for other pamphlets see Jones, *Catalogue* 355–73. Cp. i 410–29*n*.
i 83–4. 'Besides there is nothing so powerful to strengthen our Faith and Hope, as to have this always settl'd in our mind, that there is nothing which God *cannot* do: For whatsoever we ought to believ, tho it be great, tho it be wonderful, tho it exceeds the Order and Measure of things; yet humane Reason easily and without any doubting, yields and assents to it, when once it owns that God is *Almighty*' (*A Catechism for the Curats, Compos'd by the Decree of the Council of Trent* (1687) 23).
i 86. That these senses are deceived when contemplating the body of Christ in the mass was a topic in Catholic devotion, e.g. in the Eucharistic hymn 'Adoro te devote, latens Deitas', often attributed to St Thomas Aquinas and included in missals as part of the communicant's private prayers: *Visus, tactus, gustus in te fallitur / Sed auditu solo tuto creditur: / Credo, quidquid dixit Dei Filius* ('Sight, touch, taste are deceived in [approaching] you, but the hearing alone may safely be believed; I believe whatever the Son of God has spoken').
i 87. Superior faculties] 'Reason' *MS.*
i 88. subservient organs] 'The Senses' *MS.*
i 90. winking] emitting intermittent flashes of light (*OED* 2c).

    Can they who say the host should be descried
    By sense, define a body glorified,
95 Impassible, and penetrating parts?
    Let them declare by what mysterious arts
    He shot that body through th' opposing might ⎫
    Of bolts and bars impervious to the light, ⎬
    And stood before his train confessed in open sight. ⎭
100   For since thus wondrously he passed, 'tis plain
    One single place two bodies did contain,
    And sure the same omnipotence as well
    Can make one body in more places dwell.
    Let reason then at her own quarry fly,
105 But how can finite grasp infinity?
       'Tis urged again that faith did first commence

---

i 93. host] the consecrated wafer in the mass.   *descried*] discerned.
i 94. a body glorified] the body of Christ after his resurrection.
i 95. Impassible] incapable of suffering or pain.   *penetrating*] occupying the same
space as [another body]: for two material bodies to occupy the same space was
traditionally thought impossible (*OED* penetration 1b).   *parts*] places (*OED* 3, 13).
i 96–103. According to John xx 19 and 26, Christ twice appeared to the disciples
after the resurrection, when they were gathered behind closed doors. D. argues
that since, in Jesus' appearance to his disciples, one place contained two physical
bodies (Jesus and the door), God's omnipotence can as easily make one body (that
of Christ) occupy more than one place during the mass. This was a frequently
cited (and frequently contested) example in discussions of transubstantiation, as
in *The Catholick Letter to the Seeker* (1688) 14–16: 'as all things are possible to
God; so, whether *Christ*, who is perfect *God*, may not be *Intire* in the *Sacrament*,
and in many places, at one and the same *Time*, is the *Quaere?*'; after citing John
xx 19, the tract continues: '*Christ* may as well be *Intire* in the *Sacrament*, as be
Intire when he passeth thro' *Walls* and *Doors*, that are close; as also it is proved,
That *Christ* may be in more places than *One*, at the same *Time*'.
i 99. confessed] revealed.
i 104. i.e. let reason pursue only those subjects which are appropriate for it.
i 105. Echoes *RL* l. 40.
i 106–9. D. rejects the Protestant argument that since the Christian faith is founded
upon miracles which were originally confirmed by the sense perceptions of the
disciples who witnessed them, our sense perceptions can appropriately be relied
upon in rejecting the supposed miracle of transubstantiation, where no change
in the bread is perceptible to sight, touch or taste. Edward Stillingfleet commented:
'My Senses plainly tell me, what I see and feel and taste is as much Bread after
Consecration as it was before; how then comes it to pass that my Judgment that
it was Bread before, was very good; but although there be the very same Evidence
afterwards, without the least alteration to Sense, yet then I am to judge just contrary, *i.e.* that it is not Bread, which I see and feel and taste just as I did before?
. . . For the Question is not about external appearances, but about the Judgment
of the Mind upon the Evidence of Sense . . . We do not pretend to judge by our
Senses of Invisible Substances under outward appearances; but of the Truth of a

By miracles, which are appeals to sense,
And thence concluded that our sense must be
The motive still of credibility.
110   For latter ages must on former wait,
And what began belief must propagate.
     But winnow well this thought, and you shall find
'Tis light as chaff that flies before the wind.
Were all those wonders wrought by power divine
115   As means or ends of some more deep design?
Most sure as means, whose end was this alone,
To prove the godhead of th' eternal Son.
God thus asserted, man is to believe
Beyond what sense and reason can conceive;
120   And for mysterious things of faith rely
On the proponent, heaven's authority.
If then our faith we for our guide admit,

---

bodily Substance by all the Appearances of a body, under all the Circumstances necessary for the right judgment of Sense' (*A Vindication of the Answer to Some Late Papers* (1687) 4–5). On the Catholic side Cressy wrote: 'I was satisfyed that they were extreamly mistaken who thought that there was no absolute certainty in any knowledge, excepting onely such as wee receive either immediately by our senses, or by evident discourse and demonstration of reason. For on the contrary I found that knowledge from report or Tradition might in some cases be as truely certaine as that from sence or demonstration' (*Exomologesis* 296). Cp. *A Catechism for the Curats* 142: 'Wherefore that there might never any distrust or doubt of this *Effect*, arise in the minds of the Faithful; When the Sacraments *began* to be administered, it pleas'd the most merciful God by the evidence of *Miracles* to shew what the Sacraments *inwardly effected*, that we might most constantly believe, the same things to be always *inwardly wrought*, tho they were far enough distant from our *Senses*'.

i 109. *motive*] moving or inciting cause (*OED* 4b).

i 118–21. i.e. since the divinity of Christ has been established by miracles, in other areas of Christian belief man must likewise be prepared to trust his faith and rely upon the authority of heaven rather than his own reason or senses.

i 118. i.e. 'Christ's true nature as God having been made clear in this way, man is to believe . . .' (not 'God asserted that man is to believe . . .'). *asserted*] declared (*OED* 7), probably also with some element of the meaning 'declare or claim one's rights' (*OED* 3, 4, 5).

i 121. *proponent*] one who brings forward an argument or proposition: i.e. heavenly authority has demonstrated the divinity of Christ through various miracles. The *OED* cites this line as its first example of *proponent* as an adjective, but that interpretation ignores the comma in *1687* and would require the unidiomatic phrase 'the proponent heaven'; it seems better to treat it as a noun in apposition either (1) to *heaven's authority*, so that the line means 'on the source of the doctrine, that is, the authority of heaven'; or (2) to *heaven*, so that the line means 'on the proponent's – that is, heaven's – authority'. Gardiner 105 says that *proponent* echoes the Latin scholastic term for the church's authority in matters of faith, *Regula proponens*.

Vain is the farther search of human wit,
As when the building gains a surer stay
125   We take th' unuseful scaffolding away:
Reason by sense no more can understand;
The game is played into another hand.
Why choose we then like bilanders to creep ⎤
Along the coast, and land in view to keep, ⎬
130   When safely we may launch into the deep? ⎦
In the same vessel which our Saviour bore, ⎤
Himself the pilot, let us leave the shore, ⎬
And with a better guide a better world explore. ⎦
Could he his godhead veil with flesh and blood,
135   And not veil these again to be our food?
His grace in both is equal in extent,
The first affords us life, the second nourishment.
And if he can, why all this frantic pain ⎤
To construe what his clearest words contain, ⎬
140   And make a riddle what he made so plain? ⎦

i 123. Vain] devoid of value, futile (*OED* 1); foolish (*OED* 3); conceited (*OED* 4). *wit*] intelligence.

i 124. stay] support.

i 125. unuseful] useless (very common in the seventeenth century).

i 127. i.e. 'the course of play in the game allows another player [here, faith] to use his strong hand of cards'. *another hand*] 'Divine Revelation' *MS.*

i 128. bilanders] A two-masted merchant vessel used in Holland for coastal and canal traffic (*OED*). The Netherlands were staunchly Protestant, and their Stadtholder William of Orange, husband of the heir presumptive to the English throne, Princess Mary, was already seen by some as a possible defender of English Protestantism against James II (see iii 1121*n*).

i 131–2. Alluding to Matthew xiv 22–33. When the disciples are in a ship on the Sea of Galilee, Jesus comes to them by walking on the water; but when Peter tries to reach Jesus he begins to sink because he has insufficient faith, and is saved by Jesus grasping him.

i 134–5. veil with flesh] In the incarnation. *veil these again*] In the mass. The idea echoes the eucharistic hymn 'Adoro te devote, latens Deitas' (cp. i 86*n*): *In cruce latebat sola Deitas, / At hic latet simul et humanitas / . . . Jesus, quem velatum nunc aspicio* ('On the cross only the Deity was concealed, but here the humanity also lies hidden . . . Jesus, whom I now see veiled').

i 137. i.e. the incarnation provides us with eternal life (because in Christian doctrine through the incarnation Christ takes upon him man's sinful nature which is redeemed in the crucifixion), while the mass provides us with spiritual nourishment.

i 138. pain] trouble, effort (*OED* 5).

i 139. construe] accented on the first syllable in the seventeenth century. *his clearest words*] At the Last Supper Jesus took bread, gave it to the disciples, and said, 'Take, eat; this is my body' (Matthew xxvi 26). The church regarded this action as instituting the mass, and the Catholic doctrine of transubstantiation took literally the words 'This is my body': cp. Bossuet quoted in i 428–9*n*.

> To take up half on trust, and half to try,
> Name it not faith, but bungling bigotry.
> Both knave and fool the merchant we may call ⎫
> To pay great sums, and to compound the small. ⎪
145 For who would break with heaven, and would not ⎬
>   break for all? ⎪
> ⎭
> Rest then, my soul, from endless anguish freed,
> Nor sciences thy guide, nor sense thy creed.
> Faith is the best ensurer of thy bliss:
> The bank above must fail before the venture miss.
150 But heaven and heaven-born faith are far from thee,
> Thou first apostate to divinity;
> Unkennelled range in thy Polonian plains:
> A fiercer foe, th' insatiate Wolf, remains.
>   Too boastful Britain, please thyself no more

i 141. half on trust] 'Incarnation' MS.   half to try] 'real Presence' MS.   try] put to the test to ascertain the truth (OED 5c).

i 143–4. i.e. a Protestant who accepts the major counter-rational doctrines of Christianity such as the incarnation and resurrection, and yet baulks at lesser ones such as transubstantiation, is acting as foolishly and dishonestly as the merchant who pays off his large debts in full, but negotiates with his smaller creditors for a partial repayment of his debts to them.   compound] settle a debt by agreeing to a partial payment (OED 8).

i 145. i.e. who would quarrel with (OED break 34) heaven, and yet suppose that he could avoid going completely bankrupt (OED break 11b)?

i 147. Nor . . . nor] neither . . . nor.   sciences] areas or modes of human knowledge (OED 2, 3).

i 149. The bank above] 'the word of God' MS.   fail] become bankrupt.

i 150–2. Addressed to the Socinian (see i 53n).   first apostate] D. associates the Socinian with Satan, since neither would accept Christ as the Son of God (for Satan's reaction see PL v 600–65). Milton calls Satan 'apostate' in PL i 125. MS glosses first apostate as 'Arius'.   Polonian] Fausto Sozzini spent his later life in Poland, where Unitarian doctrines spread, though not without opposition.

i 153. Wolf] the Presbyterians (the description extends to l. 234). Presbyterianism is a form of church government by presbyters (ministers) rather than by bishops or through self-governing congregations. Claiming to recover the practice of the early Christians, Presbyterianism flourished in Calvin's Geneva, and in sixteenth-century Scotland. It was adopted by the English Parliament in 1646, but its implementation was patchy, since many independent or gathered congregations resisted incorporation into a state church. In the Bible the wolf is the enemy of the flock and persecutor of the church: Jesus warned, 'Beware of false prophets, which come to you in sheep's clothing, but inwardly they are ravening wolves' (Matthew vii 15; Kinsley). Franzius says that 'Hereticks are often compared to Wolves' (168–70). Butler had said that the Presbyterian was 'of a mungrel, diverse kind, / Clerick before, and Lay behind / . . . A Sheep without, a Wolf within' (Hudibras I iii 1225–32; Kinsley). Gardiner 64 notes that because of his gender the Wolf can never be the bride of Christ (cp. i 1n), whereas the Panther could.

155   That beasts of prey are banished from thy shore:
        The Bear, the Boar, and every salvage name,
        Wild in effect, though in appearance tame,
        Lay waste thy woods, destroy thy blissful bower,
        And muzzled though they seem, the mutes devour.
160   More haughty than the rest, the wolfish race
        Appear with belly gaunt, and famished face:
        Never was so deformed a beast of grace.
        His ragged tail betwixt his legs he wears
        Close clapped for shame, but his rough crest he rears,
165   And pricks up his predestinating ears.
        His wild disordered walk, his haggard eyes,
        Did all the bestial citizens surprise.
        Though feared and hated, yet he ruled awhile
        As captain or companion of the spoil.

i 156. salvage] This seventeenth-century spelling of savage recalls its etymological origin in the Latin silva ('wood').

i 158. blissful bower] The wording recalls Spenser's Bowre of Blisse (FQ II xii).

i 159. muzzled] By legal restrictions such as the Test Act, which required holders of public offices to be communicant members of the Church of England (see ii 30n). mutes] The dissenting sects, thus restricted.

i 161. 'When they are once satisfied, they endure hunger a great time, for their bellies standeth out, their tongue swelleth, their mouth is stopped' (Topsel 571).

i 162. i.e. 'Never was a beast which claimed divine grace so deformed'. grace] See i 47n.

i 163–5. As Williams observes, the ragged tail suggests the Geneva gown (a black preaching gown worn by ministers in the reformed churches to emphasize the ministry of the word rather than that of the sacraments, for which vestments are worn); and the rough crest is the black skull-cap which covered their short-cropped hair so closely that the ears became prominent. As a result of their appearance, Presbyterians (and Parliamentarians in the Civil War) were nicknamed 'prick-ears' (OED prick-ear 2). ragged tail] An emblem of the Presbyterians' bruising encounter with the restored monarchy and Church of England after 1660 (Works). Topsel notes that 'when they are in danger to be taken by the hunters, they bite off the tip of their tails' (579; Works). clapped] pressed (OED 14).

i 165. The wolf has 'short prickt ears' (Swan 447). predestinating] Most Presbyterians were Calvinists, believing that men are predestined before their birth either to salvation or to damnation, and are therefore unable to affect their eternal fate by their mode of life.

i 166. haggard eyes] 'Their eyes are yellow, black, and very bright, sending forth beams like fire, and carrying in them apparent tokens of wrath and malice' (Topsel 571). haggard] wild-looking, especially as a result of hunger or fatigue (OED 5).

i 167. surprise] alarm, terrify (OED v. 5; cp. sb. 4a for the sense, which was stronger than in modern usage).

i 169. captain or companion] As captain during the Civil War, and companion to the government and other sects during the Commonwealth (Williams). spoil] the action of pillaging or plundering (OED 2).

170   Full many a year his hateful head had been
      For tribute paid, nor since in Cambria seen:
      The last of all the litter 'scaped by chance,
      And from Geneva first infested France.
      Some authors thus his pedigree will trace,
175   But others write him of an upstart race;
      Because of Wyclif's brood no mark he brings
      But his innate antipathy to kings.
      These last deduce him from th' Helvetian kind
      Who near the Leman Lake his consort lined;
180   That fiery Zwinglius first th' affection bred,
      And meagre Calvin blessed the nuptial bed.

i 170–8. D. suggests two alternative origins for English Presbyterianism: (i) in native, Anglo-Saxon heresies; (ii) in the Switzerland of Zwingli and Calvin.
i 170–1. The Anglo-Saxon King Edgar is said to have required Ludwal, King of Wales, to provide an annual tribute of 300 wolves; after three years no wolves were left. *Works* notes that Thomas Fuller records that in the fourth and fifth centuries three heresies were found in Britain, Arianism (see i 53*n*), Pelagianism (see i 47*n*), and predestination (see i 165*n*); says that '*Naturalists* dispute how *Wolves* had their first *being* in *Britain*'; and wonders 'how these *Heretics* (*mystical Wolves not sparing the Flock*) first entered into this *Island*' (*The Church History of Britain* (1655) 25). *Cambria*] Wales; but here also early Britain more generally; 'England' *MS.*
i 172. last of all the litter] 'Calvin' *MS.*   *'scaped*] Calvin escaped from France in 1534.
i 173. Calvinism spread from Geneva into France, where by 1561 there were 2,000 Calvinist churches.
i 175. upstart race] J. R. Mason compares Milton: 'a race of upstart creatures' (*PL* ii 834).
i 176. Wyclif] John Wyclif (*c.* 1330–84), English theologian and reformer, who argued that the Bible was the sole criterion of Christian doctrine, that the authority of the Pope was ill-founded in scripture, and that the doctrine of transubstantiation was philosophically unsound and encouraged a superstitious attitude to the Eucharist. He was not hostile to kings, but his teachings were commonly (though erroneously) associated with the Peasants' Revolt of 1381.
i 178. Helvetian] Swiss.   *kind*] race.
i 179. Leman Lake] Lake Geneva.   *lined*] copulated with (used of a dog or wolf) (*OED*).
i 180. fiery] Includes the implications 'impassioned preacher' and 'lustful'. *Zwinglius*] The Latin form of the name of Ulrich Zwingli (1484–1531), Swiss reformer a generation before Calvin. He insisted that the Gospels were the sole basis for Christian teaching, and developed a purely symbolic interpretation of the Eucharist, denying any form of the bodily presence of Christ in it.
i 181. meagre] lean, emaciated.   *Calvin*] John Calvin (1509–64), French theologian and reformer, who instituted a rigid puritanical regime in Geneva which was enforced by banishment, torture and execution. Theologically he promoted the doctrine of predestination (see i 165*n* above), which was highly influential on English Protestantism. Calvinism was the dominant theology of the Church of England in the late sixteenth and early seventeenth centuries, though by the Restoration it was confined principally to Nonconformist sects, while the Church of England developed more moderate doctrines.

In Israel some believe him whelped long since   *Vid. Pref.*
When the proud Sanhedrim oppressed the prince.   *to Heyl.*
Or, since he will be Jew, derive him higher,   Hist. of
185   When Corah with his brethren did conspire   Presb.
    From Moses' hand the sovereign sway to wrest,
    And Aaron of his ephod to divest:
    Till opening earth made way for all to pass,
    And could not bear the burden of a class.
190   The Fox and he came shuffled in the dark,
    If ever they were stowed in Noah's ark.
    Perhaps not made: for all their barking train
    The Dog (a common species) will contain,

i 182. marginal note. 'Intending a compleat History of the *Presbyterians*, in all the Principles, Practices, and most remarkable Proceedings of that dangerous Sect; I am to take a higher aim then the time of *Calvin* (though he be commonly pretended for the Founder of it) and fetch their Pedigree from those whose steps they follow . . . I know that some out of pure zeal unto the Cause would fain intitle them to a descent from the Jewish *Sanhedrim*, ordained by God himself in the time of *Moses*: And that it might comply the better with their ends and purposes, they have endeavoured to make that famous Consistory of the Seventy Elders, not only a co-ordinate power with that of *Moses*, and after his decease with the Kings and Princes of that State in this Publick Government; but a Power Paramount and Supreme, from which lay no appeal to any but to God himself: A power by which they were enabled not onely to control the actions of their Kings and Princes, but also to correct their persons' (Peter Heylyn, *Aërius Redivivus, or, The History of the Presbyterians*, 2nd edition (1672) sig. A2^{r-v}).
i 183. Sanhedrim] The highest court of justice in Jerusalem.
i 184. higher] further back, from an earlier time (*OED* high *adv.* 4b).
i 185–8. Corah (or 'Korah') and his associates rebelled against Moses and Aaron, challenging their status as leaders by saying, 'Ye take too much upon you, seeing all the congregation are holy'; but the earth opened and swallowed them up (Numbers xvi 3). Heylyn suggests that Presbyterianism originated in this rebellion (A2^v). D. used the name Corah for Titus Oates in *AA* ll. 632–77.
i 187. ephod] Jewish priestly garment; hence the priestly office itself (*OED* 2).
i 189. class] classis: see 'To the Reader' ll. 59–60*n* above.
i 190. shuffled] huddled up together (*OED*, citing only D. and Oldham, 1683–5).
i 192. Perhaps not made] i.e. not made by God as distinct species, but the mongrel result of cross-breeding.
i 193. Dog] Franzius says that the dog can represent either the elect or heathens (177–9). Topsel reports that 'there be some have thought that Dogs and Wolves are one kinde; namely, that vulgar Dogs are tame Wolves, and ravening Wolves are wilde Dogs. But *Scaliger* hath learnedly confuted this opinion . . . for he saith, that there are divers wild Dogs that are not Wolves, and so have continued for many years in a hill called *Mountfalcon*, altogether refusing the society and service of men . . . For Dogs it hath been seen, that they have lived in a kinde of society and fellowship with Wolfs, but it was to steal and devour in the night time, like as Theeves do cover their malice and secret grudges one to other, when they are going about to rob true men'. Topsel also reports that 'Wolves do engender not only among themselves, but among other beasts . . . as of Dogs and Wolves

And some wild curs, who from their masters ran
195   Abhorring the supremacy of man,
In woods and caves the rebel-race began.
    O happy pair, how well have you increased!
What ills in church and state have you redressed!
With teeth untried, and rudiments of claws,
200   Your first essay was on your native laws:
Those having torn with ease, and trampled down,
Your fangs you fastened on the mitred crown,
And freed from God and monarchy your town.
What though your native kennel still be small,
205   Bounded betwixt a puddle and a wall,
Yet your victorious colonies are sent
Where the north ocean girds the continent.
Quickened with fire below, your monsters breed
In fenny Holland and in fruitful Tweed;
210   And like the first, the last affects to be
Drawn to the dregs of a democracy.
As where in fields the fairy rounds are seen,
A rank, sour herbage rises on the green,
So, springing where these midnight elves advance,

---

cometh the *Lupus Canarius*, or Panther' (570–2). And Swan says that the Panther 'is very fierce and wilde, insomuch that some have therefore called him a *Dogwolf*' (443). *MS* glosses *Dog* as 'The Atheist'.

i *196.* Cp. *AA* l. 55.

i *197. happy pair*] Ironically echoing Milton's description of Adam and Eve in paradise (*PL* iv 534). *MS* glosses the pair as 'Arius & Presbetry'.

i *200. essay*] attempt; accented on the second syllable.

i *202. mitred crown*] Scott notes that the Bishop of Geneva exercised both spiritual and temporal jurisdiction, until expelled by the citizens in 1528.

i *205. puddle*] Lake Geneva.   *wall*] the Alps.

i *207. north ocean*] North Sea.

i *209.* Calvinism took hold in both Holland and Scotland (*Tweed*) in the 1560s, becoming the dominant religion in both countries.

i *210–11.* The power of the people was strong in both Holland and Scotland. The former was a republic, and in the latter the Calvinist Church maintained a resolute independence from the monarchy, and during the Civil War attempted to persuade Parliament to adopt its doctrine and practice in England. *first . . . last*] Holland . . . Scotland. *affects*] has a natural tendency (*OED* 4).

i *211.* Echoes *AA* l. 227 (see *n*). *democracy*] generally pejorative in the seventeenth century, meaning 'mob rule'. *MS* glosses it as 'a Commonwealth'.

i *212–13.* Fairy rounds or rings are circular patches of grass differing in colour from the surrounding grass; the effect was attributed in folklore to fairies dancing, but is caused by the growth of fungi. The lines echo *The Tempest*: 'you demi-puppets that / By moonshine do the green sour ringlets make, / Whereof the ewe not bites; and you whose pastime / Is to make midnight mushrooms' (V i 36–9; Williams).

215 Rebellion prints the footsteps of the dance.
   Such are their doctrines, such contempt they show ⎤
   To heaven above, and to their Prince below, ⎬
   As none but traitors and blasphemers know. ⎦
   God like the tyrant of the skies is placed,
220 And kings like slaves beneath the crowd debased.
   So fulsome is their food, that flocks refuse
   To bite, and only dogs for physic use.
   As where the lightning runs along the ground,
   No husbandry can heal the blasting wound,
225 Nor bladed grass, nor bearded corn succeeds,
   But scales of scurf, and putrefaction breeds:
   Such wars, such waste, such fiery tracks of dearth
   Their zeal has left, and such a teemless earth.
   But as the poisons of the deadliest kind
230 Are to their own unhappy coasts confined,
   As only Indian shades of sight deprive,
   And magic plants will but in Colchos thrive,
   So presbyt'ry and pestilential zeal
   Can only flourish in a commonweal.
235 From Celtic woods is chased the wolfish crew;

i 215. 'Presbytry began by rebellion in Geneva Holld & Scotland' *MS.*

i 219. 'by Predestination' *MS.*

i 221–2. fulsome] disgusting, offensive (*OED* 5). Franzius says that wolves and foxes would eat almost anything when hungry. *flocks refuse / To bite*] Echoes 'the ewe not bites' (see i 212–13*n* above). *dogs for physic use*] 'The Dogge hauing surfetted, to procure his vomitte eateth grasse, and findeth remedy' (Lyly, *Works*, edited by R. W. Bond, i 208; Williams).

i 226. scurf] mould (*OED* 3).

i 228. teemless] not bringing forth young or fruit, barren (*OED*'s only example).

i 229–32. Cp. 'Could you shed venom from your reverend shade, / Like Trees, beneath whose arms 'tis death to sleep' (*Aureng-Zebe* IV i 360–1). The reference is to the upas tree from Java (in the East Indies), which was supposed to spread its poison over 15–18 miles: it was fatal to venture under its shade. The Royal Society was interested in poisons which were supposedly specific to certain locations: *PTRS* ii (1667) 417.

i 232. Colchos] Colchis, a province east of the Black Sea; particularly associated in classical legend with Medea, who was an expert in poisons.

i 233. zeal] a characteristic associated with extreme Protestants: cp. *To His Sacred Majesty* l. 80; and *Albion and Albanius* III i 20, where Albion faces 'Rebellion arm'd with zeal'.

i 234. commonweal] republic.

i 235. Celtic woods] France. After the revocation of the Edict of Nantes (see 'To the Reader' ll. 39–40*n*) many Huguenots fled to England to escape persecution. They were Calvinists, and so *wolfish.* *crew*] collection of men or animals (*OED* 3, 3b); again at i 450.

But ah, some pity e'en to brutes is due!
Their native walks, methinks, they might enjoy,
Curbed of their native malice to destroy.
Of all the tyrannies on human kind,
240   The worst is that which persecutes the mind.
Let us but weigh at what offence we strike,
'Tis but because we cannot think alike.
In punishing of this, we overthrow
The laws of nations and of nature too.
245   Beasts are the subjects of tyrannic sway,
Where still the stronger on the weaker prey.
Man only of a softer mould is made,
Not for his fellows' ruin, but their aid:
Created kind, beneficent and free,
250   The noble image of the Deity.
       One portion of informing fire was given
To brutes, th' inferior family of heaven:
The smith divine, as with a careless beat,

i 244. The law of nations, or *jus gentium*, was originally assembled by Roman
jurists from the customs of foreign nations who had been absorbed into the empire;
it was expanded by medieval and Renaissance lawyers to include other, non-
western cultures. The law of nature, or *jus naturale*, was associated with that natural reason which underlay custom and the law of nations (*The Cambridge History
of Political Thought 1450–1700*, edited by J. H. Burns (1991) 69). For D.'s interest
in the law of nature see 'Palamon and Arcite' ii 337*n*.
i 247. *mould*] See i 11*n*.
i 249–50. D.'s vision of human nature here is opposed to the Calvinist assertion
that man is by nature corrupt and is incapable of acting for good without divine
grace (cp. i 47*n*), and is also opposed to the Hobbesian notion that in the state
of nature man seeks only his own benefit regardless of others.
i 250. 'And God said, Let us make man in our image' (Genesis i 26).
i 251. *informing*] imparting life or spirit to (*OED* 3c); cp. 'o'erinformed' in *AA* l. 158.
fire] animating or life-giving force; cp. Virgil's *aurai simplicis ignem* ('the fire of a
pure soul': *Aen.* vi 747), and D. in 'The First Book of Ovid's *Metamorphoses*',
where he says that man was created 'with particles of Heav'nly Fire' (l. 101).
The idea that animals have a portion of heavenly spirit is classical: Plato in the
Timaeus (39e etc.) imagines the creator fashioning various kinds of creatures with
heavenly fire; Aristotle distinguished three kinds of soul, vegetative, sensitive and
intellective, the first two of which were possessed by animals (*De Anima* ii 3);
and Pythagoras taught that souls passed by transmigration from one body into
another, including the bodies of animals (Ovid, *Met.* xv 165–8). Virgil said *esse
apibus partem divinae mentis* ('there is in bees a part of the divine mind' (*Geo.* iv
220); D. when translating this passage adds that bees are 'Endu'd with Particles
of Heavenly Fires' ('The Fourth Book of the *Georgics*' l. 323)).
i 253–9. Williams noted a parallel in Sylvester's translation of Du Bartas' *Divine
Weeks and Works* (1608): God accomplished the rest of creation 'in an instant',
but when it came to creating man, 'As if he would a Councell hold, he cyteth

Struck out the mute creation at a heat;
255   But when arrived at last to human race,
The godhead took a deep considering space;
And, to distinguish man from all the rest,
Unlocked the sacred treasures of his breast;
And mercy mixed with reason did impart,
260   One to his head, the other to his heart:
Reason to rule, but mercy to forgive;
The first is law, the last prerogative.
And like his mind his outward form appeared, ⎫
When issuing naked to the wondering herd   ⎬
265   He charmed their eyes, and for they loved, they feared. ⎭
Not armed with horns of arbitrary might,   ⎫
Or claws to seize their furry spoils in fight, ⎬
Or with increase of feet t' o'ertake 'em in their flight. ⎭
Of easy shape, and pliant every way,   ⎫
270   Confessing still the softness of his clay, ⎬
And kind as kings upon their coronation day, ⎭
With open hands, and with extended space
Of arms, to satisfy a large embrace.
Thus kneaded up with milk, the new-made man

/ His sacred Power, his Prudence he inviteth, / Summons his Love, His Justice he adjournes, / Calleth his Goodnes, and his Grace returnes, / To (as it were) consult about the birth / . . . when in man he meant / In mortall limbes immortall life to place, / Hee seem'd to pawse' ('The Sixth Day of the First Weeke' ll. 470–92). Cp. *Threnodia Augustalis* ll. 435–45.

i *254. mute creation*] Milton says that the beasts were 'created mute' (*PL* ix 557; J. R. Mason).   *at a heat*] in a single operation of heating (*OED* 8b); in a single intense effort (*OED* 9).

i *262. prerogative*] special power and privilege to act, esp. the king's power to act without the specific authorization of the law or consent of Parliament.

i *265. for*] because.   *feared*] regarded with reverence and awe (*OED* 6).

i *266. arbitrary might*] [royal] power exercised without legal grounds or parliamentary consent. There had been frequent allegations that Charles II and James II were intent on arbitrary government: cp. *AA* ll. 212–13n, 329–30n, 701n.

i *268. increase of feet*] Jokingly, this line has an extra foot; indeed, it would be a fourteener if one printed *t' o'ertake* in full as *to overtake*.   *increase*] The noun was accented on the second syllable.

i *270. Confessing*] revealing.   *clay*] earth, thought of as the material of the human body, as in Genesis ii 7 (*OED* 4); cp. *AA* l. 158.

i *271*. As Scott observed, a coronation day was often marked by some act of grace or general pardon.

i *274. kneaded*] Closer to Ovid's *finxit* ('fashioned'), in the account of the creation of man by Prometheus (*Met.* i 84), than to 'formed' in Genesis ii 7.   *milk*] Perhaps recalling the 'milk of human kindness' (*Macbeth* I v 17), where milk signifies the natural human feelings imbibed at the mother's breast.

275   His kingdom o'er his kindred world began:
       Till knowledge misapplied, misunderstood,
       And pride of empire soured his balmy blood.
       Then first rebelling, his own stamp he coins;
       The murtherer Cain was latent in his loins;
280   And blood began its first and loudest cry
       For diff'ring worship of the Deity.
       Thus persecution rose, and farther space
       Produced the mighty hunter of his race.
       Not so the blessèd Pan his flock increased,
285   Content to fold 'em from the famished beast:
       Mild were his laws, the Sheep and harmless Hind

i 275. God gave man 'dominion over the fish of the sea, and over the fowl of
the air, and over every living thing that moveth upon the earth' (Genesis i 28).
i 276. knowledge] God commanded Adam not to eat 'of the tree of the knowledge of good and evil' (Genesis ii 17).
i 277. pride of empire] Pride and the desire to extend man's power are not given
as motives for the Fall in Genesis, but Milton has the serpent offer Eve the prospect
that they will become gods by eating the forbidden fruit, and she subsequently
contemplates being equal or superior to Adam (*PL* ix 712–15, 820–5). Adam blames
Eve's pride at *PL* x 874. Pride and ambition caused Satan's fall from heaven (*PL*
iv 40).   *balmy*] mild (i.e. temperate, not over-heated) (*OED* 5).
i 278. his own stamp he coins] i.e. he makes the die from which his coins will be
cast: as a rebel king, Adam sets up his own mint. The image of coining is also
linked to l. 279, as it was used for procreation: men committing fornication 'do
coin heaven's image / In stamps that are forbid' (*Measure for Measure* II iv 45–6).
i 279–81. Cain, eldest son of Adam and Eve, likewise rebelled against God's commands: he killed his brother Abel because Abel's offering of sheep pleased God,
whereas Cain's offering of crops did not. Abel's blood cried to God (Genesis
iv 2–10).
i 282. space] interval of time (*OED* 4).
i 283. Nimrod was 'a mighty hunter' (Genesis x 9). Biblical commentators had
seen him as the archetype of the tyrant, and Milton wrote that he 'Will arrogate
dominion undeserved / Over his brethren' (*PL* xii 27–8; see Fowler's edition for
a note on political interpretations of Nimrod). See also *HP* iii 1273–4*n*.
i 284. Pan] Commonly identified with Christ. 'E. K.' in Spenser's *The Shepheardes
Calender* (gloss to 'Maye' l. 54) explains: 'Great pan is Christ, the very God of
all shepheards, which calleth himselfe the greate and good shepherd [John x 11].
The name is most rightly . . . applyed to him, for Pan [πᾶν, 'all'] signifieth all
or omnipotent, which is onely the Lord Iesus . . . Plutarch . . . [in *De Defectu
Oraculorum* 418] sayth, that about the same time, that our Lord suffered his most
bitter passion for the redemtion of man, certein passengers sayling from Italy to
Cyprus and passing by certain Iles called Paxae, heard a voyce calling alowde
. . . that the great Pan was dead'. Cp. Milton, 'On the Morning of Christ's Nativity'
ll. 89–90.
i 286. Sheep] The ordinary follower of Christ; from John x 1–16, where Jesus
calls himself the good shepherd, and warns against false pastors, and predators who
climb into the sheepfold.

Were never of the persecuting kind.
Such pity now the pious pastor shows,
Such mercy from the British Lion flows,
290   That both provide protection for their foes.
        O happy regions, Italy and Spain,
Which never did those monsters entertain!
The Wolf, the Bear, the Boar can there advance
No native claim of just inheritance;
295   And self-preserving laws, severe in show,
May guard their fences from th' invading foe.
Where birth has placed 'em let 'em safely share
The common benefit of vital air;
Themselves unharmful, let them live unharmed,
300   Their jaws disabled, and their claws disarmed:
Here only in nocturnal howlings bold,
They dare not seize the Hind, nor leap the fold.
More powerful, and as vigilant as they,
The Lion awfully forbids the prey.
305   Their rage repressed, though pinched with famine sore,
They stand aloof, and tremble at his roar;
Much is their hunger, but their fear is more.

i 288. pious pastor] Innocent XI (1611–89), Pope since 1676. Noted for his piety and generosity, he was opposed to Louis XIV's revocation of the Edict of Nantes, and to James II's attempts to use royal power to promote the interests of Catholics in England, especially his *Declaration for Liberty of Conscience*.
i 289. mercy] Seen by D. as characteristic of the Stuarts: cp. *Astraea Redux* ll. 258–65*n*.
i 290. Innocent XI by opposing the revocation of the Edict of Nantes was protecting Huguenots; James II in his *Declaration for Liberty of Conscience* was protecting dissenters.
i 291–6. Protestantism never took hold in either Italy or Spain, and in both countries the Inquisition was active in suppressing heresy. Line 295 claims that the Inquisition's severity (which horrified Protestants, and terrified travellers to Catholic countries) was more apparent than real.
i 296. fences, 302. fold] See ii 313*n*.
i 298. Noyes compares Virgil: *diis sedem exiguam patriis litusque rogamus / innocuum, et cunctis undamque auramque patentem* (*Aen.* vii 229–30: 'we ask a safe landing place, and a narrow space for our household gods, and water and air which are common to all'; D. translates the last phrase as 'The common Water and the common Air' ('The Seventh Book of the *Aeneis*' l. 314)). The Latin *innocuum* means not only 'safe' but also 'harmless, innocuous', hence D.'s *unharmful* in l. 299.
i 301. nocturnal howlings] Nonconformist meetings were sometimes held at night, and were characterized by the groans of those moved by the Spirit.
i 304. awfully] inspiring awe.
i 306. Topsel says of the lion: 'It is also said, that when the Beasts do hear his voice, all of them do keep their standing and dare not stir a foot . . . for by terrour and dread they stand amazed' (362; *Works*).

    These are the chief; to number o'er the rest,
    And stand like Adam naming every beast,
310 Were weary work, nor will the Muse describe
    A slimy-born and sun-begotten tribe,
    Who, far from steeples and their sacred sound,
    In fields their sullen conventicles found:
    These gross, half-animated lumps I leave,
315 Nor can I think what thoughts they can conceive.
    But if they think at all, 'tis sure no higher
    Than matter, put in motion, may aspire.
    Souls that can scarce ferment their mass of clay, ⎫
    So drossy, so divisible are they,   ⎬
320 As would but serve pure bodies for allay: ⎭
    Such souls as shards produce, such beetle things
    As only buzz to heaven with evening wings;
    Strike in the dark, offending but by chance,
    Such are the blindfold blows of ignorance.
325 They know not beings, and but hate a name,
    To them the Hind and Panther are the same.

i 309. Adam names the animals in Genesis ii 19–20.

i 311. 'Enthusiasticks & Phanaticks' *MS.* It was a commonplace that some creatures, such as reptiles and insects, were generated from inorganic matter (especially mud) by the action of the sun: cp. Ovid, *Met.* i 416–37, and D.'s translation, 'The First Book of Ovid's *Metamorphoses*' ll. 558–85; also *All for Love* (1678) V i 153–6; Shakespeare, *Antony and Cleopatra* II vii 26–7.

i 312–13. Many Nonconformist meetings were held out of doors: one of the illustrations to Bunyan's *The Life and Death of Mr Badman* (1680) shows 'A Protestant Meeting' taking place in the corner of a field. Quakers derided churches as 'steeple-houses', Fox recording of a visit to Nottingham: 'the great steeple-house struck at my life when I spied it, a great idol and idolatrous temple' (*Journal* 39).

i 313. conventicles] Stressed at this period on the first and third syllables (*OED*; cp. 'Prologue to *The Disappointment*' l. 64).

i 314. lumps] bodies without souls: see *AA* l. 172n.

i 318. ferment] cause any movement in, impart any life to (*OED* fermentation 1c, for examples of various senses). *clay*] See i 270n.

i 319. drossy] impure. *divisible*] material, divisibility being a criterion of matter (Christie; this sense not in *OED*).

i 320. allay] alloy.

i 321. shards] patches of cow dung (*OED sb.²*). A shard-beetle is a beetle found under cow dung (*OED sb.²* b). Thomas Muffet noted the common belief that 'Beetles first breed from dung' (in Topsel 1010). D. uses similar imagery for Protestant sects in *RL* ll. 417–22.

The Panther sure the noblest, next the Hind,
And fairest creature of the spotted kind;
O, could her inborn stains be washed away,
330   She were too good to be a beast of prey!
How can I praise, or blame, and not offend,
Or how divide the frailty from the friend?
Her faults and virtues lie so mixed, that she
Nor wholly stands condemned, nor wholly free.
335   Then like her injured Lion, let me speak,
He cannot bend her, and he would not break.

i 327. The Panther] The Church of England. Topsel discusses this animal under the heading 'Of the Panther, commonly called a Pardal, a Leopard, and a Libbard', and his comment about the difficulty of classifying and naming this creature is apt for a church which D. would have regarded as harbouring various doctrines and parties, and shifting its appearance from time to time: 'There have been so many names devised for this one beast, that it is grown a difficult thing, either to make a good reconciliation of the Authors which are wed to their several opinions, or else to define it perfectly, and make of him a good methodical History' (447). He describes the Panther as 'fierce and cruel . . . very violent . . . wrathful and angry' (448), but also as 'wanton, effeminate' (451). In addition, deceit is a principal characteristic: when the Egyptians 'will signifie a cunning man covering the secret corruption and evil disposition of his minde, pretending good, and yet intending evil, they picture a Panther' (451–2). Swan treats the Panther as an emblem of 'fair tongues and false hearts' (443). Physiologus (for whom see i 1n) interpreted the Panther as an allegory of Christ. For the Panther as the offspring of dogs and wolves see i 193n. D. transfers to the Church of England the image of the beast in Revelation xiii 2, which had regularly been used by Protestants to designate the Church of Rome: 'And the beast which I saw was like unto a leopard, and his feet were as the feet of a bear, and his mouth as the mouth of a lion' (cp. i 401n, i 537n). The Panther had been used to represent the Pope in *The Fanaticks Dream* [1680] and *The Panther-Prophecy* (1662) (see Paul Hammond, *N & Q* ccvii (1982) 55–7).
i 328. fairest creature] But the Panther's attractions are dangerous: 'by his savour or sweet smell, [he] draweth unto him an innumerable company of wilde Goats, Harts, Roes, and Hindes, and such other Beasts, and so upon a sudden leapeth down upon them, when he espyeth his convenient time'. The danger is not readily apparent, for the panther uses cunning and dissimulation to catch his prey: he shams death, or turning aside his head so as not to frighten other creatures he offers 'the more beautiful parts of his body, as an alluring bait'; and 'when they go, they hide their nails within the skin of their feet, as it were in sheaths, never bringing them forth but when they are in their prey' (Topsel 450–1).
i 329. 'Can the Ethiopian change his skin, or the leopard his spots? then may ye also do good, that are accustomed to do evil' (Jeremiah xiii 23). This proverb was also applied to the panther rather than the leopard: Tilley L 206.
i 332. frailty] moral weakness, liability to error (*OED* 2).
i 334. Nor . . . nor] Neither . . . nor.

Unkind already, and estranged in part,
The Wolf begins to share her wandering heart;
Though unpolluted yet with actual ill,
340   She half commits who sins but in her will.
If, as our dreaming Platonists report,
There could be spirits of a middle sort,
Too black for heaven, and yet too white for hell,
Who just dropped halfway down, nor lower fell,
345   So poised, so gently she descends from high,
It seems a soft dismission from the sky.
Her house not ancient, whatsoe'er pretence
Her clergy heralds make in her defence:

i 337. Unkind] ungrateful (*OED* 3a), devoid of natural goodness (*OED* 3c), unnaturally cruel or hostile (*OED* 5).

i 338–40. As *Works* notes, the panther and the wolf were both thought to be lecherous and promiscuous: Franzius reported that the female panther was very lecherous (65). See also Topsel, cited in i 193n.

i 340. Christie compares Juvenal: *nam scelus intra se tacitum qui cogitat ullum,* / *facti crimen habet* (*Sat.* xiii 209–10: 'he who secretly contemplates any crime in his heart has all the guiltiness of the deed'). Cp. also Matthew v 28: 'whosoever looketh on a woman to lust after her hath committed adultery with her already in his heart'.

i 341–4. In Plato's *Symposium* (202d–e) Diotima tells Socrates that there are spirits which are halfway between god and man. Augustine discusses them in *De Civitate Dei* viii 14. Milton also imagines the possibility of 'middle spirits . . . / Betwixt the angelical and human kind' (*PL* iii 461–2). The Cambridge Platonist Henry More discusses whether the guardian angels of nations hostile to the Jews can be as good as the guardian angels who protect the Jews (*A Plain and Continued Exposition of the Several Divine Visions of the Prophet Daniel* (1681) 145–58). In *King Arthur* (1691) II i 13–15 Philidel says that he is 'An Airy Shape, the tender'st of my kind, / The last seduc'd, and least deform'd of Hell; / Half white, and shuffl'd in the Crowd, I fell'.

i 346. soft] slow (*OED* 5).   *dismission*] deprivation of position or dignity, discharge from service (*OED* 3).

i 347–50. The comparatively recent origin of the Church of England was insisted upon by Catholic writers, who argued that since it could not be traced back further than the Reformation, it lacked any claim to be the church founded by Christ. Anglican writers insisted that the Reformation simply purged the church of abuses and accretions in doctrine and practice which had no warrant in scripture, and that the Church of England preserved the apostolic succession (whereby bishops, as they are consecrated by other bishops and succeed to ancient sees, theoretically form an unbroken chain back to the first apostles). Edward Stillingfleet argued in *Origines Britannicae* (1685) that Christianity had been established in Britain at the time of the apostles, and that the early church here was independent of papal authority.

i 348. heralds] Heralds are responsible for tracing genealogies, and thus for establishing a person's entitlement to noble rank.

> A second century not halfway run
350 Since the new honours of her blood begun.
> A Lion old, obscene, and furious made
> By lust, compressed her mother in a shade;
> Then by a left-hand marriage weds the dame,
> Cov'ring adult'ry with a specious name:
355 So Schism begot, and Sacrilege and she,
> A well-matched pair, got graceless Heresy.

i 349–50. The Act of Supremacy which established Henry VIII as 'supreme head' of the Church was passed in 1534, but repealed by Mary; a new Elizabethan Act of Supremacy in 1559 made the monarch 'supreme governor' in all ecclesiastical matters.   *honours*] title of rank, degree of nobility (*OED* 5).

i 351–4. The *Lion old* is Henry VIII (1491–1547). D. does not specify who, allegorically, the *mother* of the Panther was; historically it was Henry's relationship with Anne Boleyn which prompted his wish to have his marriage with Catherine of Aragon annulled, and so precipitated the breach with Rome. The secret marriage of Henry and Anne on 25 January 1533 preceded the declaration by Archbishop Cranmer on 23 May that the King's marriage to Catherine had been invalid, a verdict which was itself contentious in both civil and canon law. The child of Henry and Anne was the Protestant heroine Elizabeth I (born 7 September 1533), so D.'s careful indefinition here associates the Panther with Elizabeth. See the quotation from D.'s *Defence of the Third Paper* in iii 203–11n. Topsel writes: 'betwixt the Lions and the Pardals there is such a confused mixed generation as is betwixt Asses and Mares' (447). He also says that the variously named cats 'are all one kinde of Beast, and differ in quantity only through adulterous generation' (448).

i 351. furious] fiercely passionate, raging, frantic.

i 352. compressed] copulated with (*OED* 6).

i 353. left-hand marriage] a morganatic marriage between a king or nobleman and a woman of lower social standing, so called because the man took the bride with his left hand rather than his right; an ambiguous, fictitious or illegal marriage; an ill-omened, inauspicious marriage (*OED* left-handed 5, 3, 4).   *dame*] lady, woman of rank (but not royal) (*OED* 7).

i 354. Cp. Virgil, writing of the union of Dido and Aeneas: *coniugium vocat, hoc praetexit nomine culpam* (*Aen.* iv 172: 'she calls it marriage, and under that name conceals the guilt'). D. later translated the line as: 'But call'd it Marriage, by that specious Name, / To veil the Crime and sanctifie the Shame' ('The Fourth Book of the *Aeneis*' ll. 249–50). As George Loane noted (*N & Q* clxxxv (1943) 276) D.'s phrase *specious name* probably derives from Ovid: *coniugiumne putas speciosaque nomina culpae / imponis, Medea, tuae?* ('do you think it to be marriage, Medea, and do you attach specious names to your crime?': *Met.* vii 69–70).

i 355–6. D. presents an allegorical narrative in which the child of Henry VIII's illicit union, Schism, joins with Sacrilege to give birth to Heresy; this makes Anglican doctrines not simply heretical but the result of a schism produced by lust, and of sacrilege prompted by greed, rather than reformed doctrine adopted for theological reasons. The grim trinity of Schism, Sacrilege and Heresy recalls Milton's allegory of Satan, Sin and Death in *PL* ii 727–814, and the scriptural passage which lies behind it from James i 15: 'Then when lust hath conceived, it bringeth forth sin: and sin, when it is finished, bringeth forth death'.   *Schism*] The separation

God's and kings' rebels have the same good cause
To trample down divine and human laws:
Both would be called reformers, and their hate
360 Alike destructive both to church and state.
The fruit proclaims the plant: a lawless prince ⎫
By luxury reformed incontinence; ⎬
By ruins, charity; by riots, abstinence; ⎭
Confessions, fasts and penance set aside: ⎫
365 O with what ease we follow such a guide, ⎬
Where souls are starved, and senses gratified! ⎭

---

of the Church of England from Rome. *Sacrilege*] The dissolution of the monasteries with the appropriation of their goods, and the spoliation of many parish churches (described in Eamon Duffy's *The Stripping of the Altars* (1992)). Cressy calls Henry VIII a 'Sacrilegious Tyrant' and says that England has been guilty of sacrilege ever since the schism of the Reformation (*Exomologesis* sig. aiij^r, 16–23). *graceless*] To D., Protestantism, despite its characteristic insistence on salvation by God's grace rather than human merit, itself lacks grace. *got*] begot.

i *357. good cause*] Echoing 'the Good Old Cause', a description given to Protestant republicanism of the 1650s and its later manifestations in the Whig party after the Restoration (cp. *AA* l. 82*n*).

i *361*. 'Ye shall know them by their fruits' (Matthew vii 16).

i *362. luxury*] lust. *incontinence*] sexual licence; an accusation made (with some justification) against the clergy and monastic orders of the pre-Reformation church.

i *363. By ruins, charity*] The dissolution (and physical ruin) of the monasteries, and of other collegiate foundations and chantries, resulted in the loss of much charitable provision for the poor and sick. *riots*] debauchery, extravagance (*OED* 1); noisy feasting (*OED* 2). *abstinence*] one of the practices of the Catholic Church, e.g. abstinence from meat on Fridays; monastic orders often practised abstinence more extensively than the laity.

i *364. Confessions*] The Catholic practice of making private (auricular) confession to a priest was dropped by the Protestant churches. Since regular confession was required of communicants, and normally led to the performance of acts of penance, it was an important part of the spiritual discipline of the church which D. contrasts here with the laxity of Henry VIII, and, by extension, of Protestantism in general. *fasts*] Fasting is designed to strengthen the spiritual life by weakening the attraction of the pleasures of the senses. The Catholic Church observed fasts on days such as Good Friday, Ash Wednesday, and the vigils before major feast days. The Anglican Book of Common Prayer did in fact include fast days in its calendar, and these continued to be observed by some in the seventeenth-century Church of England. *penance*] Penance is one of the seven sacraments of the Catholic Church. After confessing his sins and receiving absolution, the penitent performs some act of penance (e.g. the recitation of prayers, physical discipline, going on pilgrimage) both to make amends for the sin and to learn to control the passions which led to it. Along with auricular confession, penance was rejected by Protestant churches; indeed, the sale of indulgences (which granted remission from the temporal penalty due to forgiven sins) had been one of the scandals which provoked the Reformation in Germany.

Where marriage pleasures midnight prayer supply, ⎫
And matin bells (a melancholy cry)   ⎬
Are tuned to merrier notes: 'increase and multiply'. ⎭
370 Religion shows a rosy-coloured face,   ⎫
Not hattered out with drudging works of grace;   ⎬
A downhill reformation rolls apace.   ⎭
What flesh and blood would crowd the narrow gate, ⎫
Or till they waste their pampered paunches wait? ⎬
375 All would be happy at the cheapest rate.   ⎭
     Though our lean faith these rigid laws has given,
The full-fed Mussulman goes fat to heaven;
For his Arabian prophet with delights
Of sense allured his eastern proselytes.
380 The jolly Luther, reading him, began
T' interpret scriptures by his Alcoran,

---

i 367. The Catholic Church forbad clergy to marry, and members of monastic orders took a vow of chastity. After the Reformation, many clergy and former members of the dissolved monastic orders married (see i 384*n*). *midnight prayer*] The Catholic monastic office of Matins was originally performed at midnight, though under the Rule of St Benedict it was prescribed for 2 a.m. *supply*] take the place of.

i 369. '*increase and multiply*'] God's command to Adam and Eve in Genesis i 28.

i 371. hattered out] worn out, exhausted with drudgery (*OED* 2; first example). *works of grace*] The performance of spiritual disciplines and charitable works was an important element of both Catholic and Protestant practice; but that element in Protestant theology which insisted that salvation could not be earned by man's actions, but is bestowed (or withheld) by God's will irrespective of man's merits, lent itself to the inference that it was unnecessary to attempt to perform any righteous acts.

i 373. narrow gate] 'Strait is the gate, and narrow is the way, which leadeth unto life' (Matthew vii 14).

i 377–87. The Moslem paradise included 'Virgins sumptuous in apparel, and beautiful as the light . . . made on purpose to entertain the *Musulmin*' (Lancelot Addison, *The First State of Mahumedism* (1679) 121); cp. 'Epilogue to *Constantine the Great*' ll. 40–5; and John Ogilby, *Africa* (1670) 37. For a contemporary Catholic association of Islam with Antichrist, see Anne Barbeau Gardiner, *Restoration* xv (1991) 89–98.

i 377. Mussulman] Muslim. *fat*] For the sexual connotations see i 45*n*.

i 378. Arabian prophet] Muhammad.

i 380. Martin Luther (1483–1546) was the leader of the Reformation in Germany. *jolly*] lustful (*OED* 7).

i 381. Alcoran] The Koran (the usual seventeenth-century form of the word). Luther was interested in the Koran, and published a translation of it with a prologue and epilogue of his own in 1542 (*Luther's Works*, edited by Jaroslav Pelikan and Helmut T. Lehmann, 55 vols (1955–76) xliii 235 n. 24). He thought

To grub the thorns beneath our tender feet,
And make the paths of paradise more sweet;
Bethought him of a wife ere halfway gone,
385 For 'twas uneasy travailing alone;
And in this masquerade of mirth and love
Mistook the bliss of heaven for Bacchanals above.
Sure he presumed of praise who came to stock
Th' ethereal pastures with so fair a flock,
390 Burnished and battening on their food, to show
The diligence of careful herds below.
    Our Panther, though like these she changed her
      head,
Yet, as the mistress of a monarch's bed,
Her front erect with majesty she bore,
395 The crozier wielded and the mitre wore.

---

it blasphemous, and a work of 'mere human reason, without the Word of God and His Spirit', but his dictum that 'To fight against the Turks is to fight against God's visitation upon our iniquities' was condemned as heretical by the Pope. He also said that the Turk might be rightly regarded as a divinely constituted authority, at least by his own subjects: cp. *The Medal* l. 104 (George W. Forell, *Church History* xiv (1945) 256–71, at 263 and 257; Harvey Buchanan, *Archiv für Reformationsgeschichte* xlvii (1956) 145–60, at 150). D. associates Luther and Islam again at ii 116–36.

i 382. *grub*] grub up, remove.

i 384. Luther married the former nun Catherine von Bora in 1525, more than halfway through his life.

i 385. *travailing*] This is the spelling of *1687*, which in modern spelling could be either 'travailing' (labouring) or 'travelling' (i.e. on the Christian path). *Works* rightly suspects a sexual innuendo in *travailing*: it frequently refers to vigorous sexual activity (see Gordon Williams, *A Dictionary of Sexual Language and Imagery in Shakespearean and Stuart Literature* (1994) 1417).

i 387. *Bacchanals*] drunken revelry (from Bacchus, god of wine).

i 388. *presumed of*] expected, looked for (*OED* 7).

i 390. *Burnished*] grown plump (*OED* v.²). *battening*] feeding (greedily) (*OED*).

i 391. *herds*] herdsmen, shepherds (*OED* sb.²).

i 392. *these*] German Protestant churches and English Nonconformist sects. *changed her head*] rejected the Pope as head of the church.

i 394. *front*] forehead, face (*OED* 1, 2); also with implications of confidence (*OED* 3), and effrontery and impudence (*OED* 4).

i 395–9. The Church of England, by retaining episcopacy, claimed to be continuing unbroken the ancient traditions of the catholic church. The *crozier* and *mitre* are emblems of episcopacy; the former is the crook which symbolizes the bishop's pastoral care for his flock.

Her upper part of decent discipline
Showed affectation of an ancient line;
And fathers, councils, church, and church's head
Were on her reverend phylacteries read.
400   But what disgraced and disavowed the rest
Was Calvin's brand, that stigmatized the beast.
Thus, like a creature of a double kind,
In her own labyrinth she lives confined.
To foreign lands no sound of her is come,

i 396–400. upper part . . . the rest] D. imagines the Church of England as an allegorical figure, noble and decent to the waist, but indecent and bestial below. In
this she resembles Milton's Sin (*PL* ii 650–3), Spenser's Error (*FQ* I i 14), and
Phineas Fletcher's Hamartia (Error or Sin): 'A woman seemed she in her upper
part; / To which she could such lying gloss impart, / That thousands she had
slain with her deceiving art. // The rest (though hid) in serpents' form arrayed,
/ With iron scales, like to a plaited mail: / Over her back her knotty tail displayed, / Along the empty air did lofty sail: / The end was pointed with a double
sting, / Which with such dreaded might she wont to fling, / That nought could
help the wound, but bloud of heav'nly king' (*The Purple Island* (1633) xii 27–31;
from Fowler's note on *PL* ii 650–66).
i 396. decent] seemly, fitting, appropriate (*OED* 1).
i 397. affectation] studied display (*OED* 3, citing this line); false display, pretence
(*OED* 5).
i 399. In Revelation xiii 1 the beast has 'upon his heads the name of blasphemy'.
phylacteries] small leather boxes containing four texts of scripture written in Hebrew
letters on vellum, worn on the forehead by Jews during prayer. Because of the
association of the phylacteries with the Pharisees' outward displays of holiness (see
Matthew xxiii 5), they came to stand for ostentatious and hypocritical displays
of piety (*OED* 1b, citing this line). The word is usually stressed on the second
syllable, but Christie points out that here it is stressed on the third syllable, as in
the Greek φυλακτήριον. *MS* reads this as a specific reference to the '39 articles'.
i 400. disgraced] marred the grace of, disfigured (*OED* 1), with reference here to
both physical and spiritual grace.   *disavowed*] denied, refused to acknowledge as
valid (*OED* 2).
i 401. Referring to the beast of Revelation xiii, and those men who carry his
'mark'; cp. i 537*n*.   *Calvin's brand*] See i 181*n*.   *stigmatized*] branded with a hot
iron, a punishment carried out on the faces of criminals to mark their infamy.
i 402–3. In Greek legend the Minotaur was a creature with the head of a bull
and the body of a man, which lived in the labyrinth on Crete. It was the offspring of a sexual union between Pasiphae (wife of King Minos) and a bull.
Alexander Ross records an allegorical interpretation of the Minotaur: '*Pasiphae*
or knowledge of man fell in love with the Bull, that is, with Satan and his
cunning suggestions, and by this means the *Minotaur*, or monster of sin, was
procreated, being the deformed issue of Satan, and mans corrupted nature, and so
his soul and knowledge became a captive, and was inclosed in the labyrinth . . .
till Christ came . . . who killed the *Minotaur* of sin' (Ross 293).
i 404. The Church of England's failure to win converts abroad shows that it fails
the test of universality, which was one of the four notes (distinguishing marks)
of the church: see further ii 266–7*n* and 526*n*.

405   Humbly content to be despised at home.
       Such is her faith; where good cannot be had,
       At least she leaves the refuse of the bad.
       Nice in her choice of ill, though not of best,
       And least deformed because reformed the least.
410   In doubtful points betwixt her differing friends,

i 405. 'A good example of Dryden's παρὰ προσδοκίαν [contrary to expectations] sarcasms. We should have expected "admired" ' (Williams).

i 408. Nice] refined, discriminating.

i 410–29. This passage focuses on the Church of England's attempt to accommodate different doctrines of the Eucharist. Debate hinged on how to interpret the significance of the Last Supper (Matthew xxvi 26–8), and in particular Jesus' words, 'Take, eat, this is my body'. The medieval church agreed that the consecration of the bread and wine effected a change in their 'substance' into the body and blood of Christ, whereas their 'accidents' (outward appearance) remained unchanged: this was the doctrine of transubstantiation, which continued to be maintained by the Roman Catholic Church after the Reformation: see i 83–6*n*. Early Protestant teaching on the Eucharist was not unanimous. Luther argued for consubstantiation, whereby after consecration the substance of the bread and wine and the substance of Christ's body and blood coexist; Zwingli maintained that the Eucharist was a purely commemorative rite, with no change occurring to the elements; Calvin taught that although no change occurred to the bread and wine, the communicant received the power of the body and blood of Christ. In the Communion Service according to the 1662 Book of Common Prayer, the prayer of consecration, the words of administration, and the prayers of thanksgiving are carefully worded so as to avoid any precise description of the nature of the consecrated elements, but permit a range of interpretation from transubstantiation to Calvinist doctrine, and such a range of belief persisted within the seventeenth-century Church of England. (The Nonconformist sects placed little emphasis on the Eucharist, and generally held it as a commemoration of the Last Supper and the ensuing Passion.) Transubstantiation, however, is apparently denied in no. 28 of the Thirty-Nine Articles of Religion in the Anglican Book of Common Prayer: 'to such as rightly, worthily, and with faith, receive the same, the Bread which we break is a partaking of the Body of Christ . . . Transubstantiation (or the change of the substance of Bread and Wine) in the Supper of the Lord, cannot be proved by holy Writ; but it is repugnant to the plain words of Scripture, overthroweth the nature of a Sacrament, and hath given occasion to many superstitions. The Body of Christ is given, taken, and eaten, in the Supper, only after an heavenly and spiritual manner'. (The Anglican Articles of Religion were frequently the focus of controversy between Protestants and Catholics: see Tavard 113–42.) In the Catechism in the Book of Common Prayer (in words echoed by D. in ll. 417–22) a sacrament is defined as 'an outward and visible sign of an inward and spiritual grace', and in the case of the Communion 'the inward part, or the thing signified' is said to be 'The Body and Blood of Christ, which are verily and indeed taken and received by the faithful'. D.'s argument rests on the premise that if the bread and wine are signs of the body and blood of Christ, then logically they cannot be transubstantiated into or consubstantial with that body and blood, since a sign is normally considered to be other than that which it represents: a sign cannot also be the substance signified. See further Donald R. Benson, *JHI* xliii (1982) 195–208.

Where one for substance, one for sign contends,
Their contradicting terms she strives to join,
Sign shall be substance, substance shall be sign.
A real presence all her sons allow,
415   And yet 'tis flat idolatry to bow,
Because the godhead's there they know not how.
Her novices are taught that bread and wine
Are but the visible and outward sign
Received by those who in communion join.
420   But th' inward grace, or the thing signified,
His blood and body who to save us died,
The faithful this thing signified receive.
What is't those faithful then partake or leave?
For what is signified and understood
425   Is, by her own confession, flesh and blood.
Then, by the same acknowledgement, we know
They take the sign and take the substance too.
The literal sense is hard to flesh and blood,
But nonsense never can be understood.
430   Her wild belief on every wave is tossed,

i 414. real presence] A term used in Anglican Eucharistic theology to maintain that the body and blood of Christ are truly present in the consecrated elements, rather than only being symbolized by them. It avoids the question of how that presence is conceptualized.

i 415. Roman Catholic devotion included bowing or genuflecting to the consecrated elements during the mass, and when the host was carried in procession on the feast of Corpus Christi. These practices were condemned as idolatrous by Protestants: the Articles of Religion say that 'the Sacrament of the Lord's Supper was not by Christ's ordinance reserved, carried about, lifted up, or worshipped'.

i 417. Her novices] children who learn the catechism as part of their preparation for confirmation.

i 428–9. The Roman Catholic position is authoritatively explained by Bossuet: 'The real presence of the Body and Blood of our Saviour is solidly established by the words of the Institution [i.e. Matthew xxvi 26–8], which we understand literally . . . It is their parts, who have recourse to the figurative sense, and who take by-paths, to give a reason for what they do . . . So that we rest precisely upon his words, not troubling our selves how he will execute what he has said. He who does what he will, by speaking does what he pleases; and it was more easie for the Son of God to force the Laws of Nature to verify his word, than it is for us to accommodate our understandings to these kind of violent Interpretations, which break the Laws of common Discourse' (James Benigne Bossuet, *An Exposition of the Doctrine of the Catholic Church in Matters of Controversie* (1685) 18–20).

i 430. 'For he that wavereth is like a wave of the sea driven with the wind and tossed' (James i 6).

But sure no church can better morals boast.
True to her king her principles are found;
O that her practice were but half so sound!
Steadfast in various turns of state she stood,
435 And sealed her vowed affection with her blood;
Nor will I meanly tax her constancy ⎫
That interest or obligement made the tie, ⎬
Bound to the fate of murdered monarchy. ⎭
Before the sounding axe so falls the vine
440 Whose tender branches round the poplar twine.
She chose her ruin, and resigned her life,
In death undaunted as an Indian wife.
A rare example, but some souls we see
Grow hard and stiffen with adversity:
445 Yet these by Fortune's favours are undone, ⎫
Resolved into a baser form they run, ⎬
And bore the wind, but cannot bear the sun. ⎭
Let this be nature's frailty, or her fate,
Or *Isgrim's counsel, her new-chosen mate;   *The Wolf.
450 Still she's the fairest of the fallen crew,
No mother more indulgent but the true.

i 434–8. Most Anglican clergy were loyal to Charles I during the Civil War, many being ejected from their livings during the Commonwealth. The restoration of the monarchy in 1660 was accompanied by the re-establishment of the Church of England and of episcopal authority.

i 436. tax] reproach.

i 437. interest] self-interest.   *obligement*] compulsion (*OED* 3, citing only Milton's *Of Reformation*).

i 439–40. For the practice of training vines around poplars cp. 'Horace: *Epode* II' ll. 18–19. For political and ecclesiastical applications of such arboreal imagery cp. contemporary engravings of the parable of Jotham (from Judges ix) in which the vine refuses to rule the other trees; and of the tree of the catholic church, its branches and false offshoots (*ΒΑΣΙΛΙΚΑ. The Workes of King Charles the Martyr* (1662) plates after 51 and 412).

i 442. Alluding to the Indian practice of suttee, in which a widow immolates herself on her husband's funeral pyre.

i 443–6. The idea had previously been used in *Astraea Redux* ll. 95–6.

i 446. Resolved] dissolved, melted (*OED* 5).

i 447. In one of Aesop's fables the sun and the wind agree to test which of them is the stronger by trying to remove a cloak from a traveller; the sun wins. *the wind*] 'Cromwell' *MS*. *the sun*] The favourable conditions which the Church of England enjoyed after 1660.

i 449. Isgrim] A name for the wolf found in *Reynard the Fox*, a work said to have been admired by D. (Malone I i 512–13).

i 451. i.e. only the true mother, the Church of Rome, would be more forgiving. For the church as mother see Epigraph, *n*.

Fierce to her foes, yet fears her force to try,
Because she wants innate authority;
For how can she constrain them to obey
455   Who has herself cast off the lawful sway?
Rebellion equals all, and those who toil
In common theft will share the common spoil.
Let her produce the title and the right
Against her old superiors first to fight;
460   If she reform by text, ev'n that's as plain
For her own rebels to reform again.
As long as words a different sense will bear,
And each may be his own interpreter,
Our airy faith will no foundation find:
465   The word's a weathercock for every wind.
The Bear, the Fox, the Wolf by turns prevail,
The most in power supplies the present gale.
The wretched Panther cries aloud for aid

i 453. The question of authority was one of the principal points debated between Protestants and Catholics (for the books on this topic see Jones, *Catalogue* 218–97). The Roman Catholic Church claimed her authority to be derived from Christ's commission to Peter (see i 493–6n below) by unbroken apostolic succession and continuity of teaching. Protestants claimed that scripture was the sole authority for doctrine, yet could not demonstrate that their interpretations of scripture were authoritative: their claims to be guided by the Holy Spirit were unverifiable, and led to the proliferation of mutually contradictory teachings. Cressy commented: 'hitherto never has there beene made an agreement in any one controversy among them [the Protestant churches] . . . if two *Protestants* quarrell, each of them will interpret and iudge both for himselfe and his adversary too, there being no umpire betweene them, nor nothing to oblige them to Communion' (*Exomologesis* 104). *wants*] lacks.
i 454–5. obey / . . . sway] These rhymes echo Marvell's lines on Cromwell in 'An Horatian Ode': 'How fit he is to sway / That can so well obey' (ll. 83–4). For D.'s repeated use of Marvell's poem when writing about subjects rebelling against their kings see *AM* ll. 849–60n.
i 456. equals] equalizes, brings [down] to the same level (*OED* 1).
i 462–7. The problem of disparate interpretations of scripture among Protestants had troubled D. earlier, in *RL* ll. 400–26.
i 468–71. The Church of Rome held that tradition, especially as embodied in the church fathers and the councils, provided a secure guide in matters of doctrine and the interpretation of scripture. Anglican theologians respected the fathers, and upheld the authority of the first four (or sometimes six) ecumenical councils, but no. 21 of the Articles of Religion said that 'General Councils . . . may err, and sometimes have erred . . . Wherefore things ordained by them as necessary to salvation have neither strength nor authority, unless it may be declared that they be taken out of holy Scripture'. Cp. *RL* ll. 334–41n.

To church and councils, whom she first betrayed;
470   No help from fathers or tradition's train,
       Those ancient guides she taught us to disdain;
       And by that scripture which she once abused
       To reformation, stands herself accused.
       What bills for breach of laws can she prefer,
475   Expounding which she owns herself may err?
       And after all her winding ways are tried,   ⎫
       If doubts arise she slips herself aside,   ⎬
       And leaves the private conscience for the guide. ⎭
       If then that conscience set th' offender free,
480   It bars her claim to church authority.
       How can she censure, or what crime pretend,
       But scripture may be construed to defend?
       Ev'n those whom for rebellion she transmits
       To civil power, her doctrine first acquits,
485   Because no disobedience can ensue
       Where no submission to a judge is due;
       Each judging for himself, by her consent,
       Whom thus absolved she sends to punishment.
       Suppose the magistrate revenge her cause,
490   'Tis only for transgressing human laws.
       How answ'ring to its end a church is made
       Whose power is but to counsel and persuade?
       O solid rock on which secure she stands!

i 470. fathers] This could also be modernized as *fathers'*.   *train*] long line.
i 474. bills] indictments, statements of a legal charge.   *prefer*] bring forward.
i 475. owns] admits.
i 481. what crime pretend] what can she claim to be a crime.
i 482. construed] accented on the first syllable in this period (cp. *AA* l. 38).
i 483–5. Calvinist political thought authorized subjects to resist an ungodly ruler: see *RL*, Preface l. 402*n*. The Church of England, however, generally taught submission to the legally constituted civil powers, e.g. in no. 37 of the Articles of Religion, and in the Elizabethan Homily against Rebellion.
i 483. transmits] hands over, i.e. for punishment.
i 493–6. According to Matthew xvi 18–19, Christ said to Peter: 'Thou art Peter, and upon this rock I will build my church; and the gates of hell shall not prevail against it. And I will give unto thee the keys of the kingdom of heaven: and whatsoever thou shalt bind on earth shall be bound in heaven: and whatsoever thou shalt loose on earth shall be loosed in heaven'. (There is a play here in the Greek on the name 'Peter' and πέτρος, a rock.) Cp. also the parable of the house built on sand and the house built upon a rock (Matthew vii 24–7; and cp. *HP* ii 105*n*). This text was frequently cited by Roman Catholic apologists as evidence for the supremacy of the Pope, as the heir of St Peter: recent discussions

Eternal house not built with mortal hands!
495 O sure defence against th' infernal gate,
A patent during pleasure of the state!
      Thus is the Panther neither loved nor feared,
A mere mock queen of a divided herd,
Whom soon by lawful power she might control,
500 Herself a part submitted to the whole.
Then, as the moon who first receives the light
By which she makes our nether regions bright,
So might she shine, reflecting from afar
The rays she borrowed from a better star:
505 Big with the beams which from her mother flow,
And reigning o'er the rising tides below:
Now mixing with a salvage crowd she goes,
And meanly flatters her inveterate foes;
Ruled while she rules, and losing every hour
510 Her wretched remnants of precarious power.
      One evening while the cooler shade she sought,
Revolving many a melancholy thought,
Alone she walked, and looked around in vain
With rueful visage for her vanished train:
515 None of her sylvan subjects made their court,
Levees and couchees passed without resort.

---

by Catholics included Thomas Godden, *A Sermon of St. Peter* (1686), who took
Matthew xvi 18 as his text, and William Clenche, *St. Peter's Supremacy Faithfully
Discuss'd* (1686); an Anglican rejoinder was Symon Patrick, *A Sermon Preached upon
St. Peter's Day* (1687); for others on this topic see Jones, *Catalogue* 257–97.
  i 494. 'We have a building of God, an house not made with hands, eternal in
the heavens' (2 Corinthians v 1).
  i 496. *patent*] [royal] document conferring a privilege or right.   *during pleasure*]
Public officials are often appointed 'during the King's pleasure', i.e. for as long
as the King wishes (*OED* pleasure 5b).
  i 499–506. If the Church of England submitted herself to the authority of Rome,
and became a part of the Catholic (*whole*, i.e. universal) Church, she would be
able to exercise genuine authority over the dissenters, just as the moon shines
with the light which she reflects from the sun; and like the moon controlling
the tides, she would be able to control the rising tides of Nonconformity. For
the lunar imagery cp. *RL* ll. 1–11.
  i 507, 548. *salvage*] See i 156n.
  i 512. *Revolving*] considering, pondering (*OED* 4b).
  i 515. *sylvan subjects*] 'Dissenters' MS.   *sylvan*] of the woods (see i 312–13n).
  i 516. *Levees and couchees*] morning and evening receptions, especially those held
by princes and noblemen for their associates and clients.   *resort*] attendance.

So hardly can usurpers manage well
Those whom they first instructed to rebel:
More liberty begets desire of more,
520   The hunger still increases with the store.
Without respect they brushed along the wood, ⎤
Each in his clan, and filled with loathsome food, ⎬
Asked no permission to the neighbouring flood. ⎦
The Panther, full of inward discontent,
525   Since they would go, before 'em wisely went:
Supplying want of power by drinking first,
As if she gave 'em leave to quench their thirst.
Among the rest, the Hind with fearful face
Beheld from far the common watering place,
530   Nor durst approach; till with an awful roar
The sovereign Lion bade her fear no more.
Encouraged thus she brought her younglings nigh,
Watching the motions of her patron's eye,
And drank a sober draught; the rest amazed
535   Stood mutely still, and on the stranger gazed;
Surveyed her part by part, and sought to find ⎤
The ten-horned monster in the harmless Hind, ⎬
Such as the Wolf and Panther had designed. ⎦
They thought at first they dreamed, for 'twas offence
540   With them to question certitude of sense,
Their guide in faith; but nearer when they drew ⎤
And had the faultless object full in view, ⎬
Lord, how they all admired her heavenly hue! ⎦

i 517. hardly] with difficulty.
i 522. clan] group, party (contemptuously) (OED 2).   loathsome food] i.e. heretical
doctrines.
i 523. to] i.e. to go to.   flood] river, stream (OED 2).
i 526. supplying] making up for.
i 530. awful] awe-inspiring.
i 537. ten-horned monster] The Roman Catholic Church was frequently identified
by Protestants with the beast of the apocalypse: 'And I stood upon the sand of
the sea, and saw a beast rise up out of the sea, having seven heads and ten horns,
and upon his horns ten crowns, and upon his heads the name of blasphemy'
(Revelation xiii 1).
i 538. designed] identified by a description, sign or distinguishing feature (OED
1).
i 540. Alluding to Protestant reliance upon the evidence of the senses when describing the nature of the consecrated bread and wine in the Eucharist (see i 106–9n).
i 543. hue] form, appearance (OED 1).

Some, who before her fellowship disdained,
545 Scarce, and but scarce, from inborn rage restrained,
Now frisked about her, and old kindred feigned.
Whether for love or interest, every sect
Of all the salvage nation showed respect:
The viceroy Panther could not awe the herd,
550 The more the company, the less they feared.
The surly Wolf with secret envy burst,
Yet could not howl, the Hind had seen him first:
But what he durst not speak, the Panther durst.
     For when the herd, sufficed, did late repair
555 To ferny heaths, and to their forest lair,
She made a mannerly excuse to stay,
Proffering the Hind to wait her half the way:
That since the sky was clear, an hour of talk
Might help her to beguile the tedious walk.
560 With much good will the motion was embraced,
To chat awhile on their adventures past:
Nor had the grateful Hind so soon forgot
Her friend and fellow-sufferer in the plot.
Yet wondering how of late she grew estranged,
565 Her forehead cloudy, and her count'nance changed,

i 546. Some Nonconformist sects found themselves making common cause with
the Roman Catholics for liberty of worship and the freedom to hold public office,
while still being opposed to their theology; see 'To the Reader' l. 23n.
i 549. viceroy] The Church of England cannot subdue the sects because she has
neither the spiritual authority of the Pope nor the temporal power of the King;
since the King is head of the Church of England, the church herself is inevitably
only a viceroy.
i 551–2. 'If a Wolf first see a man, the man is silent, and cannot speak, but if the
man see the Wolf, the Wolf is silent and cannot cry' (Topsel 573; Works). The
idea was proverbial in both classical and Renaissance times (Franzius 161; Tilley
W 621). envy] enmity, hostile feeling (OED 1).
i 554. sufficed] having drunk sufficiently.
i 557. Proffering] offering. wait] escort, attend upon, accompany respectfully (OED 10).
i 559. beguile] pass pleasantly (OED 5).
i 560. motion] proposal.
i 563. plot] The Popish Plot (1678) was supposedly a conspiracy to assassinate
Charles II, overthrow the government, and impose Catholicism. It was largely
fabricated by Titus Oates with assistance from William Bedloe. Over a period of
three years many Catholics were tried and some 35 executed; Anglicans were
also caught up in the terror, and many (like D. at that time) doubted Oates's
claims and were sympathetic to his victims. See AA ll. 108n, 632–77n. However,
MS glosses this as 'Oliver's Usurpation'.
i 565. cloudy] sullen, frowning (OED 6).

She thought this hour th' occasion would present
To learn her secret cause of discontent,
Which well she hoped might be with ease redressed, ⎤
Considering her a well-bred civil beast, ⎟
570 And more a gentlewoman than the rest. ⎬
After some common talk what rumours ran, ⎟
The lady of the spotted muff began. ⎦

The Hind and the Panther

The Second Part

'Dame,' said the Panther, 'times are mended well
Since late among the Philistines you fell;
The toils were pitched, a spacious tract of ground
With expert huntsmen was encompassed round;
5   Th' enclosure narrowed, the sagacious power
Of hounds and death drew nearer every hour.
'Tis true, the younger Lion 'scaped the snare,

---

i 572. *muff*] Since muffs were made of fur, D. imagines the Panther as already
provided with a fashionable spotted muff, as her paws are covered in fur. The
conceit associates the Church of England with worldly luxury, contrasting with
the Hind's *heavenly hue* (l. 543).

The Second Part
ii 1. *Dame*] Lady, Madam; a respectful (though perhaps somewhat archaic) mode
of address; the word declined in its social application from the nobility to the
bourgeoisie in the course of the seventeenth century (*OED* 5).
ii 2. *late*] lately.   *Philistines*] Biblically, the enemies of the Israelites; here the enemies of the Roman Catholics, particularly during the Popish Plot (see i 563n).
ii 3–6. The imagery is biblical: 'The sorrows of death compassed me, and the
floods of ungodly men made me afraid . . . the snares of death prevented me' (Psalm
xviii 4–5).
ii 3. *toils*] nets set up to enclose an area into which the quarry can be driven.
ii 5–6. *sagacious power / Of hounds*] Williams compares Virgil, *odora canum vis* ('smelling
power of dogs': *Aen.* iv 132).   *sagacious*] acute in perception by smell (*OED* 1).
ii 7. *the younger Lion*] James II, who at the time of the Popish Plot was Duke of
York and the younger brother of the reigning King Charles II. (For James as a lion
see i 41n.) He was in danger of being associated with the Plot, since the discovery
of the correspondence of his former secretary Edward Coleman revealed that
the latter had been plotting with various parties abroad for the re-establishment
of Catholicism in England. James managed to dissociate himself from Coleman,
who was executed on 3 December 1678. (Coleman had been an undergraduate
contemporary of D. at Trinity College, Cambridge.) Cp. *RL*, Preface l. 208n.

But all your priestly calves lay struggling there,
As sacrifices on their altars laid,
10   While you their careful mother wisely fled,
Not trusting destiny to save your head.
For, whate'er promises you have applied
To your unfailing church, the surer side
Is four fair legs in danger to provide;
15   And whate'er tales of Peter's chair you tell,
Yet, saving reverence of the miracle,
The better luck was yours to 'scape so well.'
     'As I remember,' said the sober Hind,
'Those toils were for your own dear self designed
20   As well as me; and with the self-same throw
To catch the quarry and the vermin too
(Forgive the slanderous tongues that called you so).
Howe'er you take it now, the common cry
Then ran you down for your rank loyalty;
25   Besides, in popery they thought you nursed,
(As evil tongues will ever speak the worst)
Because some forms, and ceremonies some
You kept, and stood in the main question dumb.

---

ii 8. priestly calves] Five Jesuit priests, including the Provincial of the English Jesuits Thomas Whitbread, were executed on 20 June 1679. In all, some fifteen priests were executed during the Popish Plot scare, and others died in prison. *calves*] applied to young deer in their first year of life (*OED* 3).

ii 10. It is difficult to substantiate the Panther's insinuation that the Catholic Church deserted her priests, or the priests their people. Certainly many English priests worked abroad, and there was no hierarchy based in England.

ii 15. Peter's chair] Roman Catholic teaching holds that pronouncements made by the Pope *ex cathedra* (from the chair [of St Peter]) are infallible.

ii 16. saving reverence] An apologetic phrase used to introduce an expression which might cause offence (*OED* reverence 5).   *miracle*] i.e. of infallibility; but the Panther is mischievously stretching the idea to include invulnerability.

ii 20. throw] cast of the net (*OED* 7b, citing this example).

ii 21. quarry . . . vermin] The Hind is the *quarry*, which is pursued by the hounds, whereas the Panther belongs to the category of *vermin*, noxious creatures which are not hunted as game but destroyed as a nuisance because they themselves prey on game.

ii 22. slanderous tongues] 'Presbyterians' *MS*.

ii 23. cry] public voice, popular opinion (*OED* 7b, 8); yelping of hounds in the chase (*OED* 12); pack of hounds (*OED* 13).

ii 24. rank] stout, strong (*OED* 2); absolute, downright (*OED* 15); highly offensive (*OED* 14).

ii 27–8. Some forms and ceremonies used by the Roman Catholic Church were retained or adapted by the Church of England in its worship. The phrasing of l. 27 echoes the heading of the prefatory explanation in the Book of Common

Dumb you were born indeed, but thinking long
30 The Test it seems at last has loosed your tongue;
And to explain what your forefathers meant
By real presence in the sacrament
(After long fencing, pushed against a wall)
Your salvo comes: that he's not there at all.
35 There changed your faith, and what may change
     may fall.
Who can believe what varies every day,
Nor ever was, nor will be, at a stay?'
     'Tortures may force the tongue untruths to tell,
And I ne'er owned myself infallible,'
40 Replied the Panther. 'Grant such presence were,
Yet in your sense I never owned it there.

Prayer, 'Of Ceremonies, why some be abolished, and some retained'. On the *main question* of the doctrine of the Eucharist, the Church of England was hardly silent, but gave no clear and single answer. It referred matters of doctrine to scripture for settlement, but that provided only a *dumb rule* (ii 203) which required interpretation.

ii 30. The Test Act of 1673 required holders of public office to abjure the doctrine of transubstantiation; this was made more explicit in the 1678 Act, which required this oath: 'I, A.B., do solemnly and sincerely in the presence of God profess, testify and declare that I do believe that in the sacrament of the Lord's Supper there is not any transubstantiation of the elements of bread and wine into the body and blood of Christ at or after the consecration thereof by any person whatsoever; and . . . I do make this declaration and every part thereof in the plain and ordinary sense of the words read unto me, as they are commonly understood by English Protestants, without any evasion, equivocation or mental reservation whatsoever' (*English Historical Documents* 392). The terms of this oath not only precluded Catholics from taking it (as intended), but also ruled out certain Anglican interpretations of Eucharistic doctrine (cp. i 410–29*n*).

ii 33. *fencing*] evading (*OED* fence 1d).

ii 34. *salvo*] explanation of a difficulty (*OED* 3). *Works* explains *salvo* as 'a quibbling evasion or riddling rejoinder', but the Hind's point here is the opposite, namely that the Panther, after much evasion, has been compelled to deliver a clear answer to this difficult question. The *OED*'s citations suggest that the word was predominantly used in a pejorative sense, i.e. for a dishonest or unsatisfactory way of resolving a difficulty or discharging an obligation.

ii 37. *at a stay*] in an unchanging state (*OED* 7). The *OED* notes the influential usage of *stay* from 'Man that is born of a woman . . . never continueth in one stay' (Service for the Burial of the Dead in the Book of Common Prayer). The implication of the Hind's comment is therefore that the Church of England's doctrines are both changeable and human, whereas those of the Church of Rome are unchanging and God-given.

ii 39. *owned*] claimed (*OED* 3c or 5).

ii 41. *owned*] acknowledged as a fact, admitted to be true (*OED* 5).

A real virtue we by faith receive,
And that we in the sacrament believe.'
    Then said the Hind, 'As you the matter state,
45   Not only Jesuits can equivocate;
For "real", as you now the word expound,
From solid substance dwindles to a sound.
Methinks an Aesop's fable you repeat:
You know who took the shadow for the meat.
50   Your church's substance thus you change at will,
And yet retain your former figure still.
I freely grant you spoke to save your life,

ii 42. virtue] strength or power to live a good life (*OED* 9c). The Articles of Religion say that through sacraments such as the Eucharist, God 'doth work invisibly in us, and doth not only quicken, but also strengthen and confirm our Faith in him' (no. 25). Gardiner 239–40 notes that the word *virtue* (which is italicized in *1687*) had a special place in debates over the Real Presence. Originating with Zwingli (see i 180*n*, 410–29*n*), the term denoted that the presence of Christ in the sacrament was virtual or figurative.

ii 43. i.e. 'and that [virtue] we believe to be inherent in the sacrament'.

ii 45. The Jesuits were considered notorious for equivocation, i.e. answering questions with ambiguous words or attaching mental reservations to their answers. Cp. *RL*, Preface ll. 219–20*n*. D. purchased a tract against Jesuit equivocation by the Benedictine John Barnes, *Dissertatio contra Aequivocationes* (1625), at auction in 1680 (Birrell 199). Another Benedictine, Corker, wrote: 'The Doctrine of *Equivocation* or Mental Reservation, however wrongfully Imposed on the *Catholick Religion*, is notwithstanding, neither taught, nor approved by the Church, as any part of her Belief. On the contrary, *Simplicity and Godly Sincerity* are constantly recommended by her as truly *Christian Vertues*, necessary to the Conservation of *Justice, Truth, and Common Society*' (*Roman-Catholick Principles* 11–12). Cp. ii 678.

ii 46–7. To the Hind, *real* in the doctrine of the 'real presence' signifies the actual physical presence of the substance of Christ's body and blood; the Panther is using *real* to mean 'spiritually true'. Cp. Woodhead quoted in i 83–6*n*.

ii 48–9. In Aesop's fable of the dog and the shadow, the dog, which is carrying a shoulder of mutton in its mouth, lets it fall as it tries to seize the reflection of the meat in the water.   *shadow*] reflected image (*OED* 5a); delusive image, unsubstantial object (*OED* 6).

ii 50–1. i.e. the Church of England has not only changed from defining the real presence as substantial to seeing it as figurative; this is part of a larger change, for it has retained its previous Catholic appearance (*former figure* here referring to its preservation of episcopacy and certain elements of Catholic worship) while changing its *substance* (its doctrine).

ii 52–5. D. refers to the plight of the Church of England under Mary I, when many Protestants recanted and embraced Catholic doctrine in the face of torture and execution. However, *MS* in its gloss on l. 53 interprets this as a reference to the Civil War and Commonwealth: 'The Presbyter. were for turning out Bps'.

For then you lay beneath the butcher's knife.
Long time you fought, redoubled battery bore,
55   But, after all, against yourself you swore;
Your former self—for every hour your form
Is chopped and changed, like winds before a storm.
Thus fear and interest will prevail with some,
For all have not the gift of martyrdom.'
60   The Panther grinned at this, and thus replied,
'That men may err was never yet denied.
But if that common principle be true,
The cannon, dame, is levelled full at you.
But shunning long disputes, I fain would see
65   That wondrous wight Infallibility.
Is he from heaven, this mighty champion, come,
Or lodged below in subterranean Rome?
First seat him somewhere, and derive his race,
Or else conclude that nothing has no place.'
70   'Suppose (though I disown it),' said the Hind,
'The certain mansion were not yet assigned,
The doubtful residence no proof can bring

ii 57. St Paul wrote that the ministry was established so that 'we henceforth be no more children, tossed to and fro, and carried about with every wind of doctrine' (Ephesians iv 14; *Works*).
ii 58. Cp. iii 384 and *AA* l. 724.
ii 60. *grinned*] bared her teeth in pain or anger (*OED* 1a).
ii 61. *That men may err*] A common proverb (Tilley E 179).
ii 63. *cannon*] Punning on 'canon', in the sense of *common principle* (*OED* 2) (Williams).
ii 65. *wight*] person.
ii 67. *subterranean Rome*] In his book *Roma Sotterranea* (1632; revised by Paulus Aringhus as *Roma Subterranea Novissima*, 2 vols (1659); English translation 1659) Antonio Bosio described and illustrated the catacombs of Rome in which the early Christians hid, worshipped, and buried their dead. This work was cited in controversies between Catholics and Protestants as to whether their churches were being faithful to the practices of the early church. Evelyn describes a visit to these catacombs in his diary for 1 May 1645. Aringhus' book emphasizes links between the Roman Catholic Church and classical Rome, e.g. visually in its frontispiece (for which see Hammond 132 and plate 5), and in a picture of the First Roman Council being held in the Baths of Trajan (ii 182–3), and by recording the establishment of the papacy in Rome and the rebellion of the Church of England under Henry VIII (ii 29, 155–6).
ii 69. An adaptation of the Aristotelian principle that things which exist are somewhere, and the non-existent nowhere (*Physics* 208a).
ii 71. *mansion*] place of abode (*OED* 2).
ii 72–3. i.e., that we are unable to locate the place of something is no proof that it does not exist.

Against the plain existence of the thing.
Because philosophers may disagree   ⎫
75   If sight b' emission or reception be,   ⎬
Shall it be thence inferred I do not see? ⎭
But you require an answer positive,   ⎫
Which yet, when I demand, you dare not give, ⎬
For fallacies in universals live.   ⎭
80   I then affirm that this unfailing guide
In pope and general councils must reside;
Both lawful, both combined: what one decrees, ⎫
By numerous votes the other ratifies: ⎬
On this undoubted sense the church relies. ⎭

ii 74–6. D.'s contemporaries still debated whether sight happened by the eye emitting a beam which struck the object, or the object emitting a beam which was received by the eye. Cp. 'Sigismonda and Guiscardo' l. 64*n*. Cp. Thomas White: 'The *Platonists* and *Peripateticks* are divided about *the manner of vision*; *Aristotle* teaching, that the object works upon the eye; *Plato*, that the eye sends out a line of Spirits or rays to the object: Yet nothing were more ridiculous than to affirm, the *Platonists* saw in one fashion, the Peripateticks in another' (*An Apology for Rushworth's Dialogues* (1654) 38–9; Hamm).

ii 79. For this principle of argument cp. *AM*, 'Account' l. 98*n*.

ii 80–95. The Hind refers to four ways in which theologians have located infallibility: (i) in the pronouncements of the Pope ratified by a general council (ll. 80–4), which is the Hind's preferred explanation; (ii) and (iii) in either the Pope acting alone or a council acting alone (ll. 85–6), which the Hind rejects as too narrow a location for such authority; (iv) in the pronouncements of the Pope once they are ratified by a council and accepted by the church at large (ll. 87–92), which the Hind rejects as too wide a definition, since the wider church is represented by the council and so obliged to accept its decisions. The fourth of these interpretations was that promoted by the Gallican (French) clergy in 1682, when the French Assembly said that the primacy of the see of Rome was limited by general councils and the bishops, whose assent was needed before papal decrees could be regarded as authoritative. The problem had been raised by Protestant writers; Cressy cites this argument from William Chillingworth's *The Religion of Protestants* (in order to rebut it): 'Some of you say the Pope alone without a Councell may determine all Controversies: but others deny it. Some that a Generall Councell without a Pope may doe so: Others deny this. Some, both in coniunction are infallible determiners: others againe deny this. Lastly some among you hold the acceptation of the decrees of Councells by the universall Church to be the onely way to decide controversies' (*Exomologesis* 442). John Gother stated the basic Catholic position: 'He believes that the Pastors and Prelates of his Church are *Fallible* . . . but that the whole Church can fail, or be deceiv'd in any one Point of Faith, this he believes impossible; knowing it to be built on *better promises*; such as secure her from all *Error*, and danger of *Prevarication*' (*A Papist Mis-represented and Represented* (1685) 36). For contemporary discussions of infallibility see Jones, *Catalogue* 218–48.

85   'Tis true, some doctors in a scantier space
      (I mean in each apart) contract the place;
      Some, who to greater length extend the line,
      The church's after-acceptation join.
      This last circumference appears too wide:
90   The church diffused is by the council tied,
      As members by their representatives
      Obliged to laws which prince and senate gives.
      Thus some contract, and some enlarge the space; ⎤
      In pope and council who denies the place,   ⎟
95   Assisted from above with God's unfailing grace? ⎦
      Those canons all the needful points contain,
      Their sense so obvious, and their words so plain,
      That no disputes about the doubtful text
      Have hitherto the labouring world perplexed.
100   If any should in after-times appear,
      New councils must be called to make the meaning clear;
      Because in them the power supreme resides,
      And all the promises are to the guides.

ii 85–6. For the phrasing cp. Isaac Barrow: 'I know there are within the Roman communion great store of divines, who do contract the papal sovereignty within a much narrower compass' (*A Treatise of the Pope's Supremacy* (1680) xv; Kinsley).
ii 85. *doctors*] i.e. of divinity.
ii 88. *after-acceptation*] subsequent acceptance.
ii 90–2. 'Councils (wherein are some Dissenters) if accepted by a much Major part of the Church diffusive, do conclude the whole and oblige Obedience' (Woodhead, *A Rational Account* (1673) 21–2; Hamm).
ii 92. *prince and senate gives*] In the English constitution laws are made by the crown in Parliament, hence *prince and senate* is a single entity and takes a singular verb.
ii 93–5. i.e. some theologians take a broader view of the location of infallibility than others, but no one denies that it is located in Pope and council inspired from heaven by God's infallible grace.
ii 96–9. This argument echoes the Protestant claim that scripture contains all that is necessary for salvation and is sufficiently clear in all crucial matters: the Anglican Articles of Religion say that 'Holy Scripture containeth all things necessary to salvation: so that whatsoever is not read therein, nor may be proved thereby, is not to be required of any man, that it should be believed as an article of the Faith, or be thought requisite or necessary to salvation' (no. 6). (See also *HP* ii 108–10, 143–4; *RL* ll. 297–300 and *nn.*) But whereas disputes over the meaning of scripture have been legion (ii 111–27), no such disputes have arisen about the interpretation of ecclesiastical canons.   *canons*] pronouncements of ecclesiastical councils.
ii 103. Christ's promises of divine guidance (e.g. Matthew xvi 18–19, xxviii 19–20; John xiv 16–18) were given to his disciples, who were themselves to become the *guides* of the church, and whose successors were the popes and bishops of the Catholic Church. Woodhead says: 'As concerning our Saviour's *Promises* (from which is collected the Church's *Indefectibility*) all, or most of them are expressly made to the *Guides* of the *Church*; and therefore to the *Church*, as a *Guide*' (*The Guide in Controversies* (1667) 2).

This may be taught with sound and safe defence:
105   But mark how sandy is your own pretence,
Who setting councils, pope and church aside
Are every man his own presuming guide.
The sacred books, you say, are full and plain,
And every needful point of truth contain;
110   All who can read, interpreters may be.
Thus though your several churches disagree,
Yet every saint has to himself alone
The secret of this philosophic stone.
These principles your jarring sects unite,
115   When differing doctors and disciples fight.
Though Luther, Zwinglius, Calvin, holy chiefs
Have made a battle-royal of beliefs,
Or like wild horses several ways have whirled
The tortured text about the Christian world;
120   Each Jehu lashing on with furious force,
That Turk or Jew could not have used it worse.
No matter what dissension leaders make,
Where every private man may save a stake;
Ruled by the scripture and his own advice,

ii 104. *defence*] justification by argument.
ii 105. *sandy*] In Matthew vii 24–7 Christ says that the man who follows his teachings is like one who builds his house upon a rock, whereas the man who hears but ignores them 'shall be likened unto a foolish man, which built his house upon the sand', which soon falls when the rain and winds beat against it. Since the rock is elsewhere a symbol of the secure foundations of the [Catholic] church (see i 493–6*n*), the house built upon sand is for D. a natural symbol of Protestantism. The image is used again at ii 588–90.   *pretence*] claim (*OED* 1); at this date not necessarily an implicitly false claim (again at ii 154).
ii 107. *presuming*] presumptuous.
ii 111. *several*] separate, individual.
ii 112. *saint*] A description applied to themselves by some Nonconformist groups when claiming to be specially endowed with divine grace.
ii 113. *philosophic stone*] The hypothetical philosopher's stone was said by alchemists to convert base metals into gold; numerous charlatans claimed to have discovered it. A definitive Protestant interpretation of scripture would convert argument into truth; like the philosopher's stone it is often claimed, and is similarly elusive.
ii 114. *jarring*] bickering, wrangling (*OED* 12).
ii 120. *Jehu*] 'The driving is like the driving of Jehu the son of Nimshi; for he driveth furiously' (2 Kings ix 20).
ii 123. *save a stake*] ensure that he does not lose what he has wagered (i.e. his soul). The individual may think that by exercising his own judgement in the interpretation of scripture irrespective of what conflicting Protestant leaders may say, he is securing his own salvation; but he is not, and the stakes are too high for a man to take such a risk.

125   Each has a blind by-path to paradise;
       Where driving in a circle slow or fast,
       Opposing sects are sure to meet at last.
       A wondrous charity you have in store,   ⎫
       For all reformed to pass the narrow door: ⎬
130   So much that Mahomet had scarcely more.   ⎭
       For he, kind prophet, was for damning none,
       But Christ and Moses were to save their own.
       Himself was to secure his chosen race,
       Though reason good for Turks to take the place,
135   And he allowed to be the better man
       In virtue of his holier Alcoran.'
            'True,' said the Panther, 'I shall ne'er deny
       My brethren may be saved as well as I:
       Though Huguenots contemn our ordination,
140   Succession, ministerial vocation,
       And Luther, more mistaking what he read,
       Misjoins the sacred body with the bread;
       Yet, lady, still remember I maintain
       The word in needful points is only plain.'
145   'Needless or needful I not now contend,
       For still you have a loophole for a friend,'
       Rejoined the matron, 'but the rule you lay   ⎫
       Has led whole flocks, and leads them still, astray ⎬
       In weighty points, and full damnation's way.   ⎭

ii 125. blind] dark, without light (OED 6); secret, obscure, intricate and twisting, difficult to trace (OED 7, 8); leading nowhere (OED 11). by-path] private path; side path leading away from the highroad. OED cites Thomas More (1528) on evil people leading the flock out of the highway to heaven on a 'bypath to helward'.
ii 128. charity] Christian love; described by St Paul in 1 Corinthians xiii.
ii 129. narrow door] See i 373n.
ii 130–2. In the Koran God promises salvation to the followers of Jesus (Sura 3) and Moses (Sura 7), who were both true prophets.
ii 131. kind] Each of the Suras of the Koran opens with the words 'In the Name of God, the Merciful, the Compassionate'.
ii 133–6. According to the Koran, Muhammad is God's supreme Prophet; his followers will be admitted to paradise (Sura 47). chosen] The Jews were called God's chosen people (cp. ii 393). allowed] acknowledged.
ii 139–40. Huguenot (French Protestant) ministers received classical rather than episcopal ordination (see 'To the Reader' ll. 59–60n), and were appointed by local congregations governed by elders. They rejected the notion of apostolic succession (see i 347–50n). Cp. ii 456–8.
ii 141–2. For Luther's Eucharistic doctrine of consubstantiation see i 410–29n.
ii 143–4. See ii 96–9n.
ii 147. the rule] that scripture may properly be interpreted by individuals.

150   For did not Arius first, Socinus now,
        The Son's eternal godhead disavow,
        And did not these by gospel texts alone
        Condemn our doctrine, and maintain their own?
        Have not all heretics the same pretence
155   To plead the scriptures in their own defence?
        How did the Nicene council then decide
        That strong debate? Was it by scripture tried?
        No, sure; to those the rebel would not yield,
        Squadrons of texts he marshalled in the field;
160   That was but civil war, an equal set
        Where piles with piles, and eagles eagles met.
        With texts point-blank and plain he faced the foe:
        And did not Satan tempt our Saviour so?
        The good old bishops took a simpler way:
165   Each asked but what he heard his father say,
        Or how he was instructed in his youth,
        And by tradition's force upheld the truth.'
           The Panther smiled at this, 'And when,' said she,
        'Were those first councils disallowed by me?
170   Or where did I at sure tradition strike,
        Provided still it were apostolic?'

ii 150–67. For Arius, Socinus, and the Council of Nicaea see i 53*n*.

ii 153. our doctrine] the doctrine of the Trinity.

ii 156–7. Cressy asks whether Protestants can claim that 'the doctrine of Faith concerning the *Blessed Trinity* is as evidently and intelligibly stated in Scripture, as in the first *Councell of Nicée*' (*Exomologesis* 397; Hamm).

ii 160. set] match, contest (*OED* 25b).

ii 161. From Lucan: *pares aquilas et pila minantia pilis* (*De Bello Civili* i 7: 'eagles [i.e. Roman legionary standards] were matched against each other, and pilum threatened pilum'). The Catholic writer Abraham Woodhead uses the same quotation in *The Protestant's Plea for the Socinian* (1686) 18: 'if a Catholick producing the Nicene Council be rencountred by an Arian producing the Council of Ariminum which was far more numerous, here are *aquilis aquilae & pila minantia pilis*' (*Works*; cp. Hamm 412). *piles*] javelins, the weapons of the Roman foot soldiers (*OED sb.*[1] 1c, rendering the Latin *pilum*). Thomas May draws attention to this word in his translation of Lucan (1627): 'Piles against Piles, 'gainst Eagles Eagles fly', adding the note: 'If any man quarrell at the word *Pile*, as thinking it scarce English, I desire them to give a better word' (*OED*).

ii 162. point-blank] aiming straight at the target (*OED* 1); plain (*OED* 2).

ii 163. In Luke iv 10–11 the devil tempts Jesus by quoting scripture to him.

ii 168–9. See i 468–71*n*.

ii 170–1. Anglican theologians would argue that some of the doctrines and practices claimed by the Church of Rome to be sanctioned by tradition could not be traced back by *sure* and certain tradition to *apostolic* times, but were later accretions.

       'Friend,' said the Hind, 'you quit your former ground,
       Where all your faith you did on scripture found;
       Now 'tis tradition joined with holy writ,
175   But thus your memory betrays your wit.'
         'No,' said the Panther, 'for in that I view
       When your tradition's forged, and when 'tis true.
       I set 'em by the rule, and as they square
       Or deviate from undoubted doctrine there,
180   This oral fiction, that old faith declare.'
         Hind: 'The council steered, it seems, a different
           course,
       They tried the scripture by tradition's force;
       But you tradition by the scripture try;
       Pursued by sects, from this to that you fly,
185   Nor dare on one foundation to rely.
       The word is then deposed, and in this view
       You rule the scripture, not the scripture you.'
       Thus said the dame, and smiling, thus pursued:
       'I see tradition then is disallowed,
190   When not evinced by scripture to be true,
       And scripture, as interpreted by you.
       But here you tread upon unfaithful ground,
       Unless you could infallibly expound;
       Which you reject as odious popery,
195   And throw that doctrine back with scorn on me.
       Suppose we on things traditive divide,
       And both appeal to scripture to decide;
       By various texts we both uphold our claim,
       Nay, often ground our titles on the same:
200   After long labour lost, and time's expense,
       Both grant the words, and quarrel for the sense.
       Thus all disputes for ever must depend,

ii *175. wit*] intelligence.
ii *176–80.* The Panther's position is that the veracity of church tradition is tested by seeing whether such teachings square with scripture; this is in line with the Anglican Articles of Religion (see i 468–71*n*).   *rule*] criterion, test (*OED* 10), i.e. of scripture.   *oral*] As in *RL* l. 271 (see *n*) D. assumes that the 'unwritten' tradition of the church was an *oral* tradition.
ii *182. tried*] tested.
ii *189.* The Hind continues to speak.
ii *192. unfaithful*] treacherous, not firm (*OED* 2b); the Panther's position also lacks faith.
ii *196. traditive*] transmitted by tradition.
ii *202. depend*] be in suspense, be undetermined (*OED* 7).

For no dumb rule can controversies end.
Thus when you said tradition must be tried
205   By sacred writ, whose sense yourselves decide,
You said no more but that yourselves must be
The judges of the scripture sense, not we.
Against our church tradition you declare,
And yet your clerks would sit in Moses' chair.
210   At least 'tis proved against your argument
The rule is far from plain, where all dissent.'
      'If not by scriptures, how can we be sure,'
Replied the Panther, 'what tradition's pure?
For you may palm upon us new for old:
215   All, as they say, that glitters is not gold.'
      'How but by following her,' replied the dame,
'To whom derived from sire to son they came;
Where every age does on another move,
And trusts no farther than the next above;
220   Where all the rounds like Jacob's ladder rise,
The lowest hid in earth, the topmost in the skies.'
      Sternly the salvage did her answer mark,
Her glowing eyeballs glittering in the dark,

---

ii 203. *dumb rule*] scripture, which of itself has no voice (and implicitly needs
to be interpreted by the church). Cp. 'the rule is mute' (*RL* l. 315). An earlier,
anonymous, convert had explained that Catholics 'confesse a plaine, easie and
infallible rule, must guide in matters of Faith: they say moreouer that cannot be
any dead or dumbe writing, be it neuer so sacred: for nothing can be written
so plaine but in many clawses or passages it will beare seuerall constructions'
(*An Epistle of A Catholicke Young Gentleman* (1623) 24).
ii 209. Jesus said, 'The scribes and the Pharisees sit in Moses' seat: All therefore
whatsoever they bid you observe, that observe and do: but do not ye after their
works: for they say, and do not' (Matthew xxiii 2–3). *clerks*] clergymen (*OED*
1), scholars (*OED* 4).
ii 212–21. 'A Catholique does not onely or cheifly beleive *the Churches authority*
because to his private understanding and reason the Scripture seemes to say so:
but because he knowes that the present Catholique Church teacheth so both by
profession and practise, and that shee teacheth this as a Catholique Tradition beleived
and practised in all ages: then which it is impossible there should be any testimony
more assured and infallible' (Cressy, *Exomologesis* 468–9; Hamm).
ii 215. Proverbial: Tilley A 146.
ii 217. *they*] traditions.
ii 218. *move*] advance (*OED* 16); appeal to (*OED* 12).
ii 220–1. Jacob dreamed that a ladder was set up on earth, whose top reached
heaven (Genesis xxviii 12).   *rounds*] rungs of a ladder (*OED* 3).
ii 223. Topsel says that 'the greater Pardal hath . . . bright seeing eyes, the apples
whereof do glister under their eye-lids' (449; *Works*).

And said but this: 'Since lucre was your trade,
225 Succeeding times such dreadful gaps have made
'Tis dangerous climbing: to your sons and you
I leave the ladder, and its omen too.'
      Hind: 'The Panther's breath was ever famed for
            sweet,
But from the Wolf such wishes oft I meet:
230 You learned this language from the blatant beast,
Or rather did not speak, but were possessed.
As for your answer, 'tis but barely urged:
You must evince tradition to be forged,
Produce plain proofs, unblemished authors use,
235 As ancient as those ages they accuse.
Till when 'tis not sufficient to defame:
An old possession stands till elder quits the claim.
Then for our interest, which is named alone
To load with envy, we retort your own.
240 For when traditions in your faces fly,
Resolving not to yield, you must decry.
As when the cause goes hard, the guilty man
Excepts, and thins his jury all he can;
So when you stand of other aid bereft,

ii *224. lucre*] The sale of indulgences by the Roman Catholic Church in the six-teenth century had been one of the causes of the Reformation in Germany.
ii *226–7.* Alluding to the ladder on which a condemned man stood when being hanged.
ii *228.* See i 328*n*.
ii *229. Wolf*] the Presbyterians; see i 153*n*.
ii *230. blatant beast*] In Spenser (*FQ* V xii 37) the Blatant Beast represents slander. As Kinsley notes, it is described in *FQ* VI vi 12 as a 'hellish Dog', which assists D.'s association of it here with the Wolf.   *blatant*] The word was coined by Spenser, perhaps from the Latin *blaterare* or *blatire*, both meaning 'to babble'.
ii *231.* Nonconformist Protestants often claimed that their utterances were in-spired by the Holy Spirit; by contrast, *possessed* implies a diabolical source.
ii *232. barely urged*] simply alleged.
ii *233. evince*] prove by argument and evidence (*OED* 4).
ii *237.* i.e. a person's long-standing possession of a property (here, the Roman Catholic Church's claim to define tradition) remains valid until someone with a prior claim makes that possession void.   *quits*] removes (*OED* 9); not 'renounces', as *Works* says, which would invert the meaning of the line.
ii *238–9.* i.e. in reply to your accusation that self-interest (which you focus upon in order to stir up ill-will against us) motivates our attitude to tradition, we retort that self-interest motivates yours.   *envy*] opprobrium, unpopularity (*OED* 1c).
ii *240. in your faces fly*] are directly opposed to your position (*OED* face *sb* 4b).
ii *243. Excepts*] objects to [individual jurors] (*OED* 2).   *thins*] reduces in number (*OED* 3a; its first example since 1440).

245   You to the twelve apostles would be left.
        Your friend the Wolf did with more craft provide
        To set those toys, traditions, quite aside:
        And fathers too, unless when, reason spent,
        He cites 'em but sometimes for ornament.
250   But, madam Panther, you, though more sincere
        Are not so wise as your adulterer:
        The private spirit is a better blind
        Than all the dodging tricks your authors find.
        For they who left the scripture to the crowd,   ⎫
255   Each for his own peculiar judge allowed;   ⎬
        The way to please 'em was to make 'em proud.   ⎭
        Thus with full sails they ran upon the shelf;
        Who could expect a cozenage from himself?
        On his own reason safer 'tis to stand
260   Than be deceived and damned at second hand.
        But you who fathers and traditions take,
        And garble some, and some you quite forsake,
        Pretending church authority to fix,
        And yet some grains of private spirit mix,

ii 245. In ii 168–71 the Panther had claimed to respect councils which were 'apostolic', i.e. maintained the teaching of the apostles and the early fathers. The Hind now misrepresents this position and charges the Panther with recognizing the authority only of Jesus' twelve original apostles (which would thus exclude St Paul, as well as all the early church councils).   *twelve*] as on a jury.

ii 246–7. Presbyterian doctrine was based solely on scripture, and accorded no authority to church tradition.   *toys*] trifles, pieces of nonsense (*OED* 5).

ii 248. when, reason spent] when his rational arguments have been exhausted.

ii 250. sincere] The meanings here include 'pure, unadulterated'.

ii 251. your adulterer] The Wolf, who (a) adulterates pure, traditional doctrine; (b) is sexually promiscuous (see i 193*n*, 338–40*n*, 351–4*nn*, 355–6*n*).

ii 252–60. Cp. *RL* ll. 398–426.

ii 252–3. Williams suggests a recollection of the fable of the fox and the cat, in which the fox boasts that he knows many ways to escape capture (but is nevertheless caught and killed) while the cat knows only one, taking refuge up a tree. The moral is: '*Much Knowledge makes some Mad; / One good Art's better than a thousand bad*' (John Ogilby, *The Fables of Aesop* (1668) 142–3).   *private spirit*] individual judgement, supposedly inspired by the Holy Spirit, on which Presbyterians rely.   *blind*] pretence (*OED* 6).

ii 254. crowd] A pejorative synonym for 'people': cp. *AA* ll. 68, 765; *RL* l. 417.

ii 255. peculiar] particular, individual.

ii 257–8. Echoes *RL* ll. 425–6: 'The danger's much the same, on several shelves / If others wreck us, or we wreck ourselves'.   *shelf*] submerged sandbank or ledge of rock.   *cozenage*] cheat.

ii 263. i.e. claiming to establish and define the authority of the church, as in no. 20 of the Articles of Religion.

265   Are like a mule made up of differing seed,
       And that's the reason why you never breed:
       At least, not propagate your kind abroad,
       For home-dissenters are by statutes awed.
       And yet they grow upon you every day,
270   While you (to speak the best) are at a stay,
       For sects that are extremes abhor a middle way.
       Like tricks of state, to stop a raging flood,
       Or mollify a mad-brained senate's mood:
       Of all expedients never one was good.
275   Well may they argue (nor can you deny),
       "If we must fix on church authority,
       Best on the best, the fountain not the flood,
       That must be better still, if this be good.
       Shall she command who has herself rebelled?
280   Is Antichrist by Antichrist expelled?

ii 265–7. The failure of the Church of England to attract foreign converts is a sign of its lack of true doctrine and authority. Cp. i 404 and see ii 526n. Mules are sterile.

ii 268. Several statutes regulated and constrained dissenters, both Nonconformist and Catholic: the Act of Uniformity (1662) enforced the use of the Book of Common Prayer and provided for the expulsion of dissenting ministers from their livings; the Five Mile Act (1665) prevented Nonconformist preachers from coming within five miles of any city or town; the Conventicle Act (1670) provided for anyone attending Nonconformist meetings to be fined; and the Test Acts (1673, 1678) imposed an oath denying various Roman Catholic doctrines on anyone holding public office.

ii 270. at a stay] See ii 37n.

ii 275–85. In this passage the Hind speaks for the Nonconformist sects, imagining their arguments against associating with the Church of England.

ii 277. Best on the best] i.e. it is best to settle on the best authority. Joshua Bassett, in his account of his conversion to Catholicism, writes: 'as in matters of Fact, we ought to believe the most, and most proper, and credible Witnesses; so in matters of Opinion, we are obliged to submit to the *most*, and most *Excellent Authors*: Now sure, these *praestantissimi Auctores*, are those who write with *best Authority*, and have Commission from the Highest Powers, so to do' (*Reason and Authority, or, The Motives of a Late Protestants Reconciliation to the Catholic Church* (1687) 9–10). *fountain*] source (*OED* 1); i.e. the Roman Catholic Church. In the Vulgate text of Psalm xlii (there numbered xli) the hart seeks the *fontes* (see i 1n). *flood*] stream, river (*OED* 2).

ii 278. That . . . this] fountain . . . flood.

ii 280. An audacious reversal of the widespread Protestant allegation that the Roman Catholic Church was Antichrist. (Antichrist is named only in the Epistles of John, but has commonly been associated with the beast in Revelation xiii.) Since Antichrist was defined as one who denies that Jesus was God incarnate (1 John ii 22, iv 3, and 2 John 7), the Hind (speaking here in the voice of the Nonconformists) implies that the Church of England is powerless to act against heretics (e.g. Socinians

Did we a lawful tyranny displace
To set aloft a bastard of the race?
Why all these wars to win the book, if we ⎱
Must not interpret for ourselves, but she? ⎰
285   Either be wholly slaves or wholly free."
For purging fires traditions must not fight,
But they must prove episcopacy's right.
Thus those led horses are from service freed,
You never mount 'em but in time of need.
290   Like mercenaries hired for home defence,
They will not serve against their native prince.
Against domestic foes of hierarchy
These are drawn forth to make fanatics fly,
But when they see their countrymen at hand ⎱
295   Marching against 'em under church command, ⎰
Straight they forsake their colours and disband.'
        Thus she; nor could the Panther well enlarge
With weak defence against so strong a charge,
But said, 'For what did Christ his word provide
300   If still his church must want a living guide?
And if all saving doctrines are not there,
Or sacred penmen could not make 'em clear,

who deny the divinity of Christ: see i 53n) because she is herself heretical (cp.
i 453n, ii 150–5). The line also draws upon Jesus' reply when he was accused of
casting out devils by diabolical means: 'And if Satan cast out Satan, he is divided
against himself' (Matthew xii 26).
ii *281–2. lawful tyranny*] Roman Catholic Church (the Hind is still speaking in
the voice of the Nonconformists).   *bastard*] Church of England.
ii *283. wars to win the book*] The struggles during the Reformation to have the
Bible translated into English and widely circulated.
ii *286–7.* The Hind (now speaking on her own behalf again) asks why the Church
of England accepts traditions when they authorize episcopacy (which it keeps)
but not when they authorize the doctrine of Purgatory or *purging fires* (which it
denies). Article 22 says that Purgatory 'is a fond thing vainly invented, and grounded
upon no warranty of Scripture'.
ii *288–9.* i.e. just as horses which are led (for ploughing or drawing carts) rather
than ridden are not used for military service except in emergencies, so the Church
of England only resorts to invoking tradition when other arguments fail.
ii *290–1.* i.e. just as mercenaries who are hired to defend another country will
not fight against their own ruler, so traditions will not allow themselves to be
enlisted in arguments against the Church of Rome.
ii *293. These*] traditions.
ii *297. enlarge*] give free vent to thoughts in speech (*OED* 5).
ii *300. want*] have need of.
ii *301. saving doctrines*] doctrines necessary for the salvation of believers. Article 6
says that 'Holy Scripture containeth all things necessary to salvation'.

From after-ages we should hope in vain
For truths which men inspired could not explain.'
305   'Before the word was written,' said the Hind,
'Our Saviour preached his faith to human kind;
From his apostles the first age received
Eternal truth, and what they taught, believed.
Thus by tradition faith was planted first,
310   Succeeding flocks succeeding pastors nursed.
This was the way our wise Redeemer chose, ⎫
(Who sure could all things for the best dispose) ⎬
To fence his fold from their encroaching foes. ⎭
He could have writ himself, but well foresaw
315   Th' event would be like that of Moses' law:
Some difference would arise, some doubts remain,
Like those which yet the jarring Jews maintain.
No written laws can be so plain, so pure,
But wit may gloss and malice may obscure;
320   Not those indited by his first command:
A prophet graved the text, an angel held his hand.
Thus faith was, ere the written word appeared,
And men believed not what they read, but heard.

ii 305–88. The Hind argues for the superiority of oral over written tradition: it
was the means of communication chosen by Jesus, and is less susceptible than
written words to textual corruption and to disputes over interpretation. Cp. ii
176–80*n.* The Roman Catholic Church maintained that the rule of faith was comprised in 'the Doctrines delivered by Christ and his Apostles immediately to the
Church', which are 'conteyned not onely in Scripture, but likewise in unwritten Traditions' (Cressy, *Exomologesis* 123; Hamm).
ii 313. Cp. Milton's description of Satan entering Eden: 'Leaps o'er the fence with
ease into the fold' (*PL* iv 187; J. R. Mason). Cp. *HP* i 296; 'The Cock and the
Fox' ll. 493–4*n.*
ii 315–17. The Mosaic law or Torah, as recorded in the Pentateuch, prompted
extensive debate among Jewish rabbis: the school of Hillel favoured a liberal
interpretation, while the school of Shammai insisted on a strict interpretation.
Discussions of the law are recorded in the Talmud. *event*] outcome. *jarring*]
bickering, wrangling (*OED* 12).
ii 319. wit] cleverness, ingenuity (*OED* 5).
ii 320–1. i.e. even the laws (the Ten Commandments and other laws and ordinances) supposedly dictated to Moses by God have not been immune from disputed interpretations. The biblical account says both that 'Moses wrote all the
words of the Lord' and that the tablets of stone containing God's commands 'were
the work of God, and the writing was the writing of God, graven upon the tables';
after destroying the original tablets of stone, Moses made replacements and 'wrote
upon the tables the words of the covenant, the ten commandments' (Exodus xxiv
4, xxxii 16, xxxiv 28). *indited*] dictated, spoken to be written down (*OED* 1);
dictated, commanded as a law (*OED* 2). *graved*] engraved, carved (*OED* 6).

But since th' apostles could not be confined
325   To these or those, but severally designed
Their large commission round the world to blow,
To spread their faith they spread their labours too.
Yet still their absent flock their pains did share,
They hearkened still, for love produces care.
330   And as mistakes arose, or discords fell,
Or bold seducers taught 'em to rebel,
As charity grew cold, or faction hot,
Or long neglect their lessons had forgot,
For all their wants they wisely did provide,
335   And preaching by epistles was supplied:
So great physicians cannot all attend,
But some they visit, and to some they send.
Yet all those letters were not writ to all,
Nor first intended, but occasional:
340   Their absent sermons; nor if they contain
All needful doctrines, are those doctrines plain.
Clearness by frequent preaching must be wrought,
They writ but seldom, but they daily taught.
And what one saint has said of holy Paul,
345   "He darkly writ", is true applied to all.
For this obscurity could heaven provide ⎫
More prudently than by a living guide, ⎬
As doubts arose, the difference to decide? ⎭
A guide was therefore needful, therefore made,
350   And, if appointed, sure to be obeyed.
Thus with due reverence to th' apostles' writ,
By which my sons are taught, to which submit,
I think those truths their sacred works contain
The church alone can certainly explain,

---

ii 324–45. Written teaching (the gospels and epistles) originated in the practical need of the apostles to reach a wider audience than was possible by preaching.
ii 325. severally] separately, individually.
ii 326. blow] proclaim, spread abroad (OED 13).
ii 338–9. The epistles were not originally intended for a general readership, but were addressed to specific individuals and churches in response to particular needs and occasions (occasional). Cp. PL viii 555–6.
ii 344–5. 2 Peter iii 16 says of St Paul's epistles: 'in which are some things hard to be understood, which they that are unlearned and unstable wrest, as they do also the other scriptures, unto their own destruction'.
ii 346–8. Woodhead said that Christ's words 'do promise to the world's end not a Rule only, but Persons, sent to preserve us from every wind of Doctrine' (A Rational Account 8; Hamm).

355   That following ages, leaning on the past,
      May rest upon the primitive at last.
      Nor would I thence the word no rule infer,
      But none without the church interpreter.
      Because, as I have urged before, 'tis mute,
360   And is itself the subject of dispute.
      But what th' apostles their successors taught, ⎫
      They to the next, from them to us is brought, ⎬
      Th' undoubted sense which is in scripture sought. ⎭
      From hence the church is armed, when errors rise, ⎫
365   To stop their entrance and prevent surprise; ⎬
      And, safe entrenched within, her foes without defies. ⎭
      By these all festering sores her councils heal, ⎫
      Which time or has disclosed, or shall reveal, ⎬
      For discord cannot end without a last appeal. ⎭
370   Nor can a council national decide ⎫
      But with subordination to her guide ⎬
      (I wish the cause were on that issue tried). ⎭
      Much less the scripture: for suppose debate
      Betwixt pretenders to a fair estate
375   Bequeathed by some legator's last intent
      (Such is our dying Saviour's testament):
      The will is proved, is opened, and is read;
      The doubtful heirs their differing titles plead,
      All vouch the words their interest to maintain,
380   And each pretends by those his cause is plain.
      Shall then the testament award the right?
      No, that's the Hungary for which they fight,
      The field of battle, subject of debate,

ii 356. *primitive*] earliest, original; and so implicitly purest (*OED* 1).
ii 359. Cp. ii 203.
ii 365. *surprise*] sudden military attack against an unprepared position (*OED* 1).
ii 367–72. General councils of the church settle matters of doctrine and identify heresy, but national councils can make no decision in such matters which is not subject to the agreement of the universal church.
ii 368. *or . . . or*] either . . . or.
ii 372. *the cause*] the dispute between the Church of England and the Roman Catholic Church.
ii 374. *pretenders*] claimants.
ii 378. *doubtful*] uncertain (*OED* 2); apprehensive (*OED* 5).
ii 379. *vouch*] cite in support of their own views (*OED* 2d).
ii 382. Throughout the seventeenth century the Hapsburg and Ottoman empires had contended for control over Hungary, with intermittent warfare since 1661. In 1686 the coalition organized by Pope Innocent XI captured Buda from the Turks, and on 12 August 1687 the Grand Vizier was defeated at the battle of Mohacs.

    The thing contended for, the fair estate.
385   The sense is intricate, 'tis only clear
    What vowels and what consonants are there.
    Therefore 'tis plain its meaning must be tried
    Before some judge appointed to decide.'
      'Suppose,' the fair apostate said, 'I grant
390   The faithful flock some living guide should want,
    Your arguments an endless chase pursue:
    Produce this vaunted leader to our view,
    This mighty Moses of the chosen crew.'
      The dame, who saw her fainting foe retired,
395   With force renewed to victory aspired,
    And looking upward to her kindred sky,
    As once our Saviour owned his deity,
    Pronounced his words: '*She whom ye seek am I*'.
    Nor less amazed this voice the Panther heard
400   Than were those Jews to hear a God declared.
    Then thus the matron modestly renewed:
    'Let all your prophets and their sects be viewed,

ii *385. intricate*] obscure (*OED* 2).

ii *389. apostate*] one who has renounced their former belief.

ii *394. fainting*] losing heart, giving way (*OED* 1).

ii *398–400*. When Judas and a group of officers came to arrest Jesus, he 'said unto them, Whom seek ye? They answered him, Jesus of Nazareth. Jesus saith unto them, I am he . . . As soon then as he had said unto them, I am he, they went backward, and fell to the ground' (John xviii 4–6). Jesus here is not simply identifying himself by name: he is, as the Hind says, claiming divinity, because according to the Greek text of the NT he says ἐγώ εἰμί (literally 'I I-am' rather than 'I am he'), which echoes God's description of himself in the OT: 'And God said unto Moses, I AM THAT I AM: and he said, Thus shalt thou say unto the children of Israel, I AM hath sent me unto you' (Exodus iii 14). The Hind's words also recall the poem's first epigraph. D. repeats the phrase in 'The First Book of the *Aeneis*' l. 834, when the cloud dissolves revealing Aeneas, who says to Dido, 'He whom you seek am I'.

ii *401. modestly*] 1687b; modesty 1687a. *renewed*] resumed her speech.

ii *402*. There was little agreement on doctrine or practice among Protestant churches and sects, and their councils were often bitter and divisive. The Synod of Dort (1618–19), primarily an assembly of the Dutch Reformed Church and convened by the States General of the United Provinces, but also including delegations from Switzerland, the Palatinate, and England, led to the triumph of Calvinism over Arminianism; at the end of it 200 Arminian clergy were deprived, Hugo Grotius was sentenced to life imprisonment, and Oldenbarnevelt beheaded. The Westminster Assembly (1643) produced violent controversies between irreconcilable Protestant groups, and its documents were never widely accepted in England. The Savoy Conference (1661), which revised the Book of Common Prayer, resulted in the defeat of the Presbyterians, around 2000 of whom were deprived of their livings. Cp. Cressy, quoted in i 453*n*.

And see to which of 'em yourselves think fit
The conduct of your conscience to submit:
405   Each proselyte would vote his doctor best,
With absolute exclusion to the rest.
Thus would your Polish Diet disagree,
And end as it began, in anarchy.
Yourself the fairest for election stand,
410   Because you seem crown-general of the land,
But soon against your superstitious lawn
Some Presbyterian sabre would be drawn:
In your established laws of sovereignty   ⎫
The rest some fundamental flaw would see, ⎬
415   And call rebellion gospel-liberty.   ⎭
To church decrees your articles require
Submission modified, if not entire;

ii 404. conduct] direction, guidance (*OED* 5).

ii 405. doctor] learned theologian (*OED* 5a).

ii 407–15. The Panther's position is appropriately likened to the constitutional arrangements in Poland, which gave the people (both individually and collectively) a degree of control over the conduct of affairs by king and parliament which was unique in seventeenth-century Europe. The Polish parliament (the Seym) required unanimity for its resolutions, and could not proceed in the face of a formal veto by one of its members. Its proceedings were notoriously thrown into disarray in 1652 when one deputy exercised his veto and then left. A proposal to change to voting by a two-thirds majority was made in 1658 but defeated. The crown of Poland was elective, and any member of the Polish nobility or a foreign ruling house was eligible. On the death of King Michal in 1673 the leading candidate to succeed him was the *crown-general* (a Polish title: *OED* 34) Jan Sobieski, who had just become a national hero by defeating the Turks at Chocim. The Polish nobility had the constitutional right to organize armed resistance to the king in cases of national emergency. Religious toleration was enshrined in the Polish constitution. For the story that Shaftesbury had been a candidate for the throne of Poland see *The Medal*, 'Epistle' l. 12*n*.   *Diet*] congress.

ii 411. superstitious] The Anglican episcopacy was regarded as a superstitious institution by Protestant sects because not warranted by scripture; but also by the Roman Catholic Church because it held that Anglican bishops were invalidly consecrated and not part of the apostolic succession. For the contemporary controversy over the validity of Anglican orders see Jones, *Catalogue* 206–17.   *lawn*] fine linen used for bishops' sleeves.

ii 412. sabre] Poland adopted some eastern styles of dress and weaponry.

ii 415. As in *AA* l. 52.

ii 416–17. Article 20 says: 'The Church hath power to decree Rites or Ceremonies, and authority in Controversies of Faith: And yet it is not lawful for the Church to ordain any thing that is contrary to God's Word written, neither may it so expound one place of Scripture, that it be repugnant to another. Wherefore, although the Church be a witness and a keeper of holy Writ, yet, as it ought not to decree any thing against the same, so besides the same ought it not to enforce any thing to be believed for necessity of Salvation'.

Homage denied, to censures you proceed,
But when Curtana will not do the deed,
420   You lay that pointless clergy-weapon by,
And to the laws, your sword of justice, fly.
Now this your sects the more unkindly take
(Those prying varlets hit the blots you make)
Because some ancient friends of yours declare
425   Your only rule of faith the scriptures are,
Interpreted by men of judgement sound,
Which every sect will for themselves expound;
Nor think less reverence to their doctors due
For sound interpretation, than to you.
430   If then by able heads are understood
Your brother-prophets who reformed abroad,
Those able heads expound a wiser way,
That their own sheep their shepherd should obey.
But if you mean yourselves are only sound,   ⎫
435   That doctrine turns the reformation round,   ⎬
And all the rest are false reformers found: ⎭
Because in sundry points you stand alone,   ⎫
Not in communion joined with anyone,   ⎬
And therefore must be all the church, or none.   ⎭
440   Then, till you have agreed whose judge is best,

ii 419. Curtana] the pointless sword, representing mercy, carried alongside the sword
of justice before the kings of England at their coronation (*OED*). *MS* glosses this
as 'Excommunication'.
ii 423. varlets] knaves, rogues (*OED* 2). Foxe in his *Acts and Monuments* (1581–2)
uses the phrase 'verlet heretiques' (*OED*).   *hit the blots*] take exposed pieces in
backgammon; hence to take advantage of weak points in an opponent's case (*OED*
blot *sb²*).
ii 427. i.e. every sect will interpret 'men of sound judgement' to refer to them.
ii 433. It is not clear which is the subject and which the object here. The line
could mean (a) 'the sheep should obey their shepherd', i.e. the continental reformers required congregations to obey the authority of the church (thus *Works*):
an example would be Calvin's theocratic Geneva. But the logic of the passage, and
the emphasis in *their own*, points to it meaning more caustically (b) 'the shepherd
should obey his own sheep', i.e. Protestant leaders have to follow their own congregations: (i) because in Protestantism each believer has the right to interpret
scripture; (ii) because in many Protestant denominations hierarchical organization
is weak or non-existent; (iii) because many continental congregations elected their
own ministers after assessing their preaching skills. Much depends on whether
wiser in l. 432 is ironic or not, but (b) fits better with ll. 434–6, which argue that
if the Church of England insists that she alone provides sound teaching, that contradicts the principles of the Reformation: the word *But* in l. 434 introduces a
contrast between continental subservience and Anglican assertiveness.

Against this forced submission they protest:
While sound and sound a different sense explains,
Both play at hard-head till they break their brains,
And from their chairs each other's force defy,
445   While unregarded thunders vainly fly.
I pass the rest, because your church alone
Of all usurpers best could fill the throne.
But neither you, nor any sect beside   ⎫
For this high office can be qualified,   ⎬
450   With necessary gifts required in such a guide. ⎭
For that which must direct the whole, must be ⎫
Bound in one bond of faith and unity;   ⎬
But all your several churches disagree.   ⎭
The consubstantiating church and priest
455   Refuse communion to the Calvinist;
The French reformed from preaching you restrain,   ⎫
Because you judge their ordination vain;   ⎬
And so they judge of yours, but donors must ordain. ⎭
In short, in doctrine or in discipline
460   Not one reformed can with another join,
But all from each as from damnation fly;
No union they pretend but in non-popery.
Nor, should their members in a synod meet,

ii 442. See ii 385–6.
ii 443. hard-head] a contest of butting with the head (OED 2).
ii 444. chairs] Contrasting with the chair of St Peter, from which the Pope makes
pronouncements ex cathedra.
ii 447. throne] of St Peter.
ii 454–5. Lutherans refused communion to the Calvinists because they had a different Eucharistic theology: see i 410–29n.
ii 456–8. The validity of Huguenot ordination was not recognized by the Church
of England (see ii 139–40n). Some Huguenot refugees were appointed to livings
in England after receiving ordination from a bishop. Works notes that Catholic
ideas about Anglican and Huguenot principles of church government had been
set out in Abraham Woodhead, A Brief Account of Ancient Church-Government (1665,
reprinted 1685).
ii 458. donors] those having the right of presentation to a benefice (OED dona-
tion 1b).
ii 459–62. Cp. Thomas White: reformers 'were necessarily to be distinguish'd by
the Opinions they held; having no one thred, on which all their particular Tenets
might be strung and depend, but the Letter, which without a determinate sense, is
nothing; all the Rule they generally agreed in being only not to admit that of
the Catholick Church; leaving themselves no positive Rule or Principle, nor any
thing universally accepted by their whole Body, but this destroying negative, Not
to be a Papist' (Rushworth's Dialogues (1654) Preface; Hamm).
ii 463–8. Cp. ii 402n.

<pre>
          Could any church presume to mount the seat
465   Above the rest, their discords to decide:
          None would obey, but each would be the guide;
          And face to face dissensions would increase,
          For only distance now preserves the peace.
          All in their turns accusers and accused:
470   Babel was never half so much confused.
          What one can plead, the rest can plead as well, ⎫
          For amongst equals lies no last appeal,   ⎬
          And all confess themselves are fallible.   ⎭
          Now since you grant some necessary guide,
475   All who can err are justly laid aside:
          Because a trust so sacred to confer   ⎫
          Shows want of such a sure interpreter,   ⎬
          And how can he be needful who can err?   ⎭
          Then, granting that unerring guide we want,
480   That such there is you stand obliged to grant.
          Our Saviour else were wanting to supply
          Our needs, and obviate that necessity.
          It then remains, that church can only be
          The guide which owns unfailing certainty;
485   Or else you slip your hold, and change your side,
          Relapsing from a necessary guide.
          But this annexed condition of the crown,   ⎫
          Immunity from errors, you disown.   ⎬
          Here then you shrink, and lay your weak pretensions ⎭
               down.
490   For petty royalties you raise debate,   ⎫
          But this unfailing, universal state   ⎬
          You shun; nor dare succeed to such a glorious weight; ⎭
          And for that cause those promises detest
          With which our Saviour did his church invest:
</pre>

ii 470. It was at Babel that the single universal language of mankind was replaced by many mutually incomprehensible languages (Genesis xi 1–9).

ii 487. annexed condition of the crown] condition which is attached to the supreme authority.

ii 490. royalties] See 'To the Reader' l. 46*n.*

ii 492. glorious weight] the responsibility of being the unerring guide, but with echoes of St Paul's description of the heavenly reward: 'For our light affliction, which is but for a moment, worketh for us a far more exceeding and eternal weight of glory' (2 Corinthians iv 17).

ii 493. promises] See i 493–6*n.*

495 But strive t' evade, and fear to find 'em true,
     As conscious they were never meant to you:
     All which the mother-church asserts her own,
     And with unrivalled claim ascends the throne.
     So when of old th' Almighty Father sate
500 In council to redeem our ruined state,
     Millions of millions at a distance round,   ⎫
     Silent the sacred consistory crowned,   ⎬
     To hear what mercy mixed with justice could propound. ⎭
     All prompt with eager pity to fulfil
505 The full extent of their Creator's will:
     But when the stern conditions were declared,
     A mournful whisper through the host was heard,
     And the whole hierarchy with heads hung down
     Submissively declined the ponderous proffered crown.
510 Then, not till then, th' eternal Son from high
     Rose in the strength of all the Deity,
     Stood forth t' accept the terms, and underwent ⎫
     A weight which all the frame of heaven had bent, ⎬
     Nor he himself could bear, but as omnipotent.   ⎭
515 Now to remove the least remaining doubt,
     That ev'n the blear-eyed sects may find her out,
     Behold what heavenly rays adorn her brows,   ⎫
     What from his wardrobe her belov'd allows   ⎬
     To deck the wedding day of his unspotted spouse. ⎭
520 Behold what marks of majesty she brings,
     Richer than ancient heirs of eastern kings;

ii 499–514. Alluding to *PL* iii 56–343, in which God in heavenly council asks who will be prepared to redeem mankind through their own death. Much of the vocabulary of this passage is Miltonic, echoing Book iii or other comparable portions of *PL*: *Almighty Father* (*PL* iii 56); *ruined* ('ruin' is frequent in *PL* for the Fall, e.g. ix 906, 950); *millions* (often applied to the angels, e.g. i 609, iv 677); *silent* ('silence was in heaven': iii 218); *mercy and justice* (iii 132, 407); *pity* (iii 402, 405); *stern* (frequently, e.g. viii 333); *hierarchy* (vii 192); *rose* (of the Son, vi 746); *deity* (iii 187, x 65); *frame of heaven* (iii 395 etc.); *omnipotent* (iii 372).
ii 499. *sate*] sat.
ii 502. *consistory*] company surrounding a throne (*OED* 4); accented on the first syllable.
ii 508. *hierarchy*] the collective body of angels, angelic host (*OED* 1).
ii 518–19. The image of the church as the bride of Christ derives from an allegorical interpretation of the Song of Solomon (see Gardiner *passim*); cp. also Revelation xxi 2, 9, and Spenser, *FQ* I xii 21–3.

Her right hand holds the sceptre and the keys,
To show whom she commands, and who obeys;
With these to bind, or set the sinner free,
525   With that t' assert spiritual royalty.
  'One in herself, not rent by schism, but sound, *Marks*
Entire, one solid shining diamond,   *of the*
Not sparkles shattered into sects like you,   *Catholic*
One is the church, and must be to be true: *Church*
530   One central principle of unity.   ⎤ *from the*
  'As undivided, so from errors free, ⎬ *Nicene*
As one in faith, so one in sanctity.   ⎦ *Creed.*
Thus she, and none but she, th' insulting rage
Of heretics opposed from age to age;

ii 522–5. See i 493–6n. The *keys* are the symbol of St Peter, and hence of the papacy.

ii 524. See ii 402n.

ii 525. *spiritual*] Stressed on the second syllable (again at ii 618).

ii 526. *marginal note*] The 'marks' or 'notes' of the church were those distinguishing features which marked it out as being the true church. These characteristics were defined by the Nicene Creed: *Credo in unam, sanctam, catholicam et apostolicam ecclesiam* ('I believe in one, holy, catholic and apostolic church'). The marks of the true church had formed an important element in Roman Catholic apologetics, especially in Bellarmine's *De Notis Ecclesiae*, where they are defined thus: (1) the name 'catholic'; (2) antiquity; (3) uninterrupted duration; (4) amplitude, or the multitude and variety of believers; (5) the succession of bishops in the Roman Church from the apostles to the present; (6) agreement in doctrine with the ancient church; (7) the unity of its members one with another, and with the head; (8) the holiness of its teaching; (9) the efficacy of its teaching; (10) the holiness of life of its founders; (11) the glory of its miracles; (12) its prophetic light; (13) the testimony of its adversaries; (14) the unfortunate end of its opponents; (15) the worldly happiness of those who defend it (Bellarmine, *Opera Omnia*, 12 vols (1870–74) ii 361–407). These notes were much discussed in contemporary controversial literature: a substantial rebuttal of Bellarmine by various Anglican writers appeared as *The Notes of the Church . . . Examined and Confuted* (serially published from April to August 1687); see further Jones, *Catalogue* 437–40. Bassett records that after studying Bellarmine he found the marks of the true church in the Church of Rome (*Reason and Authority* 13–14). However, as D.'s marginal note makes clear, in the present passage the number and order of these notes of the church follow the Nicene Creed rather than Bellarmine, thus relying on a document accepted by all Christians rather than a partisan treatise. D. discusses the first of the marks, unity, in ll. 526–30; the second, sanctity, in ll. 532–47; the third, universality, in ll. 548–75; and the fourth, apostolicity, in ll. 578–611.

ii 527. Cp. Spenser's description of Arthur's shield, 'all of Diamond perfect pure and cleene / It framed was, one massie entire mould' (*FQ* I vii 33; Kinsley). The diamond symbolizes fortitude because of its hardness.

ii 528. *sparkles*] small diamonds (*OED* 4).

ii 533. *insulting*] scornful, boasting (*OED* 1); attacking (*OED* 3).

535   Still when the giant brood invades her throne ⎫
       She stoops from heaven, and meets 'em half way ⎬
          down, ⎪
       And with paternal thunder vindicates her crown. ⎭
       But like Egyptian sorcerers you stand, ⎫
       And vainly lift aloft your magic wand, ⎬
540   To sweep away the swarms of vermin from the land: ⎭
       You could like them, with like infernal force
       Produce the plague, but not arrest the course.
       But when the boils and botches with disgrace
       And public scandal sat upon the face,
545   Themselves attacked, the Magi strove no more, ⎫
       They saw God's finger, and their fate deplore; ⎬
       Themselves they could not cure of the dishonest sore. ⎭
          'Thus one, thus pure, behold her largely spread
       Like the fair ocean from her mother bed;
550   From east to west triumphantly she rides,
       All shores are watered by her wealthy tides;
       The gospel sound diffused from pole to pole,
       Where winds can carry, and where waves can roll;
       The self-same doctrine of the sacred page
555   Conveyed to every clime in every age.
          'Here let my sorrow give my satire place
       To raise new blushes on my British race;

---

ii 535–7. The giants attacked heaven, and were beaten back by the thunderbolts
of Jupiter, the *pater omnipotens*, 'almighty father' (Ovid, *Met.* i 151–5; Virgil, *Geo.*
i 281–3).   *paternal*] Because the thunder is that of God, her father, not the church
herself.   *vindicates*] defends against encroachment (*OED* 4).

ii 538–47. In Exodus vii–ix Moses and Aaron bring miraculous plagues on Egypt,
while the Egyptian magicians attempt to match them; though the magicians
successfully create plagues, they cannot remove them, and when they are themselves afflicted with boils 'the magicians could not stand before Moses because of
the boils'.

ii 543. *botches*] sores, ulcers.

ii 545. *Magi*] magicians.

ii 546. *deplore*] lament.

ii 547. *dishonest*] shameful (*OED* 1); hideous (*OED* 3).

ii 548–75. This passage discussing the mark of catholicity or universality follows
Bellarmine's understanding of the church's 'amplitude' (his mark no. 4: see ii
526n above).

ii 552. 1687 begins new paragraph here.   *gospel sound*] *Ed.*; Gospel-sound *1687bc*;
Golspel's-sound *1687a*.

ii 556. The Hind's sorrow (at what Britain has done) now provides a place for
her to speak satirically.

Our sailing ships like common shores we use,
And through our distant colonies diffuse
560 The draughts of dungeons, and the stench of stews;
Whom, when their home-bred honesty is lost,
We disembogue on some far Indian coast:
Thieves, panders, palliards, sins of every sort,
Those are the manufactures we export;
565 And these the missionaires our zeal has made,
For with my country's pardon be it said,
Religion is the least of all our trade.
    'Yet some improve their traffic more than we,
For they on gain, their only god, rely,
570 And set a public price on piety.
Industrious of the needle and the chart,
They run full sail to their Japonian mart:
Prevention fear, and, prodigal of fame,
Sell all of Christian to the very name;
575 Nor leave enough of that to hide their naked shame.
    'Thus of three marks which in the creed we view,
Not one of all can be applied to you:
Much less the fourth; in vain, alas, you seek
Th' ambitious title of "apostolic".
580 Godlike descent! 'Tis well your blood can be

ii 558–67. The British practice of transporting criminals to the colonies is contrasted with the religious zeal of other (Catholic) countries in sending missionaries abroad. In 1688 D. would publish his translation of *The Life of St Francis Xavier*, the Spanish Jesuit who had led missions to India, the East Indies, and Japan.
ii 558. shores] sewers.
ii 560. draughts] currents, streams (*OED* 23); selections or detachments of people (*OED* 34; first recorded in 1703); sewers (*OED* 45). stews] brothels.
ii 562. disembogue] discharge.
ii 563. palliards] professional beggars or vagabonds (*OED*).
ii 565. missionaires] missioners, i.e. missionaries, esp. Jesuit ones. The French spelling perhaps reminds readers that most missions were being undertaken from the continent.
ii 568. some] the Dutch; cp. *AM* ll. 1–16; 'Prologue to *Amboyna*' ll. 18–19.
ii 572–5. The Dutch had a monopoly on trade with Japan, where Christianity was proscribed. In order to trade, Dutch merchants had to deny their faith.
ii 573. Prevention] being anticipated or forestalled. prodigal of fame] heedless of their reputation.
ii 579. apostolic] Though the *OED* provides no evidence for this, the word must be stressed on the second syllable rather than the third (as in its root ἀπόστολος), both here and in ii 613.

Proved noble in the third or fourth degree,
For all of ancient that you had before
(I mean what is not borrowed from our store)
Was error fulminated o'er and o'er:
585   Old heresies condemned in ages past
By care and time recovered from the blast.
       "Tis said with ease, but never can be proved,
The church her old foundations has removed,
And built new doctrines on unstable sands:
590   Judge that, ye winds and rains; you proved her, yet
          she stands.
Those ancient doctrines charged on her for new,
Show when, and how, and from what hands they grew.
We claim no power when heresies grow bold
To coin new faith, but still declare the old.
595   How else could that obscene disease be purged
When controverted texts are vainly urged?
To prove tradition new, there's somewhat more
Required than saying 'twas not used before.
Those monumental arms are never stirred
600   Till schism or heresy call down Goliah's sword.
       'Thus what you call corruptions are in truth
The first plantations of the gospel's youth,
Old standard faith: but cast your eyes again
And view those errors which new sects maintain,
605   Or which of old disturbed the church's peaceful reign,
And we can point each period of the time,

ii 581. Proved to be only three or four steps (i.e. generations: OED degree 3) removed from true nobility: i.e. from the time in the early sixteenth century when the Church of England was part of the Catholic Church.
ii 584. fulminated] denounced by ecclesiastical censure (OED 8).
ii 587–9. D. refers to the Protestant charge that the Church of Rome had departed from the pure doctrine found in scripture by adding new dogmas. For the image see ii 105n.
ii 588. removed] shifted to another place.
ii 590. proved] tested.
ii 591. charged on her for] laid to her charge as being (OED charge 16).
ii 599–600. The sword of Goliath, which was kept wrapped in cloth behind the ephod in the care of a priest, was used by David as a last resort when fleeing from Saul (1 Samuel xxi 9). Cp. RL, 'Preface' l. 22. monumental] kept as a memorial (OED 2). The meaning 'colossal' seems to be nineteenth century, but may be implied here.
ii 603. standard] exemplar of correctness and perfection (OED 10); tree remaining when a coppice has been cut down (OED 20), continuing the image of plantation.

When they began, and who begot the crime;
Can calculate how long th' eclipse endured,
Who interposed, what digits were obscured:
610   Of all which are already passed away
We know the rise, the progress and decay.
      'Despair at our foundations then to strike
Till you can prove your faith apostolic,
A limpid stream drawn from the native source,
615   Succession lawful in a lineal course.
Prove any church opposed to this our head,
So one, so pure, so unconfinedly spread,
Under one chief of the spiritual state,
The members all combined, and all subordinate;
620   Show such a seamless coat, from schism so free,
In no communion joined with heresy;
If such a one you find, let truth prevail.   ⎫
Till when your weights will in the balance fail: ⎬
A church unprincipled kicks up the scale.   ⎭
625   'But if you cannot think (nor sure you can
Suppose in God what were unjust in man)
That he, the fountain of eternal grace,   ⎫
Should suffer falsehood for so long a space   ⎬
To banish truth, and to usurp her place;   ⎭
630   That sev'n successive ages should be lost,

---

ii 608. th' eclipse] 'Heresy' MS.

ii 609. digits] twelfth parts of the diameter of the sun and moon, used to measure the magnitude of an eclipse (*OED* 4).

ii 620. seamless coat] Like that of Christ in John xix 23; a traditional symbol of the unity of the church.

ii 623–4. The Church of England is weighed in the balance (cp. Daniel v 27), and because the weights in its pan are too light the pan rises. Milton uses the same image for Satan's powerlessness in *PL* iv 997–1004, and D. returns to the image at iii 313.   *unprincipled*] not grounded upon something (here, on apostolic foundations) (*OED* 1, citing only two examples from Milton); without sound and fixed principles (*OED* 2).

ii 625–35. The Hind says that the Catholic Church cannot have been corrupt (as the reformers maintained) because it is unthinkable that God should have permitted mankind to suffer under error for such a long period.

ii 628. space] period of time.

ii 630. sev'n] *1687bc*; nine *1687a*. D.'s correction. If *ages* here means 'centuries' (*OED* 10c), the seven or nine ages would be the seven or nine centuries during which God allowed the 'errors' of Catholicism to flourish before they were corrected. The beginning of Catholic Christianity in England may be dated to the arrival of St Augustine from Rome in AD 597, so D.'s original phrasing *nine . . . ages* would indicate a period of 'error' finishing with Luther (1483–1546) or the Henrician

And preach damnation at their proper cost;
That all your erring ancestors should die,
Drowned in th' abyss of deep idolatry;
If piety forbid such thoughts to rise,
635 Awake, and open your unwilling eyes:
God has left nothing for each age undone,   ⎫
From this to that wherein he sent his son: ⎬
Then think but well of him, and half your work is done. ⎭
    'See how his church, adorned with every grace, ⎫
640 With open arms, a kind forgiving face,   ⎬
Stands ready to prevent her long-lost son's embrace. ⎭
Not more did Joseph o'er his brethren weep,
Nor less himself could from discovery keep,
When in the crowd of suppliants they were seen,
645 And in their crew his best belovèd Benjamin.
That pious Joseph in the church behold,   ⎫   *The*
To feed your famine and refuse your gold;   ⎬   *renunciation of*
The Joseph you exiled, the Joseph whom   ⎪   *the Benedictines*
    you sold.'   ⎭   *to the abbey*
                                                    lands.

Reformation *c.* 1530; the revised phrasing *seven . . . ages* terminates that period with
Wyclif (*c.* 1330–1384), which is consistent with the claim in ii 582–6 that Protestant
doctrines are revivals of older heresies. See also iii 435*n.* Seven is also a sacred
and symbolic number (there are seven sacraments, seven deadly sins); it is used
repeatedly in Revelation (seven plagues, seven angels, a beast with seven heads);
and in biblical usage it denotes perfection.

ii 631. *proper*] own.

ii 634. *piety*] reverence for one's ancestors, as well as for God.

ii 640–1. Alluding to the parable of the prodigal son welcomed home by his father
(Luke xv 11–32).

ii 641. *prevent*] anticipate.   *son*] 'Engd.' MS.

ii 642–8. Joseph, sold into slavery in Egypt by his brothers, became ruler of the
country. When his brothers came to Egypt to buy corn in time of famine, Joseph
wept to see them, especially his beloved younger brother, Benjamin. He
returned the money with which they had bought the corn, and disclosed himself to them (Genesis xxxvii, xlii–xlv).

ii 646. *marginal note*] The English Benedictine monks had renounced their title to
the abbey lands which had been confiscated and sold during the Reformation:
the declaration was made by Dom Philip Ellis in a sermon preached before James
II on 13 November 1686 (*A Sermon Preach'd before the King* (1686); Saslow, cited
in l. 650*n*). Owners of such property had feared that it would be appropriated
and returned to the religious orders.

ii 647. *feed your famine*] i.e. spiritually through the ministry of Catholic priests in
England, who were supported financially by the Roman Catholic community.
Anglican clergy were supported by income from land and endowments, and by
compulsory tithes levied on agricultural produce.

Thus, while with heavenly charity she spoke,
650   A streaming blaze the silent shadows broke;
Shot from the skies a cheerful azure light,
The birds obscene to forests winged their flight,
And gaping graves received the wandering guilty sprite.
Such were the pleasing triumphs of the sky
655   For James his late nocturnal victory;
The pledge of his Almighty Patron's love,
The fireworks which his angel made above.
I saw myself the lambent easy light   *Poeta loquitu*
Gild the brown horror and dispel the night;
660   The messenger with speed the tidings bore,
News which three labouring nations did restore,
But heaven's own nuncius was arrived before.

ii 649. *charity*] Christian love (*OED* 1); especially here the desire to see others
saved (cp. *RL* ll. 198, 212).
ii 650. For the image of heavenly light signifying divine approval cp. *Astraea Redux*
ll. 288–91, *AM* ll. 1085–8, and Virgil, *Aen.* ii 692–8 (Edward L. Saslow, *SEL* xx
(1980) 373–84, an essay on this passage).
ii 652. *obscene*] ill-omened, inauspicious (*OED* 3; a Latinate sense from *obscenus*,
as in Virgil's *obscoenae volucres*, 'ill-omened birds' in *Aen.* iii 262; these are the
Harpies, for which see *HP* iii 960*n*).
ii 653. *sprite*] spirit, ghost.
ii 654–62. This passage refers to the Battle of Sedgemoor during the night of 5–6
July 1685, in which the Protestant forces of the Duke of Monmouth were defeated
by the army of James II. No contemporary account has been found which refers
to any aerial lights (e.g. a comet or the aurora borealis), though the passage clearly
implies that D. saw such a phenomenon, which he interpreted as a heavenly sign
of the victory.
ii 654. *triumphs*] a triumph was a procession through Rome staged by a general
returning from victory; hence the word came to mean a spectacle (*OED* 4) and
specifically a triumphal arch (*OED* 7).
ii 658. *marginal note*. Poeta loquitur] The poet speaks.
ii 658. *lambent*] playing lightly over a surface like tongues of fire.   *easy*] moving
gently, unhurried (*OED* 5).
ii 659. *brown*] dark (*OED* 1); cp. Milton's 'brown as evening' (*PL* ix 1088).
horror] roughness, ruggedness (*OED* 1), perhaps applied here to a turbulent sky.
Milton associates *horror* with darkness in *PL* ii 220: 'This horror will grow mild,
this darkness light'. D. uses the phrase *brown horror* again in 'The Seventh Book
of the *Aeneis*': 'a Wood, / Which thick with Shades, and a brown Horror, stood'
(ll. 40–1). In Latin *horror* includes the sense 'source or cause of horror or terror'
(*OLD* 7). The light as it gilds the darkness dispels the source of terror, i.e. allays
D.'s fears about the survival of Catholicism in England.
ii 661. *three . . . nations*] England, Scotland and Ireland.   *labouring*] distressed,
troubled (*OED* 15).
ii 662. *nuncius*] messenger (a rare word). Galileo called his book of 1610 on the
Copernican system *Sidereus Nuntius* ('the starry messenger'). The word 'angel' derives
from the Latin *angelus*, also meaning 'messenger'. D.'s choice of *nuncius* may recall

By this the Hind had reached her lonely cell,
And vapours rose, and dews unwholesome fell;
665 When she, by frequent observation wise,   ⎫
As one who long on heaven had fixed her eyes,   ⎬
Discerned a change of weather in the skies;   ⎭
The western borders were with crimson spread,
The moon descending looked all flaming red;
670 She thought good manners bound her to invite
The stranger dame to be her guest that night.
'Tis true, coarse diet and a short repast,   ⎫
She said, were weak inducements to the taste   ⎬
Of one so nicely bred, and so unused to fast;   ⎭
675 But what plain fare her cottage could afford,
A hearty welcome at a homely board,
Was freely hers; and, to supply the rest,
An honest meaning and an open breast.
Last, with content of mind, the poor man's wealth,

nuncio, the title of the papal representative at a foreign court. For the arrival of the papal nuncio Ferdinand, Count d'Adda, in November 1685, see *POAS* iv 109, 114–15.

ii *663–722.* The scene of the Hind welcoming the Panther into her humble abode links D.'s specifically theological concerns with his larger interest in hospitality, rural simplicity, and the life of the happy man: see 'Horace: Odes III xxix', 'Horace: Epode II', 'To John Driden', 'Baucis and Philemon'.

ii *663. cell*] hermit's dwelling (*OED* 3; cp. ii 699); humble dwelling, cottage (*OED* 3c; cp. ii 675); den of a wild beast (*OED* 3c).

ii *667–9.* Saslow 377 notes that proverbial English weather lore says 'Pale moon doth rain, red moon doth blow', and compares *Cleomenes* (1692) IV ii 6–10: 'For what I see, or only think I see, / Is like a Glimps of Moon-shine, streak'd with red; / A shuffled, sullen, and uncertain Light, / That Dances thro' the Clouds, and shuts again; / Than 'ware a rising Tempest on the Main'. The prevailing winds in England are westerly, so a change of weather often comes from that quarter. The *change of weather* which the Hind discerns implies that circumstances after James's *Declaration for Liberty of Conscience* will be more favourable to her, and threatening to the Panther.

ii *672–4. repast* / . . . *taste* / . . . *fast*] Probably a perfect rhyme, each word being pronounced with a short 'a'.   *nicely*] in a refined way.   *unused to fast*] Roman Catholics observed regular fasts (see i 364*n*), but these were a less important feature of Anglican discipline.

ii *677. supply*] make up for what was lacking.

ii *678.* Rebutting the frequent Protestant charge that Catholic apologists used dissimulation and equivocation (cp. ii 45*n*).

ii *679.* Cp. Lucretius: *divitiae grandes homini sunt vivere parce / aequo animo* ('the greatest riches of man are to live on little, with a contented mind': *De Rerum Natura* v 1118–19; Williams). Cp. also 'Content with poverty' in 'Horace: Odes III xxix' l. 86. The phrase *content of mind* recurs in 'To Mr Henry Higden' l. 27.

680   A grace-cup to their common patron's health.
        This she desired her to accept and stay,
        For fear she might be wildered in her way,
        Because she wanted an unerring guide;
        And then the dewdrops on her silken hide
685   Her tender constitution did declare ⎤
        Too ladylike a long fatigue to bear, ⎬
        And rough inclemencies of raw nocturnal air. ⎦
        But most she feared that travelling so late, ⎤
        Some evil-minded beasts might lie in wait, ⎬
690   And without witness wreak their hidden hate. ⎦
            The Panther, though she lent a listening ear,
        Had more of Lion in her than to fear:
        Yet wisely weighing, since she had to deal
        With many foes, their numbers might prevail,
695   Returned her all the thanks she could afford,
        And took her friendly hostess at her word:
        Who entering first her lowly roof (a shed ⎤
        With hoary moss and winding ivy spread, ⎬
        Honest enough to hide an humble hermit's head) ⎦
700   Thus graciously bespoke her welcome guest: ⎤
        'So might these walls, with your fair presence blessed, ⎬
        Become your dwelling-place of everlasting rest, ⎦
        Not for a night, or quick-revolving year,
        Welcome an owner, not a sojourner.

ii 680. *grace-cup*] cup of liquor drunk after grace is said, or before retiring for the night (*OED*). For the theological debates over *grace* see i 47n.   *common patron*] James II.
ii 682. *wildered*] led astray, lost (*OED* 1); perplexed (*OED* 1b).
ii 683. *wanted*] lacked.
ii 684. *dewdrops*] Gardiner 18 says that the dewdrops in The Song of Solomon were interpreted allegorically as imperfectly obedient churches afflicting the head of Christ.
ii 689. *evil-minded beasts*] Protestant sects.
ii 692. See i 351–4n.
ii 695. *could afford*] was capable of giving (*OED* 6).
ii 697. *lowly roof (a shed*] A recollection of Adam's description of his dwelling as a 'lowly roof' when he receives Raphael (*PL* v 463), and also of Milton's observation that 'honest-offered courtesy / . . . is sooner found in lowly sheds / With smoky rafters, than in tap'stry halls / And courts of princes' (*A Masque* ll. 321–4) (J. R. Mason).   *shed*] hut, cottage, poor dwelling (*OED* 2a); hiding-place, lair or nest of an animal (*OED* 2b).
ii 698. *hoary*] ancient (*OED* 1c).
ii 699. *Honest*] respectable, decent (*OED* 2b); not seeming other than it is, genuine, unsophisticated (*OED* 4c).
ii 704. *sojourner*] temporary resident, guest; a biblical word: e.g. 'Hear my prayer, O Lord . . . for I am a stranger with thee, and a sojourner, as all my fathers were' (Psalm xxxix 12).

705   This peaceful seat my poverty secures,
          War seldom enters but where wealth allures;
          Nor yet despise it, for this poor abode
          Has oft received, and yet receives a god;
          A god victorious of the Stygian race
710   Here laid his sacred limbs, and sanctified the place:
          This mean retreat did mighty Pan contain; ⎤
          Be emulous of him, and pomp disdain,   ⎬
          And dare not to debase your soul to gain.' ⎦
              The silent stranger stood amazed to see
715   Contempt of wealth, and wilful poverty:
          And though ill habits are not soon controlled,
          Awhile suspended her desire of gold;

ii *707–13*. Echoes Virgil, *Aen.* viii 362–5, where King Evander is addressing Aeneas as they approach his modest home: *ut uentum ad sedes, 'haec' inquit 'limina uictor / Alcides subiit, haec illum regia cepit. / aude, hospes, contemnere opes et te quoque dignum / finge deo, rebusque ueni non asper egenis.'* ('When they came to the house, [Evander] said, "The victorious Hercules passed across this threshold, and this palace received him. Guest, dare to despise wealth and make yourself also worthy of the god; come, and do not disdain poverty."'). D. translated the lines thus: 'Mean as it is, this Palace, and this Door, / Receiv'd *Alcides*, then a Conquerour. / Dare to be poor: accept our homely Food / Which feasted him; and emulate a God' ('The Eighth Book of the *Aeneis*' ll. 477–80, with verbal echoes of Cowley's translation of these lines in his essay 'Of Agriculture', *Essays* 408). D. said of Virgil's *aude, hospes, contemnere opes, et te quoque dignum finge / deo*: 'For my part I am lost in the admiration of it: I contemn the World, when I think on it, and my self when I Translate it' ('Dedication of the *Aeneis*': *Works* v 335). For an earlier use of this passage see 'To the Earl of Roscommon' ll. 77–8.
ii *708*. The Hind's cell receives a god through transubstantiation in the mass. The reception of a god by a mortal (or *theoxeny*) is also the theme of 'Baucis and Philemon'.
ii *709. A god victorious*] Hercules, who overcame the dog Cerberus in the underworld, is paralleled with Christ, who harrowed hell. Typologically Hercules, who conquered various beasts, may be interpreted to represent 'spiritual fortitude' which gains a reward 'above the starry heaven'; also 'every good Christian, *who must be a valiant Champion, to encounter against the Snakes of malice and envy, the Lion of anger, the Boar of Wantonness . . . and the Devil that great Dragon*'; also 'a good King, who ought to subdue all monsters, cruelty, disorder, and oppression in his Kingdom, who should support the Heaven of the Church with the Shoulders of Authority'; but '*Hercules* was persecuted and maligned'. Finally, 'Our blessed Saviour is the true *Hercules* . . . who was persecuted out of malice, and exposed to all dangers . . . he subdued the roaring Lion . . . that tyrant and devourer of mankinde, the devil' (Ross 168–71). *of*] over. *Stygian*] from the Styx, the river of the classical underworld.
ii *711. Pan*] Christ: see i 284*n*.
ii *715. wilful*] voluntary, chosen out of free will (*OED* 4).
ii *717. gold*] the endowments of the established church (Williams).

But civilly drew in her sharpened paws,
Not violating hospitable laws,
720   And pacified her tail, and licked her frothy jaws.
        The Hind did first her country cates provide,
        Then couched herself securely by her side.

The Hind and the Panther

The Third Part

Much malice mingled with a little wit
Perhaps may censure this mysterious writ,
Because the Muse has peopled Caledon
With panthers, bears, and wolves, and beasts unknown,
5   As if we were not stocked with monsters of our own.
Let Aesop answer, who has set to view
Such kinds as Greece and Phrygia never knew;
And Mother Hubberd in her homely dress
Has sharply blamed a British Lioness,
10   That queen whose feast the factious rabble keep,
Exposed obscenely naked and asleep.
Led by those great examples, may not I
The wanted organs of their words supply?
If men transact like brutes, 'tis equal then

ii 720. *pacified*] calmed the excitement of (*OED* 1).
ii 721. *cates*] choice delicacies.

The Third Part
iii 2. *writ*] written work, book (*OED* 1b, last example).
iii 3. *Caledon*] Britain: see i 14*n*.
iii 6. *Aesop*] Legendary figure, said to be a native of Phrygia in Asia Minor, to whom the authorship of ancient Greek beast fables was attributed.
iii 8. *Mother Hubberd*] Spenser's poem *Mother Hubberds Tale* (1591) tells of a lion (possibly representing Queen Elizabeth) who sheds his crown and sceptre and even his hide because of the heat, and has them stolen by an ape and fox (cp. i 39*n*). The lion is *sharply blamed* by Mercury who rouses him from his trance.
iii 10. In the reign of Charles II the Accession Day of Elizabeth I, 17 November, was the occasion for Protestant street demonstrations, which during the Popish Plot years included pope-burning processions: see 'Prologue to *The Loyal Brother*'.
iii 13. *wanted*] lacking (again at iii 29).
iii 14. *transact*] manage their affairs (*OED* 1).

15 For brutes to claim the privilege of men.
      Others our Hind of folly will indict,
    To entertain a dangerous guest by night:
    Let those remember that she cannot die
    Till rolling time is lost in round eternity;
20 Nor need she fear the Panther, though untamed,
    Because the Lion's peace was now proclaimed;
    The wary salvage would not give offence
    To forfeit the protection of her prince,
    But watched the time her vengeance to complete
25 When all her furry sons in frequent senate met.
    Meanwhile she quenched her fury at the flood,
    And with a lenten salad cooled her blood.
    Their commons, though but coarse, were nothing scant,
    Nor did their minds an equal banquet want.
30   For now the Hind, whose noble nature strove
    T' express her plain simplicity of love,
    Did all the honours of her house so well
    No sharp debates disturbed the friendly meal:
    She turned the talk, avoiding that extreme,

iii 19. *round*] Eternity is envisaged as a circle, perfect and without beginning or end. Kinsley compares Henry Vaughan: 'I saw Eternity the other night / Like a great *Ring* of pure and endless light' ('The World', from *Silex Scintillans* (1655)). Cp. also Cowley's 'The Muse': 'thy *Immortal Rhyme* / Makes this one short *Point* of *Time*, / To fill up half the *Orb* of *Round Eternity*'. Cowley's note on these lines reads: 'There are two sorts of *Eternity*; from the *Present backwards* to *Eternity*, and from the *Present forwards*, called by the Schoolmen *Aeternitas a parte ante*, and *Aeternitas a parte post*. These two make up the whole *Circle of Eternity*, which the *Present Time* cuts like a *Diameter*, but Poetry makes it extend to all *Eternity to come*, which is the *Half-Circle*' (*Poems* 186).
iii 21. *the Lion's peace*] James II's recent *Declaration* (see headnote).
iii 22. *salvage*] See i 156n.
iii 23. James in his *Declaration* promised to 'protect and maintain our archbishops, bishops and clergy, and all other our subjects of the Church of England in the free exercise of their religion as by law established, and in the quiet and full enjoyment of all their possessions, without any molestation or disturbance whatsoever' (*English Historical Documents* 396).
iii 25. *furry*] Williams suggests a reference to the fur hoods of graduates worn by clergy. *frequent*] crowded (*OED* 1; citing 'frequent Senate' in *The State of Innocence* I i 68). *senate*] convocation, the governing body of the Church of England.
iii 26. *flood*] river.
iii 27. *lenten*] Lent, the principal time for fasting, began in 1687 on 9 February; Easter fell on 27 March. If D. wrote or revised this portion of the poem after the publication of the *Declaration* on 4 April, Lent would be fresh in his mind.
iii 28. *commons*] allowance of food.

35   To common dangers past, a sadly pleasing theme;
      Remembering every storm which tossed the state
      When both were objects of the public hate,
      And dropped a tear betwixt for her own children's fate.
          Nor failed she then a full review to make
40   Of what the Panther suffered for her sake:
      Her lost esteem, her truth, her loyal care,
      Her faith unshaken to an exiled heir,
      Her strength t' endure, her courage to defy,
      Her choice of honourable infamy.
45   On these, prolixly thankful, she enlarged,
      Then with acknowledgements herself she charged:
      For friendship, of itself an holy tie,
      Is made more sacred by adversity.
      Now should they part, malicious tongues would say
50   They met like chance companions on the way,
      Whom mutual fear of robbers had possessed:
      While danger lasted, kindness was professed,
      But that once o'er, the short-lived union ends,
      The road divides, and there divide the friends.
55   The Panther nodded when her speech was done,
      And thanked her coldly in a hollow tone;
      But said her gratitude had gone too far
      For common offices of Christian care.
      If to the lawful heir she had been true,
60   She paid but Caesar what was Caesar's due.
      'I might,' she added, 'with like praise describe
      Your suffering sons, and so return your bribe;
      But incense from my hands is poorly prized,
      For gifts are scorned where givers are despised.

---

iii 35. *common dangers past*] the Commonwealth and Protectorate, when both
Anglicans and Catholics suffered as the various sects triumphed.
iii 40. *for her sake*] The Panther suffered for the sake of the Hind in so far as the
Church of England suffered for her adherence to the Stuart monarchy; the Hind
implicitly makes that cause her own.
iii 42. *exiled heir*] Charles II, when heir to the throne, spent most of the period
1646–60 in exile; James II when heir withdrew to Brussels or Scotland for
several periods during the Exclusion Crisis (1679–81). Kinsley notes that during
James's exile in Scotland in 1680, the Anglican bishops in the House of Lords
resolutely voted against Exclusion.
iii 58. *offices*] services (*OED* 1), duties (*OED* 2).
iii 60. As Jesus commanded in Matthew xxii 21.

65 I served a turn, and then was cast away;
    You like the gaudy fly your wings display,
    And sip the sweets, and bask in your great patron's day.'
        This heard, the matron was not slow to find
    What sort of malady had seized her mind;
70 Disdain, with gnawing envy, fell despite,
    And cankered malice stood in open sight:
    Ambition, interest, pride without control,
    And jealousy, the jaundice of the soul;
    Revenge, the bloody minister of ill,
75 With all the lean tormentors of the will.
    'Twas easy now to guess from whence arose
    Her new-made union with her ancient foes,
    Her forced civilities, her faint embrace,
    Affected kindness with an altered face:
80 Yet durst she not too deeply probe the wound,
    As hoping still the nobler parts were sound;
    But strove with anodynes t' assuage the smart,
    And mildly thus her med'cine did impart:
        'Complaints of lovers help to ease their pain;
85 It shows a rest of kindness to complain,
    A friendship loath to quit its former hold,
    And conscious merit may be justly bold.
    But much more just your jealousy would show
    If others' good were injury to you.
90 Witness, ye heavens, how I rejoice to see
    Rewarded worth, and rising loyalty.

iii 65. Leaders of the Church of England had supported James's right to succeed
to the throne, but soon found that the new king was aggressive in promoting
the interests of Roman Catholics (see iii 91–3*n*).
iii 66. fly] butterfly (*OED* 1).
iii 67. sweets] sweet food or drink (*OED* 1b); fragrant flowers (*OED* 7).
iii 70. fell] fierce, savage. *despite*] contempt.
iii 72. interest] self-interest, esp. financial.
iii 77. Anglican alliances with the Nonconformists against James's plans to
advance Catholicism.
iii 80. wound] Pronounced in the seventeenth century to form a perfect rhyme
with *sound*.
iii 82. anodynes] drugs which alleviate pain.
iii 85. a rest of kindness] that kindness still remains.
iii 91–3. James's efforts to promote Roman Catholics to important positions in
the army and the universities – by intimidatory and sometimes illegal means –
were causing controversy. His request to Parliament that Roman Catholics be
allowed to serve as commissioned officers in the army (despite the Test Acts)
caused widespread concern, and was opposed in the House of Lords by the Bishop

Your warrior offspring that upheld the crown,
The scarlet honours of your peaceful gown,
Are the most pleasing objects I can find,
95   Charms to my sight, and cordials to my mind.
When virtue spooms before a prosperous gale
My heaving wishes help to fill the sail,
And if my prayers for all the brave were heard,
Caesar should still have such, and such should still
       reward.
100   'The laboured earth your pains have sowed and
             tilled:
'Tis just you reap the product of the field.
Yours be the harvest, 'tis the beggar's gain
To glean the fallings of the loaded wain;
Such scattered ears as are not worth your care,   ⎫
105   Your charity for alms may safely spare,   ⎬
And alms are but the vehicles of prayer.   ⎭

---

of London, who saw this as a serious attack on the Church of England. In April
and May 1687 James's High Commission tried to force Cambridge to admit a
Benedictine monk to the degree of MA without requiring the customary oaths
of adherence to the Church of England; the Vice-Chancellor was deprived of
his office for refusing. In April 1687 James tried to force Magdalen College Oxford
to elect as its President a Roman Catholic who was ineligible according to its
statutes.

iii *92. upheld*] As *Works* notes, the past tense here is significant.

iii *93.* scarlet doctoral gowns.

iii *95. cordials*] invigorating medicines or drinks.

iii *96. spooms*] runs before the sea or wind.

iii *97. heaving*] causing something to swell out (*OED* 6); unfurling (*OED* 10).

iii *99. Caesar*] James II.

iii *100–8.* The Hind's acceptance that the Panther possesses church properties
which were once her own is a position adopted by moderate Catholics nervous
about the consequences of James's designs to advance and establish Catholicism.
After James's *Declaration for Liberty of Conscience* the Catholic vicar-apostolic, John
Leyburn, issued a pastoral letter saying that since the church's historic resources
had 'fallen into other hands than those they were intended for', the church was
now 'reduced . . . unto its prime [i.e. primitive] condition, and accordingly may
by the rules of justice, as well as pietie, require to be maintained after the prime
method', with the clergy 'contribut[ing] their labour in a more than ordinary
measure' and the gentry 'inlarg[ing] their charityes so far as may be necessary for
a decent maintenance of those who undergoe it' (Bossy 71).

iii *102–3.* The Hind compares herself to Ruth gleaning corn after the reapers (Ruth
ii); she was interpreted as a type of the true church (*Works*).   *harvest*] 'Church
Lands' *MS*.

iii *104–5.* Contrast the emphasis on true charitable almsgiving in *Eleonora* ll. 12–64.

iii *106. vehicles of*] means of expression for (*OED* 3; first example).

My daily bread is literally implored,
I have no barns nor granaries to hoard;
If Caesar to his own his hand extends,
110   Say which of yours his charity offends:
You know he largely gives to more than are his friends.
Are you defrauded when he feeds the poor?
Our mite decreases nothing of your store.
I am but few, and by your fare you see
115   My crying sins are not of luxury.
Some juster motive sure your mind withdraws,
And makes you break our friendship's holy laws,
For barefaced envy is too base a cause.
      'Show more occasion for your discontent:
120   Your love, the Wolf, would help you to invent
Some German quarrel, or, as times go now,
Some French, where force is uppermost, will do.
When at the fountain's head, as merit ought
To claim the place, you take a swilling draught,
125   How easy 'tis an envious eye to throw,
And tax the sheep for troubling streams below;
Or call her (when no farther cause you find)
An enemy professed of all your kind.
But then perhaps the wicked world would think
130   The Wolf designed to eat as well as drink.'
      This last allusion galled the Panther more,

iii *107*. As in the Lord's Prayer (Matthew vi 11).
iii *108*. *no barns nor granaries*] 'no Benefices' *MS*.
iii *111*. *largely*] generously.
iii *115*. *crying*] crying out for punishment, notorious (*OED* 3).
iii *120*. *Wolf*] Presbyterians: see i 153*n*.
iii *121–2*. Germany was a collection of Lutheran, Calvinist and Catholic states, and during the seventeenth century the Counter-Reformation had made considerable headway there. Anglicans had been much concerned about the fate of German Protestants (especially those in the Palatinate) during the Thirty Years War (1618–48), and there had been calls for England to intervene militarily. In 1687 Europe was temporarily at peace, but the League of Augsburg (1686) against Louis XIV anticipated further expansionist moves by France, which had a powerful army. Louis's claim to the Palatinate would renew war in 1688.   *German quarrel*] Williams notes that this adapts the French usage *querelle d'Allemand*, a quarrel entered into on a slight occasion.
iii *123–30*. In Aesop's fable the wolf drinking upstream from the lamb accuses it of fouling the water; when the lamb protests, the wolf devours it (*Fables of Aesop*, tr. John Ogilby (1668) 36–7; *Works*). Ogilby interprets the moral of the story thus: '*They that have Power to do, may, when they will, / Pick Quarrels, and, pretending Justice, kill. / Who hunt for Blood and Spoyl, need not invent / New Crimes, but lay their own on th' innocent*' (37).

Because indeed it rubbed upon the sore;
Yet seemed she not to winch, though shrewdly pained,
But thus her passive character maintained.
135   'I never grudged (whate'er my foes report)
Your flaunting fortune in the Lion's court.
You have your day, or you are much belied,
But I am always on the suffering side.
You know my doctrine, and I need not say
140   I will not, but I cannot, disobey.
On this firm principle I ever stood:
He of my sons who fails to make it good
By one rebellious act renounces to my blood.'
'Ah,' said the Hind, 'how many sons have you
145   Who call you mother, whom you never knew!
But most of them who that relation plead
Are such ungracious youths as wish you dead.
They gape at rich revenues which you hold,
And fain would nibble at your grandame gold;
150   Enquire into your years, and laugh to find
Your crazy temper shows you much declined.
Were you not dim and doted, you might see
A pack of cheats that claim a pedigree,
No more of kin to you, than you to me.

iii 133. winch] wince, flinch (OED).   shrewdly] intensely, seriously (OED 5).
iii 134. passive character] The Church of England had, since the reign of Charles
I, largely maintained the doctrine of passive obedience or non-resistance to a lawful sovereign (see iii 139–43). Scott aptly quotes the decision of the University
of Oxford in 1683 to ban all books which teach the lawfulness of resistance to
legitimate rulers, and to insist that all its tutors 'diligently instruct and ground
their scholars in that most necessary doctrine, which in a manner is the badge
and character of the church of England, of submitting to every ordinance of man
for the Lord's sake . . . Teaching, that this submission and obedience is to be clear,
absolute, and without exception' (Scott x 241–2). But by 1687 this stance was
being sorely tested by James's actions (see iii 65n, 91–3n) and had begun to be
discarded by some (see iii 948–51).
iii 143. renounces to] makes renunciation of (OED 6).
iii 147. ungracious youths] clergy who are members of the established Church
of England, but are sympathetic to Presbyterianism. 'Presby. Bpˢ & Clergy' MS.
ungracious] despite their insistence on grace: see i 47n.
iii 148. revenues] stressed on the second syllable in the seventeenth century.
iii 149. grandame gold] hoarded (i.e. ancestral, inherited) wealth (OED 5).
grandame] grandmother.
iii 150–1. Unlike the immortal Hind (i 1), the Panther is part of a mortal cycle of
growth and decay (Gardiner 7). crazy] infirm, frail (OED 2). temper] bodily
constitution (OED 8).
iii 152. dim] not seeing clearly (OED 4). doted] foolish, senile (OED).

155   Do you not know, that for a little coin,
       Heralds can foist a name into the line?
       They ask you blessing but for what you have, ⎫
       But once possessed of what with care you save, ⎬
       The wanton boys would piss upon your grave. ⎭

160   Your sons of latitude that court your grace, ⎫
       Though most resembling you in form and face, ⎬
       Are far the worst of your pretended race; ⎭
       And but I blush your honesty to blot,
       Pray God you prove 'em lawfully begot:
165   For in some popish libels I have read
       The Wolf has been too busy in your bed;
       At least their hinder parts, the belly piece,
       The paunch, and all that Scorpio claims, are his.
       Their malice, too, a sore suspicion brings,
170   For though they dare not bark, they snarl at kings.
       Nor blame 'em for intruding in your line:
       Fat bishoprics are still of right divine.
          Think you your new French proselytes are come
       To starve abroad, because they starved at home?
175   Your benefices twinkled from afar,
       They found the new Messiah by the star:

---

iii 156. Heralds (see i 348*n*) can forge a genealogy, as they did for Titus Oates
(see *AA* l. 641*n*).

iii 157. They ask you blessing] i.e. like a dutiful son to his father.

iii 160. sons of latitude] The Latitudinarians were a group within the Church of England
who emphasized rational enquiry and were open to accommodation with the
Nonconformists rather than insisting upon niceties of church government and liturgical practice. The tendency is first seen in the Cambridge Platonists, and after
the Restoration is exemplified by John Tillotson, Edward Stillingfleet and Gilbert
Burnet. Their beliefs are set out by Simon Patrick in *A Brief Account of the New
Sect of Latitude-Men* (1662). See also *Philosophy, Science, and Religion in England
1640–1700*, ed. Richard Kroll, Richard Ashcraft and Perez Zagorin (1992), and
W. M. Spellman, *The Latitudinarians and the Church of England 1660–1700* (1993). In
his contribution to *A Defence of the Papers* (1686) D. had said that 'a Latitudinarian
. . . is no otherwise different from a Presbyterian, than *by whatsoever Titles and Dignities
he is distinguish'd*' (*Works* xvii 304). For D.'s earlier comments see *RL*, Preface
ll. 88–9*n*. *MS* glosses *sons of latitude* as 'Trimmers', a term used of political mod-
erates who would not align themselves with either Whigs or Tories, and which
had come to be used abusively by Tories about those whom they thought covertly
sympathetic to the Whigs or simply opportunistic and unprincipled. *MS* thus associates religious latitude with lack of political principle.

iii 162. your pretended race] those who claim (or those whom the Panther claims)
to be part of the Church of England.

iii 168. all that Scorpio claims] Astrologically, Scorpio was said to rule the groin.

iii 173. French proselytes] the Huguenots (see ii 456–8*n*).

Those Swisses fight on any side for pay,
And 'tis the living that conforms, not they.
Mark with what management their tribes divide: ⎫
180 Some stick to you, and some to t' other side,   ⎬
That many churches may for many mouths provide. ⎭
More vacant pulpits would more converts make,
All would have latitude enough to take;
The rest unbeneficed your sects maintain, ⎫
185 For ordinations without cures are vain,   ⎬
And chamber practice is a silent gain.   ⎭
Your sons of breadth at home are much like these,
Their soft and yielding metals run with ease,
They melt and take the figure of the mould,
190 But harden and preserve it best in gold.'
   'Your Delphic sword,' the Panther then replied,
'Is double-edged, and cuts on either side.
Some sons of mine who bear upon their shield
Three steeples argent in a sable field

---

iii 177. Swisses] Swiss mercenaries. The Huguenots were not literally Swiss, but their doctrines originated in Calvin's Geneva.

iii 178. living] benefice.   *conforms*] to Anglican doctrine and practice.

iii 179. management] contrivance, ingenuity (implicitly deceitful) (*OED* 2).

iii 180. t' other side] the Nonconformist sects.

iii 181. There is an implicit contrast here with the celibate priesthood of the Roman Catholic Church.

iii 184. Huguenots without Anglican benefices are maintained financially by the Nonconformist sects.

iii 185. A priest must be ordained to the 'cure [i.e. care] of souls' in a specified parish or other ecclesiastical office. The Hind implies that ordination which carries no such appointment is not only invalid but useless to the Huguenots because unpaid.

iii 186. chamber practice] legal work carried out in a lawyer's chambers rather than in court; here with the implication that the rewards which Nonconformist ministers gain from carrying out their religious duties in private homes (particularly in bedchambers) are not spoken about.

iii 187. sons of breadth] Latitudinarians.

iii 188. yielding] *1687a errata, 1687bc*; easie *1687a text*. Probably D.'s revision to avoid an overlooked repetition.

iii 191. Delphic sword] one fashioned for many uses (Aristotle, *Politics* 1252b).

iii 193–217. This passage refers to the controversy over the Duchess of York's paper (see 'To the Reader' l. 85*n*), and makes the Panther voice some of Stillingfleet's accusations against D. (Scott).

iii 194. The three silver steeples on a black background do not correspond to any particular ecclesiastical arms, but symbolize the financial allure of the established church in hard times; *three* suggests an allusion to the common practice of pluralism (holding more than one benefice simultaneously): Stillingfleet himself was at this date both Dean of St Paul's Cathedral and Rector of St Andrew's Holborn

195 Have sharply taxed your converts, who unfed
     Have followed you for miracles of bread;
     Such who themselves of no religion are,
     Allured with gain, for any will declare.
     Bare lies with bold assertions they can face,
200 But dint of argument is out of place:
     The grim logician puts 'em in a fright,
     'Tis easier far to flourish than to fight.
     Thus our eighth Henry's marriage they defame, ⎫
     They say the schism of beds began the game, ⎬
205 Divorcing from the church to wed the dame: ⎭

(*DNB*). The phrase also has echoes of the 30 pieces of silver which Judas received
for betraying Jesus (Matthew xxvi 14–15). *Works* notes that Stillingfleet had said
that those who defended the Royal Papers regarded themselves as 'a sort of Heralds
in Controversie, whose bearing the Royal Arms, will keep them from being touched
themselves' (*Vindication* 1).
iii *195. converts*] Stillingfleet in the *Vindication* had emphasized D.'s status as a new
convert.
iii *196*. Stillingfleet had asked whether D. 'was out of the Temptation of changing his Religion for Bread?' (*Vindication* 105).
iii *197*. Stillingfleet had misquoted *AA* l. 99 ('For priests of all religions are alike';
recte 'the same') and asked: 'Why should not one who believes no religion declare
for any?' (*Vindication* 2).
iii *199–201*. Cp. Stillingfleet: 'If bold sayings and confident declarations will do
the business, he is never unprovided; but if you expect any reason from him, he
begs your pardon; he finds how ill the Character of a grim logician suits with
his inclination' (*Vindication* 116). The phrase 'grim *Logician*' had been used by D.
in his *Defence of the Papers*, where he says that although the author of the *Answer*
had asserted that 'there is nothing to be done, no satisfaction to be had in Matters of Religion without Dispute', other Anglicans thought that '*The itch of Disputation
is the Scab or Tetter of the Church*. Now if the Learned avail themselves so little of
Dispute, that it is as rare as a Prodigie for one of them to convince another, what
shall become of the Ignorant, when they are to deal with those fencers of Divinity
. . . And yet such poor People have Souls to save as precious in the sight of God
as the grim *Logicians*' (*Works* xvii 297).
iii *200. dint*] force.
iii *202*. In the *Defence of the Papers* (in a passage not thought to be written by D.)
Stillingfleet had been said to have 'a mind to flourish, before he offered to pass'
(2). Stillingfleet took up this charge in his *Vindication* (1). *flourish*] brandish a
weapon (*OED* 9); make a display, show off (*OED* 10).
iii *203–11*. In his *Defence* D. had written: 'Now the immediate Cause which produc'd the Separation of *Harry* the Eighth from the Church of *Rome*, was the refusal
of the Pope to grant him a Divorce from his first Wife, and to gratifie his Desires
in a Dispensation for a second Marriage . . . the King only knew whether it was
Conscience and Love, or Love alone, which mov'd him to sue for a Divorce:
But this we may say, that if Conscience had any part in it, she had taken a long
Nap of almost Twenty years together before she awaken'd, and perhaps had slept
on till Doomsday, if *Anne Bullen*, or some other fair Lady, had not given her a

Though largely proved, and by himself professed,
That conscience, conscience would not let him rest,
I mean not till possessed of her he loved,
And old, uncharming Catherine was removed.
210　For sundry years before did he complain,
And told his ghostly confessor his pain.
With the same impudence, without a ground,
They say, that look the Reformation round,
No *Treatise of Humility* is found.
215　But if none were, the gospel does not want:
Our Saviour preached it, and I hope you grant
The sermon in the mount was Protestant.'
　　'No doubt,' replied the Hind, 'as sure as all
The writings of Saint Peter and Saint Paul.
220　On that decision let it stand or fall.
Now for my converts, who you say unfed
Have followed me for miracles of bread:
Judge not by hearsay, but observe at least
If since their change their loaves have been increased.
225　The Lion buys no converts: if he did,

Jog; so the satisfying of an inordinate and a brutal Passion cannot be deny'd to
have had a great share at least, in the production of that Schism which led the
very way to our pretended Reformation' (*Works* xvii 316–17).
iii 206. *largely*] at length, fully (*OED* 3).
iii 207. *conscience, conscience*] In Shakespeare's *Henry VIII* the King says: 'Would
it not grieve an able man to leave / So sweet a bedfellow? But conscience, conscience; / O 'tis a tender place, and I must leave her' (II ii 141–3; Williams).
iii 209. *uncharming*] *OED*'s first example.
iii 211. Stillingfleet says of Henry VIII: 'he affirms, *That he moved it himself in
Confession to the Bishop of* Lincoln, *and appeals to him concerning the Truth of it in
open Court*' (*Vindication* 111). *ghostly*] spiritual. *confessor*] stressed on the first
syllable in the seventeenth century.
iii 212–17. For the debate over a Protestant *Treatise of Humility* see 'To the Reader'
ll. 98–9n. D. adapts here Stillingfleet's remark: 'I would desire him not to end
with such a bare-faced Assertion of a thing so well known to be false . . . Suppose
we had not such particular Books, we think the Holy Scripture gives the best
Rules and Examples of Humility of any Book in the World' (*Vindication* 118).
iii 215. *want*] lack.
iii 224. D. himself did not benefit financially from his conversion to Catholicism.
Under James II his official pension as Poet Laureate and Historiographer Royal
was payed more promptly than under Charles II, but was still in arrears, and on
27 May 1687 D. petitioned for the payment of £716 13s 9d still owing from the
reign of Charles II and for £75 owed from James. The money was never paid
(Winn 530). If James were to be succeeded by a Protestant (see iii 228n), D.
would suffer from the re-imposition of the penal sanctions against Roman
Catholics, e.g. exclusion from all public offices and double taxation.

Beasts would be sold as fast as he could bid.
Tax those of interest who conform for gain,
Or stay the market of another reign.
Your broad-way sons would never be too nice
230   To close with Calvin if he paid their price,
But raised three steeples higher would change their note,
And quit the cassock for the canting coat.
Now, if you damn this censure as too bold,
Judge by yourselves, and think not others sold.
235   'Meantime my sons accused by fame's report
Pay small attendance at the Lion's court,
Nor rise with early crowds, nor flatter late
(For silently they beg who daily wait).
Preferment is bestowed that comes unsought,
240   Attendance is a bribe, and then 'tis bought.
How they should speed? Their fortune is untried,
For not to ask is not to be denied.
For what they have, their God and King they bless,
And hope they should not murmur, had they less.
245   But if reduced subsistence to implore,
In common prudence they would pass your door;
Unpitied Hudibras, your champion friend,
Has shown how far your charities extend.
This lasting verse shall on his tomb be read:
250   "He shamed you living, and upbraids you dead."

---

iii 227. Tax] accuse.
iii 228. i.e. those who remain Protestants in the hope of prospering under a Protestant successor to James II, whose heir presumptive at this date was the Protestant Princess Mary.   *stay*] wait for and take part in (*OED* 17).
iii 229. broad-way sons] Latitudinarians, associated here with the road to hell, for 'broad is the way, that leadeth to destruction' (Matthew vii 13).   *nice*] scrupulous.
iii 230. close] make a bargain.
iii 231. raised three steeples higher] if their income were raised (see iii 194n).
iii 232. cassock] the dress of an Anglican clergyman.   *canting coat*] Geneva gown or coat of a dissenting minister (*OED* canting[2] 3, citing this example).   *canting*] using specialized or affected phrasing; applied particularly to Puritan and Presbyterian preaching styles (*OED* cant[3] 6).
iii 247. Hudibras] Samuel Butler (1613–80), author of *Hudibras* (1663–78), which included satire against Presbyterians. He notoriously died in poverty, although his work had been well received at court and he had been granted a royal pension: cp. Oldham, 'Spencer's Ghost' ll. 175–90; and D.'s letter to Laurence Hyde *c.* August 1683 asking for the payment of his own pension: 'Tis enough for one Age to have neglected Mr Cowley, and sterv'd Mr Buttler' (*Letters* 21).

'With odious atheist names you load your foes;
Your liberal clergy why did I expose?
It never fails in charities like those.
In climes where true religion is professed,
255   That imputation were no laughing jest.
But *imprimatur* with a chaplain's name
Is here sufficient licence to defame.
What wonder is't that black detraction thrives?
The homicide of names is less than lives,
260   And yet the perjured murtherer survives.'
    This said, she paused a little, and suppressed
The boiling indignation of her breast;
She knew the virtue of her blade, nor would
Pollute her satire with ignoble blood.
265   Her panting foes she saw before her lie,
And back she drew the shining weapon dry:
So when the generous Lion has in sight
His equal match, he rouses for the fight,
But when his foe lies prostrate on the plain,
270   He sheathes his paws, uncurls his angry mane,
And pleased with bloodless honours of the day
Walks over and disdains th' inglorious prey.
So James, if great with less we may compare,
Arrests his rolling thunderbolts in air,
275   And grants ungrateful friends a lengthened space
T' implore the remnants of long-suffering grace.
    This breathing-time the matron took, and then

---

iii 251. See iii 197n.

iii 256–7. Stillingfleet's *Vindication* appeared with the *imprimatur* of the Archbishop of Canterbury's chaplain.

iii 260. *perjured murtherer*] MS interprets this specifically as a reference to 'Dʳ Oates'.

iii 262. *indignation*] anger (often of a superior) at injustice or misconduct (*OED* 2).

iii 263. *virtue*] superiority, efficacy, power (*OED* 9).   *blade*] For the image of satire as a blade cp. 'Discourse Concerning Satire' (*Poems* iii 421).

iii 267. *generous*] noble.

iii 269–72. 'The *Lyon* never makes a prey of those who lye flat on their faces . . . He can contract his nails and hide them as it were in his flesh' (Franzius 42, 46; *Works*). Cp. *AA* ll. 447–54 and *nn*.

iii 273. A formula from Milton (e.g. *PL* ii 921–2: 'to compare / Great things with small'), and originally from Virgil (*Geo.* iv 176: *si parva licet componere magnis*).

iii 276. *long-suffering grace*] Echoes Exodus xxxiv 6: 'The Lord God, merciful and gracious, longsuffering, and abundant in goodness and truth'; cp. *Astraea Redux* l. 265.

Resumed the thread of her discourse again:
'Be vengeance wholly left to powers divine,
280   And let heaven judge betwixt your sons and mine:
If joys hereafter must be purchased here
With loss of all that mortals hold so dear,
Then welcome infamy and public shame,
And last, a long farewell to worldly fame.
285   'Tis said with ease, but O, how hardly tried ⎫
By haughty souls to human honour tied!   ⎬
O sharp convulsive pangs of agonizing pride! ⎭
Down then thou rebel, never more to rise,   ⎫
And what thou didst, and dost so dearly prize, ⎬
290   That fame, that darling fame, make that thy sacrifice. ⎭
'Tis nothing thou hast giv'n; then add thy tears
For a long race of unrepenting years:
'Tis nothing yet, yet all thou hast to give;
Then add those maybe years thou hast to live.
295   Yet nothing still: then poor and naked come,   ⎫
Thy father will receive his unthrift home,   ⎬
And thy blessed Saviour's blood discharge the mighty ⎟
    sum.   ⎭
     'Thus,' she pursued, 'I discipline a son
Whose unchecked fury to revenge would run:
300   He champs the bit, impatient of his loss,
And starts aside, and flounders at the cross.

iii 279. 'Vengeance is mine; I will repay, saith the Lord' (Romans xii 19).
iii 281–97. As becomes clear at iii 298, this speech is directed partly at D. himself, and thus like i 72–8 forms an autobiographical reflection on his own pride and the difficult spiritual process which has led him to accept the authority of the Roman Catholic Church, to distance himself from some of his earlier work, and to eschew revenge for scandalous attacks on his character. For D.'s refusal to retaliate to such abuse cp. 'To Mr Henry Higden' ll. 22–36 and 'Discourse Concerning Satire' (*Poems* iii 406–7).
iii 281–6. Cp. D. on the Duchess of York: 'The loss of Friends, of worldly Honours, and Esteem, the Defamation of ill Tongues, and the Reproach of the Cross, all these, though not without the struglings of Flesh and Blood, were surmounted by her; as if the Saying of our Saviour were always sounding in her Ears, *What will it profit a man to gain the whole world, and lose his Soul!*' (*Works* xvii 291).
iii 285. hardly] with difficulty.
iii 295–6. Recalling the parable of the prodigal son (Luke xv 11–32). *unthrift*] spendthrift, prodigal (*OED* 3).
iii 298. a son] D. himself, but also 'any Catholic brought by priestly admonitions through penance and contrition to forgiveness' (*Works*).
iii 301. flounders] rears, shies (*OED* 1, citing this example). *cross*] thwarting (*OED* 27); trial or affliction to be borne in a Christian spirit (*OED* 10).

Instruct him better, gracious God, to know
As thine is vengeance, so forgiveness too.
That suffering from ill tongues he bears no more
305   Than what his sovereign bears, and what his Saviour
             bore.
        'It now remains for you to school your child,
    And ask why God's anointed he reviled.
    A king and princess dead! Did Shimei worse?
    The curser's punishment should fright the curse:
310   Your son was warned, and wisely gave it o'er,
    But he who counselled him has paid the score:
    The heavy malice could no higher tend,
    But woe to him on whom the weights descend:
    So to permitted ills the demon flies,
315   His rage is aimed at him who rules the skies.
    Constrained to quit his cause, no succour found,
    The foe discharges every tire around,
    In clouds of smoke abandoning the fight,
    But his own thundering peals proclaim his flight.
320   'In Henry's change his charge as ill succeeds: ⎫
    To that long story little answer needs;   ⎬
    Confront but Henry's words with Henry's deeds. ⎭

iii 306, 310. your child . . . your son] Stillingfleet.
iii 307. God's anointed] Charles II.
iii 308. princess] Anne Hyde, Duchess of York.   *Shimei*] He cursed King David, and was killed: see 2 Samuel xvi 5–13 and 1 Kings ii 36–46. For D.'s earlier application of the story of Shimei see *AA* ll. 584–629.
iii 311. Scott thought that Bishop Gilbert Burnet was the person who counselled Stillingfleet, but *Works* points out that Burnet had left the country before the controversy over the royal papers arose. The reference remains obscure.
iii 313. From *PL* iv 996–1004, where the weights in the scales descend against Satan; cp. *HP* ii 623–4.
iii 314–15. In *PL* God permits Satan's scheme to tempt Adam and Eve, which is inspired by his rage against God himself.
iii 316. Stillingfleet was forced to admit the authenticity of the Duchess's paper, having at first questioned it (Williams).
iii 317. tire] simultaneous discharge of a battery of ordnance; broadside (*OED*).
iii 320–7. In her paper, the Duchess had explained that her conversion to Rome had been prompted by reading Peter Heylyn's *Ecclesia Restaurata* (3rd edition 1674), which argued that Henry VIII's motive for breaking with Rome was simply his desire for a divorce, a motive which the Duchess described as 'most Abominable' (*Works* xvii 519). D. had repeated and amplified this view in his *Defence*, while Stillingfleet maintained that Henry was motivated by conscience alone in the conduct of his private affairs (see iii 203–11*nn* above). Stillingfleet had also said that the cause (conscience) was distant from the political effects of Henry's action, and remarked that D. 'takes a leap from *Causes* to *Effects*' (*Vindication* 116).

Were space allowed, with ease it might be proved
What springs his blessèd reformation moved.
325 The dire effects appeared in open sight,
Which from the cause he calls a distant flight,
And yet no larger leap than from the sun to light. }
        'Now last your sons a double paean sound,
A *Treatise of Humility* is found.
330 'Tis found, but better it had ne'er been sought
Than thus in Protestant procession brought.
The famed original through Spain is known,
Rodriguez' work, my celebrated son,
Which yours by ill translating made his own, }
335 Concealed its author and usurped the name,
The basest and ignoblest theft of fame.
My altars kindled first that living coal:
Restore, or practise better what you stole.
That virtue could this humble verse inspire:
340 'Tis all the restitution I require.'
        Glad was the Panther that the charge was closed,
And none of all her favourite sons exposed.
For laws of arms permit each injured man
To make himself a saver where he can.
345 Perhaps the plundered merchant cannot tell
The names of pirates in whose hands he fell,
But at the den of thieves he justly flies,
And every Algerine is lawful prize;
No private person in the foe's estate
350 Can plead exemption from the public fate.
Yet Christian laws allow not such redress;
Then let the greater supersede the less.

---

iii 328–40. See 'To the Reader' ll. 98–105 and iii 212–17 above.
iii 328. double paean] That of Stillingfleet in his *Vindication* (118) and another unnamed author referred to by D. in 'To the Reader' l. 102 (*Works*).
iii 337. The image is from Isaiah vi 6.
iii 343–51. i.e. according to the ordinary customs of war, D. would be justified in seizing whatever goods he could from his enemies (in this case, their reputations) in compensation for injuries received, even if the individuals whose property is seized by the injured party were not themselves responsible for his loss; however, D. is instead following Christian teaching, which requires one to turn the other cheek when attacked (Luke vi 29).
iii 344. make himself a saver] compensate himself for a loss (*OED* saver 2).
iii 348. Algerine] Algerian ship. Algeria was a notorious base for pirates.
iii 349. estate] state, country (*OED* 10).

But let th' abettors of the Panther's crime
Learn to make fairer wars another time.
355   Some characters may sure be found to write ⎫
Among her sons, for 'tis no common sight, ⎬
A spotted dam, and all her offspring white. ⎭
    The salvage, though she saw her plea controlled,
Yet would not wholly seem to quit her hold,
360   But offered fairly to compound the strife,
And judge conversion by the convert's life.
''Tis true,' she said, 'I think it somewhat strange
So few should follow profitable change:
For present joys are more to flesh and blood
365   Than a dull prospect of a distant good.
'Twas well alluded by a son of mine
(I hope to quote him is not to purloin)
Two magnets, heaven and earth, allure to bliss,
The larger loadstone that, the nearer this:
370   The weak attraction of the greater fails,
We nod awhile, but neighbourhood prevails:
But when the greater proves the nearer too,
I wonder more your converts come so slow.
Methinks in those who firm with me remain,
375   It shows a nobler principle than gain.'
    'Your inference would be strong,' the Hind replied,
'If yours were in effect the suffering side:
Your clergy sons their own in peace possess,
Nor are their prospects in reversion less.

---

iii 353. the Panther's crime] 'Calumny & Slander' *MS.*
iii 355. characters] satirical sketches.
iii 358. her plea] See iii 191–217.   *controlled*] overruled (*OED* 5b; antedating its first example from 1724).
iii 359. hold] grip (*OED* 2); animal's place of refuge (*OED* 9); fortified defensive position (*OED* 10).
iii 360. compound] settle (*OED* 6).
iii 361. Cp. i 78.
iii 365. dull] dim, unclear (*OED* 7).
iii 366. alluded] expressed figuratively or fancifully (*OED* 3).
iii 368–73. The source of this image has not been identified, though Henry Vaughan describes heaven's attraction for the soul in terms of a magnet in 'The Star' and 'The Query' (*Silex Scintillans* II (1655)).
iii 371. nod] incline, tend (i.e. towards heaven) (*OED* 5, citing only Jonson).
iii 372. i.e. when heavenly and earthly rewards coincide.
iii 379. reversion] right of succession; i.e. the prospects for the Anglican clergy after James is succeeded by a Protestant monarch.

380   My proselytes are struck with awful dread,
       Your bloody comet-laws hang blazing o'er their head;
       The respite they enjoy but only lent,
       The best they have to hope, protracted punishment.
       Be judge yourself, if interest may prevail,
385   Which motives, yours or mine, will turn the scale.
       While pride and pomp allure, and plenteous ease, ⎫
       That is, till man's predom'nant passions cease,   ⎬
       Admire no longer at my slow increase.   ⎭
         'By education most have been misled,
390   So they believe because they so were bred.
       The priest continues what the nurse began,
       And thus the child imposes on the man.
       The rest I named before, nor need repeat,
       But int'rest is the most prevailing cheat,
395   The sly seducer both of age and youth;
       They study that, and think they study truth.
       When int'rest fortifies an argument,   ⎫
       Weak reason serves to gain the will's assent,   ⎬
       For souls already warped receive an easy bent. ⎭
400   'Add long prescription of established laws,
       And pique of honour to maintain a cause,
       And shame of change, and fear of future ill,
       And zeal, the blind conductor of the will;
       And chief among the still-mistaking crowd,   ⎫
405   The fame of teachers obstinate and proud,   ⎬
       And more than all, the private judge allowed; ⎭

---

iii 381–2. According to the statute 27 Eliz. I, c. 2 (1585), it was high treason for a Roman Catholic priest to be on English soil, and a felony for anyone to assist him; both offences carried the death penalty. This law was suspended by James's *Declaration for Liberty of Conscience* but not repealed, and was likely to be enforced under a Protestant successor. Gardiner 148 notes that the statute 13 Eliz. I, c. 2 made it high treason for someone to be reconciled to Rome, as D. and his sons had been.   *comet-laws*] The laws bode disaster, as a comet was supposed to do.

iii 383. protracted] deferred, postponed (*OED* 3).

iii 384. See ii 58*n*.

iii 388. Admire] wonder.

iii 389–90. Works notes that the Duchess recalled that she had been 'always Bred up in the Church of *England*, and as well Instructed in the Doctrine of it, as the best Divines, and her Capacity could make her' (*Works* xvii 519).

iii 393. named before] In iii 378–88.

iii 401. pique of honour] offence taken on a point of honour.

iii 403. zeal] See i 233*n*.

iii 406. The Protestant churches allowed private judgement in matters of faith: cp. ii 252–60.

Disdain of fathers which the dance began,
And last, uncertain whose the narrower span,
The clown unread, and half-read gentleman.'
410   To this the Panther, with a scornful smile:
'Yet still you travail with unwearied toil,
And range around the realm without control
Among my sons, for proselytes to prole,
And here and there you snap some silly soul.
415   You hinted fears of future change in state:
Pray heaven you did not prophesy your fate.
Perhaps you think your time of triumph near,
But may mistake the season of the year;
The Swallows' fortune gives you cause to fear.'

iii 407. fathers] church fathers: cp. i 468–71*n*, ii 245*n*.   *dance*] course of action, game (*OED* 5).

iii 408. span] intellectual range (*OED* 5, first example 1858).

iii 409. clown] ignorant, uncultured man (*OED* 2).

iii 413. prole] prowl (the seventeenth-century spelling is preserved for the pronunciation).

iii 414. silly] helpless, defenceless (*OED* 1b); unsophisticated, ignorant (*OED* 3).

iii 419–638. The fable of the Swallows presents a complex challenge to the reader, for (as *Works* observes) it provides an allegory of contemporary disputes among English Catholics which is diplomatically veiled, while also being related maliciously by the Panther, who gives it an ominous conclusion; and yet the whole story nevertheless reflects creditably upon the Roman Catholic Church: 'thus the Panther is made to praise unawares the Roman as the true Church and even to forecast, for all her vision of slaughter of the Catholic Swallows, eventual Roman triumph' (*Works*). Local details rebound upon the Panther, such as the representation of the Anglican clergy as Ravens (see iii 475–6*n*). *Works* notes that the fable has a source in 'The Parliament of Birds' in Ogilby's *The Fables of Aesop* 95–100, where contradictory advice is offered by the Swallow and the Linnet (equivalent to D.'s Martin). Man has grown linen, which the birds must destroy if they are not to be caught. The Linnet argues that man is no danger, while the Swallow foresees disaster and makes a pact with man. The rest of the birds are captured by man. Sir Thomas Browne records that swallows 'were sacred unto the Penates or houshold gods of the ancients' (*Pseudodoxia Epidemica* i 435). Franzius says that the swallow is the bird which announces the arrival of the most beautiful time of the year, and that swallows love their nests. Typologically the swallow represents the church in several respects: it hibernates in winter as the church endures times of persecution; just as the swallow is said to desert buildings which are liable to collapse, so the church takes note of the instability of worldly affairs, in order not to be burdened by such cares; as the swallow does not harm other birds, so the church does not harm its neighbours; and as the swallow takes very great care of its young, so the church must take great pains that many from all nations are gained for Christ (*Historia Animalium* (1687) 418–28).

The time scheme of the fable is difficult to interpret. Scott thought that it referred to the meeting at the Savoy in 1686, and that the proposed flight of the swallows

420   'For charity,' replied the matron, 'tell
        What sad mischance those pretty birds befell.'
            'Nay, no mischance,' the salvage dame replied, ⎫
        'But want of wit in their unerring guide,   ⎪
        And eager haste, and gaudy hopes, and giddy pride. ⎬
425   Yet, wishing timely warning may prevail,   ⎭
        Make you the moral, and I'll tell the tale.
            'The Swallow, privileged above the rest
        Of all the birds, as man's familiar guest,

---

was to refuge in France or Ireland. Williams concurred. But Bredvold (178) argued
that the reference was more generally to the discussions which had been held
since the accession of James. The overall thrust of the fable warns Catholics not
to be too ambitious in their demands for public rights, and to make a reasonable
accommodation with the Anglican establishment. As well as being the Panther's
malicious message, this would also have been D.'s own modest message to the
Catholic community: cp. D.'s letter quoted in iii 461n below. The anti-clerical
thrust of the fable, especially in the depiction of the Martin, is consonant both
with D.'s lifelong distrust of clergy (of whatever denomination), and with the
leading Catholic laity's fear that the revival of a Catholic establishment would
not only alienate Anglicans but also introduce an unwelcome increase in clerical
power (see Bossy 71).
    The structure of the fable may be analysed thus:
        427–44: Roman Catholic priests in England enjoy a good life, but the clim-
        ate begins to change and they sense that harder times are approaching.
        445–60: Efforts to avoid persecution by flying south.
        461–96: The Martin's advice.
        497–522: The wiser sort of Swallows' advice.
        523–42: Catholics make their way at court.
        543–87: Illusory public triumph of the Swallows.
        588–94: James's maintenance of an army.
        595–638: Tragic end of the Swallows.
iii 423. wit] intelligence.
iii 424. gaudy] excessively extravagant.   giddy] elated to thoughtlessness (Johnson).
iii 427–44. Roman Catholic priests in England enjoy a good life, but the climate
begins to change and they sense that harder times are approaching. The time
scheme here is difficult to interpret. The present tense in iii 429–32 describes the
Swallow's general characteristics. The phrase long possessed (iii 435) suggests the
long period which ended with the Reformation: this turned out to have been
merely a temporary residence (summer seat) rather than permanent possession, for
the Roman Catholic clergy were forced to leave England in the reign of Elizabeth
(see iii 381–2n). But the main implication is that the period of comfort enjoyed
by Catholics since the accession of James two years earlier is drawing to a close
(as the Panther had implied in iii 415–19). The relation between the narrative
time within the fable and historical time experienced by D. and his readers is not
simple or single.
iii 427. Swallow] The Roman Catholic Church as a whole, but particularly the
clergy. MS interprets the Swallow specifically as 'Religious Orders'.
iii 428. familiar] relating to the household (OED 1); domesticated, tame (OED 3).

Pursues the sun in summer brisk and bold,
430   But wisely shuns the persecuting cold;
Is well to chancels and to chimneys known,
Though 'tis not thought she feeds on smoke alone.
From hence she has been held of heavenly line,
Endued with particles of soul divine.
435   This merry chorister had long possessed
Her summer seat, and feathered well her nest:
Till frowning skies began to change their cheer,
And time turned up the wrong side of the year;
The shedding trees began the ground to strow
440   With yellow leaves, and bitter blasts to blow.
Sad auguries of winter thence she drew,
Which by instinct, or prophecy, she knew:
When prudence warned her to remove betimes
And seek a better heaven, and warmer climes.
445   'Her sons were summoned on a steeple's height,
And, called in common council, vote a flight;
The day was named, the next that should be fair: ⎤
All to the general rendezvous repair,   ⎟
They try their fluttering wings, and trust themselves ⎬
    in air.   ⎟
                                               ⎦
450   But whether upward to the moon they go,   ⎤
Or dream the winter out in caves below,   ⎬
Or hawk at flies elsewhere, concerns not us to know. ⎦

iii 432. smoke] With an allusion to Catholic use of incense.
iii 434. From Horace, *divinae particulam aurae* ('fragment of the divine spirit': *Serm.*
II ii 79; Williams).
iii 435. long possessed] '900 years' *MS*; cp. ii 630*n*.
iii 437. 'yᵉ. Eng. Reformation' *MS.   cheer*] countenance, aspect (*OED* 2).
iii 438. From Horace: *inversum contristat Aquarius annum* ('Aquarius saddens the
upturned year': *Serm.* I i 36; Williams). Cp. 'Horace: *Epode* II' l. 46.
iii 442. instinct] stressed on the second syllable in the seventeenth century.
iii 445–60. Efforts to avoid persecution by flying south. Bredvold (172) notes that
in March 1686 the Florentine ambassador Terriesi reported that some English
Catholics were so alarmed at the likely outcome of James's policies that they were
considering selling up and moving abroad.
iii 445. on a steeple's height] Probably the Savoy, where Roman Catholic services
were held in the royal chapel.
iii 450–2. Seventeenth-century writers were uncertain as to where swallows win-
tered; some thought that they congregated at the bottom of ponds, while others
said that 'they repair into those countreys where they may rest upon the sides of
such warm mountains as lie open to the heat of the shining sunne' (Swan 407).
iii 452. hawk] hunt on the wing (*OED* 2).

'Southwards, you may be sure, they bent their flight,
And harboured in a hollow rock at night;
455   Next morn they rose and set up every sail,
The wind was fair, but blew a mackerel gale:
The sickly young sat shivering on the shore,
Abhorred salt water never seen before,
And prayed their tender mothers to delay
460   The passage, and expect a fairer day.
'With these the Martin readily concurred,
A church-begot and church-believing bird;
Of little body but of lofty mind,
Round bellied, for a dignity designed,
465   And much a dunce, as Martins are by kind;

iii 453. Southwards] To northern France, where there were colleges at St Omer
and Douai which were founded to educate English Catholics; or to Italy, where
there was an English College in Rome; or to Spain, where Titus Oates had spent
a notorious period at Salamanca.
iii 456. mackerel gale] strong breeze which ruffles the water, so favouring the catching of mackerel (*OED*).
iii 460. expect] await.
iii 461. Martin] A bird of the swallow family; here the bold, ambitious Catholic
party at court, and particularly Edward Petre (1631–99), vice-provincial of the
English Jesuits and head of the Chapel Royal (cp. iii 941, 988). He was one of
a group of Catholic advisers around James who recklessly promoted sectarian interests, alarming the more moderate Catholics such as D. Burnet commented: 'Many
of the Papists, that were men of quiet or of fearful tempers, did not like these
methods. They thought the Priests went too fast, and the King was too eager in
pursuing every thing that was suggested by them. One Peter, descended from a
noble family, a man of no learning, nor any way famed for his virtue, but who
made all up in boldness and zeal, was the Jesuit of them all that seemed animated
with the most courage . . . That Jesuit gave daily new proofs of a weak and ill
governed passion, and discovered all the ill qualities of one, that seemed raised
up to be the common incendiary, and to drive the King and his party to the
precipice' (Burnet ii 366, 455). D. himself was anxious about James's over-
eagerness in promoting Catholic interests, writing to Etherege on 16 February
1687: 'Oh that our Monarch wou'd encourage noble idleness by his own example,
as he of blessed memory did before him for my minde misgives me, that he will
not much advance his affaires by Stirring' (*Letters* 27). *MS* glosses *Martin* as 'Priests'.
Raymond A. Anselment points out that the swallow family had traditionally
been considered intelligent, and suggests that in making the Martin dull D. may
be drawing upon the polemical characterization of Martin Marprelate as a dull
buffoon (*RES* xvii (1966) 256–67).
iii 464. dignity] high office. James made Petre a Privy Councillor, and unsuccessfully attempted to persuade the Pope to allow him to be appointed Archbishop
of York, and to make him a cardinal.
iii 465. Williams suggests that this may be a jibe at Martin Luther (by D., undermining the Panther's comment). *kind*] nature.

Yet often quoted canon laws, and code,   ⎫
And fathers which he never understood: ⎬
But little learning needs in noble blood.   ⎭
For, sooth to say, the Swallow brought him in
470 Her household chaplain, and her next of kin.
In superstition silly to excess,
And casting schemes by planetary guess:
In fine, short winged, unfit himself to fly,
His fear foretold foul weather in the sky.
475   'Besides, a Raven from a withered oak
Left of their lodging was observed to croak.
That omen liked him not, so his advice   ⎫
Was present safety, bought at any price   ⎬
(A seeming pious care that covered cowardice). ⎭
480 To strengthen this, he told a boding dream
Of rising waters, and a troubled stream,
Sure signs of anguish, dangers and distress,
With something more not lawful to express:
By which he slyly seemed to intimate
485 Some secret revelation of their fate.
For, he concluded, once upon a time
He found a leaf inscribed with sacred rhyme,

iii 466. code] collection of statutes in Roman law.
iii 468. needs] is required.
iii 471. silly] feeble-minded, credulous (*OED* 4).
iii 472. D. himself practised astrology (see *Letters* 93–4 and 'To the Memory of Anne Killigrew' ll. 41–3*n*). *schemes*] horoscopes showing the disposition of the planets and signs of the zodiac at the moment for which the horoscope is drawn.
iii 473. In fine] in conclusion.
iii 475–6. Williams cites Virgil: *ante sinistra cava monuisset ab ilice cornix* (*Ecl.* ix 15: 'a crow had warned me before, from a hollow oak on the left'). The *Raven* represents the leaders of the Anglican Church, whose sermons, speeches and publications should have warned Catholics that their ambitious designs would not go unresisted. The raven is an ill-omened bird: 'this fowl doth greatly above all others covet mens carcases, and (as some think) by a singular instinct and natur-all gift, it hath understanding of mans death, presaging it a few days before'; the raven 'and the like birds are emblemes of such as want naturall affection'; 'the fox and this bird are very friendly'; the Romans 'supposed that the raven did presage which side should perish in battell . . . he is fitly called the devils bird' (Swan 395–8). Franzius cites the raven as an instance of God's providence some-times turning evil to good ends (*Historia Animalium* 365).
iii 478. The Martin's advice is that Catholics should grasp whatever public offices they can, to make themselves secure; but to D. this is merely a short-term (and short-sighted) policy because it alienates the Protestant establishment, which might be expected to recover its full power after the death of James.
iii 482. signs] *1687bc*; sign *1687a*. Possibly D.'s revision.

Whose antique characters did well denote
The Sibyl's hand of the Cumaean grot:
490 The mad divineress had plainly writ
A time should come (but many ages yet)
In which sinister destinies ordain
A dame should drown with all her feathered train,
And seas from thence be called the Chelidonian main.
495 At this some shook for fear, the more devout
Arose, and blessed themselves from head to foot.
    "Tis true, some stagers of the wiser sort
Made all these idle wonderments their sport:
They said their only danger was delay,
500 And he who heard what every fool could say
Would never fix his thoughts, but trim his time away.
The passage yet was good; the wind, 'tis true,
Was somewhat high, but that was nothing new,
Nor more than usual equinoxes blew.
505 The sun, already from the scales declined,
Gave little hopes of better days behind,
But change from bad to worse of weather and of wind.
Nor need they fear the dampness of the sky
Should flag their wings, and hinder them to fly:
510 'Twas only water thrown on sails too dry.

iii 488. antique] Stressed on the first syllable in the seventeenth century.
iii 489. The Cumaean Sybil dwelt in a cave at the entrance of which she placed leaves inscribed with her prophecies. Every gust of wind would disarrange the leaves, making the prophecies unintelligible (*Aen.* iii 441–57, vi 77–97).
iii 490. mad divineress] From Virgil's *insanam vatem* (*Aen.* iii 443).
iii 492. sinister] unfavourable (*OED* 6); stressed on the second syllable in the seventeenth century.
iii 494. Chelidonian] From the Greek χελιδών, swallow. Classical literature commonly offers etymological myths to explain place names, as in the case of the Icarian Sea, where Icarus is said to have drowned when he fell from the sky.
iii 496. blessed themselves] made the sign of the cross.
iii 497. stagers] veterans (*OED* 1b, citing this example). They represent the old Catholic families.
iii 501. trim] waste time in indecision (*OED* 16b; only example). For its political sense, implying unprincipled timeserving, cp. iii 160n, iii 666n, and 'Epilogue to *The Duke of Guise*' l. 23.
iii 504. equinoxes] equinoctial gales (*OED* 4, sole example).
iii 505. the scales] Libra, the sign of the zodiac which the sun enters at the autumnal equinox in September (Williams).
iii 506. behind] following, later (*OED* 3b).
iii 509. flag] impede, make incapable of soaring (*OED* 5).

But least of all philosophy presumes
Of truth in dreams, from melancholy fumes.
Perhaps the Martin, housed in holy ground,
Might think of ghosts that walk their midnight round,
515   Till grosser atoms tumbling in the stream
Of fancy, madly met and clubbed into a dream.
As little weight his vain presages bear,
Of ill effect to such alone who fear.
Most prophecies are of a piece with these,
520   Each Nostradamus can foretell with ease,
Not naming persons, and confounding times,
One casual truth supports a thousand lying rhymes.
    'Th' advice was true, but fear had seized the most,
And all good counsel is on cowards lost.
525   The question crudely put, to shun delay,
'Twas carried by the major part to stay.
    'His point thus gained, Sir Martin dated thence
His power, and from a priest became a prince.
He ordered all things with a busy care, ⎫
530   And cells and refectories did prepare, ⎬
And large provisions laid of winter fare. ⎭
But now and then let fall a word or two ⎫
Of hope, that heaven some miracle might show, ⎬
And for their sakes the sun should backward go, ⎭
535   Against the laws of nature upward climb,
And mounted on the ram renew the prime:
For which two proofs in sacred story lay,

---

iii 511–12. Cp. 'The Cock and the Fox' ll. 140–59.   *presumes / Of*] relies upon
(*OED* 7).

iii 515–16. Cp. 'The Cock and the Fox' ll. 325–41; *The State of Innocence* III iii
5–9.

iii 520. *Nostradamus*] Michel de Nostradame (1503–66), author of the prophetic *Centuries* (1555), which are worded sufficiently vaguely to admit many
applications.

iii 522. *casual*] produced by chance.

iii 527. *Sir*] A title placed before the Christian name of priests (*OED* 4); somewhat archaic by this date, and probably facetious.

iii 530. Roman Catholic schools quickly began to flourish under James, with no
fewer than twelve being opened by the Jesuits (A. C. F. Beales, *Education under
Penalty* (1963) 245–55).   *refectories*] stressed on the first syllable.

iii 536. The Ram is the first of the signs of the zodiac, which the sun enters at
the vernal equinox (Williams).   *prime*] spring (*OED* 7); beginning of a new age
(*OED* 6).

Of Ahaz' dial, and of Joshua's day.
In expectation of such times as these
540 A chapel housed 'em, truly called of ease:
For Martin much devotion did not ask;
They prayed sometimes, and that was all their task.
'It happened (as beyond the reach of wit
Blind prophecies may have a lucky hit)
545 That this accomplished, or at least in part,
Gave great repute to their new Merlin's art.
Some *Swifts, the giants of the Swallow kind,   *Otherwise
Large-limbed, stout-hearted, but of stupid mind,   called
(For Swisses or for Gibeonites designed)   Martlets.
550 These lubbers, peeping through a broken pane
To suck fresh air, surveyed the neighbouring plain,
And saw (but scarcely could believe their eyes)
New blossoms flourish, and new flowers arise,
As God had been abroad, and walking there
555 Had left his footsteps, and reformed the year.

iii 538. The shadow on the dial of Ahaz went back ten degrees as a sign that God would heal Hezekiah (2 Kings xx 11). The sun and moon stood still for Joshua until the Israelites had completed the slaughter of their enemies (Joshua x 12–14); but as *Works* notes, the allusion shows that Martin's hopes are misplaced, for 'there was no day like that before it or after it, that the Lord hearkened unto the voice of a man'. *Joshua's*] Stressed on the second syllable.
iii 540. A chapel of ease is a secondary church built for the convenience of parishioners living at a distance from the parish church. Scott suggests an allusion to the Chapel Royal, where Catholic priests exercised their functions.
iii 546. *Merlin*] The enchanter; see Geoffrey of Monmouth, *History of the Kings of Britain*, and Spenser, *FQ* III iii.
iii 547. *Swifts*] As *Works* argues, these are probably not the Irish Catholics (as Scott and Kinsley suggested) but English Catholics foolishly encouraged by events in Ireland (see iii 551–60). *MS* simply glosses *Swifts* as 'Priests'.
iii 549. *Swisses*] Swiss mercenaries.   *Gibeonites*] The Gibeonites were condemned to servitude as hewers of wood and drawers of water (Joshua ix 22–7).
iii 550. *lubbers*] idle, clumsy fellows.
iii 551–60. The *neighbouring plain* is probably Ireland. Richard Talbot (1630–91), Earl of Tyrconnel, was given command of the army in Ireland at the beginning of James's reign, and used his position to discharge Protestant soldiers and admit Catholics to positions of civil and military power. In January 1687 he was appointed viceroy, and pursued his programme of advancing Catholics in public office. This would appear to be a promising development to some English Catholics (here, the unimaginative Swifts), but to the more cautious and thoughtful ones (including D.) it would seem a reckless use of power which was all too likely to invite retribution on the accession of a Protestant monarch. This was, therefore, not a true spring.

The sunny hills from far were seen to glow ⎫
With glittering beams, and in the meads below ⎪
The burnished brooks appeared with liquid gold ⎬
   to flow. ⎭
At last they heard the foolish cuckoo sing,
560   Whose note proclaimed the holy day of spring.
      'No longer doubting, all prepare to fly
And repossess their patrimonial sky.
The priest before 'em did his wings display, ⎫
And, that good omens might attend their way, ⎬
565   As luck would have it 'twas St Martin's day. ⎭
      'Who but the Swallow now triumphs alone?
The canopy of heaven is all her own,
Her youthful offspring to their haunts repair,
And glide along in glades, and skim in air,
570   And dip for insects in the purling springs,
And stoop on rivers to refresh their wings.
Their mothers think a fair provision made
That every son can live upon his trade,
And now the careful charge is off their hands
575   Look out for husbands, and new nuptial bands.
The youthful widow longs to be supplied, ⎫
But first the lover is by lawyers tied ⎬
To settle jointure-chimneys on the bride. ⎭
So thick they couple, in so short a space,
580   That Martin's marriage-offerings rise apace.
Their ancient houses, running to decay,
Are furbished up, and cemented with clay.

---

iii 559. *cuckoo*] Proverbially stupid.
iii 560. *holy day*] holiday.
iii 562. *patrimonial sky*] 'England' *MS*.
iii 565. *St Martin's day*] This falls on 11 November, so those English Catholics who interpret current developments as signs of spring are obviously deluded. A St Martin's summer is a late spell of fine weather on the brink of winter; the season is also ominous because Martinmas is the time when animals were slaughtered (cp. the proverb 'His Martinmas will come, as it does to every hog').
iii 566. *triumphs*] Stressed on the second syllable.
iii 570. *purling*] rippling, murmuring.
iii 571. *stoop*] descend from a height (*OED* 5).
iii 574. *careful*] requiring care.
iii 576. *supplied*] In both financial and sexual senses.
iii 578. *jointure*] an estate which the wife will possess after the death of her husband.
iii 581. *ancient houses*] 'Cath. Chappels' *MS*.
iii 582. *cemented*] Stressed on the first syllable.

They teem already; store of eggs are laid,
And brooding mothers call Lucina's aid.

585   Fame spreads the news, and foreign fowls appear ⎤
      In flocks to greet the new-returning year,   ⎬
      To bless the founder, and partake the cheer.   ⎦
         'And now 'twas time (so fast their numbers rise)
      To plant abroad and people colonies;

590   The youth drawn forth, as Martin had desired
      (For so their cruel destiny required)
      Were sent far off on an ill-fated day;   ⎤
      The rest would need conduct 'em on their way,   ⎬
      And Martin went, because he feared alone to stay. ⎦

595   'So long they flew with inconsiderate haste
      That now their afternoon began to waste;
      And, what was ominous, that very morn
      The sun was entered into Capricorn;
      Which by their bad astronomer's account

600   That week the virgin balance should remount;
      An infant moon eclipsed him in his way,
      And hid the small remainders of his day:
      The crowd, amazed, pursued no certain mark,
      But birds met birds, and jostled in the dark;

605   Few mind the public in a panic fright,
      And fear increased the horror of the night.
      Night came, but unattended with repose,   ⎤
      Alone she came, no sleep their eyes to close,   ⎬
      Alone and black she came, no friendly stars arose. ⎦

---

iii 584. 'New Converts' *MS. Lucina*] Roman goddess of childbirth.

iii 585. foreign fowls] 'Catholicks from abroad' *MS.*

iii 587. the founder] 'K. Jam. 2ᵈ' *MS.*

iii 595. inconsiderate] ill-considered.

iii 598. Capricorn] the winter solstice.

iii 600. virgin balance] Libra, which the sun enters at the equinox in September (cp. iii 505). Gardiner 86 suggests an allusion to Astraea, goddess of justice: the Catholics imagine that ancient justice has returned to the world.

iii 601. infant moon] Gardiner 86 suggests an allusion to the crescent moon, symbol of the Ottoman empire.

iii 603. amazed] stunned by a blow (*OED* 1); bewildered, confused (*OED* 2); terror-stricken (*OED* 3).

iii 604. Echoes D. and Lee's *Oedipus*: 'But Gods meet Gods, and justle in the dark!' (IV i 626).

iii 605. the public] the common good.

iii 607–8. Echoes the Virgilian formula *nox erat* (e.g. *Aen.* iv 522; cp. D.'s translation: ''Twas dead of Night, when weary Bodies close / Their Eyes in balmy Sleep, and soft repose' ('The Fourth Book of the *Aeneis*' ll. 757–8)).

610   'What should they do, beset with dangers round,
           No neighb'ring dorp, no lodging to be found,
           But bleaky plains, and bare unhospitable ground?
           The latter brood, who just began to fly,
           Sick-feathered, and unpractised in the sky,
615   For succour to their helpless mother call;
           She spread her wings, some few beneath 'em crawl,
           She spread 'em wider yet, but could not cover all.
           T' augment their woes, the winds began to move
           Debate in air for empty fields above,
620   Till Boreas got the skies, and poured amain
           His rattling hailstones mixed with snow and rain.
            'The joyless morning late arose, and found
           A dreadful desolation reign around,
           Some buried in the snow, some frozen to the ground:
625   The rest were struggling still with death, and lay
           The Crows' and Ravens' rights, an undefended prey;
           Excepting Martin's race, for they and he
           Had gained the shelter of a hollow tree,
           But soon discovered by a sturdy clown,
630   He headed all the rabble of a town
           And finished 'em with bats, or poled 'em down.
           Martin himself was caught alive, and tried
           For treasonous crimes, because the laws provide
           No Martin there in winter shall abide.
635   High on an oak which never leaf shall bear,
           He breathed his last, exposed to open air;
           And there his corpse, unblessed, are hanging still,

iii 611. *dorp*] village.

iii 612. *bleaky*] bleak (*OED*'s first example).

iii 613–17. The passage reflects D.'s fear that the Catholic Church will be unable to protect her adherents if and when persecution returns to England (*Works*).

iii 613. *latter brood*] 'late Converts' *MS*.   *latter*] more recent (*OED* later; for the relationship of 'latter' and 'later' see *OED s.v.* latter).

iii 614. *Sick-feathered*] with young or ungrown feathers (*OED* sick 7b).

iii 619. *Debate*] strife, conflict (*OED* 1).

iii 620. *Boreas*] the north wind. 'Persecution' *MS*.   *got*] got possession of.   *amain*] violently.

iii 626. *Crows . . . Ravens*] See iii 475–6n.

iii 629. *clown*] countryman.

iii 631. *bats*] sticks, clubs.   *poled*] struck with a pole (*OED* 4; first example 1753).

iii 632–4. See iii 381–2n.

iii 635. *an oak*] the gallows.

iii 637. *corpse*] Often considered as plural in the seventeenth century: cp. 'remains' (*OED*).   *unblessed*] The bodies of executed criminals were not given Christian burial.

To show the change of winds with his prophetic bill.'
The patience of the Hind did almost fail,
640   For well she marked the malice of the tale,
Which ribald art their church to Luther owes,
In malice it began, by malice grows:
He sowed the serpent's teeth, an iron harvest rose.
But most in Martin's character and fate
645   She saw her slandered sons, the Panther's hate,
The people's rage, the persecuting state:
Then said: 'I take th' advice in friendly part,
You clear your conscience, or at least your heart:
Perhaps you failed in your foreseeing skill,
650   For Swallows are unlucky birds to kill:
As for my sons, the family is blessed
Whose every child is equal to the rest:
No church reformed can boast a blameless line,
Such Martins build in yours, and more than mine:
655   Or else an old fanatic author lies
Who summed their scandals up by centuries.
But through your parable I plainly see
The bloody laws, the crowd's barbarity,
The sunshine that offends the purblind sight:
660   Had some their wishes, it would soon be night.
Mistake me not, the charge concerns not you,
Your sons are malcontents, but yet are true,

---

iii 638. An adaptation of the belief that the kingfisher if hanged by the bill turns its breast to the quarter from which the wind blows (Browne, *Pseudodoxia Epidemica* i 196–8).

iii 641. Some of Luther's writings are remarkable for their obscene and scatological abuse of his opponents. His *Table Talk* includes vulgar epigrams and miniature beast-fables (see Roland Bainton, *Here I Stand* (1951, 1983) 295–6).

iii 643. After killing the dragon, Cadmus sowed its teeth in the earth, from which sprang up armed men (Ovid, *Met.* iii 101–10). One interpretation of this story is that 'the destruction of one Heretick [is] the generation of many, as we see in the Arrian heresie, being overthrown by the *Nicene* Synod, of which, as out of the Dragons teeth, arose [many sects]' (Ross 52).

iii 650. 'We commonly refrain from killing Swallows, and esteem it unlucky to destroy them' (Browne, *Pseudodoxia Epidemica* i 435).

iii 655–6. John White (1590–1645) was a Puritan writer who in *The First Centurie of Scandalous Malignant Priests* (1643) catalogued the scandals of the Church of England and argued for the expulsion of Anglican clergy from their benefices.

iii 659. sunshine] Implicitly the King's favour towards Catholics, which some Protestants would like to see ended through his removal or death; 'K. Ja's reign' *MS. purblind*] partially blind (*OED* 2); stupid, obtuse (*OED* 3).

iii 662. true] i.e. loyal Englishmen.

As far as non-resistance makes 'em so,
But that's a word of neutral sense you know,
665 A passive term which no relief will bring,
But trims betwixt a rebel and a king.'
    'Rest well assured,' the Pardalis replied,
'My sons would all support the regal side,
Though heaven forbid the cause by battle should
    be tried.'
670   The matron answered with a loud 'Amen',
And thus pursued her argument again:
'If, as you say, and as I hope no less,
Your sons will practise what yourself profess,
What angry power prevents our present peace?
675 The Lion, studious of our common good,
Desires (and kings' desires are ill withstood)
To join our nations in a lasting love;
The bars betwixt are easy to remove,
For sanguinary laws were never made above.
680 If you condemn that prince of tyranny
Whose mandate forced your Gallic friends to fly,
Make not a worse example of your own,
Or cease to rail at causeless rigour shown,
And let the guiltless person throw the stone.
685 His blunted sword your suffering brotherhood
Have seldom felt; he stops it short of blood:
But you have ground the persecuting knife,
And set it to a razor edge on life.
Cursed be the wit which cruelty refines,
690 Or to his father's rod the scorpion joins;
Your finger is more gross than the great monarch's
    loins.
    But you perhaps remove that bloody note,

---

iii 663. non-resistance] See iii 134*n*.
iii 666. trims] moves according to self-interest; cp. iii 501*n*.
iii 667. Pardalis] Latin for a female panther.
iii 679. sanguinary laws] See iii 381–2*n*.
iii 680–1. Louis XIV, whose revocation of the Edict of Nantes in 1685 caused
Huguenots to flee France.
iii 684. As Christ said: John viii 7.
iii 685. blunted sword] See ii 419*n*.
iii 690–1. The images come from 1 Kings xii 10–11.
iii 691. gross] thick. *great monarch*] Perhaps referring back to Louis XIV (thus *MS*).
iii 692. note] stigma, reproach (*OED* 8).

And stick it on the first reformers' coat.
O let their crime in long oblivion sleep,
695 'Twas theirs indeed to make, 'tis yours to keep.
Unjust or just is all the question now,
'Tis plain that not repealing, you allow.
    'To name the Test would put you in a rage,
You charge not that on any former age,
700 But smile to think how innocent you stand,
Armed by a weapon put into your hand.
Yet still remember that you wield a sword
Forged by your foes against your sovereign lord,
Designed to hew th' imperial cedar down,
705 Defraud succession and disheir the crown.
T' abhor the makers, and their laws approve,
Is to hate traitors, and the treason love.
What means it else, which now your children say,
"We made it not, nor will we take away"?
710   'Suppose some great oppressor had by sleight ⎫
Of law disseized your brother of his right, ⎬
Your common sire surrendering in a fright; ⎭
Would you to that unrighteous title stand,
Left by the villain's will to heir the land?
715 More just was Judas, who his Saviour sold: ⎫
The sacrilegious bribe he could not hold, ⎬
Nor hang in peace before he rendered back the gold. ⎭
What more could you have done, than now you do,
Had Oates and Bedloe and their plot been true?
720 Some specious reasons for those wrongs were found, ⎫
The dire magicians threw their mists around, ⎬
And wise men walked as on enchanted ground. ⎭

---

iii 693. reformers'] Reformers 1687, which could be a singular or plural possess-
ive, were it not for *their* in the next line. *MS* interprets it as a reference to
'Q. Elizabeth'.
iii 697. allow] approve.
iii 698. Test] See ii 30*n*.
iii 704. imperial cedar] Symbolizes the King of Israel in 2 Kings xiv 9.
iii 705. disheir] deprive of an heir; *OED*'s only example.
iii 711. disseized] dispossessed.
iii 713. stand [to]] abide by, adhere to (*OED* 76i).
iii 714. Left] i.e. if you (rather than your elder brother) were left. heir] inherit.
iii 716–17. Matthew xxvii 3–5.
iii 719. See i 563*n*.

But now when Time has made th' imposture plain, ⎫
(Late though he followed Truth, and limping held ⎪
   her train) ⎬
725 What new delusion charms your cheated eyes again? ⎭
The painted harlot might awhile bewitch,
But why the hag uncased, and all obscene with itch?
   'The first reformers were a modest race,
Our peers possessed in peace their native place:
730 And when rebellious arms o'erturned the state,
They suffered only in the common fate.
But now the sovereign mounts the regal chair,
And mitred seats are full, yet David's bench is bare.
Your answer is, they were not dispossessed,
735 They need but rub their metal on the Test
To prove their ore: 'twere well if gold alone
Were touched and tried on your discerning stone,
But that unfaithful Test unfound will pass
The dross of atheists, and sectarian brass:
740 As if th' experiment were made to hold
For base productions, and reject the gold:

iii 723–4. Truth is usually, allegorically, the daughter of Time.
iii 726–7. In *FQ* I viii 46 Duessa is stripped and her ugliness revealed; since she
represents the false church, and the passage echoes the account of the whore in
Revelation xvii 16, D. is reapplying to the Popish Plot that imagery which had
originally been applied by Protestants to the Church of Rome.   *uncased*] stripped
of clothes.
iii 729. The Test Act of 1563 required an oath of allegiance to the Queen
and abjuration of the temporal authority of the Pope from all holders of lay or
ecclesiastical office except peers; but peers were not exempt from the Test Acts
of 1673 and 1678. James hoped that Catholic peers excluded by the Test Act
would be restored to the House of Lords (W. A. Speck, *Reluctant Revolutionaries*
(1988) 51).
iii 730–1. The Civil War and the ensuing Republic, when the House of Lords
was abolished.
iii 733. mitred seats] the seats of the Anglican bishops in the House of Lords.   *David's
bench*] the bench where the (Catholic) peers most loyal to the King would sit if
they had not been excluded by the Test Acts.   *David*] Applied now to James II,
as D. had earlier applied the name to Charles II in *AA*. For the use of King
David as a type of English kingship see *AA*, headnote, *Sources*.
iii 735–41. The image is that of a touchstone (smooth, dark quartz or jasper) which
tests the quality of gold and silver alloys by the colour of the streak produced by
rubbing them on it.
iii 738–9. The Test Acts were designed primarily to exclude Roman Catholics,
and therefore imposed an oath denying transubstantiation, which atheists and
Protestant Nonconformists could happily swear.
iii 739. sectarian brass] See *AA* l. 633*n*, for *brass* used of Titus Oates.

Thus men ungodded may to places rise,
And sects may be preferred without disguise:
No danger to the church or state from these,
745   The papist only has his writ of ease.
No gainful office gives him the pretence
To grind the subject or defraud the prince.
Wrong conscience, or no conscience, may deserve
To thrive, but ours alone is privileged to starve.
750   ' "Still thank yourselves," you cry, "your noble race
We banish not, but they forsake the place.
Our doors are open": true, but e'er they come
You toss your censing Test, and fume the room,
As if 'twere Toby's rival to expel,
755   And fright the fiend who could not bear the smell.'
To this the Panther sharply had replied,
But having gained a verdict on her side
She wisely gave the loser leave to chide;
Well satisfied to have the butt and peace,
760   And for the plaintiff's cause she cared the less,
Because she sued *in forma pauperis*;
Yet thought it decent something should be said,
For secret guilt by silence is betrayed.
So neither granted all, nor much denied,
765   But answered with a yawning kind of pride:
'Methinks such terms of proffered peace you bring

iii *742. ungodded*] ungodly (*OED*'s last example).
iii *745. writ of ease*] certificate of discharge from office.
iii *746. pretence*] [opportunity to pursue his] purpose, aim (*OED* 3).
iii *748–9. deserve / . . . starve*] A perfect rhyme in the seventeenth century, the 'er' being pronounced 'ar'. The spelling in *1687* is *sterve*, which is an obsolete form of *starve* (rather than a different word, as *Works* says).   *starve*] die a lingering death, esp. from hunger (*OED* 1).
iii *753–5*. Alluding to the apocryphal Book of Tobit, in which Tobias marries Sara, who had previously been given to seven men, all of whom were killed by a jealous spirit; Tobias burned the heart and liver of a fish and made smoke, which drove the spirit away (Tobit viii 3; cp. *PL* iv 166–71).
iii *759. butt*] of wine, representing the substantial benefit of peace. In the D.–Davenant *Tempest*, Trincalo asks, 'Peace, or War?' and Mustacho replies, 'Peace, and the Butt' (IV ii 17–18). Cp. 'Prologue to *The Mistakes*' l. 35.
iii *760. the plaintiff*] the Hind.
iii *761. she*] the Hind.   in forma pauperis] Latin for 'in the character of a poor person'. Someone could bring or defend an action *in forma pauperis* when they were unable to pay the legal expenses, and arrangements were made for them to receive legal services free.
iii *766–80*. In *Aen.* vii 213–48 (D.'s 'The Seventh Book of the *Aeneis*' ll. 290–340) Aeneas' ambassador Ilioneus tells King Latinus that the Trojan exiles have

As once Aeneas to th' Italian king:
By long possession all the land is mine, ⎫
You strangers come with your intruding line, ⎬
770 To share my sceptre, which you call to join. ⎭
You plead like him an ancient pedigree,
And claim a peaceful seat by fate's decree.
In ready pomp your sacrificer stands,
T' unite the Trojan and the Latin bands,
775 And that the league more firmly may be tied,
Demand the fair Lavinia for your bride.
Thus plausibly you veil th' intended wrong,
But still you bring your exiled gods along;
And will endeavour in succeeding space
780 Those household poppets on our hearths to place.
Perhaps some barbarous laws have been preferred;
I spake against the Test, but was not heard;
These to rescind, and peerage to restore, ⎫
My gracious sovereign would my vote implore: ⎬
785 I owe him much, but owe my conscience more.' ⎭

---

arrived in Italy by the will of Jupiter, and that they wish Latinus to give them land for themselves and their household gods. Latinus agrees, and offers Aeneas his daughter Lavinia in marriage. The Virgilian allusions create a parallel between the exiled Trojans (who will be the founders of Rome) and the Roman Catholics. The Panther presents both as intruders, but the Trojans and their household gods are actually returning, by divine command, to their original homeland, the country which Dardanus had left to found Troy. The Panther's parallel therefore works ultimately to the Hind's advantage.

iii 768. Cp. *Rex arva Latinus et urbes / iam senior longa placidas in pace regebat* (*Aen.* vii 45–6); '*Latinus* old and mild, had long possess'd / The *Latian* Scepter, and his People bless'd' ('The Seventh Book of the *Aeneis*' ll. 68–9).

iii 771–2. Cp. *a Jove principium generis: Jove Dardana pubes / gaudet avo: rex ipse Jovis de gente suprema / Troius Aeneas tua nos ad limina misit* (*Aen.* vii 219–21); 'The God began our Line, who rules above, / And as our Race, our King descends from *Jove*: / And hither are we come, by his Command, / To crave Admission in your happy Land' ('The Seventh Book of the *Aeneis*' ll. 298–301).

iii 773. *your sacrificer*] James II.

iii 774. i.e. to unite Anglicans and Catholics. The question of whether the two churches were capable of agreeing doctrinally and so uniting was aired in several pamphlets in 1687, beginning with *An Agreement between the Church of England and Church of Rome*: see Jones, *Catalogue* 179–81.

iii 776. *Lavinia*] Probably representing the right to hold public office.

iii 779. *space*] time.

iii 780. *poppets*] idols (*OED* 2c); a contemptuous reference to the Catholic use of images in worship.

iii 781. *preferred*] brought forward, introduced (*OED* 4).

iii 785. This was a genuine dilemma for many Anglican clergy.

'Conscience is then your plea,' replied the dame,
'Which well informed will ever be the same.
But yours is much of the chameleon hue,
To change the dye with every different view.
790 When first the Lion sat with awful sway,
Your conscience taught you duty to obey:
He might have had your statutes and your Test,
No conscience but of subjects was professed.
He found your temper, and no farther tried,
795 But on that broken reed your church relied.
In vain the sects assayed their utmost art
With offered treasure to espouse their part,
Their treasures were a bribe too mean to move his
     heart.
But when by long experience you had proved
800 How far he could forgive, how well he loved;
A goodness that excelled his godlike race,
And only short of heaven's unbounded grace,
A flood of mercy that o'erflowed our isle,
Calm in the rise, and fruitful as the Nile;
805 Forgetting whence your Egypt was supplied,
You thought your sovereign bound to send the tide:
Nor upward looked on that immortal spring,

iii 787. well informed] well instructed, i.e. by an authoritative religious teacher. The Hind says that when individuals' consciences are properly directed by church teaching, they will reach the same conclusion. But different Anglicans reach different conclusions: therefore their claim to be acting according to conscience is defective.

iii 790–8. On the death of Charles II the Church of England supported the accession of James II according to the prevailing law of succession. In his first speech to the Privy Council James promised to uphold the rights of the Church of England (see iii 953–4*n*), and relations between King and Church were initially good. The Hind says that James might have insisted upon the repeal of the Test Act, but did not (iii 792). At that stage, the only conscientious duty which the Church of England professed was the duty of the subject to obey the King (iii 793). James discovered the Church's true character and did not press her any further (iii 794). The Church relied for her protection on that insubstantial support the Test Act [instead of making a proper accommodation with James] (iii 795). Meanwhile the Nonconformist sects made overtures to James, but he resisted their blandishments [it is not clear what the *treasure* was which D. says they offered] (iii 796–8).

iii 790. awful] awesome, majestic.

iii 801. D. repeatedly stresses that mercy and forgiveness were characteristics (even failings) of the Stuarts: cp. i 289*n*. *godlike*] An epithet applied to Charles II as King David in *AA* l. 14.

iii 804–5. Egyptians relied upon regular inundations by the Nile to irrigate and fertilize their fields.

But vainly deemed he durst not be a king:
Then conscience, unrestrained by fear, began
810   To stretch her limits, and extend the span,
Did his indulgence as her gift dispose,
And made a wise alliance with her foes.
Can conscience own th' associating name
And raise no blushes to conceal her shame?
815   For sure she has been thought a bashful dame.
But if the cause by battle should be tried,
You grant she must espouse the regal side:
O Proteus conscience, never to be tied!
What Phoebus from the tripod shall disclose
820   Which are in last resort your friends or foes?
Homer, who learned the language of the sky,
The seeming Gordian knot would soon untie;
Immortal powers the term of conscience know,
But interest is her name with men below.'
825   'Conscience or interest be 't, or both in one,'
The Panther answered in a surly tone,
'The first commands me to maintain the crown,
The last forbids to throw my barriers down.
Our penal laws no sons of yours admit,
830   Our Test excludes your tribe from benefit.
These are my banks your ocean to withstand,

iii 811. indulgence] Probably simply 'tolerance, good nature' rather than a reference to James's *Declaration for Liberty of Conscience* (or Declaration of Indulgence)
of April 1687.
iii 812. her foes] the Nonconformists.
iii 813. 'Conscience', which had led the Church of England to support James on
his accession, is now invoked as the reason for opposing him.   associating name]
Recalling that 'Associations' had been formed in defence of Protestantism by the
Whigs, in opposition to Charles II: see *The Medal*, 'Epistle to the Whigs' l. 44n.
iii 818. Proteus was a sea god. When Menelaus seized him, Proteus changed into
various shapes in order to escape, but Menelaus held him and forced him to answer
questions (Homer, *Odyssey* iv 351–480).
iii 819. Phoebus] Apollo.   tripod] the three-legged seat of the prophetess who spoke
the unerring words of Apollo's oracle at Delphi.
iii 821–4. For Homer's perception of the difference between human and divine
names for things cp. *Iliad* i 403–4 (Scott): ὃν Βριάρεων καλέουσι θεοί, ἄνδρες
δέ τε πάντες / Αἰγαίων ('whom the gods call Briareus, but all men Aegaeon').
iii 822. Gordian knot] intricate knot by which Gordius tied his wagon to a beam;
proverbially, an insoluble difficulty.
iii 830–4. The Panther's rhetoric of inundation has a contemporary parallel, in
that Protestant preachers had begun to warn about 'the approaching Innundation'
(Gardiner 211–12, citing W[illiam] D[arrell], *The Lay-Mans Opinion* (1687) 6–7).

Which proudly rising overlooks the land;
And once let in, with unresisted sway
Would sweep the pastors and their flocks away.
835 Think not my judgement leads me to comply
With laws unjust, but hard necessity.
Imperious need which cannot be withstood
Makes ill authentic, for a greater good.
Possess your soul with patience, and attend:
840 A more auspicious planet may ascend;
Good fortune may present some happier time
With means to cancel my unwilling crime,
(Unwilling, witness all ye powers above)
To mend my errors and redeem your love:
845 That little space you safely may allow;
Your all-dispensing power protects you now.'
       'Hold!' said the Hind, ''tis needless to explain;
You would postpone me to another reign;
Till when you are content to be unjust:
850 Your part is to possess, and mine to trust:
A fair exchange proposed, of future chance
For present profit and inheritance.
Few words will serve to finish our dispute:
Who will not now repeal would persecute;
855 To ripen green revenge your hopes attend,
Wishing that happier planet would ascend:
For shame, let conscience be your plea no more, ⎤
To will hereafter proves she might before;   ⎬
But she's a bawd to gain, and holds the door. ⎦
860   'Your care about your banks infers a fear
Of threatening floods, and inundations near;
If so, a just reprise would only be
Of what the land usurped upon the sea;

iii 836. But *necessity* is commonly a Machiavellian excuse, and 'the tyrant's plea' (*PL* iv 393–4).
iii 838. *authentic*] authoritative, entitled to obedience (*OED* 1).
iii 839. From Luke xxi 19: 'in your patience possess ye your souls'.   *attend*] wait.
iii 840. The Panther is probably referring to the expectations of a Protestant successor to James II, since at the date of the poem the heir presumptive was his daughter Mary, who was married to William of Orange. The implication is that under a Protestant ruler the Church of England would feel more secure, and so might be able to dispense with the anti-Catholic laws.
iii 846. *all-dispensing power*] The king's power of granting dispensations from the laws.
iii 862. *reprise*] taking back.

And all your jealousies but serve to show
865   Your ground is, like your neighbour-nation, low.
T' intrench in what you grant unrighteous laws
Is to distrust the justice of your cause,
And argues that the true religion lies
In those weak adversaries you despise.
870   'Tyrannic force is that which least you fear,
The sound is frightful in a Christian's ear;
Avert it, heaven, nor let that plague be sent
To us from the dispeopled continent.
     'But piety commands me to refrain:
875   Those prayers are needless in this monarch's reign.
Behold, how he protects your friends oppressed, ⎫
Receives the banished, succours the distressed! ⎬
Behold, for you may read an honest, open breast. ⎭
He stands in daylight, and disdains to hide ⎫
880   An act to which by honour he is tied: ⎬
A generous, laudable, and kingly pride.   ⎭
Your Test he would repeal, his peers restore,
This when he says he means, he means no more.'
    'Well,' said the Panther, 'I believe him just,
885   And yet—' 'And yet, 'tis but because you must:
You would be trusted, but you would not trust.'
The Hind thus briefly, and disdained t' enlarge

---

iii 864. jealousies] anxiety to preserve, vigilance in guarding (*OED* 3).
iii 865. i.e. like the Netherlands, to which many Anglicans were looking as a potential source of assistance.
iii 870–8. Continental Europe had been *dispeopled* (i) through the revocation of
the Edict of Nantes in 1685, which forced many Huguenots to seek refuge in
England, where James allowed them to settle; (ii) in the barbaric Thirty Years
War (1618–48), which had devastated central and eastern Europe; (iii) in the wars
between Louis XIV and the Dutch. *Tyrannic force* had been deployed particularly
by Louis XIV against Protestants.
iii 876–7. Gilbert Burnet, who was no friend to James, recorded that he 'was
very kind to the Refugees. He was liberal to many of them. He ordered a brief
for a charitable collection over the Nation for them all: Upon which great sums
were sent in' (Burnet ii 355; Scott). *Works* notes that James's *Declaration for Liberty
of Conscience* asserted that constraint of conscience was contrary 'to the interests
of government, which it destroys by spoiling trade, depopulating countries and
discouraging strangers' (*English Historical Documents* 396).
iii 878. James was regarded by contemporaries as a man of his word. The Earl of
Ailesbury called him 'a prince that had all the moral virtues . . . the most honest
and sincere man I ever knew' (David Ogg, *England in the Reigns of James II and William
III* (1955) 140). Cp. *Threnodia Augustalis* ll. 484–7; 'Epilogue to *Albion and Albanius*'.
iii 880. An act] James's use of his dispensing power to exempt Catholics from the
provisions of the Test Act (*Works*).

On power of kings, and their superior charge,
As heaven's trustees before the people's choice:
890 Though sure the Panther did not much rejoice
To hear those echoes giv'n of her once loyal voice. }
    The matron wooed her kindness to the last,
But could not win; her hour of grace was past.
Whom thus persisting, when she could not bring
895 To leave the Wolf, and to believe her king,
She gave her up, and fairly wished her joy
Of her late treaty with her new ally:
Which well she hoped would more successful prove
Than was the Pigeons' and the Buzzard's love.
900 The Panther asked what concord there could be
Betwixt two kinds whose natures disagree?
The dame replied, "'Tis sung in every street,
The common chat of gossips when they meet.
But since unheard by you, 'tis worth your while
905 To take a wholesome tale, though told in homely style.
    'A plain, good man, whose name is understood
(So few deserve the name of plain and good)
Of three fair lineal lordships stood possessed,
And lived, as reason was, upon the best;
910 Inured to hardships from his early youth,

---

iii 889. D. insists (as in *AA*) that kings rule by divine appointment, and are responsible to God (as *heaven's trustees*) for their conduct in ruling their kingdom; they are not chosen by (or responsible to) the people.   *before*] rather than (*OED* 11).
iii 892–8. the matron . . . she] the Hind.   *her*] the Panther['s].
iii 897. ally] Stressed on the second syllable.
iii 899–1288. The Hind's fable of the Pigeons and the Buzzard offers a rejoinder to the Panther's fable of the Swallows. *Works* suggests that Chaucer's *The Nun's Priest's Tale* and the Aesopian fable 'Of the Doves and Hawks' (Ogilby, *Fables* 51–2) provided D. with source material. In *Aesop's Fables With their Morals, in Prose and Verse* (1651) the moral of this fable is: '*Let it grieve no man too much of his own condition: for* (as Horace *saith*) nothing is every way happy. *I indeed would not wish my lot to be changed, so that it be tolerable. Many having gotten a new condition have wished the old again*' (30). The Pigeons represent the Church of England; *MS* says that they are specifically the 'High Church' party, and that the Buzzard represents Presbyterians. For the Buzzard see iii 1121*n.*
iii 901. kinds] species.
iii 906. plain, good man] James II.
iii 908. three fair lineal lordships] the kingdoms of England, Scotland and Ireland.
iii 909. the best] England.
iii 910–14. James was born in 1633, and in his early youth had suffered the hardships of the Civil War, and the execution of his father in 1649. He had served with the French army 1652–5 and the Spanish forces 1657–8; from the beginning of Charles II's reign he took an active interest in naval matters, and in 1665

Much had he done and suffered for his truth:
At land and sea, in many a doubtful fight,
Was never known a more adventurous knight,
Who oftener drew his sword, and always for the right.

915   'As Fortune would (his fortune came, though late)
He took possession of his just estate;
Nor racked his tenants with increase of rent,
Nor lived too sparing, nor too largely spent;
But overlooked his hinds; their pay was just,
920   And ready, for he scorned to go on trust:
Slow to resolve, but in performance quick;
So true, that he was awkward at a trick.
For little souls on little shifts rely,
And coward arts of mean expedients try:
925   The noble mind will dare do anything but lie.
False friends, his deadliest foes, could find no way
But shows of honest bluntness to betray;
That unsuspected plainness he believed,
He looked into himself, and was deceived.
930   Some lucky planet sure attends his birth,
Or heaven would make a miracle on earth;

fought in the naval battles against the Dutch (see *AM* ll. 73–4). During the Exclusion Crisis James withdrew to Brussels and then to Scotland between March
1679 and April 1682. For D.'s earlier estimate of James see *Threnodia Augustalis*,
esp. ll. 429–64.
iii 915. *late*] James was 51 when he succeeded to the throne.
iii 917. At first James did not increase taxation, merely receiving (first by proclamation, then by vote of the House of Commons) the same revenues as
Charles II. But on 30 May 1685 James asked for, and received, additional duties,
and more were levied after the landing of Monmouth. These additional grants
brought in £400,000 per year beyond the £1.5 million which Charles had been
receiving annually.
iii 918. Economy was one of the keynotes of James's new government.
iii 919. *overlooked*] supervised, superintended (*OED* 6). *hinds*] farmhands (again
at iii 984).
iii 920. D.'s own salary was paid more promptly under James than under Charles
(Winn 530).
iii 921–5. Cp. Burnet's character of James: 'he has not the king's [i.e. Charles II's]
wit nor quickness, but that is made up by great application and industry . . . He
has naturally a candour and a justice in his temper very great, and is a firm friend,
but a heavy enemy . . . He understands business better than is generally believed,
for though he is not a man of wit or fancy, yet he generally judges well when
things are laid before him . . . He is a prince of great courage and very serene in
action, and naturally hates a coward' (Burnet's MS note *c.* 1683, in *A Supplement
to Burnet's History*, ed. H. C. Foxcroft (1902) 50–1; Kinsley).
iii 924. *coward*] cowardly.

For prosperous honesty is seldom seen,
To bear so dead a weight, and yet to win.
It looks as Fate with nature's law would strive,
935   To show plain dealing once an age may thrive:
And, when so tough a frame she could not bend,
Exceeded her commission to befriend.
    'This grateful man, as heaven increased his store,
Gave God again, and daily fed his poor.
940   His house with all convenience was purveyed:
The rest he found, but raised the fabric where he
    prayed,
And in that sacred place his beauteous wife
Employed her happiest hours of holy life.
    'Nor did their alms extend to those alone
945   Whom common faith more strictly made their own:
A sort of Doves were housed too near their hall,

---

iii 932–3. i.e. honesty seldom seems to bring prosperity, because it is itself a heavy handicap in life's race. The failure of honesty is so common that it is virtually a law of nature (iii 934).

iii 936. i.e. when Fate could not change James's unbending honesty, she went beyond her commission and befriended him.

iii 940. purveyed] furnished, supplied (*OED* 6).

iii 941. James's new Roman Catholic chapel in Whitehall was first used on Christmas Day 1686. Evelyn attended service there on 29 December and recorded in his *Diary*: 'Nothing can be finer than the magnificent Marble work & Architecture at the End, where are 4 statues representing st Joh: st. Petre, st. Paule, & the Church, statues in white marble, the worke of Mr Gibbons, with all the carving & Pillars of exquisite art & greate cost: The history or Altar piece is the Salutation, The Volto, in *fresca*, the Asumption of the blessed Virgin according to their Traditions with our B: Saviour, & a world of figures, painted by *Verio*'. For details of the chapel see *Survey of London*, ed. Montagu H. Cox and Philip Norman, vol. 13 (1930) 105–10. A satirical account of the chapel is given in *A View of the Religion of the Town, or, A Sunday-Morning's Ramble* (n.d.). The chapel fell into disuse after 1688, and was destroyed in the fire at Whitehall in 1698.

iii 942. James's Catholic wife, Queen Mary of Modena.

iii 946. a sort of Doves] The Anglican clergy: implicitly only a kind of dove, not true doves, who would represent the true church (Franzius, *Historia Animalium* 375–9). Pigeons were said to be vain (Swan 409). Brabazon Aylmer, a notable publisher of Protestant theology, operated from a shop at the sign of 'The Three Pigeons'. Gardiner 83–4 notes that the image of the dove is poignant because it is the endearment which the bridegroom uses for his bride in The Song of Solomon v 2: the Panther might have been the bride of Christ, but has chosen not to be. Gardiner also notes that in ancient animal symbolism the dove is like the panther in having the gift of eloquence, which in this case is misused. *sort*] kind, species (*OED* 1); group, flock (*OED* 17); multitude, great number (*OED* 18).

    Who cross the proverb and abound with gall.
    Though some, 'tis true, are passively inclined,
    The greater part degenerate from their kind;
950 Voracious birds that hotly bill and breed,
    And largely drink, because on salt they feed.
    Small gain from them their bounteous owner draws,
    Yet, bound by promise, he supports their cause,
    As corporations privileged by laws.
955   'That house which harbour to their kind affords
    Was built long since, God knows, for better birds;
    But fluttering there they nestle near the throne,
    And lodge in habitations not their own,
    By their high crops and corny gizzards known.
960 Like harpies they could scent a plenteous board,
    Then to be sure they never failed their lord.
    The rest was form, and bare attendance paid,
    They drank and ate, and grudgingly obeyed.

iii 947. Doves or pigeons were proverbially (though wrongly) said to have no gall (Tilley D 574; Browne, *Pseudodoxia Epidemica* i 168–71). *cross*] contradict (*OED* 14c). *gall*] bitterness, rancour (*OED* 3).

iii 948. See iii 134*n*.

iii 950. Unlike Roman Catholic priests, Anglican clergy were not required to be celibate.

iii 951. salt] Williams suggests a reference to the Anglican clergy's receipt of money from the established church's endowments and tithes ('salary', the priest's stipend, comes from the Latin *salarium*, 'salt money'). This implictly contrasts with the Roman Catholic clergy's greater dependence on donations from the faithful. Salt is also a symbol of hospitality (*OED* 2b), which implies that the clergy feed off other people. See also iii 992*n*.

iii 953–4. James had promised the Privy Council on his accession that 'he would endeavour to maintaine the Government both in Church & state as by Law establish'd, its Principles being so firme for Monarchy, & the members of it shewing themselves so good & Loyal subjects; & that as he would never depart from the just rights & prerogative of the Crown, so would he never Invade any mans propriety: but as he had often adventured his life in defence of the Nation, so he would still proceede, & preserve it in all its lawfull rites & libertyes' (Evelyn, *Diary* 6 February 1685; cp. *London Gazette* no. 2006 (5–9 February 1685)).

iii 954. The rights and privileges of corporations and municipalities were protected by charters.

iii 955–6. At the Reformation the Church of England took over the medieval churches and cathedrals, and associated domestic quarters, which had been built for the Catholic Church.

iii 959. crops] enlargements of the gullet, where the food is prepared for digestion in the stomach. *Works* notes that this suggests the chesty appearance of pigeons, and an air of pride.

iii 960. In *Aen.* iii 209–62 the harpies (monstrous birds with the faces of women, who befoul everything) snatch the food away from Aeneas and his companions.

The more they fed, they ravened still for more,
965 They drained from Dan, and left Beersheba poor;
All this they had by law, and none repined,
The preference was but due to Levi's kind;
But when some lay preferment fell by chance,
The gourmands made it their inheritance.
970 When once possessed, they never quit their claim,
For then 'tis sanctified to heaven's high name;
And hallowed thus they cannot give consent
The gift should be profaned by worldly management.
     'Their flesh was never to the table served,
975 Though 'tis not thence inferred the birds were starved,
But that their master did not like the food,
As rank, and breeding melancholy blood.
Nor did it with his gracious nature suit,
Ev'n though they were not Doves, to persecute:
980 Yet he refused (nor could they take offence)
Their glutton kind should teach him abstinence.
Nor consecrated grain their wheat he thought,
Which new from treading in their bills they brought:
But left his hinds each in his private power,
985 That those who like the bran might leave the flour.

iii 965. Dan and Beersheba represent the two extremities of Palestine (1 Samuel iii 20).
iii 966. repined] complained.
iii 967. Levi's kind] The descendents of Levi provided the Jewish priesthood.
iii 969. gourmands] gluttons.
iii 974-5. served / . . . starved] A perfect rhyme: cp. iii 748-9n.
iii 977. Burton includes pigeons among fowl whose flesh is 'hard, black, unwhole-some, dangerous, melancholy meat' (*Anatomy of Melancholy* 1.2.2.1; Williams). Swan said: 'These fowls be naturally very hot and moist, wherefore they be not good for those that be cholerick or enclined to any fevers: but to them which be flegmat-ick and pure melancholy, they are very wholesome, and be easily digested' (409). *rank*] grossly fat (*OED* 6); with an offensively strong smell (*OED* 12b). Other meanings which might be suggested secondarily are 'proud, rebellious' (*OED* 1; last example 1560) and 'lustful, licentious' (*OED* 13). For the latter cp. Swan 408, where pigeons are said to breed twelve times a year.
iii 981-3. James refused to have Anglican clergy preach to him, and did not regard their teaching as true doctrine but as *new*. The imagery of l. 982 suggests that he specifically did not consider the bread which Anglican clergy consecrated in the eucharist to be truly the Body of Christ; indeed, he refused to receive the Anglican sacrament at his coronation (Burnet ii 308). This was justified because Anglican orders were regarded as invalid by Roman Catholics.   *treading*] thresh-ing (*OED* 9).
iii 985. Reverses the proverbial phrase 'take the flour and leave the bran' (cp. *Coriolanus* I i 144-5).

He for himself, and not for others chose,
Nor would he be imposed on, nor impose;
But in their faces his devotion paid,
And sacrifice with solemn rites was made,
990 And sacred incense on his altars laid.
      'Besides these jolly birds, whose crops impure
Repaid their commons with their salt manure,
Another farm he had behind his house,
Not overstocked, but barely for his use;
995 Wherein his poor domestic Poultry fed,
And from his pious hands received their bread.
Our pampered Pigeons with malignant eyes
Beheld these inmates and their nurseries:
Though hard their fare (at evening and at morn

iii 986–7. James is not applying the principle, common in Europe, that the people must follow their prince's religion (*cuius regio, eius religio*). Ironically James is thus putting into practice, both for himself and for his Protestant subjects, that exercise of individual judgement which Protestants claimed to value, and which some Catholics thought inconsistent with the Protestant sects' intolerance of other views; cp. Cressy: 'For what is more unreasonable then that Sects, whose essentiall grounds are Scripture alone, with a renouncing of all visible authority to interpret it, should yet assume to themselves an authority to inforce their opinions upon the consciences of others?' (*Exomologesis* 11).

iii 988. Mass was celebrated openly in the Chapel Royal (see iii 941*n*); but *in their faces* perhaps suggests that this is an unwisely provocative act.

iii 991. jolly] lustful (*OED* 7); cp. i 380.

iii 992. commons] daily allowance of food. *salt manure*] ''Tis salt, which . . . renders the dung of Pigeons . . . so eminently effectual' (John Evelyn, *Philosophical Discourse of Earth* (1676) 101; *Works*). Another meaning of *salt* is 'lecherous'.

iii 994. barely] merely, simply (*OED* 4).

iii 995. domestic Poultry] The Roman Catholic clergy, particularly those who served as James's domestic chaplains. Franzius says that the cock represents the diligent priest, but his characterization of the bird includes other features which probably appealed to D., who was somewhat cynical about clergy: the cock will not tolerate rivals on its patch, and dispatches them aggressively; it is greedy and lustful. But it is devoted to its offspring, and is a vigilant guard, so that the image of a cock was placed on the top of ancient temples. Just as the cock rouses men at daybreak and summons them to work, so the Christian priest should warn men of the Last Judgement and rouse them to repentance; and as the cock warned St Peter of his fall, so the priest should warn men of their sins (Franzius, *Historia Animalium* 327–9). Gardiner notes an allusion to Jesus' words in Matthew xxiii 37: 'O Jerusalem . . . how often would I have gathered thy children together, even as a hen gathereth her chickens under her wings, and ye would not!'

iii 998. nurseries] In addition to the new Catholic schools (see iii 530*n*) new religious houses were opened by the Benedictines, Franciscans and Dominicans (Beales, *Education under Penalty* 245–55).

1000   A cruse of water and an ear of corn)
        Yet still they grudged that modicum, and thought
        A sheaf in every single grain was brought;
        Fain would they filch that little food away,
        While unrestrained those happy gluttons prey.
1005   And much they grieved to see so nigh their hall
        The bird that warned St Peter of his fall;
        That he should raise his mitred crest on high,
        And clap his wings, and call his family
        To sacred rites; and vex th' etherial powers
1010   With midnight matins, at uncivil hours:
        Nay more, his quiet neighbours should molest
        Just in the sweetness of their morning rest.
            'Beast of a bird, supinely when he might
        Lie snug and sleep, to rise before the light:
1015   What if his dull forefathers used that cry,
        Could he not let a bad example die?
        The world was fall'n into an easier way,
        This age knew better than to fast and pray.
        Good sense in sacred worship would appear
1020   So to begin, as they might end the year.
        Such feats in former times had wrought the falls

iii *1000. cruse*] small drinking vessel. The word recalls the widow's cruse which
was miraculously replenished (1 Kings xvii 16).
iii *1006.* See Matthew xxvi 74–5.
iii *1010.* See i 367*n.*
iii *1013. supinely*] lazily.
iii *1019.* D. suggests that Restoration Anglicanism is characterized by *good sense*
not only in its emphasis upon reason and toleration, but in its slackness in spiritual discipline: latitude (iii 160, 229) and laziness go together.
iii *1020.* Broadly this means that Anglicans make no distinction between feasting
and fasting, but the exact interpretation is debatable. *Works* suggests that since
the year began in the old-style calendar with Lent, D. means that Protestants
celebrate Lent with the same revelry which marked the end of the old year. But
in the old calendar the year began on Lady Day (25 March), which is usually
closer to Easter than to Ash Wednesday (in 1687 Easter fell on 27 March o.s.).
If the year is taken to begin on 1 January (which was commonly observed
as New Year's Day in this period, e.g. by Pepys), then it begins and ends with
feasting, as the new year begins during the twelve days of Christmas; implictly,
then, the Anglican year would be one long revel. The liturgical year, however,
begins on Advent Sunday, which inaugurates a season of penitential preparation
for Christmas, and ends with the thanksgivings for harvest and the associated
fairs; in this case, Anglicans would begin Advent with feasts rather than fasts.
iii *1021. such feats*] *Works* interprets this to refer to ll. 1019–20, i.e. to revelry and
luxurious living; this would make the Hind admit that the monastic orders in
England had been dissolved at the Reformation because their life was corrupt

Of crowing Chanticleers in cloistered walls.
Expelled for this, and for their lands, they fled,
And sister Partlet with her hooded head
1025 Was hooted hence, because she would not pray abed.
The way to win the restive world to God
Was to lay by the disciplining rod,
Unnatural fasts, and foreign forms of prayer:
Religion frights us with a mien severe.
1030 'Tis prudence to reform her into ease,
And put her in undress to make her pleas:
A lively faith will bear aloft the mind,
And leave the luggage of good works behind.
    'Such doctrines in the Pigeon-house were taught.
1035 You need not ask how wondrously they wrought;
But sure the common cry was all for these
Whose life and precept both encouraged ease.
Yet fearing those alluring baits might fail,
And holy deeds o'er all their arts prevail,
1040 (For vice, though frontless, and of hardened face,
Is daunted at the sight of awful grace)
An hideous figure of their foes they drew,
Nor lines, nor looks, nor shades, nor colours true;
And this grotesque design exposed to public view.

and indulgent. But *such feats* could refer back to ll. 1005–16, i.e. to the Catholic clergy's observance of spiritual discipline, here characterized as *feats* which others cannot emulate; according to this reading the Hind is suggesting that the religious orders were dissolved because their godly life irritated the lax and greedy Henry VIII and his courtiers, who were shamed by the monks' example (cp. ll. 1040–1) and also wanted their lands (l. 1023). The latter reading seems preferable, and is consistent with ll. 1024–5.

iii 1022–4. *Chanticleer* and *Partlet* are the cock and hen in Chaucer's 'The Nun's Priest's Tale' (later translated by D. as 'The Cock and the Fox'), and here represent the monks and nuns of the pre-Reformation church. *MS* glosses them specifically as 'Monks' and 'Nuns'.

iii 1026. *restive*] inactive, inert (*OED* 1); obstinate, fixed (*OED* 2); refractory, resisting control (*OED* 3).

iii 1031. *undress*] partial dress, of a kind not usually worn in public; dress which is not formal or ceremonial.

iii 1032–3. Referring to the Protestant doctrine that salvation is by faith alone, not by good works, which are important in Catholic teaching.

iii 1036. *common cry*] See ii 23n.

iii 1040. *frontless*] shameless.

iii 1041. *awful*] awesome, awe-inspiring.

iii 1042–4. Protestants' representations of Catholics, their beliefs and practices had often been grotesque: e.g. the Pope-burning processions, Oldham's *Satyrs upon*

1045 One would have thought it some Egyptian piece, ⎫
     With garden-gods and barking deities,   ⎬
     More thick than Ptolemy has stuck the skies.   ⎭
     All so perverse a draft, so far unlike,
     It was no libel where it meant to strike:
1050 Yet still the daubing pleased, and great and small
     To view the monster crowded Pigeon Hall.
     There Chanticleer was drawn upon his knees
     Adoring shrines, and stocks of sainted trees,
     And by him a misshapen, ugly race;
1055 The curse of God was seen on every face:
     No Holland emblem could that malice mend,
     But still the worse the look, the fitter for a fiend.
        'The master of the farm, displeased to find
     So much of rancour in so mild a kind,
1060 Enquired into the cause, and came to know

---

the Jesuits (1681), and much of the verbal and visual propaganda of the Popish
Plot and Exclusion Crisis. Contrast i 33–4. This greatly concerned Catholic
apologists: Bossuet said, 'the major part, who know nothing of our Doctrine,
but as represented to them by their Ministers under the most hideous Ideas,
know it not again when shewn in its natural dress' (*An Exposition of the Doctrine
of the Catholic Church* (1685) 2). Corker commented on the 'Feigned *Idolatries,
Superstitions,* and *Abuses,* [which] are . . . laid to the Charge of *Roman Catholicks,*
whereby to render both their *Faith* and *Persons* Odious to many, (otherwise
Well-meaning) People, who not sufficiently examining the Truth of Things,
but taking all for granted, Judge nothing *Ill enough* can be said or done against
Men so Principled' (*Roman-Catholick Principles* (1680) 3). John Gother in *A Papist
Mis-represented and Represented* (1685) presented in parallel columns a distorted
Protestant view of Catholic tenets, and the Catholic interpretation.
iii *1045–6.* The Egyptian god Anubis was represented with the head of a dog.
Works quotes John Gother citing the accusation against Catholics that the 'second
Council of Arles, cap. 23. sheweth it to be a custom of Pagans, to worship Trees
or Stones, or Fountains, yet our English Papists cease not to go on Pilgrimage
to St Winifrides well, nor to worship Stocks and Stones' (*Papists Protesting against
Protestant Popery* (1686) 14). Gardiner 202–5 notes that Stillingfleet's book *A Discourse
Concerning the Idolatry of the Church of Rome* (1671) had mocked Catholic devotional practices, and had been influential in encouraging others to do likewise.
iii *1045. some*] *1687bc*; an *1687a.* Probably D.'s revision.
iii *1047. Ptolemy*] Egyptian author (*fl.* AD 146–70) of influential works in math-
ematics, astronomy and geography. His model of the universe included, besides
the sun and moon, all the important stars visible from Alexandria, and proposed
a theory of heavenly spheres nested one inside the other.
iii *1053. stocks*] tree trunks (*OED* 1).
iii *1056.* Holland was noted for satirical caricatures of a political or religious nature.
mend] improve upon.
iii *1059. kind*] race, breed (again at iii 1072).

The passive church had struck the foremost blow,
With groundless fears and jealousies possessed,
As if this troublesome, intruding guest
Would drive the birds of Venus from their nest;
1065   A deed his inborn equity abhorred:
But int'rest will not trust, though God should plight
        his word.
        'A law, the source of many future harms,
        Had banished all the poultry from the farms:
        With loss of life, if any should be found
1070   To crow or peck on this forbidden ground.
        That bloody statute chiefly was designed
        For Chanticleer the white, of clergy kind;
        But after-malice did not long forget
        The lay that wore the robe and coronet;
1075   For them, for their inferiors and allies,
        Their foes a deadly shibboleth devise:
        By which unrighteously it was decreed
        That none to trust or profit should succeed
        Who would not swallow first a poisonous wicked
              weed;
1080   Or that to which old Socrates was cursed,
        Or henbane juice to swell 'em till they burst.
        The patron (as in reason) thought it hard
        To see this inquisition in his yard,
        By which the sovereign was of subjects' use debarred.
1085   'All gentle means he tried, which might withdraw
        Th' effects of so unnatural a law:
        But still the Dove-house obstinately stood

iii 1061. passive] See iii 134*n.*
iii 1062. jealousies] suspicions (*OED* 5).
iii 1064. birds of Venus] doves; in this case, the Pigeons, who are lascivious (*Works*).
iii 1066. int'rest] i.e. self-interest.
iii 1067–72. See iii 381–2*n.*
iii 1072. white] Because of his priestly vestments; and cp. i 1*n.*
iii 1073–4. See iii 729*n.*
iii 1075. allies] Stressed on the second syllable.
iii 1076. shibboleth] A test, requiring a correct utterance: in Judges xii 6 Ephraimites
who failed to pronounce the word 'Shibboleth' correctly were killed.
iii 1078. trust or profit] The Test Act of 1673 applied specifically to anyone who
'shall receive any pay, salary, fee or wages by reason of any patent or grant from
his Majesty, or shall have command or place of trust from or under his Majesty'
(*English Historical Documents* 389).
iii 1080–1. Or . . . Or] Either . . . Or.
iii 1080. Socrates was executed by the Athenians in 399 BC by drinking hemlock.

Deaf to their own, and to their neighbours' good:
And which was worse (if any worse could be)
1090   Repented of their boasted loyalty:
Now made the champions of a cruel cause,
And drunk with fumes of popular applause;
For those whom God to ruin has designed,
He fits for fate, and first destroys their mind.
1095   'New doubts indeed they daily strove to raise,
Suggested dangers, interposed delays,
And emissary Pigeons had in store
Such as the Meccan prophet used of yore,
To whisper counsels in their patron's ear,
1100   And veiled their false advice with zealous fear.
The master smiled to see 'em work in vain,
To wear him out, and make an idle reign:
He saw, but suffered their protractive arts,
And strove by mildness to reduce their hearts;
1105   But they abused that grace to make allies,
And fondly closed with former enemies;
For fools are double fools endeavouring to be wise.
      'After a grave consult what course were best,

iii 1088. neighbours'] Neighbours in *1687* might also be modernized as *neighbour's.*
iii 1089. Echoes 'And which is worse, if worse then this can be', from Orrery's
The Black Prince (in his *Two New Tragedies* (1672) 18); the line is also echoed in
'Amaryllis' l. 67, and was parodied in Rochester's *Timon* (in MS 1674, printed
1680) ll. 117–18.
iii 1092. Echoes the description of the ambitious statesman in 'Lucretius: Against
the Fear of Death' l. 203.
iii 1093–4. Proverbial: *quem Jupiter vult perdere, dementat prius.*
iii 1095–6. Burnet says that the Anglican pamphlet offensive against the Catholics
'was managed with that concert, that for the most part once a week some new
book or sermon came out' (ii 369).
iii 1098. It was a common sixteenth- and seventeenth-century story that
Muhammad trained a dove or pigeon to pick food from his ear, and then claimed
that the dove brought divine inspiration (see *1 Henry VI* i ii 140).
iii 1104. reduce] subdue, win over.
iii 1106. fondly] foolishly.
iii 1108. consult] consultation, esp. a secret, seditious meeting (*OED* 2); stressed
on the second syllable.
iii 1108–33. This speech proposes that an invitation be sent to *the noble Buzzard*
(iii 1121) to take over the government. It is not clear whether D. has a particular Anglican in mind as the speaker of this proposal. Some discussions were taking place in 1686–7 about the possibility of making an invitation to William of
Orange, who was keeping in close touch with various parties in England (Stephen
B. Baxter, *William III* (1966) 229–31). The passage begins as reported speech, but
slides into direct speech around l. 1121.

> One more mature in folly than the rest
> 1110 Stood up, and told 'em, with his head aside,
> "That desperate cures must be to desperate ills applied;
> And therefore since their main impending fear
> Was from th' increasing race of Chanticleer,
> Some potent bird of prey they ought to find,
> 1115 A foe professed to him, and all his kind:
> Some haggard Hawk, who had her eyrie nigh,
> Well-pounced to fasten, and well-winged to fly;
> One they might trust their common wrongs to wreak:
> The Musket and the Kestrel were too weak,
> 1120 Too fierce the Falcon, but above the rest
> The noble Buzzard ever pleased me best;

iii 1116. *haggard*] caught when adult, therefore wild, untamed (*OED* 1); also used of a trained hawk which has reverted to being wild (as in *Othello* III iii 264). *eyrie*] nest of a bird of prey.

iii 1117. *Well-pounced*] with sharp talons (*OED*'s first example of the adjective *pounced*; from 'pounce' *OED sb.*¹ 2: claw, talon).

iii 1118. *wreak*] avenge (*OED* 5).

iii 1119. *Musket*] male sparrowhawk (*OED*).   *Kestrel*] The spelling in *1687* is *Coystrel*, a variant form of the word.

iii 1121. *Buzzard*] An inferior kind of hawk, useless for falconry (cp. iii 1123). Hastings says it is 'More pity that the eagles should be mew'd, / While kites and buzzards prey at liberty' (*Richard III* I i 132–3). The proverb 'Between hawk and buzzard' means 'between a good and a bad thing of the same kind', since the hawk is the true sporting bird, and the buzzard a lazy, inferior bird of the same species (*OED* buzzard 1b). The buzzard is also proverbially stupid and ignorant (*OED* 2). Two identifications have been proposed for the Buzzard:

(1) Gilbert Burnet (1643–1715), a Protestant, born in Edinburgh; of Whig sympathies during the Exclusion Crisis, and strongly distrusted by James. He published *The History of the Reformation of the Church of England* (1679–81) and several anti-Catholic tracts, and preached a notable sermon against popery on 5 November 1684 on the text 'Save me from the lion's mouth: for thou hast heard me from the horns of the unicorns' (Psalm xxii 21). At the accession of James he moved to Paris, and after a visit to Italy moved to The Hague at the invitation of William of Orange, whose confidant he became. His travels were described in *Some Letters* (dated 1686; appearing in January or February 1687), which achieved a *succès de scandale* in England because of their outspoken account of life in Catholic countries with authoritarian governments. Burnet also published *Reflections on Mr Varillas's History of the Revolutions* (1686), for which see 'To the Reader' l. 76n above. In April 1687 (the citation is dated 19 April) James accused Burnet of high treason for corresponding and associating with rebels on the continent. His *Six Papers*, published at some point in 1687 (the volume includes letters dated May and June 1687) collects various polemical tracts, including 'Reasons against the Repealing the Acts of Parliament concerning the *TEST*', and 'Reflections on His Majesties Declaration for *Liberty of Conscience*'. Even if D. had not read these papers, he would have known of Burnet's position as a

prominent opponent of James's ecclesiastical policy who was waiting for an opportunity to return to England. In 1688 Burnet landed with William at Torbay,
and was rewarded for his support with the bishopric of Salisbury. See further
T. E. S. Clarke and H. C. Foxcroft, *A Life of Gilbert Burnet* (1907), and for Burnet's
own view of events, see his *History of His Own Time*. Details which suggest Burnet
are: (i) the alliteration of 'Burnet' and 'Buzzard', pointed out derisively in *The
Hind and the Panther Transvers'd*; (ii) *MS* glosses the Buzzard here as 'D^r. Burnet'
(though at l. 899 *MS* had seen the Buzzard as representing the Presbyterians generally); (iii) the indications in ll. 1146–7 that the Buzzard is a theologian: Burnet
was Professor of Divinity at Glasgow 1669–74; (iv) the indications in ll. 1151–6
that the Buzzard is dependent upon others for advancement: Burnet ingratiated
himself with Charles II, James when Duke of York, the Earl of Lauderdale, and
others who were influential in Scottish affairs, before developing his connections
with William of Orange; (v) the Buzzard vilifies those who had supported him
and whom he had previously flattered, including kings (ll. 1163–71): Burnet
forefeited the favour of Charles II by sending him a letter criticizing his personal
behaviour and his government; (vi) the Buzzard exposes those who had been
kind to him (l. 1168): Burnet acknowledges 'how much I was once in his [James's]
favour, and how highly I was obliged to him' (Burnet ii 295), but when James
charged Burnet with treason, Burnet threatened to publish an account of his
political activities which would prove damaging to James; see also iii 1179–86*n*;
(vii) the Buzzard leaves *his native clime* (l. 1152) as Burnet left Scotland to pursue
his career in England; (viii) he has a *fluent tongue* (l. 1154), which was true of
Burnet: Evelyn recorded that Burnet preached 'with such a floud of Eloquence,
& fullnesse of matter as shew'd him to be a person of extraordinary parts'
(*Diary*, 15 November 1674; *Works*); (ix) he is *by reverse of fortune chased away*
(l. 1159), as Burnet was compelled to leave England for the continent in 1685.

(2) William of Orange (1650–1702), King of England from 1689. Details
which suggest William are: (i) he *in time of war has done us harm* (l. 1125) by fighting against England in the Third Dutch War (1672–4); (ii) as a Protestant who
was strongly opposed to Catholicism his differences from the Church of England were only minor (ll. 1126–7); Burnet records a conversation with William
in 1686 in which they explored William's agreements and disagreements with the
Church of England (Burnet ii 391–2); (iii) he is already a ruler (*potentate*: l. 1130)
as Stadhouder and as Prince of Orange, is being offered the *sovereign sway* (l. 1131)
and invited to *succeed* (l. 1135), and is *crowned* (ll. 1139–40).

It is possible that D. intended a composite portrait of the Buzzard as both
king and theologian, taking character traits from two historical figures to form a
single image for the political and ecclesiastical threat to James.

Works suggests that the character of the Buzzard (from l. 1141 onward) was a
late addition by D., as the extended characterization (in the mode of *AA*) inter-
rupts the Hind's narrative of the Pigeons; *Works* believes that this may have been
prompted by the publication in April 1687 of Burnet's arguments against repealing the Test Act (in his *Six Papers*), though it is unlikely that the *Six Papers* were
published as early as April (see above). Even so, D. would have been well aware
of Burnet's position, and could have had some inkling of the coming charges
against him. It is also worth noting that l. 1141 comes at the top of p. 137 in
1687a, which is the first page of a new gathering (sig. T1^r); the incorrect catchword 'As' at the foot of p. 136 suggests that a different line was originally intended
to start p. 137; and there are several press corrections on p. 137 (in ll. 1147–54)
which suggest that D. revised this passage as *1687a* was going through the press,
which is another reason for thinking that it was a late addition. It does not seem

       Of small renown, 'tis true, for not to lie
       We call him but a Hawk by courtesy.
       I know he haunts the Pigeon-house and farm,
1125   And more, in time of war has done us harm;
       But all his hate on trivial points depends:
       Give up our forms, and we shall soon be friends.
       For Pigeons' flesh he seems not much to care,
       Crammed chickens are a more delicious fare;
1130   On this high potentate without delay
       I wish you would confer the sovereign sway:
       Petition him t' accept the government,
       And let a splendid embassy be sent."
           'This pithy speech prevailed, and all agreed,
1135   Old enmities forgot, the Buzzard should succeed.
           'Their welcome suit was granted soon as heard, ⎫
       His lodgings furnished, and a train prepared,   ⎬
       With 'B's upon their breast, appointed for his guard. ⎭
       He came, and crowned with great solemnity,
1140   "God save King Buzzard" was the general cry.
           'A portly prince, and goodly to the sight,
       He seemed a son of Anak for his height,
       Like those whom stature did to crowns prefer,
       Black-browed, and bluff, like Homer's Jupiter:
1145   Broad-backed and brawny, built for love's delight,

---

possible to determine the extent of this additional passage, or to know what, if
anything, it replaced.
iii 1129. *Crammed*] stuffed.
iii 1141. *portly*] dignified, majestic (*OED* 1); corpulent (*OED* 1b).   *goodly*] of good
appearance (*OED* 1); of considerable size (*OED* 2); cp. iii 1143*n*, and also *MF*
l. 25 (of Shadwell).
iii 1142. *son of Anak*] In Numbers xiii 33 some Israelites report: 'we saw the giants,
the sons of Anak, which come of the giants'.
iii 1143. I Samuel ix 2 says that Saul, when selected to be king over Israel, was
'a choice young man, and a goodly: and there was not among the children of
Israel a goodlier person than he: from his shoulders and upward he was higher
than any of the people'.   *prefer*] promote.
iii 1144. Homer describes how Zeus (Jupiter to the Romans) 'nodded his dark
brows' (κυανέῃσιν ἐπ' ὀφρύσι νεῦσε: *Iliad* i 528).   *bluff*] with a broad face or
forehead (*OED* 1c).
iii 1145–6. Burnet had a reputation for being emotionally involved with women
under his spiritual direction, and at the time of writing it had become known
that he was engaged to a Dutch heiress. (The marriage was politically important
because it gave him Dutch nationality.) For his correspondence with Anne Wharton
in 1682–3 see *The Surviving Works of Anne Wharton*, edited by G. Greer and S.
Hastings (1997) 339–63. A forthright comment on Burnet's behaviour appears in
BL MS Harley 7319, fol. 97ʳ (dated 1682): 'Is F-king a Crime, / When Ballocks

A prophet formed to make a female proselyte.
A theologue more by need than genial bent,
By breeding sharp, by nature confident.
Int'rest in all his actions was discerned,
1150   More learn'd than honest, more a wit than learn'd.
Or forced by fear, or by ambition led,
Or both conjoined, his native clime he fled;
But brought the virtues of his heaven along,
A fair behaviour, and a fluent tongue.
1155   And yet with all his arts he could not thrive,
The most unlucky parasite alive.
Loud praises to prepare his paths he sent,
And then himself pursued his compliment:
But, by reverse of fortune chased away,
1160   His gifts no longer than their author stay:
He shakes the dust against th' ungrateful race,
And leaves the stench of ordures in the place.

---

divine / Freely scatter their seed o'r the Nation? / For *Burnet's* stiff Tarse, / In
each Pious Arse / Rubs up a devout Meditation'.

iii 1145. Broad-backed and brawny] For the sexual connotations cp. Rochester: 'With
brawny back, and leggs and Potent Prick' (*Tunbridge Wells* l. 156).

iii 1147. theologue] theologian. *genial*] by natural disposition (*OED* 6). *genial*]
1687a corrected, 1687bc; nat'ral *1687a uncorrected.* Probably D.'s revision to avoid
repetition with 'nature' in l. 1148.

iii 1148. nature] *1687a corrected, 1687bc;* Nation *1687a uncorrected.* Probably the correction of a typesetter's error.

iii 1149. Int'rest] self-interest (rather than principle).

iii 1151. Or . . . or] Either . . . or. *ambition*] *1687a corrected;* his Profit *1687a uncorrected, 1687bc.* D.'s revision. Kinsley and *Works* follow *1687bc* in not adopting this
reading from the corrected state of *1687a,* but *Works* admits that this alteration
may have been overlooked in the preparation of *1687b* rather than deliberately
rejected. It seems best to regard this revision as having the same status as the
other press corrections on this page.

iii 1152. both conjoined, his native] *1687a corrected, 1687bc;* both, his own unhappy
1687a uncorrected. D.'s revision.

iii 1153. heaven] native climate (*OED* 2b).

iii 1154. behaviour] manners, deportment. *fluent*] *1687a corrected, 1687bc;* flatt'ring
1687a uncorrected. D.'s revision.

iii 1157. Alluding to John the Baptist: Matthew iii 3.

iii 1161. From Matthew x 14.

iii 1162. In this respect the Buzzard acts like a harpy (cp. iii 960*n*; *Works*). *Works*
also cites Burnet's description of a Venetian palace whose beauty is 'much pre-
judiced by the beastliness of those that walk along, and that leave their Marks
behind them, as if this were rather a common House of office, than so Noble a
Palace' (*Some Letters* 129–30).

Oft has he flattered and blasphemed the same,
For in his rage he spares no sovereign's name:
1165   The hero and the tyrant change their style
By the same measure that they frown or smile.
When well received by hospitable foes,
The kindness he returns is to expose;
For courtesies, though undeserved and great,
1170   No gratitude in felon minds beget:
As tribute to his wit, the churl receives the treat.
His praise of foes is venomously nice,
So touched, it turns a virtue to a vice:
A Greek, and bountiful, forewarns us twice.
1175   Sev'n sacraments he wisely does disown,
Because he knows confession stands for one;
Where sins to sacred silence are conveyed,
And not for fear or love to be betrayed:
But he, uncalled, his patron to control,

---

iii 1165. hero . . . tyrant] James II could be regarded as a hero for his military service, but as a tyrant for his extra-constitutional attempts to promote the interests of Roman Catholics.

iii 1167. hospitable foes] 'the Pope & Cardinals' *MS*.

iii 1171. treat] entertainment of food and drink.

iii 1172–3. 'It is a general and just objection to the Bishop's historical characters, that they are drawn up with too much severity, and that the keenness of party has induced him, in many cases, to impose upon the reader a caricature for a resemblance' (Scott). *nice*] careful, precise.

iii 1174. Echoing *timeo Danaos et dona ferentes* ('I fear Greeks, especially when they bear gifts': *Aen.* ii. 49). This is Laocoön's warning to the Trojans, who are about to be persuaded by the duplicitous Greek Sinon to take the wooden horse within their walls. The line is italicized in *1687*, marking it as a *sententia* (as it is also in Virgil).

iii 1175–8. The Roman Catholic Church holds that there are seven sacraments (baptism, confirmation, the Eucharist, penance, extreme unction, ordination, and matrimony); the Church of England distinguishes between the two sacraments said to have been ordained by Christ (baptism and the Eucharist) and the other five 'commonly called Sacraments . . . [which] are not to be counted for Sacraments of the Gospel' (Article 25). Confession is part of the sacrament of penance, and the priest to whom confession is made is absolutely prohibited from disclosing any part of it.

iii 1179–86. During the parliamentary examination of Lauderdale's conduct in Scotland in 1675 Burnet testified against his former patron with ambiguous evidence. Burnet himself admitted: 'I was much blamed for what I had done. Some, to make it look the worse, added, that I had been his Chaplain, which was false; and that I had been much obliged to him, tho' I had never received any real obligation from him, but had done him great services, for which I had been very unworthily requited. Yet the thing had an ill appearance, as the disclosing of what had pass'd in confidence' (Burnet i 534). *MS* is probably mistaken in glossing *his patron* as 'K. Ja. 2', though see iii 1121*n* for Burnet and James.

1180   Divulged the secret whispers of his soul:
        Stood forth th' accusing Satan of his crimes,
        And offered to the Moloch of the times.
        Prompt to assail, and careless of defence,
        Invulnerable in his impudence,
1185   He dares the world, and eager of a name
        He thrusts about, and jostles into fame.
        Frontless and satire-proof he scours the streets,
        And runs an Indian muck at all he meets.
        So fond of loud report, that not to miss ⎫
1190   Of being known (his last and utmost bliss) ⎬
        He rather would be known for what he is. ⎭
            'Such was, and is, the captain of the Test, ⎫
        Though half his virtues are not here expressed; ⎬
        The modesty of Fame conceals the rest. ⎭
1195   The spleenful Pigeons never could create
        A prince more proper to revenge their hate:
        Indeed, more proper to revenge than save;
        A king whom in his wrath th' Almighty gave:
        For all the grace the landlord had allowed ⎫
1200   But made the Buzzard and the Pigeons proud; ⎬
        Gave time to fix their friends, and to seduce the crowd. ⎭

iii *1179. control*] take to task (*OED* 3); overpower, overmaster (*OED* 5).
iii *1181. accusing*] The Greek διάβολος (hence the English 'diabolical') means 'falsely accusing, slandering'. *Satan*] The original Hebrew means 'the adversary, one who plots'.
iii *1182. Moloch*] A Canaanite god, to whom children were sacrificed as burnt offerings (*OED*; *PL* i 392–6n); here, Parliament. *MS* glosses this as 'Pr.^ce of Orange'.
iii *1187. Frontless*] shameless.
iii *1188. runs an Indian muck*] runs madly, thirsting for blood. The *OED*'s first example is from Marvell: 'like a raging *Indian* (for in *Europe* it was never before practised) he runs a *Mucke* (as they cal it there) stabbing every man he meets' (*The Rehearsal Transpros'd* (1672), ed. D. I. B. Smith (1971) 28).
iii *1191. for what he is*] 'a Knave' *MS*.
iii *1192. captain of the Test*] Burnet took a prominent part in the controversy over the possible repeal of the Test Act. See iii 1121n.
iii *1195. spleenful*] passionately angry.
iii *1198.* When the Israelites insisted on having a king, instead of having God to reign over them, God was displeased and gave them Saul, after warning them that a king would treat them tyrannically (1 Samuel viii). In the fable 'Of the Frogs desiring a King' (Ogilby, *The Fables of Aesop* 31–2) the frogs are eventually sent a predatory stork as their king. Restoration satire had used this fable with various political applications (see *POAS* i 189, 251, 281; ii 343).

They long their fellow-subjects to enthral,
Their patron's promise into question call,
And vainly think he meant to make 'em lords of all.
1205   'False fears their leaders failed not to suggest,
As if the Doves were to be dispossessed;
Nor sighs, nor groans, nor goggling eyes did want,
For now the Pigeons too had learned to cant.
The house of prayer is stocked with large increase,
1210   Nor doors, nor windows can contain the press;
For birds of every feather fill th' abode,
Ev'n atheists out of envy own a God:
And reeking from the stews adulterers come
Like Goths and Vandals to demolish Rome.
1215   That conscience which to all their crimes was mute
Now calls aloud, and cries to persecute.
No rigour of the laws to be released,
And much the less, because it was their lord's request:
They thought it great their sovereign to control,
1220   And named their pride "nobility of soul".
    ''Tis true, the Pigeons and their prince-elect
Were short of power their purpose to effect;
But with their quills did all the hurt they could,
And cuffed the tender chickens from their food:
1225   And much the Buzzard in their cause did stir,
Though naming not the patron, to infer
With all respect, he was a gross idolater.

---

iii 1202. *enthral*] enslave.

iii 1203–4. Some Anglicans alleged that James was in breach of his promise to maintain the Church of England (see iii 953–4*n*), and this was said particularly of the
Declaration for Liberty of Conscience, as it suspended the church's legal safeguards against
dissent. D.'s phrasing reminds his readers that James's promise had not been to
make the Church of England *lords of all*, simply to preserve it as the established church.

iii 1207. *want*] lack.

iii 1208. *cant*] use affected religious language; esp. of Nonconformists.

iii 1209, 1248, 1265. *increase*] stressed on the second syllable.

iii 1210. *press*] crowd.

iii 1213. *stews*] brothels.

iii 1217. *released*] alleviated, removed (*OED* 2).

iii 1226–7. 'I hope none will be wanting in all possible respect to his sacred person; and as we ought to be infinitely sorry to find him engaged in a religion
which we must believe idolatrous, so we are far from the ill-manners of reflecting on his person, or calling him an idolator' (Burnet, 'Reasons against Repealing
the Act of Parliament Concerning the Test' in *Six Papers* (1687) 6; Williams).

'But when th' imperial owner did espy
That thus they turned his grace to villainy,
1230 Not suffering wrath to discompose his mind, ⎤
He strove a temper for th' extremes to find, ⎬
So to be just, as he might still be kind. ⎦
Then all maturely weighed, pronounced a doom
Of sacred strength for every age to come.
1235 By this the Doves their wealth and state possess,
No rights infringed, but licence to oppress:
Such power have they as factious lawyers long
To crowns ascribed, that kings can do no wrong.
But since his own domestic birds have tried
1240 The dire effects of their destructive pride,
He deems that proof a measure to the rest, ⎤
Concluding well within his kingly breast ⎬
His fowl of nature too unjustly were oppressed. ⎦

iii 1228–55. This passage refers to James's *Declaration for Liberty of Conscience* issued on 4 April 1687, so these lines would have been written at a late stage in the poem's composition. The provisions of the *Declaration* to which D. refers are: (1) 'we do declare that we will protect and maintain our archbishops, bishops and clergy, and all other our subjects of the Church of England in the free exercise of their religion as by law established, and in the quiet and full enjoyment of all their possessions, without any molestation or disturbance whatsoever' (cp. iii 1235–6); (2) 'we do freely give them leave to meet and serve God after their own way and manner, be it in private houses or places purposely hired or built for that use . . . And that all our subjects may enjoy such their religious assemblies with greater assurance and protection, we have thought it requisite, and do hereby command, that no disturbance of any kind be made or given unto them' (cp. iii 1244–9) (*English Historical Documents* 395–7).
iii 1228. imperial owner] In the opening of his *Declaration* James refers to 'the imperial crown of these kingdoms' (395).
iii 1230. suffering] allowing.
iii 1231. temper] compromise, settlement (*OED* 2).
iii 1232. as] that.
iii 1233. maturely weighed] Cp. 'we are the more confirmed by the reflections we have made upon the conduct of the four last reigns' (*Declaration* 396). *doom*] verdict, judgment.
iii 1234. for every age to come] Cp. 'the free exercise of their religion for the time to come' (*Declaration* 395).
iii 1236. but licence] except their licence.
iii 1239. his own domestic birds] the Catholics. *tried*] demonstrated by experience (*OED* 13); had experience of, undergone (*OED* 14).
iii 1240. their] the Anglicans'.
iii 1241. proof] demonstration (*OED* 2). *measure*] basis upon which one may estimate what is to be expected of someone (*OED* 3). *the rest*] the Nonconformists.
iii 1243. fowl of nature] wild fowl (contrasting with the *domestic birds*): the Nonconformists. *too*] also (not 'too unjustly').

He therefore makes all birds of every sect ⎫
1245 Free of his farm, with promise to respect ⎬
Their several kinds alike, and equally protect. ⎭
His gracious edict the same franchise yields ⎫
To all the wild increase of woods and fields, ⎬
And who in rocks aloof, and who in steeples builds. ⎭
1250 To Crows the like impartial grace affords,
And Choughs and Daws, and such republic birds.
Secured with ample privilege to feed,
Each has his district, and his bounds decreed:
Combined in common interest with his own,
1255 But not to pass the Pigeons' Rubicon.
      'Here ends the reign of this pretended Dove, ⎫
All prophecies accomplished from above, ⎬
For Shiloh comes the sceptre to remove. ⎭
Reduced from her imperial high abode,
1260 Like Dionysius to a private rod:

iii 1245. Free] allowed the use and enjoyment of (*OED* 29b, first example).
iii 1246. several] separate, individual.
iii 1247. franchise] freedom, esp. from arrest (*OED* 1, 3).
iii 1248–9. Cp. i 37, 312–13*nn*.
iii 1248. increase] population.
iii 1250–1. Crows . . . Choughs . . . Daws] Various kinds of Nonconformist sects, specifically those of republican tendencies originating in the 1640s and 1650s. *Choughs*] Applied loosely to smaller members of the crow family, particularly to jackdaws.   *Daws*] jackdaws; applied to foolish and lazy people (*OED* 2, 3).
iii 1255. Rubicon] the stream which marked the boundary between Italy and Cisalpine Gaul. Roman generals were not allowed to cross it at the head of their armies when returning home, as this would constitute a rebellion against the authority of the Roman Senate. When Julius Caesar crossed it in 49 BC he precipitated civil war.
iii 1258. In Genesis xlix 9–10 Jacob prophesies: 'Judah is a lion's whelp: from the prey, my son, thou art gone up: he stooped down, he couched as a lion, and as an old lion; who shall rouse him? The sceptre shall not depart from Judah, nor a lawgiver from between his feet, until Shiloh come; and unto him shall the gathering of the people be.' Shiloh was interpreted as a reference to the Messiah.
iii 1260. Dionysius was tyrant of Syracuse 367–357 BC; after political upheavals he retired to private life in Corinth in 344 BC. Cicero says that Dionysius became a schoolmaster at Corinth, because he could not do without the right to rule (*Tusculan Disputations* III xii 27).

The passive church, that with pretended grace ⎫
Did her distinctive mark in duty place,   ⎬
Now touched, reviles her maker to his face. ⎭
   'What after happened is not hard to guess: ⎫
1265 The small beginnings had a large increase,   ⎬
And arts and wealth succeed (the secret spoils of peace). ⎭
'Tis said the Doves repented, though too late,
Become the smiths of their own foolish fate:
Nor did their owner hasten their ill hour,
1270 But sunk in credit, they decreased in power:
Like snows in warmth that mildly pass away,
Dissolving in the silence of decay.
   'The Buzzard, not content with equal place,
Invites the feathered Nimrods of his race
1275 To hide the thinness of their flock from sight,
And all together make a seeming goodly flight.
But each have separate interests of their own:
Two tsars are one too many for a throne.
Nor can th' usurper long abstain from food:
1280 Already he has tasted Pigeons' blood,
And may be tempted to his former fare
When this indulgent lord shall late to heaven repair.
Bare benting times and moulting months may come,
When lagging late they cannot reach their home;

---

iii 1261. passive] See iii 134*n*.
iii 1263. touched] put to the test, made trial of (used of testing the purity of gold or silver) (*OED* 8). *maker*] *Works* notes that since the Church of England is a secular creation, her *maker* is not God but the King of England, now James II. The implicit contrast is with the divinely instituted Church of Rome (for this claim see i 493–6*n*).
iii 1266. The *Declaration* had said that persecution spoiled trade (396).
iii 1268. Proverbially each man is the smith of his own fortune: *Faber quisquis fortunae suae* (Francis Bacon, 'Of Fortune' in his *Essayes*, ed. Michael Kiernan (1985) 122).
iii 1273–4. For Nimrod see i 283*n*. In *not content with equal place* D. is echoing Milton's description of Nimrod as 'not content / With fair equality' (*PL* xii 25–6) (J. R. Mason).
iii 1278. Peter the Great and his half-brother Ivan had been proclaimed joint tsars of Russia in 1682, as a compromise between two rival factions.
iii 1282. Cp. Horace addressing Augustus: *serus in coelum redeas* ('late may you return to heaven': *Carm.* I ii 45) (Williams); and cp. *AA* l. 350.
iii 1283. benting times] the time when pigeons are reduced to feeding on bents (reedy grasses or hard stalks) (*OED*). The idea was proverbial: 'The pigeon never knows woe but when she does a-benting go': Tilley P 316 (Kinsley).

1285   Or rent in schism (for so their fate decrees)
       Like the tumultuous college of the bees,
       They fight their quarrel, by themselves oppressed:
       The tyrant smiles below, and waits the falling feast.'
           Thus did the gentle Hind her fable end,
1290   Nor would the Panther blame it, nor commend;
       But with affected yawnings at the close,
       Seemed to require her natural repose.
       For now the streaky light began to peep,
       And setting stars admonished both to sleep.
1295   The dame withdrew, and, wishing to her guest
       The peace of heaven, betook herself to rest.
       Ten thousand angels on her slumbers wait,
       With glorious visions of her future state.

iii 1286. Virgil describes civil war in a beehive in *Geo.* iv 67–90, vividly translated by D. in an expanded passage which highlights the political implications
('The Fourth Book of the *Georgics*' ll. 92–136).
iii 1289. *gentle*] noble.
iii 1294. From Virgil: *suadentque cadentia sidera somnos* ('and setting stars persuade
to sleep': *Aen.* iv 81; *Works*).

17 A Song for St Cecilia's Day

Date and publication. A Song for St CECILIA's Day, 1687 was first printed 'for
T. Dring, in *Fleetstreet*' as a single folio half-sheet which was distributed at the
celebrations of the feast of St Cecilia (22 November) in 1687, when the poem
was performed in a musical setting by Draghi (see below). The text is printed
on one side in a double column; the verso is blank. Only one copy of the first
edition (now in the BL) seems to have survived. The poem was reprinted in *EP*
without substantive change. There is one late seventeenth-century MS of the poem
alone (Beal DrJ 188), apparently copied from one of the printed editions. There
are also five MSS which contain the poem together with its musical setting, three
in the BL (see Beal DrJ 189–91), one in BodL (MS Tenbury 1226) and one in
the West Sussex Record Office, Chichester (Cap. VI/1/1, fols. 24ʳ–63ʳ) (the last
two not listed by Beal). The Chichester MS gives a list of singers, probably
for the first performance. BL MS Royal College of Music 1106, fols. 29–74 (Beal
DrJ 191) seems to be derived from a performance in 1694 or 1695 (see Peter
Holman, *Four and Twenty Fiddlers: The Violin at the English Court, 1540–1690* (1993)
326–7). The present text is based on *1687*. [handwritten marginal notes]

Context. The earliest recorded English celebrations of the feast of St Cecilia took
place in London in 1683. They appear to have been established by the Musical
Society, a body of professional and amateur music lovers about which little is
known outside the context of the St Cecilia 'music feasts'. Each year four members of the Society (later six, then eight) were appointed stewards and made the
necessary arrangements. The celebrations involved a performance of a specially
commissioned ode, a banquet at Stationers' Hall (from 1684), and (from 1693) a
church service at St Bride's, Fleet Street, with a sermon in defence of church
music. [handwritten marginal note] The odes were performed by the combined choirs of St Paul's Cathedral,
Westminster Abbey and the Chapel Royal, supplemented by male singers
attached to the theatres, and accompanied by an instrumental ensemble probably
comprising members of the King's Band of Music and the theatre orchestras. Texts
of the odes were distributed at the performances. Poets and composers of the odes
performed between 1683 and 1686 were as follows: 1683 ('Welcome to all the
pleasures'): text by Christopher Fishbourne, music by Henry Purcell; 1684 ('Begin
the song'): text by John Oldham, music by John Blow; 1685 ('Tune the viol,
touch the lute'): text by Nahum Tate, music by William Turner; 1686 ('From those
pure, those blest abodes'): text by Thomas Flatman, music by Isaac Blackwell. In
1686 there were also Cecilian celebrations at Oxford, where the text of the ode
('Io! with triumphant noise') was written by Thomas Fletcher, a New College
undergraduate. For D.'s ode for the 1697 celebration see *Alexander's Feast*.

The music for D.'s ode in 1687 (which included for the first time parts for
trumpets and flutes as well as for strings and continuo) was by Giovanni Battista
Draghi (*c.* 1640–1708), an Italian composer often known in England as 'Signor
Baptist'. Draghi had come to England under Charles II's auspices, and was appointed
organist of James II's Roman Catholic chapel in 1687. His talents were admired
by both Pepys (12 February 1667) and Evelyn (25 June 1684, 28 January 1685,
14 March 1685), who described him as an 'excellent & stupendious Artist'. The
present setting marked a turning-point in the history of the English musical ode.
It was preceded by a descriptive Italianate prelude, rather than the customary French
overture. Its massive choruses (based on complex Italianate counterpoint, rather

than French dance patterns), its florid and extensive solos, five-part string writing and adventurous use of trumpets were all unprecedented in a work of this
kind. Draghi's setting was to be a crucial influence on the development of Henry
Purcell, and in particular on his *Hail, Bright Cecilia*, the Cecilian ode for 1692
(see Holman, *Four and Twenty Fiddlers* 427–8). Draghi's setting of D.'s poem is
notable for its frequent verbal repetitions, and for its attempts to 'underlay' (translate into musical terms) the sense and expressive effects of its text (for some illustrations see notes below, and Ernest Brennecke, Jnr, *PMLA* xlix (1934) 1–34).
Draghi does not consistently follow the contours of D.'s poetic structure. Thus,
while stanzas II, III, IV, VII, and the Grand Chorus in D.'s text are each set as
discrete musical numbers, stanza I is broken up into four separate movements,
and stanzas V and VI are combined in one and preceded by a purely instrumental
sinfonia. There is an unpublished modern edition of Draghi's score by Charles
Biklé (University of Michigan MA thesis, 1974), and Richard Platt is preparing
an edition for publication. The setting was recorded in 1995 by the Parley of
Instruments and the Playford Consort (with soloists), directed by Peter Holman
and Richard Wistreich (Hyperion CDA 66770). On the St Cecilia celebrations,
see further Malone I i 254–307; William Henry Husk, *An Account of the Musical
Celebrations on St Cecilia's Day* (1857), containing texts of all the extant odes to
1687 except Flatman's (for which see David Hopkins, *RES* xlv (1994) 486–95);
Richard Luckett, 'The Legend of St Cecilia and English Literature: A Study',
unpublished University of Cambridge PhD thesis, 1971; Charles Biklé, 'The Odes
for St Cecilia's Day in London, 1683–1703', unpublished University of Michigan
PhD thesis, 1982.

Sources. A Song for St Cecilia's Day has no single source, but draws eclectically on
various materials and traditions which can be classified for convenience as follows:
(i) legends of St Cecilia, connecting her with music and in particular with the
invention of the organ; (ii) traditional beliefs about the relation of musical to cosmic
harmony and creation, and about the affective powers of music; (iii) earlier poetic
treatments of these subjects, including earlier Cecilian odes.

   (i) St Cecilia was a Roman martyr of the third century, of whom little is known.
Her association with music (of which she came to be regarded as the patron saint)
appears to date from the fifteenth or sixteenth century, and derives from a misunderstanding of some words from her *Acts*, a heavily fictionalized account of
her life, dating from shortly before AD 500. (These *Acts* form the basis for Chaucer's
Second Nun's Tale.) Cecilia, we are there told, was given in marriage against her
will to a pagan youth named Valerian. On the wedding day, *cantantibus organis,
illa in corde suo soli Domino decantabat* ('while the pipes [organs] were playing for
the festivities, Cecilia offered her silent prayer to God'). The phrase *cantantibus
organis* was misinterpreted to mean 'she sang to the accompaniment of the organ'.
As a result, the organ became regarded as Cecilia's emblem, and in time the instrument became popularly regarded as her invention. The *Acts* relate that after her
marriage Cecilia informed her husband that an angel was keeping guard over her,
and, if Valerian attempted to consummate the marriage, he would experience
God's punishment. If he respected her virginity, however, he would be rewarded
by divine grace. Valerian declared that he would only be convinced if he could
see the angel. Cecilia told him that he could only see the angel if he were instructed
and baptized, and sent him to Pope Urban for this purpose. On his return he
saw the angel offering Cecilia and himself floral crowns. Luckett 264 and *Works*
note that D. seems to have been the first English writer to combine the story
of Cecilia's association with the organ with the story of her guardian angel, by

suggesting that it was specifically by means of her organ-playing that she first attracted the angel to earth. D.'s knowledge of the St Cecilia legend seems neither to have been particularly deep, nor to have been derived from one particular source (Luckett 225, 280). D.'s enemy Luke Milbourne (see Malone I i 259*n*) sneered at the poet for his ignorance in calling St Cecilia the inventress of the organ. But, as Luckett argues, there is no reason to suppose that D. was ignorant of the general opinion of musicians in his day (for which see Malone I i 258*n*) that the organ was of Greek or Hebrew origin. D.'s treatment of the St Cecilia legend is fully in line with the increasingly playful and literary way in which saints' lives were treated in late seventeenth-century England (Luckett 170).

(ii) D. draws on various ideas and images of music which are ultimately classical in origin but which, mediated and elaborated by early Christian and medieval authorities and by the French and Italian academicians of the sixteenth century, became part of the staple of musical discussion in the Renaissance and beyond. These can be broadly classified in two main groups. The first saw music as both an illustration and an embodiment of God's primal harmonizing act at the creation. According to this body of thought (which is ultimately Pythagorean and Platonic in origin), the universe is to be seen as a divinely ordered set of mathematical and harmonious correspondences; and the human mind's susceptibility to music is to be understood as a response to, and an epitome of, the larger patterning of the divine creation as manifested in such phenomena as the 'music of the spheres'. The correspondences of microcosmic and macrocosmic music were thought to be epitomized most concentratedly in the 'diapason' or octave, a musical interval which was the most perfect concord and the basic unit of all complex harmonies, and also (according to Pythagorean tradition) a symbol of the perfect concord of spiritual and physical elements in man, man being the culmination and epitome of God's harmonious creation, and the most harmonious of God's creatures because most like him. Since the diapason was, at least in theory, infinitely repeatable upwards and downwards on the scale of musical pitch, it was thought to form an image of the boundless eternal concord of God himself, the alpha and omega of all cosmic harmony. (See further, Leo Spitzer, *Traditio* ii (1944) 409–64, iii (1945) 307–64; Frances A. Yates, *The French Academies of the Sixteenth Century* (1947) 38; James Hutton, *English Miscellany* ii (1951) 1–63; Gretchen Ludke Finney, *Musical Backgrounds for English Literature, 1580–1650* (1961); John Hollander, *The Untuning of the Sky: Ideas of Music in English Poetry, 1500–1700* (1961); Jay Arnold Levine, *PQ* xliv (1965) 38–50.)

D. also draws on a body of beliefs and images concerning the emotional and ethical effects said to have been produced by the modes, rhythms and instrumentation of music in ancient times. Drawing on such classical myths as the stories of Orpheus and Amphion, and on historical or quasi-historical narratives by Plutarch, Dionysius of Halicarnassus, Quintilian and others, writers on music from Boethius onwards had marvelled at the miraculous affective power of ancient music, and had speculated on ways in which this might best be replicated in the modern world. Some Renaissance theorists had attempted to posit correspondences between the ancient Greek modes (and the musical instruments with which they were associated) and the scales of modern music, though there was disagreement about precisely which modern scale was the equivalent of each Greek mode. Others had attempted to establish a close causal relationship between poetic or musical rhythm and emotional effect. See further, D. P. Walker, *Music Review* ii (1941) 1–13, 111–21, 220–7, 288–307, iii (1942) 55–71; Yates, *The French Academies* 38–48; James Kinsley, *RES* iv (1953) 263–7; James Winn, *Unsuspected Eloquence: A History of the Relations between Poetry and Music* (1981) 163–79.

Some scholars have argued that theories of cosmic proportion and musical effect exercised a controlling influence on the style and organization of D.'s poem. Alastair Fowler and Douglas Brooks (in *Silent Poetry*, edited by A. Fowler (1970) 185–200) argue that every aspect of the poem is organized according to elaborate patterns of numerical symbolism and proportion, in which the key numbers are 10 (symbolizing the tetractys or sum of the numbers 1 to 4, which in Pythagorean philosophy constitutes the source of all things), 7 (symbolizing the corporeal nature of the world), 9 (symbolizing the spirituality of heaven), 8 and 15 (symbolizing the number of notes in one and two octaves), and 4 (symbolizing the elements or temperaments, and mirrored by the effects of particular instruments). For a useful summary, see Roger Bray, *Music and Letters*, lxxviii (1997) 319–21. Luckett (261) and Winn (*Unsuspected Eloquence* 227) are sceptical about the more extreme claims made by such critics. It is clear, however, that D. did pay at least some attention in this poem to questions of numerical patterning and organization: stanzas IV–VII, for example, have four, five, six and seven lines respectively, and the poem has eight stanzas in all – the number of tones in the diapason. H. Neville Davies (*JWCI* xxix (1966) 282–5) and Luckett (261–2) question the suggestion of D. T. Mace (*JWCI* xxvii (1964) 251–92) that the present poem and D.'s second Cecilian ode, *Alexander's Feast* (1697), are designed to implement mechanistic theories about the affective powers of poetic rhythm specifically derived from the writings of the humanist Isaac Vossius (1618–89).

(iii) Given the widespread currency in the seventeenth century of the ideas and images of music outlined above, it is often difficult to be sure which of the many poems and passages whose vocabulary and conceptions resemble those of 'A Song for St Cecilia's Day' should be considered direct sources for the poem. Commentators have noted similarities of thought and phrasing in a wide variety of seventeenth-century poems, including Ben Jonson's 'An Ode, or Song, by All the Muses' (esp. ll. 19–24), Milton's 'At a Solemn Music' and 'On the Morning of Christ's Nativity' (esp. ll. 117–32), Marvell's 'Musick's Empire' and ll. 49–66 of *The First Anniversary*, Cowley's digression on music in Book i of *The Davideis* (*Poems* 253–4), Katherine Philips's 'L'Accord du Bien', and Thomas Mace's 'Great God' (*Musick's Monument* (1676) 269). As Earl Miner has pointed out (*Dryden's Poetry* (1967) 278–84; *Works*), D.'s first stanza is indebted to the vocabulary of Epicurean atomism, which had become part of the staple of hexaemeral writing. There are sometimes close similarities between D.'s language and the accounts of chaos and creation by Lucretius, Ovid, Du Bartas and Milton (see ll. 2, 3, 4, 8, 9nn below).

Some of D.'s phrasing shows him to be echoing specific predecessors. The notes below list borrowings from Jonson's 'The Musicall Strife', Milton's 'L'Allegro', 'Comus' and *PL*, Cowley's 'The Resurrection', and John Norris's 'The Consummation', as well as from the previous Cecilian odes by Tate, Fletcher and Flatman. D. had previously treated the Last Judgement (the subject of ll. 59–63) in ll. 178–95 of 'To the Memory of Anne Killigrew', and his treatment of celestial harmony in ll. 1–4 of the 'Song' is recalled in ll. 20–2 of 'An Ode on the Death of Mr Henry Purcell'.

It is not known whether it was during his preparations for the writing of the present poem or at some other date that D. meditated using Spenser's description of Apollo's singing at the wedding of Peleus and Thetis (*FQ* VII vii 12–13) as the 'Groundwork for a Song on St Cecilias Day' and annotated his copy of the 1679 edition of Spenser accordingly (see Osborn 243–4). Although he never made use of the Apollo story itself, the ravishing 'delight' of 'Musicks wondrous might' is central to stanzas II–VI of 'A Song for St Cecilia's Day' and was to be the main subject of *Alexander's Feast*.

Reception. D.'s poem was echoed in several of the later St Cecilia odes, particularly the anonymous ode of 1696 (on which see David Hopkins, *RES* xlv (1994) 486–95). It is unfortunate for the student of D. and Draghi that the one surviving eyewitness account of the first performance makes no mention of either the words or music of 'A Song for St Cecilia's Day'. The MS autobiography of the politician, physician and spiritualist Goodwin Wharton (1653–1704) merely records that on this occasion Wharton 'saw no mortal worth noting, but as he mused about St Cecilia, the Lord promised that she would appear to him' (see J. Kent Clarke, *Goodwin Wharton* (1984) 211–12).

A Song for St Cecilia's Day, 1687

I

From harmony, from heavenly harmony
    This universal frame began:
When Nature underneath a heap
    Of jarring atoms lay,

¶**17.** *1–15.* As Winn demonstrates, 'the complex pattern of rhyming in the first stanza shows how poetry can use mathematical "proportion" to represent the ordering of chaos. For the first six lines, which vary in metrical length, the poem appears to be unrhymed, but with the command that Chaos order itself, each line finds a rhyme, and the rhyming lines turn out to match their partners in length, producing a highly symmetrical facsimile of the "universal Frame"' (*When Beauty* 123–4).
1–2. Set by Draghi as a separate movement for soloists, semi-chorus, full chorus, strings, and continuo, with an instrumental introduction and concluding symphony.   *heavenly harmony*] The uncreated divine music of the angels or heavenly Muses which, according to medieval and Renaissance musical theory, lies beyond and behind *musica mundana* (the music of the spheres, or concord of the elements and seasons), *musica humana* (the harmony which unites the incorporeal activity of reason with the body) and *musica instrumentalis* (the actual instrumental or vocal music which is audible to human beings), and of which the three latter are imperfect reflections (see Levine 39, drawing on Finney x and Hutton 45).
2. This universal frame] The universe, regarded as a structure (*OED* 8). D. echoes *PL* v 153–4: 'These are thy glorious works, parent of good, / Almighty, thine this universal frame' (J. R. Mason).
3–4. Set by Draghi as a recitative for bass soloist, strings, and continuo. In the Chichester and Royal College MSS, the soloist is named as the Rev. John Gostling (*c.* 1650–1733), Gentleman of the Chapel Royal from 1679, a singer renowned for the range and resonance of his voice (particularly in the lower register), for whom Purcell wrote several of his most demanding bass parts.
3. underneath] In Draghi's setting, the bass soloist here descends to C.   *heap*] Used to describe the agglomerations of the atomic particles of Epicurus in Thomas Creech's translation of Lucretius (1683 edition 153) and by D. ('Lucretius: Against the Fear of Death' ll. 117–18; *Works*).
4. jarring] (i) grating, discordant (*OED* 1); (ii) colliding with one another (*OED* 2);

God's?

an echo of the last Judgment?

4 humours?
each in its right place?

5   And could not heave her head,
    The tuneful voice was heard from high,
      'Arise, ye more than dead.'
    Then cold, and hot, and moist, and dry,
    In order to their stations leap,
10   And music's power obey.
    From harmony, from heavenly harmony

word 'harmony' acts as a diapason?

    This universal frame began:
    From harmony to harmony

as God's creation (though he did it take 8 days.)

    Through all the compass of the notes it ran,
15   The diapason closing full in man.

(iii) quarrelling, fighting (*OED* 3). The adjective is used of the elements in chaos in Sylvester's translation of Du Bartas ('The First Day of the First Weeke' l. 252) and of the 'seeds' of chaos in D.'s translation of 'The First Book of Ovid's *Metamorphoses*' l. 13. In Draghi's score, the word is set to a rapid running figure.
5. *heave her head*] lift up, raise up (*OED* 1) her head. A Miltonic expression: cp. 'L'Allegro' l. 145 (Hales; *Works*), 'Comus' l. 884, *PL* i 211 (J. R. Mason).
6. *was heard from high*] Set by Draghi to a rising arpeggio.
7–10. Set by Draghi for boy soprano soloist and continuo (l. 7), then for alto, tenor, and bass soloists (ll. 8–10), followed by an orchestral ritornello.
7. The Creator's command is cast in terms which look forward to the Last Judgement (the subject of ll. 59–63), when 'the trumpet shall sound and the dead shall be raised incorruptible' (1 Corinthians xv 52). As Levine (40, citing Harry Bober) notes, 'it was a Christian commonplace to "unite to the theme of the Beginning eschatological references to the End"'. *Arise*] Set to a rapid ascending figure.
8. The emergence or contention of these four elements is a feature of the creation story in Ovid (*Met.* i 19–20, translated by D. in 'The First Book of Ovid's *Metamorphoses*' ll. 23–4), Sylvester's Du Bartas ('The First Day of the First Weeke' ll. 252–4) and Milton (*PL* ii 898–9). Earl Miner (*Dryden's Poetry* 280) notes that Walter Charleton had attempted a synthesis of Lucretian atomic theory with the doctrine of the four elements in his *Physiologia Epicuro-Gassendo-Charltoniana* (1654): 'Patrons of Atoms do not . . . deny the Existence of those four Elements [which he terms Heat, Cold, Humidity, and Siccity] admitted by most Philosophers: but allow them to be *Elementa Secundaria*, Elements, Elementated, *i.e.* consisting of Atoms, as the First and Highest Principles'. Draghi's setting imitates the sense of D.'s text by having the soloists enter one by one, over a steadily 'walking' bass.
9. stations] appointed positions (*OED* 9, citing this example). *leap*] D. uses the word of the Lucretian atoms in 'Lucretius: Against the Fear of Death' l. 20.
11–15. Set by Draghi for soloists, semi-chorus, full chorus, strings, and continuo, recapitulating material from the setting of ll. 1–2.
13. From harmony to harmony] As Hollander (405–7) notes, 'harmony' here probably signifies 'chord'; D. is thus likening God's creation to a harmonic progression over a thoroughbass (a bass line in which harmonies were indicated for the continuo player by a series of figures).
14. compass] range of tones in the musical scale (*OED* 10).
15. Set by Draghi to a much-repeated descending phrase, treated in imitative

effective power

II

What passion cannot music raise and quell! *ends where it begins?*
When Jubal struck the chorded shell, *from Genesis to Genesis?*
His listening brethren stood around
And wondering, on their faces fell *fit for worship?*
20 To worship that celestial sound. *... of worshipping too?*
Less than a god they thought there could not dwell *idolatry?*
Within the hollow of that shell
That spoke so sweetly and so well. *the rhyme dominates: like the monotonous*
What passion cannot music raise and quell! *ringing of a bell?*
or the diapason again?

---

counterpoint. *diapason*] octave (the most perfect harmony). For the significance
of the term, see headnote, and the diagram depicting man as the culmination of
God's harmonious creation from Robert Fludd's *Utriusque Cosmi Maiori scilicet et
Minori Metaphysica, Physica, atque Technica Historia* (1617), reproduced in Earl Miner,
Dryden's Poetry 282. Scott suggested an echo of Spenser's arithmological account
of the composition of humours and faculties in the human body (*FQ* II ix 22): *Castle of Alma?*
'All which compacted made a goodly diapase'. Thomas Mace, addressing God
(*Musick's Monument* (1676) 269), sees the diapason as a symbol of divine perfec-
tion in man: '*I've almost Run my* Round; *'tis wellnigh past,* / I *Joy to think of* Thee,
(*My* First; *My* Last) / *A* Unison *(at First) I was in* Thee; / *An* Octave *(now at last)
I hope shall be,* / *To* Round Thy Praises *in* Eternity, / *In th*' Unconceiv'd Harmonious
Mystery'. Cp. also Milton, 'At a Solemn Music' l. 23.
16–24. Set by Draghi for alto soloist (in the RCM MS, John Abell, a Gentleman
of the Chapel Royal), and strings.
16. Perhaps echoing Tate's 1685 Cecilia Ode: 'What charms can Music not
impart' (*Works*). *raise*] Set by Draghi to a rising melisma. The phrase descends
again on 'and quell'. *quell*] kill, destroy (*OED* 1).
17–24. Jubal, son of Lamech, was 'the father of all such as handle the harp and
organ' (Genesis iv 21). Du Bartas associates Jubal with the invention of the lute,
adapting material from the Homeric hymn to Hermes, the legendary inventor
of the lute in classical mythology. In Du Bartas' version, Jubal, seeking to imitate
the hammering of Tubal and his associates 'In milder notes and with a sweeter
voice', finds 'An open *Tortoise* lying on the ground, / Within the which there
nothing else remained / Save three drie sinewes on the shell stiffe-strained'. With
this instrument he 'makes woodes harken, and the winds be mute; / The hils to
daunce, the heav'ns to retro-grade, / Lyons be tame, and tempests quickly vade'
('The Handy-Crafts: The IIII Part of the 1 Day of the II Week', tr. Sylvester,
ll. 539–56). *chorded*] stringed (*OED*'s first example).
18. around] Set by Draghi to a florid, circling, running phrase.
19. faces fell] Set by Draghi to a run descending to F.
21–2. In the Homeric story of the invention of the lute, the poet remarks of
Hermes that 'God in him did sing' ('A Hymne to Hermes' tr. George Chapman
l. 111; *Chapman's Homer*, edited by Allardyce Nicoll (1967) ii 548).
23. spoke] resounded, reverberated (*OED* 7a).

see the clause: first use in this role

III

a particular humour, or a
particularly military mode

25   The trumpet's loud clangour
     Excites us to arms,
   With shrill notes of anger
     And mortal alarms.
  The double, double, double beat

30   Of the thundering drum

hadn metre here?

      Cries, 'Hark the foes come;
  Charge, charge, 'tis too late to retreat!'

IV

the melancholic?

   The soft complaining flute
   In dying notes discovers

or he who plays it?

25–47. Fowler and Brooks note (187) that 'stanzas iii–vi describe music conducive to the 4 temperaments, the choleric, melancholic, phlegmatic and sanguine: equivalents in man of the 4 concordant elements that separate from chaos to form the macrocosm'. Levine (44) cites various contemporary sources which show that 'it was a commonplace in musical speculation to compare the various notes, modes or instruments to the warring elements which were divinely harmonized by God in the creation of earthly music . . . Like the atoms . . . the instruments of stanzas ii–vi must be harmonized into a full concert'.

25–32. Set by Draghi in majestic military triple time, for alto and bass soloists, full chorus, trumpets, drums, strings, and continuo.

25–30. The trumpet and drum were traditionally thought to encourage the choleric temperament. D. imitates metrically the musical *promptitude* which theorists like Marin Mersenne thought characterized choleric music (Fowler and Brooks 188).

25. clangour] resonant, ringing sound.

27. shrill notes] The texts accompanying the musical setting of D.'s poem in the three BL MSS read 'Shrills full'; the Chichester MS reads 'shirls full'. Both 'shrill' and its metathetic variant 'shirl' could be used substantively to signify a shrill sound, cry, or whistle (*OED* shrill *sb.*, shirl *sb.*).   anger] Set by Draghi to a rapid running phrase for both soloists.

28. mortal alarms] fears that one is in danger of death.

29–30. Identical wording occurs in l. 4 of the second song from *King Arthur* (*Works*). Draghi sets *thundering* to a rapid semiquaver scale, in which the bass soloist descends to D.

33–6. Set by Draghi for alto solo, two flutes and continuo, over a ground bass in languid triple time.

33. flute] Associated by some musical theorists with the Lydian mode in Greek music, the mode thought by some to be appropriate to the melancholy temperament (Fowler and Brooks 189). However, in *Alexander's Feast* ll. 98–9 the Lydian mode is associated with pleasure and relaxation. The *flute / lute* rhyme is found in the Cecilian odes by Oldham and Tate.

34. dying] (i) amorously pining (of lovers) (*OED* die 7); (ii) fading, melting away (of notes played on the flute) (*OED* 11).   discovers] reveals, discloses (*OED* 3).

35   The woes of hopeless lovers,
      Whose dirge is whispered by the warbling lute.

                              V

          Sharp violins proclaim
          Their jealous pangs and desperation,   *as if their own feelings? a powerful means of communication?*
          Fury, frantic indignation,
40   Depth of pains, and height of passion,
          For the fair, disdainful dame.   *always a love are pains for? we must hear the loss though the needs is the pain?*

                              VI

          But O, what art can teach,
          What human voice can reach   *human voice is singly or monotonous in contrast to the powerful work of the organ?*
          The sacred organ's praise?
45   Notes inspiring holy love,   *inspire further piety through their beauty?*
          Notes that wing their heavenly ways
          To mend the choirs above.   *could suggest the myth?*

                              VII

          Orpheus could lead the savage race,

36. warbling] Used by Sylvester ('The Handy-Crafts' l. 550) when describing Jubal's invention of the lute (*Works*). The texts of two of the musical MSS (Beal DrJ 190 and Chichester) substitute *warbled* for *whispered* and *whispering* for *warbling* in this line. *lute*] Cp. ll. 17–24*n*.

37–47. Set by Draghi for alto and bass soloists and continuo (ll. 37–41; this section includes much brisk passage-work), then for alto, tenor and bass soloists and continuo (ll. 42–3), with a final ritornello for strings.

37–41. Fowler and Brooks (189) note that sharp sounds were frequently associated with the phlegmatic temperament. Bertrand H. Bronson (*Stuart and Georgian Moments*, edited by Earl Miner (1972) 144) notes that violins, for which Charles II had developed a particular liking in France, and whose use he encouraged at the Restoration, would have struck many English listeners as noticeably brighter-toned than the reedier, more muted viols with which they were familiar.

42–7. Fowler and Brooks (189) suggest that the organ, the most inclusive instrument (because of the variety of its stops and tone colours), is to be seen as appropriate to the sanguine temperament, the best-balanced and best-tempered constitution. For St Cecilia's association with the organ, see headnote.

47. mend] improve (i.e. make even more harmonious) (*OED* 10). As *Works* notes, the thought echoes 'To the Memory of Anne Killigrew' l. 38, and anticipates 'An Ode on the Death of Mr Henry Purcell' ll. 22–5.

48–54. Set by Draghi for bass soloist with strings.

48–50. Stanza 2 of Fletcher's Ode (reprinted in Husk 149–51) contains a passage describing Orpheus charming the beasts and trees with his music (Brennecke 7–8). Orpheus was a standard *exemplum* of the power of music (e.g. *The Two Gentlemen of Verona* III ii 77–80; *Henry VIII* III i 3–14; Hales).

48. the savage race] the wild beasts (*OED* savage 1).

And trees unrooted left their place,
50   Sequacious of the lyre:
But bright Cecilia raised the wonder higher;
When to her organ vocal breath was given
An angel heard, and straight appeared,
Mistaking earth for heaven.

GRAND CHORUS

55   As from the power of sacred lays
The spheres began to move,
And sung the great Creator's praise
To all the bless'd above;
So when the last and dreadful hour

50. Sequacious of] ready to follow (*OED* 1, citing this example). Hales notes that Ovid (*Met.* xi 2) wrote of the 'saxa sequentia' and Sidonius (*Carmina* xvi 3) of the 'saxa sequacia' ('following rocks') which responded to Orpheus' singing.

51–4. For Cecilia, the angel and the invention of the organ, see headnote, and cp. *Alexander's Feast* ll. 161–70.

51. bright] Previously used of Cecilia in the odes by Fishbourne, Tate, and Flatman.   *raised the wonder higher*] Set by Draghi to an ascending phrase.

52. vocal] The organ, being powered by wind pumped through the pipes, was thought to be the instrument closest to the human voice (see Marin Mersenne, *Harmonie Universelle: The Books on Instruments*, tr. Roger E. Chapman (1957) 412). In Sylvester's Du Bartas God's universal harmony is imagined as the animation-by-breathing of a huge cosmic organ ('The Columnes: The IIII Part of the II Day of the II Week' ll. 719–30).   *breath*] Set by Draghi to a lengthy running phrase, requiring considerable breath control from the soloist.

54. The identical line occurs (in a similar context) in Ben Jonson's 'The Musicall Strife' l. 24 (W. A. Eddy, *MLN* xlvi (1931) 40).   *earth*] Here the bass soloist in Draghi's setting descends to a C, and then (on the repetition) to a sustained G. On *heaven* the singer rises to a top E♭.

55–63. Set by Draghi for soloists, semi-chorus, full chorus, strings, trumpets, drums, and continuo.

55–8. A reference to the 'music of the spheres', the harmonic consonance of the songs of the angels who, in the Christianized Ptolemaic astronomy, were thought to control each of the heavenly spheres which bore the planets. This harmony was thought to be both the product and the reflection of the primal, uncreated, divine music, and to fill the heavens with a song inaudible to human ears.

59–63. Noyes noted echoes of Cowley, 'The Resurrection' ll. 19–25: 'Till all *gentle Notes* be drown'd / In the *last Trumpets* dreadful sound. / That to the *Spheres* themselves shall *silence* bring, / Untune the *Universal String*. / Then all the wide extended *Sky*, / And all th'*harmonious Worlds* on high, / And *Virgils* sacred *work* shall dy' (*Poems* 182).

59. Cp. also John Norris, 'The Consummation': 'The last and dreadful Scene of Fate' (*A Collection of Miscellanies* (1687) 138; Luckett).

60   This <u>crumbling pageant</u> shall devour,   *destroys itself? whilst the current celebration or the world?*

      The trumpet shall be heard on high,   *as in 3*

      The dead shall live, the living die,

      And <u>music shall untune the sky.</u>   *what a future image! as if untuning the strings? going back to chaos?*

60. *This crumbling pageant*] (i) (in general) the world and the larger universe; (ii) (more specifically) the St Cecilia feast. Luckett (263) comments: 'The Cecilian Feast was itself a "Pageant", and the last stanza of the ode combines the vast image of music destroying both itself and the universe with a scarcely less mistakeable *memento mori* for the "Masters and Lovers of Musick" assembled on the benches and "scaffolds" of Stationers' Hall'. Cowley's image of the 'untuning' of the world (see ll. 59–63*n*) is echoed in John Norris's 'The Consummation' (see l. 59*n*), which also contains (139) the following lines: 'The Father of Mankind's amaz'd to see / The Globe too narrow for his Progeny. / But 'tis the *closing* of the Age, / And all the *Actors* now at once must grace the *Stage*'. Luckett (*Proceedings of the British Academy* lxvii (1981) 292–3) suggests that these lines may have prompted D. to remember Prospero's invocation of 'the great globe itself' (both the world, and Shakespeare's playhouse) which 'shall dissolve' like the 'insubstantial pageant' of the masque performed before Ferdinand and Miranda (*The Tempest* IV i 151–6). *devour*] 'Time devours all things' was proverbial (Tilley T 326; Shakespeare, *Sonnet* xix; Ovid, *Met.* xv 234).

62. *the living die*] Here, in Draghi's setting, the bass soloist descends to E♭, then C, on a repetition of *die*.

63. *untune*] By heralding the Last Judgement, and thus the end of all things, the last trumpet will terminate the music of the spheres, ushering in eternity. The image is used by both Cowley and Norris (see ll. 59–63, 50*nn*).

18 The Tenth Satire of Juvenal

Date and publication. The Satires of Decimus Junius Juvenalis. Translated into English Verse by Mr. Dryden, and Several Other Eminent Hands. Together with the Satires of Aulus Persius Flaccus Made English by Mr. Dryden. With Explanatory Notes at the end of each Satire. To which is Prefix'd a Discourse concerning the Original and Progress of Satire. Dedicated to the Right Honourable Charles Earl of Dorset, &c. By Mr. Dryden was published in folio by Tonson in 1692 (advertised in *The London Gazette* 24–7 October). The title page is dated 1693. A second edition appeared in 1697, but there is no evidence that D. revised the text for this publication. The translation of 'The Tenth Satire' was one of the three Juvenal translations by D. entered by Tonson on the *SR* on 9 February 1691, and therefore, presumably, one of the four which had been completed by February 1692 (see Peter Motteux in the *Gentleman's Journal* for that month). The present text is based on *1693*, with paragraphing introduced at l. 112 and overridden at ll. 116, 190.

Context. The Satires of Juvenal and Persius presents a complete English translation of two of the three extant verse-satirists of ancient Rome. D. translated Juvenal's *Satires* i, iii, vi, x and xvi himself, as well as the whole of Persius (*Satire* ii incorporating a passage by one of his sons). The remaining satires by Juvenal were translated by poets of D.'s circle, including both his sons. The sixteen *Satires* of Juvenal (*fl.* early second century AD) pillory a variety of vices (strategically located in the recent Roman past), using a style which mingles pithy epigram, vivid visual effect, obscenely scurrilous sarcasm, and rhetorical grandeur. Their targets include the hypocrisy of self-appointed moralists, the depravities of life at Rome, the lusts of women, aristocratic pride, legacy-hunting, the depravities of perverted sexuality, and (in *Satire* x) the delusory nature of human wishes. The 'Discourse Concerning the Original and Progress of Satire' prefixed to D.'s translation contains, in addition to a lengthy discussion of the origins, history, and styles appropriate to the genre, a sustained comparison of Juvenal, Persius, and Horace, in which Juvenal is praised for his 'vigorous and masculine wit': 'he gives me as much pleasure as I can bear. He fully satisfies my expectation; he treats his subject home: his spleen is raised, and he raises mine; I have the pleasure of concernment in all he says; he drives his reader along with him, and when he is at the end of his way, I willingly stop with him. If he went another stage, it would be too far; it would make a journey of a progress, and turn delight into fatigue. When he gives over, 'tis a sign the subject is exhausted, and the wit of man can carry it no farther' (*Poems* iii 412).

From his Argument, it is apparent that D. had a particular admiration for the tenth satire. John Harvey (see below, under *Sources*) reports that he had heard that when allotting contributors D. 'was resolved to pitch upon the Translation of the Tenth *Satyr*' for himself (sig. B1ʳ). The translation contains interpolations which relate to D.'s political preoccupations and situation after 1689 (see Winn 457–8 and in *Eighteenth-Century Life* xii (1988) 76–87; Kirk Combe, *MPh* lxxxvii (1989); Rachel Miller, *PQ* lxviii (1989) 53–75; William Myers, *Dryden* (1973) 152–8), but its perspectives on its subject matter are not narrowly Jacobite, and the version manifests important connections with other aspects of D.'s poetic thought in the 1680s and 1690s, particularly the various kinds of philosophical accommodation with the vicissitudes and disappointments of the world articulated and embodied in the translations from Lucretius and Horace in *Sylvae* (1685), in 'To

Mr Henry Higden' (1687), in the Dedicatory Epistles to *Don Sebastian* and *Amphitryon* (both 1690), and later in 'Palamon and Arcite' (1700) (see Paul Hammond, *MLR* lxxx (1985) 769–85; David Hopkins, *Translation and Literature* iv (1995) 31–60).

Sources. While working on his translations of Juvenal, D. made use of the footnotes and *interpretationes* (running paraphrases in Latin prose) in the editions by Cornelius Schrevelius (first published 1648; D. uses material not incorporated until the edition of 1684), Ludovicus Prateus (1684), and Henricus Christianus Henninius (1685). He also drew on the two complete earlier English translations of Juvenal by Barten Holyday (1673) and Sir Robert Stapylton (1647, revised 1660: quotations below from 1647 unless otherwise stated). For a general account of the various seventeenth-century editions of Juvenal and D.'s use of them, see *Works* iv; Alexander Lindsay, 'Dryden and Juvenal' (unpublished PhD thesis, Trinity College, Dublin, 1983). For description and discussion of the various seventeenth-century English translations of Juvenal, see G. L. Broderson, *Phoenix* vii (1953) 57–76; R. Selden, *MLR* lxviii (1973) 481–93; *Works* iv 592–4; Lindsay 53–85, 111–42; William Kupersmith, *Roman Satirists in Seventeenth-Century England* (1985). D. also made use in this poem of the following individual renderings of Juvenal's tenth satire: W[illiam] B[arksted], *That Which Seems Best is Worst. Exprest in a Paraphrastical Transcript of Iuvenals Tenth Satyr* (1617); Sir John Beaumont, 'Juvenal. Sat. 10' in *Bosworth-field* (1629); Henry Vaughan, 'Juvenal's Tenth Satire Translated' in *Poems with the Tenth Satire of Juvenal Englished* (1646); Anon. [Epistle Dedicatory by Edward Wetenhall], *The Wish, being the Tenth Satyr of Juvenal, Paraphrastically rendered in Pindarick Verse* (1675); Henry Higden, *A Modern Essay on the Tenth Satyr of Juvenal* (1686); Thomas Shadwell, *The Tenth Satyr of Juvenal, English and Latin, the English by Tho Shadwell* (1687). D. also made prepublication use of J[ohn] H[arvey], *The Tenth Satyr of Juvenal Done into English Verse*, not published till 22 June 1693 but written ten years earlier and submitted to Tonson around 1687, when its author heard that a translation of Juvenal by several hands was being planned. (For details of this version's publication and authorship, see Harold F. Brooks, *PQ* xlviii (1969) 12–19; for D.'s use of Harvey, see David Hopkins, *N & Q* ccxl (1995) 54–6.) D. also seems to have made occasional use of the French prose translations of J. Tarteron (1689), La Valterie (1680–1), and M. de Marolles (1653) (Lindsay). D. frequently borrows phrasing, diction, rhymes, and end-words from his English sources, the more significant of which are noted below. Of all the versions, he seems to have been most significantly influenced by that of Higden, for which he had written a commendatory poem in 1687. Despite its occasional trivializing tendencies (it is in octosyllabics, and contains several passages the tone of which approaches burlesque), Higden's version seems to have given D. crucial clues on how to find viable English equivalents for the characteristic wit, visual detail, and control of climaxes, without which, in his view, little sense could be conveyed of the larger aesthetic and emotional effects of Juvenal's work (see David Hopkins, *Translation and Literature* iv (1995) 46–52).

The Tenth Satire of Juvenal

Argument of the Tenth Satire

The poet's design in this divine satire is to represent the various wishes and desires of mankind,[1] and to set out the folly of 'em. He runs through all the several heads of riches, honours, eloquence, fame for martial achievements, long life, and beauty;[2] and gives instances in each, how frequently they have proved the ruin[3] of those that owned them. He concludes, therefore, that since we generally choose so ill for ourselves, we should do better to leave it to the gods to make the choice for us. All we can safely ask of heaven lies within a very small compass: 'tis but health of body and mind; and if we have these, 'tis not much matter what we want besides, for we have already enough to make us happy.

The Tenth Satire

Look round the habitable world, how few
Know their own good, or knowing it, pursue.
How void of reason are our hopes and fears!
What in the conduct of our life appears
5   So well designed, so luckily begun,
But, when we have our wish, we wish undone?
   Whole houses, of their whole desires possessed,
Are often ruined at their own request.

¶**18.** *Argument.* [1] *the various . . . mankind*] Thus in Harvey. [2] *riches . . . beauty*] Translating Schrevelius: *divitias, honores, eloquentiam, gloriam bellicam, longam vitam, pulchritudinem.* [3] *proved the ruin*] Cp. Harvey: '*prove the ruin*'.
1. the habitable world] D. generalizes Juvenal's references to Cadiz, the East, and the Ganges.
2. or . . . pursue] D.'s addition.
4. conduct] a term applicable both to the management of one's affairs (*OED* 7, 8a) and to the design and execution of works of art (*OED* 6d, first instance cited 1758, but for D.'s uses see Jensen 33). Cp. *designed* in l. 5.
5–6. Cp. Barksted: 'What in conceit hath ere so well begun, / Which hath not in the end been wisht vndone?' *luckily*] successfully, prosperously (*OED* 1). Cp. Shadwell: '*luckily begun*'.
7. houses] i.e. families. Thus in Holyday.
8. at their own request] i.e. as the result of their own wishes, granted them by the gods.

In wars and peace things hurtful we require,
10 When made obnoxious to our own desire.
        With laurels some have fatally been crowned;
    Some who the depths of eloquence have found
    In that unnavigable stream were drowned.
    The brawny fool who did his vigour boast,
15   In that presuming confidence was lost:
    But more have been by avarice oppressed,
    And heaps of money crowded in the chest:
    Unwieldy sums of wealth, which higher mount
    Than files of marshalled figures can account;
20 To which the stores of Croesus, in the scale,
    Would look like little dolphins, when they sail
    In the vast shadow of the British whale.
        For this, in Nero's arbitrary time,

9–10. Cp. Wetenhall: 'The easie Gods, granting what men require, / . . . / . . . / Ruine whole families at their own desire'. *peace*] For Juvenal's *toga* ('in times of the toga, the garment of peace'). *require*] ask for (*OED* 5a). *obnoxious*] exposed to the ill effects of (*OED* 1).

11. D.'s addition. James Winn (*Eighteenth-Century Life* xii (1988) 78) notes the personal resonance. D. had been deprived of his position as Poet Laureate in 1689, and had been succeeded by Shadwell, who had died on 19 November 1692. *fatally*] Cp. Harvey: 'fatal Dangers'.

13. *drowned*] D.'s development of Juvenal's *torrens dicendi copia* ('a torrential fluency of speech'). Thus in Wetenhall.

14. *The brawny fool*] 'Milo of Crotona, who, for a trial of strength going to rend an oak, perished in the attempt; for his arms were caught in the trunk of it, and he was devoured by wild beasts' (D.'s note). The equivalent note in Higden is similarly phrased. *brawny*] Thus in Wetenhall, Shadwell. In Roscommon's *Essay on Translated Verse* (2nd edition (1685) 6) Milo is referred to as '*Crotona*'s brawny Wrestler' (Lindsay).

15. *presuming*] presumptuous; D.'s addition.

16. *avarice*] D.'s addition. Thus in Harvey. *oppressed*] Cp. Schrevelius: *opprimit* ('oppresses').

18–19. D.'s expansion of Juvenal's *cuncta exuperans patrimonia census* ('a fortune exceeding other men's patrimonies'), perhaps prompted by Higden's mention of the rich men's 'Estate's audit'.

20. *Croesus*] Juvenal does not mention Croesus. Prateus and Henninius suggest that Juvenal's lines may allude to Midas, the legendary king of Phrygia, who was granted his wish that all he touched might turn to gold.

21–2. Cp. Stapylton: 'as our *Dolphins* faile / To match the hugenesse of the *British Whale*'. *the vast shadow of*] D.'s addition. *British whale*] Prateus and Henninius, citing Pliny, claim that whales found in the British ocean were bigger than any in the Mediterranean.

23. *arbitrary*] D.'s addition. The adjective suggested absolutism. Cp. *AA* l. 701*n*.

When virtue was a guilt, and wealth a crime,
25   A troop of cut-throat guards were sent to seize
The rich men's goods, and gut their palaces:
The mob, commissioned by the government,
Are seldom to an empty garret sent.
The fearful passenger who travels late,
30   Charged with the carriage of a paltry plate,
Shakes at the moonshine shadow of a rush,
And sees a red-coat rise from every bush;
The beggar sings ev'n when he sees the place
Beset with thieves, and never mends his pace.
35   Of all the vows, the first and chief request
Of each is to be richer than the rest:
And yet no doubts the poor man's draught control,
He dreads no poison in his homely bowl;
Then fear the deadly drug, when gems divine
40   Enchase the cup and sparkle in the wine.

24. D.'s addition.   *and wealth a crime*] Cp. Wetenhall: '(Under whom to be wealthy
was a crime)' (rhyming with 'time'; similar rhyme in Higden).
25. A troop . . . guards] For Juvenal's *tota cohors* ('a whole cohort'). 'Troops' in
Shadwell; 'Guards' in Higden. For the seventeenth-century associations of *guards*
(the élite troops of the later Stuart monarchy, prominent on state occasions and
in their suppression of public insurrections), see Ogg 253–4; Tim Harris, *London
Crowds in the Reign of Charles II* (1987) 82.
26. D. generalizes Juvenal's proper names.
27. For Juvenal's *miles* ('a soldier'). D.'s interpolation possibly alludes to the
accusations of state-orchestrated violence levelled during the Exclusion Crisis of
1681–3 (see Harris, *London Crowds* 171). He may also be thinking of the riots of
winter 1688–9 in which the London mob, prompted by *The Prince of Orange's Third
Declaration* (28 November 1688; supposedly by William, but actually by the political agitator Hugh Speke), ransacked Catholic houses and chapels on the pretext of
searching for arms (see Luttrell i 485–6, 490; Maccubbin and Hamilton-Phillips 85).
28. empty] D.'s addition.
29. passenger] traveller (*OED* 1a).
30. Charged] entrusted. Cp. Higden: 'with a Charge of Plate'.   *carriage*] transport
(*OED* 1).
32. D.'s addition.   *red-coat*] During the Civil War period the term was most
commonly applied to parliamentary troops (*OED* 1). D.'s allusion may be retro-
spective, or may refer to the government soldiers of his own day.   *from every
bush*] Cp. Higden: 'Each Bush'.
34. mends his pace] walks faster (to avoid being attacked) (*OED* 12e).
37. control] restrain, restrict (*OED* 4b).
39. Then] Emphatic: 'That is the time to fear . . .'.   *divine*] D.'s addition. Thus
in Vaughan.
40. Enchase] are set in the precious metal of (*OED* 2c).   *sparkle*] For Juvenal's
ardebit ('shall glow'). Thus in Holyday, Stapylton, Vaughan, Higden, Shadwell,
Harvey.

Will you not now the pair of sages praise,
Who the same end pursued by several ways?
One pitied, one contemned, the woeful times;
One laughed at follies, one lamented crimes.
45   Laughter is easy; but the wonder lies
What stores of brine supplied the weeper's eyes.
Democritus could feed his spleen, and shake
His sides and shoulders till he felt 'em ache;
Though in his country town no lictors were,
50   Nor rods, nor axe, nor tribune did appear,
Nor all the foppish gravity of show
Which cunning magistrates on crowds bestow.
    What had he done, had he beheld on high
Our Praetor seated in mock majesty,

---

41. pair of sages] The first sage is '*Democritus*, the *Abderite*, the *laughing Philosopher*, who being asked why he did nothing but laugh, answered, he could not chuse, having for his continuall *object man* so full of *ignorance*, all whose designes discovered him to be a child againe, Till at last he killed himselfe with cares; Which never came neare *his* chearfull heart, else he would scarce have lived to be 109. yeares old, as *Laertius* sayes he was'. The second sage is '*Heraclitus* the *Ephesian*, the *weeping Philosopher*' (Stapylton). D. had explicitly identified himself with Democritus in the Epistle Dedicatory to *Amphitryon* (1690), where he remarked: 'The Merry Philosopher, is more to my Humour than the Melancholick; and I find no disposition in my self to Cry, while the mad World is daily supplying me with such Occasions of Laughter' (*Works* xv 224).
42. several] separate, different.
43. contemned] treated with scorn, despised (*OED* 1).
46. Cp. Higden: 'What sowrce could constant Tears supply' (rhyming with 'Eye').
47. feed] For Juvenal's *agitare* ('agitate'). Cp. Higden: 'To feed the sluces of each Eye'.   *spleen*] The spleen was regarded both as the seat of melancholy and moroseness (*OED* 1b) and as the seat of laughter (*OED* 1c) (see Dustin Griffin, *EIC* xl (1990) 124–35). In 'To Mr Henry Higden' (l. 39) D. uses the term to denote the moroseness, gloom or depression (*OED* 7c) which is relieved and purged by the comic laughter provoked by the satirist. Cp. Schrevelius, Henninius: *ex splene risum dicunt gigni* ('they say that the spleen is the source of laughter'). 'Spleen' is also used by Beaumont, Holyday, Wetenhall, Higden.
48. till he felt 'em ache] D.'s addition.
49. lictors] Schrevelius and Henninius explain that the *fasces* (bundles of ceremonial rods, usually with an axe) were carried before Roman magistrates in procession by the lictors (ceremonial attendants) as symbols of their power.
50. tribune] raised platform, rostrum (*OED sb.*[2] 3; first example cited 1762), from which the Roman magistrates passed judgement; a translation of Juvenal's *tribunal*.
51–2. D.'s addition.   *foppish*] foolish (*OED* 1; without any suggestion of dandyish affectation (*OED* 2)).
54. in mock majesty] D.'s addition. The Praetor's conduct is unintentionally parodic of genuine 'majesty'.

55   His chariot rolling o'er the dusty place,
      While with dumb pride and a set formal face,
      He moves in the dull ceremonial track,
      With Jove's embroidered coat upon his back:
      A suit of hangings had not more oppressed
60   His shoulders than that long, laborious vest;
      A heavy gewgaw (called a crown) that spread
      About his temples, drowned his narrow head,
      And would have crushed it with the massy freight,
      But that a sweating slave sustained the weight:
65   A slave in the same chariot seen to ride,
      To mortify the mighty madman's pride.
      Add now th' imperial eagle, raised on high,
      With golden beak, the mark of majesty;
      Trumpets before, and on the left and right
70   A cavalcade of nobles, all in white:
      In their own natures false and flattering tribes,

55. *place*] In Juvenal, the Circus, where the Praetor is presiding at the games.
56. *with . . . face*] D.'s addition.
57. *dull*] D.'s addition.
58. *Jove's embroidered coat*] Thus in Shadwell; 'Jove's Coat . . . rich imbroyer'd' in Holyday. The commentators explain that those who triumphed wore a heavily embroidered tunic or garment which at other times was kept in the temple of Jupiter.
59. *suit of hangings*] wall tapestry, in D.'s time often massively large, densely woven and thus extremely heavy. For Juvenal's *pictae Sarrana . . . aulaea togae* ('a curtain-like toga of Tyrian embroidery'). Cp. Beaumont: 'hangings'.
60. *laborious*] the product of much labour and craftsmanship (*OED* 2b).   *vest*] coat, robe. For Juvenal's *tunica* ('tunic'). Cp. Henninius, Prateus: *veste*.
61. *gewgaw*] gaudy ornament (*OED* 1, citing this example).
62. *drowned*] smothered (*OED* 6).
63. *massy*] weighty, solid (*OED* 1).   *freight*] load, burden (*OED* 2b).
66. *mortify*] counteract, neutralize the effect of (*OED* 2). As the commentators explain, one of the functions of the Praetor's slave was to admonish him with reminders of his own frail humanity.   *the mighty madman's pride*] D.'s addition.
67. *th' imperial eagle*] 'The armes of the Empire, carried upon the top of the *Praetors* Ivory-scepter' (Stapylton). Holyday provides a pictorial illustration, and notes that the eagle 'was of Gold'.
70. *cavalcade*] For Juvenal's *praecedentia longi / Agminis officia* ('a train of attendants walking in front'). Thus in Higden.   *nobles*] For Juvenal's *quirites* ('Roman citizens'). Juvenal refers to the *sportula*, the basket of victuals and money distributed by Roman nobles to their poorer clients and dependants. D. elevates the social status of the attendants and adds l. 71 to introduce a characteristic jibe at servile and corrupt courtiers, particularly those who had supported and profited from William III's accession.
71. *tribes*] (i) the three traditional divisions of the Roman patricians (*OED* 2a); (ii) groups (*OED* 4).

But made his friends by places and by bribes.
   In his own age, Democritus could find
Sufficient cause to laugh at human kind.
75 Learn from so great a wit: a land of bogs,
With ditches fenced, a heaven fat with fogs,
May form a spirit fit to sway the state,
And make the neighbouring monarchs fear their fate.
   He laughs at all the vulgar cares and fears;
80 At their vain triumphs, and their vainer tears:
An equal temper in his mind he found,
When Fortune flattered him, and when she frowned.

72. places] official positions or appointments (*OED* 14). D.'s addition, a term with contemporary resonance: on the notorious 'place-selling' of William III's regime, see *POAS* v 100–12.
74. Sufficient cause] A philosophical term (see *OED* 2c, quotation from Hobbes, 1656).
75–6. a land . . . fenced] D.'s expansion of Juvenal's *vervecum in patria* ('in a land of sheep-heads'), alluding to William III and Holland. Juvenal's reference is to Abdera in Thrace, the birthplace of Democritus, whose 'inhabitants are barbarous and gross-witted Clowns, their brains being like their country, ever in fog' (Stapylton). Since *vervex* means literally a castrated male sheep and figuratively a dull, stupid person, D.'s additions suggest both William III's alleged impotence and his homeland, proverbially regarded by the English as a land of dullards (see Hammond 187).
77–8. fit . . . fate] D.'s addition, alluding to William III's military exploits. Though puny in stature and asthmatic as a child, William had early proved an astute and able military commander, rescuing the United Provinces from conquest by Louis XIV in the Franco-Dutch War (1672–9), and establishing himself as the leader of European resistance to French military aggression. His long-term ambition, finally achieved by the deposition of James II in 1688, had been to bring England into his anti-French front. D.'s allusion may have been partly influenced by Prateus' and Henninius' cross-reference to Horace's suggestion (*Epistles* II i 244) that Alexander the Great showed such crass literary judgement that he might have been born in Boeotia, the proverbial home of the dimwitted (William was frequently likened to Alexander in contemporary panegyric: see headnote to *Alexander's Feast*).
79–80. Cp. Wetenhall: 'He laugh't at all the Vulgar's cares, / Laugh't at their laughter; ay, laught at their very tears'; Shadwell: 'He laugh'd at *Vulgar business*, *Vulgar cares*, / He both their *joy* derided, and their *Tears*'; Harvey: 'He laugh't at Mortal Man's fantastick Cares, / His vain rejoycings and his fruitless Tears'.
vulgar] common, prevalent (*OED* 6d).   *and fears*] D.'s addition. Thus in Beaumont, Holyday, Stapylton, Vaughan.   *triumphs*] For Juvenal's *gaudia* ('joys'). Thus in Vaughan.
81. equal temper] calm equanimity, composure (*OED* temper 3).
82. When Fortune flattered him] Juvenal makes no mention of Fortune's flattery. For D.'s reflections on the vicissitudes of Fortune, and the individual's power to distance himself from Fortune's realm, see 'Horace: *Odes* I ix'; 'Horace: *Odes* III xxix' (especially ll. 83–7 and *n*); Epistle Dedicatory to *Don Sebastian* (*Works* xv 60); Paul Hammond, *MLR* lxxx (1985) 769–85.

'Tis plain from hence that what our vows request
Are hurtful things, or useless at the best.
85   Some ask for envied power, which public hate
Pursues, and hurries headlong to their fate:
Down go the titles, and the statue crowned
Is by base hands in the next river drowned.
The guiltless horses and the chariot wheel
90   The same effects of vulgar fury feel:
The smith prepares his hammer for the stroke,
While the lunged bellows hissing fire provoke.
Sejanus, almost first of Roman names,
The great Sejanus crackles in the flames:
95   Formed in the forge, the pliant brass is laid   ⎫
On anvils; and of head and limbs are made   }
Pans, cans, and piss-pots, a whole kitchen trade. ⎭

83. *our vows*] D. generalizes Juvenal's reference to inscribing vows on wax tablets which were placed on the knees of statues of the gods.

85. *which*] whom (*OED* 9). *public hate*] D.'s addition.

87. *titles*] inscriptions, name-plates (on statues) (*OED* 1a; last example given, 1645). Thus in Beaumont, Shadwell. Holyday explains: 'before the Statues of eminent persons there was placed a *Plate* or Table of Brass, containing all the Honours of him, whose Statue it was'.

87–8. *crowned . . . drowned*] D.'s addition. Stapylton and Vaughan have 'crown(s)' as a rhyme word. Holyday notes that 'the Poet spake before of the drawing of *Sejanus* in *statue* with a halter; but . . . here he speaks of the drawing of *Sejanus* himself *unco*, as he speaks, with a hook', and describes the Roman custom of dragging 'great offenders' to the *Scalae Gemoniae* ('Gemonian steps') on the banks of the Tiber, and then casting them 'headlong into the River'. D. seems to apply this custom to the statue.

90. *vulgar*] of the mob. *fury*] Cp. Stapylton: 'the fury of the *People*'.

91. D.'s addition.

92. *lunged*] D.'s addition. *provoke*] stimulate (*OED* 4).

93. *Sejanus*] Lucius Aelius Sejanus (*d.* AD 31). 'Sejanus was Tiberius' first favourite, and while he continued so had the highest marks of honour bestowed on him: statues and triumphal chariots were everywhere erected to him. But as soon as he fell into disgrace with the emperor, these were all immediately dismounted, and the Senate and common people insulted over him as meanly as they had fawned on him before' (D.'s note).

94. Cp. Shadwell: 'And great *Sejanus* crackled in the flame'.

96. *and limbs*] D.'s addition.

97. *piss-pots*] Thus in Higden. Schrevelius, Henninius and Prateus, and the Latin texts printed at the foot of Higden's page and facing Shadwell's translation, all read *patellae* ('small pans'). Higden's translation, however, anticipates or intuits the nowadays generally accepted reading *matellae* ('chamber pots'): Cp. Shadwell: '*Chamber-pots*'.

     Adorn your doors with laurels, and a bull,
     Milk-white and large, lead to the Capitol.
100   Sejanus with a rope is dragged along,
     The sport and laughter of the giddy throng.
     'Good Lord,' they cry, 'what Ethiop lips he has;
     How foul a snout, and what a hanging face!
     By heaven, I never could endure his sight!
105   But say, how came his monstrous crimes to light?
     What is the charge, and who the evidence—
     The saviour of the nation and the prince?'
     'Nothing of this; but our old Caesar sent
     A noisy letter to his parliament.'
110   'Nay, sirs, if Caesar writ, I ask no more;
     He's guilty, and the question's out of door.'
     How goes the mob (for that's a mighty thing)?

98–9. These lines, as the commentators explain, have been read both as an iron-ical address by the poet to the mob, and as the mob's imagined congratulation of Tiberius for effecting Sejanus' downfall. *Milk-white*] Thus in Stapylton, who comments: 'the colour *Jupiter* most affected in the bulls sacrificed to him, as being the same wherein he disguised himself when he was a *bull* for *Europa's* sake'. *Capitol*] the Capitoline Hill, seat of the temple of Jupiter.

101. giddy] carried away by excitement (*OED* 3a). D.'s addition. Thus in Harvey.
102. Cp. Harvey: 'Crys one, what ugly pouting Lips he has!' (rhyming with 'face'). *Good Lord*] D.'s addition. *Ethiop*] black, negroid (*OED* B 2); D.'s addition.
103. How foul a snout] D.'s addition. *hanging*] (i) gloomy, downcast; (ii) fit to be hanged (a common pun: *OED* 4). D.'s addition. Thus in Shadwell. Cp. Higden: 'hangingly'.
106. evidence] witness, provider of testimony (*OED* 7). Cp. Shadwell: 'who the Evidence'.
107. D.'s addition, with a possible glance at William III, who claimed that he 'came to save [England's] religion and liberties', and who was regularly referred to in loyalist sermons and panegyrics of the late 1680s and early 1690s as the 'deliverer', 'redeemer' and 'restorer' of the English nation from popish tyranny (see David Hopkins, *Translation and Literature* iv (1995) 38, 59). Jacobite satire of the period identified William with Tiberius (see *POAS* v 121). The title 'saviour of the nation' had, however, also been applied to Titus Oates by his supporters during the Exclusion Crisis (Hammond 189).
108. Nothing of this] Literally translating Juvenal's *nil horum*. The commentators and translators interpret Juvenal's second speaker either (i) to be suggesting that Sejanus was not brought down by the normal processes of detection, trial and conviction, or (ii) to be suggesting that nobody asked the questions raised by the first speaker, or (iii) to be dismissing the first speaker's questions as irrelevant.
109. noisy] slanderous, defamatory, rumour-mongering (*OED* noise 2a; the adjec-tive is D.'s coinage (*OED*)). *to his parliament*] D.'s addition. Thus in Higden.
111. out of door] irrelevant (*OED* 5a).
112–13. for . . . king] D.'s addition. *trump*] one of the highest-ranking suit in a card game (*OED* 1a), hence 'dominant, in the ascendant'.

When the king's trump, the mob are for the king;
They follow Fortune, and the common cry
115   Is still against the rogue condemned to die.
But the same very mob, that rascal crowd,
Had cried 'Sejanus' with a shout as loud,
Had his designs, by Fortune's favour blessed,
Succeeded, and the prince's age oppressed.
120   But long, long since, the times have changed their face,
The people grown degenerate and base;
Not suffered now the freedom of their choice
To make their magistrates, and sell their voice.
       Our wise forefathers, great by sea and land,
125   Had once the power and absolute command;
All offices of trust themselves disposed,
Raised whom they pleased, and whom they pleased deposed;
But we who give our native rights away,
And our enslaved posterity betray,
130   Are now reduced to beg an alms, and go
On holidays to see a puppet-show.

---

115. still] always.
116. rascal] composed of low-class rabble (*OED adj.* 1); D.'s addition.
117. with . . . loud] D.'s addition.
118. Fortune's] D.'s substitution for Juvenal's *Nurscia* (modern texts: *Nortia*), the Etruscan goddess of Fortune (Sejanus was from Etruria).
120–1. the . . . base] D.'s addition.
122. suffered] allowed.
123. and sell their voice] For Juvenal's *suffragia . . . vendimus* ('we sell our votes'). Cp. Barksted: 'now the peoples voices are not sold'; Beaumont: 'To sell our voyces'; Stapylton: 'the selling of our voice' (rhyming with 'choice'). *voice*] vote.
124. wise, great . . . land] D.'s additions.
127. D.'s addition, alluding to the belief that 'as far back into the misty Saxon past as men could delve, the rights of the English people had been known, ascertained and respected, kings had been elected . . . and the people's will had been expressed in popular assemblies' (J. P. Kenyon, *Stuart England* (1978) 30). Such sentiments were the particular hallmark of those at the other end of the political spectrum from D., the radical 'True Whigs' and 'Commonwealth men' (see the sources cited by David Hopkins, *Translation and Literature* iv (1995) 40–1, 59).
129. D.'s addition, suggesting the Jacobite conviction that in accepting William III, the English people had violated constitutional legality and willingly subjected themselves to a foreign tyranny (see Tim Harris, *Politics under the Later Stuarts* (1993) 213).
130–1. beg . . . show] D.'s modernizing substitution for Juvenal's *panem et circenses* ('bread and circuses'). Open-air puppet-plays were regularly performed in London, both before and after the Restoration (see Pepys, 9 May 1662; *LS* xliv). For D.'s contempt for puppet-shows, see *2AA* l. 454.

'There was a damned design,' cries one, 'no doubt;
For warrants are already issued out:
I met Brutidius in a mortal fright,
135   He's dipped for certain, and plays least in sight;
I fear the rage of our offended prince,
Who thinks the senate slack in his defence.
Come, let us haste, our loyal zeal to show,
And spurn the wretched corpse of Caesar's foe:
140   But let our slaves be present there, lest they
Accuse their masters, and for gain betray.'
      Such were the whispers of those jealous times,
About Sejanus' punishment and crimes.
      Now tell me truly, wouldst thou change thy fate,
145   To be, like him, first minister of state?
To have thy levees crowded with resort

132. There . . . one] D.'s addition.   *design*] scheme, plot (*OED* 1, 5) (i.e. against Tiberius).
133. D.'s semi-modernizing substitution for Juvenal's *perituros audio multos* ('I hear many are about to perish') and *magna est fornacula* ('there is a large furnace ready'). Cp. Higden: 'Warrants are out to seise / Many and great Accomplices'.
134–7. The equivalent passage in Juvenal, as the commentators explain, is somewhat obscure. D. follows the interpretation according to which Brutidius (a friend of the speaker) is fearful of being associated with Sejanus' conspiracy, and Tiberius (compared by Juvenal with Ajax, enraged at Ulysses' receipt of Achilles' arms) is about to purge the senate for its alleged neglect of his interests. The absence of speech marks in *1693* leaves it uncertain precisely how many speakers are involved. Some commentators attribute Juvenal's equivalent for D.'s ll. 136–41 to Brutidius. Others differentiate the *one* of D.'s l. 132 from the *I* of l. 134, seeing Juvenal's passage as a dialogue. The present text, like those of Noyes and Walker, attributes the whole passage to the speaker mentioned in l. 132.
134. I met Brutidius] Thus in Shadwell.
135. dipped] implicated, involved (*OED* 7a).   *plays least in sight*] operates as far from view as possible (*OED* play 1; Johnson sight 2, citing this example).
138–9. Cp. Beaumont: 'Let us run headlong, trampling *Caesars* foe, / While on the banke he lies, our fury show'.   *our loyal zeal to show*] D.'s addition.
139. spurn] trample, kick (*OED* 5). Thus in Shadwell.
141. for gain betray] D.'s addition.
142. of those jealous times] D.'s addition.   *jealous*] suspicious, fearful (*OED* 5).
143. punishment and crimes] D.'s addition.
144–9. D. reshapes Juvenal's original with one eye on modern conditions.
144. fate] appointed lot (*OED* 3b).
145. first . . . state] The term was frequently used in later seventeenth-century political commentary, without implying any specific constitutional status (Ronald Hutton, privately). Cp. D.'s use in *Don Sebastian* I i 65–6. Cp. Higden: 'Favourite and Prime-Minister'; Harvey: 'One of our chiefest Ministers of State'.
146–7. D.'s addition, expressing characteristic contempt for courtiers. Cp. l. 70*n*.
levees] morning assemblies held by princes or men of power (*OED* 2).   *resort*] assembly, gathering (*OED* 5b).

Of a depending, gaping, servile court;
Dispose all honours of the sword and gown,
Grace with a nod, and ruin with a frown;
150　　To hold thy prince in pupillage and sway,
That monarch whom the mastered world obey,
While he, intent on secret lusts alone,
Lives to himself, abandoning the throne;
Cooped in a narrow isle, observing dreams
155　　With flattering wizards, and erecting schemes?
　　　I well believe thou wouldst be great as he;
For every man's a fool to that degree:
All wish the dire prerogative to kill;
Ev'n they would have the power who want the will:
160　　But wouldst thou have thy wishes understood,
To take the bad together with the good?

148. Dispose all honours] Cp. Higden: 'Stand possest / Of Honours, Power and Interest; / Dispose supream Commands at will'.　*honours of the sword and gown*] i.e. military and legal positions.
149. D.'s addition.
150. in pupillage] as if he were a minor or ward (*OED* 1).
151. D.'s addition.
152. intent . . . alone] D.'s addition. Schrevelius refers to Capri as a seat *arcanae libidinis* ('of secret lust').
153. abandoning the throne] D.'s addition.
154. Cooped in a narrow isle] 'The island of Capreae [Capri], which lies about a league out at sea from the Campanian shore, was the scene of Tiberius' pleasures in the latter part of his reign. There he lived for some years with diviners, sooth-sayers, and worse company, and from thence despatched all his orders to the Senate' (D.'s note). Prateus has a very similar note.　*narrow*] D. adopts the alternative read-ing *angusta rupe* ('the narrow rock'), given by the commentators. Schrevelius', Henninius' and Prateus' texts all read *Augusta* ('Augustan' or 'imperial').
observing dreams] D.'s addition. Cp. Henninius: *somniaque, & prodigia interpretari* ('and to interpret dreams and prodigies').
155. flattering] D.'s addition.　*wizards*] For Juvenal's *grege Chaldeo* ('with a Chaldean herd', i.e. a band of Chaldean astrologers). Thus in Barksted, Higden. *and erecting schemes*] D.'s addition. *Schemes* are astrological diagrams showing the positions of the planets (*OED* 2b). For the phrase, cp. *An Evening's Love* IV i 340. *erecting*] the technical term for devising such diagrams (*OED* 8b).
157. D.'s addition.
158–9. Cp. Beaumont: 'This thou defend'st for those that have no will, / To make men die would have the power to kill'; Shadwell: 'I grant that those may wish the *power* to kill, / Who are too merciful to have the *will*'. Higden has the same rhyme a few lines earlier. The thought and rhyme are echoed in 'The Sixth Satire of Juvenal' ll. 314–15. *prerogative*] The term is used principally of spe-cifically royal powers (*OED* 1).　*want*] lack.
160–1. i.e. would you wish to be exposed to the pains and dangers as well as the pleasures of high office?

Wouldst thou not rather choose a small renown,
To be the mayor of some poor paltry town;
Bigly to look, and barbarously to speak;
165　To pound false weights, and scanty measures break?
Then grant we that Sejanus went astray
In every wish, and knew not how to pray;
For he, who grasped the world's exhausted store,
Yet never had enough, but wished for more,
170　Raised a top-heavy tower, of monstrous height,
Which mouldering, crushed him underneath the weight.
　　What did the mighty Pompey's fall beget,
And ruined him who, greater than the great,
The stubborn pride of Roman nobles broke,
175　And bent their haughty necks beneath his yoke?
What else but his immoderate lust of power,
Prayers made and granted in a luckless hour?

163. mayor] D.'s semi-modernizing substitution for Juvenal's small-town Latin officials (ll. 100–2). Thus in Higden.
164–5. Cp. Holyday: 'And at empty *Ulubrae* freely speak, / Though a course *Aedile*, and false measures break'. For the wording, rhyme and thought, cp. 'The First Satire of Persius' ll. 265–6 (*Works*).
164. D.'s addition. *Bigly to look*] Cp. Higden (earlier): 'Thus haughty Mayor without a Charter / Looks big, as if install'd o' th' Garter'. *Bigly*] boastfully, pompously (*OED* 2).
165. Cp. Higden: 'Condemn light weights, & break false measures'. *pound*] break up, crush (*OED* 1; Johnson 1, citing this example). *measures*] measuring vessels (*OED* 4). In smaller Italian towns the *aedile* (a low-ranking magistrate) had jurisdiction over weights and measures, and the authority to destroy those which did not comply with the correct standards. The mayor sometimes performed the same function in English towns (Chris Cook and John Wroughton, *English Historical Facts, 1603–1688* (1980) 98).
168–9. D.'s reshaping, echoing Nature's rebuke in 'Lucretius: Against the Fear of Death' ll. 138–40, 153–4. Cp. Wetenhall (later): 'When she [Nature] has giv'n him all this store, / And she, though liberal, can give no more'.
170–1. The earlier translators all follow Juvenal in having Sejanus destroyed by falling from, or with, the tower, not being crushed beneath it. In the light of ll. 168–9*n*, it seems likely that D. is partially assimilating Sejanus' fate to that of Tantalus in 'Lucretius: Against the Fear of Death' l. 186. *height, weight*] Listed as a true rhyme by Bysshe. *mouldering*] crumbling (*OED* 1a).
172. the mighty] D.'s addition. *Pompey's fall*] After his defeat by Julius Caesar at the battle of Pharsalia (48 BC), Pompey fled to Egypt where he was 'slain by *Achilles* eunuch to *Ptolomy* perfidiously pretending to receive *Pompey* as a friend' (Stapylton).
173–4. '*Julius Caesar* after he had reduced the State of *Rome*, to his arbitrary power, [was] slain in the Senate by *Brutus*, &c.' (Stapylton). *him*] 'Julius Caesar, who got the better of Pompey that was styled "the Great"' (D.'s note). *greater than the great*] D.'s addition.

For few usurpers to the shades descend
By a dry death, or with a quiet end.
180   The boy who scarce has paid his entrance down
To his proud pedant, or declined a noun
(So small an elf that, when the days are foul,
He and his satchel must be borne to school),
Yet prays and hopes and aims at nothing less,
185   To prove a Tully, or Demosthenes:
But both those orators, so much renowned,
In their own depths of eloquence were drowned:
The hand and head were never lost of those
Who dealt in doggerel, or who punned in prose.
190   'Fortune foretuned the dying notes of Rome,
Till I, thy consul sole, consoled thy doom.'

178–9. Cp. Beaumont: 'Few Tyrants can to *Pluto's* Court descend, / Without
fierce slaughter, and a bloody end'; Holyday: 'few Kings descend / Unslain; few
Tyrants with a dry death End'. *usurpers*] For Juvenal's *reges et . . . tyranni* ('kings
and tyrants'). Applicable to William III (Rachel Miller 61), but '*usurpe*' is also in
Stapylton. *dry*] without bloodshed (*OED* 11f).
180. entrance] entrance fee (*OED* 2d). In Juvenal the schoolboy makes a small contribution to the treasury of Minerva, goddess of arts and wisdom, at her festival
(19–23 March), in the hope that she will give him eloquence. Holyday notes
that on the first day of the festival 'Schoolmasters receiv'd their *Minerval* or Pay'.
181. D.'s addition. *declined*] recited the various cases of, in order (*OED* 20a).
182–3. foul, school] Listed as a true rhyme by Bysshe. *elf*] little thing (*OED* 3b).
when . . . foul] D.'s anglicizing addition. *He and*] In Juvenal only the satchel is
carried.
184. and hopes . . . less] D.'s expansion.
185. 'Demosthenes and Tully both died for their oratory. Demosthenes gave
himself poison to avoid being carried to Antipater, one of Alexander's captains
who had then made himself master of Athens. Tully was murdered by M.
Antony's order, in return for those invectives he had made against him' (D.'s
note). *Tully*] the Roman politician, orator and philosopher Marcus Tullius Cicero
(106–43 BC). After Julius Caesar's assassination in 44 BC, he opposed Mark
Antony in a series of *Philippics* (see l. 196*n*) for which he was proscribed, then
executed. *Demosthenes*] the Athenian orator (385–322 BC) who in his *Philippics*
(see l. 196*n*) strove unsuccessfully to warn the Athenians against the hostile intentions of Philip of Macedon, father of Alexander the Great. After the Macedonian
victory in 322 BC he committed suicide.
188. hand and head] As the commentators explain, Cicero's hand and head were
cut off and nailed to the *rostrum* from which he had delivered his orations.
189. D.'s expansion. *doggerel*] bad or trivial verse (*OED* B). On the connections
between doggerel and punning, cp. 'Prologue to *The Kind Keeper*' ll. 3, 7; on
English writers of doggerel, cp. *2AA* l. 411. *in prose*] Cp. Higden: 'Had happily
his Genius chose / To've writ such inoffensive prose'.
190–1. 'The Latin of this couplet is a famous verse of Tully's, in which he sets
out the happiness of his own consulship – famous for the vanity and the ill

His fate had crept below the lifted swords,
Had all his malice been to murther words.
I rather would be Maevius, thrash for rhymes
195   Like his, the scorn and scandal of the times,
Than that Philippic, fatally divine,
Which is inscribed the second, should be mine.
    Nor he, the wonder of the Grecian throng,
Who drove them with the torrent of his tongue,
200   Who shook the theatres and swayed the state
Of Athens, found a more propitious fate;
Whom, born beneath a boding horoscope,
His sire, the blear-eyed Vulcan of a shop,
From Mars his forge sent to Minerva's schools,
205   To learn th' unlucky art of wheedling fools.

---

poetry of it; for Tully, as he had a good deal of the one, so he had no great share
of the other' (D.'s note). Cicero's line *O fortunatam natam me Consule Romam*
('O fortunate Roman state, born during my consulship') comes, as the commentators note, from his poem celebrating the defeat of Catiline's conspiracy in 63–62
BC. It was derided by Cicero's enemies for its vanity and inept assonance, for
both of which D. finds English equivalents. *Fortuned*, as a transitive verb meaning 'determined the fate of' (*OED* 1), was archaic usage by D.'s day.
192. lifted] D.'s addition.
193. For Juvenal's *si sic / omnia dixisset* ('if all his sayings had been like that'). Cp.
Shadwell's torture of words in *MF* l. 208.
194. Maevius] Juvenal mentions no particular hack poet. D. imports the name of
a poetaster (of whom nothing is known) attacked by Virgil (*Ecl.* iii 90) and Horace
(*Epode* x).   *thrash*] Cp. *MF* l. 52.
196. that Philippic] 'The orations of Tully against M. Antony were styled by him
Philippics, in imitation of Demosthenes, who had given that name before to those
he made against Philip of Macedon' (D.'s note). Holyday explains that the second
Philippic was 'the best Oration, that e're [Cicero] made' and that it 'unhappily
cost him his life'.
200. theatres] Holyday argues that the reference is to those meetings of the
Athenian assembly which were held in the theatre when 'weighty affairs of the
Commonwealth' were being debated. D.'s translation allows (but does not insist
upon) an additional reference to the theatres of his own day (cp. l. 205n).
202. beneath a boding horoscope] For Juvenal's *diis . . . adversis . . . fatoque sinistro* ('with
the gods and an unpropitious fate against him'). For the connections in D.'s mind
between astrology and adverse fortune, see Paul Hammond, *MLR* lxxx (1985)
784–5 and Simon Bentley and Paul Hammond, *Restoration* ix (1985) 56–60:
D. had himself been born under the adverse sign of Saturn.
203–4. 'That *Demosthenes* his Father was a Cutler or one that made Swords, *Juvenal*
here affirms' (Holyday). Vulcan was the god of blacksmiths, Minerva (whom Juvenal
had mentioned earlier: see l. 180n) was the goddess of eloquence.
205. th' . . . fools] D.'s expansion, consonant with his own sense of the thankless
task of trying to please the theatre audiences of his own day (see David Hopkins,
John Dryden (1986) 91–4).

With itch of honour and opinion vain,
All things beyond their native worth we strain;
The spoils of war, brought to Feretrian Jove:
An empty coat of armour hung above
210   The conqueror's chariot, and in triumph borne;
A streamer from a boarded galley torn;
A chap-fall'n beaver loosely hanging by
The cloven helm; an arch of victory,
On whose high convex sits a captive foe,
215   And sighing casts a mournful look below:
Of every nation each illustrious name
Such toys as these have cheated into fame,
Exchanging solid quiet to obtain
The windy satisfaction of the brain.
220   So much the thirst of honour fires the blood;
So many would be great, so few be good:
For who would Virtue for herself regard,

206–7. D.'s addition.   *itch of honour*] Thus (earlier) in Vaughan. *Itch* is a favourite word of D.'s for uncontrollable desires: cp. 'Epilogue at Oxford' (1673) l. 10; 'Prologue to *The Loyal General*' l. 4; *RL* l. 410; 'The Sixth Satire of Juvenal' ll. 525, 762.   *vain*] useless, worthless (*OED* 1).   *native*] natural (*OED* 1).   *worth*] importance (Johnson 3).

208–16. 'This is a mock-account of a Roman triumph' (D.'s note).

208. *brought . . . Jove*] D.'s addition, with no precedent in the commentaries of Holyday, Stapylton, Schrevelius, Henninius or Prateus. Cp. 'Heroic Stanzas' l. 77 and *n.* Jupiter Feretrius was, in fact, only the recipient of *spolia optima* (spoils taken by a Roman general from an enemy commander whom he had killed in battle) and not, as D. here implies, of all battle spoils (Christie).

209–10. *hung . . . chariot*] Juvenal refers to an enemy chariot, part of the spoils.

212. *chap-fall'n*] hanging down like a drooping lower jaw (*OED* 1b, citing this example), perhaps recalling Shakespeare, *Hamlet* V i 212: 'Quite chap-fallen!' (of Yorick's skull).   *beaver*] the lower part of a face-guard on a helmet. Thus in Holyday, Shadwell.

214. *convex*] vault, arch (*OED* B1).

215. D.'s expansion of Juvenal's *tristis* ('sad').

217. *toys*] trifles, things of no importance (*OED* 5). Cp. (in a similar context) 'Lucretius: The Beginning of the Second Book' l. 44.

218–19. Substantially D.'s addition: Juvenal merely says that such triumphs provide a justification for all the commander's toil and peril.

218. *solid quiet*] For *quiet* as a key recurrent desideratum in D., cp. *RL* l. 450, 'Horace: *Odes* III xxix' l. 85, 'Horace: *Epode* II' l. 3, 'To Mr Henry Higden' l. 27, 'Discourse Concerning Satire' (*Poems* iii 407), 'The Second Book of the *Georgics*' l. 700.

219. Perhaps suggested by Vaughan's 'air, and empty fame'.   *windy*] worthless, flimsy (*OED* 5), inflated, conceited (*OED* 7).

220. *fires the blood*] D.'s addition.

Or wed without the portion of reward?
Yet this mad chase of fame, by few pursued,
225   Has drawn destruction on the multitude;
This avarice of praise in times to come,
Those long inscriptions crowded on the tomb,
Should some wild fig-tree take her native bent
And heave below the gaudy monument,
230   Would crack the marble titles, and disperse
The characters of all the lying verse:
For sepulchres themselves must crumbling fall
In time's abyss, the common grave of all.
    Great Hannibal within the balance lay,
235   And tell how many pounds his ashes weigh
Whom Afric was not able to contain,
Whose length runs level with th' Atlantic main,
And wearies fruitful Nilus to convey

223. wed] For Juvenal's *amplectitur* ('embraces'). The Latin commentators do not interpret Juvenal's word as implying courtship, but such a suggestion is found in both Wetenhall and Higden.   *portion*] dowry (*OED* 3).

224. mad chase of fame] D.'s addition. Cp. D.'s recent, related references to 'the madness of the dance' created by the 'ambitious meteors' of the court, and the 'mad World' which provokes his Democritean mirth, in the Dedications to *Don Sebastian* and *Amphitryon* (*Works* xv 60, 224).

228–31. Cp. 'The First Satire of Persius' ll. 57–8 and D.'s *n.*

228. take her native bent] D.'s addition. Cp. Henninius: *Caprifici, cujus ea est natura, ut saxa distrahat, & monumenta dissolvat* ('the wild fig-tree, whose nature is to break rocks asunder, and destroy tombs').

229. gaudy] D.'s addition.

230–1. and . . . verse] D.'s addition, glancing at his own career as a writer of panegyric (Lindsay).   *characters*] lettering in which it is inscribed.

233. D.'s addition. Cp. Milton: 'this wild abyss / The womb of nature and perhaps her grave' (*PL* ii 910–11; Lindsay).

234–72. Hannibal (274–182 BC) was 'that famous Generall of the *Carthaginians*, who not contenting himself to have enlarged their *Empire* to the *Atlantick* sea, which bounds *Africa* on the *North*, and to *Nile* where it terminates on the East, undertook, and almost compleated, the conquest of *Spaine*, and *Italy*' (Stapylton). After crossing the Alps and defeating the Romans at the battle of Cannae (216 BC), Hannibal was driven from Italy by Roman armies commanded by P. Cornelius Scipio, and finally defeated at the battle of Zama (202 BC). He eventually took refuge at the court of Prusias, king of Bithynia, where he swallowed poison to avoid capture by the Romans.

237. level with] alongside (*OED* 3a).   *Atlantic*] For Juvenal's *Mauro . . . oceano* ('the Moorish sea'). Thus in Holyday, Harvey, Wetenhall; *Mari Atlantico* ('the Atlantic sea') in Schrevelius, Henninius, Prateus.

238. The fancy of the personified Nile being exhausted by having to carry his waters such a distance is D.'s addition.

His sun-beat waters by so long a way,
240 Which Ethiopia's double clime divides,
And elephants in other mountains hides.
Spain first he won, the Pyreneans passed,
And steepy Alps, the mounds that nature cast;
And with corroding juices as he went
245 A passage through the living rocks he rent.
Then like a torrent rolling from on high,
He pours his headlong rage on Italy,
In three victorious battles overrun;
Yet still uneasy cries, 'There's nothing done,
250 Till level with the ground their gates are laid,
And Punic flags on Roman towers displayed!'
     Ask what a face belonged to this high fame;
His picture scarcely would deserve a frame:

239. *sun-beat*] For Juvenal's *tepenti* ('warm'). Cp. Beaumont: '*Nilus* heated with the Sunny beames'.
240. *double clime*] D.'s addition. Henninius explains that there was *duplex Aethiopia* ('a double Ethiopia'), one part stretching west to the Atlantic, the other eastward towards Arabia.
241. *in . . . hides*] D.'s addition.
242. *Pyreneans*] Pyrenees.
243. *steepy*] precipitous.   *the . . . cast*] D.'s addition.
244–5. Cp. Holyday: 'when *Hannibal*'s forces were to make a passage through a rock, they cut down huge trees, made a great pile of them, set them on fire, using the advantage of the wind, . . . and that with vinegar pour'd upon the fire they did rot the stones'.   *living*] in their natural position or site (*OED* 2d(c)). D.'s addition.
246–8. Expanding Juvenal's *jam tenet Italiam* ('now he grasps Italy'). Cp. Nathaniel Lee's Hannibal: 'I, who have such dreadful Battles gain'd, / That torrent like which from some mountain falls, / Ran from the Cloudy Alps to Romes proud Walls' (*Sophonisba* V i 4–6). A variant of D.'s 'Prologue at Oxford, 1680' had been printed in the second edition of this play (1681).
248. *three victorious battles*] As Prateus explains, Hannibal defeated the Romans in two battles near the rivers Ticinus and Trebia, and a third at Cannae, before marching on Rome itself.
250–1. *level with the ground, on Roman towers*] D.'s additions, the latter his substitution for *media . . . Subura* ('in the middle of the Suburra'). Cp. Higden: 'Brake down *Romes* Gates, level her Towers'. Modern commentators note that the Suburra was Rome's red-light district, and thus see the allusion as an example of Juvenalian bathos (Stapylton and Higden compare the Suburra to Cheapside). Schrevelius and Henninius describe the Suburra as the *nobilissimus vicus* ('noblest neighbourhood') of Rome. D.'s translation is non-committal on the issue. *Punic*] Carthaginian.
252–5. Juvenal makes the different point that the one-eyed Hannibal was a particularly suitable subject for caricature. D.'s intepretation is unprecedented among the English translators.

A sign-post dauber would disdain to paint
255　The one-eyed hero on his elephant.
Now what's his end, O charming Glory, say:
What rare fifth act to crown this huffing play?
In one deciding battle overcome,
He flies, is banished from his native home;
260　Begs refuge in a foreign court, and there
Attends, his mean petition to prefer;
Repulsed by surly grooms, who wait before
The sleeping tyrant's interdicted door.
　　What wondrous sort of death has heaven designed, ⎫
265　Distinguished from the herd of human kind, ⎬
For so untamed, so turbulent a mind? ⎭
Nor swords at hand, nor hissing darts afar,
Are doomed t' avenge the tedious, bloody war;
But poison, drawn through a ring's hollow plate,
270　Must finish him: a sucking infant's fate.

254. *sign-post dauber*] Also the object of D.'s contempt in the 'Epistle to the Whigs', prefixed to *The Medal*, ll. 15–17; 'To Mr Lee, on his *Alexander*' ll. 51–2.
257. D.'s addition, possibly with an ironical glance at his own heroic plays. *huffing*] swaggering, inflated (*OED* 2); see George Villiers, Duke of Buckingham's parody of Almanzor's 'huff' in *The Conquest of Granada* (*The Rehearsal*, edited by D. E. L. Crane (1976) 49, 94). Higden refers to Hannibal as 'this grum bulk of Huff and Storm' and to the 'Catastrophe of Fate' which destroyed him (for the possible theatrical overtones of 'catastrophe', see *OED sb.* 1).
258. *one deciding battle*] At Zama (see ll. 234–72n). D.'s addition.
259–63. Juvenal's presentation of Hannibal's offhand reception by Prusias (see ll. 234–72n) seems to have no direct parallel in the ancient historical sources. D. slightly heightens Juvenal's emphasis on Hannibal's humiliation: *pace* Rachel Miller (*PQ* lxviii (1989) 61), there would seem to be no simple implied parallel with James II's reception by Louis XIV, which was effected with conspicuous graciousness and generosity.
262. D.'s addition. *grooms*] Used specifically for officials of the royal bedchamber (*OED* groom 4; bedchamber (quotation of 1685)). Perhaps suggested by Higden: 'And there for audience suppliant sit / Till the Kings *Levè* will admit'.
263. *interdicted door*] D.'s addition. *interdicted*] to which entry was prohibited.
264–6. D.'s addition.
266. *Untamed* is used of the Panther in *HP* iii 20, *turbulent* of Achitophel in *AA* l. 153.
267. *at hand, hissing, afar*] D.'s additions. *darts*] spears, arrows (*OED* 1a).
268. *tedious*] D.'s addition.
269. *drawn through, hollow plate*] D.'s additions. Schrevelius refers to the *palea* ('hollow chamber' (literally 'husk, chaff')) of the ring in which the poison was hidden.
270. *a . . . fate*] D.'s addition.

Go, climb the rugged Alps, ambitious fool,
To please the boys, and be a theme at school!
   One world sufficed not Alexander's mind;
Cooped up, he seemed in earth and seas confined,
275   And, struggling, stretched his restless limbs about
The narrow globe to find a passage out;
Yet, entered in the brick-built town, he tried
The tomb, and found the strait dimensions wide.
Death only this mysterious truth unfolds:
280   The mighty soul how small a body holds.
   Old Greece a tale of Athos would make out,

271–2. Cp. Holyday: 'Go Mad-man; Pass the dire *Alpes*; to please fools! / To be a Declamation for the Schools'; Stapylton: 'Go climbe the horrid *Alpes* vain-glorious foole, / To please the *boyes*, and be their theame at schoole'; Shadwell: 'Run o're the rugged *Alps*, thou hot-brain'd Fool! / To be declaim'd on, and please Boys at School'. *theme*] subject of a school composition exercise (*OED* 3). Thus in Stapylton, Beaumont.

273. Alexander's] Alexander the Great (Alexander III of Macedon (356–323 BC)), whose conquests reached as far as India. Higden notes: ''tis said, *Alexander* hearing a Philosopher endeavouring to prove that there were many Worlds, he burst into tears, to his Friends complaining that he had not as yet Conquered One among so many'.

274. Cooped up] For Juvenal's *clausus* ('enclosed'). Thus in Stapylton, Harvey.

275–6. D.'s heightened emphasis on Alexander's physical frustration was perhaps inspired by Higden, who describes how Alexander 'In one poor Globe does sweat and squeeze, / Wedg'd in and crampt in *Little-Ease*'.

277. the brick-built town] 'Babylon, where Alexander died' (D.'s note).

278. and . . . wide] D.'s substitution for Juvenal's *sarcophago contentus erit* ('he will be content with a tomb'). *strait*] cramped, narrow (*OED* 2). *dimensions*] Thus in Higden.

279–80. These lines both commence with quotation marks in *1693*, signalling that they are a sententious utterance.

280. Body is the subject, *soul* the object of the sentence.

281. 'Xerxes is represented in history after a very romantic manner, affecting fame beyond measure, and doing the most extravagant things to compass it. Mount Athos made a prodigious promontory in the Aegean sea. He is said to have cut a channel through it and to have sailed round it. He made a bridge of boats over the Hellespont, where it was three miles broad, and ordered a whipping for the winds and seas, because they had once crossed his designs, as we have a very solemn account of it in Herodotus. But after all these vain boasts, he was shamefully beaten by Themistocles at Salamis, and returned home, leaving most of his fleet behind him' (D.'s note). Xerxes, King of Persia, led an expedition against Greece in 480 BC, and was defeated by the Athenian commander Themistocles at a great sea battle near the island of Salamis. The events mentioned in D.'s note are narrated by Herodotus (vii 21–5, 36–7; viii 97), to whose account the seventeenth-century commentators refer.

Cut from the continent, and sailed about;
Seas hid with navies, chariots passing o'er
The channel on a bridge from shore to shore:
285   Rivers, whose depth no sharp beholder sees,
Drunk at an army's dinner to the lees;
With a long legend of romantic things,
Which in his cups the boozy poet sings.
But how did he return, this haughty brave,
290   Who whipped the winds and made the sea his slave?
(Though Neptune took unkindly to be bound, ⎫
And Eurus never such hard usage found   ⎬
In his Aeolian prisons under ground;)   ⎭
What god so mean, ev'n he who points the way,
295   So merciless a tyrant to obey?
But how returned he, let us ask again: ⎫
In a poor skiff he passed the bloody main, ⎬
Choked with the slaughtered bodies of his train. ⎭
For fame he prayed, but let th' event declare

282. *Cut from the continent*] D.'s addition (see l. 281*n*). Cp. Higden: 'We will believe
wild *Xerxes* rent / Mount *Athos* from the Continent'.
284. *from shore to shore*] D.'s addition. Thus in Shadwell, also rhyming with 'o're'.
285. *whose . . . sees*] For Juvenal's *altos* ('deep').
286. *to the lees*] D.'s addition. The story of Xerxes' troops drinking rivers dry is
told by Herodotus (vii 21).
287. *romantic*] fantastic, extravagant (*OED* 3).
289. *haughty*] D.'s addition. Cp. Prateus: *superbus* ('proud'). *brave*] warrior,
soldier (*OED* 1a).
291. *Neptune*] god of the sea.
292. *Eurus*] the east wind.
293. *Aeolian*] Aeolus was 'king of the winds, who imprisons his unruly subjects'
(Stapylton).
294. *mean*] lowly. *he . . . way*] D.'s addition. 'Mercury, who was a god of the
lowest size, and employed always in errands between heaven and hell. And mortals
used him accordingly; for his statues were anciently placed where roads met,
with directions on the fingers of 'em, pointing out the several ways to travellers'
(D.'s note). D.'s note has no precedent in the commentators. For statues of Mercury,
cp. *The Great Historical, Geographical, Genealogical and Poetical Dictionary*, revised
and corrected by Jeremy Collier, 2nd edition (1701): 'HERMES, were *Mercury*'s
Statues commonly of Marble and sometime of Brass, without Arms and Feet:
The *Grecians* and *Romans* used to set them in the cross Ways and Porches of Houses
and Temples, because *Mercury* did preside over High-ways, and was the God of
Eloquence and Truth'. D.'s reference to the use of such statues as signposts, however, has no obvious source.
297. *skiff*] small, light boat (*OED* 1). Cp. Schrevelius, Prateus: *piscatoria scapha*
('in a fishing skiff').
299. *th' event*] the outcome, result.

300 He had no mighty penn'worth of his prayer.
    'Jove, grant me length of life, and years' good store
Heap on my bending back; I ask no more!'
Both sick and healthful, old and young, conspire
In this one silly, mischievous desire;
305 Mistaken blessing, which old age they call:
'Tis a long, nasty, darksome hospital;
A ropy chain of rheums; a visage rough,
Deformed, unfeatured, and a skin of buff;
A stitch-fall'n cheek that hangs below the jaw;
310 Such wrinkles as a skilful hand would draw
For an old grandam ape, when with a grace
She sits at squat, and scrubs her leathern face.
    In youth, distinctions infinite abound;
No shape or feature just alike are found;
315 The fair, the black, the feeble, and the strong. ⎫
But the same foulness does to age belong, ⎬
The selfsame palsy, both in limbs and tongue; ⎭
The skull and forehead one bald barren plain,
And gums unarmed to mumble meat in vain:

300. For Juvenal's has . . . exegit gloria poenas *('glory exacted this price').* penn'worth] bargain (*OED* 3, Johnson 3, citing this example).

302. Heap . . . back] D.'s addition.

303. conspire] concur, agree (*OED* 4).

304. silly, mischievous] D.'s addition. Cp. Higden: 'mischief'.

306. nasty, darksome hospital] D.'s addition. Cp. Wetenhall (later): 'In age, nothing but Hospitals we find'; Wentworth Dillon: 'Old Men are only walking Hospitals' (*Horace's Art of Poetry, Made English* (1684) 13; Lindsay).

307. ropy] forming glutinous, slimy threads (*OED* 1a). *rheums*] mucus discharges from the nose, catarrh (*OED* 1–2).

308. of buff] of leather (*OED* 2a; Johnson 1, citing this example).

309. stitch-fall'n] resembling a piece of knitting in which stitches have been dropped (*OED* 13). For Juvenal's *pendentes* ('hanging').

310–11. as . . . For] D.'s addition. *grandam ape*] For Juvenal's *mater simia* ('a mother ape'). Thus in Holyday, Wetenhall, Higden. *with a grace*] beautifully, gracefully, elegantly (*OED* 1–2). D. omits Juvenal's epic periphrasis setting the ape's actions among the forests of Thabraca.

312. sits at squat, and] D.'s addition. Holyday and Prateus cite Strabo describing Libyan apes 'some . . . in trees, some sitting'. *scrubs*] scratches, rubs (*OED* 2), rather than 'rubs clean'. *leathern*] Cp. l. 308 and Barksted (earlier): 'His soft white skinne it doth like lether tan'.

316. foulness] hideousness, repulsiveness (*OED* 3).

319. mumble] chew ineffectively (because of the absence of teeth) (*OED* 3). Thus in Shadwell.

320 Besides th' eternal drivel that supplies
   The dropping beard from nostrils, mouth, and eyes.
   His wife and children loathe him, and, what's worse,
   Himself does his offensive carrion curse.
   Flatt'rers forsake him too; for who would kill
325 Himself, to be remembered in a will?
   His taste not only palled to wine and meat,
   But to the relish of a nobler treat:
   The limber nerve, in vain provoked to rise,
   Inglorious from the field of battle flies:
330 Poor feeble dotard! How could he advance
   With his blue headpiece and his broken lance?
   Add that endeavouring still without effect,
   A lust more sordid justly we suspect.
      Those senses lost, behold a new defeat,
335 The soul dislodging from another seat.
   What music or enchanting voice can cheer
   A stupid, old, impenetrable ear?
   No matter in what place or what degree
   Of the full theatre he sits to see,
340 Cornets and trumpets cannot reach his ear;
   Under an actor's nose he's never near.
      His boy must bawl to make him understand

320–1. that . . . beard] D.'s addition. 'Dropping' in Beaumont, Stapylton, Shadwell.
supplies] fills (OED 7b).   *mouth, and eyes*] D.'s addition.
323. carrion] body, carcass (OED 3a), with suggestions of 'corpse', 'putrifying flesh'
(OED 1–2).
324–5. for . . . will?] D.'s addition. The flatterer would, presumably, kill himself
by exposing himself to the old man's foulness.
326. palled] deadened (OED 31).
328–31. The fanciful likening of the old man's sexual capacities to a military defeat
is D.'s addition, developed from Higden: 'Obsequious hand cannot excite /
The baffled Craven to the fight'.   *limber*] limp, flaccid (OED 1c).   *nerve*] penis
(OED 1b, citing this example). Thus in Stapylton, Higden. Cp. 'Lucretius:
Concerning the Nature of Love' l. 22n.   *provoked*] stimulated, excited (OED 4).
dotard] senile old fool (OED A 1a). Cp. Shadwell: 'the weak Old Doting Fool'.
headpiece] helmet (OED 1), here figuratively for the tip of the penis.
332. still] always, continually.
335. D.'s addition.
337. stupid, old, impenetrable] D.'s addition.
338. degree] tier, row (OED 1b).
340. Cornets] D.'s semi-modernizing substitution for Juvenal's *cornicines* ('horn-
blowers'). Thus in Beaumont, Stapylton, Wetenhall, Higden, Shadwell.
341. D.'s addition. Cp. Higden: 'No Actors voice can reach his ear'.

The hour o' th' day, or such a lord's at hand;
The little blood that creeps within his veins
345   Is but just warmed in a hot fever's pains.
In fine, he wears no limb about him sound,
With sores and sicknesses beleaguered round:
Ask me their names, I sooner could relate
How many drudges on salt Hippia wait;
350   What crowds of patients the town doctor kills,
Or how, last fall, he raised the weekly bills;
What provinces by Basilus were spoiled;
What herds of heirs by guardians are beguiled;
How many bouts a day that bitch has tried;
355   How many boys that pedagogue can ride;
What lands and lordships for their owners know
My quondam barber, but 'His Worship' now.
    This dotard of his broken back complains;
One his legs fail, and one his shoulder pains;
360   Another is of both his eyes bereft,
And envies who has one for aiming left;

---

343. such a lord's] D.'s semi-modernizing addition.

349. drudges] those who provide sexual services for her; not in *OED*, but see
l. 495 and cp. 'The Sixth Satire of Juvenal' ll. 46, 306, 496; Rochester, 'Love to
a Woman' l. 7 ('Drudg in fair *Aurelias* womb'). *salt*] in heat (*OED adj.*²; used
of bitches; D.'s addition. *Hippia*] 'Oppia' in modern texts. The seventeenth-
century editors cross-refer to *Satire* vi (see D.'s translation, l. 116).

350–1. For D.'s doctor-hating expansion, cp. 'To John Driden of Chesterton'
ll. 71–2.

350. D. omits Juvenal's proper names here, and in ll. 353–5.

351. fall] autumn. *weekly bills*] official returns of deaths in a particular district
(*OED* bill 10).

352. For Juvenal's *quot Basilus socios . . . circumscripserit* ('how many partners [or
allies] Basilus has swindled'). The commentators identify Basilus variously. D.'s
interpretation is close to Holyday's: 'how many wealthy Provincials *Basilus* an
unjust governor has undone in his province, by turning them out of their estates
to enrich himself'.

355. ride] mount, copulate with (*OED* 3).

356. and lordships] D.'s addition. Cp. Higden: 'each Lordly Seat'.

357. quondam] one-time, former. *'His Worship'*] the official title of a mayor in
the seventeenth century, as now. Cp. l. 163 and *n.* For Juvenal's joke, cp. 'The
First Satire of Juvenal' l. 33 and D.'s *n.*

358–9. broken back, legs] D.'s substitutions. Juvenal mentions shoulder, loins and
hip. 'Back' is in Vaughan. *shoulder pains*] Eds.; Shoulders pain *1693*. Some earlier
editions emend to 'shoulders pains', which is grammatically correct seventeenth-
century usage. But the present emendation is supported by Juvenal's *umero*
('shoulder'; singular).

361. for aiming] D.'s addition.

A fifth with trembling lips expecting stands,
As in his childhood, crammed by others' hands;
One who at sight of supper opened wide ⎫
365 His jaws before, and whetted grinders tried, ⎬
Now only yawns, and waits to be supplied: ⎭
Like a young swallow, when with weary wings
Expected food her fasting mother brings.
His loss of members is a heavy curse,
370 But all his faculties decayed a worse.
His servants' names he has forgotten quite;
Knows not his friend who supped with him last night;
Not ev'n the children he begot and bred—
Or his will knows 'em not; for in their stead,
375 In form of law, a common hackney jade
Sole heir, for secret services, is made:
So lewd, and such a battered brothel-whore,
That she defies all comers at her door.
Well, yet suppose his senses are his own,
380 He lives to be chief mourner for his son:
Before his face his wife and brother burns;
He numbers all his kindred in their urns.
These are the fines he pays for living long,

363. *As in his childhood*] D.'s addition.
365. *and . . . tried*] D.'s addition. *whetted*] sharpened.
367. *with weary wings*] D.'s addition.
368. *fasting*] For Juvenal's *ieiuna* ('hungry'). Thus in Stapylton, Harvey.
369. *members*] limbs.
371–2. Cp. Barksted: 'They which did sup with him but yesternight, / Before next morning are forgotten quite'; Beaumont: 'He cannot his owne servants names recite, / Nor know his friend with whom he supt last night'; Wetenhall: 'Their dearest Friend's forgotten quite, / Although he supp'd with them last night'; Higden: 'Forget their Ancient Servants quite, / And friends with whom they supp'd last night'.
373. *begot and bred*] Thus in Beaumont ('got'), Stapylton ('got'), Vaughan, Shadwell.
375. *In form of law*] according to the rules or prescribed procedures of the law (*OED* form 11b). *hackney*] prostituted (*OED* 7c). *jade*] wench, hussy (*OED* 2).
376. *for secret services*] D.'s addition, perhaps prompted by Schrevelius' suggestion that Phiale (the whore named by Juvenal) had administered *fellatio* to the old man (*Works*). Prateus notes that she had obliged him *nefando obsequio* ('with an abominable indulgence').
377. *So . . . battered*] D.'s addition. 'Lewd' in Higden.
378. *defies*] challenges to (sexual) combat (*OED* 2).
381. *Wife* and *brother* are both the subjects of *burns*: in seventeenth-century grammar plural nouns often take singular verbs.

And dragging tedious age in his own wrong:
385 Griefs always green, a household still in tears,
Sad pomps, a threshold thronged with daily biers,
And liveries of black for length of years.
    Next to the raven's age, the Pylian king
Was longest-lived of any two-legged thing:
390 Blessed to defraud the grave so long, to mount
His numbered years, and on his right hand count
Three hundred seasons, guzzling must of wine.
But hold a while, and hear himself repine
At Fate's unequal laws, and at the clew
395 Which, merciless in length, the midmost sister drew;
When his brave son upon the funeral pyre
He saw extended, and his beard on fire,

384. *in his own wrong*] to his own detriment, harm (*OED* 5b).
385. *still*] always, constantly.
386. *pomps*] funeral processions (*OED* 2).   *a . . . biers*] D.'s addition.
388. *the Pylian king*] 'Nestor, King of Pylos, who was 300 years old, according to Homer's account – at least, as he is understood by his expositors' (D.'s note). Holyday notes that Nestor 'lived, as some say, almost 300. years, and consequently for age was the nearest to the long-liv'd crow, which some report to live 900. years'. Homer (*Iliad* i 250; *Odyssey* iii 245) says that Nestor ruled over three generations of men. Ovid (*Met.* xii 187–8) and others interpreted this as meaning three centuries. Stapylton notes that others 'say that the *Aegyptians* . . . accounted an age to be but 30 yeares, and then *Nestor* was but ninety yeares old' (Stapylton).
389. *of any two-legged thing*] D.'s addition. Cp. *AA* l. 170 and *n*, 'The Cock and the Fox' ll. 459–62.
390. *mount*] count up, represent as amounting to a certain sum (*OED* 13f).
391. 'The ancients counted by their fingers. Their lefts hands served 'em till they came up to an hundred. After that, they used their right to express all greater numbers' (D.'s note). D. summarizes the commentators' accounts of this topic (Holyday has a particularly extensive note, plus a diagram).
392. *must of wine*] new wine before it is fully fermented (*OED* 1).
393. *repine*] complain, feel discontent (*OED* 1).
394–5. 'The Fates were three sisters which had all some peculiar [i.e. particular] business assigned 'em by the poets in relation to the lives of men. The first held the distaff, the second spun the thread, and the third cut it' (D.'s note). The duties of the Fates were variously defined in antiquity. D.'s description follows that of Prateus (in a note on *Sat.* iii 27, to which cross-reference is made in his commentary on *Sat.* x) where the three Fates are named as Clotho, Lachesis and Atropos. *clew*] thread of life, spun by the Fates (*OED* 4).   *the midmost sister*] Lachesis. D.'s addition.
396–7. *his brave son*] Antilochus, slain by Memnon at the siege of Troy (as explained by the commentators). *upon . . . extended*] D.'s addition. Cp. Stapylton: 'upon his funerall pile'. Higden and Harvey refer to 'fun'ral fire'.   *his beard on fire*] By this time Antilochus 'was now grown a man and bearded' (Holyday).

He turned, and weeping, asked his friends what crime
Had cursed his age to this unhappy time.
400   Thus mourned old Peleus for Achilles slain,
And thus Ulysses' father did complain.
     How fortunate an end had Priam made,
Among his ancestors a mighty shade,
While Troy yet stood; when Hector with the race
405   Of royal bastards might his funeral grace;
Amidst the tears of Trojan dames inurned,
And by his loyal daughters truly mourned.
Had heaven so blessed him, he had died before
The fatal fleet to Sparta Paris bore.
410   But mark what age produced: he lived to see
His town in flames, his falling monarchy;
In fine, the feeble sire, reduced by Fate
To change his sceptre for a sword, too late,
His last effort before Jove's altar tries,

---

398. turned, and weeping] D.'s addition. Cp. Barksted's substantial expansion of the passage, in which Nestor 'turnes about' and his 'teares burst out'.

399. unhappy] D.'s addition. Thus in Shadwell.

400. Peleus] 'The Father of *Achilles* was so unhappy to live till old age, to bewail the death of his Son, treacherously slain by Darts by *Paris* and *Deiphobus* in *Apollo's Temple*, when he thought to have Married *Polixena*' (Shadwell).

401. Ulysses' father] For Juvenal's *alius* ('another'). The commentators refer to Laertes' laments over Ulysses' ten-year wanderings and shipwreck. Stapylton and Schrevelius, however, note that Juvenal may have deliberately refrained from naming Laertes because of the doubts expressed in antiquity about Ulysses' parentage.   *complain*] lament (*OED* 3a).

405. bastards] For Juvenal's *fratrum* ('brothers'). According to Homer (*Iliad* xxiv 495–7) Priam was the father of 50 sons, only 19 of whom were the children of his wife, Hecuba. D.'s line might also incorporate a glance at Charles II's notorious begetting of illegitimate progeny (William Myers, *Dryden* (1973) 158).

406. inurned] having had the ashes of his cremated body committed to an urn.

407. loyal] D.'s addition. A probable glance at the disloyalty of Queen Mary in acquiescing in her husband's replacement of her father as King, a subject attracting much comment in anti-Williamite polemic of the late 1680s and early 1690s (see *POAS* v 45, 52, 60, 156–7, 236, 298–302).

409. to Sparta] As the commentators note, Juvenal refers to Paris' abduction of Helen, wife of the Spartan King Menelaus, the cause of the Trojan War.

412. In fine] at last, finally (*OED* 1b).   *reduced by Fate*] D.'s addition.

413. sceptre] For Juvenal's *tiara* ('diadem').

414–17. 'Whilst Troy was sacking by the Greeks, old King Priam is said to have buckled on his armour, to oppose 'em; which he had no sooner done, but he was met by Pyrrhus and slain before the altar of Jupiter in his own palace, as we have the story finely told in Virgil's second *Aeneid*' (D.'s note).

414. effort] Stressed on the second syllable.

415   A soldier half, and half a sacrifice:
      Falls like an ox that waits the coming blow,
      Old and unprofitable to the plough.
        At least he died a man; his queen survived
      To howl, and in a barking body lived.
420   I hasten to our own; nor will relate
      Great Mithridates' and rich Croesus' fate,
      Whom Solon wisely counselled to attend
      The name of happy, till he knew his end.
        That Marius was an exile, that he fled,
425   Was ta'en, in ruined Carthage begged his bread,
      All these were owing to a life too long:
      For whom had Rome beheld so happy, young?
      High in his chariot, and with laurel crowned,

418–19. 'Hecuba, his queen, escaped the swords of the Grecians, and outlived him. It seems she behaved herself so fiercely and uneasily to her husband's murderers while she lived, that the poets thought fit to turn her into a bitch when she died' (D.'s note). Hecuba's transformation into a bitch is narrated by Ovid in *Met.* xiii 565–75, a passage cited by Prateus. *survived, lived*] Listed as a true rhyme by Bysshe.
420. our own] i.e. examples of the miseries of old age from Roman times.
421. Mithridates] 'Mithridates, after he had disputed the empire of the world for forty years together, with the Romans, was at last deprived of life and empire by Pompey the Great' (D.'s note). Mithridates, King of Pontus, was an indefatigable enemy of Rome during the first century BC. Schrevelius, Henninius and Prateus all mention his 40-year war against Rome. *Croesus*] 'Croesus, in the midst of his prosperity making his boast to Solon how happy he was, received this answer from the wise man: that no one could pronounce himself happy till he saw what his end should be. The truth of this Croesus found, when he was put in chains by Cyrus and condemned to die' (D.'s note). Croesus, King of Lydia (*c.* 560–546 BC) was renowned for his vast wealth. He led an expedition against Cyrus, King of Persia, in which he was utterly defeated. The story of his (probably unhistorical) encounter with Solon, the famous Athenian lawgiver and poet, is told by Herodotus (i 29–32).
422–3. Rhyme identical in Beaumont, Holyday, Vaughan. *attend*] wait for (*OED* 13).
424–5. Rhyme identical in Stapylton, Shadwell, Harvey; 'begs his bread' in Beaumont. *Marius*] the celebrated Roman general Gaius Marius (157–86 BC). After being captured by Sulla, he escaped and fled to Africa, where 'he was in danger of his life, and in such distress that at the remaining ruins of *Carthage* he begg'd bread: whereas if he had breathed out his triumphant Soul . . . as soon as he ended his triumph, that is, after his glorious riding with his multitude of captive *Teutons* passing before his chariot to the *Capitol*; in the very instant of his descending from his Triumph; he had been as happy, as ever was *Roman*' (Holyday).
428. with laurel crowned] D.'s addition, alluding to the wreath worn by a triumphing Roman general.

When he had led the Cimbrian captives round
430   The Roman streets; descending from his state,
      In that blessed hour he should have begged his fate;
      Then, then he might have died of all admired,
      And his triumphant soul with shouts expired.
         Campania, Fortune's malice to prevent,
435   To Pompey an indulgent fever sent;
      But public prayers imposed on heaven to give
      Their much-loved leader an unkind reprieve;
      The city's fate and his conspired to save
      The head, reserved for an Egyptian slave.
440   Cethegus, though a traitor to the state,

429. Cimbrian] The commentators refer to Marius' victory over the Cimbri, a
German tribe.
430. state] throne (*OED* 20a).
433. triumphant] For Juvenal's *opimam* ('glorious'). Thus in Holyday. Cp.
Schrevelius, Henninius: *triumphantem*.
434–9. 'Pompey, in the midst of his glory, fell into a dangerous fit of sickness
at Naples. A great many cities then made public supplications for him. He recovered, was beaten at Pharsalia, fled to Ptolemy, King of Egypt, and, instead
of receiving protection at his court, had his head struck off by his order, to please
Caesar' (D.'s note). Gnaeus Pompeius Magnus (106–48 BC) had celebrated
the most spectacular triumph that Rome had ever seen after his defeat of
Mithridates (see l. 421*n*), but was eventually defeated by Julius Caesar at the
battle of Pharsalus in 48 BC. The information in D.'s note is paralleled in the
commentators, who cite as their sources Plutarch's *Lives* and Cicero's *Tusculan
Disputations.*
434. Campania] a region of Italy, south of Latium, which includes Naples, Capua
and Pompeii.   *Fortune's malice to prevent*] D.'s addition. For Fortune, cp. l. 82
and *n.*
435. indulgent] For Juvenal's *optandas* ('desirable') (because, as the commentators
explain, if it had killed him it would have saved him his future miseries).   *fever*]
Eds.; Favour *1693.*
436–7. to . . . reprieve] D.'s addition. 'Repriev'd' in Higden.
438. the city's] The fate of Rome is seen as intimately bound up with that of
Pompey.
439. reserved . . . slave] D.'s substitution, unprecedented in the English translations
and with no obvious source in Schrevelius, Henninius or Prateus, for Juvenal's
servatum ('hitherto preserved'). Cp. Harvey (translation): 'His Head Cut off by an
Egyptian slave'; (note, earlier): '*Pompey* the Great, treacherously murthered by
Ptolomy's Eunuch, Achilles pretending to receive him as a Friend'.
440. Cethegus] 'Cethegus was one that conspired with Catiline, and was put to
death by the Senate' (D.'s note). Catiline's conspiracy against the Roman government (63 BC) was famously thwarted by Cicero, who was consul at the time.
though . . . state] D.'s addition. D. omits Juvenal's reference to Lentulus, another
of the Catilinarian conspirators.

And tortured, 'scaped this ignominious fate;
And Sergius, who a bad cause bravely tried,
All of a piece and undiminished died.
        To Venus the fond mother makes a prayer
445   That all her sons and daughters may be fair.
True, for the boys a mumbling vow she sends;
But for the girls the vaulted temple rends:
They must be finished pieces; 'tis allowed
Diana's beauty made Latona proud,
450   And pleased to see the wondering people pray
To the new-rising sister of the day.
        And yet Lucretia's fate would bar that vow;
And fair Virginia would her fate bestow
On Rutila, and change her faultless make
455   For the foul rumple of her camel back.

---

442. Sergius] i.e. Catiline (Lucius Sergius Catilina). 'Catiline died fighting' (D.'s note, translating Prateus).   *who . . . tried*] D.'s addition. According to Sallust (cited as a source by the commentators), Catiline died bravely (*Bellum Catilinae* lx 5).

443. undiminished] Prateus notes that Pompey was punished *capitis diminutione* ('by a diminution of the head').

444. fond] foolish (*OED* 2), doting (*OED* 5a). Thus in Higden, Harvey.

446. mumbling] soft, subdued (*OED* 2).

447–8. the vaulted . . . pieces] D.'s substitution for Juvenal's *usque ad delicias votorum* ('going to fanciful lengths in her prayers').   *pieces*] works of art (*OED* 17a–c).

449. Latona] 'A mortal Lady, who got with Child by *Jupiter*, brought forth Twins, one a God and the other a Goddess *viz. Apollo* and *Diana*, very handsome, yet esteemed the Goddess of Chastity' (Harvey). For Latona's pride in Diana, cp. Virgil, *Aen.* i 502 ('The First Book of the *Aeneis*' ll. 705–6).

450–1. D.'s addition, with no source in the commentators or earlier translations. *the day*] i.e. Apollo, the sun god.

452. Lucretia] 'The faire *Lucrece* ravish'd by *Sextus*, the son of *Tarquin* the *proud*' (Stapylton). As the commentators note, the story of the rape of the beautiful and virtuous Lucretia by Sextus Tarquinius is told by Livy, Seneca, Plutarch, Valerius Maximus, and Ovid.

453. Virginia] 'Virginia was killed by her own father, to prevent her being exposed to the lust of Appius Claudius, who had ill designs upon her. The story at large is in Livy's third book; and it is a remarkable one, as it gave occasion to the putting down the power of the Decemviri, of whom Appius was one' (D.'s note). Prateus gives the reference in Livy (iii 44). Henninius, Higden and Shadwell mention that Virginia's death occasioned the demise of the Decemviri, patricians appointed to codify and publish the laws of Rome in the fourth century BC.

454. Rutila] 'An ugly crooked Woman, who lived till she was 97 years old: *Pliny, lib.* 7. takes notice of her' (Shadwell; information also in Holyday, Schrevelius, Henninius, Prateus).   *make*] bodily structure (*OED* 1b).

455. rumple] fold, hump.

But for his mother's boy, the beau, what frights
His parents have by day, what anxious nights!
Form joined with virtue is a sight too rare:
Chaste is no epithet to suit with fair.
460 Suppose the same traditionary strain
Of rigid manners in the house remain—
Inveterate truth, an old, plain Sabine's heart;
Suppose that Nature, too, has done her part,
Infused into his soul a sober grace,
465 And blushed a modest blood into his face
(For Nature is a better guardian far
Than saucy pedants or dull tutors are);
Yet still the youth must ne'er arrive at man
(So much almighty bribes and presents can);
470 Ev'n with a parent, where persuasions fail
Money is impudent, and will prevail.
   We never read of such a tyrant king
Who gelt a boy deformed, to hear him sing;
Nor Nero, in his more luxurious rage,
475 E'er made a mistress of an ugly page:
Sporus, his spouse, nor crooked was nor lame, ⎫
With mountain back and belly, from the game   ⎬
Cross-barred, but both his sexes well became. ⎭

456. *the beau*] D.'s addition. Thus in Higden (earlier).
460. *traditionary*] handed down by tradition (*OED* 1).
462. The Sabines were an Italian people famous for their gravity, sobriety and chastity. Cp. 'The Sixth Satire of Juvenal' l. 236.
464. *a sober grace*] For Juvenal's *castum ingenium* ('an innocent heart'). Cp. Higden: 'All Graces that can make a Saint'.
467. *saucy, dull*] D.'s additions. *saucy*] insolent, presumptuous (*OED* 2a).
468. The youth will not reach manhood because he will be made a eunuch.
469. *can*] are capable of.
473. *gelt*] castrated (*OED* 1a). *to . . . sing*] D.'s addition. On the presence of castrato singers in D.'s London, see Pepys 7 April 1667; x 267, 281–2; Curtis A. Price, *Music in the Restoration Theatre* (1979) 112–13.
474. *in . . . rage*] D.'s addition. *luxurious*] lascivious, lecherous (*OED* 1). *rage*] sexual passion (*OED* 6b).
476. *Sporus, his spouse*] D.'s addition. Schrevelius mentions Sporus, the youth castrated and 'married' by Nero in AD 67. Cp. 'The First Satire of Juvenal' l. 95 and D.'s *n*. *nor . . . nor*] neither . . . nor.
477. *mountain back and belly*] For Juvenal's *utero pariter, gibboque tumentem* ('swelling equally in his belly and his hump'). Perhaps recalling Ben Jonson's reference to his 'mountaine belly' in 'My Picture Left in Scotland' l. 17, also echoed in *MF* l. 193.
477–8. *from . . . became*] D.'s addition. *the game*] sexual activity (*OED* 3b). *Cross-barred*] prevented, obstructed (*OED* 2).

           Go, boast your springal, by his beauty cursed
480   To ills, nor think I have declared the worst:
           His form procures him journey-work, a strife
           Betwixt town-madams and the merchant's wife:
           Guess, when he undertakes this public war,
           What furious beasts offended cuckolds are.
485   Adult'rers are with dangers round beset:
           Born under Mars, they cannot 'scape the net,
           And from revengeful husbands oft have tried
           Worse handling than severest laws provide:
           One stabs, one slashes, one, with cruel art,
490   Makes colon suffer for the peccant part.
               But your Endymion, your smooth, smock-faced boy,
           Unrivalled shall a beauteous dame enjoy?
           Not so: one more salacious, rich, and old
           Outbids, and buys her pleasure for her gold:
495   Now he must moil and drudge for one he loathes;
           She keeps him high in equipage and clothes;

479. springal] young man (*OED* 1, citing this example).
480. nor . . . worst] D.'s addition.
481–2. a strife . . . wife] D.'s semi-modernizing addition. *journey-work*] work (in this case, sexual) done for hire (*OED* 1). *strife*] object of competition, rivalry, emulation (*OED* 3). *town-madams*] kept mistresses (*OED* 3c).
486. Born under Mars] To be born under the astrological sign of Mars was to be fated to live a life of violence, danger and tumult. *'scape the net*] As the commentators explain, the allusion is to the net in which Vulcan captured his wife, Venus, and Mars in an adulterous liaison and exposed them to the sight of the gods (Homer, *Odyssey* viii 266–366; Ovid, *Met.* iv 171–89).
487. tried] experienced (*OED* 14).
490. Juvenal refers to 'the *Roman* Revenge, that used to force a *Mullet* up the Fundament of the Offender, with the Head foremost, which having Bristles on the Back, and Finns like a Pearch, was no way to be pulled out' (Higden). Holyday calls this being 'clyster'd with a Mullet' and supplies an illustration of the fish. *peccant*] erring, offending. i.e. the penis.
491. Endymion] 'A Nick name, Ironically given to this Mothers nown [i.e. own] Son, from *Endymion*, beloved by the *Moon*, as the *Poets* feign' (Shadwell). *your smooth, smock-faced boy*] D.'s addition. *smock-faced*] effeminate, with a smooth, pale face (*OED*; this cited as the first instance).
493. one . . . old] For Juvenal's *Servilia*. D.'s details are supplied by the commentators.
495. moil] toil, drudge, with associations of working in wet and mire (*OED* 3) and of burrowing (*OED* 5). D. perhaps recalls the use of the word in the notorious 'china' scene in Wycherley's *The Country Wife* (IV iii 177). *drudge*] For the sexual associations, see l. 349n. Thus in Higden.
496. D.'s addition.

She pawns her jewels and her rich attire,
And thinks the workman worthy of his hire.
In all things else immoral, stingy, mean,
500 But in her lusts a conscionable quean.
   'He may be handsome, yet be chaste,' you say:
Good observator, not so fast away!
Did it not cost the modest youth his life,
Who shunned th' embraces of his father's wife?
505 And was not t' other stripling forced to fly, ⎤
Who coldly did his patron's queen deny, ⎬
And pleaded laws of hospitality? ⎦
The ladies charged 'em home, and turned the tale;
With shame they reddened, and with spite grew pale.

497. For Juvenal's *exuet omnem / corporis ornatum* ('she will sell every ornament of her body'). Prateus specifically mentions Servilia's pearls and jewels.

498. For Juvenal's *quid enim ulla negaverit udis / inguinibus* ('for what will any woman deny to her damp crotch'), playing on Luke x 7 ('for the labourer is worthy of his hire').

500. conscionable] conscientious, scrupulous (*OED* 1).   *quean*] harlot, strumpet (*OED* 1), with a possible homophonic pun on 'queen'. Thus in Higden (later).

501. He] Ed.; She *1693, 1697, Eds.* Since (i) it is unlikely that D. would have misunderstood the masculine case-ending of Juvenal's *casto* ('chaste'; l. 324), which is confirmed by the editorial glosses, and (ii) D. has preserved throughout the remainder of this passage Juvenal's exclusive emphasis on the dangers attending *male* beauty, we emend *1693*'s 'She' on the (palaeographically defensible) hypothesis that it represents a compositor's misreading of 'He' in the manuscript. The lack of any precedent for the emendation may be explained by the fact that l. 501 as printed in *1693* seems at first sight to follow on logically from the previous paragraph.

502. D.'s addition.   *observator*] observer, reporter (*OED* 2).

503. the modest youth] 'Hippolytus, the son of Theseus, was loved by his mother-in-law [i.e. step-mother] Phaedra. But, he not complying with her, she procured his death' (D.'s note).

504. D.'s addition. Barksted, in an extensive expansion of Juvenal, tells how '*Phaedra* his fathers wife, and his step-mother, / Did fall in loue with him aboue all other; / And woo'd him oft, and oft his patience tride, / He oft refus'd, and oft her sute denide'.

505. t' other stripling] 'Bellerophon, the son of King Glaucus, residing sometime at the Court of Proetus, King of the Argives, the queen, Sthenoboea, fell in love with him. But, he refusing her, she turned the accusation upon him, and he narrowly 'scaped Proetus' vengeance' (D.'s note).

506–7. D.'s addition, probably suggested by Barksted's expansion: '*Bellerophon* would faine himselfe excuse, / His friend King *Proetus* he may not abuse'.

508. charged 'em home] incriminated them (*OED* charge 15a, home 5a).   *turned the tale*] changed (i.e. falsified) the events narrated.   *tale*] Thus modernized by Derrick, Scott, Noyes, Walker; 'Tail' in *1693*.

509. grew pale] D.'s addition.

510   'Tis dangerous to deny the longing dame:
         She loses pity who has lost her shame.
              Now Silius wants thy counsel; give advice:
         Wed Caesar's wife, or die? The choice is nice.
         Her comet-eyes she darts on every grace,
515   And takes a fatal liking to his face.
         Adorned with bridal pomp she sits in state;
         The public notaries and auspex wait;
         The genial bed is in the garden dressed,   ⎫
         The portion paid, and every rite expressed   ⎬
520   Which in a Roman marriage is professed.   ⎭
         'Tis no stol'n wedding this; rejecting awe,
         She scorns to marry but in form of law.
         In this moot case, your judgement: to refuse
         Is present death, besides the night you lose;
525   If you consent, 'tis hardly worth your pain:
         A day or two of anxious life you gain,
         Till loud reports through all the town have passed,

513. Caesar's wife] 'Messalina, wife to the emperor Claudius, infamous for her lewdness. She set her eyes upon C. Silius, a fine youth; forced him to quit his own wife and marry her with all the formalities of a wedding, whilst Claudius Caesar was sacrificing at Ostia. Upon his return, he put both Silius and her to death' (D.'s note). Prateus and Henninius both mention Claudius' absence at Ostia. Silius was consul-designate in AD 48, and is described by Tacitus (*Annales* xi 12) as *iuventutis Romanae pulcherrimus* ('the most beautiful of Roman youth').   *nice*] tricky, delicate, dangerous and uncertain, needing tactful handling (*OED* 9a, 11a–b).
514. comet-] D.'s addition, with ominous associations (cp. 'The Sixth Satire of Juvenal' ll. 533–4).
515. fatal] D.'s addition (cp. l. 514 and *n*).
517. public notaries] officials empowered to draw up marriage contracts. Thus in Stapylton, Wetenhall, Harvey. 'Notaries' in Shadwell.   *auspex*] he who is appointed 'to *divine* by the flying of the birds the future felicity' of a marriage (Stapylton).
518. genial] nuptial (*OED* 1).   *dressed*] adorned, decked out (*OED* 7). Cp. Marolles: 'On . . . dresse'; La Valterie: 'dresser' (Lindsay).
519. portion] dowry (*OED* 3).
520. professed] affirmed, declared (*OED* 4b).
521. rejecting awe] D.'s addition. D. is possibly suggesting that she rejects the possibility of intimidating the youth into complying with her wishes (by using her exalted position).
522. scorns to] disdains to, feels it beneath her to (*OED* 4).   *but*] except.   *in form of*] according to the proper procedures of (*OED* 11b).
523. moot] debatable, arguable, doubtful.
524. besides . . . lose] D.'s addition.
526. A day or two] For Juvenal's *mora parvula* ('a short delay'). Cp. Schrevelius: *unius aut alterius diei* ('of one or two days').   *anxious*] D.'s addition.

And reach the prince: for cuckolds hear the last.
Indulge thy pleasure, youth, and take thy swing;
530 For not to take is but the selfsame thing:
Inevitable death before thee lies,
But looks more kindly through a lady's eyes.
     What then remains? Are we deprived of will?
Must we not wish, for fear of wishing ill?
535 Receive my counsel, and securely move;
Entrust thy fortune to the powers above;
Leave them to manage for thee, and to grant
What their unerring wisdom sees thee want:
In goodness as in greatness they excel;
540 Ah, that we loved ourselves but half so well!
We, blindly by our headstrong passions led,
Are hot for action, and desire to wed;
Then wish for heirs; but to the gods alone ⎫
Our future offspring and our wives are known: ⎬
545 Th' audacious strumpet and ungracious son. ⎭
     Yet, not to rob the priests of pious gain,
That altars be not wholly built in vain,

---

528. for . . . last] D. generalizes Juvenal's point, which applies only to Claudius.
529. take thy swing] (i) indulge yourself, have your fling (*OED sb.*² 5); (ii) hang
yourself (*OED* swing *sb.*² 5, 8a). Cp. Higden (earlier): 'Who in all pleasures takes
his swing'.
530–2. D.'s substitution for Juvenal's *quidquid levius meliusve putaris, / praebenda
est gladio pulchra haec et candida cervix* ('whatever you judge to be the easier and
better course, a fine white neck must bow to the sword').
533. What then remains?] A repeated formula in D. to introduce a reasoned
decision, achieved in the face of perplexity. Cp. *RL* l. 427; 'Palamon and Arcite'
iii 1111.   *will*] desires, wishes, expressed as a request (*OED* 3b).
534. for . . . ill?] D.'s addition.
535. and . . . move] D.'s addition.   *move*] exist, live (*OED* 19a).
537. manage for thee] conduct your affairs (*OED* 3d, citing this example).
538. unerring] D.'s addition, echoing his earlier discussions of man's desire for an
infallible spiritual guide. Cp. *RL* l. 277; *HP* i 65.   *want*] lack.
539. D.'s addition.
541. headstrong] D.'s addition. Used of the 'Jews' in *AA* l. 45.
542. Are hot for action] D.'s addition.
545. audacious, ungracious] D.'s additions. Cp. Higden: 'Bratts unnatural, and dam'd
wife'.   *ungracious*] (i) reprobate, wicked (*OED* 1a); (ii) ungraceful, unattractive
(*OED* 5a).
546–7. D.'s substitution for Juvenal's *ut tamen et poscas aliquid voveasque sacellis /
exta et candiduli divina tomacula porci* ('so that you have something to ask for, and
to offer the holy sausages and innards of a little white pig in their shrines').

Forgive the gods the rest, and stand confined
To health of body, and content of mind;
550   A soul that can securely death defy,
And count it nature's privilege to die;
Serene and manly, hardened to sustain
The load of life, and exercised in pain;
Guiltless of hate, and proof against desire,
555   That all things weighs, and nothing can admire;
That dares prefer the toils of Hercules
To dalliance, banquets, and ignoble ease.
        The path to peace is virtue: what I show,
Thyself may freely on thyself bestow:
560   Fortune was never worshipped by the wise,
But, set aloft by fools, usurps the skies.

548. *Forgive . . . rest*] i.e. give up any claim you might have on the gods for any other benefit. D.'s addition. (For the use of *forgive* see *OED* 3a–b.)

549. *content of mind*] For Juvenal's *mens sana* ('a sound mind').

550–7. For the blend of Stoic fortitude and Epicurean insouciance in these lines, cp. Paul Hammond on 'Palamon and Arcite' in *MLR* xl (1985) 783–4.

550–1. Cp. Harvey: 'he that quits this Life, but pays / A due and priviledge which Nature has'. *securely*] D.'s addition. For the thought and tone, cp. 'Horace: *Odes* III xxix' l. 67. *death defy*] For Juvenal's *mortis terrore carentem* ('lacking fear of death'). Cp. 'Horace: *Odes* I ix' l. 19. *nature's privilege*] a special benefit or advantage granted by nature (*OED* privilege 2b).

552. *Serene and manly*] D.'s additions. 'Serene' in Wetenhall.

553. *and exercised in pain*] D.'s expansion.

555. *admire*] be surprised at, astonished (and thus unsettled) by (*OED* 1). D. echoes Horace's celebrated counsel (*Epistles* I vi 1) that *nil admirari* ('to be surprised at nothing') is the one thing that can make human beings happy. Horace's passage is juxtaposed with Juvenal's at the end of Montaigne's 'Apologie de Raimond Sebonde' (*Essais* II xii).

557. D. omits Juvenal's reference to the luxurious Assyrian king, Sardanapalus. *ignoble ease*] From Milton, *PL* ii 227. Cp. Harvey: 'soft inglorious ease'.

558. *The . . . virtue*] Identical in Stapylton.

559. Cp. Stapylton: 'What thou thy selfe maist on thy self bestow' (rhyming with 'show').

561. *set . . . fools*] Cp. Higden: 'ador'd by fools'. *usurps*] D.'s addition, with possible (but not exclusive) contemporary resonance (cp. l. 178 and 178–9n).

19 To My Dear Friend Mr Congreve

Date and publication. 'To my Dear Friend Mr. Congreve, On His COMEDY, call'd The Double-Dealer' was first printed (sigs. a2^r–a3^v) in Tonson's first quarto edition of Congreve's play, advertised in the *London Gazette* of 4–7 December 1693, but dated 1694. In a letter to William Walsh of 12 December 1693 (with which a copy of *The Double-Dealer* was included, fresh from the press), D. wrote that his 'verses' had been 'written before the play was acted' and that he had 'neither alterd them' nor his 'opinion of the play' subsequently (*Letters* 63). *The Double-Dealer* is mentioned as forthcoming in the *Gentleman's Journal* for February 1693, probably went into rehearsal in September, and was probably first performed in early November (see William Congreve, *The Double-Dealer*, edited by J. C. Ross (1981) xxx). It is referred to as a 'new play', along with D.'s poem, in the *Gentleman's Journal* of November 1693 (probably published December). D.'s poem was not reprinted in the poet's lifetime.

Context. The poet and dramatist William Congreve was born in 1670 and brought up in Ireland, where his father held a commission in the army. He received his education at Kilkenny College (a school renowned for its rigorous classical training) and at Trinity College, Dublin. In 1688 or early 1689, the Congreves came to England as refugees from James II's pro-Catholic Irish policies. When his father returned in 1690, William stayed in England, entering the Middle Temple on 21 March 1691 to study law. His main energies, however, were quickly diverted to literary pursuits. His novel *Incognita* and some poetic contributions to Gildon's *Miscellany* appeared in February and June 1692 respectively.

It is reported that when Congreve was preparing his first play, *The Old Batchelour*, for production in autumn 1692, D., probably at the suggestion of his friend the dramatist Thomas Southerne, read the work in manuscript, pronounced that 'he never saw such a first play in his life', but judged that 'the Author not being acquainted with the stage or the town, it would be pity to have it miscarry for want of a little Assistance: the stuff was rich indeed, it wanted only the fashionable cutt of the town'. Consequently, D., together with Arthur Mainwaring and Southerne, 'red it with great care', and D. 'putt it in the order it was playd' (BL Add. MS 4221, fol. 341, reprinted in *William Congreve: The Critical Heritage*, edited by Alexander Lindsay and Howard Erskine-Hill (1989) 59). On its publication in March 1693, *The Old Batchelour* was prefaced by poems in which Southerne and Bevil Higgons hailed Congreve as D.'s natural dramatic successor, a theme which is directly taken up in the present poem. Southerne's poem inverts D.'s *MF* to praise Congreve as D.'s legitimate heir (see Jennifer Brady in Hammond and Hopkins 113–39, and cp. l. 51*n* below).

Congreve had been invited to contribute a version of Juvenal's eleventh satire to D.'s *Satires of Juvenal and Persius* (published November 1692), and supplied the dedicatory poem to D.'s translation of Persius in the same volume (see Appendix B in *Poems* iv). In 1693 he contributed to *EP* versions of three of Horace's odes (two of which had appeared the previous year in Charles Gildon's *Miscellany Poems*) and some episodes from Homer's *Iliad*. In his Dedication to *EP* (*Poems* iv 224, 227), D. singled out Congreve's Homeric translations for special praise, registering the 'entire affection' which he bore Congreve. D.'s close friendship with Congreve at this period is further evidenced in several letters of 1693 (see *Letters* 54, 56, 59, 60, 62). Around this time, Congreve may also have written a first draft of his version of Book iii of *Ovid's Art of Love*. Though not published till 1709, this work was clearly being planned in the early 1690s (see *Letters* 58; Addison, *Letters*, edited by W. Graham (1941) 2; David Hopkins, *RES* n.s. xxxix (1988) 64–74).

The initial reception of Congreve's second play, *The Double-Dealer*, was considerably cooler than that which had been afforded *The Old Batchelour*, and in his letter to Walsh of 12 December 1693 D. suggested some of the reasons why: 'His Double Dealer is much censurd by the greater part of the Town: and is defended onely by the best Judges, who, you know, are commonly the fewest. Yet it gets ground daily, and has already been acted Eight times. The women thinke he has exposd their Bitchery too much; & the Gentlemen, are offended with him; for the discovery of their follyes: & the way of their Intrigues, under the notion of Friendship to their Ladyes Husbands' (*Letters* 63). D. had the satisfaction of seeing his high opinion of the play vindicated. Its reputation was powerfully assisted by a command performance from Queen Mary, probably on 13 January 1694, for which Congreve wrote a special complimentary prologue (see *Congreve: The Critical Heritage* 3, 10).

Congreve continued to enjoy close relations with D. throughout the 1690s. From late 1693 he was lodging with D.'s publisher, Tonson (see J. M. Treadwell, *N & Q* ccxx (1975) 265–9). He contributed a song to *Love Triumphant* (1694), and a prologue to John Dryden Jnr's comedy *The Husband his own Cuckold* (1695), and assisted with the contractual arrangements for D.'s *Virgil* (to which he was one of the two-guinea subscribers) and *Fables* (see *William Congreve: Letters and Documents*, edited by John C. Hodges (1964) 76, 93–7, 99–100, 103–4). D. entrusted him with the task of checking his translation of Virgil against the Latin, and recorded that Congreve had showed him 'many Faults' which he had 'endeavour'd to Correct' ('The Dedication of the *Aeneis*'; *Works* v 337). D.'s hope, expressed in the present poem, that Congreve would be his literary successor was shared by several of the writers of elegies on D.'s death: see *Luctus Britannici* (1700) 12, 35, 38, 42 [=43], 46, ^{2}2, 12, 24. Others treated the idea less reverently: see *A New Session of the Poets, Occasion'd by the Death of Mr Dryden* (1700) 6–7 (where Apollo sneers at Congreve's claim); *Epistle to Sir Richard Blackmore* (1700) 7–8 (where D.'s true heir is said to be Sir Samuel Garth). (See further Hammond 12.) In a letter to Leibniz of 6/16 December 1696, the Scots lawyer Thomas Burnett reported: 'Monsr Congrave done l'esperance baucoup de heritier della lirique de Mr Dreyden dans l'oppinione de lui même qui appelle Mr Congrave son fils ainé dans la poesie' (*Gottfried Wilhelm Leibniz: Sämtliche Schriften und Briefe, Erster Reihe*, edited by G. Utermöhlen and S. Sellschopp (1987) xiii 383; see John Barnard, *RES* n.s. l (1999) 202). After D.'s death, Congreve honoured his friend's memory by supplying a Dedication, containing a handsome encomium of D.'s work and personal character, to a six-volume edition of D.'s *Dramatick Works* (1717). On Congreve's response to D.'s poem, and related general questions of poetic inheritance, succession, and influence, see Jennifer Brady in *Literary Transmission and Authority: Dryden and Other Writers*, edited by Earl Miner and Jennifer Brady (1993) 27–54.

In 'To . . . Mr Congreve' D. returns to a subject which had preoccupied him from the beginning of his writing career: the stature and achievements of modern English dramatists when compared with those of classical antiquity, contemporary Europe, and Jacobean England. In *EDP* (1667) D. (as 'Neander') had championed the flexibility and variety of earlier English drama, praising Shakespeare's 'comprehensive Soul', natural intelligence and vivid evocative powers, Jonson's learning and mastery of dramatic decorum, and the 'gayety' and 'Pathos' of Beaumont and Fletcher. He had also lavished extravagant praise on the English dramatists of his own day, confidently proclaiming their superiority to their classical and continental rivals, and maintaining that their achievements had been surpassed only by a handful of earlier works by their fellow countrymen. In subsequent discussions – most notably the 'Prologue to *The Tempest*' (printed 1670), the 'Defence of the Epilogue' appended to *2 Conquest of Granada* (1672), the *Heads of an Answer to Rymer* (1677), the Preface to *All for Love* (1678), and the Preface to *Troilus and Cressida* (1679) – D. had continued to affirm Shakespeare's incomparable powers of invention and to praise Jonson's judicious learning, while simultaneously conceding that, from the vantage point of a more discriminating and 'refined' age, there was much in the great Jacobeans' work that now seemed obscure, far-fetched, feeble, bombastic, prolix, and carelessly constructed (see further ll. 20–1, 21, 22, 25*nn* below). On the ambivalences and complexities of D.'s presentation of Congreve's relation to his Jacobean predecessors, see further Hammond 9–16.

To My Dear Friend Mr Congreve, On his Comedy called *The Double-Dealer*

Well then, the promised hour is come at last;
The present age of wit obscures the past.
Strong were our sires; and as they fought they writ,
Conquering with force of arms and dint of wit;
5   Theirs was the giant race before the flood,
And thus, when Charles returned, our empire stood.
Like Janus he the stubborn soil manured,

¶**19**. *1. promised*] Partly alluding to God's 'promise' of the future Messiah (Alan Roper, *Dryden's Poetic Kingdoms* (1965) 179).

2. wit] literary talent, genius (*OED* 5). *obscures*] makes less glorious, beautiful or illustrious (Johnson 4).

4. dint] force, violence, bold attack (*OED* 2).

5. Alluding to the giants who were said to have inhabited the earth before Noah's flood (Genesis vi 4). The *flood* here also signifies the Interregnum (cp. 'To His Sacred Majesty' ll. 1–8).

6. our empire] (i) the realm of poetry and drama at the Restoration; (ii) the kingdom of England. Cp. 'Defence of the Epilogue': 'At his return, [Charles II] found a Nation lost as much in Barbarism as in Rebellion: and as the excellency of his Nature forgave the one, so the excellency of his manners reform'd the other' (*Works* xi 216).

7. Janus] a mythical Italian king who was said to have hospitably received Saturn (identified by the Romans with the Greek god Cronos) when the latter had been expelled by Jupiter from Crete (see Macrobius, *Saturnalia* i 9; D.'s note to 'The First Satire of Persius' l. 111). Saturn taught the Italians agriculture and civilization, encouraging them to lay aside their former barbarity and ushering in a new golden age of peace and prosperity (see 'The Eighth Book of the *Aeneis*' ll. 425–32). 'Dryden assigns to [Janus] a part that belongs rather to Saturn himself' (Noyes).

With rules of husbandry the rankness cured;
Tamed us to manners, when the stage was rude,
10   And boist'rous English wit with art indued.
Our age was cultivated thus at length,
But what we gained in skill we lost in strength.
Our builders were with want of genius cursed;
The second temple was not like the first:
15   Till you, the best Vitruvius, come at length,
Our beauties equal, but excel our strength.
Firm Doric pillars found your solid base,
The fair Corinthian crowns the higher space;
Thus all below is strength, and all above is grace.

Janus was also thought of by the Romans as a god of peace and new beginnings
(the first month of the Roman year was named after him) (see Ovid, *Fasti* i 63–290).
stubborn] Cp. *AA* l. 327 (of the English people).
8. rankness] (i) excessive coarseness, strength and vigour (in poetry and drama)
(*OED* rank 2, 5); (ii) coarseness, crudeness (in general culture) (*OED* 14); (iii)
impetuousness, violence (in politics) (*OED* 3).
9. rude] lacking in regularity, elegance, refinement and polish; strong, but rough
and rugged (*OED* 3, 8, 9, 11, 12).
10. indued] invested (*OED* 9).
12. skill] artistic expertise, understanding (combining *OED* 6 and 7).
13. Our builders] (i) the dramatists of the earlier Restoration; (ii) the architects
(real and figurative) of the early Restoration regime. Metaphors of building and
construction were common in early Restoration panegyric (see N. Jose, *Ideas of
the Restoration in English Literature, 1660–71* (1984) 36, 56–7; John Evelyn, *A Panegyric
to Charles the Second* (1661) 8, 15).   *genius*] natural qualifications (Johnson 4).
14. Alluding to the temple of Solomon, the central sanctuary of the Jewish religion which housed the Ark of the Covenant in its 'Holy of Holies' (see *AA*
ll. 801–8; Roper 17–18). The temple was destroyed, and the Ark captured, by
the Babylonians in 686 BC. After the Babylonian exile, the temple was rebuilt at
the instigation of Haggai and Zechariah (see Ezra v–vi), but the new building was
said to be 'as nothing' in comparison with the first (see Haggai ii 3; Ezra iii 12).
As Howard Erskine-Hill notes, the Restoration had been compared to the
rebuilding of the temple in contemporary panegyric (*The Art of Alexander Pope*,
edited by Howard Erskine-Hill and Anne Smith (1979) 146, 155).
15. the best Vitruvius] Vitruvius Pollio was a Roman architect and engineer
working during the second triumvirate and the reign of Augustus. His fame rests
chiefly on *De Architectura*, the sole treatise on architecture extant from the ancient
world, and a prime source of architectural ideas in the Renaissance.   *at length*]
Congreve's dramatic career commenced over 30 years after the Restoration (see
headnote).
16. Our] D. includes himself among those 'excelled' by Congreve.
17–19. D. refers to two of the orders of ancient architecture. In the Doric order
(according to Vitruvius the most ancient, and characterized by him (IV i 6) as
'strong' and 'masculine') each column was surmounted by a capital consisting of
a basin-shaped circular moulding and a plain, square slab. In the Corinthian order

20 In easy dialogue is Fletcher's praise:
      He moved the mind, but had not power to raise.
      Great Jonson did by strength of judgement please,
      Yet, doubling Fletcher's force, he wants his ease.

(the most recent and sophisticated, and characterized by Vitruvius (IV i 8) as imitating the slight figure of a maiden) the columns were taller and more slender, and the capitals were of an inverted bell shape, decorated with graceful rows of acanthus leaves. Erskine-Hill 147–8 notes (i) that it was widely believed in the seventeenth century that Solomon's temple (see l. 14*n*) had employed Corinthian columns, and (ii) that the specific combination of orders mentioned by D. had been commended by the most celebrated Italian Renaissance architectural theorist, Andrea Palladio (1508–80), and had recently been deployed by Sir Christopher Wren in his design for Chelsea Hospital (opened 1692). Wren was known as 'the English Vitruvius' (see G. Beard, *The Work of Christopher Wren* (1982) 16). *crowns*] Erskine-Hill 147–8 notes that the Corinthian order was regularly associated by architectural theorists with royalty.

20–1. John Fletcher (1579–1625) was the author (often in collaboration with Francis Beaumont (1584–1616) and others) of a large body of plays, often in the genres of tragi-comedy and comedy of manners, first performed during the reign of James I and frequently revived after the Restoration. In the 'Defence of the Epilogue' appended to *The Conquest of Granada* (1672), D. had commented on Fletcher's 'quickness and easiness', 'wit', and 'sharpness of conceit' and praised his 'Scenes of Love', while criticizing the 'Luxuriance of his Fancy', 'the redundancy of his matter', and the 'incorrectness of his language', and judging that he had failed to understand 'correct Plotting' or '*the Decorum of the Stage*' and had been deficient in matching his wit to the demands of characterization (*Works* xi 206–7, 217). In *EDP* Neander had judged that Fletcher's comedies manifest one of the 'chiefest graces' of the genre, namely 'Repartee, . . . a chace of wit kept up on both sides, and swiftly manag'd', and that Beaumont and Fletcher 'understood and imitated the conversation of Gentlemen much better [than Shakespeare]; whose wild debaucheries, and quickness of wit in reparties, no Poet before them could paint as they have done' (*Works* xvii 48, 56). *moved the mind*] In 'The Grounds of Criticism in Tragedy', prefixed to *Troilus and Cressida* (1679), D. recorded how he found Fletcher's *A King and No King* 'moving when it is read', and attributed this effect to 'the lively touches of the passions' or to the fact 'that even in imperfect Plots, there are less degrees of Nature, by which some faint emotions of pity and terror are rais'd in us' (*Works* xiii 233). *raise*] elevate (mentally or morally) (*OED* 19). In the 'Defence of the Epilogue', D. argued that, while we should 'applaud his Scenes of Love', we should concede that Fletcher 'understood not either greatness or perfect honour in the parts of any of his women' (*Works* xi 217).

22. strength of judgement] In the 'Defence of the Epilogue', D., comparing Fletcher with Jonson, noted that Fletcher 'wanted so much judgement as seldome to have written humour; or describ'd a pleasant folly'. To Jonson he ascribed 'the height and accuracy of Judgment in the ordering of his Plots, his choice of characters, and maintaining what he had chosen, to the end' (*Works* xi 217). In *EDP* Neander had argued that Jonson 'was a most severe Judge of himself as well as others' and that he 'manag'd his strength to more advantage then any who preceded him' (*Works* xvii 57).

23. wants] lacks.

In differing talents both adorned their age,
25   One for the study, t'other for the stage.
But both to Congreve justly shall submit,
One matched in judgement, both o'er-matched in wit.
In him all beauties of this age we see: ⎫
Etherege his courtship, Southerne's purity,   ⎬
30   The satire, wit, and strength of manly Wycherley. ⎭
All this in blooming youth you have achieved,
Nor are your foiled contemporaries grieved;
So much the sweetness of your manners move,

---

25. *One for the study*] By publishing his plays with theoretical prefaces, and collecting them with his poems in the imposing folio edition of 1616, Jonson had signalled that he wished his work to be read and pondered, as well as experienced in theatrical performance.

27. *One*] Jonson.   *o'er-matched*] surpassed, excelled (*OED* 1).

29. *Etherege his*] Etherege's. Sir George Etherege (?1634–91), author of the fashionable comedies *Love in a Tub* (1664), *She Wou'd if She Cou'd* (1668) and *The Man of Mode* (1676) (for the last of which D. had supplied a complimentary Epilogue). He was also a courtier and diplomat, having served as secretary to the English ambassador in Turkey (1668–71) and as James II's envoy in Ratisbon (1685–9). He was the addressee of D.'s 'To Sir George Etherege', written 1686, published 1691: see *Poems* iii 19–27. Performances of Etherege's plays at court, and at the Theatre Royal before Charles II, were frequent. Etherege was described by one contemporary as 'a man of mighty courtesy and delicate address'. Others, less charitably, identified him with Dorimant, the 'genteel rake of wit' in his own *The Man of Mode* (see Etherege i xix, xxi, xxv).   *Southerne's purity*] Thomas Southerne (1659–1746) was the author of *The Loyal Brother* (1682) (a Tory play for which D. had written a partisan Prologue and Epilogue), *The Disappointment* (1684) (for which D. had also written a Prologue), *Sir Anthony Love* (performed 1690; published 1691), and *The Wives Excuse* (performed 1690; published 1692). Southerne had also written a prefatory poem to Congreve's *Old Batchelour* (see headnote). In 'To Mr Southerne' (prefixed to *The Wives Excuse*), D. had compared Southerne (ll. 16–17) to Terence, commending Southerne's 'true' thoughts, 'clean' language, and capacity to make even 'lewdness' 'moral'. In his notice of *The Wives Excuse* in the *Gentleman's Journal* (January 1692), Peter Motteux noted that 'some that must be granted to be good Judges commend the Purity of its Language'.

30. *manly Wycherley*] D. puns on the name of Manly, the hero of *The Plain Dealer* (performed 1676; published 1677), the last comedy of William Wycherley (1641–1716). In 'The Author's Apology for Heroique Poetry; and Poetique Licence', prefixed to *The State of Innocence* (1677), D. had spoken proudly of his friendship with Wycherley, and had referred to *The Plain Dealer* as 'one of the most bold, most general, and most useful Satyres which has ever been presented on the *English* Theater' (*Works* xii 89).

32. *Nor*] Now *1694*. The misprint was repeated when the poem was reprinted in D.'s *Poems on Various Occasions* (1701), but corrected in Congreve's *Works* (1710) and in subsequent editions.   *foiled*] outdone, surpassed (*OED* 4b; first instance cited, 1687).

We cannot envy you, because we love.
35 Fabius might joy in Scipio, when he saw
A beardless consul made against the law,
And join his suffrage to the votes of Rome,
Though he with Hannibal was overcome.
Thus old Romano bowed to Raphael's fame,
40 And scholar to the youth he taught, became.
    O that your brows my laurel had sustained!
Well had I been deposed, if you had reigned;

---

34. we love] In a letter to Tonson of 30 August 1693, D. declared himself Congreve's
'true lover' (*Letters* 59). Cp. also *Letters* 60; 'Dedication to *EP*' (*Poems* iv 224).
35–8. D. alludes to events in the Second Punic War between Rome and
Carthage (218–201 BC). After the Roman defeat at Cannae in 216, the Roman
commander Fabius Maximus pursued a policy of harassing, rather than confronting,
the armies of the Carthaginian commander Hannibal in Italy. Fabius opposed the
plans of Publius Scipio Africanus Major to mount a direct assault on Africa. Scipio's
plans, however, were put into effect, and Hannibal was finally defeated in 202,
a year afer Scipio's death. Roper 176–8 notes several points of imprecision in
the analogy: (i) Scipio was not 'beardless', but a man of 31 when elected consul; (ii) Scipio was not elected consul 'against the law'; (iii) Fabius is not recorded
as specifically objecting to Scipio's being under age for the consulship; and
(iv) there was no popular vote about the invasion of Africa. Roper suggests that
(i) and (ii) can be explained by D.'s having confused Scipio Africanus Major with
his grandson, Scipio Aemilianus Africanus Numantinus (185/4–129 BC). This Scipio
was elected consul in 147 BC, despite being under age and not having held the
necessary qualifying offices (see 'The Character of Polybius'; *Works* xx 31–2, 335).
Roper also suggests, with regard to (iii) and (iv), that D. was remembering a passage in Livy (xviii 40) where Scipio is reported to have said (i) that he was made
consul to finish the war, (ii) that this could only be accomplished by invading
Africa, and (iii) that he would seek a vote to sanction the invasion if the Senate
disapproved of it. The general sense of D.'s allusion is that, had Scipio been as
attractive a figure as Congreve, even the envious Fabius Maximus would have
supported his election to the consulship, and the subsequent invasion of Africa.
with Hannibal] Roper 176 assumes that this means 'by Hannibal', and objects that,
though Fabius Maximus' delaying tactics had not succeeded in driving Hannibal
out of Italy, he had not actually been *overcome* by the Carthaginian commander.
But the phrase more probably means 'along with Hannibal', referring to Scipio's
defeat of both Fabius Maximus (in that Scipio's policy prevailed) and Hannibal
(a military defeat).
39–40. In fact, the architect and painter Giulio Romano (1499–1546) was sixteen years younger than Raphael (1483–1520), and was Raphael's chief pupil and
assistant. D. Nichol Smith (*John Dryden: Poetry and Prose* (1925) 195) suggests that
D. confused Giulio Romano with Pietro Vannucci Perugino (*c.* 1445/50–1523),
in whose studio Raphael may have worked, and who later collaborated with Raphael
on the decoration of the audience chamber of the Collegio del Cambio at Perugia.
42. deposed] After the accession of William III, D. refused to comply with the
terms offered him by the new government, whereby he could have continued
as Poet Laureate and Historiographer Royal (see Fredson Bowers, *TLS* 10 April

The father had descended for the son;
For only you are lineal to the throne.
45 Thus when the state one Edward did depose,
A greater Edward in his room arose.
But now not I, but poetry is cursed,
For Tom the Second reigns like Tom the First.

1957 244; Winn 434), and was consequently removed from both positions. On 9 March 1689 a warrant was issued for the apppointment to both posts of D.'s old antagonist Thomas Shadwell. In the lines that follow, D. develops a series of running analogies between the ideas of literary and royal succession.

43. Possibly including an allusion to the attempts, early in 1693, by the 'Compounders' (those Jacobites who wished for a restoration, but on the condition that the civil and ecclesiastical constitution of England was guaranteed) to persuade James to resign the crown in favour of the Prince of Wales, and to allow the Prince to be educated as a Protestant (see Lord Macaulay, *History of England*, edited by C. H. Firth (1913–15) v 238–42).

45–6. King Edward II (1284–1327; reigned 1307–27) was disliked for his misgovernment and for his unworthy favourites. He was eventually deposed by a rebellion of his lords and queen, and subsequently murdered. His son succeeded him as Edward III in 1327, and went on to defeat the French at the battle of Crécy (6 August 1346). As Roper 170–1 notes, the precedent of Edward II's deposition was frequently cited in parliamentary debates and pamphlets of 1689 and afterwards (see also J. P. Kenyon, *Revolution Principles: The Politics of Party, 1689–1720* (1977) 13, 61). Jennifer Brady notes that D. appeals to the reader's knowledge of the terrible brutality of Edward II's murder, to suggest the violation of his own public identity which resulted from the seizure of his own official positions after 1688 (Hammond and Hopkins 129).

48. On the death of Thomas Shadwell in 1692, the post of Historiographer Royal had passed to Thomas Rymer (?1641–1713) and the Laureateship to Nahum Tate. Two decades previously, in the Preface to his translation of Rapin's *Reflections* (1674), Rymer had praised the description of night from D.'s *Indian Emperor.* D. had, in his turn, praised Rymer's *Tragedies of the Last Age* (1677) as 'the best piece of Criticism in the English tongue', and had noted Rymer's severity and wit, and his capacity for 'finding out a poets blind sides' (see *Letters* 13–14; see also 'Heads of an Answer to Rymer' (*Works* xvii 185); 'The Vindication of *The Duke of Guise*' (*Works* xiv 316)). The two men seem to have been on good terms during the late 1670s and 1680s (see Rymer xxxvii, citing Charles Gildon, *Miscellaneous Letters and Essays, on Several Subjects* (1694) 75). In the Preface to *Troilus and Cressida*, D. referred to 'my friend Mr Rymer' (*Works* xiii 228). Though Rymer may have been the author of a scurrilous lampoon on D. in 1688 (Rymer xxxvii, 281), D. was still referring to him respectfully in the Preface to *Don Sebastian* (1690) (*Works* xv 68–9; Winn 615). But at the end of 1692, Rymer published *A Short View of Tragedy.* This volume praises classical drama at the expense of modern, and contains an attack on Shakespeare's *Othello*, together with veiled jibes at D.'s Catholicism and his Shakespeare criticism, as well as sly allusions to *The Rehearsal*, in which D. had been famously ridiculed as 'Mr Bayes' (Rymer 236, 239–40, 267). That D. had taken offence at these passages is shown by his letter to Tonson of 30 August 1693, where, after reporting the rumour that Rymer is about to attack

But let 'em not mistake my patron's part,
50   Nor call his charity their own desert.
Yet this I prophesy: thou shalt be seen
(Though with some short parenthesis between)
High on the throne of wit; and seated there
Not mine (that's little) but thy laurel wear.
55   Thy first attempt an early promise made;
That early promise this has more than paid.
So bold, yet so judiciously you dare,
That your least praise is to be regular.
Time, place, and action may with pains be wrought,

him again for the criticisms of the government in the 'Dedication to *EP*', he
remarks: 'I doubt not his malice, from a former hint you gave me: & if he be
employd, I am confident tis of his own seeking; who you know has spoken slightly
of me in his last Critique: & that gave me occasion to snarl againe' (*Letters* 59).
49. *my patron's part*] Charles Sackville, sixth Earl of Dorset (1638–1706), was the
'Eugenius' and dedicatee of D.'s *EDP*, and the dedicatee of D.'s *Juvenal*, to which
Congreve had contributed. As Lord Chamberlain (1689–97), Dorset had probably negotiated D.'s possible retention of his offices (Winn 434), and, on D.'s refusal,
had been responsible for the appointment of Shadwell, and later Tate and Rymer
(whose *Short View of Tragedy* is dedicated to him). In 1686 Dorset had abused
D. for his change of religion (see 'To Mr Bays' in *Poems*, edited by Brice Harris
(1979) 18–20), but continued to befriend him and to offer pre-publication comment on his work (see Brice Harris, *Charles Sackville, Sixth Earl of Dorset* (1940)
197–200). He had actively subsidized his old friend Shadwell when the latter fell
on hard times in the early 1680s (Winn 387). Dorset was later one of the five-
guinea subscribers to D.'s *Virgil*, and assisted financially with the poet's funeral
(see Harris, *Charles Sackville* 221).
51. *I prophesy*] Cp. the 'prophecies' of Dekker and Flecknoe in *MF* ll. 87, 138.
As *Works* notes, this passage inverts the drift of the earlier poem (Congreve being
here hailed as D.'s true successor, where in *MF* Shadwell had been hailed as the
successor of the poetaster Flecknoe).
52. *parenthesis*] interval, interlude (*OED* 2).
53. *High on the throne of wit*] Echoing *MF* l. 107 (which itself satirically echoes
the enthroning of Satan in *PL* ii 1).
55. *Thy first attempt*] *The Old Batchelour* (see headnote).
56. *this*] *The Double-Dealer*.
57. *bold*] The term could be used of both linguistic and architectural effects which
were daring, vigorous or striking (*OED* 7, 8a). Cp. ll. 15–19 and *nn*.
58–9.] In his Epistle Dedicatory to *The Double-Dealer*, Congreve wrote that he
'design'd . . . to have made a true and regular Comedy' in which 'the Mechanical
part . . . is perfect', and that he 'was resolved to preserve the three Unities of the
Drama' (sigs. A2ʳ⁻ᵛ). 'Regular' (which etymologically means 'according to the rules')
was used of both literary and architectural effects which exemplified or embodied
accepted standards of excellence (*OED* 5a). Renaissance neo-classical literary criticism developed the principle that drama should obey the three unities of time,
place, and action: i.e. that a play should represent an action which took no longer

60 But genius must be born, and never can be taught.
    This is your portion, this your native store;
    Heaven that but once was prodigal before,
    To Shakespeare gave as much; she could not give him
        more.
    Maintain your post; that's all the fame you need,
65 For 'tis impossible you should proceed.
    Already I am worn with cares and age,
    And just abandoning th' ungrateful stage:

---

to perform than the play itself (or, failing that, should be confined within a day); that a drama should have only a single location; and that the action should be unbroken (which was developed into the French practice of the *liaison des scènes*). In the 'Discourse Concerning Satire' (*Poems* iii 354–5) D. had attributed to Aristotle the belief that tragedy is 'the most perfect work of poetry . . . because it is the most united, being more severely confined within the rules of action, time, and place'. Aristotle actually stresses the need for tragedy to present a coherent sequence of related events (*Poetics* v–viii), but says nothing about the unity of time or place. In *EDP* Eugenius attributes the latter requirement to 'the *French* poets' (*Works* xvii 26), but it was the invention of the Italian commentator Lodovico Castelvetro (1505–71).

60. Proverbial: *Poeta nascitur, non fit* ('a poet is born, not made') (Tilley P 451). *Works* suggests an additional echo of Ben Jonson, 'To the Memory of . . . Mr William Shakespeare', l. 64: 'For a good *Poet's* made, as well as borne'.

61–3. For the rhyme on *more / store*, cp. 'To the Memory of Mr Oldham' ll. 11–12. For the full triple rhyme and sentiment, cp. 'Lucretius: Against the Fear of Death' ll. 138–40, and Anne Wharton, 'Elegie on John Earle of Rochester' ll. 41–3: 'He was what no man euer was before~~~ / Nor can indulgent nature giue vs more~~ / For to make him, sh' exhausted all her store~' (*The Surviving Works of Anne Wharton*, edited by G. Greer and S. Hastings (1997) 141). (Wharton's poem was first printed in 1685, but circulated widely in MS from 1680.)

61. *portion*] attribute allotted by Fate or Destiny (*OED* 4).

63. *she*] Nichol Smith 194–5 hypothesized that D. had first written 'Nature' for 'Heaven' in l. 62, but then noticed that he had just used 'native', so hastily altered the word, leaving 'she' in l. 63. For the association of Nature with Shakespeare see *MF* l. 166*n*.

65. *proceed*] progress, advance (*OED* 3).

66. For other expressions of D.'s physical, financial and mental oppressions around this date, see *Letters* 48, 49, 52, 59, 73; 'Dedication to *EP*' (*Poems* iv 207–8); 'Prologue to *Love Triumphant*'.

67. *just*] exactly at the time of speaking (*OED* 4). D. refers to *Love Triumphant*, his last play, which was in rehearsal on 12 December 1693 (see *Letters* 62), around the time *The Double-Dealer* was published. Evelyn (11 January 1694) referred to *Love Triumphant* as D.'s 'last Valedictory Play', and said that D. was 'now intending to Write no more Plays' (*Works*). See further, 'Prologue and Epilogue to *Love Triumphant*'; Winn 471–3. *ungrateful*] (i) which does not respond to cultivation (*OED* 1c) (i.e. the theatre has not provided sufficient financial or critical recompense for all the effort that D. has expended on it); (ii) unpleasant, disagreeable, distasteful (*OED* 2).

Unprofitably kept at heaven's expense,
I live a rent-charge on his providence:
70 But you, whom every Muse and Grace adorn,
Whom I foresee to better fortune born,
Be kind to my remains; and O defend,
Against your judgement, your departed friend!
Let not th' insulting foe my fame pursue,
75 But shade those laurels which descend to you;
And take for tribute what these lines express:
You merit more; nor could my love do less.

69. rent-charge] rent charged on land and paid by its occupier to maintain someone who is not that land's owner; hence also someone who is maintained by
such income. Cp. 'Prologue to *Wit without Money*' ll. 14–15.
72. Be kind to my remains] An injunction explicitly implemented in Congreve's
Dedication to Tonson's edition of D.'s *Dramatick Works* (1717) (see especially sigs.
a4ᵛ–a5ʳ). Cp. the rendering of Virgil's advice to farmers on how to deal with
older horses in 'The Third Book of Virgil's *Georgics*', first published seven months
after the present poem: 'But worn with Years, when dire Diseases come, / Then
hide his not Ignoble Age, at Home: / In peace t' enjoy his former Palms and
Pains; / And gratefully be kind to his Remains' (ll. 151–4). *remains*] literary works
left after an author's death, as in *Remains of Mr John Oldham* (1684), to which D.
contributed his memorial poem.
73. Against your judgement] 'though you may think my merits may not strictly deserve
it', or 'before you have come to a final, judicious, decision on the matter'.
74. th' insulting foe] (i) D.'s enemies; (ii) death (Hoffman 138). *insulting*] As
well as the modern meaning (*OED* 2) the word also suggests scornful exultation
(*OED* 1) and aggressive hostility (*OED* 3–4).
75. shade] protect (*OED* 2d).
77. love] Cp. l. 34n.

20 Alexander's Feast

Date and publication. First performed 22 November 1697. First printed by Jacob Tonson as a separate folio pamphlet, *Alexander's Feast; or The Power of Musick. An Ode, in Honour of St. Cecilia's Day*, probably distributed at the first performance (see further below). Reprinted in *Fables Ancient and Modern* (1700). The present text is based on that of the first edition (*1697*).

Context. On 3 September 1697 D. wrote to his sons: 'I am writeing a Song for St Cecilia's feast, who you know is the Patroness of Musique. This is troublesome, & no way beneficiall: but I coud not deny the Stewards of the feast, who came in a body to me, to desire that kindness; one of them being Mr Bridgman, whose parents are your Mothers friends' (*Letters* 93). 'The Stewards' were the eight annually appointed officials of The Musical Society, an organization of professional musicians and amateur enthusiasts that had mounted musical celebrations on St Cecilia's Day (22 November) since 1683 (see headnote to *A Song for St Cecilia's Day*). In 1697 the stewards (whose names were printed in *1697*, sig. A1ᵛ) were 'Hugh Colvill, Esq;, Capt. Thomas Newnam, Orlando Bridgman, Esq;, Theophilus Buttler, Esq;, Leonard Wessell, Esq;, Paris Slaughter, Esq;, Jeremiah Clerk, Gent. [i.e. the composer Jeremiah Clarke], and Francis Le Riche, Gent.'. Orlando Bridg[e]man (grandson of Sir Orlando Bridgeman, Lord Keeper under Charles II) had been, along with four of the other stewards, among the 'second subscribers' to D.'s *The Works of Virgil* earlier in 1697. The St Cecilia celebrations consisted of a banquet at Stationers' Hall at which a celebratory ode was performed, preceded (from 1693) by a church service at St Bride's, Fleet Street, which included a sermon in defence of church music. D. had contributed *A Song for St Cecilia's Day* to the 1687 celebrations. For authors of the St Cecilia's Day odes prior to 1687, see headnote to *A Song for St Cecilia's Day*. There were no celebrations in 1688 and 1689. Subsequent odes were written by Thomas Shadwell (1690; music by Robert King), Tom D'Urfey (1691; music by John Blow), Nicholas Brady (1692; music by Henry Purcell) and Theophilus Parsons (1693; music by Godfrey Finger), Peter Motteux (1695; music by John Blow), and Anon (1696; music by Nicola Matteis). No certain record of the ode for 1694 has survived. On the St Cecilia celebrations, see Malone I i 254–307; W. H. Husk, *An Account of the Musical Celebrations on St Cecilia's Day* (1857; includes the texts of all the odes then known); James E. Phillips Jr, ed., *Two St Cecilia's Day Sermons* (1955; includes the text of Nicholas Brady's sermon for 1697); Richard Luckett, 'The Legend of St Cecilia and English Literature: a Study', unpublished PhD thesis, Cambridge (1971) 219–82; Ruth Smith, *SEL* xviii (1978) 480–5; David Hopkins *RES* n.s. xlv (1994) 486–95 (includes texts of the odes for 1695 and 1696, the latter unknown to Husk).

    Alexander's Feast was first performed at Stationers' Hall on Monday 22 November with music (now lost) by Jeremiah Clarke, one of the Musical Society's stewards for 1697. Repeat performances were given on 9 December (at Mr Hickford's Dancing School in Panton Street) and 16 December (at York Buildings) (Husk 43–4, citing advertisements in *The London Gazette*). Derrick (i xxviii) states, on the authority of D.'s friend Walter Moyle, that the Musical Society paid D. £40 for the poem, a suggestion that was treated sceptically, but not dismissed, by Malone (I i 287). Commentators since Malone (I i 255) have assumed that the first publication of *Alexander's Feast* occurred during December, after the Stationers' Hall performance. Luckett, however, suggests (252) that Tonson's pamphlet may well have been distributed or sold at the first performance itself, in line with the practice of 'gratuitous distribution' of each year's ode which was employed at the St Cecilia celebrations between 1685 and 1690. Luckett's suggestion is supported by the fact that the St Cecilia celebrations were 'clearly an important market for publishers' (H. Edmund Poole, *Proceedings of the Royal Musical Association* ci (1974–5) 39). If the earlier publication date is correct, then D.'s letter to Tonson, asking for the correction of 'Lais' to 'Thais' (see below, 'Sources' (iv)), assigned by Ward (*Letters* 179) to December 1697 on the assumption that *Alexander's Feast* was published in that month, must have been written before 22 November.

D.'s own remarks about the composition of *Alexander's Feast* can be supplemented by two further anecdotes. Thomas Birch reports that D. 'observes in an original Letter of his [*n*: Communicated by the very learned and ingenious *Richard Graham*, Jun. Esq;] that he was almost a fortnight in composing and correcting' it (*A General Dictionary, Historical and Critical* iv (1736) 684–5; see also Osborn 13). Joseph Warton offers an account that suggests a speedier process of composition: 'Mr. St. John, afterwards Lord Bolingbroke, happening to pay a morning visit to Dryden, whom he always respected, found him in an unusual agitation of spirits, even to a trembling. On enquiring the cause, "I have been up all night, replied the old bard; my musical friends made me promise to write them an ode for their feast of St. Cæcilia: I have been so struck with the subject which occurred to me, that I could not leave it till I had completed it; here it is, finished at one sitting". And immediately he shewed him this ode, which places the British lyric poetry above that of any other nation. This anecdote, as true as it is curious, was imparted by Lord Bolingbroke to POPE, by POPE to Mr. Gilbert West, by him to the ingenious friend [*n*: Richard Berenger, Esq.] who communicated it to me' (*Essay on the Genius and Writings of Pope* (1756–82) (2nd edition 1782) ii 20–1). Malone treated this anecdote sceptically (I i 287; see also his MS *addenda* printed in Osborn 152). Scott (i 406–7) attempted to reconcile the two apparently incompatible accounts of the poem's composition by speculating that 'Dryden may have completed, at one sitting, the whole Ode, and yet have employed a fortnight, or much more, in correction'. Macdonald (60) cites *The Egoist: or Colley upon Cibber* (1743) in support of a suggestion that D. may have written for private musical performance the texts of other odes that he refrained from publishing.

Sources. There is no single source for *Alexander's Feast*. D. draws eclectically on various traditions for the different stories that are modified, connected and combined in the poem: (i) stories of Alexander the Great's grandeur and folly, particularly the legend of his supposedly divine parentage; (ii) the story of Timotheus, Alexander's court musician, and his skilful exploitation of the affective properties of the 'modes' (attunements or scales) of Greek music; (iii) the story of Alexander's reaction to the death of his enemy, Darius III, King of Persia; (iv) the story of the courtesan Thais and her part in the firing of the city of Persepolis; (v) the legend of St Cecilia, associating her with music, and in particular with the invention of the organ.

(i) *Stories of Alexander*. The main part of D.'s poem adapts an incident that occurred during Alexander the Great's conquest of Persia. The historical Alexander (*b.* 356 BC) was the son of King Philip II of Macedon (*c.* 382–336 BC). His expedition against the Persians commenced in 334 BC when he crossed the Hellespont and invaded Asia Minor. He defeated the Persian armies at the battle of Issus (333 BC), and then, after subduing Phoenicia and Egypt, met the vast

new armies that Darius III King of Persia had by now amassed, on the plains of
Gaugamela (October 331 BC). Darius was defeated, and Alexander was now the
undisputed conqueror of Asia. He adopted the habits and customs of a Persian
despot, and marched to Babylon, Susa, and Persepolis, all of which surrendered
to him without resistance. Historically, Alexander's triumphant entry of Persepolis
and the firing of that city in 331 BC pre-dated the final defeat and death of Darius
(on which see (iii) below and ll. 80–1*n*). The main ancient sources of information about Alexander (to all of which D. would have had access) were the Greek
writers Plutarch and Diodorus Siculus, and the Roman historians Justin and Quintus
Curtius. These authors, together with a body of miscellaneous supplementary anecdotes and observations from antiquity, had bequeathed a profoundly ambivalent
picture of Alexander to posterity.

On the one hand, he was portrayed as the mightiest of all conquerors, a soldier of formidable bravery, hardiness, athletic prowess, and strategic skill, who
had been constantly blessed by good fortune, and whose commanding presence
and extraordinary physical handsomeness were matched by his loyalty to his
comrades and his humanity and magnanimity towards those whom he had
defeated. On the other hand, Alexander was seen in the ancient sources as a
man of overwhelming youthful passions that had sometimes made him seem
supreme only in his frailty, conceit, and folly. It was said that he had wept when
he was told of the existence of a plurality of worlds, since he had not yet conquered one (Plutarch, *De Tranquillitate Animi* 4), or because there was only one
world for him to conquer ('The Tenth Satire of Juvenal' ll. 273–5; cp. Samuel
Butler, *Hudibras* I iii 1021–3). His drunkenness had sometimes led to an unbridled
madness (Seneca, *Epistulae Morales* lxxxiii 19). Although master of the world, he
had frequently been overcome by incapacitating anger and grief (Seneca,
Epistulae Morales cxiii 29). A pirate whom he had once captured had alleged that
Alexander's conquests were themselves no more than piracy, but on a worldwide
scale (St Augustine, *De Civitate Dei* iv 4). And when Alexander died (not in
battle, but from a fever, after a bout of heavy drinking), the mighty king had
been reduced to the same condition as his muleteer (Marcus Aurelius, *Meditations*
vi 24). Commentators' ambivalent feelings about Alexander had often focused on
the claim that he was of divine parentage, born of a union between his mother,
Olympias, and Zeus, who had visited her in the form of a serpent, to her husband's consternation (see *Plutarchs Lives, Translated from the Greek, by Several Hands*,
5 vols (1683–6) iv 259–61).

D.'s scepticism about claims made by and for 'godlike' heroes had been
revealed in the 'Life of Plutarch', when, while discussing the 'descent into minute
circumstances, and trivial passages of life' that characterizes Plutarch's biograph-
ical writing, he remarked: 'The Pageantry of Life is taken away; you see the poor
reasonable Animal, as naked as even nature made him; are made acquainted
with his passions and his follies; and find the *Demy-God a Man*' (*Works* xvii 275).
D.'s scepticism about the 'godlike' Alexander took on a particular edge in 'To
John Driden of Chesterton' (ll. 150–63), where a parallel was drawn between
Alexander's victory over Darius and William III's defeat of Louis XIV at the
siege of Namur (1695). Alexander had frequently been associated in the 1690s
with William III, both (positively) in Williamite panegyric and (negatively) in
nonjuring and Jacobite pamphlets: see Samuel Cobb, *A Pindarique Ode, Upon the
Death of the Queen* (1694) 5, and *Pax Redux* (1697) 6; *Wit and Mirth: or Pills to
Purge Melancholy*, edited by Thomas D'Urfey (1719–20) ii 281, vi 99; *Poems on
the Reign of William III*, edited by Earl Miner (1974) vi–vii, 7, 9–10; Nahum
Tate, Epistle Dedicatory to Quintus Curtius Rufus, *The Life of Alexander the*

Great . . . Translated into English by Several Gentlemen in the University of Cambridge
(1690), sig. A6ᵛ; for discussion, see Howard Erskine-Hill, *EIC* xxix (1979) 42–3,
51, and *Modern Language Studies* ix (1979) 18; W. B. Carnochan in *The English
Hero, 1660–1800*, edited by Robert Folkenflik (1982) 47; Winn 495–6. For
D.'s awareness of this tradition, cp. 'The Cock and the Fox' ll. 659–60. On D.'s
sceptical treatment of heroes, see further Michael West, *Costerus* vii (1973)
193–22; on D. and divine sexuality, see David Hopkins, *John Dryden* (1986) 128–
30; G. J. Clingham, *Modern Language Studies* xviii (1988) 171–7. The reception
history of *Alexander's Feast*, however, shows that the poem was admired during
the eighteenth century (the period of its highest popularity) more for its celebratory than for its satirical qualities (see Tom Mason and Adam Rounce in
Hammond and Hopkins 140–73).

(ii) *The Story of Timotheus*. The history of the legend of the musician
Timotheus rousing Alexander to various passions by the exercise of his art is sketched
by Nan Carpenter (*PMLA* lxxi (1956) 1141–51). The tale is Greek in origin,
and is found (with variations) in Dio Chrysostom, Suidas' *Lexicon* and Plutarch's
Moralia. The ultimate source of the specific version in which Timotheus is said
to have aroused the banqueting Alexander to take up arms by playing a melody
in the Phrygian mode, and then to have relaxed him and returned him to his
guests by changing the style of music, is apparently to be found in St Basil's
Ad Adolescentes (J. P. Migne, *Patrologia Graeca* (1857–1904) xxxi 580; English
trans. in *Source Readings in Music History* (1950) edited by Oliver Strunk, 282n).
Carpenter (1148–9n) notes that from early on the tradition had conflated two
musicians called Timotheus, one an aulos player who attended at Alexander's wedding, the other a dithyrambic poet, composer and lyre player (*c.* 450–*c.* 360 BC).
On the confusion, see also Erwin Panofsky, *JWCI* xii (1949) 80–90. D. inherits
the conflated tradition, in making his Timotheus a poet, lyre player (ll. 22, 159)
and flautist (l. 158). The story of Timotheus and Alexander became a *locus classicus*
for illustrating the power of music, and is found in numerous Renaissance
musical treatises. For continental and English versions of the story, see Carpenter;
Strunk 287, 319, 408, 574; James Kinsley, *RES* iv (1953) 263–7; Mark Van Doren,
John Dryden: A Study of his Poetry, revised edition (1946) 204–6; John Hollander,
The Untuning of the Sky (1961) 412–4; Douglas Murray, *Scriblerian* xvi (1983–4)
182. Particularly relevant to *Alexander's Feast* is the retelling of the Timotheus
story in Jeremy Collier's essay 'Of Musick'. This essay first appeared in Collier's
Miscellanies upon Moral Subjects. The Second Part (1695). The second edition of
Collier's *Miscellanies*, entitled *Essays upon Several Moral Subjects*, was advertised in
June 1697 (see *TC* iii 29). The date of Collier's essay and its witty tone both
make it a probable source for *Alexander's Feast*: 'Timotheus, a Grecian, was so
great a *Master*, that he could make a Man storm and swagger like a Tempest.
And then, by altering the *Notes*, and the *Time*, he would take him down again,
and sweeten his Humour in a trice. One time, when *Alexander* was at dinner,
this Man play'd him a *Phrygian* Air: The Prince immediately rises, snatches up
his Lance, and puts himself in a Posture of Fighting. And the Retreat was no
sooner Sounded by the Change of the Harmony, but his Arms were Grounded,
and his Fire extinct, and he sat down as orderly as if he had come from one of
Aristotle's Lectures. I warrant you *Demosthenes* would have been Flourishing about
such Business a long Hour, and may be not have done it neither. But *Timotheus*
had a nearer Cut to the Soul: He could Neck a Passion at a Stroke, and lay it
Asleep' (*Essays upon Several Moral Subjects. In Two Parts*, second edition (1697) ii
21–2). Robert Burton had similarly stressed the comedy of the story, remarking
that 'Timotheus the musician compelled Alexander to skip up and down and leave

his dinner' (*The Anatomy of Melancholy*, 2. 2. 6. 3). But D. significantly changed the traditional legend by linking the story of Timotheus with that of the firing of Persepolis (see (iv) below), thus making Timotheus' enchantments culminate not in peaceful restoration, but in an incitement to an act of wanton destruction (see Murray 182; Robert P. Maccubbin, *Mosaic* xviii (1985) 36–7). In this, D. may have remembered John Playford's suggestion of the potentially threatening power of Timotheus' skill, when Playford connected the story of the Greek musician with that of the legendary Danish harpist, Ericus, whose playing so affected the king that 'he fell upon his most trusty friends which were near him, and slew some of them with his fist for lack of another weapon; which the Musician perceiving, ended with the sober and solemn *Dorick*, which brought the King to himself, who much lamented what he had done' (*A Briefe Introduction to the Skill of Musick*, seventh edition (1674) 61).

The Timotheus story rested on the belief that each of the 'modes', the melodic scales on which ancient Greek music had been structured, had its own 'ethos', and that each scale was capable of producing a different kind of psychic tension or laxity in the listener. The ultimate source of such ideas was Plato (*Republic* iii 398–9). During the Middle Ages and Renaissance, a complex process of accommodation had taken place, whereby the names of the ancient Greek modes were applied to the scales employed in plainchant and early polyphony (see *The New Oxford Companion to Music*, edited by Denis Arnold (1983) ii 1184–7). By the seventeenth century 'garbled notions of Greek modality, traditionally handed down, had become . . . purely literary, esthetic concepts' (Hollander 305–6). Thus, while, as Playford (57) noted, 'there is scarce an author that has wrote of Musick but do give some account' of 'the five Moods used by the Grecians', the musical effects attributed to the modes were by this time purely notional (being unrelated to actual musical experience) and sometimes differed from account to account. D. probably associated the various stages of Timotheus' song with the different 'modes' and their traditionally associated 'effects', ll. 25–46 suggesting the Dorian mode (characterized by simplicity and solemnity), ll. 47–65 the Ionian (soft and convivial), ll. 73–92 the Mixolydian (pathetic and plaintive), ll. 97–122 the Lydian (see l. 97n), and ll. 123–54 the Phrygian (martial) (see Hollander 418–19; Paul Fry, *The Poet's Calling in the English Ode* (1980) 292).

(iii) *Alexander and the Death of Darius*. D.'s poem reorders the events of the historical record, so that the firing of Persepolis is made to post-date the defeat of Darius (Smith 474; Maccubbin 38; see also ll. 80–1n). Plutarch (342–3) had given the following account of Darius' death, and Alexander's magnanimous reaction: 'And at last, with much ado, [Alexander's officers] found [Darius] lying along in a Chariot, all over wounded with Darts, just at the point of Death. However, he desired they would give him some drink, and when he had drank a little cold water, he told *Polystratus* who gave it him, *That to receive such a Benefit, and not have it in his Power to return it, was the highest pitch of his misfortune.* But Alexander, said he, *whose kindness to my Mother, my Wife, and my Children, I hope the Gods will recompence, will doubtless thank you for your Humanity to me. Tell him therefore in token of my Acknowledgment, I give him this Right Hand:* At which Words he took hold of *Polystratus* his Hand, and died. When *Alexander* came up to them, he was sensibly touch'd at the unfortunate End of so Great a Man, and pulling off his own Coat, threw it upon the Body to cover it . . . *Darius* his Body was laid in State, and sent to his Mother with Pomp suitable to his quality. His Brother *Exathres*, *Alexander* receiv'd into the number of his most intimate Friends'.

(iv) *Thais and the Firing of Persepolis*. In a letter to Tonson (*Letters* 96), written either just before or just after the first performance of *Alexander's Feast* (see above),

D. wrote: 'Remember in the Copy of Verses for St. Cecilia, to alter the name
of Lais, wch is twice there, for Thais; those two Ladyes were Contemporaryes,
wch caused that small mistake'. In his original MS, D. had evidently given the
name of Alexander's mistress as 'Lais'. This was the name of at least two famous
Greek courtesans. The former lived at Corinth at the time of the Peloponnesian
war. The latter (the daughter of Timandra, rival of Phryne and model of the
painter Apelles) lived at the time of Alexander, but is not associated with him
by the ancient sources. Plutarch's sixteenth-century French translator, Jacques Amyot,
had, however, stated that Lais had been a visitor to Alexander's camp, and this may
have been the source of D.'s momentary confusion (Maccubbin 39–40). Thais
was the celebrated courtesan who accompanied Alexander on his expedition into
Asia and who, according to some sources, provoked the firing of Persepolis.
In instructing Tonson to change the name, D. was apparently more concerned
to protect himself against charges of historical inaccuracy than to preserve the
elaborate patterns of assonance and alliteration originally built around the name
'Lais' at ll. 9–11, 105, 148–9.

The story of Alexander's firing of Persepolis is told by Plutarch (*Plutarchs Lives*
iv 331–2), where Thais declares that 'it would please her . . . if while the King
look'd on, she might in sport, with her own Hands, set fire to *Xerxes* his Court',
and Alexander, 'perswaded to be of the Party, started from his Seat, and with
a Chaplet of Flowers on his Head, and a lighted Torch in his Hand, led them
the way'. The story is also recounted by Quintus Curtius (V vii 2–7), who
stresses the drunkenness of the banqueters. It also occurs, in a form that directly
connects the firing of the city with 'a victorious Festival to *Bacchus*' and with
'Songs, Pipes, and Flutes' in Diodorus Siculus (xvii 72; see *Historical Library*, tr.
G. Booth (1700) 551–2). The story of Timotheus is linked with a tale of drunken
incendiarism in Franchino Gafori's *De Harmonia Musicorum Instrumentorum* (1518)
(see John M. Steadman in *TLS* 16 December 1960, 819). D. had alluded *en
passant* to the firing of Persepolis in *The Kind Keeper* IV i 138–9.

(v) *St Cecilia and the Invention of the Organ*. For the legend of the third-century
martyr St Cecilia, and her supposed invention of the organ, see headnote to
A Song for St Cecilia's Day (under *Sources*).

Alexander's Feast was composed about a month after the publication of D.'s
The Works of Virgil and connections between the translation and ode are evident
at several points (see ll. 22, 40–1, 52, 53, 70, 132, 140*nn*). In addition to these
instances, several details in D.'s description of Alexander's feast seem indebted to
D.'s description of the feast staged by Dido for her Trojan guests (see 'The First
Book of the *Aeneis*' ll. 977–1057).

Reception. Shortly after the publication of *Alexander's Feast*, D. wrote to Tonson:
'I am glad to heare from all hands, that my Ode is esteemed the best of all my
poetry, by all the Town: I thought it so my self when I writ it but being old,
I mistrusted my own Judgment. I hope it has done you service, & will do more'
(*Letters* 98). Malone (I i 476–7) reports that Lord Chief Justice Marley, 'being
desirous of seeing the Wits, and hearing their conversation, began at an early
period to frequent Will's Coffee-House, to which they resorted. ALEXANDER'S
FEAST, not long after its appearance, being the theme of every Critick, young
Marley, among others, took an opportunity of paying his court to the author;
and happening to sit next him, congratulated him on having produced the finest
and noblest Ode that had ever been written in any language. "You are right,
young gentleman, (replied Dryden,) a nobler Ode never *was* produced, nor ever
will["].'

During the eighteenth century *Alexander's Feast* was widely admired for the 'harmony' of its 'numbers', and came to be regarded as the supreme example in English of the 'Pindaric' or 'irregular' ode (see Mason and Rounce in Hammond and Hopkins). D. had commented on the particular metrical challenges presented by the 'Pindaric' style in the Preface to *Sylvae* (*Poems* ii 256). A detailed metrical analysis of *Alexander's Feast* is provided by James Burnett, Lord Monboddo (National Library of Scotland MS 24508, ff. 115ʳ–122ᵛ; partial transcriptions in *CH* 401–3 and Mason and Rounce 165–9).

A musical setting of parts of D.'s text (ll. 1–24, 65–79, 84–122) in the hand of Charles King (1687–1748), apprentice and later brother-in-law of Jeremiah Clarke, the composer of the original setting, is preserved in the library of the Royal College of Music (MS 96, ff. 13ʳ–35ᵛ). A second setting by Benedetto Marcello (1686–1739) of 'Il Timoteo', an early eighteenth-century translation of D.'s poem by the Abbé Conti, is preserved in the BL (Egerton MS 2487, ff. 1–21). Handel's celebrated setting of D.'s poem (edited and supplemented by Newburgh Hamilton) was first performed at the Covent Garden Theatre on 19 February 1736. Thomas Clayton's setting of 1711 has not survived. In *The Laws of Poetry* (1721), Charles Gildon cited *Alexander's Feast* in illustration of his proposition that 'there is scarce one master of musick, who has set a song, composed with art and fine sense, to any tolerable tune', and commented: 'tho' [*Alexander's Feast*] has been twice set to musick by men of considerable reputation in that art, yet the notes of the musician have generally destroy'd, not only the sense, but the very harmony of the poet. I hear there is a third has undertaken it, a man of no mean fame in musical compositions, but I am afraid with not much more success than his predecessors'. Gildon is perhaps referring to King's setting.

[handwritten marginal note: Pindaric in the sense known in Queen Anne's reign, promulgated by Cowley, behind the strict hymns of Pindar's actual Odes, a new a few unread ... for medium]

Alexander's Feast, or The Power of Music

An Ode in Honour of St Cecilia's Day

I

'Twas at the royal feast, for Persia won
      By Philip's warlike son:
    Aloft in <u>awful</u> state
    The <u>godlike</u> hero sate

[handwritten margin: emperor, despot?] 5   On his <u>imperial</u> throne;
His valiant peers were placed around,

¶20. *1–2.* See headnote, *Sources* (i).
3–4. Echoing *PL* ii 1–5: 'High on a throne of royal state, . . . / Satan exalted sat' (Fry, Carnochan).
3. awful] inspiring awe.
4. sate] sat.
6. peers] aristocrats (*OED* 4a, 5); companions, fellows (*OED* 3).

Their brows with roses and with myrtles bound
   (So should <u>desert in arms</u> be crowned);
The lovely Thais by his side,
10   Sate like a blooming <u>eastern</u> bride
In flower of youth and beauty's pride.
     Happy, happy, happy pair!
     None but the brave,
     None but the brave,
15   None but the brave deserves the fair.

CHORUS

     Happy, happy, happy pair!
     None but the brave,
     None but the brave,
     None but the brave deserves the fair.

II

20   Timotheus placed on high
     Amid the tuneful choir,
     With flying fingers touched the lyre:
The trembling notes <u>ascend the sky</u>,
     And heavenly joys inspire.
25   The song began from Jove,
Who left his blissful seats above

7. *myrtles*] The myrtle was held to be sacred to Venus, and was thus, like the rose, used as an emblem of love. Cp. 'Palamon and Arcite' ii 461, 518. J. R. Mason (privately) suggests that D. might also have been thinking here of the *ovalis corona*, the myrtle crown worn by generals who entered the city in an ovation (see Valerius Maximus III vi 5; Pliny, *Naturalis Historia* XV xxxviii 125–6; Aulus Gellius V vi 20–3). In Plutarch (see headnote, *Sources* (iv)) Alexander fires Persepolis 'with a Chaplet of Flowers on his Head' (Kinsley).
9. *Thais*] See headnote, *Sources* (iv).
10. *blooming*] in the bloom of health and beauty; in the prime of youth; flourishing (*OED* 2).
11. Cp. Cowley, 'The Chronicle' ll. 34–5: 'For the gracious Princess dy'd / In her Youth and Beauties pride' (*Poems* 40). *pride*] (i) most excellent or flourishing state, prime (*OED* 9); (ii) magnificent and ostentatious adornment (*OED* 6–7; Johnson 6).
20. *on high*] presumably in a minstrels' gallery.
22. *flying fingers*] The phrase is used of Orpheus in 'The Sixth Book of the *Aeneis*' l. 879 (J. R. Mason, privately).
23. *trembling*] vibrating (*OED* 2). Cp. *MF* l. 44.
25–33. For the story of Alexander's allegedly divine birth, see headnote, *Sources* (i).
26. *seats*] mansions, dwellings (Johnson 3).

love his ?b sung on? Jove even
as the disguise
coiled? flying?

(Such is the power of mighty <u>love</u>).
A dragon's fiery form <u>belied</u> the god;
Sublime on radiant spires he rode,

    30
language of eye : riddling her of virginity?

When he to fair Olympia <u>pressed</u>,
And while he sought her snowy breast;
Then round her slender waist he curled,

relation to X? a physical, r. metrical more?

And <u>stamped an image of himself</u>, a sovereign of the world.
The listening crowd admire the lofty sound,

    35
copied by the music?

'A present deity,' they shout around;
'<u>A present deity</u>,' the vaulted roofs rebound.

is his mother: more in praising itself or him / stamping him?

With ravished ears
The monarch hears,

is v h-brisk?

<u>Assumes the god</u>,

    40
that: how he wishes it to be?

Affects to nod,
And <u>seems</u> to shake the spheres.

28. *dragon's*] that of a huge snake or python (*OED* dragon 1). *belied*] disguised (*OED* 4b).

29. *Sublime*] aloft, high up (*OED* 1). *spires*] coils (*OED* 1, citing this example). *rode*] was carried, supported, as if riding (*OED* 9).

30. *Olympia*] Olympias, wife of Philip of Macedon and mother of Alexander (see headnote, *Sources* (i)). Saintsbury suggested that D. omitted the final 's' to avoid an ugly accumulation of sibilants. *pressed*] hastened eagerly (*OED* 15).

32. *curled*] twined round (*OED* 5). Cp., in a specifically sexual context, 'Lucretius: The Beginning of the First Book' l. 53; 'Palamon and Arcite' iii 318.

33. Cp. Shakespeare's reference (*Measure for Measure* II iv 45) to those 'that do coin heaven's image / In stamps that are forbid'. *stamped*] (i) imposed traces of (figuratively) (*OED* 8g); (ii) marked with a die (literally, as in minting a coin that bears an image of the king's head) (*OED* 4b). *sovereign*] (i) ruler (*OED* A1); (ii) gold coin (*OED* A4). Cp. Pope, *The Temple of Fame* l. 152*n*: 'The *Tiara* was the *Crown* peculiar to the *Asian* Princes: [Alexander's] Desire to be thought the Son of *Jupiter Ammon* caus'd him to wear the Horns of that God, and to represent the same upon his Coins, which was continu'd by several of his Successors' (J. R. Mason, privately).

34. *admire*] wonder at, marvel at (*OED* 2).

35–41. Cp. Horace, *Carm*. III v 1–5: *Caelo tonantem credidimus Iovem / regnare; praesens divus habebitur / Augustus adiectis Britannis / imperio gravibusque Persis* ('We believe that Jove is king in heaven because we hear his thunders peal; Augustus shall be deemed a deity present on earth for adding to our empire the Britons and dread Parthians') (Hales).

39. *Assumes the god*] takes Jove-like authority and dignity to himself (*OED* 4b, 7).

40–1. For Jove's nod of ungainsayable authority, cp. 'The Ninth Book of the *Aeneis*' ll. 120–4 (J. R. Mason); 'The Tenth Book of the *Aeneis*' ll. 153–4 (Noyes); 'The First Book of Homer's *Ilias*' ll. 705–12 (Hales).

40. *Affects to nod*] (i) takes delight in nodding (*OED* affect 2d); (ii) aspires to a Jove-like nod (*OED* affect 1).

CHORUS

With ravished ears
The monarch hears,
Assumes the god,
45   Affects to nod,
And seems to shake the spheres.

III

The praise of Bacchus then the sweet musician sung,
Of Bacchus ever fair and ever young:
The jolly god in triumph comes;
50   Sound the trumpets, beat the drums;
Flushed with a purple grace
He shows his honest face;
Now give the hautboys breath; he comes, he comes.
Bacchus, ever fair and young,
55   Drinking joys did first ordain;

48. ever fair and ever young] Cp. Ovid, *Met.* iv 17–18 (addressing Bacchus): *tibi enim inconsumpta iuventa est, / tu puer aeternus, tu formosissimus alto / conspiceris caelo* ('for thine is unending youth, eternal boyhood; thou art the most lovely in the lofty sky').

49. The jolly god] Cp. 'Ovid's *Art of Love* Book 1' ll. 590–1 (of Bacchus). *jolly*] The adjective encompasses several senses besides the usual 'gay, cheerful' (*OED* 1): (i) youthful, lively (*OED* 2); (ii) convivial, jovial (*OED* 4); (iii) bold, confident (*OED* 6); healthy in appearance (*OED* 11); (iv) delightful (*OED* 13a).

50. D. replaces the cymbals with which Bacchus was usually associated (see 'Ovid's *Art of Love* Book 1' l. 605) with more martial instruments (see l. 53*n*). The line 'is undoubtedly a reminiscence of the title and opening line of Purcell's welcome song ['Sound the trumpet, beat the drum'] of 1687' (Ernest Brennecke, Jr, *PMLA* xlix (1934) 33).

52. honest] attractive, handsome; a Latinism (*OED* 2c; no example given after 1566). Virgil refers to Bacchus' *honestum caput* in *Geo.* ii 392, which is translated by D. ('The Second Book of the *Georgics*' l. 540) as 'honest face'.

53. hautboys] oboes (*OED* 1, pronounced 'ho-boys'). The oboe was a recent innovation in D.'s day, having been first used in France shortly before 1660 and introduced into England in 1674. It was recognized as being capable of encompassing a wide variety of emotions from plaintive lyricism to rustic sprightliness, but was particularly associated with military and ceremonial music (see *The New Grove Dictionary of Musical Instruments*, edited by S. Sadie (1984) ii 795–6). Peter Motteux (*Gentleman's Journal*, January 1692 7) noted that 'hautbois' were played during the banquets at the St Cecilia's Day celebrations (Maccubbin 42). They are mentioned in Shadwell's St Cecilia Ode for 1690 (Husk 156). *he comes, he comes*] Cp. 'The Sixth Book of the *Aeneis*' l. 70: 'He comes, behold the God!' (J. R. Mason, privately).

55. Cp. 'Horace: *Odes* I ix' l. 38: 'These, these are joys the gods for youth ordain'.

Bacchus' blessings are a treasure,
Drinking is the soldier's pleasure;
Rich the treasure,
Sweet the pleasure,
60   Sweet is pleasure after pain.

CHORUS

Bacchus' blessings are a treasure,
Drinking is the soldier's pleasure;
Rich the treasure,
Sweet the pleasure,
65   Sweet is pleasure after pain.

IV

Soothed with the sound the king grew vain;
Fought all his battles o'er again;
And thrice he routed all his foes, and thrice he slew the slain.
The master saw the madness rise,
70   His glowing cheeks, his ardent eyes;
And while he heaven and earth defied,
Changed his hand, and checked his pride.
He chose a mournful Muse
Soft pity to infuse;
75   He sung Darius great and good,
By too severe a fate,
Fallen, fallen, fallen, fallen,
Fallen from his high estate
And weltering in his blood;

66, 98. Soothed] encouraged (OED 4a); induced by (OED 7b).
69. The master] Timotheus, referred to by Collier (see headnote, Sources (ii)) as
'so great a Master'.
70. His . . . his] Alexander's.   ardent] blazing with mad light. 'Ardent eyes' is
a Virgilian phrase: ardentes oculos (e.g. Aen. ii 210, translated in 'The Second Book
of the Aeneis' l. 277).
71. he] Alexander.
72. his hand] Timotheus' manner or style of performance (OED 13; Johnson 16,
citing this example).   checked] restrained, controlled (OED 4).   his pride] Alexander's
pride.
75. Darius] See headnote, Sources (iii).
77. Perhaps prompted by the repetition of 'fallen' in Isaiah xxi 9; Revelation xiv
8, xviii 2 (J. R. Mason, privately).
79. weltering in] lying prostrate, soaked in (OED 1c).

80   Deserted at his utmost need,
       By those his former bounty fed;
       On the bare earth exposed he lies,
       With not a friend to close his eyes.

       With downcast looks the joyless victor sate,
85   Revolving in his altered soul
         The various turns of chance below;
       And now and then a sigh he stole,
         And tears began to flow.

          CHORUS

       Revolving in his altered soul
90   The various turns of chance below;
       And now and then a sigh he stole,
         And tears began to flow.

          V

       The mighty master smiled to see
       That love was in the next degree:
95   'Twas but a kindred sound to move,
       For pity melts the mind to love.

80–1. After his defeat at Gaugamela (see headnote, *Sources* (i)), Darius fell into the hands of a conspiracy of his former supporters, led by Bessus, satrap (provincial governor) of Bactria, who had resolved either to make themselves masters of his empire or to hand him over to Alexander, whichever seemed most expedient. In the event, Darius was killed before Alexander's arrival. For Plutarch's account of the circumstances of Darius' death and Alexander's reaction, see headnote, *Sources* (iii). Howard Erskine-Hill (44) suggests that the couplet would also have reminded a contemporary reader of the defeated and deserted James II.

85. Revolving] turning over, pondering upon (*OED* 4). *altered*] disturbed (*OED* 3). The word is used by Playford of Bonus, King of Denmark (see headnote, *Sources* (ii)).

87. a sigh he stole] he breathed a furtive sigh (*OED* steal 5c, citing this example).

94. in the next degree] (i) one step away (*OED* degree 1); D. alludes to the traditional notion that pity is only one step away from love (see, e.g., *Twelfth Night* III i 125–6); (ii) only one note in the musical scale away (*OED* degree 11a). In one of the systems of modes described by Renaissance musical theorists, and afforded the traditional Greek names, the Mixolydian mode began one tone higher than the Lydian (see Jerome and Elizabeth Roche, *A Dictionary of Early Music* (1981) 128).

95. kindred] similar or allied in character, possessing similar features (*OED* 2, citing this example).

sib.: soft sounds

Softly sweet, in Lydian measures,
Soon he <u>soothed his soul to pleasures</u>:

can wen oneself with the 'soon': too discordant?

War, he sung, is toil and trouble;

Bissn: All He world; 100 *bubble'?*   Honour but an <u>empty bubble</u>;

of breathing an desiring

Never ending, still beginning,
Fighting still, and still destroying;
If the world be worth thy winning,

mocer'g'g him to press for an second
-filles an only from 105 IV   Think, O <u>think, it worth enjoying</u>;

Lovely Thais sits beside thee,
Take the good the gods provide thee.

a fancy

the language that pleads the case:
as Alex object to Tim?   The <u>many</u> rend the skies with loud applause;

So <u>love was crowned, but music won the</u> cause.
The prince, unable to conceal his pain,

110   Gazed on the fair
Who caused his <u>care</u>,

unsupported; or longing?

ref. to 77-8: showing the change   And sighed and looked, sighed and looked,
Sighed and looked, and sighed again:

now subject to her?
a wish man?   115   At length, with love and wine at once oppressed,
The vanquished victor sunk upon her breast.

CHORUS

The prince, unable to conceal his pain,
Gazed on the fair
Who caused his care,
And sighed and looked, sighed and looked,

97. *Lydian measures*] The Lydian mode had been condemned by Plato (*Republic* iii 398d) for its laxity. But a tradition, apparently deriving from the late Roman politician and writer Cassiodorus (*c.* 490–*c.* 583), stressed the power of the Lydian mode to soothe, calm and relax the listener by penetrating his soul (see James Hutton, *English Miscellany* ii (1951) 45–6, and Milton, *L'Allegro* ll. 135–42).   *measures*] airs, tunes, melodies (*OED* 17).

99–100. Cp. *As You Like It* II vii 149–53: 'Then, a soldier, / . . . / Jealous in honour, . . . / Seeking the bubble reputation' (J. R. Mason, privately); *Macbeth* IV i 35–6: 'Double, double toil and trouble: / Fire, burn; and cauldron, bubble'; Samuel Butler, *Hudibras* II ii 385–6: '*Honor* is like that glassy Bubble / That finds *Philosophers* such trouble'.

101–2. *still . . . still . . . still*] always, ceaselessly.

105. *Thais*] See headnote, *Sources* (iv).

107. *The many*] the assembled throng of banqueters. Noyes suggests an association of *many* with *meiny* ('retinue'): cp. 'Palamon and Arcite' iii 545.

108. *So*] i.e. in the applause. *won the cause*] was the actual victor in the case (or the lawyer who was successful in pleading the case) (*OED* cause 8).

111. *care*] concern, anxiety, perturbation (*OED* 2; Johnson 1).

119. There is no correspondent rhyme word for 'looked'.

120   Sighed and looked, and sighed again:
        At length, with love and wine at once oppressed,
        The vanquished victor sunk upon her breast.

               VI

        Now strike the golden lyre again:
        A louder yet, and yet a louder strain.
125   Break his bands of sleep asunder,
        And rouse him, like a rattling peal of thunder.
            Hark, hark, the horrid sound
            Has raised up his head,
            As awaked from the dead,
130   And amazed, he stares around.
        'Revenge, revenge!' Timotheus cries,
        'See the Furies arise!
            See the snakes that they rear,
            How they hiss in their hair,
135   And the sparkles that flash from their eyes!
            Behold a ghastly band,
            Each a torch in his hand!
      Those are Grecian ghosts, that in battle were slain,
            And unburied remain
140   Inglorious on the plain.

124. yet . . . yet] even . . . even.
125. bands] chains (*fig. OED* 7).
127. horrid] hideous, dreadful, shocking (*OED* 2, Johnson 1).
130. amazed] (i) driven out of his wits, crazed (*OED* 1); (ii) terrified, horrified (*OED* 3). *stares*] glares in horror and fury (*OED* stare 3).
131, 132, 145. No inverted commas in *1697*.
132. Furies] In classical mythology, the deities whose responsibility it is to avenge crime, particularly against kindred. They are portrayed in Aeschylus as covered in black, twisted with serpents and with foul ooze dripping from their eyes (*Choephori* ll. 1048–50; *Eumenides* ll. 46–54). D. imagines the Furies with firebrands in 'Canace to Macareus' ll. 121–2. Cp. also 'Cinyras and Myrrha' ll. 24–5. Here, however, the Furies are not conceived of as punishers of the guilty but as provokers of strife. They thus resemble most closely the Furies in Virgil and Ovid who own Alecto as chief (cp. *Aen.* vii 286–571; *Met.* iv 430–530), and who are released by the gods into the world of men to inspire mortals with destructive fury. See D.'s own note on 'The Twelfth Book of the *Aeneis*' ll. 1224–5 (J. R. Mason, privately).
133. rear] lift up, cause to rise up (*OED* 2). In Virgil (*Aen.* vi 571–2) the Fury Tisiphone brandishes her snakes in her left hand.
136. ghastly] ghost-like, spectral (*OED* 2).
140. Inglorious] unremembered, obscure (*OED* 1), hence dishonoured, disgraced (*OED* 2) because they had not received a proper, dignified, burial. Cp. 'The Tenth Book of the *Aeneis*' ll. 778–9: 'Lye there, proud Man unpity'd, on the Plain: / Lye there, inglorious, and without a Tomb'.

obligation

              Give the vengeance due
                To the valiant crew.
     Behold how they toss their torches on high,
          How they point to the Persian abodes,

religious rituals too? 145   And glittering temples of their hostile gods!'
       The princes applaud, with a furious joy,
      And the king seized a flambeau, with zeal to destroy;

she gets involved in the incitement? but is it Tim.?
                Thais led the way,
                To light him to his prey,

instructions, u in control 150   And, like another Helen, fired another Troy.
of her men?

CHORUS

     And the king seized a flambeau, with zeal to destroy;
                Thais led the way,
                To light him to his prey,
     And, like another Helen, fired another Troy.

VII

155   Thus, long ago,
         Ere heaving bellows learned to blow,

the power was there even yet?
           While organs yet were mute,
        Timotheus, to his breathing flute
           And sounding lyre,
160   Could swell the soul to rage, or kindle soft desire.

---

141. vengeance] Perhaps pronounced as a trisyllabic word, to create an anapaestic rhythm. Lord Monboddo, however, scans ll. 142–3 as 'consisting each of two Trochees and a residuous Syllable'.

142. valiant] Also perhaps trisyllabic.　*crew*] band of soldiers (*OED* 1, 2).

143. high] without a correspondent rhyme word.

144. the Persian abodes] in the city of Persepolis (see headnote, *Sources* (iv)). 'Abodes / gods' is a true, not a half, rhyme in D.'s verse.

145. Diodorus Siculus (see headnote, *Sources* (iv)) attributes the firing of Persepolis, in part, to the drunken youths' desire to avenge the Persians' earlier destruction of 'the Temples of the *Grecians*'.

147. flambeau] lighted torch (*OED* 1).

148–50. Cp. headnote, *Sources* (iv). Plutarch records that Alexander 'led them the way'. In Diodorus, Thais is the first to hurl her flaming torch *after* Alexander (see headnote, *Sources* (iv)).

150. For the firing of Troy by the Greeks, see 'The Second Book of Virgil's *Aeneis*' ll. 397–428. Cp. also Virgil, 'The Fourth Pastoral' l. 43 (D.'s trans.): 'Another *Helen* [will] other Wars create' (S. R. Swaminathan, *N & Q* ccxvii (1972) 328–30).

158. breathing] giving forth sound (*OED* 7). For Timotheus' flute, see headnote, *Sources* (ii).

159. sounding] resonant, sonorous, reverberant (*OED* 1).

> At last divine Cecilia came,
> Inventress of the <u>vocal frame;</u>
> The sweet <u>enthusiast</u>, from her sacred store,
> > <u>Enlarged</u> the former narrow bounds,   *so much more depth in the organ?*
165 > > And added length to solemn sounds,
> With nature's mother wit, and arts unknown before.] *e nature + art*
> > Let old Timotheus yield the prize,
> > > Or both divide the crown;
> > He raised a mortal to the skies;   *how the greater achievement? for Tim. did*
170 > > She drew an angel down.   *prompt needless violence from Alex, & enslaved him to his will?*

GRAND CHORUS

> At last divine Cecilia came,
> Inventress of the vocal frame;
> The sweet enthusiast, from her sacred store,
> > Enlarged the former narrow bounds,
175 > > And added length to solemn sounds,
> With nature's mother wit, and arts unknown before.
> > Let old Timotheus yield the prize,
> > > Or both divide the crown;
> > He raised a mortal to the skies;
180 > > She drew an angel down.

161–2. For St Cecilia's supposed invention of the organ, see headnote to *A Song for St Cecilia's Day, Sources*.
162. *vocal*] emitting musical notes (*OED* 4c). *frame*] structure, machine (*OED* 7, citing this example).
163. *enthusiast*] one who is (really or seemingly) divinely inspired (*OED* 1).
166. Cp. Spenser, *FQ* IV x 21: 'For all that nature by her mother wit / Could frame in earth, and forme of substance base, / Was there, and all that nature did omit, / Art playing second natures part, supplyed it' (J. R. Mason, privately).
169–70. Cp. Andrew Marvell, 'Upon Appleton House' ll. 161–2: 'Your voice, the sweetest of the choir, / Shall draw heav'n nearer, raise us higher' (E. E. Duncan-Jones, privately).
170. On St Cecilia and the angel, see headnote, *Sources* (v). *She drew an angel down*] Cp. *The Spanish Friar* III iii 174 (*Works* xiv 463).

21 Palamon and Arcite

Date and publication. First printed 1700 in *Fables Ancient and Modern*. The volume was in the press by 14 December 1699, and D. expected its publication by the end of the year (see *Letters* 130, 132). But in the event it did not appear until well into 1700. It was advertised in *The Flying Post* on 5–7 March, but D. did not receive his copy until 12 March (see *Letters* 134). A second edition appeared after D.'s death, in 1713.

Context. *Fables* contained 19 translations (from Chaucer, Ovid, Homer, and Boccaccio), two new original poems ('To the Duchess of Ormonde' and 'To John Driden of Chesterton'), two poems that had appeared previously (*Alexander's Feast*, and 'The Monument of a Fair Maiden Lady'), and the originals of the Chaucerian poems translated by D. The title page contains an epigraph from Virgil, *Aen.* v 55–7: *nunc ultro ad cineres ipsius et ossa parentis / (haud equidem sine mente, reor, sine numine divum) / adsumus* ('But now we stand by the ashes and bones of my father himself, not, I think, without the purpose and holy guidance of the gods'; D.'s own translation runs: 'But since this happy Storm our Fleet has driv'n, / (Not, as I deem, without the Will of Heav'n,) / Upon these friendly Shores, and flow'ry Plains, / Which hide *Anchises*, and his blest Remains' ('The Fifth Book of the *Aeneis*' ll. 69–72).

Several of D.'s letters provide glimpses of his work in progress on *Fables*. His first mention of the volume is in a letter to his cousin Mrs Steward of 2 February 1699: 'In the mean time, betwixt my intervalls of physique and other remedies which I am useing for my gravell, I am still drudging on: always a Poet, and never a good one. I pass my time sometimes with Ovid, and sometimes with our old English poet, Chaucer; translating such stories as best please my fancy; and intend besides them to add somewhat of my own: so that it is not impossible, but ere the summer be pass'd, I may come down to you with a volume in my hand, like a dog out of the water, with a duck in his mouth' (*Letters* 109). He made a further reference to the 'Book of Miscellanyes' on which he was 'still drudging' in another letter to Mrs Steward of 4 March (*Letters* 113). On 14 July he wrote to Pepys: 'I remember last year, when I had the honour of dining with you, you were pleas'd to recommend to me, the Character of Chaucer's Good Parson. Any desire of yours is a Command to me; and accordingly I have put it into my English, with such additions and alterations as I thought fit. Having translated as many Fables from Ovid, and as many Novills from Boccace and Tales from Chaucer, as will make an indifferent large volume in folio, I intend them for the press in Michaelmas Term next' (*Letters* 115). In October 1699 (probably) D. wrote to Charles Montague, enclosing a copy of 'To John Driden of Chesterton' for Montague's comments and approval, and appealing for support for the complete translation of the *Iliad*, which, he hoped, would follow the rendering of Book I included in *Fables* (*Letters* 120–1). And in a letter to Mrs Steward of 7 November 1699 D. noted that he had shown 'To the Duchess of Ormonde' and 'To John Driden of Chesterton' to the Earl of Dorset and Charles Montague, and that they 'are of opinion that I never writt better'. Other friends, he said, 'are divided in their Judgments which to preferr: but the greater part are for those to my dear Kinsman; which I have Corrected with so much care, that they will now be worthy of his Sight: & do neither of us any dishonour after our death' (*Letters* 123–4).

In the 'Preface to *Fables*' (*Poems* v 48–53) D. describes the order in which the poems in the volume were written. He started, he says, with the rendering of

Book I of Homer's *Iliad*, proceeding to those parts of Ovid's *Metamorphoses* dealing with the Trojan War, which he followed by renderings of the opening of Ovid's Book XV, and of a number of episodes from earlier books of the *Metamorphoses*. He then turned to Chaucer, then back to Ovid again, and after that to Boccaccio, adding some 'original papers' of his own. The arrangement of signatures in the volume (recommencing with Aɪʳ at 'To the Duchess of Ormonde') indicates that the Dedication and Preface were printed, and therefore probably written, last.

D. signed the agreement with Tonson for *Fables* on 20 March 1699. The document is printed by Malone (I i 560–1) and reprinted in *Works* vii 953. By that date, Tonson already had *c.* 7500 of the projected 10,000 lines for the volume in his possession. He agreed to pay D. £250 on 25 March, and to make up the sum to £300, payable to D. or to his 'executors administrators, or assigns', on the appearance of a second edition. D.'s receipt for the first payment (which in the event was £268 15s) is dated 24 March (see *Works* vii 954). The second payment was made after D.'s death to his administratrix, Lady Ann Sylvius, and is dated 11 June 1713 (see Malone I i 561; *Works* vii 954). Derrick (I xxviii) reports, on the testimony of 'one of [D.'s] collateral descendants', that the Duchess of Ormonde rewarded the poet with £500 for *Fables*. But, in the light of the 'distressed circumstances' in which the poet died, Malone (I i 328) judged that the sum was more likely to have been £100.

Various attempts have been made to suggest an overarching architectonic or thematic design in the volume as a whole – the former is problematic, since we have no certain knowledge whether D. or Tonson was responsible for the ordering of the poems. Miner 287–323 saw *Fables* as loosely organized round a number of thematic preoccupations – love, the good life, war, fate, and determinism, with Christian consolations against life's vicissitudes being set against pagan doctrines of materialism and metempsychosis. Judith Sloman (*ECS* iv (1971) 199–211) interpreted *Fables* as a systematic attempt to demonstrate the superiority of Christian virtue and humility over the martial heroism and amoral passions of the ancient world. James D. Garrison (*SEL* xxi (1981) 409–23) judged D. to be offering a balanced view of human nature that does justice both to its violently passionate and morally pious impulses, avoiding both despair and naive idealism. Cedric Reverand II *passim* suggested that *Fables* is organized on a sceptical, exploratory, and dialectical pattern, in which the affirmations of one poem are constantly undermined by others, so that the reader is not allowed to rest secure in the consolations provided by any single system of assumptions, values, or beliefs. Such a structure, Reverand argued, reflects D.'s own sense of uncertainty at the collapse of ideals and institutions to which he had devoted himself earlier in his career.

However one interprets the design of the volume in detail, it is clear that D.'s mind returned frequently during its composition to a number of central preoccupations: the nature of true virtue and nobility; the power of love, war, fate, and fortune to ennoble, confound, demean human endeavour, or to render it ridiculous; the relation of human behaviour to that of the animals, and to the workings of 'inanimate' nature; the simultaneously destructive and renovative effects of historical and natural change; the relations between the sexes.

Source. 'Palamon and Arcite' is the first of five poems in *Fables* that D. translated from Chaucer (the others being 'The Cock and the Fox', 'The Flower and the Leaf' (no longer attributed to Chaucer by modern scholars), 'The Wife of Bath her Tale' and 'The Character of a Good Parson'). In 'Palamon and Arcite' D. translates *The Knight's Tale*, which was itself a version of Boccaccio's *Teseida*. D. used *The Workes of our Antient and Lerned English Poet, Geffrey Chaucer* edited by

Thomas Speght with notes and glossary (1598), and the texts of the first four
Chaucerian poems, based on this edition, were reprinted at the end of *Fables*, the
first time that Chaucer had been printed in modern typography rather than black-
letter. (This text often differs substantively from the readings of modern editions,
and is frequently defective metrically.) Many of Speght's notes were also used to
suggest interpretations and turns of phrase. *The Knight's Tale* had been adapted
by Shakespeare and Fletcher in *The Two Noble Kinsmen* (printed 1634), but there
is no clear evidence that D. used it. D. sometimes keeps close to Chaucer (with
occasional lines retained verbatim), sometimes omits material, but more often paraphrases and expands on the original, providing a much looser rendering than he
did with his classical translations. His major departures from Chaucer are signalled
in the notes below, but the notation 'D.'s addition' only records instances where
D.'s lines have no direct equivalent or substantial source in Chaucer, and should
be regarded as an approximate guide. For a survey of D.'s changes see W. H.
Williams, *MLR* ix (1914) 161–72. For D.'s conception of 'Palamon and Arcite'
as an epic rivalling those of Homer and Virgil see Tom Mason in *Dryden and the
World of Neoclassicism*, edited by Wolfgang Görtschacher and Holger Klein (2001)
181–92, and for a discussion of D.'s handling of classical and medieval materials
see Paul Hammond in *The Age of Projects*, edited by Maximillian E. Novak (forthcoming). In the 'Preface to *Fables Ancient and Modern*' (*Poems* v 60–83) D. compares Chaucer with Ovid, and then calls Chaucer 'the father of English poetry'
who in that respect deserves veneration alongside Homer and Virgil. 'He is the
perpetual fountain of good sense', he 'followed nature everywhere', and in *The
Canterbury Tales* he shows 'the various manners and humours (as we now call
them) of the whole English nation in his age . . . here is God's plenty'. D. finds
Chaucer's versification deficient, and justifies his project of translating him into
modern English against those critics who argue either that he was not worth the
effort, or that his original language should have been respected. For D.'s work
with Chaucer generally see T. A. Mason, 'Dryden's Chaucer' (unpublished PhD
thesis, Cambridge (1977)). In 'Palamon and Arcite' there are numerous additions
that reflect on contemporary politics, specifically the deposition of James II and
accession of the usurper William III (as D. saw him). Another, more prominent,
element in the poem is the care that D. takes in imagining the religious and philosophical world of his characters: he expands passages relating to the gods; adds
astrological detail; accentuates Chaucer's already considerable interest in issues
of free will, predestination, and foreknowledge (to which he returns in 'The
Cock and the Fox') and adds many references to Fortune (for which see Paul
Hammond, *MLR* lxxx (1985) 769–85, esp. 781–4).

Reception. Fables was received with immediate enthusiasm (see *Letters* 135), and
retained its reputation throughout the eighteenth and early nineteenth centuries
(see H. G. Wright, *RES* xxi (1945) 23–37). William Congreve reflected the common view when he wrote that D. 'was an improving Writer to his last, even to
near seventy Years of Age; improving even in Fire and Imagination, as well as
in Judgement: Witness his Ode on St. *Cecilia*'s Day, and his Fables, his latest
Performances' (Dedication to D.'s *Dramatick Works*, 6 vols (1717) i sigs. a9^{r-v}).
Fables featured prominently in the elegies on D.'s death collected in *Luctus Britannici:
or The Tears of the British Muses; for the Death of John Dryden, Esq.* (1700) and *The
Nine Muses, or Poems Written by Nine Severall Ladies upon the Death of the late famous
John Dryden, Esq.* (1700) (on the latter, see Ruth Salvaggio, *Journal of Popular Culture*
xxi (1987) 75–91). See also *To the Memory of Mr. Dryden. A Poem* (1700), and
Alexander Oldys, *An Ode, by way of Elegy, on the Universally Lamented Death of*

the Incomparable Mr. Dryden (1700). Poems specifically praising *Fables* included Elizabeth Thomas's 'To [Mr Dryden], On his Fables' (*Miscellany Poems on Several Subjects* (1722)), and Jabez Hughes's *Verses Occasion'd by Reading Mr. Dryden's Fables* (1721). The volume was imitated in such works as Thomas D'Urfey's *Tales Tragical and Comical* (1704; explicitly based on *Fables*) and the anonymous *The Landlord's Tale* (1708), a version of Ariosto's *Orlando Furioso* xxviii, strongly reminiscent of *Fables* both in style and physical presentation (modern edition in *Translation and Literature* xi (2002) 206–36).

Chaucer had not been widely appreciated in the seventeenth century, particularly because his language and versification were considered unsophisticated, although he did have some admirers, including Pepys (who suggested that D. should translate 'The Character of a Good Parson' (*Letters* 116; Pepys 14 June 1663 and *n*)). D. was innovatory in regarding Chaucer as worthy to stand alongside Homer, Virgil and Ovid (see 'Preface to *Fables*' (*Poems* v 84–5) and 'To the Duchess of Ormonde' ll. 1–6), a view that contrasts with Samuel Cobb's description of Chaucer as 'our *English Ennius* . . . unskill'd in Art. / The sparkling Diamond on his Dung-hill shines' (*Poetae Britannici* (1700) 10). D.'s translations in *Fables* were influential in raising Chaucer's reputation, and stimulated many versions of Chaucerian poems in the early eighteenth century, including some by Pope (see William L. Alderson and Arnold C. Henderson, *Chaucer and Augustan Scholarship* (1970); Tom Mason in *The Oxford History of Literary Translation in English: Volume 3: 1660–1790*, edited by Stuart Gillespie and David Hopkins (2005)). D. was seen as Chaucer's heir by R. B.: 'The *British* Lawrel by Old *Chaucer* worn, / Still *Fresh* and *Gay*, did *Dryden*'s Brow Adorn' (Nahum Tate, *Panacea: A Poem upon Tea* sig. A6ʳ). Many of the elegists in *Luctus Britannici* praised his translations from Chaucer, although William Harrison (*Woodstock Park* (1706) 4) thought that D.'s versions failed because only Chaucer's language could express his thoughts. D. was buried in Chaucer's grave.

Palamon and Arcite,
or
The Knight's Tale,
From Chaucer.
In Three Books

Book I

In days of old, there lived, of mighty fame
A valiant prince, and Theseus was his name:
A chief who more in feats of arms excelled
The rising nor the setting sun beheld.

¶21. *i* 2. *Theseus*] Legendary king of Athens, whose campaign against the Amazons resulted in the capture of their queen, Hippolyta. Chaucer calls him 'duke'; D. uses *prince* (= 'ruler') or *king*.

5   Of Athens he was lord; much land he won,
     And added foreign countries to his crown:
     In Scythia with the warrior queen he strove,
     Whom first by force he conquered, then by love;
     He brought in triumph back the beauteous dame,
10   With whom her sister, fair Emilia, came.
     With honour to his home let Theseus ride,   ⎫
     With Love to friend, and Fortune for his guide, ⎬
     And his victorious army at his side.   ⎭
     I pass their warlike pomp, their proud array,
15   Their shouts, their songs, their welcome on the way:
     But, were it not too long, I would recite   ⎫
     The feats of Amazons, the fatal fight   ⎬
     Betwixt the hardy queen and hero knight;   ⎭
     The town besieged, and how much blood it cost
20   The female army, and th' Athenian host;
     The spousals of Hippolyta the queen;
     What tilts and tourneys at the feast were seen;
     The storm at their return, the ladies' fear:
     But these and other things I must forbear.
25   The field is spacious I design to sow,
     With oxen far unfit to draw the plough:
     The remnant of my tale is of a length
     To tire your patience, and to waste my strength;
     And trivial accidents shall be forborne
30   That others may have time to take their turn;
     As was at first enjoined us by mine host,   ⎫
     That he whose tale is best, and pleases most,   ⎬
     Should win his supper at our common cost.   ⎭

---

i 7. *Scythia*] Proverbially barbarous country, roughly southern Russia north of the Black Sea.
i 8. For 'with his Wisdome, and his Chiualrie'.
i 9. *dame*] female ruler (*OED* 1), archaic or self-consciously formal by this date, so perhaps part of D.'s medievalizing vocabulary.
i 12. D.'s addition, repeated almost verbatim in 'Cymon and Iphigenia' l. 518. *to*] as.
i 14–15. D.'s addition.
i 14. *proud*] magnificent; valiant (*OED* 6b, 7).
i 22. D.'s addition, adding medieval detail.   *tourneys*] tournaments.
i 29. D.'s addition.   *accidents*] events.
i 31. D.'s addition. In the General Prologue, the Host of the Tabard Inn, Southwark, from which the pilgrims set off for Canterbury, suggests that each pilgrim tell two stories on the outward and two on the return journey, and that the teller of the best story be rewarded with dinner at the other pilgrims' expense.

And therefore where I left, I will pursue ⎫
35   This ancient story, whether false or true, ⎬
In hope it may be mended with a new. ⎭
The prince I mentioned, full of high renown,
In this array drew near th' Athenian town;
When in his pomp and utmost of his pride,
40   Marching, he chanced to cast his eye aside,
And saw a choir of mourning dames, who lay
By two and two across the common way:
At his approach they raised a rueful cry,
And beat their breasts, and held their hands on high,
45   Creeping and crying, till they seized at last
His courser's bridle, and his feet embraced.
'Tell me', said Theseus, 'what and whence you are,
And why this funeral pageant you prepare?
Is this the welcome of my worthy deeds,
50   To meet my triumph in ill-omened weeds?
Or envy you my praise, and would destroy
With grief my pleasures, and pollute my joy?
Or are you injured, and demand relief?
Name your request, and I will ease your grief.'
55   The most in years of all the mourning train
Began, but sounded first away for pain;
Then scarce recovered, spoke: 'Nor envy we
Thy great renown, nor grudge thy victory;
'Tis thine, O King, th' afflicted to redress,
60   And fame has filled the world with thy success:
We wretched women sue for that alone
Which of thy goodness is refused to none:
Let fall some drops of pity on our grief,
If what we beg be just, and we deserve relief:

i 35–6. D.'s addition.
i 39. pride] magnificence, splendour (OED 6).
i 41. choir] organized group of people (OED 6). D. uses the word for a group of
ladies again at ii 313 and in 'The Lady's Song' l. 1.
i 44. D.'s addition.
i 46. courser] large, powerful horse ridden in battle (OED 1).
i 48. D.'s addition.
i 50. weeds] dress.
i 51–2. would destroy . . . my joy] D.'s addition.
i 56. sounded] swooned, fainted.
i 59–62. For 'But we beseke you of mercy and socour. / And haue mercy on
our wo and distresse'.
i 64. D.'s addition.

65   For none of us, who now thy grace implore,
     But held the rank of sovereign queen before;
     Till, thanks to giddy Chance, which never bears
     That mortal bliss should last for length of years,
     She cast us headlong from our high estate,
70   And here in hope of thy return we wait:
     And long have waited in the temple nigh,
     Built to the gracious goddess Clemency.
     But reverence thou the power whose name it bears,
     Relieve th' oppressed, and wipe the widow's tears.
75   I, wretched I, have other fortune seen,
     The wife of Capaneus, and once a queen:
     At Thebes he fell; cursed be the fatal day!
     And all the rest thou seest in this array
     To make their moan, their lords in battle lost
80   Before that town besieged by our confederate host:
     But Creon, old and impious, who commands
     The Theban city, and usurps the lands,
     Denies the rites of funeral fires to those
     Whose breathless bodies yet he calls his foes.
85   Unburned, unburied, on a heap they lie;
     Such is their fate, and such his tyranny;
     No friend has leave to bear away the dead,
     But with their lifeless limbs his hounds are fed.'

i 66. sovereign queen] Queen who rules in her own right (like Mary II) not as a consort; for 'dutchess or a quene'.

i 67–9. For 'Now be we caytifs [wretches], as it is well isene: / Thanked be fortune, and her false whele, / That none estate assureth for to be wele [well]'.

i 73–4. D.'s addition.

i 75. have other fortune seen] D.'s addition.

i 76. Capaneus] One of the Seven against Thebes, the leaders of the army that besieged Thebes on behalf of Polynices after his brother Eteocles had refused to share the sovereignty with him. The two brothers (sons of Oedipus) killed each other, and the crown of Thebes passed to their uncle Creon. Capaneus climbed on the walls, boasting that not even Zeus could stop him, and was killed by a thunderbolt. The story is told in Aeschylus' *Seven against Thebes*, and its aftermath in Sophocles' *Antigone* and Euripides' *Suppliant Women*; in the latter the mothers of the fallen warriors, who are denied burial by Creon, appeal to Theseus to avenge them and give them a decent funeral.

i 81. Creon] He succeeded his brother-in-law Oedipus as king of Thebes.

i 82. usurps the lands] D.'s addition, with contemporary political implications.

i 84. yet] still.

i 86. tyranny] This word and its cognates recur in the poem: see i 270, ii 168, iii 228, 671, and 669–72n.

i 87. D.'s addition.

At this she screaked aloud, the mournful train
90   Echoed her grief, and grovelling on the plain
With groans, and hands upheld, to move his mind,
Besought his pity to their helpless kind!
        The prince was touched, his tears began to flow,
And, as his tender heart would break in two,
95   He sighed; and could not but their fate deplore,
So wretched now, so fortunate before.
Then lightly from his lofty steed he flew,
And raising one by one the suppliant crew,
To comfort each full solemnly he swore
100   That by the faith which knights to knighthood bore,
And whate'er else to chivalry belongs,
He would not cease, till he revenged their wrongs:
That Greece should see performed what he declared,
And cruel Creon find his just reward.
105   He said no more, but shunning all delay
Rode on, nor entered Athens on his way:
But left his sister and his queen behind,
And waved his royal banner in the wind:
Where in an argent field the god of war
110   Was drawn triumphant on his iron car;
Red was his sword, and shield, and whole attire,
And all the godhead seemed to glow with fire;
Ev'n the ground glittered where the standard flew,
And the green grass was dyed to sanguine hue.
115   High on his pointed lance his pennon bore
His Cretan fight, the conquered Minotaur:

i 89. screaked] uttered a harsh cry, screeched (_OED_).
i 92. kind] sex, gender (_OED_ 7).
_i 93._ D.'s addition.
_i 95._ D.'s addition.   _deplore_] weep for.
i 96. so fortunate before] For 'That whylom [once] were of so great estate'.
i 98. crew] company, group of people (_OED_ 3); not derogatory.
_i 101–2._ D.'s addition.
i 107. sister] sister-in-law, i.e. Emily.
i 109. argent] silver.   _field_] background colour of a flag or shield.
_i 110._ D.'s addition.   _car_] chariot.
_i 112._ D.'s addition.
_i 114._ D.'s addition.   _sanguine_] bloody.
_i 116._ The Athenians were compelled by Minos, king of Crete, to send an annual tribute of seven young men and seven young women to be sacrificed to the Minotaur (half-man, half-bull), which lived in a labyrinth. Theseus fought and killed him.

The soldiers shout around with generous rage,
And in that victory their own presage.
He praised their ardour, inly pleased to see
His host the flower of Grecian chivalry.
All day he marched, and all th' ensuing night,
And saw the city with returning light.
The process of the war I need not tell,
How Theseus conquered, and how Creon fell:
Or after, how by storm the walls were won,
Or how the victor sacked and burned the town:
How to the ladies he restored again
The bodies of their lords in battle slain,
And with what ancient rites they were interred:
All these to fitter time shall be deferred:
I spare the widows' tears, their woeful cries
And howling at their husbands' obsequies;
How Theseus at these funerals did assist,
And with what gifts the mourning dames dismissed.
    Thus when the victor chief had Creon slain,
And conquered Thebes, he pitched upon the plain
His mighty camp, and when the day returned
The country wasted, and the hamlets burned;
And left the pillagers, to rapine bred,
Without control to strip and spoil the dead.
    There, in a heap of slain, among the rest
Two youthful knights they found beneath a load oppressed
Of slaughtered foes, whom first to death they sent,
The trophies of their strength, a bloody monument.
Both fair, and both of royal blood they seemed,
Whom kinsmen to the crown the heralds deemed;
That day in equal arms they fought for fame;
Their swords, their shields, their surcoats were the same.
Close by each other laid they pressed the ground,
Their manly bosoms pierced with many a grisly wound;
Nor well alive, nor wholly dead they were,
But some faint signs of feeble life appear:

120

125

130

135

140

145

150

---

i 117–19. D.'s addition.   *generous*] high-spirited, courageous (OED 2b).   *rage*] martial
spirit (OED 9, citing this example).   *inly*] inwardly.
i 133. *assist*] be present at a ceremony (OED 4).
i 143–4, 147. D.'s additions.
i 148. *surcoats*] garments worn over armour, showing the knights' coats of arms.
i 149–50, 152–4. D.'s additions.

The wandering breath was on the wing to part,
Weak was the pulse, and hardly heaved the heart.
155   These two were sisters' sons; and Arcite one,
Much famed in fields, with valiant Palamon.
From these their costly arms the spoilers rent,
And softly both conveyed to Theseus' tent;
Whom known of Creon's line, and cured with care,
160   He to his city sent as prisoners of the war,
Hopeless of ransom, and condemned to lie
In durance, doomed a lingering death to die.
    This done, he marched away with warlike sound,
And to his Athens turned, with laurels crowned,
165   Where happy long he lived, much loved, and more
    renowned.
But in a tower, and never to be loosed,
The woeful captive kinsmen are enclosed.
    Thus year by year they pass, and day by day,
Till once ('twas on the morn of cheerful May)
170   The young Emilia, fairer to be seen
Than the fair lily on the flowery green,
More fresh than May herself in blossoms new
(For with the rosy colour strove her hue)
Waked as her custom was before the day
175   To do th' observance due to sprightly May:
For sprightly May commands our youth to keep
The vigils of her night, and breaks their sluggard sleep:
Each gentle breast with kindly warmth she moves,
Inspires new flames, revives extinguished loves.
180   In this remembrance Emily ere day
Arose, and dressed herself in rich array;
Fresh as the month, and as the morning fair:
Adown her shoulders fell her length of hair;
A ribbon did the braided tresses bind,
185   The rest was loose, and wantoned in the wind.

i 156. fields] battlefields.
i 158. softly] gently, avoiding causing injury (OED 1).
i 159. D.'s addition.
i 161. Hopeless of] without hope of.
i 162. D.'s addition.   durance] imprisonment (OED 5).
i 178. kindly] natural (OED 1), pertaining to sexual desire and procreation (not in OED, except weakly in 5b). Cp. 'Lucretius: The Beginning of the First Book' l. 27.
i 179, 182. D.'s additions.
i 185. D.'s addition.   wantoned] played, moved freely (OED 1d).

Aurora had but newly chased the night,
And purpled o'er the sky with blushing light,
When to the garden walk she took her way,   ⎱
To sport and trip along in cool of day,   ⎰
190   And offer maiden vows in honour of the May. ⎰
        At every turn she made a little stand,
And thrust among the thorns her lily hand
To draw the rose, and every rose she drew
She shook the stalk, and brushed away the dew:
195   Then particoloured flowers of white and red
She wove, to make a garland for her head:
This done, she sung and carolled out so clear
That men and angels might rejoice to hear.
Ev'n wondering Philomel forgot to sing,
200   And learned from her to welcome in the spring.
The tower, of which before was mention made,
Within whose keep the captive knights were laid,
Built of a large extent, and strong withal,
Was one partition of the palace wall:
205   The garden was enclosed within the square
Where young Emilia took the morning air.
        It happened Palamon, the prisoner knight,
Restless for woe, arose before the light,
And with his jailer's leave desired to breathe
210   An air more wholesome than the damps beneath.
This granted, to the tower he took his way,
Cheered with the promise of a glorious day:
Then cast a languishing regard around,   ⎱
And saw with hateful eyes the temples crowned   ⎰
215   With golden spires, and all the hostile ground. ⎰
        He sighed, and turned his eyes, because he knew

i *186–7.* For 'at sunne uprist'.
i *186. Aurora*] the dawn.
i *189–94.* D.'s addition.
i *197–200.* For 'And as an angel, heuenly she song'.
i *197. carolled*] sang joyfully (*OED* 2).
i *199. Philomel*] the nightingale.
i *204. partition*] part, section (*OED* 4).
i *208.* For 'wofull'.
i *209–10. desired . . . beneath*] D.'s addition. *damps*] noxious vapours (*OED* 1).
i *212–19.* For 'In which he all the noble cite sighe'.
i *214–15.* Cp. Milton: 'the glorious Temple . . . / . . . topped with golden spires' (*PR* 544–8; J. R. Mason). *hateful*] full of hate.

'Twas but a larger jail he had in view:
Then looked below, and from the castle's height
Beheld a nearer and more pleasing sight:
220 The garden, which before he had not seen, }
In spring's new livery clad of white and green,
Fresh flowers in wide parterres, and shady walks
between.
This viewed, but not enjoyed, with arms across
He stood, reflecting on his country's loss;
225 Himself an object of the public scorn,
And often wished he never had been born.
At last (for so his Destiny required)
With walking giddy, and with thinking tired,
He through a little window cast his sight,
230 Though thick of bars that gave a scanty light:
But ev'n that glimmering served him to descry
Th' inevitable charms of Emily.
      Scarce had he seen, but seized with sudden smart,
Stung to the quick, he felt it at his heart;
235 Struck blind with overpowering light he stood,
Then started back amazed, and cried aloud.
      Young Arcite heard, and up he ran with haste
To help his friend, and in his arms embraced;
And asked him why he looked so deadly wan,
240 And whence, and how his change of cheer began?
Or who had done th' offence? 'But if', said he,
'Your grief alone is hard captivity,
For love of heaven, with patience undergo
A cureless ill, since Fate will have it so:
245 So stood our horoscope in chains to lie,

i *220–2.* For 'And eke [also] the gardyn full of braunches greene'.
i *222.* Cp. Milton: 'shade / . . . and . . . walks between' (*PL* ix 1106–7; Noyes).
i *223–5.* D.'s addition, possibly with contemporary political resonance.
i *223. with arms across*] The conventional posture of the melancholy man; cp. *Threnodia Augustalis* l. 193 (*Works*).
i *227. Destiny*] For 'auenture or caas' [by chance or accident].
i *228, 231.* D.'s additions.
i *232. inevitable*] D.'s addition.
i *233–6.* For 'And therewith he blent [turned pale], and cried, ha, / As though he stongen were to the herte'. *Works* notes that D. takes 'blent' in both the senses offered in Speght's glossary, 'blind' and 'turn back'.
i *238.* D.'s addition.
i *240. cheer*] facial expression; frame of mind (*OED* 2, 3).
i *244–5.* For 'Fortune hath yeuen vs this aduersitie'.

And Saturn in the dungeon of the sky,
Or other baleful aspect, ruled our birth,
When all the friendly stars were under earth:
Whate'er betides, by Destiny 'tis done,
250   And better bear like men, than vainly seek to shun.'
'Nor of my bonds', said Palamon again,
'Nor of unhappy planets I complain;
But when my mortal anguish caused my cry,
That moment I was hurt through either eye;
255   Pierced with a random shaft, I faint away
And perish with insensible decay:
A glance of some new goddess gave the wound,
Whom, like Actaeon, unaware I found.
Look how she walks along yon shady space: ⎫
260   Not Juno moves with more majestic grace,   ⎬
And all the Cyprian Queen is in her face.   ⎭
If thou art Venus (for thy charms confess
That face was formed in heaven) nor art thou less,
Disguised in habit, undisguised in shape,
265   O help us captives from our chains to scape;
But if our doom be passed in bonds to lie
For life, and in a loathsome dungeon die,
Then be thy wrath appeased with our disgrace,
And show compassion to the Theban race,
270   Oppressed by tyrant power!' While yet he spoke,
Arcite on Emily had fixed his look;
The fatal dart a ready passage found,

i 246. Saturn] considered astrologically to be a malevolent planet; see iii 381–419.
dungeon] mansion (OED 3b); here, astrologically the house (sector of the sky) of
the ruling planet (cp. quotation from Lydgate cited in OED 3b).
i 247. aspect] in astrology the relative position of the planets (OED 4).
i 248. D.'s addition.   under earth] so not visible at the time of their birth, and
hence unable to influence their destiny.
i 249–50. For 'We mote [must] endure; this is short and playn'.
i 252, 255–6. D.'s additions.
i 256. insensible] not perceived by the senses (OED 1a), i.e. because internal.
i 258. D.'s addition.   Actaeon] He came unexpectedly on the goddess Diana while
she was bathing, and as a punishment was turned into a stag, and then torn apart
by his own hounds (Met. iii 173–252).
i 260. D.'s addition.
i 261. Cyprian Queen] Venus.
i 262. confess] reveal (OED 5).
i 264. D.'s addition; an Ovidian 'turn'.   habit] clothing.
i 266. doom] sentence.
i 272–3. For 'her bewte hurt him so'.

And deep within his heart infixed the wound:
So that if Palamon were wounded sore,
275   Arcite was hurt as much as he, or more:
Then from his inmost soul he sighed, and said,
'The beauty I behold has struck me dead;
Unknowingly she strikes, and kills by chance;
Poison is in her eyes, and death in every glance.
280   O, I must ask—nor ask alone, but move
Her mind to mercy, or must die for love.'
     Thus Arcite: and thus Palamon replies
(Eager his tone, and ardent were his eyes):
'Speak'st thou in earnest, or in jesting vein?'   ⎫
285   'Jesting', said Arcite, 'suits but ill with pain.'   ⎬
'It suits far worse', said Palamon again,   ⎭
And bent his brows, 'with men who honour weigh,
Their faith to break, their friendship to betray;
But worst with thee, of noble lineage born,
290   My kinsman, and in arms my brother sworn.
Have we not plighted each our holy oath,
That one should be the common good of both?
One soul should both inspire, and neither prove
His fellow's hindrance in pursuit of love?
295   To this before the gods we gave our hands,
And nothing but our death can break the bands.
This binds thee, then, to farther my design,
As I am bound by vow to farther thine:
Nor canst, nor dar'st thou, traitor, on the plain
300   Appeach my honour, or thy own maintain,
Since thou art of my counsel, and the friend
Whose faith I trust, and on whose care depend:

i 273. *infixed*] implanted firmly (*OED*).
i 278–9. D.'s addition, alluding to the basilisk, a snake whose glance was said to kill.
i 287–8. For 'It were . . . to the[e] no great honour / To be false, ne for to be traytour / To me'.
i 293. D.'s addition.
i 299. *on the plain*] Either (i) 'on the open field of combat' (*OED* plain *sb.*¹ 2); or (ii) 'openly, without prevarication or ambiguity' (cp. the modern idiom 'on the level'); in this second case perhaps a version of (a) *OED* plain *adj.* 11–12, 'honest, candid; free from ambiguity or evasion', or of (b) *OED* plain *sb.*¹ 4, 'open, flat surface', for which *OED* cites only literal not figurative usages. It was prompted by Chaucer's 'in the payne' ('by torture').
i 300. *Appeach*] cast an imputation on, asperse (*OED* 3).
i 301. *of my counsel*] one of my private advisers (*OED* 6).
i 302. D.'s addition.

And wouldst thou court my lady's love, which I
Much rather than release, would choose to die?
305   But thou, false Arcite, never shalt obtain
Thy bad pretence; I told thee first my pain:
For first my love began ere thine was born;
Thou, as my counsel, and my brother sworn,
Art bound t' assist my eldership of right,
310   Or justly to be deemed a perjured knight.'
      Thus Palamon. But Arcite with disdain
In haughty language thus replied again:
'Forsworn thyself: the traitor's odious name
I first return, and then disprove thy claim.
315   If love be passion, and that passion nursed
With strong desires, I loved the lady first.
Canst thou pretend desire, whom zeal inflamed
To worship, and a power celestial named?
Thine was devotion to the blessed above,
320   I saw the woman, and desired her love;
First owned my passion, and to thee commend
Th' important secret, as my chosen friend.
Suppose (which yet I grant not) thy desire
A moment elder than my rival fire;
325   Can chance of seeing first thy title prove?
And know'st thou not, no law is made for love?
Law is to things which to free choice relate;
Love is not in our choice, but in our fate:
Laws are but positive: love's power we see
330   Is Nature's sanction, and her first decree.

i 306. pretence] assertion of right, claim; purpose, object (OED 1, 3).
i 308. counsel] adviser, counsellor (OED 7b).
i 309. eldership of right] D.'s addition, perhaps with political resonance.
i 313–14. traitor, claim] D.'s language has political resonance, where Chaucer uses
'false'.
i 315–16. For 'I loued her first'.
i 317. pretend] claim.
i 325. D.'s addition.   title] claim, right.
i 327–38. For 'Loue is a gretter lawe by my pan [skull] / Than may be yeuen to
any earthly man, / And therfore posityfe lawe, and such decre / Is broken all
day for loue in eche degre. / A man mote [must] nedes loue, maugre [despite]
his heed, / He may nat fleen it though he shuld be deed, / All be she maide,
widowe, or wife'.
i 329–30. For D.'s interest in the relationship between nature and law see ii 337n.
i 329. positive] arbitrary, derived from custom rather than nature (OED 1);
'posityfe' in Chaucer.
i 330. sanction] law, decree.

Each day we break the bond of human laws
For love, and vindicate the common cause.
Laws for defence of civil rights are placed,
Love throws the fences down, and makes a general waste:
335   Maids, widows, wives, without distinction fall;
The sweeping deluge, love, comes on, and covers all.
If then the laws of friendship I transgress, ⎫
I keep the greater, while I break the less; ⎬
And both are mad alike, since neither can possess. ⎭
340   Both hopeless to be ransomed, never more
To see the sun, but as he passes o'er.
    'Like Aesop's hounds contending for the bone,
Each pleaded right, and would be lord alone:
The fruitless fight continued all the day;
345   A cur came by, and snatched the prize away.
As courtiers therefore jostle for a grant,
And when they break their friendship, plead their want,
So thou, if Fortune will thy suit advance,
Love on; nor envy me my equal chance:
350   For I must love, and am resolved to try
My fate, or failing in th' adventure die.'
    Great was their strife, which hourly was renewed,
Till each with mortal hate his rival viewed;
Now friends no more, nor walking hand in hand,
355   But when they met, they made a surly stand,
And glared like angry lions as they passed,
And wished that every look might be their last.

---

i *331. human*] Humane *1700*. The normal spelling of 'human' in the seventeenth
century was 'humane', with the accent on the first syllable, as here. During the
eighteenth century the spelling 'humane' (now accented on the second syllable)
became restricted to the sense 'showing sympathy for the needs of others'
(*OED*). D.'s meaning here is primarily 'produced by human society rather than
by nature'.
i *332. vindicate*] cite as justification (approx. *OED* 3).
i *340–1. never . . . o'er*] D.'s addition.
i *342–5.* The story is approximately the same as Aesop's fable of the lion and the bear.
i *343.* D.'s addition, perhaps with political resonance.
i *345. cur*] Thus Speght; MSS of Chaucer have 'kyte' (Kinsley).
i *346–7.* For 'at king's court . . . / Eche man for him selfe, there is none other'.
i *348–9.* For 'Loue if thou list [wish]'. D. adds the philosophical vocabulary.
i *350–1. resolved to try / My fate*] D.'s addition.
i *351. adventure*] hazardous enterprise (*OED* 5a).
i *352–7. which hourly . . . their last*] D.'s addition.

It chanced at length Perithous came, t' attend
This worthy Theseus, his familiar friend:
360   Their love in early infancy began,
And rose as childhood ripened into man;
Companions of the war; and loved so well ⎫
That when one died, as ancient stories tell, ⎬
His fellow to redeem him went to hell. ⎭
365   But to pursue my tale: to welcome home
His warlike brother is Perithous come:
Arcite of Thebes was known in arms long since,
And honoured by this young Thessalian prince.
Theseus, to gratify his friend and guest,
370   Who made our Arcite's freedom his request,
Restored to liberty the captive knight,
But on these hard conditions I recite:
That if hereafter Arcite should be found
Within the compass of Athenian ground,
375   By day or night, or on whate'er pretence,
His head should pay the forfeit of th' offence.
To this Perithous for his friend agreed,
And on his promise was the prisoner freed.
    Unpleased and pensive hence he takes his way,
380   At his own peril; for his life must pay.
Who now but Arcite mourns his bitter fate,
Finds his dear purchase, and repents too late?
'What have I gained', he said, 'in prison pent,
If I but change my bonds for banishment?
385   And banished from her sight, I suffer more
In freedom, than I felt in bonds before;
Forced from her presence, and condemned to live:
Unwelcome freedom, and unthanked reprieve!

---

i 358. *Perithous*] Close friend of Theseus; the two men were said to have ventured
down to the underworld, in one account to obtain Persephone as a bride for
Perithous, but there appears to be no classical source for Chaucer's idea that one
went to retrieve the other from death.
i 359. *familiar friend*] Biblical phrase (Psalm xli 9).
i 361–2. *And rose . . . the war*] D.'s addition.
i 365–6. *to welcome . . . come*] D.'s addition.
i 368. *Thessalian*] from Thessaly, a region of northern Greece.
i 377–8. D.'s addition.
i 379. *pensive*] sorrowful, gloomy (*OED* 3).
i 382. D.'s addition.
i 383–90. For 'Now is my prison worse than beforne, / Now is me shapen
[destined] eternally to dwell / Nought in purgatory, but in hell'.

      Heaven is not but where Emily abides,
390   And where she's absent, all is hell besides.
      Next to my day of birth, was that accursed
      Which bound my friendship to Perithous first:
      Had I not known that prince, I still had been
      In bondage, and had still Emilia seen:
395   For though I never can her grace deserve,
      'Tis recompense enough to see and serve.
      O Palamon, my kinsman and my friend,
      How much more happy fates thy love attend!
      Thine is th' adventure, thine the victory;
400   Well has thy Fortune turned the dice for thee:
      Thou on that angel's face may'st feed thy eyes,
      In prison, no, but blissful paradise!
      Thou daily seest that sun of beauty shine,
      And lov'st at least in love's extremest line.
405   I mourn in absence, love's eternal night,   ⎫
      And who can tell but since thou hast her sight, ⎬
      And art a comely, young, and valiant knight,   ⎭
      Fortune (a various power) may cease to frown,
      And by some ways unknown thy wishes crown:
410   But I, the most forlorn of human kind,
      Nor help can hope, nor remedy can find;
      But doomed to drag my loathsome life in care,
      For my reward must end it in despair.
      Fire, water, air, and earth, and force of fates
415   That governs all, and heaven that all creates,
      Nor art, nor Nature's hand can ease my grief,
      Nothing but death, the wretch's last relief:
      Then farewell youth, and all the joys that dwell

i 398. D.'s addition.
i 399. adventure] chance (OED 1).
i 404–5. D.'s addition.
i 404. i.e. you do at least love in the outer reaches: Palamon may be separated from
Emily in prison, but at least her beauty reaches him there.   line] limit, boundary
(OED 17); line on the terrestrial sphere farthest from the sun (OED 10). From
Terence, Eunuchus 640–1: certe extrema linea / amare haud nil est ('certainly to love
in the extreme line is almost nothing') (W. H. Williams, MLR vi (1911) 386).
i 408. various] changeable, fickle (OED 2); cp. varium et mutabile semper / femina
('a changeable and mutable thing is woman always': Virgil, Aen. iv 569–70).
i 410–12. D.'s addition.
i 414–19. force of fates . . . farewell] For 'Ne creature that of him maked is / That
may me heale, or done comfort in this, / Wel ought I sterue [die] in wan hope
[despair] and distresse, / Farewell my life, my lust [delight], and my gladnesse'.

With youth and life, and life itself farewell.
420   'But why, alas! do mortal men in vain
         Of Fortune, Fate, or Providence complain?
         God gives us what he knows our wants require,
         And better things than those which we desire:
         Some pray for riches; riches they obtain,
425   But watched by robbers, for their wealth are slain:
         Some pray from prison to be freed, and come
         When guilty of their vows, to fall at home;
         Murdered by those they trusted with their life,
         A favoured servant, or a bosom wife.
430   Such dear-bought blessings happen every day,
         Because we know not for what things to pray.
         Like drunken sots about the streets we roam:
         Well knows the sot he has a certain home,
         Yet knows not how to find th' uncertain place,
435   And blunders on, and staggers every pace.
         Thus all seek happiness; but few can find,
         For far the greater part of men are blind.
         This is my case, who thought our utmost good
         Was in one word of freedom understood:
440   The fatal blessing came: from prison free,
         I starve abroad, and lose the sight of Emily.'
             Thus Arcite; but if Arcite thus deplore

---

i 421. Fortune, Fate, or Providence] For 'Of purveyance [foresight, providence] of
God, or of fortune'. D.'s terms are not synonyms, and Kinsley suggests that D.
recalls Boethius' distinction between *providentia* and *fatum*: 'the mind of God has
set up a plan for the multitude of events. When this plan is thought of as in the
purity of God's understanding, it is called Providence, and when it is thought of
with reference to all things, whose motions and order it controls, it is called by
the name the ancients gave it, Fate. Providence is the divine reason itself . . . Fate
is the planned order inherent in all things subject to change through the medium
of which Providence binds everything in its allotted place' (*De Consolatione
Philosophiae* iv 6; tr. V. E. Watts). Although an allusion by D. to Boethius would
be in tune with Chaucer's admiration for him, it would also be possible to interpret *Fate* as referring to the classical idea that man's destiny is determined (in
Greek mythology, by the three Moirai who spin and cut man's thread of life).
Fate and *Providence* would thus distinguish between classical and Christian beliefs.
Fortune is a late Roman goddess who acts capriciously (Boethius ii 1; D., 'Horace:
Odes III xxxix' ll. 73–87n).
i 427. guilty of] bound to the performance of (*OED* 4; last example).
i 428–9. For 'is by his meyne [members of his household] slain'; D. adds the wife.
i 437. D.'s addition.
i 441. starve] die, esp. a lingering death, e.g. from grief (*OED* 1).
i 442–3. D.'s addition.
i 442. deplore] weep for.

His sufferings, Palamon yet suffers more.
For when he knew his rival freed and gone,
445 He swells with wrath, he makes outrageous moan;
He frets, he fumes, he stares, he stamps the ground;
The hollow tower with clamours rings around:
With briny tears he bathed his fettered feet,
And dropped all o'er with agony of sweat.
450 'Alas!' he cried, 'I wretch in prison pine,
Too happy rival, while the fruit is thine:
Thou liv'st at large, thou draw'st thy native air,
Pleased with thy freedom, proud of my despair:
Thou mayst, since thou hast youth and courage joined,
455 A sweet behaviour, and a solid mind,
Assemble ours and all the Theban race
To vindicate on Athens thy disgrace;
And after (by some treaty made) possess
Fair Emily, the pledge of lasting peace.
460 So thine shall be the beauteous prize, while I
Must languish in despair, in prison die.
Thus all th' advantage of the strife is thine,
Thy portion double joys, and double sorrows mine.'
    The rage of jealousy then fired his soul,
465 And his face kindled like a burning coal:
Now cold despair, succeeding in her stead,
To livid paleness turns the glowing red.
His blood, scarce liquid, creeps within his veins,
Like water which the freezing wind constrains.
470 Then thus he said: 'Eternal deities,
Who rule the world with absolute decrees,
And write whatever time shall bring to pass
With pens of adamant on plates of brass,
What is the race of human kind your care
475 Beyond what all his fellow-creatures are?

i *445–6.* D.'s addition.
i *449.* D.'s addition.   *dropped*] dripped.
i *453. proud of*] pleased at (*OED* 2).
i *454–5. youth . . . mind*] For 'wisedom and manhed'.
i *455. behaviour*] Meanings included 'external appearance' (*OED* 1d).   *solid mind*]
reliable judgement in practical matters (*OED* solid 12b).
i *457. vindicate*] revenge (*OED* 1).
i *465–9.* For 'and hent [seized] him by the hert / So woodly [madly] that he
likely was to behold / The boxe tree, or the assen [ash] dead and cold'.
i *467. livid*] of bluish leaden colour (*OED* 1).
i *473. adamant*] legendary hard rock or mineral.

He with the rest is liable to pain,
And like the sheep, his brother-beast, is slain.
Cold, hunger, prisons, ills without a cure,
All these he must, and guiltless oft, endure:
480   Or does your justice, power, or prescience fail,
When the good suffer, and the bad prevail?
What worse to wretched virtue could befall,
If Fate, or giddy Fortune, governed all?
Nay, worse than other beasts' is our estate:
485   Them to pursue their pleasures you create,
We, bound by harder laws, must curb our will,
And your commands, not our desires fulfil.
Then, when the creature is unjustly slain,
Yet after death at least he feels no pain;
490   But man in life surcharged with woe before,
Not freed when dead, is doomed to suffer more.
A serpent shoots his sting at unaware,
An ambushed thief forelays a traveller:
The man lies murdered, while the thief and snake,
495   One gains the thickets, and one threads the brake.
This let divines decide; but well I know,
Just or unjust, I have my share of woe:
Through Saturn seated in a luckless place,
And Juno's wrath, that persecutes my race,
500   Or Mars and Venus in a quartile, move
My pangs of jealousy for Arcite's love.'
       Let Palamon oppressed in bondage mourn,
While to his exiled rival we return.
By this the sun declining from his height,
505   The day had shortened to prolong the night:

i 476. D.'s addition.
i 477. brother-] D.'s addition, perhaps influenced by the arguments in 'Of the
Pythagorean Philosophy' ll. 256–9.
i 480–3. For 'What gouernance is in this prescience / That giltlesse turmenteth
innocence, / And encreaseth thus all my penaunce'.
i 480. prescience] foreknowledge.
i 484. D.'s addition.   estate] condition.
i 490. surcharged] overburdened.
i 493. ambushed] lying in ambush.   forelays] lies in wait for (OED 1).
i 495. brake] ferns, bracken (OED sb.¹); bushes, thickets (OED sb.²).
i 498. seated in a luckless place] placed in an unfavourable astrological position. D.'s
addition.
i 499. See ii 92–3n.
i 500. quartile] aspect of two heavenly bodies which are 90° apart from each other,
an unfavourable position astrologically. D.'s addition.

The lengthened night gave length of misery
Both to the captive lover, and the free.
For Palamon in endless prison mourns,
And Arcite forfeits life if he returns.
510 The banished never hopes his love to see,
Nor hopes the captive lord his liberty;
'Tis hard to say who suffers greater pains:
One sees his love, but cannot break his chains;
One free, and all his motions uncontrolled,
515 Beholds whate'er he would, but what he would behold.
Judge as you please, for I will haste to tell
What fortune to the banished knight befell.
      When Arcite was to Thebes returned again,
The loss of her he loved renewed his pain;
520 What could be worse, than never more to see
His life, his soul, his charming Emily?
He raved with all the madness of despair,
He roared, he beat his breast, he tore his hair.
Dry sorrow in his stupid eyes appears,
525 For wanting nourishment, he wanted tears:
His eye-balls in their hollow sockets sink,
Bereft of sleep; he loathes his meat and drink.
He withers at his heart, and looks as wan
As the pale spectre of a murdered man:
530 That pale turns yellow, and his face receives
The faded hue of sapless boxen leaves:
In solitary groves he makes his moan,
Walks early out, and ever is alone.
Nor mixed in mirth, in youthful pleasure shares,
535 But sighs when songs and instruments he hears:
His spirits are so low, his voice is drowned, ⎫
He hears as from afar, or in a swound, ⎬
Like the deaf murmurs of a distant sound: ⎭
Uncombed his locks, and squalid his attire,
540 Unlike the trim of love and gay desire;

---

i 518. Editorial paragraph.
i 522–3. D.'s addition.
i 524. *stupid*] stupified, insensible (*OED* 1b); cp. 'The Third Book of the *Georgics*'
l. 781: 'His Eyes are settled in a stupid peace'.
i 525. D.'s addition, an Ovidian 'turn'.   *wanting*] lacking.
i 531. D.'s addition, from an earlier line in Chaucer (see ll. 465–9*n* above).   *boxen*]
of the box tree.
i 534, 537–9. D.'s additions.
i 537. *swound*] swoon, fainting fit.

But full of museful mopings, which presage
The loss of reason, and conclude in rage.
    This when he had endured a year and more,
Now wholly changed from what he was before,
545   It happened once, that slumbering as he lay
He dreamt (his dream began at break of day)
That Hermes o'er his head in air appeared,
And with soft words his drooping spirits cheered:
His hat, adorned with wings, disclosed the god,
550   And in his hand he bore the sleep-compelling rod:
Such as he seemed, when at his sire's command
On Argus' head he laid the snaky wand.
'Arise', he said, 'to conquering Athens go,
There Fate appoints an end of all thy woe.'
555   The fright awakened Arcite with a start,
Against his bosom bounced his heaving heart;
But soon he said, with scarce recovered breath,
'And thither will I go, to meet my death,
Sure to be slain; but death is my desire,
560   Since in Emilia's sight I shall expire.'
By chance he spied a mirror while he spoke,
And gazing there beheld his altered look;
Wondering, he saw his features and his hue
So much were changed, that scarce himself he knew.
565   A sudden thought then starting in his mind,
'Since I in Arcite cannot Arcite find,
The world may search in vain with all their eyes,
But never penetrate through this disguise.
Thanks to the change which grief and sickness give,
570   In low estate I may securely live,
And see unknown my mistress day by day.'
He said; and clothed himself in coarse array,
A labouring hind in show. Then forth he went,
And to th' Athenian towers his journey bent.
575   One squire attended in the same disguise,

i 538. *deaf*] muffled (*OED* 5).
i 541. *museful*] absorbed in thought (*OED*, citing this example).
i 542. D.'s addition.   *rage*] madness (*OED* 1, citing this example).
i 547. *Hermes*] messenger of the gods.
i 552. *Argus*] The many-eyed watchman who guarded Io at Hera's request; Hermes lulled him to sleep and killed him. See 'The First Book of Ovid's *Metamorphoses*' ll. 856–1004.
i 556–7. D.'s addition.
i 566–8. D.'s addition. Line 566 is another Ovidian 'turn'.
i 573. *hind*] agricultural labourer.

Made conscious of his master's enterprise.
Arrived at Athens, soon he came to court,
Unknown, unquestioned in that thick resort;
Proffering for hire his service at the gate,
580 To drudge, draw water, and to run or wait.
        So fair befell him, that for little gain
He served at first Emilia's chamberlain;
And watchful all advantages to spy,
Was still at hand, and in his master's eye;
585 And as his bones were big, and sinews strong,
Refused no toil that could to slaves belong;
But from deep wells with engines water drew,
And used his noble hands the wood to hew.
He passed a year at least attending thus
590 On Emily, and called Philostratus.
But never was there man of his degree
So much esteemed, so well beloved as he.
So gentle of condition was he known,
That through the court his courtesy was blown:
595 All think him worthy of a greater place,
And recommend him to the royal grace;
That exercised within a higher sphere,
His virtues more conspicuous might appear.
Thus by the general voice was Arcite praised,
600 And by great Theseus to high favour raised;
Among his menial servants first enrolled,
And largely entertained with sums of gold:
Besides what secretly from Thebes was sent
Of his own income, and his annual rent.
605 This well employed, he purchased friends and fame,
But cautiously concealed from whence it came.
Thus for three years he lived with large increase
In arms of honour, and esteem in peace;
To Theseus' person he was ever near,
610 And Theseus for his virtues held him dear.

The end of the first book.

i 576. *conscious*] aware of a secret.
i 578. D.'s addition.   *resort*] crowd (*OED* 5).
i 593. *gentle*] noble.
i 594. *blown*] talked about (*OED* blow v.¹ 13).
i 605. D.'s addition.
i 607. *increase*] accented on the second syllable.
i 609. D.'s addition.

Book II

While Arcite lives in bliss, the story turns
Where hopeless Palamon in prison mourns.
For six long years immured, the captive knight
Had dragged his chains, and scarcely seen the light:
5   Lost liberty and love at once he bore;
His prison pained him much, his passion more:
Nor dares he hope his fetters to remove,
Nor ever wishes to be free from love.
   But when the sixth revolving year was run,
10 And May within the Twins received the sun,
Were it by chance, or forceful destiny,
Which forms in causes first whate'er shall be,
Assisted by a friend one moonless night,
This Palamon from prison took his flight:
15 A pleasant beverage he prepared before
Of wine and honey mixed, with added store
Of opium; to his keeper this he brought,
Who swallowed unaware the sleepy draught,
And snored secure till morn, his senses bound
20 In slumber, and in long oblivion drowned.
Short was the night, and careful Palamon
Sought the next covert ere the rising sun.
A thick-spread forest near the city lay,
To this with lengthened strides he took his way
25 (For far he could not fly, and feared the day):
Safe from pursuit, he meant to shun the light,
Till the brown shadows of the friendly night
To Thebes might favour his intended flight.
When to his country come, his next design

---

ii 3. *six*] 'seuen' in Chaucer; cp. ii 368.
ii 4, 7–8. D.'s additions.
ii 10. *Twins*] the astrological sign Gemini, which the sun enters on 21 May (11 May in D.'s day). D. adds the astrological detail.
ii 12. For 'As when a thing is shapen, it shal be'. *causes*] A philosophical term: Aristotle identified four causes, 'efficient', 'formal', 'material', and 'final' (see *OED* s.v. cause sb. 5). D.'s *causes first* should not be read as referring to the philosophers' 'first cause' or God (which could not be plural): D. means that before events take place, destiny first fashions the causes which will bring these events about.
ii 15–16. Speght glosses Chaucer's *clarrie* as 'wine and honey mingled' (*Works*).
ii 18. D.'s addition. *draught*] Pronounced in this period to rhyme with *brought*.
ii 27. *brown*] dark (*OED* 1).

30 Was all the Theban race in arms to join,
    And war on Theseus, till he lost his life,
    Or won the beauteous Emily to wife.
    Thus while his thoughts the lingering day beguile,
    To gentle Arcite let us turn our style,
35 Who little dreamt how nigh he was to care,
    Till treacherous Fortune caught him in the snare.
    The morning lark, the messenger of day,
    Saluted in her song the morning grey,
    And soon the sun arose with beams so bright
40 That all th' horizon laughed to see the joyous sight;
    He with his tepid rays the rose renews,
    And licks the dropping leaves, and dries the dews;
    When Arcite left his bed, resolved to pay
    Observance to the month of merry May:
45 Forth on his fiery steed betimes he rode,
    That scarcely prints the turf on which he trod:
    At ease he seemed, and prancing o'er the plains
    Turned only to the grove his horse's reins—
    The grove I named before; and lighting there
50 A woodbine garland sought to crown his hair;
    Then turned his face against the rising day,
    And raised his voice to welcome in the May.
        'For thee, sweet month, the groves green liveries wear:
    If not the first, the fairest of the year;
55 For thee the Graces lead the dancing Hours,
    And Nature's ready pencil paints the flowers:

ii 33. D.'s addition.
ii 34. turn our style] turn to another subject (*style* = stylus, pen) (*OED*'s last example).
ii 40. laughed] Attributed poetically to inanimate objects 'chiefly with reference to movement or play of light and colour which is apprehended as the expression of joyous feeling' (*OED* 1c).
ii 41. D.'s addition.
ii 42. dropping] dripping [with dew] (*OED* 1b).
ii 45. betimes] early.
ii 46. D.'s addition.
ii 49. lighting] alighting.
ii 50. woodbine] used of various climbing plants, including convolvulus, ivy, and honeysuckle; the last is probably meant here.
ii 51. against] towards.
ii 53–62. For '*Maie*, with all thy floures and thy grene, / Welcome be thou, faire freshe *Maie*, / I hope that I some grene get maie'.
ii 55. Cp. Milton: 'while universal Pan / Knit with the Graces and the Hours in dance / Led on the eternal spring' (*PL* iv 266–8; J. R. Mason).
ii 56. pencil] paintbrush.

When thy short reign is past, the feverish sun
The sultry tropic fears, and moves more slowly on.
So may thy tender blossoms fear no blight,
60   Nor goats with venomed teeth thy tendrils bite,
As thou shalt guide my wandering feet to find
The fragrant greens I seek, my brows to bind.'
    His vows addressed, within the grove he strayed, ⎫
Till Fate, or Fortune, near the place conveyed   ⎬
65   His steps where secret Palamon was laid.   ⎭
Full little thought of him the gentle knight,   ⎫
Who flying death had there concealed his flight, ⎬
In brakes and brambles hid, and shunning mortal sight. ⎭
And less he knew him for his hated foe,
70   But feared him as a man he did not know.
But as it has been said of ancient years,
That fields are full of eyes, and woods have ears;
For this the wise are ever on their guard,
For unforeseen, they say, is unprepared.
75   Uncautious Arcite thought himself alone,
And less than all suspected Palamon,
Who listening heard him, while he searched the grove,
And loudly sung his roundelay of love.
But on the sudden stopped, and silent stood,
80   As lovers often muse, and change their mood,
Now high as heaven, and then as low as hell;
Now up, now down, as buckets in a well:
For Venus, like her day, will change her cheer,
And seldom shall we see a Friday clear.

ii 58–9. The tropic is where the sun is furthest from the equator and seems to turn back towards it. The *sultry tropic* is the one which it reaches in summer. The sun's apparent north–south movement slows as it changes direction (*Works*).
ii 64. *Fate, or Fortune*] For 'by aduenture' (chance).
ii 66. D.'s addition.   *gentle*] noble.
ii 68. D.'s addition.   *brakes*] ferns, bracken (*OED sb.*¹); bushes, thickets (*OED sb.*²).
ii 70. D.'s addition.
ii 72. Proverbial (Tilley F 209).
ii 74. Also proverbial, generally in the positive version 'forewarned is forearmed' (Tilley H 54). For 'For all daie men mete at vnset steuin [unexpected time]'.
ii 78. *roundelay*] short song with a refrain (*OED*).
ii 83. *cheer*] disposition, mood; facial expression (*OED* 3a, 2a).
ii 84. For 'Selde is the *Friday* all the week alike'. Friday was often regarded as the most unlucky or inauspicious weekday, probably because it was the day of the crucifixion (Bonnie Blackburn and Leofranc Holford-Strevens, *The Oxford Companion to the Year* (1999) 580–1). The weather on Fridays was also said to be either a predictor of Sunday's weather, or particularly variable (G. L. Apperson, *English Proverbs and Proverbial Phrases* (1929)).

85   Thus Arcite having sung, with altered hue
     Sunk on the ground, and from his bosom drew
     A desperate sigh, accusing heaven and Fate,
     And angry Juno's unrelenting hate.
     'Cursed be the day when first I did appear;
90   Let it be blotted from the calendar,
     Lest it pollute the month, and poison all the year.
     Still will the jealous Queen pursue our race?
     Cadmus is dead, the Theban city was;
     Yet ceases not her hate: for all who come
95   From Cadmus are involved in Cadmus' doom.
     I suffer for my blood: unjust decree
     That punishes another's crime on me!
     In mean estate I serve my mortal foe,
     The man who caused my country's overthrow.
100 This is not all, for Juno, to my shame,
     Has forced me to forsake my former name;
     Arcite I was, Philostratus I am.
     That side of heaven is all my enemy:
     Mars ruined Thebes, his mother ruined me.
105 Of all the royal race remains but one
     Beside myself, th' unhappy Palamon,
     Whom Theseus holds in bonds, and will not free;
     Without a crime, except his kin to me.
     Yet these, and all the rest, I could endure,
110 But love's a malady without a cure:
     Fierce Love has pierced me with his fiery dart,
     He fries within, and hisses at my heart.
     Your eyes, fair Emily, my fate pursue;

ii 87–8. accusing . . . hate] D.'s addition; l. 88 echoes 'The First Book of the *Aeneis*'
l. 2.
ii 89–91. Cp. Job iii 1–6 (Noyes, citing Warton).
ii 90–1. D.'s addition.
ii 92–3. Cadmus was the legendary founder of Thebes. Juno was incensed by
Jupiter's adultery with Cadmus' sister Europa and his daughter Semele (Ovid, *Met.*
ii 833–75, iii 261–309). She destroyed Semele, and extended her hatred to their
relatives (*Met.* iii 258–9). She drove Cadmus' daughter Ino and her husband Athamas
insane (*Met.* iv 416–542; Dante, *Inferno* xxx 1–12). Cadmus' family was often
regarded as cursed: his grandson Pentheus was torn apart by Bacchantes, while
his great-grandson Laius was killed by his own son Oedipus; Oedipus' sons Eteocles
and Polynices killed each other (see i 76*n*).
ii 96–7. unjust . . . me] D.'s addition.
ii 99. D.'s addition, the wording allowing a contemporary political allusion.
ii 103, 108. D.'s additions.
ii 112. fries] burns.
ii 113. fate] death.

I suffer for the rest, I die for you.
115 Of such a goddess no time leaves record,
Who burned the temple where she was adored:
And let it burn, I never will complain,
Pleased with my sufferings, if you knew my pain.'
At this a sickly qualm his heart assailed,
120 His ears ring inward, and his senses failed.
No word missed Palamon of all he spoke,
But soon to deadly pale he changed his look:
He trembled every limb, and felt a smart,
As if cold steel had glided through his heart;
125 Nor longer stayed, but starting from his place
Discovered stood, and showed his hostile face:
'False traitor Arcite, traitor to thy blood,
Bound by thy sacred oath to seek my good,
Now art thou found forsworn for Emily,
130 And dar'st attempt her love for whom I die.
So hast thou cheated Theseus with a wile,
Against thy vow returning to beguile
Under a borrowed name: as false to me,
So false thou art to him who set thee free:
135 But rest assured, that either thou shalt die,
Or else renounce thy claim in Emily:
For though unarmed I am, and (freed by chance)
Am here without my sword or pointed lance,
Hope not, base man, unquestioned hence to go,
140 For I am Palamon thy mortal foe.'
Arcite, who heard his tale, and knew the man,
His sword unsheathed, and fiercely thus began:
'Now by the gods who govern heaven above,
Wert thou not weak with hunger, mad with love,
145 That word had been thy last, or in this grove
This hand should force thee to renounce thy love.

---

ii 115–18. D.'s addition, echoing Thomas Carew: 'Of such a Goddesse no times
leave record, / That burnt the temple where she was ador'd' ('A cruell Mistris'
ll. 17–18; Noyes citing Warton).   record] Stressed on the second syllable.
ii 119–20. Adapted from Lucretius, De Rerum Natura iii 153–6 (Kinsley).
ii 119. qualm] fit of faintness or sickness (OED 1).
ii 126. D.'s addition.   discovered] revealed.
ii 137. by chance] For 'by grace'.
ii 139. D.'s addition.   unquestioned] without being challenged or confronted
(OED question v. 1b, c).
ii 146. D.'s addition.

The surety which I gave thee, I defy;   ⎫
Fool, not to know that love endures no tie, ⎬
And Jove but laughs at lovers' perjury.   ⎭
150   Know I will serve the fair in thy despite,
But since thou art my kinsman, and a knight,
Here, have my faith: tomorrow in this grove
Our arms shall plead the titles of our love:
And heaven so help my right, as I alone
155   Will come, and keep the cause and quarrel both unknown,
With arms of proof both for myself and thee;
Choose thou the best, and leave the worst to me.
And, that at better ease thou mayst abide,
Bedding and clothes I will this night provide,
160   And needful sustenance, that thou mayst be
A conquest better won, and worthy me.'
His promise Palamon accepts, but prayed
To keep it better than the first he made.
Thus fair they parted till the morrow's dawn,
165   For each had laid his plighted faith to pawn.
O Love! Thou sternly dost thy power maintain, ⎫
And wilt not bear a rival in thy reign;   ⎬
Tyrants and thou all fellowship disdain.   ⎭
This was in Arcite proved, and Palamon,
170   Both in despair, yet each would love alone.
Arcite returned, and, as in honour tied,
His foe with bedding and with food supplied;
Then, ere the day, two suits of armour sought,
Which borne before him on his steed he brought:
175   Both were of shining steel, and wrought so pure
As might the strokes of two such arms endure.
Now, at the time, and in th' appointed place,
The challenger and challenged, face to face,
Approach; each other from afar they knew,
180   And from afar their hatred changed their hue.

ii *147. defy*] renounce, repudiate (*OED* 1b, citing only Chaucer).
ii *149.* D.'s addition. Proverbial (Tilley J 82; *Romeo and Juliet* II ii 92–3).
ii *152. faith*] promise, pledge.
ii *153. titles*] claims.
ii *156. of proof*] tried and tested (*OED* 10).
ii *158, 161, 163.* D.'s additions.
ii *165. pawn*] pledge (*OED sb.* 1).
ii *168. Tyrants*] D.'s addition.
ii *170–2.* D.'s addition.

So stands the Thracian herdsman with his spear,
Full in the gap, and hopes the hunted bear,
And hears him rustling in the wood, and sees
His course at distance by the bending trees,
185　　And thinks, 'Here comes my mortal enemy,
And either he must fall in fight, or I.'
This while he thinks, he lifts aloft his dart,
A generous chillness seizes every part,
The veins pour back the blood, and fortify the heart.
190　　　　Thus pale they meet; their eyes with fury burn;
None greets, for none the greeting will return;
But in dumb surliness, each armed with care
His foe professed, as brother of the war:
Then both, no moment lost, at once advance
195　　Against each other, armed with sword and lance:
They lash, they foin, they pass, they strive to bore
Their corslets, and the thinnest parts explore.
Thus two long hours in equal arms they stood,
And wounded wound, till both were bathed in blood;
200　　And not a foot of ground had either got,
As if the world depended on the spot.
Fell Arcite like an angry tiger fared,
And like a lion Palamon appeared:
Or as two boars whom love to battle draws,
205　　With rising bristles, and with frothy jaws,
Their adverse breasts with tusks oblique they wound;
With grunts and groans the forest rings around.
So fought the knights, and fighting must abide,

ii *182. hopes*] expects, waits for (*OED* 4).
ii *187–9.* D.'s addition.
ii *187. dart*] spear.
ii *188. generous*] strong, powerful (*OED* 6).
ii *194.* D.'s addition.
ii *196–201.* For 'Thei foinen eche at other wonder long'.
ii *196. lash*] make a sudden movement; aim a blow at, strike out violently (*OED*
1, 2a, b).   *foin*] lunge, thrust with a pointed weapon (*OED*).   *pass*] thrust, lunge
(*OED* 24, last example).   *bore*] pierce, stab with a weapon (*OED* 1b).
ii *197. corslets*] armour covering the torso.   *explore*] test, try out (senses taken from
the Latin *explorare*; *OED* 1 cites only Milton, *PL* ii 632); probe (*OED* 2b, of a
wound, first example 1767).
ii *198. in equal arms*] equally matched in battle (*OED* equal 4b).
ii *202. Fell*] fierce, savage.
ii *205–7.* For 'That frothen white as fome for ire woode [mad]'.
ii *206. adverse*] opposing.

Till Fate an umpire sends their difference to decide.
210 The power that ministers to God's decrees,
And executes on earth what heaven foresees,
Called Providence, or Chance, or Fatal Sway,
Comes with resistless force, and finds or makes her way.
Nor kings, nor nations, nor united power
215 One moment can retard th' appointed hour.
And some one day some wondrous chance appears,
Which happened not in centuries of years:
For sure, whate'er we mortals hate or love,
Or hope, or fear, depends on powers above:
220 They move our appetites to good or ill,
And by foresight necessitate the will.
In Theseus this appears, whose youthful joy
Was beasts of chase in forests to destroy;
This gentle knight, inspired by jolly May, ⎫
225 Forsook his easy couch at early day, ⎬
And to the wood and wilds pursued his way. ⎭
Beside him rode Hippolyta the queen,
And Emily, attired in lively green;
With horns, and hounds, and all the tuneful cry,
230 To hunt a royal hart within the covert nigh;
And as he followed Mars before, so now
He serves the goddess of the silver bow.
The way that Theseus took was to the wood
Where the two knights in cruel battle stood:
235 The laund on which they fought, th' appointed place

ii 209. D.'s addition.
ii 210–15. For 'The destinie, and the minister generall, / That executeth in the
worlde ouer all / The purueyance [foresight] that God hath said* beforne, / So
strong it is, that though the world had sworne / The contrary of thing be ye
[by yea] and naie'. *'seyn' [seen] in modern editions.
ii 213. resistless] irresistible.
ii 214. Nor . . . nor] neither . . . nor (again at l. 375).
ii 218–21. For 'For certainly our appetites here, / Be it of warre, peace, hate or loue,
/ All is ruled by the sight aboue'. D. also expands on Chaucer's interest in foreknowledge and predestination in 'The Cock and the Fox' ll. 508–48 (q.v.).
ii 221. necessitate] bring under necessity, compel, force (OED 1c, citing this example).
ii 224. gentle] noble (again at l. 332).
ii 226. D.'s addition.
ii 229. cry] pack of hounds (OED 13).
ii 232. goddess of the silver bow] Diana, goddess of hunting.
ii 234. D.'s addition.
ii 235. laund] glade, open space within a wood (OED).

In which th' uncoupled hounds began the chase.
Thither forthright he rode to rouse the prey,
That shaded by the fern in harbour lay;
And thence dislodged, was wont to leave the wood
240   For open fields, and cross the crystal flood.
Approached, and looking underneath the sun,
He saw proud Arcite and fierce Palamon,
In mortal battle doubling blow on blow;
Like lightning flamed their falchions to and fro,
245   And shot a dreadful gleam; so strong they struck
There seemed less force required to fell an oak.
He gazed with wonder on their equal might,
Looked eager on, but knew not either knight.
Resolved to learn, he spurred his fiery steed
250   With goring rowels to provoke his speed.
The minute ended that began the race,
So soon he was betwixt 'em on the place;
And with his sword unsheathed, on pain of life
Commands both combatants to cease their strife.
255   Then with imperious tone pursues his threat:
'What are you? Why in arms together met?
How dares your pride presume against my laws,
As in a listed field to fight your cause?
Unasked the royal grant, no marshal by,
260   As knightly rites require, nor judge to try?'
Then Palamon, with scarce recovered breath,
Thus hasty spoke: 'We both deserve the death,
And both would die; for look the world around,
A pair so wretched is not to be found.
265   Our life's a load; encumbered with the charge
We long to set th' imprisoned soul at large.

ii *236–40.* D.'s addition.
ii *238. harbour*] covert or place of retreat of wild animals (*OED* 3c).
ii *244, 599. falchions*] broad swords.
ii *245. struck*] Spelt *strook* in *1700*, suggesting a good rhyme with *oak*.
ii *247, 252, 255.* D.'s additions.
ii *258. listed*] prepared with palisades for a tournament (*OED*'s only previous example is 'listed field' in Milton, *Samson Agonistes* l. 1087 (1671)).
ii *259. marshal*] officer who supervised a tournament.
ii *263–6.* For 'Two wofyl wretches been we and caitiues [wretches], / That been encombred of our own liues'.
ii *265.* Cp. 'If life be grown a load' ('Lucretius: Against the Fear of Death' l. 135).

Now as thou art a sovereign judge, decree ⎫
The rightful doom of death to him and me: ⎬
Let neither find thy grace, for grace is cruelty. ⎭
270 Me first, O kill me first, and cure my woe,
Then sheathe the sword of justice on my foe:
Or kill him first, for when his name is heard
He foremost will receive his due reward.
Arcite of Thebes is he, thy mortal foe,
275 On whom thy grace did liberty bestow,
But first contracted, that if ever found
By day or night upon th' Athenian ground,
His head should pay the forfeit: see returned
The perjured knight, his oath and honour scorned.
280 For this is he, who with a borrowed name
And proffered service, to thy palace came,
Now called Philostratus: retained by thee, ⎫
A traitor trusted, and in high degree, ⎬
Aspiring to the bed of beauteous Emily. ⎭
285 My part remains: from Thebes my birth I own,
And call myself th' unhappy Palamon.
Think me not like that man, since no disgrace
Can force me to renounce the honour of my race.
Know me for what I am: I broke thy chain,
290 Nor promised I thy prisoner to remain:
The love of liberty with life is given,
And life itself th' inferior gift of heaven.
Thus without crime I fled; but farther know
I with this Arcite am thy mortal foe:
295 Then give me death, since I thy life pursue:
For safeguard of thyself, death is my due.
More wouldst thou know? I love bright Emily,
And for her sake, and in her sight will die:

ii 268–9. For 'Ne yeue [give] us neither mercie ne refuge'.
ii 268. doom] verdict, sentence (again at ll. 300, 307).
ii 269, 275, 327, 391. grace] mercy, forgiveness (OED 15).
ii 273. D.'s addition.
ii 275–9. For 'That fro thy land is banished on his hedde, / For which he hath deserued to be dedde'.
ii 287–8, 290–3. D.'s additions.
ii 293. without crime I fled] Chaucer says the opposite: 'That hath thy prison broke wickedly'.
ii 295–6. D.'s addition.

But kill my rival too, for he no less   ⎫
300   Deserves, and I thy righteous doom will bless,   ⎬
      Assured that what I lose, he never shall possess.' ⎭
      To this replied the stern Athenian prince,
      And sourly smiled: 'In owning your offence
      You judge yourself, and I but keep record
305   In place of law, while you pronounce the word.
      Take your desert, the death you have decreed;
      I seal your doom, and ratify the deed.
      By Mars, the patron of my arms, you die.'
          He said; dumb sorrow seized the standers by.
310   The queen above the rest, by nature good,
      (The pattern formed of perfect womanhood)
      For tender pity wept; when she began
      Through the bright choir th' infectious virtue ran.
      All dropped their tears, ev'n the contended maid,
315   And thus among themselves they softly said:
      'What eyes can suffer this unworthy sight!
      Two youths of royal blood, renowned in fight,
      The mastership of heaven in face and mind,
      And lovers, far beyond their faithless kind.
320   See their wide streaming wounds—they neither came
      From pride of empire, nor desire of fame:
      Kings fight for kingdoms, madmen for applause,
      But love for love alone, that crowns the lover's cause.'
      This thought, which ever bribes the beauteous kind,
325   Such pity wrought in every lady's mind,
      They left their steeds, and prostrate on the place

---

ii 300–1. and I . . . possess] D.'s addition.

ii 302–3. stern . . . sourly] For 'worthy'.

ii 304. record] stressed on the second syllable.

ii 305–7. D.'s addition.

ii 309–16. For 'The quene anon for very woman hedde / Gan for to wepe and so did *Emelye*, / And all the ladies in the companie'.

ii 313. choir] organized group of people (*OED* 6).   *virtue*] i.e. pity; but cp. the sense of 'power (eg. in plants) to affect the human body' (*OED* 9, 11).

ii 314. contended] striven for, disputed (*OED*'s first example).

ii 317–19. For 'For gentilmen thei were of great estate, / And nothing but for loue was this debate'.

ii 318. mastership] Perhaps (i) ascendancy (*OED* 1), i.e. their beauty and intellect show heaven's ascendancy; or (ii) masterpiece (not in *OED*), i.e. they are heaven's supreme creation (for this usage cp. *Threnodia Augustalis* l. 445, 'The Cock and the Fox' l. 470); or (iii) a misprint for 'masterpiece'.

ii 321–5. D.'s addition, with a glance at the warrior King William III in ll. 321–2.

ii 324. kind] sex, gender (*OED* 7).

From the fierce king implored th' offenders' grace.
He paused a while, stood silent in his mood,
(For yet his rage was boiling in his blood)
330   But soon his tender mind th' impression felt
(As softest metals are not slow to melt,
And pity soonest runs in gentle minds)
Then reasons with himself; and first he finds
His passion cast a mist before his sense,
335   And either made or magnified th' offence.
Offence! of what? to whom? Who judged the cause?
The prisoner freed himself by nature's laws:

ii 330–1. D.'s addition.

ii 333–40. For 'And although his ire her gilt accused, / Yet in his reason he hem both excused: / As thus: he thought well that euery man / Woll helpe himselfe in loue all that he can, / And eke deliuer himself out of prison'. D. adds the emphasis on nature's laws (see next note), and on man being born free.

ii 337. nature's laws] The idea of nature's laws interested D. throughout his career, especially towards its end. It relates to two distinct areas: (i) the principles by which the physical world operates, which can be known by the human mind's rational investigations (the principal sense in the quotation from the *Georgics* below); (ii) the principles upon which human rights and duties are founded, often appealed to as a source of authority higher than social custom or the laws of the state (as in this instance by Palamon in ii 291; and cp. *AA* l. 458). Although distinct, the two ideas are linked by the shared vocabulary, thus implying that both kinds of law are grounded in the same power (sometimes personified as the female figure of 'Nature'). Taking his bearings partly from Montaigne's essay 'Des Cannibales', which drew on the encounter with the native peoples of the Americas to question European definitions of nature and culture, the civilized and the wild, D. in his early plays explored the 'natural' life of indigenous peoples and its clash with the civilization represented by invading Spanish armies (see 'Prologue to *The Indian Queen*', esp. ll. 7–10). In *1 Conquest of Granada* he coined the phrase 'the noble savage' (later made famous in expositions of Rousseau) in a speech by Almanzor that prefigures Palamon's assertion of freedom: 'But whence hast thou the right to give me death? / Obey'd as Soveraign by thy Subjects be, / But know, that I alone am King of me. / I am as free as Nature first made man / 'Ere the base Laws of Servitude began / When wild in woods the noble Savage ran' (I i 204–9). See also *HP* i 243–50. His interest in the concept is often mediated through classical texts: D. explored the folly of man trying to evade the laws of Nature (personified) in 'Lucretius: Against the Fear of Death', and in 'The Second Book of the *Georgics*' he writes: 'Happy the Man, who, studying Nature's Laws, / Thro' known Effects can trace the secret Cause' (ll. 698–9). In *Fables* the topic is addressed particularly in 'Cinyras and Myrrha' (see headnote) when Myrrha queries why incest is prohibited for humans but not for other animals; in 'Sigismonda and Guiscardo' when Sigismonda challenges her father's views on nobility derived from blood; and in 'Of the Pythagorean Philosophy', which includes a long exposition of the laws of nature as understood by Pythagoras, particularly concerning the relationships between humans and animals. D. frequently introduces the idea of *nature's laws*, sometimes without explicit warrant in his originals: see (e.g.) 'Sigismonda and Guiscardo' l. 517, 'Theodore and Honoria' l. 219, 'Of the Pythagorean Philosophy' ll. 8, 89, 125, 150.

Born free, he sought his right; the man he freed
Was perjured, but his love excused the deed.
340　Thus pond'ring, he looked under with his eyes,
And saw the women's tears, and heard their cries,
Which moved compassion more; he shook his head,
And softly sighing to himself he said:
　　'Curse on th' unpard'ning prince, whom tears can draw
345　To no remorse, who rules by lion's law;
And deaf to prayers, by no submission bowed,
Rends all alike, the penitent and proud.'
At this, with look serene, he raised his head,
Reason resumed her place, and passion fled.
350　Then thus aloud he spoke: 'The power of Love
In earth, and seas, and air, and heaven above,
Rules, unresisted, with an awful nod,
By daily miracles declared a god:
He blinds the wise, gives eyesight to the blind,
355　And moulds and stamps anew the lover's mind.
Behold that Arcite, and this Palamon,
Freed from my fetters, and in safety gone:
What hindered either in their native soil
At ease to reap the harvest of their toil?
360　But Love, their lord, did otherwise ordain,
And brought 'em in their own despite again
To suffer death deserved; for well they know
'Tis in my power, and I their deadly foe.
The proverb holds, that to be wise and love
365　Is hardly granted to the gods above.
See how the madmen bleed: behold the gains
With which their master, Love, rewards their pains:

---

ii 340. looked under] looked down (*OED look v.* 44; only example).
ii 349. For 'when his ire was thus agone'.
ii 350–1. Recalling 'Lucretius: The Beginning of the First Book' ll. 1–3.
ii 351. D.'s addition.
ii 352. awful] awesome, awe inspiring.　*nod*] the gesture of authority attributed to Jove.
ii 354–5. D.'s addition; exemplified in 'Cymon and Iphigenia'.
ii 360–2. But Love . . . deserved] D.'s addition.
ii 361. in their own despite] in spite of themselves (*OED despite* 5f).
ii 364–5. Adapting 'Who may be a fool, but if he loue, / Behold for Goddes sake, that sitteth aboue, / See how they blede'. D. translates the aphorism *amare et sapere vix deo conceditur* ('to love and to be wise is hardly conceded to God': Publilius Syrus, *Sententiae* xxii); quoted by Speght from Seneca (Kinsley); see Tilley L 558.

For seven long years, on duty every day,
Lo their obedience, and their monarch's pay;
370   Yet, as in duty bound, they serve him on;
And ask the fools, they think it wisely done.
Nor ease, nor wealth, nor life itself regard,
For 'tis their maxim, love is love's reward.
This is not all: the fair for whom they strove
375   Nor knew before, nor could suspect their love,
Nor thought, when she beheld the fight from far,
Her beauty was th' occasion of the war.
But sure a general doom on man is passed,
And all are fools and lovers, first or last.
380   This both by others and myself I know,
For I have served their sovereign, long ago;
Oft have been caught within the winding train ⎤
Of female snares, and felt the lover's pain, ⎪
And learned how far the god can human hearts ⎬
   constrain. ⎦
385   To this remembrance, and the prayers of those
Who for th' offending warriors interpose,
I give their forfeit lives—on this accord,
To do me homage as their sovereign lord,
And as my vassals, to their utmost might,
390   Assist my person, and assert my right.'
This freely sworn, the knights their grace obtained;
Then thus the king his secret thoughts explained:
'If wealth, or honour, or a royal race,
Or each, or all, may win a lady's grace,
395   Then either of you knights may well deserve
A princess born, and such is she you serve:
For Emily is sister to the crown,
And but too well to both her beauty known:
But should you combat till you both were dead,

ii 372–3. D.'s addition. Line 373 is proverbial (Tilley L 515).
ii 376–7. D.'s addition.
ii 378. doom] sentence.
ii 381–3. Greek legend associated Theseus with several women besides Hippolyta:
he abandoned Ariadne on Naxos after she had helped him to kill the Minotaur;
he married her sister Phaedra; and he abducted Helen.
ii 390. D.'s addition. assert my right] defend (OED assert 2) my throne [against
enemies or rival claimants].
ii 394. grace] favour, acceptance.
ii 397–8. is sister . . . known] D.'s addition.

400 Two lovers cannot share a single bed:
     As therefore both are equal in degree,
     The lot of both be left to Destiny.
     Now hear th' award, and happy may it prove
     To her, and him who best deserves her love.
405 Depart from hence in peace, and free as air,
     Search the wide world, and where you please repair;
     But on the day when this returning sun
     To the same point through every sign has run,
     Then each of you his hundred knights shall bring
410 In royal lists to fight before the king;
     And then the knight whom Fate or happy Chance
     Shall with his friends to victory advance,
     And grace his arms so far in equal fight
     From out the bars to force his opposite,
415 Or kill, or make him recreant on the plain,
     The prize of valour and of love shall gain;
     The vanquished party shall their claim release,
     And the long jars conclude in lasting peace.
     The charge be mine t' adorn the chosen ground,
420 The theatre of war, for champions so renowned;
     And take the patron's place of either knight,   ⎫
     With eyes impartial to behold the fight;   ⎬
     And heaven of me so judge, as I shall judge aright. ⎭
     If both are satisfied with this accord,
425 Swear by the laws of knighthood on my sword.'
         Who now but Palamon exults with joy?
     And ravished Arcite seems to touch the sky.
     The whole assembled troop was pleased as well,
     Extolled th' award, and on their knees they fell
430 To bless the gracious king. The knights with leave
     Departing from the place, his last commands receive;
     On Emily with equal ardour look,

---

ii *403. award*] judge's decision (*OED* 1).
ii *404.* D.'s addition.
ii *407–8.* D. adds the astrological phrasing.
ii *410, 440. lists*] palisades erected for a tournament.
ii *411. Fate or happy Chance*] D.'s addition.
ii *412–22.* D.'s expansion of Chaucer.
ii *414.* i.e. to force his opponent out of the enclosure formed by the barriers.
ii *415. recreant*] one who surrenders (*OED* B 1).
ii *418. jars*] conflicts.
ii *425, 431–3, 435.* D.'s additions.

And from her eyes their inspiration took.
From thence to Thebes' old walls pursue their way,
435   Each to provide his champions for the day.
      It might be deemed on our historian's part
Or too much negligence, or want of art,
If he forgot the vast magnificence
Of royal Theseus, and his large expense.
440   He first enclosed for lists a level ground,
The whole circumference a mile around:
The form was circular, and all without
A trench was sunk, to moat the place about.
Within, an amphitheatre appeared,
445   Raised in degrees, to sixty paces reared:
That when a man was placed in one degree,
Height was allowed for him above to see.
      Eastward was built a gate of marble white,
The like adorned the western opposite.
450   A nobler object than this fabric was
Rome never saw, nor of so vast a space.
For, rich with spoils of many a conquered land,
All arts and artists Theseus could command
Who sold for hire, or wrought for better fame:
455   The master painters and the carvers came.
So rose within the compass of the year
An age's work, a glorious theatre.
Then, o'er its eastern gate was raised above
A temple, sacred to the Queen of Love;
460   An altar stood below; on either hand
A priest with roses crowned, who held a myrtle wand.
      The dome of Mars was on the gate opposed,
And on the north a turret was enclosed,

ii 437. *Or . . . or*] Either . . . or.
ii 438. *magnificence*] the Aristotelian virtue of liberality of expenditure combined with
good taste (*OED* 1); sovereign bounty or munificence (*OED* 2); again at l. 664.
ii 445. *degrees*] steps.
ii 451. *Rome*] For 'yearth'.
ii 452. D.'s addition.
ii 454. For 'That *Theseus* ne gaue him mete and wages'.
ii 456–7. For 'That Theatre to make and deuise'.
ii 460–1. *on either hand . . . wand*] D.'s addition.
ii 461. *myrtle*] The plant was held to be sacred to Venus, and an emblem of love
(William Lily, *Christian Astrology* (1647) 75).
ii 462. *dome*] temple (not in *OED*; from Latin *domus dei*, 'house of god'); cp.
AA ll. 868–9*n*.

Within the wall, of alabaster white ⎫
465   And crimson coral, for the Queen of Night, ⎬
Who takes in sylvan sports her chaste delight. ⎭
   Within these oratories might you see
Rich carvings, portraitures, and imagery,
Where every figure to the life expressed
470   The godhead's power to whom it was addressed.
In Venus' temple on the sides were seen
The broken slumbers of enamoured men;
Prayers that ev'n spoke, and pity seemed to call,
And issuing sighs that smoked along the wall;
475   Complaints, and hot desires, the lover's hell,
And scalding tears, that wore a channel where they fell;
And all around were nuptial bonds, the ties ⎫
Of love's assurance, and a train of lies, ⎬
That, made in lust, conclude in perjuries. ⎭
480   Beauty, and Youth, and Wealth, and Luxury,
And sprightly Hope, and short-enduring Joy,
And sorceries to raise th' infernal powers,
And sigils framed in planetary hours:
Expense, and Afterthought, and idle Care,
485   And Doubts of motley hue, and dark Despair;
Suspicions, and fantastical Surmise,
And Jealousy suffused with jaundice in her eyes
Discolouring all she viewed, in tawny dressed,

---

ii 465. *Queen of Night*] Diana, goddess of hunting and virginity.
ii 466, 619. *sylvan*] of the woods.
ii 470, 473. D.'s additions.
ii 474. *smoked*] rose like smoke (*OED* 2b).
ii 477–9. For 'The othes that her couenauntes assuren'.
ii 480–9. These abstract nouns (and those later at ii 561ff) are probably to be thought of as allegorical figures represented pictorially on the walls, and are therefore capitalized here. (The capitalization in *1700* is profuse, and therefore does not necessarily denote personification.)
ii 483. D.'s addition. *sigils*] occult signs in astrology supposed to have secret powers (*OED*). *planetary hours*] Astrologically each day is divided into 12 hours from sunrise to sunset, and each night into a further 12 from sunset to sunrise. Each hour is governed by a planet: the first hour after sunrise belongs to the planet after which the day is named (e.g. the Sun on Sunday), and the subsequent hours are allocated in the sequence Saturn, Jupiter, Mars, Sun, Venus, Mercury, Moon (*Riverside Chaucer*, edited by Larry D. Benson (1987) 837).
ii 485–6. D.'s addition.
ii 485. *motley*] many coloured.
ii 487–8. For 'That weared [wore] of yelowe goldes a garlande'.

Down-looked, and with a cuckoo on her fist.
490   Opposed to her, on t' other side, advance
       The costly feast, the carol, and the dance,
       Minstrels and music, poetry and play,
       And balls by night, and tournaments by day.
       All these were painted on the wall, and more,
495   With acts and monuments of times before,
       And others added by prophetic doom,
       And lovers yet unborn, and loves to come:
       For there th' Idalian mount, and Citheron,
       The court of Venus, was in colours drawn:
500   Before the palace gate, in careless dress,
       And loose array, sat portress Idleness:
       There by the fount Narcissus pined alone, ⎫
       There Samson was, with wiser Solomon,   ⎬
       And all the mighty names by love undone: ⎭
505   Medea's charms were there, Circean feasts,
       With bowls that turned enamoured youth to beasts.
       Here might be seen that beauty, wealth, and wit,

ii 489. down-looked] with downcast glance (Noyes).   *cuckoo*] symbolically (and etymologically) linked with 'cuckold'.
ii 490. D.'s addition.
ii 491. carol] ring dance accompanied by a song; feast of which this was a feature (*OED* 1).
ii 495–7. D.'s addition.
ii 495. acts and monuments] A wry allusion to John Foxe's *Actes and Monuments* (1563), a catalogue of the sufferings of Protestant martyrs under Catholic persecution.
ii 496. doom] discernment (*OED* 3b); cp. 'With sure foresight, and with unerring Doom, / He sees what is, and was, and is to come' ('The Fourth Book of the *Georgics*' ll. 565–6; *OED*'s sole example of this sense after 1496).
ii 497. And] Perhaps *And* (an easy compositorial error through dittography) should be emended to *Of*.
ii 498. Idalian mount] Mt Idalus in Cyprus was sacred to Venus.   *Citheron*] Thus spelt in *1700*. Cithaeron, a mountainous area in Greece, sacred to the Muses, where Oedipus was exposed, and where Actaeon was killed. D. repeats Chaucer's error in confusing Cithaeron with the island of Cythera, where Venus was born.
ii 502. Narcissus] He fell in love with his own reflection in a pool (*Met.* iii 407–510).
ii 503. Samson] For Chaucer's Hercules, perhaps influenced by Milton's *Samson Agonistes* (1671). He was betrayed to his enemies the Philistines by the woman he loved, Delilah (Judges xvi). See iii 416–17.   *wiser Solomon*] Solomon was renowned for his wisdom, but 'loved many strange women' (1 Kings xi 1).
ii 504. D.'s addition.
ii 505. Medea] Princess of Colchis and wife of Jason; she had magical powers.
Circean] Circe the seductive enchantress turned men into animals (*Odyssey* x 133–574, xii 8–150).
ii 506. D.'s addition.

And prowess to the power of love submit:
The spreading snare for all mankind is laid,
510 And lovers all betray, and are betrayed.
The goddess' self some noble hand had wrought;
Smiling she seemed, and full of pleasing thought:
From ocean as she first began to rise,
And smoothed the ruffled seas, and cleared the skies;
515 She trod the brine all bare below the breast,
And the green waves but ill concealed the rest;
A lute she held, and on her head was seen
A wreath of roses red, and myrtles green;
Her turtles fanned the buxom air above,
520 And by his mother stood an infant Love,
With wings unfledged, his eyes were banded o'er, ⎫
His hands a bow, his back a quiver bore,   ⎬
Supplied with arrows bright and keen, a deadly store. ⎭
    But in the dome of mighty Mars the red,

ii 510. D.'s addition; cp. 'The Secular Masque' l. 89: 'Thy lovers were all untrue'.
ii 512. D.'s addition.
ii 513–15. Venus was said to have been born from the remains of Uranus scattered in the sea, and is often depicted rising from the sea or floating in a scallop shell (e.g. in Botticelli's painting *The Birth of Venus*).
ii 514. D.'s addition.
ii 515–16. breast, / . . . rest] For the rhyme and the euphemism *the rest* cp. Marvell: 'Two hundred [years] to adore each breast: / But thirty thousand to the rest' ('To his Coy Mistress' ll. 15–16; also echoed in 'Cymon and Iphigenia' ll. 154–5).
ii 518. roses red] Venus' flowers were white roses stained red by the blood of Adonis. myrtles] See ii 461n.
ii 519. Cp. Milton: 'with quick fan / Winnows the buxom air' (*PL* v 269–70). turtles] turtle doves; emblems of love, and of fidelity to a mate. buxom] unresisting (*OED* 2; last example); amorous (*OED* 3, citing Johnson's definition (which it rejects)).
ii 520. infant Love] Cupid.
ii 521. Cupid is often represented as blind or (as here) blindfolded, to show that love is blind.
ii 524–616. Some details in the description of Mars show that Chaucer and D. were drawing on the characteristics that astrologers attributed to the planet Mars and its influence. William Lily in his widely read handbook *Christian Astrology* (1647) not only associates Mars with war but calls the man influenced by Mars 'a lover of Slaughter and Quarrels, Murder, Theevery, a promoter of Sedition, Frayes and Commotions . . . a Traytor, of turbulent Spirit, Perjured . . . neither fearing God or caring for man, Unthankful, Trecherous . . . Furious, Violent' (66; cp. ll. 560–83). Mars is associated not only with soldiers, but also with 'Cutlers of Swords and Knives' and cooks (67; cp. ll. 591, 597–9); his stone is adamant (68; cp. l. 554), his metal is iron (68; cp. l. 557) and he produces 'all hurts by Iron'

525 With different figures all the sides were spread:
    This temple, less in form, with equal grace
    Was imitative of the first in Thrace:
    For that cold region was the loved abode
    And sovereign mansion of the warrior god.
530 The landscape was a forest wide and bare,
    Where neither beast nor human kind repair;
    The fowl that scent afar the borders fly,
    And shun the bitter blast, and wheel about the sky.
    A cake of scurf lies baking on the ground,
535 And prickly stubs, instead of trees, are found,
    Or woods with knots and knares deformed and old;
    Headless the most, and hideous to behold.
    A rattling tempest through the branches went,
    That stripped 'em bare, and one sole way they bent.
540 Heaven froze above, severe, the clouds congeal,
    And through the crystal vault appeared the standing hail.
    Such was the face without, a mountain stood
    Threatening from high, and overlooked the wood:
    Beneath the louring brow, and on a bent,
545 The temple stood of Mars armipotent:
    The frame of burnished steel, that cast a glare
    From far, and seemed to thaw the freezing air.

(67; cp. ll. 566, 571, 597–9); he promotes anger (67; cp. l. 563); and 'he delighteth
in Red colour' (67; cp. l. 524). Trees associated with Mars are 'prickly' (68; cp. l.
535), and he causes 'Thunder, Lightning . . . pestilent Aires' (68; cp. ll. 538–41).
ii 526. D.'s addition.
ii 527. Thrace] An area roughly equivalent to modern Bulgaria. Its people were
viewed by the Greeks as wild and undisciplined; it was regarded as a warlike
country, and the seat of Mars.
ii 529. mansion] place where one stays or dwells (*OED* 2); in astrology, a sign of
the zodiac, for each planet except the sun and moon has two houses that it rules
(*OED svv.* mansion 5a, house 8).
ii 531. repair] go.
ii 532–4. D.'s addition.
ii 534. scurf] salty or sulphurous deposit; mould (*OED* 3).
ii 536. knares] knots in wood (*OED*'s only instance since Chaucer).
ii 540–3. D.'s addition.
ii 541. standing] vertical (*OED* 3); continuous (*OED* 13).
ii 542. face] appearance (*OED* 9).
ii 544. bent] place covered with grass (*OED* 5); hillside, rising ground (*OED* 6).
ii 545. armipotent] powerful in arms.
ii 547. D.'s addition.

A strait, long entry to the temple led,
Blind with high walls, and horror overhead.
550   Thence issued such a blast, and hollow roar,
As threatened from the hinge to heave the door;
In through that door a northern light there shone,
'Twas all it had, for windows there were none.
The gate was adamant, eternal frame!
555   Which hewed by Mars himself from Indian quarries came,
The labour of a god; and all along
Tough iron plates were clenched to make it strong.
A tun about was every pillar there,
A polished mirror shone not half so clear.
560   There saw I how the secret felon wrought,   ⎫
And Treason labouring in the traitor's thought,   ⎬
And midwife Time the ripened plot to Murder   ⎭
        brought.
There the red Anger dared the pallid Fear;
Next stood Hypocrisy, with holy leer,
565   Soft, smiling, and demurely looking down,
But hid the dagger underneath the gown:
Th' assassinating wife, the household fiend,
And far the blackest there, the traitor-friend.
On t' other side there stood Destruction bare,
570   Unpunished Rapine, and a waste of War.
Contest, with sharpened knives in cloisters drawn,
And all with blood bespread the holy lawn.

---

ii 548. strait] Spelled *streight* in *1700* (and in Chaucer), which was the seventeenth-century spelling of both the modern 'strait' and 'straight'; either modernization is possible.
ii 549. *Blind*] dark (*OED* 7); without openings for light (*OED* 10).   *horror*] roughness, ruggedness (*OED* 1); cp. *HP* ii 659*n.*
ii 554. *adamant*] legendary hard rock or mineral.
ii 555–6. D.'s addition.
ii 558. *tun*] a measure of capacity, from a wine cask containing 252 gallons.
ii 561–2. For 'compassing' (scheming).
ii 563. *dared*] terrified, made paralysed with fear (*OED* dare *v.*² 6).
ii 564, 567–8, 569–70. D.'s additions.
ii 564–6. *Works* suggests an allusion to the assassination of the French King Henri III by the monk Jacques Clément in 1589, but there is nothing in the phrasing to imply such a specific reference: the point is more generally anticlerical.
ii 571–2. D. adds *cloisters* and *holy lawn*.
ii 572. *lawn*] fine linen used for clerical surplices.

Loud Menaces were heard, and foul Disgrace, ⎫
And bawling Infamy, in language base, ⎬
575   Till sense was lost in sound, and Silence fled the place. ⎭
The slayer of himself yet saw I there,
The gore congealed was clottered in his hair:
With eyes half closed, and gaping mouth he lay,
And grim, as when he breathed his sullen soul away.
580   In midst of all the dome, Misfortune sat,
And gloomy Discontent, and fell Debate:
And Madness laughing in his ireful mood,
And armed Complaint on Theft, and cries of blood.
There was the murdered corpse, in covert laid,
585   And violent death in thousand shapes displayed:
The city to the soldier's rage resigned,
Successless wars, and Poverty behind;
Ships burnt in fight, or forced on rocky shores,
And the rash hunter strangled by the boars:
590   The new-born babe by nurses overlaid,
And the cook caught within the raging fire he made.
All ills of Mars his nature, flame and steel:
The gasping charioteer beneath the wheel
Of his own car; the ruined house that falls
595   And intercepts her lord betwixt the walls:

ii *573–5.* For 'All full of chirking [groaning] was that sory place'.

ii *577. clottered*] coagulated, clotted.

ii *579.* D.'s addition.

ii *580. sat*] Noyes suggests emending to *sate* (a common form of the past tense of 'sit': cp. iii 112, 486) for the rhyme (elsewhere D. rhymes *debate* with *gate, hate,* and *fate*: 'The Seventh Book of the *Aeneis*' ll. 218, 468, 'The Tenth Book' ll. 21, 51).

ii *581. fell*] fierce, savage. *Debate*] strife, quarrelling, conflict (*OED* 1).

ii *582. ireful*] angry.

ii *583. Complaint on Theft*] The allegorical figure of Complaint (outcry against an injury (*OED* 3)) is shouting out after a thief.

ii *587.* For 'there was nothing ilaft'. *Successless wars*] Glancing at the campaigns of William III in Europe (cp. iii 669–71n). Cp. 'The Secular Masque' l. 88: 'Thy wars brought nothing about'.

ii *589. strangled*] killed, especially by suffocation, by a wild animal (*OED* 3c). *boars*] For Chaucer's *beres*.

ii *590. nurses*] For 'Sow'.

ii *592. Mars his*] Mars'.

ii *594. car*] chariot.

ii *594–5. the ruined house . . . walls*] D.'s addition.

ii *595. intercepts*] catches someone on their way (*OED* 1); contains, encloses (*OED* 3).

The whole division that to Mars pertains,
All trades of death that deal in steel for gains
Were there: the butcher, armourer, and smith,
Who forges sharpened falchions, or the scythe.
600 The scarlet Conquest on a tower was placed,
With shouts, and soldiers' acclamations graced:
A pointed sword hung threatening o'er his head,
Sustained but by a slender twine of thread.
There saw I Mars his Ides, the Capitol,
605 The seer in vain foretelling Caesar's fall,
The last triumvirs, and the wars they move,
And Antony, who lost the world for love.
These, and a thousand more, the fane adorn,
Their fates were painted ere the men were born,
610 All copied from the heavens, and ruling force
Of the red star in his revolving course.
The form of Mars high on a chariot stood,
All sheathed in arms, and gruffly looked the god:
Two geomantic figures were displayed ⎫
615 Above his head, a warrior and a maid, ⎬
One when direct, and one when retrograde. ⎭
    Tired with deformities of death, I haste

ii 597. D.'s addition.

ii 602–3. An allusion to the sword which Dionysius of Syracuse suspended by a single thread over the head of the flatterer Damocles, who had praised the delights of monarchy.

ii 604–6. For 'the slaughter of *Julius*'. The Ides (15th) of March was the day on which the soothsayer prophesied (correctly) that Julius Caesar would be assassinated. He was killed in the Roman Capitol. After the murder the Roman world was plunged into civil war between the conspirators and the three leaders or *triumvirs* (Octavius, Antony, and Lepidus) who sought to avenge Caesar. Antony, through his love for Cleopatra, *lost the world for love* (D.'s addition; cp. the title of D.'s play on the subject: *All for Love, or, the World well Lost* (1678)).

ii 606. move] stir up, begin (*OED* 8).

ii 608. D.'s addition. *fane*] temple.

ii 611. red star] Mars.

ii 614–16. geomantic] Referring to geomancy, the art of divination by means of a handful of earth thrown down on a surface, or by lines and figures formed by putting down on paper a number of dots at random (*OED*). For details of the procedure see *Riverside Chaucer* 836.

ii 615. a warrior and a maid] 'Rubeus and Puella' (D.'s note). Noyes observes that D. adapts a note in Speght's edition: 'The names of two figures in geomancie, representing two constellations in heaven. *Puella* signifieth Mars retrograde, and *Rubeus* Mars direct'.

ii 616. direct] moving in the same direction as the sun in relation to the stars. *retrograde*] appearing to move in the opposite direction (*OED* direct 3, retrograde 1).

To the third temple of Diana chaste;
A sylvan scene with various greens was drawn,
620   Shades on the sides, and on the midst a lawn:
The silver Cynthia, with her nymphs around,
Pursued the flying deer, the woods with horns resound:
Calisto there stood manifest of shame,
And turned a bear, the northern star became:
625   Her son was next, and by peculiar grace
In the cold circle held the second place:
The stag Actaeon in the stream had spied
The naked huntress, and for seeing died:
His hounds, unknowing of his change, pursue
630   The chase, and their mistaken master slew.
Peneian Daphne too was there to see,
Apollo's love before, and now his tree:
Th' adjoining fane th' assembled Greeks expressed,

ii 616–17. one . . . death, 619–22. D.'s additions.

ii 619. sylvan scene] A Miltonic phrase (PL iv 140).

ii 620. on the midst] Works emends to in the midst, but the line makes precise sense
as it stands in 1700: 'shady groves were painted on the side walls of the temple,
and on the middle wall was painted an open space'.   lawn] open space between
woods (OED sb.² 1).

ii 621. silver] Lily (Christian Astrology 82) notes that Diana (as the Moon) is associated with silver (cp. l. 647).   Cynthia] Diana.

ii 623. Calisto] Diana's nymph Calisto was seduced by Jupiter, who assumed the
appearance of the goddess. Juno changed her into a bear, and Jupiter made her
the constellation Arctus and her son Arcas the neighbouring constellation Boötes
(Ovid, Met. ii 401–530).   manifest of] evidently guilty of (OED 2; a Latinate
construction, as in AA l. 204).

ii 625. peculiar] special.

ii 627. Actaeon] Actaeon the hunter saw Diana bathing naked, for which he
was punished by being turned into a stag, and killed by his own hounds (Met.
iii 138–252).

ii 631. Daphne] Daughter of the river god Peneus, loved by Apollo; she fled from
him, and was turned into the laurel tree, which became sacred to Apollo (Met.
i 452–567; tr. by D. in 'The First Book of Ovid's Metamorphoses' ll. 606–768).

ii 633–8. D. expands Chaucer's briefer reference. Meleager, son of Oeneus, King
of Calydon, killed a boar which had been ravaging his country and presented its
head as a trophy to Atalanta; his uncles, feeling dishonoured, snatched the prize
away, and in revenge Meleager killed one of them, Plexippus. It had been prophesied that Meleager's life would continue so long as a particular log in the house
of Meleager's mother Althaea remained unburnt; when she heard the news of
her brother's death, Althaea threw the log on the fire, causing the death of her
son. See 'Meleager and Atalanta', and Met. viii 270–546.

ii 633. Th' adjoining fane] Presumably the next chapel within the temple, not the
next temple (pace Works).   expressed] represented in sculpture or painting (OED 5).

And hunting of the Calydonian beast:
635   Oenides' valour, and his envied prize,
The fatal power of Atalanta's eyes;
Diana's vengeance on the victor shown,
The murderess mother, and consuming son;
The Volscian queen extended on the plain,
640   The treason punished, and the traitor slain.
The rest were various huntings, well designed,
And salvage beasts destroyed of every kind.
The graceful goddess was arrayed in green,
About her feet were little beagles seen
645   That watched with upward eyes the motions of their
        queen.
Her legs were buskined, and the left before
In act to shoot, a silver bow she bore,
And at her back a painted quiver wore.
She trod a waxing moon, that soon would wane,
650   And drinking borrowed light, be filled again:
With downcast eyes, as seeming to survey
The dark dominions, her alternate sway.
Before her stood a woman in her throes,
And called Lucina's aid, her burden to disclose.
655   All these the painter drew with such command,
That Nature snatched the pencil from his hand,
Ashamed and angry that his art could feign
And mend the tortures of a mother's pain.
Theseus beheld the fanes of every god,
660   And thought his mighty cost was well bestowed:
So princes now their poets should regard;

ii 639–42. D.'s addition. Camilla's father dedicated her to Diana from childhood.
She grew up to be a huntress and warrior, and fought for the Volscians against
Aeneas' Trojans. She was killed by Arruns, who was punished by being killed
by one of Diana's nymphs (*Aen.* xi 532–867).
ii 642. *salvage*] A now obsolete form of 'savage'; the spelling is kept for the pronunciation, and to signal the etymology of the word from Latin *silva* (wood).
ii 645–6. D.'s addition.
ii 646. *buskined*] clad in boots.
ii 650. D.'s addition. Cp. Milton: the moon 'With borrowed light . . . in her pale
dominion'; 'And drink the liquid light' (*PL* iii 730–2; vii 362).
ii 653. *throes*] pains of childbirth.
ii 654. *Lucina*] Diana as goddess of childbirth.
ii 656–9. D.'s addition.
ii 656. *pencil*] paintbrush.
ii 661–2. D.'s addition, with personal and political resonance.

But few can write, and fewer can reward.
　　The theatre thus raised, the lists enclosed,
And all with vast magnificence disposed,
665　We leave the monarch pleased, and haste to bring
The knights to combat, and their arms to sing.

The end of the second book.

Book III

The day approached when Fortune should decide
Th' important enterprise, and give the bride;
For now the rivals round the world had sought,
And each his number, well appointed, brought.
5　The nations far and near contend in choice,
And send the flower of war by public voice,
That after or before were never known
Such chiefs, as each an army seemed alone.
Beside the champions, all of high degree,
10　Who knighthood loved, and deeds of chivalry,
Thronged to the lists, and envied to behold
The names of others, not their own, enrolled.
Nor seems it strange, for every noble knight ⎤
Who loves the fair, and is endued with might, ⎬
15　In such a quarrel would be proud to fight. ⎦
There breathes not scarce a man on British ground
(An isle for love and arms of old renowned)
But would have sold his life to purchase fame,
To Palamon or Arcite sent his name;
20　And had the land selected of the best,
Half had come hence, and let the world provide the rest.
A hundred knights with Palamon there came,
Approved in fight, and men of mighty name;
Their arms were several, as their nations were,

ii 664. magnificence] See ii 438*n*.
iii 1–2. when Fortune . . . bride] D.'s addition.
iii 5–6, 8–9. D.'s additions.
iii 8. each an army seemed alone] From Virgil: *magnique ipse agminis instar* ('equal to a mighty army himself': *Aen.* vii 707; Christie).
iii 17–21. D.'s addition.
iii 17. An isle for love] Cp. Song XI from *King Arthur* ll. 61–4 (Kinsley).
iii 23. D.'s addition.　*approved*] tried, tested (*OED* 1).

25   But furnished all alike with sword and spear.
     Some wore coat-armour, imitating scale,
     And next their skins were stubborn shirts of mail.
     Some wore a breastplate and a light jupon,
     Their horses clothed with rich caparison:
30   Some for defence would leathern bucklers use
     Of folded hides, and others shields of Pruce.
     One hung a poleaxe at his saddle bow,
     And one a heavy mace, to stun the foe;
     One for his legs and knees provided well,
35   With jambeaux armed, and double plates of steel;
     This on his helmet wore a lady's glove,
     And that a sleeve embroidered by his love.
        With Palamon, above the rest in place,   ⎫
     Lycurgus came, the surly king of Thrace;   ⎬
40   Black was his beard, and manly was his face: ⎭
     The balls of his broad eyes rolled in his head,
     And glared betwixt a yellow and a red:
     He looked a lion with a gloomy stare,
     And o'er his eyebrows hung his matted hair:
45   Big boned, and large of limbs, with sinews strong,
     Broad shouldered, and his arms were round and long.
     Four milk-white bulls (the Thracian use of old)
     Were yoked to draw his car of burnished gold.
     Upright he stood, and bore aloft his shield,
50   Conspicuous from afar, and overlooked the field.
     His surcoat was a bear-skin on his back,
     His hair hung long behind, and glossy raven-black.

iii 25, 27. D.'s additions.
iii 27. stubborn] stiff, hard.
iii 28. jupon] either a close-fitting tunic worn under armour, or a surcoat worn
over it ('gippion' in Chaucer).
iii 29. D.'s addition.   *caparison*] ornamented cloth covering a saddle (*OED*).
iii 30. bucklers] small round shields.
iii 31. of Pruce] of Prussian or spruce fir wood (*OED*'s only example in English).
Chaucer has 'Pruce sheeld' ('Prussian shield') in modern editions, 'pruce, shield'
in Speght.
iii 35. jambeaux] armour for the legs (*OED*'s only example since Spenser, *FQ* vi
29, probably D.'s source).
iii 36-7. D.'s addition, with medieval chivalric detail.
iii 43. lion] Thus Speght; modern editions have 'grifphon' (Kinsley).
iii 47. use] custom.
iii 48. car] chariot.
iii 49-50. D.'s addition.

His ample forehead bore a coronet
With sparkling diamonds, and with rubies set:
55 Ten brace and more of greyhounds, snowy fair, ⎫
    And tall as stags, ran loose, and coursed around ⎪
        his chair,   ⎬
    A match for pards in flight, in grappling, for the bear: ⎭
    With golden muzzles all their mouths were bound,
    And collars of the same their necks surround.
60 Thus through the fields Lycurgus took his way,
    His hundred knights attend in pomp and proud array.
        To match this monarch, with strong Arcite came
    Emetrius, King of Ind, a mighty name,
    On a bay courser, goodly to behold,
65 The trappings of his horse embossed with barbarous gold.
    Not Mars bestrode a steed with greater grace;
    His surcoat o'er his arms was cloth of Thrace,
    Adorned with pearls, all orient, round, and great;
    His saddle was of gold, with emeralds set.
70 His shoulders large a mantle did attire,
    With rubies thick, and sparkling as the fire:
    His amber-coloured locks in ringlets run
    With graceful negligence, and shone against the sun.
    His nose was aquiline, his eyes were blue,
75 Ruddy his lips, and fresh and fair his hue.
    Some sprinkled freckles on his face were seen,
    Whose dusk set off the whiteness of the skin;
    His awful presence did the crowd surprise,
    Nor durst the rash spectator meet his eyes,
80 Eyes that confessed him born for kingly sway,
    So fierce, they flashed intolerable day.
    His age in nature's youthful prime appeared,

iii 56. *chair*] chariot (*OED sb.²*).
iii 57. *pards . . . bear*] Thus Speght; modern editions have 'leoun . . . deer' (Kinsley).
pards] panthers or leopards.
iii 63. *Ind*] India.
iii 64. *courser*] powerful horse ridden in a battle or tournament (*OED*).
iii 65. *barbarous gold*] From Virgil's *barbarico auro* (*Aen.* ii 504; and cp. *PL* ii 4; Kinsley).
iii 67. *Thrace*] Thus Speght; modern editions have 'Tars', i.e. Tarsia in Turkestan (Kinsley).
iii 77. D.'s addition. *dusk*] dark shade (*OED* 1, first example).
iii 78–81. For 'And as a lyon, he his eyen keste'.
iii 78. *awful*] awesome, awe inspiring. *surprise*] overpower; astonish, alarm, excite to admiration (*OED* 1b; 5).

And just began to bloom his yellow beard.
Whene'er he spoke, his voice was heard around,
85   Loud as a trumpet, with a silver sound.
A laurel wreathed his temples, fresh and green,
And myrtle sprigs, the marks of love, were mixed between.
Upon his fist he bore for his delight
An eagle well reclaimed, and lily-white.
90   His hundred knights attend him to the war,
All armed for battle, save their heads were bare.
Words and devices blazed on every shield,
And pleasing was the terror of the field.
For kings, and dukes, and barons you might see ⎤
95   Like sparkling stars, though different in degree, ⎬
All for th' increase of arms, and love of chivalry. ⎦
Before the king tame leopards led the way,
And troops of lions innocently play.
So Bacchus through the conquered Indies rode,
100   And beasts in gambols frisked before their honest god.
In this array the war of either side
Through Athens passed with military pride.
At prime they entered on the Sunday morn;
Rich tap'stry spread the streets, and flowers the posts adorn.
105   The town was all a jubilee of feasts,
So Theseus willed, in honour of his guests:
Himself with open arms the kings embraced,

iii 87. D.'s addition.   *myrtle*] See ii 461*n*.
iii 89. *reclaimed*] tamed (*OED* 3).
iii 92–3. D.'s addition, with more chivalric detail.
iii 92. *blazed*] painted (used of heraldic devices and mottoes) (*OED v.*² 5).
iii 95. D.'s addition.
iii 99–100. D.'s addition. Bacchus (the Greek god Dionysus) is often represented riding in a chariot drawn by leopards, tigers, or other wild beasts; he was said to have conquered India (Ovid, *Met.* iv 20–1, 604–5).
iii 100. *honest*] held in honour, revered (*OED* 1; last example 1692). *Works* notes that Virgil used the epithet *honestum* (honoured, handsome (*OLD* 1, 4)) for Bacchus (*Geo.* ii 392).
iii 101. *war*] soldiers in fighting array (*OED* 6b).
iii 103, 543. *prime*] the first hour of the day, six o'clock or sunrise (*OED* 2).
iii 104. D.'s addition.   *posts*] Eds; Pots *1700*. Kinsley observes that D. was familiar with the Roman custom of decorating doorposts with flowers, citing 'The Sixth Satire of Juvenal' ll. 75, 321, 'The First Book of Ovid's *Metamorphoses*' l. 761, and 'Cymon and Iphigenia' l. 561. But *ports* ('gateways': *OED* port *sb.*³ 1) is also possible.
iii 105. *jubilee*] occasion of general rejoicing (*OED* 4).
iii 107. D.'s addition.

Then all the rest in their degrees were graced.
No harbinger was needful for the night,
110 For every house was proud to lodge a knight.
     I pass the royal treat, nor must relate
The gifts bestowed, nor how the champions sate;
Who first, who last, or how the knights addressed
Their vows, or who was fairest at the feast;
115 Whose voice, whose graceful dance did most surprise,
Soft amorous sighs, and silent love of eyes.
The rivals call my Muse another way,
To sing their vigils for th' ensuing day.
     'Twas ebbing darkness, past the noon of night,
120 And Phosphor on the confines of the light
Promised the sun; ere day began to spring ⎫
The tuneful lark already stretched her wing, ⎬
And flickering on her nest, made short essays to sing: ⎭
When wakeful Palamon, preventing day, ⎫
125 Took to the royal lists his early way, ⎬
To Venus at her fane, in her own house, to pray; ⎭
There, falling on his knees before her shrine,
He thus implored with prayers her power divine:
'Creator Venus, genial power of love,
130 The bliss of men below, and gods above,
Beneath the sliding sun thou runn'st thy race,

iii *108. graced*] honoured.
iii *109–10*. D.'s addition.
iii *109. harbinger*] person sent ahead to arrange lodgings for an army or royal entourage (*OED* 2).
iii *111. treat*] entertainment (*OED* 4b).
iii *112. sate*] sat.
iii *115. surprise*] captivate (*OED* 1b).
iii *117–18*. D.'s addition.
iii *119*. This edition follows Kinsley in starting a new paragraph here rather than at l. 124 as in *1700*. *noon of night*] midnight (*OED* 4).
iii *120*. D.'s addition. *Phosphor*] the morning star, the planet Venus appearing before sunrise (*OED*).
iii *123*. D.'s addition. *flickering*] fluttering, hovering (*OED* 1), as in 'Ceyx and Alcyone' l. 484. Kinsley notes that Chaucer uses 'flikerynge' for Venus' doves earlier at l. 1962. *essays*] first tentative efforts (*OED* 7; first example from *PL*).
iii *124. preventing*] anticipating.
iii *126. fane*] temple.
iii *129–144*. D.'s addition. This invocation of Venus has verbal and rhetorical links with 'Lucretius: The Beginning of the First Book', *The State of Innocence* II iii 30, and Spenser, *FQ* IV x 44–6.
iii *129. genial*] procreative.
iii *131. sliding*] moving smoothly through the air (*OED* slide *v*. 1).

Dost fairest shine, and best become thy place.
For thee the winds their eastern blasts forbear,
Thy month reveals the spring, and opens all the year.
135   Thee, goddess, thee, the storms of winter fly,
Earth smiles with flowers renewing, laughs the sky,
And birds to lays of love their tuneful notes apply.
For thee the lion loathes the taste of blood,
And roaring hunts his female through the wood:
140   For thee the bulls rebellow through the groves,
And tempt the stream, and snuff their absent loves.
'Tis thine, whate'er is pleasant, good, or fair:
All nature is thy province, life thy care;
Thou mad'st the world, and dost the world repair.
145   Thou gladder of the mount of Citheron,
Increase of Jove, companion of the sun;
If e'er Adonis touched thy tender heart,
Have pity, goddess, for thou know'st the smart.
Alas! I have not words to tell my grief,
150   To vent my sorrow would be some relief:
Light sufferings give us leisure to complain;
We groan, but cannot speak, in greater pain.
O goddess, tell thyself what I would say;
Thou know'st it, and I feel too much to pray.
155   So grant my suit, as I enforce my might,
In love to be thy champion, and thy knight;
A servant to thy sex, a slave to thee,
A foe professed to barren chastity.
Nor ask I fame or honour of the field,
160   Nor choose I more to vanquish than to yield:
In my divine Emilia make me blest,

iii *134.* April was associated with Venus, and Roman writers derived its name either from Aphrodite (the Greek equivalent of Venus) or from *aperire*, 'to open' (Bonnie Blackburn and Leofranc Holford-Strevens, *The Oxford Companion to the Year* (1999) 140).

iii *136. laughs*] See ii 40*n.*

iii *141. tempt*] venture into (*OED* 2c).   *snuff*] detect or anticipate by inhaling the odour of (*OED* 4; first example 1697 from D.'s 'The First Book of the *Georgics*' l. 519).

iii *144. repair*] renew, renovate, revive (*OED* 3).

iii *145. Citheron*] See ii 498*n.*

iii *146. Increase*] offspring (*OED* 6); stressed on the second syllable.

iii *150–2.* D.'s addition.

iii *151–2.* Proverbial, from *curae leves loquuntur, ingentes stupent* ('light cares speak, great ones are silent': Seneca, *Phaedra* l. 607).

iii *151. leisure*] freedom, opportunity (*OED* 1).

Let Fate, or partial Chance, dispose the rest;
    Find thou the manner, and the means prepare:
    Possession more than conquest is my care.
165 Mars is the warrior's god, in him it lies
    On whom he favours to confer the prize;
    With smiling aspect you serenely move
    In your fifth orb, and rule the realm of love.
    The Fates but only spin the coarser clew,
170 The finest of the wool is left for you.
    Spare me but one small portion of the twine,
    And let the sisters cut below your line:
    The rest among the rubbish may they sweep,
    Or add it to the yarn of some old miser's heap.
175 But if you this ambitious prayer deny
    (A wish, I grant, beyond mortality)
    Then let me sink beneath proud Arcite's arms,
    And I once dead, let him possess her charms.'
      Thus ended he; then with observance due
180 The sacred incense on her altar threw:
    The curling smoke mounts heavy from the fires;
    At length it catches flame, and in a blaze expires:
    At once the gracious goddess gave the sign,
    Her statue shook, and trembled all the shrine.
185 Pleased Palamon the tardy omen took,
    For since the flames pursued the trailing smoke,
    He knew his boon was granted; but the day
    To distance driven, and joy adjourned with long delay.
      Now morn with rosy light had streaked the sky,

---

iii *162, 166.* D.'s additions.
iii *167–8.* For 'Your vertue is so great in heauen aboue'.
iii *167. aspect*] (i) countenance (*OED* 10); (ii) astrologically (a) the angular separation of one planet from another, or, more loosely, (b) the relationship of planets
to observers on earth (*OED* 4). Venus is a benign planet.
iii *168. fifth orb*] A puzzle. In the Ptolemaic system the earth is imagined to be at
the centre of a set of hollow concentric spheres, each of which is the sphere
(*OED* orb 7) of one of the planets. These spheres are (in order outwards from
the earth) the Moon, Mercury, Venus, the Sun, Mars, Jupiter, Saturn, the fixed
stars, and the *primum mobile*. Venus is therefore in the third orb from the earth.
She would be in the fifth orb if one counted only the planets, working inwards
from Saturn.
iii *169–74.* D.'s addition.
iii *169. clew*] thread (of life) (*OED* 4), spun and cut by the three Fates (l. 172).
iii *176, 180–2, 186.* D.'s additions.
iii *187. boon*] something requested in prayer (*OED* 3), an archaic word at this date.
iii *189.* Cp. Milton: 'Now Morn her rosy steps in the eastern clime' and 'ere fresh
morning streak the east' (*PL* v 1, iv 623; J. R. Mason).

190   Up rose the sun, and up rose Emily,
        Addressed her early steps to Cynthia's fane,
        In state attended by her maiden train,
        Who bore the vests that holy rites require,
        Incense, and odorous gums, and covered fire.
195   The plenteous horns with pleasant mead they crown,
        Nor wanted aught besides in honour of the moon.
        Now while the temple smoked with hallowed steam,
        They wash the virgin in a living stream;
        The secret ceremonies I conceal,
200   Uncouth, perhaps unlawful to reveal.
        But such they were as pagan use required,
        Performed by women when the men retired,
        Whose eyes profane their chaste, mysterious rites
        Might turn to scandal, or obscene delights.
205   Well-meaners think no harm, but for the rest
        Things sacred they pervert, and silence is the best.
        Her shining hair, uncombed, was loosely spread,
        A crown of mastless oak adorned her head:

iii 191. Cynthia] Diana.

iii 193. vests] robes, gowns (*OED* 1b, first example used for a woman's robe); ecclesiastical vestments (*OED* 2).

iii 194. odorous gums] Thus Milton, *PL* iv 248 (J. R. Mason).   *covered fire*] smouldering charcoal carried in an incense burner.

iii 195. horns] horn-shaped vessels for holding liquid (*OED* 12).   *crown*] fill to the brim (*OED* 8; first example 1697 from D.'s 'The Fifth Pastoral of Virgil' l. 108).

iii 197. steam] smoke.

iii 198. living] constantly flowing (*OED* 2d); also drawing on the biblical sense of the 'living water' which is the gift of the Holy Spirit (John iv 10).

iii 199–200. Cp. Milton: 'The secrets . . . / Not lawful to reveal' (*PL* v 569–70; J. R. Mason).

iii 200–4. D.'s addition. Kinsley cites D.'s note on 'The Sixth Satire of Juvenal' l. 430, which refers to the rites of the Roman fertility goddess the Bona Dea, 'at whose feasts no men were to be present'.

iii 200. Uncouth] unknown, uncertain; unfamiliar, strange, marvellous (*OED* 1, 3).

iii 201. use] custom (*OED* 7); religious ceremony (*OED* 12), normally used specifically of the Roman Catholic liturgy.

iii 203. mysterious rites] Cp. *PL* iv 742–3: 'Nor Eve the rites / Mysterious of connubial love refused'.

iii 206. D.'s addition.

iii 208. mastless] without acorns (*OED*'s only example). Speght's text here has the meaningless 'vnseriall' (misprinted 'vnferiall' in *1700*), but this is corrected in his notes: '*Vnseriall, read,* cerriall: cerrus is a kinde of tree like an Oke, and beareth maste' (sig. Bbbbiiii^r). D. therefore fuses 'maste' from Speght's note with 'un-'

When to the shrine approached, the spotless maid
210 Had kindling fires on either altar laid
(The rites were such as were observed of old
By Statius in his Theban story told).
Then kneeling with her hands across her breast,
Thus lowly she preferred her chaste request:
215   'O goddess, haunter of the woodland green,
To whom both heaven and earth and seas are seen;
Queen of the nether skies, where half the year
Thy silver beams descend, and light the gloomy sphere;
Goddess of maids, and conscious of our hearts,
220 So keep me from the vengeance of thy darts,
Which Niobe's devoted issue felt,
When hissing through the skies the feathered deaths
    were dealt,
As I desire to live a virgin life,
Nor know the name of mother or of wife.
225 Thy vot'ress from my tender years I am,
And love, like thee, the woods and sylvan game.
Like death, thou know'st, I loathe the nuptial state, ⎫
And man, the tyrant of our sex, I hate—   ⎬
A lowly servant, but a lofty mate: ⎭
230 Where love is duty, on the female side,
On theirs mere sensual gust, and sought with surly pride.

---

from his text. The reference is to the evergreen cerrial oak of southern Europe.
Cp. 'The Flower and the Leaf' l. 230.
iii 209. D.'s addition.
iii 212. Statius, *Thebaid* iv 443–68.
iii 213. D.'s addition.
iii 214. preferred] offered (*OED* 4).
iii 217–18. For 'Quene of the reigne of *Pluto*, darke and low'.
iii 217. nether skies] underworld; as in 'Ceyx and Alcyone' l. 136.
iii 219. conscious of] aware of the secrets of (*OED* 1).
iii 221–2. For 'that *Acteon* abought cruelly'. Niobe boasted of the number of her
children (seven to twelve in various sources), comparing herself with Latona, who
had only two, Apollo and Diana. At Latona's request Apollo killed all but one
of Niobe's children with arrows (*Met.* vi 146–312).
iii 221. devoted] given up to destruction (*OED* 3).
iii 225. vot'ress] one vowed to religious service.
iii 226. sylvan] of the woods.
iii 227–31. For 'Nought will I know company of man'. With D.'s expansion of
Chaucer here cp. the feminist sentiments in 'Sigismonda and Guiscardo'.
iii 229. lofty] haughty, overbearing (*OED* 2).
iii 231. gust] taste; enjoyment (*OED* 1, 4).

Now by thy triple shape, as thou art seen
In heaven, earth, hell, and everywhere a queen,
Grant this my first desire: let discord cease,
235   And make betwixt the rivals lasting peace:
Quench their hot fire, or far from me remove
The flame, and turn it on some other love.
Or if my frowning stars have so decreed
That one must be rejected, one succeed,
240   Make him my lord within whose faithful breast
Is fixed my image, and who loves me best.
But O, ev'n that avert! I choose it not,
But take it as the least unhappy lot.
A maid I am, and of thy virgin train;
245   O let me still that spotless name retain!
Frequent the forests, thy chaste will obey,
And only make the beasts of chase my prey!'
      The flames ascend on either altar clear,
While thus the blameless maid addressed her prayer.
250   When lo! the burning fire that shone so bright
Flew off, all sudden, with extinguished light,
And left one altar dark a little space,
Which turned self-kindled, and renewed the blaze:
That other victor-flame a moment stood,
255   Then fell, and lifeless left th' extinguished wood;
For ever lost, th' irrevocable light
Forsook the blackening coals, and sunk to night;
At either end it whistled as it flew,   ⎫
And as the brands were green, so dropped the dew, ⎬
260   Infected as it fell with sweat of sanguine hue. ⎭
      The maid from that ill omen turned her eyes,
And with loud shrieks and clamours rent the skies,
Nor knew what signified the boding sign,
But found the powers displeased, and feared the wrath
      divine.

---

iii 232. triple shape] Diana was regarded as having three aspects: (i) in the heavens,
as the moon and goddess of childbirth; (ii) on earth, as the goddess of chastity
and of the hunt; (iii) in the underworld, as Proserpina, wife of Pluto, associated
with the arrival and departure of spring.
iii 233, 241–3. D.'s additions.
iii 245. still] always.
iii 247. D.'s addition.
iii 250–7. For 'For right anon one of the fyres queynte [was extinguished], / And
quicked [came to life] again; and after that anon / That other fyre was queynte,
and all agon'.

265   Then shook the sacred shrine, and sudden light
       Sprung through the vaulted roof, and made the temple
          bright.
       The power, behold! the power in glory shone,
       By her bent bow and her keen arrows known;
       The rest, a huntress issuing from the wood,
270   Reclining on her cornel spear she stood.
       Then gracious thus began: 'Dismiss thy fear,
       And heaven's unchanged decrees attentive hear:
       More powerful gods have torn thee from my side,
       Unwilling to resign, and doomed a bride:
275   The two contending knights are weighed above;
       One Mars protects, and one the Queen of Love:
       But which the man is in the Thund'rer's breast;
       This he pronounced: 'tis he who loves thee best.
       The fire that once extinct revived again,
280   Foreshows the love allotted to remain.
       Farewell', she said, and vanished from the place.
       The sheaf of arrows shook, and rattled in the case.
       Aghast at this the royal virgin stood,
       Disclaimed, and now no more a sister of the wood:
285   But to the parting goddess thus she prayed: ⎫
       'Propitious still be present to my aid,   ⎬
       Nor quite abandon your once favoured maid.'   ⎭
       Then sighing she returned; but smiled betwixt,
       With hopes, and fears, and joys with sorrows mixed.
290   The next returning planetary hour
       Of Mars, who shared the heptarchy of power,
       His steps bold Arcite to the temple bent,

iii 265–6. D.'s addition.
iii 270. D.'s addition. cornel] made from Cornelian cherry (OED).
iii 272–8. For 'Among the goddes hie it is affirmed, / And by eterne word
written and confirmed, / Thou shalt ben wedded to one of tho / That haue for
thee so moch care and wo; / But vnto which of hem I may not tell'.
iii 274. doomed] decided judicially [that you are to be].
iii 277. Thund'rer] Jupiter. See 'The First Book of Homer's Ilias' l. 579n.
iii 284. D.'s addition.
iii 288–9. but smiled . . . mixed] D.'s addition.
iii 290. planetary hour] The day is Monday, so the planetary hour of Mars is the
fourth hour after sunrise (see ii 483n).
iii 291. who shared the heptarchy of power] D.'s addition. heptarchy] government by
seven rulers, specifically applied to Anglo-Saxon England (OED); here applied
to the seven heavenly bodies that rule the sky in astrology: the Sun, the Moon,
Mercury, Venus, Mars, Jupiter, and Saturn.

T' adore with pagan rites the power armipotent:
Then prostrate, low before his altar lay,
295   And raised his manly voice, and thus began to pray:
'Strong god of arms, whose iron sceptre sways
The freezing north, and Hyperborean seas,
And Scythian colds, and Thracia's wintry coast,
Where stand thy steeds, and thou art honoured most:
300   There most, but everywhere thy power is known,
The fortune of the fight is all thy own:
Terror is thine, and wild amazement flung
From out thy chariot withers ev'n the strong:
And disarray and shameful rout ensue,
305   And force is added to the fainting crew.
Acknowledged as thou art, accept my prayer,
If aught I have achieved deserve thy care:
If to my utmost power with sword and shield ⎫
I dared the death, unknowing how to yield, ⎬
310   And falling in my rank, still kept the field: ⎭
Then let my arms prevail, by thee sustained,
That Emily by conquest may be gained.
Have pity on my pains; nor those unknown
To Mars, which when a lover were his own.
315   Venus, the public care of all above,
Thy stubborn heart has softened into love;
Now by her blandishments and powerful charms
When yielded, she lay curling in thy arms,
Ev'n by thy shame, if shame it may be called,
320   When Vulcan had thee in his net enthralled,

iii 293. *armipotent*] powerful in arms.
iii 296–9. For 'O stronge God, that in the regions cold / Of *Trace*, honoured art, and lord yhold'.
iii 297. *Hyperborean*] In Greek myth an area beyond the north wind (Boreas), hence the extreme north.
iii 298. *Scythian*] See i 7n. *Thracia*] See ii 527n.
iii 302–5. D.'s addition.
iii 303. *withers ev'n the strong*] Cp. Milton: 'withered all their strength' (*PL* vi 850; J. R. Mason).
iii 308–12. For 'And that my might be worthy for to serue / Thy godhead, that I may bene one of thine'.
iii 314–22. Venus and Mars were caught in a net by her husband Vulcan while they were making love, and exhibited to the other gods (*Met.* iv 171–89); cp. 'Lucretius: The Beginning of the First Book' ll. 45–58.
iii 316–17. D.'s addition.
iii 320. *enthralled*] held in bondage.

O envied ignominy, sweet disgrace,
When every god that saw thee, wished thy place!
By those dear pleasures, aid my arms in fight,
And make me conquer in my patron's right.

325 For I am young, a novice in the trade,
The fool of love, unpractised to persuade,
And want the soothing arts that catch the fair,
But caught myself, lie struggling in the snare.
And she I love or laughs at all my pain

330 Or knows her worth too well, and pays me with disdain.
For sure I am, unless I win in arms,
To stand excluded from Emilia's charms:
Nor can my strength avail, unless by thee
Endued with force, I gain the victory.

335 Then for the fire which warmed thy generous heart,
Pity thy subject's pains, and equal smart.
So be the morrow's sweat and labour mine,
The palm and honour of the conquest thine.
Then shall the war, and stern debate, and strife

340 Immortal be the business of my life;
And in thy fane the dusty spoils among
High on the burnished roof my banner shall be hung,
Ranked with my champions' bucklers, and below,
With arms reversed, th' achievements of my foe.

345 And while these limbs the vital spirit feeds,
While day to night, and night to day succeeds,
Thy smoking altar shall be fat with food
Of incense, and the grateful steam of blood;

iii 321–2. D.'s addition, echoing *illi iacuere ligati / turpiter, atque aliquis de dis non tristibus optat / sic fieri turpis* ('there they lay disgracefully tied up, and one of the merry gods wished that he might be so disgraced': *Met.* iv 186–8).
iii 324. D.'s addition.
iii 326–8. *unpractised . . . snare*] D.'s addition.
iii 329–30. *or . . . Or*] either . . . Or.
iii 334. *Endued*] supplied.
iii 335. *generous*] courageous (*OED* 2).
iii 338. *palm*] emblem of victory.
iii 339. *debate*] strife, quarrelling, conflict (*OED* 1).
iii 344. D.'s addition. *arms reversed*] weapons carried in a position contrary to that in which they are ready for use (*OED* reverse 3b), a sign of defeat. *achievements*] shields with armorial bearings, along with other pieces of armour such as sword and helmet, often placed on a tomb.
iii 346–9. D.'s addition, with Homeric overtones.
iii 347. *fat*] dense with odours (*OED* 7c).
iii 348. *grateful*] pleasing, welcome (*OED* 1). *steam*] smell (*OED* 1b).

Burnt offerings morn and evening shall be thine,
350   And fires eternal in thy temple shine.
This bush of yellow beard, this length of hair,
Which from my birth inviolate I bear,
Guiltless of steel, and from the razor free,
Shall fall a plenteous crop, reserved for thee.
355   So may my arms with victory be blest,
I ask no more; let Fate dispose the rest.'
     The champion ceased; there followed in the close
A hollow groan, a murmuring wind arose,
The rings of iron that on the doors were hung
360   Sent out a jarring sound, and harshly rung:
The bolted gates flew open at the blast,
The storm rushed in, and Arcite stood aghast.
The flames were blown aside, yet shone they bright,
Fanned by the wind, and gave a ruffled light.
365   Then from the ground a scent began to rise,
Sweet smelling, as accepted sacrifice:
This omen pleased, and as the flames aspire
With odorous incense Arcite heaps the fire,
Nor wanted hymns to Mars, or heathen charms.
370   At length the nodding statue clashed his arms,
And with a sullen sound, and feeble cry,
Half sunk, and half pronounced the word of 'victory'.
For this, with soul devout, he thanked the god,
And of success secure, returned to his abode.
375   These vows thus granted raised a strife above
Betwixt the God of War and Queen of Love.
She granting first had right of time to plead,
But he had granted too, nor would recede.
Jove was for Venus, but he feared his wife,

---

iii 353. guiltless of] having no experience of (*OED* 3; first example from *PL* ix 392).
iii 356. let Fate dispose the rest] D.'s addition.
iii 359–60. Cp. Milton: 'every bolt and bar / Of massy iron . . . / . . . on a sudden
open fly / With impetuous recoil and jarring sound / . . . / Harsh thunder'
(*PL* ii 877–82; J. R. Mason).
iii 359. D.'s addition.
iii 364. D.'s addition.   *ruffled*] irregular, intermittent.
iii 369. wanted] were lacking.
iii 370. nodding] See ii 352n.
iii 371. sullen] deep and mournful (*OED* 3b).
iii 372. sunk] suppressed in uttering (*OED* 25c, first example 1742).
iii 377–9. D.'s addition, l. 379 recalling the domestic tensions in 'The First Book
of Homer's *Ilias*' ll. 697–765.

380   And seemed unwilling to decide the strife,
        Till Saturn from his leaden throne arose,
        And found a way the difference to compose.
        Though sparing of his grace, to mischief bent,
        He seldom does a good with good intent;
385   Wayward, but wise; by long experience taught,
        To please both parties by ill ends he sought:
        For this advantage age from youth has won,
        As not to be outridden, though outrun.
        By fortune he was now to Venus trined,
390   And with stern Mars in Capricorn was joined;
        Of him disposing in his own abode,
        He soothed the goddess, while he gulled the god:
        'Cease, daughter, to complain, and stint the strife;
        Thy Palamon shall have his promised wife,
395   And Mars, the lord of conquest, in the fight

iii 381. Saturn] Also known as Chronos (cp. l. 426), the god of time; son of Uranus (sky) and Ge (earth), he castrated his father and married his sister Rhea, who gave birth to Jupiter, Juno, and other gods. As with the depiction of Mars in ii 524–616, some details in the presentation of Saturn show that Chaucer and D. were drawing on astrological interpretations of the influence of the planet. William Lily (*Christian Astrology* (1647)) notes that Saturn 'is of a Pale, Wan, or Leaden, Ashy colour' and 'ruleth over Lead' (57, 60; cp. l. 381). He is 'slow in Motion, finishing his Course through the twelve Signes of the Zodiack in 29 yeers, 157 dayes, or thereabouts' (57; cp. l. 398). Saturn is 'Melancholick . . . Malevolent . . . malicious' (58; cp. ll. 383–4), but was also credited with the wisdom born of experience (see *Riverside Chaucer* 838); as Lily says, 'he is profound in his Imagination . . . in arguing or disputing grave' (58) and associated with 'Old men, Fathers, Grandfathers' (59; cp. ll. 387, 393, 420). He is linked with 'Miners under ground' (59; cp. l. 415) and 'Caves, Dens, Holes . . . Ruinous Buildings, Cole-mines' (60; cp. ll. 402, 414–17); with 'obscure Ayre, cold and hurtfull' (60; cp. ll. 403–4) and with 'all quartan Agues proceeding of cold, dry and melancholly Distempers . . . Rheumes, Consumptions . . . vaine feares, Fantasies' (59; cp. ll. 403, 405–7).

iii 382–5. And found . . . wise] D.'s addition.

iii 388. Proverbial in the form 'Men may the old outrun, but not outwit'. D. misconstrues Chaucer's 'out rede' as 'outride' rather than 'outwit'.

iii 389–92. D.'s addition, developing Chaucer's astrology.

iii 389. trined] linked astrologically at an angle of 120°, a benign aspect.

iii 390–1. It is not clear whether *his own abode* refers to Saturn or Mars. Lily (57) says that Capricorn is Saturn's 'Night-house', but J. C. Eade says that 'when the zodiacal signs are paired with the astrological houses and distributed among the planets, the 10th house and Capricorn fall to Mars' (*The Forgotten Sky* (1984) 210).

iii 391. abode] astrological house.

iii 393. daughter] Thus Chaucer; affectionate address to a girl by an older person (*OED* 3). Venus was actually Saturn's granddaughter (see iii 420*n*).   *stint*] bring to an end (*OED* 7).

iii 394–6. D.'s addition.

With palm and laurel shall adorn his knight.
Wide is my course, nor turn I to my place
Till length of time, and move with tardy pace.
Man feels me when I press th' ethereal plains,
400   My hand is heavy, and the wound remains.
Mine is the shipwreck in a watery sign,
And in an earthy, the dark dungeon mine.
Cold shivering agues, melancholy care,   ⎫
And bitter blasting winds, and poisoned air   ⎬
405   Are mine, and wilful death, resulting from despair. ⎭
The throttling quinsy 'tis my star appoints,
And rheumatisms I send to rack the joints:
When churls rebel against their native prince,
I arm their hands, and furnish the pretence;
410   And housing in the Lion's hateful sign
Bought senates and deserting troops are mine.
Mine is the privy poisoning, I command
Unkindly seasons, and ungrateful land.
By me kings' palaces are pushed to ground,
415   And miners crushed beneath their mines are found.
'Twas I slew Samson, when the pillared hall

---

iii 397. course] movement of a planet through the heavens (*OED* 2).
iii 398–400. D.'s addition.
iii 401–2. watery sign . . . earthy] D.'s additions, associating the zodiacal signs with the four elements or humours.
iii 403–7. For 'Mine is the strangling and the hanging by the throte'.
iii 406. quinsy] inflammation of the throat.
iii 408–9, 411. For 'The murmure, and the churles rebelling'. Alluding to the Revolution of 1688–9 when James II was deposed and succeeded by William of Orange. The commanders of James's navy refused to engage the Dutch fleet, while many officers and men deserted James's army and went over to William. William was offered the crown by the specially elected Convention Parliament in 1689. The allusion to *bought senates* may also refer to *The Danger of Mercenary Parliaments* (1698), a pamphlet by the Earl of Shaftesbury and John Toland which argued that William's government relied on bribery to promote its absolutism; see also *POAS* vi 18–19.
iii 408. churls] people from a low social class; peasants; villains (*OED* 3b, 4, 5).
iii 410. the Lion] Leo. *hateful sign*] Leo was thought to increase the destruction wrought by malevolent planets (*Riverside Chaucer* 838). 'For then is Saturne in his detriment, and in opposition to his own house' (Speght sig. Bbbbiiiiʳ).
iii 413. D.'s addition. *Unkindly*] contrary to nature; not nurturing. *ungrateful*] not yielding to cultivation (cp. *AA* l. 12).
iii 414. kings' palaces] For 'hie halles', perhaps alluding to the fire that destroyed the palace of Whitehall in 1698.
iii 416–17. See ii 503*n* and Judges xvi 21–31.

Fell down, and crushed the many with the fall.
My looking is the sire of pestilence,
That sweeps at once the people and the prince.
420 Now weep no more, but trust thy grandsire's art;
Mars shall be pleased, and thou perform thy part.
'Tis ill, though different your complexions are,
The family of heaven for men should war.'
Th' expedient pleased, where neither lost his right:
425 Mars had the day, and Venus had the night.
The management they left to Chronos' care;
Now turn we to th' effect, and sing the war.
          In Athens all was pleasure, mirth, and play,
All proper to the spring, and sprightly May;
430 Which every soul inspired with such delight
'Twas jousting all the day, and love at night.
Heaven smiled, and gladded was the heart of man,
And Venus had the world, as when it first began.
At length in sleep their bodies they compose,
435 And dreamt the future fight, and early rose.
          Now scarce the dawning day began to spring,
As at a signal given the streets with clamours ring:
At once the crowd arose; confused and high ⎫
Ev'n from the heaven was heard a shouting cry, ⎬
440 For Mars was early up, and roused the sky. ⎭
The gods came downward to behold the wars,
Sharpening their sights, and leaning from their stars.
The neighing of the generous horse was heard,
For battle by the busy groom prepared:
445 Rustling of harness, rattling of the shield,
Clattering of armour furbished for the field.
Crowds to the castle mounted up the street,
Battering the pavement with their coursers' feet.
The greedy sight might there devour the gold

iii 417. D.'s addition.   *many*] company, host (*OED* B2); cp. l. 545n.
iii 419. D.'s addition.
iii 420. *grandsire's*] Saturn was the father of Jupiter, and Jupiter the father of Venus.
iii 422. *complexions*] temperaments (*OED* 1, 3).
iii 423–6. D.'s addition.
iii 426. *Chronos'*] Saturn's.
iii 432, 439–42. D.'s additions.
iii 443. *generous*] courageous, spirited (*OED* 2, 2c).
iii 444, 447. D.'s additions.

450   Of glittering arms, too dazzling to behold,
      And polished steel that cast the view aside,
      And crested morions with their plumy pride.
      Knights with a long retinue of their squires
      In gaudy liveries march, and quaint attires.
455   One laced the helm, another held the lance,
      A third the shining buckler did advance.
      The courser pawed the ground with restless feet,
      And snorting foamed, and champed the golden bit.
      The smiths and armourers on palfreys ride,
460   Files in their hands, and hammers at their side,
      And nails for loosened spears, and thongs for shields
         provide.
      The yeomen guard the streets in seemly bands,
      And clowns come crowding on, with cudgels in their hands.
      The trumpets, next the gate, in order placed,
465   Attend the sign to sound the martial blast.
      The palace yard is filled with floating tides,
      And the last comers bear the former to the sides.
      The throng is in the midst: the common crew
      Shut out, the hall admits the better few.
470   In knots they stand, or in a rank they walk,
      Serious in aspect, earnest in their talk:
      Factious, and favouring this or t' other side,
      As their strong fancies, and weak reason, guide:
      Their wagers back their wishes: numbers hold
475   With the fair freckled king, and beard of gold:
      So vigorous are his eyes, such rays they cast,
      So prominent his eagle's beak is placed.
      But most their looks on the black monarch bend,

---

iii 452. *morions*] seventeenth-century helmets without visors (*OED*), resembling Greek helmets.
iii 453. *retinue*] stressed on the second syllable in this period.
iii 454. D.'s addition. *gaudy*] bright, festive. *quaint*] skilfully made, beautiful, elegant (*OED* 4).
iii 457. D.'s addition.
iii 459. *palfreys*] horses for ordinary riding, as distinguished from warhorses (*OED*).
iii 463. *clowns*] countrymen, peasants (*OED* 1).
iii 465, 467–9, 473. D.'s additions.
iii 474–83. D.'s expansion, with more detail of the champions' appearance.
iii 476. *such rays they cast*] Extramission (the idea that the eyes cast beams which connected with the object seen) was still a widespread theory of vision in this period. Cp. *HP* ii 72–6*n* and 'Sigismonda and Guiscardo' l. 64*n*.

His rising muscles and his brawn commend,
480 His double-biting axe and beamy spear,
Each asking a gigantic force to rear.
All spoke as partial favour moved the mind,
And safe themselves, at others' cost divined.
     Waked by the cries, th' Athenian chief arose,
485 The knightly forms of combat to dispose;
And passing through th' obsequious guards, he sate
Conspicuous on a throne, sublime in state.
There for the two contending knights he sent:
Armed cap-à-pie, with reverence low they bent;
490 He smiled on both, and with superior look
Alike their offered adoration took.
The people press on every side to see
Their awful prince, and hear his high decree.
Then signing to the heralds with his hand,
495 They gave his orders from their lofty stand.
Silence is thrice enjoined; then thus aloud
The King at Arms bespeaks the knights and listening crowd.
     'Our sovereign lord has pondered in his mind
The means to spare the blood of gentle kind;
500 And of his grace and inborn clemency
He modifies his first severe decree,
The keener edge of battle to rebate,
The troops for honour fighting, not for hate.
He wills not death should terminate their strife,
505 And wounds, if wounds ensue, be short of life.
But issues ere the fight his dread command
That slings afar, and poniards hand to hand,
Be banished from the field; that none shall dare
With shortened sword to stab in closer war;

---

iii 481. *asking*] requiring.
iii 485–94. In Chaucer, Theseus sits at a window and is reverenced by the people, not the rival knights.
iii 486. *obsequious*] obedient, dutiful (OED 1).
iii 489. *cap-à-pie*] head to foot.
iii 493. *awful*] awesome, awe inspiring.
iii 497. *King at Arms*] chief herald.
iii 499. *gentle*] noble.   *kind*] family, ancestral race (OED 11–12).
iii 500, 502–3. D.'s additions.
iii 502. *rebate*] blunt.
iii 505–6. D.'s additions.
iii 507. *poniards*] daggers.

510   But in fair combat fight with manly strength,
        Nor push with biting point, but strike at length.
        The tourney is allowed but one career
        Of the tough ash, with the sharp-grinded spear.
        But knights unhorsed may ride from off the plain,
515   And fight on foot, their honour to regain;
        Nor, if at mischief taken, on the ground
        Be slain, but prisoners to the pillar bound,
        At either barrier placed; nor, captives made,
        Be freed, or armed anew the fight invade.
520   The chief of either side bereft of life,
        Or yielded to his foe, concludes the strife.
        Thus dooms the lord: now valiant knights and young,
        Fight each his fill with swords and maces long.'
            The herald ends; the vaulted firmament
525   With loud acclaims and vast applause is rent:
        'Heaven guard a prince so gracious and so good,
        So just, and yet so provident of blood!'
        This was the general cry. The trumpets sound,
        And warlike symphony is heard around.
530   The marching troops through Athens take their way,
        The great Earl Marshal orders their array.
        The fair from high the passing pomp behold;
        A rain of flowers is from the windows rolled.
        The casements are with golden tissue spread,
535   And horses' hoofs, for earth, on silken tap'stry tread.
        The king goes midmost, and the rivals ride
        In equal rank, and close his either side.
        Next after these there rode the royal wife,
        With Emily, the cause and the reward of strife.
540   The following cavalcade, by three and three,
        Proceed by titles marshalled in degree.

iii 510. D.'s addition.
iii 512. tourney] tournament.   *allowed*] allotted.   *career*] attack on horseback, charge.
iii 514. D.'s addition.
iii 516. at mischief] at a disadvantage in a fight (*OED* 1c, last example 1579).
iii 518–19. nor . . . invade] D.'s addition.
iii 522. dooms] decides.
iii 527. provident] sparing.
iii 529. symphony] music in parts or played by a group of performers (*OED* 4a).
iii 531–5. For 'Honged with cloth of gold, and not with sarge [serge]'.
iii 531. Earl Marshal] official in charge of royal ceremonies.
iii 539. the cause and the reward of strife] D.'s addition.

Thus through the southern gate they take their way,
And at the lists arrived ere prime of day.
There, parting from the king, the chiefs divide,
545   And wheeling east and west before their many ride.
Th' Athenian monarch mounts his throne on high,
And after him the queen, and Emily.
Next these, the kindred of the crown are graced
With nearer seats, and lords by ladies placed.
550   Scarce were they seated, when with clamours loud
In rushed at once a rude promiscuous crowd;
The guards, and then each other, overbear,
And in a moment throng the spacious theatre.
Now changed the jarring noise to whispers low,
555   As winds forsaking seas more softly blow;
When at the western gate, on which the car
Is placed aloft that bears the god of war,
Proud Arcite entering armed before his train
Stops at the barrier, and divides the plain.
560   Red was his banner, and displayed abroad
The bloody colours of his patron god.
     At that self moment enters Palamon
The gate of Venus and the rising sun;
Waved by the wanton winds his banner flies,
565   All maiden white, and shares the people's eyes.
From east to west, look all the world around,
Two troops so matched were never to be found:
Such bodies built for strength, of equal age,
In stature sized, so proud an equipage,
570   The nicest eye could no distinction make
Where lay th' advantage, or what side to take.
     Thus ranged, the herald for the last proclaims
A silence, while they answered to their names:
For so the king decreed, to shun with care
575   The fraud of musters false, the common bane of war.

iii 542, 544–5. D.'s additions.
iii 545. *many*] company, host; retinue (*OED* B2, last example).
iii 548. D.'s addition.
iii 550–5. For 'Vnto the seates preaseth all the route [rabble]'.
iii 551. *promiscuous*] of different kinds mixed together (*OED* 1).
iii 556. *car*] chariot.
iii 559. D.'s addition.
iii 564. *wanton*] unrestrained, playful (*OED* 3c).
iii 570. *nicest*] most discriminating.
iii 574–5. D.'s addition.

The tale was just, and then the gates were closed,
And chief to chief, and troop to troop opposed.
The heralds last retired, and loudly cried,
'The fortune of the field be fairly tried.'
580   At this, the challenger with fierce defy
His trumpet sounds; the challenged makes reply:
With clangour rings the field, resounds the vaulted sky.
Their visors closed, their lances in the rest,
Or at the helmet pointed, or the crest,
585   They vanish from the barrier, speed the race,
And spurring see decrease the middle space.
A cloud of smoke envelops either host,
And all at once the combatants are lost:
Darkling they join adverse, and shock unseen,
590   Coursers with coursers jostling, men with men:
As labouring in eclipse, a while they stay,
Till the next blast of wind restores the day.
They look anew: the beauteous form of fight
Is changed, and war appears a grisly sight.
595   Two troops in fair array one moment showed,
The next, a field with fallen bodies strowed.
Not half the number in their seats are found,
But men and steeds lie grovelling on the ground.
The points of spears are stuck within the shield,
600   The steeds without their riders scour the field.
The knights unhorsed, on foot renew the fight,
The glittering falchions cast a gleaming light:

iii 576. *tale*] tally, enumeration (*OED* 6–7).

iii 577. D.'s addition.

iii 580. *defy*] challenge to fight (*OED*).

iii 584. D.'s addition.   *Or . . . or*] Either . . . or.

iii 585–601. For 'In goth the sharpe spurres into the side: / There se men who can iust [joust] and who can ride: / There shiueren shaftes upon sheldes thicke; / He feleth through the hert spoune [breast bone] the pricke. / Vp springeth the speres, twenty fote on hight'.

iii 587. *smoke*] dust (cp. *OED v.* 2).

iii 589. *Darkling*] in the dark.   *adverse*] in opposition.   *shock*] collide, esp. in battle (*OED* 1).

iii 591. *labouring*] plying with blows (*OED* 4, last example 1697 from D.'s 'The Third Book of the *Georgics*' l. 639), punning on Latin *laborare* ('to eclipse'); cp. *OED* labour *sb.* 7, citing only D.'s 'The Second Book of the *Georgics*' l. 679 for the meaning 'eclipse'; and cp. *PL* ii 665–6.

iii 600. *scour*] move quickly over (*OED v.*¹ 2).

iii 602. *falchions*] broad swords (*OED*).

Hauberks and helms are hewed with many a wound;
Out spins the streaming blood, and dyes the ground.
605   The mighty maces with such haste descend,
They break the bones, and make the solid armour bend.
This thrusts amid the throng with furious force:
Down goes at once the horseman and the horse;
That courser stumbles on the fallen steed,
610   And floundering, throws the rider o'er his head.
One rolls along, a football to his foes,
One with a broken truncheon deals his blows.
This halting, this disabled with his wound,
In triumph led is to the pillar bound,
615   Where by the king's award he must abide:
There goes a captive led on t' other side.
By fits they cease, and leaning on the lance
Take breath a while, and to new fight advance.
        Full oft the rivals met, and neither spared
620   His utmost force, and each forgot to ward.
The head of this was to the saddle bent,
That other backward to the crupper sent:
Both were by turns unhorsed, the jealous blows
Fall thick and heavy, when on foot they close.
625   So deep their falchions bite, that every stroke
Pierced to the quick, and equal wounds they gave and took.
Borne far asunder by the tides of men,
Like adamant and steel they meet again.
        So when a tiger sucks the bullock's blood, ⎫
630   A famished lion issuing from the wood   ⎬
Roars lordly fierce, and challenges the food. ⎭
Each claims possession, neither will obey,
But both their paws are fastened on the prey:
They bite, they tear, and while in vain they strive,

iii 603. *Hauberks*] coats of chain mail.
iii 604. *spins*] gushes, spurts (*OED* 8).
iii 615. *award*] decision.
iii 620–2. D.'s addition.
iii 623. *jealous*] wrathful, furious (*OED* 1, last example 1661); afraid of losing
something to a rival (*OED* 4b).
iii 624. D.'s addition.
iii 627–8. D.'s addition.
iii 628. *adamant*] loadstone, magnet (*OED* 3, last example 1656).
iii 629–35. Chaucer compares Arcite with a tiger deprived of its cub, and Palamon
with a lion hunting its prey.

635   The swains come armed between, and both to
       distance drive.
       At length, as Fate foredoomed, and all things tend
   By course of time to their appointed end,
   So when the sun to west was far declined,
   And both afresh in mortal battle joined,
640   The strong Emetrius came in Arcite's aid,
   And Palamon with odds was overlaid:
   For turning short, he struck with all his might
   Full on the helmet of th' unwary knight:
   Deep was the wound, he staggered with the blow,
645   And turned him to his unexpected foe,
   Whom with such force he struck, he felled him down,
   And cleft the circle of his golden crown.
   But Arcite's men, who now prevailed in fight,
   Twice ten at once surround the single knight:
650   O'erpowered at length, they force him to the ground,
   Unyielded as he was, and to the pillar bound;
   And King Lycurgus, while he fought in vain
   His friend to free, was tumbled on the plain.
       Who now laments but Palamon, compelled
655   No more to try the fortune of the field!
   And worse than death, to view with hateful eyes
   His rival's conquest, and renounce the prize!
       The royal judge on his tribunal placed,
   Who had beheld the fight from first to last,
660   Bad cease the war, pronouncing from on high
   Arcite of Thebes had won the beauteous Emily.
   The sound of trumpets to the voice replied, ⎫
   And round the royal lists the heralds cried, ⎬
   'Arcite of Thebes has won the beauteous bride.' ⎭
665   The people rend the skies with vast applause,
   All own the chief, when Fortune owns the cause.
   Arcite is owned ev'n by the gods above,
   And conquering Mars insults the Queen of Love.

iii *636. as Fate foredoomed*] D.'s addition.
iii *641–51.* D.'s expansion of Chaucer.
iii *641. overlaid*] overwhelmed, overpowered (*OED* 7a).
iii *656–7, 662–4.* D.'s additions.
iii *665.* Echoes *Alexander's Feast* l. 107 (Christie).
iii *666–72.* D.'s addition.
iii *668. insults*] triumphs scornfully over (*OED* 2b, first example 1775).

> So laughed he when the rightful Titan failed,
> 670 And Jove's usurping arms in heaven prevailed;
> Laughed all the powers who favour tyranny,
> And all the standing army of the sky.
> But Venus with dejected eyes appears,
> And weeping on the lists distilled her tears;
> 675 Her will refused, which grieves a woman most,
> And in her champion foiled, the cause of love is lost.
> Till Saturn said, 'Fair daughter, now be still,
> The blustering fool has satisfied his will:
> His boon is given, his knight has gained the day
> 680 But lost the prize: th' arrears are yet to pay.
> Thy hour is come, and mine the care shall be
> To please thy knight, and set thy promise free.'
>   Now while the heralds run the lists around,
> And 'Arcite, Arcite' heaven and earth resound,
> 685 A miracle (nor less it could be called)
> Their joy with unexpected sorrow palled.

iii 669–72. With contemporary resonance, recalling the deposition of James II. The Titans, led by Chronos (Saturn), were overthrown by Zeus (Jupiter) (Hesiod, *Theogony* ll. 617–735).

iii 671. tyranny] Not only (i) cruel or despotic rule (*OED* tyranny 2, 3a), but also (ii) rule by one who seizes the sovereign power without legal right, i.e. a usurper (*OED* tyrant 1). D. regarded William III as a tyrant in this latter sense. Cp. i 86*n*.

iii 672. standing army] The Parliament of 1697–8 had refused to accept William III's request that a large standing army be maintained. He had argued that despite the Treaty of Ryswick in 1697 peace in Europe was precarious, but there was concern about the huge cost of maintaining an army, and reluctance to countenance further involvement in continental wars. Many feared that such an army would be used for internal repression and the implementation of autocratic rule rather than for defence. It was also argued that a standing army (which included Dutch soldiers and other mercenaries) should be replaced by reformed local militias. See Lois Schwoerer, *No Standing Armies!* (1974). Opposition to a standing army was rehearsed in pamphlets such as *An Argument showing that a Standing Army is Incompatible with a Free Government* (1697) and *A Short History of Standing Armies in England* (1698). Ironically, Daniel Defoe in his answer to the latter pamphlet quoted D. to disparage his opponents' methods of argument: 'Disputants, when reasons fail, / Have one sure Refuge left, and that's to rail' (from the 'Epilogue to *All for Love*' ll. 1–2; [Daniel Defoe], *A Brief Reply to the History of Standing Armies in England* (1698) 15). See also *POAS* vi 161.

iii 674. distilled] let fall in drops (*OED* 2).

iii 675–6. D.'s addition.

iii 680–2. For 'thou shalt be eased sone [soon]'.

iii 682. set . . . free] discharge, release from the obligations relating to (cp. *OED* free *v*. 2).

iii 686. D.'s addition.

The victor knight had laid his helm aside,
Part for his ease, the greater part for pride:
Bare-headed, popularly low he bowed,
690   And paid the salutations of the crowd.
Then spurring at full speed, ran endlong on
Where Theseus sat on his imperial throne;
Furious he drove, and upward cast his eye
Where next the queen was placed his Emily;
695   Then passing, to the saddle bow he bent;
A sweet regard the gracious virgin lent
(For women, to the brave an easy prey,
Still follow Fortune, where she leads the way).
Just then, from earth sprung out a flashing fire,
700   By Pluto sent, at Saturn's bad desire;
The startling steed was seized with sudden fright,
And bounding, o'er the pummel cast the knight:
Forward he flew, and pitching on his head
He quivered with his feet, and lay for dead.
705   Black was his count'nance in a little space,
For all the blood was gathered in his face.
Help was at hand; they reared him from the ground,
And from his cumbrous arms his limbs unbound;
Then lanced a vein, and watched returning breath;
710   It came, but clogged with symptoms of his death.
The saddle bow the noble parts had pressed,
All bruised and mortified his manly breast.
Him still entranced, and in a litter laid,
They bore from field, and to his bed conveyed.
715   At length he waked, and with a feeble cry
The word he first pronounced was 'Emily'.
        Meantime the king, though inwardly he mourned,
In pomp triumphant to the town returned,
Attended by the chiefs who fought the field
720   (Now friendly mixed, and in one troop compelled);
Composed his looks to counterfeited cheer,

---

iii 688. D.'s addition.   *pride*] See iii 770*n*.
iii 689–90. For 'for to shewe his face'.
iii 689. Echoing *AA* l. 689 (Monmouth courting the crowd).
iii 690. paid] requited, returned (*OED* 3).
iii 691. endlong on] right along, straight on (*OED* 3).
iii 692. D.'s addition.
iii 697. to the brave an easy prey] D.'s addition.
iii 707–10. D.'s addition.
iii 713. D.'s addition.   *entranced*] thrown into a trance, unconscious (*OED* 1).
iii 720–1. D.'s addition.

And bade them not for Arcite's life to fear.
But that which gladded all the warrior train,
Though most were sorely wounded, none were slain.
725 The surgeons soon despoiled 'em of their arms,
And some with salves they cure, and some with charms;
Foment the bruises, and the pains assuage,
And heal their inward hurts with sovereign draughts of sage.
The king in person visits all around,
730 Comforts the sick, congratulates the sound;
Honours the princely chiefs, rewards the rest,
And holds for thrice three days a royal feast.
None was disgraced, for falling is no shame,
And cowardice alone is loss of fame.
735 The vent'rous knight is from the saddle thrown,
But 'tis the fault of Fortune, not his own.
If crowns and palms the conquering side adorn,
The victor under better stars was born.
The brave man seeks not popular applause,
740 Nor overpowered with arms deserts his cause;
Unshamed, though foiled, he does the best he can:
Force is of brutes, but honour is of man.
    Thus Theseus smiled on all with equal grace,
And each was set according to his place.
745 With ease were reconciled the differing parts,
For envy never dwells in noble hearts.
At length they took their leave, the time expired,
Well pleased, and to their several homes retired.
    Meanwhile the health of Arcite still impairs,
750 From bad proceeds to worse, and mocks the leeches' cares:
Swoll'n is his breast, his inward pains increase,
All means are used, and all without success.

---

iii 720. compelled] gathered into a company by force (*OED* 3); but perhaps closer to the Latin *compellere*, 'drive together, round up' (*OLD* 1), which does not necessarily imply the use of force.
iii 725. D.'s addition.
iii 727. foment] bathe with warm or medicated lotions (*OED* 1).
iii 728. sovereign] efficacious, potent (*OED* 3). *sage*] The herb was regarded as having healing properties.
iii 735–42. D.'s addition.
iii 739. popular applause] A phrase also used of demagoguery in 'Lucretius: Against the Fear of Death' l. 203 and *HP* iii 1092.
iii 748. several] separate, individual.
iii 750. leeches'] doctors'; cp. 'To John Driden of Chesterton' l. 79*n*.
iii 751–2. D.'s addition.

The clotted blood lies heavy on his heart,
Corrupts, and there remains in spite of art:
755   Nor breathing veins nor cupping will prevail,
All outward remedies and inward fail.
The mould of nature's fabric is destroyed,
Her vessels discomposed, her virtue void:
The bellows of his lungs begins to swell,   ⎫
760   All out of frame is every secret cell,   ⎬
Nor can the good receive, nor bad expel.   ⎭
Those breathing organs thus within oppressed
With venom soon distend the sinews of his breast.
Nought profits him to save abandoned life,
765   Nor vomits upward aid, nor downward laxative.
The midmost region battered and destroyed,
When nature cannot work, th' effect of art is void:
For physic can but mend our crazy state,
Patch an old building, not a new create.
770   Arcite is doomed to die in all his pride,   ⎫
Must leave his youth, and yield his beauteous bride, ⎬
Gained hardly, against right, and unenjoyed.   ⎭
When 'twas declared all hope of life was past, ⎫
Conscience, that of all physic works the last, ⎬
775   Caused him to send for Emily in haste.   ⎭
With her, at his desire, came Palamon;

---

iii 755. breathing veins] opening veins to draw off blood; a common treatment. Cp. 'Heroic Stanzas' l. 48*n*. *cupping*] drawing blood by scarifying the skin and applying a hot cup or glass.
iii 756–7. D.'s addition.
iii 757. mould] earth regarded as the material of the human body (*OED* mould¹ 4; last example 1629, but cp. *AA* l. 368*n*); bodily form (*OED* mould³ 10).
iii 758. discomposed] disarranged; disturbed in health (*OED* 2, 2b). *virtue*] power or efficacy inherent in something (*OED* 11).
iii 760. D.'s addition. *cell*] cavity within the body, e.g. the ventricles of the heart (*OED* 11a).
iii 763. D.'s addition.
iii 765. laxative] The spelling *Laxatife* in *1700* provides a good rhyme.
iii 768–9. D.'s addition.
iii 768. crazy] frail, diseased (*OED* 2). *state*] suggests a political analogy: cp. *AA* ll. 801–3, 809–10.
iii 770. pride] feeling of superiority, self-esteem (*OED* 1); ostentation, display (*OED* 6), both senses also present in l. 688; most flourishing state or condition (*OED* 9).
iii 771–4. D.'s addition.
iii 772. hardly] with difficulty.

Then on his pillow raised, he thus begun:
'No language can express the smallest part
Of what I feel, and suffer in my heart,
780   For you, whom best I love and value most,
But to your service I bequeath my ghost,
Which from this mortal body when untied,
Unseen, unheard, shall hover at your side;
Nor fright you waking, nor your sleep offend,
785   But wait officious, and your steps attend.
How I have loved, excuse my faltering tongue,
My spirits feeble, and my pains are strong:
This I may say, I only grieve to die
Because I lose my charming Emily:
790   To die when heaven had put you in my power,
Fate could not choose a more malicious hour!
What greater curse could envious Fortune give,
Than just to die when I began to live!
Vain men, how vanishing a bliss we crave,
795   Now warm in love, now withering in the grave!
Never, O never more to see the sun!
Still dark, in a damp vault, and still alone!
This fate is common; but I lose my breath
Near bliss, and yet not blessed before my death.
800   Farewell, but take me dying in your arms,
'Tis all I can enjoy of all your charms.
This hand I cannot but in death resign;
Ah, could I live! But while I live 'tis mine.
I feel my end approach, and thus embraced
805   Am pleased to die; but hear me speak my last.
Ah! my sweet foe, for you, and you alone,
I broke my faith with injured Palamon.
But love the sense of right and wrong confounds,
Strong love and proud ambition have no bounds.
810   And much I doubt, should heaven my life prolong,

iii *777.* D.'s addition.
iii *781. ghost*] spirit (again at ll. 988, 1110).
iii *782–6.* D.'s addition.
iii *785. officious*] dutiful.
iii *787. feeble*] Possibly an adjective (supply 'are'), but more probably an intransitive
verb, 'become feeble' (*OED*'s last example is from 1496).
iii *790–3, 796–9.* D.'s additions.
iii *797. Still*] always, for ever (*OED* 3).
iii *801–4, 808–22, 830–3.* D.'s additions.

I should return to justify my wrong:
For while my former flames remain within,
Repentance is but want of power to sin.
With mortal hatred I pursued his life,
815 Nor he, nor you, were guilty of the strife;
Nor I, but as I loved: yet all combined—
Your beauty, and my impotence of mind,
And his concurrent flame that blew my fire:
For still our kindred souls had one desire.
820 He had a moment's right in point of time:
Had I seen first, then his had been the crime.
Fate made it mine, and justified his right,
Nor holds this earth a more deserving knight
For virtue, valour, and for noble blood,
825 Truth, honour, all that is comprised in good.
So help me heaven, in all the world is none
So worthy to be loved as Palamon.
He loves you too, with such a holy fire
As will not, cannot but with life expire.
830 Our vowed affections both have often tried,
Nor any love but yours could ours divide.
Then by my love's inviolable band,
By my long suffering, and my short command,
If e'er you plight your vows when I am gone,
835 Have pity on the faithful Palamon.'
          This was his last, for death came on amain,
And exercised below his iron reign;
Then upward to the seat of life he goes;
Sense fled before him; what he touched, he froze.
840 Yet could he not his closing eyes withdraw,
Though less and less of Emily he saw:
So speechless for a little space he lay,
Then grasped the hand he held, and sighed his soul away.
          But whither went his soul, let such relate
845 Who search the secrets of the future state.

---

iii *830–1. vowed affections . . . divide*] Echoes 'Nisus and Euryalus' l. 250.
iii *832. band*] bond.
iii *836. amain*] rapidly.
iii *837.* D.'s addition.
iii *838–9. he*] death.
iii *840. he*] Arcite.
iii *844–53.* For 'His spirite chaunged, and out went there, / Whetherwarde
I cannot tell, ne where: / Therefore I stint, I am no diuinistre [theologian]; /

Divines can say but what themselves believe;
Strong proofs they have, but not demonstrative:
For were all plain, then all sides must agree,
And faith itself be lost in certainty.
850 To live uprightly then is sure the best,
To save ourselves, and not to damn the rest.
The soul of Arcite went where heathens go
Who better live than we, though less they know.
     In Palamon a manly grief appears:
855 Silent he wept, ashamed to show his tears;
Emilia shrieked but once, and then oppressed
With sorrow, sunk upon her lover's breast,
Till Theseus in his arms conveyed with care
Far from so sad a sight the swooning fair.
860 'Twere loss of time her sorrow to relate:
Ill bears the sex a youthful lover's fate
When just approaching to the nuptial state.
But like a low-hung cloud it rains so fast
That all at once it falls, and cannot last.
865 The face of things is changed, and Athens now,
That laughed so late, becomes the scene of woe:
Matrons and maids, both sexes, every state,
With tears lament the knight's untimely fate.
Not greater grief in falling Troy was seen
870 For Hector's death, but Hector was not then.
Old men with dust deformed their hoary hair,
The women beat their breasts, their cheeks they tear.
'Why would'st thou go', with one consent they cry,
'When thou hadst gold enough, and Emily!'
875   Theseus himself, who should have cheered the grief
Of others, wanted now the same relief.

Of soules finde I not in this registre; / Ne me leste not thilke opinion to tell /
Of hem, though they writen where thei dwell. / *Arcite* is cold, that *Mars* his soule
gie [guide]'. For D.'s attitude to the question of the salvation of pagans see *RL*
'Preface' ll. 48–50, 130–75, Poem ll. 186–211 and *nn*.
iii 847. *demonstrative*] proving conclusively (*OED* 4).
iii 854–5. For 'houlen [howled] *Palamon*'.
iii 857, 863–6. D.'s additions.
iii 871–2. *with dust . . . tear*] D.'s addition, recalling scenes of mourning in Homer
and Virgil.
iii 875–6. D.'s addition.

Old Egeus only could revive his son,
Who various changes of the world had known,
And strange vicissitudes of human fate,
880   Still altering, never in a steady state:
Good after ill, and after pain, delight,
Alternate, like the scenes of day and night:
'Since every man who lives is born to die,
And none can boast sincere felicity,
885   With equal mind what happens let us bear,
Nor joy, nor grieve too much for things beyond our care.
Like pilgrims to th' appointed place we tend,
The world's an inn, and death the journey's end.
Ev'n kings but play, and when their part is done,
890   Some other, worse or better, mount the throne.'
With words like these the crowd was satisfied,
And so they would have been had Theseus died.
    But he, their king, was labouring in his mind ⎫
A fitting place for funeral pomps to find,   ⎬
895   Which were in honour of the dead designed.   ⎭
And after long debate, at last he found
(As love itself had marked the spot of ground)
That grove for ever green, that conscious laund,
Where he with Palamon fought hand to hand:
900   That where he fed his amorous desires
With soft complaints, and felt his hottest fires,
There other flames might waste his earthly part,
And burn his limbs, where love had burned his heart.
    This once resolved, the peasants were enjoined

---

iii 879. vicissitudes] alterations (*OED* 3).
iii 882. D.'s addition.
iii 884–6. D.'s addition.
iii 884. sincere] unmixed (*OED* 2); cp. *AA* l. 43.
iii 885. equal] with strength adequate to the occasion (*OED* 3b, first example from D.'s 'The Second Book of the *Georgics*' l. 304); tranquil, undisturbed (*OED* 9), as in 'The Tenth Satire of Juvenal' l. 81.
iii 888. inn] temporary dwelling-place (*OED* 3), often used figuratively, e.g. for the body or the world as the temporary lodging of the soul.
iii 889–90, 892. D.'s additions (the former with political resonance).
iii 898. conscious] aware of secrets (*OED* 1).   *laund*] open space between woods, glade (*OED*).
iii 902–3. For 'He would make a fire, in which the offis / Funerall he might hem all accomplis'.

905   Sere wood, and firs, and doddered oaks to find.
        With sounding axes to the grove they go,
        Fell, split, and lay the fuel on a row,
        Vulcanian food: a bier is next prepared
        On which the lifeless body should be reared,
910   Covered with cloth of gold, on which was laid
        The corpse of Arcite, in like robes arrayed.
        White gloves were on his hands, and on his head
        A wreath of laurel mixed with myrtle spread.
        A sword keen-edged within his right he held,
915   The warlike emblem of the conquered field;
        Bare was his manly visage on the bier,
        Menaced his count'nance, ev'n in death severe.
        Then to the palace hall they bore the knight
        To lie in solemn state, a public sight.
920   Groans, cries, and howlings fill the crowded place,
        And unaffected sorrow sat on every face.
        Sad Palamon above the rest appears,
        In sable garments dewed with gushing tears;
        His auburn locks on either shoulder flowed,
925   Which to the funeral of his friend he vowed:
        But Emily, as chief, was next his side,
        A virgin widow, and a mourning bride.
        And that the princely obsequies might be
        Performed according to his high degree,
930   The steed that bore him living to the fight   ⎫
        Was trapped with polished steel, all shining bright, ⎬
        And covered with th' achievements of the knight. ⎭
        The riders rode abreast, and one his shield,
        His lance of cornel wood another held;

iii 905. Sere] dry.   *doddered*] having lost their tops and branches through age and decay; D.'s coinage in 'Virgil's Ninth Eclogue' (1684) l. 12; also used in 'The Fifth Satire of Persius' l. 80. Thomas Sternberg suggests that the word had Northamptonshire associations (*The Dialect and Folk-Lore of Northamptonshire* (1851) 188–9).
iii 906. D.'s addition.
iii 908. Vulcanian] for Vulcan, god of fire.
iii 909. D.'s addition.
iii 913. laurel . . . myrtle] emblems of the victor and the lover.
iii 915, 917, 921, 925. D.'s additions.
iii 927. D.'s addition.   *mourning bride*] Capitalized and italicized in *1700* as *Mourning Bride*, thus alluding to Congreve's play *The Mourning Bride* (1697).
iii 931. trapped with] adorned with trappings of (*OED*).
iii 932. achievements] See iii 344*n.*
iii 934. cornel] See iii 270*n.*

935   The third his bow, and glorious to behold
      The costly quiver, all of burnished gold.
      The noblest of the Grecians next appear,
      And weeping, on their shoulders bore the bier;
      With sober pace they marched, and often stayed,
940   And through the master street the corpse conveyed.
      The houses to their tops with black were spread,
      And ev'n the pavements were with mourning hid.
      The right side of the pall old Egeus kept,
      And on the left the royal Theseus wept:
945   Each bore a golden bowl of work divine,
      With honey filled, and milk, and mixed with ruddy wine;
      Then Palamon the kinsman of the slain,
      And after him appeared th' illustrious train:
      To grace the pomp came Emily the bright,
950   With covered fire, the funeral pile to light.
      With high devotion was the service made,
      And all the rites of pagan honour paid.
      So lofty was the pile, a Parthian bow
      With vigour drawn must send the shaft below.
955   The bottom was full twenty fathom broad,
      With crackling straw beneath in due proportion strowed.
      The fabric seemed a wood of rising green,
      With sulphur and bitumen cast between
      To feed the flames: the trees were unctuous fir, ⎫
960   And mountain ash, the mother of the spear; ⎬
      The mourner yew, and builder oak were there; ⎭
      The beech, the swimming alder, and the plane,
      Hard box, and linden of a softer grain,
      And laurels, which the gods for conquering chiefs
        ordain.
965   How they were ranked shall rest untold by me,

---

iii 940. *master street*] main or principal street (*OED*'s sole example is from Chaucer).
iii 949. *pomp*] ceremonial procession (*OED* 2).
iii 950. *covered fire*] See iii 194n.
iii 952–5. D.'s addition.
iii 953. *Parthian*] The Parthians were proverbially skilled archers.
iii 958. D.'s addition. *bitumen*] stressed on the second syllable.
iii 959–64. D. halves the number of trees, and adds the epithets, imitating Spenser, *FQ* I i 8–9, esp. 'The builder Oake . . . / The Laurell, meed of mightie Conquerours / . . . The Firre that weepeth still'. Kinsley suggests that *the swimming alder* derives from Virgil's *alnos primum fluuii sensere cauatas* ('the rivers first felt the hollow alders': *Geo.* i 136).

With nameless nymphs that lived in every tree;
Nor how the dryads, and the woodland train,
Disherited, ran howling o'er the plain;
Nor how the birds to foreign seats repaired,
970 Or beasts, that bolted out and saw the forest bared;
Nor how the ground, now cleared, with ghastly fright
Beheld the sudden sun, a stranger to the light.
  The straw, as first I said, was laid below,
Of chips and sere wood was the second row;
975 The third of greens, and timber newly felled;
The fourth high stage the fragrant odours held,
And pearls, and precious stones, and rich array,
In midst of which, embalmed, the body lay.
The service sung, the maid with mourning eyes
980 The stubble fired; the smouldering flames arise.
This office done, she sunk upon the ground,
But what she spoke, recovered from her swound,
I want the wit in moving words to dress,
But by themselves the tender sex may guess.
985 While the devouring fire was burning fast,
Rich jewels in the flame the wealthy cast,
And some their shields, and some their lances threw,
And gave the warrior's ghost a warrior's due.
Full bowls of wine, of honey, milk, and blood,
990 Were poured upon the pile of burning wood,
And hissing flames receive, and hungry lick the food.
Then thrice the mounted squadrons ride around
The fire, and Arcite's name they thrice resound:
'Hail and farewell' they shouted thrice amain,
995 Thrice facing to the left, and thrice they turned again:
Still as they turned they beat their clattering shields,
The women mix their cries, and clamour fills the fields.
The warlike wakes continued all the night,

---

iii *967. dryads*] tree nymphs.
iii *972. sudden*] appearing unexpectedly (*OED* 1d).
iii *974. sere*] dry.
iii *982. swound*] swoon, faint.
iii *983–5.* D.'s addition.
iii *983. want*] lack.
iii *988, 991.* D.'s additions.
iii *994.* D.'s addition. The Romans greeted the dead body three times with *ave atque vale* ('hail and farewell'); cp. 'To the Memory of Mr Oldham' l. *22n.   amain*] with all their might.

And funeral games were played at new-returning light.
1000 Who naked wrestled best besmeared with oil,
Or who with gauntlets gave or took the foil,
I will not tell you, nor would you attend,
But briefly haste to my long story's end.
    I pass the rest; the year was fully mourned,
1005 And Palamon long since to Thebes returned,
When by the Grecians' general consent
At Athens Theseus held his parliament.
Among the laws that passed, it was decreed
That conquered Thebes from bondage should be freed,
1010 Reserving homage to th' Athenian throne,
To which the sovereign summoned Palamon.
Unknowing of the cause, he took his way,
Mournful in mind, and still in black array.
    The monarch mounts the throne, and placed on high
1015 Commands into the court the beauteous Emily.
So called, she came; the senate rose and paid
Becoming reverence to the royal maid,
And first soft whispers through th' assembly went;
With silent wonder then they watched th' event.
1020 All hushed, the king arose with awful grace,
Deep thought was in his breast, and counsel in his face.
At length he sighed, and having first prepared
Th' attentive audience, thus his will declared:
    'The cause and spring of motion, from above
1025 Hung down on earth the golden chain of love:

---

iii *1001. gauntlets*] In 'The Fifth Book of the *Aeneis*' l. 88 D. used *gauntlet* to translate the Latin *cestus*, a leather thong weighted with iron and lead, wound round the hand by Roman boxers. This nonce usage is repeated here. *foil*] in wrestling, a throw that does not result in a fall (*OED sb.*[2]).

iii *1005, 1016–19.* D.'s additions.

iii *1019. event*] outcome.

iii *1020. awful*] awesome, awe inspiring.

iii *1024–1118.* The major philosophical speech that Chaucer gives to Theseus (ll. 2987–3069) is based partly on Boethius' *De Consolatione Philosophiae* ii m. 8; iv pr. 6 and m. 6; iii pr. 10. D.'s own version blends Christian ideas with echoes of Lucretius (cp. 'Lucretius: Against the Fear of Death' and 'From Lucretius: Book the Fifth') and Ovid (cp. 'Of the Pythagorean Philosophy') in his handling of the topic of man's place in a universe of continual change.

iii *1024. cause*] The First Cause, or creator of the universe.

iii *1025. golden chain*] For Chaucer's 'faire chaine'. Zeus (*Iliad* vii 18–27) claimed that he could hang the other gods, the earth, and the sea from Olympus by a golden chain, and Milton imagines the earth hanging by a golden chain in *PL* ii 1051: see Fowler's note on this line for allegorical interpretations of the golden chain.

Great was th' effect, and high was his intent,
When peace among the jarring seeds he sent.
Fire, flood, and earth, and air by this were bound,
And love, the common link, the new creation crowned.
1030 The chain still holds, for though the forms decay,
Eternal matter never wears away:
The same first mover certain bounds has placed
How long those perishable forms shall last,
Nor can they last beyond the time assigned
1035 By that all-seeing and all-making mind.
Shorten their hours they may, for will is free,
But never pass th' appointed destiny.
So men oppressed, when weary of their breath,
Throw off the burden, and suborn their death.
1040 Then since those forms begin, and have their end,
On some unaltered cause they sure depend:
Parts of the whole are we, but God the whole,
Who gives us life, and animating soul.
For nature cannot from a part derive
1045 That being which the whole can only give:
He perfect, stable; but imperfect we,
Subject to change, and different in degree:

Milton interprets this chain as 'the universal concord and sweet union of all things which Pythagoras poetically figures as harmony' (Prolusion II, cited by Fowler).
iii 1026. high] of great consequence, serious (OED 6b); difficult to perform or comprehend (OED 6c, and cp. Psalm cxxxix 6 AV).
iii 1027. D.'s addition. jarring] discordant (OED 1); striking with concussion (OED 2); clashing (OED 3). seeds] atoms. This sense is not in OED, but D. uses it thus in 'Lucretius: Against the Fear of Death' l. 35 to translate semina, Lucretius' term for atoms. Cp. A Song for St Cecilia's Day l. 4.
iii 1028. The four elements thought to make up the physical world.
iii 1030–1. D.'s addition.
iii 1030, 1033, 1040, 1051. forms] particular manifestations (OED 5).
iii 1035. D.'s addition.
iii 1036. for will is free] D.'s addition.
iii 1037. appointed destiny] D.'s addition.
iii 1038–9. D.'s additions, recalling 'Lucretius: Against the Fear of Death' l. 137.
iii 1039. suborn] procure secretly or unlawfully (OED 3). Cp. The State of Innocence V i 189–90: 'Those who, by lingring sickness, lose their breath; / And those who, by despair, suborn their death' (Kinsley).
iii 1040–1. For 'thilke mouer stable is and eterne'.
iii 1042–3. For 'euery part is deriued from his hoole': D. adds God.
iii 1043. animating soul] an interlingual play on the Latin anima, 'soul'.
iii 1047–53. For 'Discending so till it be corrumpable'.
iii 1047–9. See iii 1076–7n.

Plants, beasts, and man; and as our organs are
We more or less of his perfection share.
1050   But by a long descent th' ethereal fire
Corrupts, and forms—the mortal part—expire:
As he withdraws his virtue, so they pass,
And the same matter makes another mass.
This law th' omniscient power was pleased to give,
1055   That every kind should by succession live:
That individuals die his will ordains,
The propagated species still remains.
The monarch oak, the patriarch of the trees,
Shoots rising up, and spreads by slow degrees:
1060   Three centuries he grows, and three he stays,
Supreme in state, and in three more decays.
So wears the paving pebble in the street,
And towns and towers their fatal periods meet.
So rivers, rapid once, now naked lie,
1065   Forsaken of their springs, and leave their channels dry.
So man, at first a drop, dilates with heat,
Then formed, the little heart begins to beat;
Secret he feeds, unknowing in the cell,
At length, for hatching ripe, he breaks the shell,
1070   And struggles into breath, and cries for aid;
Then, helpless, in his mother's lap is laid.
He creeps, he walks, and issuing into man
Grudges their life from whence his own began.
Retchless of laws, affects to rule alone,
1075   Anxious to reign, and restless on the throne.

iii *1050. ethereal*] heavenly: first used in this sense in *PL* viii 646 (*OED*).
iii *1052. virtue*] power inherent in a supernatural being (*OED* 1), here the power that sustains life.
iii *1053*. A Lucretian idea (see 'Lucretius: Against the Fear of Death') but also recalling *Met.* xv (see 'Of the Pythagorean Philosophy').
iii *1055. kind*] species.
iii *1056–7*. D.'s addition.
iii *1058. monarch, patriarch*] D.'s additions; so too is *supreme in state* in l. 1061.
iii *1059*. D.'s addition.
iii *1060–1*. D. specifies the length of time.
iii *1064. naked*] i.e. the river bed is no longer covered with water.
iii *1066–77*. D.'s addition. Cp. 'From Lucretius: Book the Fifth'; 'Of the Pythagorean Philosophy' ll. 324–53.
iii *1068. cell*] See iii 760n.
iii *1074. Retchless*] reckless. *affects*] aims, aspires (*OED* 1b).

First vegetive, then feels, and reasons last,
Rich of three souls, and lives all three to waste.
Some thus; but thousands more in flower of age,
For few arrive to run the latter stage.
1080 Sunk in the first, in battle some are slain,
And others whelmed beneath the stormy main.
What makes all this but Jupiter the king,
At whose command we perish, and we spring?
Then 'tis our best, since thus ordained to die,
1085 To make a virtue of necessity.
Take what he gives, since to rebel is vain;
The bad grows better, which we well sustain;
And could we choose the time, and choose aright,
'Tis best to die our honour at the height,
1090 When we have done our ancestors no shame,
But served our friends, and well secured our fame.
Then should we wish our happy life to close,
And leave no more for Fortune to dispose:
So should we make our death a glad relief
1095 From future shame, from sickness, and from grief;
Enjoying while we live the present hour,
And dying in our excellence and flower.
Then round our deathbed every friend should run,
And joy us of our conquest, early won;

---

iii 1076–7. Renaissance philosophy, drawing on Aristotle (*De Anima* ii 3), taught that the soul had three faculties (sometimes referred to as three souls): vegetal (in plants), sensitive (in animals), and rational (in man), each faculty including the lower one, so that man alone possesses all three. D. sees the growth of the human being as the gradual acquisition of the three souls.

iii 1078. i.e. some die thus, in old age, when all the faculties have wasted away, but more die in their prime (*flower of age*: *OED* flower 11a).

iii 1079. D.'s addition.

iii 1081. whelmed] drowned (*OED* 4).

iii 1083. For 'That is prince, and cause of al thing'.

iii 1084. since thus ordained to die] D.'s addition.

iii 1087–8. D.'s addition.

iii 1087. sustain] endure (*OED* 8).

iii 1090. ancestors] For 'frends'.

iii 1092–6. D.'s addition, with an echo of 'Horace: *Odes* III xxix' l. 50.

iii 1098. run] hasten, be active; have resort [to] (*OED* 3a, c).

iii 1099–1101. D.'s addition.

iii 1099. joy] congratulate (*OED* 5b).

1100   While the malicious world with envious tears
        Should grudge our happy end, and wish it theirs.
        Since then our Arcite is with honour dead,
        Why should we mourn that he so soon is freed,
        Or call untimely what the gods decreed?
1105   With grief as just a friend may be deplored
        From a foul prison to free air restored.
        Ought he to thank his kinsman or his wife
        Could tears recall him into wretched life?
        Their sorrow hurts themselves, on him is lost,
1110   And worse than both, offends his happy ghost.
        What then remains, but after past annoy
        To take the good vicissitude of joy?
        To thank the gracious gods for what they give,
        Possess our souls, and while we live, to live?
1115   Ordain we then two sorrows to combine,
        And in one point th' extremes of grief to join,
        That thence resulting joy may be renewed,
        As jarring notes in harmony conclude.
        Then I propose that Palamon shall be
1120   In marriage joined with beauteous Emily,
        For which already I have gained th' assent
        Of my free people in full parliament.
        Long love to her has borne the faithful knight,
        And well deserved, had Fortune done him right:
1125   'Tis time to mend her fault, since Emily
        By Arcite's death from former vows is free;

---

iii 1104–5. D.'s addition.
iii 1105. deplored] wept for (*OED* 1).
iii 1108. D.'s addition.
iii 1111. what then remains] See 'The First Book of Homer's *Ilias*' ll. 85–6n.   *annoy*]
trouble (*OED*, citing this example).
iii 1112. vicissitude] natural process of change (D.'s addition).
iii 1114. D's addition. Cp. 'In your patience possess ye your souls' (Luke xxi 19).
while we live, to live] This echoes the Latin tag *dum vivimus, vivamus* ('while we
live, let us live'). Robert South cited it as an example of the levity of pre-Christian
morality (*Twelve Sermons Preached upon Several Occasions: The Second Volume* (1694)
351), but Jeremy Taylor had argued that it could be taken as an initial step towards
a truly Christian attitude: 'For he that by a present and a constant holiness secures
the present, and makes it useful to his noblest purposes, he turns his condition
into his best advantage, by making his unavoidable fate become his necessary religion' (*The Rule and Exercises of Holy Dying* (1651) 19) (Tom Mason, privately).
iii 1116, 1118, 1124–6, 1129. D.'s additions.

If you, fair sister, ratify th' accord,
And take him for your husband, and your lord.
'Tis no dishonour to confer your grace
1130   On one descended from a royal race:
And were he less, yet years of service past
From grateful souls exact reward at last:
Pity is heaven's and yours: nor can she find
A throne so soft as in a woman's mind.'
1135   He said; she blushed; and as o'erawed by might
Seemed to give Theseus what she gave the knight.
Then turning to the Theban, thus he said:
'Small arguments are needful to persuade
Your temper to comply with my command;'
1140   And speaking thus, he gave Emilia's hand.
Smiled Venus, to behold her own true knight   ⎫
Obtain the conquest, though he lost the fight,   ⎬
And blessed with nuptial bliss the sweet laborious ⎪
      night.   ⎭
Eros and Anteros on either side,
1145   One fired the bridegroom, and one warmed the bride;
And long-attending Hymen from above
Showered on the bed the whole Idalian grove.
All of a tenor was their after-life,
No day discoloured with domestic strife,
1150   No jealousy, but mutual truth believed,
Secure repose, and kindness undeceived.
Thus heaven beyond the compass of his thought
Sent him the blessing he so dearly bought.
      So may the Queen of Love long duty bless,
1155   And all true lovers find the same success.

The end of the third book.

iii *1133–4.* For 'Let see now of your womanly pite'.
iii *1135–6, 1141–9.* D.'s additions.
iii *1144. Eros and Anteros*] While Eros is the god of passionate sexual love, Anteros represents reciprocated love.
iii *1146. Hymen*] god of marriage.
iii *1147. Idalian grove*] Mt Idalus in Cyprus was sacred to Venus.
iii *1149.* Cp. 'Baucis and Philemon' ll. 171–2.
iii *1151–2, 1154–5.* D.'s additions.

22 To John Driden of Chesterton

Date and publication. First printed 1700 in *Fables Ancient and Modern* (see headnote to 'Palamon and Arcite' for further details).

Context. D.'s first recorded mention of the poem occurs in a letter to Charles Montague of ? October 1699 (*Letters* 120–1). D. and Montague (1661–1715), the future Earl of Halifax and current First Lord of the Treasury, had enjoyed complex literary and personal relations since the 1680s (for a full account, see David Hopkins, *RES* n.s. li (2000) 83–9). Although very different in their politico-religious affiliations, D. and Montague were on sufficiently friendly terms in October 1699 for D. to seek Montague's assurance that 'To John Driden of Chesterton' contained no material of a potentially inflammatory nature. D. writes as follows: 'These verses had waited on you with the former ['To Her Grace the Duchess of Ormonde', sent earlier to Montague]; but they then wanted that Correction, which I have since given them, that they may the better endure the Sight of so great a Judge & Poet. I am now in feare that I have purged them out of their Spirit; as our Master Busby, usd to whip a Boy so long, till he made him a Confirmd Blockhead. My Cousin Driden saw them in the Country; & the greatest Exception He made to them, was a Satire against the Dutch valour, in the late Warr. He desir'd me to omit it, (to use his Own words) out of the respect He had to his Sovereign. I obeyd his Commands; & left onely the praises, which I think are due to the gallantry of my own Countrymen. In the description which I have made of a Parliament Man, I think I have not onley drawn the features of my worthy Kinsman, but have also given my Own opinion, of what an Englishman in Parliament oughto be; & deliver it as a Memorial of my own Principles to all Posterity. I have consulted the Judgment of my Unbyassd friends, who have some of them the honour to be known to you; & they think there is nothing which can justly give offence, in that part of the Poem. I say not this, to cast a blind on your Judgment (which I cou'd not do, if I indeavourd it) but to assure you, that nothing relateing to the publique shall stand, without your permission. For it were to want Common sence, to desire your patronage, & resolve to disoblige you: and as I will not hazard my hopes of your protection by refusing to obey you in any thing, which I can perform with my conscience, or my honour; So I am very confident you will never impose any other terms on me' (*Letters* 120–1). In a letter to Mrs Steward of 7 November 1699, D. wrote: 'the Earl of Dorsett, & your Cousin Montague have both seen the two poems, to the Duchess of Ormond, & my worthy cousin Driden: And are of opinion that I never writt better. My other friends, are divided in their Judgments which to preferr: but the greater part are for those to my dear Kinsman; which I have Corrected with so much care, that they will now be worthy of his Sight: & do neither of us any dishonour after our death' (*Letters* 123–4). After the publication of *Fables*, D. wrote again to Mrs Steward: 'The Town encourages them [my new Poems] with more Applause than any thing of mine deserves; And particularly My Cousin Driden accepted One from me so very Indulgently, that it makes me more & more in Love with him' (Letter of 12 March 1700; *Letters* 134). And in a third letter to the same recipient of 11 April 1700 D. wrote: 'I have always thought my Verses to my Cousin Driden were the best of the whole; & to my comfort the Town thinks them so; & He, which pleases me most is of the same Judgment as appears by a noble present he has sent me, which surprisd me, because I did not in the least expect it' (*Letters* 135). Malone (I i 326–8) reports the family tradition that the 'present' was a gift of £500, but judges that a sum of £100 was more likely.

John Driden (*c.* 1641–1708) of Chesterton, Huntingdonshire (near Peterborough), was the poet's first cousin, the son of Sir John Dryden, second Baronet of Canons Ashby, Northants (D.'s father's brother) and his wife Honor. John Driden's sister, also Honor, had been the addressee of an early verse letter by D. (see 'To Honor Dryden'). A wealthy landowner, Driden had been educated at Wadham College Oxford and the Middle Temple, and had served in a variety of local offices during the reign of Charles II: as justice of the peace, commissioner for recusants, deputy lieutenant and sheriff for Cambridgeshire and Huntingdonshire. At the time of the first Declaration of Indulgence, he had professed loyalty to James II, but seems to have shared some of the sentiments of his father (a keen Parliamentarian during the Civil War) and to have had few qualms about accepting the Revolution in 1688–9. He was elected one of the knights of the shire in the general election of 1690. His political affiliations seem to have repeatedly puzzled the compilers of parliamentary lists, and little detailed information about his convictions and principles has survived, beyond the suggestions contained in D.'s poem. In 1690 Lord Carmarthen listed him as doubtful, but probably a supporter of the Court. In 1691 he was described as a member of the Country party (see below l. 128*n*), but a doubtful one, and two years later he was included again among the followers of the Court. In the mid-1690s he seems to have temporarily grown tired of Parliament, and to have devoted himself principally to rural pursuits. He returned to the House in 1699, apparently as a supporter of the Country party. Subsequent parliamentary lists indicate fairly consistent inclination towards the Whigs. He was renowned in his lifetime as a philanthropist, having donated benefactions amounting to some £16,000 (see *History of Parliament: The House of Commons 1690–1715, III: Members A–F*, edited by Eveline Cruickshanks, Stuart Handley, and D. W. Hayton (2002) 921–2).

John Driden's Whig sympathies, and his specific objections to the 'Satire against the Dutch valour' which had been included in the first draft of D.'s poem, might seem at first sight to make him an unlikely recipient of an epistle embodying D.'s own 'opinion, of what an Englishman in Parliament oughto be' and constituting a 'Memorial of [D.'s] own Principles to all Posterity'. At this date, however, party affiliations were often less significant than ad hoc alignments over particular issues, and it was often observed that contemporary politicians seemed to be behaving in ways that ran quite counter to expectations – with Tories, for example, seeming to act and speak on occasion like 'Republicans' and 'Commonwealthmen' (see Jay Arnold Levine, in *Dryden's Mind and Art*, edited by Bruce King (1969) 115–16, citing Luke Milbourne and Richard Blackmore). The controversy over William's standing army precipitated a 'fragmentation of Whiggery' between 1697 and 1699 (see Craig Rose, *England in the 1690s* (1999) 93–9). D.'s common ground with his cousin on this and other matters (see *Letters* 124) makes it easier for him to present Driden as 'neither Whig nor Tory, Court nor Country, but a personification of Albion itself' (Levine 120). From several passing references in his letters, D. seems to have kept in regular touch with Driden and his affairs (see *Letters* 101, 112, 129, 131, 135, plus the additional letter of 18 February 1699 in *The Clark Newsletter* v (1983) 1–3). Malone (I i 233) records an anecdote that D. wrote 'the first lines' of his translation of Virgil 'on a pane of glass in one of the windows' of John Driden's house.

Form and sources. 'To John Driden' combines elements from several different literary modes and traditions of thought. Its principal model is Horace's second epode, a translation of which D. had published in *Sylvae* (1685), which had spawned a rich tradition of poems of rural content and retirement in the seventeenth century (see Maren-Sofie Røstvig, *The Happy Man*, second edition, 2 vols (1962–71); H. A. Mason, *CQ* viii (1978) 11–55 and ix (1980) 218–71) – poems that had often combined, as in 'To John Driden', the Horatian theme of rural content with images of Edenic perfection (see Levine 121–2). 'To John Driden', significantly, has no equivalent of the conclusion of Horace's epode, in which the rural ideal is undercut (or at least complicated) by being retracted by its speaker, the usurer Alfius / Morecraft. D.'s poem has also been located in the tradition of seventeenth-century 'country house poems', as 'an encomium . . . with many estate poem features', in which 'Driden's benefactions are treated as extensions of his hospitality' (*The Country House Poem*, edited by Alastair Fowler (1994) 393). As befits the encomiastic mode, D. is concerned not so much with realistic portraiture as with 'a persistent exemplification of the ideal' (James Kinsley, *ES* xxxiv (1953) 62). The imagery of 'To John Driden' constantly draws on and develops analogies between individual virtue and the health of the state that ultimately derive from Plato's *Republic* and Aristotle's *Rhetoric* (see Levine 122–5). The poem's rhetorical structure is organized in the manner recommended by Aristotle for the *dispositio* of a deliberative oration: exordium (introduction, designed to capture the audience's attention) (ll. 1–6), statement (ll. 7–116), proof (ll. 117–94), and epilogue (ll. 195–209) (Levine 125). In its general design and intent, it also bears some resemblance to 'a common journalistic practice of the age: that of issuing just prior to the assembling of a parliament tracts variously called a letter or advice to a member of parliament setting forth a course of action to be followed with respect to the issues that were to be raised' (Alan Roper, *Dryden's Poetic Kingdoms* (1965) 133).

To My Honoured Kinsman, John Driden of Chesterton in the County of Huntingdon, Esquire

How blessed is he who leads a country life
Unvexed with anxious cares, and void of strife!
Who, studying peace and shunning civil rage,
Enjoyed his youth, and now enjoys his age:
5   All who deserve his love, he makes his own,
And to be loved himself, needs only to be known.

¶22. *1–4.* Closely based on Horace, *Epode* ii 1–8 (D.'s translation ll. 1–17).
1. blessed is he] A recurrent formulation in the AV of the Bible (*Works*), as well as a translation of Horace's *Beatus ille.*
2. anxious cares] A key phrase in Milton: cp. *PL* viii 184: 'the sweet of life, from which / God hath bid dwell far off all anxious cares' (J. R. Mason). Cp. 'Horace: *Epode* II' l. 55, 'Horace: *Odes* III xxix' ll. 10, 44. *void of strife*] Verbatim (also rhyming with *country life*) in 'Horace: *Epode* II' l. 4.
3. peace] Both personal tranquillity and peace for his community (Roper 125).
rage] violence (*OED* 4a); madness (*OED* 1a).

>   Just, good, and wise, contending neighbours come
> From your award to wait their final doom;
> And, foes before, return in friendship home.

10   Without their cost, you terminate the cause,
    And save th' expense of long litigious laws:
    Where suits are traversed, and so little won
    That he who conquers is but last undone.

>   Such are not your decrees; but so designed,
15 The sanction leaves a lasting peace behind:
> Like your own soul, serene—a pattern of your mind.

     Promoting concord, and composing strife,
    Lord of yourself, uncumbered with a wife;
    Where for a year, a month, perhaps a night,
20 Long penitence succeeds a short delight:
    Minds are so hardly matched, that ev'n the first,
    Though paired by heaven, in paradise were cursed.
    For man and woman, though in one they grow,
    Yet, first or last, return again to two.
25 He to God's image, she to his was made;

8. *award*] arbitrator's decision (*OED* 1).   *doom*] judgement (*OED* 2).

10. *cause*] case, legal action (*OED* 8). Horace's happy man also avoids 'The clamours of contentious law' ('Horace: *Epode* II' l. 14).

12. *traversed*] disputed, contradicted (*OED* 12a; legal).

13. *undone*] ruined (*OED* ppl. a.² 1).

14. *decrees*] legal decisions (*OED* 1).

15. *sanction*] legal decision, enacted as either a penalty or a reward (*OED* 2a–b). *lasting peace*] Perhaps to be implicitly contrasted with the precarious peace that followed the Treaty of Ryswick (1697) (Robert Cummings, *Seventeenth-Century Poetry: An Annotated Anthology* (2000)).

16. *pattern*] likeness, copy (*OED* 4).

18. *Lord of yourself*] Cp. John Oldham, 'A Satyr Address'd to a Friend' l. 121: 'Lord of my self, accountable to none' (Oldham 229); John Norris, 'The Retirement', st. iv: 'Lord of my self, accountable to none, / Like the first Man in *Paradise*, alone' (*A Collection of Miscellanies*, third edition (1699) 20) (Levine); Charles Dryden, 'On the Happyness of a Retir'd Life . . . Sent to his Father from ITALY' (*The Annual Miscellany* (1694) 199): 'Lords of themselves, and of their Passions grown'.

19–20. Kinsley compares John Donne, 'Love's Alchymie' ll. 11–12: 'So, lovers dreame a rich and long delight, / But get a winter-seeming summers night'. Cp. also the proverbial 'Marry in haste and repent at leisure' (Tilley H 196) (Robert Cummings).

21. *hardly*] uneasily, painfully (*OED* 5); with difficulty (*OED* 6).

23. *in one*] A biblical idea. *Works* compares Matthew xix 5–6; Genesis ii 24; cp. also Mark x 7–8; 1 Corinthians vi 16; Ephesians v 31.

25. Cp. *PL* iv 299: 'He for God only, she for God in him' (J. R. Mason) (drawing on 1 Corinthians xi 7–8), and Genesis i 26: 'And God said, Let us make man in our image'.

So, farther from the fount the stream at random strayed.
　　How could he stand, when put to double pain
He must a weaker than himself sustain?
Each might have stood perhaps, but each alone;
30　Two wrestlers help to pull each other down.
　　Not that my verse would blemish all the fair; ⎫
But yet if some be bad, 'tis wisdom to beware, ⎬
And better shun the bait than struggle in the snare. ⎭
Thus have you shunned, and shun the married state,
35　Trusting as little as you can to Fate.
　　No porter guards the passage of your door,
T' admit the wealthy and exclude the poor;
For God, who gave the riches, gave the heart
To sanctify the whole, by giving part;
40　Heaven, who foresaw the will, the means has wrought,
And to the second son a blessing brought;
The first-begotten had his father's share,
But you, like Jacob, are Rebecca's heir.
　　So may your stores and fruitful fields increase,

26. Cp. 'On the Death of a Very Young Gentleman' ll. 31–2.

27–9. Echoing several passages in *PL* referring to Adam and Eve's and the angels' capacity to 'stand' against temptation (see *PL* iii 98–9, 102; iv 59–60; v 568; vi 908–9, 911–12; J. R. Mason).　*stand*] remain steadfast (*OED* 9b).

31. blemish] defame, cast a slur upon (*OED* 4c).

33. Works compares 'Palamon and Arcite' iii 328 and *HP* ii 7–8.

35. For D.'s thoughts on Fate and related concepts, see Paul Hammond, *MLR* lxxx (1985) 769–85.

36–7. Fowler compares Robert Herrick, 'A Panegyrick to Sir Lewis Pemberton' ll. 13–18: 'For no black-bearded *Vigil* from thy doore / Beats with a button'd-staffe the poore: / But from thy warm-love-hatching gates each may / Take friendly morsels, and there stay / To Sun his thin-clad members, if he likes, / For thou no Porter keep'st who strikes'.

38. riches] For John Driden's wealth (in sharp contrast to the 'humble poverty' of the countryman in 'Horace: *Epode* II'), see headnote.

39. Works suggests a reference to 'Hebrew sacrifices in which the entire offering was holy even though only part of it was presented to the deity' (see, e.g., Leviticus vi 14–18).

41. the second son] John Driden was his father's second son by his third marriage. Robert, the first son, had inherited the baronetcy and family seat, but John had inherited his Chesterton estate from his mother. D. alludes to the story of Jacob and Esau (Genesis xxv–xxviii). Jacob, the second son of Isaac, was the favourite of his mother Rebekah, who helped him to trick Isaac into giving his paternal blessing to Jacob rather than to Jacob's elder brother, Esau. As Winn points out (504) the analogy is inexact and may reflect D.'s hostility to his cousin Robert (for which, see the letter from Lady Dryden to Malone, quoted in Osborn 254–7).

45   And ever be you blessed, who live to bless.
      As Ceres sowed, where'er her chariot flew,
      As heaven in deserts rained the bread of dew,
      So free to many, to relations most,
      You feed with manna your own Israel host.
50   With crowds attended of your ancient race,
      You seek the champaign sports, or sylvan chase;
      With well-breathed beagles you surround the wood,
      Ev'n then industrious of the common good;
      And often have you brought the wily fox
55   To suffer for the firstlings of the flocks;
      Chased ev'n amid the folds, and made to bleed,
      Like felons, where they did the murderous deed.
      This fiery game your active youth maintained;
      Not yet by years extinguished, though restrained:
60   You season still with sports your serious hours;
      For age but tastes of pleasures, youth devours.
      The hare in pastures or in plains is found,
      Emblem of human life, who runs the round,
      And, after all his wandering ways are done, ⎫
65   His circle fills, and ends where he begun,   ⎬
      Just as the setting meets the rising sun.   ⎭

---

46. After the recovery of Proserpina, Ceres ordered Triptolemus to scatter seed from her chariot in the untilled earth, and in fields which had long lain fallow (Ovid, *Met.* v 645–7).

47. *the bread of dew*] manna, the food sent by God to the Children of Israel in the desert (Exodus xvi 13–15).

48. *to relations most*] For John Driden's generosity to D., see headnote.

50–66. For the hunting pursuits of Horace's countryman (including the pursuit of hares) cp. 'Horace: *Epode* II' ll. 45–53. On hunting as a theme in the country house poem, see Fowler 6, 60.

50. *ancient*] For the earlier history of the Dryden family, see Winn 2–3.

51. *champaign*] of the open field (*OED* B2).   *sylvan*] of the woods (*OED* B1).

52. *well-breathed*] well exercised, so as not to get out of breath.

53. *industrious of*] painstakingly attentive to (*OED* 2).

55. *the firstlings of the flocks*] Biblical diction, indicating a sacrificial offering (see, e.g., Genesis iv 4).

57. *felons*] Cp. (of a fox) 'The Cock and the Fox' l. 727.

60. *season*] intersperse with something that imports relish (*OED* 1b, citing this example).

63. *runs the round*] Used by Nature of her activity in 'Lucretius: Against the Fear of Death' l. 140.

65. Alluding to the proverbial observation that the hunted hare will always return to its form (nest or lair). See *The Oxford Dictionary of Proverbs*, edited by F. P. Wilson, third edition (1970) *s.v.* hare.

    Thus princes ease their cares; but happier he
Who seeks not pleasure through necessity,
Than such as once on slippery thrones were placed,
70   And chasing, sigh to think themselves are chased.
    So lived our sires, ere doctors learned to kill,
And multiplied with theirs the weekly bill.
The first physicians by debauch were made:
Excess began, and sloth sustains the trade.
75   Pity the generous kind their cares bestow
To search forbidden truths (a sin to know),
To which if human science could attain,
The doom of death, pronounced by God, were vain.
In vain the leech would interpose delay;
80   Fate fastens first, and vindicates the prey.

67–70. A. W. Verrall 43–4 suggested an allusion to the exiled James II, hunting in the forest of St Germain and sighing to think of himself *chased* from his kingdom. The lines may equally allude to William III, by whom, reported Gilbert Burnet, 'hunting . . . was so used . . . that it was become necessary', and who had recently found himself *chased* (by plotters against his life) in the very kingdom from which he had *chased* James (Levine 126).

69. slippery thrones] Cp. Cowley's reference to 'the slippery tops of humane State' ('Seneca, ex Thyeste, Act. 2. Chor.' l. 1; *Essays* 399) (Robert Cummings).

71. sires] forefathers (*OED* 6).   *doctors*] As Levine notes (126–7, citing Halifax, Charles Davenant, and the *Somers Tracts*), D.'s digression on doctors draws on the analogy, frequently adduced in the political literature of the 1690s, between the 'health' of the individual and that of the body politic. On the personal level, D. notes that regular 'exercise' through hunting 'will be the better' for John Driden's 'health' (*Letters* 112) (Robert Cummings).

72. weekly bill] The 'bill of mortality' or official return of deaths published weekly from 1592 by the London Company of Parish Clerks (*OED* bill *sb.*³ 10).

73. In Ecclesiasticus xxxvii 29–xxxviii 15 warnings against 'excess of meats' and 'surfeiting' are juxtaposed with the instruction to 'honour a physician' (*Works*).

75. Pity] 'It is a pity that' (Christie).

76. a sin to know] The 'physician's search after forbidden knowledge is a recapitulation of Adam's sin in Paradise' (Levine 128). Cp. *PL* iv 517 (J. R. Mason).

77. science] knowledge (*OED* 2).

78. doom] sentence (*OED* 2).   *pronounced by God*] See Genesis iii 19.

79. leech] physician (*OED sb.*¹), often understood as referring to the treatment prescribed by doctors by which blood-sucking leeches were *fastened* to patients.

80. vindicates] claims possession of (*OED* 5).

What help from art's endeavours can we have?
Gibbons but guesses, nor is sure to save;
But Maurus sweeps whole parishes, and peoples every
    grave;
And no more mercy to mankind will use,
85 Than when he robbed and murdered Maro's Muse.
Would'st thou be soon dispatched, and perish whole?
Trust Maurus with thy life, and M—lb—rne with thy soul.
    By chase our long-lived fathers earned their food;
Toil strung the nerves, and purified the blood:
90 But we, their sons, a pampered race of men,
Are dwindled down to threescore years and ten.

---

82. Gibbons] William Gibbons (1649–1728), Fellow of the Royal College of
Physicians, and one of D.'s doctors. He is referred to in 'The Third Satire of
Persius' (l. 126) and thanked in the 'Postscript to the Reader' attached to D.'s
Aeneis (*Works* vi 810) for having helped D. to recover 'in some measure the health
which I had lost by too much application to this Work'. Kinsley notes that Gibbons
was satirized as 'Mirmillo' in *The Dispensary* by D.'s friend Sir Samuel Garth (see
iii 53–4; *POAS* vi 94).

83. Maurus] Sir Richard Blackmore (1654–1729), Whig physician, and author of
the epic poems *Prince Arthur* (1695) and *King Arthur* (1697), in the first of
which D. had been libelled as '*Laurus*', 'An old, revolted, unbelieving Bard',
'Distinguished by his louder craving Tone', who 'did the Voice of modest Poets
drown' (167). In the Preface to *Prince Arthur* Blackmore had railed against the
'general *Confederacy*' of contemporary poets and dramatists (among whom D. is
clearly included) 'to expose *Religion* and *Virtue*, and bring *Vice* and *Corruption of
Manners* into Esteem and Reputation' (second edition (1695) sig. Aᵛ). Blackmore
also abused D. (along with Samuel Garth) in *A Satyr Against Wit* (dated 1700,
published November 1699), associating 'wit' with debauchery, immorality, and
the subversion of true learning. A further attack on D. by Blackmore appeared
in the Preface to *A Paraphrase on the Book of Job* (1700), where D. is implicitly
insulted by Blackmore's suggestion that Homer and Virgil have never been 'well
Translated into the English *Language*' (sigs. aᵛ, bᵛ, dᵛ).

85. Maro's] Virgil's. D. refers to Blackmore's attempts at Virgilian epic.

87. M—lb—rne] Luke Milbourne (1649–1720), a clergyman and minor poet, who
had published an unsuccessful translation of Book I of Virgil's *Aeneid* in 1688. In
Notes on Dryden's Virgil. In a Letter to a Friend (1698), he had attacked D. acri-
moniously for misunderstanding Virgil's meaning. Milbourne's volume included
a version of Book I of the *Georgics*, designed to show up D.'s version, and accompanied by an insulting expression of thanks to D. 'that his Mistakes, have given
me an opportunity to dive farther into *Virgil's meaning*, and to admire *his beauties* more than I have ever done before' (206).

89. strung] gave tone to (*OED* 3a, citing this example). *nerves*] sinews, muscles
(*OED* 1a).

91. threescore years and ten] The duration of a man's life as prescribed by Psalm
xc 10. The reported age of Methuselah (969 years: Genesis v 27) shows the Hebrew
belief that in the distant past men lived much longer.

Better to hunt in fields, for health unbought,
Than fee the doctor for a nauseous draught.
The wise, for cure, on exercise depend;
95   God never made his work for man to mend.
        The tree of knowledge, once in Eden placed,
Was easy found, but was forbid the taste:
O had our grandsire walked without his wife,
He first had sought the better plant of life!
100   Now both are lost: yet, wandering in the dark,
Physicians, for the tree, have found the bark;
They, labouring for relief of human kind,⎫
With sharpened sight some remedies may find;⎬
Th' apothecary-train is wholly blind.⎭
105   From files a random recipe they take,
And many deaths of one prescription make.
Garth, generous as his Muse, prescribes and gives;
The shopman sells, and by destruction lives:

92. unbought] Horace's countryman is content to eat the 'unbought dainties of
the poor' ('Horace: Epode II' l. 72). Fowler compares Ben Jonson, 'To Sir Robert
Wroth' l. 14 (in which Wroth lives 'with unbought provision blest'), and notes
that D. is here 'reapplying the estate poem commonplace: here health, not provisions, are unbought' (Fowler 393).
96–7. For the vocabulary, particularly the importance of taste, cp. PL i 2; iv 423–4,
513–15; ix 751–3, 925 (J. R. Mason).
97. forbid the taste] forbidden to be tasted.
98. walked without his wife] Cp. Andrew Marvell, 'The Garden' ll. 57–8: 'Such
was that happy garden-state, / While man there walked without a mate'.
99. the better plant of life] The Tree of Life from which Adam and Eve are allowed
to eat (Genesis ii 16, iii 22; PL iv 419–26).
101. the bark] 'The bark of various species of the Cinchona tree, from which quin-
ine is procured, formerly ground into powder and taken as a febrifuge [cooling
drink to take away fever]' (OED 7; a medical usage).
104. Th' apothecary-train] Apothecaries were a medical underclass, the activities
of which had originally been restricted to the preparation and sale of drugs for
medicinal purposes. Towards the end of the seventeenth century apothecaries were
seeking the right to become independent medical practitioners, a move that was
fiercely opposed by loyalists within the College of Physicians (see Harold J. Cook
in Maccubbin and Hamilton-Phillips 186–94).
105. files] strings or wires on which documents are threaded for reference (OED
sb.² 3a; Johnson 2, citing this example).
107. Garth] Sir Samuel Garth (1661–1719), doctor, poet, and friend of D. Garth
was a loyal member of the College of Physicians and opposed the 'Apothecaries'
Physicians' who had colluded with the apothecaries in attempting to block a scheme
to establish a free clinic for the poor of London. The quarrel is the subject of
Garth's mock-heroic poem The Dispensary (1699; POAS vi 58–128, 722–50).
108. shopman] apothecary.

Ungrateful tribe! who, like the viper's brood,
110 From Med'cine issuing, suck their mother's blood!
Let these obey, and let the learned prescribe,
That men may die without a double bribe;
Let them but under their superiors kill,
When doctors first have signed the bloody bill;
115 He 'scapes the best who, nature to repair,
Draws physic from the fields, in draughts of vital air.
    You hoard not health for your own private use,
But on the public spend the rich produce.
When, often urged, unwilling to be great,
120 Your country calls you from your loved retreat,
And sends to senates, charged with common care,
Which none more shuns, and none can better bear.
Where could they find another formed so fit
To poise with solid sense a sprightly wit?
125 Were these both wanting (as they both abound)
Where could so firm integrity be found?
    Well born and wealthy, wanting no support,
You steer betwixt the country and the court;
Nor gratify whate'er the great desire,
130 Nor grudging give what public needs require.

109–10. Noyes compares Joshua Sylvester, *Du Bartas his Divine Weekes and Workes* (First Week, Sixth Day, ll. 250–1): 'Thou mak'st th' ingratefull *Viper* (at his birth) / His dying Mother's belly to gnaw forth'.
111. obey] i.e. maintain their traditional subordination to the Physicians.
112. double bribe] payment to both apothecary and physician. *Works* compares Gomez's complaint against such charges in *The Spanish Friar* IV i 99–101.
114. bloody bill] fatal prescription.
116. physic] medicine (*OED* 2).   *vital*] life giving (*OED* 2c).
121. senates] i.e. parliament.
122. shuns] i.e. from reticence or modesty.
124. wit] intelligence.
125. wanting] lacking.
127. Well born and wealthy] See headnote.
128. the country and the court] Labels used in the late seventeenth century for two political tendencies, characterized respectively by (i) a professed concern for the 'public good' of the country as a whole, local loyalties, and a hostility to the military and fiscal powers of central government; (ii) support for, and involvement with, the policies and ambitions of the crown and its ministers. Both labels denoted loose, and sometimes shifting, groups of men holding similar views, rather than political parties in the modern sense. For Driden's allegiances, see headnote.
129–30. Nor . . . Nor] Neither . . . Nor.

Part must be left, a fund when foes invade,
And part employed to roll the watery trade:
Ev'n Canaan's happy land, when worn with toil,
Required a sabbath year to mend the meagre soil.
135   Good senators (and such are you) so give
That kings may be supplied, the people thrive:
And he, when want requires, is truly wise, ⎫
Who slights not foreign aids, nor overbuys, ⎬
But on our native strength in time of need relies. ⎭
140 Münster was bought, we boast not the success;
Who fights for gain, for greater makes his peace.
Our foes, compelled by need, have peace embraced;
The peace both parties want is like to last:
Which, if secure, securely we may trade;
145 Or, not secure, should never have been made.
Safe in ourselves, while on ourselves we stand,

131. Part] i.e. of government revenue.   *fund*] government money set aside for the specific purpose of national defence (as opposed to aggressive war-mongering abroad).

132. roll] keep moving (*OED* 3).   *the watery trade*] The fleet was vital for the protection of British shipping against piracy. The provisioning of the fleet had been in severe crisis in 1697 (see Craig Rose 142–3). For D.'s interest in maritime trade, cp. *AM* ll. 617–56; 'To Dr Charleton' ll. 21–6; Dedication to *All for Love* (*Works* xiii 6).

133. Canaan's happy land] The 'promised land' given to the Israelites by God (Numbers xiv 8; Deuteronomy xxvi 9).

134. sabbath year] Alluding to God's command (Exodus xxiii 10–11; Leviticus xxv 3–4) that the Israelites should sow their land for six years, but 'let it rest' in the seventh.

138. slights] disdains (*OED* 3a).   *overbuys*] buys at too high a price (*OED* 1, citing this as its last example).

139. During 'King William's War' of 1689–97 the English army had expanded to some 66,000 men, and there were also several thousand foreign troops in English pay (see John Childs, *The British Army of William III, 1689–1702* (1987) 103). On 16 December 1698 the Commons voted to reduce the army to 7000 men, all of whom had to be English (Luttrell iv 319), a move that led to the disbandment of William III's Dutch Guards.

140. Münster] Bernhard von Galen, Bishop of Münster, whom Charles II had paid to fight as an ally during the second Dutch War (see *AM* l. 145*n*).

141. D.'s remark does not apply to von Galen, who did not make peace 'for gain', but because his English subsidies had dried up.

142. A reference to the Treaty of Ryswick, which ended 'King William's War'. The French, under the pressure of severe financial difficulties, had opened negotiations in 1696, and concluded terms of peace on 6 July 1697. Spain and the Emperor initially refused to agree with them, but soon gave way, and three treaties were concluded on 21 September between France, Holland, Spain, and England.

144. securely we may trade] After the defeat of the French fleet at Barfleur in May 1692, the French navy had concentrated on raiding British and Dutch commercial vessels.

> The sea is ours, and that defends the land.
> Be then the naval stores the nation's care,
> New ships to build, and battered to repair.
> 150   Observe the war in every annual course;
> What has been done was done with British force:
> Namur subdued is England's palm alone;
> The rest besieged, but we constrained the town:
> We saw th' event that followed our success;
> 155   France, though pretending arms, pursued the peace,
> Obliged by one sole treaty to restore
> What twenty years of war had won before.
> Enough for Europe has our Albion fought:
> Let us enjoy the peace our blood has bought.
> 160   When once the Persian king was put to flight,
> The weary Macedons refused to fight:
> Themselves their own mortality confessed,
> And left the son of Jove to quarrel for the rest.
>   Ev'n victors are by victories undone;
> 165   Thus Hannibal, with foreign laurels won,
> To Carthage was recalled, too late to keep his own.

147. The sea is ours] Despite the contraction of the army (see l. 139*n*) the British navy had been maintained at 10,000 men (*Works*, citing Luttrell iv 322).

152–3. A reference to the two-month siege and final capture (in September 1695) of the frontier fortress town of Namur, reckoned among William III's greatest victories. The siege involved both British troops and allies from Brandenburg, Liège, Bavaria, and Holland. As *Works* notes (citing Luttrell iii 498), the English and Scots losses in the initial assault on the town were reckoned at 440 and the Dutch at about 160. Christie suggests that it was probably at this point in the poem that the uncomplimentary lines on the Dutch, suppressed in response to John Driden's comments (see headnote), were originally included.

154. event] outcome, consequence (*OED* 3a).

155. pretending arms] claiming to pursue the war.

156. one sole treaty] The Treaty of Ryswick, actually three treaties (see l. 142*n*). *to restore*] The treaties obliged the French to surrender all conquests made since the Treaties of Nijmegen (1678–9), except Strasbourg and a number of other small territories.

158. Europe] i.e. the anti-French European interest. *Albion*] An ancient term for Britain, embodying suggestions of the 'ancient constitution' and English sea power (see Elizabeth Duthie, *ELH* xlvii (1980) 684–5). D.'s allegorical opera on the Restoration was entitled *Albion and Albanius* (1685).

160–3. D. seems to refer to the incident narrated by Plutarch (*Lives* (1683–6) iv 327–8) in which Alexander the Great's Macedonian army refused to cross the Ganges after the defeat of the Persian king, Darius. For Alexander's claims to be the son of Jove, see *Alexander's Feast*, headnote, *Sources*.

165–6. In 203 BC Hannibal, after his Italian conquests, was recalled to Africa to defend Carthage. The following year he was defeated by Roman forces under

While sore of battle, while our wounds are green,
Why should we tempt the doubtful die again?
In wars renewed uncertain of success;
170   Sure of a share as umpires of the peace.
        A patriot both the king and country serves;
Prerogative and privilege preserves:
Of each our laws the certain limit show;
One must not ebb, nor t' other overflow:
175   Betwixt the prince and parliament we stand,
The barriers of the state on either hand:
May neither overflow, for then they drown the land.
When both are full, they feed our blessed abode,
Like those that watered once the paradise of God.
180   Some overpoise of sway by turns they share,
In peace the people, and the prince in war;
Consuls of moderate power in calms were made;
When the Gauls came, one sole dictator swayed.

Scipio Africanus at the battle of Zama. *Works* notes that the incident is narrated
in Plutarch's 'Life' of Fabius Maximus. It is referred to in the 'Dedication of the
Aeneis' (*Works* v 277).

167. green] fresh, recent (*OED* 10a).

168. doubtful die] risky throw of dice (*OED* die 1a), hence hazardous chance
(*OED* 2a).

170. umpires] parties to or agents of the settlement (*OED* 1).

171. patriot] A hotly contested title in seventeenth-century political rhetoric, claimed
by the Whigs during the Exclusion Crisis (see *AA* ll. 179 and *n*, 965–6) but rightly
applied, according to D., only to 'such . . . under whom we see their Country
Flourish' ('Dedication of the *Georgics*'; *Works* v 141). The term is used satirically
by Daniel Defoe of those parliamentarians who opposed William III's policies:
see 'An Encomium upon a Parliament' l. 1 (*POAS* vi 49).

172. prerogative] the rights of the sovereign (*OED* 1a).   *privilege*] the rights enjoyed
by parliament (*OED* 4a).

173. our laws] The subject of the sentence.

174–9. Fowler compares D.'s imagery of uncontrolled floods as an emblem of
civil imbalance with that of Sir John Denham, *Cooper's Hill* (1642) ll. 343–58.

176. barriers] river banks.

177–8. Denham's Thames is 'without ore-flowing full' (*Cooper's Hill* l. 192).

178–9. feed . . . watered] 'And a river went out of Eden to water the garden' (Genesis
ii 10). Cp. *PL* iv 223–30, 237–41 (J. R. Mason).

179. the paradise of God] Cp. 'for blissful paradise / Of God the garden was'
(*PL* iv 208–9) (J. R. Mason).

180. overpoise] preponderant weight (*OED*, quoting Johnson).   *sway*] power, rule
(*OED* 6a).

183. dictator] In republican Rome, the dictatorship was an ad hoc magistracy that
entrusted sole power to one individual in times of national emergency. The most
celebrated Roman dictator, appointed specifically to repel the invading Gauls,
was Marcus Furius Camillus (*c.* 334 BC). Normally supreme authority in republican Rome was invested in two annually elected consuls.

Patriots in peace assert the people's right,
185 With noble stubbornness resisting might;
No lawless mandates from the court receive,
Nor lend by force, but in a body give.
Such was your generous grandsire; free to grant
In parliaments that weighed their prince's want:
190 But so tenacious of the common cause,
As not to lend the king against his laws;
And in a loathsome dungeon doomed to lie, ⎫
In bonds retained his birthright liberty,   ⎬
And shamed oppression, till it set him free. ⎭
195   O true descendant of a patriot line,
Who, while thou shar'st their lustre, lend'st 'em thine,
Vouchsafe this picture of thy soul to see;
'Tis so far good, as it resembles thee;
The beauties to th' original I owe,
200 Which when I miss, my own defects I show:
Nor think the kindred Muses thy disgrace;
A poet is not born in every race.
Two of a house few ages can afford,
One to perform, another to record.
205 Praiseworthy actions are by thee embraced,
And 'tis my praise to make thy praises last.
For ev'n when death dissolves our human frame, ⎫
The soul returns to heaven from whence it came; ⎬
Earth keeps the body, verse preserves the fame. ⎭

186. mandates] commands (*OED* 1).
187. by] as a result of.
188. your generous grandsire] Sir Erasmus Dryden (1553–1632) of Canons Ashby
(also D.'s grandfather), imprisoned (1604–5) for petitioning on behalf of puritan
preachers, and (1627–8) for refusing to pay the forced loan levied on his subjects
by Charles I (Winn 4–5). The example has a contemporary resonance, since William
III had recently (4 January 1699) threatened to abdicate, in the face of extensive
cuts imposed on his military spending by parliament.   *generous*] noble (*OED* 1a).
201. i.e. Do not consider it any defect in you that you are not a poet like me.
202. race] family.
206. my praise] i.e. to my credit.
207–9. Used as an epigraph (forming, in effect, D.'s epitaph on himself) on the
title page of *Luctus Britannici: or The Tears of the British Muses; for the Death of John
Dryden, Esq.* (1700) (Levine).
208–9. Cp. *Eleonora* ll. 375–6; John Donne, 'The First Anniversary' ll. 473–4:
'Verse hath a middle nature, heaven keepes Soules, / The Grave keepes bodies,
Verse the Fame enroules'; Sir John Denham, 'To Sir Richard Fanshaw upon his
Translation of *Pastor Fido*' ll. 23–4: 'They but preserve the Ashes, thou the Flame,
/ True to his sense, but truer to his fame'.
208. Works compares Ecclesiastes xii 7: 'Then shall the dust return to the earth
as it was: and the spirit shall return to God who gave it'.

23 Sigismonda and Guiscardo

Date and publication. First printed 1700 in *Fables Ancient and Modern* (see headnote to 'Palamon and Arcite' for further details).

Source. D. translates the first story from day IV of Boccaccio's *Il Decamerone* (1349–51). Scholars have been unable to identify the edition from which D. worked. The Italian text is quoted here from *Tutte le Opere*, edited by Vittore Branca, vol. 4 (1976), with translations adapted from the version by G. H. McWilliam (1972). For D.'s critical opinion of Boccaccio, see 'Preface to *Fables*' (*Poems* v 83–4). It is not known when D. became interested in Boccaccio, but he was evidently discussing the Italian literature and philosophy of love in 1691 with William Walsh, who in a letter mentioned, among several other texts, Mario d'Esquicola's *Della Natura d'Amore*, in which the *Decameron* features prominently (*Letters* 45; Richard Bates, unpublished PhD thesis, Cambridge 1983). Boccaccio was quite widely known in seventeenth-century England, both in the original and in translation: for the history of his reception see Herbert G. Wright, *Boccaccio in England from Chaucer to Tennyson* (1957). This particular story was frequently translated and adapted in the sixteenth century: in prose by William Painter in *The Palace of Pleasure* (1566–7), as a verse drama by R. Wilmot and others (*Gismond of Salern* (1567–8), revised as *The Tragedie of Tancred and Gismund* (1591)), in verse by William Walter in *Guystarde and Sygysmonde* (1532), and in an anonymous undated MS play (*Ghismonda*, edited by Herbert G. Wright (1944)). There is no solid evidence, however, that D. used any of these versions. (There are minor coincidences of vocabulary between D. and Walter, including some rhymes (see ll. 318–19*n*, 431–2*n*), but the evidence does not seem strong enough to conclude that D. actually consulted his version.) Kinsley suggests that D. drew on William Chamberlayne's *Pharonnida* (1659), but the parallels adduced are unconvincing. He did draw occasionally on the complete translation of *The Decameron*, probably by John Florio (1620; frequently reprinted, reaching a fifth edition in 1684), but his debts are generally rather minor appropriations of vocabulary or phrasing, and are not particularly significant. Some are recorded in the notes below. The French translation of *Le Decameron* by Antoine le Maçon (1545, frequently reprinted) is generally too close to the Italian for one to be able to identify any use that D. might have made of it, but very occasional turns of phrase raise the possibility that he consulted the later and slightly freer French translation, *Contes et Nouvelles de Bocace Florentin* (1697): see l. 43*n*. In turning Boccaccio's prose narrative into verse, D. often translates rather loosely, so the notes below which record D.'s additions should be taken as approximate indications of passages which have no direct source in the Italian, while passages not so marked are often fairly free paraphrases. For D.'s association of Sigismonda's speech on the nature of true nobility with the comparable speech by the Wife of Bath, see the 'Preface to *Fables*' (*Poems* v 83–4). A notable change that D. makes to the original is the introduction of the priest (see ll. 94–6, 151–2, 163–73*nn*), so that the relationship between Sigismonda and Guiscardo is a secret marriage rather than an illicit sexual affair. This might have been in order to make the poem less objectionable to moralists (see D.'s reply to Jeremy Collier's criticism of the immorality of his earlier work in 'Cymon and Iphigenia' ll. 1–41, and 'Preface to *Fables*' *Poems* v 88–90), but if so, the hastiness of the marriage and the embarrassment of the priest are a mischievous addition.

Sigismonda and Guiscardo

From Boccace

While Norman Tancred in Salerno reigned,
The title of a gracious prince he gained;
Till turned a tyrant in his latter days,
He lost the lustre of his former praise;
5   And from the bright meridian where he stood,
Descending, dipped his hands in lovers' blood.
    This prince, of Fortune's favour long possessed,
Yet was with one fair daughter only blessed;
And blessed he might have been with her alone:
10 But O! how much more happy had he none!
She was his care, his hope, and his delight,
Most in his thought, and ever in his sight:
Next, nay, beyond his life, he held her dear;
She lived by him, and now he lived in her.
15 For this, when ripe for marriage, he delayed
Her nuptial bands, and kept her long a maid,
As envying any else should share a part
Of what was his, and claiming all her heart.
At length, as public decency required,

¶**23**. *Title. Boccace*] Boccaccio: the spelling in *1700* might suggest that D. may have used a French version of the *Decameron*, but Boccaccio's name was regularly anglicized as 'John Boccace' by Thomas Rymer, Thomas Pope Blount, and other seventeenth-century writers.
1. Norman] D.'s addition. The medieval Norman kingdom of Sicily comprised not only the island of Sicily but the mainland south of Naples, including the city of Salerno.
3. turned a tyrant] D.'s addition; he adds *tyrant* again at ll. 108, 119, 131, 288, 595. See 'Palamon and Arcite' i 86*n*.
4–5. D.'s addition.
5. meridian] the point at which the sun attains its highest altitude; so figuratively the highest point of someone's achievement before decline sets in (*OED* 2).
7. D.'s addition. *Fortune*] a common motif in *Fables*; cp. 'Palamon and Arcite', *passim*, and Paul Hammond, *MLR* lxxx (1985) 769–85. Florio has 'it fortuned'.
9. D.'s addition.
10, 12, 14. Ovidian 'turns' of thought: with l. 12 cp. 'Ceyx and Alcyone' l. 217.
11–14. D.'s expansion of Boccaccio.
16. bands] union (*OED* bond *sb.*[1] 7b).
17–18. D.'s addition.
17. As] as if, as it were (*OED* 10a).
19–24. For 'alla fine a un figliuolo del duca di Capova datala' ('in the end, having been given to a son of the Duke of Capua'). D. heightens Tancred's possessiveness and reluctance.

20   And all his vassals eagerly desired,
      With mind averse, he rather underwent
      His people's will, than gave his own consent.
      So was she torn, as from a lover's side,
      And made almost in his despite a bride.
25   Short were her marriage joys, for in the prime
      Of youth her lord expired before his time,
      And to her father's court in little space ⎫
      Restored anew, she held a higher place, ⎬
      More loved, and more exalted into grace. ⎭
30   This princess fresh and young, and fair, and wise,
      The worshipped idol of her father's eyes,
      Did all her sex in every grace exceed,
      And had more wit beside than women need.
        Youth, health, and ease, and most an amorous ⎫
          mind,   ⎬
35   To second nuptials had her thoughts inclined, ⎪
      And former joys had left a secret sting behind. ⎭
      But prodigal in every other grant,
      Her sire left unsupplied her only want,
      And she, betwixt her modesty and pride,
40   Her wishes, which she could not help, would hide.
        Resolved at last to lose no longer time,
      And yet to please herself without a crime,
      She cast her eyes around the court, to find
      A worthy subject suiting to her mind,
45   To him in holy nuptials to be tied,

21. *underwent*] submitted himself to (*OED* 6a).
24. *in his despite*] despite him, against his will (again at l. 198).
27–9. D.'s expansion of 'rimase vedova e al padre tornossi' ('she was left a widow and returned to her father').
27. *space*] extent of time.
29. *grace*] [her father's] favour.
30. *fresh*] blooming, looking healthy or youthful (*OED* 9b).
31. D.'s addition.
33. *wit*] intelligence.
34–6. D.'s addition.
36. *sting*] wound inflicted on the mind or heart; appetite, stimulus, incitement (*OED* 5a).
37. *prodigal*] lavish, generous.
40–2. D.'s addition.
43. The 1697 French translation has: 'Aprés avoir jetté les yeux sur tous les Cavaliers de la Cour'.
44–6. Boccaccio writes: 'avere . . . occultamente un valoroso amante' ('to have secretly a worthy lover'). D. adds the idea of a marriage.

A seeming widow, and a secret bride.
Among the train of courtiers, one she found
With all the gifts of bounteous Nature crowned;
Of gentle blood, but one whose niggard Fate
50   Had set him far below her high estate:
Guiscard his name was called, of blooming age,
Now squire to Tancred, and before his page.
To him, the choice of all the shining crowd,
Her heart the noble Sigismonda vowed.
55   Yet hitherto she kept her love concealed,
And with close glances every day beheld
The graceful youth; and every day increased
The raging fire that burned within her breast:
Some secret charm did all his acts attend,
60   And what his fortune wanted, hers could mend:
Till, as the fire will force its outward way,
Or, in the prison pent, consume the prey,
So long her earnest eyes on his were set:
At length their twisted rays together met,
65   And he, surprised with humble joy, surveyed
One sweet regard, shot by the royal maid.

48–50. For 'uom di nazione assai umile ma per vertù e per costumi nobile' ('a man of very humble birth, but noble in virtue and manners').
49. *gentle*] honourable, of the gentry (*OED* 2a): Guiscardo is not one of the nobility, but is a 'gentleman'. Cp. l. 489.
53. D.'s addition. *of*] from among.
55–64. D.'s expansion of: 'più che altro le piacque, e di lui tacitamente, spesso vedendolo, fieramente s'accese, ognora più lodando i modi suoi' ('By seeing him often, she fell madly and secretly in love with him, and she increasingly admired his ways').
56. *close*] secret.
58. The image (though commonplace) may derive from Florio: 'her affection being but a glowing sparke at the first, grewe like a Bauin [bundle of firewood] to take flame' (Kinsley).
60. *wanted*] lacked.
64. In the Renaissance there were two theories of vision: extramissive (in which the eye was thought to send out a beam that connected with the object seen), and intramissive (in which the object seen sent out a beam that connected with the eye). The former theory was particularly useful to poets describing love (cp. Donne, 'The Ecstasy' ll. 7–8), and persisted in such contexts after it had been abandoned as a scientific theory. Cp. *HP* ii 72–6*n*, 'Palamon and Arcite' iii 476.
65–70. D.'s expansion of: 'E il giovane, il quale ancora non era poco avveduto, essendosi di lei accorto, l'aveva per sì fatta maniera nel cuor ricevuta, che da ogni altra cosa quasi che da amor lei aveva la mente rimossa' ('As for the young man himself, not being slow to take a hint, from the moment he perceived her interest in him he lost his heart to her so completely that he could think of virtually nothing else').

Not well assured, while doubtful hopes he nursed,
A second glance came gliding like the first,
And he who saw the sharpness of the dart,
70   Without defence received it in his heart.
In public, though their passion wanted speech,
Yet mutual looks interpreted for each:
Time, ways, and means of meeting were denied,
But all those wants ingenious Love supplied:
75   Th' inventive god, who never fails his part,
Inspires the wit, when once he warms the heart.
   When Guiscard next was in the circle seen
Where Sigismonda held the place of queen,
A hollow cane within her hand she brought,
80   But in the concave had enclosed a note:
With this she seemed to play, and, as in sport,
Tossed to her love in presence of the court.
'Take it,' she said, 'and when your needs require,
This little brand will serve to light your fire.'
85   He took it with a bow, and soon divined
The seeming toy was not for nought designed;
But when retired, so long with curious eyes
He viewed the present, that he found the prize.
Much was in little writ, and all conveyed ⎫
90   With cautious care, for fear to be betrayed   ⎬
By some false confidant, or favourite maid. ⎭
The time, the place, the manner how to meet,
Were all in punctual order plainly writ:
But since a trust must be, she thought it best ⎫
95   To put it out of laymen's power at least,   ⎬
And for their solemn vows prepared a priest. ⎭

71–2. For 'In cotal guisa adunque amando l'un l'altro segretamente' ('and so they
were secretly in love with each other').
72. *mutual looks*] 'mutually' (Florio).
73. D.'s addition.
74–6. Boccaccio attributes the idea to Sigismonda, rather than to the god Love.
The idea of love inspiring and energizing the mind recurs in 'Cymon and Iphigenia',
esp. ll. 27–32, 117–28. With l. 75 cp. 'The Art of Poetry' l. 519 (Richard Bates).
77–8. D.'s addition.
79. *hollow cane*] Thus Florio.
80. *concave*] cylindrical cavity (*OED* 1b).
86. *toy*] trifle, thing of little value (*OED* 5, 7).
87. *curious*] careful, attentive; inquisitive, eager to learn (*OED* 1a, 3a; 5a).
93. *punctual*] dealing with a matter point by point; detailed and precise (*OED* 6).
94–6. D.'s addition, introducing the priest, who is not in the original.

Guiscard (her secret purpose understood)
With joy prepared to meet the coming good;
Nor pains nor danger was resolved to spare,
100 But use the means appointed by the fair.
Near the proud palace of Salerno stood
A mount of rough ascent, and thick with wood;
Through this a cave was dug with vast expense,
The work it seemed of some suspicious prince,
105 Who, when abusing power with lawless might,
From public justice would secure his flight.
The passage made by many a winding way
Reached ev'n the room in which the tyrant lay.
Fit for his purpose, on a lower floor
110 He lodged, whose issue was an iron door,
From whence, by stairs descending to the ground,
In the blind grot a safe retreat he found.
Its outlet ended in a brake o'ergrown
With brambles, choked by time, and now unknown.
115 A rift there was, which from the mountain's height
Conveyed a glimmering and malignant light,
A breathing place to draw the damps away,
A twilight of an intercepted day.
The tyrant's den, whose use though lost to fame,
120 Was now th' apartment of the royal dame;
The cavern only to her father known,
By him was to his darling daughter shown.
Neglected long she let the secret rest,
Till Love recalled it to her labouring breast,

102–6. D.'s addition, making the point that the cave was dug for political reasons, and forming another reference to tyranny (see l. 3n).
107–18. D.'s expansion: Boccaccio just says that the staircase led to Sigismonda's room on the ground floor; D. adds Tancred's knowledge of it.
112. blind] dark (OED 6a); secret, obscure (OED 8a); concealed from sight (OED 9a). grot] cave.
113. brake] clump of bushes, thicket. o'ergrown] 'ouer-growne' (Florio).
116. glimmering] faint or intermittent (OED glimmer v. 2a). malignant] scanty (not in OED; from the Latin malignus (see OLD malignus 2, 'poor, scanty, small in extent')). Christie notes the echo of Virgil's sub luce maligna (Aen. vi 270: 'under a scanty light').
118. twilight] dim light (OED 2, first example from Milton, PL i 597). intercepted] cut off (OED, citing this example).
119. fame] common talk (OED 1a).
124. labouring] struggling with emotion (OED 3).

125   And hinted as the way by heaven designed
       The teacher, by the means he taught, to blind.
       What will not women do, when need inspires
       Their wit, or love their inclination fires!
       Though jealousy of state th' invention found,
130   Yet love refined upon the former ground.
       That way the tyrant had reserved to fly
       Pursuing hate, now served to bring two lovers nigh.
           The dame, who long in vain had kept the key,
       Bold by desire explored the secret way;
135   Now tried the stairs, and wading through the night
       Searched all the deep recess, and issued into light.
       All this her letter had so well explained,
       Th' instructed youth might compass what remained:
       The cavern mouth alone was hard to find,
140   Because the path, disused, was out of mind:
       But in what quarter of the copse it lay,
       His eye by certain level could survey:
       Yet (for the wood perplexed with thorns he knew)
       A frock of leather o'er his limbs he drew,
145   And thus provided, searched the brake around
       Till the choked entry of the cave he found.
           Thus, all prepared, the promised hour arrived,
       So long expected, and so well contrived.
       With Love to friend, th' impatient lover went,
150   Fenced from the thorns, and trod the deep descent.
       The conscious priest, who was suborned before,

125–32. D.'s addition.
129. jealousy] anxiety to guard something; suspicion, mistrust (OED 3, 5).   invention]
contrivance, scheme (OED 8).
138. compass] manage.
139–42. D.'s addition.
140. out of mind] 'out of memory' (Florio).
142. level] estimate (not in OED, but cp. OED level v.¹ 8b, 'to guess'; and OED
sb. 1a, the instrument used in surveying).
143. perplexed] entangled (OED 3). J. R. Mason suggests that D. echoes Milton's
usage in Comus l. 37 and PL iv 176.
144. frock] long coat, tunic (OED 2a, citing this example).
145–6. Boccaccio has Guiscardo descending into the cavern by a rope.
147–9. D.'s addition, possibly drawing on Florio: 'this long desired, and now obtained
meeting'.
149. With Love to friend] Echoes 'Palamon and Arcite' i 12.   to] as.
151–2, 163–73. D. adds all the material concerning the priest. The passage reworks
the account of a secret marriage in Don Sebastian III i 38–47 (Richard Bates).
151. conscious] sharing a [guilty] secret (OED 1); again at ll. 231, 720.   suborned]

Stood ready posted at the postern door;
The maids in distant rooms were sent to rest,
And nothing wanted but th' invited guest.
155 He came, and knocking thrice, without delay,
The longing lady heard, and turned the key;
At once invaded him with all her charms,
And the first step he made was in her arms.
The leathern outside, boisterous as it was,
160 Gave way, and bent beneath her strict embrace:
On either side the kisses flew so thick
That neither he nor she had breath to speak.
The holy man, amazed at what he saw,
Made haste to sanctify the bliss by law,
165 And muttered fast the matrimony o'er
For fear committed sin should get before.
His work performed, he left the pair alone, ⎫
Because he knew he could not go too soon, ⎬
His presence odious when his task was done. ⎭
170 What thoughts he had beseems not me to say, ⎫
Though some surmise he went to fast and pray, ⎬
And needed both, to drive the tempting thoughts away. ⎭
     The foe once gone, they took their full delight;
'Twas restless rage and tempest all the night;
175 For greedy love each moment would employ,
And grudged the shortest pauses of their joy.
     Thus were their loves auspiciously begun,
And thus with secret care were carried on.
The stealth itself did appetite restore,
180 And looked so like a sin, it pleased the more.

---

commissioned, procured (often with implications of bribery, or the commission
of an illegal act: OED 1); again at l. 718.
152. postern door] private or side door (OED).
154–5. D.'s addition.
154. wanted] was lacking.
157–62. For 'insieme maravigliosa festa si fecero' ('they gave each other a raptur-
ous greeting').
157. charms] A stronger word in Restoration usage than now, often connoting
'sexual attractions': cp. Rochester: '*Naked* she lay clasp'd in my longing Armes, /
I fill'd with Love, and she all over Charmes' ('The Imperfect Enjoyment' ll. 1–20).
159. boisterous] rough, strong, stiff (OED 2, last example).
160. strict] tight (OED 1).
174–6. For 'con grandissimo piacere gran parte di quel giorno si dimorarono' ('they
stayed for a great part of that day with great pleasure').
177–80. D.'s addition. Line 180 repeats the idea in 'Cinyras and Myrrha' l. 263.

      The cave was now become a common way,
      The wicket, often opened, knew the key;
      Love rioted secure, and long enjoyed,
      Was ever eager, and was never cloyed.
185   But as extremes are short, of ill and good,
      And tides at highest mark regorge the flood,
      So Fate, that could no more improve their joy,
      Took a malicious pleasure to destroy.
      Tancred, who fondly loved, and whose delight
190   Was placed in his fair daughter's daily sight,
      Of custom, when his state affairs were done,
      Would pass his pleasing hours with her alone;
      And, as a father's privilege allowed,
      Without attendance of th' officious crowd.
195   It happened once, that when in heat of day
      He tried to sleep, as was his usual way,
      The balmy slumber fled his wakeful eyes,
      And forced him, in his own despite, to rise:
      Of sleep forsaken, to relieve his care
200   He sought the conversation of the fair:
      But with her train of damsels she was gone,
      In shady walks the scorching heat to shun.
      He would not violate that sweet recess,
      And found besides a welcome heaviness
205   That seized his eyes, and slumber, which forgot
      When called before to come, now came unsought.

182–4. D.'s addition.

183. rioted] revelled, indulged to excess (*OED* 1).

185–8. For 'Ma la fortuna, invidiosa di così lungo e di così gran diletto, con doloroso avvenimento la letizia de' due amanti rivolse in tristo pianto' ('But Fortune, envious of such continued and intense pleasure, with an unhappy occurrence turned the joy of the two lovers into wretched weeping').

186. regorge] swallow again, i.e. the tide at its highest point appears to swallow up the flood water as it retreats (*OED* 2, sole example before 1894, but cp. the intransitive usage 1b, 'flow back again' from 1654).

188. malicious pleasure] Cp. Fortune's 'malicious joy' in 'Horace: *Odes* III xxix' l. 73. Florio has 'malicious'.

189–94. D.'s expansion.

189. fondly] 'Fond' was a strong word at this date: 'infatuated', 'mad', 'over-affectionate, doting' (*OED* 2, 3, 5a); again at l. 441.

194. officious] doing their duty (*OED* 2); not pejorative.

196–9. D.'s addition.

203. sweet recess] Used in *PL* ix 456, xi 303–4 (J. R. Mason). Cp. 'The Cock and the Fox' l. 598. *recess*] retirement, privacy.

204–6, 210. D.'s additions.

From light retired, behind his daughter's bed
He for approaching sleep composed his head;
A chair was ready, for that use designed,
210 So quilted, that he lay at ease reclined;
The curtains closely drawn, the light to screen,
As if he had contrived to lie unseen:
Thus covered with an artificial night,
Sleep did his office soon, and sealed his sight.
215 With heaven averse, in this ill-omened hour
Was Guiscard summoned to the secret bower,
And the fair nymph, with expectation fired,
From her attending damsels was retired;
For, true to love, she measured time so right
220 As not to miss one moment of delight.
The garden, seated on the level floor,
She left behind, and locking every door
Thought all secure; but little did she know,
Blind to her fate, she had enclosed her foe.
225 Attending Guiscard in his leathern frock
Stood ready, with his thrice repeated knock.
Thrice with a doleful sound the jarring grate
Rung deaf and hollow, and presaged their fate.
The door unlocked, to known delight they haste,
230 And panting in each other's arms, embraced;
Rush to the conscious bed, a mutual freight,
And heedless press it with their wonted weight.
  The sudden bound awaked the sleeping sire,
And showed a sight no parent can desire:
235 His opening eyes at once with odious view

211. The curtains closely drawn] 'the Curtaines close drawne' (Florio).
213. D.'s addition.
214. office] function.
215. For 'per isventura' ('unfortunately'). D.'s emphasis on supernatural forces is a characteristic motif in *Fables*.
219–21. D.'s addition.
221. seated] situated (*OED* seat *v.* 5, citing this example). *on the level floor*] i.e. the garden was on the same level as her bedroom (*OED* level *adj.* 3a).
224. blind to her fate] D.'s addition.
226–8. D.'s addition, again introducing an ominous note.
228. deaf] hollow, not having its usual character (*OED* 6a, rather than 'muffled' (*OED* 5), as *Works* has it: the disturbing aspect of the sound is not its low volume but its strange character).
231. conscious] aware of a [guilty] secret. *freight*] load, burden (*OED* 2b).

The love discovered, and the lover knew:
He would have cried, but hoping that he dreamt,
Amazement tied his tongue, and stopped th' attempt.
Th' ensuing moment all the truth declared,
240   But now he stood collected, and prepared,
For malice and revenge had put him on his guard.
    So, like a lion that unheeded lay,
Dissembling sleep, and watchful to betray,
With inward rage he meditates his prey.
245   The thoughtless pair, indulging their desires,
Alternate kindled and then quenched their fires;
Nor thinking in the shades of death they played,
Full of themselves, themselves alone surveyed,
And, too secure, were by themselves betrayed.
250   Long time dissolved in pleasure thus they lay,
Till nature could no more suffice their play;
Then rose the youth, and through the cave again
Returned; the princess mingled with her train.
    Resolved his unripe vengeance to defer,
255   The royal spy, when now the coast was clear,
Sought not the garden, but retired unseen
To brood in secret on his gathered spleen,
And methodize revenge: to death he grieved,
And, but he saw the crime, had scarce believed.
260   Th' appointment for th' ensuing night he heard,
And therefore in the cavern had prepared
Two brawny yeomen of his trusty guard.

239–40. D.'s addition.
240. stood collected] Cp. Milton's classical orator who 'Stood in himself collected' (*PL* ix 673; J. R. Mason).
242–4. D.'s addition.
245–52. For 'I due amanti stettero per lungo spazio insieme' ('the two lovers remained together for a long time'). Line 249 may derive from Florio's reference to 'their ouer-confident trust'.
249. secure] free from care, overconfident (*OED* 1).
250. dissolved] Often used in Restoration poetry for lovers in the state of orgasm and post-coital oblivion; cp. 'Lucretius: Concerning the Nature of Love' l. 82*n*.
254–9. For 'da una finestra di quella si calò nel giardino e senza essere da alcun veduto, dolente a morte, alla sua camera si tornò' ('through a window he lowered himself into the garden without being seen by anyone, and, grieved to death, returned to his own apartment').
257. spleen] bad temper, passionate indignation (*OED* 6–8).
258. methodize] put into a methodical arrangement (*OED* 1, citing this example).
260–9. D.'s expansion.
260–2. For the rhyme see ll. 286–7*n*.

Scarce had unwary Guiscard set his foot
Within the farmost entrance of the grot,
265 When these in secret ambush ready lay,
And rushing on the sudden seized the prey:
Encumbered with his frock, without defence, ⎫
An easy prize, they led the prisoner thence, ⎬
And, as commanded, brought before the prince. ⎭
270 The gloomy sire, too sensible of wrong
To vent his rage in words, restrained his tongue,
And only said, 'Thus servants are preferred,
And trusted, thus their sovereigns they reward.
Had I not seen, had not these eyes received
275 Too clear a proof, I could not have believed.'
He paused, and choked the rest. The youth, who saw
His forfeit life abandoned to the law,
The judge th' accuser, and th' offence to him
Who had both power and will t' avenge the crime,
280 No vain defence prepared; but thus replied:
'The faults of Love by Love are justified:
With unresisted might the monarch reigns,
He levels mountains, and he raises plains;
And not regarding difference of degree
285 Abased your daughter, and exalted me.'
This bold return with seeming patience heard,
The prisoner was remitted to the guard.
The sullen tyrant slept not all the night,

270–1. For 'il quale, come il vide, quasi piagnendo disse' ('he, when he saw him, said weeping').
270. *sensible*] aware, conscious.
272–3. D. gives a more general application to the first part of Tancred's speech: 'la mia benignità verso te non avea meritato l'oltraggio e la vergogna la quale nelle mie cose fatta m'hai' ('my benevolence towards you did not merit the outrage and the shame which you have committed against me'). *preferred / . . . reward*] A good rhyme, since *preferred* was pronounced (and sometimes spelt) *prefarred*.
272. *preferred*] promoted.
276–80. *He paused . . . prepared*] D.'s addition.
281–5. D.'s expansion of 'Amor può troppo più che né voi né io possiamo' ('love is too powerful for either you or I to resist'). Cp. Arcite's speech in 'Palamon and Arcite' i 326–36.
284. *degree*] social rank.
286–7. *heard / . . . guard*] A good rhyme, since *heard* was pronounced (and sometimes spelt) *hard*. Cp. ll. 260–2 and *prepared / . . . heard* in ll. 292–3.
286. D.'s addition.
288–96. D.'s addition. In Boccaccio, Guiscardo is apprehended after leaving Sigismonda; in D.'s version he never reaches her (Kinsley).

But lonely walking by a winking light,
290   Sobbed, wept, and groaned, and beat his withered breast,
But would not violate his daughter's rest;
Who long expecting lay, for bliss prepared,
Listening for noise, and grieved that none she heard;
Oft rose, and oft in vain employed the key, ⎫
295   And oft accused her lover of delay,   ⎬
And passed the tedious hours in anxious thoughts away. ⎭
      The morrow came, and at his usual hour
Old Tancred visited his daughter's bower;
Her cheek (for such his custom was) he kissed,
300   Then blessed her kneeling, and her maids dismissed.
The royal dignity thus far maintained,
Now left in private, he no longer feigned,
But all at once his grief and rage appeared,
And floods of tears ran trickling down his beard.
305   'O Sigismonda,' he began to say: ⎫
Thrice he began, and thrice was forced to stay, ⎬
Till words with often trying found their way: ⎭
'I thought, O Sigismonda (but how blind
Are parents' eyes, their children's faults to find!)
310   Thy virtue, birth, and breeding were above
A mean desire, and vulgar sense of love:
Nor less than sight and hearing could convince ⎫
So fond a father, and so just a prince,   ⎬
Of such an unforeseen, and unbelieved offence. ⎭
315   Then what indignant sorrow must I have
To see thee lie subjected to my slave!

---

289. winking] intermittent, twinkling (*OED* 2c).
299–303. D.'s addition.
300. It was common for fathers to give their children a blessing on meeting or parting (cp. Polonius and Laertes in *Hamlet* I iii 57).
304. Cp. Florio: 'the teares trickling downe his aged white beard'.
306–7. D.'s addition, echoing *PL* i 619–21 (J. R. Mason).
308–9. but how . . . to find] D.'s addition.
310–46. D. rearranges the order of some of the material in Tancred's speech.
311. For 'che tu di sottoporti a alcuno uomo, se tuo marito stato non fosse' ('that you would think of yielding to a man who was not your husband'). *mean, vulgar*] of low social status.
313–16. D.'s addition.
313. fond] See l. 189*n* (again at l. 329).
316. subjected] Not only socially 'subordinate to' (*OED* 2), but literally 'lying underneath' (*OED* 1).

A man so smelling of the people's lee,
The court received him first for charity;
And since with no degree of honour graced,
320 But only suffered where he first was placed—
A grovelling insect still; and so designed
By Nature's hand, nor born of noble kind:
A thing by neither man nor woman prized,
And scarcely known enough to be despised.
325 To what has heaven reserved my age? Ah! why
Should man, when Nature calls, not choose to die,
Rather than stretch the span of life, to find
Such ills as Fate has wisely cast behind
For those to feel whom fond desire to live
330 Makes covetous of more than life can give!
Each has his share of good, and when 'tis gone
The guest, though hungry, cannot rise too soon.
But I, expecting more, in my own wrong
Protracting life, have lived a day too long.
335 If yesterday could be recalled again,
Ev'n now would I conclude my happy reign:
But 'tis too late, my glorious race is run,
And a dark cloud o'ertakes my setting sun.
Hadst thou not loved, or loving, saved the shame,
340 If not the sin, by some illustrious name,
This little comfort had relieved my mind:
'Twas frailty, not unusual to thy kind.

317–24. For 'giovane di vilissima condizione, nella nostra corte quasi come per Dio da piccol fanciullo infino a questo dì allevato' ('a young man of the basest condition, whom we took into our court and raised from early childhood mainly out of charity').
317. lee] (now always 'lees', pl.) sediment deposited in wine, dregs; often used metaphorically (OED 1, citing this example; see also its quotation from Estcourt (1706), under 2b, which seems an echo of D.'s line).
318–19. Walter has 'for charitye' (as a rhyme) and 'degree'.
320. suffered] tolerated.
322. kind] race, family.
325–38. For 'di che io, in questo poco di rimanente di vita che la mia vecchiezza mi serba, sempre sarò dolente di ciò ricordandomi' ('the memory of it will always torment me during what little remains of my old age').
325–32. Introduced from Lucretius: cp. 'Lucretius: Against the Fear of Death' ll. 121–31.
339–46. For 'E or volesse Idio che, poi che a tanta disonestà conducer ti dovevi, avessi preso uomo che alla tua nobilità decevole fosse stato' ('Since you felt bound to bring so much dishonour upon yourself, in God's name you might at least have chosen someone whose rank was suited to your own').
342. frailty] See l. 385n. kind] [female] sex (again at l. 403).

But thy low fall beneath thy royal blood
Shows downward appetite to mix with mud:
345   Thus not the least excuse is left for thee,
Nor the least refuge for unhappy me.
        'For him I have resolved: whom by surprise
I took, and scarce can call it in disguise;
For such was his attire, as with intent
350   Of nature, suited to his mean descent:
The harder question yet remains behind,   ⎫
What pains a parent and a prince can find   ⎬
To punish an offence of this degenerate kind. ⎭
        'As I have loved, and yet I love thee more
355   Than ever father loved a child before,
So that indulgence draws me to forgive;
Nature, that gave thee life, would have thee live.
But as a public parent of the state,
My justice, and thy crime, requires thy fate.
360   Fain would I choose a middle course to steer;
Nature's too kind, and Justice too severe:
Speak for us both, and to the balance bring
On either side the father and the king.
Heaven knows, my heart is bent to favour thee;
365   Make it but scanty weight, and leave the rest to me.'
        Here stopping with a sigh, he poured a flood
Of tears, to make his last expression good.
        She, who had heard him speak, nor saw alone
The secret conduct of her love was known,
370   But he was taken who her soul possessed,
Felt all the pangs of sorrow in her breast;
And little wanted, but a woman's heart

344. *mud*] figuratively, the dregs, the lowest or worst layer (*OED* 2b).
348–50. *and scarce . . . descent*] D.'s addition.
351–3. D.'s expansion of 'ma di te sallo Idio che io non so che farmi' ('but God knows what I am to do with you').
357. D.'s addition.
358. D.'s image.
359. *fate*] death; again at ll. 382, 401.
361. Florio has: 'whereas Nature pleadeth pardon for the one, yet iustice standeth vp against the other, and vrgeth cruell seuerity against thee'.
362–5. *and to . . . to me*] D.'s addition.
365. i.e., however meagre her argument in defence of her conduct, Tancred will strengthen it by adding his fatherly feelings in its support.
367. Boccaccio says: 'come farebbe un fanciul ben battuto' ('like a child who has been soundly beaten').
370. For 'Guiscardo'.

With cries and tears had testified her smart;
But inborn worth, that Fortune can control,
375 New strung and stiffer bent her softer soul;
The heroine assumed the woman's place,
Confirmed her mind, and fortified her face.
Why should she beg, or what could she pretend,
When her stern father had condemned her friend!
380 Her life she might have had, but her despair
Of saving his had put it past her care.
Resolved on fate, she would not lose her breath,
But rather than not die, solicit death.
Fixed on this thought, she not, as women use,
385 Her fault by common frailty would excuse,
But boldly justified her innocence,
And while the fact was owned, denied th' offence:
Then with dry eyes, and with an open look,
She met his glance mid-way, and thus undaunted spoke:
390   'Tancred, I neither am disposed to make
Request for life, nor offered life to take:
Much less deny the deed; but least of all
Beneath pretended justice weakly fall.
My words to sacred truth shall be confined,
395 My deeds shall show the greatness of my mind.
That I have loved, I own; that still I love,
I call to witness all the powers above.
Yet more I own: to Guiscard's love I give
The small remaining time I have to live;
400 And if beyond this life desire can be,
Not fate itself shall set my passion free.

374–7. For 'ma pur questa viltà vincendo il suo animo altiero, il viso suo con maravigliosa forza fermò' ('But her proudness of heart more than made up for her shattered spirits, and by a miraculous effort of will, she remained impassive').
374. control] overpower, master (*OED* 5); *worth* is the subject, *Fortune* the object.
377. Confirmed] made firm.
378. pretend] claim.
379. friend] lover, sexual partner (*OED* 4).
383. D.'s addition.
384. use] are accustomed to do.
385–7. D.'s addition.
385. frailty] Often used to excuse (or denounce) the propensity of women to seek sexual pleasure: cp. Hamlet's denunciation of Gertrude's remarriage: 'Frailty, thy name is woman' (I ii 146), and Angelo's enticement to Isabella in *Measure for Measure*: 'women are frail' (II iv 123).
393. pretended justice] D.'s idea.

'This first avowed; nor folly warped my mind,
Nor the frail texture of the female kind
Betrayed my virtue: for too well I knew
405 What honour was, and honour had his due:
Before the holy priest my vows were tied,
So came I not a strumpet, but a bride:
This for my fame, and for the public voice.
Yet more, his merits justified my choice,
410 Which had they not, the first election thine,
That bond dissolved, the next is freely mine.
Or grant I erred (which yet I must deny)
Had parents power ev'n second vows to tie,
Thy little care to mend my widowed nights
415 Has forced me to recourse of marriage rites,
To fill an empty side, and follow known delights.
What have I done in this deserving blame?
State laws may alter, Nature's are the same;
Those are usurped on helpless womankind,
420 Made without our consent, and wanting power to bind.
   'Thou, Tancred, better shouldst have understood
That as thy father gave thee flesh and blood,
So gav'st thou me: not from the quarry hewed,
But of a softer mould, with sense endued,

402–20. For 'la mia feminile fragilità, quanto la tua poca sollecitudine del mari-tarmi e la virtù di lui' ('not my womanly frailty, but your lack of concern to marry me, and his virtue').
402–3. nor . . . Nor] neither . . . Nor.
403. texture] disposition, character (*OED* 5).
408. fame] reputation.
410. election] choice.
419–20. These lines draw on Montaigne's essay 'Sur des vers de Virgile', perhaps in the translation by Charles Cotton (*Essays,* 3 vols (1685–6) iii 113): 'Women are not to blame at all, when they refuse the Rules of Life that are introduc'd into the world; forasmuch as the Men made them without their Consent' (Richard Bates, *N & Q* ccxxxi (1986) 44). Cp. *The Wild Gallant* II i 305–6.
419. usurped] inflicted, imposed (*OED* 5, citing this example). Montaigne also refers to the 'Usurpation of sovereign Authority . . . over the women' in the same essay (iii 170; Bates, thesis).
422. flesh and blood] Thus Florio.
424–7. D.'s addition.
424. Cp. 'The Wife of Bath her Tale' l. 90 (Bates, thesis). *sense*] This word has a complex semantic field, but among the relevant meanings here are 'capacity for feeling' (*OED* 5), 'faculty of the mind or soul' (7), 'reason' (10b), 'natural intelligence, soundness of judgment' (11a), 'recognition of a duty or virtue as a standard for one's conduct' (15b), 'emotional consciousness' (16a): Sigismonda is claiming a finer-grained awareness of the intellectual, moral, and emotional bases of action than Tancred has.

425   Ev'n softer than thy own, of suppler kind,
      More exquisite of taste, and more than man refined.
      Nor need'st thou by thy daughter to be told,
      Though now thy sprightly blood with age be cold,
      Thou hast been young, and canst remember still
430   That when thou hadst the power, thou hadst the will;
      And from the past experience of thy fires
      Canst tell with what a tide our strong desires
      Come rushing on in youth, and what their rage
        requires.
        'And grant thy youth was exercised in arms,
435   When love no leisure found for softer charms,
      My tender age in luxury was trained,
      With idle ease and pageants entertained;
      My hours my own, my pleasures unrestrained.
      So bred, no wonder if I took the bent
440   That seemed ev'n warranted by thy consent;
      For when the father is too fondly kind,
      Such seed he sows, such harvest shall he find.
      Blame then thyself, as reason's law requires
      (Since Nature gave, and thou foment'st my fires);
445   If still those appetites continue strong,
      Thou may'st consider, I am yet but young.
      Consider too, that having been a wife,
      I must have tasted of a better life,
      And am not to be blamed, if I renew,
450   By lawful means, the joys which then I knew.
      Where was the crime, if pleasure I procured,
      Young, and a woman, and to bliss inured?

---

426. exquisite] careful, precise, exact (*OED* 2); stressed on the first syllable.
430–3. For 'chenti e quali e con che forza vengano le leggi della giovanezza' ('the nature and power of the laws of youth').
430. will] sexual appetite.
431–2. Walter has the same rhymes (in the singular).
433. rage] violent sexual passion (*OED* 6b).
434. exercised in arms] Thus Florio.
435–40. For 'gli ozii e le dilicatezze' ('idleness and luxury').
437. pageants] empty shows (*OED* 4a).
441–5. For 'sì come da te generata' ('I was fathered by you').
442. Proverbial: Galatians vi 7; Tilley S 687.
450–1. lawful and *Where was the crime*] D.'s additions; Boccaccio's heroine (who is not married to Guiscardo) calls it 'natural peccato' ('natural sin').
452. inured] accustomed.

That was my case, and this is my defence:
I pleased myself, I shunned incontinence,
455   And, urged by strong desires, indulged my sense. }
      'Left to myself, I must avow, I strove
From public shame to screen my secret love;
And, well acquainted with thy native pride,
Endeavoured what I could not help, to hide:
460   For which a woman's wit an easy way supplied. }
How this, so well contrived, so closely laid,
Was known to thee, or by what chance betrayed,
Is not my care: to please thy pride alone
I could have wished it had been still unknown.
465   'Nor took I Guiscard by blind fancy led,
Or hasty choice, as many women wed,
But with deliberate care, and ripened thought,
At leisure first designed, before I wrought:
On him I rested, after long debate,
470   And not without considering, fixed my fate:
His flame was equal, though by mine inspired
(For so the difference of our birth required):
Had he been born like me, like me his love
Had first begun what mine was forced to move:
475   But thus beginning, thus we persevere; }
Our passions yet continue what they were, }
Nor length of trial makes our joys the less sincere. }
      'At this my choice, though not by thine allowed
(Thy judgement herding with the common crowd)
480   Thou tak'st unjust offence; and, led by them,

453–5. D.'s expansion.
454. incontinence] promiscuous sex.
455. sense] desire for sensual pleasure.
458. D.'s addition.
460. a woman's wit] For 'pietoso Amore e benigna fortuna' ('compassionate Love and benign Fortune').
463–4. to please . . . unknown] D.'s addition.
465–6. blind fancy and hasty choice] For 'per accidente' ('at random').
465. fancy] caprice, whim; capricious personal inclination, esp. in love (OED 7a, 8a, b).
471–7. D.'s addition.
477. trial] experience (OED 7).   sincere] pure, unmixed (OED 2).
478. allowed] approved.
479. For 'la volgare opinione' ('the common opinion').
480–9. D.'s expansion of Boccaccio's point that Tancred's objection is merely to Guiscardo's rank.

Dost less the merit than the man esteem.
Too sharply, Tancred, by thy pride betrayed,
Hast thou against the laws of kind inveighed;
For all th' offence is in opinion placed,
485   Which deems high birth by lowly choice debased:
This thought alone with fury fires thy breast
(For holy marriage justifies the rest),
That I have sunk the glories of the state,
And mixed my blood with a plebeian mate:
490   In which I wonder thou shouldst oversee ⎫
Superior causes, or impute to me   ⎬
The fault of Fortune, or the Fates' decree. ⎭
Or call it heaven's imperial power alone,
Which moves on springs of justice, though unknown;
495   Yet this we see, though ordered for the best,
The bad exalted, and the good oppressed;
Permitted laurels grace the lawless brow,
Th' unworthy raised, the worthy cast below.
    'But leaving that: search we the secret springs,
500   And backward trace the principles of things,
There shall we find, that when the world began,
One common mass composed the mould of man;
One paste of flesh on all degrees bestowed,
And kneaded up alike with moistening blood.
505   The same Almighty Power inspired the frame
With kindled life, and formed the souls the same:

483. *kind*] nature (*OED* 4a); Sigismonda implicitly contests Tancred's adherence to *kind* in *OED*'s sense 2a, 'one's status conferred by birth'.
489. *plebeian*] not of noble rank (*OED* A b); often used derogatorily (*OED* A c, B c). Cp. l. 49*n*.
490–5. D.'s expansion of Boccaccio's point that Tancred should blame Fortune.
490. *oversee*] overlook, disregard (*OED* 6).
494, 499. *springs*] forces by which an action is produced; causes; impelling agencies (*OED sb.*¹ 23, figurative use of the metal coils); cp. *Astraea Redux* l. 168.
497–8. In part an autobiographical allusion to D.'s loss of the laureateship in 1689, and his displacement by Shadwell.
497. D.'s addition.
501–9. For 'tu vedrai noi d'una massa di carne tutti la carne avere e da uno medesimo creatore tutte l'anime con iguali forze, con iguali potenze, con iguali vertù create' ('you will see that we are all of one flesh, and that our souls were created by a single maker, with equal force, with equal power, with equal virtue').
502. *mould*] earth regarded as the material of the human body (*OED sb.*¹ 4; last example from Milton 1629).
503. *paste*] the material of which a person is said to be made (*OED* 4).   *degrees*] social ranks.

The faculties of intellect and will
Dispensed with equal hand, disposed with equal skill, }
Like liberty indulged with choice of good or ill.
510   Thus born alike, from virtue first began
The difference that distinguished man from man:
He claimed no title from descent of blood,
But that which made him noble, made him good:
Warmed with more particles of heavenly flame, }
515   He winged his upward flight, and soared to fame;
The rest remained below, a tribe without a name. }
            'This law, though custom now diverts the course,
As Nature's institute, is yet in force,
Uncancelled, though disused: and he whose mind
520   Is virtuous, is alone of noble kind;
Though poor in fortune, of celestial race,
And he commits the crime who calls him base.
            'Now lay the line, and measure all thy court
By inward virtue, not external port,
525   And find whom justly to prefer above
The man on whom my judgement placed my love:
So shalt thou see his parts and person shine,
And thus compared, the rest a base degenerate line.
Nor took I, when I first surveyed thy court,
530   His valour or his virtues on report,
But trusted what I ought to trust alone,
Relying on thy eyes, and not my own:
Thy praise (and thine was then the public voice)
First recommended Guiscard to my choice:
535   Directed thus by thee, I looked, and found
A man, I thought, deserving to be crowned;

512, 514–16. D.'s additions. With l. 514 cp. 'The First Book of Ovid's *Metamorphoses*' l. 101 (on men), 'The Fourth Book of the *Georgics*' l. 323 (on bees), and 'The Cock and the Fox' l. 462 (on a cock).

518. institute] established law (*OED* 2a). See 'Palamon and Arcite' ii 337*n*.

520. kind] This usage seems to combine the senses 'nature' and 'race, family'; cp. l. 483*n*.

521. D.'s addition.

523. lay the line] lay down a measuring tape (*OED* line *sb.*² 4a). D.'s image.

524. port] manner in which one bears oneself, mien; style of living, social position (*OED sb.*⁴ 1a, 2a).

527. parts] abilities.

531–2. For 'tue parole e de' miei occhi' ('your words and my eyes').

535–40. D.'s expansion.

536. crowned] honoured, rewarded (*OED* 11).

First by my father pointed to my sight,
Nor less conspicuous by his native light:
His mind, his mien, the features of his face,
540 Excelling all the rest of human race:
These were thy thoughts, and thou could'st judge aright,
Till interest made a jaundice in thy sight.
        'Or should I grant thou didst not rightly see,
Then thou wert first deceived, and I deceived by thee.
545 But if thou shalt allege, through pride of mind,
Thy blood with one of base condition joined,
'Tis false: for 'tis not baseness to be poor;
His poverty augments thy crime the more,
Upbraids thy justice with the scant regard
550 Of worth: whom princes praise, they should reward.
Are these the kings entrusted by the crowd
With wealth to be dispensed for common good?
The people sweat not for their king's delight,
T' enrich a pimp, or raise a parasite:
555 Theirs is the toil, and he who well has served
His country, has his country's wealth deserved.
        'Ev'n mighty monarchs oft are meanly born,
And kings by birth to lowest rank return;
All subject to the power of giddy Chance,
560 For Fortune can depress, or can advance:
But true nobility is of the mind,
Not given by Chance, and not to Chance resigned.
        'For the remaining doubt of thy decree,
What to resolve, and how dispose of me,
565 Be warned to cast that useless care aside:
Myself alone will for myself provide.
If in thy doting and decrepit age,

541–2. D.'s addition.
542. *interest*] regard for one's self, self-interest (*OED* 5). *jaundice*] This medical
condition can produce yellow or disordered vision (*OED* 3, citing this example).
545. *through pride of mind*] D.'s addition.
548–56. D.'s expansion of 'con tua vergogna si potrebbe concedere, ché così hai
saputo un valente uomo tuo servidore mettere in buono stato' ('to your shame
it [the charge of poverty] might be conceded, for the small rewards you have
bestowed on such a worthy man your servant'). The politically charged language
of ll. 550–6, with possible contemporary application, is his own.
550. Cp. 'Palamon and Arcite' ii 661–2.
558. D. varies Boccaccio's point that many ploughmen and shepherds were once
wealthy.
559–62, 566. D.'s additions. The former is another passage on Fortune, the latter
another Ovidian 'turn'.

Thy soul, a stranger in thy youth to rage,
Begins in cruel deeds to take delight,
570   Gorge with my blood thy barbarous appetite:
For I so little am disposed to pray
For life, I would not cast a wish away.
Such as it is, th' offence is all my own,
And what to Guiscard is already done,
575   Or to be done is doomed by thy decree, ⎱
That, if not executed first by thee, ⎰
Shall on my person be performed by me. ⎰
        'Away, with women weep, and leave me here,
Fixed like a man to die without a tear;
580   Or save or slay us both this present hour,
'Tis all that Fate has left within thy power.'
        She said: nor did her father fail to find,
In all she spoke, the greatness of her mind;
Yet thought she was not obstinate to die,
585   Nor deemed the death she promised was so nigh.
Secure in this belief, he left the dame,
Resolved to spare her life, and save her shame;
But that detested object to remove,
To wreak his vengeance, and to cure her love.
590   Intent on this, a secret order signed,
The death of Guiscard to his guards enjoined;
Strangling was chosen, and the night the time,
A mute revenge, and blind as was the crime:
His faithful heart, a bloody sacrifice,
595   Torn from his breast to glut the tyrant's eyes,
Closed the severe command: for (slaves to pay)
What kings decree, the soldier must obey:
Waged against foes, and when the wars are o'er,
Fit only to maintain despotic power:
600   Dang'rous to freedom, and desired alone

---

570. D. strengthens Boccaccio's 'usa in me la tua crudeltà' ('turn your cruelty on me').
579, 581. D.'s additions.
580, 633. Or . . . or] Either . . . or.
585. D.'s addition.
593. D.'s addition.   blind] secret, out of sight (OED 8a).
594–5. For 'trattogli il cuore a lui il recassero' ('take out his heart and bring it to him').
596–603. D.'s addition.
598–601. See 'Palamon and Arcite' iii 669–72n.
598. waged] hired for military service (OED 7, last example 1652–62).

By kings who seek an arbitrary throne:
Such were these guards, as ready to have slain
The prince himself, allured with greater gain:
So was the charge performed with better will
605 By men inured to blood, and exercised in ill.
    Now, though the sullen sire had eased his mind,
The pomp of his revenge was yet behind,
A pomp prepared to grace the present he designed.
A goblet rich with gems, and rough with gold,
610 Of depth and breadth the precious pledge to hold,
With cruel care he chose: the hollow part
Enclosed, the lid concealed the lover's heart.
Then of his trusted mischiefs, one he sent,
And bad him with these words the gift present:
615 'Thy father sends thee this, to cheer thy breast,
And glad thy sight with what thou lov'st the best;
As thou hast pleased his eyes, and joyed his mind,
With what he loved the most of human kind.'
    Ere this, the royal dame, who well had weighed
620 The consequence of what her sire had said,
Fixed on her fate, against th' expected hour
Procured the means to have it in her power.
For this she had distilled with early care
The juice of simples friendly to despair,
625 A magazine of death; and thus prepared,
Secure to die, the fatal message heard,
Then smiled severe; nor with a troubled look
Or trembling hand the funeral present took;
Ev'n kept her count'nance when the lid removed
630 Disclosed the heart, unfortunately loved.

---

601. *arbitrary throne*] absolute monarchy, government without regard to Parliament or law.
605–8. D.'s addition.
607. *pomp*] ostentatious display (*OED* 3). *yet behind*] still to come.
610, 747. *pledge*] The heart in the goblet is Guiscardo's pledge of his love and faithfulness to her; but D. seems also to be playing on other uses of the word: (i) token of mutual love or hostage given to fortune (normally applied to a child: *OED* 2d); (ii) assurance of allegiance or goodwill made through the drinking of a health (*OED* 4).
611. *cruel care*] D.'s paradox.
613. *mischiefs*] persons who cause harm (*OED* 7).
619–20. *who well . . . had said*] D.'s addition.
624. *simples*] plants used for medicinal purposes.
626. *Secure*] certain (*OED* 2a); free from anxiety (*OED* 1).
630. *unfortunately loved*] D.'s phrase.

She needed not be told within whose breast
It lodged; the message had explained the rest.
Or not amazed, or hiding her surprise,
She sternly on the bearer fixed her eyes;
635   Then thus: 'Tell Tancred, on his daughter's part
The gold, though precious, equals not the heart:
But he did well to give his best, and I,
Who wished a worthier urn, forgive his poverty.'
    At this, she curbed a groan that else had come,
640   And pausing, viewed the present in the tomb:
Then to the heart adored devoutly glued
Her lips, and raising it, her speech renewed:
'Ev'n from my day of birth to this, the bound
Of my unhappy being, I have found
645   My father's care and tenderness expressed:
But this last act of love excels the rest;
For this so dear a present, bear him back
The best return that I can live to make.'
    The messenger dispatched, again she viewed
650   The loved remains, and sighing, thus pursued:
'Source of my life, and lord of my desires,
In whom I lived, with whom my soul expires;
Poor heart, no more the spring of vital heat,
Cursed be the hands that tore thee from thy seat!
655   The course is finished which thy Fates decreed,
And thou from thy corporeal prison freed:
Soon hast thou reached the goal with mended pace,
A world of woes dispatched in little space:
Forced by thy worth, thy foe in death become
660   Thy friend, has lodged thee in a costly tomb;
There yet remained thy funeral exequies,
The weeping tribute of thy widow's eyes,
And those indulgent heaven has found the way
That I, before my death, have leave to pay.

633. D.'s addition.
638–40. D.'s addition.
641. glued] attached, esp. in affection (*OED* 2, citing this example).
651–3. For 'dolcissimo albergo di tutti i miei piaceri' ('sweetest lodging of all my joys').
656. D.'s addition.
657. For the image cp. 'To the Memory of Mr Oldham' ll. 7–10*n*.   *with mended pace*] To 'mend one's pace' is to travel faster (*OED v.* 12e).
658. A world of woes] J. R. Mason compares Milton's 'a world of woe' (*PL* ix 11).

665 My father ev'n in cruelty is kind,
     Or heaven has turned the malice of his mind
     To better uses than his hate designed;
     And made th' insult which in his gift appears
     The means to mourn thee with my pious tears;
670 Which I will pay thee down, before I go,
     And save myself the pains to weep below—
     If souls can weep; though once I meant to meet
     My fate with face unmoved, and eyes unwet,
     Yet since I have thee here in narrow room
675 My tears shall set thee first afloat within thy tomb:
     Then (as I know thy spirit hovers nigh)
     Under thy friendly conduct will I fly
     To regions unexplored, secure to share
     Thy state; nor hell shall punishment appear,
680 And heaven is double heaven if thou art there.'
          She said: her brim-full eyes that ready stood,
     And only wanted will to weep a flood,
     Released their watery store, and poured amain,
     Like clouds low hung, a sober shower of rain;
685 Mute, solemn sorrow, free from female noise
     Such as the majesty of grief destroys:
     For bending o'er the cup, the tears she shed
     Seemed by the posture to discharge her head,
     O'erfilled before; and oft (her mouth applied
690 To the cold heart) she kissed at once, and cried.
     Her maids, who stood amazed, nor knew the cause
     Of her complaining, nor whose heart it was,
     Yet all due measures of her mourning kept,

665. D.'s paradox; cp. *cruel care* in l. 611.
667–9. D.'s addition.
668. *insult*] outrage (*OED sb.* 2, first example from Milton, 1671); scornful triumph (cp. *OED v.* 1). The noun is stressed on the second syllable.
671–2. *And save . . . can weep*] D.'s addition.
674–5. D.'s addition.
677. *conduct*] guidance, leading (*OED* 1).
678. *secure*] certain (*OED* 2a).
679–80, 682. D.'s additions.
683. *amain*] at once (*OED* 2b (no example between 1600 and 1821) rather than the more usual meaning 'with full force' (*OED* 1), which would contradict *sober*).
684. Boccaccio says 'like water from a fountain'.   *sober*] quiet, gentle (often used of rain: *OED* 6a).
686, 688–9. D.'s additions.
692. *whose heart it was*] 'what heart it was' (Florio).

Did office at the dirge, and by infection wept;
695   And oft enquired th' occasion of her grief
      (Unanswered but by sighs) and offered vain relief.
      At length, her stock of tears already shed,
      She wiped her eyes, she raised her drooping head,
      And thus pursued: 'O ever-faithful heart,
700   I have performed the ceremonial part,
      The decencies of grief: it rests behind,
      That as our bodies were, our souls be joined:
      To thy whate'er abode my shade convey,
      And as an elder ghost direct the way.'
705   She said, and bad the vial to be brought,
      Where she before had brewed the deadly draught;
      First pouring out the med'cinable bane,
      The heart her tears had rinsed she bathed again;
      Then down her throat the death securely throws,
710   And quaffs a long oblivion of her woes.
          This done, she mounts the genial bed, and there
      (Her body first composed with honest care)
      Attends the welcome rest: her hands yet hold
      Close to her heart the monumental gold;
715   Nor farther word she spoke, but closed her sight,
      And quiet, sought the covert of the night.
          The damsels, who the while in silence mourned,
      Not knowing, nor suspecting death suborned,
      Yet, as their duty was, to Tancred sent,
720   Who, conscious of th' occasion, feared th' event.
      Alarmed, and with presaging heart he came,

---

694. *Did office*] officiated.   *infection*] influence of sympathy (OED 9).
701. *decencies*] proper observances (OED 4, citing this line).   *rests*] remains.
703–4. D.'s addition.
706. *draught*] Often pronounced *drawt* in this period, so a good rhyme (see OED).
707. *med'cinable bane*] D.'s paradox.
710. D.'s addition.
711. *genial*] relating to marriage (OED adj.¹ 1); D.'s addition.
712. *honest*] honourable, respectable, decent; chaste (OED 2, 3b).
713. *Attends*] waits for.
714. *monumental*] serving as a tomb (OED 1, 2).
715–16. For 'senza dire alcuna cosa aspettava la morte' ('without saying a word waited for death').
715. *sight*] eyes (OED 9a).
716. *covert*] covering, protection (OED 1, 2).
718. *suborned*] procured (OED 1).
720. *conscious*] sharing a [guilty] secret (OED 1).   *event*] outcome.

And drew the curtains, and exposed the dame
To loathsome light; then with a late relief
Made vain efforts to mitigate her grief.
725 She, what she could, excluding day, her eyes
Kept firmly sealed, and sternly thus replies:
    'Tancred, restrain thy tears, unsought by me,
And sorrow, unavailing now to thee:
Did ever man before afflict his mind
730 To see th' effect of what himself designed?
Yet if thou hast remaining in thy heart
Some sense of love, some unextinguished part
Of former kindness, largely once professed, ⎤
Let me by that adjure thy hardened breast ⎬
735 Not to deny thy daughter's last request: ⎦
The secret love which I so long enjoyed,
And still concealed to gratify thy pride,
Thou hast disjoined; but, with my dying breath,
Seek not, I beg thee, to disjoin our death:
740 Where'er his corpse by thy command is laid,
Thither let mine in public be conveyed;
Exposed in open view, and side by side,
Acknowledged as a bridegroom and a bride.'
    The prince's anguish hindered his reply;
745 And she, who felt her fate approaching nigh,
Seized the cold heart, and heaving to her breast,
'Here, precious pledge,' she said, 'securely rest.'
These accents were her last; the creeping death
Benumbed her senses first, then stopped her breath.
750   Thus she for disobedience justly died;
The sire was justly punished for his pride;
The youth, least guilty, suffered for th' offence
Of duty violated to his prince;
Who late repenting of his cruel deed,
755 One common sepulchre for both decreed;
Entombed the wretched pair in royal state,
And on their monument inscribed their fate.

722–3. D.'s addition.
724. efforts] Stressed on the second syllable.
725–6. D.'s addition.
734. adjure] entreat solemnly.
737–9, 743, 747, 750–3, 757. D.'s additions.

24 Baucis and Philemon
(from Ovid's *Metamorphoses* VIII)

Date and publication. First printed 1700 in *Fables Ancient and Modern* (see head-note to 'Palamon and Arcite' for further details).

Context. For D.'s account of the composition of this poem in relation to that of the other contributions to *Fables*, see 'Preface to *Fables*' (*Poems* v 47–8). In the same Preface, D. praised Ovid's understanding of 'the manners; under which name I comprehend the passions and in a larger sense the description of persons and their very habits. For an example, I see Baucis and Philemon as perfectly before me as if some ancient painter had drawn them' – echoing Daniel Crispinus' commentary on *Met.* viii 645: *Annon ea cura mores totamque aniculae rationem ob oculos ponit Poeta, ut ipsam coram cernere videaris?* ('Has not the poet set before one's eyes the behaviour and characteristics of an old woman with the kind of care that one seems to see her face to face?').

    D. had included comments on Ovid in the 'Account of the Ensuing Poem' prefixed to *AM*, where he had commented on the Roman poet's skill in presenting 'the movements and affections of the mind, either combating between two contrary passions, or extremely discomposed by one' and of provoking 'concernment' for his female characters (ll. 167–71, 189–91). He had also incorporated a translation of *Met.* i 533–42 in *AM* itself (see ll. 521–8 and *n*). In 1680 he had contributed a Preface and three translations (one in collaboration with the Earl of Mulgrave) to *Ovid's Epistles*, a composite translation of the *Heroides*. The Preface to that collection contained an extensive discussion of Ovid's style, including criticisms of his self-indulgence, prolixity and 'prodigality of . . . wit', which echo strictures on the Roman poet traceable back to his own lifetime (see *Poems* i 380–2), and which were also alluded to in the 'Preface to *Sylvae*' (see *Poems* ii 240). In the 'Discourse Concerning Satire' D. had commented appreciatively on the 'turns on the words' (rhetorical figures involving obtrusive verbal repetition) which are so prominent a characteristic of Ovid's style (see *Poems* iii 441–5), but in the 'Dedication to *Examen Poeticum*' he repeated the traditional criticisms of Ovid while simultaneously asserting that the translations from Ovid included in *EP* appeared to him 'to be the best of all my endeavours in this kind', perhaps because Ovid accorded more with his 'genius' than other writers whom he had translated (see *Poems* iv 218–19). D. seems to have been planning a complete collaborative translation of the *Metamorphoses* in the early 1690s, a project that was postponed when D. embarked on his translation of Virgil, but put into effect posthumously in the version edited by Sir Samuel Garth (1717): see *Poems* iv 204–5; David Hopkins, *RES* n.s. xxxix (1988) 64–74, li (2000) 83–9. In the 'Preface to *Fables*' D. included an extensive comparison of Ovid with Chaucer, in which he again repeated the traditional criticisms of Ovid's 'boyisms' and inappropriate displays of wit in serious circumstances (see *Poems* v 54–67), while frequently imitating these very features of Ovid's style in his own versions. On the relation between D.'s critical and creative responses to Ovid, see further David Hopkins in *Ovid Renewed*, edited by Charles Martindale (1988) 167–90, 276–9.

Sources. D. translates *Met.* viii 611–724. Bottkol established that, when composing his translations from Ovid, D. consulted the variorum edition by Borchard

Cnipping (1670) and the Delphin edition by Daniel Crispinus (1689; revision by
John Freind, 1696), the latter including a Latin *interpretatio* (running prose paraphrase). He also made use of the edition by Cornelius Schrevelius (1662). He
drew on the previous complete English translations of the *Metamorphoses* by Arthur
Golding (1567) and George Sandys (in both the 1626 and 1632 editions, the latter
containing an extensive allegorical commentary: see David Hopkins, *N & Q* ccxxi
(1976) 552–3). The only previous English versions of this episode were those of
Golding and Sandys, but a number of details in D.'s translation (see ll. 34, 129,
134, 138, 175–6 and *nn*) suggest that he had read Jean de la Fontaine's French
version, first published in *Ouvrages de prose et de poésie des sieurs de Maucroix et de
la Fontaine, tome 1* (1685) and reprinted in *Fables choisis* (1694). D. also coloured
his depiction of Baucis and Philemon's banquet with echoes of Milton's *PL* (see
ll. 52, 89, 108–9, 111, 163 and *nn*; David Hopkins, *N & Q* ccxxvii (1982) 503–4).
Ovid's episode had frequently been likened by allegorizing commentators to the
passage in Genesis xix in which Lot entertains two angels hospitably in Sodom,
as a reward for which his family is rescued from the general destruction of the
city (see W. Stechow, *JWCI* iv (1941) 103–13; M. Beller, *Philemon und Baucis in
der europäischen Literatur* (1967)). This interpretation is mentioned in the editions
used by D. (see Sandys's exposition: 1632 edition, 296) and has left its mark on
his translation (see ll. 75, 146 and *nn*), but D. does not impose any overall Christian
interpretation on Ovid's tale (see Reverand 84–6, 90).

Reception. There were two early parodies of D.'s poem: Matthew Prior, 'The Ladle'
(first published in *Miscellany Poems: The Fifth Part* (1704)), and Jonathan Swift,
'Baucis and Philemon' (originally written *c.* 1706; first published in *Miscellany
Poems: The Sixth Part* (1709)). On the latter, see E. Rothstein in *The Augustan
Milieu: Essays Presented to Louis A. Landa*, edited by H. K. Miller, E. Rothstein,
and G. S. Rousseau (1970) 205–24.

Baucis and Philemon, Out of the Eighth
Book of Ovid's *Metamorphoses*

The author, pursuing the deeds of Theseus, relates how he, with
his friend Perithous, were invited by Achelous, the river god, to
stay with him till his waters were abated. Achelous entertains them
with a relation of his own love to Perimele, who was changed into
an island by Neptune, at his request. Perithous, being an atheist,
derides the legend, and denies the power of the gods to work
that miracle. Lelex, another companion of Theseus, to confirm
the story of Achelous, relates another metamorphosis, of Baucis
and Philemon into trees, of which he was partly an eye-witness.

¶24. *D.'s headnote. Perithous*] Thus spelt by *1700* and Crispinus (text); *Pirithous*
in Crispinus' *Interpretatio* and notes, and in Cnipping and Schrevelius.   *miracle*]
From Ovid's *factum mirabile* ('miraculous occurrence').

Thus Achelous ends; his audience hear
With admiration, and admiring, fear
The powers of heaven; except Ixion's son,
Who laughed at all the gods, believed in none;
5 He shook his impious head, and thus replies:
'These legends are no more than pious lies:
You attribute too much to heavenly sway,
To think they give us forms, and take away.'
  The rest, of better minds, their sense declared
10 Against this doctrine, and with horror heard.
Then Lelex rose, an old experienced man,
And thus with sober gravity began:
'Heaven's power is infinite: earth, air, and sea,
The manufacture mass, the making power obey.
15 By proof to clear your doubt: in Phrygian ground
Two neighbouring trees, with walls encompassed round,
Stand on a moderate rise, with wonder shown,
One a hard oak, a softer linden one;
I saw the place and them, by Pittheus sent
20 To Phrygian realms, my grandsire's government.
Not far from thence is seen a lake, the haunt
Of coots, and of the fishing cormorant.

2. D. adds the 'turn' on *admiration/admiring.*
2–3. fear / The powers of heaven] D.'s expansion, drawing out the implications of Ovid's *credentes* ('believers'). *Ixion's son*] Perithous.
5. shook his impious head] D.'s addition.
6. pious lies] For Ovid's *ficta* ('fictions'); 'lyes' in Sandys.
9. of better minds] D.'s addition.
12. with sober gravity] D.'s addition, perhaps prompted by Schrevelius' note: *Sententia gravi viro maxime conveniens* ('A pronouncement fully befitting a serious man').
13. infinite] For Ovid's *immensa* ('immeasurable'). Cp. Crispinus, *Interpretatio: infinita.*
13–14. earth, air, and sea . . . obey] For Ovid's *et quicquid superi voluere, peractum est* ('and whatever the gods decree is done').
14. manufacture] Noyes and *Works* emend to *manufactur'd,* but the attributive use of *manufacture* (in the sense of 'something made by art or handicraft') is acknowledged by Johnson (2) and *OED* (2a), both of which cite this example.
17. with wonder shown] D.'s addition.
18. hard, softer] D.'s additions.
19. and them] D.'s addition.
20. my] D.'s error. Ovid refers to Phrygia as *Pelopeia . . . arva* ('the land of Pelops'). As Cnipping and Crispinus explain, Pelops' father Tantalus had also been king of Phrygia. D. mistakenly makes Tantalus Lelex's grandfather. *government*] kingdom (*OED* 5, citing this example).
21. lake] For Ovid's *stagnum* ('marsh'); Crispinus, *Interpretatio: lacus.*
22. fishing] D.'s addition, from Sandys: 'Where Cootes and fishing Cormorants abound'.

Here Jove with Hermes came, but in disguise
Of mortal men concealed their deities;
25 One laid aside his thunder, one his rod,
And many toilsome steps together trod;
For harbour at a thousand doors they knocked,
Not one of all the thousand but was locked.
At last an hospitable house they found,
30 A homely shed; the roof, not far from ground,
Was thatched with reeds and straw together bound.
There Baucis and Philemon lived, and there
Had lived long married, and a happy pair;
Now old in love; though little was their store,
35 Inured to want, their poverty they bore,
Nor aimed at wealth, professing to be poor.
For master or for servant here to call
Was all alike, where only two were all.
Command was none where equal love was paid,
40 Or rather both commanded, both obeyed.
    'From lofty roofs the gods repulsed before,
Now stooping, entered through the little door;
The man (their hearty welcome first expressed)
A common settle drew for either guest,
45 Inviting each his weary limbs to rest.
But ere they sat, officious Baucis lays

---

25. thunder] D.'s addition. Jove lays aside his thunderbolts, just as Hermes lays aside his winged staff.

26. D.'s addition.

30. shed] cottage, poor dwelling (*OED* 2a, citing this example).   *not far from ground*] D.'s addition.

34. old in love] D.'s expansion of Ovid's *consenuere* ('grew old together'). La Fontaine had similarly stressed the couple's love: 'Ni le temps ni l'hymen n'éteignirent leur flamme . . . / L'amitié modéra leurs feux sans les détruire'.

36. Nor aimed at wealth] D.'s addition.   *professing*] declaring themselves (*OED* 2), perhaps also with suggestions of commitment to a quasi-religious vow (*OED* 1c); stronger than Ovid's *fatendo* ('acknowledging').

41. D.'s addition.

43. their hearty welcome first expressed] D.'s addition.

44. common] shared; D.'s addition.   *settle*] long, high-backed, wooden bench with locker under the seat (*OED* 3, citing this example).   *either guest*] i.e. both guests (*OED* either 1b).

45. weary] D.'s addition, rendering Schrevelius' gloss: *propter lassitudinem gravia* ('heavy through weariness').

46. ere they sat] D.'s addition.   *officious*] obliging, kind (*OED* 1; non-pejorative), rendering Crispinus, *Interpretatio: officiosa* (which glosses Ovid's *sedula* ('attentive, painstaking')).

Two cushions stuffed with straw, the seat to raise;
Coarse, but the best she had; then rakes the load
Of ashes from the hearth, and spreads abroad
50   The living coals; and, lest they should expire,
With leaves and barks she feeds her infant fire;
It smokes; and then with trembling breath she blows,
Till in a cheerful blaze the flames arose.
With brushwood and with chips she strengthens these,
55   And adds at last the boughs of rotten trees.
The fire thus formed, she sets the kettle on;
Like burnished gold the little seether shone;
Next took the coleworts which her husband got
From his own ground, a small well-watered spot;
60   She stripped the stalks of all their leaves; the best
She culled, and then with handy care she dressed.
High o'er the hearth a chine of bacon hung;
Good old Philemon seized it with a prong,
And from the sooty rafter drew it down,
65   Then cut a slice, but scarce enough for one;
Yet a large portion of a little store,
Which for their sakes alone he wished were more.
This in the pot he plunged without delay,

47–8. Expanding Ovid's *textum rude* ('a rough covering'). Cp. Sandys: '*Baucis* straw-stuft cushions layd'. Golding has 'quishons'.

50–1. *living, infant*] D.'s animistic additions, taking the hint from Ovid's *suscitat* ((i) 'restores to health' (*OLD* 3); (ii) 'kindles' (*OLD* 4)), and *nutrit* ('feeds').

52. *trembling*] For Ovid's *anili* ('of an old woman'). Cp. La Fontaine: 'haletant'.

53. *cheerful*] D.'s addition.

54. *chips*] small pieces of wood (*OED* 1a).

55. D.'s addition; from La Fontaine: 'Des branches de bois sec aussitôt s'enflammèrent'.

56. *kettle*] pot, cauldron (*OED* 1a); thus in Sandys.

57. Ovid simply says that the cauldron was *aeno* ('a bronze [vessel]'). *seether*] utensil for boiling (*OED* 2, citing this as its only example).

58. *coleworts*] cabbages; for Ovid's *holus* ('vegetable'); cp. Golding: 'Coleworts'; Sandys: 'cole-flowrs'.

60–1. For Ovid's *truncat holus foliis* ('she strips the vegetable of the leaves').

61. *handy*] dexterous (*OED* 4).

62. *High o'er the hearth*] D.'s addition.   *chine*] joint, consisting of the backbone and adjoining meat (*OED* chine *sb.²* 3b).

63. *Good old*] D.'s addition.

65. *but scarce enough for one*] For Ovid's *exiguam* ('small').

66–7. D.'s expansion of Ovid's *diu servato* ('stored for a long time').

68–9. *without delay . . . drain the salt away*] D.'s addition.

To tame the flesh, and drain the salt away.
70 The time between, before the fire they sat,
And shortened the delay by pleasing chat.
'A beam there was, on which a beechen pail
Hung by the handle, on a driven nail;
This filled with water, gently warmed, they set ⎤
75 Before their guests; in this they bathed their feet, ⎬
And after with clean towels dried their sweat: ⎦
This done, the host produced the genial bed, ⎤
Sallow the feet, the borders, and the stead, ⎬
Which with no costly coverlet they spread, ⎦
80 But coarse old garments; yet such robes as these
They laid alone at feasts, on holidays.
The good old housewife, tucking up her gown,
The table sets; th' invited gods lie down.
The trivet table of a foot was lame,
85 A blot which prudent Baucis overcame,
Who thrusts beneath the limping leg a sherd,
So was the mended board exactly reared;
Then rubbed it o'er with newly gathered mint,

69. *tame*] reduce the intense flavour of, temper, mellow (*OED* 3, citing this example).
70. *before the fire they sat*] D.'s addition.
72–5. D. translates Ovid ll. 652–55a, printed in the seventeenth-century texts, but relegated to a footnote by Loeb. Loeb's l. 655 does not appear in the seventeenth-century texts, but is given in a footnote by Cnipping and Schrevelius.
72. *A beam there was, on which*] D.'s addition.
73. *driven*] D.'s addition.
75. *feet*] For Ovid's *artus* ('limbs'), reflecting the paralleling of Ovid's story with that of Lot (see headnote), in which (Genesis xix 2) Lot invites the visiting angels to wash their feet. Cp. Schrevelius: *pedes* ('feet'); Golding, Sandys: 'feete'. Crispinus (*ad loc*) refers to the regular washing of feet in scripture.
76. D.'s addition.
77–80. Cp. Sandys: 'A couerlet, vs'd but at feasts, they spred: / Though course, and old; yet fit for such a bed'.
77. *genial*] nuptial (*OED* 1); D.'s addition.
78. *Sallow*] of willow wood (*OED* 2). In Ovid, the bed has a sedge mattress. *borders*] sides (*OED* 1), edgings (*OED* 5a); D.'s addition.   *stead*] frame (*OED* 8); cp. Cnipping, Schrevelius: *bedsted* (given in English); Sandys: 'bed-steede'.
81. *alone*] only.   *holidays*] spelt *Holydays* in *1700*.
82. *good old housewife*] For Ovid's *anus* ('old woman').
84. *trivet*] three footed (*OED* 4, citing this example).   *lame*] For Ovid's *inpar* ('unequal, unsteady'). Thus in Sandys.
85. D.'s addition.
86. *limping*] D.'s addition.
87. *reared*] built up (*OED* 7a).
88. *newly gathered*] For Ovid's *virentes* ('green').

A wholesome herb, that breathed a grateful scent.
90 Pallas began the feast, where first was seen
The parti-coloured olive, black and green;
Autumnal cornels next in order served,
In lees of wine well pickled and preserved;
A garden salad was the third supply,
95 Of endive, radishes, and succory;
Then curds and cream, the flower of country fare, ⎫
And new-laid eggs, which Baucis' busy care   ⎬
Turned by a gentle fire, and roasted rare.   ⎭
All these in earthen ware were served to board; ⎫
100 And next in place an earthen pitcher, stored ⎬
With liquor of the best the cottage could afford. ⎭
This was the table's ornament and pride,
With figures wrought; like pages at his side
Stood beechen bowls, and these were shining clean,
105 Varnished with wax without, and lined within.
By this the boiling kettle had prepared,
And to the table sent the smoking lard;
On which with eager appetite they dine,
A savoury bit, that served to relish wine;

89. D.'s addition. Schrevelius notes that *mentha suavissimi odoris est herba* ('mint is a herb of the most pleasant smell'). Crispinus notes that mint leaves *attritu gratum odorem emitterent* ('give off a pleasant smell when rubbed'). *grateful*] pleasing to the senses (*OED* 1).

90. *Pallas*] Athene was said to have created the olive tree.

91. *parti-coloured*] some of one, some of another colour; thus in Sandys.

92. *Autumnal cornels*] 'A red fruite with a hard shell growing on a thick shrub, for the most part in mountanous places' (Sandys).

93. *pickled*] Thus in Cnipping, Schrevelius (in English); *pickle* in Golding, Sandys.

94. D.'s expansion. *supply*] provision of food (*OED* 9).

95. *succory*] chicory (*OED* 1).

96. *curds*] Rendered as 'cheese' by Sandys and the commentators. *the flower of country fare*] D.'s addition.

97. *new-laid*] D.'s addition. *Baucis' busy care*] D.'s addition.

98. *rare*] left soft in cooking, underdone (*OED adj.*[2]); thus in Golding, Sandys.

100–2. *stored / With liquor . . . ornament and pride*] D.'s addition.

103. *like pages at his side*] D.'s addition.

104. *and these were shining clean*] D.'s addition.

106–11. D.'s expansion of Ovid's *parva mora est, epulasque foci misere calentes, / nec longae rursus referuntur vinae senectae* ('very shortly the hearth produced its hot feast, and wine of no great age was brought out').

107. *lard*] fat bacon (*OED* 1, citing this example); from Crispinus' *lardum*, for Ovid's *epulas* ('feast').

108–9. *eager appetite, savoury*] Drawing on the vocabulary and resonances of *PL* ix 739–41; v 303–5 (David Hopkins, *N & Q* ccxxvii (1982) 503–4).

110   The wine itself was suiting to the rest,
       Still working in the must, and lately pressed.
       The second course succeeds like that before,
       Plums, apples, nuts, and of their wintry store
       Dry figs and grapes, and wrinkled dates were set
115   In canisters, t' enlarge the little treat;
       All these a milk-white honeycomb surround,
       Which in the midst the country banquet crowned.
       But the kind hosts their entertainment grace
       With hearty welcome, and an open face;
120   In all they did, you might discern with ease
       A willing mind, and a desire to please.
         'Mean time the beechen bowls went round, and still,
       Though often emptied, were observed to fill;
       Filled without hands, and of their own accord
125   Ran without feet, and danced about the board.
       Devotion seized the pair, to see the feast
       With wine, and of no common grape, increased;
       And up they held their hands, and fell to prayer,
       Excusing as they could their country fare.
130   'One goose they had, 'twas all they could allow, ⎫
       A wakeful sentry, and on duty now,   ⎬
       Whom to the gods for sacrifice they vow: ⎭
       Her with malicious zeal the couple viewed;

---

111. working in the must] fermenting (*OED* must 1c). Again the vocabulary and associations are Miltonic: cp. *PL* v 344–7.

113. of their wintry store] D.'s addition.

115. canisters] baskets (*OED* 4). *t' enlarge the little treat*] D.'s addition.

117. the country banquet crowned] D.'s addition.

119. With . . . an open face] frankly (*OED* open a. 5b).

120. D.'s addition.

122. beechen] D.'s addition.

124–5. and of their own accord . . . about the board] D.'s addition. Robert Cummings suggests that D. is remembering the moving tripods made by Homer's Hephaestus (*Iliad* xviii 372–8).

127. and of no common grape] D.'s addition.

129. Cp. La Fontaine: 'Grand Dieu, dit Philémon, excusez notre faute'.

130. One goose they had] Verbatim in Sandys. *'twas all they could allow*] D.'s addition.

131. For Ovid's *minimae custodia villae* ('the guardian of their tiny estate'). Crispinus' note reminds the reader of Plutarch's account of how the geese on the Capitol gave warning of the Gauls' attack on Rome. Sandys notes that a goose is 'wakefull and crying out at euery noise'. Cp. 'Ceyx and Alcyone' l. 276.

133. with malicious zeal the couple viewed] D.'s addition.

She ran for life, and limping they pursued;
135 Full well the fowl perceived their bad intent,
And would not make her masters' compliment;
But persecuted, to the powers she flies,
And close between the legs of Jove she lies.
He with a gracious ear the suppliant heard,
140 And saved her life; then what he was declared,
And owned the god. "The neighbourhood," said he,
"Shall justly perish for impiety:
You stand alone exempted; but obey
With speed, and follow where we lead the way;
145 Leave these accursed, and to the mountain's height
Ascend, nor once look backward in your flight."
'They haste, and what their tardy feet denied,
The trusty staff (their better leg) supplied.
An arrow's flight they wanted to the top,
150 And there secure, but spent with travel, stop;
Then turn their now no more forbidden eyes;
Lost in a lake the floated level lies:
A watery desert covers all the plains,
Their cot alone, as in an isle, remains:

134–8. Cp. La Fontaine: 'Elle en veut faire un mets, et la poursuit en vain; / La volatille échappe à sa tremblante main; / Entre les pieds des Dieux elle cherche un asile'. Robert Cummings notes that Otto van Veen's illustration of the scene (in *Horatii Emblemata* (1612) 87) depicts the goose at Jupiter's feet.
134. limping] Ovid merely says that they were *tardos aetate* ('slow through age').
135–6. For Ovid's *eluditque diu* ('he eluded them for a long time').
138. D.'s addition.
139. with a gracious ear the suppliant heard] D.'s addition. Cp. Schrevelius: *Supplex & hospes non violandus; protegendus potius* ('A suppliant and guest is not to be harmed, but rather protected').
141, 193. neighbourhood] people living nearby (*OED* 6a).   *owned*] confessed himself to be.
143–4. obey / With speed] D.'s addition.
145. D.'s substitution for Ovid's *vestra tecta* ('your dwelling').
146. nor once look backward in your flight] D.'s addition, glancing at the story of Lot (Genesis xix 17; see headnote): 'Escape for thy life; look not behind thee, neither stay thou in all the plain: escape to the mountain, lest thou be consumed'.
148. trusty, their better leg] D.'s additions.
149. wanted to] fell short of (*OED* 2d).
150. D.'s addition.   *travel*] Spelt thus in *1700*, but could also be modernized as *travail*, since the two words shared the same spelling in this period.
151. now no more forbidden eyes] D.'s addition, again glancing at the story of Lot.
152. floated] flooded (*OED* 10).   *level*] plain (*OED* 6).
153. D.'s addition.
154. cot] cottage (*OED* sb. 1).   *as in an isle*] D.'s addition.

155 Wondering with weeping eyes, while they deplore
Their neighbours' fate, and country now no more,
Their little shed, scarce large enough for two,
Seems, from the ground increased, in height and bulk to
      grow.
A stately temple shoots within the skies,
160 The crotches of their cot in columns rise;
The pavement polished marble they behold,
The gates with sculpture graced, the spires and tiles of gold.
      'Then thus the sire of gods, with look serene:
"Speak thy desire, thou only just of men;
165 And thou, O woman, only worthy found
To be with such a man in marriage bound."
      'A while they whisper; then, to Jove addressed,
Philemon thus prefers their joint request:
"We crave to serve before your sacred shrine,
170 And offer at your altars rites divine;
And since not any action of our life
Has been polluted with domestic strife,
We beg one hour of death, that neither she
With widow's tears may live to bury me,
175 Nor weeping I, with withered arms may bear
My breathless Baucis to the sepulchre."
      'The godheads sign their suit. They run their race

155. *deplore*] lament (*OED* 1).
156. *and country now no more*] D.'s addition.
158. D.'s addition.
159. In Ovid, the cottage *vertitur in templum* ('is changed into a temple').
160. *crotches*] forked supports (*OED* 3, citing this example); thus in Sandys.
161. *polished*] D.'s addition.
162. *the spires and tiles of gold*] For Ovid's *stramina flavescunt aurataque tecta videntur* ('the straw grew yellow and gilded roofs appear') (printed as parts of two separate lines in the seventeenth-century editions).
163. *with look serene*] Miltonic; cp. *PL* x 1094 (J. R. Mason).
164–5. *only, only*] D.'s additions.
167. *A while they whisper*] For Ovid's *cum Baucide pauca locutus* ('when he had spoken a few words with Baucis'); cp. Sandys: 'They talke a while alone'.
168. *prefers*] puts forward (*OED* 1a).
171–2. For Ovid's *et quoniam concordes egimus annos* ('and since we have spent our years in harmony'). Cp. 'Palamon and Arcite' iii 1149.
173–6. *that neither she / With widow's tears . . . to the sepulchre*] D.'s expansion of Ovid's *ne coniugis umquam / busta meae videam, neu sim tumulandus ab illa* ('that I may never see my wife's tomb, nor be buried by her'). For the imagined tears, cp. La Fontaine: 'D'autres mains nous rendraient un vain et triste office: / Je ne pleurerais point celle-ci, ni ses yeux / Ne troubleraient non plus de leurs larmes ces lieux'.
177. *The godheads sign their suit*] Cp. Sandys: 'Their sute is sign'd'.   *sign*] confirm (*OED* 4a).   *suit*] petition (*OED* 11a).

In the same tenor all th' appointed space;
Then, when their hour was come, while they relate
180 These past adventures at the temple gate,
Old Baucis is by old Philemon seen
Sprouting with sudden leaves of sprightly green;
Old Baucis looked where old Philemon stood,
And saw his lengthened arms a sprouting wood;
185 New roots their fastened feet begin to bind,
Their bodies stiffen in a rising rind;
Then, ere the bark above their shoulders grew,
They give and take at once their last adieu;
At once, "Farewell, O faithful spouse," they said;
190 At once th' encroaching rinds their closing lips invade.
Ev'n yet an ancient Tyanaean shows
A spreading oak that near a linden grows;
The neighbourhood confirm the prodigy:
Grave men, not vain of tongue, or like to lie.
195 I saw myself the garlands on their boughs,
And tablets hung for gifts of granted vows;
And offering fresher up, with pious prayer,
"The good," said I, "are God's peculiar care,
And such as honour heaven, shall heavenly honour
        share." '

---

178. *in the same tenor*] continuing in the same way (*OED* tenor 2a).
180. *adventures*] marvels (*OED* 5a).
181, 183. Old (first); Old, old (both)] D.'s additions.
182. *sudden, of sprightly green*] D.'s additions.   *sprightly*] quick-growing (*OED* 1c, only example from Evelyn, 1693); cheerful (*OED* 1a, 3a).
184–6. D.'s addition.
186. *rind*] bark (*OED* 1a).
187. *shoulders*] For Ovid's *vultus* ('faces').
188. D.'s expansion.
190. *encroaching, closing*] D.'s additions.   *invade*] penetrate (*OED* 2).
191. *Tyanaean*] inhabitant of Tyana, 'A city of *Phrygia*' (Sandys).
192. D.'s substitution for Ovid's *de gemino vicinos corpore truncos* ('the neighbouring trees formed from their two bodies' (or 'growing from one double trunk')). Cp. Crispinus: *Mutatus enim est Philemon in quercum; Baucis in tiliam* ('For Philemon is changed into an oak, Baucis into a linden (lime) tree'). Cnipping and Schrevelius have similar notes.
193. *The neighbourhood*] D.'s addition.   *prodigy*] miracle, marvel (*OED* 3).
194. Cp. Sandys: 'Old men, nor like to lye, nor vaine of tongue'.
197. *with pious prayer*] D.'s addition.
198. D. follows Crispinus' and Cnipping's reading: *Cura pii Dis sunt* ('The pious are the care of the gods'). Schrevelius and Loeb read: *cura deum di sint* ('let those beloved of the gods be gods').

25 Cinyras and Myrrha
(from Ovid's *Metamorphoses* X)

Date and publication. First printed 1700 in *Fables Ancient and Modern* (see headnote to 'Palamon and Arcite' for further details). The present text is based on that of *1700*, with paragraphing added at ll. 35, 102, 184, 214, 264, 354, 380.

Context. From the beginning of his career, D. had shown a particular interest in Ovid's story of Myrrha as a notable example of the poet's capacity to depict women in the throes of conflicting passions (see 'An Account of the Ensuing Poem' prefixed to *AM* ll. 189–97). Like a number of his predecessors and contemporaries, D. was also fascinated by the subject of incestuous passion and by the ways in which incest might be thought of as both an expression of, and an outrage against, divine and natural law. (In this respect, the poem resonates with others in *Fables* – most notably 'Palamon and Arcite' (see ii 337*n*), 'Sigismonda and Guiscardo' and 'The Wife of Bath her Tale' – in its exploration of the conflicts between 'nature' and human social norms.) The subject of incest is treated at length in the epistle of 'Canace to Macareus' in *Ovid's Epistles* (1680), on four occasions in the plays – in *Aureng-Zebe* (1676), *Oedipus* (with Lee, 1679), *Don Sebastian* (1690) and *Love Triumphant* (1694) – and, in a comic context, in 'The Cock and the Fox'. The treatment in *Aureng-Zebe*, in particular, anticipates 'Cinyras and Myrrha' in a number of respects (see ll. 61, 71–3, 88, 97 and *nn*), and may itself have been influenced by Ovid's episode, which D. would have known since boyhood. The shapings and emphases of D.'s rendering bring out the problematic nature of Myrrha's passion. D.'s heightened stress on the complicity of both Cinyras and the nurse in the incestuous act (see ll. 247–57 and *nn*) reinforces Myrrha's assertions (which themselves parallel arguments offered in antiquity by the Sophists and Cynics, and, nearer D.'s time, by Montaigne and other French sceptical writers) that, in treating certain bonds and prohibitions as absolutes and calling them Natural Law, human societies are improperly imputing a universal validity to what are merely their own current practices. However, D.'s treatment also stresses Myrrha's guilty revulsion against a passion that she feels to be a 'crime' and a 'sin', and her consciousness of the 'impious' confusion of human relationships and categories that is the result of an incestuous union (see ll. 37–8, 83–97 and *nn*). See further, David Hopkins, *MLR* lxxx (1985) 786–801. For the larger context, see Richard McCabe, *Incest, Drama, and Nature's Law, 1550–1700* (1993); R. S. White, *Natural Law in English Renaissance Literature* (1996). At several points in his version D. heightens the dramatic vividness of the story (see, e.g., ll. 152–6 and *nn*). He also frequently imitates the 'turns' (artful play on repeated words and phrases) that he thought to be a particular characteristic of Ovid's style (see 'Discourse Concerning Satire' (*Poems* iii 441–5); 'Preface to *Fables*' (*Poems* v 48)), on several occasions adding examples of his own that have no precedent in the Latin (see, for example, ll. 48, 71, 78, 101, 127, 141, 277 and *nn*). The connection of 'Cinyras and Myrrha' with 'Pygmalion and the Statue' (the poem that precedes it in *Fables*) may have been influenced by Montaigne's mention of the episode in 'Of the Affection of Fathers to their Children': 'I make no great Question whether *Phidias*, or any other excellent Statuary, would be so solicitous of the Preservation and Continuance of his Natural Children, as he would be of a rare Statue, which with long labour and study, he had perfected according to Art. And to those furious and irregular Passions that have sometimes flam'd in Fathers towards their own Daughters, and in Mothers towards their own Sons, the like is also found in this other sort of Parentry: Witness what is related of *Pygmalion*, who having made the Statue of a Woman of singular Beauty, fell so passionately in love with this Work of his, that the Gods, in favour of his Passion, must inspire it with Life' (*Essays*, tr. Charles Cotton, 3 vols (1685–6) ii 122–3).

Sources. D. translates *Met.* x 298–524. For the editions and earlier English trans-lations of the complete *Metamorphoses* recurrently used by D., see headnote to 'Baucis and Philemon'. For this version he also made use of two earlier separate renderings of the episode, James Gresham's *The Picture of Incest* (1626) and Charles Hopkins's 'The Story of Cinyras and Myrrha' in *Epistolary Poems, on Several Occasions* (1694) (see David Hopkins, *N & Q* ccix (1974) 419–20). He may have also used Henry Austin's *The Scourge of Venus* (second edition 1614), although the parallels between this work and his version are not conclusive.

Reception. An anonymous version of the same Ovidian episode, indebted in small details to D.'s version, was included in Tonson's *Poetical Miscellanies: The Fifth Part* (1704). Even clearer traces of D.'s translation are to be found in 'The Passion of Myrrha' in Samuel Cobb's *Poems on Several Occasions* (1710).

Cinyras and Myrrha, Out of the Tenth Book of Ovid's *Metamorphoses*

There needs no connection of this story with the former, for the beginning of this immediately follows the end of the last; the reader is only to take notice that Orpheus, who relates both, was by birth a Thracian, and his country far distant from Cyprus where Myrrha was born, and from Arabia whither she fled. You will see the reason of this note, soon after the first lines of this fable.

> Nor him alone produced the fruitful queen,
> But Cinyras, who like his sire had been
> A happy prince, had he not been a sire.
> Daughters and fathers, from my song retire:

¶25. *D.'s headnote. the former*] This poem was preceded in *Fables* by 'Pygmalion and the Statue'.
1. *him*] Paphos, son (in seventeenth-century editions of Ovid) of Pygmalion, King of Cyprus, and his statue-turned-maiden, and brother to Cinyras (see 'Pygmalion and the Statue' ll. 99–101). *the fruitful queen*] i.e. the statue; D.'s expansion of Ovid's *hac* ('this woman').
2. *sire*] father (*OED* 6).

5   I sing of horror; and could I prevail,
     You should not hear, or not believe my tale.
     Yet if the pleasure of my song be such
     That you will hear, and credit me too much,
     Attentive listen to the last event,
10 And with the sin believe the punishment:
     Since Nature could behold so dire a crime,
     I gratulate at least my native clime
     That such a land, which such a monster bore,
     So far is distant from our Thracian shore.
15 Let Araby extol her happy coast,
     Her cinnamon and sweet amomum boast,
     Her fragrant flowers, her trees with precious tears,
     Her second harvests and her double years;
     How can the land be called so blessed that Myrrha
       bears?
20 Nor all her odorous tears can cleanse her crime;
     Her plant alone deforms the happy clime.

---

5. I sing of horror] Cp. Sandys: 'I sing of Horror! Daughters, farre, ô farre / From hence remove! and You, who fathers are!' *could I prevail*] D.'s addition.

8. credit] believe; a Latinism, thus in Sandys. Cp. Ovid ll. 302–3: *nec credite factum: / vel, si credetis, facti quoque credite poenam* ('do not give credence to this story, and believe that it never happened; or, if you do believe it, believe also in the punishment of the deed').

9. the last event] the metamorphosis with which the tale concludes. *event*] outcome (*OED* 3; a Latin sense).

10. Cp. Gresham: 'Yet with the fact beleeve the punishment'.

12. gratulate] compliment, congratulate (*OED* 3), rendering Ovid's *gratulor* (l. 306). *clime*] region of the earth (*OED* 2).

13. such a monster] Cp. Crispinus: *tantum monstrum*; Sandys: 'such a cursed Monster'.

14. our Thracian shore] For Ovid's *gentibus Ismariis* ('Ismarian people'). Sandys explains that Ismarus was 'a Mountaine of *Thrace*', the home of Orpheus, in Ovid the narrator of the story (see D.'s headnote).

16. sweet amomum] an odoriferous plant, yielding spice, the precise identification of which in antiquity was uncertain (*OED*).

18. D.'s addition. Cp. Diodorus Siculus, *Historical Library* II liv 5, tr. G. Booth (1700): 'That Part [of Arabia] bordering upon the Ocean lyes about *Arabia* the *Happy*, and there (by many Rivers falling down together) are made many large Ponds and Lakes up and down the Country: And because large Tracts of Ground are water'd by the Rivers and the Rains that fall in the Summer time, they have a double Harvest' (81). *double years*] double yields of the normally expected year's produce (*OED* year 4).

21. D.'s addition. *Her plant*] myrrh, the resin-producing tree into which Myrrha is transformed (ll. 336–53).

Cupid denies to have inflamed thy heart,
Disowns thy love, and vindicates his dart:
Some Fury gave thee those infernal pains,
25 And shot her venomed vipers in thy veins.
To hate thy sire had merited a curse,
But such an impious love deserved a worse.
The neighbouring monarchs, by thy beauty led,
Contend in crowds, ambitious of thy bed:
30 The world is at thy choice, except but one,
Except but him thou canst not choose alone.
She knew it too, the miserable maid,
Ere impious love her better thoughts betrayed,
And thus within her secret soul she said:
35 'Ah Myrrha! whither would thy wishes tend?
Ye gods, ye sacred laws, my soul defend
From such a crime as all mankind detest,
And never lodged before in human breast!
But is it sin? Or makes my mind alone
40 Th' imagined sin? For Nature makes it none.
What tyrant then these envious laws began,

22–3. Cp. Sandys: '*Cupid* denies t'have us'd his darts therein: / And vindicates his flames from such a Sinne'. In l. 389, however, it is implied that Venus (mother of Cupid) was indeed responsible for Myrrha's passion.
23. *vindicates*] clears from censure (*OED* 3), a Latinism; thus in Gresham, Sandys.
24. *Some Fury*] Cp. Cnipping: *Una ex furiis*.
25. *vipers*] Cp. Crispinus: *viperis*. The Furies, avengers of crimes committed against kindred, were often described and depicted as having flaming torches in their hands and serpents twined in their hair. Cp. *Alexander's Feast* ll. 132–7.
27. *impious*] contrary to piety (see l. 45*n*), and thus meriting the most severe punishment.
29. *ambitious of*] eager to attain (*OED* 2).
30. *The world*] For Ovid's *Oriente* ('the East').
31. D.'s reinforcing addition.
32. *miserable*] D.'s addition, perhaps prompted by Ovid's *miseram* (l. 334) (*Works*).
34. *secret*] not expressed, concealed; known only to her, inmost (*OED* 1f). Myrrha's speech is not uttered aloud.
35. *Ah Myrrha*] D.'s addition.
36. *defend*] (i) protect (*OED* 4); (ii) prohibit (*OED* 3e).
37–8. *as all mankind detest . . . human breast*] D.'s addition; Myrrha contradicts this assertion in ll. 57–62.
39–40. *Or makes my mind alone / Th' imagined sin*] D.'s addition.   *Nature*] For Ovid's *pietas* (l. 324); thus in Golding. On the problematic centrality of 'Nature' in the poem, see headnote.
41–2. D.'s addition.
41. *envious*] malicious, spiteful (*OED* 2); for Ovid's *malignas* and (l. 331) *invida* ('jealous').

Made not for any other beast but man?
The father-bull his daughter may bestride,
The horse may make his mother-mare a bride;
45　What piety forbids the lusty ram
Or more salacious goat to rut their dam?
The hen is free to wed the chick she bore,
And make a husband whom she hatched before.
All creatures else are of a happier kind, ⎫
50　Whom nor ill-natured laws from pleasure bind, ⎬
Nor thoughts of sin disturb their peace of mind. ⎭
But man a slave of his own making lives;
The fool denies himself what Nature gives:
Too busy senates, with an over-care

43–8. D. introduces a farmyard vocabulary (*bestride, rut, hatched*), perhaps prompted by the earthy language ('cover', 'leapes', 'tups', 'beestrydes', 'bucke', 'tread', etc.) of Golding and Gresham.

45. piety] faithfulness to the duties and affections owed mutually by parents and children (a sense of the Latin *pietas*: *OED* 3). The words *pious* and *impious* recur throughout the poem. *ram*] D.'s addition.

46. salacious] lustful, lecherous (*OED* 1; first citation, 1661).

47. hen / chick] For Ovid's *ales* ('bird'), perhaps (as *Works* suggests) with a glance at Chanticleer's incest in 'The Cock and the Fox' ll. 55–66.

48. husband] D.'s addition, the alliteration with 'hatched' producing something of the effect of an Ovidian 'turn'. *hatched before*] Thus in Golding; 'hatch'd' in Gresham.

49. happier] more fortunate (*OED* 2). *kind*] race, species.

50. nor] neither. *ill-natured*] evil, malignant (*OED* 1), for Ovid's *invida* ('envious') translated earlier (l. 41). *bind*] constrain with legal authority (*OED* 16); thus in Sandys.

51. D.'s addition, referring to a phenomenon recurrently treated in his work. Cp., for example, 'Prologue at Oxford' (1674) ll. 1–4, 'Lucretius: Concerning the Nature of Love' ll. 110–15 (specifically concerning the mental unease caused by sexual desire), 'Horace: *Epode* II' ll. 3–4, 'To Mr Henry Higden' ll. 22–8, 'The Tenth Satire of Juvenal' l. 549, 'The Fifth Satire of Persius' l. 221, 'The Second Book of the *Georgics*' ll. 698–701, 'The Fourth Book of the *Aeneis*' ll. 769–71. See, further, 'Horace: *Odes* III xxix' l. 10n.

52–7. D. expands Ovid's ll. 329–31, heightening Myrrha's condemnation of Man's folly and malice in rejecting Nature's gifts. Cp. Hopkins: 'But, foolish Man, against himself conspires, / Inventing Laws, to curb his free desires. / Industrious, to destroy his own content, / He makes those bars, which Nature never meant'.

54. senates] legislative bodies (*OED* 1). *over-care*] Cp. *Secret Love* I iii 82–3: 'If they have err'd, 'twas but an over-care; / An ill-tim'd Duty'; 'Prologue to *Tyrannic Love*' ll. 12–13: 'Poets, like lovers, should be bold and dare; / They spoil their business with an over-care'. As *Works* points out, D. responds to both main senses of Ovid's *cura*: (i) concern, anxiety (*OLD* 5–6); (ii) administration (*OLD* 7).

55　To make us better than our kind can bear,
Have dashed a spice of envy in the laws,
And straining up too high, have spoiled the cause.
Yet some wise nations break their cruel chains,
And own no laws but those which love ordains:
60　Where happy daughters with their sires are joined,
And piety is doubly paid in kind.
O that I had been born in such a clime,
Not here, where 'tis the country makes the crime!
But whither would my impious fancy stray?
65　Hence hopes, and ye forbidden thoughts away!
His worth deserves to kindle my desires,
But with the love that daughters bear to sires.
Then had not Cinyras my father been,
What hindered Myrrha's hopes to be his queen?
70　But the perverseness of my fate is such,
That he's not mine, because he's mine too much:
Our kindred blood debars a better tie;
He might be nearer, were he not so nigh.
Eyes and their objects never must unite,
75　Some distance is required to help the sight.

55. *kind*] nature (*OED* 3).
56. *envy*] malice (*OED* 1a).
57. *straining up*] forcing up to an excessively demanding level (*OED* 11j).
58–9. *break their cruel chains . . . love ordains*] D.'s addition. Cp. Arcite in 'Palamon and Arcite' i 326–36.
60–1. Cp. Hopkins: 'Where Men, and Women, all in common joyn'd, / With doubled Love, exalt their gen'rous Kind'.
61. *piety*] Cp. the Empress Nourmahal in *Aureng-Zebe* IV i 131–5: 'Custom our Native Royalty does awe; / Promiscuous Love is Nature's General Law: / For whosoever the first Lovers were, / Brother and Sister made the second Pair, / And doubled, by their love, their piety'.　*in kind*] (i) in the very commodity in question (i.e. parents/children) (*OED* 15); (ii) naturally (*OED* 4b); (iii) by one's kindred (*OED* 11).
62. *in such a clime*] Thus in Hopkins.
64. *impious*] D.'s addition.
69. *queen*] Ovid's Myrrha simply wishes *Cinyrae concumbere* ('to sleep with Cinyras').
71–3. Line 71 is a 'turn'. Cp. Sandys: 'Now, in that mine, not mine: proximitie / Dis-joynes us; neerer, were we not so nigh'; Hopkins: 'Engag'd already, in too strict a tye, / I might be nearer, were I not so nigh'. Cp. Nourmahal in *Aureng-Zebe* III i 360–1: 'Why was that fatal knot of Marriage ti'd, / Which did, by making us too near, divide?'
74–5. D.'s addition.

Fain would I travel to some foreign shore, ⎫
Never to see my native country more,   ⎬
So might I to myself myself restore;   ⎭
So might my mind these impious thoughts remove,
80 And, ceasing to behold, might cease to love.
But stay I must, to feed my famished sight,
To talk, to kiss—and more, if more I might:
More, impious maid! What more canst thou design? ⎫
To make a monstrous mixture in thy line,   ⎬
85 And break all statutes human and divine?   ⎭
Canst thou be called (to save thy wretched life)
Thy mother's rival, and thy father's wife?
Confound so many sacred names in one,

76. to some foreign shore] D.'s addition.

78. D.'s addition, another 'turn'. The present text combines *1700*'s 'my self' as one word, although the seventeenth-century spelling perhaps suggests a subtly different relation between speaker and 'self' than that conveyed by the modern reflexive pronoun. For earlier uses of the doubled pronoun to represent the mind torn by passion, cp. Shakespeare, *Lucrece* ll. 157, 160, 998 (Eric Langley, privately).

79–80. For Ovid's *dum scelus effugiam* ('if only I could flee the crime').

81. For Ovid's *retinet malus ardor amantem, / ut praesens spectem Cinyram tangamque* ('but a wicked passion keeps the lover here, that I might see Cinyras in person, and touch him').

81–2. Cp. Sandys: 'To feast my hungrie eyes with his deare sight, / Talke, touch, and kisse; or more, if more I might'; Hopkins: 'Talk, touch, and kiss, do more, if more I might'.

84. D.'s addition. *monstrous*] (i) manifesting itself as a congenital abnormality or unnatural monster (*OED* 1–2); (ii) atrocious, horrible (*OED* 6). *mixture*] Contemporary senses of the word included 'sexual intercourse' (*OED* 1e).

85. all statutes human and divine] D.'s expansion of Ovid's *et iura et nomina* ('both obligations and names').

86. (to save thy wretched life)] D.'s addition.

87, 89. Cp. Hopkins: 'Your Father's Whore, a Mother to the Son, / Born of your Mother; Sister to your own'.

87. rival] Translating Ovid's *paelex* ('mistress installed as a rival or in addition to a wife'). *wife*] For Ovid's *adultera* ('mistress').

88. names] The confusion of names (and the relational categories they imply) was regarded by some ancient writers as the prime factor that made the perpetrators of incestuous acts effectively inhuman. See, e.g., Cicero, *Pro Cluentio* 199 (on the marriage of his client's mother to her son-in-law): *Atque etiam nomina necessitudinum, non solum naturae nomen et iura mutavit: uxor generi, noverca filii, filiae pellex: eo iam denique adducta est, uti sibi praeter formam nihil ad similitudinem hominis reservavit* ('Nay, more; as the wife of her son-in-law, the step-mother of her son, the rival of her daughter, she has changed not merely the names and ordinances which nature gives, but even the name we give to relationships; and she is come at last to such a pass that she has lost all semblance of humanity save only her outward form'). The same topic is treated in *Oedipus* (V i 155, 162) and *Aureng-Zebe* (III i 364–9).

Thy brother's mother, sister to thy son?
90   And fear'st thou not to see th' infernal bands,
     Their heads with snakes, with torches armed their hands;
     Full at thy face th' avenging brands to bear,
     And shake the serpents from their hissing hair?
     But thou in time th' increasing ill control,
95   Nor first debauch the body by the soul;
     Secure the sacred quiet of thy mind,
     And keep the sanctions Nature has designed.
     Suppose I should attempt, th' attempt were vain,
     No thoughts like mine his sinless soul profane,
100 Observant of the right; and O, that he
     Could cure my madness, or be mad like me!'
         Thus she; but Cinyras, who daily sees
     A crowd of noble suitors at his knees,
     Among so many knew not whom to choose,
105 Irresolute to grant or to refuse.
     But, having told their names, enquired of her
     Who pleased her best, and whom she would prefer?
     The blushing maid stood silent with surprise,
     And on her father fixed her ardent eyes,
110 And looking sighed; and as she sighed, began
     Round tears to shed, that scalded as they ran.

90. *th' infernal bands*] the Furies. See l. 24*n*.
93. *their hissing hair*] Thus in Sandys; *hissing* is D.'s addition.
94–5. For Ovid's *dum corpore non es / passa nefas, animo ne concipe* ('while you have
not yet allowed wickedness in your body, do not conceive it in your mind').
95. *debauch*] seduce, corrupt, deprave (*OED* 2).
96. D.'s addition. Cp. l. 51*n*.
97. *the sanctions Nature has designed*] those natural considerations that lead human
beings to obey particular moral laws or to recognize particular distinctions and
categories (*OED* sanction 3). Cp. 'The Fifth Satire of Persius' ll. 141–2; 'Palamon
and Arcite' i 229. Cp., also, Zayda's protest against Nourmahal's declaration of
incestuous love (*Aureng-Zebe* III i 350–3): 'If contradicting int'rests could be mixt,
/ Nature her self has cast a bar betwixt. / And, ere you reach to this incestuous
Love, / You must Divine and Humane rights remove'.
99. *profane*] defile, pollute (*OED* 1b).
101. *cure my madness*] D.'s addition; the play on 'madness'/'mad' is another 'turn'.
102. *Thus she; but Cinyras*] Thus in Sandys.
103–4. *at his knees / Among so many*] D.'s addition.
105. D.'s expansion.
108. *blushing*] D.'s addition.   *with surprise*] D.'s addition, from Crispinus' *Interpretatio*:
stupens ('surprised').
110. *And looking sighed; and as she sighed*] D.'s addition, with an added Ovidian 'turn'.
111. *scalded*] Replacing Ovid's *tepido* ('lukewarm') (l. 360). Cp. Golding: 'scalding
teares'.

The tender sire, who saw her blush and cry,
Ascribed it all to maiden modesty,
And dried the falling drops, and yet more kind
115 He stroked her cheeks, and holy kisses joined.
She felt a secret venom fire her blood,
And found more pleasure than a daughter should;
And, asked again, what lover of the crew
She liked the best, she answered, 'One like you.'
120 Mistaking what she meant, her pious will
He praised, and bad her so continue still;
The word of 'pious' heard, she blushed with shame
Of secret guilt, and could not bear the name.
'Twas now the mid of night, when slumbers close
125 Our eyes, and soothe our cares with soft repose;
But no repose could wretched Myrrha find,
Her body rolling as she rolled her mind;
Mad with desire, she ruminates her sin,
And wishes all her wishes o'er again;
130 Now she despairs, and now resolves to try;
Would not, and would again, she knows not why;
Stops, and returns, makes and retracts the vow;
Fain would begin, but understands not how.

112. The tender sire] For Ovid's *Cinyras*.
114. yet more kind] D.'s addition. Cp. l. 61n.
115. holy] D.'s addition.
116. D.'s addition; love is described as a 'venom' in 'Lucretius : Concerning the Nature of Love' l. 24.
118. crew] company, group of people (*OED* 3a).
119. One like you] Cp. Sandys: 'Once more asked, who / She best could like: repli'd, One, like to you'.
122. Ovid's Myrrha lowers her eyes to the ground, rather than blushing.
123. could not bear the name] D.'s addition (cp. l. 88n).
124. 'Twas now the mid of night] Identical in Sandys.
124–5. close / Our eyes and *with soft repose* are D.'s additions. Cp. 'The Fourth Book of the *Aeneis*' ll. 757–8: ''Twas dead of night, when weary bodies close / Their eyes in balmy sleep, and soft repose'.
126–33. D. imitates and extends the mimetic rhetorical patterning of Ovid's ll. 370–2: *furiosaque vota retractat. / et modo desperat, modo vult temptare, pudetque, / et cupit, et, quid agat, non invenit* ('She renews her mad prayers, is filled now with despair, now with lust to try, feels now shame and now desire, and finds no plan of action').
127. D.'s addition, another 'turn'. *rolling / rolled*] Cp. Crispinus, Schrevelius: *revolvit*; Hopkins: 'So roll the thoughts in her uncertain mind'.
128. ruminates] meditates upon (*OED* 1a).
130. try] make the attempt (*OED* 15).
131. Would not, and would again] in turn does not wish, then wishes [*sc.* to do it].

As when a pine is hewed upon the plains,
135   And the last mortal stroke alone remains,
Labouring in pangs of death, and threatening all,
This way and that she nods, considering where to fall;
So Myrrha's mind, impelled on either side,
Takes every bent, but cannot long abide:
140   Irresolute on which she should rely,
At last, unfixed in all, is only fixed to die.
On that sad thought she rests; resolved on death,
She rises, and prepares to choke her breath;
Then while about the beam her zone she ties,
145   'Dear Cinyras, farewell,' she softly cries,
'For thee I die, and only wish to be
Not hated, when thou know'st I die for thee:
Pardon the crime, in pity to the cause.'
This said, about her neck the noose she draws.
150   The nurse, who lay without, her faithful guard,
Though not the words, the murmurs overheard,
And sighs, and hollow sounds: surprised with fright,
She starts, and leaves her bed, and springs a light,
Unlocks the door, and entering out of breath
155   The dying saw, and instruments of death.
She shrieks, she cuts the zone with trembling haste,

134. pine] For Ovid's *trabs* ('tree'); from Crispinus' *Interpretatio: pinus.*   *upon the plains*]
D.'s addition.
135. mortal] D.'s addition.
136–7. Labouring, pangs, threatening and *considering* are D.'s animistic expansions.
139. Takes every bent] twists and bends in every direction (*OED* bent 6).
141. unfixed in all] D.'s addition, forming another 'turn' with *fixed*.
142. On that sad thought she rests] D.'s expansion.
143. prepares to choke her breath] Cp. Sandys: 'Resolv'd to choake her hated breath'.
144. zone] girdle (*OED* 3), directly from Ovid's *zona*.
145. Identical in Sandys.
146–7. and only wish to be / Not hated] D.'s addition.
148. D.'s addition.
149. Cp. Golding: 'about her necke shee draws'; Sandys: 'That said, the noose
about her neck she drawes'.
152–6. D. adds a number of touches (the nurse's *fright*, her leaving *her bed*, her
springing a light, her breathlessness, her *trembling haste*) to enhance the dramatic
vividness of the scene.
152. hollow] muffled, sepulchral (*OED* 4).
153. springs a light] produces a light quickly and unexpectedly (Johnson, spring 2,
citing this example).
155. The dying] D.'s addition.

And in her arms her fainting charge embraced;
Next (for she now had leisure for her tears)
She weeping asked, in these her blooming years,
160 What unforseen misfortune caused her care
To loathe her life, and languish in despair?
The maid, with downcast eyes, and mute with grief
For death unfinished, and ill-timed relief,
Stood sullen to her suit; the beldam pressed
165 The more to know, and bared her withered breast;
Adjured her by the kindly food she drew
From those dry founts, her secret ill to show.
Sad Myrrha sighed, and turned her eyes aside;
The nurse still urged, and would not be denied;
170 Nor only promised secrecy, but prayed
She might have leave to give her offered aid.
'Good will,' she said, 'my want of strength supplies,
And diligence shall give what age denies:
If strong desires thy mind to fury move,
175 With charms and medicines I can cure thy love;
If envious eyes their hurtful rays have cast,
More powerful verse shall free thee from the blast;
If heaven offended sends thee this disease,
Offended heaven with prayers we can appease.
180 What then remains, that can these cares procure?
Thy house is flourishing, thy fortune sure:
Thy careful mother yet in health survives,

---

157. Cp. Hopkins: 'Closely her Aged Arms her Charge embrace'. *fainting*] D.'s addition.

160–1, 164–5, 168–9. Same rhymes in Sandys.

160. care] Perhaps 'the object of her care' (*OED* 5), i.e. Myrrha (for a similar sense, see 'The First Book of Homer's *Ilias*' l. 501). Alternatively, D.'s nurse may be asking what misfortune caused Myrrha such care that she loathed her life (cp. the use of *cares* in l. 180).

161. Ovid's nurse (l. 388) simply asks *laquei . . . causam* ('the reason for the noose').

164. sullen] stubbornly unresponsive (*OED* 1b). *beldam*] aged woman (*OED* 2).

166. Adjured] entreated earnestly (*OED* 2). *the kindly food she drew*] Cp. Hopkins: 'whence your first Food you drew'. *kindly*] nutritious (*OED* 5b).

169. urged] pleaded insistently (*OED* 3). *would not be denied*] Cp. Sandys: 'would not be so denied'.

176. envious] malicious. *rays*] See 'Sigismonda and Guiscardo' l. 64*n*.

177. verse] i.e. of the charms (l. 175). *blast*] curse (*OED* 6c).

180. that can these cares procure] D.'s addition.

181. is flourishing] Cp. Crispinus: *florens*.

182. careful] attentive (*OED* 3); D's addition. *in health*] Thus in Golding.

And, to thy comfort, thy kind father lives.'
   The virgin started at her father's name,
185 And sighed profoundly, conscious of the shame;
Nor yet the nurse her impious love divined,
But yet surmised that love disturbed her mind.
Thus thinking, she pursued her point, and laid
And lulled within her lap the mourning maid;
190 Then softly soothed her thus: 'I guess your grief:
You love, my child; your love shall find relief;
My long-experienced age shall be your guide;
Rely on that, and lay distrust aside:
No breath of air shall on the secret blow,
195 Nor shall (what most you fear) your father know.'
Struck once again, as with a thunderclap,
The guilty virgin bounded from her lap,
And threw her body prostrate on the bed,
And, to conceal her blushes, hid her head:
200 There silent lay, and warned her with her hand
To go; but she received not the command,
Remaining still importunate to know.
Then Myrrha thus: 'Or ask no more, or go;
I prithee go, or staying spare my shame;
205 What thou wouldst hear, is impious ev'n to name.'
At this, on high the beldam holds her hands,
And trembling both with age and terror stands;
Adjures, and falling at her feet intreats,

183. to thy comfort] D.'s addition.   *kind*] D's addition. Cp. l. 61*n*.
185. conscious of the shame] D.'s addition.   *conscious*] guiltily aware (*OED* 4b).
191. my child] D.'s addition.
193. Rely on that] D.'s addition.
194. D.'s addition.
195. (what most you fear)] D.'s addition.
196. as with a thunderclap] D.'s addition.
198. her body prostrate] Cp. Sandys: 'her prostrate body'.
199. to conceal her blushes] D.'s addition.
200. with her hand] In Ovid (l. 411), Myrrha addresses the nurse directly, without the manual gesture. D. postpones Myrrha's request until slightly later than its position in Ovid.
201. received] gave heed to (*OED* 1d).
202. importunate] persistent, pertinacious (*OED* 4).
203. Or . . . or] Either . . . or.
206. beldam] See l. 164*n*; thus in Gresham.   *on high, holds*] For Ovid's *tendit* ('stretches out'). Cp. Crispinus, *Interpretatio*: *tollit* ('lifts').
208. Adjures] See l. 166*n*.

Soothes her with blandishments, and frights with threats
210 To tell the crime intended, or disclose
What part of it she knew, if she no farther knows;
And last, if conscious to her counsel made,
Confirms anew the promise of her aid.
    Now Myrrha raised her head; but soon oppressed ⎫
215 With shame, reclined it on her nurse's breast; ⎬
Bathed it with tears, and strove to have confessed: ⎭
Twice she began, and stopped; again she tried;
The faltering tongue its office still denied.
At last her veil before her face she spread, ⎫
220 And drew a long preluding sigh, and said, ⎬
'O happy mother, in thy marriage bed!' ⎭
Then groaned, and ceased; the good old woman shook,
Stiff were her eyes, and ghastly was her look:
Her hoary hair upright with horror stood,
225 Made (to her grief) more knowing than she would.
Much she reproached, and many things she said
To cure the madness of th' unhappy maid;
In vain: for Myrrha stood convict of ill,
Her reason vanquished, but unchanged her will;
230 Perverse of mind, unable to reply,
She stood resolved or to possess, or die.

209. blandishments] flattering words (*OED* 1).
211. D. adds an Ovidian 'turn' on *knew / knows*.
212. conscious to] sharing in the knowledge of (*OED* 5); from Ovid's *conscia* (l. 416).
215–16. on her nurse's breast / . . . *confessed*] Cp. Sandys: 'her Nurses brest / With weeping bathes: oft strove to have confest'.
217–18. Expanding Ovid's *saepe tenet vocem* ('she often held her words back').
220. preluding] preparatory (*OED* 1); D.'s addition.
221. happy] See l. 49*n*; Cp. Sandys: 'And said, ô Mother, happy in thy bed'.
223. D.'s addition. *Stiff*] rigid, fixed (*OED* 1), possibly suggested by Ovid's *rigidis* ('stiff') applied to the nurse's hair. *ghastly*] pale (*OED* 2). Cp. Sandys: 'with a gastly looke'.
224. hoary hair] Thus in Golding, Austin, Sandys; cp. Hopkins: 'Her hoary Hairs upright with horrour rise'.
225. D.'s addition. Cp. 'Ceyx and Alcyone' l. 463.
226. Much she reproached, and] D.'s addition.
227. unhappy] ill-fated (*OED* 2). D.'s addition. As *Works* points out, the word conveys the ominous sense of Ovid's *diros . . . amores* ('ill-fated love').
228. convict] proved guilty (*OED* 2, citing this example).
229–30. D.'s addition, drawing out the psychological significance of Myrrha's response.
231. Cp. Sandys: 'But stands resolv'd, or to possesse, or die'.

At length the fondness of a nurse prevailed
Against her better sense, and virtue failed:
'Enjoy, my child, since such is thy desire,
235   Thy love,' she said (she durst not say, 'thy sire').
'Live, though unhappy, live on any terms;'
Then with a second oath her faith confirms.
  The solemn feast of Ceres now was near,
When long white linen stoles the matrons wear;
240   Ranked in procession walk the pious train,
Offering first-fruits, and spikes of yellow grain:
For nine long nights the nuptial bed they shun,
And sanctifying harvest, lie alone.
  Mixed with the crowd, the queen forsook her lord,
245   And Ceres' power with secret rites adored.
The royal couch now vacant for a time,
The crafty crone, officious in her crime,
The cursed occasion took: the king she found
Easy with wine, and deep in pleasures drowned,
250   Prepared for love; the beldam blew the flame,
Confessed the passion, but concealed the name.
Her form she praised; the monarch asked her years,
And she replied, 'The same thy Myrrha bears.'

232–3. D's addition.
234. since such is thy desire] D.'s addition.
236. D.'s addition.
237. second] D.'s addition. *confirms*] ratifies, makes valid (as in the case of a charter or vow) (*OED* 2).
238. solemn] holy (*OED* 1). Cp. Crispinus: *solennia . . . sacra.* *Ceres*] goddess of the generative power of nature, especially the harvest.
239. stoles] For Ovid's *veste* ('clothing') (l. 432); *stoles* are ecclesiastical vestments, consisting of linen strips and reaching to the knees (*OED* 2). Cp. Sandys: 'long linnen stoles'.
241. and] As *Works* points out, not additive: the ears of corn in this instance *are* the first fruits. *spikes*] ears of corn (*OED sb.* 1); from Ovid's *spicea.*
243. D.'s elaboration.
244. forsook her lord] D.'s elaboration.
247. officious] unduly zealous (*OED* 3). Cp. Crispinus: *perversè officiosa.*
248. occasion] opportunity (*OED* 1).
249. Easy] (i) comfortable, luxurious (*OED* 2); (ii) compliant, easily aroused (*OED* 12); for Ovid's *gravem* ('heavy').
249–50. and deep . . . blew the flame] D.'s addition.
251. concealed the name] Ovid's nurse gives a false name.
252. Her form she praised] Cp. Crispinus: *praedicat formam.*

Wine and commended beauty fired his thought;
255 Impatient, he commands her to be brought.
Pleased with her charge performed, she hies her home,
And gratulates the nymph, the task was overcome.
Myrrha was joyed the welcome news to hear;
But clogged with guilt, the joy was unsincere:
260 So various, so discordant is the mind,
That in our will a different will we find.
Ill she presaged, and yet pursued her lust,
For guilty pleasures give a double gust.
    'Twas depth of night; Arctophylax had driven
265 His lazy wain half round the northern heaven,
When Myrrha hastened to the crime desired;
The moon beheld her first, and first retired;
The stars amazed ran backward from the sight,
And (shrunk within their sockets) lost their light.

254–5. Wine and commended beauty . . . Impatient] D.'s addition. For the emphasis on Cinyras' lecherous susceptibility, cp. ll. 249–50 and *nn.* Cp. Hopkins: 'And, all inflam'd, commands her to be brought'.

256. Pleased with her charge performed] D.'s addition.

257. gratulates] See l. 12*n.*

259. unsincere] not pure, not unmixed (*OED* 2). Cp. 'Lucretius: Concerning the Nature of Love' l. 42.

260–3. D. expands in the manner of ll. 229–30. With line 260, cp. Gresham: 'the various discords of her minde'; Sandys: 'such discord rackt her minde'.

261. D.'s addition.

262. and yet pursued her lust] For Ovid's *sed tamen et gaudet* ('but she rejoiced too').

263. D.'s addition. *Works* compares the proverb: 'stolen fruit is sweet' (Tilley F 779). Cp. *The Assignation* III iii 72–3: 'Thus dangers in our Love make joyes more dear; / And Pleasure's sweetest when 'tis mixt with fear'. *gust*] relish, enjoyment (*OED* 4).

264. Arctophylax] The northern constellation Boötes. Boötes was often thought of as the driver of the Great Bear (the latter constellation seeming like a large waggon, drawn by two oxen). Cp. Cnipping, Schrevelius: *Bootes, qui & Arctophylax appellatur* ('Boötes, who is also called Arctophylax') (Bottkol).

265. lazy] D.'s addition. *wain*] waggon; the Great Bear was known as 'Charles's Wain' (for the possible origins of the term see *OED*). *half round the northern heaven*] Ovid says that Boötes has driven his waggon *obliquo . . . temone* ('with its slanting yoke') *inter . . . triones* ('between the oxen'), referring to the positions of different constellations at midnight, as they appear in the northern hemisphere.

268–9. For Ovid's *tegunt nigrae latitantia sidera nubes* ('black clouds hid the skulking stars').

269. sockets] holders (the stars being imagined as candles, held in candlesticks) (*OED* 3). For the fancy (D.'s addition, prompted by Ovid's animistic *latitantia* ('skulking'), cp. *AM* ll. 1162–4.

270   Icarius first withdraws his holy flame;
       The virgin sign, in heaven the second name,
       Slides down the belt, and from her station flies,
       And night with sable clouds involves the skies.
       Bold Myrrha still pursues her black intent;   ⎫
275   She stumbled thrice (an omen of th' event);   ⎬
       Thrice shrieked the funeral owl, yet on she went, ⎭
       Secure of shame, because secure of sight;
       Ev'n bashful sins are impudent by night.
       Linked hand in hand, th' accomplice and the dame,
280   Their way exploring, to the chamber came;
       The door was ope, they blindly grope their way,
       Where dark in bed th' expecting monarch lay;
       Thus far her courage held, but here forsakes;
       Her faint knees knock at every step she makes.
285   The nearer to her crime, the more within

270–1. Cp. Sandys: 'This *Icarius* was a Guest to *Bacchus*, who gave him a Borachio of wine, and bad him communicate it to others. Certaine shepheards, in his returne into *Attica*, drinking thereof immoderately, intoxicated fell on the Earth: and imagining that he had poysoned them, slew him with their staves. His dog *Nerea*, by running before and howling, shew'd *Erigone* her father where he lay unburied: who after she had interred him, ascended the mountaine *Hymettus*, and there hung her selfe. It is fained that *Iupiter*, at the intreaty of *Bacchus*, changed them both into Constellations: calling *Erigone*, Virgo; one of the six Northerne signs, who carries in her left hand an eare of corne with a starre of the first magnitude; and her father *Bootes*; between whose legs shines the eminent *Arcturus*, which in revenge of his murder ariseth in tempests'.

270. holy flame] For Ovid's *vultus* ('face').

271. For Ovid's *Erigoneque pio sacrata parentis amore* ('and you, Erigone, deified for your pious love of your father').

272. D.'s addition.   *the belt*] a strip or ring of small stars (*OED* 2c); perhaps, here, the tail of stars adjoining the constellation Virgo.

273. sable] black (*OED* B2b).   *involves*] enwraps (*OED* 1).

274. D.'s addition.

275. th' event] the outcome (*OED* 3).

277. Secure of shame] free from the apprehension of shame (*OED* secure 1b, citing this example). The 'turn' on *secure* is D.'s addition.   *secure of sight*] protected from being seen (*OED* secure 3, sight 10).

278. D.'s addition. As *Works* notes, *impudent* is suggested by Ovid's *pudorem* ('shame'). *bashful*] shamefaced (*OED* 2).

279–80. In Ovid it is only Myrrha who feels the way.

281. The door was ope] Thus in Golding.   *they blindly grope their way*] Cp. Golding: 'the darke blynd way did grope'; Gresham: 'groping out the blind way'; Sandys: 'And groping with the other hand, explores / Her blinde accesse'.

282. D.'s addition. Cp. ll. 254–5n.

283. D.'s expansion.

She feels remorse, and horror of her sin;
Repents too late her criminal desire,
And wishes that unknown she could retire.
Her lingering thus, the nurse (who feared delay
290 The fatal secret might at length betray)
Pulled forward, to complete the work begun,
And said to Cinyras, 'Receive thy own.'
Thus saying, she delivered kind to kind,
Accursed, and their devoted bodies joined.
295 The sire, unknowing of the crime, admits
His bowels, and profanes the hallowed sheets;
He found she trembled, but believed she strove ⎫
With maiden modesty against her love, ⎬
And sought with flattering words vain fancies to remove. ⎭
300 Perhaps he said, 'My daughter, cease thy fears'
(Because the title suited with her years);
And, 'Father,' she might whisper him again,
That names might not be wanting to the sin.
Full of her sire, she left th' incestuous bed,
305 And carried in her womb the crime she bred.
Another, and another night she came,
For frequent sin had left no sense of shame,
Till Cinyras desired to see her face
Whose body he had held in close embrace,

287. too late] D.'s addition.
288. Cp. Sandys: 'and would unknown retire'; Hopkins: 'and wou'd, unknown, retire'.
289–90. who feared . . . at length betray] D.'s addition.
290. fatal] that will lead to disaster (*OED* 6).
291. to complete the work begun] D.'s substitution for Ovid's *alto . . . lecto* ('to the tall bed').
292. Receive thy own] Thus in Sandys.
293. kind to kind] Cp. l. 61*n*.
294. devoted] (i) doomed (*OED* 3); (ii) closely attached to one another (*OED* 2), from Ovid's *devota* (l. 464), which also contains both meanings (see *OLD*).
295. unknowing of the crime] D.'s addition.
296. His bowels] his own child (*OED* 5); thus in Golding, Gresham, Sandys. *the hallowed sheets*] For Ovid's *obsceno . . . lecto* ('into the lewd bed'), later translated by D. (as an addition) as *th' incestuous bed* (l. 304). *profanes*] Cp. l. 99*n*; again at l. 330.
303. names] Cp. l. 88*n*.
304. Full of] pregnant by (*OED* 1e), rendering Ovid's *plena patris* (l. 469). Cp. Hopkins: 'Full of her Father, now she leaves his Bed'.
307. D.'s addition, with *frequent* suggested by Ovid's *post tot concubitus* ('after so many copulations').

310   And brought a taper; the revealer, light,
       Exposed both crime and criminal to sight.
       Grief, rage, amazement could no speech afford,
       But from the sheath he drew th' avenging sword;
       The guilty fled; the benefit of night,
315   That favoured first the sin, secured the flight.
       Long wandering through the spacious fields, she bent
       Her voyage to th' Arabian continent;
       Then passed the region which Panchaea joined,
       And flying left the palmy plains behind.
320   Nine times the moon had mewed her horns; at length
       With travel weary, unsupplied with strength,
       And with the burden of her womb oppressed,
       Sabaean fields afford her needful rest;
       There, loathing life, and yet of death afraid,
325   In anguish of her spirit, thus she prayed:
       'Ye powers, if any so propitious are
       T' accept my penitence, and hear my prayer,
       Your judgements, I confess, are justly sent;
       Great sins deserve as great a punishment;
330   Yet since my life the living will profane,
       And since my death the happy dead will stain,

311. *criminal*] For Ovid's *natam* ('daughter'), forming a 'turn' with *crime*.
312. *rage, amazement*] D.'s additions.
313. *avenging*] For Ovid's *nitidum* ('bright'). Cp. *PL* vi 277–8: 'There mingle broils, / Ere this avenging sword begin thy doom' (J. R. Mason).
315. *That favoured first the sin*] D.'s addition.   *secured the flight*] Cp. Hopkins: 'secur'd her flight'.
316. *through the spacious fields*] Cp. Sandys: 'through spacious fields'.
317. *voyage*] journey (*OED* 1).
318. *Panchaea*] an island east of Arabia, noted for its aromatic spices.
320. *mewed her horns*] As the months pass, the moon sheds the pointed extremities of its crescent (*OED* horn 17), just as a stag 'sheds' (*OED* mew 2, citing this example) its antlers.
322–3. Cp. Hopkins: 'Till, with the Burden in her Womb opprest, / Her staggering Limbs requir'd their needful rest'.
322. *the burden of her womb*] Thus in Golding.   *oppressed*] physically weighed down (*OED* 1).
323. *Sabaean fields*] Like Panchaea, Sabaea was a region of Arabia Felix (Sandys, marginal note).   *needful*] D.'s addition.
325. *In anguish of her spirit*] For Ovid's *nescia voti* ('not knowing what to pray for').
326. *so propitious*] Cp. Crispinus: *propitii*.
327. *accept my penitence, and*] D.'s addition.
328–9. For Ovid's *nec triste recuso / suppliciam* ('I do not refuse harsh punishment'). The 'turn' on *Great / as great* is D.'s addition.
331. *happy*] D.'s addition.

A middle state your mercy may bestow,
Betwixt the realms above, and those below:
Some other form to wretched Myrrha give,
335   Nor let her wholly die, nor wholly live.'
      The prayers of penitents are never vain;
At least, she did her last request obtain;
For while she spoke, the ground began to rise,
And gathered round her feet, her legs, and thighs;
340   Her toes in roots descend, and spreading wide
A firm foundation for the trunk provide;
Her solid bones convert to solid wood,
To pith her marrow, and to sap her blood;
Her arms are boughs, her fingers change their kind,
345   Her tender skin is hardened into rind.
And now the rising tree her womb invests,
Now, shooting upwards still, invades her breasts,
And shades the neck; when, weary with delay,
She sunk her head within, and met it half the way.
350   And though with outward shape she lost her sense,
With bitter tears she wept her last offence;
And still she weeps, nor sheds her tears in vain,
For still the precious drops her name retain.
      Meantime the misbegotten infant grows,
355   And, ripe for birth, distends with deadly throes
The swelling rind, with unavailing strife
To leave the wooden womb, and pushes into life.

334. wretched] D.'s addition. Cp. l. 32*n*.
339. Ovid does not specifically mention *feet* or *thighs*.
342. solid bones convert to solid wood] D.'s addition.
343. Cp. Sandys: 'To pith her marrow, into sap her blood'; Hopkins: 'To pith her marrow'.
344. change their kind] For Ovid's *ramos in parvos* [*it*] ('changes into small branches').
345. tender] D.'s addition.   *rind*] bark (*OED* 1).
346. invests] envelops, clothes (*OED* 1).
347. shooting upwards still] D.'s addition.   *still*] continuously.
350. Cp. Sandys: 'Though sense, with shape, she lost'.
351. bitter tears] Thus in Sandys.   *bitter*] renders Ovid's *tepidae* ('warm').   *her last offence*] D.'s addition.
352. nor sheds her tears in vain] D.'s addition.
353. As myrrh, a resinous gum used in perfumes and incense.
355. ripe] Cp. 'Palamon and Arcite' iii 1069.   *distends*] Cp. Schrevelius: *distentam*. *deadly*] D.'s addition.
357. pushes into life] D. expands, in a manner paralleled in his other depictions of childbirth. Cp. 'Palamon and Arcite' iii 1069–70; 'Of the Pythagorean Philosophy' ll. 330–3.

The mother-tree, as if oppressed with pain,
Writhes here and there to break the bark, in vain;
360 And, like a labouring woman, would have prayed,
But wants a voice to call Lucina's aid;
The bending bole sends out a hollow sound,
And trickling tears fall thicker on the ground.
The mild Lucina came uncalled, and stood
365 Beside the struggling boughs, and heard the groaning wood;
Then reached her midwife-hand to speed the throes,
And spoke the powerful spells that babes to birth disclose.
The bark divides the living load to free,
And safe delivers the convulsive tree.
370 The ready nymphs receive the crying child,
And wash him in the tears the parent plant distilled.
They swathed him with their scarves, beneath him spread
The ground with herbs, with roses raised his head.
The lovely babe was born with every grace,
375 Ev'n Envy must have praised so fair a face:
Such was his form, as painters when they show
Their utmost art on naked Loves bestow:
And that their arms no difference might betray,
Give him a bow, or his from Cupid take away.
380   Time glides along with undiscovered haste,

361. wants] lacks (*OED* 1).   *Lucina*] the goddess of childbirth (either Juno or Diana).
363. on the ground] The tears of Ovid's Myrrha fall on the tree itself.
364. uncalled] D.'s addition.
366. midwife] D.'s addition.   *throes*] Thus in Golding.
370. the ready nymphs] The Naiads, here imagined as Lucina's assistants in child-birth.   *the crying child*] Adonis.
371. distilled] let fall in drops (*OED* 2).
372. They swathed him with their scarves] D.'s addition.   *scarves*] strips of fine silk, worn loosely over the shoulders (*OED* 3).
373. with roses raised his head] D.'s addition.
374. D.'s expansion.
375. Envy] Livor or Invidia, the personification of Envy, is imagined by Ovid (*Met.* ii 760–4) as inhabiting a gloomy, chill cave, shrouded in fogs, and filthy with black blood.
376–7. when they show / Their utmost art] D.'s addition.
377. Loves] Cupid-like love deities, as imagined by mythologists and depicted by painters (*OED* 5b).
378. difference] Cp. Crispinus: *differentiam*. As *Works* points out, D. exploits the heraldic sense of *difference*: 'an alteration of or addition to a coat of arms, to distinguish a junior member or branch of a family from the chief line' (*OED* 4b).
379. bow] For Ovid's *pharetras* ('quiver').
380. Cp. Sandys: 'Time glides away with undiscovered hast'.   *undiscovered*] un-observed, not noticed (*OED* 4).

The future but a length behind the past,
So swift are years: the babe whom just before
His grandsire got, and whom his sister bore,
The drop, the thing which late the tree enclosed,
385 And late the yawning bark to life exposed,
A babe, a boy, a beauteous youth appears,
And lovelier than himself at riper years.
Now to the Queen of Love he gave desires,
And with her pains revenged his mother's fires.

381. D.'s substitution for Ovid's *fallitque* ('and cheats on').
383. whom his sister bore] Thus in Sandys.
384. The drop] D.'s addition. Cp. 'Palamon and Arcite' iii 1066–7; 'Of the Pythagorean Philosophy' ll. 324–5. *tree enclosed*] Thus in Sandys.
385. yawning] D.'s addition. *to life exposed*] for Ovid's *genitus* ('born'). Cp. 'From Lucretius: Book the Fifth' l. 65.
388–9. Venus fell in love with Adonis, on account of his extraordinary beauty. After he had been killed by a boar, to Venus' great grief, the goddess transformed his blood into an anemone flower (*Met.* x 525–739).
389. with her pains] D.'s addition. *his mother's fires*] Thus in Sandys.

26 The First Book of Homer's *Ilias*

Date and publication. First printed 1700 in *Fables Ancient and Modern* (see headnote to 'Palamon and Arcite' for further details). The present text is based on that of *Fables*, with paragraphing overridden at l. 114.

Context. In the 'Preface to *Fables*' (*Poems* v 48, 55–6) D. explains that the present poem was the first of the translations in the volume to be completed, having been designed as 'an essay' to a projected complete version of Homer's epic, and being appropriately complemented in *Fables* by renderings of episodes from Ovid recounting later events in the Trojan War. In a letter to Charles Montague probably dating from October 1699, D. wrote: 'My thoughts at present are fixd on Homer: And by my translation of the first Iliad; I find him a Poet more according to my Genius than Virgil: and consequently hope I may do him more justice, in his fiery way of writeing; which, as it is liable to more faults, so it is capable of more beauties, than the exactness, & sobriety of Virgil. Since 'tis for my Country's honour as well as for my own, that I am willing to undertake this task; I despair not of being encouragd in it, by your favour' (*Letters* 121). D.'s letter might suggest that he was still working on the version of 'The First Book' after the completion of the versions from Chaucer and Ovid (by 14 July 1699: see *Letters* 115). His wording, however, is also compatible with the possibility that the translation of Book I was already complete, and that his mind was now concentrated on soliciting patronage for the complete translation – his experiences with Book I having convinced him that he was poetically and temperamentally fit for the task. His new-found sense of artistic affinity with Homer, who, he says, has now displaced Virgil from the summit of his literary affections, is confirmed in the 'Preface to *Fables*' (*Poems* v 56; for commentary, see Robin Sowerby in *Translation and Literature* v (1996) 26–50). D.'s translation of 'The First Book', however, contains many echoes of his own rendering of Virgil's *Aeneid*, and his diction and style were clearly influenced by his experience of fashioning an appropriate English idiom for Homer's greatest Roman disciple.

Sources. D. translates the complete Greek text of Book I of the *Iliad*. Verbal details in his rendering reveal his debts to the Latin commentary and translation by Spondanus (Jean de Sponde, 1583), together with a range of other renderings in several languages. These include the *ad verbum* Latin version of Andreas Divus (1537) and the more artistic Latin versions by Lorenzo Valla (1474), V. Obsopoeus (1527), Joachim Camerarius (1538), Helius Eobanus Hessus (1540), and Constantinus Pulcharelius (1619). (On the history and development of the *versio Latina* [literal prose rendering] of Homer, see Robin Sowerby, *Illinois Classical Studies*, xxi (1996) 161–202.) Among English translations, D. drew on the complete versions of George Chapman (in all three versions: 1598, 1610 and 1611), John Ogilby (1660, revised 1669), and Thomas Hobbes (1676), plus the version of Book I by Thomas Grantham (1660), and the burlesque rendering of Books I and II by James Scudamore (1664).

There are also close and extensive resemblances between his translation and the version of *Iliad* i 1–412 by Arthur Maynwaring (or Mainwaring) (1668–1712), published in Tonson's *Poetical Miscellanies: The Fifth Part* (1704). If Maynwaring's version was composed shortly before its publication, these would simply reveal Maynwaring's indebtedness to D.'s version. However, many of the items in Tonson's fifth miscellany date from before 1704, and the high incidence of borrowings in Maynwaring's translation from D.'s *Aeneis*, together with a conspicuous absence of parallels with D.'s most creative embellishments of Homer, suggest the possibility that (as H. A. Mason argued in an unpublished paper) Maynwaring's translation was composed after D.'s *Aeneis* and before *Fables*, and was consulted by D. in manuscript when composing 'The First Book of Homer's *Ilias*'. There are certainly close connections between D. and Maynwaring in the late 1680s and 1690s. In his early years Maynwaring composed fierce Jacobite satires, including a poem in D.'s manner (see [John Oldmixon], *The Life and Posthumous Works of Arthur Maynwaring, Esq.* (1715) 9–10) and *Suum Cuique* (1689), one of the most outspoken attacks on William III (see *POAS* v 117–22). Maynwaring's *The King of Hearts* (1690) contains many echoes of *AA* and was attributed to D. by Tonson and others: D. is said to have to 'disown'd it' and to have named its true author (Oldmixon, *Life* 14). *Tarquin and Tullia* (1689), another of Maynwaring's Jacobite satires, was attributed to D. in 1704 (Macdonald 320–1). Maynwaring kept a commonplace book that included notes and quotations from D. (Oldmixon, *Life* 5–7), mentioned D. to Boileau (Oldmixon, *Life* 17), and collaborated with D. in helping Congreve to get *The Old Batchelour* staged (Macdonald 54). Since it seems impossible to be certain whether Maynwaring's translation of Homer pre- or post-dates D.'s, we cite the closest parallels between the two versions in our notes. These may constitute source material, or may, alternatively, provide a striking illustration of the early influence of D.'s translation.

French versions used by D. include those of S. Du Souhait (1540), Hughes Salel (1580), Salomon Certon (1615), and the Abbé de la Valterie (1681). He also drew on the Italian versions by Luigi Groto (1570) and (in burlesque) by G. F. Loredano (1654). For a fuller account of D.'s relation to the tradition of Homeric scholarship and reception, see *Poems* iv 313–15 and Robin Sowerby, 'Dryden and Homer' (unpublished PhD thesis, Cambridge 1975). The notes below illustrate some of D.'s more significant uses of his sources, plus his echoes of other classical and English poets.

Reception. Several of the elegists in *Luctus Britannici* and *The Nine Muses* (both 1700) commented specifically on the promise of 'The First Book', and regretted that D. had not lived to complete his English *Iliad* (see *Luctus Britannici* 10, 14–15, 35–6, 53; *The Nine Muses* 4, 10). In the Preface to his own translation of the *Iliad*, Alexander Pope noted: 'had he [D.] translated the whole Work, I would no more have attempted *Homer* after him than *Virgil*' (*Poems*, edited by J. Butt et al., 11 vols. (1939–69) vii 22).

The First Book of Homer's *Ilias*

The Argument

Chryses, priest of Apollo, brings presents to the Grecian princes to ransom his daughter Chryseis, who was prisoner in the fleet. Agamemnon, the general, whose captive and mistress the young lady was, refuses to deliver her, threatens the venerable old man, and dismisses him with contumely. The priest craves vengeance of his god, who sends a plague among the Greeks: which occasions Achilles, their great champion, to summon a council of the chief officers. He encourages Calchas, the high priest and prophet, to tell the reason why the gods were so much incensed against them. Calchas is fearful of provoking Agamemnon, till Achilles engages to protect him. Then, emboldened by the hero, he accuses the general as the cause of all, by detaining the fair captive, and refusing the presents offered for her ransom. By this proceeding, Agamemnon is obliged, against his will, to restore Chryseis, with gifts, that he might appease the wrath of Phoebus; but at the same time, to revenge himself on Achilles, sends to seize his slave Briseis. Achilles, thus affronted, complains to his mother Thetis; and begs her to revenge his injury, not only on the general, but on all the army, by giving victory to the Trojans, till the ungrateful king became sensible of his injustice. At the same time, he retires from the camp into his ships, and withdraws his aid from his countrymen. Thetis prefers her son's petition to Jupiter, who grants her suit. Juno suspects her errand, and quarrels with her husband for his grant, till Vulcan reconciles his parents with a bowl of nectar, and sends them peaceably to bed.

> The wrath of Peleus' son, O Muse, resound,
> Whose dire effects the Grecian army found,
> And many a hero, king, and hardy knight,

¶**26**. *The Argument*. D.'s 'Argument' is similar in phrasing at various points to Spondanus' *Argumentum* (a Latin translation of the Greek Ὑπόθεσις attached to early texts of Homer), and to analogous material in Chapman, Divus, Du Souhait, Grantham, Ogilby, Maynwaring.   *contumely*] scornful rudeness (*OED* 1). *sensible*] aware (*OED* 11a).

1. *Peleus' son*] Achilles.

3. *many a hero, king, and hardy knight*] For Homer's πολλὰς δ' ἰφθίμους ψυχὰς ('many brave souls'). Cp. John Oldham, 'Bion, A Pastoral' l. 154 (of Spenser): 'He sung of Hero's, and of hardy Knights'.

Were sent, in early youth, to shades of night:
5   Their limbs a prey to dogs and vultures made;
So was the sovereign will of Jove obeyed:
From that ill-omened hour when strife begun,
Betwixt Atrides great, and Thetis' godlike son.
What power provoked, and for what cause, relate,
10   Sowed in their breasts the seeds of stern debate:
Jove's and Latona's son his wrath expressed,
In vengeance of his violated priest,
Against the king of men; who, swoll'n with pride,
Refused his presents, and his prayers denied.
15   For this the god a swift contagion spread
Amid the camp, where heaps on heaps lay dead.
For venerable Chryses came to buy,
With gold and gifts of price, his daughter's liberty.
Suppliant before the Grecian chiefs he stood,
20   Awful, and armed with ensigns of his god:

---

4. in early youth] D.'s addition. Cp. de la Valterie: 'dans la fleur de leur âge'.

5. vultures] For Homer's οἰωνοῖσί τε πᾶσι ('birds of every kind'); thus in Chapman 1611; 'vautours' in de la Valterie.

6. sovereign] D.'s addition; for *sovereign will* (of God) cp. Milton, *PL* vii 79; xi 83 (J. R. Mason).

7–8. Cp. Chapman 1611: 'from whom, first strife begunne, / Betwixt *Atrides*, King of men, and *Thetis* godlike Sonne'.   *ill-omened*] D.'s addition. For the phrase *ill-omened hour*, cp. 'The Fourth Book of the *Aeneis*' ll. 245–6; 'Sigismonda and Guiscardo' l. 215.   *Atrides*] Agamemnon, son of Atreus.

10. The sowing metaphor is D.'s addition. Cp. Maynwaring: 'What unrelenting God, / In Friendly Breasts, those Seeds of Discord sow'd'.   *debate*] strife, contention (*OED* 1a).

11. Jove's and Latona's son] Apollo. Spondanus, Chapman 1611, and Ogilby similarly use the Latin forms for Homer's Greek names (Zeus, Leto).

13. king of men] For Homer's Ἀτρεΐδης ('the son of Atreus'), translating ἄναξ ἀνδρῶν in Homer's l. 7 (omitted by D. in his l. 8). The phrase is used of Agamemnon by Diomedes in 'The Eleventh Book of the *Aeneis*' l. 411.

13–14. swoll'n with pride . . . and his prayers denied] D.'s addition. For *his prayers denied* cp. Obsopoeus: *despecta precamina Chrysae* ('the despised prayers of Chryses').

15. swift] For Homer's κακήν ('evil').

16. heaps on heaps] D.'s addition. Cp. 'The Seventh Book of the *Aeneis*' l. 745; 'The Twelfth Book of the *Aeneis*' l. 775.

17–18. Cp. Chapman 1611: '*Chryses* the Priest, came to the fleete, to buy / For presents of vnvalued price, his daughters libertie'.

17. venerable] D.'s addition.

19–20. D.'s addition, anticipating the ensuing scene. Cp. Groto: *in suon supplice* ('in a supplicating tone').

20. Awful] awe inspiring (*OED* 1).   *ensigns*] signs, tokens (*OED* 2); thus in Hobbes, Maynwaring.

Bare was his hoary head; one holy hand
Held forth his laurel crown, and one his sceptre of command.
His suit was common; but above the rest
To both the brother-princes thus addressed:
25   'Ye sons of Atreus, and ye Grecian powers,
So may the gods who dwell in heavenly bowers
Succeed your siege, accord the vows you make,
And give you Troy's imperial town to take;
So, by their happy conduct, may you come
30   With conquest back to your sweet native home;
As you receive the ransom which I bring,
Respecting Jove and the far-shooting king,
And break my daughter's bonds at my desire,
And glad with her return her grieving sire.'
35   With shouts of loud acclaim the Greeks decree
To take the gifts, to set the damsel free.
The king of men alone with fury burned,

21. *Bare was his hoary head*] D.'s addition.   *holy*] D.'s addition. Cp. Eobanus: *sacra ferens manibus* ('holding holy objects in his hands').
22. *laurel crown*] For Homer's στέμματ᾽ ('ribbons'); thus in Chapman (all versions); *corona* in Spondanus; *couronne* in Certon, Du Souhait, de la Valterie; *Laurel* in Ogilby. In Homer the ribbons are held χρυσέῳ ἀνὰ σκήπτρῳ ('on a staff of gold') rather than in the other hand.   *of command*] D.'s addition. Cp. 'The Flower and the Leaf' l. 189.
24. *both the brother-princes*] For Homer's Ἀτρεΐδα . . . δύω ('the two sons of Atreus'), i.e. Menelaus, the abduction of whose wife Helen had caused the Trojan War, and his brother Agamemnon, the Greek commander-in-chief. Cp. Eobanus: *geminos fratres* ('twin brothers'); Ogilby: 'The Royall Brothers'; Certon: 'les Atrides Germains'.
27. D.'s expansion. Cp. Groto: *Cosi uoto uostro ui succeda* ('so that any vow of yours may succeed').   *accord*] grant (*OED* 10).
28. Cp. Maynwaring: 'Assist your Arms, King *Priam*'s Town to take'.
29–30. For Homer's ἐὺ δ᾽ οἴκαδ᾽ ἱκέσθαι ('and return safely home'). Cp. Chapman 1611: 'And grant ye happy conduct home'. For *sweet*, cp. Groto: *alme* ('sweet, propitious').
32. *the far-shooting king*] Apollo. Homer's epithet (ἑκηβόλον) thus translated by Chapman and (earlier) Ogilby.
33. *break my daughter's bonds*] For Homer's λύσαιτε ('set free'). Cp. Maynwaring: 'free from servile Bonds a Beauteous Dame'.
34. D.'s addition. Cp. Eobanus: *reddendum misero . . . parenti* ('to be returned to her wretched parent').
35. *loud acclaim*] A Miltonism: cp. *PL* ii 520; iii 397; vi 23; x 455 (J. R. Mason).
36. *to set the damsel free*] For Homer's αἰδεῖσθαί θ᾽ ἱερῆα ('to respect the priest'). Cp. Hobbes: 'and set my Daughter free'.
37. Homer says that Chryses' words οὐκ Ἀτρεΐδῃ Ἀγαμέμνονι ἥνδανε θυμῷ ('did not please the heart of Agamemnon, son of Atreus'). In Du Souhait, Agamemnon's words are 'poussé de fureur & de colere' ('forced out by fury and wrath').

And haughty these opprobrious words returned:
'Hence, holy dotard, and avoid my sight,
40 Ere evil intercept thy tardy flight!
Nor dare to tread this interdicted strand, ⎫
Lest not that idle sceptre in thy hand   ⎬
Nor thy god's crown my vowed revenge withstand. ⎭
Hence on thy life! The captive maid is mine,
45 Whom not for price or prayers I will resign;
Mine she shall be, till creeping age and time
Her bloom have withered, and consumed her prime:
Till then my royal bed she shall attend,
And having first adorned it, late ascend:
50 This for the night; by day, the web and loom, ⎫
And homely household task, shall be her doom, ⎬
Far from thy loved embrace, and her sweet native home.' ⎭
He said; the helpless priest replied no more,
But sped his steps along the hoarse-resounding shore.
55 Silent he fled; secure at length he stood,

38. opprobrious] vituperative, abusive (*OED* 1). Used later (by Jove of Juno) in
Ogilby.
39. holy] D.'s addition.   *dotard*] aged imbecile (*OED* 1a); thus in Chapman (all
editions), Ogilby.   *and avoid my sight*] D.'s addition. Cp. Valla: *Abi . . . a conspectu
meo* ('go away from my sight'); Groto: *Leuati . . . dal mio cospetto* ('get out of my
sight').
40. D.'s substitution for Homer's μή μ' ἐρέθιζε, σαώτερος ὥς κε νέηαι ('do not
anger me, so that you may go the safer') a few lines later.
41. this interdicted strand] For Homer's κοίλησιν . . . παρὰ νηυσὶ ('by the hollow
ships').   *interdicted*] forbidden.
42. idle] useless, ineffective (*OED* 3a). D.'s addition.
44–5. For Homer's τὴν δ' ἐγὼ οὐ λύσω ('but her I will not release'); *captive
maid* in Maynwaring.
46–7. D's elaboration. Homer's Agamemnon simply says that Chryseis will stay
with him in Argos until old age comes upon her.
46. creeping] Cp. Obsopoeus: *tarda* ('slow').
49. D.'s addition. Cp. Grantham: 'adorn my Bed with Gallantrie'; Maynwaring:
'My Bed she shall adorn'. In *AA* (l. 15) Charles II's mistresses 'like slaves his bed
. . . did ascend'.   *late*] afterwards.
50. D. adds the *night/day* contrast.
51. And homely household task] D.'s addition.
52. thy loved embrace, sweet] D.'s additions.
53. the helpless priest] For Homer's ὁ γέρων ('the old man'); *helpless* is D.'s regular
word for the plight of women, children, and the aged: cp. 'The First Book of the
Aeneis' l. 683; 'The Second Book' l. 812; 'The Twelfth Book' l. 859.
54. hoarse-resounding] For Homer's πολυφλοίσβοιο ('loud-resounding'). For *hoarse*,
used of the sea, cp. *PL* ii 287, 661; 'Virgil's Ninth Pastoral' l. 51.

Devoutly cursed his foes, and thus invoked his god:
  'O source of sacred light, attend my prayer,
God with the silver bow, and golden hair,
Whom Chrysa, Cilla, Tenedos obeys,
60 And whose broad eye their happy soil surveys;
If, Smintheus, I have poured before thy shrine
The blood of oxen, goats, and ruddy wine,
And larded thighs on loaded altars laid,
Hear, and my just revenge propitious aid:
65 Pierce the proud Greeks, and with thy shafts attest
How much thy power is injured in thy priest!'
  He prayed, and Phoebus hearing urged his flight,
With fury kindled, from Olympus' height;

56. *Devoutly cursed his foes*] D.'s addition. Cp. de la Valterie: 'il fit mille imprécations
contre eux' ('he made a thousand imprecations against them').   *thus invoked his god*]
Verbatim in Maynwaring, rhyming with *stood.   his god*] For Homer's Ἀπόλλωνι
ἄνακτι τὸν ἠΰκομος τέκε Λητώ ('the lord Apollo, whom fair-haired Leto bore').
57. *O source of sacred light*] D.'s addition. Cp. 'Veni Creator Spiritus' l. 7. Homer uses
ζαθέην ('holy') of Cilla. Ovid's Phaethon (*Met.* ii 35) addresses Apollo as *o lux
immensi publica mundi* ('O common light of this vast world') (Sowerby).
58. *and golden hair*] D.'s addition. Cp. Groto: *crin d'oro* ('golden hair'). Ovid depicts
Apollo with golden hair in *Met.* xi 165.
59. Repeated (slightly varied) at ll. 616–18 below. Cp. also 'The First Book of Ovid's
Metamorphoses' l. 693.   *Chrysa*] 'a City of *Cilicia*, not far from *Thebes*, famous for
the Temple of *Apollo Smintheus*' (Ogilby).   *Cilla*] 'a City of the same Province,
built by *Pelops* in memory of *Cillos*, who drove his chariot' (Ogilby).   *Tenedos*]
'An Island between *Lesbos* and the *Hellespont*, lying against *Troy*, distant from the
Sigeïan shore about 12 miles, from *Lesbos* 56' (Ogilby).
60. D.'s expansion of Homer's ἀμφιβέβηκας ('you have protected'); cp. Spondanus:
tueris ('you have looked over').
61. *Smintheus*] A cult title of Apollo, possibly derived from σμίνθος ('mouse').
Ogilby reports a story from Eustathius, according to which, interpreting the
enigmatic words of an oracle, the Teucri erected a temple to Apollo where they
had been assaulted by a plague of mice 'with his *Statue* pressing a Mouse under
his Feet'. The title may, alternatively, derive from *Sminthe*, a town near Troy.
61–2. *poured . . . the blood*] D.'s subsitution for Homer's ἔρεψα ('have roofed over').
and ruddy wine] D.'s addition. Cp. l. 636 below.
63. *larded thighs*] Cp. l. 632n.   *on loaded altars*] D.'s addition. Cp. 'The Eleventh
Book of the *Aeneis*' l. 72.
64. For Homer's τόδε μοι κρήηνον ἐέλδωρ ('fulfil for me this wish').   *propitious*]
favourable, gracious (*OED* 1: adj. as adv.); cp. 'Palamon and Arcite' iii 286.
65–6. Freely paraphrasing Homer's τίσειαν Δαναοὶ ἐμὰ δάκρυα σοῖσι βέλεσσιν
('let the Danaans pay for my tears by your arrows'). Cp. Valla: *Immitte tua tela in
Graios* ('send your arrows against the Greeks'); Groto: *Qual sia lo tuo poter lor nostra,
e quanto* ('[show them] what kind of power you have, and how much').
67. *urged his flight*] D.'s addition. Cp. Groto: *Indi à uolar sollecito si mosse* ('then he
hastened to fly').   *urged*] hastened (*OED* 5).

His quiver o'er his ample shoulders threw,
70 His bow twanged, and his arrows rattled as they flew.
Black as a stormy night, he ranged around
The tents, and compassed the devoted ground;
Then with full force his deadly bow he bent,
And feathered fates among the mules and sumpters sent,
75 Th' essay of rage; on faithful dogs the next,
And last, in human hearts his arrows fixed.
The god nine days the Greeks at rovers killed,
Nine days the camp with funeral fires was filled;
The tenth, Achilles, by the queen's command
80 Who bears heaven's awful sceptre in her hand,
A council summoned; for the goddess grieved
Her favoured host should perish unrelieved.
  The kings, assembled, soon their chief enclose;
Then from his seat the goddess-born arose,

70. In Homer, the arrows rattle in Apollo's quiver. For arrows *rattling* in flight, cp. *PL* vi 546 (J. R. Mason).

71. *stormy*] D.'s addition.

71–2. *he ranged around . . . the devoted ground*] D.'s addition. Cp. Chapman 1611: 'he rang'd the host'; Maynwaring: 'rang'd apart'.

72. *devoted*] doomed (*OED* 3); thus in Maynwaring.

73. *with full force*] D.'s addition.

74. *feathered fates*] For Homer's βέλος ἐχεπευκές ('a bitter arrow').   *and sumpters*] D.'s addition.   *sumpters*] baggage horses, beasts of burden (*OED* 2, citing this example).

75. *Th' essay of rage*] D.'s addition.   *essay*] proof (*OED* 1); specimen (*OED* 2, first example).   *faithful*] For Homer's ἀργούς ('swift').

77. *at rovers*] at individually selected targets, or randomly (*OED* rover 1a–b; an archery term, also used in 'Discourse Concerning Satire' (*Poems* iii 322)). Cp. Chapman 1611: 'he rang'd the host, and rou'd'; Maynwaring: 'when the Darts nine Days had rov'd'.

78. *funeral fires*] For Homer's πυραὶ νεκύων ('pyres of the dead'). Cp. Hobbes: 'the fire of Funerals'.

79. *the queen's*] Hera / Juno's.

80. D.'s addition. In 'The Fourth Book of the *Aeneis*' (ll. 354–5) Mercury 'grasps within his awful Hand / The mark of Sov'raign Pow'r, his Magic Wand'.   *awful*] awesome, awe inspiring (*OED* 1).

81–2. Cp. Ogilby: '*Juno* griev'd / To see the *Grecians* perish unreliev'd'.   *unrelieved*] D.'s addition.   *favoured*] D.'s addition. Cp. Maynwaring: 'Men . . . to whom her Heart inclin'd'.

83. *their chief enclose*] D.'s addition. Spondanus notes that it was then the custom *etiamsi reges essent, vt eos circumstaret populus, & æqualiter ab omnibus exaudirentur* ('even if they were kings, that the people stood around them, and they were heard equally by all').

84. *the goddess-born*] Achilles. D. translates the epithet διογενής ('heaven-born') from later in Homer (l. 489) rather than the epithet given here: πόδας ὠκὺς ('swift of feet'). Cp. ll. 449, 504, 661.

85   And thus undaunted spoke: 'What now remains,
     But that once more we tempt the watery plains,
     And wandering homeward seek our safety hence,
     In flight at least if we can find defence?
     Such woes at once encompass us about,
90   The plague within the camp, the sword without.
     Consult, O king, the prophets of th' event;   ⎫
     And whence these ills, and what the god's intent,   ⎪
     Let them by dreams explore; for dreams from Jove are ⎬
        sent.   ⎪
     What want of offered victims, what offence   ⎭
95   In fact committed could the sun incense
     To deal his deadly shafts? What may remove
     His settled hate, and reconcile his love?
     That he may look propitious on our toils,
     And hungry graves no more be glutted with our spoils.'
100   Thus to the king of men the hero spoke,
     Then Calchas the desired occasion took:
     Calchas the sacred seer, who had in view

85. undaunted] D.'s addition.
85–6. What now remains, / But] Homer's Achilles simply begins νῦν . . . ὀίω ('now . . .
I think'). D.'s formula is found in *PL* x 502–3 (J. R. Mason), and is used several
times by D. to denote a hard-won decision: cp. *RL* l. 427; 'Palamon and Arcite'
iii 1111.
86. tempt] set out adventurously on, with possible risk (*OED* 2c).
87. wandering homeward] Cp. Maynwaring: 'To wander homewards through the
doubtful Main'.
89. For the idea of woes *encompassing* mortals (D.'s addition) cp. 'To the Memory
of Mr Oldham' l. 25.
90. within, without] D.'s additions.   *sword*] For Homer's πόλεμός ('war'). Cp.
Scudamore: 'Plague, and Sword'.
91. th' event] the future outcome (*OED* 3a).
92–3. Cp. Scudamore: '(For dreames from *Jupiter* are sent,) / So we may know
Phoebus's intent'.
92. and what the god's intent] D.'s addition.
94. want] lack, deficiency.   *offered victims*] For Homer's ἑκατόμβης ('hecatomb':
an offering of a hundred oxen). Cp. Chapman 1598: 'offered sheepe'.
94–5. offence / In fact committed] For Homer's εὐχωλῆς ('vow'; i.e. broken).
95. Cp. Chapman 1611: 'Why *Phoebus* is so much incenst'.
96–7. Cp. Maynwaring: 'If humble Victims will this Plague remove, / Appease
the Godhead, and regain his Love'.
98–9. Freely paraphrasing Homer's αἴ κέν πως ἀρνῶν κνίσης αἰγῶν τε τελέιων/
βούλεται ἀντιάσας ἡμῖν ἀπὸ λοιγὸν ἀμῦναι ('in the hope that perhaps he
might accept the savour of lambs and unblemished goats, and be minded to ward
off destruction from us').
101. the desired occasion took] For Homer's ἀνέστη ('he rose'). For the formula,
cp. *AA* l. 1208; 'The Ninth Book of the *Aeneis*' l. 82; 'The Eleventh Book of
the *Aeneis*' l. 697; 'Cinyras and Myrrha' ll. 247–8.

Things present and the past, and things to come foreknew;
Supreme of augurs, who by Phoebus taught
105 The Grecian powers to Troy's destruction brought.
Skilled in the secret causes of their woes,
The reverend priest in graceful act arose,
And thus bespoke Pelides: 'Care of Jove,
Favoured of all th' immortal powers above,
110 Wouldst thou the seeds deep sown of mischief know,
And why provoked Apollo bends his bow?
Plight first thy faith, inviolably true,
To save me from those ills that may ensue.
For I shall tell ungrateful truths to those
115 Whose boundless power of life and death dispose;
And sovereigns, ever jealous of their state,
Forgive not those whom once they mark for hate;
Ev'n though th' offence they seemingly digest,

104–5. Cp. Maynwaring: 'Who safe to *Troy* the *Graecian* Navy brought / By that Prophetick Art which *Phoebus* taught'.   *Supreme*] For Homer's ἄριστος ('best'). Cp. Chapman 1611: 'of Augures, the supreme'.   *to Troy's destruction*] Homer simply says Ἴλιον εἴσω ('to Troy').

106. D.'s addition. Cp. Maynwaring: 'To learn the Cause of our Impending Woes'.

107–8. The reverend priest . . . thus bespoke Pelides] For Homer's ὅ σφιν ἐϋφρονέων ἀγορήσατο καὶ μετέειπεν ('he with good intent addressed their assembly and spoke among them').

107. The reverend priest] Loredano says that Calchas displayed *una bella reverenza*. *in graceful act*] Cp. Belial in *PL* ii 108–9 (J. R. Mason).   *act*] With suggestions of an oratorical or theatrical performance (although not necessarily of insincerity) (*OED* 7d).

108. bespoke] addressed (*OED* 6).   *Pelides*] Achilles (son of Peleus).   *Care of*] A person particularly protected by.

109. D.'s addition.

110–11. the seeds deep sown . . . bends his bow] For Homer's μῆνιν Ἀπόλλωνος ἑκατηβελέταο ἄνακτος ('the wrath of Lord Apollo who smites from far off'). Cp. Groto: *contra noì parco / Di uotar la faretra, e tender l'arco* ('[Apollo] does not refrain from emptying his quiver and drawing his bow against us').

112. faith] assurance, promise (*OED* 8a).   *inviolably true*] D.'s elaboration. Cp. de la Valterie: 'par un serment inviolable'.

113. from those ills that may ensue] D.'s addition. Cp. Groto: *al gran periglio . . . / Che può seguirmi* ('from the great danger that might follow'); cp. Ogilby: 'from all danger'.

114. ungrateful] unpleasant, distasteful (*OED* 2); thus in Maynwaring.

115. of life and death] D.'s expansion.

116. ever jealous of their state] D.'s addition.   *jealous*] watchful, suspiciously careful (*OED* 3).

117. Cp. Chapman 1611: 'When a king hath once markt for his hate'.

118–19. Cp. Chapman 1611: 'though that day his wrath seemes to digest / Th' offence he takes; yet euermore he rakes vp in his brest / Brands of quicke anger'.

Revenge, like embers raked within their breast,
120 Bursts forth in flames, whose unresisted power
Will seize th' unwary wretch, and soon devour.
Such, and no less, is he on whom depends
The sum of things, and whom my tongue of force offends.
Secure me then from his foreseen intent,
125 That what his wrath may doom, thy valour may prevent.'
To this the stern Achilles made reply:
'Be bold, and on my plighted faith rely,
To speak what Phoebus has inspired thy soul
For common good, and speak without control.
130 His godhead I invoke; by him I swear
That while my nostrils draw this vital air,
None shall presume to violate those bands,
Or touch thy person with unhallowed hands;
Ev'n not the king of men that all commands.'
135 At this, resuming heart, the prophet said:

119–25. Considerably expanding Homer's ll. 81–3: εἴ περ γάρ τε χόλον γε
καὶ αὐτῆμαρ καταπέψῃ, / ἀλλά τε καὶ μετόπισθεν ἔχει κότον, ὄφρα τελέσσῃ
/ ἐν στήθεσσιν ἑοῖσι. σὺ δὲ φράσαι εἴ με σαώσεις ('For even if he swallows
down his anger for the one day, still afterwards he holds resentment in his heart
until he fulfils it. Consider, then, if you will keep me safe').
120. unresisted] irresistible.
123. The sum of things] the highest public good (*OED* 13b). Cp. *PL* vi 673 (J. R.
Mason). *of force*] inevitably, necessarily (*OED* 19a).
125. doom] decree, pronounce as a judgement (*OED* 5). *thy valour may prevent*]
Thus (with *will* for *may*) in Chapman 1611.
126. stern] D.'s replacement for Homer's πόδας ὠκύς ('swift of foot'). Thus in
Ogilby, Maynwaring. Used of Achilles by Milton in *PL* ix 5, and by D. in 'The
Third Satire of Juvenal' l. 443; used of Aeneas by D. in 'Tenth Book of the *Aeneis*'
l. 843; 'The Twelfth Book' l. 1284.
127. on my plighted faith rely] D.'s expansion. *faith*] assurance, promise (*OED* 8a).
128. what Phoebus has inspired thy soul] For Homer's θεοπρόπιον ὅ τι οἶσθα
('any oracle you know'). Cp. de la Valterie: 'dites hardiment ce qu' Apollon vous
inspirera' ('state forthrightly what Apollo will inspire you to say').
129. For common good] D.'s addition. *without control*] unrestrainedly, freely (*OED*
2); D.'s expansion.
131. while my nostrils draw this vital air] For Homer's ἐμεῦ ζῶντος καὶ ἐπὶ χθονὶ
δερκομένοιο ('while I live and have sight on earth'). Cp. Pulcharelius: *vitali potiar
dum luminis aura* ('while I enjoy the vital air of light').
132. to violate those bands] D.'s addition. Cp. Obsopoeus: *Nemo te . . . violabit* ('no-one
will violate you'). For *bands*, cp. l. 22n.
133. unhallowed] D.'s substitution for Homer's βαρείας ('heavy'). For the phrase,
cp. 'The Twelfth Book of Ovid's *Metamorphoses*' l. 346.
134. that all commands] D.'s addition. Cp. Certon: 'commande a toute ceste armee'
('commands this whole army').

'Nor hecatombs unslain, nor vows unpaid,
On Greeks accursed this dire contagion bring,
Or call for vengeance from the bowyer king;
But he the tyrant, whom none dares resist,
140 Affronts the godhead in his injured priest:
He keeps the damsel captive in his chain,
And presents are refused, and prayers preferred in vain.
For this th' avenging power employs his darts,
And empties all his quiver in our hearts;
145 Thus will persist, relentless in his ire,
Till the fair slave be rendered to her sire,
And ransom-free restored to his abode,
With sacrifice to reconcile the god;
Then he, perhaps, atoned by prayer, may cease
150 His vengeance justly vowed, and give the peace.'
      Thus having said, he sate. Thus answered then,

---

136. hecatombs] See l. 94*n.*   *unslain*] D.'s addition.   *unpaid*] D.'s addition. Thus in
Chapman 1611.

137–8. D.'s expansion. Homer's Calchas says that Apollo οὐ . . . ἐπιμέμφεται ('does
not blame us') for these things.

138. the bowyer king] Apollo. D. translates the epithet ἑκηβόλος ('who shoots from
afar') from later in Homer (l. 96).

139. the tyrant, whom none dares resist] D.'s political expansion. Homer's Calchas
simply names Agamemnon. For D.'s insertion of *tyrant* into his translations, see
'Palamon and Arcite' i 86*n.*

140. injured] wronged (*OED* 1). Valla and Pulcharelius both refer to the *iniuria*
('wrongs') done to Chryses.

141. in his chain] D.'s addition.

142. presents] gifts, offered as a ransom (*OED sb.*² 2); thus (in sing.) in Chapman
1611.   *and prayers preferred in vain*] D.'s addition.   *preferred*] offered (*OED* 4); thus
in Chapman 1611.

143. th' avenging power] substituted for Homer's epithet (for which see l. 138*n.*).

143–4. employs his darts . . . in our hearts] For Homer's ἄλγε' ἔδωκεν ('has given woes').
Cp. Chapman 1611: 'This is cause, why heauens farre-darter darts, / These plagues
amonst vs; and this still, will emptie in our hearts / His deathfull quiuer'.   *darts*]
arrows.

145. For Homer's οὐδ' ὅ γε πρὶν λοιμοῖο βαρείας χεῖρας ἀφέξει [Spondanus'
text; Loeb has different readings] ('nor will he remove his heavy hands from the
plague, until . . .').

146. fair] For Homer's ἑλικώπιδα κούρην, glossed by Spondanus as *nigris oculis
puellae* ('girl with black eyes') and by Camerarius as *nigris oculis decoram puellam*
('beautiful girl with black eyes').

150. justly vowed, and give the peace] D.'s addition. Cp. Valla: *Ibi tum nostra expiatione,
tum Chrysae precibus Phoebi pacem consequemur* ('Then by our expiation and our
prayers to Chryses, we might obtain the peace of Apollo').

Upstarting from his throne, the king of men,
His breast with fury filled, his eyes with fire,
Which rolling round he shot in sparkles on the sire:
155 'Augur of ill, whose tongue was never found
Without a priestly curse or boding sound!
For not one blessed event foretold to me
Passed through that mouth, or passed unwillingly;
And now thou dost with lies the throne invade,
160 By practice hardened in thy slandering trade;
Obtending heaven for whate'er ills befall,
And sputtering under specious names thy gall.
Now Phoebus is provoked, his rites and laws
Are in his priest profaned, and I the cause;
165 Since I detain a slave, my sovereign prize,
And sacred gold, your idol-god, despise.
I love her well; and well her merits claim
To stand preferred before my Grecian dame:
Not Clytemnestra's self in beauty's bloom
170 More charmed, or better plied the various loom:
Mine is the maid, and brought in happy hour
With every household grace adorned, to bless my nuptial
     bower.

152. *from his throne*] D.'s addition.   *the king of men*] For Homer's ἥρως Ἀτρεΐδης
εὐρὺ κρείων Ἀγαμέμνων ('the warrior, son of Atreus, wide-ruling Agamemnon').
Cp. l. 13*n*.
153. *breast*] For Homer's φρένες ('mind', 'heart', lit. 'midriff').
154. For Homer's Κάλχαντα πρώτιστα κάκ᾽ ὀσσόμενος προσέειπε ('to Calchas
first he spoke, with an evil look'). Cp. Chapman 1610: 'his eyes like burning fire
/ Cast sparkles from his bended browes, all blowen out of his Ire'.
156. *boding*] ominous. Thus in Maynwaring.
158. *or passed unwillingly*] D.'s addition.
159. Homer's Agamemnon simply says that Calchas utters his prophecies among
the Danaans.   *with lies*] Cp. Groto: *mendace lingua* ('with lying tongue'). Eobanus'
Agamemnon accuses Calchas of uttering *conficta . . . mendacia* ('invented lies').
160–2. D.'s addition, considerably intensifying Agamemnon's contempt for Calchas.
161. *Obtending*] offering as justification (*OED* 1, citing this example).
162. *gall*] Cp. Chapman 1611: 'prophetique gall'.
163. *Now*] i.e. 'according to you'.
166. Homer's Agamemnon simply refers to his unwillingness to accept ἀγλά᾽ ἄποινα
('the glorious ransom') for Chryseis.
169–70. Homer's Agamemnon refers to Chryseis' δέμας ('build'), φυήν ('stature'),
φρένας ('mind'), and ἔργα ('works, accomplishments').
170. *various*] (i) moving in different directions (in the act of weaving) (*OED* 1c);
(ii) generating multicoloured products (*OED* 4a).
171–2. Homer's Agamemnon simply says that he wishes to keep Chryseis οἴκοι
('at home'). For the collocation of *brought*, *adorned*, and *nuptial bower*, cp. *PL* iv
712–14; viii 50; ix 1030–1; xi 280 (J. R. Mason).

Yet shall she be restored, since public good ⎫
For private interest ought not be withstood, ⎬
175 To save th' effusion of my people's blood. ⎭
But right requires, if I resign my own,
I should not suffer for your sakes alone;
Alone excluded from the prize I gained,
And by your common suffrage have obtained.
180 The slave without a ransom shall be sent:
It rests for you to make th' equivalent.'
      To this the fierce Thessalian prince replied:
'O first in power, but passing all in pride,
Griping, and still tenacious of thy hold,
185 Wouldst thou the Grecian chiefs, though largely souled,
Should give the prizes they had gained before,
And with their loss thy sacrilege restore?
Whate'er by force of arms the soldier got,
Is each his own, by dividend of lot:
190 Which to resume were both unjust and base,
Not to be borne but by a servile race.

173–4. D. adds the *private/public* contrast. Cp. l. 129. Du Souhait (marginal note) similarly contrasts 'le bien du public' and 'leur interest particulier'. Cp. also Chapman 1598, 1610: 'our common good'.

175. effusion] shedding (*OED* 1).

177. for your sakes alone] D.'s addition.

179. suffrage] consent, approval (*OED* 5a).

180–1. Homer's Agamemnon says that it is not fitting for his prize to go elsewhere. Cp. Du Souhait: 'c'est à vous autres Grecs à preuoir qu'en perdant Criseide, ie sois recompensé' ('it is for you other Greeks to see to it that, in losing Chryseis, I am recompensed'). De la Valterie's Agamemnon says that he will give up Chryseis 'sans rançon' ('without a ransom').

182. the fierce Thessalian prince] For Homer's ποδάρκης δῖος Ἀχιλλεύς ('noble Achilles, swift of foot'). Achilles' home was Phthia in Thessaly.

183–4. For Homer's φιλοκτεανώτατε πάντων ('most covetous of all men').

183. in pride] Cp. Groto: *di superbia acceso* ('fired by pride').

184. griping] clutching tightly, avaricious (*OED* 1).

185. largely souled] noble, generous.

187. D.'s addition. *restore*] make amends for (*OED* 2a, last example 1642).

188. by force of arms the soldier got] For Homer's ἐξεπράθομεν ('we pillaged'); cp. Du Souhait: 'par le droit des armes' ('by right of arms').

189. dividend] share (falling to each) (*OED* 3). Spoils of war were divided by *lots* (pieces of wood bearing the mark of the various competitors) being placed in a helmet and shaken: the spoils went to the warrior whose *lot* fell out first (see *OED* lot 1a). Ogilby and Maynwaring have *dividend*.

190. resume] take back (*OED* 3a); thus in Hobbes, Maynwaring.

191. D.'s substitution for Homer's ἀλλὰ σὺ μὲν νῦν τήνδε θεῷ προές ('but do you now give her back to the god').

But this we can: if Saturn's son bestows
The sack of Troy, which he by promise owes,
Then shall the conquering Greeks thy loss restore,
195   And with large interest make th' advantage more.'
      To this Atrides answered: 'Though thy boast
Assumes the foremost name of all our host,
Pretend not, mighty man, that what is mine,
Controlled by thee, I tamely should resign.
200   Shall I release the prize I gained by right
In taken towns, and many a bloody fight,
While thou detain'st Briseis in thy bands,
By priestly glossing on the god's commands?
Resolve on this (a short alternative):
205   Quit mine, or, in exchange, another give;
Else I, assure thy soul, by sovereign right
Will seize thy captive in thy own despite;
Or from stout Ajax or Ulysses bear
What other prize my fancy shall prefer:
210   Then softly murmur, or aloud complain,
Rage as you please, you shall resist in vain.
But more of this in proper time and place;

192. But this we can] D.'s addition.   *Saturn's son*] Zeus; named in Homer.
193. which he by promise owes] D.'s addition, drawing on Chapman 1611: 'when
Iupiter bestowes / The sacke of well-wall'd Troy on vs; which by his word, he
owes'. Zeus had promised Agamemnon that he would return home having sacked
Troy (*Iliad* ix 19–20).
195. For Homer's τριπλῇ τετραπλῇ ('threefold and fourfold').
198. Pretend] plan, intend (*OED* 8), with a suggestion of the trickery and deceit
attributed to Achilles by Homer's Agamemnon. Cp. de la Valterie: 'Ne prétendez-
pas, Achille, que j'abandonne lâchement mes droits' ('Do not deceive yourself
that I will abandon my rights in a cowardly manner').
199. Controlled] dominated, commanded (*OED* 4).
200–3. Mostly D.'s addition. Homer's Agamemnon refers (without naming her)
to the γέρας ('prize') that Achilles will retain, even if Agamemnon loses his.
201. In taken towns] Cp. de la Valterie: 'à la prise de tant de Villes' ('at the capture
of so many cities').
203. By] because of, by means of.   *glossing on*] interpretation of (*OED* 1b); cp.
Chapman 1611: 'glosse'.
204–5. Resolve on this . . . Quit mine] D.'s addition. Chapman 1611 has 'Resolve this'.
206. assure thy soul, by sovereign right] D.'s addition.
207. in thy own despite] in contemptuous defiance of you (*OED* despite 5); D.'s
addition.
210–11. Expanding Homer's ὁ δὲ κεν κεχολώσεται ὅν κεν ἵκωμαι ('he will
be angry, to whomever I come'). Chapman 1611 has 'rage'.
212. in proper time and place] For Homer's αὖτις ('later'). Cp. Certon: 'en autre
temps' ('at another time').

To things of greater moment let us pass.
A ship to sail the sacred seas prepare,
215 Proud in her trim, and put on board the fair,
With sacrifice and gifts, and all the pomp of prayer.
The crew well chosen, the command shall be
In Ajax; or if other I decree,
In Creta's king, or Ithacus, or if I please in thee:
220 Most fit thyself to see performed th' intent
For which my prisoner from my sight is sent
(Thanks to thy pious care) that Phoebus may relent.'
At this Achilles rolled his furious eyes,
Fixed on the king askant, and thus replies:
225 'O impudent, regardful of thy own,
Whose thoughts are centred on thyself alone,
Advanced to sovereign sway for better ends
Than thus like abject slaves to treat thy friends!
What Greek is he that, urged by thy command,
230 Against the Trojan troops will lift his hand?
Not I! Nor such enforced respect I owe;
Nor Pergamus I hate, nor Priam is my foe.

213. D.'s addition. *moment*] importance (*OED* 4).
215. *Proud in her trim*] D.'s addition. *Proud*] stately, majestic (*OED* 6b).
216. For Homer's reference to a hecatomb (cp. l. 94*n*). Cp. Grantham: 'Sacrifice';
Maynwaring: 'with Pomp of Sacrifice'.
217. *well chosen*] Homer refers to ἐρέτας ἐπιτηδὲς ('a due number of rowers').
Cp. Chapman 1610: 'chosen rowers'.
218. *if other I decree*] D.'s addition.
219. *Creta's king*] Named by Homer as Idomeneus. Cp. Maynwaring: '*Creta*'s'.
Ithacus] For Homer's δῖος Ὀδυσσεὺς ('noble Odysseus'). Thus in Chapman 1611,
Ogilby, Grantham. Odysseus was king of Ithaca. *if I please*] D.'s addition. Cp.
Hobbes: 'if you please'.
220–2. *Most fit thyself . . . thy pious care*] For Homer's πάντων ἐκπαγλότατ' ἀνδρῶν
('most daunting of men'). Camerarius suggests that Agamemnon speaks here with
ironical intent. Chapman 1611 translates in that spirit; his Agamemnon comments
that it would be 'fittest' for Achilles to 'see, these holy acts performd / For which
thy cunning zeale so pleades'.
223–4. *rolled his furious eyes . . . askant*] Strengthening Homer's ὑπόδρα ἰδὼν ('with
a stern glance'). Cp. Satan's response to Abdiel in *PL* vi 149–50.
225. Cp. Chapman 1611: 'of no good but thine owne / Euer respectfull'. O
impudent] Cp. Spondanus: *impudentia*; Salel: 'impudent'; Chapman 1611: 'impudent';
Hobbes: 'impudence'.
227–8. D.'s contemptuous addition.
229. *What Greek is he*] Following Salel's 'Qui est le Grec, qui'.
230. Homer does not specifically name the Trojans. Cp. Hobbes: 'Against the *Trojans*'.
231–5. A free rendering of Homer's ll. 152–7.
231. *Nor such enforced respect I owe*] D.'s addition.
232. *Pergamus*] Troy (thus called after its citadel).

What wrong from Troy remote could I sustain, ⎫
To leave my fruitful soil and happy reign,   ⎬
235   And plough the surges of the stormy main?   ⎭
Thee, frontless man, we followed from afar,
Thy instruments of death, and tools of war.
Thine is the triumph, ours the toil alone;
We bear thee on our backs, and mount thee on the throne.
240   For thee we fall in fight; for thee redress
Thy baffled brother, not the wrongs of Greece.
And now thou threaten'st with unjust decree
To punish thy affronting heaven on me;
To seize the prize which I so dearly bought,
245   By common suffrage given, confirmed by lot.
Mean match to thine: for still above the rest
Thy hooked rapacious hands usurp the best,
Though mine are first in fight, to force the prey,
And last sustain the labours of the day.
250   Nor grudge I thee the much the Grecians give,
Nor murmuring take the little I receive;
Yet ev'n this little thou, who wouldst engross
The whole, insatiate, enviest as thy loss.
Know, then, for Phthia fixed is my return: ⎫
255   Better at home my ill-paid pains to mourn,   ⎬
Than from an equal here sustain the public scorn.' ⎭

234. Cp. Maynwaring: 'Nor fruitful *Phthia*'s happy Soil'.
236. *frontless*] shameless (*OED* 1). Thus in Chapman 1611.   *from afar*] D.'s addition.
237. D.'s addition.
238–40. *ours the toil . . . fall in fight*] D.'s addition. Cp. 'The Eleventh Book of the *Aeneis*'
l. 571 (Drances to Turnus): 'We, but the Slaves who mount thee to the Throne'.
241. *Thy baffled brother*] Homer's Achilles simply names Menelaus.   *baffled*] dishonoured (*OED* 1).   *not the wrongs of Greece*] Replacing Homer's πρὸς Τρώων
('from the Trojans').
242. *with unjust decree*] D.'s addition.
243. D.'s addition; i.e. 'to punish me for the fact that you have affronted heaven'.
244. Cp. Hobbes: 'Which by my labour I have dearly bought'.
245. Homer's Achilles says that his prize was given to him by υἷες Ἀχαιῶν ('the
sons of the Achaeans').
246–7. *for still, above the rest . . . usurp the best*] D.'s addition.
250–1. The stress on Achilles' uncomplaining response is D.'s. Cp. de la Valterie:
'sans en murmurer' ('without muttering about it').
252–3. D.'s addition.   *engross*] monopolize (*OED* 4).
254–5. Cp. Maynwaring: ''Tis better to return / To Native *Greece*, than here Oppression mourn'.
255. *my ill-paid pains to mourn*] Replacing Homer's ἴμεν ('to go').
256. Homer's Achilles declares that he does not intend to accumulate wealth for
Agamemnon. D. adds Achilles' reference to Agamemnon as *an equal*.

The king, whose brows with shining gold were bound,
Who saw his throne with sceptred slaves encompassed round,
Thus answered stern: 'Go, at thy pleasure, go!
260   We need not such a friend, nor fear we such a foe.
There will not want to follow me in fight:
Jove will assist, and Jove assert my right.
But thou of all the kings, his care below,
Art least at my command, and most my foe.
265   Debates, dissensions, uproars are thy joy;
Provoked without offence, and practised to destroy.
Strength is of brutes, and not thy boast alone;
At least 'tis lent from heaven, and not thy own.
Fly then, ill-mannered, to thy native land,
270   And there thy ant-born Myrmidons command.
But mark this menace: since I must resign

257–8. *The king . . . encompassed round*] For Homer's ἄναξ ἀνδρῶν Ἀγαμέμνων ('Agamemnon, lord of men'). Cp. de la Valterie: 'Agamemnon qui se voyoit à la teste de tant d'autres Princes' ('Agamemnon who saw himself at the head of so many other princes'). For subordinate princes as *sceptred slaves*, cp. *All for Love* III i 142.
259. *stern*] D.'s addition.
260. *nor fear we such a foe*] D.'s addition. Cp. Hobbes: 'nor your anger fear'; Grantham: 'Nor fear thy wrath'.
261. i.e. I will not lack followers in battle.
262. For Homer's μάλιστα δέ μητίετα Ζεύς ('and above all Zeus, the lord of counsel').
263. *his*] i.e. Jove's. Chapman 1611 refers to '*Ioue*-kept kings'.
264. For Homer's ἔχθιστος δέ μοί ἐσσι ('are most hateful to me'). Cp. Grantham: 'but thou my greatest Foe'.
265. *Debates, dissensions, uproars*] A politicized rendering of Homer's ἔρις ('strife'), πόλεμοι ('wars'), μάχαι ('battles'). Cp. de la Valterie: 'les querelles, & les dissensions'; Maynwaring: 'Faction'.   *Debates*] strifes, contentions (*OED* 1a).
266. D.'s addition.
267. *is of brutes*] D.'s addition. For the sentiment, cp. 'Palamon and Arcite' iii 742; *Cleomenes* V ii 153 (*Works*); 'Dedication to *Fables*' (*Poems* v 44).
268. Cp. Chapman 1611: 'God gaue thee it; and so tis not thine owne'.
269. *ill-mannered*] D.'s addition.
270. *ant-born*] D.'s addition. Ogilby's note offers two alternative explanations. According to the first, the Myrmidons were so called 'from *Myrmex* an *Athenian* Virgin, whom *Ceres* (displeased that she had communicated the invention of the Plough) transformed into an Ant, from whom a multitude of the same *species* proceeding, they were upon the wish of *Æacus* (wanting Associates) turned into men'. Alternatively, according to Ovid (*Met.* vii 615–60), Jupiter, out of pity for Aeacus, transformed 'all the Pismires' of Aegina into men, 'who thence were called *Myrmidons*, Μύρμηξ signifying an Ant or Pismire'.
271. *menace*] threat (*OED* a). Cp. de la Valterie: 'voicy la menace que j'ay à vous faire' ('this is the threat I have to offer you').

My black-eyed maid to please the powers divine,
A well-rigged vessel in the port attends,
Manned at my charge, commanded by my friends;
275   The ship shall waft her to her wished abode,
Full fraught with holy bribes to the far-shooting god.
This thus dispatched, I owe myself the care
My fame and injured honour to repair;
From thy own tent, proud man, in thy despite
280   This hand shall ravish thy pretended right.
Briseis shall be mine, and thou shalt see   ⎫
What odds of awful power I have on thee,   ⎪
That others at thy cost may learn the difference of ⎬
   degree.'   ⎪
At this th' impatient hero sourly smiled;   ⎭
285   His heart impetuous in his bosom boiled,
And jostled by two tides of equal sway,
Stood for a while suspended in his way
Betwixt his reason and his rage untamed,
One whispered soft, and one aloud reclaimed:

272. my black-eyed maid] For Homer's Χρυσηΐδα ('the daughter of Chryses'),
translating Homer's earlier epithet (see l. 146*n*). Thus in Chapman 1598, 1610;
Maynwaring.   *the powers divine*] Only Apollo in Homer; thus in Maynwaring.
273. well-rigged] D.'s addition.   *in the port attends*] D.'s addition.
274. Cp. Ogilby: 'In mine owne Ship, well man'd, with choisest Friends'.
276. D.'s addition. For *far-shooting*, cp. l. 32, l. 138*n*.
277–8. D.'s addition.
279. tent] For Homer's κλισίηνδε ('hut'), glossed as *tentorium* by Spondanus, and
translated as *tent* in Chapman 1611.
280. pretended] to which you make false claim (*OED* 2).
282. Cp. de la Valterie: 'que j'ay plus de pouvoir icy que vous' ('that I have more
power here than you').   *odds . . . on*] superiority over (*OED* 4).   *awful*] inspiring
awe; D.'s addition.
283. degree] rank (*OED* 4a).
284. impatient] D.'s addition, translating Horace's *impiger*, used of Achilles in *Ars
Poetica* l. 12 (quoted in 'Preface to *Fables*' (*Poems* v 59)). The epithet is repeated
in 'The Twelfth Book of Ovid's *Metamorphoses*' l. 136.   *sourly smiled*] Homer
says that ἄχος γένετ' ('grief came upon him'). For the formula, cp. Theseus in
'Palamon and Arcite' ii 303; Mezentius in 'The Tenth Book of the *Aeneis*' l. 1046.
285–93. D. expands Homer's description of Achilles' ἦτορ ('heart') torn between
the desires (i) to draw his sword on Agamemnon and kill him, and (ii) to check
his χόλον ('bile') and curb his θυμόν ('spirit') (ll. 188–92), depicting Achilles'
state as a conflict between reason and passion. Cp. Spondanus: *Certamen istud in
Achille fuit Rationis & partis irascibilis* ('This contest in Achilles was between reason
and the irascible part'); Chapman 1598, 1610: 'His rationall and angrie parts, a
doubtfull strife possest'; Ogilby: 'Whilst thus his Reason combated with Rage'.
For a similar dilemma, cp. Turnus in 'The Twelfth Book of the *Aeneis*' ll. 967–74.
289. reclaimed] cried loudly (*OED* 8, rare example); protested (*OED* 7).

290   That only counselled to the safer side,
        This to the sword his ready hand applied.
        Unpunished to support th' affront was hard,
        Nor easy was th' attempt to force the guard;
        But soon the thirst of vengeance fired his blood:
295   Half shone his falchion, and half sheathed it stood.
           In that nice moment, Pallas from above,
        Commissioned by th' imperial wife of Jove,
        Descended swift (the white-armed queen was loath
        The fight should follow, for she favoured both);
300   Just as in act he stood, in clouds enshrined
        Her hand she fastened on his hair behind;
        Then backward by his yellow curls she drew,
        To him, and him alone, confessed in view.
        Tamed by superior force, he turned his eyes,
305   Aghast at first, and stupid with surprise;
        But by her sparkling eyes and ardent look,
        The virgin-warrior known, he thus bespoke:
          'Com'st thou, celestial, to behold my wrongs?
        Then view the vengeance which to crimes belongs.'

---

293. D. adds the suggestion that Agamemnon was surrounded by guards.

294. D.'s addition. Spondanus writes of Achilles' *pars irascibilis* prompting him *ad vindictam* ('to vengeance'). De la Valterie refers to Achilles' desire for 'sa vengeance'.

295. The antithesis on *half* is D.'s addition. Cp. Ogilby: 'His Sword halfe out'. *falchion*] sword.

296. In that nice moment] Cp. de la Valterie: 'en ce moment'.   *nice*] crucial, dangerous (*OED* 11a).

297. th' imperial wife of Jove] For Homer's θεὰ Ἥρη ('the goddess Hera'). Chapman notes that '*Iuno* is Goddess of state'.

298. swift] D.'s addition. Cp. Certon: 'promptement'.

300. D.'s addition.

302. backward, she drew] D.'s additions. Cp. Groto: *a dietro il tira* ('she pulls it back'). *curls*] For Homer's κόμης ('hair'). Thus in Chapman 1611.

303. confessed] revealed (*OED* 5).

304. Tamed by superior force] D.'s addition.

305. For Homer's θάμβησεν ('he was struck with wonder').   *stupid*] stunned (*OED* 1).

306. and ardent look] D.'s expansion. Cp. Chapman 1611: 'ardor'; Groto: *A i fochi ardenti* ('with ardent (fiery) eyes').

307. The virgin-warrior] Homer simply names her as Pallas Athene. Cp. Obsopoeus: *Bellipotens uirgo* ('The virgin powerful in war'); Certon: 'la Deesse guerriere' ('the warrior goddess').

308–9. A freely compressed rendering of Homer's ll. 202–5.

308. celestial] For Homer's αἰγιόχοιο Διὸς τέκος ('aegis-bearing daughter of Zeus'). Cp. Groto: *celeste* ('celestial one').   *my wrongs*] Homer's Achilles refers to Agamemnon's ὕβριν ('insolence').

309. vengeange, crimes] Both in Maynwaring (with no strict equivalent in Homer); Chapman 1611 has *revenge*.

310   Thus he. The blue-eyed goddess thus rejoined:
         'I come to calm thy turbulence of mind,
         If reason will resume her sovereign sway,
         And sent by Juno, her commands obey.
         Equal she loves you both, and I protect;
315   Then give thy guardian gods their due respect,
         And cease contention; be thy words severe,
         Sharp as he merits, but the sword forbear.
         An hour unhoped already wings her way
         When he his dire affront shall dearly pay;
320   When the proud king shall sue, with treble gain,
         To quit thy loss, and conquer thy disdain.
         But thou, secure of my unfailing word,
         Compose thy swelling soul, and sheathe the sword.'
             The youth thus answered mild: 'Auspicious maid,
325   Heaven's will be mine, and your commands obeyed.

---

310. blue-eyed] For Homer's γλαυκῶπις. Thus in Maynwaring. The translation
of the term is disputed by modern scholars (see the edition of *Iliad* I by Simon
Pulleyn (2000) 183–4), but *blue-eyed* was the standard seventeenth-century rendering (for other examples in D., see 'The Last Parting of Hector and Andromache'
l. 19; 'The Second Book of the *Aeneis*' l. 243; 'The Twelfth Book of Ovid's
Metamorphoses' l. 208).

311–12. Echoing Milton's description of the usurpation of the 'sway' of
'sovereign reason' in *PL* ix 1120–31 (J. R. Mason).

313. Juno] For Homer's λευκώλενος Ἥρη ('white-armed Hera').   *her commands
obey*] D.'s addition.

315. D.'s addition. Cp. Chapman 1611: 'Come, giue vs both respects'.

316. contention] For Homer's ἔριδος ('strife'). Cp. Spondanus: *contentione*; Chapman
1611: 'contention'.

317. Sharp as he merits] D.'s addition.

318. unhoped] not hoped for (*OED* 2). D.'s addition.

319. D.'s addition. Cp. Scudamore: 'This combate he shall dearly rue'.

320–1. Homer makes no specific mention of Agamemnon's pride or Achilles'
disdain.

320. with treble gain] Cp. Chapman 1611: 'Will treble . . . in gaine'; Hobbes: 'with
triple gain'; Maynwaring: 'With trebble Gain'.

321. quit] pay for (*OED* 4); repay (*OED* 10).   *disdain*] indignation, anger arising
from offended dignity (*OED* 2, last example 1677).

322. secure of my unfailing word] D.'s addition.

323. swelling] D.'s addition. Cp. Hobbes (earlier): 'This swell'd *Achilles* choler to
the height'.   *sheathe the sword*] For Homer's πείθεο δ᾽ ἡμῖν ('obey us'). Cp. Ogilby:
'sheath thy Sword'.

324. The youth] For Homer's πόδας ὠκὺς Ἀχιλλεύς ('Achilles swift of foot').
mild] D.'s addition. The formula is Miltonic: cp. *PL* v 371; vii 110; ix 226; x 67
(J. R. Mason).   *Auspicious maid*] For Homer's θεά ('goddess'). Cp. Ogilby: 'Bless'd
Mayd'.

325. Heaven's will] D.'s Christian colouring (cp. *RL* l. 121), also deployed in a
classical context in 'The Third Book of the *Aeneis*' l. 480.

The gods are just, and when subduing sense
We serve their powers, provide the recompense.'
He said; with surly faith believed her word,
And in the sheath, reluctant, plunged the sword.

330   Her message done, she mounts the blessed abodes,
And mixed among the senate of the gods.
    At her departure his disdain returned;
The fire she fanned with greater fury burned,
Rumbling within till thus it found a vent:

335   'Dastard and drunkard, mean and insolent;
Tongue-valiant hero, vaunter of thy might,
In threats the foremost, but the lag in fight!
When didst thou thrust amid the mingled preace,
Content to bide the war aloof in peace?

340   Arms are the trade of each plebeian soul;
'Tis death to fight, but kingly to control;

326–7. Cp. de la Valterie: 'les Dieux aiment une parfaite obéïssance, & ne manquent point à la recompenser'.

326. The gods are just] Homer's Achilles refers to the gods' willingness to listen to human beings. *subduing sense*] Cp. Chapman 1611: 'Who subdues his earthly part'.

328. with surly faith] D.'s addition.

329. reluctant] D.'s addition.

330. Her message done] D.'s addition.   *the blessed abodes*] Homer refers to the house of aegis-bearing Zeus. Cp. Ogilby: 'she mounts to thundring *Jove*'s aboads' (rhyming with 'gods'). D. also uses the phrase of Olympus in 'The First Book of Ovid's *Metamorphoses*' l. 215; 'The Second Book of the *Aeneis*' l. 393; 'The Tenth Book' l. 8.

331. the senate of] D.'s addition, also used of the Olympians in 'The Tenth Book of the *Aeneis*' l. 6.

332–4. A free rendering of Homer's ll. 223–4, which simply say that Achilles addressed Agamemnon ἀταρτηροῖς ἐπέεσσιν ('with hurtful words') and that he οὔ πω λῆγε χόλοιο ('did not yet cease from his anger'). The metaphor in l. 334 is frequent in D.: cp. l. 444 below; *The Medal* ll. 295–6; *Eleonora* l. 245; 'Of the Pythagorean Philosophy' ll. 457, 518; 'The Wife of Bath her Tale' ll. 178, 190. It is used in the description of Turnus' outburst of fury against Drances ('The Eleventh Book of the *Aeneis*' l. 584), where Drances is also described as a 'Tongue-valiant Lord' (l. 514) and 'ever foremost in a Tongue debate' (l. 588).

335–6. Apart from *drunkard*, D.'s addition. For *tongue-valiant*, see ll. 332–4*n* and 'The Speeches of Ajax and Ulysses' l. 147.

335. mean and insolent] Cp. de la Valterie: 'lâche et insolent'.

337. Paraphrasing Homer, whose Achilles (l. 225) says that Agamemnon has the face of a dog, but the heart of a deer.

338. preace] battle-throng (*OED* 1b; a variant of *press*: the older spelling is here preserved for the rhyme). Thus in Chapman 1611.

339. D.'s addition.   *bide*] *Eds*; bid *1700*: endure, undergo (*OED* 9).

340. D.'s addition.

341–3. Freely paraphrasing Homer, whose Achilles (ll. 229–30) taunts Agamemnon with taking back the gifts of anyone who opposes him.

Lord-like at ease, with arbitrary power,
To peel the chiefs, the people to devour:
These, traitor, are thy talents; safer far
345   Than to contend in fields, and toils of war.
Nor couldst thou thus have dared the common hate,
Were not their souls as abject as their state.
But by this sceptre solemnly I swear
(Which never more green leaf or growing branch shall bear:
350   Torn from the tree, and given by Jove to those
Who laws dispense, and mighty wrongs oppose)
That when the Grecians want my wonted aid,
No gift shall bribe it, and no prayer persuade.
When Hector comes, the homicide, to wield
355   His conquering arms, with corpse to strew the field,
Then shalt thou mourn thy pride, and late confess
My wrong, repented when 'tis past redress.'
He said; and with disdain in open view

342. *arbitrary power*] This and similar phrases were regularly used in the seventeenth century to denote absolutist ambition (see, e.g., *AA* ll. 212, 330, 701, 762; *The Medal* ll. 142, 249, 314; *HP* i 266). D. had used the phrase in connection with the tyranny of the Roman kings and of Mezentius ('The Eighth Book of the *Aeneis*' ll. 438, 531).

343. *peel*] rob, plunder (*OED* 1). Cp. de la Valterie: 'Vous n'estes propre qu'à piller les peuples' ('You are only good at plundering people').   *devour*] Cp. Spondanus: *populivorator* ('devourer of the people').

344–5. D.'s addition, recapitulating Achilles' earlier arguments; *safer far* and *fields* in Chapman 1611.

346–7. D.'s expansion. Homer's Achilles simply says that if Agamemnon did not rule over οὐτιδανοῖσιν ('nonentities') this would be his last outrage. Groto's Achilles says that Agamemnon's subjects are *Più pusilli di quel, che conuerrebbe* ('more cowardly than they should be').

348–9. Cp. Ogilby: 'Now solemnly I by this Scepter swear, / Which ne're will burgeon more, nor branches bear'; Maynwaring: 'But by this awful Scepter now I swear / (Which ne'er again will happy Branches bear[)]'.

350. D. omits Homer's details (ll. 236–7) of the sceptre's mountain origins and former leaves and bark.   *Torn from the tree*] From Du Souhait: 'apres auoir esté arraché de son arbre'.

351. *and mighty wrongs oppose*] D.'s addition.

353. Homer's Achilles simply says (ll. 240–1) that Agamemnon will not be able to help the Greeks in their distress.

354. *the homicide*] From *homicida*, Spondanus' rendering of Homer's ἀνδροφόνοιο ('man-slaying').

354–5. *to wield / His conquering arms*] D.'s addition.

355. *corpse*] A plural form (*OED* 2c).

357. *My wrong*] i.e. the wrong done to me.   *when 'tis past redress*] Drawing on Homer's ll. 240–1 (cp. l. 353*n*).

358. *with disdain in open view*] D.'s addition. Cp. Maynwaring: 'in Disdain'.

Against the ground his golden sceptre threw,
360   Then sate; with boiling rage Atrides burned,
And foam betwixt his gnashing grinders churned.
   But from his seat the Pylian prince arose,
With reasoning mild, their madness to compose;
Words, sweet as honey, from his mouth distilled;
365   Two centuries already he fulfilled,
And now began the third; unbroken yet,
Once famed for courage, still in council great.
   'What worse,' he said, 'can Argos undergo,
What can more gratify the Phrygian foe,
370   Than these distempered heats, if both the lights
Of Greece their private interest disunites?
Believe a friend, with thrice your years increased,
And let these youthful passions be repressed.
I flourished long before your birth; and then ⎱
375   Lived equal with a race of braver men   ⎬
Than these dim eyes shall e'er behold again. ⎭

360. boiling] D.'s addition.
361. D.'s addition. *grinders*] teeth (*OED* 1a). The description resembles those of Lycaon ('The First Book of Ovid's *Metamorphoses*' ll. 309–10), the boar in 'The Fourth Book of the *Georgics*' l. 400, Alecto ('The Seventh Book of the *Aeneis*' l. 633), and the Calydonian boar ('Meleager and Atalanta' ll. 26–7).
362. Pylian prince] Nestor, King of Pylos.
363. D.'s addition, drawing on Homer's description of Nestor's sweetness of speech and clear-voiced oratory (ll. 247–8). Cp. Maynwaring: 'but *Nestor* rose / With mild Discourse their Fancy to compose'.
364. Cp. Groto: *che stillaua* ('which distilled').
365. centuries] For Homer's γενεαί ('generations', sometimes calculated by the Greeks as three to a century). D. remembers Ovid's account of Nestor (see 'The Twelfth Book of Ovid's *Metamorphoses*' ll. 258–60; see also 'The Tenth Satire of Juvenal' l. 388*n*).
366–7. unbroken yet . . . in council great] D.'s addition, drawing on information provided by Homer elsewhere in the episode. With l. 367, cp. Chapman 1611: 'You, that all our host excell, / In councell'.
366. unbroken] not impaired or weakened (*OED* 3).
368. Argos] For Homer's Ἀχαιΐδα γαῖαν ('the land of Achaea').
369. the Phrygian foe] Cp. Maynwaring: 'the *Phrygian* King'. Phrygia is 'A realme in Asia the lesse, hauing on the east, Cappadocia: on the south, Lycaonia: on the west, Troas: on the north, Galatia' (Thomas Cooper, *Thesaurus Linguae Romanae & Britannicae* (1565)).
371. their private interest disunites] Homer's Nestor refers to their mutual strife.
372–3. For Homer's ἀλλὰ πίθεσθ' ('but do as I say'). Cp. Chapman 1611: 'repell / These young mens passions'.
374. I flourished long before your birth] Homer's Nestor simply says that Agamemnon and Achilles are both younger than he.
375. a race of] D.'s addition. Thus in Maynwaring.
376. dim] D.'s addition.

Caeneus and Dryas, and, excelling them,
Great Theseus, and the force of greater Polypheme.
With these I went, a brother of the war,
380 Their dangers to divide, their fame to share;
Nor idle stood with unassisting hands
When salvage beasts, and men's more salvage bands,
Their virtuous toil subdued: yet those I swayed
With powerful speech: I spoke, and they obeyed.
385 If such as those my counsels could reclaim,
Think not, young warriors, your diminished name
Shall lose of lustre by subjecting rage
To the cool dictates of experienced age.
Thou, king of men, stretch not thy sovereign sway
390 Beyond the bounds free subjects can obey;
But let Pelides in his prize rejoice,
Achieved in arms, allowed by public voice.
Nor thou, brave champion, with his power contend
Before whose throne ev'n kings their lowered sceptres bend;
395 The head of action he, and thou the hand;
Matchless thy force, but mightier his command.
Thou first, O king, release the rights of sway;

377–8. D. omits Homer's mention of Perithous and Exadius. For Caeneus, see 'The Twelfth Book of Ovid's *Metamorphoses*' ll. 609–701.
378. the force of greater] For Homer's ἀντίθεον ('godlike').
379–81. A loose paraphrase of Homer's ll. 269–70. Homer's Nestor simply says that he answered the summons to join with the others.
382. salvage beasts] Homer specifically mentions the centaurs (for whom see 'The Twelfth Book of Ovid's *Metamorphoses*'). *more salvage*] D.'s addition.
385–8. D. expands Nestor's plea (Homer l. 274) that they should listen to his advice, just as the others did.
387–8. Cp. Maynwaring: 'Let me prevail to calm your fatal Rage, / Obey the Dictates of maturer Age'.
389–90. stretch not . . . free subjects can obey] D.'s political emphasis. Homer's Nestor simply advises Agamemnon not to take Briseis. Cp. Maynwaring: 'Stretch not, Atrides, your Prerogative'.
391. For Homer's ἀλλ' ἔα ('but leave her'). Cp. Groto: *fa ch' ei goda in pace* ('make him rejoice in peace').
392. Achieved in arms] D.'s addition. *allowed*] granted as his share (OED 12a). *public voice*] For Homer's reference to the sons of the Achaeans.
393. brave champion] For Homer's Πηλεΐδη ('son of Peleus'). *contend*] Cp. Obsopoeus, Valla: *contendere*; Du Souhait: 'en contention'; Certon: 'contendre'.
394. In Homer, the sceptre (*sing.*) is Agamemnon's. D. adds the idea of other kings bowing their sceptres in deference to him.
395. D.'s addition.
396. Cp. Chapman 1611: 'Yet he of force, is mightier'.
397. release the rights of sway] Homer's Nestor asks Agamemnon to check his temper. *release*] relinquish (OED 4a).

Power self-restrained the people best obey.
Sanctions of law from thee derive their source;
400   Command thyself, whom no commands can force.
The son of Thetis, rampire of our host,
Is worth our care to keep; nor shall my prayers be lost.'
    Thus Nestor said, and ceased. Atrides broke
His silence next, but pondered ere he spoke:
405   'Wise are thy words, and glad I would obey,
But this proud man affects imperial sway,
Controlling kings, and trampling on our state;
His will is law, and what he wills is fate.
The gods have given him strength; but whence the style
410   Of lawless power assumed, or licence to revile?'
    Achilles cut him short, and thus replied:
'My worth, allowed in words, is in effect denied;
For who but a poltroon, possessed with fear,
Such haughty insolence can tamely bear?

398–9. D.'s politicizing addition.

399. Sanctions] decrees (*OED* 1).

400. whom no commands can force] D.'s addition. Cp. Groto: *Hor prima tu, che gli altri regger uuoi / Reggi te stesso* ('you who want to govern others, first govern yourself and your appetites').

401. rampire] person resembling a rampart (*OED* 2, citing this example). For Homer's ἕρκος ('bulwark'). Cp. Salel, Du Souhait, de la Valterie: 'rampart'. *of our host*] For Homer's πολέμοιο κακοῖο ('of evil war'). Cp. Salel: 'de tout le camp Gregeois'; Du Souhait: 'de tous les Grecs'; de la Valterie: 'de nostre Camp'.

402. D.'s expansion.

403. Thus Nestor said, and ceased] D.'s addition. Cp. de la Valterie: 'Aprés qu'il eût cessé de parler'.

403–4. broke / His silence . . . ere he spoke] Homer merely says that he replied.

405. and glad I would obey] D.'s addition. Groto's Agamemnon says that Nestor's words *Mertano ubbidienza* ('merit obedience').

406. proud] D.'s addition. *imperial*] D.'s addition. Cp. Eobanus: *imperium*; Groto: *impero*.

407. trampling on our state] Homer's Agamemnon simply claims that Achilles wants to give orders to all. Cp. Ogilby: 'Would on us trample too'; Grantham: 'but he will bear the sway / Over us all, and domineer as King'.

408. D.'s addition, drawing on Milton's God at *PL* vii 173: 'what I will is fate' (J. R. Mason). Cp. also Chapman 1611: 'giue to all / His hote will for their temperate law'.

409–10. Cp. Chapman 1611: 'If the Gods haue giuen him the great stile / Of ablest souldier; made they that, his licence to reuile / Men with vile language'.

410. lawless power assumed] D.'s addition.

412. D.'s expansion. *in effect*] in fact, in reality (*OED* 8).

413. poltroon] spiritless coward, mean-spirited wretch; for Homer's οὐτιδανὸς ('nonentity'). Cp. Certon: 'poltron'.

414. Such haughty insolence] For Homer's ὅττι κεν εἴπῃς ('whatever you say'). Cp. Eobanus: *superbi / Facta hominis* ('the deeds of a proud man'); Groto: *tanta insolenza* ('such insolence'); *e così altero* ('and so haughty'). *tamely*] D.'s addition.

415   Command thy slaves; my freeborn soul disdains
        A tyrant's curb, and restiff breaks the reins.
        Take this along: that no dispute shall rise
        (Though mine the woman) for my ravished prize;
        But she excepted, as unworthy strife,
420   Dare not, I charge thee dare not, on thy life,
        Touch ought of mine beside, by lot my due,
        But stand aloof, and think profane to view:
        This falchion else, not hitherto withstood,
        These hostile fields shall fatten with thy blood.'
425   He said, and rose the first; the council broke,
        And all their grave consults dissolved in smoke.
        The royal youth retired, on vengeance bent;
        Patroclus followed silent to his tent.
        Meantime, the king with gifts a vessel stores,
430   Supplies the banks with twenty chosen oars;
        And next, to reconcile the shooter god,

415. thy slaves] For Homer's ἄλλοισιν ('others').
415–16. my freeborn soul . . . breaks the reins] For Homer's οὐ γὰρ ἐγώ γ᾽ ἔτι σοὶ
πείσεσθαι ὀίω ('for I think I shall obey you no longer'). Cp. Chapman 1611:
'my free Spirit'. D. uses very similar vocabulary of the proud colt in 'The Third
Book of the *Georgics*' ll. 323–4. Cp. also Almanzor in *The Conquest of Granada* I
i 6–8: 'But know, that I alone am King of me. / I am as free as Nature first
made man / 'Ere the base Laws of Servitude began'.
416. restiff] resisting control (*OED* 1b).
417. along] in addition (*sc.* to what I have already said) (not in *OED*, but see
Johnson 5, citing this example). Cp. Grantham: 'but this from me take'.
418. ravished] seized from me (*OED* 1). Homer's Achilles explains that in seizing
Briseis, Agamemnon is only taking back what he gave.
419. as unworthy strife] D.'s addition.
420. Cp. Chapman 1598, 1610: 'Dare not to touch'; Maynwaring: 'But Tyrant,
on thy Life'.
421. by lot my due] D.'s addition.
422. D.'s addition.
423–4. Paraphrasing Homer's αἶψά τοι αἷμα κελαινὸν ἐρωήσει περὶ δουρί
('at once your dark blood will spurt around my spear').
426. consults] discussions (*OED* 1); stressed on the second syllable.   *dissolved in
smoke*] came to nothing (*OED* smoke 4g). D.'s addition. Cp. Du Souhait (later):
'leur dessein passant en fumée'.
427. The royal youth] For Homer's Πηλείδης ('the son of Peleus').   *on vengeance
bent*] D.'s addition.
428. Patroclus] Homer refers to the son of Menoetus and Achilles' men.   *silent*]
D.'s addition.
429. with gifts] D.'s addition. Thus in Maynwaring.
430. banks] benches for rowers in a galley (*OED* 3).   *oars*] oarsmen (*OED* 3b;
first quotation 1749); thus in Ogilby.
431. shooter] D.'s addition (cp. l. 138*n*).

Within her hollow sides the sacrifice he stowed;
Chryseis last was set on board, whose hand
Ulysses took, entrusted with command;
435   They plough the liquid seas, and leave the lessening
land.
Atrides then, his outward zeal to boast,
Bade purify the sin-polluted host.
With perfect hecatombs the god they graced,
Whose offered entrails in the main were cast;
440   Black bulls and bearded goats on altars lie,
And clouds of savoury stench involve the sky.
These pomps the royal hypocrite designed
For show, but harboured vengeance in his mind;
Till holy malice, longing for a vent,
445   At length discovered his concealed intent.
Talthybius, and Eurybates the just,
Heralds of arms, and ministers of trust,
He called, and thus bespoke: 'Haste hence your way,
And from the goddess-born demand his prey.

432. hollow] D.'s addition, translating the epithet (κοίλησιν) used earlier (l. 26) by Homer.   *the sacrifice*] For Homer's Χρυσηίδα καλλιπάρηον ('the fair-cheeked daughter of Chryseis'). Cp. Groto: *l' almo sacrificio* ('the sweet sacrifice').

433–4. whose hand / Ulysses took] D. adds the visual detail.

435. plough] For Homer's ἐπέπλεον ('sailed over'); *ploughed* in Chapman, Maynwaring. *and leave the lessening land*] D.'s addition.

436. his outward zeal to boast] D.'s addition.

437. sin-polluted] D.'s addition. Cp. Chapman 1598, 1610: 'purgde from polluted blood'; Maynwaring: 'he purify'd the Coast / From foul Pollutions of his sinful Hoast'.

438. perfect] Thus in Chapman; cp. Spondanus: *perfectas*.   *graced*] For Homer's ἔρδον ('they sacrificed'). Thus in Chapman 1611.

439. main] open ocean (*OED* 5a).

440. black, bearded] D.'s additions.

441. involve] envelop (*OED* 1).   *stench*] Only given in pejorative senses in *OED*, but Johnson (2), citing this example, notes that he found it 'used once for a good smell'.

442–5. D.'s pejorative expansion. Homer (ll. 318–19) says that Agamemnon did not cease from the strife with which he had threatened Achilles.

442. pomps] celebrations (*OED* 1), perhaps with suggestions of specious or ostentatious display (*OED* 3).

443. vengeance] Thus in Maynwaring.

444. longing for a vent] Cp. ll. 332–4*n*; cp. Chapman 1611: 'vented'.

446. the just] D.'s addition.

447. Heralds of arms] The term has specific English associations, signifying officers entrusted with delivering royal proclamations and messages (*OED* herald 1a, d). *ministers of trust*] For Homer's ὀτρηρὼ θεράποντε ('zealous squires'); thus in Chapman 1611.

450   If yielded, bring the captive; if denied,
       The king (so tell him) shall chastise his pride,
       And with armed multitudes in person come
       To vindicate his power, and justify his doom.'
          This hard command unwilling they obey,
455   And o'er the barren shore pursue their way,
       Where quartered in their camp the fierce Thessalians lay.
       Their sovereign seated on his chair they find,
       His pensive cheek upon his hand reclined,
       And anxious thoughts revolving in his mind.
460   With gloomy looks he saw them entering in
       Without salute; nor durst they first begin,
       Fearful of rash offence and death foreseen.
       He soon the cause divining, cleared his brow,
       And thus did liberty of speech allow:
465   'Interpreters of gods and men, be bold;
       Awful your character, and uncontrolled:
       Howe'er unpleasing be the news you bring,

---

450. the captive] Homer specifies Briseis καλλιπάρῃον ('with fair cheeks').

451. chastise his pride] D.'s addition.

452–3. D.'s substitution for Homer's τό οἱ καὶ ῥίγιον ἔσται ('and it shall be even the worse for him'). Cp. Chapman 1611: 'with multitudes'; Maynwaring: 'will in Person come, / By force of Conquest to revoke her Doom'.

453. vindicate] maintain, defend against encroachment (*OED* 4).   *doom*] judgement, decision (*OED* 2).

455. barren] For Homer's ἁλὸς ἀτρυγέτοιο ('of the untiring sea'); thus in Chapman 1598, 1610; Ogilby.

457. on his chair] Homer describes Achilles as sitting beside his hut and his black ship.

458–9. D.'s addition; l. 459 is taken almost verbatim from 'The Sixth Book of the *Aeneis*' l. 454 (Aeneas in Hades).

458. pensive] full of anxious thought (*OED* 2; stronger than in modern usage); thus in Ogilby, Maynwaring.

459. revolving] turning over, considering (*OED* 4).

461. salute] greeting (*OED* 1). Thus in Chapman 1598, 1610. Homer says that they neither addressed nor questioned Achilles.

462. Homer says that they were seized with fear and awe of Achilles.

463. divining] intuiting (*OED* 2).   *cleared his brow*] i.e. stopped frowning (see *OED* brow 3a). D.'s addition; for the idiom, cp. Deucalion in 'The First Book of Ovid's *Metamorphoses*' l. 524; Groto: *e'l ciglio leua* ('and he lifts his brow').

464. For Homer's φώνησέν τε ('and said'). Cp. Drances in 'The Eleventh Book of the *Aeneis*' l. 346: *det libertatem fandi* ('let him give liberty of speech').

465. Homer's Achilles addresses them as messengers of Zeus and men. Cp. Chapman 1598, 1610: 'of gods'; de la Valterie: 'divins Interpretes des Dieux & des hommes'.
be bold] Homer's Achilles invites them to draw near.

466–7. D.'s addition.

466. awful] awe inspiring.

I blame not you, but your imperious king.
You come, I know, my captive to demand;
470   Patroclus, give her to the herald's hand,
But you authentic witnesses I bring
Before the gods, and your ungrateful king,
Of this my manifest: that never more
This hand shall combat on the crooked shore:
475   No; let the Grecian powers, oppressed in fight,
Unpitied perish in their tyrant's sight.
Blind of the future, and by rage misled,
He pulls his crimes upon his people's head;
Forced from the field in trenches to contend,
480   And his insulted camp from foes defend.'
He said, and soon obeying his intent,
Patroclus brought Briseis from her tent,
Then to th' entrusted messengers resigned:
She wept, and often cast her eyes behind,

468. Cp. Chapman 1611: 'I nothing blame you, but your king.'   *your imperious king*] Homer names Agamemnon.
470. to the herald's hand] For Homer's σφωιν ('to these two'). Cp. Maynwaring: 'Patroclus, lead her to their awful Hands'.
471. authentic] authoritative (*OED* 1a); D.'s addition.
472. ungrateful] harsh, disagreeable (*OED* 20; in addition to the more usual meaning: *OED* 1).
473–4. Homer's Achilles implies, but does not state explicitly, his resolve never to fight again for the Greeks.
473. manifest] public declaration (*OED* 2, citing this example).
474. the crooked shore] D.'s addition. Cp. l. 660 below. For the phrase, cp. 'The Third Book of the *Aeneis*' l. 311; 'The Seventh Book' l. 200.
475–6. D.'s addition, making clear the 'moral' of the *Iliad*, as stated by Horace (*Epist.* I ii 14): *quidquid delirant reges, plectuntur Achivi* ('whatever folly the kings commit, the Achaeans pay the price'). Cp. Maynwaring: 'When e'er the *Grecian* Pow'rs, oppress'd with Woes'.
477. Blind of the future] A Latinism: cp. Lucan, *De Bello Civile* ii 14 (*caeca futuri*); Claudian, *De Raptu Proserpinae* i 138 (*caecae futuri*). For the expression, cp. 'Cymon and Iphigenia' l. 324.
478. D.'s addition.
479. Homer makes no explicit reference at this point to an attack on the camp, or to the Greeks fighting in trenches. De la Valterie refers to 'les Troyens, qui viendront les attaquer jusques dans leur Camp'.
480. insulted] attacked, assaulted (*OED* 4).
483. th' entrusted messengers] D.'s expansion.
484–6. Homer describes Briseis as going with the heralds unwillingly, and makes no mention of her tears, her looking back, or her love for Achilles. Briseis weeps in Chapman 1598, 1610. Her backward look incorporates memories of Orpheus (see 'The Fourth Book of the *Georgics*' l. 708) and Andromache ('The Last Parting of Hector and Andromache' l. 191). Cp. also Groto: *A dietro il uiso uolge* ('she turned her face behind').

485 Forced from the man she loved; they led her thence,
     Along the shore, a prisoner to their prince.
        Sole on the barren sands the suffering chief
     Roared out for anguish, and indulged his grief;
     Cast on his kindred seas a stormy look,
490 And his upbraided mother thus bespoke:
        'Unhappy parent of a short-lived son,
     Since Jove in pity by thy prayers was won
     To grace my small remains of breath with fame,
     Why loads he this embittered life with shame,
495 Suffering his king of men to force my slave,
     Whom, well deserved in war, the Grecians gave?'
        Set by old Ocean's side the goddess heard,
     Then from the sacred deep her head she reared;
     Rose like a morning mist, and thus begun
500 To soothe the sorrows of her plaintive son:
        'Why cries my care, and why conceals his smart?
     Let thy afflicted parent share her part.'
        Then sighing from the bottom of his breast,
     To the sea goddess thus the goddess-born addressed:
505 'Thou know'st my pain, which telling but recalls;

487. Sole] Homer says that Achilles drew apart from his companions. Cp. Valla: *solus.*
on the barren sands] Cp. l. 455. For Homer's θῖν᾽ ἔφ᾽ ἁλὸς πολιῆς ('on the shore
of the grey sea').
488. Homer's Achilles weeps and prays to his mother. Cp. Groto: *alto sospira* ('with
a deep sigh').   *indulged*] gave way to (*OED* 3).
489. kindred] (i) because they match Achilles' mood (*stormy* is D.'s addition);
(ii) because they are the abode of his mother, the sea nymph Thetis, the daughter
of Nereus, called 'Ocean' by D. (see l. 497 and *n*). Homer's sea is οἴνοπα
('wine-dark').
492–3. D. adds the suggestion that it was as a result of Thetis' prayers that Zeus
had granted Achilles fame as compensation for the shortness of his life.
494. Homer's Achilles complains that Zeus has not honoured him at all.
496. D.'s expansion. Homer's Achilles refers to his γέρας ('prize'). Cp. Valla: *quod
mihi consensus Graiorum honoris ac praemij causa donauerat* ('which the consensus
of the Greeks gave me as a mark of honour and reward'); Chapman 1611: 'that
prize . . . / That all the Greeks gaue'.
497. old Ocean] For Homer's πατρὶ γέροντι ('the old man, her father'). Cp.
Chapman 1598, 1610: 'old *Oceanus*'. Modern commentators identify Thetis'
father as Nereus.
499–500. and thus begun . . . her plaintive son] In Homer (ll. 360–1) Thetis sits down
in front of him, strokes him with her hand, and addresses him by name.
501. my care] the person dear to me, for whom I care (*OED* 5a).
502. Cp. Maynwaring: 'And let thy tender Parent beare her share'.
503. For Homer's βαρὺ στενάχων ('groaning deeply'). Cp. Chapman 1611, Ogilby:
'sighing'; Obsopoeus, Eobanus: *imo de pectore* ('from the bottom of his breast').

By force of arms we razed the Theban walls;
The ransacked city, taken by our toils,
We left, and hither brought the golden spoils:
Equal we shared them; but before the rest,
510   The proud prerogative had seized the best.
Chryseis was the greedy tyrant's prize,
Chryseis, rosy-cheeked, with charming eyes.
Her sire, Apollo's priest, arrived to buy,
With proffered gifts of price, his daughter's liberty.
515   Suppliant before the Grecians' chiefs he stood,
Awful, and armed with ensigns of his god;
Bare was his hoary head; one holy hand
Held forth his laurel crown, and one his sceptre of command.
His suit was common, but above the rest
520   To both the brother-princes was addressed.
With shouts of loud acclaim the Greeks agree
To take the gifts, to set the prisoner free.
Not so the tyrant, who with scorn the priest
Received, and with opprobrious words dismissed.
525   The good old man, forlorn of human aid,
For vengeance to his heavenly patron prayed:
The godhead gave a favourable ear,
And granted all to him he held so dear;

---

506. Theban] Ogilby explains that the reference is to the Thebes 'in *Troas*, so called from that adjoyning Mountain, now *Adramyttium*, where reigned *Eetion* the Father of *Andromache*, married to *Hector*'.
507. ransacked] Thus in Chapman 1598, 1610.   *taken by our toils*] D.'s expansion. Cp. Maynwaring: 'what by their Toils they got'.
508. We left] D.'s addition.   *golden*] D.'s addition.
509. before the rest] D.'s addition.
510. proud] D.'s addition.   *prerogative*] royal power, monarchical right (*OED* 1a); Homer names Agamemnon.
511. the greedy tyrant's] D.'s addition.
512. rosy-cheeked] For Homer's καλλιπάρῃον ('fair-cheeked').   *with charming eyes*] D.'s addition. Cp. l. 741 below (of Juno); 'The Tenth Book of the *Aeneis*' l. 862 (also of Juno).
513–20. A very close repetition of ll. 17–24 above (as in Homer's original).
513. Her sire] Homer names Chryses.
521–2. A close repetition of ll. 35–6.
521. With shouts of loud acclaim] A Miltonic formula: cp. *PL* ii 520, iii 397, vi 23, x 455 (J. R. Mason).
523. the tyrant] Homer names Agamemnon, son of Atreus.
524. opprobrious] contemptuous, abusive (*OED* 1).
525. good] D.'s addition. Thus in Maynwaring.   *forlorn of human aid*] D.'s addition.
526. For vengeance] Homer describes Chryses as χωόμενος ('angry').
526, 527. his heavenly patron, The godhead] Homer names Apollo.

In an ill hour his piercing shafts he sped,
530 And heaps on heaps of slaughtered Greeks lay dead,
While round the camp he ranged: at length arose
A seer who well divined, and durst disclose
The source of all our ills: I took the word,
And urged the sacred slave to be restored,
535 The god appeased: the swelling monarch stormed,
And then the vengeance vowed he since performed.
The Greeks, 'tis true, their ruin to prevent,
Have to the royal priest his daughter sent;
But from their haughty king his heralds came,
540 And seized by his command my captive dame,
By common suffrage given; but thou be won,
If in thy power, t' avenge thy injured son!
Ascend the skies, and supplicating move
Thy just complaint to cloud-compelling Jove.
545 If thou by either word or deed hast wrought
A kind remembrance in his grateful thought,
Urge him by that; for often hast thou said
Thy power was once not useless in his aid,
When he who high above the highest reigns,

529–30. Cp. Chapman 1611: 'The God, an ill shaft sent abrode, / That tumbl'd downe the Greekes in heapes'.
530. heaps on heaps] Cp. l. 16.
532–3. disclose / The source of all our ills] Homer's Achilles says that Calchas declared the oracles of Apollo.
533. took the word] began speaking (OED word 28b, citing only 'The Eleventh Book of the Aeneis' l. 510 between 1557 and 1808).
534. the sacred slave to be restored] D.'s addition.
535–6. Cp. Ogilby: 'Atrides rising then extreamly storm'd / And what he raging threatned hath perform'd'; Maynwaring: 'And urg'd our brutal Chief, who loudly storm'd / To threaten Vengeance, which he since perform'd'; Chapman 1598, 1610: 'performd'.
535. the swelling monarch] In Homer, Agamemnon quickly stands up.
537. their ruin to prevent] D.'s addition.
539. from their haughty king] D.'s addition.
540. by his command] D.'s addition.   my captive dame] Homer names the daughter of Briseus.
541. common suffrage] Cp. l. 245 and n.
542. injured] wronged (OED 1); D.'s addition.
543. the skies] Homer names Olympus.
543–4. move / Thy just complaint, cloud-compelling] D.'s additions, the last rendering νεφεληγερέτα in Homer, l. 511.
547. Urge him by that] D.'s addition.
549. he who high above the highest reigns] Homer refers to the son of Cronos, lord of the dark clouds. Cp. Ecclesiastes v 8: 'he that is higher than the highest' (of God).

550   Surprised by traitor gods, was bound in chains;
      When Juno, Pallas, with ambition fired,
      And his blue brother of the seas conspired,
      Thou freed'st the sovereign from unworthy bands,
      Thou brought'st Briareus with his hundred hands
555   (So called in heaven, but mortal men below
      By his terrestrial name Aegeon know;
      Twice stronger than his sire, who sate above
      Assessor to the throne of thundering Jove).
      The gods, dismayed at his approach, withdrew,
560   Nor durst their unaccomplished crime pursue.
      That action to his grateful mind recall,
      Embrace his knees, and at his footstool fall;
      That now, if ever, he will aid our foes;
      Let Troy's triumphant troops the camp enclose;
565   Ours, beaten to the shore, the siege forsake,
      And what their king deserves, with him partake;
      That the proud tyrant at his proper cost
      May learn the value of the man he lost.'
        To whom the mother-goddess thus replied,
570   Sighed ere she spoke, and while she spoke she cried:

550. *traitor gods*] Homer refers to the other Olympians.

551–2. Cp. Maynwaring: 'When *Juno, Pallas, Neptune*, all conspir'd, / You, *Thetis*, you, with just Resentment fir'd'.

552. *his blue brother of the seas*] Homer names Poseidon.

553–6. Cp. Maynwaring: 'To save the Godhead from ignoble Bands, / Brought up *Briareus* with his Hundred Hands; / Immortals by that Name the Gyant know, / Called Great *Ægëon* in the World below'.

553. *unworthy*] D.'s addition.

557. *his sire*] Cp. Ogilby: 'This *Ægeon* was a Sea-Deity the Son (as some say) of *Neptune*, or (as others) of *Cælum* and *Tellus*'.

558. *Assessor to*] one who shares, or sits beside in (*OED* 1); used of the Son in *PL* vi 679 (J. R. Mason).

559–60. Cp. Maynwaring: 'Then all the Rebel Deities withdrew, / Nor durst their bold, unfinish'd Plot pursue'.

559. *dismayed*] overcome with fear (*OED*); thus in Chapman 1611.

560. Homer says that the gods did not bind Zeus.

561. *grateful*] D.'s addition.

562. *at his footstool fall*] Homer's Achilles asks Thetis to sit by Zeus' side. Cp. Chapman 1598, 1610: 'at his foote'.

565. *the siege forsake*] D.'s addition.

567. *the proud tyrant*] Homer refers to the son of Atreus, wide-ruling Agamemnon. *proper*] own.

568. *the man he lost*] For Homer's ἄριστον Ἀχαιῶν ('the best of the Achaeans').

569. *the mother-goddess*] Homer names Thetis.

570. *Sighed ere she spoke*] D.'s addition. For the formula, cp. 'The Last Parting of Hector and Andromache' l. 147; 'The Twelfth Book of Ovid's *Metamorphoses*' l. 714.

'Ah, wretched me! by Fates averse decreed
To bring thee forth with pain, with care to breed!
Did envious heaven not otherwise ordain,
Safe in thy hollow ships thou shouldst remain,
575   Nor ever tempt the fatal field again;
But now thy planet sheds his poisonous rays,
And short and full of sorrow are thy days.
For what remains, to heaven I will ascend,
And at the Thunderer's throne thy suit commend.
580   Till then, secure in ships, abstain from fight;
Indulge thy grief in tears, and vent thy spite.
For yesterday the court of heaven with Jove
Removed; 'tis dead vacation now above.
Twelve days the gods their solemn revels keep,
585   And quaff with blameless Ethiops in the deep.
Returned from thence, to heaven my flight I take,
Knock at the brazen gates, and Providence awake;

571. wretched me] D.'s addition. Cp. Obsopoeus: *miserum*; Du Souhait: 'miserable';
Grantham: 'Woe's me'.   *by fates averse*] For Homer's κακῇ αἴσῃ ('to an evil
destiny'). Cp. Obsopoeus: *fatis . . . malignis* ('by malign fates').
572. with care to breed] D.'s addition. Cp. Obsopoeus: *sedula cura* ('with diligent
care'); Ogilby: 'And bred with paines'.
573. envious] malicious (*OED* 2).
574. Safe] For Homer's ἀδάκρυτος καὶ ἀπήμων ('without tears and without
grief'). Cp. Obsopoeus: *immunis*.   *hollow*] D.'s addition. Cp. l. 432*n*.
575. D.'s addition. Cp. Grantham: 'And by no means go to the War again'.
576. D.'s astrological elaboration of Homer's reference to Achilles' αἶσα ('destiny').
Cp. 'The Cock and the Fox' ll. 679–84.
578. heaven] Homer refers to snowy Olympus.
579. the Thunderer] Homer refers to Zeus who delights in the thunderbolt. Cp.
ll. 751, 765 below. *Works* notes the use of the formula in *PL* (ii 28, vi 491) and
elsewhere in D. (*Astraea Redux* l. 42; 'Palamon and Arcite' iii 277).
580. Cp. Ogilby: 'And from the Field and bloody Fights abstaine'.
581. Homer's Thetis simply exhorts Achilles to continue his wrath.
582. the court of heaven] Homer refers to the gods. Cp. Ogilby: 'Jove's Celestial
Court'. Cp. the comparison of Olympus with the Louvre in 'The First Book of
Ovid's *Metamorphoses*' ll. 222–7.
583. Removed] changed its residence (*OED* 8b).   *'tis dead vacation now above*] D.'s
addition.   *dead vacation*] The seventeenth-century term for the periods of the year
when the law courts and theatres were inactive (see *LS* lxvii–lxx; *Works* on 'Prologue
to *Marriage A-la-Mode*' l. 18; 'The Sixth Satire of Juvenal' l. 100).
584. their solemn revels keep] D.'s elaboration. For the wording, cp. Shakespeare's
descriptions of the fairies' and Theseus and Hippolyta's feasting in *A Midsummer
Night's Dream* II i 18; IV i 184; V i 355–6.
585. blameless] For Homer's ἀμύμονας ('excellent'); thus in Chapman 1611.
586. Returned] i.e. when Zeus has returned.
587. and Providence awake] D.'s addition, with Christian resonance (cp. l. 686 below).

Embrace his knees, and suppliant to the sire,
Doubt not I will obtain the grant of thy desire.'
590   She said; and parting left him on the place,
Swoll'n with disdain, resenting his disgrace;
Revengeful thoughts revolving in his mind,
He wept for anger, and for love he pined.
    Meantime with prosperous gales Ulysses brought
595   The slave, and ship with sacrifices fraught,
To Chrysa's port; where entering with the tide
He dropped his anchors, and his oars he plied,
Furled every sail, and drawing down the mast,
His vessel moored, and made with hawsers fast.
600   Descending on the plain, ashore they bring
The hecatomb to please the shooter king.
The dame before an altar's holy fire
Ulysses led, and thus bespoke her sire:
'Reverenced be thou, and be thy god adored!
605   The king of men thy daughter has restored,
And sent by me with presents and with prayer;
He recommends him to thy pious care,
That Phoebus at thy suit his wrath may cease,
And give the penitent offenders peace.'
610   He said, and gave her to her father's hands,
Who glad received her, free from servile bands.

---

589. of thy desire] D.'s addition. Cp. Chapman 1611: 'thy desires grant'; de la Valterie: 'ce que vous desirez'.

591–3. A substantial elaboration of Homer's registration of Achilles' anger at the seizure of Briseis (ll. 429–30).

591. resenting his disgrace] Cp. Maynwaring: 'resenting bold Injustice done'.

592. revolving in his mind] A regular formula in D. for brooding cogitation. Cp. l. 459 above, and examples in D.'s *Aeneis*: 'The Third Book' l. 137; 'The Fourth Book' ll. 406, 564; 'The Sixth Book' l. 271; 'The Twelfth Book' l. 968.

594. with prosperous gales] D.'s addition. *prosperous*] favourable (*OED* 2); thus in Ogilby.

596. with the tide] D.'s addition.

600. the plain] i.e. the shore.

601. the shooter king] Cp. l. 32*n*.

602. holy fire] D.'s addition. Cp. Certon: 'le Saint Autel'.

606. with presents and with prayer] Homer refers to a holy hecatomb. Cp. Groto: *con doni . . . e con preci* ('with presents and with prayers').

608–9. Cp. ll. 149–50. Line 609 replaces Homer's reference to the woes and lamentation that Apollo has brought upon the Argives.

608. at thy suit] D.'s addition.

611. free from servile bands] D.'s addition. Cp. Maynwaring: 'To free from servile Bonds'.

This done, in order they with sober grace
Their gifts around the well-built altar place;
Then washed, and took the cakes, while Chryses stood
615　With hands upheld, and thus invoked his god:
　　　'God of the silver bow, whose eyes survey ⎫
　　　The sacred Cilla, thou whose awful sway ⎬
　　　Chrysa the blessed, and Tenedos obey, ⎭
　　　Now hear, as thou before my prayer hast heard
620　Against the Grecians and their prince preferred.
　　　Once thou hast honoured, honour once again
　　　Thy priest, nor let his second vows be vain;
　　　But from th' afflicted host and humbled prince
　　　Avert thy wrath, and cease thy pestilence.'
625　Apollo heard, and conquering his disdain
　　　Unbent his bow, and Greece respired again.
　　　　Now when the solemn rites of prayer were past,
　　　Their salted cakes on crackling flames they cast;
　　　Then, turning back, the sacrifice they sped,
630　The fatted oxen slew, and flayed the dead;
　　　Chopped off their nervous thighs, and next prepared
　　　T' involve the lean in cauls, and mend with lard.
　　　Sweetbreads and collops were with skewers pricked

612. *in order they with sober grace*] For Homer's ἐξείης ('in good array').
614. *cakes*] For Homer's οὐλοχύτας ('barley grains'). Cp. Chapman 1611: 'salt cakes'. As *Works* points out, D. frequently uses the term of sacrifices in his Virgil translations.
616–18. A slightly varied reprise of ll. 58–60 above.
618. *the blessed*] D.'s addition. Thus in Ogilby.
620. *and their prince*] D.'s addition.　*preferred*] offered, presented (*OED* 4).
622. *nor let his second vows be vain*] D.'s addition.
624. *cease*] For Homer's ἄμυνον ('ward off'). Cp. Salel: 'cessa'; Du Souhait: 'faisant cesser'.
625–6. *conquering his disdain . . . Greece respired again*] Homer says that Apollo heard him. Cp. Groto: *sdegno* ('disdain').
628. *on crackling flames*] D.'s addition.
630. *fatted*] D.'s addition. Homer does not state explicitly that the sacrificial victims are oxen.
631. *nervous*] muscular (*OED* 2).　*thighs*] Cp. Ogilby: 'this part alone of the Sacrifice was totally burnt, being wrapped in a double Caul or Leaf of fat, to cause them to burn the clearer, it being esteemed ominous and of an ill presage if they smothered onely, and did not consume with a light flame. The other parts being roasted, were eaten by the Priests and Sacrificers, e're they departed the Temple'.
632. *involve*] roll, enwrap (*OED* 1).　*cauls*] fatty membranes (*OED* 5a). Thus in Ogilby, Scudamore.　*mend*] improve (*OED* 10a).
633. *Sweetbreads and collops*] Cp. Chapman 1611: 'sweet-breads prick'.　*collops*] slices of meat (*OED* 2).　*were with skewers pricked*] D.'s addition. Cp. Scudamore: 'with skew'rs they stuck the cawle'.

About the sides, imbibing what they decked.
635 The priest with holy hands was seen to tine
The cloven wood, and pour the ruddy wine.
The youth approached the fire, and as it burned,
On five sharp broachers ranked, the roast they turned;
These morsels stayed their stomachs, then the rest
640 They cut in legs and fillets for the feast;
Which drawn and served, their hunger they appease
With savoury meat, and set their minds at ease.
    Now when the rage of eating was repelled,
The boys with generous wine the goblets filled:
645 The first libations to the gods they pour,
And then with songs indulge the genial hour;
Holy debauch! till day to night they bring,
With hymns and paeans to the bowyer king.
At sunset to their ship they make return,
650 And snore secure on decks till rosy morn.

634. D.'s addition.   *imbibing*] soaking up (*OED* 4).   *decked*] adorned (*OED* 2).
635. The priest with holy hands] For Homer's ὁ γέρων ('the old man'). Cp. Chapman 1611: 'The Priest'.   *tine*] kindle; a variant of *tind* (*OED* 1) used by Milton (*PL* x 1075).
636. cloven wood] Homer's priest burns the meat on billets of wood. Cp. Hobbes: 'on a fire of cloven wood'.
637. approached the fire, and as it burned] Homer's youths are simply described as beside the priest. Cp. de la Valterie: 'chacun s'approcha' ('each one approached him').
638. sharp] D.'s addition.   *broachers*] spits (*OED* 2, citing this example). Cp. Scudamore: 'broach'.   *turned*] D.'s addition. Cp. Chapman 1611: 'And turnd (in fiue ranks) spits'.
640. in legs and fillets] D.'s addition.
641. drawn] i.e. from the spits.
642. savoury meat] *Works* compares Genesis xxvii 4, 7 etc.   *and set their minds at ease*] Homer says that their hearts did not lack anything of the shared banquet.
643. rage of] desire for, appetite for (*OED* 7a).
644. generous] abundant (*OED* 4a); rich, invigorating (*OED* 5). D.'s addition. Cp. Grantham: 'with generous Wine'.
645. libations] drink offerings.
646. indulge] give themselves up to (*OED* 3).   *genial*] festive (*OED* 2).
647. Holy debauch!] D.'s addition, one of many couplings of *holy* with an unlikely noun. Cp. 'Virgil's Fifth Pastoral' l. 46 (Bacchus' 'holy Revels'); 'The Third Book of the *Georgics*' l. 735 (a priest as 'holy Butcher'); 'The Second Book of the *Aeneis*' l. 749 (Priam 'Slidd'ring thro' . . . holy Mire'); 'The Fifth Book' l. 433 (Nisus falling in 'holy Gore'); 'The Tenth Book' l. 752 (a priest as 'holy Coward'); 'The Twelfth Book' l. 459 ('holy Poniard'); 'Palamon and Arcite' ii 564; 'The Cock and the Fox' l. 482; 'The Wife of Bath her Tale' l. 39 (the 'holy leer' of priests).
648. bowyer king] See l. 138*n*.
650. snore secure] Homer merely says that they slept. Cp. Scudamore: 'snort'. Cp. the Rutulians who 'supinely snore' after their banquet ('The Ninth Book of the *Aeneis*' l. 424).   *on decks*] Homer says that they slept by the stern cables of the ship. Cp. Ogilby: 'on their Decks'.

    The skies with dawning day were purpled o'er;
    Awaked, with labouring oars they leave the shore;
    The power appeased, with winds sufficed the sail,
    The bellying canvas strutted with the gale;
655 The waves indignant roar with surly pride,
    And press against the sides, and beaten off divide.
    They cut the foamy way, with force impelled
    Superior, till the Trojan port they held;
    Then hauling on the strand their galley moor,
660 And pitch their tents along the crooked shore.
    Meantime the goddess-born in secret pined,
    Nor visited the camp, nor in the council joined;
    But keeping close, his gnawing heart he fed
    With hopes of vengeance on the tyrant's head;
665 And wished for bloody wars and mortal wounds,
    And of the Greeks oppressed in fight to hear the dying
        sounds.
    Now when twelve days complete had run their race,
    The gods bethought them of the cares belonging to their
        place.
    Jove at their head ascending from the sea,

651. *purpled*] Miltonic; cp. *PL* vii 29–30 (J. R. Mason). Homer refers to the dawn
as ῥοδοδάκτυλος ('rosy-fingered').
652. Homer simply says that they set sail for the Achaeans' camp.
653. *The power*] Homer names Apollo.   *appeased*] D.'s addition. Thus in Ogilby.
sufficed] provided (with adequate supplies of wind) (*OED* 9).
654. *strutted*] bulged, swelled (*OED* 2a). Cp. Chapman 1611: 'strooted with the gale'.
655. *indignant, with surly pride*] D.'s animistic additions.
656. *against the sides*] For Homer's ἀμφὶ . . . στείρῃ ('around the keel'). Cp. Chapman
1598: 'about her sides'; Hobbes: 'on both sides'.   *and beaten off divide*] D.'s addition.
657. Cp. Ogilby: 'Cutting deep Furrowes through the foamy Flood'.
657–8. *with force impelled / Superior*] D.'s elaboration.
659. *strand*] coast, shore (*OED* 1a).
660. Homer says that they scattered among the huts and ships. For *crooked shore*,
cp. l. 474n. For *tents*, cp. de la Valterie: 'dans leurs tentes'.
661. *in secret pined*] For Homer's μήνιε ('raged'). Cp. Chapman 1611: 'his lou'd
heart pin'd'.
663. *keeping close*] Cp. Chapman 1611: 'But kept close'.   *close*] to himself (*OED* 4).
663–4. *his gnawing heart . . . on the tyrant's head*] Homer says that Achilles allowed
his heart to waste away. Cp. Obsopoeus: *aluit sub pectore flammas* ('he nourished
flames under his breast').
665. *bloody*] D.'s addition.   *mortal wounds*] For Homer's αὐτήν ('battle-shout').
666. D.'s addition. Cp. Eobanus: *Tristia bella avidus gemitusque audire cadentum* ('keen
to hear the sorrows of war and the groans of the fallen'). Groto interprets similarly.
668. *bethought them . . . to their place*] Homer says that they all came to Olympus.
669. *ascending from the sea*] D.'s addition.

670   A shoal of puny powers attend his way.
      Then Thetis, not unmindful of her son,
      Emerging from the deep to beg her boon,
      Pursued their track, and wakened from his rest,
      Before the sovereign stood, a morning guest.
675   Him in the circle but apart she found;
      The rest at awful distance stood around.
      She bowed, and ere she durst her suit begin,
      One hand embraced his knees, one propped his chin;
      Then thus: 'If I, celestial sire, in ought
680   Have served thy will, or gratified thy thought,
      One glimpse of glory to my issue give,
      Graced for the little time he has to live.
      Dishonoured by the king of men he stands;
      His rightful prize is ravished from his hands.
685   But thou, O father, in my son's defence,
      Assume thy power, assert thy providence.
      Let Troy prevail, till Greece th' affront has paid
      With doubled honours, and redeemed his aid.'
        She ceased; but the considering god was mute,

670. D.'s addition. Cp. Ogilby: 'Attending *Jove*'; Maynwaring: 'Where humble Gods Jove's awful Throne attend'.
672–4. *to beg her boon . . . stood, a morning guest*] Homer says that she mounted up to Olympus early in the morning.
676. D.'s addition.   *awful*] reverential, profoundly respectful (*OED* 6).
677. Homer says that she sat down before him.
679–80. Homer's Thetis speaks of having helped Zeus ἢ ἔπει ἢ ἔργῳ ('either in word or deed').
679. *celestial sire*] For Homer's Ζεῦ πάτερ ('father Zeus'). Cp. Chapman 1598, 1610: 'Celestiall *Ioue*'.
681. *One glimpse of*] D.'s addition.   *glimpse*] momentary shining, flash (*OED* 1, citing this example).
682. Cp. Hobbes: 'Short time the Fates have given him to live' (rhyming with 'give').
684. *ravished*] seized. Cp. Certon: 'rauissant'; Du Souhait: 'rauy'.   *from his hands*] D.'s expansion.
685. *O father*] Homer's Thetis addresses him as Olympian Zeus, μητίετα ('lord of counsel').
685–6. *in my son's defence . . . assert thy providence*] Homer's Thetis simply begs Zeus to show Achilles honour. Cp. l. 587 and *n.*
687. *Let Troy prevail*] Thus in Ogilby.
688. *doubled, and redeemed his aid*] D.'s expansions.   *redeemed*] brought back, regained (*OED* 1a,b).
689–90. Cp. Scudamore: 'Thus when she had propos'd her suite / Cloudy *Jove* sate a good while mute'.
689. *considering*] Rendering Homer's earlier epithet for Zeus (see l. 685*n*), rather than νεφεληγερέτα ('cloud-gatherer'), the epithet given at this point in Homer.

690 Till she, resolved to win, renewed her suit,
      Nor loosed her hold, but forced him to reply:
      'Or grant me my petition, or deny;
      Jove cannot fear; then tell me to my face
      That I of all the gods am least in grace.
695 This I can bear.' The cloud-compeller mourned,
      And sighing first, this answer he returned:
          'Know'st thou what clamours will disturb my reign,
      What my stunned ears from Juno must sustain?
      In council she gives licence to her tongue,
700 Loquacious, brawling, ever in the wrong;
      And now she will my partial power upbraid,
      If, alienate from Greece, I give the Trojans aid.
      But thou depart, and shun her jealous sight;
      The care be mine to do Pelides right.
705 Go then, and on the faith of Jove rely,
      When nodding to thy suit he bows the sky.
      This ratifies th' irrevocable doom,
      The sign ordained, that what I will shall come;
      The stamp of heaven, and seal of fate.' He said,

690. resolved to win] D.'s addition.
691. but forced him to reply] Homer says that she asked him a second time. Cp.
Certon: 'le pressoit de respondre'.
692. Or . . . or] Either . . . or.   *grant*] Homer's Thetis asks Jove to nod assent.
693. to my face] D.'s addition.
695. This I can bear] D.'s addition.
696. sighing first] Homer says that Zeus was greatly troubled. Cp. Groto: *Dopo un
sospir* ('after a sigh').
697. my reign] D.'s addition.
698. stunned] D.'s addition.
699. In council] For Homer's ἐν ἀθανάτοισι θεοῖσι ('among the immortal gods').
700. D.'s addition.   *brawling*] quarrelling, scolding (*OED* brawl *v.*[1] 1a, b).   *ever in
the wrong*] Cp. Zimri in *AA* l. 547.
701. partial] biased (*OED* 1).
702. alienate from Greece] D.'s addition.   *alienate*] withdrawn in affection from
(*OED* 1).
703. jealous] D.'s addition.
704. The care be mine] I will see to it (*OED* care 4a).
705. faith] pledge (*OED* 8a). Cp. Scudamore: 'My nod, on that you may rely'.
706. he bows the sky] D.'s addition. For Jove's nod shaking the firmament, cp. 'The
First Book of Ovid's *Metamorphoses*' l. 231. As *Works* notes, the Psalmist invites
God to 'bow' his heavens (Psalm cxliv 5).
707–8. Cp. Chapman 1611: 'Which is the great signe of my will . . . / Irreuocable'.
707. doom] decree (*OED* 1).
709. For Jove's nod as the *seal* of his decrees (D.'s addition), cp. 'The Twelfth
Book of the *Aeneis*' l. 297.

710   And shook the sacred honours of his head:
       With terror trembled heaven's subsiding hill,
       And from his shaken curls ambrosial dews distil.
       The goddess goes exulting from his sight,
       And seeks the seas profound, and leaves the realms of light.
715   He moves into his hall; the powers resort,
       Each from his house, to fill the sovereign's court;
       Nor waiting summons, nor expecting stood,
       But met with reverence, and received the god.
       He mounts the throne; and Juno took her place,
720   But sullen discontent sate louring on her face.
       With jealous eyes at distance she had seen
       Whispering with Jove the silver-footed queen;
       Then impotent of tongue, her silence broke,
       Thus turbulent in rattling tone she spoke:

710. the sacred honours] Homer refers to Zeus' dark brows and divine locks. For *honours* (= adornments) *of his head*, cp. *MF* l. 134, 'The First Book of Ovid's *Metamorphoses*' l. 768; 'The Tenth Book of the *Aeneis*' l. 172. The usage is Virgilian (e.g. *Aen.* i 591).

711. With terror] D.'s addition.   *heaven's subsiding hill*] Homer refers to great Olympus. *subsiding*] sinking, tending downwards (Johnson, citing this example).

712. dews distil] D.'s addition. Cp. *PL* v 56–7 (J. R. Mason).   *distil*] drop.

713. exulting] D.'s addition.

714. profound] For Homer's βαθεῖαν ('deep'). Cp. Spondanus, Obsopoeus: *profundum*; Certon, de la Valterie: 'profond'.

716. Each from his house] Homer says that the gods rose together from their seats. Cp. 'The First Book of Ovid's *Metamorphoses*' l. 215, where the gods 'issue from their blessed abodes' to attend Jove's 'council'. D. colours the scene with recollections of more modern courts, as had de la Valterie when describing the gods revering Zeus, 'leur Roy' 'sur son Trône d'or'. *House* can also signify a temple (*OED* 2b) and (significantly in the light of D.'s association of the Olympian gods with the signs of the zodiac in 'Palamon and Arcite') an astrological seat or sign (*OED* 8a).

718. with reverence] Cp. Groto (marginal note): *Riuerenza* ('bow'); Loredano: *e fecer reverenza* (Sowerby).

719–20. and Juno took her place . . . on her face] D.'s addition.

720. louring] Cp. Scudamore: 'lowred' (of Jove).

721. With jealous eyes at distance] D.'s additions. Cp. Chapman 1598, 1610: 'her ielous view'.

722. Whispering] Homer's Hera sees that Thetis has taken counsel with Zeus. Cp. Groto: *Murmure bisbigliar* ('whispering and murmuring').

723. D.'s addition.   *impotent of*] not able to restrain (*OED* 3).

724. turbulent in rattling tone] Homer says that she addresses Zeus κερτομίοισι ('with heart-cutting words'). For *turbulent*, cp. Achitophel at *AA* l. 153.   *rattling*] scolding (*OED* 7a).

725   'Author of ills, and close contriver Jove,
         Which of thy dames, what prostitute of love,
         Has held thy ear so long, and begged so hard
         For some old service done, some new reward?
         Apart you talked, for that's your special care:
730   The consort never must the council share.
         One gracious word is for a wife too much;
         Such is a marriage vow, and Jove's own faith is such.'
             Then thus the sire of gods, and men below:
         'What I have hidden, hope not thou to know.
735   Ev'n goddesses are women; and no wife
         Has power to regulate her husband's life.
         Counsel she may; and I will give thy ear
         The knowledge first of what is fit to hear.
         What I transact with others, or alone,
740   Beware to learn, nor press too near the throne.'
             To whom the goddess with the charming eyes:
         'What hast thou said, O tyrant of the skies?
         When did I search the secrets of thy reign,

725. Author of ills] D.'s addition. Cp. *PL* ii 381; vi 262 (of Satan) (J. R. Mason).
and close contriver Jove] D.'s addition. Cp. Shakespeare, *Macbeth* III v 8 (of Hecate):
'The close contriver of all harms'.   *close*] secretive (*OED* 7).
726–8. D.'s freely expansive rendering of Homer's l. 540: τίς δὴ αὖ τοι, δολομῆτα,
θεῶν συμφράσσατο βουλάς ('who of the gods, crafty one, has been taking
counsel with you?'). D. gives Juno a tone similar to that of Ovid's goddess, upbraid-
ing her husband over his liaison with the 'Strumpet' and 'triumphant Whore'
Callisto in *Met.* ii (see Addison's translation in *Ovid's Metamorphoses, in Fifteen
Books*, edited by Samuel Garth (1717) 56–7).
730–2. D. adds the stress on Juno's grievances as a neglected wife. Cp. Ogilby:
'I of your secret counsells must not share.'
732. faith] fidelity, loyalty (*OED* 10); pledge, promise (*OED* 8a).
734. What I have hidden] Homer's Zeus simply refers to his μύθους ('words'). D.'s
passage is coloured with echoes of Raphael's warnings against any attempt to 'search'
for 'secrets' that God has chosen to 'hide from common sight': cp. *PL* vii 118–25;
viii 66–75, 167–8 (J. R. Mason).
735–7. Ev'n goddesses are women . . . counsel she may] D.'s generalizing expansion.
Homer's Zeus tells Hera that his words will prove harsh for her, even though she
is his wife. Zeus in Chapman 1611 refers to 'what fits thy womans eare to heare'.
739. with others] D.'s addition.
740. nor press too near the throne] D.'s expansion. Cp. Salel: 'Tu ne doibs point plus
auant me presser' ('You should not press me any further').
741. Identical line in 'The Tenth Book of the *Aeneis*' l. 862.   *the goddess with the
charming eyes*] For Homer's βοῶπις πότνια Ἥρη ('the ox-eyed, queenly Hera').
742. O tyrant of the skies] For Homer's αἰνότατε Κρονίδη ('most dread son of
Cronos'). Juno's characterization of Jove parallels Achilles' of Agamemnon (l. 511),
and D.'s of the Presbyterians' conception of God (*HP* i 219).
743. Cp. de la Valterie: 'vous ay-je demandé jamais vos secrets?'

Though privileged to know, but privileged in vain?
745 But well thou dost, to hide from common sight
Thy close intrigues, too bad to bear the light.
Nor doubt I but the silver-footed dame,
Tripping from sea, on such an errand came,
To grace her issue at the Grecians' cost,
750 And for one peevish man destroy an host.'
　　To whom the Thunderer made this stern reply:
'My household curse, my lawful plague, the spy
Of Jove's designs, his other squinting eye!
Why this vain prying, and for what avail?
755 Jove will be master still, and Juno fail.
Should thy suspicious thoughts divine aright,
Thou but becom'st more odious to my sight
For this attempt; uneasy life to me,
Still watched and importuned, but worse for thee.
760 Curb that impetuous tongue, before too late
The gods behold, and tremble at thy fate;
Pitying, but daring not in thy defence
To lift a hand against omnipotence.'
　　This heard, th' imperious queen sate mute with fear,

744. D.'s addition.
745–6. Homer's Hera accuses Zeus of planning, untroubled, whatever he likes.
748. D.'s addition. Homer's Hera expresses her fear that Thetis has beguiled Zeus.
749. issue] See l. 681*n*.
750. for one peevish man] D.'s addition.
752–3. A free expansion of Homer's δαιμονίη, αἰεὶ μὲν ὀίεαι, οὐδέ σε λήθω ('You are incredible! You are always imagining things, and I can keep nothing from you'). Cp. Groto: *Così dunque tu nuoi femmina ria / I mei consigli andar sempre spiando* ('So then, wretched female, you always want to spy on my thoughts').
752. lawful] Because she is Jove's wife.
755. D.'s addition. *still*] always.
756–7. Homer's Jove says that if Hera is right, his desires will nevertheless prevail. D. follows Spondanus: *Suspicione tua nihil proficies . . . quin & eo nomine magis odiosa esse mihi incipis* ('You will not accomplish anything by your suspicion, . . . no, you will be more odious to me on that account').
758–9. uneasy life to me . . . but worse for thee] D.'s expansion.
760. Curb that impetuous tongue] Cp. Chapman 1611: 'curbe your tongue'. *impetuous*] D.'s addition.
761. and tremble at thy fate] D.'s addition.
762. Pitying] D.'s addition.
763. omnipotence] Homer's Jove threatens to lay irresistible hands on Hera. Milton's God is referred to as 'the omnipotent' (*PL* i 49; vi 136) (J. R. Mason).
764. imperious] D.'s replacement for Homer's repeated epithets (for which see l. 741*n*). *sate mute*] D.'s addition. A Miltonism: cp. *PL* ii 420; iii 217; ix 1064 (J. R. Mason).

765   Nor further durst incense the gloomy Thunderer:
       Silence was in the court at this rebuke,
       Nor could the gods abashed sustain their sovereign's look.
         The limping smith observed the saddened feast,
       And hopping here and there (himself a jest)
770   Put in his word, that neither might offend,
       To Jove obsequious, yet his mother's friend:
       'What end in heaven will be of civil war,
       If gods of pleasure will for mortals jar?
       Such discord but disturbs our jovial feast;
775   One grain of bad embitters all the best.
       Mother, though wise yourself, my counsel weigh;
       'Tis much unsafe my sire to disobey;
       Not only you provoke him to your cost,
       But mirth is marred, and the good cheer is lost.

765. Homer describes Hera as curbing her dear heart. Cp. Hobbes: 'And take heed you no farther me incense'.

767. Homer simply says that the gods were troubled.

768. *The limping smith*] Homer refers to Hephaestus, the famed craftsman. Cp. Ogilby: '*Vulcan* was twice cast out of Heaven: once by his Mother *Juno*, presently after his Birth, for his Deformity, by which Fall he was maimed, albeit the *Scholiast* makes him born lame: again by *Jupiter*, upon this occasion. *Hercules*, after the sacking of *Troy*, for the Cheat put upon him by *Laomedon*, (who, instead of the immortal Horses he had promised him, put him off with mortal) was driven in his return by a Tempest, procured by *Juno*'s implacable hatred, upon the Island *Cos*, whose Inhabitants, affrighted, as at the sight of some savage Beast, forced him with Stones from their Walls: for which inhospitable Treatment he took and sacked their City. *Jupiter*, coming to the knowledge of what had passed after he awaked, (*Juno* having cast him into a sleep, the better to compasse her ends) highly incensed, hung her up in her own Element, the Air, and taking *Vulcan* by the Leg, who attempted to unbind her, threw him out of Heaven into the Island *Lemnos*, thence ever after held sacred to him'.

768–9. *observed the saddened feast . . . himself a jest*] D.'s addition, perhaps prompted (*Works*) by the gods' later mirth (Homer ll. 599–600) when they see Hephaestus' bustling and puffing.

770–1. Homer refers to Hephaestus' attempts to calm Hera.

772. *civil war*] D.'s addition.

773. *gods of pleasure*] D.'s addition.   *jar*] wrangle, bicker (*OED* 12). For the collocation with *civil war*, cp. 'Prologue to *Marriage A-la-Mode*' ll. 3–4; 'The Fourth Book of the *Georgics*' ll. 94–5.

774. Cp. Ogilby: 'And discord spoile the Musick of our Feast'.   *jovial*] For Homer's ἐσθλῆς ('good').

775. Homer's Hephaestus notes that the feast will be spoilt since the worse prevails. *Works* notes that D.'s formulation is close to several proverbial phrases: Tilley A 294, C 585, E 246, S 308, S 774, W 240.

777–9. D.'s addition. With l. 778, cp. Eobanus: *ne patrem forte lacessas* ('lest you provoke my father by chance').

780 Tempt not his heavy hand, for he has power
To throw you headlong from his heavenly tower;
But one submissive word which you let fall
Will make him in good humour with us all.'
He said no more, but crowned a bowl unbid;
785 The laughing nectar overlooked the lid;
Then put it to her hand, and thus pursued:
'This cursèd quarrel be no more renewed:
Be, as becomes a wife, obedient still;
Though grieved, yet subject to her husband's will.
790 I would not see you beaten; yet afraid
Of Jove's superior force, I dare not aid.
Too well I know him, since that hapless hour
When I and all the gods employed our power
To break your bonds; me by the heel he drew,
795 And o'er heaven's battlements with fury threw.
All day I fell; my flight at morn begun,
And ended not but with the setting sun.

780. Tempt not his heavy hand] Homer's Hephaestus floats the possibility that Zeus might be minded to cast the gods from Olympus.
781. headlong] D.'s addition. Cp. *PL* i 45; vi 864.   *from his heavenly tower*] For Homer's ἐξ ἑδέων ('from our seats').
782. one submissive word] For Homer's ἐπέεσσι . . . μαλακοῖσιν ('gentle words').
784. crowned] filled to overflowing (*OED* 8). D.'s addition. Thus in Chapman 1611; Eobanus: *coronant.*   *unbid*] D.'s addition.
785. D.'s addition. *Laughing* and *overlooked* are common images in this context. Cp. Spenser, *FQ* II xii 548: 'the Rubine, laughing sweetly red'; Richard Crashaw, 'Psalme 23' l. 56: 'How my cup o'erlooks her Brims' (*Poems*, edited by L. C. Martin (1957) 104); Charles Cotton, 'Ode' ('Come, let us drink away the time') ll. 34–5: 'Fill up the Goblet, let it swim / In foam, that overlooks the brim' (*Poems*, edited by John Buxton (1958) 222).
787–9. Homer's Hephaestus exhorts his mother to endure, despite her grief.
791. dare] D.'s intensification.
792. hapless] unfortunate. For the story, see l. 768*n*.
793. and all the gods] For Homer's ἄλλοτ' ('on another occasion'). Cp. Chapman 1611: 'other Gods'.
794–9. D. echoes Milton's description of the fall of Mulciber (*PL* i 740–6), which had in turn echoed this moment in Homer: 'Men called him Mulciber; and how he fell / From heaven, they fabled, thrown by angry Jove / Sheer o'er the crystal battlements: from morn / To noon he fell, from noon to dewy eve, / A summer's day; and with the setting sun / Dropped from the zenith like a falling star, / On Lemnos the Ægæan isle'.
794. To break your bonds] For Homer's ἀλεξέμεναι ('to help').   *heel*] For Homer's ποδὸς ('foot'). Thus in Chapman 1611.
795. with fury] D.'s addition.
796. my flight at morn begun] D.'s addition.

Pitched on my head, at length the Lemnian ground
Received my battered skull, the Sinthians healed my wound.'
800   At Vulcan's homely mirth his mother smiled,
And smiling took the cup the clown had filled.
The reconciler bowl went round the board,
Which, emptied, the rude skinker still restored.
Loud fits of laughter seized the guests, to see
805   The limping god so deft at his new ministry.
The feast continued till declining light;
They drank, they laughed, they loved, and then 'twas night.
Nor wanted tuneful harp, nor vocal choir:
The Muses sung, Apollo touched the lyre.
810   Drunken at last, and drowsy, they depart,
Each to his house, adorned with laboured art
Of the lame architect. The thundering god,
Ev'n he withdrew to rest, and had his load;
His swimming head to needful sleep applied,
815   And Juno lay unheeded by his side.

798. on my head] D.'s addition.

799. Sinthians] The inhabitants of Lemnos (see l. 768*n*).

800. homely mirth] D.'s addition.   *his mother*] Homer names Hera.

801. clown] jester (*OED* 3).

802–3. A free rendering of Homer's description (ll. 597–8) of Hephaestus pouring wine for the gods, from left to right. Cp. Chapman 1611: 'The sweete-peace-making-draught went round'.

802. reconciler] D.'s addition. Cp. Certon: 'Vulcan intervient & la reconcilie'.

803. skinker] tapster, potman (*OED* 1). Chapman 1611 (marginal note): 'Vulcan skinker to the Gods'; Hobbes: 'To see the lame and sooty *Vulcan* skink'.   *still*] continuously. Cp. Eobanus: *pleno iterum cratere exhausta refundens* ('refilling the bowl when it was drained').

805. Homer simply refers to Hephaestus ποιπνύοντα ('puffing') through the palace. *ministry*] service, function (*OED* 2). Groto's gods delight to see Hephaestus *amministrarsi* ('administer') the drinks.

807. Homer says that their hearts lacked nothing of the shared feast.

808. wanted] lacked.

810. Drunken at last] D.'s addition.

811. laboured] accomplished with great skill (*OED* 3).

812. architect] D.'s addition. Used of Mulciber in *PL* i 732 (J. R. Mason). Cp. also Valla: *domos, quas . . . Vulcanus architectatus est* ('the palaces of which Vulcan was the architect').

813. had his load] has as much drink as he could take (*OED* 5a). Cp. 'Virgil's Sixth Pastoral' l. 21 (of Silenus). Homer says that Zeus goes to his usual sleeping place.

814. swimming] D.'s addition. Cp. Scudamore: 'with a giddy head'.   *needful*] For Homer's γλυκὺς ('sweet').

815. unheeded] D.'s addition.

27 The Cock and the Fox

Date and publication. First printed 1700 in *Fables Ancient and Modern* (see headnote to 'Palamon and Arcite' for further details). Numerous textual problems in this poem suggest that D. did not read proofs, perhaps because of ill health.

Sources. D. translates Chaucer's *The Nun's Priest's Tale*. For D.'s versions of Chaucer see headnote to 'Palamon and Arcite'. His adaptation of the original shows that he was particularly interested in the issues of astrology, predestination, foreknowledge, and freewill that the story raises. In addition, several passages deploy vocabulary from Milton's *PL*, as recorded in the notes. For these see further T. A. Mason, 'Dryden's Chaucer' (unpublished PhD thesis, Cambridge (1977)), and Taylor Corse, *Milton Quarterly* xxvii (1993) 109–18.

The Cock and the Fox
or
The Tale of the Nun's Priest

There lived, as authors tell, in days of yore
A widow somewhat old, and very poor:
Deep in a dell her cottage lonely stood,
Well thatched, and under covert of a wood.
5   This dowager, on whom my tale I found,
Since last she laid her husband in the ground,
A simple sober life in patience led,   *fu non ill'vila effuts the in the original*
And had but just enough to buy her bread:
But housewifing the little heaven had lent,
10   She duly paid a groat for quarter rent,
And pinched her belly with her daughters two
To bring the year about with much ado.

¶**27**. *1.* D.'s addition.
3. dell] Noyes, Kinsley (cp. 'dale' in Chaucer); Cell *1700*, Scott, *Works*. *OED* cell *sb.*[1] 3c offers the meaning 'lonely nook' (adopted as a gloss here by *Works*), but its examples refer either to a building (such as a cottage) or to the den of a beast (cp. *HP* ii 663), not to a location in which a building might stand, which is what is required here. D. often uses *cell* for a rural cottage (usually contrasted with a court: see 'Epilogue Spoken to the King' l. 11; *Secret Love* III i 185; *Tyrannic Love* III i 48) but not for a valley.
8. D.'s addition.
9. housewifing] managing the household thriftily.
10. D.'s expansion of Chaucer's 'rent'.   *quarter rent*] rent due every three months.
11. daughters] Eds; daughter *1700*.
12. D.'s addition.   *bring the year about*] complete the year (*OED* bring 11b), i.e. survive for a whole year.

>The cattle in her homestead were three sows,
>An ewe called Mally, and three brinded cows;
15 Her parlour window stuck with herbs around
>Of savoury smell, and rushes strewed the ground.
>A maple dresser in her hall she had,
>On which full many a slender meal she made;
>For no delicious morsel passed her throat:
20 According to her cloth she cut her coat.
>No poignant sauce she knew, no costly treat,
>Her hunger gave a relish to her meat.
>A sparing diet did her health assure,
>Or sick, a pepper posset was her cure.
25 Before the day was done, her work she sped,
>And never went by candle light to bed.
>With exercise she sweat ill humours out,
>Her dancing was not hindered by the gout.
>Her poverty was glad, her heart content,
30 Nor knew she what the spleen or vapours meant.
>Of wine she never tasted through the year,
>But white and black was all her homely cheer:
>Brown bread and milk (but first she skimmed her bowls)
>And rashers of singed bacon on the coals.
35 On holy days, an egg or two at most,
>But her ambition never reached to roast.

13. *cattle*] livestock (*OED* 4).
14. *brinded*] brown; streaked or spotted (*OED*).
15–16. D.'s addition.
17. *a maple dresser*] For 'Well sooty was her boure'.
20. Proverbial (Tilley C 472). For 'Her diet was accordaunt to her cote [small farm]'.
21. *poignant*] piquant (*OED* 2).   *treat*] feast (*OED* 4).
22. D.'s addition.
24–6. D.'s addition.
24. *posset*] drink of hot milk mixed with ale or wine and spices, as a remedy for colds (*OED*).
25. *sped*] finished (*OED* 8–9).
27. *sweat*] past tense.
29–30. D.'s addition.
29. *glad*] borne with cheerfulness (*OED* 2b; only example is 'glad poverte' from Chaucer's 'The Wife of Bath's Tale' l. 1183; cp. D.'s 'The Wife of Bath her Tale' l. 465).
30. *spleen*] ill humour, irritability (*OED* 6).   *vapours*] hypochondria, hysteria (*OED* 3b).
34. *singed*] The bacon is cut from the carcass of a pig that has been passed over a flame to remove the bristles (*OED* singe 1a).
35. *holy days*] *Holy-Days* in *1700* might also be modernized as 'holidays'.
36. D.'s addition.

A yard she had with pales enclosed about,
Some high, some low, and a dry ditch without.
Within this homestead lived without a peer
40 For crowing loud, the noble Chanticleer:
So hight her cock, whose singing did surpass
The merry notes of organs at the mass.
More certain was the crowing of this cock
To number hours, than is an abbey clock;
45 And sooner than the matin bell was rung,
He clapped his wings upon his roost, and sung:
For when degrees fifteen ascended right,
By sure instinct he knew 'twas one at night.
High was his comb, and coral red withal,
50 In dents embattled like a castle wall;
His bill was raven black, and shone like jet,
Blue were his legs, and orient were his feet:
White were his nails, like silver to behold,
His body glittering like the burnished gold.
55 This gentle cock for solace of his life
Six misses had beside his lawful wife;
Scandal that spares no king, though ne'er so good,
Says they were all of his own flesh and blood:
His sisters both by sire and mother's side,
60 And sure their likeness showed them near allied.

41. hight] was called (*OED* 5). Thus Chaucer; the word was archaic by D.'s day.
42. merry] pleasant, sweet sounding; thus in Chaucer (of music or voices: *OED* 3; last example 1535, but cp. Shakespeare, *Love's Labours Lost* (*c.* 1594–5) V ii 907). Again at ll. 578, 622.
43. this] *Works*; a *1700*, Kinsley; the *Scott, Noyes*.
45–6. D.'s addition.
45. matin] Matins is the monastic office sung at midnight or daybreak; in the Anglican church it is the service of morning prayer; also in poetic use (*OED* 2a) the morning song of birds.
47–8. 'Fifteene degrees of the equinoctiall rise euery equall houre: so that when 15 degrees were ascended in the Horizon after midnight (for so he meaneth) then it is one of the clocke, about the which time is the first cocke, as they call it' (Speght sig. Bbbbvi').
48. instinct] stressed on the second syllable.
50. dents] indentations (*OED sb.*² 1, last example).   *embattled*] crenellated.
52. orient] shining, esp. bright red like the dawn (*OED* 2b).
55. solace] delight, recreation, enjoyment (*OED* 2).
56–67. For 'Seuen hennes, to done his pleasaunce, / Which were his susters and his paramours, / And wonder like to him, as of colours'. There may be allusions here to rumours about Charles II's relations with his sister the Duchess of Orleans, and to the cousinhood of William and Mary.
56. misses] mistresses.

But make the worst, the monarch did no more
Than all the Ptolemies had done before:
When incest is for int'rest of a nation,
'Tis made no sin by holy dispensation.
65   Some lines have been maintained by this alone,
Which by their common ugliness are known.
        But passing this as from our tale apart,
Dame Partlet was the sovereign of his heart:
Ardent in love, outrageous in his play,
70   He feathered her a hundred times a day:
And she that was not only passing fair,
But was withal discreet and debonair,
Resolved the passive doctrine to fulfil,
Though loath, and let him work his wicked will.
75   At board and bed was affable and kind,   ⎫
According as their marriage vow did bind,   ⎬
And as the church's precept had enjoined.   ⎭
Ev'n since she was a sennight old, they say,   ⎫
Was chaste, and humble to her dying day,   ⎬
80   Nor chick nor hen was known to disobey.   ⎭
        By this her husband's heart she did obtain:

62. Ptolemies] Greek rulers of Egypt in the last three centuries BC, some of whom married their own sisters.
63–6. Kinsley suggests that this refers to Henry VIII, who was given a papal dispensation to marry his brother's widow, Catherine of Aragon. Henry's second thoughts about the legality of this marriage were instrumental in his break with Rome and the establishment of the Church of England (see *HP* i 351–4*n*). Line 66 probably refers to the 'Habsburg lip', a protruding lower jaw in the Austrian and Spanish royal families, which was a notorious instance of hereditary deformity resulting from inbreeding.
69. D.'s addition.
70. feathered] Thus Chaucer: covered her with his feathers while copulating (*OED* 6, citing only this example and Chaucer); again at l. 437.
72. debonair] Thus Chaucer: kindly, courteous, pleasant (*OED*).
73–7. D.'s addition.
73. passive doctrine] An allusion to the doctrine of passive obedience, whereby a subject is supposed not to rebel against (while not actively supporting) a ruler whom he regards as illegal or oppressive. It was preached by some Anglican clergy after the Revolution of 1688–9, who urged the people not to resist William III even though they did not regard him as the legitimate ruler.
75. board and bed] The standard phrase 'bed and board', deriving from the pre-Reformation marriage service (*OED* bed 1c), denoted full marital relationships, sexual and domestic, between man and wife.   *kind*] includes the meaning 'sexually compliant' (*OED* 6).
78. sennight] week.
79–80, 82–6. D.'s additions.

What cannot beauty joined with virtue gain!
She was his only joy, and he her pride;
She, when he walked, went pecking by his side:
85   If spurning up the ground he sprung a corn,
The tribute in his bill to her was borne.
But O! what joy it was to hear him sing
In summer, when the day began to spring,
Stretching his neck, and warbling in his throat,
90   *Solus cum sola* then was all his note.
For in the days of yore the birds of parts
Were bred to speak and sing, and learn the liberal arts.
     It happed that perching on the parlour beam
Amidst his wives, he had a deadly dream,
95   Just at the dawn, and sighed, and groaned so fast
As every breath he drew would be his last.
Dame Partlet, ever nearest to his side,
Heard all his piteous moan, and how he cried
For help from gods and men; and sore aghast
100 She pecked and pulled, and wakened him at last.
'Dear heart,' said she, 'for love of heaven declare
Your pain, and make me partner of your care.
You groan, sir, ever since the morning light,
As something had disturbed your noble sprite.'

85. spurning] trampling, stirring with the foot (*OED* 5b, citing this example).
89–90. D.'s addition.
90. Solus cum sola] 'A man and a woman alone together'. Thomas Coryate heard
men and women sing this song as they bathed together in the hot baths at Baden,
Switzerland, and found it 'sweet & most amorous' (Thomas Coryate, *Coryats Crudities*
(1611) 404; *Works*). There was also a lute piece by John Dowland called *Solus
cum sola* (see Diana Poulton, *John Dowland* (1982) 121). The phrase was part of
a medieval Latin proverb, *Solus cum sola in lecto non presumuntur orare Pater noster*
('a man and a woman alone in bed together are not assumed to be praying "Our
Father"'): see Hans Walter, *Proverbia Sententiaeque Latinitatis Medii Aevi* v (1967)
no. 87a.   *note*] song, esp. of a bird (*OED* note *sb.*[2] 3); possibly punning on the
medieval meaning of *note* as 'occupation' (*OED* note *sb.*[1] 2, last example 1513).
91–2. For 'For that time, as I haue vnderstond, / Beestes and birdes could speake
and sing'.
91. parts] abilities, accomplishments.
92. liberal arts] the medieval scholastic curriculum, comprising the *trivium* (grammar,
logic, and rhetoric) and the *quadrivium* (arithmetic, geometry, music, and astronomy)
(*OED* art 7a).
96. D.'s addition.
99. For . . . men] D.'s addition.
100, 102. D.'s additions.
104. D.'s addition.   *As*] As if.   *sprite*] spirit.

105   'And, madam, well I might,' said Chanticleer,
        'Never was shrovetide cock in such a fear.
        Ev'n still I run all over in a sweat,
        My princely senses not recovered yet.
        For such a dream I had of dire portent
110   That much I fear my body will be shent:
        It bodes I shall have wars and woeful strife,
        Or in a loathsome dungeon end my life.
        Know, dame, I dreamt within my troubled breast ⎫
        That in our yard I saw a murderous beast   ⎬
115   That on my body would have made arrest.   ⎭
        With waking eyes I ne'er beheld his fellow,
        His colour was betwixt a red and yellow;
        Tipped was his tail, and both his pricking ears,
        With black, and much unlike his other hairs;
120   The rest, in shape a beagle's whelp throughout,
        With broader forehead and a sharper snout:
        Deep in his front were sunk his glowing eyes,
        That yet methinks I see him with surprise.
        Reach out your hand: I drop with clammy sweat,
125   And lay it to my heart, and feel it beat.'
           'Now fie for shame,' quoth she, 'by heaven above
        Thou hast for ever lost thy lady's love;
        No woman can endure a recreant knight:
        He must be bold by day, and free by night.
130   Our sex desires a husband or a friend
        Who can our honour and his own defend;
        Wise, hardy, secret, liberal of his purse;
        A fool is nauseous, but a coward worse;

106–8. D.'s addition.
106. *shrovetide cock*] Shrove Tuesday was celebrated with cock-fighting and cock-throwing (Bonnie Blackburn and Leofranc Holford-Strevens, *Oxford Companion to the Year* (1999) 606).
109. *portent*] stressed on the second syllable.
110–11. D.'s addition.
110. *shent*] injured; destroyed (*OED* 3).
115. *made arrest*] seized (*OED* arrest *sb.* 7, citing Chaucer).
116, 120. D.'s additions.
122. *front*] face.
123. *surprise*] alarm, terror (*OED* 4a).
124–5. D.'s addition.
124. *drop*] drip (*OED* 2).
128. *recreant*] cowardly.
129. D.'s addition, except for *free*: eager, willing (*OED* 20b).
130. *friend*] lover (D.'s addition, as is l. 131).
133. For 'ne no foole'.

No bragging coxcomb, yet no baffled knight.
135 How dar'st thou talk of love, and dar'st not fight?
How dar'st thou tell thy dame thou art afeared:
Hast thou no manly heart, and hast a beard?
    'If aught from fearful dreams may be divined,
They signify a cock of dunghill kind.
140 All dreams, as in old Galen I have read,
Are from repletion and complexion bred:
From rising fumes of indigested food,
And noxious humours that infect the blood.
And sure, my lord, if I can read aright,
145 These foolish fancies you have had tonight
Are certain symptoms (in the canting style)
Of boiling choler, and abounding bile:
This yellow gall that in your stomach floats
Engenders all these visionary thoughts.
150 When choler overflows, then dreams are bred
Of flames and all the family of red:
Red dragons and red beasts in sleep we view,
For humours are distinguished by their hue.
From hence we dream of wars and warlike things,
155 And wasps and hornets with their double wings.
    'Choler adust congeals our blood with fear,
Then black bulls toss us, and black devils tear.
In sanguine airy dreams aloft we bound;
With rheums oppressed we sink in rivers drowned.

---

134. For 'ne none auantour [boaster]'. *coxcomb*] fool; from the fool's cap or 'cocks-comb' (*OED*), an obvious joke here. *baffled*] disgraced, dishonoured (*OED*).
138–9. D.'s addition.
140. Galen] Greek physician (AD 129–*c.*199), whose writings were the cornerstone of medical theory through the Middle Ages. D.'s addition.
141. repletion] Thus Chaucer ('repleccions'): overeating. *complexion*] Thus Chaucer ('commpleccions'): the combination of the four bodily humours, according to medieval physiology.
146. D.'s addition. *canting*] using jargon.
147. choler] one of the four humours, supposed to cause irascibility (*OED*); *bile* and *yellow gall* are synonyms.
148–9, 153. D.'s additions.
156. Choler adust] black bile, another of the humours, thought to cause melancholy (*OED*).
158–9. D.'s addition, to complete the list of the four humours.
158. sanguine] The predominance of the blood over the other three humours was said to cause a *sanguine* disposition, courageous, hopeful and amorous (*OED*).
159. rheums] phlegm, the fourth of the humours, cold and moist, leading to indolence and apathy (*OED*).

160   'More I could say, but thus conclude my theme:
       The dominating humour makes the dream.
       Cato was in his time accounted wise,
       And he condemns them all for empty lies.
       Take my advice, and when we fly to ground ⎫
165   With laxatives preserve your body sound,   ⎬
       And purge the peccant humours that abound. ⎭
       I should be loath to lay you on a bier,
       And though there lives no 'pothecary near
       I dare for once prescribe for your disease,
170   And save long bills, and a damned doctor's fees.
           'Two sovereign herbs which I by practice know,
       And both at hand (for in our yard they grow)
       On peril of my soul shall rid you wholly
       Of yellow choler, and of melancholy;
175   You must both purge and vomit, but obey,
       And for the love of heaven make no delay.
       Since hot and dry in your complexion join,
       Beware the sun when in a vernal sign;
       For when he mounts exalted in the ram,
180   If then he finds your body in a flame,
       Replete with choler, I dare lay a groat
       A tertian ague is at least your lot:
       Perhaps a fever (which the gods forfend)
       May bring your youth to some untimely end.
185   And therefore, sir, as you desire to live,
       A day or two before your laxative
       Take just three worms, nor under nor above,

161. D.'s addition.
162. Cato] See ll. 203–4n.
166. peccant] morbid, causing disorder of the bodily system (OED 3).
167. D.'s addition.
168. 'pothecary] Apothecaries were pharmacists, dispensing drugs, but from c. 1700 they gradually became general medical practitioners (OED). Cp. l. 407n.
170. D.'s addition. For other sceptical remarks about doctors cp. ll. 401–7 and 'To John Driden of Chesterton' ll. 71–2, 92–3.
171. sovereign] especially efficacious (OED 3).
173–4. D.'s addition.
178. in a vernal sign] During the spring, which was regarded as beginning on 10 or 11 March, at the beginning of the astrological sign Aries (the ram of l. 179) (J. C. Eade, The Forgotten Sky (1985) 120).
179. D.'s addition.
182. tertian] occurring on alternate days (OED).
184–5. D.'s addition.
187. under] Scott, Noyes, Christie, Works; over 1700, Kinsley.

Because the gods unequal numbers love.
These digestives prepare you for your purge
190   Of fumitory, centaury, and spurge,
And of ground ivy add a leaf or two,
All which within our yard or garden grow.
Eat these, and be, my lord, of better cheer:
Your father's son was never born to fear.'
195   'Madam,' quoth he, 'gramercy for your care,
But Cato, whom you quoted, you may spare:
'Tis true, a wise and worthy man he seems,
And (as you say) gave no belief to dreams;
But other men of more authority,
200   And, by th' immortal powers, as wise as he,
Maintain with sounder sense that dreams forbode,
For Homer plainly says they come from God.
Nor Cato said it, but some modern fool
Imposed in Cato's name on boys at school.
205   'Believe me, madam, morning dreams foreshow
Th' events of things, and future weal or woe.
Some truths are not by reason to be tried,
But we have sure experience for our guide.
An ancient author, equal with the best,
210   Relates this tale of dreams among the rest.
'Two friends, or brothers, with devout intent
On some far pilgrimage together went.
It happened so that when the sun was down
They just arrived by twilight at a town;

188. D.'s addition, drawing on Virgil, *Ecl.* viii 75 (Christie).
189. digestives] medicines promoting digestion; stressed on the first and third syllables.
190. fumitory, centaury] From Chaucer: herbs regarded as having hot and dry qualities (*Riverside Chaucer* 938).   *spurge*] D.'s addition; plant of the genus *Euphorbia*, thought to have medicinal qualities (*OED*).
195. gramercy] Thus Chaucer: thank you.
200, 202–4. D.'s additions.
202. Homer plainly says] *Iliad* i 63, and D.'s 'The First Book of Homer's *Ilias*' l. 93.
203. Nor Cato said it] Chanticleer points out that the Cato cited by Partlet is not Marcus Porcius Cato, the Censor (234–149 BC), but 'Dionysius Cato', supposed author of the medieval school text *Disticha de Moribus ad Filium*, which advises one to take no heed of dreams (*Riverside Chaucer* 844, 937).
206. events] outcomes.   *weal*] happiness.
207. D.'s addition, recalling the Hind's arguments in *HP* ii 105–25.
209. An ancient author] Cicero, *De Divinatione* i 27 is the source of the following two stories (Christie). The vagueness is Chaucer's. Speght notes: 'Namely *Valerius Maximus* in his first booke and the seuenth chapter telleth this history of two Arcadians trauelling to Megara' (sig. Bbbbvi[r]).

215   That day had been the baiting of a bull,
      'Twas at a feast, and every inn so full
      That no void room in chamber or on ground,
      And but one sorry bed was to be found:
      And that so little it would hold but one,
220   Though till this hour they never lay alone.
          'So were they forced to part; one stayed behind,
      His fellow sought what lodging he could find:
      At last he found a stall where oxen stood,
      And that he rather chose than lie abroad.
225   'Twas in a farther yard without a door,
      But for his ease, well littered was the floor.
          'His fellow, who the narrow bed had kept,
      Was weary, and without a rocker slept:
      Supine he snored, but in the dead of night
230   He dreamt his friend appeared before his sight,
      Who with a ghastly look and doleful cry
      Said, "Help me, brother, or this night I die:
      Arise and help, before all help be vain,
      Or in an ox's stall I shall be slain."
235   'Roused from his rest he wakened in a start,
      Shivering with horror, and with aching heart;
      At length to cure himself by reason tries: ⎫
      'Twas but a dream, and what are dreams but lies? ⎬
      So thinking changed his side, and closed his eyes. ⎭
240   His dream returns; his friend appears again: ⎫
      "The murd'rers come; now help, or I am slain."   ⎬
      'Twas but a vision still, and visions are but vain. ⎭
          'He dreamt the third: but now his friend appeared
      Pale, naked, pierced with wounds, with blood besmeared.
245   "Thrice warned, awake," said he, "relief is late;
      The deed is done; but thou revenge my fate.
      Tardy of aid, unseal thy heavy eyes,
      Awake, and with the dawning day arise;
      Take to the western gate thy ready way,

215–16, 218–20. D.'s additions.
224. D.'s addition.   abroad] in the open air (OED 3).
226. D.'s addition.   littered] covered with straw (OED 5; first example).
228–9. D.'s additions.
228. rocker] nurse or attendant who rocks a child in a cradle (OED sb.¹ 1).
231, 236–7. D.'s additions.
240–2. For 'Thus twise in his slepe dremed he'.
244–7. For 'and said I now am slawe: / Beholde my bloody woundes, depe and wide'.

250 For by that passage they my corpse convey:
My corpse is in a tumbril laid, among
The filth and ordure, and enclosed with dung.
That cart arrest, and raise a common cry:
For sacred hunger of my gold I die."
255 Then showed his grisly wounds, and last he drew
A piteous sigh, and took a long adieu.
  'The frighted friend arose by break of day,
And found the stall where late his fellow lay.
Then of his impious host enquiring more,
260 Was answered that his guest was gone before.
"Muttering he went," said he, "by morning light,
And much complained of his ill rest by night."
This raised suspicion in the pilgrim's mind,
Because all hosts are of an evil kind,
265 And oft, to share the spoil, with robbers joined.
  'His dream confirmed his thought: with troubled look
Straight to the western gate his way he took.
There, as his dream foretold, a cart he found,
That carried compost forth to dung the ground.
270 This when the pilgrim saw, he stretched his throat
And cried out "Murther!" with a yelling note.
"My murthered fellow in this cart lies dead:
Vengeance and justice on the villain's head!
You magistrates who sacred laws dispense,
275 On you I call to punish this offence."
  'The word thus given, within a little space
The mob came roaring out, and thronged the place.
All in a trice they cast the cart to ground,
And in the dung the murthered body found,
280 Though breathless, warm, and reeking from the wound.
Good heaven, whose darling attribute we find
Is boundless grace and mercy to mankind,

---

250. D.'s addition.
251. *tumbril*] cart, esp. one used for dung (*OED* 3).
254. *sacred hunger of my gold*] From Virgil's *auri sacra fames* (*Aen.* iii 57). *sacred*]
accursed (*OED* 6, citing this example).
259, 262, 264–5. D.'s additions.
279. *found*] Eds; bound 1700.
280. D.'s addition. *reeking*] bleeding (*OED* 2c).
281. *darling*] favourite (*OED* B).
282–4. D.'s addition. The idea that *grace* is *boundless* counters the Protestant (esp.
Calvinist) insistence that God's grace is limited to the elect. Cp. ll. 508–22n.

Abhors the cruel, and the deeds of night
By wondrous ways reveals in open light.
285 Murther may pass unpunished for a time,
But tardy justice will o'ertake the crime;
And oft a speedier pain the guilty feels:
The hue and cry of heaven pursues him at the heels,
Fresh from the fact, as in the present case: ⎫
290 The criminals are seized upon the place, ⎬
Carter and host confronted face to face. ⎭
Stiff in denial, as the law appoints
On engines they distend their tortured joints:
So was confession forced, th' offence was known,
295 And public justice on th' offenders done.
     'Here may you see that visions are to dread:
And in the page that follows this, I read
Of two young merchants, whom the hope of gain
Induced in partnership to cross the main:
300 Waiting till willing winds their sails supplied, ⎫
Within a trading town they long abide, ⎬
Full fairly situate on a haven's side. ⎭
     'One evening it befell that, looking out,
The wind they long had wished was come about:
305 Well pleased they went to rest, and if the gale
'Till morn continued, both resolved to sail.
But as together in a bed they lay,
The younger had a dream at break of day.
A man, he thought, stood frowning at his side, ⎫
310 Who warned him for his safety to provide, ⎬
Not put to sea, but safe on shore abide. ⎭
"I come, thy genius, to command thy stay: ⎫
Trust not the winds, for fatal is the day, ⎬
And death unhoped attends the watery way." ⎭

287–9. D.'s addition.
289. fact] crime.
292. D.'s addition.
293. engines] machines (of torture).
295. For 'And were honged by the necke bone'.
304. come about] turned to a different quarter (*OED* 49b).
312. genius] guardian spirit.
313–14. For 'If thou to morow wende, / Thou shalt be dreint, my tale is at an ende'.
314. unhoped] unexpected (*OED* 1a; only seventeenth-century example is from D.'s 'The Tenth Book of the *Aeneis*' l. 990, but cp. *Astraea Redux* l. 140).

315   'The vision said; and vanished from his sight.
        The dreamer wakened in a mortal fright;
        Then pulled his drowsy neighbour, and declared
        What in his slumber he had seen and heard.
        His friend smiled scornful, and with proud contempt
320   Rejects as idle what his fellow dreamt.
        "Stay who will stay: for me no fears restrain,
        Who follow Mercury the god of gain.
        Let each man do as to his fancy seems:
        I wait not, I, till you have better dreams.
325   Dreams are but interludes which fancy makes: ‖
        When monarch reason sleeps, this mimic wakes,
        Compounds a medley of disjointed things,
        A mob of cobblers, and a court of kings.
        Light fumes are merry, grosser fumes are sad;
330   Both are the reasonable soul run mad.
        And many monstrous forms in sleep we see
        That neither were, nor are, nor e'er can be.
        Sometimes forgotten things long cast behind
        Rush forward in the brain, and come to mind.
335   The nurse's legends are for truths received,
        And the man dreams but what the boy believed.
           ' "Sometimes we but rehearse a former play: ⎫
        The night restores our actions done by day,   ⎬
        As hounds in sleep will open for their prey.   ⎭
340   In short, the farce of dreams is of a piece,
        Chimeras all, and more absurd, or less.
        You, who believe in tales, abide alone:

315. D.'s addition.
320–41. For 'No dreme (q[uo]d. he) may so my herte agaste, / That I woll let for to do my thinges: / I set not a strawe for thy dreminges, / For sweuens [dreams] ben but vanities and iapes: / Men meten [think] all day of oules and of apes, / And eke of many a mase therewithall, / And dremen of a thing that neuer was, ne shall'.
322. Mercury was the god of merchants and thieves.
325–6. Drawing on Milton's account of how 'mimic fancy wakes' in dreams (*PL* v 110; J. R. Mason).
325. interludes] farcical plays (*OED* 1).
326. mimic] burlesque actor (*OED* 1).
329. fumes] noxious vapours supposed to rise from the stomach to the brain (*OED* 4).
330. reasonable soul] See 'Palamon and Arcite' iii 1076–7*n.*
332. Almost verbatim from 'Lucretius: Against the Fear of Death' l. 225.
337. rehearse] repeat (*OED* 1b).

Whate'er I get this voyage is my own."
          'Thus while he spoke he heard the shouting crew
345   That called aboard, and took his last adieu.
       The vessel went before a merry gale,
       And for quick passage put on every sail.
       But when least feared, and ev'n in open day,
       The mischief overtook her in the way:
350   Whether she sprung a leak, I cannot find,
       Or whether she was overset with wind,
       Or that some rock below her bottom rent,
       But down at once with all her crew she went.
       Her fellow ships from far her loss descried,
355   But only she was sunk, and all were safe beside.
          'By this example you are taught again
       That dreams and visions are not always vain:
       But if, dear Partlet, you are yet in doubt,
       Another tale shall make the former out.
360   'Kenelm, the son of Kenulph, Mercia's king,
       Whose holy life the legends loudly sing,
       Warned in a dream, his murther did foretell
       From point to point as after it befell;
       All circumstances to his nurse he told
365   (A wonder, from a child of seven years old).
       The dream with horror heard, the good old wife
       From treason counselled him to guard his life,
       But close to keep the secret in his mind,
       For a boy's vision small belief would find.
370   The pious child, by promise bound, obeyed,
       Nor was the fatal murther long delayed:

343–4. D.'s addition.
346–8. D.'s addition.
346. merry] favourable (*OED* 1d); cp. 'Horace: *Odes* III xxix' l. 101.
350–1. D.'s addition.
351. overset] overturned, capsized (*OED* 3).
355. D.'s addition.
360. Mercia] The Old English kingdom of Mercia occupied the area now known as the Midlands.
361–75. For '*Kenelm* mette [dreamt] a thing, / A little er he were murdered on a day: / His murder in this vision he say [saw]: / His norice [nurse] him expounded it euery dele [part] / His sweuen [dream], and badde him keepe him wele / Fro trayson, but he was but seuen yere olde, / And therefore little tale [heed] he thereof tolde / Of any dreme, so holy was his herte: / By God, I had rather than my sherte, / That ye haue herde his legend, as haue I'.
366. wife] woman of humble rank or employment (*OED* 1).

By Quenda slain he fell before his time,
Made a young martyr by his sister's crime.
The tale is told by venerable Bede,
375 Which at your better leisure you may read.
     'Macrobius too relates the vision sent
To the great Scipio with the famed event;
Objections makes, but after makes replies,
And adds that dreams are often prophecies.
380 'Of Daniel you may read in holy writ,   ⎫
     Who, when the king his vision did forget,   ⎬
     Could word for word the wondrous dream repeat. ⎭
Nor less of patriarch Joseph understand,
Who by a dream enslaved th' Egyptian land:
385 The years of plenty and of dearth foretold,
When for their bread, their liberty they sold.
Nor must th' exalted butler be forgot,
Nor he whose dream presaged his hanging lot.
     'And did not Croesus the same death foresee,
390 Raised in his vision on a lofty tree?
The wife of Hector in his utmost pride
Dreamt of his death the night before he died.

---

372. Quenda] D. took the name of Kenelm's sister Quenda (not in Chaucer's text) from Speght's note (sig. Bbbbvi').

374. Bede] Kinsley notes that Kenelm (son of Kenulf, King of Mercia, d. 821) lived after Bede (*c*.673–735).

376. Macrobius] Cicero's *Somnium Scipionis*, originally the final chapter in his *De Republica*, was edited with a commentary by Macrobius (early fifth century AD). P. Cornelius Scipio Aemelianus dreamt of his future, which included the possibility of death at the hands of his kinsmen (VI xii).

377. event] outcome.

378. D.'s addition.

380–2. See Daniel ii. Lines 381–2 are D.'s addition.

383–8. See Genesis xl–xli, xlvii. Joseph correctly interpreted the dream of Pharaoh's butler as signifying that he would be restored to the king's favour, and his baker's dream as signifying that he would be hanged. He interpreted the king's dream as presaging seven years of plenty followed by seven years of famine, so the king laid in stocks of corn. When the famine arrived, the people exchanged their livestock, and eventually their land, for bread: 'the Egyptians sold every man his field, because the famine prevailed over them: so the land became Pharaoh's' (Genesis xlvii 20).

384–6. D.'s addition, with contemporary political implications in l. 386.

389–90. At the end of *The Monk's Tale* Chaucer recounts that Croesus, King of Lydia, had a dream that foretold his death by hanging.

391–5. Andromache's dream is not given in classical sources for the Trojan war; Chaucer takes it from Dares Phrygius, *De Excidio Troiae Historia*.

391. pride] most flourishing state or condition (*OED* 9).

Well was he warned from battle to refrain,
But men to death decreed are warned in vain:
395   He dared the dream, and by his fatal foe was slain.
     'Much more I know, which I forbear to speak,
For see, the ruddy day begins to break:
Let this suffice, that plainly I foresee
My dream was bad, and bodes adversity.
400   But neither pills nor laxatives I like:
They only serve to make a well man sick.
Of these his gain the sharp physician makes,
And often gives a purge, but seldom takes:
They not correct but poison all the blood,
405   And ne'er did any but the doctors good.
Their tribe, trade, trinkets, I defy them all,
With every work of 'Pothecaries' Hall.
     'These melancholy matters I forbear;
But let me tell thee, Partlet mine, and swear,
410   That when I view the beauties of thy face,
I fear not death, nor dangers, nor disgrace.
So may my soul have bliss, as when I spy
The scarlet red about thy partridge eye,
While thou art constant to thy own true knight,
415   While thou art mine, and I am thy delight,
All sorrows at thy presence take their flight.
For true it is, as *in principio*,
Mulier est hominis confusio.
Madam, the meaning of this Latin is
420   That woman is to man his sovereign bliss.
For when by night I feel your tender side,
Though for the narrow perch I cannot ride,
Yet I have such a solace in my mind,
That all my boding cares are cast behind;

---

395. dared] defied.
401–7. 'For they ben venemous, I wete it wele: / I hem defie, I loue hem neuer a dele'.
407. 'Pothecaries' Hall] Apothecaries' Hall, the headquarters of the Apothecaries' Company, and scene of the controversy recorded in Samuel Garth's poem *The Dispensary* (1699). Cp. 'To John Driden of Chesterton' ll. 104*n*, 107*n*.
411, 414–17. For 'It maketh al my drede for to dien'.
417. in principio] 'in the beginning' (the opening of John i 1).
418. Mulier est hominis confusio] 'woman is man's confounding', a widespread medieval saying (see *Riverside Chaucer* 939).
420. sovereign] chief, principal.
422. ride] copulate.

425   And ev'n already I forget my dream.'
       He said, and downward flew from off the beam;
       For daylight now began apace to spring,
       The thrush to whistle, and the lark to sing;
       Then crowing clapped his wings, th' appointed call
430   To chuck his wives together in the hall.
           By this the widow had unbarred the door,
       And Chanticleer went strutting out before,
       With royal courage, and with heart so light,
       As showed he scorned the visions of the night.
435   Now roaming in the yard he spurned the ground,
       And gave to Partlet the first grain he found.
       Then often feathered her with wanton play,
       And trod her twenty times ere prime of day;
       And took by turns and gave so much delight
440   Her sisters pined with envy at the sight.
           He chucked again when other corns he found,
       And scarcely deigned to set a foot to ground,
       But swaggered like a lord about his hall,
       And his seven wives came running at his call.
445   'Twas now the month in which the world began
       (If March beheld the first created man),
       And since the vernal equinox, the sun

428. D.'s addition.
430. chuck] call together by making a clucking noise (*OED* 2; only transitive example).
431–2. D.'s addition.
433. courage] spirit (*OED* 3); pride, boldness (*OED* 3b; last example 1608); lust, sexual vigour (*OED* 3e, last example 1615).
435–6. D.'s addition.
435. spurned] See l. 85*n.*
438. trod] copulated with (*OED* 8). *prime*] the first hour of the day, six o'clock or sunrise (*OED* 2).
439–40. D.'s addition.
443. For 'As royal as a prince in his hall'.
445–6. According to medieval belief, the world was created at the vernal equinox (*Riverside Chaucer*).
447–8. This is a crux in Chaucer. The text in Speght reads: 'When . . . / . . . March . . . / Was complete, and passed were also, / Sith *March* began twenty daies and two'. Modern editors of Chaucer say that the date intended is 3 May (the same day as the fight of Palamon and Arcite), i.e. 32 days after the end of March, not 22 days after its beginning: the error may be Chaucer's or a scribe's. Speght's note draws attention to an error here: 'This place is misprinted, as well in misnaming of the signe, as the misreckoning the degrees of the sun: for that the two and twenty of March, the sunne is in Aries, and that but eleuen degrees or thereabouts, and hath in all but thirty degrees' (sig. Bbbbvi^r). Aries begins to be in the ascendant at the vernal equinox.

In Aries twelve degrees or more had run,
When casting up his eyes against the light,
450 Both month and day and hour he measured right,
And told more truly than th' Ephemeris,
For art may err, but nature cannot miss.
     Thus numbering times and seasons in his breast,
His second crowing the third hour confessed;
455 Then turning, said to Partlet, 'See, my dear,
How lavish Nature has adorned the year:
How the pale primrose and blue violet spring,
And birds essay their throats disused to sing:
All these are ours, and I with pleasure see
460 Man strutting on two legs, and aping me!
An unfledged creature of a lumpish frame,
Endued with fewer particles of flame:
Our dame sits cowering o'er a kitchen fire,
I draw fresh air, and Nature's works admire:
465 And ev'n this day in more delight abound
Than since I was an egg I ever found.'
     The time shall come when Chanticleer shall wish
His words unsaid, and hate his boasted bliss:
The crested bird shall by experience know ⎤
470 Jove made not him his masterpiece below, ⎬
And learn the latter end of joy is woe.   ⎦
The vessel of his bliss to dregs is run,
And heaven will have him taste his other tun.
     Ye wise draw near, and hearken to my tale,

451–2. For 'He knew by kinde [nature], and by none other lore'.
451. Ephemeris] astronomical almanac showing the predicted positions of the heavenly bodies (*OED* 3).
453–4. D.'s addition.
453. times and seasons] Biblical (e.g. Acts i 7).
454. confessed] declared, announced (approx. *OED* 1 or 5).
456–66. For 'Herken how these blisful birdes sing, / And see the fresh floures how they gan spring: / Full is mine hert of reuel, and solas'.
458. essay] try.
460–1. See *AA* ll. 170, 172*nn.*
462. flame] soul; cp. *AA* ll. 156–8*n.*
467–70. D.'s addition.
471. Proverbial: Tilley J 85.
472–3. D.'s addition.
473. other tun] D. alludes to *Iliad* xxiv 527–8, where on Zeus' floor there are two urns, one with blessings and one with evils (Noyes, citing Joseph Warton). *tun*] barrel; any large vessel (*OED* 1, 1b).

475   Which proves that oft the proud by flattery fall:
        The legend is as true, I undertake,
        As *Tristram* is, and *Launcelot of the Lake*,
        Which all our ladies in such reverence hold
        As if in *Book of Martyrs* it were told.
480   A fox full fraught with seeming sanctity,
        That feared an oath, but like the devil would lie,
        Who looked like Lent, and had the holy leer,
        And durst not sin before he said his prayer:
        This pious cheat, that never sucked the blood
485   Nor chawed the flesh of lambs—but when he could—
        Had passed three summers in the neighbouring wood;
        And musing long whom next to circumvent,
        On Chanticleer his wicked fancy bent;
        And in his high imagination cast
490   By stratagem to gratify his taste.
           The plot contrived, before the break of day
        Saint Reynard through the hedge had made his way;
        The pale was next, but proudly with a bound

---

475. D.'s addition. The subtitle to the reprint of Chaucer's text in *Fables* 611 says: 'The Moral whereof is, *To embrace True Friends, and to beware of Flatterers*'.

477. Tristram] D.'s addition. The legends of Tristram (or Tristan) and Lancelot are parts of the Arthurian cycle.

479. D.'s addition, an anti-Protestant allusion. John Foxe's *Actes and Monuments* (1563), commonly known as the *Book of Martyrs*, catalogued the sufferings of Protestants under the Marian persecutions. D. impugns its veracity. The allusion prepares for a pun on *fox* in l. 480.

480–5. For 'A col [black-tipped] fox (ful of sleight and iniquitie)', adding an extended emphasis on religious hypocrisy.

480. full fraught with] Milton's phrase for Satan in *PL* ii 1054 (J. R. Mason).

481. Quakers and other Nonconformists refused to swear oaths (cp. *HP* i 38). The devil was said to be the father of lies (John viii 44).

485. chawed the flesh of lambs] Echoes Milton (*PL* iii 434), where Satan like a Tartar will 'gorge the flesh of lambs' (J. R. Mason). The imagery recalls Jesus' instruction to his disciples to 'feed my lambs', i.e. his followers (John xxi 15).   *chawed*] by-form of 'chewed' (*OED*).

487–8. D.'s addition.

487. circumvent] capture by stratagem; outwit (*OED* 1, 3).

490. D.'s addition.

492. Saint Reynard] D.'s addition.   *Saint*] a designation claimed by Puritans: cp. *AA* l. 529.

493–4. D.'s addition, echoing Milton: Satan 'in contempt, / At one slight bound high overleaped all bound . . . / Leaps o'er the fence' (*PL* iv 180–1, 186; J. R. Mason). The imagery in Milton relates partly to the corruption of the church. Cp. *HP* ii 313*n*.

He leapt the fence of the forbidden ground;
495 Yet fearing to be seen, within a bed
Of coleworts he concealed his wily head;
There skulked till afternoon, and watched his time
(As murd'rers use) to perpetrate his crime.
     O hypocrite, ingenious to destroy,
500 O traitor, worse than Sinon was to Troy,
O vile subverter of the Gallic reign,
More false than Gano was to Charlemagne!
O Chanticleer, in an unhappy hour
Didst thou forsake the safety of thy bower!
505 Better for thee thou had'st believed thy dream,
And not that day descended from the beam!
     But here the doctors eagerly dispute:
Some hold predestination absolute:

---

494. forbidden] Also Miltonic: 'the fruit / Of that forbidden tree' (*PL* i 1–2).
496. coleworts] cabbages.
498. use] are accustomed to do.
499. D.'s addition.
500. Sinon's lying tale persuaded the Trojans to break down the walls of their city to bring in the wooden horse, which was full of Greek soldiers (*Aen.* ii 57–198).
501. D.'s addition, punning on Latin *gallus* ('cock'), and glancing at Louis XIV's grandiose monarchy. The cock is the emblem of France. See Charles H. Hinnant, *SP* lxv (1968) 647–56.
502. Gano] Ganelon was a paladin of Charlemagne who was led by jealousy of Roland to collude with the Moors in an attack on Charlemagne's forces at Roncesvalles (AD 778). He persuaded Charlemagne that the small rearguard under Roland was sufficient to hold off the Moors; but it was not, and Roland and a large part of Charlemagne's army were killed.
507. doctors] learned theologians.
508–22. D.'s considerable expansion of Chaucer's 'But what that God afore wote [knows], must nedes bee', prompted in part by the discussion of foreknowledge in *PL* iii. These issues were much debated, and the quotations below from contemporary texts are offered as illustrative analogues, not sources. If D. were acquainted with French Catholic thought, he would have known that these questions of predestination and freewill were much debated between Jansenists and their opponents (the former held a position closer to that of Calvin than the central Catholic tradition). The argument is:
(a) some scholars maintain that man's life is completely predetermined [by God] (l. 508);
(b) others maintain that God foresees what will happen (l. 509), and
(c) that this foreknowledge in itself determines what will happen (l. 510; cp. 'Palamon and Arcite' ii 220–1; but contrast the argument in *PL* iii 114–19, and the classic Augustinian position that God knows all things before they happen, but that we act according to our free will (*De Civitate Dei* v 9));
(d) specifically, that it binds the human will (l. 511). In this case,

Some clerks maintain that heaven at first foresees,
510   And in the virtue of foresight decrees.
If this be so, then prescience binds the will,
And mortals are not free to good or ill:

(e) man's good or evil actions are not the result of his free will [but are determined by God] (l. 512).
(f) That which God foresees will happen, he must also cause to happen (l. 513);
otherwise
(g) [if, as a result of man acting freely, things turned out differently from how
they were foreseen by God, then] his foreknowledge would be false (l. 514).
(h) This would be as bad for men as if there were no divine foreknowledge
(l. 515). Cp. 'If it be said, We cannot understand how any thing can be certain,
and yet contingent; or how a voluntary action can be foreseen, which depends
upon free choice, and that at any time until it be effected, may be either done
or let alone. Let such persons try how they can clear the inconveniences of an
ignorant and imperfect Deity, which will lie hard upon them if they grant not
Divine prescience' (*An Occasional Discourse, Concerning God's Fore-knowledge, and
Man's Free-Agency* (1687) sig. A3ʳ). For
(i) God is made the author of human sin (l. 516) [because he wills everything
that happens]. Cp. 'If there be not in Man a free Election, where is sin? for where
there is no choice, how can any one choose amiss?' (*An Occasional Discourse* sig.
A3ʳ). Augustine insists that the fact that God foreknew that a man would sin does
not make him sin: a man does not sin unless he himself wills it (*De Civitate Dei*
v 10).
(j) And to maintain that would be blasphemous, for one could say no worse of
the devil (ll. 517–18).
(k) For God cannot be just if he punishes man for sin, or rewards man for good
deeds, when those actions are the result of divine will rather than human choices
(ll. 519–22). The unspoken conclusion is that predestination is therefore morally
untenable.
It is not clear what *As bad* in l. 515 refers to. D.'s narrator may be arguing that
the absence of divine foreknowledge would be as bad *for us* as God having false
foreknowledge (because both would radically diminish man's concept of God).
Nor is it clear whether proposition (i) (l. 516), which makes God the author of
sin, depends logically on the previous line: *For* suggests such a connection, but
logically God would be the author of human sin if he determined what will
happen (argument (d)), but would not be if he had no or only faulty foreknowledge
(arguments (g) and (h)). Lines 514–16 may be three free-standing thoughts, as
the terminal colons (in *1700*, and kept here) suggest, rather than steps in a logical
argument. Although the narrator here cannot simply be assumed to be voicing
D.'s own opinions, D.'s Catholic faith leads him to stress man's free will (as Noyes
pointed out), and in ll. 517–22 the argument exposes the moral implications of
Calvin's doctrine of predestination, which was a principal element in seventeenth-
century Protestantism. D. had always taken a generous stance on the availability
of salvation, as his attitude to non-Christians in *RL* ll. 186–223 shows. See also
'Palamon and Arcite' iii 844–53.
509. clerks] scholars.
510. virtue] divine power (*OED* 1); inherent nature or quality (*OED* 8).
511. prescience] foreknowledge.

For what he first foresaw, he must ordain,
Or its eternal prescience may be vain:
515   As bad for us as prescience had not been:
For, first or last, he's author of the sin.
And who says that, let the blaspheming man
Say worse ev'n of the devil, if he can.
For how can that eternal power be just
520   To punish man, who sins because he must?
Or how can he reward a virtuous deed
Which is not done by us, but first decreed?
    I cannot boult this matter to the bran,
As Bradwardine and holy Austin can:
525   If prescience can determine actions so

514. *its*] heaven's.
515. *been*] The spelling *bin* in *1700* here and in l. 559 (but not l. 549, which has *been*) indicates seventeenth-century pronunciation and provides a perfect rhyme.
516. *he's*] God is.
523. *boult . . . to the bran*] sift the flour from the bran.
524. *Bradwardine*] Thomas Bradwardine (*c*.1295–1349), Archbishop of Canterbury, whose principal work was *De Causa Dei contra Pelagium*. He insisted on the necessity of grace, and the irresistible efficacy of the divine will that lies behind all actions. *Austin*] St Augustine (354–430), whose immensely influential theological writings argued that no good act can be performed without divine grace. God predestined the elect to salvation, and either consigned the rest to damnation or permitted (without actually decreeing) their damnation. This doctrine would be developed in a more extreme form by Calvin. But Augustine also insisted on the freedom of the human will, and therefore man's responsibility for sin: see the quotations above.
525–51. Another substantial expansion of Chaucer: 'Whether that goddes worthy foreweting [foreknowledge], / Straineth [constrains] me nedely [of necessity] to do a thing: / (Nedely clepe [call] I simple necessity) / Or if the free choice be graunted me / To do the same thing, or to do it nought, / Though God forewote it, or [before] it was wrought: / Or of his weting straineth neuer a dele [not at all] / But by necessitie conditionele, / I wol not haue to done of such mattere'. The structure of the argument is as follows:
(a) [The narrator does not know whether] God's foreknowledge predetermines our actions (ll. 525–6), which is called 'simple' or 'strict necessity' (l. 529);
(b) or whether God's foreknowledge leaves us free to act as we will (ll. 527–8).
(c) 'Simple necessity' compels us to act as God foresees by constraining the human will (ll. 531–5).
(d) 'Conditional necessity' does not constrain the will, but leaves us free to act or not. God foresees what we will decide, but has no influence on that decision (ll. 536–9; cp. *PL* iii 114–19).
(e) Man was originally created free (Genesis ii 16); God's foreknowledge is subordinate to that initial gift of freedom (ll. 540–1).
(f) The narrator does not wish to argue about whether God *could* have created man as a wholly free agent, because human beings cannot claim to understand divine power (ll. 542–5).

That we must do because he did foreknow;
Or that foreknowing, yet our choice is free,
Not forced to sin by strict necessity:
This strict necessity they 'simple' call,
530 Another sort there is, 'conditional':
The first so binds the will, that things foreknown
By spontaneity, not choice, are done:
Thus galley slaves tug willing at their oar,
Consent to work, in prospect of the shore—
535 But would not work at all, if not constrained before.
That other does not liberty constrain,
But man may either act, or may refrain.
Heaven made us agents free to good or ill,
And forced it not, though he foresaw the will.
540 Freedom was first bestowed on human race,

(g) God created man in his own image (Genesis i 26), and as God is free, so
man too must be free (ll. 546–8). Cp. Nathaniel Whaley: 'When God therefore
said, *Let us make Man in our Image, after our Likeness*, (Gen. 1. 26) 'tis plain that
this was done with the Approbation of all his Attributes; and that there was nothing to [ob]struct his making Man a reasonable and free Agent, and endowing
him with divine and virtuous Principles, because this was to make him after the
Image of his Maker' (*A Discourse Shewing the Consistency of God's Infinite Goodness
with his Foreknowledge of the Fall of Man* (1698) 123).
(h) It might have been better for man to have been compelled to be good, instead of
being (as he is) free to sin, but the narrator does not wish to debate this (ll. 549–51).
Cp. 'What could Man under a necessity of always doing good, signifie, more than
a good Watch? which tho' it moves regularly, yet is it altogether in-voluntary,
cannot do otherwise, knows not that it moves at all; and consequently is incapable of praise or encouragement, reward or punishment' (*An Occasional Discourse* 25).
531–5. 'The distinction is between (i) deliberate, rational choice of a course of action,
and (ii) "spontaneous" or unreflective action in inevitable circumstances. The slaves
do not initially choose whether to row or not; but constrained to work, they
pull "willingly" under the natural prompting of a "prospect of the Shore"' (Kinsley).
532. spontaneity] D. appears to alter the currently accepted meaning of the word,
which is 'spontaneous, or voluntary and unconstrained, action' (*OED* 1, first
example from Cartwright (1651): 'Bernard doth agree with Calvin in making the
freedome of mans will to consist in a spontaneity, and a freedom from coaction').
D. argues that according to the theory of 'simple necessity', man's will is so constrained by God that his actions (which are foreknown by God) are performed
without any process of deliberation and choice. His usage of *spontaneity* may be
influenced by its Latin origins in *sponte*, which means 'by the will': in the case of
simple necessity, the will is already bound, and so the act is carried out *by spontaneity*
in the sense of 'by the [previously bound] will' rather than as a result of reflection
and decision. Or he may mean that under such constraints as the rowers experience, the body acts as if by reflex rather than by the direction of the mind.
536. That other] The doctrine of conditional necessity.

And prescience only held the second place.
   If he could make such agents wholly free,
I not dispute: the point's too high for me;
For heaven's unfathomed power what man can sound,
545   Or put to his omnipotence a bound?
He made us to his image all agree: ⎫
That image is the soul, and that must be ⎬
Or not the Maker's image, or be free.   ⎭
   But whether it were better man had been
550   By nature bound to good, not free to sin,
I waive, for fear of splitting on a rock:
The tale I tell is only of a cock,
Who had not run the hazard of his life
Had he believed his dream, and not his wife:
555   For women, with a mischief to their kind,
Pervert with bad advice our better mind.
A woman's counsel brought us first to woe,
And made her man his paradise forgo,
Where at heart's ease he lived, and might have been
560   As free from sorrow as he was from sin.
For what the devil had their sex to do,
That, born to folly, they presumed to know,
And could not see the serpent in the grass?
But I myself presume, and let it pass.
565   Silence in times of suffering is the best:
'Tis dangerous to disturb a hornet's nest.
In other authors you may find enough,
But all they say of dames is idle stuff,
Legends of lying wits together bound:
570   The Wife of Bath would throw 'em to the ground.

548. Or . . . or] Either . . . or.
555–6. For 'Womens counsailes ben oft ful colde [fatal]'.
555. mischief] hurtful character or influence; wickedness; cause or source of harm or evil (*OED* 6, 7, 8). *to their kind*] intrinsic to their nature (*OED* 3) or gender (*OED* 7).
557–8. In Genesis iii.
560. D.'s addition.
561–6. For 'If I counsaile of wemen should blame, / Passe ouer, I said it in my game'.
565–6. With application to D.'s own circumstances as a Jacobite and Catholic.
568–70. D.'s addition.
568. dames] ladies.
570. The Wife of Bath] One of the Canterbury pilgrims, whose prologue and tale (for D.'s translation of the latter, see *Poems* v 499–518) illustrate her vigorous defence of women.

These are the words of Chanticleer, not mine:
I honour dames, and think their sex divine.
   Now to continue what my tale begun.
Lay madam Partlet basking in the sun,
575 Breast-high in sand; her sisters in a row
Enjoyed the beams above, the warmth below.
The cock, that of his flesh was ever free,
Sung merrier than the mermaid in the sea.
And so befell that, as he cast his eye
580 Among the coleworts on a butterfly,
He saw false Reynard where he lay full low;
I need not swear he had no list to crow,
But cried 'Cock, cock,' and gave a sudden start,
As sore dismayed, and frighted at his heart:
585 For birds and beasts, informed by nature, know
Kinds opposite to theirs, and fly their foe.
So Chanticleer, who never saw a fox,
Yet shunned him as a sailor shuns the rocks.
   But the false loon, who could not work his will
590 By open force, employed his flattering skill.
'I hope, my Lord,' said he, 'I not offend;
Are you afraid of me, that am your friend?
I were a beast indeed to do you wrong—
I, who have loved and honoured you so long.
595 Stay, gentle sir, nor take a false alarm,
For on my soul I never meant you harm.
I come no spy, nor as a traitor press
To learn the secrets of your soft recess:

572. For 'I can of women no harm deuine [discover].'
576. D.'s addition.
578. merrier] See l. 42n.
582. list] desire.
585–6. In medieval thought, each creature had its contrary, towards which it felt
a natural antipathy.
586. Kinds] natures; species.
588–90. D.'s addition.
589. loon] worthless person, rogue (OED, citing this example).
594–5. D.'s addition.
595. gentle] noble.
597–8. Cp. Milton: 'I come no spy, / With purpose to explore or to disturb /
The secrets of your realm' (PL ii 970–2 (Satan to Chaos); J. R. Mason).
598. recess] retirement, privacy; place of retirement, private space (OED 2b, 5;
also in PL iv 708, ix 456, xi 304).

Far be from Reynard so profane a thought;
600 But by the sweetness of your voice was brought,
     For as I bid my beads, by chance I heard
     The song as of an angel in the yard:
     A song that would have charmed th' infernal gods,
     And banished horror from the dark abodes:
605 Had Orpheus sung it in the nether sphere,
     So much the hymn had pleased the tyrant's ear
     The wife had been detained, to keep the husband there.
        'My Lord, your sire familiarly I knew,
     A peer deserving such a son as you:
610 He, with your lady-mother (whom heaven rest)
     Has often graced my house, and been my guest:
     To view his living features does me good,
     For I am your poor neighbour in the wood,
     And in my cottage should be proud to see
615 The worthy heir of my friend's family.
        'But since I speak of singing, let me say
     (As with an upright heart I safely may)
     That, save yourself, there breathes not on the ground
     One like your father for a silver sound.
620 So sweetly would he wake the winter day
     That matrons to the church mistook their way,
     And thought they heard the merry organ play.
     And he to raise his voice with artful care
     (What will not beaux attempt to please the fair?)
625 On tiptoe stood to sing with greater strength,
     And stretched his comely neck at all the length;
     And while he pained his voice to pierce the skies,

599. D.'s addition. *so*] *Eds*; *to 1700*.
601. D.'s addition. Reynard claims to be a pious Catholic, saying his rosary.
603–7. D.'s addition. Orpheus was famed for his skill as a musician, and his song could charm the beasts. When his wife Eurydice died, he went down to the underworld to retrieve her, but lost her for ever by turning to look at her on the way back. See 'The Fourth Book of the *Georgics*' ll. 651–767.
604. *horror*] roughness, ruggedness (*OED* 1); cp. 'Palamon and Arcite' ii 549*n*.
605. *Orpheus*] *Eds*; *Orphans 1700*.
606. *the tyrant*] Minos, ruler of the underworld.
609, 611–15. D.'s additions.
617. D.'s addition. *upright heart*] A biblical expression, esp. in the Psalms (e.g. Psalm vii 10).
620–2. D.'s addition.
622. *merry*] See l. 42*n*.
624. D.'s addition.

As saints in raptures use, would shut his eyes,
That the sound striving through the narrow throat
630   His winking might avail to mend the note.
By this, in song he never had his peer,
From sweet Cecilia down to Chanticleer;
Not Maro's Muse who sung the mighty man,
Nor Pindar's heavenly lyre, nor Horace when a swan.
635   Your ancestors proceed from race divine,
From Brennus and Belinus is your line,
Who gave to sovereign Rome such loud alarms
That ev'n the priests were not excused from arms.
   'Besides, a famous monk of modern times
640   Has left of cocks recorded in his rhymes
That of a parish priest the son and heir
(When sons of priests were from the proverb clear)
Affronted once a cock of noble kind,
And either lamed his legs, or struck him blind;
645   For which the clerk his father was disgraced,
And in his benefice another placed.
Now sing, my Lord, if not for love of me,

628. As saints in raptures use] D.'s addition.   *use*] are accustomed to do.
629. D.'s addition.
630. winking] closing both eyes.   *mend*] make more excellent (*OED* 10a).   *note*] song.
632–8. D.'s addition.
632. Cecilia] Patron saint of music, celebrated in D.'s *A Song for St Cecilia's Day* (1687) and *Alexander's Feast* (1697).
633. Maro] Virgil (Publius Vergilius Maro), whose *Aeneid* begins *arma virumque cano* ('I sing the arms and the man').
634. swan] singer, poet (*OED* 2c).
636. Brennus was the leader of the Gauls who sacked Rome in 390 BC (Livy v 38). As Scott notes, D. continues the pun from l. 501, making Chanticleer a descendant of the Gauls. Geoffrey of Monmouth (iii 1–10) makes Brennius [*sic*] and his brother Belinus Britons.
638. Priests were customarily not required (and according to some theologians not permitted) to bear arms (see Aquinas, *Summa Theologica* II. ii. q. 40 art. 2).
639. 'Nigellus Wireker, Monke of Canterbury . . . was not afraid to write of the faults of curates, & the mispending of churchgoods . . . He did write in verse . . . a booke vnder the title of Brunellus, called *Speculum stultorum* ['The Mirror of Fools']' (Speght sig. Bbbbvi'). The story is that 'a young man named Gundulfus broke a cock's leg by throwing a stone at it. Later, when Gundulfus was to be ordained and receive a benefice, the cock crowed so late that Gundulfus over-slept and lost his living' (*Riverside Chaucer*).
642. D.'s addition. When priests (as in the Roman Catholic Church) were required to be celibate, their sons would be bastards (cp. Tilley S 630).
643. Affronted] attacked (*OED* 3b, citing this example).   *kind*] race.
645. D.'s addition.

Yet for the sake of sweet Saint Charity;
Make hills, and dales, and earth, and heaven rejoice,
650   And emulate your father's angel-voice.'
        The cock was pleased to hear him speak so fair,
And proud beside, as solar people are;
Nor could the treason from the truth descry,
So was he ravished with this flattery;
655   So much the more as from a little elf
He had a high opinion of himself:
Though sickly, slender, and not large of limb,
Concluding all the world was made for him.
        Ye princes raised by poets to the gods,
660   And Alexandered up in lying odes,
Believe not every flattering knave's report:
There's many a Reynard lurking in the court,
And he shall be received with more regard,
And listened to, than modest truth is heard.
665   This Chanticleer, of whom the story sings,
Stood high upon his toes, and clapped his wings;
Then stretched his neck, and winked with both his eyes,
Ambitious, as he sought th' Olympic prize.
But while he pained himself to raise his note,
670   False Reynard rushed and caught him by the throat;
Then on his back he laid the precious load,
And sought his wonted shelter of the wood.

---

648. Saint Charity] Thus capitalized in *1700*, but not a saint's name, although often used in mild oaths as if it were (cp. *Hamlet* IV v 58). Chaucer's 'saint charitie' means 'holy charity'.
649. D.'s addition.   *hills . . . rejoice*] The 'hills rejoice' in Psalm lxv 12.
651–3. D.'s addition.
652. solar people] People governed astrologically by the sun (as Chanticleer is: see l. 680). William Lily says that the sun signifies 'Kings, Princes, Emperours, &c.'; in its positive influence such a man is 'of great Majesty and Statelinesse, Industrious to acquire Honour', but negatively he is 'Arrogant and Proud . . . cracking of his Pedigree, he is Pur-blind in Sight and Judgment'; and one of the sun's birds is the cock (*Christian Astrology* (1647) 70–2).
655–60. D.'s addition.
655. elf] child, small animal (*OED* 3b).
657. slender] weak, not robust (*OED* 1b).
660. William III was likened to Alexander in several flattering poems: see head-note to *Alexander's Feast*.
662–4. Echoes 'Prologue to His Royal Highness' ll. 14–16 (Christie).
668–9. D.'s addition.
668. as] as if.

Swiftly he made his way, the mischief done,
Of all unheeded, and pursued by none.
675 Alas, what stay is there in human state,
Or who can shun inevitable fate?
The doom was written, the decree was passed,
Ere the foundations of the world were cast!
In Aries though the sun exalted stood,
680 His patron planet to procure his good,
Yet Saturn was his mortal foe, and he
In Libra raised, opposed the same degree:
The rays both good and bad, of equal power,
Each thwarting other, made a mingled hour.
685 On Friday morn he dreamt this direful dream,
Cross to the worthy native in his scheme!
Ah, blissful Venus, goddess of delight,
How couldst thou suffer thy devoted knight
On thy own day to fall by foe oppressed,
690 The wight of all the world who served thee best?
Who true to love, was all for recreation,
And minded not the work of propagation.
Gaufride, who could'st so well in rhyme complain

673. D.'s addition.
675–84. For 'O destinie, that maist not be eschued'.
675. stay] permanent state or condition (OED 7b).
676–8. Cp. 'strict Fate had cast too deep / Her dark foundations' (PL vi 869–70;
J. R. Mason); and 'the kingdom prepared for you from the foundation of the
world' (Matthew xxv 34; T. A. Mason).
679–84. Although Chanticleer's ruling planet, the Sun, is propitiously exalted in
the sign of Aries, the malevolent planet Saturn (for which see 'Palamon and Arcite'
ii 381n, 397–419) is equally elevated opposite in the sign of Libra, and so their
contrary effects cause mixed fortunes.
685. Friday (the day dedicated to Venus: Latin Veneris dies, French 'vendredi') was
often regarded as an unpropitious day, being the day when the expulsion from
paradise and the crucifixion were said to have taken place; see also ll. 697–8.
686. D.'s addition. native] one born under a particular planet (OED 2). scheme]
horoscope (OED 2b).
690. wight] man.
691–2. For 'More for delite than the worlde to multiplie'. D.'s version keeps
Chaucer's sense if we take minded not to mean 'paid no heed to' rather than 'did
not object to': i.e. Chanticleer was sexually active for the sheer pleasure of it
(recreation) rather than to produce offspring (propagation).
693–8. Geoffrey of Vainsauf in his Poetria Nova (c.1210) has an extravagant lament
on the death of King Richard I (Cœur de Lion), who was fatally wounded on
a Friday.
693. complain] lament (OED, last example).

The death of Richard with an arrow slain,
695   Why had not I thy Muse, or thou my heart,
To sing this heavy dirge with equal art!
That I like thee on Friday might complain,
For on that day was Cœur de Lion slain.
     Not louder cries when Ilium was in flames
700   Were sent to heaven by woeful Trojan dames,
When Pyrrhus tossed on high his burnished blade, ⎫
And offered Priam to his father's shade,   ⎬
Than for the cock the widowed poultry made.   ⎭
Fair Partlet first, when he was borne from sight,
705   With sovereign shrieks bewailed her captive knight,
Far louder than the Carthaginian wife
When Asdrubal her husband lost his life,
  ·   When she beheld the smouldering flames ascend,
And all the Punic glories at an end:
710   Willing into the fires she plunged her head,
With greater ease than others seek their bed.
Not more aghast the matrons of renown
When tyrant Nero burned th' imperial town
Shrieked for the downfall in a doleful cry,
715   For which their guiltless lords were doomed to die.
     Now to my story I return again:
The trembling widow and her daughters twain
This woeful cackling cry with horror heard
Of those distracted damsels in the yard,
720   And starting up, beheld the heavy sight
  ·   How Reynard to the forest took his flight,

696. D.'s addition. *equal*] appropriate, matching.
701–2. Pyrrhus, son of Achilles, killed the Trojan King Priam, telling him to complain of his behaviour to his father in the underworld (*Aen.* ii 526–58).
705. *sovereign*] principal, greatest (*OED* 2).
706–11. Hasdrubal (not, *pace Works*, the brother of Hannibal) was the ruler of Carthage when it was captured and burnt by the Romans in 146 BC. He surrendered and spent the rest of his life in captivity in Italy; his wife killed herself. Chaucer's idea that Hasdrubal committed suicide may be a conflation of this story with that of an earlier Hasdrubal who killed himself in 202 BC. For Chaucer's sources see *Riverside Chaucer* 940.
709. *Punic*] Carthaginian.
711. D.'s addition.
712–15. In AD 64 a fire, which the Emperor Nero was rumoured to have started, devastated Rome. He blamed it on the Christians, and had many of them burned alive.

And 'cross his back, as in triumphant scorn,
The hope and pillar of the house was borne.
'The fox, the wicked fox!' was all the cry;
725 Out from his house ran every neighbour nigh;
The vicar first, and after him the crew
With forks and staves the felon to pursue.
Ran Coll our dog, and Talbot with the band,
And Malkin with her distaff in her hand;
730 Ran cow and calf, and family of hogs
In panic horror of pursuing dogs,
With many a deadly grunt and doleful squeak,
Poor swine, as if their pretty hearts would break.
The shouts of men, the women in dismay,
735 With shrieks augment the terror of the day.
The ducks that heard the proclamation cried,
And feared a persecution might betide,
Full twenty mile from town their voyage take,
Obscure in rushes of the liquid lake.
740 The geese fly o'er the barn, the bees in arms
Drive headlong from their waxen cells in swarms.
Jack Straw at London stone with all his rout
Struck not the city with so loud a shout;
Not when with English hate they did pursue
745 A Frenchman, or an unbelieving Jew:

723. D.'s addition; cp. his description of Shadwell as 'Rome's other hope, and
pillar of the state' (*MF* l. 109).
725–7. For 'And eke with staues many another man'. *crew*] band of armed men
(*OED* 2).
732, 735. D.'s additions.
736–9. For 'The Duckes cried as men would them quell'.
739. Obscure] remote from observation; inconspicuous (*OED* 5, 6).   *liquid*] watery
(*OED* 1b).
741. waxen cells] Milton's phrase in *PL* vii 491 (J. R. Mason).
742–3. Jack Straw was one of the leaders of the Peasants' Revolt in 1381, whose
victims included prosperous Flemings engaged in the wool trade.
742. London stone] The milliarium of Roman London, from which distances
were measured, which stood by St Swithun's church in Cannon Street. D. has
conflated the story of Jack Straw with that of Jack Cade, who in 1450 led his
rebels to London stone and asserted his claim to be Lord Mortimer, an episode
dramatized by Shakespeare in *2 Henry VI* IV vi. (*Works*).
744–5. For 'Whan that they would any *Flemming* kill'.

Not when the welkin rung with 'One and all,'   ⎫
And echoes bounded back from Fox's Hall: ⎬
Earth seemed to sink beneath, and heaven above to fall. ⎭
With might and main they chased the murderous fox
750   With brazen trumpets and inflated box
To kindle Mars with military sounds,
Nor wanted horns t' inspire sagacious hounds.
　　But see how Fortune can confound the wise,
And, when they least expect it, turn the dice.
755   The captive cock, who scarce could draw his breath,
And lay within the very jaws of death,
Yet in this agony his fancy wrought,
And fear supplied him with this happy thought:
'Yours is the prize, victorious Prince,' said he,
760   'The vicar my defeat, and all the village see.
Enjoy your friendly Fortune while you may,
And bid the churls that envy you the prey
Call back their mongrel curs, and cease their cry: ⎫
"See, fools, the shelter of the wood is nigh,   ⎬
765   And Chanticleer in your despite shall die.   ⎭
He shall be plucked, and eaten to the bone."'
　　' 'Tis well advised, in faith it shall be done.'
This Reynard said; but as the word he spoke
The prisoner with a spring from prison broke,
770   Then stretched his feathered fans with all his might,
And to the neighbouring maple winged his flight.
　　Whom when the traitor safe on tree beheld,

746–8. D.'s addition.

746. *'One and all'*] A rallying cry (Tilley O 51).

747. *Fox's Hall*] A pun on Vauxhall, the pleasure garden south of the Thames (*Works*). The line also echoes *MF* l. 48.

750. *inflated box*] pipes made of boxwood which they blew into; for Chaucer's staves of boxwood. *OED* (*s.v.* inflated 1) cites this example with the gloss 'filled with wind'.

751–2. D.'s addition.

752. *sagacious*] acute in perception by smell (*OED* 1); cp. *HP* ii 5.

755–61. For 'This Cocke that laie vpon the Foxe backe, / In all his drede vnto the Foxe he spake'.

759–60. Scott notes that these lines parody Virgil: *vicisti et victum tendere palmas / Ausonii videre* ('you are the victor, and the Ausonians have seen me stretch forth my hands as the vanquished': *Aen.* xii 937–8; Turnus to Aeneas).

763. D.'s addition.

769–70. For 'The Cock brake from his mouth deliuerly'.

He cursed the gods, with shame and sorrow filled:
Shame for his folly, sorrow out of time
775 For plotting an unprofitable crime.
Yet mast'ring both, th' artificer of lies
Renews th' assault, and his last battery tries:
   'Though I,' said he, 'did ne'er in thought offend,
How justly may my Lord suspect his friend!
780 Th' appearance is against me, I confess,
Who seemingly have put you in distress:
You, if your goodness does not plead my cause,
May think I broke all hospitable laws
To bear you from your palace yard by might,
785 And put your noble person in a fright:
This, since you take it ill, I must repent,
Though heaven can witness with no bad intent
I practised it to make you taste your cheer
With double pleasure, first prepared by fear.
790 So loyal subjects often seize their prince, ⎫
Forced (for his good) to seeming violence,   ⎬
Yet mean his sacred person not the least offence. ⎭
Descend; so help me Jove as you shall find
That Reynard comes of no dissembling kind.'
795   'Nay,' quoth the cock, 'but I beshrew us both
If I believe a saint upon his oath:
An honest man may take a knave's advice,
But idiots only will be cozened twice.

773–94. For 'Alas (qd. he) O *Chaunteclere*, alas, / I haue (qd. he) doe to you trespas, / In as much as I made you aferde, / Whan I you hent, and brought out of your yerde. / But sir, I did it not in no wicked entent: / Come down, and I shal tel you what I ment, / I shall you say sothe, God helpe me so'.
774. out of time] too late (*OED* time 44).
776. artificer of lies] Milton calls Satan 'artificer of fraud' (*PL* iv 121; J. R. Mason).
788. cheer] hospitable entertainment; food provided as hospitality (*OED* 5, 6).
790–3. Possibly a glance at the enforced abdication of James II in 1688, but more applicable to the rhetoric used in the Civil War, when Parliamentarians initially insisted that they were fighting not against the person of the king, but against his bad advisers.
794. kind] race, species.
795. beshrew] curse.
796–9. If . . . bewared] For 'If thou begyle me ofter than ones'.
796. See l. 492n.
798. cozened] cheated.

Once warned is well bewared: no flattering lies ⎫
800   Shall soothe me more to sing with winking eyes ⎬
And open mouth, for fear of catching flies. ⎭
Who blindfold walks upon a river's brim
When he should see, has he deserved to swim?'
'Better, Sir Cock, let all contention cease;
805   Come down,' said Reynard, 'let us treat of peace.'
'A peace with all my soul,' said Chanticleer,
'But with your favour, I will treat it here.
And lest the truce with treason should be mixed,
'Tis my concern to have the tree betwixt.'

The Moral

810   In this plain fable you th' effect may see
Of negligence, and fond credulity;
And learn besides of flatt'rers to beware,
Then most pernicious when they speak too fair.
The cock and fox the fool and knave imply;
815   The truth is moral, though the tale a lie.
Who spoke in parables I dare not say, ⎫
But sure he knew it was a pleasing way ⎬
Sound sense by plain example to convey. ⎭
And in a heathen author we may find ⎫
820   That pleasure with instruction should be joined: ⎬
So take the corn, and leave the chaff behind. ⎭

799. bewared] warned (*OED* II, citing this example).
801–3. D.'s addition.
804–9. For 'Naie (qd. the foxe) but God yeue him mischance, / That is so indiscrete of gouernaunce / That iangleth, whan that he should haue pees'.
805. treat of] negotiate, discuss (*OED* 1, 2).
811. fond] foolish.
813, 816–20. D.'s additions.
820. From Horace: *omne tulit punctum qui miscuit utile dulci* ('he gains every prize who mixes instruction with pleasure': *Ars Poetica* l. 343).

28 The Secular Masque from *The Pilgrim*

Date and publication. First printed in *The Pilgrim, a Comedy: As it is Acted at the Theatre-Royal, in Drury-Lane. Written Originally by Mr. Fletcher, and now very much Alter'd, with several Additions. Likewise A Prologue, Epilogue, Dialogue, and Masque, Written by the late Great Poet Mr. Dryden, just before his Death, being the last of his Works*, published by Benjamin Tooke in 1700 (two issues); advertised in *The London Gazette* 13–17 June; *TC* June (siglum: *1700*). The second issue (Macdonald 94b) has a separate half-title for 'A Dialogue, and Secular Masque, in the Pilgrim. Written by the Late Famous Mr. Dryden.', and separate pagination, which suggests that some copies of the song and masque were sold separately, perhaps at the performance. Macdonald records no evidence of such separate sales, but there is a separate copy of the second issue of the song and masque, without the play, in the Brotherton Collection, Leeds University Library. The play proper ends with a speech by the Governor designed to introduce the 'Secular Masque': 'I hope before you go, Sir, you'l share with us, an Entertainment the late great Poet of our Age prepar'd to Celebrate this Day. Let the Masque begin' (42). On 11 April 1700 D. had written to Mrs Steward: 'Within this moneth there will be playd for my profit, an old play of Fletchers, calld the Pilgrim, corrected by my good friend Mr Vanbrook; to which I have added A New Masque, & am to write a New Prologue & Epilogue' (*Letters* 136). John Fletcher's play, revised by Sir John Vanbrugh, was performed by Christopher Rich's company at Lincoln's Inn Fields; the first performance was probably on Monday 29 April 1700, as it was reported that because D. died on the third day (1 May) the share of the profits which would have accrued to him fell to his family (*LS* 527). (One BL copy (841.c.7(1)) has a MS note on the title page: 'the 5. of May / monday', which may preserve a correct memory of the day of the week, although the date itself cannot be that of the first performance.) Colley Cibber (who, unusually, spoke both the Prologue and the Epilogue) records that Vanbrugh revised the play 'to assist the benefit Day of Dryden' (*Apology*, cited in *LS* 528). D.'s contributions to *The Pilgrim* (omitting the song) were collected posthumously in *The Comedies, Tragedies, and Operas . . . With A Secular Masque*, 2 vols (1701; Macdonald 107a ii, published by Daniel Brown, a set of sheets from Tonson's 1701 edition of the collected plays expanded to include the 'Secular Masque'). The present text follows *1700*.

The music for the 'Secular Masque' was composed at least partly by Daniel Purcell: his setting of ll. 1–44 survives in BL MS Add 29378, fols. 194ʳ–205ᵛ, and the settings of ll. 1–6 (Janus' song, performed by Mr Freeman), 13–25 (Momus and Janus, by Freeman and William Pate) and 27–32 (Diana's song, by Mrs Erwin) were printed in *A Collection of New Songs . . . Compos'd by Mr Daniel Purcell. Perform'd in the New Revised Comedy call'd the Pilgrim . . . 1700* (published June 1700). These songs (which were printed on one side of the paper only for the convenience of musicians) also survive as separate sheets extracted or reprinted from the *Collection*. Purcell's setting of ll. 1–6 was also printed in *Mercurius Musicus* for May 1700. Godfrey Finger set Venus' song (ll. 72–7), which was printed (as 'Sung by Mrs Campion') in *A Collection of the Choicest Songs and Dialogues Compos'd by the most Eminent Masters of the Age* (*c.* 1705), and also as a single printed sheet. In addition, BodL MS Mus. Sch. C. 107 preserves an anonymous setting of countertenor and tenor parts for the choruses in ll. 21, 35–6, and countertenor parts for ll. 37–40, 41–4, 57, 62. For later musical settings see Day 184–5.

The Secular Masque

Enter Janus.

Janus.   Chronos, Chronos, mend thy pace,
            An hundred times the rolling sun

¶28. The precise implications of the allegory have been disputed, but Diana (ll. 27–44) clearly represents the early part of the century, and as Winn suggests (511) 'since James I was an inveterate hunter and Elizabeth "the virgin Queen", the virgin huntress Diana may stand for both monarchs'. Mars (ll. 45–71) represents the period of the Civil War. Venus (ll. 72–81) as goddess of love symbolizes the reigns of Charles II and James II, and their addiction to pleasure, the passing of which (under the rule of William and Mary) Chronos laments in ll. 82–5. (Diana, Venus, and Mars are also the three deities to whom the protagonists pray in 'Palamon and Arcite'.) Momus, the satirical commentator, derides the idealizing potential in all three representations: Diana's 'chase had a beast in view' (l. 87), i.e. the Elizabethan cult of chastity was hypocritical, and James was as interested in the sexual pursuit of young men as in hunting animals; Mars' wars achieved nothing, since the monarchy was restored, although there may (as Winn suggests) be an additional glance at the recently concluded European wars in which William III had taken a leading role, and which had proved so expensive for England; and Venus' lovers were unfaithful. Momus' cynicism should not, of course, be attributed in any simple way to D. himself.

Title. Secular] occurring or celebrated once in a century or age (*OED* 5). In ancient Rome, games continuing for three days and nights were celebrated every 120 years, and a hymn or *carmen saeculare* was composed to be sung at these games. Horace's *Carmen Saeculare* is evoked by D.'s title, but D.'s masque bears an ironic relation to Horace's text: it has none of Horace's serious religious tone and concern for the future of Rome. Like D., Horace invokes Diana, but this is to stress the chastity of the boys and girls who hymn the gods, and of Aeneas, Rome's progenitor. D.'s ironic account of recent and contemporary history contrasts with Horace's view of (or prayer for) the present: *iam Fides et Pax et Honos Pudorque / priscus et neglecta redire Virtus / audet, apparetque beata pleno / Copia cornu* (ll. 57–60: 'Now we have Faith and Peace and Honour and Chastity; and ancient Virtue, once neglected, dares to return; and blessed Abundance appears with her full horn'). D.'s work also forms a contrast with (and perhaps replies to) Matthew Prior's long and effusive praise of William III, *Carmen Seculare, for the Year 1700. To the King*, published on 1 January 1700, which particularly celebrated his military victories, but also praised his encouragement of 'Some that to Morals shall recal the Age, / And purge from vitious Dross the sinking Stage' (ll. 444–5). A song with some similar secular motifs is found next to D.'s 'Secular Masque' in *Mercurius Musicus* for May 1700, entitled 'A Song Sett by Mr. Goudge; The Words by Mr. Clark': ' 'Tis said the War's over, / all Battles are done, / still the Fates only / know what yet is to come: / let the true Sons of *Mars*, / this Liberty

Around the radiant belt has run
In his revolving race.

5   Behold, behold, the goal in sight,
Spread thy fans, and wing thy flight.

Enter Chronos with a scythe in his hand, and a great globe
on his back, which he sets down at his entrance.

Chronos.   Weary, weary of my weight,
Let me, let me drop my freight,
And leave the world behind.

10   I could not bear
Another year
The load of humankind.

Enter Momus laughing.

Momus.   Ha! ha! ha! Ha! ha! ha! well hast thou done
To lay down thy pack,

15   And lighten thy back,
The world was a fool e'er since it begun,
And since neither Janus, nor Chronos, nor I
Can hinder the crimes,
Or mend the bad times,

20   'Tis better to laugh than to cry.

Cho. of all 3.   'Tis better to laugh than to cry.

Janus.   Since Momus comes to laugh below,
Old Time begin the show,
That he may see in every scene

25   What changes in this age have been.

Chronos.   Then goddess of the silver bow, begin.

Horns or hunting music within.

Enter Diana.

Diana.   With horns and with hounds I waken the day,
And hie to my woodland walks away;

---

prize, / as a Furlow to Bask / in their Mistresses Eyes; / the Wheel will turn
round, / while Cloth's a Spinning, / thus things seem to end, / when they're
but a beginning' (32–3, omitting repetitions).

s.d. Janus] The god with two faces, guardian of gates and doors, so appropriately
the figure who introduces this masque, which looks backwards and forwards. Prior's
poem also opened with Janus.

1. *mend thy pace*] move faster (*OED* mend 12e).

3. *radiant belt*] the zodiac.

6. *fans*] wings (*OED* 4, citing 'The Cock and the Fox' l. 770).

6. *s.d. Chronos*] Time.

12. *s.d. Momus*] god of ridicule, driven out of heaven for criticizing the gods.

26. *s.d. Diana*] goddess of hunting and chastity.

		I tuck up my robe, and am buskined soon,
30		And tie to my forehead a waxing moon.
		I course the fleet stag, unkennel the fox,
		And chase the wild goats o'er summits of rocks,
		With shouting and hooting we pierce
		through the sky,
		And Echo turns hunter, and doubles the cry.
35	*Cho. of all.*	With shouting and hooting we pierce
		through the sky,
		And Echo turns hunter, and doubles the cry.
	Janus.	Then our age was in its prime,
	Chronos.	Free from rage .
	Diana.	——————And free from crime.
	Momus.	A very merry, dancing, drinking,
40		Laughing, quaffing, and unthinking time.
	Cho. of all.	Then our age was in its prime,
		Free from rage, and free from crime,
		A very merry, dancing, drinking,
		Laughing, quaffing, and unthinking time.

Dance of Diana's attendants.
Enter Mars.

45	*Mars.*	Inspire the vocal brass, inspire;
		The world is past its infant age:
		Arms and honour,
		Arms and honour,
		Set the martial mind on fire,
50		And kindle manly rage.
		Mars has looked the sky to red,
		And Peace, the lazy good, is fled;
		Plenty, Peace, and Pleasure fly;
		The sprightly green

29. *buskined*] shod in buskins (leather boots).
30. *moon*] a symbol of Diana.
31. *course*] chase with dogs, keeping the quarry in sight (rather than follow a scent) (*OED* 1). *unkennel*] dislodge a fox from its hole (*OED* 1).
34. Alan Roper (*MLQ* xxiii (1962) 29–40) notes an echo of Virgil: *et vox assensu nemorum ingeminata remugit* (*Geo.* iii 45, translated by D. as: 'From Hills and Dales the chearful cries rebound: / For Eccho hunts along; and propagates the sound': 'The Third Book of the *Georgics*' ll. 77–8).
37. *prime*] beginning (*OED* 6); state of greatest perfection or vigour (*OED* 9b).
45. *inspire*] breathe into.
52. *good*] This is the reading of *1700* ('Good'), but Scott's emendation to 'God' is attractive.

55		In woodland walks no more is seen;
		The sprightly green has drunk the Tyrian dye.
	Cho. of all.	Plenty, Peace, *etc.*
	Mars.	Sound the trumpet, beat the drum,
		Through all the world around;
60		Sound a reveille, sound, sound,
		The warrior god is come.
	Cho. of all.	Sound the trumpet, *etc.*
	Momus.	Thy sword within the scabbard keep,
		And let mankind agree;
65		Better the world were fast asleep,
		Than kept awake by thee.
		The fools are only thinner,
		With all our cost and care;
		But neither side a winner,
70		For things are as they were.
	Cho. of all.	The fools are only, *etc.*
		Enter Venus.
	Venus.	Calms appear when storms are past,
		Love will have his hour at last:
		Nature is my kindly care,
75		Mars destroys, and I repair;
		Take me, take me, while you may,
		Venus comes not every day.
	Cho. of all.	Take her, take her, *etc.*
	Chronos.	The world was then so light,
80		I scarcely felt the weight;
		Joy ruled the day, and Love the night.
		But since the queen of pleasure left the
		ground,
		I faint, I lag,
		And feebly drag
85		The ponderous orb around.
	Momus.	All, all of a piece throughout;
	Pointing to Diana	Thy chase had a beast in view;
	to Mars	Thy wars brought nothing about;
	to Venus	Thy lovers were all untrue.

56. *Tyrian dye*] purple, blood red.
74–5. Cp. 'Palamon and Arcite' iii 143–4 (Roper).
74. *kindly*] nurturing growth (*OED* 5b).
82. Alluding also to the exile of James II's Queen Mary (Scott).
86. *all of a piece throughout*] Reused from 'Epitaph on Sir Palmes Fairborne' l. 15.
87. *in view*] i.e. the quarry was kept in sight, rather than being hunted by its scent.

90	*Janus.*	'Tis well an old age is out,
	Chronos.	And time to begin a new.
	Cho. of all.	All, all of a piece throughout;
		Thy chase had a beast in view;
		Thy wars brought nothing about;
95		Thy lovers were all untrue.
		'Tis well an old age is out,
		And time to begin a new.

Dance of huntsmen, nymphs, warriors, and lovers.

Index of Titles for *The Poems of John Dryden* (Volumes I–V)

The titles of poems included in the present selected edition are set in bold type, and in these cases the page reference is to the present volume.